ASPEN PUBLISHERS

Mandated Benefits
2009 Compliance Guide

by RSM McGladrey, Inc.

Mandated Benefits 2009 Compliance Guide is a comprehensive and practical reference manual covering key federal regulatory issues that must be addressed by human resources (HR) managers, benefits specialists, and company executives in all industries. Frequent changes in employment laws, coupled with the need to recruit and retain top talent while simultaneously holding down costs, present these professionals with an array of challenges on a daily basis.

Mandated Benefits 2009 Compliance Guide helps take the guesswork out of managing employee benefits and human resources by clearly and concisely describing the essential requirements and administrative processes necessary to comply with each regulation. The *Guide* offers suggestions for protecting employers against the most common litigation threats and recommendations for handling various types of employee problems.

Throughout the *Guide* are numerous exhibits, useful checklists and forms, and do's and don'ts. A list of HR audit questions at the beginning of each chapter serves as an aid in evaluating a company's level of regulatory compliance.

It is critical that employers remember that any federal law regulating administration of employment, compensation, or employee benefits represents the minimum requirements for compliance. A state may pass legislation to modify a federal law and increase the benefit's entitlement, but no state may reduce the entitlement to a benefit below the federal minimum.

If a company finds that the current administration for any benefit or employment requirement does not meet at least the federal law, the mismatch should be looked into promptly. There are significant fines and penalties associated with failure to comply with required employee benefits and human resources regulations.

Highlights of the 2009 Guide

The *2009 Compliance Guide* contains the following major additions and revisions:

- Chapter 3 adds the definition of the regular rate of pay for non-exempt employees and new information on compensation for volunteers.

- Chapter 4 has been updated with recent case law on the classification of independent contractors.

Wolters Kluwer
Law & Business

- Chapter 5 contains (1) highlights of the Genetic Information Nondiscrimination Act (GINA); (2) information on ERISA requirements for bonding, plan administrators, written plan document and record retention; (3) summary of the newly enacted amendments to the Mental Health Parity Act; and (4) electronic notification for Medicare Part D Notices.

- Chapter 6 adds the definition and examples of supplemental excepted benefits under HIPAA.

- Chapter 7 includes additional information on covered employers, open enrollment and leaves of absence.

- Chapter 8 has been updated with new proposed and final regulations for the Pension Protection Act of 2006, as well as an entirely new section on fiduciary responsibilities.

- Chapter 10 adds new information on financial and retirement planning education.

- Chapter 11 has been updated with descriptions of partial day absences and exempt employee status and the Department of Labor's description of a bona fide sick leave plan.

- Chapter 12 has added information on (1) dependent care flexible spending accounts; (2) the IRS definition of dependent; (3) definition of and rulings on medical care expenses; (4) the Heroes Earnings Assistance and Relief Tax Act of 2008 (HEART Act) exception to the use it or lose it rule; and (5) the requirement for plan sponsors to treat employee contributions to the health plan as plan assets. Additionally, the chapter contains new proposed and final guidance on Health Savings Accounts (HSAs), and final regulations on the coordination of retirees' health care coverage with Medicare as a result of the final ruling on the *Erie County* and *AARP v. EEOC* cases.

- Chapter 13 has included information on the recently enacted ADA Amendments Act of 2008 (ADAAA).

- Chapter 14 has been updated to include information on the new proposed FMLA regulations and the new military family leave, including updates to the relevant forms in the chapter's exhibits.

- Chapter 16 has been significantly revised for clarity. In addition, the Form I-9 section has been expanded and new sections on the government's E-Verify program and on-boarding have been added.

- Chapter 18 contains new information on GINA, AAPs for veterans under VEVRAA, as amended and the Vets-100 report.

- Chapter 19 includes updated research on telecommuting.

- Chapter 20 has added information on GINA and recent case law involving the privacy of text messages.

- Chapter 22 has been updated with a new section on OSHA enforcement.

- Chapter 24 has been revised with updated information on social security mismatch letters, and the structure of employee files.

- Chapter 27 has been updated with information on the tax consequences of COLI policies and a correction program for nonqualified plans' operational failures.

All chapters have been updated with new information, applicable regulatory changes, relevant court cases, and updated statistics and survey information.

12/08

For questions concerning this shipment, billing, or other customer service matters, call our Customer Service Department at 1-800-234-1660.

For toll-free ordering, please call 1-800-638-8437.

Mandated Benefits

2009 Compliance Guide

ASPEN PUBLISHERS

Mandated Benefits

2009 Compliance Guide

RSM McGladrey, Inc.

™ Wolters Kluwer

Law & Business

AUSTIN   BOSTON   CHICAGO   NEW YORK   THE NETHERLANDS

This publication is designed to provide accurate and authoritative information in regard to the subject matter covered. It is sold with the understanding that the publisher is not engaged in rendering legal, accounting, or other professional services. If legal advice or other professional assistance is required, the services of a competent professional person should be sought.

—From a *Declaration of Principles* jointly adopted by
a Committee of the American Bar Association and
a Committee of Publishers and Associations

Printed in the United States of America

1 2 3 4 5 6 7 8 9 0

ISBN 978-0-7355-7389-5

About Wolters Kluwer Law & Business

Wolters Kluwer Law & Business is a leading provider of research information and workflow solutions in key specialty areas. The strengths of the individual brands of Aspen Publishers, CCH, Kluwer Law International and Loislaw are aligned within Wolters Kluwer Law & Business to provide comprehensive, in-depth solutions and expert-authored content for the legal, professional and education markets.

CCH was founded in 1913 and has served more than four generations of business professionals and their clients. The CCH products in the Wolters Kluwer Law & Business group are highly regarded electronic and print resources for legal, securities, antitrust and trade regulation, government contracting, banking, pension, payroll, employment and labor, and healthcare reimbursement and compliance professionals.

Aspen Publishers is a leading information provider for attorneys, business professionals and law students. Written by preeminent authorities, Aspen products offer analytical and practical information in a range of specialty practice areas from securities law and intellectual property to mergers and acquisitions and pension/benefits. Aspen's trusted legal education resources provide professors and students with high-quality, up-to-date and effective resources for successful instruction and study in all areas of the law.

Kluwer Law International supplies the global business community with comprehensive English-language international legal information. Legal practitioners, corporate counsel and business executives around the world rely on the Kluwer Law International journals, loose-leafs, books and electronic products for authoritative information in many areas of international legal practice.

Loislaw is a premier provider of digitized legal content to small law firm practitioners of various specializations. Loislaw provides attorneys with the ability to quickly and efficiently find the necessary legal information they need, when and where they need it, by facilitating access to primary law as well as state-specific law, records, forms and treatises.

Wolters Kluwer Law & Business, a unit of Wolters Kluwer, is headquartered in New York and Riverwoods, Illinois. Wolters Kluwer is a leading multinational publisher and information services company.

ASPEN PUBLISHERS SUBSCRIPTION NOTICE

This Aspen Publishers product is updated on a periodic basis with supplements to reflect important changes in the subject matter. If you purchased this product directly from Aspen Publishers, we have already recorded your subscription for the update service.

If, however, you purchased this product from a bookstore and wish to receive future updates and revised or related volumes billed separately with a 30-day examination review, please contact our Customer Service Department at 1-800-234-1660 or send your name, company name (if applicable), address, and the title of the product to:

ASPEN PUBLISHERS
7201 McKinney Circle
Frederick, MD 21704

Important Aspen Publishers Contact Information

- To order any Aspen Publishers title, go to *www.aspenpublishers.com* or call 1-800-638-8437.
- To reinstate your manual update service, call 1-800-638-8437.
- To contact Customer Care, e-mail *customer.care@aspenpublishers.com*, call 1-800-234-1660, fax 1-800-901-9075, or mail correspondence to Order Department, Aspen Publishers, PO Box 990, Frederick, MD 21705.
- To review your account history or pay an invoice online, visit *www.aspenpublishers.com/payinvoices*.

RSM. McGladrey

RSM McGladrey is the professional services firm for companies on the move. Whether it's accounting, tax or business consulting, we're focused on listening to your needs, then designing solutions that fit—with your budget, your timeline, your corporate culture and vision. We provide assurance services through McGladrey & Pullen LLP, a leading national CPA firm. RSM McGladrey and McGladrey & Pullen have an alternative practice structure. Though separate and independent legal entities, they can work together to serve clients' business needs. When considered together, the companies rank as the fifth largest U.S. provider of accounting, tax and business consulting services, with nearly 8,000 professionals and associates in nearly 100 offices nationwide.

RSM McGladrey is dedicated to providing the best locally-based, personalized service to every client. Our business consulting services include the following:

◆ *Human Resources*

We are consultants to large and small companies—some of them publicly held, others closely held—covering many industries. We also serve the human resources (HR) functions of major corporations. Some of our clients have limited HR management capabilities. Others lack the time or formal systems usually needed to effectively manage their human resources. Whatever your organization's situation or size, we can help you to establish HR processes and practices that are responsive to both organization and employee needs. We provide Compensation, Performance Management and Employee Welfare Benefits Consulting; Executive Search and Personnel Selection; and Human Resource Strategy, Organization Planning, Design and Structuring, HR Compliance, Employment Survey, and HR Staff Augmentation Services.

◆ *Business Planning*

When it is time to plan for the future, our business planning consultants pinpoint issues that could detract from your company's focus on profitable growth. Our role is to help your people develop your business plan and use it as a management tool.

◆ *Information Technology*

Our Integrated Technology Solutions Group has more than 400 consultants who are exclusively dedicated to helping clients address their information technology issues. We partner with our clients to achieve their strategic business objectives through innovative solutions that align people, processes, and technology.

◆ *Financial Management*

Our financial management consultants highlight profit improvement opportunities. We evaluate the financial prospects of a new business or product. And we perform business valuations for valuation planning, estate and tax transfers, and mergers and acquisitions. Our objective is to help you with the effective management of your financial resources.

◆ *Operations*

Your company could be pouring profits down the drain—in ways you may not realize. Hidden causes for lost productivity can be identified so your company can achieve its objectives more economically. Our operations consultants can help you address operational problems, large or small, that could be key factors in your productivity and profitability.

To learn more, contact:
RSM McGladrey, Inc.
(800) 274-3978
Please visit our Web site at
www.rsmmcgladrey.com

About the Authors

This manual represents the collective effort of the following consultants at RSM McGladrey, Inc., each of whom is a contributing author:

Susan Bock, CEBS, SPHR, a Human Resources Consultant, has more than 25 years of HR experience in the banking, construction, distribution, government, health care, manufacturing, and not-for-profit industries. Her experience covers all of the major areas of HR, including recruiting, compensation, legal compliance, employee relations, and training. She has specialized in benefits planning, development, and compliance. Ms. Bock earned a Master of Human Resources Management degree from the University of Utah and a Bachelor of Arts in Psychology from Miami University.

Maryellen Galuchie, CPA, is a Managing Director in the Southern California Group of RSM McGladrey, Inc. and a partner with McGladrey & Pullen, LLP, overseeing the firm's Southern California Consulting Practice. With over 25 years of experience, she directs a multi-disciplined team of consultants on major projects. Ms. Galuchie is directly responsible for providing financial management and business advisory services. Her practice involves a wide range of industries, including manufacturing, distribution, construction, and professional services, with particular emphasis on the following practice areas: business valuation and planning, financial operations and controls analysis, mergers and acquisition assistance and business process improvement. She earned a Bachelor of Arts in Business Administration from California State University, Fullerton.

Steve Levin is a Managing Director with RSM McGladrey Retirement Resources in the Fort Lauderdale, Florida, office. Prior to joining RSM McGladrey, Mr. Levin practiced law in the Twin Cities for more than 13 years, specializing in tax, retirement plans, benefits, and business planning issues. He currently assists clients in the areas of executive deferred compensation, qualified retirement plans, leveraged ESOPs, and other tax and ERISA matters. Mr. Levin earned a Master of Law degree in Taxation from New York University, a Juris Doctor degree from the University of Nebraska, and a Bachelor of Arts degree from the University of Minnesota.

Bill O'Malley is a tax partner with McGladrey & Pullen, LLP, having joined McGladrey in 1984 after working for a law firm in Chicago. He focuses his practice on employee benefit tax issues including representing clients before the Internal Revenue Service in audit, self-correction and determination letter matters. Mr. O'Malley has a law degree from The John Marshall Law School (Chicago, Illinois) and a Bachelor of Arts degree from Quincy University. Mr. O'Malley has also passed the CPA examination and has received the Certified Pension Consultant designation from the American Society of Pension Professionals and Actuaries.

Diane Uyematsu, SPHR, is a Human Resources consultant. With more than 25 years of HR experience, Ms. Uyematsu provides human resources consulting services in compensation, performance management, benefits, training, management development, legal compliance, and general human resources for employers in the manufacturing, distribution, finance, education, construction, government, and not-for-profit sectors. Ms. Uyematsu earned a Bachelor of Arts in Business Administration from the University of Redlands and a Master of Business Administration degree from Chapman University.

ACKNOWLEDGMENTS

We wish to thank the following individual, who is not affiliated with RSM McGladrey, Inc., for his important contributions to the 2009 Edition:

Terry L. Tyson, CSA, CMSP, has been a safety professional for more than 25 years. Mr. Tyson works primarily in the mining, construction, and transportation industries. He is a past Vice President and President of the United Safety Associates and has served on various industry councils and committees within the American Society of Safety Engineers, Associated General Contractors, National Stone, Sand & Gravel Association, Pacific Safety Council, and National Safety Council. Mr. Tyson is certified by the National Safety Council as a Certified Safety Administrator, and as a Certified Mine Safety Professional by the International Society of Mine Safety Professionals. He earned a Bachelor of Arts degree from the University of California, Riverside.

We wish to acknowledge the unique contribution of Susan Bock, who served as the overall editor and project manager for the 2009 Edition, and Diane Uyematsu, who assisted in editorial and project management. We also thank many other members of the RSM McGladrey team whose support made the writing of this manual possible.

RSM McGladrey, Inc.

Contents

*A complete table of contents for each chapter is
included at the beginning of the chapter.*

Chapter 1
Human Resources Management: Strategy and Structure

Chapter 2
Organization Development: Planning and Evaluation

Chapter 3
Pay Practices

Chapter 4
Payroll Administration

Chapter 5
Health Care Benefits

Chapter 6
Health Insurance Portability and Accountability Act (HIPAA)

Chapter 7
Medical and Health Care Continuation Coverage/COBRA

Chapter 8
Pensions and Other Savings Plans

Chapter 9
Life Insurance and Disability and Income Protection Benefits

Chapter 10
Supplemental Benefits

Chapter 11
Time Away from Work

Chapter 12
Managing the Benefits Package

Chapter 13
The Americans with Disabilities Act

Chapter 14
Family and Medical Leave

Chapter 15
Integrating ADA, FMLA, Workers' Compensation, and Related Requirements

Chapter 16
The Interview and Selection Process

Chapter 17
Layoffs and Termination

Chapter 18
Equal Employment Opportunity and Affirmative Action Plan

Chapter 22
Workplace Health and Safety

Chapter 23
Substance Abuse in the Workplace

Chapter 24
Recordkeeping

Chapter 25
Human Resources Risk Management

Chapter 26
Special Human Resources Situation: Merger or Acquisition

Chapter 27
Nonqualified Deferred Compensation Plans

Appendix A
Quiz: How Many of These Acronyms/Abbreviations Do You Know?

Glossary

Index

Chapter 1
Human Resources Management: Strategy and Structure

§ 1.01   AUDIT QUESTIONS

1. Does the Human Resources (HR) department play a role in implementing the strategic vision and mission of the company?

2. Does the top HR officer serve as a confidant to the CEO?

3. Does the top HR officer understand business administration and the basics of finance or accounting, or both?

4. Is the HR department staffed and organized to deliver the appropriate level of service to meet the company's expectations?

5. Is there a job description for every position?

Note: Consistent "yes" answers to the above questions suggest that the organization is applying effective management practices and/or complying with federal regulations. "No" answers indicate that problem areas exist and should be addressed immediately.

This chapter describes the role of HR as a strategic partner in maximizing the long-term success of a business. It presents the general principles of planning HR department structure and staffing and describes two HR-level service models—maintenance and full range—to help determine the optimum HR setup within a company. It describes the typical HR staff hiring progression, shows representative activities and levels, and lists typical expectations of the HR staff. The chapter also touches on four common strategic initiatives faced by HR managers and refers readers to the appropriate chapter in the book for more in-depth information.

In December 2007, Deloitte Consulting, LLP released the results of its HR Transformation survey of 150 large global organizations. Of these participants, 84 percent are currently transforming their human resources departments or are planning to do so. While the changes to the HR department often occur due to a new Chief Executive Officer or new head of HR, 85 percent of the respondents cite cost savings or efficiency as the business reason for making changes. Only 30 percent of the respondents are or will transform the HR department to reduce administrative tasks in order to free up HR to take on a more strategic role.

This chapter is written for the reasonably experienced HR practitioner who is responsible for setting up or reorganizing an HR department. A company's top HR officer may be the HR director or the HR manager (these terms are used interchangeably). Whoever is the most senior HR officer has the responsibility of setting up or organizing the HR department.

The information contained herein will be useful for any company executive who wishes to broaden his or her knowledge of how to manage the HR function. After reviewing this information, the company executive will have a better understanding of the strategy underlying HR staffing and service models and what HR can provide in terms of support for the strategic objectives of the company. However, because every company has its unique growth strategy and desired HR service level and unique employee programs and services, each firm's approach to HR staffing will differ.

Appendix 1-A provides a basic organization chart for an HR department, a list of typical HR activities, and descriptions of typical roles and responsibilities by function for a sample organization.

§ 1.02   HUMAN RESOURCES: A STRATEGIC PARTNER IN BUSINESS MANAGEMENT

Within the HR function is a dizzying array of responsibilities for an HR manager. The main issue is determining where the HR manager should focus his or her attention to do the most good for the company. There is no one right answer; the correct choices are relative to the long- and short-range needs of the organization and an understanding of the risks associated with each choice.

What *is* clear, however, is that selecting the traditional, somewhat insular focus on compliance and recordkeeping is no longer an option. Instead, the top HR officer must think much more globally to become a true strategic partner in business management.

For many chief executive officers (CEOs), the relationship they develop with their senior HR officers becomes one of the most significant relationships they have. The quality that CEOs tend to value most in their top HR officers is honesty. But to be both honest and valuable, HR managers must be functioning effectively at the highest level. The balancing act of the top HR officer becomes one of serving as a sounding board and confidant to the CEO while simultaneously developing a trust relationship with employees.

To serve as a strategic business partner, the HR manager must understand the long-range vision and mission of the company, *actively participate* in planning activities, and be able to provide ''what if'' assessments for various scenarios, such as anticipating the changing demographics and expectations of the workforce five or six years in the future.

Following is a summary of the critical skills an HR manager needs to join the strategic ranks of his or her organization:

1. *Be familiar with the corporate business plan.* The top HR officer must be familiar with the corporate business plan. He or she should study it carefully to find out exactly where the organization is headed.

2. *Have a good grasp of financial issues.* To be effective in strategic and business planning, the HR manager needs a good grasp of financial issues beyond the HR department budget. For example, he or she should understand basic accounting concepts such as variable versus fixed costs. Often, HR professionals are not well enough versed in the fundamentals of finance to grasp the workings of the plan. If an HR manager does not have a good knowledge of business essentials, he or she may want to consider getting some training.

3. *Open discussion with senior management if there is no formal business plan.* If there is no formal business plan, the HR manager is encouraged to broach discussions with the CEO, president, and other members of senior management. A unified sense of direction and purpose is a critical component to ensuring the long-term survival of any business.

4. *Be visionary and persuasive.* Initiating discussions about strategic and/or business planning will give the HR leader an opportunity to exercise another key skill—the ability to be persuasive and move the organization forward by influencing key decisions. HR leaders must be prepared to "push the envelope"—to take calculated risks and be visionary when necessary.

5. *Be prepared to lead the development of the HR strategic plan.* The most important HR document after the business plan is the HR strategic plan. The HR manager should be prepared to lead the development of this plan.

6. *Demonstrate passion and enthusiasm for the mission of HR.* A passion for the mission of HR is critical for success. At the heart of a successful HR professional is someone who truly cares about employees at all levels and wants to see them succeed and build better lives as a result of working at the company. Such a passion affords HR the opportunity to be a strong, positive influence for change within the organization.

§ 1.03   ORGANIZATION OF THE HR DEPARTMENT

If they have not already done so, HR managers must begin exercising a more strategic role in the organization by refining the structure and function of the HR department. The goal is to ensure that HR systems and processes are aligned with the mission, values, and vision of the corporation.

[A]   HR Department Design

To best understand HR department design, it is necessary to borrow from an architectural design concept: form follows function. To determine the appropriate structure of the HR department, first it is necessary to determine the overall expectations of the HR function, the level of HR service desired in the company, and the impact of the company's configuration and growth strategies. The determination process should be a group effort involving the organization's top management. Top management's "buy in" to the level of desired HR service is critical to its ongoing support of the HR function. Once the design of the HR department is determined, it will be possible to accurately assess the number of people required in HR to deliver the chosen level of service.

[B] Defining Desired Level of Service

To help define the desired level of service, company management is encouraged to define explicitly the following key aspects of HR philosophy:

- *Human resources management goal.* What is the goal of HR in the company?
  Example: The overall executive HR goal is to establish a professional, businesslike approach to HR management while maintaining a feeling of care and respect for employees.

- *People management goal.* What is the overall goal for how employees should perceive the company?
  Example: The overall HR goal for the company is to create a dedicated team of career-minded employees who work together to build the organization. Senior management wants employees to enjoy their work, feel a sense of ownership in the company, and have confidence in senior management's ability to lead.

- *Employee productivity and motivation.* How should employees view their personal job responsibilities?
  Example: Employees should be motivated. They should understand that personal ownership in the success of the organization brings increased personal responsibility. Further, employees should understand that their personal responsibility for increased productivity ultimately comes in the form of providing good customer service, for both internal and external customers.

Optimally, the HR function is then structured to support the defined management goals.

[C] "Expected Level of Service" Approach to HR Department Staffing

The key variable affecting the staff to HR ratio is the expected level of service and support to be provided by the HR department. There are two levels of HR service in an organization: maintenance management and full-range management. Understanding these two levels and explicitly defining the level of service expected from HR within the company are critical to determining the appropriate HR department staffing. These two structures represent significantly different expectations for how HR will operate within an organization. Understanding this is key to ensuring HR can meet the level of service expectations held by management.

[1] Maintenance Level

At this level, the HR department is primarily concerned with maintenance, regulatory compliance, and administrative tasks. HR is reactive, responding upon demand to legal changes and management and employee needs, but seldom initiating activity. At the maintenance level, HR plays a less strategic role in the organization. At this level, the structure and staffing are designed to be reactive and are focused primarily on compliance and risk management.

At the maintenance level, core functions should be designed to minimize liability for the company. The HR department is expected to provide administrative support for management and employees and provide some counsel to management in appropriate personnel actions. Administrative support includes providing timely response to employee requests for information and prompt filing of documents and preparation of various HR reports.

Typical HR maintenance activities include:

- Interpreting policy and answering employee questions or concerns regarding such areas as benefits and payroll

- Administering employee benefits and insurance

- Processing new hires and terminations

- Maintaining employee files

- Tracking basic personnel data such as vacation and leave of absence

- Preparing government-required reports and distribution of HR-related memoranda

- Conducting some activities to minimize risk to the organization and initiating performance improvement activities to a limited extent

- Administering a salary program

- Providing basic level of counsel to individual managers and supervisors on issues related to performance of subordinates

- Screening employment candidates and checking references

[2]   Full-Range Service Level

At the full-range service level, the focus of HR activities broadens to include development and implementation of programs that support the overall growth of the organization, productivity improvement, and employee relations. The HR department initiates activities to minimize risk to the organization and drives a range of performance improvement activities. In this mode HR is positioned—indeed, generally expected—to participate as a high-level strategic partner in supporting the organization's short- and long-range business and personnel objectives.

Typical full-range HR service activities include:

- Participating in business planning activities and providing "what if" assessments on various scenarios (e.g., organic growth or merger)

- Coordinating and/or conducting training in management and supervisory skills as well as technical training

- Designing and implementing employee performance improvement and communications programs

- Initiating organizational development activities such as career planning and succession charting

- Providing in-depth counsel to managers and supervisors regarding subordinate performance problems

- Providing statistical and other data to determine trends and identify problems as they emerge among the employee population

The benefits of the full-range service approach include increased protection of the organization as a result of the reduced potential for liability, reduced turnover, improved employee relations, better trained managers and supervisors, and reduced costs of workers' compensation. However, increased manpower costs are needed to support this level of service.

[D] Employee to HR Staff Ratios

The rule of thumb that many companies use in staffing their HR departments is a commonly accepted industry ratio of one HR professional for each 100 employees, or 1 to 100. That ratio, however, is the minimum HR staffing requirement to fulfill an organization's *basic* (maintenance level) HR needs, and it does not take into account that a part-time employee may require the same level of HR support as a full-time employee. Further, the rule-of-thumb ratio assumes that every company employs fully qualified and trained HR professionals performing with average competency.

[1] Industry Variables

Although comprehensive industry surveys report that the most common ratio of full-time professional HR staff to number of employees served is 1 to 100, the ratio varies somewhat by industry. The industry variables that affect HR staffing include (1) the level of regulatory oversight; (2) the type, extent, and frequency of required employee training; and (3) the type and extent of required recordkeeping and reporting. As reported in the HR Department Benchmarks and Analysis Survey 2005-2006, a survey conducted by the Bureau of National Affairs, Inc. (BNA), the average HR to staff ratio for companies of all sizes in the health care sector is less than 1.0 to 100, while the ratio for services and other nonmanufacturing companies is over 1.2 to 100.

[2] Organization Size

Another variable that affects the size of the HR Department is the total number of employees in the organization. Generally, as firms increase in size, the ratio of HR employees to total employees decreases. As reported in the SHRM Human Capital Benchmarking Study (Society for Human Resources Management, 2007), in companies with less than 100 employees the median ratio was 2.4 HR employees to total employees; in companies with 250 to 499 employees, the ratio was 0.94; and in companies with 7,500 or more employees, the ratio was 0.72.

[3] Company Variables

In addition to industry variables, company variables must be considered when performing a staffing analysis. Just as there is no standard company, there is no one-size-fits-all HR staffing ratio. The attainment of a company's desired service level is the ultimate standard against which HR staffing decisions are judged. Failure to consider the following factors unique to a company will impact the ability of its HR department to meet actual company needs:

- Centralization or decentralization of the HR function (and corresponding responsibility for administration of HR duties)

- Number of locations

- Geographic distribution of the employees served

- Outsourced services

- Amount of automation

- Relative sophistication of the employees

- Relative complexity of the company's strategic mission and objectives for the HR function (desired service level)

- Relative revenue and size—the risk of employment liability increases with assets and the number of employees

[4] Non-HR Functions Performed by HR

When determining the optimum HR staff level, management must (1) account for the non-HR activities handled by the HR function and (2) understand how standard ratios for HR staff per employee are affected by company-specific attributes. Many HR managers will consider the sample HR job profiles (see **Appendix 1-A**) incomplete because they do not list *all* the duties performed by their departments. Many HR departments manage at least one general administrative function. Such functions include managing security and property protection, overseeing the company's credit union, handling the mail and phones, and providing in-house medical and travel services.

[5] Multiple Locations

Companies with multiple geographically dispersed sites faced unique HR challenges. The critical objective is to ensure that the HR staff at a site or a division is adequate to ensure that the site or division is consistent in applying and interpreting the corporate HR policy. In a complex, multilayered organization, a higher level of HR involvement is required to ensure that all divisional HR actions are consistent with company policy and in compliance with state and federal law. Ultimately, each site requires an individual with day-to-day responsibility for HR administration. At smaller sites, that person is often the site manager, who may have a clerk helping with personnel files and employee-related functions. At larger sites, the on-site HR staff may begin to mirror the corporate HR staff. A company may be able to delay hiring HR staff for each of its sites or divisions if it automates a significant portion of its HR administration by implementing a human resources information system (HRIS).

Employers with separate strategic business units or profit centers (i.e., divisions) or multistate or international divisions are advised to assign divisional HR responsibilities to HR professionals who are familiar with the local laws and regulations, following the same staffing guidelines as those described in the preceding paragraphs. If a division is too small to support a full-time HR manager, the company may wish to engage a part-time (or contractual) HR professional.

[6] Merger or Acquisition

A merger or an acquisition presents the potential for major upheaval in virtually all existing systems, processes, and procedures in both the acquiror and the acquiree. Buying a complete business assumes the purchase of the acquiree's staff along with its other assets. Growth by acquisition has two simultaneous effects on the acquiror's HR department. First, HR must fully integrate the acquiree's employees both administratively and culturally. (For example, no matter what the HR level of service strategy practiced by the acquiror is, it is usually HR's task to educate new employees so they understand the firm's business mission and objectives.) Second, each acquisition is followed by a sudden spike in time- and labor-intensive recruitment activities. It is an industry rule of thumb that 95 percent (or more) of the employees acquired in a merger or acquisition leave the company within the first year or upon the termination of their incentive compensation agreements, if such financial advantages were offered to them for staying for a designated period of time. These employees must be replaced, and their replacements must be integrated into the company.

If a company has a strategy of growth by acquisition, its management should recognize that following an acquisition, HR programs and services will go through an adjustment because the maintenance-level HR activities will increase exponentially, albeit temporarily. Thus, following an acquisition, a company would be wise to bring in temporary outside HR assistance, or suspend "nonessential" activities, or otherwise plan for the unavoidable impact on HR staff. If a company plans to acquire new companies on a fairly regular basis (say, every other year), it would make sense to selectively expand its HR staff to ensure that there is sufficient support for maintaining the company's desired HR service level at the same time as the assimilation or replacement of newly acquired employees is proceeding. (See **Chapter 26** for general guidance in managing a merger or an acquisition.)

[E] Typical HR Department Structure

Responsibility for HR administration is generally concentrated in one department. This most often includes responsibility for all aspects of the function, including employment, training, safety programs, benefits, compensation, employee relations (or labor relations), personnel file maintenance, employee programs and services, and termination-related activities. It may also include retiree program administration, if applicable.

Less frequent, although becoming more common, is HR responsibility for risk management and other corporate insurance/liability programs. A variable in many organizations is responsibility for payroll. Often payroll administration falls under the finance/accounting department. In many organizations payroll processing is outsourced to a vendor.

In small organizations (revenues under $20 million) responsibility for HR is often retained by the president/owner or given to the controller or top financial executive, who may have a clerk assisting him or her with employee files and other administrative functions.

In small to midsized organizations (revenues between $20 million and $80 million), where there is a formal HR department, the top position in HR is often at midmanagement level, reporting to a vice president of administration or the head of finance/accounting. The number of HR staff varies with the number of employees and the sophistication and complexity of the organization. It should be recognized, however, that the chain of command in smaller companies is often more flexible than in large organizations. Thus, even if the head of HR does not report directly to the president/owner, generally there is still a direct line of communication for critical issues between HR and the top level of the company.

In large organizations (revenues of $80 million and up) there is more variation. In general, the larger the company, the higher the level of the top HR person. Large companies tend to recognize that their increased size increases their potential for litigation, which elevates the significance of HR risk management. In most $150 million-plus companies the hierarchy of positions in HR parallels that of any other corporate function: vice president, HR (reporting to the president/owner), director of HR, HR manager, and a mixture of staff, some exempt and some nonexempt.

[F]   Common Roles and Responsibilities

Drafting job descriptions is an efficient method of clarifying roles and responsibilities of each position. A description should also include the level of technical skill, education, and experience required of the average competent employee to perform the job, as well as a representative list of desirable characteristics and work style attributes required for success in each position.

Appendix 1-A provides an organization structure and summary list of duties and responsibilities normally assigned to the positions of HR director, employee relations and training manager, employment and benefits representative, compensation and benefits assistant, and payroll assistant. The sample job summaries are constructed assuming a single-site $150 million manufacturing company with 400 employees. The desired service level is full-range. These job responsibilities may be combined as appropriate to the size and complexity of the organization.

[G]   Common Expectations of HR Staff

All HR staff members are commonly expected to display the types of abilities listed as minimum qualifications for success:

- Maintain confidentiality.

- Earn respect of employees.

- Be technically skilled.

- Commit to his or her job.

- Have a service orientation.

- View employees as customers.

- Give employees direction to solve problems.

- Deliver on commitments.

- Be accountable.

- Respond to senior management's special requirements accurately and quickly.

- Consistently follow established policies and procedures.

- Serve all levels of employees equally well.

§ 1.04   HR STAFF ASSESSMENT

Once the jobs have been defined, it is important to assess the ability of the HR department to deliver what is required to meet the needs of the organization. One way to assess an organization's HR staff is to meet with each staff member to discuss the technical aspects of the person's job and his or her HR-related education and experience. In these meetings it is also key to discuss the individual's future career objectives within or outside the HR function and his or her own perception of his or her work style, strengths, and areas for improvement. These meetings are often conducted by an outside HR expert.

Job assignment recommendations that come out of the meetings with the HR employees should be based on the following:

- Evaluation of each staff member's current position, related education and experience, and stated career objectives

- Consideration of each person's self-assessment

- Interviewer's judgment of the employee's individual work style, strengths, areas of needed improvement, and technical skill

- The technical skills, desirable characteristics, and work style attributes required for each position in the HR function

If employees have gaps in education, skill, and experience, management must actively take steps to remedy the situation. This can often be accomplished through training seminars, enrolling in a certificate program, or spending one-on-one time with an experienced HR consultant. However, if a realistic appraisal shows that an employee is a poor fit within HR, and it is not a training issue, or so much training is needed that it is not feasible to bring the person up to speed in a reasonable period of time, consider moving the employee to another department or laying him or her off. It may sound harsh, but unqualified HR staff can inflict considerable harm on an organization.

§ 1.05 ELEMENTS OF STRATEGIC PLANNING IN HUMAN RESOURCES

An HR strategic plan is really a high-level organization development (OD) project. It integrates company culture and vision with HR policies, procedures, systems, staffing, and structure and provides the high-level framework for how HR is supposed to function within an organization.

The HR strategic plan should reflect the long-term goals and objectives of company management by describing specifically how HR supports the company's strategic business plan. This level of alignment can be most effectively accomplished when the HR plan is drafted in conjunction with the conduct of a company-wide OD project. (For more information on how to conduct an OD project, see **Chapter 2**.)

Appendix 1-A
Human Resources Organization Chart and Summary Job Descriptions

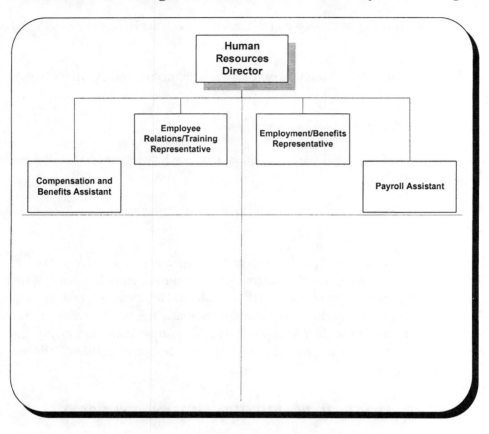

The incumbents of the following jobs must be able to perform satisfactorily each of the essential duties in their job descriptions. The requirements listed for each position are representative of the knowledge, skill, and abilities required by the industry. Reasonable accommodations may be made to enable individuals with disabilities to perform the essential functions.

* * * * *

HUMAN RESOURCES DIRECTOR

Reports to: President

Status: Exempt

ESSENTIAL DUTIES AND RESPONSIBILITIES

Creates policy and directs and coordinates HR management activities, such as employment, compensation, employee relations, benefits, training, performance appraisal, and employee services, by performing the following duties personally or through subordinate supervisors.

Writes directives advising department managers of company policy regarding equal employment opportunities, compensation, employee benefits, training, and development and performance appraisal programs.

Confers with senior management to ensure HR staffing and career development plans support the strategic objectives of the company. Oversees the recruitment and job placement activities.

Formulates compensation guidelines and policy. Determines appropriate salary level for each position based on market rate data.

Confers with management to determine employee training needs. Recommends appropriate instructional methods, such as company-sponsored group instruction, self-study, or other external workshops or seminars. Directs development of management training manuals and other educational materials.

Consults legal counsel to ensure that policies comply with federal and state law. Explains to employees company and governmental rules, regulations, and procedures, and the need for compliance.

Develops and maintains a human resources information system that meets top management information needs.

Oversees the analysis, maintenance, and communication of records required by law or local governing bodies, or other departments in the organization. Implements appropriate procedures to maintain confidentiality of protected information.

Meets with management to discuss possible HR actions to be taken. Alternately, represents management and/or acts as employees' advocate in problem resolution. May inspect any operation or administrative departments or workstations to ensure that required changes are implemented.

Oversees issuance of HR policies to operational and administrative managers. Reviews and approves revisions of employee handbook. Recommends to management for approval.

EDUCATION AND EXPERIENCE

Bachelor of science (or bachelor of arts) degree in human resources or the equivalent; three years of HR management experience; total of five years of related experience or equivalent combination of education and experience. Master's degree desirable.

OTHER SKILLS AND ABILITIES

Familiarity with application of employment law in company industry. Ability to interact well with all levels of employees. Good organization. Good listening and communication skills. Ability to see the big picture without loss of detail and to remain calm in stressful or demanding situations.

EMPLOYEE RELATIONS AND TRAINING MANAGER

Reports to: Human Resources Director

Status: Exempt

ESSENTIAL DUTIES AND RESPONSIBILITIES

Understands and interprets HR policies and procedures and interprets the intent, spirit, and terms of each to employees and managers. Explains to employees company and governmental rules, regulations, and procedures, and the need for compliance.

Counsels management in application of effective employee relations policies and practices. Verifies adherence to employee relations policies and practices by monitoring day-to-day implementation of policies concerning wages, hours, and working conditions.

Recommends revisions or drafts new employee relations policies and procedures as required. Presents to the HR Director for approval.

Meets with management to discuss possible HR actions to be taken. Alternately, represents management and/or acts as employee advocate in grievance resolution. Inspects all departments or workstations to ensure that required changes are implemented. Prepares reports on employees' comments and actions taken.

Gathers employees' feedback regarding factors that affect employee morale, motivation, and efficiency. Provides feedback, analysis, and recommendations to management. Coordinates employee achievement and recognition programs and employee recreational programs.

Screens, counsels, and recommends employees for participation in training and education programs. Coordinates employee participation in established training courses offered through community schools, professional service providers, and other vendors.

Coordinates use of management training manuals, reference library, and other educational materials. Maintains records and prepares statistical reports to evaluate success of training and development programs, and monitors progress of participants. Recommends program changes.

EDUCATION AND EXPERIENCE

Bachelor's degree or equivalent, or five years of related experience, or equivalent combination of education and experience.

OTHER SKILLS AND ABILITIES

Familiarity with application of employment law. Ability to interact well with all levels of employees. Good listening and communication skills. Well organized. Creative problem-solving skills. Ability to remain calm in stressful or demanding situations.

EMPLOYMENT AND BENEFITS REPRESENTATIVE

Reports to: Human Resources Director

Status: Exempt

ESSENTIAL DUTIES AND RESPONSIBILITIES

Develops and implements programs to attract, retain, and motivate employees; works in conjunction with employee relations.

Represents the company at unemployment hearings. Contests invalid claims.

Coordinates the compensation and benefit programs of the company to attract, retain, and motivate employees.

Interprets employee benefit policies and procedures to employees and managers. Assists in resolving problems with claims. Maintains insurance and payroll service contacts to investigate discrepancies and provide information on nonroutine situations.

Implements company policies and procedures on recruitment, testing, selection, and job placement. Works with management to define job selection criteria. Responsible for sourcing qualified applicants, conducting screening interviews, checking references, and ensuring background investigation is conducted.

Ensures preparation of job descriptions for all positions. Determines appropriate salary level according to compensation guidelines and policy formulated by the HR Director. Recommends compensation and benefits status for candidates.

Conducts analysis of job descriptions to determine appropriate salary level according to compensation guidelines and policy formulated by the HR Director. Approves compensation and benefits status changes.

Analyzes turnover statistics and assesses reasons for turnover. Makes recommendations regarding methods of controlling excessive turnover.

Interprets company compensation guidelines and policy to managers and employees. Reviews and recommends approval of salary increases permitted within budgetary limits and according to established compensation policies. Resolves problems with recommended increase amounts.

Analyzes company compensation policies in relation to governmental wage and hour regulations and prevailing rates for similar jobs in comparable industries or geographic areas, and recommends changes as appropriate to establish and maintain competitive rates.

Enrolls new employees in benefit plans and conducts benefits orientation. Visits different departments, as necessary, during open enrollment periods.

Participates in, or reviews, the investigation of accidents and injuries, and cooperates in the preparation of materials and evidence for use in hearings, litigation, and insurance investigations. Reviews or prepares reports for insurance carrier or as required by regulatory agencies. Notifies the coordinator of the safety program about significant accidents or trends that may be relevant to address in the safety program.

Oversees the administration of workers' compensation program, including working with insurance carriers to cut down on lost employee time and cut back on unjust claims. Contests invalid claims.

EDUCATION AND EXPERIENCE

Bachelor's degree or equivalent, or two to five years of related experience and/or training, or equivalent combination of education and experience.

OTHER SKILLS AND ABILITIES

Familiarity with application of employment law. Ability to interact well with all levels of employees. Well organized. Detail oriented and analytical.

COMPENSATION AND BENEFITS ASSISTANT

Reports to: Human Resources Director

Status: Nonexempt

ESSENTIAL DUTIES AND RESPONSIBILITIES

Assists in administration of the compensation and benefit programs of the company.

Assists in the preparation of job descriptions and maintains master files.

Distributes and follows up on the performance appraisal and other performance rating forms and reviews forms for completeness.

Processes approved salary changes and maintains the compensation rate and range structure.

Assists in the enrollment of new employees in benefit plans and removes ineligible employees from the rolls. Verifies accuracy of billing; visits departments as necessary during open enrollment periods.

Provides general benefit policy, procedure, and coverage information to all employers and managers.

Maintains vendor contact to investigate discrepancies and provide information on routine situations; assists in resolving routine employee problems regarding insurance claims.

Maintains workers' compensation records; prepares records as required.

Maintains unemployment insurance records; prepares records as required.

Administers the COBRA program: enrolls eligible employees, tracks payments, removes ineligible employees.

Aids in the evaluation of existing employee benefits with those of other employers by analyzing other plans, surveys, and other sources of information.

EDUCATION AND EXPERIENCE

Associate's degree or equivalent; three years of related experience or equivalent combination of education and experience.

OTHER SKILLS AND ABILITIES

Ability to work with database programs. Strong analytical skills. Well organized and detail-oriented. Interacts well with employees at all levels. Ability to remain calm in stressful or demanding situations.

PAYROLL ASSISTANT

Reports to: Human Resources Director

Status: Nonexempt

ESSENTIAL DUTIES AND RESPONSIBILITIES

Compiles payroll data to maintain payroll records. Processes payroll and sales commissions.

Provides general administrative support to the HR department.

Compiles payroll data from timesheets and other records (e.g., hours worked; commissions earned; taxes, insurance, and other monies to be withheld; employee identification numbers).

Prepares computer input forms, enters data into computer files, or computes wages and deductions, and posts to payroll records. Prepares periodic reports of earnings, taxes, and deductions. Keeps records of leave pay and nontaxable wages.

Records data affecting net wages (e.g., exemptions, insurance coverage, and loan payments) for each employee to update master payroll records.

Records data concerning transfer of employees between departments.

Prorates expenses to be debited or credited to each department for cost accounting records.

Reviews wages computed and corrects errors to ensure accuracy of payroll. Prepares and issues paychecks. Resolves problems involving pay amounts.

Prepares commission reports and issues checks. Resolves problems involving pay amounts.

Maintains the HR information system (HRIS). Enters new employees into, and removes termination employees from, the HRIS. Maintains employee history files and other related records. Follows proper procedures to ensure the protection of confidential information.

EDUCATION AND EXPERIENCE

High school graduate or equivalent, or six months to one year of related experience and/or training, or equivalent combination of education and experience.

OTHER SKILLS AND ABILITIES

Ability to work with database program. Strong analytical skills. Well organized and detail-oriented. Interacts well with employees at all levels. Remains calm in stressful or demanding situations.

Chapter 2
Organization Development: Planning and Evaluation

§ 2.01   AUDIT QUESTIONS

1. Does the company have a defined philosophy and process of managing growth and change within the organization?

2. Does the organization have clearly defined duties, responsibilities, and reporting relationships for each position?

3. Does the organization have a well-defined succession plan?

4. Are the organization's goals and objectives clearly defined and effectively communicated to all employees?

Note: Consistent "yes" answers to the above questions suggest that the organization is applying effective management practices and/or complying with federal regulations. "No" answers indicate that problem areas exist and should be addressed immediately.

A successful human resources (HR) department is expected to go beyond its tactical HR function and contribute strategically to maximizing the long-term success of the business. HR's contribution includes (1) systematically assessing the effectiveness of the company's organizational structures and systems and (2) establishing a plan for gaining employees' acceptance and adoption of change in the company's culture and structure and in their roles and responsibilities. This contribution to long-term business success is the process known as *organization development* (OD).

OD is the assessment of the major elements that define an organization: its people, its culture, its systems, its strategic management and management style, its skills, and its technology. The way in which these elements are displayed in an organization's structure, positions, and functional responsibilities and the way in which the elements fit together determine the organization's overall effectiveness. Individual OD initiatives should be linked to the business's overall strategy and objectives.

OD is a huge topic. An in-depth discussion could fill many volumes. This chapter begins by briefly discussing the broad charter of OD and presents various OD processes that effectively facilitate change and growth within a company. It describes typical OD project objectives and benefits and representative steps in project scoping, planning, and execution and describes several of the basic OD tools.

§ 2.02 WHAT IS ORGANIZATION DEVELOPMENT?

OD is a major element of the HR strategic planning process. In *Organizational Development: A Process of Learning and Changing* (Addison Wesley, 1987), W. Warner Burke defined OD as "a planned process of change in an organization's culture through the utilization of behavioral science, technologies, research and theory...." In 1969, Professor Warren Bennis of the University of Southern California's Marshall School of Business defined OD as "a response to change, a complex educational strategy intended to change the beliefs, attitudes, values, and structure of organizations so they can better adapt to new technologies, markets, and challenges, and the dizzying rate of change itself." Although there is no universally accepted definition, it is clear that OD is focused on change management.

The primary purpose of OD is to increase the effectiveness of the organization and improve problem solving and adaptability by identifying processes or behaviors that help or hinder growth and development. OD attempts to increase employee awareness, participation, and influence at an individual level, with the overall goal of better integrating individual and organizational goals. Inherent in ensuring that the organization's employees, systems, and processes remain in alignment is the ability to effectively anticipate and manage change. Thus, the major characteristics of OD are:

- Planned change—Systematic, organized, specific

- Comprehensive change—Involves total organization or an identifiable unit

- Emphasis on work groups—Mostly aimed at groups, not individuals; tends toward a "sociological flavor"

- Long-term change—May take months or years for full acceptance; not a quick fix

- Participation of change—Usually involves outside "third party" to address sensitive agent issues

- Emphasis on intervention—Results in active intervention in ongoing activities; change or action research agent is involved in hands-on implementation of change activities

Exhibit 2.1 shows various tools used to gauge the alignment of each major element to the vision, values, and mission of the organization. (There are many effective tools and techniques beyond those specifically described herein and which the reader is encouraged to explore.)

[A]   Indicators of Need for OD

It is possible to directly or indirectly identify the need for an OD study by observing one or more of the following symptoms, each of which may be an indication of an organization problem:

- Lack of key organization documents such as organization charts and position descriptions

- Organization resistance to change and new ideas

- High turnover of personnel

- Lack of clearly defined position duties, responsibilities, and reporting relationships

- Lack of a succession plan or shortage of leadership skills

- Requests for review by regulatory authorities/agencies

- Confusion regarding management roles and accountability

- Lack of clearly defined organization goals and objectives

- Difficulty managing the growth of the business

- Addition of new products, services, or locations or acquisition of other entities

- Low organization performance or profitability

[B]   OD Project Objectives

An overall organization planning and evaluation study is generally conducted for the following purposes:

- To analyze and assess the company's mission, objectives, goals, and key strategies vis-à-vis the overall strategic direction and priorities of the organization, and to determine the extent of the match with day-to-day practices, systems, and policies

- To analyze and evaluate the existing organization structure

- To assess the capabilities of managerial and key nonmanagerial personnel

- To analyze the roles and responsibilities performed within the organization as a whole or within selected functional areas

- To evaluate alternative structures and appropriate alignment within the organization relative to its vision, mission, and key strategies

- To develop recommendations related to other areas where management and organizational change are needed, in addition to revising functional and position requirements as needed

- To develop planning tools to assist the client with implementing the revised organization structure, management and staff changes, and other recommended organization improvements

The most critical systems that must be coordinated to facilitate effective organization change are performance management systems, reward systems, and information systems.

§ 2.03 FORMS OF OD

Organization planning and evaluation can take many forms but typically involve one of the following three levels of the organization: top management, departmental, or total organization.

[A] Top Management Study

A study of top management is an analysis of roles and duties performed at a top, or "summary," level to determine the functions that should be included in the organization and the relative emphasis they should receive. The intent of such a study is to develop recommendations relative to broad functional content within, and relationships between, all management positions down to a selected level of management, and to develop a plan indicating the sequence of steps necessary to ensure an orderly transition from the present to the proposed structure.

A top management study is very general, having as its primary objective the simplification and clarification of top management positions, and their responsibilities and relationships.

[B] Supplementary or Departmental Study

A departmental study typically encompasses the following:

- Analysis of roles and responsibilities in terms of required functions and emphasis in specific areas or departments of the organization

- Development of recommendations related to the functional content within, and relationships between, all positions within the department or function

- Development of a plan indicating the sequence of all steps necessary to ensure an orderly transition from the present to the proposed structure, phased in both time and content with the operating changes recommended by some other study if appropriate

Such a study might be either summary or detailed but would be limited to designated areas of the total structure.

[C] Total Organization Study

A total organization study would include the following:

- Analysis of the needs of the total organization in terms of required functions and relative emphasis of each

- Analysis of the needs of the organization in terms of organizational relationships and management tools necessary for achieving motivation and coordination throughout (e.g., procedure and policy manual, performance evaluation, business planning process, or information systems)

- Development of recommendations related to the functional content within and relationships between all major positions, committees, and teams

- Development of recommendations related to statements of objectives, standards of managerial performance, planning and budgeting tools, and policies and procedures

- Development of a plan indicating the sequence of all steps necessary to ensure an orderly transition from the present to the proposed structure, and involving plans for the development of objectives, standards, plans, budgets, policies, and procedures appropriate to the proposed structure

A total organization study goes a step beyond providing an organization structure for accomplishing work. It includes providing some of the incentives and tools that are also necessary to help manage the organization and meet the organization's goals.

Almost regardless of scope, OD planning projects are process-oriented and integrative in nature because they require the following:

- Identification or development of company goals and objectives

- Assessment of organization strengths and weaknesses

- Recognition of business strategy

- Evaluation of functional needs and capabilities

- Assessment of management talent and processes

§ 2.04   THE BENEFITS OF OD

The benefits to companies undertaking OD often include the following:

- More clearly defined strategic direction, company goals, and objectives

- An orderly, well-planned analysis of alternative organization structures

- Identification of functional areas and activities that need to be added and/or emphasized

- Appraisal of personnel capabilities relative to present and future organization needs

- Recommendations regarding present, interim, and proposed organization changes such as changes in reporting relationships, the need for new positions, the need for new people skills, redefined job positions, increased emphasis in certain activity areas, or changes in levels of authority

- Recommendations regarding strategic alignment of the major elements of organizational effectiveness

- Improved communications within the organization

- Initiation of organizational changes needed to improve performance and help achieve profitable growth

- Participation in an organization development process

[A] Demonstrating the Measurable Value of OD

For OD initiatives to achieve their potential, the recommendations to conduct the OD study must be tied directly to the company's business goals. The HR department can increase management's understanding and support for OD by clearly demonstrating to executives the business rationale for the recommendations and how success will be measured. Thus, the OD initiatives guidance document must delineate specific goals and strategies for achieving the results expected and must link each initiative to the company's strategic plan and goals.

Creating demonstrable linkage between the strategic plan, individual OD initiatives, and measurable results is somewhat of a paradigm shift in traditional HR management. In the past, HR managers tended to view such activities as a series of isolated initiatives, and wrote goals with words like "increase," "improve," and "reduce," without a solid target or number attached. Within HR, the perception that many aspects of HR are not measurable persists. This mindset must change if HR managers are to effectively present the benefits of OD planning and its implementation.

In addition, it is critical to measure the "right" results. For example, if an organization initiates changes that result in reducing from 20 to 10 the number of employees taking customer calls at a call center, it has achieved a decrease; however, did the organization measure the impact of such reduction on the quality of customer service? How does the organization know if the staff decrease has helped it or hurt it? The measurements must account for actual success in achieving the business goal. Even the traditionally "softer" goals, such as improved employee morale, are quantifiable. A well-drafted employee attitude survey should provide statistical data concerning specific aspects of employee morale.

Business managers are driven by numbers and results. For OD to be accepted as part of the overall process of managing a business, the deliverables must be quantifiable. Any initiatives recommended by HR must provide meaningful cost-benefit analysis and clearly measurable outcomes. Incomplete or erroneous data can sideline HR from assuming a strategic position in the organization.

[B] OD Planning in Relation to the HR Strategic Plan

It is important to understand that OD planning exists within the HR strategic plan; there are not two plans. Interlacing OD goals, objectives, and expected measurable outcomes within the HR strategic plan helps ensure that HR considers the impact of changes on the whole organization. A word of caution: industry averages should not be used to quantify the expected results. Every company is unique, and HR needs to know the numbers for its own company to be able to develop legitimate goals.

To ensure that HR considers all key issues prior to the recommendation of an OD initiative, it is important to have the plan reviewed by key persons outside the HR function. One of the most essential departments that HR works with is finance. The finance department is a key resource, so it should be part of the planning team right from the beginning. Finance personnel are trained to accurately estimate costs and quantify and qualify outcomes. Their support is essential for obtaining management's support for OD recommendations. Depending on the organization, other departments may be equally key.

This holistic planning approach helps build key management support, eliminates surprises, and reduces uncertainty about the strategy and success of the OD initiatives.

§ 2.05   PLANNING AN OD PROJECT

OD planning may be done formally or fairly informally, depending on the needs and sophistication of the organization. OD projects can vary greatly in scope while remaining conceptually similar. The actual size of the project needed to accomplish the objective may be difficult to define at the outset. It is possible that even a modest change in project objectives can significantly modify the time and resources required for the project's completion. Thus, in-depth initial project planning is very critical. Careful definition of the project's scope and objectives will allow the HR manager to establish realistic expectations for senior management in terms of time, cost, and expected outcome. The definition of project scope will also allow the HR manager to determine at the beginning whether to handle the project internally or bring in outside assistance.

The major factors contributing to the size and scope of an OD project are the following:

- *Size and complexity of the organization.* The more complex an organization, the larger potential scope of an OD project. A complex organization structure is defined as an organization with (1) multiple business entities, (2) multiple operating locations, and/or (3) a broad geographic distribution. The number of divisions and related subsidiaries and an organization's ownership structure significantly affect the number of positions and levels in that organization. Extensive product or service offerings affect the number of organization levels.

- *Level of the organization structure analyzed.* The level of the organization structure analyzed affects the complexity of the overall project inasmuch as higher job levels in an organization typically have more diversified responsibilities and reporting relationships.

- *Orientation of the project to overall organization needs or an individual function.* In most cases, variations in overall needs and needs of an individual function (e.g., accounting, manufacturing) will affect the scope of the project more from the time required to complete than from the conceptual standpoint.

- *Number of positions analyzed and evaluated.* The number of positions analyzed and evaluated directly impacts the estimated time required for data collection and analysis. Similarly, the number of positions analyzed impacts the amount of time needed to develop project documents.

- *Required technical capabilities.* HR managers may not possess the requisite expertise and qualifications for conducting organization planning. When the technical capabilities to conduct OD are lacking internally, consultants must be brought in, adding significantly to project expenses.

- *Identification of critical issues.* It is important to identify in advance any critical issues affecting the company's ownership, management, and industry that should receive special attention during the project.

§ 2.06   SELECTING THE PROJECT LEADER

Ideally, only experienced HR practitioners should be in charge of OD projects because of the extensive cross-functional, top management involvement necessary to successfully undertake OD planning and evaluation. Similarly, the process-intensive nature of OD projects requires that experienced personnel conduct the data-gathering interviews.

Often, the OD project leader is the company's HR manager (or top HR officer). If an HR manager does not possess the requisite skills, however, consultants should be brought in. In working with the consultants, the HR manager or other officer will gain valuable experience for the future. A third party can be particularly effective when a study touches on sensitive issues that require full and impartial exploration.

The criteria for selection of an OD project leader are as follows:

1. The leader should be comfortable working in ambiguous situations and be able to work with large amounts of qualitative information.

2. The leader must be seen as being objective and fair, not simply a representative of senior management. He or she should be able to deal effectively with "politically sensitive" feedback and should be recognized for his or her ability to maintain confidentiality and objectivity. The project leader must be seen as a change agent, capable of helping to facilitate the more challenging aspects of the change process.

3. The project leader must be qualified to envision what steps are necessary in the present to meet the challenges presented in the future, so he or she can draw valid conclusions, make recommendations, and draft guidance documents. He or she must be able to analyze the gap between the current status of the organization's structure, processes, information system, skills, and experience and the status required to meet the future business objectives driving the planning process. For example, if a company wants to add a new line of business, the OD project leader must consider factors such as numbers of new employees needed, levels of education, required skills, specialized training, language fluency, department structure, division location, and other issues related to managing growth.

§ 2.07   CONDUCTING AN OD PROJECT

An OD planning and evaluation project normally involves the following series of major work steps, with various checkpoints for management to make decisions regarding organization structure, new policies and procedures, and implementation.

[A]   Determining Project Scope

Clarify the goals and objectives of the project. Define the size of the project, including the organization level and positions to be reviewed. Determine if outside assistance is needed; this can often be determined by the perceived sensitivity of the issues to be discussed. Review of very sensitive issues often benefits from outside involvement. Obtain management approval to proceed.

[B]   Data Collection

It is important to collect all available documents, which may include:

- Detailed company, division/subsidiary, and departmental organization charts

- Position descriptions for all departmental positions

- Past organization charts depicting changes in organization structure

- Any special company-wide or departmental organization studies for the last five years

- Company personnel manual

- Company policy and procedures manual

- Departmental procedures manual

- Company strategic plan, including statements of mission, vision, values, objectives, and goals

- Company wage and salary administration plan and performance evaluation program

- Basic information on current departmental employees, including length of service, positions held, age, compensation levels, and classification

[C] Obtaining Direct Feedback

The data collection process encompasses obtaining direct feedback from employees and, in some cases, customers. Data collection tools that a company might use include employee surveys, position description questionnaires, organization needs assessment surveys, and situation analysis forms. These tools can assist in assessing group and individual perceptions of key issues such as quality of leadership, organizational climate, and overall satisfaction with the company. The research data requirements must be identified. The project leader must determine, for example, whether comparative industry data are relevant and, if they are, determine the methods of obtaining them.

[D] Conducting Interviews

Conduct personal interviews with senior managers and other key personnel. Before initiating such interviews, a schedule should be prepared and a consistent project introduction for participating employees drafted. During the interviews, discuss with management the business strategy, company goals and objectives, vision, values, and corporate mission. Determine the consistency and clarity of the interviewees' awareness of the vision, mission, objectives, and goals.

Document each interviewee's perception of his or her department, job function and major responsibilities, reporting relationships (both formal and informal), key aspects or duties of the position that are not performed, how his or her position has changed or is changing, and problems associated with the job, the department, or the organization as a whole.

The OD project leader should also develop a summarized personal evaluation of the interviewee's background, capabilities, insights, and experience as soon as possible after the interview while the conversation is still fresh in his or her mind.

[E] Assessing the Data

The data gathered must be analyzed, and critical issues and needs must be determined. The project leader should identify the strengths and weaknesses of the organization, critical organization issues and needs, and areas where the perceptions, roles, and functions are out of strategic alignment. In addition, management and nonmanagement positions must be analyzed.

[F] Preparing Recommendations

The OD project leader prepares preliminary recommendations for short- and long-term organization structure, prioritizes the recommendations, and reviews them with management. While plan recommendations vary greatly from project to project, at a minimum they include a revised organization structure and summaries of major job responsibilities for positions being analyzed, including management and linear responsibility charts. It is useful to illustrate the current organization charts and position responsibilities along with the recommended changes.

[G] Implementation

Results of the OD study are presented to participants and all affected employees, and implementation of the recommendations begins.

[H] Additional Projects

A number of subprojects can arise from an OD study that are especially sensitive and time-consuming or require specialized expertise. Examples include succession planning, executive search, management assessment, strategic planning, change management, reengineering, operations planning, information technology, and technical assistance in HR processes such as development of compensation structures.

§ 2.08 OD PROJECT SUCCESS DETERMINANTS

Following are the key project management points to consider in undertaking an OD project:

- Successful completion of OD projects is as dependent upon good communications and extensive cross-functional involvement as it is upon the ultimate technical quality of the project.

- Effective strategic planning is not an individual effort—it needs teamwork. Cross-functional involvement builds organizationwide consensus and "ownership" of the final product.

- All affected employees need to be involved, even if on a superficial basis.

- Employee understanding of the need and likely benefits resulting from the project must be assured.

- Outside consultants should not make bottom-line recommendations regarding job assignments or terminations for specific people.

- The HR manager must have good interviewing skills, be prepared for interviews, and through the interviews gain the employees' confidence to assure the collection of valid data.

- The HR manager must maintain a sufficiently broad perspective on the organization's business situation and origination needs to permit effective analysis and evaluation.

- The evaluation process should not occur only at the end of a project; continued analysis and formulation of ideas throughout the course of a project are critical to the development of successful recommendations.

§ 2.09 DECLINING AN OD PROJECT

By its nature OD work creates an expectation of change. Thus, the goals and objectives of the project should be geared to match management's level of commitment to change. Corporate top management must be closely involved and fully supportive of an OD project for it to succeed. If the organizational culture is such that business risk and organizational change are approached with caution, it will necessarily have an impact on the speed and the degree to which the company is willing to implement the project's final recommendations. An OD project should be performed only when top management is enthusiastically committed to supporting the project and implementing the outcome.

The HR manager is also advised to evaluate senior management's reasons for embarking on an OD study. If the HR manager determines that the study is to be conducted for one of the following purposes, he or she is advised not to proceed with the project:

- To validate a conclusion already reached by top management or staff

- To rubber-stamp a finding or recommendation previously made

- To establish an excuse to terminate an employee or group of employees

The negative implications of proceeding under these circumstances are obvious. In some states, such as California, there may even be legal ramifications. *Constructive discharge* is established under certain circumstances when an organization uses subterfuge to cloud the real reasons for termination of an otherwise protected employee (i.e., one who is in a protected classification or has a contractual employment relationship with the company).

Exhibit 2.1
Basic Organization Development Tools

Chapter 3
Pay Practices

§ 3.01 AUDIT QUESTIONS

1. Are males and females in the company paid equally for equal work?

2. Do jobs classified as exempt in the company meet the revised (in 2004) exemption requirements?

3. Does the company correctly pay exempt employees on a salaried basis?

4. Does the company pay nonexempt employees time and a half for hours worked over 40 hours in a workweek?

5. Does the company pay nonexempt employees for noncommute travel time that is considered work time?

6. Has the company posted notices regarding minimum wage, overtime, equal pay, and child labor restrictions?

Note: Consistent "yes" answers to the above questions suggest that the organization is applying effective management practices and/or complying with federal regulations. "No" or "not sure" answers indicate that problem areas exist and should be addressed immediately.

This chapter reviews mandated benefits that relate to pay practices. Specific topics discussed include wage and hour laws governing minimum wage, tip income, overtime, company-required training and meetings outside of working hours, travel time, and equal pay.

Given the uncertain labor market, companies are trying to identify new and innovative approaches to compensating key employees. Whether a company is creating new compensation strategies, revising current strategies, or staying with the old strategies, it is important to regularly review the organization's pay practices in light of the law.

In 2004, the U.S. Department of Labor (DOL) published significant changes to the Fair Labor Standards Act of 1938 (FLSA), which governs many pay practices and is one of the more difficult laws with which to comply when seeking to create new and innovative compensation programs. To fully comprehend the scope of the FLSA and other laws affecting pay practices requires some study on the part of employers. This chapter attempts to provide an overview of the key aspects of pay practice compliance.

Before examining the specifics of the laws governing pay practices, it is important to understand the differences between the two types of pay discrimination:

1. *Valuation discrimination.* Relates to the pay that minorities and women receive for the jobs they perform. The Equal Pay Act of 1963 establishes that it is discriminatory to pay those in protected classes less than white males performing equal work (i.e., doing the same work and expected to produce the same results). This definition of pay discrimination is based on the standard of equal pay for equal work.

2. *Access discrimination.* Relates to the staffing and allocation decisions made by employers (e.g., recruiting, hiring, promoting, training, and laying off employees). Access discrimination denies particular jobs, promotions, or training opportunities to qualified applicants or employees in protected classes.

§ 3.02   THE EQUAL PAY ACT OF 1963

The Equal Pay Act, the first modern statute aimed at eliminating discrimination in the job market, and Title VII of the Civil Rights Act of 1964 are the two major laws prohibiting pay discrimination. Title VII prohibits employers from basing employment decisions (including decisions regarding pay) on race, color, creed, religion, or sex. In addition, the Equal Pay Act requires employers to examine equal jobs within their organizations to ensure that males and females performing those jobs are paid equally, based on equal skill, effort, responsibility, and working conditions. If a company pays men and women differently for the same work, the only way to justify those pay differences is under one of the following four affirmative defenses:

1. Seniority—rewarding length of service with an organization

2. Merit—rewarding individual competence and performance in a job

3. Incentive—rewarding quantity or quality of production, commissions, piece-rate systems, or goal-attainment systems

4. Factors other than gender—including shift differentials, experience, ability, temporary assignments, and bona fide training programs (programs established either formally or informally covering a

specific course of activity for a defined period of time, systematically applied in a nondiscriminatory manner, and communicated to all covered employees)

In recent years, factors other than gender (e.g., ability, training, and work experience) have been interpreted as a broad exception that could include business reasons advanced by the employer. Because the courts have not provided legal clarification of this notion, however, the definition of *factors other than gender* is still somewhat clouded, although pay differences for equal work opportunity can be justified for demonstrated business-related reasons.

In *Warren v. Solo Cup Co.*, [516 F.3d 627 (7th Cir. 2008)] the court concluded that education and job skills could be a rationale for higher pay, even if those factors were not required for the job. A woman tool crib attendant was paid less than a male in the same position, even though she had worked for the company longer. She had a high school education and marginal computer skills, while her fellow employee had multiple advanced degrees and excellent computer skills. The appeals court noted that even if these factors are not included in a job description, employers may consider these skills when making compensation decisions.

Although the law seems simple on the surface, its provisions have had to be clarified in a number of court cases, especially the definition of *equal*. The following paragraphs attempt to present the issues involved in determining what is considered equal work within the scope of the law.

[A] Equal Work

After years of judicial indecision, guidelines for defining work were established in a 1970 case, *Schultz v. Wheaton Glass Co.* [421 F.2d 259 (3d Cir. 1970)]. Those guidelines are still used today. In *Schultz*, the court ruled that the equal work standard required only that jobs be substantially, not identically, equal. Furthermore, it ruled that the occasional extra duties performed by the men in this case did not justify their being paid 10 percent more than the women were paid. Thus, "substantially equal work" has become the basis for determining whether jobs are equal.

In addition, the courts have generally held that the actual work performed is the appropriate information to use when reaching a decision on whether jobs are substantially equal. This rule was established in several cases in which the duties that employees fulfilled differed from those in the written job descriptions.

[B] The Four Components of Equal Work

The DOL provides the following definitions of the four components of work:

1. *Skill.* Experience, training, education, and ability as measured by the performance requirements of a particular job

2. *Mental or physical effort.* The amount or degree, not type, of effort expended in the performance of a job

3. *Responsibility.* The degree of accountability required in the performance of a job

4. *Working conditions.* The physical surroundings and hazards of a job, including such factors as inside versus outside work, heat, cold, noise, and poor ventilation

To support a claim of unequal work, an employer must prove that the following conditions exist:

- The level of skill, effort, and responsibility is substantially greater in one of the jobs being compared.

- The tasks involving the extra skill, effort, and responsibility consume a significant amount of time for all employees whose additional wages are in question.

- The extra skill, effort, and responsibility have a value commensurate with the questioned pay differential, as determined by the employer's own evaluation.

A subsequent court ruling held that shift differentials are not illegal. However, if differentials are paid, the employer must clearly state that the purpose is to compensate workers for unusual conditions, and the extra pay must be separate from the base wage for the job.

[C] Reverse Discrimination

Several cases have dealt with the issue of reverse discrimination against men when pay for women is adjusted. In these cases, men have claimed that, simply because they were men, they were paid less than women doing similar work. In one case, the University of Nebraska created a model to calculate salaries on the basis of values estimated for a faculty member's education, field of specialization, years of direct experience, years of related experience, and merit. Based on these qualifications, the university granted raises to approximately 30 women whose salaries were less than the amount computed by the model. However, the university did not grant such increases to more than 90 men whose salaries were also below the amount the model set for them on the basis of their qualifications. The court declared this system a violation of the Equal Pay Act. It held that the university was, in effect, using a new system to determine a salary schedule based on specific criteria; to refuse to pay employees of one gender the minimum required by these criteria was illegal.

In another case, the male faculty of Northern Illinois University (NIU) sued to have a model the university had developed to adjust female faculty salaries applied to male faculty as well. This case differs from that involving the University of Nebraska in that the regional civil rights office had found reasonable cause to believe that the university was discriminating against the female faculty. Instead of disputing this finding, the university sought to correct the salary differences on the basis of a model similar to the one used at the University of Nebraska. However, the NIU model was used to allocate a one-time salary adjustment to correct the results of past discrimination against women. The model was not used to make a permanent change in the compensation system. The court ruled that it did not have to be applied to men. In contrast, the Nebraska salary model was not designed to correct past discrimination; it was a new way of calculating salaries and therefore had to be applied to all faculty members equally.

With respect to compensation management, court decisions, when viewed collectively, have provided reasonably clear directions. The design of pay systems must incorporate a policy of equal pay for substantially equal work. The determination of substantially equal work must be based on the actual work performed and must reflect the skill, effort, and responsibility required of employees and working conditions.

It is legal to pay men and women who perform substantially equal work differently if the pay system is designed to recognize, in a nondiscriminatory manner, differences in performance, seniority, quantity and quality of results, or certain factors other than gender. Furthermore, to minimize the possibility of reverse discrimination suits, if a new pay system is designed, it must be applied equally to all employees. On the other hand, if a one-time adjustment is made to correct past inequities, it need only apply to the affected group.

Employers must not be complacent about discrimination in dissimilar jobs (i.e., jobs that are not substantially equal). For example, if almost all female employees in Company A work in one job classification—office and clerical—and the employer grants cost-of-living increases semiannually to employees in all job classes except those in office and clerical, because jobs in that classification are not substantially equal to jobs in other classifications, the Equal Pay Act does not apply. Nevertheless, the office and clerical employee group can still charge Company A with pay discrimination under Title VII of the Civil Rights Act, which prohibits discrimination on the basis of race, color, sex, religion, or national origin in any employment condition, including hiring, firing, promotion, transfer, compensation, and admission to training programs. Title VII was later amended to expand coverage to include private employers of more than 15 persons. The pregnancy amendment of 1978 made it illegal to discriminate on the basis of pregnancy, childbirth, or related conditions.

§ 3.03   FEDERAL WAGE AND HOUR LAWS

Enacted in 1938, the FLSA is administered by the DOL's Wage and Hour Division. The statute governs the procedural aspects of paying employees, sets overtime pay and minimum wage requirements, and sets standards for recordkeeping and child labor. Although the FLSA has been revised several times, its provisions often seem out of date compared with modern-day employment practices. However, significant changes to the overtime exemption rules were made in 2004. (See discussion of these changes at **Sections 3.03[H] and 3.03[I]**.)

A company is subject to the FLSA if it:

1. Produces or handles goods for interstate commerce

2. Met one of the following criteria before April 1, 1990:

   a. Engaged in retail or service business with gross annual sales of $362,500

   b. Conducted other business with gross annual sales of $250,000

   c. Was a construction or cleaning company, a hospital, a certain health care institution, a school, or a government agency

3. Did not exist before April 1, 1990, or did not meet the previous criteria—or, if it did, it had gross annual sales of at least $500,000

Certain classifications of employees are not subject to federal minimum wage requirements; they are called exempt employees. Exempt employees are not eligible for overtime pay. Employees who are subject to federal minimum wage requirements are nonexempt employees; they are eligible for overtime pay. The remaining sections of this chapter discuss child labor, minimum wage, overtime, and provisions relating to exempt and nonexempt employees.

[A] Child Labor

Under the FLSA, employers are allowed to hire children under age 18, but many restrictions determine the type of work they can do and the hours they are allowed to work. In addition, state laws regulate child labor. Employers should be familiar with both federal and state laws, because they must follow the more stringent set. For example, if children are allowed to work until 9:00 P.M. under the federal law, but only until 7:00 P.M. under the state law, state law applies because it is more stringent.

Unless otherwise exempt, minors may not be paid less than the statutory minimum wage (see **Section 3.03[D]**). Minors also must be paid overtime, as appropriate.

The DOL has released a proposal to update the FLSA regulations governing the employment of teenage workers. The key proposals provide restrictions on the types of hazardous jobs available to teenagers, such as fighting forest fires, riding on forklifts as passengers, and loading and operating non-paper products balers and compactors. The proposals would expand opportunities for 14- to 15-year olds in certain areas such as information technologies, but also prohibit them from door-to-door sales. The DOL requested comments on the proposed regulations by July 16, 2007. As of this writing, no further action has been taken. For current information, including comments received as well as proposed regulations, visit the Web site *www.youthrules.dol.gov*. Current occupational restrictions can be found in the Code of Federal Regulations, Title 29, Part 570, Subpart E.

In other recent legislative action, the Genetic Information Nondiscrimination Act, passed May 21, 2008, amends Section 16(e) of the FLSA. For each violation of the child labor laws that results in the death or serious injury to an employee under age 18, the employer may be assessed $50,000.

The DOL's Wage and Hour Division has produced a self-assessment tool for non-agricultural employers to gage compliance with FLSA's youth employment provisions. This checklist can be accessed at *www. youthrules.dol.gov*.

[B] Minimum Wage

The FLSA established a minimum wage rate that must be paid to nonexempt employees for each hour worked. *Minimum wage* is defined as a gross hourly wage before deductions. Although the law establishes a minimum wage, it does not set maximums. Any business that is involved in interstate commerce, regardless of its revenue size, is subject to the FLSA.

The federal minimum wage increased to $6.55 per hour on July 24, 2008, and will increase to $7.25 per hour on July 24, 2009.

Each state may set its own minimum wage requirements, which may be higher or lower than the federal government's. An employer must determine which law to follow; if the federal and state rates differ, an employer must use the higher standard. For example, if ABC Company's state minimum wage is $6.75 per hour and ABC is subject to both federal and state law, ABC must pay its employees $6.75 per hour rather than the current federal minimum wage of $6.55 per hour. In a state that has a minimum wage of $6.15 per hour, a company that is subject to both federal and state law must pay the federal rate of $6.55 per hour. That company may pay the lower state minimum wage if it does not meet the minimum requirements of the FLSA.

In addition to state minimum wages, cities may also pass minimum wage or living wage laws. Minimum wage laws generally apply to all employees who work in that city, while living wage laws are typically required for those who work on specific government (e.g., city) contracts.

In September 2005, the California Superior Court made the first class action living wage decision in the country. [Amaral v. Cintas Corp., Cal. Super. Ct. C.A. No. HG03 103046, 2005] Cintas Corp. had a contract with the City of Hayward to clean city uniforms. The City of Hayward stipulates as part of their contracts that workers will be paid, at minimum, a specific wage. Cintas paid the workers the living wage for hours worked on the contract, but not for other work performed. A class of 219 workers filed suit, claiming that Cintas had violated the City of Hayward ordinance. The court in this case held that those employees that worked on the city contract should be paid the living wage for all hours worked. Other employees who did not work on the city contract did not need to be paid the living wage. Back wages and interest totaled $1.1 million.

Companies must be aware of the minimum wage requirements of the states and the cities in which they are located (see **Appendix 3-A**), as well as any other state, county, or city regulations that affect pay.

[C]   Alternatives to Paying Employees on an Hourly Basis

Some employees are not paid on an hourly basis; they may be paid instead for piecework or by commission. When an employee is not paid on an hourly basis, the employer should compute the employee's total wages for the workweek and divide this amount by the number of hours worked during that week to determine an average hourly wage. This rate should be compared with the required minimum wage, and, if it is below the minimum, the employer must make up the difference. For example, if an employee who is paid 60 cents for each piece completes 400 pieces in a 40-hour workweek, the company's calculation is $0.60 times 400 equals $240, and $240 divided by 40 hours equals $6 per hour. If the company is subject to federal minimum wage requirements, it is required to pay the employee an additional $0.55 per hour for the 40 hours worked in that week.

Under federal law, tipped employees, such as wait staff, are defined as employees who customarily receive more than $30 per month in tips. The employer may meet federal minimum wage requirements by paying a basic wage and add that to the tips employees receive from customers. Employers must provide a minimum cash wage of $2.13 an hour to tipped employees. If the employer does combine basic wages and tips, it must be sure the employee is notified in advance and that the employee is receiving at least the minimum wage when basic wages and tips are combined. Many states have a maximum amount in tips that can be applied against minimum wage requirements. The company should be aware of such requirements within the state.

Federal law states that minimum wage need not be paid in cash; it may be paid through board, lodging, meals, or other facilities furnished by the employer for the benefit of the employee. The company should take note of state requirements that may specify exact amounts that may be deducted.

[D]   Subminimum Wages

Under federal law, three categories or types of workers may be paid a wage lower than the required minimum wage of $6.55 per hour: (1) apprentices; (2) workers with disabilities; and (3) students. The below-minimum-wage rate is usually calculated as a percentage of the federal minimum rate, typically 50 percent to 85 percent. The employer must first obtain a special certificate from the DOL's Wage and

Hour Division in its area before paying this rate. Some states have restrictions regarding subminimum wages for minors, learners, or apprentices, and some restrict the length of time that subminimum wages can be paid. The company usually must obtain approval from the state's labor department.

[E]   Overtime

The law says that the workweek consists of 40 hours and requires companies to pay overtime to an employee at one and one-half times the employee's regular rate of pay whenever he or she works more than 40 hours in a week (see **Section [F]** Regular Rate of Pay below). The FLSA does not require that overtime be paid for hours worked in excess of 8 hours per day or on weekends or holidays. Some state laws, on the other hand, may provide workers with greater overtime protection.

A workweek consists of seven consecutive 24-hour periods and need not coincide with the calendar week. The workweek may begin on any day and at any hour of the day that the employer chooses, but it must begin and end at the same time, on the same day each week. Employers may change their definition of the workweek as long as the change is permanent and is not done to evade the overtime requirements of the law. Each workweek stands alone and cannot be averaged over a period of several weeks. If, for example, a nonexempt employee works 30 hours one week and 50 hours the next, the company cannot consider this as an average of 40 hours a week and avoid the payment of overtime.

In hospitals, overtime may be computed on a 14-day basis, provided the hospital and the employee agree before performing the work. Time and one-half must be paid for all hours more than 8 in one day, or more than 80 in 14 days.

Overtime payments to employees can be made at the end of the next regular pay period. If the correct amount of overtime cannot be determined by that next regular pay period, the law allows it to be paid as soon after the next regular pay period as is practicable. Employees who are eligible for overtime payment are considered nonexempt (i.e., not exempt from the provisions of the FLSA).

The DOL has introduced a new on-line tool for calculating overtime pay, available to both employers and employees. The user inputs various factors including regular pay, shift differentials, commissions, hours worked, and method of paying employees, and the required overtime pay is calculated. It is available at *www.dol.gov/elaws.*

[F]   "Regular Rate" of Pay

For purposes of properly calculating overtime pay, the FLSA has defined an employee's "regular rate" of pay: "The regular hourly rate of pay of an employee is determined by dividing his total remuneration for employment (except statutory exclusions) in any workweek by the total number of hours actually worked by him in that workweek for which such compensation was paid." [29 C.F.R. § 778.109] The "regular rate" of pay includes bonuses, shift premiums, and incentives that are non-discretionary.

There are certain payments that do not need to be included in regular rate calculations. These "statutory exclusions" are found in Section 7(e) of the FLSA. In general, these are payments that are not dependent on the individual's hours worked, production, or efficiency. Specific exclusions include:

- Gifts, such as a holiday bonus

- Payments made for occasional periods when no work is performed due to vacation, holiday, illness or failure of the employer to provide sufficient work

- Reasonable expenses that are reimbursed by the employer for travel or purchasing work-related supplies

- Payments made to a third party for a bona fide retirement plan, or health or life insurance

- Extra compensation paid at a "premium rate," such as week-end pay, as long as it is paid at no less than time and one-half

- Value or income from employer-provided grants or rights provided through a stock option, stock appreciation right, or employee stock purchase plan meeting certain criteria.

For a complete list of exclusions, refer to the DOL website at *www.dol.gov/elaws*.

In spite of the detailed wording within the FLSA about what is and is not included in the "regular rate" of pay, there are many gray areas. Some issues have been raised in court cases, while others have been determined on an individual basis through DOL opinion letters.

For example, one recent case addressed the issue of including flex credits in calculating overtime. In *Abarca v. Manheim Services Corp.* [2007 U.S. Dist. LEXIS 4656 (N.D. Ill. Jan. 19, 2007)], the court determined that the employer's contribution of flex credits did not need to be added to the "regular rate" of pay because it fell into the exclusion for bona fide retirement, life, health insurance and similar plans.

In another example, the DOL determined in an opinion letter that the employer's "stay-on" bonuses (offered to encourage employees to remain at the company for a specific period of time) were non-discretionary and therefore needed to be included in the overtime calculation [FLSA 2005-47].

> **Example.** A non-exempt employee with a standard 40-hour workweek works 50 hours in one week. His base pay is $10 per hour. This week, he is given a production bonus of $50. To calculate his "regular rate" of pay, first determine total compensation before the overtime premium. Total compensation is calculated at 50 hours × $10 per hour = $500.00, plus $50 bonus equals **$550**. The "regular rate" of pay is total compensation divided by total hours worked, or $550 divided by 50 hours, or $11 per hour. The premium rate is one-half the "regular rate," or $5.50 per hour. The premium earned is $5.50 × 10 hours = **$55**. This employee's total pay for the week is $550 + $55 = $605.

[G] Waiving Rights to Overtime

Employees may not waive their rights to be compensated for overtime hours worked and may not agree to be paid a lower overtime rate than required by law. This means that covered employers are liable for any overtime payments to workers, even if the worker tells the employer that it is not necessary to pay him or her for overtime hours worked.

[H] Exempt Employees

The FLSA has defined certain occupations and industries that are exempt from the overtime provisions. Employees in these positions are commonly called exempt employees. Exempted are:

- White-collar workers (e.g., executives, professionals, administrators, or outside salespeople)

- Farm workers employed by employers using less than 500 "man days" in any quarter of the previous year

- Sea workers on foreign vessels or employees in fishing operations

- Employees of certain small newspapers

- Employees of certain amusement or recreational establishments

- Switchboard operators with small telephone companies

- Employees of certain small retail or service establishments

- Babysitters employed on a casual basis

- Companions

- Local seasonal harvesters under age 17

- Employees of gas stations with annual sales of less than $250,000

- Home workers making evergreen wreaths

- Live-in domestic workers and domestic workers not covered by the Social Security Act or employed more than 40 hours per week by one employer

- Motor vehicle sales and service personnel

- Employees of small loggers

- Employees of maple sapping companies

- Employees of certain country elevators

- Announcers and editors at certain small broadcast stations

- Employees of motor carriers, airlines, and railroads

- Taxi drivers

- Certain drivers and helpers on local delivery

- Movie theater employees

[I]   White Collar Exemptions

In April 2004, the DOL published new regulations for employers to use in determining exempt status. These "Fair Pay" rules, effective August 23, 2004, create new definitions and increase the salary level test for exemptions.

It is critical that employers conduct a thorough review of their exempt employee positions to ensure that they satisfy the new guidelines. The duties and responsibilities of the job, as well as the pay level, determine whether a position is exempt. (See **Exhibit 3.1** for a checklist identifying workers who may qualify for exemption from overtime pay.)

Five work categories fall into the "white collar" exemptions. Historically, a position had to satisfy both a "short test" and a "long test" to qualify as exempt. The new rules establish one standard test for each exemption.

In addition to the "duties" test discussed below, employees in all categories, except outside sales, must be paid a minimum salary to be classified as exempt. To be considered exempt, an employee must be paid at least $455 per week. This amount is considerably larger than the prior minimum salary requirements: $155 per week for executive and administrative employees and $170 per week for professionals.

The Fair Pay rules establish a new definition of *primary duty*. Prior to the change, an exempt employee could spend no more than 20 percent of his or her time on nonexempt duties. Under the current regulation, *primary duty* is defined as the employee's "main, major, or most important duty." An employee must now spend at least 50 percent of his or her time on exempt duties to qualify for a white collar exemption.

[1] Executive Work

Work that qualifies for exemption under the executive category must meet the following requirements:

- The work involves, as a primary duty, the management of an enterprise or a recognized department or subdivision.

- The work involves supervision of two or more employees.

- The work includes hiring and firing, or effectively recommending decisions to hire and fire.

[2] Professional Work

Work that qualifies for exemption under the professional category must meet the following requirements:

Learned Professional

- The work requires advanced scientific, academic, or other specialized knowledge that is typically gained through a prolonged course of specific instruction and study and not from general academic education.

- The work requires consistent exercise of discretion and judgment.

- The work is primarily intellectual in character.

Creative Professional

- The work must be original and creative in character in a recognized artistic field, and its result must depend on invention, imagination, or talent.

[3] Administrative Work

Work that qualifies for exemption under the administrative category must meet the following requirements:

- The work involves, as a primary duty, the performance of office or nonmanual work directly related to management policies or general business operations, or it must be performed in the administration of a school system, educational establishment or institution, and be directly related to academic instruction or training.

- The work regularly involves the exercise of discretion and independent judgment.

[4] Outside Sales

Outside sales employees are exempt from overtime requirements if they meet the following requirements:

- They are employed to make sales or obtain orders from customers for services to be performed by others, rather than to service or deliver products.

- They regularly work away from the employer's place of business.

[5] Computer Professionals

Computer professionals are exempt from overtime if they meet the following requirements:

- They have as primary duties work that involves systems analysis techniques and procedures; user systems design, development, or testing; and/or operating systems design, development, or testing.

- They are paid on a salary basis, or not less than $27.63 per hour if not paid on a salary basis.

[6] Other Categories

In addition to the categories of workers described in the preceding sections, the following categories of individuals may receive an exempt classification:

- *Business Owners.* An individual must own at least 20 percent of the business and be actively engaged in the management of the company to be classified as exempt.

- *Highly Compensated Employees.* Employees who earn $100,000 or more per year and regularly perform at least one of the exempt duties outlined in the executive, professional, or administrative categories may be classified as exempt. They must also meet the weekly salary level and salary status tests.

When determining whether a job meets the above exemptions, it is helpful to understand how the DOL approaches exemptions. In reviewing a position, the DOL assumes that the job falls within the scope of the law; thus, the incumbent(s) would receive the FLSA's protection (i.e., be classified as nonexempt). The burden is on the employer to prove that the position meets the exemption requirements.

Many employees mistakenly associate an exempt position with status or prestige. Such an association makes the FLSA classification an employee relations and political issue instead of a government-mandated approach to paying employees. Managers must understand and represent jobs in the company accurately, or risk making erroneous classifications under the FLSA as well as having personal liability. They must apply strictly the definitions of exempt and nonexempt employees and not allow cultural influences to play a role in the job classification decision.

[J] Paying Employees on a Salary Basis

Employees who qualify for exemption under the executive, professional, administrative, and highly compensated employee categories of the FLSA must be paid on a salaried basis. The level of fixed compensation is a predetermined amount that is paid each pay period, regardless of the number of days or hours worked by the employee. Under the federal guidelines, teachers and those practicing law and medicine are not subject to the salary basis requirement. Computer professionals must be compensated either on a salary basis or paid no less than $27.63 per hour.

An employer's decision to pay an employee on a salaried basis does not automatically make that employee exempt from overtime under the FLSA. For example, a secretary may be paid a salary of $550 per week but is still considered nonexempt under the law. The company must pay time and one-half for all hours worked over 40 in a workweek, and the company must maintain FLSA-required records. Overtime is calculated by dividing the salaried rate by 40 hours to determine an hourly equivalent: $550 divided by 40 equals $13.75 per hour. This secretary would earn $20.63 per hour ($13.75 × 1.5) for all hours worked over 40 per week. An hourly rate for a tipped employee is calculated by adding actual weekly earnings to the tip credit, and dividing that number by the hours worked. Overtime pay is computed at one and one-half times that hourly rate for all hours worked over 40 per week.

Exemption status may be at risk if an employer withholds pay in increments of less than a full day. For example, the company may not withhold pay for an absence of less than a day for illness, personal reasons, jury duty, or temporary military leave. Employers, however, may withhold pay without jeopardizing an employee's exemption status for the following reasons:

- Absence of a full day for personal reasons other than sickness or accident

- Absence of a day or more for sickness or disability, if part of a bona fide plan providing wage replacement benefits

- Penalties for violating major, life-threatening safety rules

- Initial and final weeks of employment

- Absence under the Family and Medical Leave Act (FMLA)

- Disciplinary suspensions of one or more days if following a written policy

The Fair Pay rules include regulations regarding pay deductions. An employer that practices improper deductions may lose the exemption for all employees in the same position classification reporting to the same manager. However, the regulations also provide for a "safe harbor." If the improper deductions are inadvertent, the exemption will not be lost if the employer (1) has a clearly communicated policy that prohibits improper deductions, including a complaint procedure; (2) reimburses the affected employees; and (3) does not continue the improper deductions going forward.

Despite past rulings by the Wage and Hour Division allowing employers to require employees to substitute paid leave for the above-listed absences without losing their exemption for that week, the courts have not been unanimous in decisions on this issue. The DOL has confirmed that such deductions from bona fide benefit plans are permissible. The basis of the ruling is that such substitutions (i.e., of accumulated leave time for compensation) result in the exempt employee receiving payment in an amount equal to his or her guaranteed salary.

[K] Defining Hours Worked

Employers are required to pay nonexempt employees for time spent for the benefit of the employer, or working time, even if such time was not specifically requested. Nonexempt employees must be compensated at their regular hourly rate for such time or at overtime rates if the employee has worked more than 40 hours in the workweek. Examples of activities that are generally considered to constitute working time are:

- Break or rest periods of 20 minutes or less

- Meal periods of less than 30 minutes, or if the employee is unable to leave his or her work area

- On-call waiting time if the employee's freedom is restricted (e.g., an employee required to stay on the company's premises)

- On-duty waiting time if such waiting is required by the employer (e.g., a machine operator waiting for his or her machine to be repaired)

- Travel time from one location or job site to another during the workday

- Changing clothes or cleaning up, if it is necessary to performance on the job (e.g., an employee who must wear protective clothing because of materials that he or she may come in contact with when performing the job)

- Training or meeting time, if such training or meeting benefits the employer or the employee's current job or takes place during working hours

- Volunteer work, if it is performed at the employer's request or for the benefit of the employer

A recent case reaffirmed the concept that changing clothes or putting on or taking off protective gear, if it is an "integral and indispensable" part of the employee's "principal work activity," is compensable. In *IBP, Inc. v. Alvarez* [126 S. Ct. 514, 163 L. Ed. 2d 288 (2005)], the Supreme Court said that "walking time" between the changing area and the workstation is also compensable. Waiting time before changing clothes is not compensable.

In 2007, both the Second and Eleventh Circuit Courts addressed the issue of compensable time for employees that must go through security screens on their way to their job sites. The courts agreed that employees going through badge inspection, metal detectors, and employer-provided transportation to the job site do not need to be compensated for that time. Under the Portal-to-Portal Act, the security screening time is an extension of commute time. [Gorman v. Consolidated Edison, 488 F.3d 586 (2d Cir. 2007); Bonilla v. Baker Concrete Construction, Inc., 487 F.3d 1340 (11th Cir. 2007)]

Employers must compensate nonexempt employees for all hours worked at either straight time or overtime rates, as applicable, even if the employee volunteers to perform the work or takes work home. Activities not generally considered work time and not compensated under federal law include:

- Commuting time between personal residence and work

- Personal absences, such as sick time, holidays, funeral leave, or time off due to inclement weather

- Medical attention during nonworking hours

- Jury duty that is required by a civil authority

- Preemployment testing

[1] Travel Time

Whether time spent traveling is considered work time, and therefore subject to minimum wage and overtime pay requirements, depends on the type of travel involved. The Portal-to-Portal Act of 1947 defines whether time spent traveling is considered work time.

Travel time is considered work time in the following instances, with certain exceptions:

1. Travel over a substantial distance to perform emergency work for a customer of the employer after the end of the employee's workday. (However, the Wage and Hour Division has not addressed whether travel to and from the regular workplace in an after-hours emergency is considered work time.)

2. Travel as part of the employee's principal activity, such as travel from one office or job site to another during the workday. If an employee is required to report to a meeting place to receive instructions, pick up tools, or perform other work there, travel from the designated place to the workplace is part of the day's work and must be counted as such.

3. Travel away from home when it "cuts across the employee's workday." In such situations, the employee is considered to be substituting travel for other duties. The time counted includes hours worked on regular workdays during normal work hours as well as corresponding hours on nonwork days. For example, if an employee regularly works from 8:00 A.M. to 5:00 P.M. Monday through Friday and must work on a weekend, travel time during these hours is work time on Saturday and Sunday. Regular meal period time is not counted. Time spent in travel away from home outside of regular work hours as a passenger on an airplane, train, boat, bus, or automobile is not considered work time.

[2] Callback Pay or Report-In Pay

Callback pay pertains to employees who are called back to work after leaving the work premises. There is no federal law that guarantees an employee a minimum number of hours of work when called back. Only the actual time worked need be counted as hours worked under the FLSA. The employee must be paid at his or her base rate or overtime rate, if applicable.

Federal law does not require employers to pay employees if they report in at the company's regular starting time but are unable to work due to some unusual condition at their place of employment.

Whether the time spent waiting for a call to work should be treated as hours worked depends on whether the time can be used effectively for the employee's personal purposes, such as whether an employee who is waiting at home can conduct his or her normal activities. This varies on a case-by-case basis.

[L] Compensatory Time Off

Some companies prefer to give compensatory time off (sometimes known as comp time) in lieu of paying overtime when nonexempt employees work more than 40 hours in a workweek. Unlike federal, state, and local government employers, private employers are not allowed to provide comp time under the FLSA.

However, a private employer may be able to achieve its objective of controlling payroll costs while complying with the FLSA by scheduling employees' hours to "make up" for any overtime worked within the same pay period. That is, an employer with a two-week pay period may maintain payroll costs at a level equal to two 40-hour weeks by giving the employee time off in the week following a week when overtime was worked. To maintain the same payroll costs, the time off must be paid at a rate of one and one-half hours for each hour worked in excess of 40 hours in the immediately preceding workweek.

> **Example.** Karen, a nonexempt employee, is paid $10 an hour. Karen works two hours of overtime during the first week of the two-week pay period. Her employer gives her three hours of time off (two hours of overtime at time and one-half) during the second week of the pay period. For the first week, Karen is paid for 40 hours at $10 an hour plus two hours at $15 an hour (i.e., $400 + $30 = $430). For the second week, she is paid for 37 hours at her regular rate (i.e., 37 hours × $10 per hour = $370). Karen's total pay for the pay period equals $800 ($430 + $370), which is the same as her pay for a regular pay period. By giving Karen time off equal to one and one-half times the number of hours of overtime worked in the first week, Karen's employer keeps the payroll at the same level, as if no overtime had been worked.

This approach, while legal under the FLSA, can be difficult to administer and document, especially in a company that has semimonthly payroll periods. It may also lead to dissatisfaction among employees.

[M] Volunteers

The 1985 FLSA Amendments clarified the definition of volunteers. Subsequent DOL opinion letters have added to our understanding of this definition. In essence, an employee is considered a volunteer and not subject to minimum wage and other FLSA requirements if:

- The volunteer work is performed without expectation or receipt of compensation by the volunteer, although the volunteer can be paid "a nominal fee to perform such services"

- The volunteer work is provided freely and without coercion from the employer

- The employee is not volunteering the same services to the employer that he or she is employed to perform

If employees are working for a charitable cause at the request of the employer and during regular working hours, it is likely that they would not be considered volunteers and therefore subject to FLSA requirements.

To review recent DOL opinion letters, visit their Web site at *www.dol.gov/esa/whd/opinion/flsa.htm*. Relevant letters include FLSA 2006-38, FLSA 2005-51, FLSA 2005-33, and FLSA 2005-32.

[N] Posting of Notices

Employers covered under the FLSA must post notices that outline employees' rights under the Act, including minimum wage, overtime, equal pay, and child labor restrictions. Notices must be posted in enough conspicuous places that employees can see them as they enter and leave the workplace.

As a result of the recent federal minimum wage increase, there is a new federal minimum wage poster. It is available on the DOL's Web site at *www.wagehour.dol.gov*.

[O] Opinion Letters

The DOL routinely answers questions posed by employers seeking clarification on wage and hour issues. These answers are in the form of "opinion letters" and are published on the DOL's Web site (*www. wagehour.dol.gov*). While they are not legally binding opinions, they provide useful information about the DOL's position on the subjects addressed.

Some of the interesting conclusions published in the last few years:

- "Registered Professionals"—those employed as stockbrokers, financial advisors, and financial consultants—may qualify for the administrative exemption outlined in the FLSA regulations (FLSA2006-43, published November 27, 2006).

- "Information Technology Support Specialists"—sometimes titled "Help Desk" specialists or technicians—are generally not exempt from the FLSA overtime requirements (FLSA2006-42, published October 26, 2006).

- Cash shortages deducted from an exempt employee's commission payments, rather than from base salary, do not affect the exempt status of an employee, as long as the salary test is met (FLSA2006-24, published July 6, 2006).

Employers should carefully review the facts in the cases noted above before making decisions about their own employee situations.

[P] Class Action Litigation

The number of wage and hour claims and lawsuits have risen dramatically in the last few years. Between 2004 and 2006 alone, the number of federal wage and hour cases increased by 86 percent, and the number of multi-plaintiff wage and hour cases increased by 70 percent, as reported by the law firm Epstein, Becker & Green. These claims, which are filed as class actions in state court, or collective actions in federal court, have cost employers millions of dollars in judgments and settlements.

Recent examples of class action or collective action lawsuits include:

- Family Dollar stores received a judgment of $35.6 million for failure to pay overtime to store managers, determined to be improperly classified as exempt.

- Three state courts have ruled against Wal-Mart in three separate wage and hour class action lawsuits. In the most recent case in Minnesota, where Wal-Mart was charged with failing to provide rest breaks, the judge awarded $6.5 million to the class. Previously, in California and Philadelphia, the judgments were $172 million and $78 million, respectively.

- Staples settled a lawsuit after eight years of litigation for $38 million. The retailer was charged with improperly classifying their store managers as exempt.

- Lawsuits have been filed against multiple pharmaceutical companies, including Johnson & Johnson, Novartis and Eli Lilly & Co., alleging misclassification of sales representatives as exempt, thereby denying proper overtime pay.

While many of the cases cited above are in the appeal process, it is safe to say that facing litigation—especially where a class of employees is created—is a time-consuming and expensive proposition. All employers, regardless of size and industry, should ensure that they are in compliance with federal and state wage and hour laws.

Exhibit 3.1   Mandated Benefits: 2009 Compliance Guide

Exhibit 3.1
Checklist for Identifying Exempt Workers

Answering "yes" to all questions in any one category indicates that the employee meets the legal requirements to be considered exempt from overtime within that category.

Executive	Yes	No
Is the employee's primary duty the management of a customarily recognized department, area, or subdivision?	☐	☐
Does the employee regularly direct the work of two or more employees?	☐	☐
Do this employee's recommendations regarding hiring and termination of other employees carry weight?	☐	☐
Does the employee spend at least 50 percent of his or her time on exempt duties?	☐	☐
Is the employee regularly paid a weekly salary of at least $455?	☐	☐

Professional	Yes	No

Does the employee's primary duty require one of the following:

- Advanced knowledge in a field of science or learning, which is predominantly intellectual in character and which requires consistent exercise of discretion and judgment? or,

- Originality and creativity in a recognized field of artistic endeavor? or,

	Yes	No
• Teaching, tutoring, or instructing?	☐	☐
Does the employee spend at least 50 percent of his or her time on exempt duties?	☐	☐
Is the employee regularly paid a weekly salary of at least $455?	☐	☐

Administrative	Yes	No
Is the employee's primary duty office or nonmanual work that is directly related to management policies or general business operations (which may include academic instruction in an educational establishment) of the employer or the employer's customers?	☐	☐
Does the employee regularly exercise discretion and independent judgment in matters of significance?	☐	☐
Does the employee spend at least 50 percent of his or her time on exempt duties?	☐	☐
Is the employee regularly paid a weekly salary of at least $455?	☐	☐

Outside Sales   **Yes**   **No**

Does the salesperson sell somewhere other than the company's place of business?   ☐   ☐

Does the salesperson make sales or get orders or contracts for a product, a service, or the use of
facilities provided by the company?   ☐   ☐

Does the employee spend at least 50 percent of his or her time on exempt duties?   ☐   ☐

Appendix 3-A
Pay Practices by State

This appendix contains a state-by-state listing of requirements for minimum wage, subminimum wage, tip credit, overtime, and callback pay. The information in this appendix is effective January 1, 2009, as known October 2008.

Most, but not all, employers are covered under the federal minimum wage law. If for some reason an employer is not covered by the federal minimum wage law, the minimum wage in that state can be different. Employers are advised to contact the wage and hour office within their state to verify the state minimum wage.

Subminimum Wage

Some states have provisions to pay less than the minimum wage under certain conditions, such as paying a training wage for a specified period. In these states, an inquiry about the minimum wage may be answered in terms of the lowest wage an employer may pay, which might refer to the training wage. Therefore, employers are advised to clarify whether a minimum wage amount quoted by a representative of the state's wage and hour office pertains to the lowest wage an employer may pay an employee barring any exceptions to the state statute.

Appendix 3-A (cont'd)

ALABAMA	
Minimum Wage	The state has no minimum wage regulation. Employers are governed by federal law.
Subminimum Wage	No state subminimum wage regulation.
Tip Credit	No state tip credit regulation.
Overtime	State law regulates overtime pay only for law enforcement officers, who must receive time and one-half in excess of 8 hours per day or 40 hours per week, or one and one-half times rate in compensatory time. Officers must choose between overtime pay or compensatory time by the last day of the calendar month in which the overtime hours are worked. If they choose pay, it must be paid out by the next pay period. Compensatory time can be taken at any time during the calendar year in which it is earned.
Callback Pay	There is no state provision.

Appendix 3-A (cont'd)

ALASKA	
Minimum Wage	$7.15. The wage applies to employers and employees who are covered by the federal minimum wage law. Occupations and industries exempt from Alaska minimum wage include agriculture and aquatic workers, domestic workers, government employees, newspaper carriers, minors under age 18 who are employed fewer than 30 hours per week, certain security guards and caretakers, rock hunters, workers who serve as substitute parents of institutionalized children, hand pickers of shrimp, workers in certain computer operations, outside salesmen, or any salesmen working on a straight commission basis, independent cab drivers, a person holding a license under AS 08.54 and who is employed by a registered guide or master guide under AS 08.54, and employees in a bona fide executive, professional or administrative capacity as defined by regulations of the Commissioner of Labor. Public school bus drivers must be paid twice the statutory minimum wage. Exempt employees in retail and service establishments who spend up to 40 percent of their time performing nonexempt duties must be paid two times the state wage for the first 40 hours of employment each week.
Subminimum Wage	The state commissioner of labor may allow for employment at wages below the minimum for learners and apprentices, for the physically or mentally disabled, and for those employed by certain residential drug or alcohol treatment programs.
Tip Credit	Tips or gratuities may not be credited toward the minimum hourly wage.
Overtime	The overtime pay rate is one and one-half times the employee's pay rate for hours worked in excess of 8 hours per day and 40 hours per workweek. Employers who are covered by both Alaska and federal law must comply with the state law to the extent it is more generous to the employee.

Under a voluntary flexible work-hour plan approved by the Alaska Department of Labor, a 10-hour day, 40-hour workweek may be instituted with premium pay after 10 hours a day instead of after 8 hours.

Overtime pay does not apply to: employees of organizations that employ fewer than four employees; to any individual employed as a seaman, outside buyer of poultry or dairy (in its raw or natural state), line haul truck driver (for trips exceeding 100 road miles), medical service provider or community health aides; specific conditions within agricultural, mining, publishing, forestry, timber, lumber, switchboard operations and communication provider industries; and other exempted retail or service establishments. |
| **Callback Pay** | There is no state provision. |

Appendix 3-A (cont'd)

ARIZONA	
Minimum Wage	$7.25. The minimum wage will be increased annually every January 1st by the increase in the cost of living.
Subminimum Wage	The scale of wage rates below regular fair rates may be recommended by a wage board for learners, apprentices, and disabled workers.
Tip Credit	The rate is $3.00 per hour less than the minimum wage for any employee who customarily and regularly receives tips or gratuities, if the employer can establish by its records that for each week, when adding tips received to wages paid, the employee received not less than the minimum wage for all hours worked.
Overtime	No state overtime law applies; employers are governed by federal law. Employers not covered by federal law are not obligated to pay overtime for hours in excess of 40; however, they may do so at their discretion. Some public employees are covered.
Callback Pay	There is no state provision.
ARKANSAS	
Minimum Wage	$6.25 (applicable to employers of four or more employees).
Subminimum Wage	The Director of the Department of Labor may permit a lower-than-minimum-wage rate for minors, apprentices, learners, full-time students, and handicapped workers. The rate must be at least 85 percent of minimum wage for full-time students at state-accredited schools who work 20 hours or fewer per week, or 40 hours or fewer during vacation.
Tip Credit	Employees engaged in occupations in which gratuities have been recognized as part of remuneration for hiring purposes are entitled to allowance for gratuities in amount not exceeding 58 percent of minimum wages. Tips must be sufficient to bring the server's wages up from $2.62 per hour to $6.25 per hour.
Overtime	The rates are time and one-half for over 40 hours per week for most employees and time and one-half for over 48 hours per week for employees of hotels, motels, restaurants, and tourist attractions with sales of less than $500,000.
Callback Pay	Employees must be paid their regular rate or the applicable overtime rate. When on duty for more than 24 hours, and living at their place of work, employees must be paid for at least 8 hours in each 24-hour period. When required to be on duty for less than 24 hours per day, employees must be compensated for all hours on duty, even if the employee is allowed to sleep or use the time for his or her own purposes.

Appendix 3-A (cont'd)

CALIFORNIA	
Minimum Wage	$8.00.
Subminimum Wage	$4.25 for first 90 consecutive calendar days of employment for those under age 20. Learners 18 or older may be paid 85 percent of minimum wage for the first 160 hours. Student employees and camp and program counselors may be paid a weekly salary of 85 percent of minimum wage. Minors may be paid 85 percent of minimum wage if the number of minors employed at this lesser rate does not exceed 25 percent of the persons regularly employed in the establishment. An employer of fewer than 10 persons may employ three minors at 85 percent of minimum wage. This 25 percent rule does not apply during school vacations. Disabled workers may be paid less than minimum wage if licenses are obtained.
Tip Credit	The state does not authorize a tip credit.
Overtime	Employers, with certain exceptions, are required to pay overtime for: • Any work in excess of eight hours in one workday, and • Any work in excess of 40 hours in any workweek, and • The first eight hours worked on the seventh day of work in any workweek at the rate of no less than one and one-half times the regular rate of pay for an employee. Further, it requires that (a) any work in excess of 12 hours in one day and/or (b) any work in excess of eight hours on any seventh day of a workweek be compensated at the rate of no less than twice the regular rate of pay for an employee. Overtime requirements do not apply to teachers at private elementary or secondary academic institutions where pupils are enrolled in grades K through 12. Refer to state regulations for a complete description of exceptions.
Callback Pay	Employees required to return to work a second time in any workday must be paid for at least two hours of work, whether or not they actually work that long. Exceptions are household workers (e.g., butlers, maids, and chauffeurs).

Appendix 3-A (cont'd)

COLORADO	
Minimum Wage	$7.28. The minimum wage will be adjusted annually for inflation as measured by the Consumer Price Index for the state.
Subminimum Wage	The following employees may be paid at 85 percent of the minimum: minors supported by a parent and disabled individuals with authorization by the state labor authorities.
Tip Credit	Employers may pay a cash wage of at least $4.00 per hour if they claim a tip credit against their minimum wage. If tips and employers' cash of $4.00 do not equal minimum wage, the employers must make up the difference.
Overtime	Wages are paid at a rate of one and one-half times the rate for hours worked in excess of 12 a day and 40 a workweek (defined as 168 hours or seven consecutive 24-hour periods). Minors under the age of 18 are paid time and one-half for hours in excess of 8 per day and 40 per workweek.
Callback Pay	There is no state provision.

Appendix 3-A (cont'd)

CONNECTICUT	
Minimum Wage	$8.00; $8.25 effective January 1, 2010. The minimum wage rate cannot be less than one-half of one percent more than the federal minimum wage.
Subminimum Wage	Apprentices, learners, disabled workers, and minors can be paid below the minimum with the approval of the state commissioner of labor. Apprentices, learners, and persons under age 18 can be paid no less than 85 percent of minimum wage for first 200 hours of employment, with commissioner approval. Except in institutional training programs, post-training minimum increases to state minimum wage.
	Minors between the ages of 16 and 18 who are employees of the state or a political subdivision and agricultural workers between the ages of 14 and 18 must be paid 85 percent of the minimum wage. Agricultural workers between the ages of 14 and 18 who did not work eight or more weeks in the preceding years must be paid a minimum wage of not less than 75 percent of the minimum wage rate.
Tip Credit	Gratuities are not to exceed 31 percent of minimum wage for persons in hotel and restaurant industry and not to exceed $2.48 per hour in any other industry. For bartenders who customarily and regularly receive gratuities, a tip credit of 11 percent will apply. All other tipped employees have a maximum tip credit of $0.35 per hour.
Overtime	One and one-half times hourly pay rate for hours in excess of 40 in a workweek. Employees in restaurant and hotel restaurant occupations who work a seventh consecutive day must be paid not less than one and one-half times the applicable minimum wage for all time worked on the seventh consecutive day. For hospitals, eight hours per day or 80 hours per 14-day pay period. There are specific overtime payment calculations for certain public employees. Effective October 1, 2005, hospitals will not be able to require a registered nurse, licensed practical nurse, or registered nurse's aide to work in excess of his or her scheduled work shift, if that workshift was determined and provided at least 48 hours prior to the start of the scheduled shift. Exceptions apply.
Callback Pay	Employees subject to call for emergency service or who must keep the employer informed of their whereabouts and are contacted by the employer and assigned to duty yet not specifically required to be subject to call must be paid for their time.
	A minimum of four hours of pay at the regular rate is required for employees in beauty shops and laundry, cleaning, and dyeing occupations, regardless of whether work was assigned.
	Mercantile trade employees must be paid for a minimum of four hours when requested or approved to report to work. This can be waived if the employee works less than the four hours and signs a mutual agreement, but the employee must be paid a minimum of twice the applicable minimum hourly rate. Restaurant and hotel employees asked to report to work must be paid at least two hours at their regular rate of pay.

Appendix 3-A (cont'd)

DELAWARE	
Minimum Wage	$7.15. The state minimum wage is automatically replaced with the federal minimum wage if it is higher than the state minimum.
Subminimum Wage	Student learners may be paid no less than 85 percent of minimum wage. Apprentices may be paid no less than 50 percent of the journeyman rate. Disabled employees may be paid not less than 50 percent of minimum wage, and severely handicapped workers may be paid not less than 25 percent of minimum wage. Minors under age 18 who have worked for the employer less than 90 days may be paid $3.35 per hour.
Tip Credit	Up to $3.92 in tips or gratuities may be credited toward the minimum hourly wage for employees who regularly receive more than $30 per month in tips. The amount may not be less than $2.23.
Overtime	The state has no overtime regulations. Employers are governed by federal law.
Callback Pay	There is no state provision.

DISTRICT OF COLUMBIA	
Minimum Wage	$7.25; $8.25 effective July 24, 2009. The minimum wage cannot be less than $1.00 higher than the federal minimum wage. Rates may be reduced by $0.50 per hour if health benefits are provided. Rates are reduced for certain industries; employers should contact their state wage and hour office to verify. Minors, students at institutions of higher learning, and workers under 21 may be paid $5.15 for 90 days.
Subminimum Wage	Upon approval, subminimum wages may be paid to handicapped workers and workers under 18 years old.
Tip Credit	Tips or gratuities may be credited toward 55 percent of minimum hourly wage. Minimum cash wage of $2.77 per hour is required.
Overtime	District regulations are the same as federal law.
Callback Pay	Employers who call employees in to work must pay the employee for at least four hours, even if they are unable to provide work or provide fewer than four hours of work.

FLORIDA	
Minimum Wage	$7.21. The rate will be increased annually based on the Consumer Price Index.
Tip Credit	For tipped employees meeting eligibility requirements for the tip credit under the FLSA, employers may count tips actually received as wages under the FLSA, but the employer must pay tipped employees a direct wage in an amount equal to the minimum wage of $6.79 minus $3.02 (which, as required by Florida's Constitution, is the 2003 tip credit existing under the FLSA), or a direct hourly wage of $3.77 as of January 1, 2008.
Overtime	The state has no overtime regulations. Employers are governed by federal law.
Callback Pay	There is no state provision.

Appendix 3-A (cont'd)

GEORGIA	
Minimum Wage	$5.15 (applicable to employers of 6 or more employees). The state minimum wage is automatically replaced by the federal minimum wage if it is higher than the state minimum.
Subminimum Wage	Upon approval, certain organizations and businesses that employ disabled workers, and others who cannot compete effectively, may pay subminimum wages. Minimum wage of $4.25 per hour may be paid to employees younger than 20 years of age for first 90 days of employment.
Overtime	The state has no overtime regulations. Employers are governed by federal law.
Callback Pay	There is no state provision.

HAWAII	
Minimum Wage	$7.25. An employee earning a guaranteed monthly compensation of $2,000 or more is exempt from the state minimum wage law.
Subminimum Wage	Upon approval, subminimum wages may be paid to learners, apprentices, disabled workers, part-time workers, certain students, and paroled wards of state youth correctional facilities.
Tip Credit	$0.25 an hour less than minimum wage is allowed for employees regularly receiving more than $20 per month in tips, if combined wages and tips are at least $0.50 an hour more than minimum wage. Minimum cash wage of $7.00 per hour is required.
Overtime	With certain exceptions, employers must pay one and one-half times the employee's regular rate of pay for hours worked over 40 in a workweek. Refer to state regulations for a list of exceptions.
Callback Pay	There is no state provision.

IDAHO	
Minimum Wage	$6.55; $7.25 effective July 24, 2009.
Subminimum Wage	Upon approval, subminimum wages may be paid to disabled workers, apprentices, and learners for up to one year. Trainees may receive $4.25 for the first 90 days.
Tip Credit	Tips or gratuities may be credited toward 35 percent of the minimum hourly wage for employees regularly receiving more than $30 per month in tips. Minimum cash wage of $3.35 per hour is required. Total rate with tips and cash wage cannot be less than minimum wage.
Overtime	Private employers are governed by federal law. State employees must be paid at one and one-half times their regular rate of pay.
Callback Pay	There is no state provision.

Appendix 3-A (cont'd)

ILLINOIS	
Minimum Wage	$7.75; $8.00 effective July 1, 2009; $8.25 effective July 1, 2010 (applicable to employers with four or more employees, excluding family members).
Subminimum Wage	At no time shall the wages paid to any employee under 18 years of age be more than $0.50 less than the wage required to be paid to employees who are at least 18 years of age. Upon approval, subminimum wages may be paid to disabled workers. Learners may be paid 70 percent of minimum wage up to six months after beginning employment.
Tip Credit	Tips or gratuities may be credited toward 40 percent of minimum hourly wage. A minimum actual wage of $4.65 for employees over 18 and $4.35 for employees under 18 is required.
Overtime	The overtime pay rate is one and one-half times the employee's regular rate for hours worked in excess of 40 hours per week. Certain employers and employees are exempt.
Callback Pay	There is no state provision.
INDIANA	
Minimum Wage	$6.55; $7.25 effective July 24, 2009 (applicable to employers of two or more employees).
Subminimum Wage	Employees under age 20 may be paid $4.25 per hour for the first 90 consecutive calendar days of employment.
Tip Credit	Employers of tipped employees must pay a cash wage of at least $2.13 per hour if they claim a tip credit against their minimum wage obligation. If an employee's tips combined with the employer's cash wage of at least $2.13 per hour do not equal the minimum hourly wage, the employer must make up the difference.
Overtime	Employers who are not exempt from the federal Fair Labor Standards Act must pay at least 1.5 times the regular rate of pay for all hours worked over 40 in a work week. Tipped employees must receive at least $8.78 an hour for all hours worked over 40 in a work week.
Callback Pay	There is no state provision.
IOWA	
Minimum Wage	$7.25. The state minimum wage is automatically replaced with the federal minimum wage if it is higher than the state minimum.
Subminimum Wage	All new hires may be paid $4.25 per hour for the first 90 consecutive calendar days of employment.
Tip Credit	Tips or gratuities may be credited toward 40 percent of minimum hourly wage for employees who regularly receive more than $30 per month in tips. Minimum cash wage of $4.35 per hour is required.
Overtime	The state has no overtime regulations. Employers are governed by federal law.
Callback Pay	There is no state provision.

Appendix 3-A (cont'd)

KANSAS	
Minimum Wage	$2.65.
Subminimum Wage	Upon approval, subminimum wages may be paid to disabled workers, learners, apprentices, and patient workers.
Tip Credit	Tips or gratuities may be credited toward 40 percent of minimum hourly wage for employees who regularly receive and keep their tips. Minimum cash wage of $1.59 per hour is required.
Overtime	Time and one-half for hours worked over 46 in a workweek.
Callback Pay	There is no state provision.
KENTUCKY	
Minimum Wage	$6.55; $7.25 effective July 1, 2009. The federal minimum wage is adopted as the state's minimum wage. Individuals engaged in providing companionship services who are employed by a third-party employer or agency, and some employees of retail stores, service industries, hotels, motels, and restaurant operations are exempt from minimum wage.
Subminimum Wage	Upon approval, subminimum wages may be paid to disabled workers, apprentices, learners, and sheltered workshop employees.
Tip Credit	Tips or gratuities may be credited toward 50 percent of minimum hourly wage for employees regularly receiving more than $30 per month in tips. Minimum cash wage of $2.13 per hour is required.
Overtime	The state law is the same as federal law, for the first 40 hours in the first six days of work in a week. Overtime pay must be paid for all hours worked on the seventh day, if 40 hours have been worked in the six previous days. Certain employees in specific industries, such as retail, hospitality, and transportation, are exempt from overtime.
Callback Pay	There is no state provision.
LOUISIANA	
Minimum Wage	The state has no minimum wage regulation. Employers are governed by federal law.
Subminimum Wage	There is no state provision.
Tip Credit	There is no state provision.
Overtime	The state has no overtime regulations. Employers are governed by federal law.
Callback Pay	There is no state provision.

Appendix 3-A (cont'd)

MAINE	
Minimum Wage	$7.25; $7.50 effective October 1, 2009. The state minimum wage is automatically replaced with the federal minimum wage if it is higher than the state minimum.
Subminimum Wage	Upon approval, subminimum wages may be paid to disabled workers, learners, and apprentices for a period not to exceed 1 year. Subminimum wage may not be less than 85 percent of minimum wage for persons under age 19 who are enrolled in an educational institution.
Tip Credit	If notified in advance, tips or gratuities may be credited toward 50 percent of minimum hourly wage for employees who regularly receive at least $20 per month in tips. Minimum cash wage of $3.50 per hour is required.
Overtime	With certain exceptions, employers must pay one and one-half times the employee's regular rate of pay for hours worked over 40 in a workweek. Refer to state regulations for a list of exceptions.
Callback Pay	There is no state provision.

Appendix 3-A (cont'd)

MARYLAND	
Minimum Wage	$6.15. The state minimum wage is automatically replaced with the federal minimum wage if it is higher than the state minimum. The following workers are exempt from Maryland's minimum wage provisions: certain agricultural workers; executives, administrative and professional employees; employees of educational, charitable, religious, and other non-profit organizations where the employee is working as a volunteer; employees of restaurants, cafés, drive-ins, taverns, and drug stores that sell food and drink for consumption on the premises where the annual gross income is not more than $250,000; employees of motion picture and drive-in theaters; employees under 16 years of age working not more than 20 hours per week; outside salespersons and individuals compensated on a commission basis; individuals 62 years of age and working not more than 25 hours a week; employees of establishments engaged in canning, packing or freezing or the first processing of seasonal fruits, vegetables, poultry and seafood; the immediate family of the employer; those employees enrolled in a special educational program and non-administrative employees of organized camps.
Subminimum Wage	Upon approval, subminimum wages may be paid to disabled workers. Apprentices and learners may not be paid less than 80 percent of the minimum wage. Employees under 20 years old may be paid no less than $4.25 per hour for no longer than their first 90 days of employment.
Tip Credit	$3.28 per hour and employers must make up the difference if their gratuities do not bring them at least minimum wage for employees who regularly receive at least $30 per month in tips.
Overtime	The following workers and employers are exempt from Maryland's overtime provisions: certain agricultural workers; executives, administrative and professional employees; employees of educational, charitable, religious, and other non-profit organizations where the employee is working as a volunteer; employees of restaurants, cafés, drive-ins, taverns, and drug stores that sell food and drink for consumption on the premises where the annual gross income is not more than $250,000; employees of motion picture and drive-in theaters; employees under 16 years of age working not more than 20 hours per week; outside salespersons and individuals compensated on a commission basis; individuals 62 years of age and working not more than 25 hours a week; employees of establishments engaged in canning, packing or freezing or the first processing of seasonal fruits, vegetables, poultry and seafood; the immediate family of the employer; those employees enrolled in a special educational program and non-administrative employees of organized camps; and employers covered by certain railroad requirements of the Department of Transportation, the Federal Motor Carrier Act and the Interstate Commerce Commission; employers operating a hotel, motel, restaurant, gas service station, an amusement or recreational establishment, including certain swimming pools; employers operating a bona fide private country club; employers operating a non-profit entity providing in-home care services for the sick, aged or individuals with disabilities; employers operating a theater, music festival, musical pavilion, theatrical show or non-profit concert promotion; employers who employ certain mechanics, parts-persons, or salespersons who primarily sell or service automobiles, farm equipment, trailers or trucks; employers who operate a taxicab business.
Callback Pay	There is no state provision.

Appendix 3-A (cont'd)

MASSACHUSETTS	
Minimum Wage	$8.00. The minimum wage cannot be less than $0.10 higher than the federal minimum wage.
Subminimum Wage	Upon approval, subminimum wages may be paid to minors and disabled workers. Students may be paid at 80 percent of minimum wage. Apprentices and learners may not be paid less than 80 percent of minimum wage. In retail, merchandising, or laundry occupations, subminimum wage applies only to the first 80 hours. Ushers, ticket sellers, and ticket takers must be paid $1.25, and janitors and caretakers can be paid no less than $36 per week. Agricultural workers may be paid $1.60 per hour.
Tip Credit	Tips or gratuities may be credited toward 50 percent of minimum hourly wage for employees who regularly receive at least $30 per month in tips. Minimum cash wage of $2.63 per hour is required.
Overtime	With certain exceptions, employers must pay one and one-half times the employee's regular rate of pay for hours worked over 40 in a workweek. Refer to state regulations for a list of exceptions.
Callback Pay	Anyone reporting to work must be paid a minimum of three hours' wages, whether any work is actually assigned. People who are required to remain on duty or call to attend to emergencies must be paid at least four hours' wages, whether or not they actually have to respond to a call.
MICHIGAN	
Minimum Wage	$7.40 (applicable to employers of two or more employees 16 years of age or older).
Subminimum Wage	Upon approval, subminimum wages may be paid to disabled workers, apprentices, and learners. Also, Michigan provides for an hourly training wage of $4.25 per hour for the first 90 days of employment of a new employee 16 to 19 years old. A youth subminimum wage may be paid to a minor age 16 or 17 that is 85 percent of the adult minimum wage.
Tip Credit	A tip credit of $2.50 per hour is allowed for employees earning at least $30 per month in tips. Minimum cash wage of $2.65 per hour is required.
Overtime	With certain exceptions, employers must pay one and one-half times the employee's regular rate of pay for hours worked over 40 in a workweek. Refer to state regulations for a list of exceptions.
Callback Pay	There is no state provision.

Appendix 3-A (cont'd)

MINNESOTA	
Minimum Wage	$6.15. For small employers (enterprises with annual receipts of less than $625,000), minimum wage is $5.25 per hour.
Subminimum Wage	With permit from the State Labor Standards Division, minimum wage is $4.90 an hour for first 90 consecutive days of employment for workers under age 20. With permit from the State Labor Standards Division, employers can pay a disabled worker a minimum wage of at least 50 percent of standard minimum. The number of people who may be so employed by an employer, the length of the learning period, and occupations in which such employees may work may be limited by the state's approval.
Tip Credit	Tips or gratuities may not be credited toward minimum wage.
Overtime	Overtime rates are time and one-half for hours worked in excess of 48 in a workweek.
Callback Pay	There is no state provision.

MISSISSIPPI	
Minimum Wage	The state has no minimum wage regulations. Employers are governed by federal law.
Subminimum Wage	There is no state provision.
Tip Credit	There is no state provision.
Overtime	The state has no overtime regulations. Employers are governed by federal law.
Callback Pay	There is no state provision.

MISSOURI	
Minimum Wage	$7.05. (Retail or service businesses with less than $500,000 in gross annual sales are exempt.) State law excludes from coverage any employment that is subject to the federal FLSA. The minimum wage rate will increase or decrease on January 1 of each year based on the change in the cost of living as measured by the Consumer Price Index.
Subminimum Wage	The state requires a subminimum wage of not less than $0.90 less than the minimum wage for employees under 20 years of age. A training wage may be paid for the first 90 days of employment.
Tip Credit	A tip credit of 50 percent is allowed. The total rate with tips and cash wage cannot be less than $6.65 per hour.
Overtime	With certain exceptions, employers must pay one and one-half times the employee's regular rate of pay for hours worked over 40 in a workweek. Refer to state regulations for a list of exceptions.
Callback Pay	There is no state provision.

Appendix 3-A (cont'd)

MONTANA	
Minimum Wage	$6.55. Employers with gross annual sales of $110,000 or less can pay $4.00 an hour. However, if an individual employee is producing or moving goods between states or otherwise covered by the Fair Labor Standards Act, that employee must be paid the greater of either the federal minimum wage or Montana's minimum wage. The minimum wage will be adjusted annually for inflation as measured by the Consumer Price Index.
Subminimum Wage	Training wage is not allowed.
Tip Credit	Tips or gratuities may not be credited toward minimum wage.
Overtime	The state law requires time and one-half to be paid for hours worked in excess of 40 in a workweek.
Callback Pay	On-call employees who must remain on the employer's premises, or so close to the premises that they cannot use the time for their own purposes, must be paid for that time. Employees who are called to work and then required to wait on the employer's premises until work is provided must be paid for that time.
NEBRASKA	
Minimum Wage	$6.55; $7.25 effective July 24, 2009 (applicable to employers with four or more employees).
Subminimum Wage	The state law sets subminimum wage at 75 percent of minimum wage for student learners, upon approval. Trainees less than 20 years of age who are not seasonal or migrant workers may be paid $4.25 for the first 90 days of employment.
Tip Credit	Up to $4.42 of an employee's tips or gratuities may be credited toward the minimum hourly wage. A minimum wage of $2.13 is required.
Overtime	The state law is the same as federal law.
Callback Pay	There is no state provision.

Appendix 3-A (cont'd)

NEVADA	
Minimum Wage	$6.85 if the employee does not receive qualified benefits; $5.85 if the employee receives qualified benefits. The minimum wage will be adjusted annually for inflation as measured by the Consumer Price Index, but not more than 3 percent in any one year.
Subminimum Wage	The wages are 85 percent of minimum wage for minors under the age of 18; $4.75 for agricultural workers who are under the age of 18 (set by the commissioner).
Tip Credit	Tips or gratuities may not be credited toward minimum hourly wage.
Overtime	Any employee who earns less than one and one-half times the applicable minimum wage must receive overtime for any hours worked over 8 in a 24-hour period. Thus, daily overtime is required if an employee receives qualified benefits and earns less than $8.775 per hour or if an employee does not receive qualified benefits, and earns less than $10.275 per hour. By mutual employer/employee agreement, a scheduled 10-hour day for four days a week may be worked without premium pay after 8 hours. Overtime pay on either a daily or weekly basis is not applicable to employees of companies having a gross annual sales volume of less than $250,000.
Callback Pay	There is no state provision.

NEW HAMPSHIRE	
Minimum Wage	$7.25. The state minimum wage is automatically replaced with the federal minimum wage if it is higher than the state minimum.
Subminimum Wage	The state law grants not less than 75 percent of minimum wage for workers under age 16. For disabled employees, students in work-study programs, or employees in sheltered work programs, subminimum rates may be paid upon approval.
Tip Credit	Tips or gratuities may be credited toward 55 percent of minimum hourly wage for employees of restaurants, hotels, motels, inns, and cabins who regularly receive more than $30 per month in tips. Minimum cash wage of $3.26 per hour is required.
Overtime	With certain exceptions, employers must pay one and one-half times the employee's regular rate of pay for hours worked over 40 in a workweek. Refer to state regulations for a list of exceptions.
Callback Pay	Employees asked to report to work must be paid at least two hours at their regular rate of pay, unless the employer makes a good faith effort to notify them not to report. All other federal provisions apply.

Appendix 3-A (cont'd)

NEW JERSEY	
Minimum Wage	$7.15.
Subminimum Wage	Upon approval, employers are allowed to pay 85 percent of minimum wage for full-time students employed by the university or college where they are enrolled. Apprentices, disabled workers, and learners may be paid wages lower than minimum wage upon approval.
Tip Credit	Maximum tip credit is $5.02, and may include tips, food, and lodging.
Overtime	With certain exceptions, employers must pay one and one-half times the employee's regular rate of pay for hours worked over 40 in a workweek. Refer to state regulations for a list of exceptions.
Callback Pay	Employees asked to report to work must be paid at least one hour at their regular rate of pay, unless the employer has already made available the minimum number of hours agreed upon before the day in question.
NEW MEXICO	
Minimum Wage	$7.50. Small employers with less than $500,000 in gross annual receipts and not engaged in interstate commerce pay a minimum of $4.25 per hour. An employer furnishing food, utilities, supplies, or housing to an employee who is engaged in agriculture may deduct the reasonable value of the furnished items from any wages due.
Subminimum Wage	State law allows subminimum wages not less than 50 percent of minimum wage upon approval for disabled workers. Subminimum wage is allowed for students regularly enrolled in a primary or secondary school who work after school hours or on vacations; persons age 18 or younger who are not students in a primary, secondary, vocational, or training school; and persons age 18 or younger who are not graduates of a secondary school.
Tip Credit	The rate is $2.13 per hour for all employees who regularly make at least $30 per month in tips. Total rate with tips and cash wage cannot be less than minimum wage.
Overtime	With certain exceptions, employers must pay one and one-half times the employee's regular rate of pay for hours worked over 40 in a workweek. Refer to state regulations for a list of exceptions.
Callback Pay	There is no state provision.

Appendix 3-A (cont'd)

NEW YORK	
Minimum Wage	$7.15. The state minimum wage is automatically replaced with the federal minimum wage if it is higher than the state minimum.
Subminimum Wage	The state law allows subminimum wage for persons employed as part of a rehabilitation program approved by the state. The state may authorize payment at less than the minimum wage for apprentices and learners, disabled individuals, minors for a period not extending beyond 17 consecutive weeks at a camp or resort, residential employees, and seasonal workers.
Tip Credit	Up to $2.55 may be credited toward the minimum hourly wage for food service workers; credit ranges from $1.10 (for chambermaids in resort hotels) to $2.85 (for all other resort hotel workers).
Overtime	With certain exceptions, employers must pay one and one-half times the employee's regular rate of pay for hours worked over 40 in a workweek. Refer to state regulations for a list of exceptions.
Callback Pay	Employees asked or required to report to work must be paid for at least four hours or for the number of hours in the shift if the scheduled shift is shorter than four hours. The hourly rate must be at or above the minimum wage. An employee in the restaurant or hotel industry who is asked or required to report to work must be paid for at least three hours.
NORTH CAROLINA	
Minimum Wage	$6.55; $7.25 effective July 24, 2009. The state minimum wage is automatically replaced with the federal minimum wage if it is higher than the state minimum.
Subminimum Wage	Employers may pay 85 percent of minimum wage to those certified as economically disadvantaged, for up to 52 weeks, and 85 percent of minimum for people employed at amusement parks and seasonal recreation establishments. Full-time students, learners, apprentices, and messengers may be paid at 90 percent of the current rate. Employers can pay subminimum wages for disabled employees, upon approval.
Tip Credit	Maximum tip credit allowed is $4.42 ($5.12 effective July 24, 2009). Employee must receive a minimum cash wage of $2.13 per hour.
Overtime	The state law is the same as federal law. Overtime pay is required after 45 hours in a week in seasonal amusements or recreational establishments.
Callback Pay	There is no state provision.

Appendix 3-A (cont'd)

NORTH DAKOTA	
Minimum Wage	$6.55; $7.25 effective July 24, 2009.
Subminimum Wage	Upon approval, subminimum wages may be paid to students in vocational education and to disabled workers.
Tip Credit	Tips or gratuities may be credited toward 33 percent of minimum hourly wage for employees who regularly receive more than $30 per month in tips. Minimum cash wage of $4.39 per hour is required; $4.86 effective July 24, 2009.
Overtime	With certain exceptions, employers must pay one and one-half times the employee's regular rate of pay for hours worked over 40 in a workweek. Refer to state regulations for a list of exceptions.
Callback Pay	There is no state provision.

OHIO	
Minimum Wage	$7.30. The federal minimum wage may be paid for employees of businesses with annual gross receipts of $250,000 or less or for employees under the age of 16; $2.80 for some agricultural workers. The minimum wage will be adjusted annually for inflation as measured by the Consumer Price Index.
Subminimum Wage	Apprentices may be paid 85 percent of minimum wage for a period of up to 90 days, upon approval. Disabled employees may be paid a subminimum wage, upon approval.
Tip Credit	Employees who regularly receive at least $30 per month in tips may be paid a minimum wage of $3.65 per hour. Including tips added to the cash wage, employees' hourly pay cannot be less than the regular minimum wage.
Overtime	The overtime pay rate is one and one-half times the employee's pay rate for hours worked in excess of 40 hours per work week. Hospitals, nursing homes, and day care centers are permitted to pay time and one-half in excess of 80 hours in a two-week period and for hours worked in excess of 8 in a workday. Premium pay is not required for businesses with less than $150,000 in sales per year.
Callback Pay	There is no state provision.

OKLAHOMA	
Minimum Wage	$6.55; $7.25 effective July 24, 2009. Employers with fewer than 10 employees grossing $100,000 or less per year pay a minimum of $2.00 per hour. The federal minimum wage is adopted as the state's minimum wage.
Subminimum Wage	Upon approval, subminimum wages may be paid to apprentices, learners, messengers, disabled workers, state and local government employees, and students employed at institutions of higher learning.
Tip Credit	Tips, gratuities, food, and lodging may be credited toward 50 percent of minimum hourly wage. Minimum cash wage of $3.28 per hour is required.
Overtime	There is no state provision.
Callback Pay	There is no state provision.

Appendix 3-A (cont'd)

OREGON	
Minimum Wage	$8.40. The rate will be adjusted annually for inflation by a calculation using the U.S. City Average Consumer Price Index for All Urban Consumers for All Items. The wage amount established will be rounded to the nearest five cents.
Subminimum Wage	Upon approval, student learners in vocational training programs and disabled workers may be paid 75 percent of the minimum wage.
Tip Credit	Tips or gratuities may not be credited toward the minimum hourly wage.
Overtime	The state law is the same as federal law, except overtime pay is required after 10 hours a day in nonfarm canneries, driers, or packing plants and in mills, factories, or manufacturing establishments (excluding sawmills, planing mills, shingle mills, and logging camps). Employees who are performing work that meets the state definition of ''agriculture'' are exempt from overtime pay. In some cases, they may also be exempt from the minimum wage.
Callback Pay	Under state law, employers must provide adequate work to people who are required to report to work. Employees must work or be paid for at least one-half a normal day's wages.

Appendix 3-A (cont'd)

PENNSYLVANIA	
Minimum Wage	$7.15; $7.25 effective July 24, 2009.
Subminimum Wage	Upon approval, students and learners may be paid 85 percent of minimum wage. Disabled workers may also be paid a subminimum wage, upon approval. A training wage of $6.55 may be paid for 60 days to workers under 20 years of age; after July 23, 2009, the training wage will not be allowed.
Tip Credit	Maximum tip credit is $4.32 ($4.42 effective July 24, 2009) for employees who regularly receive at least $30 per month in tips. Minimum cash wage of $2.83 per hour is required.
Overtime	With certain exceptions, employers must pay one and one-half times the employee's regular rate of pay for hours worked over 40 in a workweek. Refer to state regulations for a list of exceptions.
Callback Pay	There is no state provision.
RHODE ISLAND	
Minimum Wage	$7.40. Minimum wage commencing every July 1st shall be adjusted by a cost of living index for the period of March 31 through April 1 of the previous year as calculated for the northeast region of the United States Department of Labor.
Subminimum Wage	Upon approval, payment is as follows: at least 75 percent of minimum wage for minors ages 14 to 15 working 24 hours or less a week and full minimum age for those working more than 24 hours; at least 90 percent of minimum wage for full-time students under age 19 working for nonprofit organizations. Less than the minimum wage can be paid for learners and apprentices for the first 90 days of employment, and for the disabled, with license from the Director of Labor. Employers should verify these reduced wages with the state wage and hour office.
Tip Credit	Maximum tip credit is $4.51 per hour. This does not apply to table busers, unless they are directly tipped by customers. Minimum cash wage of $2.89 per hour is required.
Overtime	With certain exceptions, employers must pay one and one-half times the employee's regular rate of pay for hours worked over 40 in a workweek. Refer to state regulations for a list of exceptions. The state prohibits a health care facility from requiring nurses to work overtime in excess of a pre-determined shift, and in no case over 12 hours.
Callback Pay	Employers who call an employee in to work or permit an employee to show up for work must pay the employee for at least three hours of work, even if none was provided.
SOUTH CAROLINA	
Minimum Wage	The state has no minimum wage regulation. Employers are governed by federal law.
Subminimum Wage	There is no state provision.
Tip Credit	There is no state provision.
Overtime	The state has no overtime regulations. Employers are governed by federal law.
Callback Pay	There is no state provision.

Appendix 3-A (cont'd)

SOUTH DAKOTA	
Minimum Wage	$6.55; $7.25 effective July 24, 2009.
Subminimum Wage	Upon approval, subminimum wages may be paid to handicapped workers, learners, and apprentices. Minors under age 18 may be paid 75 percent of minimum wage rates. Any employee 18 or 19 years old may be paid an opportunity wage, as defined in FLSA.
Tip Credit	Maximum tip credit is $4.42 per hour for employees who regularly receive at least $35 per month in tips. Tip credit may include tips, food and lodging.
Overtime	The state has no overtime regulations. Employees are governed by federal law.
Callback Pay	There is no state provision.

TENNESSEE	
Minimum Wage	The state has no minimum wage regulation. Employers are governed by federal law.
Subminimum Wage	There is no state provision.
Tip Credit	There is no state provision.
Overtime	The state has no overtime regulations. Employees are governed by federal law.
Callback Pay	There is no state provision.

TEXAS	
Minimum Wage	$6.55; $7.25 effective July 24, 2009. The federal minimum wage is adopted as the state's minimum wage.
Subminimum Wage	Upon receipt of a medical certificate, employees who are impaired by age or disability may be paid 60 percent of minimum wage if employer obtains a medical certificate within 90 days of employment.
Tip Credit	Maximum tip credit is $4.42 per hour ($5.12 effective July 24, 2009) for employees who regularly earn more than $20 per month in tips. Minimum cash wage of $2.13 is required.
Overtime	The state has no overtime regulations. Employers are governed by federal law.
Callback Pay	There is no state provision.

UTAH	
Minimum Wage	$6.55; $7.25 effective July 24, 2009. The federal minimum wage is adopted as the state's minimum wage.
Subminimum Wage	Upon approval, subminimum wages may be paid to handicapped workers and learners. Learners may be paid lower rates for the first 160 hours of employment. Minors must be paid at least $4.25 per hour for the first 90 days of employment.
Tip Credit	Maximum tip credit is $4.42 per hour ($5.12 effective July 24, 2009) for employees who regularly earn more than $30 per month in tips. Minimum cash wage of $2.13 is required.
Overtime	The state has no overtime regulations. Employers are governed by federal law.
Callback Pay	There is no state provision.

Appendix 3-A (cont'd)

VERMONT	
Minimum Wage	$8.06. The minimum wage will be increased each year by 5 percent or the percentage increase of the Consumer Price Index, whichever is smaller. The state minimum wage is automatically replaced with the federal minimum wage if it is higher than the state minimum.
Subminimum Wage	Upon approval, subminimum wages may be paid to handicapped workers and learners. The learning rate is 85 percent of minimum for 30 days or 240 hours, whichever comes first.
Tip Credit	Employees must be paid a minimum of $3.91 per hour. The tip credit will be increased each year by 5 percent or the percentage increase of the Consumer Price Index, whichever is smaller. Employees must earn more than $120 per month in tips.
Overtime	With certain exceptions, employers must pay one and one-half times the employee's regular rate of pay for hours worked over 40 in a workweek. Refer to state regulations for a list of exceptions.
Callback Pay	There is no state provision.

VIRGINIA	
Minimum Wage	$6.55; $7.25 effective July 24, 2009. The federal minimum wage is adopted as the state's minimum wage.
Subminimum Wage	The state law follows the FLSA requirements of training wage.
Tip Credit	Tips or gratuities may be credited toward the minimum hourly wage. Employers are permitted to take a credit in the amount of any tips received by the employee. An employee claiming that his or her hourly rate, including tips, is below the minimum must be able to demonstrate that the amount of tips actually received was less than the credit taken.
Overtime	The state has no overtime regulations. Employers are governed by federal law.
Callback Pay	There is no state provision.

WASHINGTON	
Minimum Wage	$8.55. The minimum wage will be increased by the rate of inflation every year. The new wage will be announced each September and become effective on the first day of the next year.
Subminimum Wage	Minors (age 14 and 15) may be paid 85 percent of the minimum wage.
Tip Credit	Tips or gratuities may not be credited toward the minimum hourly wage.
Overtime	With certain exceptions, employers must pay one and one-half times the employee's regular rate of pay for hours worked over 40 in a workweek. Refer to state regulations for a list of exceptions. Employees may request compensatory time off in lieu of overtime pay at a rate of 1.5 hours of compensatory time for every one hour worked above 40 hours per week. Compensatory time off in lieu of overtime pay is not allowed in industries or enterprises that are subject to the FLSA.
Callback Pay	There is no state provision.

Appendix 3-A (cont'd)

WEST VIRGINIA	
Minimum Wage	$7.25 (applicable to employers of six or more employees). The state minimum wage is automatically replaced with the federal minimum wage if it is higher than the state minimum.
Subminimum Wage	Employees under 20 years of age may be paid a training wage of $5.15 per hour for their first 90 days of employment.
Tip Credit	Maximum tip credit is 20 percent of minimum wage, or $1.45 per hour. Minimum cash wage of $5.80 per hour is required.
Overtime	With certain exceptions, employers must pay one and one-half times the employee's regular rate of pay for hours worked over 40 in a workweek. Refer to state regulations for a list of exceptions.
Callback Pay	There is no state provision.

WISCONSIN	
Minimum Wage	$6.50.
Subminimum Wage	Opportunity employees under 20 years old may be paid $5.90 for the first 90 days of employment. Less than minimum wage may also be paid to student workers, apprentices, and disabled workers.
Tip Credit	Minimum hourly wage for tipped employees is $2.33. It is $2.13 for opportunity employees.
Overtime	With certain exceptions, employers must pay one and one-half times the employee's regular rate of pay for hours worked over 40 in a workweek. Refer to state regulations for a list of exceptions.
Callback Pay	There is no state provision.

WYOMING	
Minimum Wage	$5.15.
Subminimum Wage	Employees working 20 or fewer hours per week are exempt from the state minimum wage. Employees under 20 years of age may be paid a training wage of $4.25 per hour for the first 90 consecutive days of employment.
Tip Credit	Cash wages may not be less than $2.13 per hour. If the cash wages combined with the tips received by the employee during a pay period do not equal at least the applicable minimum wage, the employer shall pay the difference to the employee. Tip credit may only be used if employee receives a minimum of $30 per month in tips.
Overtime	The state makes no general provisions. State and county employees are entitled to one and one-half times regular wages for hours worked in excess of 8 per day or 40 per week.
Callback Pay	There is no state provision.

Chapter 4
Payroll Administration

§ 4.01 AUDIT QUESTIONS

1. Does the company withhold for child support over any other legal process?

2. Does the company report newly hired employees to the state's child support enforcement agency?

3. Does the company require a Form W-5 before providing an advance payment of an employee's earned income credit?

4. Does the company check employment status against the Internal Revenue Service Common Law Rules before classifying a new worker as an independent contractor?

5. Does the company retain payroll tax records for at least three years?

Note: Consistent "yes" answers to the above questions suggest that the organization is applying effective management practices and/or complying with federal regulations. "No" answers indicate that problem areas exist and should be addressed immediately.

This chapter discusses payroll administration issues, such as required records, required and prohibited deductions, garnishments, reporting requirements, and requirements for termination pay. Various laws govern this area, both federal and state, and it is important to monitor these laws for changes that affect payroll administration.

§ 4.02 PERMISSIBLE METHODS OF WAGE PAYMENTS

Almost all states permit payment for wages by cash (U.S. currency only) or check that is negotiable within the state. The federal Fair Labor Standards Act (FLSA) requires that employees receive the minimum wage in cash or a negotiable instrument. (See **Chapter 3** for further discussion of minimum wage requirements.) Other methods, such as a draft voucher or scrip, are permitted in some states.

Most states allow direct deposit of employee wages if the employer has obtained advanced written consent from the employee. Employee participation in a direct deposit program must be voluntary. The employee must be permitted to select the financial institution in which the deposits will be made and, in some states, allowed to terminate direct deposit authorization at any time. Some states specify county or place where payment must be negotiable.

A relatively new alternative to the direct deposit method of paperless payment is the debit card. Employers can set up a personal account for the employee that can be accessed by a payroll debit card. The debit card, in addition to being much less labor intensive for the employer, is extremely advantageous for employees who do not have—or cannot open—a bank account. For those without a bank account, the debit card may assess low or no fees, in contrast to check cashing fees which can be as much as 6 percent of the check value. The disadvantage of the debit card is the ease with which it can be lost or stolen.

Payroll debit cards are covered by the Federal Reserve Board's consumer protection regulation governing electronic fund transfers (Regulation E). Such accounts are defined by this regulation as "accounts directly or indirectly established through an employer to which transfers of the consumer's wages or other compensation are made on a recurring basis." Generally, Regulation E requires financial institutions to provide periodic statements of the account transactions; however, these will not be required of payroll card accounts if the institution:

1. makes balance information available to the consumer through a readily available telephone line;

2. makes an electronic history available to the consumer, through, for example, an Internet Web site; this history must cover a period of at least 60 days preceding the date the consumer electronically accesses the account; and

3. upon the consumer's oral or written request, promptly provides a written history of the consumer's account transactions covering a period of at least 60 days prior to the request.

Regulation E further provides that the electronic or written history of the account transactions must include information about any fees for electronic fund transfers imposed during the 60-day period. The regulation also provides for an error resolution process; institutions can comply if they allow a consumer to report an error up to 120 days after the date the transaction allegedly in error was credited or debited to the consumer's account.

State regulations may dictate how debit cards can be used. For example, many states require that employees be offered at least one no-fee method of getting cash. States generally mandate disclosure of fees and the terms and conditions regarding the use of the payroll card. And, most states require that payroll debit cards and direct deposit programs be voluntary—employees can't be required to participate. For specific information regarding direct deposit, debit cards or any other method of payment, contact the state's wage and hour division.

§ 4.03 PAYMENT FREQUENCY

The FLSA does not specify the frequency with which payment must be made, except that payment must be made "customarily and regularly" in the occupation engaged. Although the FLSA does not specify payment frequency, employers must establish a frequency for payment and maintain it once it has been determined. Changes in payment frequency (e.g., going from weekly to biweekly intervals) are allowed so long as they are permanent changes and not the result of an intention to avoid compliance with the FLSA. Specific requirements regarding the frequency of payment for employee wages are set by state statutes. These laws require that workers receive their regular wages at a minimum of certain intervals, usually biweekly or semimonthly. Some states allow other pay frequencies for administrative, executive, or professional employees, or dictate payment frequency for specific occupations (e.g., agricultural employees).

Violations of payment frequency requirements may have both civil and criminal consequences (e.g., fines and imprisonment).

§ 4.04 GARNISHMENTS AND CHILD SUPPORT WITHHOLDING

A *garnishment* is a court order to an employer, called the garnishee, to withhold a sum of money from an employee's earnings for payment of a debt to a third party. Garnishments typically relate to an employee's obligations for child support, alimony, federal or state taxes, or other debts.

The federal Consumer Credit Protection Act (CCPA) establishes limits on the amount that can be deducted weekly from an employee's wages due to garnishment. Wage garnishment law does not affect voluntary wage assignments. Instructions for withholding for support and nonsupport orders often differ from state to state; therefore, it is important to check state law whenever faced with a garnishment order. CCPA supersedes less restrictive state laws (i.e., laws that provide less protection to the employee).

The CCPA established that the maximum per week that an employer may garnish from an employee's wages is the lesser of (1) 25 percent of the employee's disposable earnings or (2) the amount of disposable earnings in excess of 30 times the effective federal minimum wage per the CCPA.

Disposable wages include regular wages, commissions, bonuses, and payments to pension or retirement programs minus mandated withholdings (e.g., federal and state taxes, Social Security, and Medicare payments). Tips are not considered earnings for purposes of wage garnishment. State laws may include variations to disposable wages (e.g., union dues).

[A] Exceptions

Support orders (e.g., child support and/or alimony), state or federal tax indebtedness, or bankruptcy court orders may dictate an exception to these limits. Withholding for child support takes priority over any other legal process carried out under state law against the same wages. This means that withholding for child support must be done first, then the deductions for other withholding orders may be made from the remaining unprotected wages.

Employers must report newly hired employees to their state child support enforcement agency (or other appropriate state agency) so that any child support withholding orders may be placed into effect with the employer. Under these rules, the maximum amount that may be withheld for support is (1) 50 percent of disposable earnings in the case of an absent parent who has a second family or (2) 60 percent of disposable earnings if there is no second family. These limits are each increased by 5 percent (to 55 percent and 65 percent) if payments are in arrears for more than 12 weeks.

The Welfare Reform Act of 1996 established four basic standards for child support that all states must follow:

1. Employers must report new hires to the state child support enforcement agency for a determination of whether the employee is subject to a withholding order.

2. Employers must begin withholding no later than the first pay period that occurs after 14 days from the mailing date on a notice sent to it by the state's child support enforcement agency.

3. Employers must remit withheld amounts to the state within seven days of the date the employee is paid.

4. States must recognize child support withholding orders issued by agencies in other states.

Following a court or agency order, employers may have the responsibility of arranging for health insurance for children of noncustodial parents. Some states require the employer to enroll children in the employer's health plan and withhold appropriate premiums from the employee's wages.

Some states dictate the timing when withholding must be made and payment sent, set priorities for different types of garnishments, and define allowable fees an employer may deduct for each type of payment. Generally, when an employer receives multiple garnishment orders, the creditors are paid one at a time, in the order in which the documents are received.

The CCPA prohibits discharge of an employee whose wages have been garnished "for any one indebtedness." For a garnishment to be considered a second or successive garnishment, it must be separate and distinct from the debt that formed the basis of the first garnishment. An employee may be lawfully discharged for multiple garnishments; however, caution is advised. Terminations of employment that result in disparate impact (unintended discriminatory effect) on a protected class may violate fair employment laws and result in fines of up to $1,000, imprisonment for up to one year, or both, for willful violations.

An employer who receives notice of a wage claim is best advised to handle the claim as quickly and as accurately as possible. The best way to ensure the speedy and accurate processing of a wage claim is to establish a standard procedure to be followed whenever a wage claim is received.

For more information about federal wage garnishment law, log on to the Department of Labor website: *www.dol.gov*.

§ 4.05   DEDUCTIONS

By law, certain deductions must be made from employees' gross wages. Required federal deductions include Social Security and Medicare (FICA) and federal income tax. Most states have additional required deductions for state and/or local income taxes.

[A]   Federal Insurance Contributions Act

FICA provides for a tax on employee income for the purposes of Old-Age, Survivors, and Disability Insurance (OASDI) or Social Security and Hospital Insurance (Medicare). FICA for 2008 comprises a combined tax of 7.65 percent of employee wages—6.2 percent for Social Security and 1.45 percent for Medicare. These percentages will remain the same in 2009. Employees and employers must each pay this tax. All covered wages are subject to Medicare taxes. The 2009 taxable wage base for Social Security is $106,800. Employers should be aware that the Social Security taxable wage base generally changes each year and that they are required to match an employee's FICA tax.

[B]   Federal Income Tax

The federal government provides tables that show various ranges of income and the dollar amounts to be withheld for each range from each employee's compensation. To know how much income tax to withhold from employees' wages, the employer should have a Form W-4, Employee's Withholding Allowance Certificate, on file for each employee.

[1]   Supplemental Wages

Employers should be aware of the new requirements for income tax withholding on supplemental wage payments that occurred with the passing of the American Jobs Creation Act of 2004. *Supplemental wages* are those that are not "regular" wages. *Regular wages* are defined as amounts paid by an employer for a payroll period either at a regular hourly, daily or similar periodic rate or in a predetermined fixed amount for the current payroll period. Wages that vary from period to period are generally supplemental wages. The final regulations issued by the Department of Treasury and the Internal Revenue Service (IRS) on July 25, 2006 (26 C.F.R. Part 31 [T.D. 9276] RIN 1545-BD96) provide examples of supplemental wages including bonuses, back pay, commissions, wages paid under reimbursement or other expense allowance arrangements, nonqualified deferred compensation includible in wages, wages paid as non-cash fringe benefits, and sick pay paid by a third party as an agent of the employer. Tips and overtime, although classified as supplemental wages, may be treated as regular wages by the employer.

For supplemental wages of $1,000,000 or less, the employer has the option of using either the aggregate procedure or the flat rate method of withholding. Under the aggregate procedure, employers calculate the amount of withholding due by aggregating the amount of supplemental wages with the regular wages paid for the current payroll period or for the most recent payroll period of the year of the payment, and treat the aggregate as if it were a single wage payment for the regular payroll period. By utilizing the flat rate method of withholding, the employer ignores the amount of regular wages as well as the withholding allowances claimed by the employee on the Form W-4 and uses the flat rate percentage specified in the regulations. In order to utilize the flat rate method of withholding, generally the employer must have withheld income taxes from regular wages paid the employee and the supplemental wages are either (a) not paid at the same time as regular wages or (b) separately stated on the employer's payroll records. For supplemental payments made after December 31, 2004, the flat tax rate is 28 percent. This rate may change if income tax rates change. The American Jobs Creation Act of 2004 sets the withholding amount for supplemental wages in excess of $1 million at the highest income tax rate (35 percent in 2007). For current information, visit the IRS Web site: *www.irs.gov*.

[2]   Foreign Persons

Generally, employers are required to withhold federal income tax at the rate of 30 percent from paychecks of foreign persons paid out of a U.S. payroll. There are certain reductions in that tax rate based on tax treaties with the home country of the foreign person. Withholdings should be reported on Form 1042-S, Foreign Person's U.S. Source Income Subject to Withholding, and Form 1042, Annual Withholding Tax

Return for U.S. Source Income of Foreign Persons. For information on employer requirements, refer to the IRS Fact Sheet on U.S. Tax Withholding on Payments to Foreign Persons, March 21, 2008.

[3]   Earned Income Credit

Some low-income taxpayers may be eligible for earned income credit (EIC) under Section 32 of the Internal Revenue Code (Code). The EIC is a credit that not only reduces the tax owed, but can also result in a refund even if no tax is owed. Each year, employers are required to notify each employee who worked during the year and from whom no federal income tax was withheld that they may be eligible for the EIC. However, the notice is not required to be given to an employee who claimed exemption from withholding on Form W-4 Employee's Withholding Allowance Certificate. The notice is printed on the back of Copy B of Form W-2 Wage and Tax Statement. If the Form W-2 is not prepared for an employee to whom a notice is required, the employer may provide the employee with a copy of Notice 797, or with their own written statement that includes the same wording as Notice 797. Notice 797 is available on the IRS Web site. Certain employees may receive advance payments of the EIC through their employer's payroll by filing Form W-5, but they must certify they have at least one qualifying child for the taxable year. Employees who do not file Form W-5 cannot receive advance payment of EIC. The maximum amount of EIC that may be paid in advance by the employer is $1,712 for 2007; the actual amount an employee may receive depends on the number of qualifying children the employee has. Unlike a Form W-4, which stays in effect until a new one is filed to replace it, a Form W-5 remains in effect only until the end of the calendar year to which it applies, or until the employee revokes it or replaces it with a new Form W-5.

[4]   Withholding Compliance

The IRS has established a Withholding Compliance Program to identify those employees with withholding compliance problems. Based on Forms W-2 "Wage and Tax Statement," the IRS will identify those employees with serious under-withholding of federal income tax. The IRS may issue a "lock-in letter" to the employer specifying the maximum number of withholding allowances permitted for the employee. The IRS has outlined employer responsibilities when a lock-in letter is issued, which include:

- Furnish a copy of the proposed lock-in letter to the employee immediately upon receipt.

- Impose the new withholding rate 60 days after the date on the original letter and maintain that rate.

- If the employee is no longer employed, fax a signed note on company letterhead to the IRS stating the employee is no longer employed by the business.

- If there is an acquisition or merger of the business, continue the lock-in process on gained employees based on the transferred W-4 and lock-in letter from the predecessor employer.

- Ensure safeguards are in place to prevent employees from increasing their allowances electronically.

- Maintain the withholding amount specified in the lock-in letter.

- Remind employees that the notice they received tells them how to contact the IRS if they want to change the withholding status and allowances from single/zero and that they will need the following information available when they call or write:
  - Form W-4 and worksheets;

- Most current pay stub for each job;

- Number of allowance claimed on current Forms W-4; and

- The Social Security numbers and dates of birth for any children and proof of any deductions they want to use to claim additional withholding allowances.

Employers are reminded that they must maintain the withholding amount specified in the lock-in letter. Penalties may apply if the employer fails to honor the lock-in requirement and they could be liable for the amount of tax that should have been withheld.

For current tax tables, contact your regional IRS office and ask for Circular E, Employer's Tax Guide. The IRS offers valuable information, including forms and publications, on its Web site: *www.irs.gov.*

[C]   State Income Tax

States generally provide tax tables that show various ranges of income and the dollar amounts or percentage to be withheld for each range from each employee's compensation. To use the tax tables correctly, every employee must complete an exemption form. A Form W-4 remains in effect until the employee submits a new one. At least annually, it is a good idea to remind employees to advise the human resources (HR) department if their number of exemptions change as a result of marriage or the adoption or birth of a child.

Some states use the federal exemption form, W-4, and others have developed their own similar forms. Employers should take care to use the correct form, as some states will not accept a W-4 if they have a special form of their own. Furthermore, some states do not require individual income tax.

To obtain state income tax tables, employers should contact their state Department of Revenue or visit its Web site or the Web site of their state Department of Taxation. The IRS Web site—*www.irs.gov*— maintains links to state Web sites.

Many states require in-state employers to withhold state income tax for services performed in the state by resident and nonresident employees. Nonresidents are generally subject to withholding on wages they receive for services rendered in the taxing state. When a nonresident employer performs services in a third state, it is generally required to follow the rules of either the employee's state of residence or the rules of the third state in regard to withholding.

Some states have established reciprocity agreements that do not require withholding on a resident of another state if the other state reciprocates (e.g., Ohio has reciprocity agreements with Indiana, Kentucky, Michigan, Pennsylvania, and West Virginia).

[D]   Permitted Deductions

State laws vary regarding the types of deductions that are permitted from an employee's wages. Deductions for state and federal taxes are allowed without employee authorization. Generally, deductions pursuant to a court order or the employee's advanced written authorization are allowed.

The following deductions are permitted by law:

- Union dues and initiation fees

- Employee contributions to insurance premiums

- Repayment of loans from credit unions

- Employee contributions to flexible spending accounts

- Deductions for payment of U.S. savings bonds

- Contribution to a state employee retirement fund

- Employee contributions to charitable organizations

Federal law allows certain deductions that may reduce the employee's pay below minimum wage. Overtime pay is excluded in this formula, so the amount that may be deducted is calculated on the basis of a 40-hour workweek, regardless of the amount of overtime worked. (See **Appendix 3-A**, for specific laws within each state.) Such deductions include the following:

1. *Deductions that benefit the employee.* Such deductions include employee contributions for health and life insurance, pension plans, and welfare plans. These deductions may reduce wages below minimum if the employee gives the employer permission to make such deductions and if the employer derives no profit or benefit.

2. *Meals, lodging, and other facilities.* The fair value or reasonable cost of meals, living quarters, or other facilities may be credited as part of minimum wage. Fair value must not include any profit to the employer.

3. *Transportation provided by the employer.* Transportation may be credited against minimum wage but only if travel time does not count as time worked and is not required by or necessary to the employer.

4. *Fuel and merchandise.* Minimum wage may be credited for residential heating and cooking fuel, or general merchandise provided by a company store, but only if it is reasonably related to board or lodging.

5. *Instructional costs.* Colleges that provided tuition to their student employees may credit this against minimum wage.

6. *Paycheck advances.* Advances may be deducted even if they reduce wages below the minimum wage because advances are considered wages given at an earlier time. Any deductions for interest or administrative costs, however, cannot reduce wages below the minimum wage.

Other deductions that are allowable, but may not cause wages to fall below the FLSA minimum wage, include:

1. *Shortages.* Employers have limited rights under federal law to recover cash shortages from cashiers or others who handle money. State laws are often more restrictive.

2. *Damages.* Employers may deduct for damages to company property caused by gross negligence or dishonest, willful acts by employees.

3. *Employee loans.* On a negative payback basis, employers may deduct only the regular amount, not the full balance due.

4. *Uniforms.* Employers may deduct the cost of employee uniforms, even if the uniforms are required by the employer.

5. *Customer tips.* Tips that are included as part of a charge on a customer's credit card are often advanced to the employee. If the tip charge is not collectible, the employer may deduct the amount of the tip from the employee's next paycheck.

For protection, an employer should receive advanced written authorization from employees regarding the conditions of deductions and the treatment of the final paycheck upon the employee's termination.

[E] Definition of Employee Versus Independent Contractor

It is up to the employer to classify an individual as an employee or independent contractor. If an employer fails to classify a worker properly, the employer may be liable for penalties on payments that should have been made, or may make payments in excess of the amount required by payroll tax laws.

Generally, independent contractor status is preferred by the person or business for whom services are performed because that person is not required to withhold income taxes and employee Social Security taxes and must pay Social Security and Federal Unemployment Tax Act (FUTA) taxes. On the other hand, a worker who incurs substantial amounts of unreimbursed travel expenses because of his or her job will probably prefer independent contractor status because the travel expenses will be fully deductible as a business expense under Code Section 162.

A common-law test can be used to determine whether an individual is an employee or an independent contractor. Under the test, an individual is an employee if he or she is under the direction and control of the party for whom services are being performed. The employer must be able to direct and control not only the result to be obtained from the individual's services but also the means used to achieve those results for an employer-employee relationship to exist under common law. In other words, the employer must have the right to dictate what is to be done and how it is to be done. Former employees who have been rehired by their former employer as consultants will be treated as employees or independent contractors for employment tax purposes, depending upon their situation after being rehired.

In a private letter ruling, the IRS held that where six retired employees were rehired as consultants, four were independent contractors because they (1) had no set work schedules, (2) were free to follow their own established routines and schedules, and (3) could provide similar services to other firms. The other two were held to be employees because the employer had significant control over how, when, and where their services were to be performed.

The IRS utilizes the following three categories of evidence to determine the degree of control and independence of workers:

1. *Behavioral control.* Facts that show whether the business has a right to direct and control how the worker does the task for which the worker is hired. This category includes facts and evidence related to:

   a. Instructions the business gives the worker

   b. Training the business gives the worker

2. *Financial control*. Facts that show whether the business has the right to control the business aspects of the worker's job. This category includes facts and evidence related to:

   a. Extent of unreimbursed business expenses

   b. Extent of the worker's investment

   c. Extent to which the worker makes services available to the relevant market

   d. How the business pays the worker

   e. Extent to which the worker can realize profit or loss

3. *Type of relationship*. Facts that show the type of relationship between the worker and the business. This category includes facts and evidence related to:

   a. Written contracts describing the relationship the parties intended to create

   b. Whether the business provides the worker with employee-type benefits, such as insurance, a pension plan, vacation pay or sick pay

   c. The permanency of the relationship

   d. The extent to which the services performed by the worker is a key aspect of the regular business of the company

No one factor is necessarily controlling, and all evidence regarding the relationship is considered. The relative importance of any one factor may vary depending on the occupation and the situation under consideration. (See IRS Publication 15-A "Employer's Supplemental Tax Guide.")

The IRS will rule on the status of a worker when an employer cannot clearly determine whether a worker is an employee or an independent contractor. Employers may file Form SS-8, "Determination of Worker Status for Purposes of Federal Employment Taxes and Income Tax Withholding," with the IRS to request a determination. This form, as well as Publication 15-A referred to above, is available on the IRS Web site: *www.irs.gov*.

States may have their own rules for determining whether an individual is an employee or an independent contractor. These requirements may be even more stringent than the IRS's; therefore, employers should ensure that any individuals classified as independent contractors can meet the tests of their state and the IRS.

Form W-9, Request for Taxpayer Identification Number and Certification, is used to obtain a correct taxpayer identification number (TIN) from a recipient of a reportable payment, such as an independent contractor. The IRS requires an employer to withhold a flat 31 percent backup withholding rate from the independent contractor's reportable payments (payments of $600 or more made in the course of a trade or business, beginning with the first payment that reaches the $600 threshold) (1) if the contractor fails to furnish his or her TIN number to the employer, or (2) if requested by the IRS because the payee has furnished the employer with an incorrect TIN, or (3) if the recipient notifies the employer that he or she is subject to backup withholding.

When an employer misclassifies a worker as an independent contractor, the employer is still responsible for paying the employee's federal income tax withholding (and usually state income tax withholding) and the employee's share of payroll taxes (such as FICA), even if it was not withheld from the worker's pay. These amounts are in addition to the employer's share of FICA and FUTA. The IRS provides some relief for employers who have misclassified a worker. Code 3509 provides the employer with the opportunity to correct the tax treatment of misclassified workers and provides for a reduced rate for the employee's share of FICA taxes and for the federal income tax that should have been withheld. The employer's share of FICA is not reduced, nor is the FUTA rate reduced.

A number of recent cases highlight the need for employers to make careful decisions about who they classify as independent contractors. In *Friendly Cab Co. Inc. v. National Labor Relations Board*, [512 F. 3d 1090 (9th Cir. 2008)] the Ninth Circuit held that the 90+ cab drivers were employees, due to the control the company had over the drivers. Among the facts leading to the court's ruling: the drivers were not allowed to operate an independent cab business; they were required to follow strict company rules and dress code requirements; and they were required to accept vouchers from regular company patrons. One result of this ruling is that the cab drivers now have a right to unionize.

In December, 2007, the IRS found that FedEx Corporation owed $319 million in taxes and penalties for 2001, due to the misclassification of drivers as independent contractors. FedEx is appealing the decision. The Company is also defending against dozens of lawsuits brought by current and former truck drivers, claiming that they are employees, not independent contractors.

§ 4.06 EMPLOYER RESPONSIBILITIES

For each new employee, an employer must verify that the employee is legally eligible to work in the United States by completing the U.S. Citizenship and Immigration Services (USCIS) Form I-9, Employment Eligibility Verification. Form I-9 may be obtained from any USCIS office or downloaded from the agency's Web site: *http://uscis.gov*. (Call the USCIS at 800-375-5283 for further information.)

Employers are also required to do the following:

- Record each new employee's name and Social Security number.

- Ask each new employee to complete a current Form W-4. (Form W-4 remains in effect until the employee replaces it with a new one.)

- Withhold federal and state income tax based on employee's filing status and withholding allowances in accordance with tax tables from the IRS publication, Circular E.

- Withhold each employee's share of Social Security and Medicare taxes under the Federal Insurance Contributions Act (FICA). (Employers are required to match employee FICA tax, which includes 6.2 percent Social Security tax, on a base wage basis up to $106,800, effective January 1, 2009, and 1.45 percent Medicare tax. All covered wages are subject to Medicare tax.)

- Deposit withheld income tax, Social Security and Medicare taxes, employer's Social Security and Medicare taxes, minus any advance earned income credit. (Due dates for deposits depend on the employer's schedule—monthly or semiweekly.)

- Deposit quarterly (by April 30, July 31, October 31, and January 31 of each year) FUTA tax in an authorized financial institution if undeposited amount is over $100. FUTA requires that tax be paid on the first $7,000 earned by an employee. The tax through 2009 is 6.2 percent. Some employers may be entitled to a credit from FUTA through a state program. State Unemployment Tax Act (SUTA) regulatory schemes differ greatly in the rates they impose and in the wage base they tax. Because the taxable wage base usually changes each year, the HR department should contact the state's wage and hour division to ascertain the current year's taxable wage base.

- File Form 941, Employer's Quarterly Federal Tax, and deposit any undeposited income, Social Security, and Medicare taxes.

On an annual basis, employers are required to do the following:

- Remind employees to submit a new Form W-4 if they need to change their withholding.

- Remind each employee to complete a new Form W-4 claiming exemption from income tax withholding if the number of exemptions has changed.

- Reconcile Form 941 with Form W-2 and the transmittal Form W-3 (Transmittal of Wage and Tax Statements) with the Social Security Administration if his or her number of exemptions has changed.

- Furnish each employee with a Form W-2.

- File copy A of Form W-2 and the transmittal Form W-3 with the Social Security Administration.

- Furnish each employee with a Form 1099-R for distributions from pensions, annuities, retirement or profit-sharing plans, IRAs, and insurance contracts, or a Form 1099-MISC for miscellaneous income for independent contractors.

- File Form 940 or Form 940-EZ, Employer's Annual FUTA Tax Return, by January 31. If all FUTA deposits were made when due, the employer has until February 10 to file the appropriate forms.

- File Form 945 for non-payroll income tax withholding, which include pensions, annuities, IRAs, military retirement, gambling winnings, Indian gaming profits, voluntary withholding on certain government payments, and backup withholding.

Employers should be aware that they are responsible for payment of payroll taxes, even if they use an outside payroll service bureau. In a recent case, a payroll service collected money from the employer to pay payroll taxes, but then filed fraudulent tax forms and kept much of the money collected. The employer owed not only the back taxes, but interest on the delinquent taxes. [Pediatric Affiliates, P.A. v. U.S., 230. Fed. Appx. 167 (3rd Cir. 2007)]

§ 4.07 REPORTING REQUIREMENTS

[A] Federal Withholding

In general, employers must deposit income tax withheld and both the employer and employee Social Security and Medicare taxes (minus any advance EIC payments) by mailing or delivering a check, money order, or cash to an authorized financial institution or Federal Reserve Bank. Some taxpayers are required to deposit by electronic funds transfer. (Employers who deposited total federal tax deposits (including employment tax, excise tax, and corporate income tax) of more than $200,000 in 1999 or who were required to deposit by electronic funds transfer in 2000 must make electronic deposits for all depository tax liabilities that occur after 2000.) Employers who are not required to deposit by electronic funds transfer are nevertheless encouraged to do so. The Electronic Federal Tax Payment System (EFTPS) is a free service. More information about EFTPS can be found on its Web site: *www.eftps.com.*

There are two deposit schedules: monthly and semiweekly. Before the beginning of each calendar year, an employer must determine which of the two deposit schedules it is required to use. The deposit schedule required is based on the employer's total tax liability reported on Form 941 during a four-quarter lookback period, which runs from the previous period of July 1 to June 30. Basically, an employer is a monthly schedule depositor for a calendar year if its total taxes on Form 941 for the lookback period were $50,000 or less; an employer is a semiweekly schedule depositor if its taxes for the lookback period exceeded $50,000.

However, regardless of whether an employer (including a new employer) is determined to be a monthly depositor or a semiweekly depositor, if that employer on any day has $100,000 or more of employment taxes accumulated, those taxes must be deposited by the close of the next banking day. Once an employer who is determined to be a monthly depositor becomes subject to the $100,000 on one day exception, it immediately becomes a semiweekly depositor for the remainder of that calendar year and the following calendar year.

An employer must file Form 941, Employer's Quarterly Federal Tax Return, and deposit any undeposited income, Social Security, and Medicare taxes by the end of each quarter—April 30, July 31, October 31, and January 31. An employer may pay such taxes quarterly with Form 941 or once a year with Form 945 if its total tax liability for the quarter is less than $1,000. If an employer deposited all taxes when due, it has 10 additional days from the above due dates to file the return.

[B] State Withholding

States have established schedules for submitting reports and payments of personal income taxes withheld from employee compensation to the state. Filing (i.e., report submission) requirements may be annual, quarterly, monthly, or more frequently. Some states do not have an individual income tax and therefore have no withholding requirements. Generally an employer determines the applicable schedule based on how much income tax the employer withholds.

Quarterly periods end on March 31, June 30, September 30, and December 31. Reports are usually due in the month following the end of the period if filing is required on a quarterly or monthly basis. Some states have more frequent filing requirements or just simply mandate that employers follow their federal income tax withholding schedule and reporting requirements.

States have established forms to use for reporting and making payments. Payments are generally payable to the employer's state Department of Revenue.

Penalties for noncompliance with the withholding laws generally include fines, which are based on the amount of money that was not reported or not paid to the state when due.

§ 4.08 UNCLAIMED WAGES—EMPLOYER REQUIREMENTS

Unclaimed wages, according to federal law, must be reported on the employee's W-2 form. State laws determine an employer's action for unclaimed wages or paychecks not cashed. State laws also define the period of time that must pass before wages are considered abandoned or unclaimed.

Unclaimed wages are treated like abandoned property. Money from accounts set up to pay employee benefits (e.g., vacation and profit-sharing amounts) is considered unclaimed wages in some states. Generally, states provide longer periods of waiting time for abandoned benefits than abandoned wages.

When the statutory period has passed, the employer is required to treat unclaimed wages in the following manner:

1. Attempt to contact the former employee. This requirement applies to unclaimed wages exceeding a specified amount in most states.

2. Submit a report to inform the designated state agency or official about the former employee and unclaimed wages.

3. Deliver the sum of unclaimed wages to the state administrator, who will attempt to notify the employee through publication in newspaper.

Violation of the delivery requirements is considered more severe than failing to meet reporting requirements. Penalties become more severe if an employer fails to deliver the amount once the state official has requested such action.

Each state has determined the amount of time that must pass before wages may be considered abandoned, threshold amounts, employer's responsibilities for contacting former employees, and reporting and delivering unclaimed wages.

§ 4.09   COMBINED ANNUAL WAGE REPORTING PROGRAM

The Social Security Administration (SSA) and the IRS routinely share tax information received from the employee and the employer. The Combined Annual Wage Reporting (CAWR) is a program to match documents and resolve discrepancies. When discrepancies are noted, tax examiners are assigned to research and resolve the issues. If necessary, they will contact the employer for additional information by issuing Letter 99C, Wage Discrepancy Per SSA; Information/Verification Requested. The employer has 45 days to respond. If there is no response, the case will be closed and the employer will be liable for the penalties outlined in the notice.

§ 4.10   RECORDKEEPING REQUIREMENTS

State laws often identify which employee records an employer must maintain, along with the length of time these records must be retained. These records include personal data, wage and payment history, and work schedules. Recordkeeping requirements often vary for adult employees and minors, with additional requirements for minors. To meet the special recordkeeping requirements for minors, most employers have one set of records with required information for minors only.

Federal regulations require all payroll tax records be kept at one or more convenient and safe locations accessible to IRS officers. These records must be available for inspection at all times. The employer must retain these records for a period of four years, beginning with the due date of the tax for the return period or the date of actual payment, whichever is later. The Department of Labor (DOL) requires that payroll data records be maintained for a minimum of three years and that the records on which wage computations are determined (e.g., time cards, time sheets) must be maintained for a minimum of two years.

Most employers still maintain paper records, but many are considering electronic storage. The DOL has adopted the IRS's standards for electronically stored payroll records. These standards emphasize controls for system integrity, accuracy, and reliability; prevention and detection of unauthorized creation, alteration, and deletion of or addition to the records; regular inspections of the system; retrieval systems for storing data that include an indexing system; and the ability to create accurate, legible, and complete hard copies of the electronically stored records. One example of a records management resource to use when formulating an electronic records management practice is the National Archives and Record Administration's "Standards for the Creation, Use, Preservation, and Disposition of Electronic Records," available on the Web site *www.nara.gov*.

[A]   General Recordkeeping

General recordkeeping requirements for all employees include the following:

- The employer identification number (EIN)

- The employee's full name as used for Social Security records and, on the same records, the employee's identifying symbol or number, if one is used in place of his or her name on any time, work, or payroll records

Other recordkeeping information includes:

- Employee's home address, including zip code

- Employee's date of birth, if he or she is under the age of 19

- Employee's sex, which may be indicated by the use of Mr., Mrs., or Ms.

- Copies of employee's income tax withholding allowance certificates (Forms W-4, W-4P, W-4S, and W-4V)

- Occupation in which the employee is employed

- Dates of employment

- Time of day and the day of the week on which the employee's workweek begins

- Hours worked by the employee each workday and the total hours worked each workweek

[B]   Deductions Data

Deductions data that employers are required to record include the following:

- Records of the total amount of additions to or deductions from the wages paid to the employee each pay period and in individual employee accounts, and the dates, accounts, and nature of the items that make up the total additions or deductions

- Dates and amounts of tax deposits made

[C]   Wage Data

Wage data that employers are required to record include the following:

- The regular hourly rate of pay for any week when overtime is worked and overtime excess compensation is owed under the FLSA, the basis on which wages are paid, and the amount and nature of each payment that is excluded from the regular rate

- Each employee's total daily or weekly straight-time earnings or wages (i.e., the total earnings or wages owed to the employee for the hours worked during the workday or workweek, including all earnings or wages due for any overtime worked but exclusive of any premium for overtime)

- Each employee's total of overtime premiums for the workweek (i.e., the compensation for overtime worked that is over and above the straight-time earnings or wages also earned during the overtime period)

- Total wages paid to each employee each pay period, including annuity and pension payments

- Date of every payment made to each employee and the pay period covered by the payment

- Records of allocated tips

- Records of fringe benefits provided to employees, including substantiation

- Periods for which employees were paid while absent due to sickness or injury and the amount and weekly rate of payments the employer or third-party payers made to them

- Records of retroactive payment of wages

[D] Exempt Versus Nonexempt Employee Time-Keeping Requirements

The FLSA governs the procedural aspects of paying employees, including minimum wage and overtime requirements. Certain classifications of employees are not subject to federal minimum wage requirements or eligible for overtime pay; these employees are called exempt employees. Employees who are subject to federal minimum wage requirements and are eligible for overtime pay are called nonexempt. The definition of exempt employment is clearly spelled out by the FLSA. (See **Chapter 3** for further information on the FLSA.)

For nonexempt employees, an employer should maintain time-keeping records, which include the number of hours worked, the pay rate, and the overtime pay per week or per pay period.

Regarding exempt employees, employers are not required to maintain records of regular hourly rate of pay, hours worked in a workday, total daily or weekly straight-time earnings, total premium pay for overtime hours, or total additions to or deductions from wages paid each pay period. Employers must maintain records on wages paid in sufficient detail to permit calculation for each pay period of the employee's total remuneration for employment, including fringe benefits and perquisites. The total may be shown as the dollar amount of earnings per month, per week, or per month plus commissions. Keeping records on vacations and other paid time off taken by exempt employees while preserving their exempt status is important, particularly in states where accrued, unused vacation must be paid out at termination.

[E] Minimum Wage

The FLSA establishes a minimum wage rate that must be paid to nonexempt employees for each hour worked. Effective July 24, 2008, the federal minimum wage is $6.55 per hour. The minimum wage will increase to $7.25 on July 24, 2009. Any business involved in interstate commerce is subject to the minimum wage law.

States may set their own minimum wage rate, which may be higher than the federal minimum wage rate. An employer must use the higher standard if federal and state rates differ. Companies should be aware of the state minimum wage requirements in states where they operate. (See **Appendix 3-A**.)

[F] Overtime Pay

The FLSA states that the workweek consists of 40 hours worked within any seven consecutive 24-hour days and that companies must pay overtime at one and one-half times a nonexempt employee's regular rate of pay whenever he or she works more than 40 hours in a week. The FLSA does not require that overtime be paid for hours worked in excess of eight hours per day or on weekends or holidays. Some state laws, on the other hand, may provide workers with greater overtime protection.

Overtime payments to employees may be made at the end of the next regular pay period or as soon as is practical after the pay period in which the overtime was incurred. As noted above, employers should maintain time-keeping records for hours worked per week and the amount of overtime paid in each pay period. (See **Chapter 3** for more information on overtime pay and calculations.)

[G] Time Cards

To conform to FLSA requirements regarding overtime, minimum wage, and meal periods, employers must keep accurate records of hours worked by nonexempt employees. Such records must be in ink or other indelible form, such as a stamped time card from a time clock. A manual recording system may be used as long as it is accurate. It is highly recommended that time cards be signed by both the employee and the supervisor.

[H] Family and Medical Leave Act

To comply with the Family and Medical Leave Act (FMLA), employers must maintain certain records for three years. Required records include the employee's name, address, wages paid, hours worked, and dates on which designated FMLA leave are taken. An employer's HR department is required to maintain additional records (see **Chapter 14**).

§ 4.11 RECORDS PRESERVATION

Federal agencies and individual states have record retention requirements that have to be followed. Some requirements apply only to government contractors or subcontractors or may be dependent on the number of employees.

The DOL requires that employers preserve payroll records for three years from the last date of entry. Records that should be maintained for two years include basic employment and earnings records (i.e., time and earning cards with starting and stopping time for individual employee), wage rate tables, and records of additions to or deductions from wages.

The IRS requires that records containing employees' names, addresses, Social Security numbers, dates of employment, and wage and tax deposit data be available for review for at least four years. When similar records are required under more than one law, information should be retained for the longer required period. For this reason, companies should investigate such requirements in the states where they do business.

It is recommended that employers establish a system for consistently auditing and destroying records when the retention period has passed. Be aware, however, that when a discrimination charge or lawsuit has been filed, all records related to the charge must be kept until "final disposition" of the charge or lawsuit. (See **Chapter 24** for further discussion of recordkeeping.)

§ 4.12 TERMINATION AND FINAL WAGES

State law regulates the payment of final wages payment due on termination or death of an employee (see **Exhibit 4.1**). The specified period between separation of employment and the due date of final wages may vary depending on the type of separation. There may be different rules for certain types of employers. For example, for discharged employees in California, wages are due and payable immediately. Certain seasonal employers may pay wages within 72 hours and by mail if the employee requests. Motion picture and oil drilling industry employers may pay wages within 24 hours.

[A] Involuntary Termination

When termination of employment is involuntary, state laws provide that final wages be paid in a specified period of time that varies from immediately to the earlier of 15 days or the next regular payday. An extension may be provided to calculate commission or some other basis that requires an accounting before the final payment can be determined.

[B] Voluntary Termination

State laws generally allow a longer time for paying final wages to employees who voluntarily terminate their employment. This time may vary by type of employer or classification of wages (e.g., commissions).

[C] Death of an Employee

Upon the death of an employee, many states require earned wages and benefits to be paid to the employee's spouse, adult children, parents, or siblings, in that order. Certain payments may be made without the need for formal probate or other administrative or judicial procedures.

[D] Strike or Layoff

When there is a strike or layoff, some states require payment of earned wages to affected employees within a specified period of time through the day the employees went on strike. Union contracts may provide for different due dates for final wages than the statutes specify.

[E] Permitted Deductions

For its protection, an employer should obtain written authorization from employees regarding the conditions of deductions and the treatment of the final paycheck upon termination of employment.

[F] W-2 Forms

Upon oral or written request by an employee, an employer must issue the employee a Form W-2 within 30 days of the request or within 30 days of the last payment of wages, whichever is later. Because federal and state laws governing payroll administration change from time to time, an employer should take care to monitor the federal laws and the laws in each state where it does business.

Exhibit 4.1   Mandated Benefits: 2009 Compliance Guide

Exhibit 4.1
Wage Payments Due on Termination or Death of Employee

	Involuntary Termination	Resignation	Severance Pay	Vacation Pay	Death	Citations to Authority
AL	—	—	—	—	All wages are payable to the decedent's spouse or to the guardian of the employee's minor children.	Ala. Code § 43-8-115.
AK	All wages, salaries, and other compensation due the employee are payable within 3 working days at the usual place of payment or other place agreed on by the employer and the employee.	All wages, salaries, and other compensation due the employee are payable by the next regular payday that is at least 3 days after the employer receives notice and at the usual place of payment or other place agreed on by the employer and the employee.	—	If vacation is a payment agreed to by employer, it must be paid upon termination of employment.	—	Alaska Stat. §§ 23.05.140, 23.05.170; *United Food & Commercial Workers Union, Local No. 1496 v. D&A Supermarkets, Inc.*, 688 P.2d 165 (Alaska 1984).
AZ	Wages must be paid within 3 working days or by the end of the next pay period, whichever is sooner.	Wages must be paid by the regular payday for the pay period during which the resignation occurred. The employee may request payment by mail.	—	If vacation is promised in a company policy or by practice, or if company policy provides for payment of accrued fringe benefits (sick pay, severance pay, commissions, and bonuses), vacation (and all accrued fringe benefits) must be paid upon termination of employment.	The employer must pay wages of up to $5,000 to surviving spouse.	Ariz. Rev. Stat. Ann. §§ 14-3971, 23-350, 23-353.
AR	Wages must be paid within 7 days. If the employer is a railroad, wages must be paid on the day of discharge. The railroad employee may request that wages be sent to any station, in which case the wages must be paid within 7 days.	—	—	—	—	Ark. Code Ann. § 11-4-405.

	Involuntary Termination	Resignation	Severance Pay	Vacation Pay	Death	Citations to Authority
CA	Wages are due and payable immediately. Certain seasonal employers may pay wages within 72 hours and by mail if the employee requests. Motion picture and oil drilling industry employers may pay wages by the next payday or within 24 hours, respectively.	If the employee gave no notice, wages must be paid within 72 hours; employee may elect to have the wages mailed. If the employee gave 72 hours' notice, the wages must be paid on the final work day.	—	Vested but unused vacation time must be paid as wages on termination if employer contract or policy provides for paid vacation. Forfeiture of vacation time on termination is prohibited by law.	The employer should pay wages and unused vacation pay or other compensation of up to $5,000 to surviving spouse, conservator, or guardian.	Cal. Lab. Code §§ 201, 201.5, 201.7, 202, 209, 227.3; Cal. Prob. Code § 13600.
CO	Wages are due and payable immediately. If the accounting unit is not regularly scheduled to be operational, wages must be paid within 6 hours of the start of the next regular workday. If accounting unit is located off-site, wages must be paid within 24 hours after start of next regular workday.	Wages must be paid on the next regular payday at work site, at employer's local office, or by mail.	—	Unused vested vacation, unused floating holidays and optional paid holidays must be paid at the time of termination.	Wages owed to employee at employee's death must be paid to employee's personal representative. If there is no personal representative, wages should be paid to employee's surviving spouse or next legal heir. Payments must be made upon request. Payments must be acknowledged in writing by representative, spouse, or legal heir.	Colo. Rev. Stat. Ann. §§ 8-4-101, 8-4-109.
CT	Wages must be paid on the next business day.	Wages must be paid on the next regular payday, through the regular channels, or by mail.	—	If employer, under policy or collective bargaining agreement, provides for payment of accrued fringe benefits on termination, and employee has not received benefits at time of termination, he or she must be compensated for vacation, sick leave, and other benefits in the form of wages.	Employer may pay up to $20,000 in unpaid wages to a spouse, next of kin, or partner in a civil union.	Conn. Gen. Stat. Ann. §§ 31-71c, 31-76k, 45a-273.

Exhibit 4.1　　　　　　　　　　　　　　　　　　Mandated Benefits: 2009 Compliance Guide

Exhibit 4.1 (cont'd)
Wage Payments Due on Termination or Death of Employee

	Involuntary Termination	Resignation	Severance Pay	Vacation Pay	Death	Citations to Authority
DE	Wages must be paid on the next regular payday. In the case of a suspension or layoff, wages must be paid on the next regular payday. The employee may request payment by mail.	Wages must be paid on the next regular payday. The employee may request payment by mail.	—	If company policy, employment contract or collective bargaining agreement provide for vacation pay, accrued vacation pay must be paid upon termination.	If the wages owed are not in excess of $300, wages should be paid to the surviving children under age 21 and their parent or guardian; the spouse; children over age 21; or parents of the employee, in that order.	Del. Code Ann. tit. 19, §§ 1103, 1106.
DC	Wages must be paid on the next working day. If the employee was in charge of accounts, the employer has 4 days to determine the accuracy of the employee's accounts and pay the wages due.	Wages must be paid on the earlier of the next regular payday or 7 days from the date of termination.	—	There is no statute to require payment of vacation upon termination; however, courts have interpreted that wages due upon termination include accrued vacation pay.	—	D.C. Code Ann. § 32-1303.
FL	—	—	—	—	The employer should pay the spouse, children over age 18, or parents of the employee any wages or traveling expenses due the employee. Traveling expenses so exempted from administration must not exceed the sum of $300.	Fla. Stat. Ann. § 222.15.

	Involuntary Termination	Resignation	Severance Pay	Vacation Pay	Death	Citations to Authority
GA	—	—	—	—	The employer must pay up to $2,500 of the wages due the employee (if employer is the state, all wages must be paid) to the beneficiary specified by the employee. If the employee has not specified a beneficiary, wages should be paid to the spouse, minor children, or guardian of the minor children of the employee.	Ga. Code Ann. §§ 29-5-12, 34-7-4.
HI	Wages should be paid at the time of discharge unless the conditions prevent immediate payment, in which case wages must be paid on the working day following the discharge. In the case of a layoff for any reason, wages must be paid on the next regular payday. The employee may request payment by mail.	Wages must be paid on the next regular payday. If the employee gives at least 1 pay period's notice, wages must be paid on the last working day. If the employer requests advance notice and advance notice is given, the employee must be paid for the entire notice period, until employment is terminated, as long as the employee does not voluntarily terminate employment or is not terminated for cause before the last day of the notice period. The employee may request payment by mail.	Any employer of 50 or more employees that relocates outside the state, closes, or partially closes must pay eligible employees a dislocated worker allowance equal to the difference between the employee's average weekly wage and unemployment compensation benefits for 4 weeks.	Vacation pay accrues until date of termination. Employers must post their vacation pay policy in a place where all employees can view it.	The employer should pay wages, vacation, and sick pay not exceeding $2,000 to the employee's spouse (or adult child if there is no surviving spouse) on proof of relationship.	Haw. Rev. Stat. Ann. §§ 388-3, 388-4, 388-41, 394B-10.
ID	Wages must be paid on the earlier of the next regular payday or 10 days from the date of discharge or *(continued)*	Wages must be paid on the earlier of the next regular payday or 10 days from the date of resignation, weekends and holidays excluded. If the *(continued)*	—	There is no statute to require payment of vacation upon termination; however, courts have interpreted that wages due *(continued)*	—	Idaho Code § 45-606.

Exhibit 4.1   Mandated Benefits: 2009 Compliance Guide

Exhibit 4.1 (cont'd)
Wage Payments Due on Termination or Death of Employee

	Involuntary Termination	Resignation	Severance Pay	Vacation Pay	Death	Citations to Authority
ID *(continued)*	layoff, weekends and holidays excluded. If the employee makes a written request for earlier payment, wages must be paid within 48 hours of the receipt of the request, weekends and holidays excluded.	employee makes a written request for earlier payment, wages must be paid within 48 hours of the receipt of the request, weekends and holidays excluded.		upon termination include accrued vacation pay.		
IL	Wages must be paid at the time of separation if possible, and in no case later than the next regularly scheduled payday. The employee may request that payment be sent by mail. If workers are laid off, the employer must pay all wages earned up until that point at the next regular payday.	Wages must be paid at the time of separation if possible, and in no case later than the next regularly scheduled payday. The employee may request that payment be sent by mail.	—	Earned but unused vacation time must be paid unless otherwise provided for in a collective bargaining agreement.	—	820 Ill. Comp. Stat. Ann. 115/4, 115/5.
IN	Wages must be paid on the next regular payday. Provision does not apply to railroads in their payments to employees.	Wages must be paid at the next usual and regular payday. If the employee leaves without notice and no address is known to the employer, the employer has 10 days from the time wages are demanded or until the employee provides an address.	—	There is no statute to require payment of vacation upon termination; however, courts have interpreted that wages due upon termination include accrued vacation pay.	45 days after the death of the employee, the employer should pay sums owed to surviving heirs if affidavit meeting statutory guidelines is presented.	Ind. Code Ann. §§ 22-2-5-1, 22-2-9-2, 29-1-8-1.

	Involuntary Termination	Resignation	Severance Pay	Vacation Pay	Death	Citations to Authority
IA	Wages must be paid on the next regular payday. The employer has 30 days from the date of termination to calculate commissions.	Wages must be paid on the next regular payday. The employer has 30 days to calculate commissions. If an employer actively recruits non-English-speaking residents of states more than 500 miles from the place of employment and the employee resigns within 4 weeks of the start of employment and requests transportation home within 3 days of the resignation, the employer must provide the transportation at no cost to the employee.	—	If vacation pay is due an employee under an agreement or employer policy, employee must be paid for accrued vacation.	—	Iowa Code Ann. §§ 91A.2, 91A.4, 91E.3.
KS	Wages must be paid on the next regular payday. The employee may request payment by mail.	Wages must be paid on the next regular payday. The employee may request payment by mail.	—	There is no statute to require payment of vacation upon termination; however, courts have interpreted that wages due upon termination include accrued vacation pay.	In the absence of notice of probate proceedings and upon proper demand, wages should be paid to the employee's spouse, adult children, parents, and siblings, or the person who paid the funeral expenses, in that order.	Kan. Stat. Ann. §§ 44-315, 44-318.
KY	All wages earned are payable not later than the next normal pay date following the date of separation or 14 days following separation, whichever is later. Employees not paid at a fixed time must be paid at any time or within 14 days after request.	All wages earned are payable not later than the next normal pay date following the date of separation or 14 days following separation, whichever is later. Employees not paid at a fixed time must be paid at any time or within 14 days after request.	—	Vested vacation pay must be paid upon termination of employment.	—	Ky. Rev. Stat. Ann. §§ 337.010, 337.055.

Exhibit 4.1   Mandated Benefits: 2009 Compliance Guide

Exhibit 4.1 (cont'd)
Wage Payments Due on Termination or Death of Employee

	Involuntary Termination	Resignation	Severance Pay	Vacation Pay	Death	Citations to Authority
LA	Wages must be paid on or before the next regular payday or not later than 15 days following the date of discharge, whichever occurs first. The employee may request payment by mail, and if so, must leave a self-addressed, stamped envelope with the employer for the mailing.	Wages must be paid on the earlier of the next regular payday or 15 days from the date of resignation. The employee may request payment by mail, and if so, must leave a self-addressed, stamped envelope with the employer for the mailing.	—	If employer's policy provides for accrual of paid vacation, accrued but unused vacation must be paid upon termination of employment.	The employer may pay up to $6,000 in wages and other benefits due the deceased employee to the employee's spouse. If the employee had no spouse, or divorce proceedings had begun, amounts owed should be paid to the employee's adult children.	La. Rev. Stat. Ann. §§ 9:1515, 23:631.
ME	Wages must be paid on the earlier of the next regular payday or 2 weeks from the date of discharge. An employer engaged in any manufacturing or mechanical business may contract with employees to have them give 1 week's notice or forfeit 1 week's pay. In such a case, the employer is required to give the same notice or pay the employee for an additional week, but not if the employee is fired for cause.	Wages must be paid on the earlier of the next regular payday or 2 weeks from the date of resignation. An employer engaged in any manufacturing or mechanical business may contract with employees to have them give 1 week's notice or forfeit 1 week's pay. In such a case, the employer is required to give the same notice or pay the employee for an additional week, but not if the employee is fired for cause.	Any industrial or commercial facility that has employed 100 employees in the preceding 12 months and that relocates 100 miles from original location or terminates business must pay 1 week's pay for each year worked for employees employed for at least 3 years.	If the employee receives paid vacation under the employer's policy, vacation pay has the same status as earned wages.	—	Me. Rev. Stat. Ann. tit. 26, §§ 625, 625-B, 626. Severance not preempted by ERISA. *Fort Halifax Packing Co. v. Coyne*, 482 U.S. 1 (1987).

	Involuntary Termination	Resignation	Severance Pay	Vacation Pay	Death	Citations to Authority
MD	Wages must be paid on or before the day the employee would have been paid for that work if the employee had not been discharged. Wages include all compensation due an employee, including bonuses, commissions, and fringe benefits. Sales representatives must be paid all commissions due under a terminated contract within 45 days after payment would have been due if the contract had not terminated.	Wages must be paid on or before the day the employee would have been paid for that work if the employee had not resigned. Wages include all compensation due an employee, including bonuses, commissions, and fringe benefits. Sales representatives must be paid all commissions due under a terminated contract within 45 days after payment would have been due if the contract had not terminated.	—	Employers may follow company policy regarding the payment of vacation pay upon termination, except that employees must be notified in writing if vacation pay will be lost upon termination. If employees are not so notified, vacation pay may not be forfeited.	—	Md. Code Ann., Lab. & Empl. §§ 3-501, 3-504, 3-505, 3-604.
MA	Wages must be paid on the day of discharge, except that Boston employers may make payment as soon as they have complied with laws requiring payrolls and accounts to be certified. If a manufacturing employer requires an employee to forfeit wages on resignation, the employer must forfeit an equal amount when the employer terminates an employee without notice.	Wages must be paid on the next regular payday, or on the following Saturday if there is no regular payday.	Buyer of company must pay 2 weeks' pay for each year of service to employees with 3 or more years of service who are terminated within 2 years of the transfer of control. Payments apply to employers with 50 or more full-time employees who are terminated within 24 months after corporate takeover.	Payment upon termination must include any holiday or vacation payments due the employee under an oral or written agreement.	If 30 days have passed since the death of the employee and an administrator has not made written demand on the employer for payment, wages of up to $100 owed to the employee may be paid to the employee's spouse. If there is no spouse, payment should be made to the children of the employee.	Mass. Gen. Laws Ann. ch. 149, §§ 148, 159, 178A, 183. Note: The U.S. Court of Appeals, 1st Circuit, has held that the Massachusetts statute on severance pay is preempted by ERISA. *Simas v. Quaker Fabric Corp. of Fall River*, 6 F.3d 849 (1st Cir. 1993).

Exhibit 4.1 (cont'd)
Wage Payments Due on Termination or Death of Employee

	Involuntary Termination	Resignation	Severance Pay	Vacation Pay	Death	Citations to Authority
MI	Wages must be paid as soon as the amount owed can, with due diligence, be determined. If the employee is under a contract and the amount owed cannot be determined until the end of the contract period, an estimate should be paid at the time of discharge, with an adjustment at the end of the contract period. *(continued)*	Wages must be paid as soon as the amount owed can, with due diligence, be determined. Certain agricultural employees must be paid within 3 days of resignation. If the employee is under a contract and the amount owed cannot be determined until the end of the contract period, an estimate should be paid at the time of resignation, with an adjustment at the end of the contract period.	—	Employer must pay value of fringe benefits if so provided in written contract or written policy.	Wages and fringe benefits should be paid to the employee's designee, spouse, children, parents, or siblings, in that order.	Mich. Comp. Laws Ann. §§ 408.474, 408.475, 408.480. Mich. Admin. Code §§ 408.9005, 408.9007.
MN	If the employer is a public service corporation, wages must be paid at the time of discharge. If the employment is transitory, wages must be paid within 24 hours. For other employers, wages must be paid within 24 hours of demand by the employee. If payment not made within 24 hours of demand, earned wages and commissions will continue for up to 15 days. If the employee *(continued)*	If the employment is transitory, wages must be paid within 24 hours. For other employment, wages must be paid not later than the next regularly scheduled payday, unless the payday occurs less than 5 days from resignation, in which case full payment may be delayed until the second regularly scheduled payday, but not more than 20 days from resignation. If the employee is under contract and gives 5 days' notice, wages must be paid within 24 hours. If the employee was in charge of accounts, the employer has 10 days to audit the accounts *(continued)*	—	If vacation pay is provided under an employment agreement or employer policy, employee must be paid for vacation pay.	The employer should pay wages owed, up to $10,000, to the surviving spouse.	Minn. Stat. Ann. §§ 181.08, 181.11, 181.13, 181.14, 181.58, 181.74, 181.87, 181.145.

	Involuntary Termination	Resignation	Severance Pay	Vacation Pay	Death	Citations to Authority
MN *(continued)*	was in charge of accounts, the employer has 10 days to audit the accounts and pay the wages owed. The employee may request payment by mail. Any payment guarantees for migrant workers do not apply if the worker is discharged before the completion of a 2-week period. If the employee works on commission, or is a migrant worker, wages must be paid within 3 days.	and pay the wages owed. The employee may request payment by mail. Any payment guarantees for migrant workers do not apply if the worker resigns before the completion of a 2 week period. If the employee works on commission and does not give notice, the employer has 6 days to pay wages owed. If commissioned salesperson gives 5 days' notice, wages must be paid within 3 days.				
MS	—	—		If the state is the employer, accrued leave must be paid when the employee leaves for any reason.	The employer must pay wages or other compensation owed an employee to the spouse, adult children, parents, or adult siblings of the employee, in that order. The employer should pay the amounts owed to the chancery clerk if none of the surviving members of the above groups are adults. If the estate is administered upon, the employer should not pay amounts owed until further direction. If the employer is the state, accumulated personal leave must be paid.	Miss. Code Ann. §§ 25-3-97, 91-7-323, 91-7-329.

Exhibit 4.1   Mandated Benefits: 2009 Compliance Guide

Exhibit 4.1 (cont'd)
Wage Payments Due on Termination or Death of Employee

	Involuntary Termination	Resignation	Severance Pay	Vacation Pay	Death	Citations to Authority
MO	Wages must be paid on the day of discharge. The employee may request that wages be paid by mail, in which case amounts are due to the employee within 7 days of request. These rules do not apply in the case of an employee who works on commission or a similar basis when an audit is necessary to determine the amount due.	—	—	—	—	Mo. Rev. Stat. § 290.110.
MT	Unpaid wages are due and payable immediately on separation unless the employer has a written personnel policy governing the employment that extends the time for payment of final wages to the next regular payday or to within 15 days of separation. If the employee was discharged for cause, wages must be paid immediately, but if theft charges are pending, the employer may apply to the court for an order staying payment of wages.	Wages must be paid by the earlier of the next regular pay day or 15 days from the date of resignation.	—	There is no statute to require payment of vacation upon termination; however, the Montana attorney general has interpreted that wages due upon termination includes earned vacation pay.	—	Mont. Code Ann. §§ 39-3-201, 39-3-205.

	Involuntary Termination	Resignation	Severance Pay	Vacation Pay	Death	Citations to Authority
NE	Wages must be paid on the earlier of the next regular payday or 2 weeks from the date of discharge. Commissions are due at the next regular payday. If the employer is a political subdivision and notice of the discharge was given 1 week before the next meeting of the governing body, wages must be paid within 2 weeks of the meeting. If less than 1 week of notice was given, wages must be paid within 2 weeks of the next meeting.	Wages must be paid on the earlier of the next regular payday or 2 weeks from the date of resignation. Commissions are due at the next regular payday. If the employer is a political subdivision and notice of the discharge was given 1 week before the next meeting of the governing body, wages must be paid within 2 weeks of the meeting. If less than 1 week of notice was given, wages must be paid within 2 weeks of the next meeting.	—	When there is an agreement between the employer and the employee that vacation pay will be treated as wages, and the employee has met the terms of the agreement, then vacation pay is to be paid upon termination of employment. Wages include sick leave and other fringe benefits when an agreement between employer and employee so provides.	—	Neb. Rev. Stat. Ann. §§ 48-1229, 48-1230.
NV	Wages are due and payable immediately, unless the state is the employer.	Wages must be paid on the earlier of the next regular payday or 7 days from the date of resignation, unless the state is the employer.	—	—	40 days after death of the employee, the employer should pay amounts owed to heirs (spouse, children, grandchildren, parents, siblings, or guardian) if those amounts are less than $10,000.	Nev. Rev. Stat. Ann. §§ 146.080, 608.012, 608.020, 608.030.
NH	Wages must be paid within 72 hours. In the case of a layoff for any reason, wages must be paid on the next regular pay day. The employee may request payment by mail.	Wages must be paid on the next regular payday, but if the employee gave 1 pay period's notice, wages must be paid within 72 hours. The employee may request payment by mail.	—	Final wages include vacation if vacation pay is due an employee under an employer policy or practice.	The employer should pay wages and commissions of up to $500 to surviving spouse.	N.H. Rev. Stat. Ann. §§ 275:42-275:44, 560:20.

Exhibit 4.1   Mandated Benefits: 2009 Compliance Guide

Exhibit 4.1 (cont'd)

Wage Payments Due on Termination or Death of Employee

	Involuntary Termination	Resignation	Severance Pay	Vacation Pay	Death	Citations to Authority
NJ	Wages must be paid by the regular payday for the pay period during which the discharge took place. If the employee is compensated by an incentive system, the employer should pay an approximation until the exact amount can be determined. The employee may request payment by mail. If the employment is suspended as a result of a labor dispute that involves employees in the employer's payroll department, the employer has an extra 10 days to pay wages.	Wages must be paid by the regular payday for the pay period during which the resignation took place. If the employee is compensated by an incentive system, the employer should pay an approximation until the exact amount can be determined. The employee may request payment by mail.	—	—	Absent notice of probate, the employer should pay all wages due to the spouse, children age 18 and older, parents, siblings, or person paying funeral expenses of the employee, in that order.	N.J. Stat. Ann. §§ 34:11-4.3, 34:11-4.5.
NM	Wages must be paid within 5 days. If the employee works on commission or a similar basis, wages must be paid within 10 days.	Wages must be paid on the next regular payday.	—		The employer must pay amounts owed to the employee's surviving spouse.	N.M. Stat. Ann. §§ 45-3-1301, 50-4-4-50-4-6.

	Involuntary Termination	Resignation	Severance Pay	Vacation Pay	Death	Citations to Authority
NY	Wages due on the regular payday. The employee may request payment by mail. When a contract between a sales representative and a principal is terminated, all earned commissions are due within 5 days of termination, or if not due at the time of termination, within 5 days after commissions become due.	If an employee resigns, wages must be paid by the regular payday. When a contract between a sales representative and a principal is terminated, all earned commissions are due within 5 days of termination or 5 days after becoming due if not due at the time of termination. The employee may request payment by mail.	—	Final wages include vacation if vacation pay is provided under an employer policy.	The employer should pay wages and pension, retirement, or death benefits of up to $15,000 to surviving spouse, adult child, parent, sibling, niece, nephew, or person paying funeral expenses of the employee, in that order.	N.Y. Lab. Law §§ 190, 191, 191-c; N.Y. Surr. Ct. Proc. Act Law § 1310.
NC	Wages must be paid on or before the next regular payday. The employee may request payment by mail. If the wages are based on commissions, bonuses, or similar systems, the wages must be paid on the first regular payday after they become calculable. Wages include sick pay, vacation pay, and any other such sums an employer has a practice of paying.	Wages must be paid on or before the next regular payday. The employee may request payment by mail. If the wages are based on commissions, bonuses, or similar systems, the wages must be paid on the first regular pay day after they become calculable. Wages include sick pay, vacation pay, and any other such sums an employer has a practice of paying.	—	Employers may follow company policy regarding the payment of vacation pay upon termination, except that employees must be notified in writing or by way of a posted notice if vacation pay will be lost upon termination (or other reasons). If employees are not so notified, vacation pay may not be forfeited.	—	N.C. Gen. Stat. §§ 95-25.2, 95-25.7.

Exhibit 4.1   Mandated Benefits: 2009 Compliance Guide

Exhibit 4.1 (cont'd)
Wage Payments Due on Termination or Death of Employee

	Involuntary Termination	Resignation	Severance Pay	Vacation Pay	Death	Citations to Authority
ND	Railroad employees must be paid at the time of discharge or on demand. Other employees must be paid at the earlier of 15 days after discharge or the next regular payday. The employee may request payment by mail. An employee who is discharged for cause is entitled to such proportion of compensation as the service rendered bears to the service intended.	Wages must be paid on the next regular payday. An employee who resigns for cause is entitled to such proportion of compensation as the service rendered bears to the service contemplated.	—	Vacation pay is included in final wages, if employee has been employed for at least one year and has earned the time off. Vacation pay may not be forfeited upon termination, unless policy or employment contract requires that employee take vacation by a certain date or lose the vacation and employee has had opportunity to take earned vacation.	The employer should pay amounts owed to surviving spouse or next eligible heirs.	N.D. Cent. Code §§ 34-01-12, 34-03-09, 34-14-03, 49-10.1-15.
OH	—	—	—	—	An employer may pay all wages due the employee to the employee's spouse, adult children, or parents, in that order, without requesting an estate tax release, or letters of administration or testamentary, when wages do not exceed $2,500.	Ohio Rev. Code Ann. §§ 2113.04, 4113.15.

	Involuntary Termination	Resignation	Severance Pay	Vacation Pay	Death	Citations to Authority
OK	Wages must be paid on the next regular payday. The employee may request payment by mail or direct deposit.	Wages must be paid on the next regular payday. The employee may request payment by mail. Wages include holiday, vacation, and severance pay. Payment by mail must be postmarked by the next regular payday date.	—	Final wages include vacation pay if vacation is included in employer's established policy or is agreed to by employee and employer.	The employer should pay amounts owed, up to $3,000, to surviving spouse, or if no surviving spouse, to dependent child, guardian of child, or conservator of estate.	Okla. Stat. Ann. tit. 40, §§ 165.1, 165.3, 165.3a.
OR	If the employee is discharged or leaves by mutual agreement, wages must be paid no later than the end of the first business day after discharge. Employee may request payment by mail or direct deposit.	If the employee gives 48 hours' notice (excluding weekends and holidays), wages must be paid by the last day of employment. If 48 hours' notice is not given, wages must be paid by the earlier of the next regular payday or 5 working days from the date of resignation. The employee may request payment by mail. The employer and employee may agree to have payment made by direct deposit.	—	There is no statute to require payment of vacation upon termination; however, the courts have interpreted that wages due upon termination includes earned vacation pay. Also, the Or. Rev. Stat. defines wages as including the "cash value of all compensation paid in any medium other than cash."	The employer should pay wages of up to $10,000 to the spouse, or if there is no surviving spouse, to the dependent children or their guardian in equal shares.	Or. Rev. Stat. §§ 652.140, 652.170, 652.190. Or. Admin. Rules §§ 839-001-0410–839-001-0450.
PA	Wages must be paid on the next regular payday on which such wages would otherwise be due. The employee may request payment by mail. There will be no violation of this statute if, because of an industrial dispute or other circumstances beyond the control of the *(continued)*	Wages must be paid on the next regular payday on which such wages would otherwise be due. The employee may request payment by mail. There will be no violation of this statute if, because of an industrial dispute or other circumstances beyond the control of the employer, the employer cannot prepare the payroll.	Buyer of company must pay 1 week's severance for each year of service to each employee with 2 or more years of service who is terminated within 2 years of transfer of control of company.	Wages include fringe benefits, such as vacation and holiday pay, when company policy or practice is to provide vacation pay.	The employer should pay wages owed of up to $5,000 to surviving spouse, child, parent, or sibling of the employee, in that order.	15 Pa. C.S. §§ 2581, 2582; 20 Pa. C.S. § 3101; 43 Pa. C.S. §§ 260.2, 260.5.

Exhibit 4.1

Mandated Benefits: 2009 Compliance Guide

Exhibit 4.1 (cont'd)
Wage Payments Due on Termination or Death of Employee

	Involuntary Termination	Resignation	Severance Pay	Vacation Pay	Death	Citations to Authority
PA (continued)	employer, the employer cannot prepare the payroll.					
RI	Wages must be paid on the next regular payday at the regular place of employment. If the employer is liquidating the business, wages must be paid within 24 hours.	Wages must be paid on the next regular payday. If the employer is liquidating the business, wages must be paid within 24 hours.	Buyer of company must pay 2 weeks' severance pay for each year of service to employees with 3 or more years of service who are terminated within 2 years after transfer of control; within 1 year preceding transfer of control; or during period when buyer increases ownership of voting securities from 5% to 50%.	If the employee had 1 year of service, any vacation pay earned under an employer agreement, company policy or collective bargaining is payable and must be paid by the next regular pay day.	Anytime after 30 days from the employee's death the employer may pay wages, in the following order, to the employee's spouse, adult children, parents, or siblings, or to the person who paid for the funeral, provided the employer knows of no will or similar document and wages do not exceed $150.	R.I. Gen. Laws §§ 28-7-19.2, 28-14-4-28-14-6. Note: Severance pay requirement held to be preempted by ERISA. *United Paperworkers International Union Local 1468 v. Imperial Home Decor Group*, 76 F. Supp. 2d 179 (D.R.I. 1999).
SC	Wages must be paid within 48 hours of the time of discharge or at the next regular payday, but not to exceed 30 days from the time of discharge.	Wages must be paid within 48 hours of the time of resignation or at the next regular payday, but not to exceed 30 days from the time of written notice.	—	Wages due upon termination include vacation pay, holiday pay, sick pay, and other compensation due the employee under employer policy or contract.	—	S.C. Code Ann. §§ 41-10-10, 41-10-50.
SD	Wages must be paid at the next regular payday or as soon thereafter as the employee returns all of the employer's property.	Wages must be paid at the next regular payday or as soon thereafter as the employee returns all of the employer's property.	—	—	—	S.D. Codified Laws §§ 60-11-10-60-11-12.

	Involuntary Termination	Resignation	Severance Pay	Vacation Pay	Death	Citations to Authority
TN	Wages must be paid by the later of the next regular payday or 21 days.	Wages must be paid by the later of the next regular payday or 21 days.	—	Employer may follow its own vacation payment policy.	The employer should pay wages of up to $10,000 to the employee's designee or the surviving spouse. If there is no surviving spouse, the employer may pay the wages to the employee's surviving children.	Tenn. Code Ann. §§ 30-2-103, 50-2-103(g).
TX	Railroad employees must be paid within 6 days of discharge. Wages must be paid to other employees within 6 days.	Wages must be paid on the next regular payday.	—	If employer has policy that it will pay employee for unused vacation leave and sick leave, it must pay for these benefits upon termination.	—	Tex. Lab. Code Ann. § 61.014; Tex. Rev. Civ. Stat. Ann. art. 6431.
UT	Wages must be paid within 24 hours, unless wages are determined by commission and require accounting.	If there is no written contract, wages and any deposits paid to the employer must be paid at the next regular payday unless wages are paid by commission and require accounting.	—	If employer has policy that it will pay employee for unused vacation leave, it must pay for these benefits upon termination.	30 days after the death of the employee, the employer should pay amounts owed to heirs if affidavit is presented, as provided by statute.	Utah Code Ann. §§ 34-28-5, 75-3-1201.
VT	Wages must be paid within 72 hours.	Wages must be paid on payday; if there is no regular payday, on the following Friday.	—	If employer has written policy that it will pay employee for accrued vacation, it must pay for these benefits upon termination.	—	Vt. Stat. Ann. tit. 21, § 342.
VA	Wages must be paid on or before the next regular payday.	Wages must be paid on or before the next regular payday.	—	—	The employer should pay up to $5,000 of wages owed to the employee's spouse, or distributees of decedent if there is no surviving spouse.	Va. Code Ann. §§ 40.1-29, 64.1-123.

Exhibit 4.1   Mandated Benefits: 2009 Compliance Guide

Exhibit 4.1 (cont'd)
Wage Payments Due on Termination or Death of Employee

	Involuntary Termination	Resignation	Severance Pay	Vacation Pay	Death	Citations to Authority
WA	Wages must be paid at the end of the established pay period, except in the case of an employee working for multiple employers that cooperate to pay wages, or if union contract provides otherwise.	Wages must be paid at the end of the established pay period, except in the case of an employee working for multiple employers that cooperate to pay wages, or if union contract provides otherwise.	—	—	The employer should pay wages owed up to $2,500 to the employee's spouse, parents, or children, in that order. If there is a community- property agreement between the employee and the surviving spouse, the employer must pay all wages due or the portion governed by the community-property agreement to the spouse.	Wash. Rev. Code Ann. §§ 49.48.010, 49.48.120.
WV	Wages must be paid within 72 hours. In the case of a layoff, wages must be paid on the next regular payday. The employee may request payment by mail.	Wages must be paid on the regular payday. If the employee gave 1 pay period's notice, wages are due at the time of resignation. The employee may request payment by mail.	—	Wages include all fringe benefits, including vacation pay.	The employer should pay wages owed of up to $800 to the employee's spouse, adult children, parents, siblings, or person paying funeral expenses, in that order.	W. Va. Code Ann. §§ 21-5-4, 21-5-8a.
WI	If the employee is not under a contract or on commission payment basis, wages must be paid by the earlier of the next regular pay-day or 1 month (3 months for logging operation and farm *(continued)*	If the employee is not under a contract or on a commission payment basis, wages must be paid by the earlier of the next regular payday or 1 month (3 months for logging operation and farm labor employees). Migrant workers must be paid *(continued)*	—	Employee must be paid for unused vacation and sick leave.	The employer should pay the full amount owed to the employee's spouse, children, or other dependents living with the employee, parents, or siblings, in that order.	Wis. Stat. Ann. §§ 103.93, 109.03.

	Involuntary Termination	Resignation	Severance Pay	Vacation Pay	Death	Citations to Authority
WI *(continued)*	labor employees). Migrant workers must be paid in full within 3 days after the termination of employment. If the employer liquidates or ceases business operations in whole or in part, wages must be paid within 24 hours.	in full within 3 days after the termination of employment.				
WY	Wages must be paid within 5 working days. If the employee is paid on a commission basis, wages must be paid after an audit is completed. In the case of a layoff, wages must be paid on the next regular payday. The employee may request payment by mail.	Wages must be paid within 5 working days. If the employee is paid on a commission basis, wages must be paid after an audit is completed.	—	There is no statute to require payment of vacation upon termination; however, the Wyoming attorney general has interpreted that vacation pay is additional or deferred wages and are due upon termination if there is an agreement between the employee and employer that provides for vacation pay. Additional requirements must be met in the agreement.	—	Wyo. Stat. Ann. §§ 27-4-101, 27-4-104.

Source: John F. Buckley & Ronald M. Green, *2008 State by State Guide to Human Resources Law* (New York: Aspen Publishers, Inc. 2008).

Chapter 5
Health Care Benefits

§ 5.01 AUDIT QUESTIONS

1. Has the company updated its summary plan description to include the "Statement of ERISA Rights" information required by the Health Insurance Portability and Accountability Act of 1996 (HIPAA)?

2. If the company's health plan has reduced covered services or benefits, has it provided plan participants with a summary of material modifications no later than 60 days after the effective date of those changes?

3. Has the company developed and implemented clear procedures to meet the notification, determination, and administration requirements of the Omnibus Budget Reconciliation Act of 1993 related to qualified medical child support orders?

4. Does the company's group health plan restrict the hospitalization period after childbirth for the mother or newborn to no less than 48 hours for a vaginal delivery and no less than 96 hours for a cesarean delivery?

5. Does the group health plan provide coverage for reconstructive surgery after a mastectomy, if the plan covers mastectomies?

6. Does the company provide annual written notice of the group health plan's coverage of reconstructive surgery after mastectomy?

7. Does the company avoid requesting genetic information about employees and/or their family members prior to or as a condition of enrolling them in the group health plan?

Note: Consistent "yes" answers to the above questions suggest that the organization is applying management practices and/or complying with federal regulations. "No" answers indicate that problem areas exist and should be addressed immediately.

There is no federal law that requires private employers to provide group health care or related benefits to their employees. Although several proposals have been made to change this situation, at present comprehensive federal health care reform legislation is not a reality. Many of the issues in proposals that have been discussed, however, will be reopened or debated again, and more proposals are expected in the future.

This chapter discusses the impact of existing federal legislation on employers that choose to provide employee health care and related benefits, proposed, incremental federal health care reform legislation, and ways in which some states regulate employer health care benefits within their boundaries.

The following federal laws in one way or another have an impact on employers' group health plans:

- The Employee Retirement Income Security Act of 1974

- Title VII of the Civil Rights Act of 1964

- Amendments to Title VII

- The Pregnancy Discrimination Amendment to Title VII

- The Health Maintenance Organization Act of 1973

- The Americans with Disabilities Act of 1990

- The Family and Medical Leave Act of 1993

- The Consolidated Omnibus Budget Reconciliation Act of 1985

- The Omnibus Budget Reconciliation Act of 1993

- The Health Insurance Portability and Accountability Act of 1996

- The Mental Health Parity Act of 1996

- The Newborns' and Mothers' Health Protection Act of 1996

- The Women's Health and Cancer Rights Act of 1998

- The Medicare Prescription Drug Improvement and Modernization Act of 2003

- The Uniformed Services Employment and Reemployment Rights Act of 1994

- The Genetic Information Nondiscrimination Act

Each of these laws is discussed in the following sections, except for the Health Insurance Portability and Accountability Act of 1996 and the Consolidated Omnibus Budget Reconciliation Act of 1985. (See **Chapter 6** for a discussion of the Health Insurance Portability and Accountability Act of 1996 and **Chapter 7** for a discussion of the Consolidated Omnibus Budget Reconciliation Act of 1985.)

§ 5.02 THE EMPLOYEE RETIREMENT INCOME SECURITY ACT

In 1974, Congress passed a comprehensive employee benefits law known as the Employee Retirement Income Security Act (ERISA). Many of ERISA's requirements apply to employers' qualified plans, such as pension plans and 401(k) plans. ERISA was enacted to implement a federal regulatory framework for pension and welfare benefit plans with the primary purpose of protecting employees' rights with regard to such plans. ERISA was drafted to supersede all state laws that relate to employee benefits plans. The significance of ERISA, for the purposes of this chapter, lies in its preemption provisions.

[A] The ERISA Preemption

Because benefits administrators must consider all the state-mandated benefits that can potentially apply to an employee, they should be familiar with the concept of the ERISA preemption. The preemption applies to all state laws that relate to employee benefit plans, not just state laws relating to the specific subjects of ERISA. Specifically, ERISA may preempt a state law mandating a particular benefit, as a consequence of which the particular benefit may not truly be mandated. The resulting preemption of state law is significantly broad. Congress believed that it was essential to eliminate the threat of inconsistent state and local regulation of employee benefit plans, and broad preemption was the only weapon to eliminate the threat completely.

One important exception to ERISA's preemption is known as the *savings clause,* which provides that nothing in ERISA is to be construed to exempt or relieve any person from any state law that regulates insurance, banking, or securities. The reference to insurance is significant and is explored in detail later in this chapter.

In general, state wage withholding laws are also preempted by ERISA. Many, if not all, states prohibit employers from withholding any money from employees' paychecks without their specific written consent. However, courts have generally held that ERISA preempts these laws as they apply to ERISA employee benefit plans. Thus, if an employer requires the employee to contribute to the cost of benefits under an ERISA benefit plan, the employer is not required to obtain the employee's written consent to deduct that contribution from the employee's paycheck (although notification of the withholding is required in the SPD).

[B] ERISA Coverage

ERISA applies to both employee pension benefit plans and employee welfare benefit plans. The term *employee pension benefit plan* includes any plan, fund, or program that provides retirement income to employees or results in a deferral of income by employees for periods extending to the termination of employment or beyond. The term *employee welfare benefit plan* includes any plan, fund, or program that provides medical, surgical or hospital care benefits, sickness, accident, disability, death, unemployment or vacation benefits, apprenticeship or other training, day care centers, scholarships, prepaid legal services, or holiday, severance, or similar benefit plans. These arrangements must be sponsored by an employer or an employee organization. ERISA covers nearly every employee benefit plan, with some exemptions.

[C] ERISA Exemptions

Plan sponsors or plans that fall within certain significant exemptions are not subject to ERISA. In addition, such plan sponsors and plans are not subject to preemption. Arrangements or plans that are exempt from ERISA coverage include:

- Any arrangement that does not cover employees. (Under ERISA, a 100 percent shareholder in a corporation and his or her spouse are not considered employees; this is true even if the spouses are treated as common-law employees for payroll tax purposes.)

- A partner in a partnership, without regard to the percentage of the business owned, in contrast to the treatment of partners under other employment law areas, such as the Age Discrimination in Employment Act of 1967 (ADEA).

- A sole proprietor and his or her spouse.

Thus, any plan that covers only the persons listed above is not an ERISA plan.

Employee benefit plans that are exempt from ERISA include those of any governmental unit—the federal government, a state government, or any political subdivision, agency, or instrumentality of such governments.

Note: Because local school districts are governmental units, their benefit plans are not subject to ERISA.

The employee benefit plan of a church is similarly exempt from ERISA. The term *church* means an organized body of a single church, a convention or association of churches, or a tax-exempt organization controlled by a church.

[D] ERISA Applications

In applying the ERISA preemption to the plan sponsor's advantage, it is necessary to first understand what plans or other arrangements are subject to ERISA. Answering the following questions should help the benefits administrator determine the relevance of ERISA exemptions to the company:

- *Is the organization's arrangement a plan?* The courts have constructed a number of standards for defining whether a set of facts constitutes a plan. Basically, the arrangement must specify the intended benefits, who would be eligible to receive such benefits, the source of the financing of the benefits, and the procedures for receiving the benefits. For example, the Supreme Court has upheld a state severance pay statute as not being an ERISA plan because it required employers to provide a onetime severance payment to employees in the event of a plant closing. The Court ruled that ERISA covers benefit plans, not simply benefits. Further, the Court held that the statutory requirement of a one-time, lump-sum payment triggered by a single event did not require companies to establish a plan. A plan would be created only if it were necessary to establish ongoing administrative procedures to keep track of employees and their eligibility for benefit payments. Thus, it failed the requirement that required procedures for the administration of the plan.

  ERISA requires that a plan be in writing. Violating this rule does not result in the arrangement's losing its ERISA protection. However, penalties may be assessed for rule violation. This holding is also true for the other parts of the definition of an ERISA plan. If the employer fails to specify the funding source, the plan may still be an ERISA plan.

- *Does the plan involve an employer or an employee organization?* The law requires some employer involvement in the arrangement to create an ERISA plan. Thus, a group insurance program may not be considered an employee benefit plan if any of the following conditions apply:

— The employer makes no contributions toward premiums.

— Participation is completely voluntary for employees.

— The employer's sole functions are, without endorsing the program, to allow the insurer to publicize it to employees, to collect premiums through payroll deductions, and to remit them to the insurer.

— The employer receives no consideration in connection with the program other than reasonable compensation for administrative services rendered in connection with payroll deductions.

Whether an employer's involvement in a group insurance program is sufficient to create a plan is frequently litigated. For example, in *Gray v. Prudential Ins. Co. of Am.*, [2006 U.S. Dist. LEXIS 46714 (E.D. Ark. 2006)] the court found the disability plan in question did not meet the voluntary plan safe harbor because (i) the employer's logo was found on the cover page of the plan and in the SPD; (ii) the employer held the insurance contract (vs. individual contracts for each employee); (iii) the employer determined the eligibility of individual employees; and (iv) the employer was listed as the agent of service for legal process.

A plan may be subject to ERISA even if the persons covered are not the employees of the plan sponsor. The most obvious example is a collectively bargained plan. Although the union sponsors the plan, the covered participants are not limited to employees of the union. Less obvious are employee associations. For example, the Department of Labor (DOL) has ruled that a police benevolence arrangement is an ERISA plan, even though it is not sponsored by the police department but is simply a voluntary arrangement of employees that offers ERISA-covered benefits.

- *Is the plan specifically exempted from ERISA?* As previously noted in this section, some plan sponsors are exempt from ERISA. In addition, some plan types are exempt from ERISA. For example, an arrangement whose sole purpose is to comply with state workers' compensation, unemployment compensation, or disability insurance laws is generally not subject to ERISA. Other statutory exemptions exist for plans maintained outside the United States for nonresident aliens or an unfunded excess benefit plan.

In addition, DOL regulations exempt from the definition of employee benefit plan certain payroll practices (e.g., direct payment for sick leave, holidays, and vacation). A minor change in this area can make a plan exempt from or subject to ERISA. For example, if an employer pays for vacation pay out of its checking account, the plan is exempt from ERISA. If the employer funds the vacation pay plan through a voluntary employee beneficiary association (VEBA) or other arrangement that gives the plan assets, the plan becomes subject to ERISA. This is a special rule for vacation pay plans.

In order for a payroll practice that provides disability or sick pay benefits to be exempt from ERISA, it must provide payment of the employee's normal compensation from the employer's general assets. Various courts have ruled benefit plans that pay less than the employee's normal compensation will also be exempt from ERISA if the amount paid is "related to" the employee's normal compensation. Thus, if the plan pays 60 percent of the employee's base salary while an employee is absent from work due to illness or injury, and the payments are made by the employer out of its general assets (e.g., through payroll), the plan will not be considered an ERISA plan. In order to maintain this ERISA exemption, it is important that there is no insurance contract that pays the benefits. Another requirement for the payroll practice exemption is that payments cannot be made to former employees. It is recommended that all references to ERISA be removed from the communication material about the plan.

Another example of an exempt plan is a bonus program. For example, an employer may provide a deferred-bonus arrangement under which an employee must remain employed for three years from the date of the bonus accrual to receive the bonus amount. Such an arrangement is not an ERISA plan, because the payment is made after a fixed period rather than as a result of separation from service or retirement. However, if an employee covered by a deferred-bonus arrangement is age 62 and is expected to retire at age 65, the arrangement might be an ERISA plan, because payment is, in fact, due at retirement.

- *Does the plan relate to an ERISA benefit?* Most benefits administrators seem to understand which of their benefits fall under the retirement benefits of ERISA, but they cannot as easily identify which company benefits are actually welfare benefits as defined by ERISA and which are simply fringe benefits. In addition to group health plans, welfare benefits include medical, dental, and vision benefits; life insurance; other death benefits, such as travel accident and accidental death and dismemberment plans; disability plans; severance pay plans; prepaid legal service plans; and funded scholarship plans.

  For example, a cafeteria plan that allows employees to direct their salary deferrals among health insurance premiums, disability insurance premiums, dependent care expenses, and additional time off is not an ERISA welfare benefit plan. The health and disability provisions within the cafeteria plan are ERISA plans, but the cafeteria plan is simply a payroll practice facilitating the funding of these arrangements and not a plan in the ERISA context. This is true even though a Form 5500 series report is required for the cafeteria plan. That filing is required by the Internal Revenue Code (Code), not by ERISA.

  Further, some arrangements may or may not be subject to ERISA because some minor portion of the benefits provided are ERISA benefits. For example, many employers sponsor employee assistance programs (EAPs). EAPs are designed to help employees with personal or business-related problems, such as balancing their checkbooks, dealing with excess consumer debt, marital strife, and chemical dependency. An EAP is a fringe benefit in general parlance, but it is an ERISA welfare plan only if it covers an ERISA benefit. Thus, an EAP that provides only financial counseling is not an ERISA plan because financial counseling is not a covered benefit. If an EAP offers counseling for chemical dependency treatment, however, it might be considered an ERISA plan if the chemical dependency treatment is considered sickness coverage. (See **Chapter 10**.)

- *Does the state law relate to an ERISA employee benefit plan?* Preemption is not limited to state laws that conflict with ERISA or state laws that actually affect or regulate plan terms. Even state laws designed to protect employee benefit plans are preempted. However, not every conceivable cause of action that may be brought against ERISA plans is preempted. For example, a state action that affects plans in a tenuous, remote, or peripheral manner may stand.

The guidelines are obviously not clear-cut. Plan administrators need expert assistance to determine whether many arrangements are ERISA plans. The purpose of this chapter is to demonstrate how expansive the definition is and to act as a warning that plans may unexpectedly be subject to or exempt from ERISA requirements. If they are exempt, the ERISA preemption does not apply. In general, the interpretations of the Supreme Court have been consistent with the intent of the preemption provision and have given the provision broad effect.

[E] The Savings Clause

Even if the benefits administrator determines that the employer's plan is an ERISA plan and that preemption may apply, he or she must consider the savings clause, which is a significant factor pertaining to many mandated benefits tied to insurance products. The savings clause is one exception to ERISA's preemption. Generally, it states that ERISA does not exempt the employer from state laws that govern insurance, banking, or securities. Thus, because of the savings clause, ERISA does not preempt state insurance laws. ERISA does not preempt state statutes that require insurance policies to include particular provisions, even if a policy is sold to an ERISA-covered employee benefit plan. As a consequence, state statutes that require health insurance policies to include specific benefits (e.g., for mental health, the treatment of drug and alcohol abuse, or payment for services rendered by chiropractors) or to include specific terms (e.g., preexisting condition limits) still apply to policies sold to ERISA-covered plans.

[F] Using the ERISA Preemption to the Employer's Advantage

Although ERISA's requirements can be burdensome, at least they are uniform among all states and are fairly well understood. Accordingly, the benefits administrator may prefer to have the employee benefit arrangements be subject to ERISA exclusively rather than to a host of state laws. If the benefit is not part of an ERISA-covered plan, there may be some strategies available to achieve protection.

For example, the most common strategy is to use a self-insured medical plan to avoid state-mandated health benefits. As states have become more active in mandated health benefits legislation, more employers have turned to self-insured medical plans to avoid mandated benefits. This strategy is effective because of an exception to an exception. Specifically, whereas the savings clause excepts state insurance laws from ERISA preemption, the deemer clause excepts self-insured plans from the savings clause, by providing that an employee benefit plan is not deemed to be engaged in the business of insurance. By definition, a self-insured program does not use an insurance contract, and because the self-insured plan is not treated as engaged in the business of insurance, there is no insurance for a state law to regulate. Accordingly, state statutes mandating the inclusion of certain benefits in health insurance policies may not be applied to self-insured medical plans. Self-insured plans are an important alternative to state-mandated health benefits. Whether to implement a self-insured plan is discussed in detail in the following section.

For the benefits administrator to exercise the ERISA preemption, the plan must be subject to ERISA. For example, a self-insured plan of a governmental unit is exempt from ERISA, and its plan therefore is not exempt from state laws mandating certain benefits.

A plan administrator may also use ERISA to avoid other types of state mandates. For example, California mandates vesting of vacation pay. If vacation pay qualifies as a payroll practice, it is not subject to ERISA, and ERISA cannot preempt this state mandate. However, if the employer were to provide vacation pay through a VEBA, the funded vacation-pay program becomes an ERISA-protected employee benefit plan. ERISA would then preempt this particular state mandate, and the employer would not need to vest vacation pay. Of course, there are pros and cons to using a VEBA; the benefits administrator should consult with a competent benefits consultant before developing an ERISA plan for the first time.

[G] Self-Insured Health Plans

If an employer provides employees with medical coverage out of its general assets, the health plan is self-insured. A self-insured health plan passes all risks to the employer; however, such mechanisms as stoploss coverage can be obtained to control the risk.

Stop-loss, or excess-loss, insurance is purchased from an insurance carrier. This type of coverage limits a self-funded plan's liability if claims exceed a specified dollar amount over a set period of time. Coverage may be purchased on an aggregate (i.e., whole group) or specific (i.e., participant or family) basis, or both.

A second advantage of self-insurance is the employer's ability to limit liability to the claims experience of its own employees. Yet another advantage is unilateral decision making; the employer has the ability to design and modify the plan without the restrictions, delays, and costs involved in obtaining the approval of another party, such as an insurer or regulatory agency.

Of the many factors that affect an employer's decision to self-insure, the most important is the employer's ability to assume the risks involved. In general, smaller employers simply cannot afford to assume the risks. An employer contemplating self-insurance primarily to avoid state mandates should consider the following issues:

- Are the benefits mandated by the state costly?

- Would the benefits offered by a self-insured plan be different from state-mandated benefits (i.e., are the mandated benefits too popular to eliminate)?

- What is the likelihood of an increasing number of mandated benefits in that state?

- If the employer operates in more than one state, will compliance with state mandates be complicated by the employer's multistate operations?

Before a plan administrator finalizes any decision to self-insure, he or she should review the caveats. ERISA does not preempt all state laws. For example, ERISA does not preempt laws enabling a state to obtain Medicaid reimbursements and state criminal laws of general application. Self-insured plans are subject to state garnishment laws and state contract and tort laws. They must meet the self-insured plan criteria to be treated as such for purposes of ERISA preemption. Although an otherwise self-insured plan's purchase of stop-loss or excess risk insurance generally should not convert it to an insured plan for preemption purposes, at least in cases when policy proceeds are payable directly to the plan, some court decisions have decided differently. The cases appear to turn largely on whether the stop-loss insurance constitutes catastrophic protection for the plan or more closely resembles a group insurance policy with a high deductible. The closer to the former, the more likely that preemption is found. Two factors come into play here: (1) whether the trigger is determined on an aggregate claim or individual participant claim basis (i.e., a stop-loss threshold), and (2) whether policy proceeds are payable to the plan or the participant once the trigger is reached (i.e., the trigger point).

A federal district court case from Maryland highlights this issue. Maryland's insurance commissioner issued a regulation that attempted to define when stop-loss insurance purchased by a self-funded plan would be treated as an insured plan. In doing so, the state was trying to direct the terms of the stop-loss policies. If a policy did not meet the specific requirements, the state would treat the policy as an insured plan and subject it to the state-mandated benefits. The state, in effect, was trying to regulate certain self-insured plans by means of this regulation. The district court found, however, that the regulation was preempted by ERISA's deemer clause. [American Med. Sec. Inc. v. Bartlett, 915 F. Supp. 740 (D. Md. 1996)] A similar conclusion was reached by the Missouri Court of Appeals in *Associated Industries of Missouri v. Angoff* [937 S.W.2d 277 (Mo. App. 1996)].

(See **Chapter 12** for further discussion of decision making regarding self-insuring health benefits.)

[H] The Downside of the ERISA Preemption

The decision to convert a plan to an ERISA plan should not be made without expert assistance because the ERISA preemption comes with costs. For example, if an unfunded vacation pay plan is converted to a funded arrangement to obtain ERISA status, the employer may incur significant costs. The unfunded plan is not subject to annual filings with the DOL and the Internal Revenue Service (IRS). A trust agreement must be established and operated for an ERISA plan. If an ERISA plan covers more than 100 participants, an annual audit must be performed. These costs could exceed the savings associated with not vesting the vacation pay.

In addition to incurring the out-of-pocket costs, converting the plan to an ERISA arrangement changes enforcement procedures. Any disputes over the plan must go to federal court rather than state court. This may or may not be to the employer's advantage, depending on the circumstances. Plan administrators should discuss the implications with legal counsel before proceeding.

[I] ERISA Reporting Requirements

ERISA requires a plan administrator to disclose to participants certain plan information, including the actual plan documents, the summary plan document, trust agreements (if any), the latest annual report, and any collective bargaining agreements or contracts under which the plan was established. Participants or beneficiaries may make a written request for the information, and any requested document(s) must be copied or made available within 30 days. This is known as the general disclosure requirement.

In addition to the general disclosure requirement, employers' group health plans must provide four basic reporting documents: the summary plan description (SPD), Form 5500, the summary annual report (SAR), and the summary of material modifications (SMM). Failure to provide the required documents in a timely manner can result in a $110 per day penalty, up to a maximum of $1,100.

Generally, employers can provide the required documents by first class mail to participants and beneficiaries (see **Section [5]** below for information on electronic disclosures). Because litigants in benefit disputes often claim that they did not receive the required notices, plan sponsors are encouraged to document their mailing processes in writing and ensure that proof of mailing is maintained throughout the ERISA-required recordkeeping period.

[1] Summary Plan Description (SPD)

The purpose of the SPD is to provide adequate information to plan participants and beneficiaries to ensure that they understand material provisions of the plan. The SPD must be provided to each plan participant. Plan participants are employees or former employees who are or may become eligible for benefits under the group health plan. Beneficiaries who are or may become eligible for benefits must also receive an SPD. SPDs must be provided to COBRA qualified beneficiaries, covered retirees, and other former employees who are or may become eligible for benefits.

For a new plan, the SPD must be provided within 120 days of the date the plan becomes subject to the requirement or the date of plan adoption. For new participants in the plan, notification must take place within 90 days of the effective date of plan participation. An updated SPD must be provided every five years if the plan has been amended and every 10 years with no plan amendments. The updated SPD must be provided to each participant and beneficiary within 210 days following the last day of the fifth or tenth plan year.

In addition to automatically providing each participant with a copy of the SPD upon a new plan or new plan participation, participants and beneficiaries have rights to receive copies as follows: (i) an SPD must be provided for review purposes immediately upon their request; and (ii) within 30 days of receipt of a written request, plan sponsors must provide the participant or beneficiary with a copy of the SPD. The requirement to provide immediate access to the SPD for examination by a participant or beneficiary also applies to any bargaining agreement, trust agreement, contract or other instrument that governs the plan. The Taxpayer Relief Act of 1997 (TRA '97) eliminated the requirement that SPDs be filed with the DOL. However, if the DOL requests, the employer must furnish any documents relating to its plan within 30 days. Failure to provide SPDs and other required notices can result in a $110 per day penalty, up to a maximum of $1,100.

The SPD must be written in language understood by the average participant. It should be written simply and clearly and in a manner not meant to confuse the reader. Confusing language can lead to legal claims, as evidenced by the case of *Watts v. BellSouth Telecommunications, Inc.* [316 F.3d 1203 (11th Cir. 2003)]. One page of the plan's SPD stated that an employee should submit an appeal of a denied claim in writing within 60 days, whereas another page of the SPD stated, "If you have a claim for benefits which is denied or ignored, in whole or in part, you may file suit in a state or federal court." These conflicting statements led the employee to believe that she could pursue either, neither, or both remedies. The court agreed and allowed the employee to pursue her claim in court, even though the employee did not exhaust the plan's appeals procedures. The court in this case advised the plan to revise its SPD language to make it clear to participants that they must exercise all of the plan's appeal rights and that the claims must have been denied, in whole or in part, before the participants can file a lawsuit.

ERISA, as amended by HIPAA and per the DOL's most recent regulations, requires that the SPD include the following information:

- Type of plan (e.g., group health plan)

- Cost sharing provisions, including premiums, deductibles, coinsurance, and copayments (while the specific premium amounts need not be disclosed, the SPD must describe the circumstances under which and the extent to which participants and beneficiaries will be responsible for premiums, deductibles, copayments, and so forth)

- Annual or lifetime caps or other limits on benefits under the plan

- The extent to which preventive services are covered under the plan

- Whether, and under what circumstances, existing and new drugs are covered under the plan

- Whether, and under what circumstances, coverage is provided for medical tests, devices, and procedures

- Provisions governing the use of network providers, the composition of the provider network, and whether, and under what circumstances, coverage is provided for out-of-network services (the listing of providers may be furnished to participants and beneficiaries as a separate document, provided that the SPD contains a general description of the provider network and indicates that provider lists are furnished, without charge, in a separate document)

- Any conditions or limits on the selection of primary care providers or providers of specialty medical care

- Any conditions or limits applicable to obtaining emergency medical care

- Any provision requiring preauthorization or utilization review as a condition to obtaining a benefit or service under the plan (the summary of these provisions must be sufficient to inform participants and beneficiaries of their rights and obligations under such provisions)

- A statement clearly identifying circumstances which may result in disqualification, ineligibility or denial, loss, forfeiture, suspension, offset, reduction or recovery (e.g., by exercise of subrogation or reimbursement rights) of any benefits that a participant or beneficiary might otherwise reasonably expect the plan to provide

- A summary of the authority of the plan sponsors or others to terminate the plan or amend or eliminate benefits under the plan and the circumstances, if any, under which the plan may be terminated or benefits may be amended or eliminated

- A summary of the benefits, rights, and obligations of participants and beneficiaries under the plan on termination of the plan or amendment or elimination of benefits under the plan

- A summary of the allocation and disposition of plan assets upon termination

- A summary of any provisions that may result in the imposition of a fee or charge on a participant or beneficiary, or on an individual account thereof, the payment of which is a condition to the receipt of benefits under the plan

- A description of the plan's procedures for qualified medical child support orders (QMCSOs) or a statement that the QMCSO procedures are available to participants and beneficiaries without charge from the plan administrator

- A description of the rights and obligations of participants and beneficiaries subject to the COBRA continuation coverage provisions (see **Chapter 7**) (It is unlikely that the COBRA notice in the SPD will be able to substitute for the initial notice required by the COBRA regulations. An SPD must be distributed within 90 days of an individual's becoming a plan participant or beneficiary; however, COBRA information must be provided when the employee and spouse begin coverage. An SPD with the COBRA notice hand-delivered to the employee at work will not meet the spousal notice requirements.)

- Inclusion in the claims procedure of any plan procedures for preauthorization, approval, or utilization review (The claims procedure may be provided as a separate document that accompanies the SPD, provided that the separate document satisfies the DOL's requirements for style and format and that the SPD contains a statement that the claims procedures are furnished automatically without charge, as a separate document.)

- A revised ERISA rights statement that includes participant rights under the COBRA continuation provisions and the portability provisions

For many group health plans, especially insured plans and health maintenance organizations (HMOs), specific benefit information is not included in current SPDs, but is included in the schedule of benefits. In its comments on the regulations, the DOL indicated that "only a general description of such benefits is required if reference is made to detailed schedules of benefits which are available, without cost to any participant or beneficiary who so requests."

In addition, HIPAA requires group health plans to include the following information in the "Statement of ERISA Rights" section of the SPD:

- The name and address of any health insurance issuer

- A description of the insurer's responsibilities for financing or administration

- The extent to which benefits are guaranteed under an insurance contract (note that this is particularly important in those cases where the plan is self-funded and an insurer is serving as a contract administrator or claims payor, rather than as an insurer)

- A notice that participants may obtain information about their benefit rights from the DOL's Employee Benefits Security Administration (EBSA) local or national office

- A description of the participants' rights to minimum hospital stays under the Newborns' and Mothers' Health Protection Act of 1996 (NMHPA) unless state law supersedes the NMHPA (e.g., when state law offers better benefits than the NMHPA), and then the SPD should reflect the state law's provisions.

A full SPD for group health plans offering coverage through a federally qualified HMO is required. Prior to the DOL's November 2000 regulations, SPDs were not required for HMO coverage.

Many employers believe that their insurance (or HMO) providers will prepare and supply the SPD for their plan. This is not necessarily the case. In *Sunderlin v. First Reliance Standard Life Insurance Co.* [235 F. Supp. 2d 222 (W.D.N.Y. 2002)], the employee (Sunderlin) became disabled, began receiving disability benefits under the employer's insurance plan, and requested a copy of the SPD when further benefits were denied. Neither the employer nor the insurance carrier provided Sunderlin with a copy of the SPD. The court ruled that it was the employer's responsibility, not the carrier's, to provide the SPD. The employer cannot delegate the duty to ensure that all ERISA-required communication material and documents are prepared appropriately and distributed to participants.

[2] Form 5500

A group health plan must file Form 5500, Annual Return/Report of Employee Benefit Plan, with the DOL and the IRS by the last day of the seventh month after the close of the plan year. Form 5558 may be filed to request a two-and-a-half-month extension. Alternatively, the extension of the plan sponsor's tax return may be used to extend the deadline for filing Form 5500, assuming that the plan year and the sponsor's tax year are the same. The extension provides only a maximum of a one-and-a-half-month extension for the corporate sponsor. To obtain a nine-and-a-half-month extension after year-end, plan administrators must file Form 5558 at the end of the original seven-month period.

Exempted are welfare benefit plans with fewer than 100 participants at the beginning of the plan year that are either unfunded or funded fully by insurance, or a combination of the two. Unfunded plans are those that pay benefits solely from the general assets of the employer or employee organization and do not pre-fund benefits through the use of a trust account, TPA account, or other means. If employee contributions are required by the plan, employee contributions must apply only to the insured benefits and are remitted directly to the insurer. Generally, unfunded plans do not have any plan assets at any time during the plan year.

The financial statements of welfare benefit plans must be audited by an independent qualified public accountant if:

1. A Form 5500 must be filed for the plan,

2. There are 100 or more participants in the plan on the first day of the plan year (counting newly eligible participants), and

3. The plan is funded.

A plan is considered funded if it uses a separate plan account to receive contributions or pay benefits. If the account belongs to the plan sponsor (e.g., employer or employee organization) and deposits are made to the account only when claims are ready to be paid, the plan will (generally) be considered unfunded.

If a VEBA (or Section 501(c)(9)) or grantor trust is used, the plan is funded.

Under a special transition rule, plans with 80 to 120 (inclusive) participants at the beginning of the plan year may elect to delay the audit requirements if there were fewer than 100 participants at the beginning of the preceding plan year.

Failure to file the Form 5500 can result in a civil penalty of up to $1,100 per day.

Participants and beneficiaries have a right to examine and receive copies of the Form 5500: (i) the Form 5500 must be provided for review purposes immediately upon request; and (ii) within 30 days of receipt of a written request, plan sponsors must provide the participant or beneficiary with a copy of the Form 5500.

For plan years beginning on or after January 1, 2009, the Form 5500 must be filed electronically. The DOL believes that a completely electronic filing system will reduce errors, lower annual reporting costs, and provide for more timely enforcement. Although not developed as of this writing, the DOL's system for receiving electronic filing of Form 5500 will provide for a secure Internet-based filing method and will support approved privately developed filing methods. In preparing for the all electronic filing of the Form 5500, the DOL published a final rule revising the annual reporting and disclosure regulations. [72 Fed. Reg. 64,710 (Nov. 16, 2007)] On that same date, the DOL and IRS published a notice of adoption of revisions to the Form 5500 that reflected the changes adopted in the final rule. [72 Fed. Reg. 64,731 (Nov. 16, 2007)]

[3] Summary Annual Report (SAR)

The purpose of the SAR is to provide plan participants and beneficiaries a summary of the financial information included on Form 5500. The SAR must be furnished annually to plan participants and beneficiaries on or before the last day of the ninth month after the close of the plan or fiscal year, or on or before the last day of the second month following the filing of Form 5500. If the plan has an extension for filing Form 5500, the same extension will apply to the SAR. If the plan is exempt from filing Form 5500, it is also exempt from providing the SAR.

SARs must be provided to participants (but not beneficiaries) in fully insured health plans. COBRA beneficiaries, however, including spouses and dependents, are considered participants in the group health plan, and therefore would receive the SAR. Health flexible spending accounts (health FSAs) are exempt from the SAR requirement if they are totally unfunded welfare plans, that is, plans that pay the benefits totally from the employer's general assets. Note that for this purpose, employees' salary reduction contributions are considered paid from the employer's general assets. A cafeteria plan (other than the health FSA) is not a welfare benefit plan under ERISA, and is therefore exempt from the SAR requirement.

[4] Summary of Material Modifications (SMM)

The purpose of the SMM is to provide information to plan participants and beneficiaries on any material changes to the SPD. The SMM must be provided in writing to participants no later than 210 days after the close of the plan year in which the modification or change was adopted. A material modification includes any change that is important to plan participants. Material modifications (in addition to those listed below) would likely include a change in the name or address of the plan sponsor or plan administrator, a change in the plan requirements (e.g., eligibility, funding, or both), and a change in plan trustees, if applicable. Although beneficiaries are not required to be automatically provided with an SMM, if they make a written request, an SMM then must be provided within 30 days.

HIPAA requires that a notice of "material reductions in covered services or benefits provided under a group health plan" must be furnished to participants and beneficiaries no later than 60 days after the effective date of those changes, unless summaries of modifications or changes are provided to participants and beneficiaries on a regular basis no less than every 90 days. The final DOL regulations discussed in the preceding section also defined a "material reduction in covered services or benefits" to mean any modification to the plan or change in the information required to be included in the SPD that, independently or in conjunction with other contemporaneous modifications or changes, would be considered by the average plan participant to be an important reduction in covered services or benefits. Examples of "reductions in covered services or benefits" include elimination of benefits; reduction of benefits; increased premiums, deductibles, coinsurance, copayments, or other amounts to be paid by a participant or beneficiary; reduction of the service area covered by an HMO; or establishment of new conditions or requirements (i.e., preauthorization requirements) to obtain services or benefits under the plan.

SMMs, like SPDs, must be written so as to be understood by the average plan participant. It is recommended that SMMs be written so they "fit" with the SPD they are modifying. The DOL has not prepared regulations regarding the content of the SMM, but typically SMMs would include the name of the health plan and SPD that they are modifying; a description of the change; any language that is to be substituted or added to the SPD; directions that the SMM should be read in conjunction with the SPD and should be kept with the SPD; and the name of a contact person where participants can obtain additional information.

TRA '97 eliminated the requirement for group health plans to file SMMs with the DOL. If the DOL requests, however, an employer must furnish any documents relating to its plan within 30 days. Failure to do so can result in a $110 per day penalty, up to a maximum of $1,100.

Cafeteria plans that are not welfare plans are subject to alternative reporting requirements. The plan administrator should contact a benefits consultant for information regarding additional reporting requirements.

[5]   Electronic Disclosure

The EBSA issued final rules establishing safe harbor standards for using electronic media to distribute required communication to participants. [29 C.F.R. § 2520.107-1] Most of ERISA Title I disclosures may be furnished electronically, including (this list is not all inclusive):

* Summary plan description

* Summary of material modifications

* Summary annual report

* Form 5500

* COBRA notifications

To meet the safe harbor standards, the plan administrator must take steps to reasonably ensure that the transmitted documents are actually received by the participants and the confidentiality of personal information is protected. Participants must receive a notice of the significance of the document (if this is not otherwise apparent from the electronically transmitted document), and of the right to receive a paper version of the document, upon request.

Documents may be transmitted electronically to employees at work, or "any location where the participant is reasonably expected to perform his or her duties as an employee," such as to a home worksite or while traveling, provided they have access to the employer's or plan sponsor's electronic information system.

Documents may also be provided to participants, beneficiaries and other persons (such as alternate payees) who consent to receiving documents electronically through independent means (e.g., through a personal e-mail account) provided that:

* The recipient affirmatively consents to receiving the document electronically

* The recipient provides an address for receiving the document, and

* Before consenting, the intended recipient is provided clear information that describes:

  — The types of documents to be provided electronically

  — Any hardware or software required for accessing the documents

  — The right to request a paper version of the document and its cost, if any

  — The right to withdraw electronic consent at any time

  — Procedures for withdrawing consent

  — Procedures for updating the recipient's electronic address

In October 2006, the IRS and the Treasury Department issued final regulations for electronic distribution of notices and the transmission and receipt of elections to and from plan participants. [71 Fed. Reg. 61,877 (October 20, 2006)] Under the final regulations, electronic media include Web sites, e-mail, telephonic systems, and CD-ROMs. The proposed regulations would provide safe harbor guidelines that would apply to any notice, election, or similar communication provided to a beneficiary or participant in any of the following welfare benefit plans (certain qualified retirement plans are also included in the proposed regulations):

- Accident and health plans (Code Sections 104(a)(3) or 105)

- Cafeteria plans (Code Section 125)

- Educational assistance programs (Code Section 127)

- Qualified transportation fringe benefit programs (Code Section 132)

- Archer Medical Savings Accounts (Code Section 220)

- Health Savings Accounts (Code Section 223)

The final guidelines do not pertain to any of the ERISA Title I and Title IV required notices. The guidelines for electronic disclosure described in the EBSA final rules will continue to apply to those communications.

The final regulations conform the IRS and Treasury Department rules on electronic distribution to the Electronic Signatures in Global and National Commerce Act (E-SIGN). The final regulations allow plan sponsors to choose between complying with the E-SIGN requirements ("the consumer consent method") or with rules that are substantially similar to the current retirement plan rules for electronic transmission ("the alternative method"). The alternative method essentially requires that the recipient effectively be able to access the electronic medium and be advised that he or she can request a paper copy at no charge. Under the consumer consent method, the participant must consent to receive the communication electronically before an applicable notice is provided using an electronic medium.

[J] Other ERISA Requirements

ERISA has many other requirements. Some of them are briefly described here.

[1] Bonding

Section 412 of ERISA requires that anyone who "handles" funds of employee benefit plans must be bonded in an amount no less than ten percent of the value of the funds handled, up to a maximum of $500,000 per plan. In this context, "funds handled" is defined as the value of the plan's assets. The ERISA bond protects the employee benefit plans whereas a fiduciary liability policy seeks to protect the individual and corporate fiduciaries in the event they are sued for an alleged breach of their fiduciary duties (see **Section 8.04[G]** for further information about fiduciary responsibilities). Often, this bonding requirement is met by endorsing the employer's ERISA benefit plans as Named Insureds on the organization's employee dishonesty/fidelity insurance policy (sometimes referred to as the organization's crime policy).

[2] Written Plan Document

ERISA requires all employee benefit plans to be maintained pursuant to a written document. If the group health plan is insured, the insurance policy or contract issued by the carrier which incorporates the certificate of insurance and schedule of benefits may be able to be used as the written plan document. However, one of ERISA's requirements for a plan document is the designation of a named fiduciary and most insurance contracts do not include this information. Other beneficial information found in a plan document, but not included in most insurance contracts is the designation of how many benefit plan(s) an employer sponsors and which benefits are included in each benefit plan. The designation of how many and what benefits are included in each plan is important for COBRA purposes (see **Chapter 7**).

[3] Plan Administrator

The plan document should also designate the Plan Administrator. The Plan Administrator is responsible for ensuring that the ERISA plan meets its plan disclosure and other ERISA compliance requirements. If the plan document does not clearly identify the Plan Administrator, ERISA provides a default rule: the plan sponsor is the Plan Administrator. Plan Administrators are fiduciaries of the ERISA plan and thus can be financially liable when the compliance requirements are not met. Note that the named Plan Administrator is not a plan's third party administrator (TPA) unless the contract between the plan sponsor and the TPA specifically indicates that the TPA agrees to be the Plan Administrator.

Identification of the Plan Administrator can be significant in the event of a lawsuit where request for plan disclosures was not sent to the Plan Administrator. In *Player v. Northrop Grumman Corp.*, [2006 U.S. Dist. LEXIS 62521 (D. Ut. Aug. 31, 2006)] the claimant sent a request for plan documents to the company's human resources director, who only provided a copy of the summary of the plan's benefits. The plan document clearly identified the Plan Administrator as the employer's benefits committee, but the claimant did not request the documents from it. The court ruled that the plan could not be penalized for not providing the requested documents, as the proper Plan Administrator was not contacted for those documents.

[4] Non-Retaliation

Section 510 of ERISA prohibits employers from terminating an employee or otherwise discriminating or retaliating against a plan participant for exercising his or her rights under the employee benefit plan or ERISA.

[5] Record Retention

Plan Administrators have record keeping responsibilities under ERISA. Records that must be maintained include information necessary to substantiate the information on Forms 5500 and all information related to benefit claims. For all practical purposes, claims and other ERISA benefit plan records must be maintained for eight years. However, ERISA does not specify a statute of limitations for benefit claims, so courts look to state law for the longest period of time that a participant or beneficiary has to file a legal claim. In some cases, this may be longer than eight years, so Plan Administrators should confer with appropriate legal advisors to determine how long benefit claim records should be maintained.

Claims may be maintained in electronic format as long as DOL and Code rules relating to the security, accessibility, legibility and usability are followed. In addition to the DOL's and Code's guidance in this area, the Electronic Signatures in Global and National Commerce Act (E-SIGN) provides additional standards for the use of electronic records.

The DOL has created website guidance to assist employers and plan sponsors in determining their recordkeeping and reporting requirements. The Recordkeeping, Reporting and Notices Advisor (available at *www.dol.gov/elaws/firststep/*) summarizes the recordkeeping requirements of ERISA, COBRA, HIPAA portability, the Newborns' and Mothers' Health Protection Act, the Women's Health and Cancer Rights Act, FMLA and USERRA. (This website also provides an Employment Law Overview Advisor and a Poster Advisor.)

§ 5.03   TITLE VII OF THE CIVIL RIGHTS ACT OF 1964

Title VII prohibits discrimination in employment on the basis of race, color, religion, sex, or national origin; it specifically applies to terms and conditions of employment, including benefits. Two federal laws that have been passed since 1964 expand the scope of Title VII and further restrict apparent discrimination in conditions of employment. These laws are the Pregnancy Discrimination Amendment to Title VII (PDA) and the Health Maintenance Organization Act (HMO Act).

[A]   The Pregnancy Discrimination Amendment to Title VII

This amendment specifically prohibits discrimination in employment, including conditions of employment, related to pregnancies. Under the PDA, employers that offer group health plans must offer coverage of pregnancy and related conditions under the same terms as those offered for other, similar disabilities. The PDA does permit group health plans to exclude charges for an employee's daughter's pregnancy and related charges, as long as daughters of male employees are treated the same as those of female employees.

A growing body of court cases has applied the PDA to contraceptive coverage under the health plan. Most recently, a district court in Nebraska ruled that the PDA applies to contraceptive coverage because the law applies to "women affected by pregnancy," not just pregnant women. The court ruled that not providing coverage for contraceptives affects the health of women only and, therefore, is illegal under the PDA. However, in 2007 the Eighth Circuit (the first federal appellate court to address whether the PDA requires coverage for contraception) ruled that the PDA "does not encompass contraception." [*In re* Union Pac. R. R. Employment Practices Litig., 2007 U.S. App. LEXIS 5914 (8th Cir. 2007)] The Eighth Circuit based its ruling on an analogous ruling it made in an earlier case on infertility. The court concluded that "contraception is not 'related to' pregnancy for PDA purposes because, like infertility treatments, contraception is a treatment that is only indicated prior to pregnancy." The dissent on this ruling noted that it is inconsistent with the U.S. Supreme Court's holding in *Johnson Controls*, which held that discriminating against women on the basis of "potential pregnancy" violated Title VII. Rulings from other circuit courts will be likely in the future.

The PDA is a federal law. Any applicable state law that requires better coverage for employees overrides the PDA. In Illinois, for example, an employer is prohibited from denying coverage for a dependent child's maternity charges if maternity benefits are offered under the insured's group health policy.

Many states impose similar nondiscrimination prohibitions on group health plans that are offered in the state, under department of insurance or other governing agency requirements. Such state requirements apply to insured plan contracts offered to employers in the state but generally do not apply to self-funded plans governed by ERISA.

[B]   The Health Maintenance Organization Act

The HMO Act, enacted in 1973 and amended in 1988, originally required certain private employers that offer group health benefits to their employees to offer those employees a choice between a "qualified" HMO and other health plan options. The HMO Act has two requirements:

1. Employers who allow employees to contribute their share of other plan premiums through payroll deduction must allow employees to make HMO contributions through payroll deduction as well. (This requirement was intended to make HMOs accessible to employees who chose this new type of health care coverage.)

2. Employers cannot create contribution requirements for participation in a qualified HMO that financially discriminate against employees who elect the HMO.

Before October 24, 1995, the HMO Act included a "dual-choice" requirement. Specifically, employers of 25 or more employees that offered a group health benefit plan to their employees and that were subject to requirements of the Fair Labor Standards Act of 1938 (FLSA) regarding minimum wage and overtime pay were obligated to offer their employees an HMO if a federally qualified HMO made a written request to the employer to do so. Since the expiration of this requirement, employers may decide whether offering an HMO is appropriate in light of their own business and employee-relations issues.

The HMO Act was intended to encourage creation of HMOs as a means of controlling rising health care costs, and it has done that. Since passage of this act, HMOs and other managed care health plans have proliferated. Point-of-service (POS) plans, preferred provider organizations (PPOs), and physician hospital organizations (PHOs), in addition to a variety of HMO structures, have been created as managed care alternatives to traditional, full-choice, fee-for-service (i.e., indemnity) health care plans. Even major insurance companies, known for offering traditional indemnity health care plans, have created successful managed care plan alternatives.

Traditionally, HMOs have been fundamentally different from insurance companies in that they arrange for both the offering and the financing of medical care. The linkage between offering and financing medical care provides the potential for additional cost savings as compared to insurance company indemnity coverage. The downside associated with HMOs is that employees are frequently confronted with a limited number of options with respect to how and where they may obtain medical care. To understand how these restrictions work, it is necessary to understand the HMO's structure. Within any particular service area, an employer may find that more than one form of HMO is available. Each form has its own name and acronym, but HMOs generally fit into one of two basic categories: the group practice model or the individual practice association.

[1]   The Group Practice Model

In this type of HMO, physicians are employed by or are under contract to the plan, and most medical services are provided at a central location. The group practice model is also known as a closed-panel program or staff-model HMO. The Group Health Association, Inc., in Washington, D.C., and Group Health of Puget Sound are examples of staff-model HMOs. Kaiser Permanente in California is an example of a group-model HMO. To the consumer, there is little apparent difference between staff-model and group-model HMOs. In either case, covered persons obtain the majority of their care from a well-defined structure of physicians and other professionals who service only members of the HMO.

[2] The Individual Practice Association

An individual practice association (IPA) is a network model or an open-panel program. An IPA contracts with a variety of physicians and other providers who are in practice in the general community. The medical professionals do not restrict their practice to participants in the HMO. The advantage of an IPA is that it represents enough numbers to be able to negotiate a discounted rate for its members. Two well-known examples of network-model HMOs are Group Health, Inc., of Minneapolis, Minnesota, and PacifiCare Health Systems of California.

Although some employers may view offering employees an HMO option as a government-imposed burden, HMOs offer a number of advantages:

1. An HMO offers a choice between alternatives, which is consistent with the growing desire among employees for more flexibility in benefit plans.

2. Because the HMO concept is based on preventive medicine, an HMO increases the likelihood of early diagnosis and treatment, thereby reducing the possibility of more costly serious illnesses.

3. The HMO has a direct incentive to keep members well, to avoid hospitalization unless necessary, and to keep costs to a minimum level.

4. HMO members receive comprehensive health care, usually in an efficient, service-integrated facility.

Employers are also working on their own, or in cooperation with other businesses, to take control of group health care plans and costs. Voluntary business coalitions have been developed in at least 33 states, and the number is growing.

HMOs have expanded their membership by demonstrating success at providing quality health care, acceptable employee service, and lower costs than competing indemnity health plans. As of January 1, 2002, total enrollment in HMOs nationwide was 26 percent of the U.S. population, a 34.5 percent increase over 1996. However, this was an 8 percent decrease from 2001.

[3] Managed Care Issues

Increased HMO enrollment has led to more scrutiny, and public outrage against questionable managed care practices has prompted legislation on patients' rights in more than 30 states. This trend continues in state legislatures, as well as at the federal level. Several states permit HMO members to sue their HMOs for negligence and malpractice in state courts. In *Aetna Health Inc. v. Davila* [124 S. Ct. 2488 (2004)], the U.S. Supreme Court ruled unanimously that HMO enrollees' claims regarding denial of benefits or negligence fall within the scope of ERISA and, therefore, must be pursued in federal court. This ruling invalidated patients' rights laws enacted in at least 10 states: Arizona, California, Georgia, Maine, New Jersey, North Carolina, Oklahoma, Texas, Washington, and West Virginia.

For several years, patients' rights legislation has been proposed in Congress. In 2003, three bills were introduced in the House of Representatives and in the U.S. Senate, but none has been signed into law as of this writing.

Employers, insurance groups, and HMOs see legislation as a nonreasoned response to these concerns. "Easy" political solutions, they say, will not make health care better. Employer groups generally believe that all the necessary legislation is in place; what is needed is enforcement. Other critics of recent legislation argue that market forces will correct health care quality problems. Legislation (of mandated care) will stifle creativity and raise the costs of providing health care: those costs will ultimately be passed on to employers and consumers. The Congressional Budget Office reported that the House and Senate bills introduced in 2001 would have increased insurance premiums by 2.9 to 4.2 percent on average. Increases generally hit small employers harder. According to the Employer Health Benefits 2006 Annual Survey, conducted by the Kaiser Family Foundation and the Health Research and Educational Trust, 74 percent of the small employers surveyed cited high costs as the major reason for not offering group health coverage. The survey also noted that only 60 percent of all small firms (those with 200 or fewer employees) offered health benefits to their employees, compared with 98 percent of firms with more than 200 employees. This percentage may drop even further if patients' rights bills allowing liability for employers are passed. According to the Health Care Expectations: Future Strategy and Direction survey conducted by Hewitt Associates, 46 percent of U.S. employers would drop coverage if such legislation is passed.

Regardless of the ultimate outcome of patients' rights legislation, employers must make insurers, HMOs, and other managed care organizations accountable for quality and for presenting quality information to participants so that they can make informed choices.

§ 5.04 THE AMERICANS WITH DISABILITIES ACT

The ADA, enacted in 1990, was designed to protect people with disabilities in employment, in access to public services, and in various other related areas. Specific ADA provisions related to employers' group health care plans are discussed in this chapter. (See **Chapter 13** for a detailed discussion of the ADA.)

Relying on guidance issued by the Equal Employment Opportunity Commission (EEOC), plan administrators should consider the list of ADA do's and don'ts (see **Exhibit 5.1**) as they review their group health plan provisions.

[A] Case Law and Group Benefits

In *John Doe and Richard Smith v. Mutual of Omaha Insurance Co.* [179 F.3d 557 (7th Cir. 1999), *cert. denied,* 2000 WL 12573 (U.S. 2000)], the Seventh Circuit Court of Appeals ruled that the ADA "does not apply to insurance policies." The case resulted from a lawsuit filed by two HIV-infected individuals who were covered by separate Mutual of Omaha health insurance policies. Both policies limited coverage for HIV infections and other AIDS-related conditions to a specified lifetime cap. The individuals sued, alleging discrimination on the basis of disability, and the district court agreed. The circuit court concluded that the insurance company did not refuse to sell insurance policies, but the policies might be less valuable to persons with AIDS than to those with other diseases or disabilities. The court added that the ADA "does not require a seller to alter his product to make it equally valuable to the disabled and to the non-disabled, even if the product is insurance."

The Sixth Circuit Court of Appeals ruled that the ADA may invalidate the terms of an employer's long-term disability (LTD) policy. [Parker v. Metropolitan Life Ins. Co., 99 F.3d 181, 1996 U.S. App. LEXIS 27624 (6th Cir. 1996)] An employee of Schering-Plough became totally disabled as a result of severe depression. The terms of the employer's LTD policy, under which the employee began receiving benefits, provided that benefits for mental or nervous disorders would continue beyond a 24-month period only if the individual were confined to a hospital or institution. The employee sued under Title III of the ADA.

Ruling in the employee's favor, the court said insurance services clearly fall within ADA protections. The court said, "Because [the employee] suffers from a 'nervous/mental' [rather than a physical] disability, the plaintiff is receiving a 'good' or 'service' that is different ... from those provided to other individuals." The ruling returned the case to the trial court, where the employee was required to show that the distinction between mental and physical disabilities in LTD coverage was unjustified. The trial court also had to determine whether Schering-Plough was a proper defendant, because Title III of the ADA does not govern terms and conditions of employment.

In another case, the U.S. District Court for the Southern District of New York found, on appeal, that an employee with a mental disability who was unable to perform the essential functions of his job was a qualified individual under Title I of the ADA, and thus his claim of benefit discrimination could be brought to trial if settlement efforts failed. The court's decision meant that an employer may be sued for benefit discrimination under the ADA even if the claimant is unable to perform the essential duties of his or her job. At issue in this case was whether the employer's LTD coverage was discriminatory.

In another case, the U.S. Court of Appeals for the District of Columbia Circuit found that the ADA does not mandate that mental health benefits be treated the same as those for physical illness. [Modderno v. King, 82 F.3d 1059 (D.C. Cir. 1996), *cert. denied,* 117 S. Ct. 772 (1997)] The court in *Modderno* affirmed the dismissal of a complaint filed by the former spouse of a Foreign Service officer who claimed she was prematurely released from hospitalization for mental illness because the Federal Employee Health Benefits Plan set a lifetime cap for mental health benefits at $75,000. The judge found that the health plan drew no distinction between disabling and nondisabling mental illness, but rather between mental and physical illness. Of course, under the Mental Health Parity Act of 1996, effective January 1, 1998, decisions in similar cases may be different.

[B]   EEOC Compliance Manual

In October 2000, the EEOC published a new section in its Compliance Manual, covering how antidiscrimination laws apply to health and welfare benefit plans. The guidance indicates that any differences in benefits must not be based on disability, but allows for a limited exception: differences may be disability-based if they are justified by actuarial data or are necessary to avoid prohibitive increases in premiums for other employees. According to the manual, differences in benefits are disability-based if they pertain to:

- A single disability (e.g., all physical and mental disorders are covered except psychosis);

- A group of disabilities (e.g., the maximum coverage for a heart disease is one million dollars, but for all other conditions, the maximum is ten million dollars); or

- Disabilities in general (e.g., a retirement plan that provides different benefits for disabled participants than for non-disabled participants).

Health and welfare plans may have broad differences that apply to dissimilar conditions, and affect both disabled and non-disabled employees without running afoul of the ADA.

§ 5.05   THE FAMILY AND MEDICAL LEAVE ACT

In 1993, Congress passed the FMLA. Among its provisions, the FMLA requires that covered employers that offer group health coverage to their employees continue to provide that coverage while an eligible employee is on FMLA leave. (See **Chapter 14** for an extensive discussion of the FMLA provisions.) Such benefits must continue to be offered to employees on FMLA leave under the same terms and conditions as before the leave began. An employer may require an employee to pay his or her pre-leave share of premium costs throughout an FMLA leave.

Employers are faced with at least two conflicting, practical concerns in administering required benefit provisions under the FMLA:

1. Employees who return from an FMLA leave must be allowed to return to their benefit plans as though they had never left employment. No restrictions can be imposed for preexisting conditions, and no waiting period may be imposed.

2. Employers may discontinue the group health coverage of employees on FMLA leave who do not pay their share of premiums during the leave.

These two FMLA provisions cause most employers to continue paying an employee's full premium costs, regardless of whether the employee is paying his or her share throughout the FMLA leave. Unless the employer can negotiate with the insurance carrier, this is the one way an employer can ensure that, when the employee returns from FMLA leave, the insurance company will pose no restrictions on the employee's eligibility for group health plan coverage.

HR departments must communicate the FMLA's benefit provisions to employees who request an FMLA leave. They should also inform eligible employees that, should they not pay their share of premiums during an FMLA leave, their employer may require them to refund its excess contributions upon their return from leave. If an employee does not return from leave, under certain circumstances, the employer may collect the contribution it paid for that employee's benefits premiums during the leave period.

§ 5.06 THE CONSOLIDATED OMNIBUS BUDGET RECONCILIATION ACT

In 1985, federal legislation was passed regarding continuation of group health care benefits to certain employees. The law, known as COBRA, has been amended since its passage to expand required continuation coverage.

COBRA requires that a private employer with 20 or more employees and sponsoring a group health plan must extend coverage to its employees and their dependents in situations in which those individuals might otherwise lose their coverage. COBRA applies whether the employer's plan is insured or self-funded.

Employees who lose their jobs, experience a significant reduction in their hours of work that results in loss of benefit eligibility, or lose eligibility for health care benefits for other reasons may continue their coverage in their employers' plans via COBRA continuation. It is vital that the language in the group health plan include a clear definition of the qualifying events that trigger COBRA eligibility under the plan. Dependents covered under the group plan who lose coverage may also elect to continue their coverage under the plan, under certain conditions. COBRA imposes several specific notification requirements on covered employers and provides for significant penalties to be imposed on covered employers that do not meet its requirements. Case law since 1985 has clearly interpreted the law in favor of covered employees and their dependents. It is therefore imperative that employers ensure their procedures comply with

COBRA by following a standard process for each COBRA-eligible individual. (See **Chapter 7** for an extensive discussion of COBRA.)

§ 5.07   THE OMNIBUS BUDGET RECONCILIATION ACT

Under the Omnibus Budget Reconciliation Act of 1993 (OBRA '93), group health plans are required to cover adopted children and children placed for adoption with no preexisting condition limitations and on the same terms as those that apply to natural children. OBRA also requires group health plans to maintain coverage for pediatric vaccines at the level of coverage that was provided on May 1, 1993.

The federal Office of Child Support Enforcement has developed an employer services Web site—*www.acf. hhs.gov/programs/cse/newhire/employer/home.htm*—that provides information to employers on child support, state-by-state practices, publications, as well as contact information.

[A]   Qualified Medical Child Support Orders

OBRA '93 requires employer-sponsored group health plans to provide benefits to noncustodial participants' children, if so ordered pursuant to a QMCSO. This provision is intended to lessen the federal government's matching-funds contributions to state Medicaid programs by shifting more of the health care costs of children of divorced or separated parents into the private sector whenever possible.

QMCSOs may be made pursuant to a state domestic relations law or to enforce a state law relating to medical child support. The child receiving the benefit is called the alternate recipient. To be qualified and binding on a group health care plan, a QMCSO must create or recognize the alternate recipient's right to receive the benefits for which a participant or beneficiary is eligible. The QMCSO must also clearly specify the following:

- The name of the issuing state agency

- The name and last known mailing address of the participant and the name and mailing address of each alternate recipient covered by the order (or the mailing address of the state official or agency as a substitute for the alternate recipient's address)

- A reasonable description of the type of coverage the plan is to provide to each alternate recipient or the manner in which the coverage is to be determined

- The period to which the QMCSO applies

- Each health care plan to which the QMCSO applies

Any payments for benefits made by a group health plan under a QMCSO or reimbursement for expenses paid by the child or the child's custodial parent or legal guardian must be made either to the child or to the child's custodial parent or legal guardian.

[1]   National Medical Support Notice

In 2001, the Department of Health and Human Services (DHHS) and the DOL issued the final version of a standardized QMCSO known as the National Medical Support Notice (NMSN). Most state agencies were to begin using the notice by October 1, 2001, to notify employers that the group health plan of a noncustodial parent or employee must cover that parent's child or children. According to the final rules published by DHHS and DOL, a properly completed NMSN will constitute a valid QMCSO.

The notice has two parts (1) Part A: Notice to Withhold for Health Care Coverage including an employer response section, and (2) Part B: Medical Support Notice to Plan Administrator. The notice comes with instructions to the employer and to the plan administrator including the plan administrator response section. The employer receives and reviews both parts of the notice and determines whether it is a valid QMCSO. If it is not valid, or if coverage is not available to the children (e.g., if family coverage is not available through the health plan or the employee works only part-time and part-time employees are not eligible for coverage), the employer returns Part A and the employer response section of the notice to the issuing agency. If the NMSN is valid and coverage is available, the employer sends Part B to the plan administrator within 20 days of the date of the NMSN. The plan administrator must notify the issuing agency within 40 days of the date of the NMSN and all appropriate recipients that the child is (children are) or will be enrolled in the plan and the date of enrollment. If more than one option is available for the dependent, the plan administrator must be informed about available coverage options. The plan administrator also notifies the employer of the amount of the employee contribution for the dependent coverage, if any. The employer must then determine whether enrollment can be completed based on any withholding restrictions on the employee's pay; if so, the employer returns the employer response section of Part A to the issuing agency to inform it that the dependent will not be enrolled.

Federal law requires that alternate recipients be enrolled in available group health plan coverage, even if the parent-employee has not enrolled. If the group health plan does not provide for dependent-only coverage, then the plan administrator must enroll both the parent-employee and the alternate recipient child(ren).

The use of the NMSN should simplify the administration of QMCSOs for employers, state agencies, and plan administrators. For employers, the biggest advantage of the notice is that the determination of whether it is a valid QMCSO is made much simpler than had been the case before this model notice was developed.

[2] Notification

On receipt of any medical child support order, the plan administrator must notify all concerned parties of the order. The plan administrator must also notify the parties of the plan's procedures for determining whether the order is qualified and of reasonable procedures for administering the benefits under the order, if it is found to be qualified. The determination must be made within a reasonable period (see **Section 5.07[A][1]**). The participant and each alternate recipient child must be notified of the determination once it has been made. The cost of coverage for the alternate recipient must be the same as the cost for children of other plan participants.

[3] Other Requirements

Employers must also notify the issuing agency when the parent-participant terminates from employment. Notification can be via a copy of the employee's COBRA or HIPAA notice. Note that alternate recipients are treated as qualified beneficiaries under COBRA continuation coverage rules, and should receive their own COBRA notice when the parent's coverage terminates.

If a parent-participant is temporarily laid off and loses plan coverage, the QMCSO must be retained—the time period varies from state to state, but is often 90 days. If the parent-participant is rehired during the mandated time period, the employer must reactivate the health coverage under the original QMCSO.

If the parent-participant's group health plan coverage is subject to a waiting period that is longer than 90 days from the date the administrator receives Part B of the NMSN, the employer must notify the plan administrator as soon as the waiting period has been completed.

Plan administrators must continue coverage for the alternate recipient until the employer receives written notice that the QMCSO is no longer in effect or the child receives comparable coverage elsewhere.

[4] Written Procedures

The plan administrator should establish written procedures that specify how the administrator:

- Determines whether the order is qualified

- Notifies individuals affected by the order

- Segregates amounts payable under the order

- Distributes benefits under the QMCSO

- Enrolls the alternate recipients in the plan on the earliest possible date following the determination that the order is a QMCSO

The written procedures must permit the child to designate a representative to whom all copies of notices concerning the QMCSO must be sent.

Alternate recipients under QMCSOs are generally considered beneficiaries under the plan for purposes of ERISA. For reporting and disclosure purposes, however, alternate recipients under a medical child support order, whether or not they are qualified, are treated as participants under the plan and must receive summary plan descriptions.

Group health plan documents must be amended to reflect the QMCSO rules. Employers should review plan documents or obtain assistance from a benefits consultant or attorney to review plan documents to determine compliance with this rule.

§ 5.08 THE MENTAL HEALTH PARITY ACT

Effective for health plan years beginning on or after January 1, 1998, the Mental Health Parity Act (MHPA) amended ERISA to prohibit annual or lifetime dollar limits on mental health treatments, unless the same dollar limits also apply to medical and surgical benefits under the employer's health plan. The MHPA does not require the employer's group health plan to provide any mental health benefits, nor does it place any restrictions on the terms or conditions relating to the amount, duration, or scope of the mental health benefits under the plan (e.g., cost sharing, limits on the number of visits or days of coverage, and requirements relating to medical necessity). For purposes of the MHPA, mental health benefits do not include benefits for the treatment of substance abuse or chemical dependency.

The MHPA applies to both insured and self-funded health plans offered by employers of at least 50 employees. It does not cover small employers (those employing an average of at least two but not more than 50 employees during a preceding calendar year and who employ at least two employees on the first day of the plan year). To qualify as a small employer, all related employers (such as members of a controlled group or an affiliated service group as defined in Code 414) must be counted. Under the current regulations, part-time employees are counted as full-time employees. The MHPA also does not apply to small plans (those plans with fewer than two participants who are current employees on the first day of the plan year).

The MHPA allows for an exemption from its requirements if an employer's insurance costs rise more than 1 percent because of such requirements. Under a Clinton administration ruling, an employer wishing to employ this exemption must comply with the law for a minimum of six months and then provide information about actual cost increases to document its self-implementing exemptions. The employer is not required to receive approval from the federal government before implementing the exemption, but 30 days' advance notice to plan participants and the government is required.

Studies done prior to the effective date of the MHPA revealed contrasting cost results. A RAND Institute study of 24 managed health care plans in the Midwest indicated that the cost of implementing the MHPA was roughly $1 per participant. This estimate contrasts significantly with a Congressional Research Service estimate that placed the cost of implementing the MHPA at $100 per enrollee per year. The RAND study cautions that its data may not necessarily be representative of all industries or for other geographic regions.

Employers were required to review and amend their group health plans to meet MHPA requirements. To guide implementation, the IRS issued interim final regulations on December 22, 1997. The interim rules indicated that a group health plan may comply with the parity requirements in any of the following ways:

- The plan may comply by not including any aggregate lifetime dollar limit or annual dollar limit on mental health benefits.

- The plan may comply by imposing a single aggregate lifetime or annual dollar limit on both medical/ surgical benefits and mental health benefits in a way that does not distinguish between the two.

- The plan may comply by imposing an aggregate lifetime dollar limit or annual dollar limit on mental health benefits that is not less than the aggregate lifetime dollar limit or annual dollar limit on medical/ surgical benefits.

- In the case of a plan under which aggregate lifetime dollar limits or annual dollar limits differ for categories of medical/surgical benefits, the plan may comply by calculating a weighted average aggregate lifetime dollar limit or weighted average annual dollar limit for mental health benefits. The weighted average must be based on a formula prescribed by the interim rules that takes into account the limits on different categories of medical/surgical benefits. In addition, benefits for treatment of substance abuse or chemical dependency may not be counted in applying an aggregate lifetime or annual dollar limit that applies separately to mental health benefits.

IRS monetary penalties of $100 per day apply to plans that fail to satisfy the requirements of the MHPA.

The interim rules described the method by which an employer can claim exemption from the MHPA under the increased cost exemption. The interim rules detailed the formula that an employer must use to determine whether its costs have increased by 1 percent or more as a result of compliance with the MHPA. Examples were given to help an employer apply the formula.

If an employer decides to exempt itself from the requirements of the MHPA because of the increased cost exemption, it must notify participants and beneficiaries. A plan may satisfy this requirement by providing participants and beneficiaries with an SMM outlining the reductions in covered services or benefits.

A plan not subject to ERISA requirements for preparing and distributing an SMM, or which chooses not to include this information in the SMM, may develop a separate notice of its exemption from the MHPA. (See **Exhibit 5.2** for a model notice, as published in the interim regulations.)

Although it was originally slated to expire on September 30, 2001, the MHPA has been extended several times. Most recently, under the Heroes Earnings Assistance and Relief Tax Act of 2008 (the "HEART" Act), the MHPA's provisions were extended to December 31, 2008. Congress has attempted to expand mental health parity many times since the passing of the MHPA. For example, in 2007, Representatives Patrick Kennedy (D-RI) and Jim Ramstad (R-MN) introduced H.R. 1424, the Paul Wellstone Mental Health and Addiction Equity Act of 2007. This bill would significantly expand benefits by requiring health plans with 50 or more participants to provide coverage for mental health and substance abuse treatment comparable to other medical/surgical services. This bill was passed by the House on March 5, 2008 and sent to the Senate. In the Senate, the bipartisan Mental Health Parity Act of 2007 (S. 558) was introduced by Pete Domenici (R-NM). This bill does not require group health plans to provide mental health coverage, but if a plan does, then the plan must provide that financial requirements (e.g., deductibles, copayments) and treatment limitations (number of visits, frequency of treatment) are comparable with medical/surgical benefits. S. 558 was passed by the Senate on September 18, 2007 and forwarded to the House. As of this writing, it is unclear whether a compromise can be reached and signed by both legislative houses by the end of the 2007–2008 congressional year.

On October 3, 2008, President Bush signed the Emergency Economic Stabilization Legislation (Pub. L. No. 110-343, Div. C). Among other provisions, this legislation expands the mental health parity requirements for group health plans. The current mental health parity provisions are made permanent as of January 1, 2009. The expanded requirements made by this legislation include: 1) financial requirements parity—deductibles, co-payments, co-insurance and out-of-pocket costs that apply to mental health benefits cannot be more restrictive than those that apply to the most common or frequent medical-surgical benefits; 2) treatment limitations parity—limits on the number of visits, days of coverage, frequency of treatment, or similar limits may not be more restrictive than those of the most common or frequent limitation for medical-surgical benefits; 3) parity for substance use disorder benefits—all current parity requirements and the new requirements under this legislation also apply to substance use disorder benefits; and 4) networks—if a plan allows participants to go out of network for medical-surgical benefits, it must also allow participants to go out of network for mental health benefits. Small employers (those with less than 50 employees) are exempt from these requirements. The cost exemption is made stricter, and plans must comply with the new requirements for the first six months of the plan year and then actuarially determine whether the plan's expenses meet the cost exemption. The new rules will go into effect for plan years that begin on or after October 3, 2010. Regulations and guidelines to assist plan sponsors in implementing the new requirements are expected from the DOL, HHS, and the Treasury department.

§ 5.09   THE NEWBORNS' AND MOTHERS' HEALTH PROTECTION ACT

Effective for health plan years beginning on or after January 1, 1998, the Newborns' and Mothers' Health Protection Act of 1996 (NMHPA) amended ERISA and the Public Health Service (PHS) Act by placing requirements on minimum length of hospital stays in connection with childbirth. Specifically, a group health plan may not restrict the hospitalization period after childbirth for the mother or for the newborn to less than 48 hours for a vaginal delivery and 96 hours for a cesarean delivery. This restriction does not apply if the decision to discharge the mother or her newborn child before the expiration of the minimum length of stay is made by the attending health care provider in consultation with the mother. That is, if the physician and mother agree, the mother, her newborn, or both may leave the hospital earlier than the required time. This decision is not permitted to be made by an insurance carrier or plan sponsor.

The NMHPA imposes several restrictions on insurers and health plans to prevent them from avoiding the restrictions. The new law does not prevent an insurer or a group health plan from imposing deductible, coinsurance, or other cost-sharing techniques regarding the hospital stay. Many states have established similar minimum-stay requirements for mothers and newborn children under health plans. The NMHPA provides that the state laws are not preempted by ERISA, provided the state law:

1. Requires at least the same time periods.

2. Follows guidelines established by professional medical associations.

3. Requires the decision to be made by the attending health care provider in consultation with the mother.

Under ERISA, the required amendments of the employer's group health plan are considered to be material modifications in the terms of the plan. As discussed in the section on reporting requirements under ERISA (see **Section 5.02[J]**), participants must be notified of material changes to the plan. The NMHPA provides that the required SMM to the plan must be provided to plan participants no later than 60 days after the first day of the first plan year in which the requirements apply. IRS penalties apply for failure to comply with the requirements of the NMHPA.

On October 27, 1998, the DOL, the IRS, and the CMS issued a Joint Interim Rule regarding implementation of NMHPA. This interim rule is designed to provide guidance to employers, as well as participants, relating to the requirements of NMHPA. The interim rule became effective January 1, 1999. It provides information on:

- *Length of stay calculations.* When delivery occurs inside the hospital, the 48- (or 96-) hour minimum stay (known as the general rule) begins at the time of delivery. When delivery occurs outside the hospital, the minimum stay begins when the mother or newborn is admitted.

- *Prohibitions.* Health plans are prohibited from denying a mother or newborn eligibility or continued eligibility to enroll or renew coverage under the terms of the plan to avoid NMHPA's requirements; providing any form of monetary payments to a mother to encourage her to accept less than the minimum stay; restricting or reducing the benefits for any portion of the 48- (or 96-) hour hospital stay that is less favorable than the benefits provided for any preceding portion of the stay; reducing the reimbursement or compensation to or otherwise penalizing the health care provider for providing care consistent with the requirements of the NMHPA; and providing incentives to health care providers to induce the mother or newborn to receive fewer benefits than those provided by the NMHPA.

- *Authorization and precertification.* Health plans are prohibited from requiring the health care provider to obtain authorization from the plan to prescribe a length of stay authorized under NMHPA; requiring precertification for a portion of a hospital stay that is subject to the general rule if precertification is not required for any preceding portion of a stay (although precertification for the entire stay and precertification for the length of stay over the 48- (or 96-) hour minimum are not prohibited); and increasing the coinsurance for a later portion of the hospital stay.

- *Notices*. Plans subject to the requirements of the PHS Act (generally state and local government plans) will also have notice requirements similar to those required by ERISA.

The interim regulations repeat that the interim rules will not apply to insurance contracts issued in those states with similar legislation that meets the NMHPA's minimum criteria as described above. Companies must determine whether they are required to comply with state law or federal law. The full text of the rule may be found on the CMS Web site: *http://www.cms.gov/hipaa/hipaa1/content/nmhpa.asp*.

§ 5.10   THE WOMEN'S HEALTH AND CANCER RIGHTS ACT

The Women's Health and Cancer Rights Act of 1998 (WHCRA) was signed into law by President Clinton on October 21, 1998. It includes specific protections for breast cancer patients who elect reconstruction in connection with a mastectomy. The WHCRA amends ERISA and the PHS Act and is administered, as are other laws discussed in this chapter, by the DOL and the Department of Health and Human Services.

The WHCRA applies to all group health plans, insured and self-funded, that provide coverage for medical and surgical benefits with respect to a mastectomy. Requirements of the WHCRA are effective for plan years beginning on or after October 21, 1998. The requirements fall into two general categories: coverage and notice.

[A]   Coverage Requirements

Revised group health plan coverage requires that plans offering coverage for mastectomy must also provide coverage for reconstructive surgery in a manner determined in consultation with the attending physician and the patient. Coverage, in compliance with the WHCRA, includes the following:

- All stages of reconstruction of the breast on which the mastectomy was performed,

- Surgery and reconstruction of the other breast to produce a symmetrical appearance, and

- Prostheses and treatment of physical complications at all stages of the mastectomy, including lymphedemas.

[B]   Notice Requirements

The WHCRA mandates three primary notices regarding required coverage. The first notice was a one-time requirement, whereby a plan must have furnished a written description of the benefits required under the WHCRA by January 1, 1999. Notice language was required to have outlined the deductible and coinsurance limits applicable to this coverage under the plan. Participant costs had to be consistent with limits established for other benefits under the plan. The second notice must also describe the benefits required under the WHCRA, but must be provided upon individual's enrollment in the plan. The third notice must contain the same information as the enrollment notice, but must be furnished annually to all plan participants.

All notices should be delivered by first-class mail or by any other means commonly used to provide similar benefits notices and information. Specifically, the regulations outline that separate notices should be provided to a plan beneficiary whose last known address is different from the last known address of the (related) covered participant. To avoid duplication of notices, either the group health plan or the insurance company or HMO may satisfy the notice requirement by providing the WHCRA notice to participants and beneficiaries. If the general plan information is provided to participants and beneficiaries in a manner that complies with the DOL's regulations on providing disclosure information, then the WHCRA required notice may be included with the general plan information.

[C]   Additional Information for Employers

In November 1998, the DOL published a revised supplement to its April 1997 pamphlet, "Questions and Answers: Recent Changes in Health Care Law." The revised supplement included information on the WHCRA as well as detailed questions and answers about regulations that had been issued relative to the HIPAA, the MHPA, and the NMHPA. The revised supplement is available on the Internet at *http://www. dol.gov/ebsa/compliance_assistance.html*, or by calling (866) 444-3272.

§ 5.11   THE MEDICARE PRESCRIPTION DRUG IMPROVEMENT AND MODERNIZATION ACT OF 2003

The Medicare Prescription Drug Improvement and Modernization Act of 2003 (also known as the Medicare Modernization Act (MMA)), enacted on December 8, 2003, provides the most sweeping changes to the Medicare program since its creation. Although most changes do not affect employers, several significant changes do affect employers, as follows:

- Addition of optional prescription drug coverage for Medicare-eligible individuals beginning in 2006

- Provision of a tax-free subsidy to qualifying employers who continue to provide drug coverage to retirees

- Creation of the Health Savings Account (HSA) allowing employees and retirees to set aside tax-free money to meet medical expenses not paid for by insurance or group health plans.

[A]   Medicare Prescription Drug Benefit

Under this new benefit, Medicare Part B enrollees and those entitled to Part A would have the option of enrolling in a Prescription Drug Plan (PDP) under the new Part D. Such coverage began on January 1, 2006. The basic benefits for 2009 will include a $295 deductible (the deductible was $275 in 2008), 25 percent coinsurance up to the initial coverage limit of $2,700 ($2,510 in 2008, catastrophic coverage after an enrollee incurs $4,350 ($4,050 in 2008) in out-of-pocket expenses, and $6,153.75 for the total covered Part D drug spending at the out-of-pocket expense threshold ($5,726.25 in 2008). The out-of-pocket limit will not include costs for benefits not provided due to use of a formulary. The catastrophic coverage will require only nominal cost sharing. Many other benefits and restrictions will apply, including access to choice of plans, "any willing provider" requirements, formulary standards, and establishment of grievance and appeal procedures. In addition, a premium, paid by the Medicare participant, will apply to the PDP. Information for employers and unions sponsoring prescription drug plans for Medicare eligible employees and retirees can be found on the HHS Web site: *http://www.cms.hhs.gov/EmplUnionPlanSponsorInfo/*.

[B] Subsidy to Employers for Retiree Drug Plans

For retirees who are not enrolled in a Part D PDP, employers and unions may receive a tax-free federal subsidy for continuing their qualified retiree prescription drug plans. The subsidy is equal to 28 percent of a qualifying retiree's allowable drug costs attributable to gross prescription drug costs between the cost threshold and the cost limit (for plan years ending in 2009 the cost threshold is $295 and the cost limit is $6,000). A qualifying retiree is an individual who is eligible for Part D coverage, is covered under the employer (or union) plan, and is not enrolled in a Part D PDP. Allowable drug costs include covered Part D drugs actually paid for by the plan sponsor, and by or on behalf of a qualifying retiree. Eligible costs do not include plan administrative costs. The employer (union) plan must be an employment-based retiree health plan that provides prescription drug coverage that has an actuarial value equal to or greater than the actuarial value of the Standard Part D Plan. Employment-based retiree health plans include ERISA group health plans, federal and state government plans, and church plans.

Early surveys of large employers with retiree health benefit plans indicated that nearly 80 percent of these employers planned on applying for the retiree drug subsidy. According to Watson Wyatt Worldwide ("The Changing Horizon of Retiree Medical Benefits," June 2006), 77 percent of employers applied for the subsidy in 2006, and 64 percent of those employers planned to do so again in 2007. In December 2006, the Kaiser Family Foundation and Hewitt Associates released the 2006 Survey on Retiree Health Benefits based on the responses of 302 large (1,000 or more employees) private-sector firms. This survey indicated that 79 percent of the respondents said it is likely that they will offer drug coverage and request the retiree drug subsidy in 2008.

Employers who wish to (continue to) provide prescription drug coverage to their retirees and receive the federal drug subsidy must prove that their PDP meets a two-prong actuarial equivalence standard. The first prong, the gross value test, requires that the expected amount of paid claims for the Medicare beneficiaries in the employer's plan be at least equal to the expected amount of paid claims for those beneficiaries under the Standard Part D Plan. The second prong, the net value test, requires that the net value of the employer's plan be at least equal to the net value of the Standard Part D Plan. In the second prong test, any retiree premium and/or contribution is subtracted from the gross value of the coverage under the employer's plan, and compared to the net value of Plan D, which is obtained by subtracting the annual Medicare beneficiaries' premium from the gross value of Plan D.

Subsidy applications are required 90 days prior to the start of the plan year. One 30-day extension may be applied for if the request for extension is received 90 days prior to the start of the plan year. Applications and requests for extensions, as well as other helpful information to employers requesting the drug subsidy, can be found at CMS's Retiree Drug Subsidy Web site: *http://rds.cms.hhs.gov*. The application must include the following:

- An actuary's certification that the plan satisfies the actuarial equivalence tests;

- A signed sponsor agreement; and

- A list of individuals the plan sponsor believes to be qualifying covered retirees enrolled in the sponsor's prescription drug plan, along with their covered spouses and dependents, and the following identifying information about the individuals:

  — Full name;

— Medicare's Health Insurance Claim number or Social Security Number;

— Date of birth;

— Gender; and

— Relationship to the Medicare beneficiary.

Other information will be required such as periodically updated enrollment information and drug cost data.

[C] Disclosure Notice

Entities (e.g., employers and unions) that provide any prescription drug coverage to Medicare beneficiaries must provide a disclosure notice as to whether the coverage is "creditable prescription drug coverage." ("Creditable" in this instance does not have the same meaning as it has under HIPAA.) Most employer/plan sponsors will have to provide this notice; however, those that contract with Medicare directly as a Part D plan, or that contract with a Part D plan to provide qualified coverage, are exempt from this requirement.

The notice provides Medicare beneficiaries with needed information relating to Medicare Part D enrollment. Beneficiaries who are not covered under creditable prescription drug coverage, and who choose not to enroll before the end of their Part D initial enrollment period, will likely pay a higher premium on a permanent basis if they subsequently enroll in Part D.

Specifically, the notice must be given to all Part D eligible individuals who are covered under, or who apply for, the entity's prescription drug coverage, regardless of whether the coverage is primary or secondary under Medicare. Active employees, retirees, COBRA beneficiaries, disabled individuals, spouses, and dependents who are Medicare beneficiaries must receive the notice. A Part D eligible individual is one who:

- Is entitled to Medicare Part A and/or enrolled in Part B; and

- Resides in the service area of a PDP or of a Medicare Advantage plan that provides prescription drug coverage (MA-PD). (For purposes of the Part D regulations, an individual who is living abroad or is incarcerated is not eligible for Part D because he or she is not considered to "reside" in the service area of a Part D plan.)

As a practical matter, most employers will provide the notice to all employees and retirees covered by their prescription drug coverage. Detailed information about Medicare Part A and Part B eligibility and enrollment is available in the CMS publication "Enrolling in Medicare"(publication number 11036), available on the Medicare Web site: *www.medicare.gov*.

According to guidance provided by CMS, plan sponsors provide "creditable" coverage if their prescription drug coverage is actuarially equivalent to the standard Part D Plan. For purposes of determining whether the employer's coverage is equivalent, only the first prong of the aforementioned two-prong test (see **Section 5.11[B]**) is required. Thus, if the plan sponsor's plan meets the first prong of the test, it is considered actuarially equivalent and would be required to provide a notice indicating that its plan is creditable under the MMA. This notice of creditable coverage is required even if the plan sponsor does not intend to apply for the federal subsidy. CMS has provided an alternative to actuarial analysis of the plan sponsor's prescription drug coverage for those plans that are not seeking the federal subsidy. Under this alternative, the coverage will be deemed creditable if it:

1. Provides coverage for brand and generic prescriptions;

2. Provides reasonable access to retail providers and, optionally, for mail-order coverage;

3. Is designed to pay on average at least 60 percent of participants' prescription drug expenses; and

4. Satisfies at least one of the following:

    a. The prescription drug coverage has no maximum annual benefit or a maximum annual benefit payable by the plan of at least $25,000, or

    b. The prescription drug coverage has an actuarial expectation that the amount payable by the plan will be at least $2,000 per Medicare eligible individual in 2006.

    c. For entities that have integrated health coverage, the integrated health plan has no more than a $250 deductible per year, has no annual benefit maximum or a maximum annual benefit payable by the plan of at least $25,000, and has no less than a $1,000,000 lifetime combined benefit maximum.

The CMS guidance defines an integrated plan as any plan of benefits where the prescription drug benefit is combined with other health coverage offered by the entity (e.g., medical, dental, vision) and the plan has the following provisions:

1. a combined plan year deductible for all plan benefits;

2. a combined annual benefit maximum for all plan benefits; and

3. a combined lifetime benefit maximum for all plan benefits.

To be considered an integrated plan and use the simplified method of determining creditable coverage status, the plan must meet all three parameters above.

The disclosure notice must be made to CMS annually, and within 30 days of termination of prescription drug benefits or upon any change in the plan that affects whether the coverage is creditable. The first notice to CMS was due on March 31, 2006 for all plan years that end in 2006. For all plan years that end in 2007 and later, the filing deadline is 60 days after the first day of the plan year. For example, if a plan year is July 1 – June 30, the notice is due to CMS by August 30. The notice must be provided by every entity that provides prescription drug coverage to Part D eligible individuals. CMS guidance indicates that employers that qualify for the retiree drug subsidy do not need to complete this notice (their application for the subsidy is, in effect, the notice to CMS); however, they must provide the notice to CMS for any Part D eligible individuals for whom they are not claiming the federal subsidy. The notice must be completed on-line and submitted electronically to CMS. It is available on the CMS Web site: *http://www.cms.hhs.gov/ CreditableCoverage/*. On this Web site, CMS has also provided a helpful User Guide and List of Commonly Asked Questions and Helpful Hints to assist entities in completing the notice to CMS.

The notice must also be provided to Part D eligible individuals, minimally, at the following times:

- Prior to the Medicare Part D annual coordinated election period—November 15th through December 31st each year. ("Prior to" is defined as within the previous 12 months);

- Prior to an individual's initial enrollment period for Part D. ("Prior to" is defined as within the previous 12 months);

- Prior to the effective date of coverage for any Medicare eligible individual who joins the plan;

- Whenever prescription drug coverage ends or changes so that it is no longer creditable or becomes creditable; and

- Upon a beneficiary's request.

If the disclosure notice is provided to all plan participants (not just to Medicare beneficiaries), CMS will consider that the conditions of the first two bullet items in the above list have been met. Because of this allowance, it is expected that most plan sponsors will provide the disclosure notice to all plan participants. In order to meet the requirements of the third bullet, most plan sponsors have included the notice with the plan's enrollment materials.

The notice need not be mailed separately; it may be provided with other plan communication materials. One notice may be sent to the participant and all dependents covered under the same plan unless it is known that the spouse or dependent resides at an address other than the participant's. In such a case, separate notices must be sent to each address. If the notice is sent with other plan materials, the disclosures must be prominent and conspicuous. The statements or a reference to the section in the document being provided to the beneficiary that contains the required statement must be prominently referenced in at least 14-point font in a separate box, bolded, or offset on the first page that begins the plan participant information being provided. An example of the reference statement is given in the CMS guidance is as follows:

> If you and/or your dependents have Medicare or will become eligible for Medicare in the next 12 months, a Federal law gives you more choices about your prescription drug coverage. Please see page xx for more details.

Notices may be provided electronically to plan participants. CMS has indicated that the electronic disclosure rules provided in ERISA (29 CFR Section 2520.104b-1(c)(1)) apply to the Part D disclosure notices (see **Section 5.02[J][5]** for these requirements). Plan sponsors who provide notices electronically must inform plan participants that they are responsible for providing a copy of the electronic disclosure notice to their Medicare-eligible dependents covered under the group health plan.

Model disclosure notices (updated for June 15, 2008 and beyond) are provided to plan sponsors at the CMS Web site. One model is provided for creditable coverage and one for non-creditable coverage. A third model, "Model Individual Personalized Disclosure Notice," is also available. This model includes personalized information about the Part D eligible individual such as name, date of birth, or unique member identification number (not a Social Security number); a statement that the plan sponsor's plan provides either creditable or non-creditable coverage; and the dates of that coverage. All three model notices are available in Spanish. CMS also provides instructions for completing the disclosure notice. If a plan sponsor wishes to use its own notice, CMS has provided content standards in its guidance. The model notices and content guidance are available on the CMS Web site: *http://www.cms.hhs.gov/CreditableCoverage/*.

Although the plan sponsor providing the prescription drug coverage is legally responsible for providing the notice, there are no preclusions from entering into an arrangement with a third-party vendor to provide the Notice. Legal experts recommend that, in such a case, appropriate indemnification language be added to the contract with the vendor.

CMS, in further guidance, indicated that disclosure notices are not required for health FSAs, Health Savings Accounts (HSAs) (see **Section 5.11[D]**), or MSAs. Health reimbursement accounts (HRAs) may be creditable coverage and would, therefore, be required to provide the disclosure notice, whether an HRA is offered as a stand-alone plan, or in conjunction with a high-deductible health plan (HDHP). The guidance provides further instructions on how to determine whether the HRA (with or without the HDHP) provides creditable coverage (as defined above). (See **Chapter 12** for a further discussion of HRAs.)

[D]   Health Savings Accounts

HSAs are defined as tax-exempt trust or custodial accounts similar to IRAs. Like MSAs (see **Chapter 6**), individuals are eligible for these tax benefits in any month in which the individual is covered under a HDHP, and not covered by any other non-HDHP plan (with some exceptions). The limits imposed on the HDHP are different for HSAs than for MSAs (for 2009):

	Individual Plan	**Family Plan**
Minimum deductible	$1,150	$ 2,300
Out-of-pocket limit	$5,800	$11,600

Health plans that apply no deductibles to preventative care will still qualify as HDHPs, as will those plans that have annual deductibles and out-of-pocket limits that are higher than the aforementioned limits for out-of-network providers.

Employer contributions to HSAs, within limits, are excluded from the employee's income for income tax purposes. If the contribution to the HSA is made by the employee, it can be deducted from the adjusted gross income, even if the employee does not itemize deductions. The maximum deduction/exclusion is the lesser of the HDHP's annual deductible or a specified limit (for 2009, $3,000 for individual coverage and $5,950 for family coverage) if the HDHP was in place for a full year.

If the employer makes the contributions to the HSAs, the contributions must be comparable for all employees with comparable coverage. Contributions will be considered comparable if they are either the same dollar amount or the same percentage of the deductible. A 35 percent excise tax will be applied to contributions that are not comparable.

HSA distributions are not required during the year of the deduction/exclusion, nor at termination of employment or upon reaching age 65. The HSA fund may accumulate year after year, and can be used to pay for retiree medical benefits (see **Chapter 12** for more information on HSAs).

§ 5.12   UNIFORMED SERVICES EMPLOYMENT AND REEMPLOYMENT RIGHTS ACT (USERRA)

The Uniformed Services Employment and Reemployment Rights Act (USERRA), enacted December 12, 1994, substantially improved reemployment rights of employed veterans. USERRA prohibits employment discrimination due to an individual being "a member of, applies to be a member of, performs, has performed, applies to perform, or has an obligation to perform, service in a uniformed service." The "uniformed services" include the Army, Navy, Marine Corps, Air Force, Coast Guard, Army National Guard, Air National Guard, the Commissioned Corps of the Public Health Service, and the reserves of the Army, Navy, Marine Corps, Air Force and Coast Guard, as well as training for or activation for intermittent disaster response to the National Disaster Medical System.

Employers must offer its employees on military leave the option to continue health benefits. If such leave is for 30 consecutive days (or less), the employee may be required to pay the employee's share (if any) of the cost of the individual and family coverage. For leaves of more than 30 days, health benefits may be continued for the length of the leave or 24 months, whichever is shorter, and the employee is responsible for 102 percent of the applicable premium. The USERRA continuation coverage period begins on the date the military leave of absence begins. It ends on the day the employee reapplies for work, the day after the employee fails to apply for reemployment or when 24 months have past, whichever is shorter.

Employers are given flexibility to develop notification and election procedures for employees to elect USERRA continuation coverage. They may elect to use the same procedures and time limits they use for COBRA continuation coverage (see **Chapter 7**) or develop other procedures, time limits, etc. The procedures and time limits must be reasonable however. (It should be noted that even employers who are not required to provide COBRA continuation coverage must provide USERRA continuation coverage.) If an employer does not develop USERRA continuation coverage procedures, employees on service leave have the option of electing USERRA continuation coverage anytime during the 24-month period when the continuation coverage must be offered. Such coverage must be retroactive to the date the employee first lost their health care coverage. Unlike COBRA, USERRA continuation coverage may be elected only by the employee. Dependents do not have an independent right to elect USERRA continuation coverage as they do for COBRA. In addition to USERRA continuation coverage, COBRA may also apply to employees (and/or their dependents) on military leave; if so, for each right and responsibility included under both laws, those which provide the service member the greater benefit must be applied.

USERRA continuation coverage cannot be terminated because a participant enrolls in another group health plan, unlike COBRA coverage. Thus, if an employee has elected USERRA continuation coverage while on a military leave of absence, and also becomes covered by the military health plan (TRICARE), as long as the employee continues to pay for the USERRA continuation coverage, such coverage cannot be terminated.

The requirements to continue health coverage when an employee is on a leave of absence under USERRA include health flexible spending accounts (FSAs). Participants may elect health FSA continuation for the 24-month USERRA continuation period; this is different than the rules under COBRA, which only require that COBRA be offered for the remainder of the calendar year in which the participant loses health coverage. There have been no regulations or guidance as to how to implement health FSA coverage during a USERRA leave of absence. Although reference to the COBRA continuation requirements and guidance can be of assistance, employers are also cautioned that the two laws are not identical, and some flexibility will be required.

See **Chapter 11** for more information about leave requirements under USERRA.

§ 5.13   GENETIC INFORMATION NONDISCRIMINATION ACT (GINA)

The Genetic Information Nondiscrimination Act (GINA) was signed into law on May 21, 2008. GINA prohibits discrimination against individuals on the basis of their genetic information in both employment and health care. The provisions relating to group health plans will become effective one year after the bill's signing, while the employment provisions will become effective 18 months after signing. GINA amends ERISA, the Public Health Service Act and the Code, as well as Title VII of the Civil Rights Act.

Although GINA will generally preempt state genetic nondiscrimination laws, state laws that are more stringent than GINA's requirements, standards or implementations will supersede GINA. GINA defines family member as: (1) the individual's spouse; (2) a dependent child of the individual, including children placed for adoption; or (3) parents, grandparents or great-grandparents. Genetic information is defined as (1) the individual's genetic tests; (2) the individual's family members' genetic tests; and (3) the manifestation of a disease or disorder in family members of an individual.

Under GINA, group health plans, insured or self-insured, may not deny enrollment or eligibility for enrollment based on an employee's or an employee's family member's genetic information. Similarly, group health plans may not adjust premiums or contribution rates based on genetic information. Group health plans may not require genetic testing of participants as a prerequisite for enrollment or eligibility for enrollment. GINA will not prevent genetic testing as part of health care or treatment.

In general GINA prevents an employer from requiring, requesting or purchasing genetic information about an employee or a family member. There are exceptions: (1) inadvertent requests for such information; (2) genetic services provided by the employer, including wellness programs; (3) when required to correctly administer leaves under FMLA; and (4) when obtained through the purchase of commercially available documents.

If an individual or family member feels that their health care rights under GINA have been violated, they may seek relief under ERISA. If health care coverage was denied, it can be reinstated back to the date of loss of coverage. Penalties against the health plan and/or employer include $100 per day during the period of noncompliance and penalties of $2,500 (for de minimis violations) up to $15,000 for a total of up to $500,000 for multiple violations.

Information on GINA's employment nondiscrimination requirements can be found in **Chapter 18.**

§ 5.14   STATE GROUP HEALTH PLAN REQUIREMENTS

Although it is not unusual for states to impose specific mandates on insurers (see below), the newest state-imposed employer mandate may have far-reaching implications; that is, if they can survive ERISA preemption. In January 2006, the State of Maryland overrode their governor's veto and passed the "Fair Share Health Care Fund Act." This legislation requires all for-profit employers with 10,000 or more employees that do not spend at least 8 percent of total wages on health insurance costs to contribute to a state fund for the uninsured. The amount of funding required would be the amount equal to the difference between what the employer spends on health insurance and 8 percent of total wages. The funding will support the operation of the state's Medicaid program. Known as a "pay or play" law, the stated aim of the legislation is to reduce the number of uninsured in the state. However, due to the size parameters included in the law, it will, in fact, only apply to one employer: Wal-Mart.

In February 2006, the Retail Industry Leaders Association filed a lawsuit against the state claiming that the law is illegal under ERISA. On July 19, 2006, a federal district court ruled in favor of the RILA, that the Fair Share Health Care Fund Act is preempted by ERISA. [Retail Industry Leaders Association v. Fielder, Civ. No. JFM-06-316 (D. Md. July 19, 2006)] In making his decision, the judge wrote "my finding that the act is preempted is in accordance with long established Supreme Court law that state laws which impose health or welfare mandates on employers are invalid under ERISA." Maryland appealed the ruling to the Fourth Circuit Court of Appeals. On January 17, 2007, the Fourth Circuit affirmed the lower court's ruling that the Maryland Fair Share Health Care Fund Act is preempted by ERISA. Maryland's Attorney General indicated that his office will not pursue an appeal of this ruling.

Two other states have also passed "pay or play" laws. Vermont enacted two bills: "An Act Relating to Health Care Affordability for Vermonters" and "An Act Relating to Catamount Health." These laws will create a health coverage program for the state's uninsured called Catamount Health. In addition to other funding, employers of greater than 8 employees will pay $1 per full-time equivalent employee per day if they do not offer health coverage. This required funding will begin in April 2007 and will also be assessed on employees who are not eligible for the employer's insurance and for any uninsured employees.

Massachusetts passed the "Massachusetts Health Care Access and Affordability Act" on April 12, 2006. Employers of greater than 10 employees working in the state who do not provide health coverage for their employees will be assessed $295 per employee per year (the "Fair Share Contribution"). The employer requirements are effective on October 1, 2006. Although no minimum plan design is mandated, employers will need to obtain a minimum participation rate of 25 percent of full-time employees and provide a minimum contribution rate of 33 percent of the cost of the coverage to avoid the "Fair Share Contribution" assessment. The legislation also requires a surcharge of non-health-care-providing employers if more than five uninsured employees utilize free public health care, or if any one uninsured employee used free care more than three times in one year. The "Free Rider Surcharge" became effective on July 1, 2007 and varies between 10 and 55 percent, based on the size of the employer, the number of uninsured employees accessing public care, and the frequency of the care provided. To avoid the surcharge, employers can implement a cafeteria plan for employees who work at least 64 hours per month. The plan must allow employees to pay for employer-provided health care on a pretax basis, or to pay for the Commonwealth Connector medical plan on a pretax basis. The mandate for the cafeteria plan is effective on October 1, 2007. It should be noted that this law requires that all individuals have health care coverage. Various options will be available for the uninsured.

As of this writing, no legal challenges have been filed against either the Vermont or Massachusetts' laws.

Other states have attempted to avoid the ERISA challenge to mandated health care coverage by requiring that employers establish a cafeteria plan under IRC Section 125. In addition to Massachusetts, Connecticut, Missouri, and Vermont have recently passed laws that require employers to provide these plans that allow employees to pay their share of the health coverage on a pretax basis.

States often impose specific requirements on the design of employer-provided group health insurance within their boundaries. Each state follows broad guidelines to develop group health insurance requirements. For example, plan administrators should be aware of the following:

- Almost every state requires mandatory coverage for alcoholism treatment. Often, the requirement is that alcoholism be treated as any other health condition covered under the plan. The requirements of the ADA place some additional limitations on treatment of alcoholism.

- Most states require some level of coverage of substance abuse treatment and place minimum benefit limitations on both outpatient and inpatient treatments.

- Many states mandate mental health coverage and list the types of related providers that must be covered (e.g., social workers, psychiatrists, and psychologists). Some states provide minimum-dollar-amount limits for both inpatient and outpatient services. As of this writing, 42 states have some form of mental health parity law.

- Specific providers, such as chiropractors, optometrists and podiatrists, are required to be eligible providers under the statutes of most states.

- Most states regulate the eligibility of employees' dependent children, supplementing the OBRA '93 requirement for adopted children and children placed for adoption. Coverage for handicapped dependents and newborns is also required by most states. For example, New Jersey requires insured medical plans to extend coverage for unmarried dependents up to the age of 30 (or adopt an alternative that provides COBRA-like coverage to dependents who lose coverage before age 30).

- Many states require coverage for certain preventive treatments, including mammograms and Pap smears for women, and well-child care and immunizations for children. Mandated coverage for PSA tests for men is becoming more prevalent, as well.

- Most states have laws that equal or improve upon the federal laws for maternity stay requirements. Similarly, states have laws that provide for breast reconstruction after mastectomies that equal or improve upon the federal law.

- Most states have mandates for providing diabetic supplies, emergency services, PKU/formula coverage, well-child care, and prostate screening.

[A] Trends in State Requirements

Although Congress may be reluctant to pass laws affecting health care coverage, state lawmakers appear not to have the same reluctance. Mandates, parity, and nondiscrimination issues have been prevalent topics in state legislatures. For example, more than half of the states now ban employment discrimination based on genetic information. At least 43 states have laws banning discrimination in health insurance. A corollary involves the privacy of genetic information; at least 30 states have special genetic privacy laws.

Contraceptive coverage is another "hot" issue among state lawmakers. As of this writing, at least 23 states have laws or regulations to guarantee the same insurance coverage of contraceptive drugs and/or services as afforded to other prescription drugs or other preventive services. Both state and federal courts have issued rulings that uphold these laws, including a 2003 California appellate court ruling that the Roman Catholic church must provide contraceptive coverage to its secular employees, and that a state law mandating such benefits does not infringe on religious freedom.

Another state trend is the requirement that group health plans and/or health insurers cover expenses related to services received in clinical trials or experimental procedures. For example, South Dakota passed a law in 2000 requiring that health insurers who cover prescription drugs must also cover experimental drugs used for the treatment of cancer or other life-threatening diseases. California, in 2001, passed legislation requiring health insurers to cover all routine medical expenses incurred by cancer patients enrolled in clinical trials. As of this writing, other states are also considering bills that would ensure complete coverage for cancer patients in experimental drug trials.

Some states have passed laws requiring insurers to cover complementary and alternative medicine (CAM), at least in part because of the growing awareness that CAM can reduce catastrophic health claims. CAM, also known as alternative therapy, is a term for such treatments as acupuncture, nutritional counseling and supplements, therapeutic massage, chiropractic care, naturopathy, hypnotherapy, meditation, aromatherapy, yoga, and herbal medicine. These treatments may also be included as a part of homeopathic medical care. For example, the U.S. Supreme Court has upheld a Washington state law that requires insurance carriers to provide access to all types of health care providers licensed or certified under state law, including chiropractors, naturopaths, acupuncturists, massage therapists, and others.

Some states are looking at restricting rather than adding requirements. Lawmakers in several states are considering a moratorium on any new mandated benefits, debating or studying whether to impose a freeze on any additional state-required insurance benefits.

Exhibit 5-1   Mandated Benefits: 2009 Compliance Guide

Exhibit 5.1
ADA Do's and Don'ts for Benefits

Do:

- Continue to offer health insurance policies that contain preexisting clauses, as long as the clauses are applied consistently, meet the requirements of HIPAA, and are not used as a method of evading ADA nondiscrimination requirements.

- Place limits on reimbursements for certain procedures or types of drugs or procedures covered by the plan. Make sure these limitations are applied equally to employees and their dependents with and without disabilities, and the limit does not target specific disabilities or an identifiable group of disabilities.

- Uniformly apply benefit provisions within the scope of EEOC guidance, even though they may not specifically address the special needs of every individual with a disability.

- Encourage voluntary medical examinations, including voluntary medical histories as a part of employee health programs. Make sure the results of these examinations are not used to limit health insurance eligibility. The employer must keep records developed in the course of these activities confidential.

- Maintain evidence to justify any disability-based distinction in the plan (e.g., actuarial data or actual or anticipated claims experience).

Don't:

- Make any employment decision or justify disparate treatment of an employee or dependent with a disability on the basis of a speculation that the individual may cause increased health insurance costs.

- Reduce the level of health insurance benefits offered simply because a dependent of any employee has a disability.

- Use voluntary medical examinations, including voluntary medical histories that are a part of an employee health program, for the purpose of limiting health insurance eligibility.

- Use any of the accepted principles of risk assessment or current insurance industry underwriting practices as a method of evading ADA nondiscrimination requirements.

Exhibit 5.2
Notice of Group Health Plan's Exemption from the Mental Health Parity Act

---

NOTICE OF GROUP HEALTH PLAN'S EXEMPTION FROM THE MENTAL HEALTH PARITY ACT

* **DESCRIPTION OF THE ONE PERCENT INCREASED COST EXEMPTION — This notice is required to be provided to you under the requirements of the Mental Health Parity Act of 1996 (MHPA) because the group health plan identified in Line 1 below is claiming the one percent increased cost exemption from the requirements of MHPA. Under MHPA, a group health plan offering both medical/surgical and mental health benefits generally can no longer set annual or aggregate lifetime dollar limits on mental health benefits that are lower than any such dollar limits for medical/surgical benefits. In addition, a plan that does not impose an annual or aggregate lifetime dollar limit on medical/surgical benefits generally may not impose such a limit on mental health benefits. However, a group health plan can claim an exemption from these requirements if the plan's costs increase one percent or more due to the application of MHPA's requirements.**

This notice is to inform you that the group health plan identified in Line 1 below is claiming the exemption from the requirements of MHPA. The exemption is effective as of the date identified in Line 4 below. Since benefits under your group health plan may change as of the date identified in Line 4 it is important that you contact your plan administrator or the plan representative identified in Line 5 below to see how your benefits may be affected as a result of your group health plan's election of this exemption from the requirements of MHPA.

Upon submission of this notice by you (or your representative) to the plan administrator or the person identified in Line 5 below, the plan will provide you or your representative, free of charge, a summary of the information upon which the plan's exemption is based.

1. Name of the group health plan and the plan number (PN): _____

2. Name, address, and telephone number of plan administrator responsible for providing this notice:

    _____

    _____

    _____

3. For single-employer plans, the name, address, telephone number (if different from Line 2), and employer identification number (EIN) of the employer sponsoring the group health plan:

    _____

    _____

    _____

4. Effective date of the exemption (at least 30 days after the notices are sent): _____

5. For further information, call: _____

Chapter 6
Health Insurance Portability and Accountability Act (HIPAA)

§ 6.01   AUDIT QUESTIONS

1. Is the company on behalf of its group health plan providing written certificates of creditable coverage or ensuring that the group health plan's provider is doing so?

2. Does the company's group health plan have written procedures for participants and beneficiaries to request certificates of creditable coverage?

3. Does the company allow special enrollment periods?

4. Has the company reviewed all of its benefits to ensure that individual eligibility for benefits is not based on such criteria as medical condition, health status, and medical history?

5. Has the company's group health plan provided all participants with a Notice of Privacy Practices, or, if fully insured, ensured that its health insurer or HMO has done so?

6. Has the company conducted a security risk analysis of the group health plan's electronic protected health information?

Note: Consistent "yes" answers to the above questions suggest that the organization is applying management practices and/or complying with federal regulations. "No" answers indicate that problem areas exist and should be addressed immediately.

The Health Insurance Portability and Accountability Act of 1996 (HIPAA) added new dimensions to employee benefits. As indicated in the title of the law, HIPAA was passed as a means to provide greater portability of employee health care coverage, particularly as individuals move from one job to another. Preexisting condition exclusions (PCEs) in employer group health plans were perceived to be arbitrary deterrents to changing jobs, in effect creating "job lock."

Unique aspects of this legislation include the new health plan portability rules, the preexisting condition exclusion, guaranteed renewability, certification of creditable coverage, excepted benefits, special enrollment periods, nondiscrimination requirements, disclosure requirements, the creation of medical savings accounts, long-term care insurance provisions and the administrative simplification requirements of privacy, security, and transaction standards. These aspects, except long-term care, are discussed in this chapter. (See **Chapter 10** for a discussion of long-term care insurance and **Chapter 7** for a discussion of changes made to COBRA by HIPAA.)

§ 6.02 HEALTH CARE PORTABILITY

Effective July 1, 1997, HIPAA created new health coverage portability provisions. The purpose of HIPAA is to ensure that employees leaving an employer's health plan have access to a new employer's plan without limitations because of preexisting conditions, waiting periods, or health status. The law applies to health plans with two or more active participants who were employees on the first day of the plan year. The portability requirements limit preexisting conditions exclusions, prohibit exclusion from coverage based on health status, and guarantee renewability of health insurance coverage.

Interim final regulations were published in April 1997 and a clarification of those rules was published in December 1997. Final regulations for health coverage portability were published in the *Federal Register* on December 30, 2004. The sections below contain the most recent regulations, which were effective February 28, 2005, and applicable to all plan years beginning on or after July 1, 2005.

Concurrent to the publication of the final regulations, new proposed regulations were published in the *Federal Register*. These proposed regulations reference creditable coverage, special enrollment periods, interaction with the Family and Medical Leave Act and special rules relating to group health plans and number of employees. Employers are not required to conform to the proposed regulations as of this writing. However, it is permissible to do so, and employers may want to consider the implications of compliance. The following sections are based on the final regulations; a brief description of the proposed regulations is included where applicable.

[A] The Preexisting Conditions Exclusion

The regulations covering the HIPAA portability provisions define a preexisting condition exclusion (PCE) as a "limitation or exclusion of benefits relating to a condition based on the fact that the condition was present before the effective date of coverage under a group health plan or group health insurance coverage, whether or not any medical advice, diagnosis, care, or treatment was recommended or received before that day." The final regulations, published on December 30, 2004, present three examples to help plan sponsors understand PCEs. (For the examples, go to the Employee Benefits Security Administration (EBSA) Web site: *http://www.dol.gov/ebsa/regs/fedreg/final/main.htm.*)

In general, HIPAA limits PCEs to 12 months. The requirements are as follows:

- Employers may have an 18-month PCE for employees who do not enroll as soon as they become eligible for benefits, but they must reduce the 12- or 18-month cap by one month for each month of prior continuous, creditable coverage. Creditable coverage is coverage that may have been provided under a previous group health plan, individual health insurance, Medicare, COBRA, or other federal health programs (see below).

- Employers cannot apply a PCE to newborns, adopted children, or pregnancies that exist on the day coverage begins.

- If there is a break in coverage of more than 63 days, prior continuous coverage does not have to be counted against the 12- or 18-month cap.

- A health plan must provide a written certificate of creditable coverage when an individual ceases health plan or COBRA coverage, or if an employee requests such certification within 24 months from the date coverage ends.

In reviewing group health plan documents, the Department of Labor (DOL) has found examples of what it calls "hidden preexisting-condition exclusions." These hidden PCEs occur when a particular benefit is restricted based on when the condition arose in relation to the effective date of coverage; they are hidden because these restrictions are not identified as PCEs. For example, a plan would violate HIPAA if it excludes benefits for cosmetic surgery that is required as a result of an injury sustained before the effective date of plan coverage. The plan must either delete the requirement that the injury take place while the participant is covered under the plan or eliminate the timing requirement such that it no longer serves as a form of a preexisting condition. Hidden PCEs may also be found in benefits with lifetime limits that include benefits received under prior health plan coverage. A plan that provides for a lower benefit limit if the injury or illness first occurred before the effective date of plan coverage is also a form of a hidden PCE.

The 2004 proposed regulations would change the timing of the 63-day break-in-coverage period. Under the proposed rule, the tolling of the break-in-coverage would be delayed if the employee did not receive the certificate of creditable coverage on or before the day coverage ends. In this case, the break-in-coverage period would not begin until the earlier of when the certificate is provided, or 44 days after the coverage ends.

Corresponding changes have been made to the COBRA health care continuation rules. Specifically, the COBRA rules coordinate with the new rules regarding PCEs (see **Chapter 7**). If a group health plan fails to comply with these new rules, a penalty may be imposed on the employer until the failure is corrected.

[B] Guaranteed Renewability

Individuals with at least 18 months of coverage under a previous plan must, after exhausting all possible avenues for health coverage, be offered the opportunity to purchase an individual policy in their state (unless the state already has a program in place to offer coverage in this situation).

[C] Certification of Creditable Coverage

HIPAA requires employers to provide employees a written certificate of coverage outlining coverage provided during the 24-month period before coverage ceased. There are three occasions when the certification statement must be given to an employee, a qualified beneficiary, or both:

1. At the time coverage ends, which can be at the same time as COBRA notification

2. At the time COBRA coverage (if elected) ends or at the end of the grace period for payment of COBRA premium

3. Upon request by an employee at any time within 24 months following the end of coverage

Employers have to provide names of dependents on the certification statement. If dependents participated in different types of benefits, separate certificates must be provided indicating which participant or beneficiary received which type of benefit. The certificate must show all periods of creditable coverage.

Creditable coverage is broadly defined to include coverage under one or more of the following:

- A group health plan, including a government or church plan

- Individual health insurance

- Medicare

- Medicaid

- Military-sponsored health care

- The program of the Indian Health Service

- A state health benefits risk pool

- The Federal Employee Health Benefits Program

- State Children's Health Insurance Program (S-CHIP)

- A public health plan (as defined in regulations)

- Any health benefit plan under Section 5(e) of the Peace Corps Act

Creditable coverage does not include accident and disability income, liability, workers' compensation, or automobile medical insurance. Coverage for limited benefits (e.g., limited dental, vision, and long-term care) or for plans under which health benefits are "incidental" is also not considered creditable (see **Section 6.02[D]** below). Waiting periods and HMO affiliation periods count as creditable coverage and need to be indicated on the certificate. Certificates must be provided when requested, even if the coverage is still in effect.

The certificates may be provided either by the employer or by the health insurance carrier, but need not be provided by both. An employee's current (i.e., new) employer may request information from a prior employer about categories of benefits, but the prior employer may charge for the costs of disclosing that information. When a health plan changes insurers under a group health plan, it is not necessary to provide certificates to the participants. However, the discontinued insurer must provide information to the plan such that the plan can prepare HIPAA certificates for the period of time under that insurer. And the insurer must provide a certificate to any participant upon request for that period of time when that insurer was the provider under the plan.

The final regulations added an educational statement on HIPAA rights to the certificate, which is provided on the new model certificate for group health plans. (See **Exhibit 6.1** for the model HIPAA certification statement included in the final regulations, and **Exhibit 6.2** for a sample form for providing information on different categories of benefits based on the model outlined in interim regulations published in the *Federal Register* on April 8, 1997.) The final regulations also require that plans have written procedures for participants and beneficiaries to request certificates of creditable coverage. The penalty for failing to provide the certificate is $100 per day per individual for each day of noncompliance. The maximum fine is the lesser of 10 percent of the plan sponsor's annual health care plan payments or $500,000.

The proposed rules add additional educational language to the certificate regarding the interaction of the HIPAA portability provisions with the Family and Medical Leave Act (FMLA), as follows:

> **Special information for people on FMLA leave.** If you are taking leave under the FMLA and you drop health coverage during your leave, any days without health coverage while on FMLA leave will not count towards a 63-day break in coverage. In addition, if you do not return from leave, the 30-day period to request special enrollment in another plan will not start before your FMLA ends. Therefore, when you apply for other health coverage, you should tell your plan administrator or health insurer about any prior FMLA leave.

In addition, the proposed regulations clarify that employers must provide automatic certificates when coverage ends during or at the end of an FMLA leave.

The proposed rules also suggest a default for determining how many plans an employer has. Under the previous regulations, it was not clear whether an employee switching between health care options under an employer's plan (e.g., from the HMO option to the PPO option) was losing coverage under one plan. If so, a certificate of creditable coverage would be required. The proposed rules clarify that, unless the plan documents state otherwise and the plans are administered according to those plan documents, various choices under an employer's sponsorship are not separate plans; rather, they are options under one plan. Therefore, when an employee switches between options, no certificate will be required.

[D] Excepted Benefits

HIPAA excepts certain benefits from coverage under the portability rules. Accident-only coverage, disability-income coverage, workers compensation, and liability insurance are all exempt from HIPAA.

Generally, all group health plans are covered, except limited scope dental and vision benefits and long-term care coverage. Excepted benefits must be provided under a separate insurance policy or contract, or are otherwise not an integral part of a plan that is subject to HIPAA. These benefits will not be considered an integral part of a plan subject to HIPAA if participants have the right not to elect coverage for the benefits, and if the participants who elect such coverage must pay an additional premium or contribution for it. Therefore, self-funded limited scope dental or vision plans that meet these two conditions of the "not an integral part of a plan" requirement will be considered an excepted benefit. Limited scope dental benefits are those that are substantially for treatment of the mouth (including any organ or structure within the mouth). Limited scope vision benefits are those that are substantially for treatment of the eye. If the benefits under a plan are excepted benefits, certificates of coverage are not required, and the coverage may not qualify as creditable coverage.

The final regulations clarify that benefits under a health care flexible spending account (FSA) are excepted benefits if:

- The health FSA meets the definition of a health FSA in Code Section 106(c)(2).

- The maximum benefit available for any participant of the FSA must not exceed two times the participant's salary reduction, or if larger, the amount of the salary reduction plus $500. The maximum benefit available is equal to the employee's salary reduction plus any employer contribution. By definition, this condition will be met if the FSA is funded only by employee contributions (salary reductions).

- The employee has other health care coverage available for the year of the employee's coverage under the FSA, and this other health care coverage cannot be limited to HIPAA excepted benefits (e.g., limited scope benefits such as dental or vision coverage). The participant does not need to have elected the other health care coverage, only that it be available to the participant if he or she elects it.

The final regulations also clarify that, generally, the HIPAA provisions for portability will apply to high deductible health plans and will not apply to health savings accounts (see **Chapter 5**). Fixed dollar indemnity plans (those that pay a fixed dollar amount per day (or other period) regardless of the amount of expenses incurred) are also excepted benefits, if:

- The benefits are provided under a separate policy, certificate, or insurance contract;

- There is no coordination of benefits between the provision of the benefits and an exclusion of benefits under any group health plan maintained by the same plan sponsor; and

- The benefits are paid without regard to whether benefits are paid for the event under any group health plan maintained by the same plan sponsor.

"Supplemental excepted benefits" are also excepted benefits under HIPAA. To qualify as excepted benefits, supplemental excepted benefits must be provided under a separate policy, certificate, or contract of insurance, and be either Medicare supplemental health insurance, TRICARE supplemental program, or "similar supplemental coverage provided to coverage under a group health plan." Similar supplemental coverage provided to coverage under a group health plan is not defined in HIPAA or its regulations, although the regulations do clarify that one requirement is that the plan must be designed to fill gaps in primary coverage, such as deductibles or coinsurance. On December 7, 2007 the DOL issued a Field Assistance Bulletin (FAB No. 2007-04) that provides assistance in determining whether a group health plan is an excepted supplemental benefit (the Treasury Department and HHS issued similar guidance). The guidance indicated that "similar supplemental coverage" will fall within an enforcement safe harbor if it is a separate policy, certificate or contract of insurance (collectively "policy") and if it satisfies all of the following requirements:

1. Independent of Primary Coverage—the policy must be issued by an entity that does not provide the primary coverage under the plan. The entities must not be under the same controlled group of corporations or part of the same group of trades or businesses under common control.

2. Supplemental for Gaps in Primary Coverage—the policy must fill gaps in primary coverage, such as deductibles or coinsurance, but the plan will not meet the safe harbor if it only becomes secondary or supplemental under a coordination-of-benefits provision.

3. Supplemental in Value of Coverage—the cost of the policy must not exceed 15 percent of the cost of the primary coverage; cost is determined in the same manner as COBRA coverage cost is determined.

4. Similar to Medicare Supplemental Coverage—the policy must not differentiate among individuals in eligibility, benefits or premiums based on any health factor of an individual or any dependent of the individual.

Questions still remain, however, about some plans that may or may not be excepted benefits. For example, the following issues are unresolved:

- EAPs may be group health plans, depending on what benefits are provided under the plan. If counseling or other direct services are provided, they will most likely fall within HIPAA coverage.

- Stand-alone retiree medical plans may be excepted because HIPAA applies to plans with two or more participants "who are active employees on the first day of the plan year."

- Stop-loss insurance may also be an exception to HIPAA coverage requirements, if the stop-loss coverage does not apply to individuals. However, requirements under HIPAA that stop-loss coverage be disclosed would still apply.

[E] Special Enrollment Periods

As of July 1, 1997, employers must allow employees to enroll in health coverage during certain special enrollment periods in addition to the initial and open enrollment periods. These special enrollment periods include loss of other coverage and upon obtaining a new dependent.

[1] Loss of Coverage

If an employee does not enroll in the employer's health plan when he or she first becomes eligible, because the employee wants to keep his or her current health coverage (e.g., COBRA coverage from a previous employer), the employer must allow the employee to enroll in the plan within 30 days of the date the other coverage is exhausted. If the employee stops paying for the COBRA coverage before it runs out, the employer could require the employee to wait to enroll during the next open enrollment period, if one exists.

Loss of coverage situations that provide for special enrollment periods include the following:

- The individual no longer resides in an HMO service area;

- The individual suffers a loss of dependent status;

- The plan no longer offers any benefits to a class of similarly situated individuals;

- A health insurance issuer ceases to operate in the group market (unless the plan otherwise provides a current right to enroll in alternative health coverage);

- The individual reaches a lifetime limit on all benefits;

- Upon any other reason for loss of coverage, the individual declines enrollment in COBRA or similar coverage; or

- There are no other coverage opportunities.

An employer may require that when coverage is declined during the initial enrollment period, the employee must put in writing that the declination is due to other coverage. The employee who then exhausts other coverage must request enrollment in the employer's health plan within 30 days of the date of the loss of the other coverage. Enrollment under this special enrollment right must be effective no later than the first day of the month following the date the enrollment is requested.

The final regulations clarify that the initial enrollment period is not the only time when an individual with other health coverage may decline coverage and still satisfy the prerequisites for special enrollment upon loss of other coverage.

The DOL presented informal guidance (American Bar Association (ABA) Joint Committee on Employee Benefits, Meeting with DOL Officials, May 18, 2005; available at the ABA's Web site: *http://www.abanet.org/jceb/2005/ qa05dol.pdf*) on participants who reach a lifetime limit on all benefits under their group health plan. The DOL indicated that such participants would be eligible to enroll in another option of the same plan, if the other option has a higher lifetime maximum, or if the benefits under the various options were not integrated (that is, the plan did not consider all benefits paid under all options to determine whether the lifetime limit was reached). Similarly, if the employer provided benefit alternatives under different plans (rather than as options under one plan), an individual who reached the lifetime limit under one plan would have special enrollment rights to enroll into another plan.

[2] New Dependents

New dependents of eligible employees by marriage, birth, adoption, or placement for adoption must be permitted to enroll in the organization's health plan if the employer is notified within 30 days of such event. The coverage becomes effective on the date of the birth, adoption, or placement for adoption. For a marriage, coverage can become effective on the date the employee notifies the plan, but no later than the first day of the first month beginning after the date the completed request for enrollment is received. It is not required to make coverage due to marriage retroactive to the date of the marriage.

Numerous court cases have dealt with the special enrollment rules as they apply to newborn coverage. Generally, when plan sponsors have provided adequate notice of the requirement to notify the plan of a newborn within the time period allowed by the group health plan (no less than 30 days from the date of birth), and enrollment notice was not provided in a timely manner, the courts have held that no special enrollment is required. Some court cases have determined what appropriate notice is. For example, in *Lindstrom v. W.J. Bauman Assoc., Ltd.* [2006 U.S. Dist. LEXIS 4498 (W.D. Wis. 2006)], the employee submitted a "medical expense reimbursement account form" that listed her newborn as a new dependent within the required time period to enroll a newborn as a special enrollee, but did not submit an "employee change form" until 45 days after the birth of her child. The court in this case found for the employer, rejecting the employee's argument that the "medical expense reimbursement account form" was the notification for enrolling her new child. The court held that the employee could not show how naming her newborn on this form provided notice to the plan administrator to enroll him on the plan.

When a special enrollment right is available due to a new dependent, the regulations require that others may be eligible for enrollment also. For example, if a child is born to or placed for adoption with an employee who had not previously enrolled in the health plan, the child, employee and spouse are all eligible for enrolling under the special enrollment rules. In *Livingston v. S.D. State Med. Holding Co.* [411 F. Supp. 1161, 2006 U.S. Dist. LEXIS 5280, 37 Employee Benefits Cas. (BNA) 1354 (D.S.D. 2006)], the court held in favor of the employee, who had not enrolled in the health plan prior to the birth of her child. Upon the child's premature birth (and within the 30-day time period), the employee requested enrollment for both herself and her newborn, but the plan denied coverage in part because the employee returned to work in a part-time status, and part-time employees were not eligible for health care benefits. The court disagreed, indicating that at the time of the birth of her child, she was full-time and eligible for benefits, and therefore she should have been allowed special enrollment rights retroactive to the date of the birth of her child.

Under the regulations, all special enrollees are required to be offered all group health plan options that are available to new enrollees. For example, if an employee is enrolled under an HMO option of the group health plan, and gives birth, the employee, the spouse and the child may all enroll in any option offered by the employer, including switching out of the HMO and into any other option available. If the health plan requires that all members of the family be enrolled in the same option, the special enrollment rules do not contradict this requirement.

[3] Notice and Enrollment Request

The final regulations require employers to provide potential enrollees with a description of their special enrollment rights. This notice must be provided at or before the time an employee is given an opportunity to elect coverage under the group health plan. The DOL has prepared the following model language that plan sponsors can use to inform employees who are declining coverage because they have other coverage:

> If you are declining enrollment for yourself or your dependents (including your spouse) because of other health insurance coverage or group health plan coverage, you may be able to enroll yourself and your dependents in this plan if you or your dependents lose eligibility for that other coverage (or if the employer stops contributing towards you or your dependents' other coverage). However, you must request enrollment within [insert "30 days" or any longer period that applies under the plan] after your or your dependents' other coverage ends (or after the employer stops contributing toward the other coverage).

> In addition, if you have a new dependent as a result of marriage, birth, adoption, or placement for adoption, you may be able to enroll yourself and your dependents. However, you must request enrollment within [insert "30 days" or any longer period that applies under the plan] after the marriage, birth, adoption, or placement for adoption.

> To request special enrollment or obtain more information, contact [insert the name, title, telephone number, and any additional contact information of the appropriate plan representative].

The proposed rules clarify that employees need only make an oral or written request for special enrollment during the 30-day window period. If a plan requires an application form to be completed to effect enrollment, the plan cannot require employees to complete the application for a special enrollment during the 30-day window period. According to the proposed rules, plans can require the applicant to complete the application within a reasonable time frame after the 30-day window period, and assuming that the employee made proper (oral or written) notice within the 30-day period.

[F] Nondiscrimination Requirements

HIPAA furthered the requirements prohibiting group health plans from discriminating on the basis of health status. Specifically, a group health plan may not establish rules for individual eligibility based on any of the following:

- Health status

- Medical condition (including both physical and mental illnesses)

- Claims experience

- Medical history

- Genetic information

- Evidence of insurability

- Receipt of health care

- Disability

The nondiscrimination requirement does not mean that a group health plan is required to provide particular benefits, procedures, treatment, or service. A group plan may establish limitations or restrictions on benefits or coverage for covered groups of individuals in similar situations, such as union status, full-time v. part-time, geographic location, or other employment status.

Group health plans may not discriminate on the basis of eligibility. Nondiscrimination on the basis of eligibility includes enrolment, effective date of coverage, waiting periods, benefits, cost-sharing methods, continuing eligibility, and termination of eligibility. The nondiscrimination rules also require that plans may not apply an actively-at-work provision to employees who are absent due to a health reason; apply nonconfinement provisions to dependents; apply evidence of insurability requirements to late enrollees or for specific options (e.g., for PPO coverage); exclude individuals from coverage because they participate in dangerous activities; and exclude individuals due to a history of health claims.

Interim regulations implementing HIPAA indicate that the prohibition on discrimination does not prevent a plan or insurance issuer from establishing premium discounts or rebates or otherwise modifying applicable copayments or deductibles in return for adherence to programs of health promotion and disease prevention that are known as bona fide wellness programs. In 2001, the DOL published proposed regulations on the establishment and implementation of wellness programs that provide financial incentives. On December 13, 2006, the Departments of Labor, Treasury, and Health and Human Services jointly issued final rules on wellness programs (71 Fed. Reg. 75,014 (December 13, 2006)). While in general the final rules are similar to the proposed rules, some important differences and clarifications were made. The final regulations are effective for plan years beginning on or after July 1, 2007. See **Chapter 10 (Section 10.09[D])** for information on the final regulations' impact on wellness programs.

These final regulations also provide additional guidance with respect to nondiscrimination rules, such as:

- Source-of-injury exclusion: plans cannot exclude treatment of an injury because the injury is the result of domestic violence or a medical condition (either mental or physical). Plans may exclude source-of-injury treatment related to high-risk activities, such as snowmobiling, horseback riding, motorcycle riding, skiing, etc., but participation in such activities may not preclude employees' eligibility to enroll in the plan.

- Actively-at-work requirements: plans cannot establish eligibility rules, individual premiums, or employee contribution rates based on whether the employee is actively at work, unless employees who are not actively at work due to health conditions are treated as if they are at work for purposes of health coverage.

Further information on the nondiscrimination requirements under HIPAA is available on the DOL's Web site: *http://www.dol.gov/ebsa/faqs/main.html*.

[G] Disclosure Requirements

As of March 1, 1998, employers are required to disclose more information in the Summary Plan Description (SPD). The timing of disclosures on reductions in benefits was also changed by HIPAA. These requirements are outlined in the **Chapter 5** section dealing with the Employee Retirement Income Security Act (ERISA) reporting requirements (see **Section 5.02[J]**). If the employer does not want to issue a completely new SPD, a Summary of Material Modification may be distributed instead.

A general notice of PCEs must be provided as part of any written application materials distributed by the plan or its health insurance issuer. If no such materials are distributed, the notice must be provided by the earliest date following an enrollment request that the plan or its insurance issuer, acting in a reasonable and prompt fashion, can provide. The notice must include the following:

- The plan's PCE limitations, including the plan's lookback period and the maximum preexisting condition exclusion period;

- An explanation of how prior creditable coverage offsets the PCE period;

- Information regarding the participant's right to demonstrate prior creditable coverage;

- A statement that the current plan will assist in obtaining a certificate from any prior plan or issuer, if necessary;

- Information regarding the participant's right to obtain a certificate of creditable coverage and to use the plan's appeal process related to prior creditable coverage decisions;

- A description of the special enrollment periods if the plan has otherwise limited enrollment periods; and

- The name of a person to contact (including an address or telephone number) to obtain additional information or assistance regarding the PCE.

The final regulations provide sample language for the general notice.

While health plan providers can include these disclosures in the summary of benefits booklets, it is the plan sponsor's responsibility to ensure compliance with the disclosure rules. If employers want their health plan providers or administrators to take on this responsibility, it is recommended that they sign written agreements with their providers and follow up to ensure that adequate notices are received by their employees.

A plan or insurance issuer, when it receives creditable coverage information, is required to make a determination regarding the amount of the individual's creditable coverage and the length of any exclusion that remains within a reasonable time following receipt of the creditable coverage information.

In addition, individual notices of a PCE are required when the plan determines that it will apply a PCE to an individual participant. For example, a plan may receive a certificate of creditable coverage that indicates that the prior coverage is not sufficient to offset the PCE period. If the plan seeks to impose the PCE, it must provide the following information in writing to the participant:

- The plan's determination of the creditable coverage period, including the last day on which the PCE applies;

- The basis for the determination, including the source and substance of any information on which the plan relied;

- An explanation of the individual's right to submit additional evidence of creditable coverage; and

- The appeal procedures established by the plan or insurance carrier.

The individual notice is not required to identify any medical conditions specific to the individual that could be subject to the exclusion.

§ 6.03   MEDICAL SAVINGS ACCOUNTS

Beginning in 1997, an entirely new benefit plan can be used to aid individuals in accumulating funds to pay medical expenses. A medical savings account (MSA) is a trust or custodial account, similar to an IRA, created for the exclusive purpose of paying the qualified medical expenses of an individual or the individual's spouse and dependents. An eligible individual is permitted a deduction from taxable income for the amount paid in cash during the tax year to an MSA. Alternatively, an employer can contribute to an MSA on behalf of an employee, and employer contributions are excludable from employees' income. HIPAA also provides that MSAs are portable. At the end of December 2002, these accounts were renamed Archer MSAs. [Pub. L. No. 106-554, 114 Stat. 2763 (Dec. 21, 2000), §§ 201, 202] For the purposes of this book, an Archer MSA will be referred to as an MSA.

MSAs are available to self-employed individuals and to employees (and their spouses) of small employers. For this purpose, a self-employed individual includes a partner in a partnership and a more-than-2-percent shareholder of an S corporation. A small employer is any employer who employed an average of 50 or fewer employees during either of the two preceding calendar years. Individuals covered under Medicare are not eligible to contribute to an MSA.

In addition, the participating individual must be covered under a high-deductible health plan (HDHP).

A participant who is an employee must be covered under an employer-sponsored HDHP with an annual deductible of $2,000 to $3,000 for individual coverage and $4,000 to $6,050 for family coverage (2009 amounts). The amounts are indexed for inflation and may change each year. Annual out-of-pocket expenses for the employee cannot exceed $4,000 for individual coverage and $7,350 for family coverage. An HDHP can be offered by insurance companies and HMOs. State insurance commissions will oversee the issuance of HDHPs. An individual who has coverage under an HDHP cannot also be covered under any health plan that is not an HDHP, except for limited permitted coverage, including:

- Medicare supplemental insurance

- Workers' compensation liability insurance

- Insurance covering liabilities relating to ownership or use of a property (such as automobile insurance)

- Insurance for a specified disease or illness

- Dental and vision care

- Long-term care

- Accident-only insurance

- Insurance paying a fixed amount per day (or other period) of hospitalization

The maximum annual MSA contribution is 65 percent of the deductible for individual coverage and 75 percent of the deductible for family coverage, up to the amount earned for the year from the employer through whom the employee has the HDHP, or, if self-employed, up to the amount of net self-employed income. Individual contributions to an MSA are deductible when determining adjusted gross income on an income tax return. Employer contributions are excluded from income, although they are required to be reported to the employee. Contributions can be made until the annual due date of the individual's tax return. Contributions must be held in a trust account at a bank, insurance company, or similar institution. The trust assets cannot be invested in life insurance contracts and cannot be commingled with other property, except in a common trust fund or common investment fund.

Distributions from an MSA for qualified medical expenses of an individual, or for the individual's family, can be made at any time and are not taxable. However, distributions that are not used for medical expenses are includable in income and are subject to an additional 15 percent tax, unless they are made after age 65, death, or disability. The individual is responsible for properly reporting the distributions and supporting a claim that a distribution is not taxable (i.e., by maintaining proper records of medical expenses).

Qualified medical expenses are any expenses for medical care as defined under the rules relating to itemized deductions for medical expenses, but only if they are not reimbursed by any other plan. They do not include any insurance premiums except for premiums for qualified long-term care insurance, COBRA continuation coverage, or coverage while the individual is receiving unemployment compensation.

Earnings on amounts in an MSA are not currently taxable, and the balance in an MSA can be carried over from year to year. In addition, MSAs are portable because they belong to the account holder, even when funded by the employer. All amounts in an MSA are 100 percent vested at all times; therefore, the balance cannot be forfeited. As with an IRA, the money in an MSA can be accumulated from year to year and earn tax-deferred income.

MSAs were a pilot program. Congress limited MSA availability to 750,000 individuals. An employer will not be affected by the 750,000 participant cutoff rule if:

1. A qualifying high-deductible health plan was offered on or before the close of the cutoff year.

2. A qualifying high-deductible health plan was offered during the employee's regularly scheduled health insurance coverage enrollment period that occurred after the close of the cutoff year.

Originally, the MSA pilot program was scheduled to expire December 31, 2000. However, each year the program has been extended; in its latest extension, the pilot program was extended until December 31, 2007. (Existing MSAs can continue to be used after the expiration date.)

§ 6.04   MEDICAL INFORMATION PRIVACY

As required by the administrative simplification provisions of HIPAA, the Department of Health and Human Services (HHS) issued a final medical information privacy regulation on December 20, 2000, with an effective date of April 14, 2003 (small health plans had one additional year). The regulation is titled "Standards for Privacy of Individually Identifiable Health Information" and is known as the privacy rule. The first in a series of guidelines was released on July 6, 2001. Further final regulations were issued on August 14, 2002. Although the initial regulation and accompanying commentary are more than 1,500 pages in length, the essential reason for the privacy rule is to ensure the confidentiality of patients' personally identifiable health information: in short, "a covered entity may not use or disclose an individual's protected health information, except as otherwise permitted or required by this [regulation]." Despite the fact that employers are generally not directly covered by the regulation (with certain exceptions, see **Section 6.04[A]**), they do need to understand the privacy rule and its ramifications for the provision of medical coverage for employees.

[A] Definitions

The following are useful definitions:

- *Covered entities.* All health plans, health care clearinghouses, and health care providers that electronically conduct certain financial and administrative transactions such as billing, submitting claims for payment, or transferring funds.

- *Health plans.* All individual and employee group health plans (both insured and self-insured); multiemployer health plans; insurance companies; HMOs; federal, state, and local government plans; and Medicare and Medicare+Choice plans. Group health plans include medical, dental and vision plans, employee assistance plans (if they provide health services, such as drug abuse counseling), wellness plans, and health flexible spending accounts. Under the HIPAA privacy rule, group health plans exclude life and disability insurance plans and workers' compensation plans.

  — *Small health plans.* Those health plans with up to $5 million dollars in annual receipts. Annual receipts are defined as the amount of total premiums paid for fully insured coverage, or the total amount of claims adjudicated through the health plan.

- *Health care clearinghouses.* Private and public entities that process health information, received from another entity, from standard to nonstandard format or vice versa.

- *Health care providers.* Doctors, hospitals, medical groups, and any person or organization that furnishes or is paid for health care in the normal course of its business.

- *Individually identifiable health information.* Health information that:

  — Is created or received by a health care provider, health plan, employer or health care clearinghouse;

  — Relates to the past, present or future physical or mental health or condition of an individual, the provision of health care to an individual, or the past, present or future payment for the provision of health care to an individual; and

  — Identifies the individual, or with respect to which there is a reasonable basis on the part of the disclosing entity for believing that the information may be used to identify the individual (including any demographic information on the individual).

- *Protected health information* (PHI). Any individually identifiable health information maintained or transmitted in any form (e.g., electronic, oral, handwritten) that is created or received by a covered entity, with the exception of:

  — Information found in education records covered by the Family Educational Rights and Privacy Act (FERPA);

  — Health care records of post-secondary degree students; and

  — Employment records held by a covered entity in its role as an employer.

Eighteen specific identifiers of health information have been delineated by the HIPAA regulations; the most typical include:

- Name

- Geographic subdivisions smaller than a state, including ZIP codes

- All forms of dates (e.g., birth date, date of death, admission date, discharge date, etc.)

- Telephone numbers

- Fax numbers

- E-mail addresses

- Social Security numbers

- Medical record numbers

- Account numbers

- Certificate and license numbers

- Vehicle identifiers and serial numbers, including license plate numbers

- Web Universal Resource Locators (URLs)

- Internet Protocol (IP) addresses

- Biometric identifiers, including finger and voice prints

- Full face photographic images

On May 21, 2008, the Genetic Information Nondiscrimination Act of 2008 (GINA) was signed into law. Among many other provisions, GINA amends HIPAA to include genetic information under the definition of PHI and subjects genetic information to the privacy rule regulations.

[B] Use and Disclosure of Protected Health Information

Covered entities may use PHI without the individual's written consent for treatment, payment, or health care operations, unless the privacy rule specifically prohibits such use. A covered entity is required to make a good faith effort to obtain from a patient a written acknowledgment that the patient has received the entity's notice of privacy practices (see **Section 6.04[C]**).

A plan sponsor's use of enrollment and disenrollment information is an exception to the general use and disclosure of PHI rules. Enrollment information includes any information about whether the individual is participating in the group health plan, or is enrolled in or has disenrolled from the health insurance or HMO offered by the plan. The group health plan may transmit enrollment and disenrollment information to the plan sponsor without the individual's written consent and without needing to amend the group health plan to allow for the transmission of this information.

Specific authorization is required when the PHI is going to be used for something other than treatment, payment, or the covered entity's health care operations (e.g., marketing purposes). Covered entities may not refuse to treat those who do not provide such written authorization. The regulation proscribes detailed requirements for the content of the forms used to obtain authorization.

The privacy rule specifically authorizes the release of PHI when there is an overriding public interest, such as reporting abuse or neglect, public health needs, judicial and law enforcement, governmental functions, medical research, and when otherwise required by law. Individuals must be able to obtain their own PHI from covered entities, and minors' PHI must be released to their parents.

The amount of PHI disclosed must be kept to the minimum necessary to meet the requirements of the request for the PHI. This requirement applies only when one covered entity is requesting PHI from another covered entity. When a covered entity makes routine and recurring requests for or disclosures of PHI (such as for the completion of claim forms), it must implement policies and procedures that limit the disclosure or request to only the PHI necessary to meet the purpose of the disclosure or request. This is intended to assist those covered entities from having to make case-by-case decisions of the minimum necessary PHI for each instance of the recurring requests or disclosures.

Group health plans must protect PHI to ensure that PHI is not used or disclosed in violation of HIPAA's privacy rules. The security rule (discussed in **Section 6.05[A]** below) is designed to protect electronic PHI, but the privacy rule's "mini-security" rule safeguards all PHI. Plan sponsors must implement appropriate administrative, technical, and physical safeguards to protect the privacy of PHI. Plan sponsors can follow the general guidelines of the security rule to guide their protection of all PHI, electronic or not.

Group health plans can share PHI with a plan sponsor (generally an employer) if there are restrictions on the plan sponsor's use of the PHI; for example, plan sponsors must restrict access to the PHI to employees who perform plan administrative functions for the sponsor. Group health plans can provide summary claims information without certain identifiers to plan sponsors for the purpose of obtaining premium quotes or for amending or terminating the plan. Group health plans and health insurance issuers may disclose PHI to a plan sponsor that is needed for plan administration functions only after the group health plan certifies in writing that the plan documents have been amended to indicate its compliance with the privacy rule. Plan sponsors may not use the PHI for taking any actions regarding any other benefit or employee benefit plan without the individual's consent. Plan sponsors may not use PHI for making employment decisions, such as terminating the employment of an employee who submits false claims to the group health plan. However, the fraudulent submission of claims can be used to terminate the employee's coverage under the plan if the plan document includes that as a possible penalty.

Individuals also have the right to request that health care providers and plans communicate health information by "alternative means" or at "alternative locations." So, for example, employees may request that their explanations of benefits be sent to their work location, rather than their home location.

The HHS has posted various forms of helpful information to covered entities on its Web site. Such information includes fact sheets, frequently asked questions (FAQs), and interactive decision tools. The HIPAA privacy Web site can be found at: *http://www.hhs.gov/ocr/hipaa*.

[C]   Notice of Privacy Practices

Individuals must also receive notice regarding covered entities' privacy practices. The notice must provide adequate information regarding the permitted uses of PHI, individual's rights (such as how to file complaints), and the covered entities' legal obligations regarding the protection of PHI. Health care providers must give the notice directly to patients as well as post the notice in their offices.

Health plans must provide the notice to all enrollees as of the compliance date, to new enrollees upon their enrollment, and within 60 days of any significant change to the covered entity's privacy policies. Health plans must inform enrollees about the availability of the notice every three years. Health plans that were required to comply with the privacy rule by April 14, 2003 (that is, those plans that are not small health plans) must have provided the notice of the availability of the notice by April 14, 2006; small health plans have until April 14, 2007 to provide this required reminder.

The notice of privacy practices may be delivered electronically only if recipients have waived their right to a paper copy and agreed to receive the notice electronically. Participants may withdraw their agreements at any time, and the notice would then need to be delivered in paper form. Plans must also deliver a paper copy of the notice if they know that the electronic version failed to reach the participant.

A group health plan that provides benefits entirely through an insurance contract with a health insurance issuer is not required to provide any notice of its privacy practices for PHI unless it receives or creates PHI other than summary claims information or individuals' enrollment information.

[D]   Business Associates

Relationships between covered entities and their business associates must meet certain requirements. A covered entity's *business associate* is any person or organization that performs a function of or a service to the covered entity that involves the use or disclosure of PHI. The organization or person must be performing the function or service for or on behalf of the covered entity in order to be considered a business associate of the covered entity. Employees of the covered entity are not business associates.

Covered entities must enter into a written contract that assures that the business associate will protect the PHI, that it will restrict the use and disclosure of PHI, and that any further disclosure of the PHI will also be confidentially maintained. A covered entity must take appropriate actions if it becomes aware that the business associate has materially breached the confidentiality of the PHI.

Disclosure of PHI between group health plans and plan sponsors (as described above) does not require a business associate contract.

[E]   Other Requirements

Covered entities must comply with administrative requirements to designate a privacy officer who will oversee compliance and act as the contact for complaints and questions, develop and implement policies and procedures that will provide the framework for the covered entity to comply with the privacy rule, and train employees on the privacy requirements.

HIPAA preempts all "contrary" state laws unless a state law is more stringent. The state law is contrary if an entity would find it impossible to comply with both the state and federal requirements or when the state law is an obstacle to the accomplishment of the purposes and objectives of HIPAA. A state law is more stringent if it further limits the use or disclosure of PHI (other than placing more limits on the rights of individuals to their own PHI), provides individuals with more access to their PHI (with exceptions for minors), provides more information about their rights, or otherwise enhances privacy protections.

Small group health plans—those with fewer than 50 participants that are fully employer administered, that is, no insurance company or TPA is involved, are exempt from the privacy rule requirements.

[F]   Challenges to the Privacy Rule

The privacy rule has been challenged on several fronts. In July 2001, several national physician groups, led by the South Carolina Medical Association and the Louisiana State Medical Society, filed a lawsuit in federal court to overturn the regulation on the basis that the issuance of the privacy rule was an unconstitutional delegation of congressional authority. However, the Fourth Circuit Court of Appeals upheld the district court's ruling that Congress did not improperly give away its authority to HHS.

In 2002, the Citizens for Health, a coalition of health care providers, organizations and patients, sued the HHS, claiming that by allowing "routine uses" of PHI without consent, HHS violated their constitutional rights to privacy and free speech. They also claimed that the rule change was outside the scope of HHS' authority and that adequate public notice was not provided. On appeal, the Third Circuit court agreed with the lower (District) court that the amended HIPAA rules do not violate constitutional rights to privacy because they do not require PHI disclosure without consent. The court also noted that HHS had balanced HIPAA's goals of privacy with health care efficiency. [Citizens for Health v. Leavitt, 428 F.3d 167 (3d Cir. 2005)]

[G]   Recommended Actions

Employers that are group health plan sponsors should investigate whether they need to revise their group health plans' privacy policies. The creation and implementation of the policies and procedures required for compliance is likely to require significant time and effort. Suggested action steps include:

1. Determine what aspects of the privacy rule, if any, may affect the employee health plan and/or the company, and how they affect it

2. Inform managers about the privacy rule and its potential effects on the organization

3. Develop a compliance plan with timelines for implementation

4. Prepare a budget for expenses associated with the implementation of the plan

5. Consider the following actions for inclusion in the plan:

a. Review and revise group health plan documents

b. Appoint a HIPAA privacy officer

c. Review and renegotiate any contracts with consultants and/or vendors that may fall within the definition of a "business associate"

d. Train employees on privacy obligations

e. Develop policies for access to and disclosure of PHI

f. Determine how violations of the privacy rule will be handled

g. Update computerized and manual information systems

§ 6.05 SECURITY AND TRANSACTION REQUIREMENTS

The administrative simplification provisions of HIPAA also require group health plans to comply with its security and electronic transaction standards. These standards were designed to make it easier and less costly for the health care industry to process health claims and other transactions while assuring patients that their health care information will remain confidential.

An example may be useful to understand the electronic interchange of data that occurs in the health care industry: Patients visit their doctors who then submit claims electronically to the patients' insurers. A health care insurer electronically transmits to its bank a payment file containing payment instructions for multiple claims from different medical providers. The bank transmits the file to its automated clearing-house, which will transmit the payments to the providers' banks. These recipient banks then transmit the electronic remittance advices, which contain PHI, to the medical providers.

Clearly it will make all these transactions smoother if there is one national standard for all of these electronic data transmissions—this is the goal of the transaction requirements of HIPAA. But it is critical that the electronic transmissions and the PHI they contain are secure. HIPAA's security rule, in concert with the privacy rule, is designed to help ensure this happens.

[A] Security Standards

In February 2003, the HHS released the final security rule (available for download at *www.cms.hhs.gov*). Compliance with the security rule was due no later than April 21, 2005 (small group health plans had one more year to comply). The Centers for Medicare and Medicaid Services (CMS) (the agency responsible for the enforcement of the non-privacy related administrative simplification standards) has posted security standard and related materials on its educational Web site: *http://www.cms.hhs.gov/EducationMaterials/*.

Essentially, group health plans (and other covered entities) must establish procedures and mechanisms to protect the confidentiality, integrity, and availability of electronic PHI. Administrative, physical, and technical safeguards are required. Four security requirements are specified:

1. Ensure the confidentiality, integrity, and availability of all electronic PHI the covered entity creates, receives, maintains, and transmits;

2. Protect against any reasonably anticipated threats or hazards to the security or integrity of such information;

3. Protect against any reasonably anticipated uses or disclosures of such information that are permitted or required under subpart E of this part [the privacy rule]; and

4. Ensure compliance by [the covered entity's] workforce.

Electronic PHI (ePHI) is PHI that is or was electronically transmitted or stored. Examples include PHI that is stored on hard drives, servers, laptops, memory sticks, and PDAs. PHI that is contained in (or attached to) e-mail is ePHI. For example, e-mails sent from the benefits department of a plan sponsor acting on behalf of the group health plan with PHI information included or attached (e.g., if a claims statement or appeal was attached) is ePHI. In the preamble to the security rule, HHS clarified that to be ePHI, the data must be or have been stored or transmitted in electronic form. Therefore PHI that is faxed back to a patient or covered entity via a "faxback" system (e.g., a request for information from a computer made via voice or telephone keypad input with the requested information returned as a fax) is ePHI, but a voice to voice discussion over the phone, paper to paper faxes, video teleconferences, and voice messages left on voice-mail are not ePHI.

Implementation of the security rule is addressed through "standards" and "implementation specifications." Standards explain what must be done, and implementation specifications describe how to do it. Implementation specifications are either required or addressable. If the implementation specification is essential, it is labeled "required." If the implementation specification is seen (by HHS) as one of several options, none of which by itself is essential, it is labeled "addressable." In some cases, the means of implementing the standard are understood within the standard itself. In these cases, there is no implementation specification. All standards must be complied with.

Flexibility is inherent in this approach to meeting the security rule's requirements. For each addressable implementation specification, the group health plan must evaluate whether it is reasonable and appropriate for its unique situation. If it is, it must implement that specification (e.g., it becomes required). If it is not, the entity must either implement an equivalent measure that is reasonable and appropriate or, if the standard can be met some other way, choose not to implement that specification or any equivalent specification. Careful and thorough documentation of the group health plan's decision-making is required. Failure to implement an equivalent measure and failure to document why implementation of the implementation specification is not reasonable and appropriate are violations of the security rule.

To determine if an implementation specification is reasonable and appropriate, group health plans may factor in cost, size, complexity, technical infrastructure, other capabilities, and the criticality (likelihood and seriousness) of potential security risks.

The Security Rule's standards and implementation specifications are as follows:

1. Security management process

    a. Risk analysis (required)

    b. Risk management (required)

    c. Sanction policy (required)

    d. Information system activity review (required)

2. Assigned security responsibility

3. Workforce security

    a. Authorization and/or supervision (addressable)

    b. Workforce clearance procedure (addressable)

    c. Termination procedures (addressable)

4. Information access management

    a. Isolating health care clearinghouse functions (required)

    b. Access authorization (addressable)

    c. Access establishment and modification (addressable)

5. Security awareness and training

    a. Security reminders (addressable)

    b. Protection from malicious software (addressable)

    c. Log-in monitoring (addressable)

    d. Password management (addressable)

6. Security incident procedures

    a. Response and reporting (required)

7. Contingency plan

    a. Data backup plan (required)

    b. Disaster recover plan (required)

    c. Emergency mode operation plan (required)

    d. Testing and revision procedures (addressable)

    e. Applications and data criticality analysis (addressable)

8. Evaluation

Covered entities must conduct a risk analysis and document this analysis in writing. A risk analysis is defined by the security rule as "an accurate and thorough assessment of the potential risks and vulnerabilities to the confidentiality, integrity and availability of ePHI held by the covered entity." As described in the preamble to the security rule, a vulnerability is a weakness in the system that can be exploited to breach the security of the information contained in the system, and risk is an assessment of the likelihood of that exploitation as well as the extent of impact that such a breach may cause. The basics of a risk analysis include:

— Identify all of the physical components that may receive, store, maintain or transmit ePHI (e.g., hardware, fax machines, physical locations, etc.);

— Identify all of the electronic systems that receive, store, maintain or transmit ePHI (e.g., e-mail systems, claims adjudication software, etc.);

— Identify and assess all security measures already in place—technical (e.g., virus protection software, firewalls, etc.), physical (e.g., locked doors and cabinets, etc.), and administrative security (e.g., password protection, access protection, etc.)

— Identify the vulnerabilities and risks to ePHI

— Compare what is already in place to the identified vulnerabilities and risks (e.g., perform a gap analysis)

— Identify new security measures that will be needed to bridge the identified gaps

— Develop appropriate policies and procedures for the new security measures

— Implement the new security measures

The plan sponsor must document in writing each step of the risk analysis, including the reasons why decisions were made.

Covered entities may permit a business associate to create, receive, maintain, or transmit ePHI on the covered entity's behalf only if it obtains satisfactory assurances that the business associate will also comply with the security rule. This requirement is written into the regulations as a "standard," and the required implementation specification is a written contract documenting the satisfactory assurances of the business associate that it will comply. Plan sponsors are ultimately responsible for any security breaches committed by a TPA or other business associate. It is incumbent upon the plan sponsor to perform security due diligence on the security measures adopted by its business associates.

In the 244-page preamble to the 45-page final rule, HHS refers to the "800 Series" of guides published by the National Institute of Standards and Technology (NIST). These guides serve as practical expansions of the final rule in assessing risk and managing security over time.

The security rule also requires that if the plan sponsor has access to its group health plan's electronic PHI, the plan document must be amended to require the employer, as plan sponsor, to: implement measures to secure the electronic PHI, implement the adequate separation (of employer as plan sponsor and as employer) requirement, require the same of all business associates, and report all security incidents to the group health plan. Because these amendments are similar to those required by the privacy rule, it is efficient and acceptable to combine all required changes into one amendment.

Remote access and storage of ePHI is becoming more commonplace. Plan sponsors must incorporate the requirements of the security rule in the management of remote access and storage. Use of home computers, laptops, flash drives, emails, smart phones, personal digital assistants and public wireless access points are all areas for concern and review. In "HIPAA Security Guidance for Remote Use of and Access to Electronic Protected Health Information," plan sponsors and other covered entities should allow remote use only if "great rigor has been taken to ensure that policies, procedures and workforce training have been effectively deployed." The CMS guidance is available at its Web site: *http://www.cms.hhs.gov/Security Standard/Downloads/SecurityGuidanceforRemoteUseFinal.pdf.*

Although fully insured health plans may have had few requirements under the privacy rule, all health plans will have to show that they meet the requirements of the security rule. If a health plan has only fully insured coverage and receives no ePHI under the plan, it may not have to do much in the way of meeting the standards or implementation specifications. However, it will have to document that it conducted a risk analysis (noting that it reviewed all electronic physical elements and systems to determine that it did not receive any ePHI), identify a security officer, develop (limited) risk management procedures, conduct periodic evaluations (to determine that nothing has changed and it is still not receiving any ePHI), and document that its business associates, if any, are in compliance with the security rule. If necessary, the group health plan's plan document may also need amending, and in that case, the plan would then need to comply with that amendment.

[B] Transaction Standards

In keeping with its goal of encouraging electronic commerce in the health care industry, ultimately simplifying the processes and thereby reducing costs, HHS published proposed rules for electronic transactions on May 31, 2002, and a final regulation on February 20, 2003. Compliance with these rules was due October 16, 2002, with small group health plans having one additional year to comply. However, non-small group health plans could have extended their compliance due date to October 16, 2003, by filing an extension prior to the original due date.

The HHS adopted standards for electronically transmitting the following administrative and financial health care transactions:

- Health claims and equivalent encounter information

- Enrollment and disenrollment data

- Health plan eligibility

- Health care payment and remittance advice

- Health plan premium payments

- Health claim status

- Referral certification and authorization

- Coordination of benefits

Note that the transaction standards apply only to electronic data interchange or EDI—when data are transmitted electronically between health care providers and insurers or clearinghouses as part of a standard transaction. However, the security standards apply to the storage of PHI, as well as its transmission.

All covered entities, including group health plans, that submit or receive these transactions electronically are required to comply with these standards. Most group health plans utilize an insurer or TPA to conduct these transactions. However, the group health plan must ensure that these entities are in compliance with the standards. Plan sponsors are encouraged to become at least somewhat knowledgeable in order to track the progress of these organizations in complying with the transaction requirements.

The standards chosen are the National Council for Prescription Drug Programs (NCPDP) for retail pharmacy transactions and ANSI ASC X12N standards, Version 4010 for all other transactions. Covered entities can obtain implementation guides from the NCPDP at *www.ncpdp.org*, and ASC X12N standards can be obtained from the Washington Publishing Company at *www.wpc-edi.com/hipaa*.

Employers are required to use standard national numbers that identify them on standard transactions. The Employer Identification Number (EIN), issued by the Internal Revenue Service, was selected as the identifier for employers and was adopted effective July 30, 2002.

The National Provider Identifier (NPI) is also required under HIPAA's administrative simplification rules. The NPI is a unique identification number for covered health care providers. Covered health care providers and all health plans and health care clearinghouses will use the NPIs in the administrative and financial transactions adopted under HIPAA. The NPI is a 10-position, intelligence-free numeric identifier (10-digit number). This means that NPIs do not carry other information about health care providers, such as the state in which they live or their medical specialty. Beginning May 23, 2007 (May 23, 2008, for small health plans), the NPI must be used in lieu of legacy provider identifiers in the HIPAA standard transactions. Covered entities may invoke contingency plans after May 23, 2007, and guidance about contingency plans may be found in the "Guidance on Compliance with the HIPAA National Provider Identifier (NPI) Rule" published on April 3, 2007, and available on the CMS Web site: *http://www.cms.hhs.gov/NationalProvIdentStand/*. CMS provides a searchable database of health care providers' NPIs on their Web site: *https://nppes.cms.hhs.gov/NPPES/NPIRegistryHome.do*.

Prior to July 5, 2005, CMS had announced a nonenforcement policy for covered entities that had not yet come into full compliance with the transaction standards, but had implemented contingency plans to do so. However, effective October 1, 2005, CMS withdrew its nonenforcement policy and will not accept non-HIPAA-compliant electronic Medicare claims; those claims will be returned to the filer to be resubmitted in compliant form and content.

§ 6.06 ENFORCEMENT AND PENALTIES

Enforcement of the privacy rule is delegated to the HHS Office of Civil Rights (OCR). CMS enforces the security rule and transaction and code set standards. Both agencies will work together to ensure enforcement of the HIPAA administrative simplification provisions.

Prior to the issuance of the final Enforcement Rule on February 16, 2006 (*Federal Register*, 45 CFR Parts 160 and 164 HIPAA Administrative Simplification: Enforcement; Final Rule, RIN 0991-AB29), the rules relating to the investigation of noncompliance and the process for imposition of civil money penalties applied only to the privacy standards. With the publication of the final Enforcement Rule, these rules now apply to all of the HIPAA administrative simplification provisions. The final rule also clarifies and elaborates upon the investigation process, the bases for liability, determination of the penalty amount, grounds for waiver, conduct of the hearing and the appeal process; all of these sections will also apply to all the administrative simplification provisions. The final Enforcement Rule went into effect on March 16, 2006.

There is no individual right of action that would permit patients (or employees) to sue for violations, but there are civil and criminal penalties for violations. Monetary penalties start at $100 per violation, up to a maximum of $25,000 per plan per violation. However, the final Enforcement Rule indicates that one act of non-compliance that violates more than one subpart of the administrative simplification rules will be treated as separate, multiple violations. So, for example, if a covered entity re-sells its used computers without scrubbing the hard drives that contain protected health information, this act may violate several separate legal obligations under the security and privacy rules. In this scenario, the covered entity will have multiple violations and could be fined up to the $25,000 maximum for each separate violation.

Individuals who knowingly violate a standard can be punished by a criminal penalty of up to $50,000 and/or imprisonment for up to one year; the penalties increase to $100,000 and/or imprisonment for up to five years for any person who violates such standards under false pretenses, and up to $250,000 and/or imprisonment of up to 10 years for violation of a standard with the intent to sell, transfer, or use PHI for commercial advantage.

Under the final Enforcement Rule, the definition of "person" has been expanded to include: "a natural person, trust or estate, partnership, corporation, professional association or corporation, or other entity, pubic or private." The term includes all States and other public entities.

Although there is no private right to sue under HIPAA, several courts have ruled that HIPAA's nondiscrimination and other portability provisions may be enforced under ERISA Section 502. [*See, e.g.*, Werdehausen v. Benicorp Ins. Co., 2007 U.S. App. LEXIS 12348 (8th Cir. 2007)] Courts have found in favor of an individual's right to sue because the portability provisions of HIPAA amended and became part of ERISA. In addition, individuals may obtain the right to sue under ERISA for the privacy and security rules if such rules were made part of the plan's written plan document.

Enforcement activities will be primarily complaint driven, and will focus on obtaining voluntary compliance through technical assistance. In June 2000, OCR posted its procedures for filing complaints regarding the privacy rule on its Web site: *www.hhs.gov/ocr/hipaa*. Information on how to file a health information privacy complaint and the health information privacy complaint form are available in eight languages: English, Chinese, Korean, Polish, Russian, Spanish, Tagalog, and Vietnamese. In March 2005, CMS released its procedures for filing complaints regarding the security rule and transaction and code set requirements, which are available on the CMS Web site—*www.cms.hhs.gov*. Within CMS, the Office of e-Health Standards and Services (OESS) will conduct onsite compliance reviews and investigations. CMS has provided a list of potential personnel to be interviewed and documents that might be requested during a HIPAA security onsite investigation or compliance review (*http://www.cms.hhs.gov/enforcement/ 025_generalenforcementinformation.asp*).

As of June 30, 2008, HHS/OCR has received 37,223 HIPAA privacy rule complaints. HHS/OCR has investigated and resolved 30,582 cases. Over 6,648 cases of privacy complaints resulted in changes in covered entities' privacy practices and other corrective actions. In another 3,290 cases, HHS' investigations found no violation had occurred. OCR referred 436 cases to the Department of Justice involving the knowing disclosure or obtaining of PHI in violation of the privacy rule. HHS/OCR reported that the compliance issues investigated most frequently in 2007 were, in order of frequency:

1. Impermissible uses and disclosures of PHI;

2. Lack of safeguards of PHI;

3. Lack of patient access to their own PHI;

4. Uses or disclosures of more than the minimum necessary PHI; and

5. Lack of proper privacy notice.

As of June 30, 2008, CMS has received 956 security and transactions and code sets complaints. The majority of the security-related complaints related to information access management; access control was the second most common type of complaint.

The DOL has established an interactive Web site to provide employers a resource for complying with various federal health benefit laws. The Health Benefits Advisor is available at *www.dol.gov/elaws/ebsa/health*. It provides information on HIPAA, as well as COBRA, Newborns' and Mothers Health Protection Act, Mental Health Parity Act, and the Women's Health and Cancer Rights Act (see **Chapter 7** for more information on COBRA, and **Chapter 5** for more information on the other Acts). In addition, OCR created a website on HIPAA privacy compliance and enforcement: *www.hhs.gov/ocr/privacy/enforcement*.

In June 2005, the Department of Justice (DOJ) published an Opinion Memorandum outlining the scope of criminal enforcement under the Administrative Simplification section of HIPAA. After reviewing the history of Congress' intent for enacting HIPAA and its regulations, as well as relevant case law, the DOJ concluded that "covered entities and those rendered accountable by general principles of corporate criminal liability may be prosecuted directly under 42 U.S.C. § 1320d-6 (the criminal enforcement section of HIPAA), and the knowingly element of the offense set forth in that provision requires only proof of knowledge of the facts that constitute the offense." Essentially, health plans (including group health plans sponsored by employers and unions), health care providers, and health care clearinghouses can be prosecuted under the criminal sanctions provisions of HIPAA. Certain directors, officers, and employees of these entities may also be directly liable in accordance with general principles of corporate criminal liability, as those principles develop in the course of specific prosecutions. It is still possible for individuals acting on behalf of the group health plan, within the scope of their duties, to be held criminally liable under HIPAA. In addition, to be held criminally liable under HIPAA, the individual or entity need only know the facts of the offense, and not necessarily that the offense is or could be contrary to the law or its regulations.

In the first HIPAA case to go to trial, the jury found an individual guilty of wrongfully obtaining individually identifiable PHI with the intent to sell, transfer, or use it for personal gain. [United States v. Ferrer, No. 06-cr-60261-JIC (Jan. 24, 2007)] The individual had paid a co-defendant (who had pled guilty and testified during the trial) for the information with the intent of committing Medicare fraud. At sentencing, he received 87 months in prison and 3 years of supervised release, and was required to pay over $2.5 million in restitution for all of the crimes for which he was convicted.

Exhibit 6.1   Mandated Benefits: 2009 Compliance Guide

Exhibit 6.1
Model Certificate of Group Health Plan Coverage

1. Date of this certificate: _____

2. Name of group health plan: _____
_____

3. Name of participant: _____

4. Identification number of participant: _____

5. Name of individuals to whom this certificate applies: _____
_____

6. Name, address, and telephone number of plan administrator or issuer responsible for providing this certificate: _____
_____

7. For further information, call: _____

8. If the individual(s) identified in line 5 has (have) at least 18 months of creditable coverage (disregarding periods of coverage before a 63-day break), check here and skip lines 9 and 10: ___

9. Date waiting period or affiliation period (if any) began:
_____

10. Date coverage began: _____

11. Date coverage ended (or if coverage has not ended, enter "continuing"): _____

[Note: separate certificates will be furnished if information is not identical for the participant and each beneficiary.]

Statement of HIPAA Portability Rights

IMPORTANT — KEEP THIS CERTIFICATE. This certificate is evidence of your coverage under this plan. Under a federal law known as HIPAA, you may need evidence of your coverage to reduce a preexisting condition exclusion period under another plan, to help you get special enrollment in another plan, or to get certain types of individual health coverage even if you have health problems.

Preexisting condition exclusions. Some group health plans restrict coverage for medical conditions present before an individual's enrollment. These restrictions are known as "preexisting condition exclusions." A preexisting condition exclusion can apply only to conditions for which medical advice, diagnosis, care, or treatment was recommended or received within the 6 months before your "enrollment date." Your enrollment date is your first day of coverage under the plan, or, if there is a waiting period, the first day of your waiting period (typically, your first day of work). In addition, a preexisting condition exclusion cannot last for more than 12 months after your enrollment date (18 months if you are a late enrollee). Finally, a preexisting condition exclusion cannot apply to pregnancy and cannot apply to a child who is enrolled in health coverage within 30 days after birth, adoption, or placement for adoption.

If a plan imposes a preexisting condition exclusion, the length of the exclusion must be reduced by the amount of your prior creditable coverage. Most health coverage is creditable coverage, including group health plan coverage, COBRA continuation coverage, coverage under an individual health policy, Medicare, Medicaid, State Children's Health Insurance Program (SCHIP), and coverage through high-risk pools and the Peace Corps. Not all forms of creditable coverage are required to provide certificates like this one. If you do not receive a certificate for past coverage, talk to your new plan administrator.

You can add up any creditable coverage you have, including the coverage shown on this certificate. However, if at any time you went for 63 days or more without any coverage (called a break in coverage) a plan may not have to count the coverage you had before the break.

→ Therefore, once your coverage ends, you should try to obtain alternative coverage as soon as possible to avoid a 63-day break. You may use this certificate as evidence of your creditable coverage to reduce the length of any preexisting condition exclusion if you enroll in another plan.

Right to get special enrollment in another plan. Under HIPAA, if you lose your group health plan coverage, you may be able to get into another group health plan for which you are eligible (such as a spouse's plan), even if the plan generally does not accept late enrollees, if you request enrollment within 30 days. (Additional special enrollment rights are triggered by marriage, birth, adoption, and placement for adoption.)

→ Therefore, once your coverage ends, if you are eligible for coverage in another plan (such as a spouse's plan), you should request special enrollment as soon as possible.

Prohibition against discrimination based on a health factor. Under HIPAA, a group health plan may not keep you (or your dependents) out of the plan based on anything related to your health. Also, a group health plan may not charge you (or your dependents) more for coverage, based on health, than the amount charged a similarly situated individual.

Right to individual health coverage. Under HIPAA, if you are an "eligible individual," you have a right to buy certain individual health policies (or in some states, to buy coverage through a high-risk pool) without a preexisting condition exclusion. To be an eligible individual, you must meet the following requirements:

- You have had coverage for at least 18 months without a break in coverage of 63 days or more;
- Your most recent coverage was under a group health plan (which can be shown by this certificate);
- Your group coverage was not terminated because of fraud or nonpayment of premiums;
- You are not eligible for COBRA continuation coverage or you have exhausted your COBRA benefits (or continuation coverage under a similar state provision); and
- You are not eligible for another group health plan, Medicare, or Medicaid, and do not have any other health insurance coverage.

The right to buy individual coverage is the same whether you are laid off, fired, or quit your job.

→ Therefore, if you are interested in obtaining individual coverage and you meet the other criteria to be an eligible individual, you should apply for this coverage as soon as possible to avoid losing your eligible individual status due to a 63-day break.

State flexibility. This certificate describes minimum HIPAA protections under federal law. States may require insurers and HMOs to provide additional protections to individuals in that state.

For more information. If you have questions about your HIPAA rights, you may contact your state insurance department or the U.S. Department of Labor, Employee Benefits Security Administration (EBSA) toll-free at 1-866-444-3272 (for free HIPAA publications ask for publications concerning changes in health care laws). You may also contact the CMS publication hotline at 1-800-633-4227 (ask for "Protecting Your Health Insurance Coverage"). These publications and other useful information are also available on the Internet at: *http://www.dol.gov/ebsa*, the DOL's interactive web pages (Health Elaws), or *http://www.cms.hhs.gov/hipaal*.

Exhibit 6.2   Mandated Benefits: 2009 Compliance Guide

Exhibit 6.2
Sample Certificate for Categories of Benefits*

INFORMATION ON CATEGORIES OF BENEFITS

1. Date of original certificate:

2. Name of group health plan providing the coverage:

3. Name of participant:

4. Identification number of participant:

5. Name of individual(s) to whom this information applies:

6. The following information applies to the coverage in the certificate that was provided to the individual(s) identified above:

    a. *MENTAL HEALTH:*

    b. *SUBSTANCE ABUSE TREATMENT:*

    c. *PRESCRIPTION DRUGS:*

    d. *DENTAL CARE:*

    e. *VISION CARE:*

For categories a through e, enter "N/A" if the individual had no coverage within the category or either (i) enter both the date that the individual's coverage within the category began and the date that the individual's coverage within the category ended (or indicate if continuing), or (ii) enter "same" if the beginning and ending dates for coverage within the category are the same as the beginning and ending dates for the coverage in the certificate.

---

* This sample certification statement is based on model certificate information provided in the interim regulations implementing the Health Insurance Portability and Accountability Act of 1996 (HIPAA). Any form should be reviewed by legal counsel for specific application to the company's health plan.

Chapter 7
Medical and Health Care Continuation Coverage/COBRA

§ 7.01 AUDIT QUESTIONS

1. Has the employer determined how many health plans it has for COBRA purposes?

2. Is an initial notice of COBRA rights (i.e., the General Notice) given to employees and their spouses when they first become eligible for coverage in the group health plan?

3. When a qualifying event occurs, are separate notices of COBRA eligibility and election given to the employee and his or her spouse?

4. Does the employer determine the appropriate COBRA premium prior to a fixed 12-month period, and maintain that premium even if the insurer or HMO raises its premiums during that 12-month period?

5. Does the employer assess an employee's leave of absence as a potential qualifying event and provide an Employer Notice of Qualifying Event or the COBRA Election Notice if applicable?

6. Is the employer complying with state-mandated continuation coverage requirements as well as COBRA?

7. If the employer sponsors an employee assistance program that offers counseling services, is the employer offering this plan as part of the COBRA election?

Note: Consistent "yes" answers to the above questions suggest that the organization is applying effective management practices and/or complying with federal regulations. "No" answers indicate that problem areas exist and should be addressed immediately.

Congress, as an issue of public policy, has desired to provide Americans with access to affordable health coverage. In the past, one of the problems for individuals with employer-sponsored health coverage was the loss of coverage associated with such events as death, divorce, reduction in hours, and termination of employment. Historically, few employers extended group coverage to the employee and his or her family members if there was a change in the employee's family status. In many cases, the high cost of insurance or the uninsurability of a family member makes health insurance coverage unaffordable outside the work setting.

To support its policy objectives, Congress enacted the Consolidated Omnibus Budget Reconciliation Act of 1985 (COBRA), a portion of which requires, with certain exceptions, that employers offer employees and family members covered under an employer-sponsored group health plan the opportunity to continue to receive the same coverage they were receiving before the occurrence of certain life events (defined in the act) that would otherwise have resulted in termination of their group health coverage.

The COBRA legislation added parallel employer requirements to both the Internal Revenue Code (Code), administered by the Internal Revenue Service (IRS), and the Employee Retirement Income and Security Act of 1974 (ERISA), which is administered by the Department of Labor (DOL).

This chapter discusses the application of COBRA rules to employer-sponsored health plans; administration issues, such as employee notification and election requirements; COBRA enforcement and penalties; state continuation of coverage rules; requirements of the Health Insurance Portability and Accountability Act of 1996 (HIPAA); and other plans affected by COBRA.

The first proposed regulations were issued in 1987 to assist employers and insurers in meeting their COBRA obligations. Throughout this chapter, these regulations will be referred to as "previously proposed regulations." In 1999, "final regulations" and "new proposed regulations" were issued. In 2001, new "final regulations" adopted the "new proposed regulations" of 1999 with very few changes. In 2003 the DOL proposed regulations on notices; these are referred to as the "2003 proposed regulations." On May 26, 2004, the final regulations regarding COBRA notices were published. This chapter incorporates and refers to these various regulations.

§ 7.02   DEFINITIONS

Several definitions are important in order to understand the COBRA requirements:

- *Qualified Beneficiary.* An individual who is provided health coverage on account of (prior) services rendered to the employer sponsoring the group health plan. All family members of such employees who are covered by the employer's health plan are also qualified beneficiaries. In order to be considered a qualified beneficiary, the individual must be covered under the group health plan on the day before the qualifying event.

  In addition, a child born to or placed for adoption with a covered employee during a period of COBRA coverage is also a qualified beneficiary only if the covered employee elects COBRA coverage during the election period and enrolls the new child within 30 calendar days of the birth or adoption.

- *Qualifying Event.* A life or work event, as enumerated in COBRA, that results in the loss of coverage under a covered group health plan.

- *Loss of Coverage.* To cease to be covered under the same terms and conditions as those in effect immediately before the qualifying event.

- *Election Period.* The period of time during which a qualified beneficiary has the right to elect COBRA continuation coverage.

- *Plan Administrator.* The person or entity responsible for administering the group health plan as defined in the group health plan's written plan document. Generally, the plan administrator for plans provided by a single employer is the employer. When a plan is provided to employees of multiple employers, such as with employee union plans, the plan administrator is the multiemployer plan, and not any of the employers who participate in the plan. COBRA responsibilities are generally assigned to the plan administrator. Therefore, throughout the rest of this chapter, we will use the term "plan administrator" to refer to the entity which has the COBRA responsibility. The reader is cautioned to remember that unless otherwise noted, the plan administrator is the employer.

§ 7.03 COVERED EMPLOYERS

In general, an employer is subject to COBRA if it maintains or contributes to a group health plan for the purpose of providing medical benefits to its employees or former employees or their families. As a result of this broad rule, virtually all employers with group health plans are covered by COBRA, except for churches, governments, and small employers.

A small-employer plan is a group health plan maintained by an employer with fewer than 20 employees on at least 50 percent of the working days during the preceding calendar year. To determine whether an employer meets this exception, all full-time and part-time common-law employees are counted; however, self-employed individuals, directors, and independent contractors are not. Part-time employees are to be counted as fractional employees based on the number of hours the part-time employee works divided by the number of hours required to be a full-time employee (not to exceed eight in one day or 40 per week). For example, an employee who works 20 hours per week in a firm that requires employees to work 40 hours to be considered full-time would be counted as a 0.5 employee or 1/2 (20/40 = 0.5). In determining whether an employer is a small employer, all employees of any other entities that constitute a "controlled group" with the employer must be included. Employees of foreign companies must also be counted. Special rules may apply if two small employer plans are merged as a result of either a stock or an asset acquisition. The IRS issued Revenue Ruling 2003-70 [2003-27 I.R.B. 8] to give employers guidance on these types of mergers and acquisitions and their effects on small employer plans. Revenue Ruling 2003-70 is available on the IRS Web site: *www.irs.gov.*

Health plans that are sponsored by a church, by an association or convention of churches or by an employer that "shares common religious bonds or convictions" with a church, association or convention are exempt from COBRA's requirements. The test for "sharing common religious bonds or convictions" is based on whether (1) the religious organization has an official role in governing the employer (for example, members of the religious organization sit on the employer's Board of Directors); (2) the religious organization provides assistance to the employer; and (3) employees or customers must be of a particular religion or denomination. Employers who wish to be exempt from COBRA based on the religious exemption may wish to obtain a private letter ruling from the IRS and an advisory opinion from the DOL. Although these determinations are not binding on courts, if an organization is sued, many courts will take such determinations into consideration.

State and local government group health plans are subject to similar health care continuation requirements under the Public Health Service Act. In addition, federal government plans are subject to continuation coverage rules under the Federal Employees Health Benefits Amendments Act.

COBRA does not directly apply to insurers or third-party administrators (TPAs). COBRA's requirements, and the liability that may arise when those requirements are not met, fall on employers as plan sponsors. Plan sponsors may want to review their contracts with insurers and TPAs to determine whether any COBRA responsibilities are delegated to insurers and/or TPAs.

§ 7.04   GROUP HEALTH PLANS

Group health plans include those providing medical, dental, vision, employee assistance, wellness, and other forms of health care coverage. This includes health flexible spending accounts (also known as cafeteria plans or Section 125 plans) and health reimbursement arrangements (see **Chapter 12**). COBRA applies to all group health plans whether fully insured, partially self-insured, or fully self-insured. The group health care plans for which COBRA coverage must be offered will depend on the number of health plans the employer maintains. COBRA regulations set the default that all types of benefits are included in one group health plan unless the documents governing the arrangement, such as the plan documents, clearly indicate that each coverage is intended to be and is operated as a separate plan. If there are no documents, or if the documents are unclear, then all health care benefits are assumed to be offered under one plan.

> **Example.** Employer A offers medical, dental, and vision benefits under one plan. A qualified beneficiary is offered COBRA coverage for all three benefits, and his or her election is either for all benefits or for none. Employer B offers medical, dental, and vision benefits as separate plans (i.e., active employees may opt in or out of any plan separately). Each plan in which qualified beneficiaries had coverage on the day before the qualifying event must be offered to them separately. If qualified beneficiary X who works for Employer B had medical and dental coverage, and a qualifying event occurs, then X may elect COBRA coverage as follows: medical alone, dental alone, neither, or both.

[A]   Other Plans Affected by COBRA

Plans other than straightforward health care benefit plans may be subject to COBRA. The key determining factor is a plan's provision of medical benefits. The following plans generally raise questions as to their coverage under COBRA:

[1]   Cafeteria Plans

As discussed in **Chapter 12**, a cafeteria plan provides employees with a choice of employee benefit selections, some of which are made available on a tax-favored basis. At least one of the choices must be cash. If any benefit option made available under the cafeteria plan, standing alone, meets COBRA's definition of a group health plan, that option is subject to COBRA. However, COBRA never applies to the cash option, as cash is not a group health plan.

> **Example.** Employer A's cafeteria plan offers a choice among cash, pretax participation in a medical plan, and pretax life insurance. COBRA applies to the medical plan, whether it is technically within the cafeteria plan or is a separate plan that is incorporated by reference. COBRA does not apply to either the cash option or the life insurance option, as neither is a "group health plan." Employees X, Y, and Z all participate in the cafeteria plan, with Employee X choosing cash, Employee Y choosing the medical plan,

and Employee Z choosing life insurance. Each of them is terminated. Only Employee Y must be offered COBRA continuation coverage, and only Employee Y must be offered the benefit of any open enrollment period occurring during the COBRA continuation period.

[2] Flexible Spending Accounts

A health care flexible spending arrangement or account, also known as a health care FSA, constitutes a group health plan subject to COBRA. Under a typical flexible spending account, the employee designates an amount of salary reduction contribution for the plan year and directs the employer to credit that amount to the FSA. Under the FSA, an individual account is credited with a certain level of contributions, either employer-paid contributions, employee-paid contributions, or both, to reimburse specified eligible expenses up to an annual dollar limit, and the individual account is debited as those expenses are reimbursed. Generally, health FSAs that meet the following two conditions are required to offer COBRA continuation coverage to a qualified beneficiary only for the plan year in which the qualifying event occurs:

1. The health FSA meets the requirements for an "excepted benefit" under HIPAA by meeting the following two requirements:

   a. The maximum benefit requirement: the maximum benefit available for any participant of the FSA must not exceed two times the participant's salary reduction, or if larger, the amount of the salary reduction plus $500. The maximum benefit available is equal to the employee's salary reduction plus any employer contribution. By definition, this condition will be met if the FSA is funded only by employee contributions (salary reductions).

   b. The availability requirement: other health care coverage must be available to the participant for the year of the participant's coverage under the FSA, and this other health care coverage cannot be limited to HIPAA excepted benefits (e.g., limited scope benefits such as dental or vision coverage). Note that the participant does not need to have elected the other health care coverage, only that it be available to the participant if he or she elects it.

2. In the plan year in which the qualifying event occurs, the maximum amount the health FSA could charge for a full plan year of COBRA continuation coverage equals or exceeds the maximum benefit available under the health FSA for the year.

The IRS believes that the second condition will be satisfied in most cases. For example, if an employee elects a $1,200 health FSA for a calendar year plan and then terminates employment, the health FSA could charge a maximum of $1,224 for a full year of such benefit under COBRA. Because the maximum payment ($1,224) exceeds the maximum benefit ($1,200), COBRA would not be required in any plan year following the qualifying event if the health FSA is excepted from HIPAA.

In addition, if a third condition is satisfied, the health FSA is not required to offer COBRA continuation coverage to a qualified beneficiary at all. That third condition is satisfied if the maximum benefit available to the qualified beneficiary under the health FSA for the remainder of the plan year does not exceed the maximum amount that the plan could require as a payment for the remainder of that year, to maintain coverage under the health FSA. For example, assume an employee elects $1,200 for a health FSA for a calendar year plan, submits $600 of health claims for reimbursement, then terminates on April 30. The maximum benefit available for the remainder of the plan year is $600, and the maximum required payment for the remainder of the plan year is $816 ($100/month $\times$ 8 $\times$ 102%). Because the maximum benefit available ($600) is less than the maximum required payment ($816), COBRA need not be offered in the plan year of the qualifying event.

For more information about FSAs, see **Chapter 12**.

[3] Health Reimbursement Arrangements

Health Reimbursement Arrangements (HRAs) are group health plans and unless other exceptions apply, COBRA will apply to these accounts. HRAs generally do not qualify for the exceptions available to health FSAs. For more information about HRAs, see **Chapter 12**.

[4] Employee Assistance Programs

An employee assistance program (EAP) is a type of employer-provided benefit that may include, among other things, counseling, referrals, and treatment for specified concerns, such as anxiety, depression, stress, alcoholism and drug abuse, work problems, marital or family problems, and child care or elder care needs. EAPs vary greatly from employer to employer, and any particular EAP may be limited or broad, depending on the types of concerns and related services that it covers.

To the extent that an EAP is maintained by an employer or employee organization and provides medical care, it is a group health plan to which COBRA applies. Assuming that the EAP satisfies the requirement of being maintained by the employer, the key issue is whether any of the benefits available through the EAP constitute medical care. The COBRA regulations define a plan as a group health plan for COBRA purposes if it provides medical care, as defined under Code Section 213(d). At least some of the services offered by the EAP may qualify as "the diagnosis, cure, mitigation, treatment, or prevention of disease" within the meaning of Code Section 213.

The IRS has yet to issue any guidance specifically addressing the potential application of COBRA to EAPs. Although the DOL does not have regulatory authority under COBRA to define what constitutes medical care for COBRA purposes, it has issued several advisory opinions analyzing whether EAPs are welfare benefit plans under ERISA. For example, DOL Advisory Opinion 91-26A (July 9, 1991) advised that an EAP that was not staffed with trained counselors and provided only referral to other services was not a welfare benefit plan under ERISA. Technically, DOL Advisory Opinions cannot be relied on by anyone other than the parties to whom they are issued. However, they provide some guidance regarding how to evaluate the services provided by an EAP for COBRA purposes.

[5] Long-Term Care Plans

HIPAA clarified that specifically defined long-term care services are considered medical expenses, effective for taxable years beginning after December 31, 1996. However, HIPAA also provided that the COBRA rules do not apply to a plan under which substantially all of the coverage is for qualified long-term care services. (See **Chapter 10** for further discussion of long-term care plans.)

[6] Individual Voluntary Plans

Individual, voluntary plans are often elected by employees to supplement other coverage they may have. These plans are often disease specific (e.g., cancer protection plan) and often pay set amounts to the covered participants when an event occurs (e.g., when cancer is diagnosed, or when a participant is in the hospital). Employers often offer these plans to employees as a way of providing additional benefits to the employee at no (or little) employer cost. Generally employers do not contribute to the premiums of these plans, but do allow the insurance plans' marketing representatives to contact employees (generally on-site) to sell these plans. Employers will also payroll deduct the premiums and then pay the insurer for those employees who have elected the voluntary plans.

Employers often believe that because they do not contribute to the plan, these are not group health plans under ERISA. However, that may not always be the case. The DOL's regulations provide a "safe harbor" for group-type plans that are employee-pay-all and have minimal employer involvement (DOL Reg. Section 2510.3-1(j). The minimal involvement allows offering payroll deductions and paying the insurance premium on behalf of those employees who have elected the voluntary insurance. However, employers should not allow the plans to be paid on a pre-tax basis (where, in addition to the possibility of losing the safe harbor protections under ERSIA, HIPAA non-discrimination provisions may be violated) nor should they become involved in "marketing" the plan. Such marketing efforts should be provided only by the insurer and its representatives.

And even if the plan escapes ERISA (and therefore COBRA requirements under ERISA) under the DOL's safe harbor regulations, the Internal Revenue Code may still apply. Under the Code, any arrangement that is not "available at the same cost to an individual but for the individual's employment-related connection to the employer or employee organization" is a group plan, and will be required to comply with COBRA. The major problem to the employer is that most of these individual voluntary plans are not written to comply with COBRA. If so, the employer will be responsible for providing the coverage under a COBRA election.

§ 7.05 ELIGIBILITY FOR COBRA COVERAGE

To be eligible for COBRA coverage:

1. The individual must be a qualified beneficiary.

2. The individual must experience an event listed in COBRA (a qualifying event).

3. The individual must lose group health plan coverage as a result of that event within a certain period of time.

For COBRA purposes, to lose coverage means to cease to be covered under the same terms and conditions as those in effect immediately before the qualifying event. Any increase in the premium or contribution that must be paid by a covered employee (or the spouse or dependent of a covered employee) as a result of a COBRA event is considered a loss of coverage.

Covered employees are those employees who provide services for an employer and were covered by the employer's health plan by virtue of providing those services. Thus, independent contractors, self-employed individuals, and directors who are covered under the group health plan are also eligible for COBRA coverage if they experience a qualifying event.

[A] Qualified Beneficiaries

Qualified beneficiaries are defined as the following:

1. a covered employee (or independent contractor, self-employed individual or director) who has coverage on the day before the qualifying event, but only for the qualifying events of termination of employment and reduction of hours;

2. spouse and/or dependent children of a covered employee who have coverage on the day before the qualifying event due to their status as a spouse or dependent child of a covered employee;

3. a child born to or adopted by a covered employee during a period of COBRA coverage; and

4. an alternate recipient (one who is receiving plan benefits required by a Qualified Medical Child Support Order (QMCSO)) (see **Section 5.07**) who loses coverage due to a qualifying event.

Qualified beneficiaries must generally be treated the same as active employees (see **Section 7.10**).

§ 7.06   QUALIFYING EVENTS

The events listed in COBRA constitute qualifying events if they result in a loss of group health plan coverage. The qualifying events for an employee who is a qualified beneficiary are:

- Termination of employment due to reasons other than the employee's gross misconduct

- Reduction in the employee's hours of employment such that loss of coverage results.

For an employee's spouse or dependent child who is a qualified beneficiary, the qualifying events are as follows:

- Termination of the employee's employment due to reasons other than the employee's gross misconduct

- Reduction in the employee's hours of employment leading to loss of coverage

- Death of the employee

- Divorce or legal separation from the covered employee

- The employee's entitlement to Medicare

- The employer's commencement of a bankruptcy proceeding under Chapter 11 (but only for those covered employees who retired on or before the date the employer commenced the bankruptcy proceedings, their spouses, and their dependent children)

- Loss of dependent-child status under the terms of the plan

The final regulations state that a reduction in hours that results from a strike, lockout, layoff, or leave of absence (other than leave under the Family and Medical Leave Act) will be a qualifying event if it results in loss of group health care coverage. Except for facts demonstrating gross misconduct, whether a termination or reduction in hours is voluntary or involuntary is not relevant to determining if a qualifying event has occurred. If an employer's policy requires an "increase in the premium or contribution that must be paid by a covered employee (or the spouse or dependent child of a covered employee)" during the strike, lockout, layoff or leave of absence, a loss of coverage, and therefore a qualifying event, will result. [26 C.F.R. § 54.4980B, 64 Fed. Reg. 5160 (Feb. 3, 1999) and 66 Fed. Reg. 1843 (Jan. 10, 2001)]

It is also not relevant if the employee and dependents are covered by another group health plan at the time of the qualifying event. Employers must offer COBRA and permit employees and their dependents to elect COBRA coverage in addition to any other coverage already in place.

Loss of coverage during open enrollment is generally not a qualifying event. Thus, if an employee drops his/her spouse and/or dependents during the employer's open enrollment period, a qualifying event has not occurred and the spouse/dependents do not have a right to elect COBRA coverage. However, if the employee drops a spouse from coverage "in anticipation of" a divorce or legal separation, the COBRA regulations indicate that COBRA must be offered to the spouse as of the date of the divorce or legal separation. Similarly, an employee may drop a dependent during open enrollment because he/she is no longer eligible for dependent coverage (for example, if the child reaches an age which is no longer covered by the plan). Even though the child was dropped during open enrollment, he or she may be eligible for COBRA coverage. In these situations, the employee, spouse or dependent-child should notify the plan of the qualifying event (see **Section 7.11**). If the employer or plan administrator is otherwise aware of these situations, they may want to provide the COBRA notice to the dropped spouse or dependent even if the spouse/dependent does not notify the plan.

If a qualifying event occurs, an employer must offer each qualified beneficiary the opportunity to elect to continue the group health plan coverage. In general, qualified beneficiaries who elect COBRA coverage must be provided with the same coverage that they received before the qualifying event. Under some circumstances, however, qualified beneficiaries must be permitted to enroll in any group health plan maintained by the employer. If the employer revises its health coverage, the employer must offer the qualified beneficiary access to the revised or replacement coverage.

[A] Gross Misconduct

The regulations are silent as to defining "gross misconduct" and there has been little guidance from the courts. A recent court case is not definitive, but does provide some assistance to employers in this area. In *Pomales v. Celulares Telefonica, Inc.*, Civ. No. 02-1256 (D.P.R. 2005); *aff'd, Pomales v. Celulares Telefonica, Inc.*, 447 F.3d 79 (1st Cir. 2006), an employee was terminated for falsifying reports and not following company policies regarding making sales to customers without deposits. The company had clearly stated rules that called for immediate termination for these actions. The employer denied COBRA to the employee on the grounds that the employee was terminated for gross misconduct. The employee sued (on this and other bases) and the district court ruled in favor of the employer. The court came to its decision by determining that, in order to be fired for gross misconduct, the employer must show that the employee engaged in job-related misconduct and was fired for that misconduct. It is important to note that the actions of the employee were those outlined in the employer's rules of conduct and that those rules clearly stated that violations of these rules would result in termination.

Another court case provides additional, although dispositive, guidance. In *Boudreaux v. Rice Palace, Inc.,* 207 U.S. Dist. LEXIS 43714 (W.D. La. 2007), the employer terminated an employee for bizarre work behavior that allegedly was due to misuse of prescription drugs and resulted in an unsafe workplace as well as non-performance of work. The terminated employee sued her employer for failure to provide a COBRA election notice (as well as other employment-related claims). The employer stated that since she had been fired for gross misconduct, it did not need to provide her with a COBRA election notice. The court referenced case law on misconduct and determined that to be gross misconduct, behavior must be more than negligent, incompetent, or unsatisfactory.... Moreover, the conduct must be intentional, willful, wanton, reckless, or in deliberate disregard of the employer's interest. The court also reviewed the state law's interpretation of gross misconduct as it applies to unemployment coverage; in this case state law stated that the misconduct must have resulted from willful or wanton disregard of the employer's interest, from a deliberate violation of the employer's rules, or from a direct disregard of standards of behavior. Although in this case a final decision was not made (the case was remanded for trial), it does provide some further potential definitions of gross misconduct. Plan sponsors are urged to obtain competent legal assistance if they wish to use the gross misconduct standard to deny a qualified beneficiary a COBRA election notice.

[B] Second Qualifying Events

It is possible that a second qualifying event may occur during the initial COBRA continuation coverage period that will extend the length of the coverage period. The following qualifying events, if they occur during the initial COBRA period, and if the initial continuation coverage was provided due to a qualifying event of termination or reduction of hours, are second qualifying events:

- The covered employee dies

- The covered employee divorces or legally separates

- The covered employee's child ceases to qualify as a dependent child under the group health plan

- The covered employee becomes entitled to Medicare (providing a second qualifying event for the covered employee's spouse and children)

These second qualifying events will extend the COBRA continuation period to a total of 36 months, counting from the time when the initial COBRA continuation period began. For example, if an initial COBRA continuation period for both employee A and spouse B began on July 1, 2006 due to the termination of employment for employee A, and on March 15, 2007, employee A and spouse B divorced, spouse B would be eligible for COBRA continuation coverage for 36 months from July 1, 2006, or until June 30, 2009.

The second qualifying rule only applies if the second qualifying event would have caused a loss of coverage if it had occurred first. The rule will apply to those qualifying beneficiaries who elected COBRA and who are still receiving COBRA coverage when the second qualifying event occurs, whether or not the covered employee elected or was receiving COBRA coverage.

[C] Alternative Coverage Due to Relocation

If a qualified beneficiary participates in a region-specific health plan (i.e., a health maintenance organization or clinic) and moves out of the service area of that plan, the qualified beneficiary must be offered the opportunity to elect any alternative coverage provided by the employer to active employees. This coverage must be effective on the earlier of the date of relocation or the first of the month following the month of the request of the qualified beneficiary for the alternative coverage. If the employer does not make group health plan coverage available to active employees in the area to which the qualified beneficiary is relocating, but does have other coverage which can be extended to that location, it must make that other coverage available to the qualified beneficiary. For example, if the qualified beneficiary is moving out of his or her current HMO's service area, no other HMO offered by the employer serves the area to which the qualified beneficiary is moving, and there is an indemnity plan that will offer coverage regardless of where the qualified beneficiary (or employee) lives, then the indemnity plan must be offered.

If the employer offers only the region-specific group health plan and the qualified beneficiary is relocating out of that plan's service area, no other coverage need be obtained for or offered to the qualified beneficiary.

[D] Leaves of Absence

In general, a leave of absence constitutes a reduction in hours, and, if accompanied by a loss of health plan coverage, will be a COBRA qualifying event. However, under specific DOL regulations for Family and Medical Leave Act (FMLA) and COBRA, leave taken under the FMLA, (see **Chapter 12**) is not a qualifying event for COBRA. If an employee does not return to work after an FMLA leave, the last day of FMLA leave is the qualifying event. This is true even if an employee has not paid the required premium during FMLA leave and loses coverage during the leave.

Leaves that extend past the FMLA required period, or that do not qualify as FMLA leaves, will generally be COBRA qualifying events. However, courts' decisions are mixed on whether non-payment of premiums during a non-FMLA leave results in a COBRA qualifying event. For example, in *Jordan v. Tyson Foods, Inc.*, 257 Fed. Appx. 972 (6th Cir. 2007), the court ruled that an employee's coverage was not lost due to the "reduction in hours" due to a short-term disability leave; it was lost due to the failure to pay the premium.

However, a different court reached a different conclusion. In *Aquilino v. Solid Waste Servs., Inc.*, 2008 U.S. Dist. LEXIS 47168 (E.D. Pa. June 12, 2008), the court ruled that a loss of coverage occurred when an employee ceased to be covered under the same terms and conditions that existed prior to the leave. The court determined that a change in the method or means by which a participant is required to make payments toward the health plan's premium is an "implicit term and condition of the health plan." Therefore, an employee experiences a COBRA qualifying event when the leave of absence requires him/her to change the method by which the employee makes premium payments (for example, if the employee is required to pay the premiums by check to the employer instead of having them deducted from his paycheck).

Employers may require COBRA coverage after the end of an FMLA leave, even if the employee has accrued enough paid time off hours to remain on paid leave. In *Mehman v. Collin County*, 2007 WL 3389929 (E.D. Tex. 2207), an employee remained on a disability leave for three months after the FMLA leave was exhausted. During this post-FMLA disability leave, the employer provided a COBRA election notice, which the employee elected and paid his COBRA premiums. When the employee returned to work, he sued the company to recover the COBRA premiums he had paid. The court agreed with the employer, rejecting the employee's contention that only unpaid leaves of absence constitute a "reduction of hours" qualifying event for COBRA.

Administering COBRA continuation coverage correctly during leaves of absence can be challenging. Employers who do not use specialized COBRA TPA services are encouraged to obtain assistance from appropriate consultants or counsel.

§ 7.07   WHEN COBRA COVERAGE BEGINS

If the qualified beneficiary elects COBRA coverage in a timely manner, continuation coverage must begin on the day the qualified beneficiary loses coverage, even if this date is prior to the date the qualified beneficiary makes the election. Generally, qualified beneficiaries have 60 calendar days to elect COBRA coverage. This election period cannot end sooner than 60 days after the qualified beneficiary would lose group health care coverage or 60 days after the qualified beneficiary receives the notice of COBRA coverage, whichever is later. The election is considered made on the date it is mailed by the qualified beneficiary.

If a qualified beneficiary does not elect COBRA coverage by the end of the election period, he or she ceases to be a qualified beneficiary. However, a qualified beneficiary may revoke any prior waiver of COBRA continuation during the 60-day election period.

A question frequently asked by employers is what to do about covering the qualified beneficiary between the date that coverage as an active employee ends and the election date. Some employers choose to continue the employee's coverage during this period, assuming that their contract and/or Summary Plan Description (SPD) allows them to retroactively cancel coverage, should the qualified beneficiary fail to elect COBRA coverage. Most employers however do not continue coverage under the active employee plan. Rather, they terminate coverage and, if necessary, will reinstate the coverage under the COBRA portion of their plan. This reinstatement is likely to be retroactive, so employers should ensure that their insurance contract, plan document and/or SPD will allow retroactive COBRA coverage.

§ 7.08   MAXIMUM LENGTH OF COBRA COVERAGE

The maximum required COBRA continuation periods, which vary according to the nature of the qualifying event, are as follows:

- 18 months, for employee termination or reduction of hours;

- 29 months, if the individual is disabled at the time of a qualifying event; and

- 36 months for any other qualifying event.

The extension of COBRA coverage to 29 months for a disabled qualified beneficiary also applies if the disability exists at any time during the first 60 calendar days of COBRA coverage. The disability determination has to be made and the notice of disability has to be given before the end of the initial 18-month COBRA coverage period, provided that the qualified beneficiary was provided notice that the notice of disability had to be provided prior to the end of the initial 18-month COBRA coverage period. The extended COBRA coverage period of 29 months also applies to each qualified beneficiary of the covered employee, even if the disabled qualified beneficiary has not elected COBRA. For example, John is a disabled qualified beneficiary who does not elect COBRA when his employment ends. However, his wife Mary does elect COBRA coverage. As long as John's disability determination was made and the notice of disability given to the plan administrator was prior to the end of the initial 18-month COBRA coverage period, Mary's COBRA coverage could continue for a total of 29 months from the original date of loss of coverage.

Note that 36 months is the longest period of COBRA coverage required under the law. Even if a qualified beneficiary has a third or more qualifying event, the 36-month period is not further extended.

[A] Medicare Entitlement and Extension of Coverage

On February 13, 2004, the IRS issued Revenue Ruling 2004-22 [2004-10 I.R.B. 553], which provides new interpretation of the COBRA extension of coverage of qualified beneficiaries (spouses and dependents who are receiving COBRA benefits) when the former employee becomes entitled to Medicare.

The facts of the case addressed by Revenue Ruling 2004-22 indicate that covered employee E and E's spouse lost coverage under the group health plan as a result of E's termination of employment. E's spouse elects and timely pays for COBRA coverage. During the initial 18 months of COBRA coverage, E becomes entitled to Medicare. E's spouse notifies the plan of E's entitlement and requests the extension of coverage to 36 months from the initial date of loss of coverage. Prior to the issuance of Revenue Ruling 2004-22, it had been standard practice to extend the initial COBRA benefit period to 36 months.

Revenue Ruling 2004-22 holds that the Medicare entitlement of a covered employee is not a second qualifying event for the qualified beneficiary, because the Medicare entitlement would not have resulted in a loss of coverage for the qualified beneficiary under the group health plan that is providing the COBRA coverage. Under the Medicare Secondary Payer provisions of the Social Security Act, plans cannot treat current employees or their dependents differently from other plan participants because the employee (or a dependent) is eligible for Medicare. That is, Medicare entitlement is not a qualifying event while the employee is an active participant in the group health plan.

The timing of Medicare entitlement is critical in this analysis. In 1996, Congress amended COBRA as part of the Small Business Job Protection Act of 1996 (SBJPA; Pub. L. No. 104-188, 110 Stat. 1755 (Aug. 20, 1996)), which resulted in the provision of 36 months of COBRA coverage to a qualified beneficiary if Medicare entitlement occurs within the 18-month period before termination of employment (or a reduction in hours leading to loss of coverage).

Revenue Ruling 2004-22 provides that if Medicare entitlement occurs after the termination of employment (or reduction in hours leading to loss of coverage), the length of the COBRA coverage period for qualified beneficiaries remains 18 months.

[B] Early Termination of Coverage

Coverage may end early if timely payment is not made, if the employer ceases to maintain any group health plan for its employees, if the qualified beneficiary becomes entitled to Medicare (i.e., enrolls in Medicare Part A or B), or becomes covered under another group health plan (that does not contain preexisting condition limitations) after his or her COBRA election date. However, for purposes of COBRA, "group health plan" excludes plans provided by a Federal or other governmental entity. Health plans provided by the military to active duty members and reservists and their families are not group health plans under COBRA. Therefore, COBRA coverage may not be terminated due to a qualified beneficiary receiving coverage under any military (or other governmental) health plan. Qualified beneficiaries, who are receiving extended COBRA coverage due to disability, may have their COBRA coverage terminated prior to the full 29-month period if they are determined to no longer be disabled.

While in general COBRA may not be terminated during an open enrollment period, under at least one circumstance this may occur. If a group health plan requires all participants, active employees, and COBRA qualified beneficiaries, to re-enroll during every open enrollment period, and the COBRA participant does not submit his/her re-enrollment materials to the plan, the COBRA coverage may be terminated. It is critical that the employer provide the same open enrollment information to the COBRA qualified beneficiaries as they do to their active employees and clearly indicate that re-enrollment is required to continue coverage. As long as the same conditions apply to both active and COBRA participants, canceling the coverage of a COBRA participant who does not re-enroll is permitted.

§ 7.09 COBRA PREMIUMS

Employers are not required to pay for COBRA coverage. This is true even if coverage under the plan was paid for entirely by the employer before the qualifying event. The cost of coverage may not exceed 102 percent of the applicable premium. This limit increases to 150 percent for the 19th through the 29th month of coverage for disabled qualified beneficiaries and their covered dependents. The applicable premium is the cost to the health plan for current plan beneficiaries, and must be determined for a 12-month period before that 12-month period begins. The COBRA cost must be fixed for this 12-month period, even if an insurer raises the rates to the employer mid-year. Thus, most employers determine the COBRA premium to match their insurer's (or HMO's) rate period.

In Revenue Ruling 96-8 [1996-1 C.B. 286], the IRS highlights the application of the above rule. The ruling does not address how to calculate the premium; rather, it discusses when employees and their family members should be charged single coverage or family coverage. Revenue Ruling 96-8 made the following conclusions:

- Two or more beneficiaries (e.g., the employee and spouse, the spouse and dependent(s), or the employee and dependent(s)) who make an election for coverage due to a life event can be charged the family rate.

- When an employee and a spouse or dependent(s) have family coverage and after the life event only one of the beneficiaries elects continuation coverage, the employer can charge only the single rate.

Revenue Ruling 96-8 addresses specific fact patterns. Many other situations need to be addressed individually. The premium may be paid by any third party, such as a hospital or a new employer, on behalf of the qualified beneficiary.

Generally, COBRA premiums must be paid on the same day as the group health plan's premium is due. However, COBRA provides two time periods ("grace periods") within which COBRA premiums must be paid. In general, qualified beneficiaries have 45 calendar days from the date of election of coverage within which to pay the premium due for the period of time from the loss of coverage date to the election date. On an ongoing basis, payments are timely if made within 30 calendar days of the due date or on a later date permitted under the plan. A failure to pay premiums in a timely manner may cause a qualified beneficiary to lose COBRA coverage. It is critical to inform qualified beneficiaries correctly about the due date(s) of their premiums. If premiums for the group health plan are due on the first of every month, then this is the due date that should be communicated to qualified beneficiaries. The 30-day period should be articulated as a grace period, not the due date. An example of correctly identifying the due date and grace period is as follows:

> The due date for your COBRA premium is the first day of every month for that month's coverage. You will be given a 30-day grace period after the first day of the month to submit your payment for that month. Premiums not received by the end of this grace period will be returned to you, and your COBRA continuation coverage will cease, as of the last day of the previous month.

If the insurer or HMO allows the employer a longer-than 30-day grace period, then this longer grace period must also be provided to the qualified beneficiary. For example, if the insurer allows the employer a 45-day grace period in which to pay the premiums, the qualified beneficiary must also be provided with a 45-day grace period in which to pay his/her COBRA premiums.

A shortfall in premium payments may lead to automatic termination of coverage in certain circumstances. COBRA regulations on this issue are based on whether or not the shortfall is insignificant. An *insignificant shortfall* in premium payments is defined as an underpayment that is less than or equal to the lesser of (1) $50 or (2) 10 percent of the required COBRA premium.

If the shortfall is *less than* the insignificant amount, the plan must notify the qualified beneficiary of the underpayment and provide him or her with the opportunity to pay the difference within 30 days of the issuance of the notice. Alternatively, the plan may choose to accept the underpayment as payment in full.

If the shortfall *exceeds* the amount defined as an insignificant shortfall, the plan may automatically terminate the qualified beneficiary's COBRA coverage after the applicable grace period. However, in order to automatically terminate the coverage, the plan must first have notified qualified beneficiaries that it will do so in its general and election notices (see **Section 7.11**).

It should be noted that any third party may pay the COBRA premium. Thus, new employers may pay the COBRA premium on behalf of their new employee. Medical providers, hospitals, nursing homes, etc., may pay the COBRA premium to ensure that coverage for their patient continues as long as possible. Plan administrators are required to answer medical providers' questions about the status of a qualified beneficiary's COBRA coverage and election rights.

§ 7.10 EQUAL TREATMENT

Qualified beneficiaries must be treated in the same manner as all other group health plan participants with respect to the coverage options, benefit limitations, and conversion rights available under the group health plan. Qualified beneficiaries are eligible to make changes to their coverage during all "open enrollment" periods that occur during their COBRA continuation coverage (e.g., they may elect other health plan options the plan sponsor provides to all other employees, such as moving from an HMO plan to the point-of-service plan and vice versa). If the plan sponsor terminates an option under which a qualified beneficiary is covered, the qualified beneficiary will have to elect one of the other remaining options provided by the plan sponsor if he/she wishes to continue COBRA coverage. The plan sponsor is not required to continue to provide a health care option simply because a qualified beneficiary has elected coverage under that particular plan.

Employers are required to provide notification of changes to the plan to qualified beneficiaries who have elected COBRA coverage. Generally, employers provide the same open enrollment communication material to qualified beneficiaries as they provide to employees.

If employers change insurance providers, the employer is responsible for ensuring that the new insurance carrier will provide COBRA coverage for existing qualified beneficiaries.

The requirement that qualified beneficiaries be treated in the same manner as other plan participants also applies to the cost of COBRA coverage. If, during the period of continuation coverage, the cost of the coverage (the total cost, including both the employer and employee's share, if any) increases or decreases, the cost to the qualified beneficiary will also increase or decrease.

Qualified beneficiaries may enroll dependents under HIPAA's special enrollment rules. Under HIPAA's special enrollment rules, employees and dependents have the right to enroll in an employer's group health plan if other health coverage or insurance ends. If the group health plan provides dependent coverage, the special enrollment rules also provide for adding spouses and/or dependents upon marriage, birth or adoption, as applicable. These special enrollment periods also apply to COBRA coverage. Thus, if a qualified beneficiary marries, the new spouse must be enrolled onto COBRA coverage, if the qualified beneficiary allows. Note that the new spouse is not technically a qualified beneficiary. If the qualified beneficiary dies during the COBRA period, the new spouse's COBRA coverage can end and she or he is not eligible for the extension due when a second qualifying event occurs. Be advised that the special enrollment rules allow for adding dependents at times other than the plan sponsor's normal open enrollment period. As described further in this **Section 7.10,** qualified beneficiaries may enroll spouses and dependents during open enrollment, if such activity is allowed for active employees.

In general, if all the employer's plans, including plans sponsored by an employer in the same controlled group, are eliminated, the employer's COBRA obligations cease, unless the employer has some other contractual or other type of obligation to provide such coverage.

§ 7.11   COBRA NOTICES

COBRA imposes specific notification requirements on employers, plan administrators, and employees. Failure to comply with all notice requirements in a timely manner can result in significant penalties for employers, including providing health care coverage where otherwise no requirement to do so would exist.

Generally, the Department of the Treasury has interpretive authority for substantive COBRA rights. However, the DOL has interpretive authority for the notice and disclosure provisions of COBRA. On May 28, 2003, the Employee Benefits Security Administration (EBSA) of the DOL published proposed regulations for 29 C.F.R. Part 2590, Health Care Continuation Coverage (RIN 1210-AA60) to provide uniformity and clarity on the various notices that the law requires employers, plan administrators, and employees to furnish. Some of the information published in the proposed regulations represented clarifications of the existing law, and EBSA expected that employers would comply immediately. EBSA published the final rule on May 26, 2004. The final rule, which made some changes to the proposed regulations, became effective on November 26, 2004. The changes must be implemented no later than the first day of the first plan year beginning on or after November 26, 2004 (e.g., plans that operate on a calendar-year basis must implement the requirements of the final regulations by January 1, 2005).

COBRA and its implementing regulations place liability on employers and plan administrators and not on insurers or TPAs. Many plan administrators contract with TPAs to help ensure that the plan meets its COBRA obligations. If the TPA does not provide the appropriate notices or otherwise fails to fulfill the plan's COBRA obligations, the employer remains responsible for these failures. Employers should ensure that their contracts with TPAs (or insurers) clearly delineate who will be responsible for providing the required notices, and what recourse will be available should the parties fail to meet their respective obligations.

(See **Exhibit 7.1** for a summary of the COBRA notice requirements and the time frame within which the notice must be provided.)

[A] General COBRA Notice

Employees and covered spouses must receive the general notice of their COBRA rights within 90 calendar days of the date they first become eligible for coverage under a group health plan. It is acceptable to provide a single general notice to both the employee and covered spouse, except in the following instances:

- The covered spouse's last known address is different from that of the employee.

- The covered spouse's coverage begins at a time different from that of the employee.

The group health plan's summary plan description (SPD) can be used in lieu of the general notice if it contains the required COBRA information. However, if the SPD is only provided to the employee at work, a separate notice must be provided to the covered spouse at his or her last known address, even if this address is the same as the employee's. The general notice may be delivered by hand or first-class mail, or, if prior approval from the participant is obtained, it may be delivered electronically. Covered dependent children do not need to receive a separate general notice.

The final rule provides a model general notice (for single-employer plans), which must be customized for each group health plan maintained by the employer. The model notice is available on EBSA's Web site: *www.dol.gov/ebsa/modelgeneralnotice.doc*. A model notice in Spanish is available at *www.dol.gov/ebsa/ modelgeneralnoticesp.doc*.

The general notice should be written in a manner that can be understood by the average plan participant and it must contain, at minimum, the following information:

- The name of the plan;

- The name, address, and telephone number of the party or parties administering continuation coverage;

- A general description of continuation coverage, including who may become qualified beneficiaries, what types of events are qualifying events, maximum coverage periods, extensions to the maximum coverage periods, and premium payment obligations;

- The plan's requirements for, and the procedures to be used by, qualified beneficiaries to provide notice of certain qualifying events such as divorce, separation, a dependent becoming ineligible for coverage as a dependent, or a determination by the Social Security Administration (SSA) that the qualified beneficiary is disabled;

- An explanation of the importance of keeping the plan's records up to date regarding the addresses of participants; and

- A statement that the notice does not fully describe continuation coverage rights and that more information is available from the plan administrator and in the SPD.

The model notice may also be used to notify participants in health flexible spending accounts (FSAs). However, the model notice will need to be modified to describe the special COBRA rules applicable to health FSAs (see **Section 7.12 [B][2]**).

[B]   Employer Notice of Qualifying Event

If the qualifying event is any of the following: termination of employment, reduction in hours of employment, death, Medicare entitlement, or the employer's bankruptcy under Chapter 11 of the Internal Revenue Code, and the employer is the plan administrator, the employer has 14 calendar days in which to notify all qualified beneficiaries of their right to elect COBRA coverage.

If an employer is not the plan administrator, the employer must notify the plan administrator if one of the above qualifying events occurs. Generally, the employer notice must be provided to the plan administrator within 30 calendar days of the date of the qualifying event. However, if the plan specifically states that continuation coverage and the applicable period for providing the employer notice begins on the date of loss of coverage, the 30-day timing requirement begins on the date of loss of coverage rather than on the date of the qualifying event. The employer notice must provide sufficient information for the plan administrator to determine the employee, the qualifying event, the date of the qualifying event, and the group health plan involved. (See **Exhibit 7.2** for a sample notice of qualifying event from employer to plan administrator.)

Once the plan administrator has received the employer notice, the plan administrator has 14 calendar days in which to notify all qualified beneficiaries of their COBRA rights.

[C]   Employee Notice of Qualifying Event

Employees and qualified beneficiaries are required to notify the plan administrator of a divorce or legal separation or a child's loss of dependent status under the plan. Under the 2004 final rule, qualified beneficiaries must also notify the plan administrator if they experience a second qualifying event, have received a determination by the SSA that they are disabled, or have received a subsequent determination by the SSA that they are no longer disabled.

In general, the employee notice must be provided within 60 calendar days of the qualifying event. However, this 60-day period does not begin until the plan administrator has provided the employee with the general notice. Also, if the plan specifically states that continuation coverage begins on the date of loss of coverage, the 60-day period begins on the date of loss of coverage, rather than on the date of the qualifying event. Since it is possible that an employee may receive a disability determination from the SSA before a qualifying event occurs, the 60-day period begins on the latest date that:

- The SSA makes a disability determination,

- A qualifying event occurs,

- The qualified beneficiary loses coverage, or

- The qualified beneficiary is informed of the employee notice procedures (see below) by receiving the general notice (or SPD, if the general notice information is included in the SPD)

If a qualified beneficiary is determined by SSA to no longer be disabled, the beneficiary must provide the notice to the plan administrator no later than 30 calendar days after the later of:

- The date of SSA's final determination, or

- The date on which the qualified beneficiary is informed of the employee notice procedures (see below) by receiving the general notice (or SPD, if the general notice information is included in the SPD)

[1] Employee Notice Procedures

Group health plans must establish reasonable procedures for an employee and/or covered dependent to notify the plan of a qualifying event. Procedures will be deemed reasonable if:

- They are described in the SPD;

- They specify the individual, by name or title, or the entity responsible for receiving the qualified beneficiary's notice;

- They describe the means by which the qualified beneficiary may give notice (e.g., orally, in writing, on a specific form, etc.);

- They describe what information is necessary for an adequate notice; and

- Otherwise comply with all COBRA regulations as they pertain to timing and content of the notices.

If the employer fails to prepare and adequately inform the employees of this notification procedure, any oral or written notice from a qualified beneficiary will be deemed acceptable, if it identifies the qualifying event and delivers the information to any person or organizational unit of the employer that usually handles the plan (such as the employee benefits unit of the employer or, if the plan is insured or administered by an insurance company, the insurance company's claims department). These procedures must also be addressed in the general notice; the model notice provided by EBSA indicates where this information (specific to each employer) should be inserted. (See **Exhibit 7.3** for a sample notice of qualifying event from employee to employer/plan administrator.)

[D] COBRA Election Notice

When a qualifying event occurs, the plan administrator must provide an election notice to the qualified beneficiaries informing them that they have a right to elect continuation coverage. When this notice must be provided depends on who provides notice of the qualifying event and whether the employer is the plan administrator, or another entity is the plan administrator.

If the employee or other qualified beneficiary is required to provide notice of a COBRA qualifying event (see **Section 7.11[C]** above), then the plan administrator has a maximum of 14 days to provide the COBRA Election Notice to the employee or other qualified beneficiary.

If the employer must provide notice of a qualifying event (see **Section 7.11[B]** above), then:

- If the employer is the plan administrator, the employer has 44 calendar days from either date of loss of coverage or date of qualifying event (as previously determined by the plan) to provide the COBRA Election Notice to the employee or qualified beneficiary

- If the employer is not the plan administrator, the employer has 30 days from the date of the qualifying event to notify the plan administrator of the qualifying event; the plan administrator then has 14 days to provide the COBRA Election Notice to the qualified beneficiaries.

The election notice must contain 14 specific information items, as follows:

1. The name of the plan and the name, address, and telephone number of those responsible for the administration of continuation coverage

2. Identification of the qualifying event

3. Identification, by status or name, of the qualified beneficiaries who are recognized by the plan as being entitled to elect continuation coverage, and the date on which coverage will terminate if continuation coverage is not elected

4. A statement that each individual who is a qualified beneficiary has an independent right to elect continuation coverage, that either a covered employee or the (former) spouse of the covered employee may elect continuation coverage on behalf of all other qualified beneficiaries, and that a parent or legal guardian may elect continuation coverage on behalf of minor child(ren)

5. An explanation of the plan's procedures for electing continuation coverage, including the time periods in which such election must be made, and the date by which the election must be made

6. An explanation of the consequences of not electing (or waiving) continuation coverage, including the potential effect on the future rights of qualified beneficiaries to group health portability, guaranteed access to individual coverage and special enrollment rights under HIPAA; this section must also include where qualified beneficiaries may obtain additional information about these rights and the plan's procedures for revoking a waiver of the right to continuation coverage before the date by which the election must be made

7. The date on which continuation coverage, if elected, will begin, and a description of the continuation coverage (which may be included in the election notice, or, alternatively, included by reference to the plan's SPD)

8. A description of the maximum length of time that continuation coverage will be provided, if elected, and the termination date, as well as an explanation of any events that might cause the coverage to be terminated earlier than the end of the maximum period

9. A description of the circumstances that will result in the extension of the maximum period of continuation coverage, including the occurrence of a second qualifying event or a determination by SSA that a qualifying beneficiary is disabled, and the length of the extension

10. If the length of the continuation coverage period is less than 36 months, a description of the plan's requirements regarding the responsibility of the qualified beneficiaries to provide notice of a second qualifying event or disability determination by SSA; the description must include the plan's procedures for providing these notices, the time periods required to provide the notices, the consequences of failing to provide the notices, and the requirement that notices must be provided if the qualified beneficiary is subsequently determined to no longer be disabled

11. The premium amount for each qualified beneficiary

12. The due date for each premium payment, the grace periods for payment, the address to which the payments should be mailed, and the consequences of nonpayment

13. An explanation of the importance of keeping the administrator informed of the current addresses of the beneficiaries

14. A statement that the election notice does not fully describe continuation coverage or other rights under the plan and that more complete information regarding such rights is available in the plan's SPD or from the plan administrator

It is not necessary to send separate notices to each qualified beneficiary who resides at the same address. However, if a spouse and/or dependent child(ren) reside at an address different than that of the employee, a separate notice must be sent to those individuals. The final rule provides a new model election notice for single employer plans, which must be customized for each type of qualifying event and for each health plan maintained by an employer. In response to Revenue Ruling 2004-22 [2004-10 I.R.B. 553], plan sponsors may wish to modify the model election notice by removing the phrase "the employee's becoming entitled to Medicare benefits" from the "How Long Will Continuation Coverage Last?" section. The similar phrase may also be removed from the "Second Qualifying Event" section. The model election notice is available in English and Spanish on the EBSA Web site: *www.dol.gov/ebsa/modelelectionnotice.doc* and *www.dol.gov/ebsa/modelelectionnoticesp.doc*.

It is not entirely clear whether a second Election Notice is required when there is a second qualifying event (see **Section 7.06[B]**). The DOL has indicated that if the Election Notice provided upon the first qualifying event included the plan's procedures for employees providing the notice of the second qualifying event, the time frame for providing that notice to the plan, and the consequences of failing to provide it, the second Election Notice generally would not be required. However, plan administrators may wish to operate conservatively and provide a second Election Notice to the qualified beneficiary upon notice of a second qualifying event.

[E]   Notice of Unavailability

If an employee or a qualified beneficiary provides notice to the plan administrator of a qualifying event, a second qualifying event, or of an SSA disability determination and the plan administrator determines that the employee or qualified beneficiary is not eligible for continuation coverage, the plan administrator must provide a notice of unavailability. This notice must be provided within the same time frame as is required for providing the election notice (i.e., for a plan administrator, 14 days after the receipt of the employee/ qualified beneficiary notice). The notice of unavailability must be written in language that can be understood by the average plan participant and must contain an explanation of why the individual is not entitled to continuation coverage. The notice must be provided to the individual who is the subject of the notice or request for COBRA coverage; this might not necessarily be the same individual who actually provided the original notice or request to the employer (e.g., if an employee (husband) provided notice of a divorce, the divorced wife is the subject of the notice, not the husband). The notice of unavailability does not need to be furnished to the individual if the qualifying event was one which the employer is required to provide notice to the plan administrator (e.g., termination of employment, reduction in work hours, death, or entitlement to Medicare). (See **Exhibit 7.4** for a sample notice of unavailability of COBRA continuation coverage.)

Although only required in the above described situations, it may be advantageous for the plan to provide a Notice of Unavailability whenever an employee or covered spouse or dependent requests coverage and it is determined that they are not eligible. Providing this notice can prevent misunderstandings and avoid the individuals believing they are entitled to a benefit for which they are not eligible.

[F]   Notice of Termination of Continuation Coverage

If continuation coverage ends earlier than the maximum period of coverage applicable to the specific qualifying event, the plan administrator must send notice to all affected qualified beneficiaries notifying them of early termination. The notice must be provided as soon as practicable after the plan administrator has determined that continuation coverage will be terminated. EBSA, in the 2004 final rule commentary, specifically indicated that the notice of termination may be provided at the same time as the HIPAA Certificate of Creditable Coverage. There is no requirement to provide the notice of termination prior to actually terminating the coverage. For example, if coverage is to terminate early due to nonpayment of a premium, the date of termination of coverage may be the end of the grace period for premium payment. In this case, the plan administrator will not determine that coverage will terminate until the end of the grace period when the payment is not received. The notice of termination should be provided as soon as practicable thereafter.

The notice of termination must be written in a manner that can be understood by the average plan participant and must include: (1) the reason that continuation coverage is/has terminated earlier than the maximum period of coverage applicable to the qualifying event; (2) the date the coverage terminated; and (3) any rights the qualified beneficiary may have under the plan or under applicable law to elect an alternative group or individual coverage, such as a conversion right.

[G] Summary Plan Description

Specific information concerning COBRA should be contained in the plan's SPD. An SPD must contain sufficient language describing COBRA rights and obligations, so that plan participants and beneficiaries understand their rights to continue coverage and the procedures they must follow to elect coverage. Inaccurate, incomplete, or misleading information in an SPD can result in liability for both the plan and the employer and can impose a COBRA obligation on the employer when the obligation otherwise would not exist. Specifically, 29 C.F.R. Section 2520.102-3(o) states that the SPD must include "information concerning qualifying events, and qualified beneficiaries, premiums, notices and election requirements and procedures, and duration of coverage."

The 2003 proposed regulations reminded employers that the Trade Adjustment Assistance Reform Act of 2002 (Trade Reform Act) [Pub. L. No. 107-210, 116 Stat. 933 (Aug. 6, 2002)] amended Section 605 of ERISA to add a new subsection (b). The new subsection provides a second 60-day COBRA election period for certain individuals who become eligible for trade adjustment assistance (TAA) pursuant to the Trade Act of 1974. One of the benefits of TAA is a potential tax credit toward the cost of COBRA coverage. EBSA indicated in its commentary that the SPD should include information on the qualified beneficiary's right to elect COBRA coverage under the Trade Reform Act, if an employee might qualify for the assistance. This Act allows qualified beneficiaries who are eligible for TAA a second COBRA election period, if they become eligible for such assistance after their initial election period has expired. The COBRA section of the SPD must also outline the procedures a qualified beneficiary must follow to inform the plan administrator of a qualifying event (see above). Further information on the Trade Reform Act of 2002 is available online at *www.doleta.gov/tradeact/2002act_index.cfm*.

[H] Documentation of Notices

Plans and employers must retain sufficient documentation regarding their procedures and actions taken in compliance with COBRA's notice requirements. In the event of a lawsuit by a qualified beneficiary claiming not to have received a COBRA notice or COBRA coverage, the plan or employer may have to prove that the notices were sent. Failure to provide the required COBRA notices to qualified beneficiaries in a timely manner may result in the imposition of various statutory penalties and an award of damages against plans, plan administrators, and employers.

COBRA regulations require that employers send the notices to the "last known" address of the qualified beneficiary. To adequately comply with the COBRA regulations, employers and plan administrators may want to include requirements in the General Notice that employees and other (potential) qualified beneficiaries must keep the plan informed of their current address. If a notice is returned as "undeliverable," plan administrators may want to research whether a more current address is available through another company department (e.g., payroll or accounts payable) or from the insurance company or HMO.

Many employers, in an effort to more fully "prove" that they provided employees with the required notices, send the notices via certified mail. The COBRA regulations require only that the notices be sent via first-class mail, and certified mail may in fact work to the employer's disadvantage. Take, for example, the case of *DeGruise v. Sprint Corp.* [23 EBC 1277 (E.D. La. 1999)] Sprint mailed the COBRA Qualifying Event Notice to its former employee, Mr. DeGruise, in a timely manner using certified mail. No one was home to sign for the package, so the U.S. Postal Service left a notice for DeGruise. When DeGruise attempted to retrieve the package from the post office, it had already been returned to Sprint. DeGruise sued Sprint for not meeting its COBRA notice obligations. In its findings, the court noted that COBRA requires only that an employer make a good faith attempt to comply with its notice requirements. It found that Sprint had in fact done so, and the fact that the package was not *delivered* to DeGruise was not due to Sprint's error or omission. The court found in favor of Sprint.

However, other courts might not take the same view. When sending a letter via certified mail, the lack of a signed certification receipt may help prove the claimant's case that the employer did not appropriately comply with COBRA. If notices are sent via first-class mail, no such proof of nondelivery is available to the potential litigant. Employers should maintain proof of *sending* the required notices such as U.S.P.S. proof of mailing certificate or a photocopy of the metered or stamped envelope, a copy of the notice, and a handwritten notation by the person doing the mailing.

In another case regarding the provision of COBRA notices, *Scott v. Suncoast Beverage Sales, Ltd.* [295 F.3d 1223 (11th Cir. 2002)], Scott, a terminated employee, claimed that he did not receive the required COBRA notification his employer, Suncoast Beverage Sales, Ltd., contracted with a third-party administrator (TPA) to send. Suncoast, however, provided no evidence that the TPA actually sent a COBRA notice to the claimant. The court found in favor of Scott. The court ruled that the employer has the responsibility to provide the COBRA qualifying event notice even if it contracts with another party to provide this service. If the employer contracted with a TPA to provide COBRA administrative services, including the mailing of required notices, the employer should ensure that the TPA follows written procedures for sending such notices, and the employer should retain evidence that the notices were in fact sent. The court added that although the employer cannot by statute remove the liability from itself to the TPA, it can include language in its contract with the TPA that provides for indemnification in the event the TPA fails to provide the required COBRA notices.

It is recommended that plan sponsors:

1. Develop written procedures for providing notices

2. Consistently comply with its own procedures

3. Maintain copies of the notices along with the address(es) to which the notices were sent, and

4. Maintain proof of mailing.

If the plan sponsor contracts with a TPA for providing notices to qualified beneficiaries, the plan sponsor should ensure that the TPA is following the above recommendations and can prove it does so in the event that a lawsuit is filed.

[I] Other Notice Requirements

Various other notice issues arise in relation to other mandated benefits. In brief, those notice requirements are as follows:

- *The Americans with Disabilities Act (ADA).* Employers covered by the ADA presumably may be required to provide reasonable accommodation to disabled employees in connection with their COBRA rights.

- *The Family and Medical Leave Act (FMLA).* A leave of absence under the FMLA does not constitute a COBRA qualifying event because no loss of coverage occurs during the FMLA leave. Under the FMLA, employers are required to continue group health coverage during the period of leave at the same level and under the same conditions that coverage would have been provided if the employee had continued in employment continuously for the duration of such leave. Accordingly, the COBRA notice should not be distributed at the beginning of the leave period, as no qualifying event will have occurred at that time. However, a qualifying event will occur on the last day of the FMLA leave if the employee does not return to work. Thus, in the case of an employee who takes a leave under the FMLA and notifies his or her employer that he or she will not be returning to work upon expiration of the leave period, the COBRA notice should be mailed after the employer learns that the employee will not be returning to work. However, the period of COBRA coverage begins on the day the employee loses coverage due to his or her failure to return to work.

- *Qualified Medical Child Support Orders (QMCSOs).* Federal law requires that group health plans honor QMCSOs by providing for the immediate enrollment of the child of a participant in the plan in accordance with the order. Such a child is designated an alternate recipient, and the law provides that he or she is a plan beneficiary for all purposes of ERISA, but for purposes of the reporting and disclosure rules of ERISA, he or she is a plan participant. As a result, plan administrators should provide these children with separate copies of the health plan's documents, including the SPD and COBRA notices.

- *HIPAA Certificate of Creditable Coverage.* HIPAA mandated some changes that affect the operation of the COBRA laws. Effective June 1, 1997, employers are required to provide a "Certificate of Group Health Plan Coverage" to employees and their beneficiaries who lose coverage under a group health plan, including COBRA. The certificate provides information on the period of "creditable coverage" the individual(s) had under the plan, including COBRA coverage. An automatic certificate must be provided when COBRA coverage lapses. The plan must also provide a certificate in a reasonable and prompt fashion on request by an individual, up to 24 months from the date of loss of coverage under COBRA. A sample certification statement is included as **Exhibit 6.2** (see **Chapter 6**).

Further information on the final regulations as well as fact sheets and sample forms on COBRA requirements can be found on the EBSA Web site: *www.dol.gov/ebsa.*

[J] Retention Period for Notices and Other COBRA Information

COBRA and its regulations do not provide specific retention period requirements for COBRA information. The recordkeeping rules of ERISA impose an eight-year retention rule for many plan records, which many plan sponsors apply to COBRA records. An alternative method might be referred to as the "statute of limitations" period. This refers to the statute of limitations under which a claimant may bring a claim under COBRA. COBRA does not have a specific statute of limitations, so the courts must look to the most analogous state-law period to determine the statute of limitations in each state. For most employment-related claims, the statute of limitations begins at the time the claimant knew or should have known that he or she had a claim. Thus, a potential qualified beneficiary may have as much as three years from the start of his or her COBRA coverage to make a claim of medical benefits, and determine that he or she is, in fact, not covered.

Employers and plan sponsors may want to determine the longest period of statute of limitations for all of the states in which the plan operates, add that to the time period the potential claimant has to make a COBRA claim (up to three years) and use that total amount of time as the minimum length of time that COBRA documents should be maintained.

§ 7.12   COBRA ENFORCEMENT AND PENALTIES

Failure to comply with any of COBRA's requirements can result in the imposition of penalties and other liability under both the Code and ERISA. Both civil and tax penalties may be levied against employers. Civil sanctions allow the plan beneficiaries themselves or the DOL to sue the plan if it does not provide required COBRA notices to employees. Beneficiaries are entitled to equitable relief if a court decides that they were wrongfully denied continuation coverage or if they were not given required notices. Generally, courts have provided such relief in the form of payment of the actual medical expenses (less COBRA premiums, deductibles, and other applicable patient-paid expenses). Courts may also include the plaintiff's attorney's fees as part of the penalty. Furthermore, employers and plan administrators may be liable for a statutory penalty of up to $110 a day for failure to provide the required COBRA notices.

A recent court case outlines how the courts may impose the statutory penalty. In *Sluka v. Landau Uniforms, Inc.*, [343 F. Supp. 649 (D.N.J. 2005)], the employer overlooked sending a terminated employee the COBRA Election Notice. The former employee sued, including a claim for the penalty. The employer countered that there had been no proof of damages and therefore the penalty should not be applied. The court disagreed with the employer, however, limited the award to $20 per day for every day that the employer had not sent the notice. The court stated that it balanced the employer's lack of malice with the need for compliance with COBRA, noting that the employer had every resource and ability to comply with the statute, and therefore should be held accountable for its failure to do so.

Tax sanctions under COBRA include a nondeductible excise tax of $100 a day for each beneficiary affected during the period of noncompliance. However, the tax penalty is limited to $200 per day per affected family. For purposes of applying the $100-a-day penalty, the period of noncompliance is measured from the date of the failure to the date when the failure is corrected or the date six months after the last day of the otherwise applicable COBRA coverage period, whichever is earlier.

Violations attributable to reasonable cause are generally not penalized if they are corrected within 30 calendar days. The IRS may also waive part or all of the tax for reasonable cause violations based on the seriousness of the violation. If an uncorrected COBRA violation is discovered during an IRS audit, however, the 30-day correction grace period is disallowed, and an excise tax is imposed.

The maximum excise tax for a single employer for all violations during a taxable year is 10 percent of total health plan contributions during the preceding year, up to $500,000. The maximum liability for a person, other than an employer, is $2 million. The limits do not apply to violations due to willful neglect. In some cases, an HMO, insurance company, or TPA may be held jointly liable with the employer for payment of COBRA excise taxes.

Plan sponsors should note that delegating the COBRA notice duty does not relieve the plan sponsor from liability under ERISA for COBRA notice violations. In view of the potentially hefty fines that could be imposed if it is determined that the plan administrator failed to provide a COBRA notice to a qualified beneficiary, administrators should be conservative in determining whether to provide the notice. For example, if an employee is allegedly terminated for gross misconduct, the plan administrator might consider providing the employee and the covered dependents with a COBRA notice that clearly states (1) that continuation coverage is contingent on a final determination that the employee was not terminated for gross misconduct and (2) that a finding of gross misconduct extinguishes any rights to COBRA continuation coverage.

The IRS does perform COBRA examinations to pursue enforcement measures. A COBRA examination is an inspection of the employer's books and records, including personnel records and correspondence, to determine compliance with the rules. Generally, a COBRA audit arises as a result of a complaint to the IRS by an employee or in the course of a routine field audit of the employer's income tax returns. The IRS has developed an internal procedures manual to perform COBRA audits. Accordingly, if the plan administrator receives notice of a COBRA audit, he or she should consult a tax advisor. Of course, a more proactive approach would be to review the COBRA procedures now to ensure that the company is meeting the COBRA requirements.

§ 7.13 STATE CONTINUATION OF COVERAGE RULES

Many states now have laws similar to COBRA that require employers to offer former employees and other beneficiaries continuation of health coverage. As of December, 2007, 39 states and the District of Columbia had expanded continuation coverage to employers with fewer than 20 employees. Most of these state laws operate independently of COBRA and differ in some way from the federal law. For example, the maximum duration of continuation coverage ranges from six to 36 months, and the cost of coverage is limited to 100 to 115 percent of the plan's premium. Few states specifically discuss how their continuation rules coordinate with the COBRA rules. Accordingly, employers must coordinate their state compliance efforts with their COBRA compliance program. Future court cases bear observation as to how the courts treat the interaction of the federal and state continuation rules.

When evaluating state continuation rules, employers should keep in mind the following general principles:

1. To the extent a state law requires coverage that is inferior to COBRA, if COBRA is applicable, it overrides the state law, as COBRA coverage satisfies the state requirement.

2. To the extent a state law requires coverage that is superior to COBRA, state law controls, because the law provides greater rights to beneficiaries.

3. In the event that a state has no continuation requirements, the COBRA rules apply.

§ 7.14 CONCLUSION

COBRA legislation has been in effect for a number of years now, and many cases have come to trial in which employees, their dependents, or the executors of the estates of former employees have sued employers for COBRA coverage. A high percentage of the cases have been settled in favor of the employee or beneficiary. To reduce or avoid potential litigation, an employer should take care to review all COBRA compliance procedures on a regular basis. In addition, if a TPA or insurance company handles the COBRA administration, the employer should review the TPA's procedures because ultimate responsibility for COBRA compliance is the employer's. Of tantamount importance is that employers and plan administrators carefully follow all employee and dependent COBRA notification procedures to the letter.

Exhibit 7.1
Summary of COBRA Notice Requirements

Notice	When Due	Who Sends	Who Receives	An Example
Initial Notice for a new plan	When group health plan becomes covered by COBRA	Employer	All participants	*www.dol.gov/ebsa/model-generalnotice.doc*
Initial Notice for a new participant	Within 90 days of the date a new participant and spouse are first covered under the plan	Employer	Employee; separate notice to spouse/children if they reside at different address	*www.dol.gov/ebsa/model-generalnotice.doc*
Employer Notice of Qualifying Event Termination, reduction in hours, death, employer's bankruptcy	Within 30 days of qualifying event	Employer	Plan Administrator, if there is one	Exhibit 7.2
Employee Notice of Qualifying Event Divorce, legal separation, loss of dependent child status, second qualifying event while covered under COBRA	Within 60 days of qualifying event	Employee	Employer, which then must notify the Plan Administrator, if there is one	Exhibit 7.3
COBRA Election Notice, if employer is plan administrator and qualifying event is listed under Employer Notice of Qualifying Event (above)	Within 44 days of qualifying event	Employer	Qualified beneficiary	*www.dol.gov/ebsa/model-electionnotice.doc*
COBRA Election Notice, if plan administrator is not employer	Within 14 days of receipt of Employer Notice of Qualifying Event	Plan Administrator	Qualified Beneficiary	*www.dol.gov/ebsa/modelelectionnotice.doc*

Exhibit 7.1   Mandated Benefits: 2009 Compliance Guide

Exhibit 7.1 (cont'd)
Summary of COBRA Notice Requirements

Notice	When Due	Who Sends	Who Receives	An Example
COBRA Election	The later of 60 days of date of COBRA Election Notice or date of loss of group health plan coverage	Qualified Beneficiary	Employer or Plan Administrator*	Included in model Election Notice (see above)
Notice of Unavailability	Within the same time frames required for COBRA Election Notice	Employer or Plan Administrator*	Employee, Dependent, or Qualified Beneficiary	Exhibit 7.4
Notice of Termination of qualified beneficiary from COBRA coverage, if coverage ends prior to maximum period of coverage	As soon as practical once it has been determined that coverage will be, or was, lost	Employer or Plan Administrator*	Qualified Beneficiary	Exhibit 7.5
Notice of Termination of group health plan	On timely basis	Employer or Plan Administrator*	Qualified Beneficiary	Exhibit 7.5
Notice of Termination of qualified beneficiary from COBRA coverage at end of maximum coverage period	Optional; no time requirements	Employer or Plan Administrator*	Qualified Beneficiary	No
Conversion Notice	The earlier of within 180 days before the anticipated termination date or immediately upon termination	Employer	Qualified Beneficiary	No

*If the plan is a multiemployer plan, the plan administrator is responsible. If the plan is a single employer plan, generally the employer is responsible. These functions/responsibilities may be delegated to a third-party administrator (TPA); however this should be verified by the contract for services between the employer and the TPA.

Exhibit 7.2
Sample Notice of Qualifying Event from Employer to Plan Administrator

[To Be Provided to Plan Administrator Upon Covered Employee's Death, Termination of Employment, Reduction in Hours of Employment, or Medicare Enrollment]

[Date]

Plan Administrator

_____ Group Health Plan

[Address]

Re: [Name and Identification (Social Security) Number of Covered Employee]

Dear [Plan Administrator]:

Please be advised that, on [insert date], the above named covered employee [died] [terminated employment (other than due to gross misconduct)] [reduced his/her hours of employment] [became enrolled in the Medicare program]. As a result, coverage under the _____ Group Health Plan for [the employee and/or the employee's spouse and/or dependent children [insert name(s), if applicable] will terminate [terminated] on [insert date].

In view of the above, as required under COBRA, please send a notice of COBRA continuation coverage rights and a COBRA election form to the above-named individual(s), who is (are) [a] qualified beneficiary(ies) under COBRA, within 14 days of the date that you receive this notice.

Sincerely,

[Employer]

Exhibit 7.3   Mandated Benefits: 2009 Compliance Guide

Exhibit 7.3
Sample Notice of Qualifying Event from Employee to Employer/Plan Administrator*

If you believe you have experienced a life event that would qualify you (or a covered dependent) to COBRA continuation coverage, complete this form and attach appropriate documentation of the event. **This form must be received (or postmarked, if mailed) by the** [*Insert name or title*] **no later than 60 days** from the date of the potential qualifying event indicated below. If this notice is not received within that time, no continuation coverage will be provided. Return the form to:

[Insert name, title, and address of contact person at Employer/Plan Administrator]

I hereby inform the [*Insert name of plan*] group health plan of a life event that may be a qualifying event under COBRA and may qualify me and/or my eligible dependents for COBRA continuation coverage.

Employee (or former employee) name: _____

Address to which COBRA Notice should be sent: _____

_____

Date of potential qualifying event:_____

Qualifying event (check all that apply):
- ☐ Divorce or legal separation
- ☐ Loss of status as a dependent child due to (check one):
  - ☐ Marriage　　　　　　　☐ Attainment of age limit
  - ☐ Loss of student status　　☐ Change in custody
- ☐ Individual on COBRA; request coverage for new child due to birth or adoption

Extension of continuation coverage for disability or second qualifying event (check all that apply):
- ☐ Disabled per Social Security Administration (attach copy of SSA letter of disability determination)
- ☐ Death of former employee on COBRA (attach copy of death certificate)
- ☐ Former employee on COBRA entitled to Medicare
- ☐ Divorce of legal separation (attach final judgment of dissolution of marriage)
- ☐ Loss of status as a dependent child due to (check one):
  - ☐ Marriage　　　　　　　☐ Attainment of age limit
  - ☐ Loss of student status　　☐ Change in custody

Please provide the information below on each individual who may be affected by the qualifying event:

Name(s), including (former) Employee	Date of Birth	Social Security Number	Gender
_____	_____	_____	____
_____	_____	_____	____
_____	_____	_____	____
_____	_____	_____	____

I hereby certify that all of the above information is true and accurate, to the best of my knowledge.

_____　　　_____

Signature　　　　　　　　　　　　　　　　　　　　Date

* To be provided to employer/Plan Administrator upon covered employee's divorce, legal separation, dependent's loss of covered status, extension of coverage due to disability, or second qualifying event.

Exhibit 7.4
Sample Notice of Unavailability of COBRA Continuation Coverage*

[*Insert date*]

To: _____

This notice is to inform you that we received your request for continuation of health care coverage or extension of your COBRA continuation coverage on [*Insert date*].

We have reviewed your request and determined that you are not eligible for the coverage you have requested due to the following reason:

☐ You failed to provide notice of the event within 60 days of the event.

☐ Your divorce from the covered employee is not yet finalized.

☐ You did not lose dependent child status under our Plan.

☐ You did not experience a second qualifying event while on COBRA continuation coverage, because the event of which you provided notice would not have caused a loss of coverage under the Plan.

☐ You did not provide notice of the determination that you were disabled within 60 days of the date the Social Security Administration made that determination.

☐ The Social Security Administration's determination was that you became disabled more than 60 days after beginning your COBRA continuation coverage.

☐ The notice of the Social Security Administration's determination of your disability does not confirm that the disability has continued through the entire period of your original COBRA continuation coverage.

☐ You failed to provide documentation of the event for which you are requesting continuation coverage/ extended continuation coverage.

☐ Other: _____

If you disagree with this decision (that COBRA is unavailable for the individual(s) named above), you may request that we reconsider our decision by filing a written appeal as follows:

1. Explain, in writing, why you believe COBRA continuation coverage should be available for the named individual(s). Provide all documentation that you believe is applicable to this situation and would provide us with additional information in considering this appeal. Include the names and addresses of all individuals that you believe should receive COBRA continuation coverage.

2. Mail the written explanation and all support documentation to: [*Insert name, title and address of contact person*].

Exhibit 7.4   Mandated Benefits: 2009 Compliance Guide

Exhibit 7.4 (cont'd)

We will respond within 14 days of our receipt of your written appeal.

If any of the individuals named in this notice do not reside with you, please notify us immediately of their address and phone number so that we may provide them with a copy of this notice.

If you have questions about this notice and its determination that you do not have rights to COBRA continuation coverage or extended COBRA continuation coverage, contact [*Insert name, title, address, and phone number of contact person*].

*To be provided to employee when employer or Plan Administrator determines that employee is not eligible for COBRA coverage.

Exhibit 7.5
Sample Notice of Termination of COBRA Continuation Coverage

[*Insert date*]

To: _____

This notice is provided to inform you that your COBRA continuation coverage terminated or will terminate before the maximum period of coverage ends as of [*Insert date*] due to (check appropriate box):

☐ Failure to make payment for continuation coverage on time or within applicable grace periods

☐ [*Insert name of employer*] (and all companies within its control groups) are no longer providing group health coverage to any of its (or their) employees

☐ You became covered, after electing this COBRA continuation coverage, by another group health plan that does not impose any pre-existing condition exclusion for a pre-existing condition that you have

☐ You became entitled to Medicare benefits after electing this COBRA continuation coverage

☐ The final determination of the Social Security Administration that the disability by which you had extended COBRA continuation coverage no longer disables the formerly disabled individual

☐ An event that would cause termination of coverage of a participant or beneficiary who was not receiving continuation coverage (e.g., fraud)

☐ Other: _____

_____

_____

[*Include, if applicable*]: You may have the right to convert your coverage to an individual policy under the insurance policy's conversion coverage. If you would like to do so, please contact [*Insert name of person or department of insurance company*] at [*Insert address and phone number*].

If you disagree with this decision (that COBRA should be terminated early for the individual(s) named above), you may request that we reconsider our decision by filing a written appeal as follows:

1. Explain, in writing, why you believe COBRA continuation coverage should not be terminated early for the named individual(s). Provide all documentation that you believe is applicable to this situation and would provide us with additional information in considering this appeal. Include the names and addresses of all individuals that you believe should continue to receive COBRA continuation coverage.

2. Mail the written explanation and all support documentation to: [*Insert name, title and address of contact person*].

We will respond within 14 days of our receipt of your written appeal.

Exhibit 7.5   Mandated Benefits: 2009 Compliance Guide

If any of the individuals named in this notice do not reside with you, please notify us immediately of their address and phone number so that we may provide them with a copy of this notice.

If you have questions about this notice and its determination that your COBRA continuation coverage will terminate prior to the maximum COBRA continuation period, you should contact [*Insert name or title of contact person at employer or the name of the Plan Administrator, telephone number and address*].

Chapter 8
Pensions and Other Savings Plans

§ 8.01   AUDIT QUESTIONS

1. If there are more than 100 participants in the retirement benefits plan, does the company have the plan audited annually?

2. Does the company annually file a Form 5500 for its benefit plan?

3. Does the company annually test both employee elective deferrals (pretax and Roth) and employee after-tax contributions for nondiscrimination?

4. Does the plan monitor participants nearing or over age 70 to prepare and calculate required minimum distributions?

5. Does each employee have a copy of the summary plan description of each plan that is sponsored?

6. Is the summary plan description current?

7. Does each participant in a participant directed individual account plan receive a statement of benefits at least quarterly?

8. Does the company deposit employee contributions to the plan within no more than seven days of the payroll date?

9. Do the company's plan fiduciaries understand their personal liability for the operation of the plan and have a due diligence process in place to manage that liability?

Note: Consistent "yes" answers to the above questions suggest that the organization is applying effective management practices and/or complying with federal regulations. "No" answers indicate that problem areas exist and should be addressed immediately.

Companies are not obligated by federal law to provide employees with retirement plans. However, more than half of all employers contribute to some sort of retirement plan for their employees. One of the most popular fringe benefits is a retirement plan in which the company places funds in trust on behalf of its employees, to pay retirement benefits at some point in the future. Retirement plans are advantageous because they add to employees' compensation in a tax-favored manner and can be a means of forced savings for employees.

§ 8.02   THE EMPLOYEE RETIREMENT INCOME SECURITY ACT

Because of misappropriations and mishandling of pension plan funds in the past, in 1974, Congress passed the Employee Retirement Income Security Act (ERISA). ERISA defines a pension plan as any plan, fund, or program established or maintained by an employer or an employee organization, or both, that provides retirement income to employees or results in the deferral of income by employees for periods extending to the termination of covered employment or beyond, regardless of the method of calculating or distributing benefits under the plan. In general, all pension plans are subject to ERISA.

Although ERISA does not require employers to establish pension plans, it exercises certain controls over plans that are established. For example, ERISA requires that employers offer qualified retirement plans to employees on a nondiscriminatory basis and imposes vesting rules and limitations on the amount of contributions employers may make.

Under ERISA, the term *pension plan* (in contrast to *welfare plan*) includes both defined benefit plans and defined contribution plans, both qualified and, in some cases where the program is not carefully designed or operated, nonqualified.

The following are exempt from ERISA's requirements:

- Government plans

- Church plans that do not elect coverage

- Plans established to comply with workers' compensation or unemployment or disability insurance laws

- Plans primarily for nonresident aliens

- Unfunded excess benefit plans

- Certain tax-sheltered annuities, which are covered by special tax rules

The U.S. Department of Labor (DOL) refers to nonqualified plans that are maintained solely for a select group of management or highly compensated employees (HCEs) as *top hat plans*. They generally are exempt from ERISA operational requirements and are able to use an alternative method of compliance with ERISA reporting requirements.

A deferred compensation retirement plan may be qualified or nonqualified. As discussed later in this chapter, a plan is qualified if it is designed and operated within the rules of Section 401(a) of the Internal Revenue Code (Code) and ERISA, if applicable. A qualified plan is tax-deductible to the employer and nontaxable to the employee, while certain Internal Revenue Service (IRS) and DOL rules apply. When benefits are later distributed, they are taxable to the employee, without further deduction to the employer. A nonqualified plan is not subject to all the same ERISA and Code rules, but it is no less legal. It must satisfy certain other requirements to meet the goals of the employer and the plan's participants.

The Pension Protection Act (PPA) of 2006 makes the most significant changes to pension plan design and operation since the enactment of ERISA. Throughout this chapter, significant changes made by the PPA are noted in each appropriate section. In addition, a general discussion of the PPA is included at the end of **Section 8.05** and **Section 8.06**. The Department of Labor provides extensive information on the PPA on its Web site: *http://www.dol.gov/ebsa/pensionreform.html*. Similarly, the IRS has a Web site devoted to the PPA: *http://www.irs.gov/retirement/article/0,,id=165131,00.html*.

§ 8.03 NONQUALIFIED PLANS

Typically, a *nonqualified deferred compensation (pension and savings) plan* is an unfunded and unsecured promise by an employer to pay compensation at some future date for current services performed by its employees. Usually, an employer will use a nonqualified plan to provide supplemental retirement benefits to its executives and owners. Many plans provide that benefits are not available to the employee until retirement, death, or disability. Generally, these benefits are paid from the employer's general assets.

Nonqualified plans are generally designed in one of two ways:

1. As an excess benefit plan, which provides benefits in excess of the maximum contributions permitted under a qualified plan and which is entirely exempt from ERISA; or

2. As a top-hat plan, eligible for alternative ERISA reporting and disclosure rules, which provides benefits for a select group of management or highly compensated employees

Two tax principles are used to determine whether a nonqualified plan allows an employee to defer taxation until he or she actually receives the money:

1. *The economic benefit doctrine.* This principle states that a transfer of property occurs when a person acquires a beneficial ownership interest in the property.

2. *The constructive receipt doctrine.* This principle states that an employee is taxed on the amounts deferred on the first date that the employee could access the funds without a substantial risk of forfeiture or other substantial restriction.

The employer is not allowed a tax deduction for nonqualified plans until the employee is taxed on the benefits. Nonqualified plans avoid some of the requirements imposed on qualified plans by ERISA, such as nondiscrimination, funding, and vesting; however, the arrangements are still subject to limited reporting and disclosure requirements and other than those plans which meet the requirements of Code Section 457(b), these plans must meet the strict form and administration rules of Code Section 409A. See **Chapter 27** for more information on nonqualified deferred compensation plans.

§ 8.04   QUALIFIED PLANS

[A]   General Qualification Requirements

Qualified plans must meet the list of requirements in Code Section 401(a) and other related sections, underlying regulations, and other rules established by law, such as the rest of ERISA.

Every qualified retirement plan must be established and maintained according to a written plan, and, except in certain situations, all plan assets must be held in trust by one or more trustees. If the assets are not held in a trust, they must be held in an insurance contract or a custodial account. The law does not require a retirement plan to obtain advance IRS approval. However, because of the complex rules governing qualified plans, and in view of the extreme importance of being certain that the plan meets statutory and administrative tests, it is highly advisable to ask the IRS for a specific ruling that the plan is qualified. Such a ruling is known as a *determination letter*.

Under the IRS's self-correction program (SCP), offered as part of the Employee Plans Compliance Resolution System (EPCRS), a plan must have either a determination letter or it must be entitled to rely on an IRS opinion letter issued to a prototype or volume submitter plan sponsor before it may take advantage of the program. For this reason, an employer that adopts an individually designed plan such as a cash balance plan is wise to file for a determination letter from the IRS when it initially adopts, amends, restates, or terminates the plan. A determination letter generally simplifies any IRS or DOL plan audit.

Banks, insurance companies, and other entities (such as law and accounting firms) are permitted to offer master, prototype and volume submitter plans—plans that have received IRS approval as being tax-qualified. Master, prototype and volume submitter plans contain standard provisions for many aspects of the plan, such as definitions, type of administration, and termination language.

Employers have limited options when choosing other features of the master or prototype plan, such as eligibility and vesting provisions, amount of contributions or benefits, and methods of payment of benefits. Many employers adopt standardized prototypes with the belief that such a plan will always be automatically qualified in form. This is not always the case, as the IRS opinion letter with respect to a standardized plan will not apply if the employer maintains more than one plan or if another company in the same controlled group maintains a separate plan. Nonstandardized prototypes and volume submitter plans offer employers more plan design options than standardized prototypes. However, adopters of such plans can rely on the prototype or volume submitter plan's opinion letter only if the employer (1) adopts a plan that is identical to the approved plan; and (2) chooses only options permitted under the terms of the approved plan. Even then, an employer will not be able to rely on a favorable opinion letter issued to the prototype in areas of coverage, participation, discrimination, or compensation definition requirements unless fail-safe or safe harbor selections are made in the adoption of the plan. Employers adopting a nonstandardized or volume submitter plan should obtain their own determination letters if they cannot rely on the preapproved plan's opinion letter. The use of a master, prototype or volume submitter plan document can be a less expensive method of implementing a qualified plan. The alternative is an individually designed and drafted custom plan.

The following rules govern qualified plans:

- Taxation of earnings on the amounts set aside is delayed until retirement payments are made.

- Employers are entitled to deduct contributions paid within certain dollar limits.

- Qualified plans may be designed to coordinate the employer's portion of Social Security contributions with plan contributions or benefits, thereby providing greater benefits to highly paid employees without disqualifying a plan as discriminatory.

- Employees are entitled to the amounts in their retirement accounts when they vest in the plan. *Cliff vesting* does not offer immediate vesting but provides 100 percent vesting after a specified time. *Graded or graduated vesting* vests employees over a longer period of time, but allows for some vesting each year after a two- or three-year period. While a more rapid vesting schedule than required may be provided by an employer's plan, a slower one may not.

- Plans normally have a trustee or fiduciary whose activities on behalf of the plan are subject to special rules regarding investments and accounting. Specific rules of conduct for fiduciaries and trustees are included in ERISA Section 404. The PPA amended certain plan fiduciary requirements. A good summary and discussion of fiduciary responsibility can be found online at *www.dol.gov/ebsa/publications/fiduciaryresponsibility.html*. The DOL has updated this information for the changes under the PPA, but the Web site does give employers general information about fiduciary responsibilities. See **Section 8.04[G]** for more information on fiduciary responsibilities.

- To remain qualified, a plan cannot discriminate in favor of HCEs. Certain employees can be excluded from a qualified plan. They include union employees covered by collective bargaining agreements, employees under age 21, employees with less than one year of service, and nonresident aliens with no earned income in the United States. By design a plan can exclude certain other classes of employees, for example, employees of Division A or hourly paid employees. While design-based exclusions are permissible, the plan must cover a sufficiently broad-based group of employees to remain qualified.

- The tax treatment of distributions from a qualified plan depends on the reason for the distribution and the amount distributed. If specific rules are not met, penalties may apply. For example, participants are generally subject to a 10 percent penalty for distributions received before age 59½.

- Programs permitting loans of plan assets to participants must be authorized and described in written plan documents. Participant loan rules specify the interest rate that can be charged (generally prevailing market rates), the type of collateral that must secure the loan, and any other restrictions such as for financial hardship only.

- Employee benefit plans subject to Title I of ERISA are protected from creditors in an employee's bankruptcy. Similarly, amounts deducted from employees' pay are protected, even if the amounts have not been deposited into a separate trust fund. (The Bankruptcy Abuse Prevention and Consumer Protection Act of 2005 (BAPCPA), enhanced the bankruptcy protections under ERISA.)

Qualified plans may be complex to establish and administer because of the many reporting requirements, discrimination and disclosure rules, and applicable dollar thresholds. Plan administrators, for example, must consider the following:

- A qualified plan requires the establishment of a funding vehicle such as a separate trust account owned by the plan and not the employer to hold the retirement funds.

- The qualified plan may need to be audited annually if it has 100 or more participants on the first day of the plan year.

- A qualified plan must file Form 5500 series reports annually with the DOL, which will forward the information to the IRS.

- Employers with qualified plans must comply with numerous DOL reporting and disclosure rules (e.g., preparing and distributing summary plan descriptions and summary annual reports on a regular basis to each participant).

Most states do not have specific laws regarding retirement plans because state laws are generally preempted by ERISA. Several states, however, have enacted state human rights and age discrimination acts that are not preempted by ERISA and may affect retirement plans. These state laws require that if there are differences in a retirement plan design or benefits based on age, sex, or other characteristics, the plan design may not be used as a subterfuge to violate state discrimination laws. Plans may not be designed to provide lesser benefits to any group on account of age, sex, or other protected classification.

Tax laws relating to qualified retirement plans change often. Therefore, before establishing or changing the company's retirement plan, employers and plan sponsors should contact an attorney and a qualified plan tax specialist.

[B] Types of Qualified Plans

Qualified retirement plans fall into two basic categories:

1. *Defined benefit plan.* A defined benefit plan promises specific benefits in specific circumstances (e.g., retirement or disability). Benefits are not necessarily the same for all participants in the plan. To determine how much employees or their beneficiaries would receive, a defined benefit plan typically uses a formula relating benefits to years of service and (usually) to the employees' salaries. Trust fund contributions are determined on an actuarial basis according to the expectations of benefits payable in the future.

2. *Defined contribution plan.* A defined contribution plan maintains individual accounts to which it allocates the employer's contributions, if any are made or required to be made, along with any employee contributions. The employee is entitled to the vested portion of the value of his or her account upon termination of employment, though the plan may delay payment until retirement age. The plan is funded through the accumulation of contributions made on behalf of participating employees, each of whom must have an individual account.

Frequently, larger employers (i.e., those with several thousand employees) sponsor defined benefit pension plans. If plan assets perform well, a defined benefit plan can offer substantial retirement benefits to long-term employees at relatively low cost to the employer. Such a plan can do so because its funding takes into account future earnings on trust assets and employee turnover. Under a defined benefit plan, employees with a short employment history may receive fairly low or no plan benefits, but employees with long service records enjoy a substantial degree of postretirement financial security. Their security, in part, arises from the extent to which ERISA has focused on regulating defined benefit plans.

In addition to requiring that most defined benefit plans participate in the Pension Benefit Guaranty Corporation insurance program, ERISA mandates that defined benefit plans satisfy rigorous funding requirements. ERISA also limits an employer's ability to reduce past benefits or future benefit accruals or to terminate an underfunded defined benefit plan.

ERISA's limitations on an employer's control over plan funding costs, coupled with the complexity of defined benefit plans, have caused most employers to shift their focus to defined contribution plans. Many such plans, also called profit-sharing or 401(k) plans, are funded with discretionary employer contributions and, sometimes, employee contributions. Under certain circumstances, employers may implement a type of defined contribution plan with a more fixed contribution obligation, popularly known as a *money purchase plan* or a *target benefit plan.*

[C] Coverage Requirements

To ensure that the tax advantages granted to qualified retirement plans benefit employees in general (rather than solely owners, officers, shareholders, or HCEs), ERISA established strict standards for coverage of employees. Under the minimum coverage provisions, plans must satisfy one of the following coverage tests:

- *Ratio test.* The percentage of non-highly compensated employees (NHCEs) must be at least 70 percent of the percentage of HCEs covered.

- *Average benefits test.* The plan must cover a group of employees that meet a nondiscriminatory classification, and the average benefit—measured as a percentage of pay—provided to NHCEs must be at least 70 percent of the average benefit provided to HCEs.

For purposes of these tests, employers may exclude employees who have not met the minimum age and service requirements, nonresident aliens whose compensation is not from U.S. sources, and employees who are members of collective bargaining units if retirement benefits have been bargained for in good faith.

The minimum coverage tests are performed on a controlled-group basis. Therefore, the employees of each entity that is part of a parent-subsidiary, brother-sister, or affiliated service group must be counted for this test. However, this does not mean that all related employers must contribute equivalent amounts to the plan or even participate in the same plan. Suppose that a controlled group exists with a parent and one subsidiary. The parent has 3 HCEs and 40 NHCEs. The subsidiary has 3 HCEs and 10 NHCEs. On a controlled-group basis, there are a total of 6 HCEs and 50 NHCEs. The parent has a plan, the subsidiary does not. The percentage of HCEs covered by the parent's plan would be 50 percent (3 ÷ 6) and the required coverage of NHCEs will be 35 percent (50% × 70%). The plan covers 80 percent of the NHCEs (40 ÷ 50) and easily passes the coverage test. However, if only the subsidiary sponsored a plan, the results would fail as the 20 percent coverage ratio (10 ÷ 50) is less than the required 35 percent.

(See **Exhibit 8.1** for worksheets for testing compliance with the minimum coverage and participation standards.)

[D] Nondiscrimination Standards

Similar to the coverage requirements outlined in the previous section, the IRS nondiscrimination regulations are designed to ensure that qualified retirement plans do not benefit only the owners or other HCEs of an employer. Thus, the nondiscrimination regulations provide that:

- The amount of contributions or benefits provided under the plan must not discriminate in favor of HCEs.

- The benefits, rights, and features of a plan—distribution options, investment alternatives, and plan loan features—must be available on a nondiscriminatory basis.

- Plan amendments and terminations may not have the effect of discriminating in favor of HCEs.

The nondiscrimination requirements can be satisfied by plan design or by the satisfaction of certain objective tests. The regulations outline when plans can be or must be aggregated, disaggregated, or restructured before the nondiscrimination tests are applied.

Unfortunately, the above summary of the discrimination requirements is greatly oversimplified. In its effort to prevent every possible form of discrimination, the IRS has generated hundreds of pages of complex regulations. More than ever, a company should ensure the competency of the individuals involved in the design and administration of its qualified retirement plan.

[E] Highly Compensated Employees

An employee is a highly compensated employee for the 2009 plan year if, at any time during the plan year or the previous plan year, the employee owned more than 5 percent of the employer (a "5 percent owner") or if the employee earned more than $105,000 in annual compensation from the employer in 2008. At the employer's election, the latter group may be limited to the top 20 percent of the workforce, ranked by pay. The $105,000 limit for the 2008 look-back year is an inflation-indexed amount.

For purposes of defining an HCE, compensation includes taxable compensation for services performed and must include salary reduction contributions or elective deferrals to a cafeteria plan, 401(k) cash or deferred arrangement, or tax-sheltered annuity (Code Section 403(b) plan).

It is important to note that former employees can be HCEs for some purposes. For example, an amendment increasing the monthly pension benefit for retirees cannot discriminate in favor of former HCEs.

The family member attribution rules must be applied when determining whether an employee is a 5 percent owner. Thus, an employee's familial relationships may result in that employee also being considered a 5 percent owner, even when he doesn't own 5 percent directly. A common example is where a 100 percent owner of corporation is employing his or her child. The child, while not necessarily owning a part of the business, is an HCE due to his relationship to the 100 percent owner.

A plan must identify and determine the number of the employer's HCEs and NHCEs on a controlled group basis, not by line of business or operating unit. For example, an employer consisting of two divisions (A and B), where each division sponsors its own plan, will need to consider the employees of A when testing Plan B and vice-versa.

If using the top-paid group election, employers may exclude from the active workforce:

- Employees who have not completed six months of service

- Employees who usually work less than 17 hours per week

- Employees who usually work less than six months per year

- Employees who have not reached age 21

- Nonresident aliens with no income from U.S. sources

- Employees covered by a collective bargaining agreement

(See **Exhibit 8.2** for a worksheet for determining who is an HCE.)

[F]   Top-Heavy Plans

In general, plans that primarily benefit *key employees* must meet certain requirements concerning vesting, minimum benefits, or contributions for employees who are not considered key employees.

- *Defined contribution plans* are considered top-heavy if more than 60 percent of the account balances have been accumulated for the benefit of key employees.

- *Defined benefit plans* are considered top-heavy if more than 60 percent of the accrued benefits have been accumulated for the benefit of key employees. To determine if a defined benefit plan is top-heavy, a uniform benefit accrual test is used.

If an employer sponsors both a defined benefit and a defined contribution plan, there are rules defining how to determine top-heavy status on an aggregated basis.

For purposes of the top-heavy rules, key employees are the following:

- Officers of the employer earning more than $150,000 (indexed for inflation).

- A 5 percent owner of the employer.

- A 1 percent owner receiving annual compensation from the employer in excess of $150,000 (not inflation adjusted).

Five percent and 1 percent owners are employees who directly or by attribution own more than 5 percent or 1 percent of the employer. In applying this definition "more than" means more than, so someone who owns exactly 5 percent or 1 percent of an employer is not a 5 percent or 1 percent owner as appropriate.

(See **Exhibit 8.3** for a sample top-heavy test.)

[G]   Fiduciary Responsibilities

ERISA's overriding goal or objective is to provide protection to the interests of retirement plan participants. All other concerns are secondary, so plan sponsors are required to act in the best interest of their plans and participants. ERISA seeks to meet this goal by placing the responsibility for successful plan administration on the fiduciaries of the plan. The DOL has provided assistance to employers and plan sponsors on its Web site in the form of an ERISA Fiduciary Advisor, available at: *http://www.dol.gov/ elaws/ERISAFiduciary.htm.*

[1]   Fiduciary Defined

Under ERISA, a fiduciary is a person who:

- Exercises discretionary authority or control over management of the plan, or exercises any authority or control over the management or disposition of its assets;

- Provides investment advice for a fee or other compensation (direct or indirect) as to any monies or other property of the plan, or has any authority or responsibility to do so;

- Has discretionary authority or discretionary responsibility in the administration of the plan;

- Is named as such by the plan sponsor in the plan document (a "named fiduciary");

- Is a named fiduciary who has been designated as having the authority to carry out certain fiduciary duties and responsibilities (a "designated fiduciary").

A person may be a limited fiduciary if he or she only has the ability to exercise authority and control over only certain aspects of a plan.

[a] Employers

The employer that sponsors the plan is almost always a fiduciary. Many employers think that they have no fiduciary responsibilities (other than a contractual obligation to remit deferrals to the insurer, mutual fund, or trust company that is providing the plan's investment vehicles). Other employers are under the impression that they have delegated all of their fiduciary liability to the service providers associated with the plan. However, most employers retain control over the administration of the plan and the management of assets. Therefore, employers are generally fiduciaries.

[b] Trustees

Trustees, whether corporate or named individuals, will always be fiduciaries. When the trustee is selecting plan investments, it is clear that they are fiduciaries. What has not always been clear is the status of directed-trustees. These trustees take action only at the direction of the participants and the plan administrator. Directed-trustees' primary responsibilities are the safeguarding of plan assets and the following of legal instructions received.

Recently, directed-trustees received a wake-up call from the Enron case. In that case, the court permitted the employee plaintiffs to name a directed-trustee as defendant in a claim for breach of fiduciary duty by permitting so much employer stock in the plan and for not stopping a blackout period that prevented participants from selling stock while its value was falling. The Department of Labor filed a friend of the court brief in the Enron case. The essence of the DOL's brief was that a directed trustee is a fiduciary and as such, it has a fiduciary duty to decide whether it is going to follow a direction provided by another fiduciary.

[c] Corporate Directors and Officers

Corporate directors typically appoint the plan trustee, the named fiduciary, and the plan administrator. Therefore, as the appointing fiduciaries, the directors retain oversight responsibilities in connection with those appointments. Similarly, the employer relative to the administration of the plan often assigns certain corporate officers duties, and to the extent that an officer accepts that assignment, it will be a fiduciary. For example, the directors may assign the company CFO to hire an investment management firm. In this regard, the CFO will have a fiduciary responsibility to conduct the search, selection, and ongoing monitoring process in a prudent fashion.

[d] The Plan Administrator

ERISA contemplates the appointment of a plan administrator. Under ERISA, the primary responsibility of the plan administrator is to administer the plan for the exclusive benefit of the participants. In doing so, the plan administrator will have the power and discretion to construe the terms of the plan and to determine all questions arising in connection with the administration, interpretation, and application of the plan. The plan administrator may be a committee, a named individual, the person holding a named title within the company, or the company itself.

[e] Investment Managers

An investment manager is someone who has the power to manage, acquire, or dispose of plan assets, and who is registered as an investment adviser. An investment manager may also be a bank or an insurance company qualified to perform services described above under the laws of more than one state. An investment manager must acknowledge in writing that it is a plan fiduciary.

[f] Other Investment Advisors

The lack of a written acknowledgment of fiduciary status will not necessarily protect an investment advisor. A person who renders investment advice for a fee or other compensation with respect to plan assets or has the authority or responsibility to do so is a fiduciary. A person renders investment advice for a fee if the person advises on the value of securities or other property or makes recommendations as to the advisability of investing in, purchasing, or selling securities or other property. If the advisor has discretionary authority or control covering the purchase or selling of securities or other property, or provides advice pursuant to an agreement that says such advice will serve as the primary basis for investment decisions and that the person renders individualized advice to the plan based on the particular needs of the plan, he/she will also be a fiduciary.

[g] The Unknowing Fiduciary

It is not necessary that any formal appointment and acceptance process take place for a person to be a fiduciary. All that is necessary is that the person function as a fiduciary by exercising discretionary control over the plan operations or its assets, or, as indicated above, provide investment advice for a fee.

[h] Individuals Who Are Not Fiduciaries

Individuals who perform ministerial functions for an employee benefit plan under the direction of or according to policies determined by others are not fiduciaries. That is because these individuals do not have discretionary authority or exercise discretionary control respecting plan management, the disposition of plan assets, and so on. Prime examples are accountants, attorneys, actuaries, and consultants that provide professional services to the plan or the plan sponsor. However, if these service providers begin to act with discretionary control, then they will be fiduciaries.

- **Participant-Directed Accounts**—Even though an individual account plan may provide that participants may exercise control over the assets of their accounts (direct the investments), any participant that takes advantage of that feature is not a fiduciary.

[i]   Persons Who Cannot Be Fiduciaries

Because the retirement plan system depends largely on the hoped for good conduct of fiduciaries, ERISA is concerned with the moral character of the individuals who serve in a fiduciary role. Accordingly, individuals convicted of certain crimes may not serve as fiduciaries of employee benefit plans. This prohibition lasts for 13 years after the later of the date of the conviction or, if imprisonment is involved, 13 years after the end of imprisonment.

The offenses that preclude an individual from serving as a fiduciary include: robbery, bribery, extortion, embezzlement, fraud, grand larceny, burglary, arson, murder, rape, kidnapping, perjury, assaulting another with intent to kill, a felony violation of federal or state drug laws, certain crimes described in the Investment Company Act of 1940, mail fraud, and acceptance of kickbacks from public works employees.

[2]   Multiple Fiduciaries—Who is Responsible for What?

Many, if not most, plans have more than one fiduciary. The multiple fiduciary scenario calls for an allocation of responsibilities amongst the various parties. The employer is the primary fiduciary. It is the employer, or more specifically the employer through its directors and officers, that selects a plan trustee (or in some cases an insurance provider), defines the terms of the plan, adopts a funding policy and method, chooses an investment provider, and appoints a plan committee to manage the plan. Decisions and appointments that have fiduciary implications include:

- **Trustee**—The employer may select an individual, a group of individuals, or a corporation with trust powers to serve as trustee. In the context of a participant-directed plan, the trustee will typically be a corporation serving as directed-trustee. This means that the trustee is not intending to be responsible for selecting or monitoring the various investment funds that participants may use to direct the investment of their accounts. This also means that the employer has not delegated the responsibility for selecting investment funds.

- **Plan Committee**—The employer may formally, though sometimes informally, select a group of employees to serve as the plan administrator. As such, these employees become responsible for managing the affairs of the plan potentially including the investment selection and retention process.

- **Co-Fiduciaries**—Plan committees are increasingly recognizing that they may not have the ability to manage the investment selection and monitoring process. Lack of knowledge or ability is not a defense for poor decisions. Accordingly, committees often seek outside investment counsel. These outside advisors may take on the duties of preparing investment policy statements, preparing performance monitoring reports, and selecting funds for the plan. When an investment advisor is providing these services, it will be a fiduciary under ERISA.

In this multiple fiduciary scenario, the employer remains the ultimate fiduciary and its board of directors needs to be cognizant of its duties to select appropriate individuals for each task and to monitor their performance.

General business law requires corporations to hold annual meetings to review the affairs of the business, appoint new directors, and so on. Complying with this annual meeting requirement is a sign of good corporate governance. This annual meeting approach of corporate law translates well to the ERISA plan. Each year, the employer should arrange for a trustees meeting. In this meeting, the fiduciaries should review the plan's investment results, the status of the administration of the plan, and any law or regulation changes.

[3] Exclusive Benefit Rule

When dealing with plan assets, fiduciaries must act for the exclusive purpose of providing participants plan benefits and incurring only reasonable expenses in the administration of the plan. This exclusive benefit rule, takes fiduciaries straight to the overriding goal of ERISA, which is to protect employees' retirement and other benefits.

[a] Plan Assets

The exclusive benefit rules refer to plan assets and it is therefore important for a fiduciary to understand what plan assets are and when these assets become plan assets. The issue of what constitutes plan assets is important for two main reasons. First, any individual who handles plan assets is a fiduciary. Second, once an individual becomes a fiduciary, he violates his fiduciary duties if he mishandles plan assets or he knowingly fails to act to prevent another from mishandling plan assets.

Except in the area of participant contributions, ERISA and the regulations do not provide a great deal of definition of the term plan assets. Amounts that employees pay to their employer for benefits, whether through payroll withholding or otherwise, are plan assets at the earliest date on which the employer can reasonably segregate the funds from the employer's general assets. With respect to employee contributions to pension type plans, the absolute latest date that these payments become plan assets and, must, therefore, be paid to the plan, is the 15th business day of the month following the month in which the contributions were withheld or received by the employer. However, no employer should focus its compliance efforts on the 15-day rule. The Department of Labor's enforcement efforts focus on the earliest date standard. Thus, any deposit later than seven days after the amounts were withheld from employees' pay runs the risk of the DOL asserting a fiduciary violation against an employer.

[b] Fees and Expenses

A fiduciary is obliged to ensure that the services provided to the plan are necessary and that the cost of those services is reasonable. The three most common types of fees paid for a plan or by plan participants are:

- Administration Fees including fees for recordkeeping, accounting, auditing, and tax compliance services;

- Investment Fees are usually the largest in terms of dollars of all fees paid by a plan. Typically, Investment Fees are an indirect charge to plan assets (most often expressed in terms of basis points—a percentage with 1 percent equaling 100 basis points); and

- Individual Participant Expenses such as loan and distribution charges.

An employer may pay the fees and expenses of the plan directly or require that the plan (and indirectly the plan participants) pay all fees associated with the plan. Most commonly, it is a combination of the employer and the plan participants bearing the costs of the plan. Employers also have a choice as to what type of service provider they will use to provide services to the plan. Some providers operate in bundled fashion where the provider, in exchange for one fee, provides for or subcontracts out all services necessary for the recordkeeping, investment management, and administration of the plan. Other employers use providers that operate in an unbundled fashion with the employer selecting different providers according to the provider's expertise.

The fees vary depending upon the size of the plan, the internal resources of an employer, and the level of services desired. Fees and expenses are one of several factors for a fiduciary to evaluate in selecting plan service providers. The important considerations are that the fiduciary fully understand the amount and types of fees the plan is paying or may be subject to (e.g., surrender charges) and that the fees are reasonable for the level of service provided.

The fees and expenses paid from plan assets have a direct bearing on the participants' ultimate investment returns. Therefore, the duties of prudence and loyalty (discussed below) require a fiduciary to analyze and monitor fees and expenses closely.

It is the fiduciaries' responsibility to ensure that the plan permits the payment only of proper expenses from plan assets. Certain expenses referred to as "settlor expenses" are the responsibility of the employer. This is a trust law concept that requires the creator of the plan and trust (the settlor) to bear certain creation costs. The method the plan uses for withdrawal of expenses should be communicated to plan participants.

[4] Fiduciary Standards and Duties

ERISA requires that a fiduciary act solely in the interest of the participants and beneficiaries. This "duty of loyalty" requires the fiduciary to be loyal to the participants when faced with any conflict of interest. The fiduciary must carry out that duty with the care, skill, prudence, and diligence under the circumstances then prevailing that a prudent man acting in a like capacity and familiar with such matters would use. In other words, the fiduciary has a "duty of prudence." To avoid the risk of large losses, the fiduciary has a duty to diversify the investments unless it would not be prudent to do so. Fiduciaries of trustee-directed plans often fail to understand this "duty of diversification." Finally, fiduciaries have a "duty to comply with the plan documents" unless it would be inappropriate to do so. These duties of loyalty, prudence, diversification, and compliance with plan documents are the basis for reviewing the decisions of any fiduciary.

Loyalty—Plan investments must be made primarily in the interest of accumulating retirement capital for the participants and beneficiaries of the Plan. A fiduciary must discharge his duties for the exclusive benefit of the plan participants and beneficiaries. This forbids not only the use of plan assets for his own benefit, but also the favoring of a third party over the interests of the plan participants, even when the fiduciary will not benefit from the transaction. This does not mean that an action by the fiduciary can never benefit the employer or another party, but it does mean that the primary reason for the action must be the benefit of the plan participants. Whenever a conflict arises, because the fiduciary also has a duty to another, such as an officer of the employer, then the duty to the plan participants takes precedence. In those cases, the fiduciary should consider seeking the advice of a competent independent party to act as fiduciary to make the decisions involved.

Prudence—Plan investments must be determined, knowledgably, to be prudent and reasonable, regardless of whether the fiduciary has actual knowledge and experience with such investments. Each plan investment must be prudent and reasonably expected to provide a return relative to the risk involved. The fiduciary must make such determinations within the facts and circumstances of the situation, but within a high standard of care of a knowledgeable investor familiar with such matters. Lack of actual knowledge is not enough to excuse the fiduciary from responsibility. As stated in one case: "a pure heart and an empty head are not enough." The fiduciary should seek counsel of knowledgeable investment advice if any doubt arises as to the prudence or reasonability of the investment.

Diversification—Fiduciaries must diversify plan investments to minimize the risk of large losses, unless it is clearly not prudent to do so. There are no specific standards, percentages, dollar amounts, or other bright line tests for diversification. In general, a disproportionate amount of plan assets should not be in any single investment or investment class, based on the facts and circumstances, which change over time. Therefore, the initial investment decision date is not the only time fiduciaries need to review diversification, and plans should monitor relative investment proportions regularly.

Compliance with Plan Documents—Plan investments and other actions must not violate any restrictions or prohibitions in the plan document. Some plan documents do not permit investment in insurance, limit percentages of investment in employer securities, or prohibit certain other types of investments. Even though participants may have the ability to direct the investment of their accounts, fiduciaries must determine that those directions are within any such plan document restrictions or limitations.

[H] Deemed IRAs

EGTRRA introduced the concept of "deemed IRAs" within employer sponsored retirement plans. For plan years that begin after January 1, 2003, qualified employer plans (401(a) qualified plans, 403(a) annuities, 403(b) plans, and governmental 457(b) plans) may allow employees to make voluntary employee contributions to a separate account or annuity under the employer's plan. Such contributions will be deemed IRA or Roth IRA contributions rather than qualified plan contributions, and will not affect qualified plan contribution or benefit limits. Under EGTRRA, deemed IRAs were only authorized until December 31, 2010; however, the PPA made this plan feature permanent.

Issues to consider regarding deemed IRAs are as follows:

- *Trustee/Issuer requirement.* The trustee of an IRA must be a bank or eligible non-bank trustee, or an insurance company must provide an underlying annuity. Qualified employer plans that employ individuals as trustees would need to appoint and pay another entity as trustee or insurer for any deemed IRAs.

- *Added fiduciary responsibility.* Many of the same fiduciary duties that apply to qualified plan assets will apply to deemed IRA assets, including liability for a co-fiduciary breach of responsibility for appointed outside trustees.

- *System issues.* Payroll and plan recordkeeping systems would need to be revised to accommodate deemed IRA contributions.

- *Forms.* Plan sponsors may need or want separate investment and distribution elections and beneficiary forms.

- *Roles and responsibilities.* Responsibility for monitoring the many new IRA contribution compliance and administrative requirements and limits will need to be clearly defined and training provided for those with these responsibilities.

- *Reporting and disclosure.* The contribution activity, investment performance, and annual valuation of the IRA assets must be tracked separately from the assets of the qualified plan, and additional forms for distribution must be provided.

Potential employee advantages include:

- Increased employee retirement savings due to the ease of making additional employee contributions to qualified employer plans (e.g., through payroll deduction)

- Employee familiarity with investment options under the plan

- Single benefit statement that includes both qualified and IRA benefit amounts

- Ability to convert plan distributions to deemed IRAs in the plan

- Additional ERISA protection afforded to deemed IRAs

- Bankruptcy protection of deemed IRAs

Potential advantages for employers include:

- Reduced plan expenses due to additional assets invested in the plan (e.g., potential for lower fees due to increased volume)

- Administrative ease due to using IRA as the default IRA for involuntary cash-outs

Potential employer disadvantages include:

- Likely negative impact of diversion of participants' elective deferrals to deemed IRAs on 401(k) nondiscrimination test results, since the majority of participants that can make deductible IRA contributions will be NHCEs

- Expense and cumbersomeness of increased administrative and reporting requirements

- Additional fiduciary responsibilities for the plan sponsor

The Treasury Regulation applicable to deemed IRAs [69 Fed. Reg. 43735 (July 22, 2004)] clarifies that a qualified employer plan and the deemed IRA are separate entities, and that each will be subject to the rules for that plan under tax law. The guidance explains the tax requirements and fiduciary and insurance implications for offering these accounts.

Although deemed IRAs appear to have numerous potential advantages for employees, they are not widely used. Because participants are not expected to put much of their retirement dollars into deemed IRAs, and plan sponsors are likely to experience additional administrative and reporting costs and added fiduciary exposures, few plan sponsors are expected to choose to add deemed IRAs to their plans.

[I] Automatic Rollover of Distributions

EGTRAA also added new rules requiring the automatic rollover of certain plan distributions. Unless a terminated participant elects a different form of distribution, and if the plan requires involuntary distributions, any vested benefit of $1,000 to $5,000 must be automatically rolled over to an IRA once the new requirements are effective.

The applicable regulations provide fiduciaries with five criteria for safe harbor compliance with the mandatory cash-out rules under Code Section 401(a)(31)(B). The five criteria are as follows:

1. The amount cashed out must exceed $1,000, but may not exceed $5,000.

2. The direct transfer must be to an IRA or annuity contract with a bank, insurance company, financial institution, or other provider of individual retirement plans.

3. The rollover must be invested in investments that:

   a. Are designed to preserve principal and provide a reasonable rate of return (such as money market or stable value funds);

   b. Seek to maintain, over time, the initial dollar amount invested;

   c. Are offered by a state or federally regulated financial institution;

   d. Do not charge fees and expenses that are in excess of those for comparable IRAs established for reasons other than automatic rollover; and

   e. Allow the participant the right to enforce the terms of the IRA agreement once the automatic rollover has taken place.

4. Automatic rollover procedure details must be disclosed to participants (via an SPD or an SMM) before any automatic rollover. The SPD or SMM must disclose the following information:

   a. The plan's automatic rollover requirements, including how the mandatory distribution will be invested;

   b. How the fees and expenses attributable to the deemed IRA will be allocated and

   c. Plan contact information.

5. The plan's fiduciary must not engage in any prohibited transactions in the selection of the individual retirement plan provider or investment products, unless such transactions fall under a statutory or administrative ERISA exemption.

The IRS provided a sample plan amendment to implement these rules. As employer's deadline to adopt a mandatory distribution amendment was the later of (1) the end of the plan year containing March 28, 2005, (2) December 31, 2005, or (3) the due date (including extensions) for the employer's tax year including March 28, 2005.

The Treasury Department is of the opinion that establishing these accounts will not violate the customer identification and verification (CIP) provisions of the Uniting and Strengthening America by Providing Appropriate Tools Required to Intercept and Obstruct Terrorism Act of 2001 (USA PATRIOT Act). The Treasury Department advised the DOL that banks and other financial institutions will not implement their CIP provisions until the IRA account holder contacts the bank to exercise control over the account. State escheat rules may still apply.

If plans do not want to establish automatic rollovers, the plan document must be revised to either eliminate all involuntary distributions, or reduce the involuntary threshold to those accounts with $1,000 or less.

[J] Rollovers to Nonspouse Beneficiaries

The PPA added Section 402(c)(11) to the Code. Beginning in 2007, if a participant in a qualified retirement plan dies leaving his or her accrued benefit under the plan to a nonspouse designated beneficiary, if the plan provides, such a designated beneficiary may be able to roll over the inherited funds into an IRA set up to receive such funds. The rollover must be accomplished by a direct trustee-to-trustee transfer (a "direct rollover"). Amounts rolled over will be non-taxable to the beneficiary in the year of the rollover. These inherited IRAs are subject to the required minimum distribution rules upon the death of a participant and, unless the five-year rule is applicable, benefits will need to commence in the year following the participant's death. Qualified plans are not required to offer a direct rollover of a distribution to a nonspouse designated beneficiary, but may do so. If so, the plan must be amended in writing to allow for such rollovers. This provision of the PPA is effective for rollovers made after December 31, 2006.

[K] Required Minimum Distributions

Code Section 401(a)(9) provides that a participant in a qualified retirement plan must commence taking required minimum distributions (RMDs) for the year in which the participant attains age 70½. If the participant is not a 5 percent owner, RMDs must commence for the year in which the participant retires. Generally, RMDs must begin not later than the April 1 following the year in which the participant attains age 70½ and then must continue each December 31 for each year thereafter. Note that if the first distribution is delayed until April 1 of the following year, two distributions will be required in that calendar year—one for the initial distribution year and one for the second distribution year.

Previously, the IRS issued final regulations that greatly simplified the calculation of RMDs and in most cases significantly reduced the amount that a participant or beneficiary must receive as a distribution to meet the RMD rules. The new regulations generally became effective January 1, 2002.

[1] Required Distributions after Age 70½

Before the new proposed IRS regulations, RMDs were calculated on the basis of the participant's age, the beneficiary's age, and whether the participant had elected at age 70½ to recalculate one or both life expectancies. Beneficiary changes after 70½ also affected the calculation.

The new rules generally use only the participant's age for calculating lifetime distributions and apply the recalculated joint life expectancy of the participant and a beneficiary 10 years younger, regardless of the actual age of the beneficiary. No recalculation decision is involved, and a Uniform Table of life expectancy factors is provided for this purpose.

Exhibit 8.4 contains the Uniform Required Minimum Distribution Table showing the life expectancy factor to be used for computing account balance benefits. The account balance at the beginning of the year is divided by the factor for the participant's age on his or her birthday during the year. A participant whose spouse is more than 10 years younger than the participant and who is the sole beneficiary of the participant's account may use the old joint life expectancy factors set forth in Treasury Regulations Section 1.401(a)(9)-9, Q&A-3, which produce an even smaller required payout.

[2] Required Distributions after Death

Distribution rules have also been simplified for beneficiaries. In general, a designated beneficiary will be able to withdraw the account over his or her remaining life expectancy. The oldest beneficiary, determined as of the end of the calendar year following the year of the participant's death, is the beneficiary whose life expectancy is used for this calculation. The single life expectancy factors found at Treasury Regulations Section 1.401(a)(9), are used to compute the fixed distribution period. Each year the distribution period is reduced by one year. Generally, distributions should begin within one year of the participant's death.

Following are the key points that a plan participant should understand when planning for his or her RMDs:

- Naming a designated beneficiary (whether individual or nonindividual) is critical to taking full advantage of the flexibility of the rules.

- Participants may make new plan distribution decisions that may affect distribution calculations for 2001 and thereafter, regardless of what decisions they may have made previously.

- Immediate qualified plan amendments make it easier for plan participants to take advantage of the new rules.

[L] Plan Asset Investment

Qualified plan assets may be invested in any reasonably prudent and diverse set of investments, such as annuity contracts, life insurance contracts, mutual funds, real estate, or any other type of property. Special tax rules may apply to investments in active business assets or debt-financed purchases, and care should be taken in how investments are made so that the investment is not a prohibited transaction. Beyond that, the investments, in the aggregate, must be sufficiently diverse to provide a reasonable net return for a reasonable assumed investment risk, all with a view to being in the best interest of the plan participants. Few other restrictions exist.

Insurance was the original funding vehicle for pension plans before ERISA, and it is still used in many plans today. However, after expressing dislike of so-called springing cash value life insurance policies for many years and threatening to disallow their use in qualified retirement plans, the IRS released guidance in 2004 on life insurance valuation. The guidance is in four parts; it consists of proposed regulations (26 C.F.R. Part 1 [REG-126967] RIN 1545-BC20), Revenue Procedure 2004-16 [2004-10 I.R.B. 559], Revenue Ruling 2004-20 [2004-10 I.R.B. 546], and Revenue Ruling 2004-21 [2004-10 I.R.B. 544]. While the rules may have a broader effect, the IRS notes that the purpose of this guidance is to stop abuses of life insurance in retirement plans that "do not reflect the underlying economics of the arrangements."

[M]   Reporting and Disclosure Requirements

ERISA reporting and disclosure requirements apply generally to all employee benefit plans, including all qualified retirement plans not otherwise exempt from ERISA.

Annual returns must be filed with the DOL and IRS, which also provide some information to the Pension Benefit Guaranty Corporation (PBGC). These returns are filed as a Form 5500, along with the appropriate schedules. These forms are generally due the end of the seventh month after the end of the plan year, but that due date may be extended by filing a Form 5558, Application for Extension of Time to File Certain Employee Plan Returns, or automatically extended with the extension of the employer's tax return if the plan year and employer tax year are the same. For plan years starting on or after January 1, 2009, the Form 5500 must be filed electronically. To ensure smooth electronic processing, the DOL has issued proposed and final changes to the content of the Form 5500. [71 Fed. Reg. 41,392 (July 21, 2006), 72 Fed. Reg. 64,710 (Nov. 16, 2007), and 72 Fed. Reg. 64,731 (Nov. 16, 2007)] The revisions include creation of a new short form for small plans whose assets are in easy-to-value investments with regulated financial institutions; providing improved information on the funding of defined benefit plans; increased transparency of plan-related fees and expenses; and providing customized information depending on the type of plan for which the Form 5500 is being filed.

Summary plan descriptions (SPDs) must be provided to participants, as well as updates to these SPDs in the form of summaries of material modifications to the plan, as they occur. Plans also must provide participants with summary annual reports (SAR), notice of filings with the IRS, notice of plan termination, and benefit statements. Although benefit statements must be provided to participants upon request, because requests cannot be more often than annual, many employers provide benefit statements annually, without request, to preempt the need to respond to statement requests individually.

Beginning with the 2008 plan year, defined benefit plans will no longer have to provide the SAR to plan participants. Instead, all single-employer plans will be required to issue and distribute a funding notice within 120 days after the close of the plan year (for plans with fewer than 100 employees, the notice can be delayed until the due date of the Form 5500). The notice must include the plan's assets and liabilities for the current year and for the three preceding years; its funded percentage (if less than fully funded); its funding policy and asset allocation; any amendments or other events that materially affect the plan's funding status; the number of active, retired, and deferred vested participants; and other information.

Distribution disclosures required include Form 1099R for the distributions themselves, filed both with the participant and with the IRS, and notices to participants who are receiving distributions that are eligible for rollover of their distribution choices. The plan may provide the notice to a participant as much as 180 days before the annuity starting date. The notice must include a description of the participant's right to defer the distribution and the consequences of failing to defer receipt of a distribution. Details to be included in these disclosures should be discussed with the administrator of the plan or the sponsor's tax advisor.

Other information that must be filed by plans may include the Form 990-T, if a plan has unrelated business income for the plan year; reports to the PBGC of reportable transactions, if and as they occur; premium returns by a defined benefit plan to the PBGC; and termination notices and reports when a defined benefit plan is terminated.

Pension benefit statement requirements under Section 105 of ERISA have been amended under the PPA for both defined contribution and defined benefit plans. For individual account plans (the usual format used for 401(k) plans), the benefit statement must be provided at least once each quarter if participants direct their investments and at least once per year if participants are not permitted to direct their investments. For defined benefit plans, a pension plan statement must be provided at least once every three years. These requirements are effective for plan years beginning after December 31, 2006. As no regulations had been provided by the DOL, guidance in the form of Field Assistance Bulletins, Nos. 2006-03 and 2007-03, were published. In this guidance, the DOL defines good faith compliance as to form of statements, manner of furnishing statements, and dates for furnishing statements.

As to the form of the document, the DOL indicated that the use of multiple documents to provide the required information would be permissible, pending further regulation or guidance. Thus, if one vendor to a plan provides the investment-related account information and the plan administrator provides the vesting information, this will be considered good faith compliance, if the participants and beneficiaries have been furnished notification that explains how and when the information required by Section 105 will be furnished or made available. This notice should be written in a manner calculated to be understood by the average plan participant and provided in advance of the date on which a plan is required to furnish the first pension benefits statement pursuant to the changes to Section 105 under the PPA.

Pension benefit statements can be furnished electronically, as well as in written or other appropriate form to the extent that such form is reasonably accessible to the participant or beneficiary. For example, current benefit statements could be provided on a continuous basis through a secure plan Web site for a participant or beneficiary who has access to the Web site. Any electronic media used to provide pension benefit statements should satisfy the DOL's requirements for distribution of electronically provided notices and material. If a plan provides participants with continuous access to benefit statement information through one or more secure Web sites, the DOL will view this as good faith compliance, provided that participants and beneficiaries have been furnished notification that explains the availability of the required pension benefit statements and how such information can be accessed by the participants and beneficiaries. In addition, the notification must apprise participants of their right to request and obtain, free of charge, a paper version of the pension benefit statement information required under Section 105. This notification should be written in a manner calculated to be understood by the average plan participant, furnished both in advance of the date on which a plan is required to furnish the first pension benefit statement pursuant to Section 105 and annually thereafter.

The DOL indicated in this guidance that plan administrators have 45 days from the end of the period to which the pension benefit statement applies in which to provide the pension benefit statement. For example, if an individual account balance plan that allows participants to direct their investments operates on a calendar year basis, the first pension benefit statement reflecting the first quarter (January 1, 2007 through March 31, 2007) was required to be provided to participants and beneficiaries by no later than May 15, 2007.

On October 12, 2007, the DOL issued Field Assistance Bulletin 2007-03 which provides guidance for non-participant-directed defined contribution plans (such as profit sharing plans). FAB 2007-03 indicates that plan sponsors of these plans have until the due date of their Form 5500 (including extensions) to provide the pension benefit statement.

Investment principles. Section 105 also requires that the pension benefit statement of an individual account plan, that permits participant investment direction include an explanation of the importance of a well-balanced and diversified investment portfolio for the participant's long-term retirement security. The pension benefit statement must include a statement of the risk that holding more than 20 percent of a portfolio in the security of one entity (such as employer securities) may not be adequately diversified. The DOL provided the following model language in its guidance:

> To help achieve long-term retirement security, you should give careful consideration to the benefits of a well-balanced and diversified investment portfolio. Spreading your assets among different types of investments can help you achieve a favorable rate of return, while minimizing your overall risk of losing money. This is because market or other economic conditions that cause one category of assets, or one particular security, to perform very well often cause another asset category, or another particular security, to perform poorly. If you invest more than 20 percent of your retirement savings in any one company or industry, your savings may not be properly diversified. Although diversification is not a guarantee against loss, it is an effective strategy to help you manage investment risk.

> In deciding how to invest your retirement savings, you should take into account all of your assets, including any retirement savings outside of the Plan. No single approach is right for everyone because, among other factors, individuals have different financial goals, different time horizons for meeting their goals, and different tolerances for risk.

> It is also important to periodically review your investment portfolio, your investment objectives, and the investment options under the Plan to help ensure that your retirement savings will meet your retirement goals.

The pension benefit statement is also required to inform participants and beneficiaries in individual account plans that permit participant investment direction of the DOL's Internet Web site for sources of information on individual investing and diversification: *http://www.dol.gov/ebsa/investing.html*.

This is only a brief summary of reporting and disclosure requirements of qualified retirement plans. Because the penalties for any failure or delinquency in reporting are substantial, a full understanding of these requirements is important, and proper procedures should be in place to fulfill these requirements.

Electronic distribution of notices. In July 2005, the IRS and the Treasury Department issued proposed regulations for the electronic distribution of notices and transmittal and receipt of elections to and from plan participants. [Fed. Reg. 40,676 (July 14, 2005)] On October 20, 2006, the final regulations were published. [71 Fed. Reg. 61,877 (October 20, 2006)] The final regulations became effective for notices provided to participants on or after January 1, 2007. Under the final regulations, electronic media include Web sites, e-mail, telephonic systems, and CD-ROMs. The final regulations provide safe harbor guidelines that apply to any notice, election, or similar communication provided to a beneficiary or participant in any of the following qualified retirement plans (certain welfare benefit plans are also included in the proposed regulations):

- Qualified retirement plan

- Annuity contract (described in Code Section 403(a) or 403(b))

- Simplified employee pension plan (described in Code Section 408(k))

- Simple retirement plan (described in Code Section 408(p))

- Eligible governmental plan (described in Code Section 457(b))

The final guidelines pertain to mandatory notices such as eligible rollover notices; notices of plan amendments that reduce or eliminate benefits; notices required by safe-harbor 401(k) plans; cash-out notices; plan loan notices; and notice of spousal consent to waive joint and survivor rule. The final regulations do not pertain to any of the ERISA Title I and Title IV required notices (e.g., summary plan description, summary of material modification, summary annual reports, and so on).

The final regulations require the electronic notices to meet certain requirements. The electronic system must be reasonably designed to:

- Provide the information in a manner no less understandable than if provided on a written paper document.

- Alert the recipient, at the time the applicable notice is provided, to the significance of the information in the notice (including the identification of the subject matter of the notice), and provide any instructions needed to access the notice, in a manner that is as readily understandable and accessible as an applicable notice provided using a written paper document.

- Maintain the electronic notice in a form that is capable of being retained and accurately reproduced for later reference.

The final regulations bring the IRS and Treasury Department's rules on electronic distribution into conformity with the Electronic Signatures in Global and National Commerce Act (E-SIGN). The final regulations allow plan sponsors to choose between complying with the E-SIGN requirements (consumer consent method) and the rules that are substantially similar to the previous retirement plan rules for electronic transmission (the alternative method). Under the consumer consent method, a notice may be provided using an electronic medium after the recipient consents to the electronic delivery of the notice. The alternative method essentially requires that the recipient be effectively able to access the electronic medium and be advised that he or she can request a paper copy at no charge.

[N] Relief for Delinquent Filings

In an effort to encourage reporting compliance, the DOL implemented the Delinquent Filer Voluntary Compliance (DFVC) Program in 1995. The DFVC was modified in 2002 and again in 2006. This program is intended to encourage plan administrators to file past-due Forms 5500 for welfare plans and retirement plans for plan years beginning on or after January 1, 1988. The penalties for filing under the DFVC Program are substantially less than the normal DOL penalties for late filing. The penalties are:

- *For large plans (100 or more participants on the first day of the plan year):*

  — $10 per day, up to a maximum of $2,000 for one annual report filed after its original due date (without regard to any extensions)

  — $4,000 for two or more annual reports filed for one plan in one submission after their original due dates (without regard to any extensions)

- *For small plans (fewer than 100 participants of the first day of the plan year or plans filing under the 80-120 rule):*

  — $10 per day, up to a maximum of $750 for one annual report filed after its original due date (without regard to any extensions)

  — $1,500 for two or more annual reports filed for one plan in one submission after their original due dates (without regard to any extensions).

  — $750 for two or more annual reports filed for one plan of a 501(c)(3) organization in one submission after their original due dates (without regard to any extensions). This includes 403(b) plans. Note, this smaller penalty amount does not apply if, as of the date the plan files under the DFVC Program, there is a delinquent Form 5500 for a plan year during which the plan was a large plan.

The fees listed above are based on the original due date of the Form 5500. When calculating the penalties, the DOL ignores any extensions that are filed on behalf of the plan. For example, a Form 5558 is filed timely for a large plan to extend the Form 5500 due date from July 31 to October 15. However, the Form 5500 isn't filed until November 15. Under the DFVC Program, the penalty is $1,070 ($10 per day, 107 days measured from the July 31 due date). Form 5558 provides no relief since the Form 5500 was not filed by the extended due date.

The IRS and the PBGC do not assess their own penalties against an employer for filing a late annual report under the DFVC Program. Therefore, the DFVC Program is more valuable than ever and should be used anytime a Form 5500 is late or missing for a retirement plan.

[O] Voluntary Correction Programs

In addition to the DFVC program described above, the DOL and IRS offer voluntary correction programs to allow plan sponsors and administrators to correct plan defects and operational errors before agency audits. Use of these self-correcting programs generally allows plan sponsors to save fees and penalties that would apply if the errors were caught during an audit by any of these agencies.

The DOL offers the Voluntary Fiduciary Correction Program (VFCP), which generally deals with delinquent participant contributions and other violations prohibited under ERISA. The VFCP was updated in 2006 and now allows for self-correction of 19 potential errors under ERISA. Violations that may be self-corrected include: delinquent participant contributions, delinquent participant loan repayments, loans with parties in interest and with non-parties in interest, purchase and/or sale of assets by plans to parties in interest, and improper payment of expenses by plan. Persons using the VFCP must fully and accurately correct violations; failure to do so may subject plans to enforcement actions including assessment of civil monetary penalties. Certain VFCP transactions may receive relief from payment of excise taxes. There is no need for plans to consult or negotiate with the Employee Benefits Security Administration (EBSA) to use the VFCP. There are four basic steps in the procedure to use VFCP (described here briefly, they are outlined more fully in the April 19, 2006 Federal Register):

- Identify any violations and determine whether they fall within the transactions covered by the VFCP;

- Follow the process for correcting specific violations (see the *Federal Register* for the details on correcting the violations);

- Calculate and restore any losses or profits with interest, if applicable, and distribute any supplemental benefits to participants; and

- File an application with the appropriate EBSA regional office that includes documentation showing evidence of corrective action taken.

The IRS offers two programs to correct plan errors: the Self Correction Program (SCP) and the Voluntary Correction Program (VCP); both are part of the Employee Plans Compliance Resolution System (EPCRS). It should be noted that failures involving misuse or diversion of plan assets are not eligible for self-correction under any EPCRS program.

Under the SCP, plan errors can be corrected without IRS involvement. There is no notification of IRS, no fees or penalties to the IRS, and any tax benefits are retained by the plan and its participants. Qualified plans, 403(b) plans, SEPs and SIMPLE IRA plans are eligible to correct insignificant failures that are operational in nature. Qualified plans and 403(b) plans are also eligible to correct significant plan failures under the SCP; however a favorable letter from the IRS is required under this situation, but is not required if only insignificant failures are being corrected. Egregious failures are not eligible for correction under the SCP by any plan.

Under the VCP, qualified plans, 403(b) plans, SEPs and SIMPLE IRA plans may correct operational, plan document and demographic failures. Although a favorable letter is not required, generally a fixed fee depending on the size of the plan will be assessed. If there is an egregious failure, a sanction of up to 40 percent of the maximum payment amount will be assessed. Written IRS approval is also required. Further information about the self-correction programs under EPCRS is available at *www.irs.gov/ep*.

§ 8.05 DEFINED BENEFIT PLANS

A defined benefit plan requires an annual employer contribution that is based on an actuarial computation to determine the amount necessary to fund a retirement benefit goal in the future. Defined benefit plans provide a predetermined fixed amount at retirement, based on such factors as the employee's years of service, average earnings during a specific period of time, and age at the time of retirement. The maximum benefit that may be funded (Section 415(b)(1)(A) limit) is limited to the lesser of 100 percent of the participant's highest three-year average compensation or an indexed dollar limit ($185,000 for 2008, $180,000 for 2007, and $175,000 for 2006). The annual contribution is determined by, among other things, the fund's past investment experience and estimated future investment experience. Under a defined benefit plan, the employer bears the risk of loss because the employee is assured of a certain benefit level upon retirement.

Most defined benefit plans are noncontributory (i.e., contributions are provided entirely by the employer). A noncontributory plan is advantageous to employees because they are not required to pay for any of the cost of the benefits and are not taxed currently on the employer's contributions. In a contributory defined benefit plan, employees contribute to the plan with after-tax dollars that are applied toward their ultimate benefit.

Defined benefit plans have the following advantages over other types of pension and savings plans:

- They allow employees to anticipate the level of benefit they will be obtaining and to budget accordingly for their own retirement.

- They allow but do not require the employer to recognize past service when it establishes the plan, thus creating significant benefits for employees whose years of service predate plan formation.

- They allow the employer to anticipate benefits on the basis of the employee's salary level shortly before retirement. Thus, if the employer has an objective to provide a certain standard of living after retirement (e.g., 60 percent of the employee's preretirement income), that level can be anticipated more easily through a defined benefit plan.

- Plan investment gains and losses, not the participant's benefit, affect the company's funding requirement. Thus, employee morale is not adversely affected by poor investment performance in the plan. Further, outstanding investment management reduces the cost to the employer of providing the benefit.

- For an employer with a typical or high employee turnover rate, a defined benefit plan can provide a substantial benefit to long-service employees at a fairly low annual contribution cost.

The disadvantages of defined benefit plans are as follows:

- Plan investment gains reduce the program cost, and unanticipated poor investment performance increases the cost of the program. At the same time, a minimum level of liquid assets must be maintained. This minimum level may hinder investment performance.

- The PBGC insures benefits for employees, but the employer must pay for this insurance. Assuming that a plan is adequately funded, the premium rate is $30 per year per participant. Since the passage of the amendments to the General Agreement on Tariffs and Trade (GATT) in 1993, the rates for a plan that becomes underfunded increase with the level of underfunding on a scale that has no ceiling.

- The employer must obtain annual actuarial valuations, so it may have a higher annual administration charge than with a comparable defined contribution plan.

- The employer must make annual contributions, on a quarterly basis in some cases, regardless of whether it has had a profitable year.

- The unfunded liability for past employee service is reflected on the balance sheet of the employer.

- The actuary determines the annual maximum deductible limit for the benefit provided by the plan. For any year in which the employer tries to fund more than this maximum, the employer will be penalized: no deduction can be taken for the excess contribution, and the employer will be liable for a 10 percent excise tax on this excess amount.

Deciding whether to implement a defined benefit plan or a defined contribution plan is not simple. Many decisions must be made before an employer installs a defined benefit plan. Given the costs and the complex legal and tax issues involved in establishing a defined benefit plan, an employer may find it worthwhile to seek the advice of a consultant or other pension professional.

[A] Minimum Participation Standards

A qualified defined benefit plan must cover the lesser of 50 persons or 40 percent of the eligible workforce. Covering refers to the number of participants who accrue a meaningful benefit under the terms of the plan for the year. IRS guidance indicates that a benefit equal to one-half of a percent of pay is a meaningful benefit.

Plans that do not provide for any current accruals (frozen plans) are not subject to these regulations. Finally, and most important, plans that cover only NHCEs are not subject to these standards. The following example illustrates the rule.

> **Example.** A parent company, P, owns one subsidiary, S. P and S each sponsor separate 401(k) plans that cover all employees of P and S, respectively. P also sponsors a defined benefit plan for its employees. S does not sponsor a defined benefit plan. P has five HCEs and 30 NHCEs. S employs 10 HCEs and 55 NHCEs. For the 2009 plan year all 35 employees of P accrued a benefit in the P defined benefit plan. Combined, P and S employ 100 employees, but only 35 employees accrued a benefit in P's defined benefit plan. P's defined benefit plan fails the rule requiring coverage of 50 employees or 40 percent of the total workforce, whichever is less.

> To correct this situation, P can amend the defined benefit plan to cover a sufficient number of S employees that will permit it to pass the test.

[B] Eligibility for Participation

The first step in designing any employee benefit plan is to decide who will be covered. This decision is particularly important for a defined benefit plan because participation by certain types of employees (older, highly paid, or with longer service) can make the plan very costly to the employer.

The Code and ERISA work together to set certain limits on an employer's discretion with respect to eligibility. The only minimum age restriction that ERISA allows is for excluding employees under the age of 21. Employers can require one year of service with the company before the employee enters the plan (or up to two years if benefits are 100 percent vested immediately). The employee may be required to work at least 1,000 hours during that year for it to count toward plan eligibility. There is no maximum age for entrance into a qualified retirement plan.

Working within these fixed rules, an employer still has some flexibility about which eligible employees are admitted to the plan, as long as the final participant group satisfies the nondiscrimination standards of the Code. The basic rule is that the plan must not discriminate in favor of HCEs. Nor may a plan exclude employees based on age or the employee's status as a less than full-time employee. The IRS will disallow any employee eligibility exclusion that is in effect a disguised age exclusion or requires an employee to work more than 1,000 hours per year to enter the plan.

As discussed above, a defined benefit plan must cover at least 40 percent of the legally eligible employees (age 21, one year of service) or 50 people, whichever is less. In addition, the percentage of NHCEs covered must be 70 percent or more of the percentage of HCEs covered by the plan. If this ratio is not met, the plan may still qualify, but it will have to demonstrate that it covers a nondiscriminatory classification of employees and the benefits provided to NHCEs are, on average, at least 70 percent of the benefit provided to HCEs.

The preceding rules highlight an important point. It is possible to exclude selected groups of employees from the plan. Too many plan sponsors believe that they have no liberty to decide which employees are covered by their qualified retirement plans. However, this is not the case. In the simplest case, if the plan covers everyone who is highly compensated, it could exclude as many as 30 percent of the non-highly compensated and still be a qualified retirement plan. For example, it is common to exclude people who are no longer employed at year-end. Another example is that of excluding the employees of a newly acquired division or an unprofitable operation, while still passing coverage and nondiscrimination rules. These are merely options for consideration, not recommendations for the exclusion of any particular group.

[C] Employee Contributions

One category of pension plans, called *contributory plans,* requires that participants bear a part of the cost. In contrast, the employer pays the entire cost of noncontributory plans.

Membership in contributory plans is usually voluntary; employees must elect to join and authorize the employer to deduct contributions from their pay. In these types of plans, credited service for purposes of determining the amount of a participant's benefit includes only the period of service during which the employee actually made contributions.

Whether a defined benefit plan should be contributory or noncontributory is an important factor in plan design. The advantages of a contributory plan are as follows:

- The employer can provide a better plan for the same cost or the same plan at a lower cost.

- Many employers firmly believe in the psychology that if employees contribute toward the cost of the plan, they will value it more.

The disadvantages of a contributory plan are as follows:

- Employee contributions are not pretax, whereas employer contributions are deductible.

- Contributory plans are unpopular with most employee groups. Furthermore, younger participants may be paying more than the total cost of the benefits they are accruing and thus subsidizing the cost of older employees' benefits.

- Contributory plans are more complicated to administer than noncontributory plans because they require additional records and the payment of refunds with interest, in the event of termination or death.

- Employers may find it difficult to satisfy the Code's new nondiscrimination requirements under these plans.

Because of the disadvantages of contributory plans, for many years the steady trend in defined benefit plans has been toward noncontributory plans. This movement has been accelerated by the growing prevalence of contributory defined contribution plans, such as 401(k) plans and other thrift or savings plans.

Many large employers have converted pension plans to a noncontributory basis and established accompanying thrift or savings plans, which employees have welcomed.

[D] Benefits Formula

Every defined benefit pension plan includes a description of how the benefit is calculated; this is commonly referred to as the *benefits formula*. The formula defines the pension that the employee will receive upon normal retirement, while some corollary of the formula defines benefits payable at other times, such as death, disability, or early retirement. The benefits formula typically includes one or more of the following parameters:

1. *Service factor.* Both employers and employees generally feel that pensions should be based, in part, on years of service because it seems only fair that an employer should provide a larger pension for a participant with 40 years of service than for a participant with five years of service.

2. *Relationship to salary.* Many pension plans base benefits on salary level so that higher-paid employees receive a larger pension. Because the pension benefit replaces pay, higher-paid employees need higher pensions to maintain their previous living standard. Under Section 415 of the Code, a life annuity pension benefit is limited to the lesser of $90,000 or 100 percent of average pay for an employee's three highest consecutive years of pay at Social Security retirement age, with significant reductions in the dollar amount in the event of early retirement. The dollar portion of this limitation is indexed to the cost of living, and, as a result, the maximum benefit has increased to $195,000 for 2009. In addition, for 2009 no more than $245,000 of compensation may be included in calculating benefits. The limitations have somewhat reduced the qualified benefit plan for executives, but many larger employers have added nonqualified plans to avoid penalizing executive groups. The need for nonqualified plans may be reduced after 2001 by the higher benefit limit and higher compensation limit enacted as part of EGTRRA.

3. *Recognition of Social Security benefits.* Social Security retirement benefits provide a level of replacement pay that may be as high as 50 percent for lower-paid employees. Because Social Security weights its benefit formula in favor of lower-paid employees, the percentage of pay replacement is typically much lower for higher-paid employees. Employers may recognize the impact of Social Security retirement coverage indirectly by setting the benefit formula at a lower level, or they can recognize Social Security benefits directly by adjusting the formula to coordinate the two benefits. The Code contains complex *permitted disparity* rules regarding the integration of Social Security benefits and qualified retirement plan benefits.

[1] Two Types of Formulas

Most defined benefit plans include one of two types of benefit formulas, *flat benefits* or *unit benefits*.

1. *Flat benefit formula.* There are two types of flat benefit formulas. One formula provides the same dollar value to all employees, with benefits prorated according to service. For example, any employee who stays with the employer until retirement age, without regard to when he or she was hired, earns the right to $300 per month for life, commencing at age 65. The other formula provides the same percentage of average annual compensation to all employees, prorated on service. For example, the plan might offer 40 percent of pay as a pension benefit. Thus, a $10,000 per year employee earns a $4,000 benefit, while an $80,000 per year employee earns a $32,000 per year benefit.

2. *Unit benefit formula.* The unit benefit formula provides benefits based on a percentage of pay per year of service or a fixed monthly benefit per year of service. For example, an employee might earn

$20 per month for each year of service. Alternatively, he or she might earn 2 percent of pay for each year of service. The number of years counted in the formula may be limited. For example, if the maximum number of years counted was 35, the first plan would provide a maximum benefit of $700 per month, and the second plan would provide a maximum benefit of 70 percent of pay.

Other terms also must be considered in setting a benefit formula. For example, several of the approaches outlined above are based on pay. There are several choices in how this pay is measured, which are discussed later in this chapter. For purposes of the benefit formula, the key variable is the period over which pay is measured.

Career average pay formulas provide the employee with a benefit based on his or her compensation for the current period worked. Thus, if the benefit formula were 40 percent of career average pay, the future benefit would be the sum of 40 percent of the average rate of compensation for each of the years of the employee's working career. However, in an inflationary economy, this formula tends to understate the amount of income that the employee might actually need to live on. Thus, employers often need to increase benefits for aging employees to maintain a comparable standard of living at retirement.

Final average pay formulas provide the employee with a benefit based on an average compensation at retirement age. Thus, these plans provide more certainty that the targeted replacement level for retirement income will be met. Rarely is the benefit based on the last year of work. Instead, most plans use an average (e.g., final three years, final five years, or five highest consecutive years during the last ten years of employment). There is a significant amount of flexibility under these formulas. As noted earlier, the benefit limitations are the lesser of $195,000 (for 2009) or 100 percent of the average pay of the three highest consecutive years. It is rare for any employer to offer a plan at 100 percent of pay, so the percentage is mostly theoretical for non-highly paid employees, and the limitation based on dollar compensation for the period worked applies more often only to the higher-paid group.

Although various combinations of these basic formulas are possible, combinations increase the complexity of the plan, making it harder for employees to understand and for the employer to administer.

[2] Cash Balance Plan Approach

Another formula for providing defined benefits to employees is the *cash balance plan* approach. Under this approach the defined benefit plan describes the participant's benefit in terms of an imaginary account. This reported account is the sum of imaginary allocations for prior plan years provided under an imaginary formula that may resemble a defined contribution plan allocation formula. In addition, this imaginary account is credited with interest on the previously allocated contribution credits, mimicking earnings in a defined contribution plan account. Benefits for the participant are expressed in terms of the present value of the projected value of the credits to the participant's account. The employer is committing to a projected benefit, in terms of a current contribution and a return on that contribution, but the present value may be determined using a different interest rate. The result is that the employer takes on the risk that investment performance will be less than the designed return. Because the contribution credit is determined each year, the benefit is based on career average pay, not final average pay, and more closely matches compensation expense for an employee with the related revenue generated by that employee for each year.

Although a subject of much negative press over the past few years, cash balance plans can provide meaningful benefits for younger employees who remain with the employer for a reasonable number of years. Meanwhile, the employer saves the cost of providing high benefits for older employees and other employees who may have worked for the employer only a short time. These cost savings are often used for enhancing other employee benefits or payments to some workers who may skip additional accruals for several years as the result of a conversion of a more traditional defined benefit plan to a cash balance plan. Negative press is generated when the transition of a plan conversion is not properly communicated to employees and those employees who may feel shortchanged by the conversion are not compensated for the projected reduction in their retirement benefit.

The PPA clarifies the legal standing of cash balance and other hybrid plans on a prospective basis. It validates the basic design of these plans and provides that conversions are valid as long as certain rules are followed. It establishes an age-discrimination standard for all defined benefit plans that clarifies current law under ERISA. The PPA's provisions for cash balance plans are effective prospectively only, that is, for plans adopted or converted after August 17, 2006.

While a cash balance approach may have several budgeting and productivity advantages for your business, the design of such a plan requires careful planning and assessment of overall benefits strategy. Particular care should be exercised if the plan is a conversion of a traditional defined benefit plan, rather than a new part of the total benefit package. Be sure to assemble your full benefits, legal, and administrative team when considering the pros and cons of this plan design.

[3] Coordination with Social Security Benefits

As discussed earlier, employers are permitted to integrate qualified retirement plans with Social Security benefits (i.e., to coordinate benefits or contributions with the employer-provided portion of Social Security benefits). Under prior law, this approach was called *Social Security integration* and that phrase is still used by some. The Code now refers to this approach as *permitted disparity*. This was not just a frivolous name change. It represents a significant change in the manner in which Social Security benefits can be included in the design of a qualified retirement plan. Under the prior Social Security integration, an employer could establish a qualified retirement plan that provided benefits only in excess of the Social Security benefits, thus leaving an employee whose income was below the Social Security level with no benefits from the employer's plan. Under the new permitted disparity, an employer can provide a greater benefit on wages in excess of the Social Security level only if it provides some basic level of benefit based on lower wages.

Thus, since the enactment of permitted disparity, there have been only two permissible means for including Social Security benefits in the design of a defined benefit plan:

1. *Step-rate retirement plans.* A plan can provide two benefit accrual rates for wages above and below some break point. However, the difference between the two rates of benefit accrual cannot exceed the lesser of the base percentage or 0.75 percent per year of service (not to exceed 35 years), subject to various reductions. The base percentage is the percentage of compensation for determining benefits for wages below the break point. For example, a plan could provide a formula of 1 percent per year of service on average base pay (the base percentage) and 1.5 percent per year of service on the excess of average pay. The difference between the two rates is 0.5 percent, which is less than 0.75 percent (the maximum rate) and less than 1 percent (the base rate). The break point for wages above and below the different rates can be some fixed wage level, or it may change with changes in the Social Security wage base.

2. *Offset retirement plans.* These plans typically provide for a projected pension benefit based on average salary and years of service reduced or "offset" by the benefit that the employee is to receive

from Social Security. The maximum offset percentage is the lesser of 0.75 percent, subject to various reductions and, at most, one-half of the gross benefit before the offset is applied. The benefit formula is typically difficult to communicate and administer.

[E] Pay for Pension Purposes

As previously indicated, a large proportion of defined benefit pension plans have pay-related benefit formulas. As pension plans first developed, employers defined pay as base salary or wages. However, this definition discriminates against lower-paid employees by omitting important elements of their compensation, such as overtime and shift differentials. At the same time, it penalizes higher-paid employees by omitting their bonuses, commissions, and incentive awards. As a consequence, many employers have moved to a definition of pay that includes all compensation, or all taxable compensation, which is more acceptable to the IRS. However, beginning in 1989, legislation limited covered compensation to $200,000, indexed for inflation (Section 401(a)(17)/404(l) annual compensation limit). Subsequent legislation reduced this level further. Beginning in 2002, EGTRRA restored the $200,000 limit. The limit is $245,000 for 2009, and is indexed for years thereafter.

For plan purposes, a plan sponsor may exclude certain elements of compensation from the definition of wages. Some exclusions are made for administrative ease, others for design considerations. For example, one acceptable formula under the final IRS regulations is to use wages subject to withholding rather than total compensation. This formula could be easier to administer because it eliminates those minor add backs (e.g., excess group-term life insurance) that are not included in the basic payroll system. From a design perspective, it may be appropriate to eliminate certain forms of incentive compensation. Those awards are frequently made only to HCEs, so they can be eliminated without worry about the nondiscrimination rules. In addition, incentive awards are made to encourage an employee to reach a specific goal. They do not need to be included in compensation for a defined benefit plan, which is usually in place to provide a basic income security package.

[F] Credited Service

Credited service, the yardstick for determining benefits under qualified retirement plans, must be defined with some precision because of its potential impact and complexity. In particular, employers must compute credited service to determine whether an employee is eligible to participate in a qualified plan under ERISA and Code provisions, whether any portion of an employee's benefit is vested, and what benefits have actually accrued to a plan participant.

For eligibility and vesting purposes, credited service is based on the employment year. For benefit accrual purposes, credited service is based on the plan participation year. These periods of service may be defined in terms of *elapsed time* between date of hire and date of termination. Usually, however, these periods are defined in terms of the number of hours of service credited to an employee during a specified computation time frame, generally, 12 consecutive months.

The employer should realize that it has some discretion in measuring a year of service if it counts hours of service. The 1,000-hour rule is a maximum for purposes of determining eligibility and vesting. That is, a plan sponsor can use fewer hours per year, but not more. Thus, an employer that relies heavily on part-time personnel and wants to compensate them for their flexibility could reduce the hour requirement to bring these people into the plan and provide for their vesting in benefits. That is optional. A special rule applies with respect to benefits accrual service. The 1,000-hour rule is most often used for accruing benefits. If an employee has less than 1,000 hours, then no year of service credit is given. However, a plan can provide for a higher number of hours during a 12-month period for a full year's credit, as long as a proportionately partial year's credit is given for periods in which an employee has less than a full year's number of hours. Generally, only very large employers use this system of more than 1,000 hours, because of the additional administration required.

- *Eligibility computation period.* To be eligible to participate in a qualified plan, employees may have to complete one year of service, usually defined as 1,000 hours of work in a 12-consecutive-month period. The initial 12-month computation period, which begins on date of hire, must be designated in the plan. An employee who completes 1,000 hours during this period meets the service requirement. If the employee does not meet the requirement, the plan may designate future 12-consecutive-month computation periods, beginning on the anniversary of the employment date of hire, or change to a 12-month period that coincides with the plan year.

- *Vesting computation period.* Under ERISA and the Code, an employee's accrued benefits derived from employer contributions must be vested under certain statutory schedules based on the employee's years of service. The computation period used to determine whether an employee has a year of service for vesting purposes must be designated in the plan. That vesting computation period may be any consecutive 12-month period, such as the plan year, calendar year, or a year based on an employment date and subsequent anniversaries of that date. An employer may require no more than 1,000 hours of service to earn a vesting year. If the computation period is based on an individual's employment anniversary date, however, the plan's vesting computation periods will not be the same for all employees, which complicates the employer's recordkeeping.

Although not as visible to the employee, the *funding* limits and requirements for *all* benefit formulas, even a flat benefit formula, must take the benefit accrual service of participants into account. An employee can accrue a benefit equal to the percentage of pay earned for the year. For example, assume that the employee enters the plan at age 25, and the benefit is estimated to be $1,000 per month, payable at age 65. That employee has 40 years from entry date to age 65. A typical accrual method would say that each year, he or she will accrue one-fortieth (1/40) of the benefit, or $25. Another accrual method is the 3 percent method. Under that approach, the employee would accrue $30 each year.

The effect of a year of benefit accrual service on the funding requirements will depend upon which accrual method is chosen and how fast the related liability and related contribution obligation are accumulating. Clearly, the selection of a method can get quite technical. In implementing a defined benefit plan, the employer should discuss these issues with an actuary to determine how they might affect costs and benefits.

[G] Vesting

Vested interest is that portion of the employee's accrued benefits in which the employee has a nonforfeitable right. An employee's vested interest typically is expressed as a percentage of accrued benefit.

If a defined benefit plan allows voluntary employee contributions, the employer must credit those contributions to a separate account. Earnings and growth attributable to those contributions also must be credited to that separate account, which must be fully vested at all times.

Benefits based on employer contributions must be fully vested once the employee reaches normal retirement age, as defined by the plan. Employers may choose between two statutory alternatives for vesting before normal retirement age—five-year cliff vesting and seven-year graduated vesting—or provide something more generous.

1. *Five-year cliff vesting.* Benefits derived from employer contributions must be 100 percent vested after five years of service.

2. *Seven-year graduated vesting.* Benefits from employer contributions are vested according to the following schedule:

Years of Service	Nonforfeitable Percentage
3	20%
4	40
5	60
6	80
7 or more	100

Under certain circumstances, other vesting rules apply. If the plan becomes top-heavy, each of the schedules above is accelerated. A top-heavy defined benefit plan is one that primarily benefits key employees (as defined and discussed earlier in this chapter under the ERISA rules). The five-year cliff vesting schedule becomes a three-year cliff vesting schedule. The seven-year graduated schedule is accelerated a year at each level to become a six-year schedule.

If a plan is fully or partially terminated, all affected employees become fully vested in their accrued benefits. In this day and age of mergers and spin-offs, employers need to be aware of the concept of a partial termination. This could happen when an employer takes an action such as spinning off a division, resulting in the termination of 20 percent or more of its employees. In that case, the IRS would probably argue that the employees who were affected must become fully vested.

Although ERISA banned "bad-boy" clauses that caused an employee who was discharged for cause to forfeit his or her entire account balance, a bad-person vesting provision is still an option. Under these rules, a person who has been found to have committed some specific offense can be subjected to the most conservative legal vesting schedule. For example, if a plan vests 20 percent per year of service and an employee is convicted of embezzlement after only three years of service, the delayed vesting schedule could provide for the five-year cliff vesting. The net result would be that this person would lose his or her entire benefit. After five years of service, this person could not be subject to a full forfeiture. This type of provision is difficult to enforce, is not permitted in a prototype plan, and can have unexpected consequences. It is not recommended, except possibly in very limited situations, such as a conviction for a work-related felony.

[H] Other Typical Plan Provisions

Other typical defined benefit plan provisions are discussed in the following subsections.

[1] Early Retirement

A defined benefit pension plan customarily sets a normal retirement age, usually 65, and any retirement before that age is designated early retirement. Generally, early retirement is permitted between the ages of 55 and 65. Either or both normal and early retirement can require a specific period of employment first. The advantage of requiring a specific period of employment is that it precludes accelerated vesting. At age 65, the longest employment period allowed is five years. Early retirement, however, can require any employment period. The early retirement benefit usually consists of the accrued benefit with an actuarial reduction, which allows the employer to provide benefit payments that start earlier and continue for a longer period of time for relatively similar costs. The actuarial reduction is substantial; for example, if the normal retirement age is 65, retirement at age 60 would reduce benefits by approximately 30 to 40 percent, and retirement at age 55 would reduce them by approximately 50 to 60 percent. Note that under EGTRRA, the benefit reduction may not be as significant, because beginning in 2002 the benefit limits will be reduced if a participant begins taking distributions at age 62, rather than at his or her Social Security retirement age. A participant is usually required to have 10 or 15 years of service before being eligible for such early retirement.

[2] Preretirement Death Benefits

ERISA requires that all qualified pension plans include a preretirement survivor annuity benefit in the event of death before retirement. The specific requirements are complex but essentially state that if a participant dies after becoming vested or eligible for early retirement, the plan must provide a lifetime pension to the participant's spouse.

If the participant dies after eligibility for early retirement, the spouse's pension must equal at least the amount that would have been received had the participant retired immediately before the date of death with a 50 percent joint and survivor annuity (JSA) in effect. Under a 50 percent JSA, the participant receives a reduced pension until death, after which the spouse receives 50 percent of the participant's benefit until death.

If the participant is vested but dies before becoming eligible for early retirement, the benefit is based on the assumption that the participant left service on the date of death, survived to the earliest retirement age, retired with a JSA at that age, and then immediately died. The spouse's benefit is then payable from the assumed date of retirement.

[3] Supplemental Death Benefits

In addition to the required spousal benefits, a plan may provide additional benefits in the event of death. These must meet the "incidental" insurance rules. Basically, a plan can provide a supplemental life insurance benefit equal to 100 times the participant's expected retirement benefit. Currently, participants are taxed on the annual insurance value provided.

[4] Postretirement Health Care Benefits

Under a fairly obscure part of the Code, Section 401(h), it is possible for the sponsor of a pension plan to fund postretirement health coverage with currently deductible dollars in a separate 401(h) account under the plan. These nonretirement benefits must be subordinate to the retirement benefit purpose of the overall plan. Therefore, the funding is limited to 25 percent of the contribution required for the pension benefits provided under the plan for the year. Thus, the permissible level of contributions is measured by actual contributions to the plan after the date the medical benefits account is established. Note, however, that even if the plan is fully funded, excess pension assets may be transferred from a defined benefit plan to a Section 401(h) account if the requirements of Code Section 420 for a qualified transfer are satisfied.

[5] Forms of Benefit Payments

Nearly all pension plans contain some provision for the payment of benefits to a spouse after the death of a retired participant. In addition, ERISA requires that qualified pension plans provide a 50 percent JSA as the usual form of benefit for participants who are married at the time of retirement. Participants generally must have the opportunity to elect another type of benefit, but a married participant who elects any benefit other than a qualified JSA must obtain the spouse's written and witnessed consent.

In addition to JSAs, other common types of benefits include period certain and life annuities and lump-sum cash options. Conversion from one form of benefit payment to another is usually calculated so that the value of all options is actuarially equivalent to the value of the benefit in the unreduced standard form of benefit payment provided in the plan. The unreduced form may be an annuity merely for the life of the participant, with no benefit payable after death. If the participant selected a different form of payment, such as the JSA, the plan would pay a reduced benefit to the participant such that the total value of the annuity is equal in actuarial value to the benefit on the unreduced form (i.e., the life annuity). Effectively, the participant is paying for the death benefit coverage with a reduction in his or her own lifetime benefit.

An employer's pension plan might allow participants to choose among the following types of benefits:

- A life annuity, which would provide the largest benefit to the participant for as long as he or she lives

- A 50, 75, 100, or other percentage JSA paying a reduced benefit amount while the participant is alive and 50, 75, or 100 percent of that payment amount to his or her surviving spouse

- Contingent annuitant options, which are similar to JSAs except that the participant can choose the annuitant

- A 5- or 10-year period certain and life annuity, which pays a pension for a given period, regardless of whether the participant is alive, and then continues payment as long as he or she lives

- Modified cash refund benefits, which are an option only if the plan includes employee contributions

A number of plans provide a cash option that allows participants to elect to take a lump sum instead of a schedule of pension payments. Although some experts believe that this option may encourage employees to squander their benefits, others feel that a cash option adds flexibility to a program, permitting rollovers to IRAs, and that denying it would be overly paternalistic.

[I]   Funding

[1]   General Concepts

It is difficult to determine a plan's exact cost at any particular time because the cost depends on many variables related to future events. For instance, the number of current participants who terminate before vesting or die before they are entitled to a death benefit affects the benefits paid (or not paid) under a plan. Consequently, employers must use certain assumptions to determine annual costs and then allocate those costs in some fashion over the period during which the benefits are earned. Under ERISA, the plan's actuary is responsible for advising the employer on this process, which is based on the actuarial cost or funding method and a set of actuarial assumptions that the employer must select.

The actuarial funding method allocates costs over a period of years by projecting into the future the benefit accruals for a group of participants. These projected costs are then discounted back to the present using a set of actuarial assumptions that are related to factors such as mortality, turnover, plan expense, salary growth, morbidity, interest, and assumed retirement age.

The result is the present value of benefits the employer expects to pay. The actuary then subtracts the value of the plan's assets from the present value of future benefits, and the remainder represents the plan's liability for benefits that are not yet funded. The portion of the unfunded liability that relates to future-year accruals is generally allocated to those years, and the portion of unfunded liability that relates to benefits already accrued (past service liability) is amortized over a specified period.

If the assumptions used by the actuary coincide exactly with future experience, the annual costs will meet future obligations. However, no matter how reasonable the actuarial assumptions may be, they almost always differ from actual experience. To reflect this, the cost method has to indicate actuarial gains and losses and then amortize them over a five-year period.

Selecting a funding method and assumptions is not a straightforward process; it requires expert actuarial assistance. During this process, the employer needs to realize that it has choices. Different funding assumptions trigger the recognition of the plan's costs at different times. Some funding methods provide only one contribution amount. Other methods provide a range of allowable contributions. Although these methods can be changed even after they are implemented, the change may require IRS approval.

[2]   Funding Requirements

All pension plans require the plan sponsor to make periodic contributions to the plan. These contributions are based on the plan's funding status and do not vary with the profitability of the plan sponsor. *Fully funded* means that the plan's obligations to pay benefits can all be satisfied by the assets that the plan already has. Generally, a fully-funded plan will not have a minimum required contribution for a plan year, though it may have an actuarially determined permitted deductible contribution amount.

To the extent that a plan is not fully funded, contributions are required. An actuary calculates the minimum required and maximum deductible amount of the contribution. Minimum contributions must be made quarterly. If the plan sponsor chooses to deposit more than the minimum required contribution, the sponsor can make that deposit at any time through the due date of the plan sponsor's income tax return, including extensions. The range between the minimum and maximum funding amounts will depend on the funding method selected.

The PPA requires most plans to become 100 percent funded over a seven-year period. In effect, the annual minimum contribution will be the normal cost (the cost of benefits accruing in the current year), plus an amount to amortize any funding shortfall over seven years. The transition from the pre-PPA 90 percent funded target to 100 percent is gradual, beginning in 2008. Avoiding a funding "shortfall" for the transition years will require a funded percentage of 92 percent for 2008, 94 percent for 2009, and 96 percent for 2010. However, if a plan has a deficit reduction contribution (DRC) for the 2007 plan year, this graded transition to 100 percent is not available. As an example, if a plan is 92 percent funded in 2008 (and did not have a DRC in 2007), it will be treated as not having a shortfall, and the minimum contribution for 2008 will be equal to the plan's normal cost. However, if the plan is 91 percent funded, the minimum contribution for 2008 will be the plan's normal cost plus a shortfall amortization (over seven years) based on the difference between 100 percent of the plan's liability and the value of plan assets.

"At-risk" plans will have accelerated contribution requirements. A plan is generally considered at-risk if it is 65 percent funded in 2008, 70 percent funded in 2009, 75 percent funded in 2010 or 80 percent funded in 2011. At-risk plans will be required to use a more conservative measurement of liability. Depending on the plan's funded percentage, at-risk plans may have additional restrictions, such as disallowing the use of credit balances, limitations on the ability to pay lump-sum benefits, and inability to amend the plan to increase benefits. In severe cases (less than 60 percent funded), a plan may be required to temporarily cease all benefit accruals. Plans with less than 500 participants (on a controlled group basis) will be exempt from the at-risk rules.

Failure to deposit contributions within eight and one-half months of year-end results in a nondeductible excise tax of 10 percent. Failure to make the appropriate quarterly deposits brings an interest penalty.

If an employer faces a severe financial hardship, it can request a waiver of the funding requirement. This is not a true waiver because the amount still must be deposited; the deposit is simply deferred. The employer can obtain this waiver by written request to the IRS.

The actuary also determines the annual maximum deductible limit for the benefit provided by the plan. For any year in which the employer tries to fund more than this maximum, the employer will be penalized: no deduction can be taken for the excess contribution, and the employer will be liable for a 10 percent excise tax on this excess amount. The PPA significantly increased the maximum deductible limits for 2006 and later. For 2006 and 2007, the deductible contribution limit is increased to 150 percent of current liability, as compared to the pre-PPA 100 percent of current liability limit. For 2008 and later, plans are permitted to deduct up to 150 percent of the target liability plus the additional liability attributable to projected pay increases.

The combined plan deductible limit for plan sponsor contributions to defined benefit and defined contribution plans has also been changed. The overall limit in such cases has been 25 percent of employee compensation (or the minimum required defined benefit plan contribution, if higher). Beginning in 2006, contributions to a defined contribution plan are only counted against the limit to the extent that they exceed 6 percent of compensation. Beginning in 2008, the combined plan limit is changed to exclude contributions to defined benefit plans that are insured by the PBGC.

[J] Accounting for Defined Benefit Pension Plans

A sponsor of a defined benefit pension plan becomes subject to Statements of Financial Accounting Standards Nos. 87, 88, and 106 as amended by No. 132 (FAS 87, FAS 88 and FAS 106). These cover the operation and termination of defined benefit plans. Because a defined benefit plan represents a commitment to provide benefits on the basis of past and future service, the resulting unfunded benefit obligation or excess funding affects the financial statements of the plan sponsor. Either a liability or an asset may be recorded. Further, a financial statement expense may be required even when the plan is fully funded, and no contribution is required. The unfunded liability for past employee service is reflected on the balance sheet of the employer.

The measurement of the impact on the accounting expense and balance sheet is based on the rigid standards set forth in the applicable statements issued by the Financial Accounting Standards Board (FASB). In many cases, the underlying methods and assumptions are different from those used by the actuary for income tax reporting and deductibility. The result is that two sets of actuarial reports are generated, and the deferred tax liability or asset is affected.

On September 29, 2006, FASB issued FAS No. 158 amending existing FAS Nos. 87, 88, 106, and 132. FAS 158 requires an employer to recognize the over- or underfunded status of a defined benefit postretirement plan as an asset or liability on its financial statements. The changes to the funded status must be recognized and reported in the year in which the changes occur. The employer must measure the funded status of a plan as of the end of its fiscal year (some limited exceptions apply). FAS 158 has two effective dates: for employers with publicly traded securities, the disclosures required under FAS 158 must be provided as of the end of the fiscal year ending after December 15, 2006, and for employers without publicly traded securities, it is effective as of the end of the fiscal year ending after June 15, 2007.

In implementing or amending a defined benefit plan, an employer needs to ascertain the effect on its financial statements before making any final decision. The results might be unexpected.

[K] Pension Benefit Guaranty Corporation

Defined benefit pension plans are subject to the jurisdiction of the PBGC, the federal agency that guarantees that all participants and beneficiaries of defined benefit pension plans will receive at least a minimal monthly benefit if the plan sponsor is unable to fund the plan adequately. This maximum insured benefit (the language "maximum insured" is from the employer's perspective) is adjusted annually for cost-of-living changes. For 2008, the insured monthly benefit was $4,312.50. Only basic benefits are insured. Supplemental death benefits and postretirement health benefits are not subject to this protection.

In return for this coverage, the plan sponsor is required to pay annual premiums. Plans covering fewer than 500 participants pay their premiums eight and one-half months after the beginning of the plan year. Plans covering 500 or more participants must file and pay the basic rate within two months of the beginning of the plan year. The variable portion, if any, is due at the usual due date of eight and one-half months after the beginning of the year. The basic premium rate is $30 per participant (an increase from the prior $19 rate; the increase is effective for plan years that begin in 2006). The variable portion depends upon whether and to what extent the plan is underfunded. The variable premium increases, with no ceiling, if the plan is seriously underfunded. The variable premium is $9 per $1,000 of unfunded vested benefits (the amount of unfunded benefits is determined under the PPA's minimum funding rules, including the at-risk rules where applicable). The variable rate for small employers (fewer than 25 employees) is $5 per participant. There is no waiver of the PBGC premium even if the plan is overfunded.

To improve accuracy and efficiency, the PBGC set up the "My Plan Administration Account" or "My PAA" Web site for receiving premiums and information filings. Use of this Web site was voluntary for plan sponsors until July 2006. Large plans (those with 500 or more participants) are required to file electronically the estimation, declaration and reconciliation of premium information through the My PAA Web site for filings due on or after July 1, 2006. Small plans (those with fewer than 500 participants) must file electronically for premiums due on or after January 1, 2007. Premiums may be paid through the secure My PAA Web site by credit card, electronic check or Automated Clearing House (ACH) transfer, or outside the My PAA site by paper check or wire transfer. Although premium payments are not yet required to be made electronically, the PBGC prefers that they are paid through the My PAA site, and may require doing so in the future. On a case by case basis, the PBGC may grant an exemption to the electronic filing requirement for good cause in appropriate circumstances. The My PAA Web site can be found at: *www. pbgc.gov*.

In addition to the annual premium payments, the PBGC requires that it be notified of certain reportable events. These are events that might indicate an emerging funding problem for the plan. They include the loss of qualified status, determination of noncompliance with the provisions of ERISA, amendments that reduce the benefits payable to people who have already retired, a substantial (more than 20 percent) decrease in the number of participants covered by the plan, failure to meet the minimum funding standards, inability to pay benefits when due, and mergers. This is not an exhaustive list of all reportable events.

The PPA changed the requirements for plan sponsors' notices of underfunded plans. Starting in 2008, all defined benefit plans that are less than 80 percent funded must send a notice to the PBGC indicating actuarial and plan sponsor financial information, as well as information about termination liabilities. The PBGC must summarize the information it receives from plan sponsors and provide annual reports to Congress.

The PBGC is also responsible for administering the termination of pension plans to ensure that participants receive their accrued benefits when the plan is terminated. Sponsors who want to terminate must file appropriate notices with the PBGC and the participants prior to the proposed termination date. The PBGC then determines whether the plan is able to provide the appropriate benefits. If there are not enough plan assets to provide the applicable benefits, the PBGC will intervene. The employer can be required to fund the plan, up to certain limits. If corporate assets are insufficient, the PBGC will assume the remaining obligation, but only to the extent of the guaranteed benefits. Benefits over the guaranteed amount are lost.

To the extent that the PBGC must fund benefits, it may impose a lien on up to 30 percent of the employer's assets to collect reimbursement for any benefit payments it makes. In addition, the PPA requires that plan sponsors be subject to termination premiums of $1,250 per participant for up to three years in the event a sponsor "dumps" pension liabilities on the PBGC and subsequently emerges from bankruptcy.

Where a plan is in significant financial difficulty, the PBGC has the authority to force its termination. The process of covering minimum guaranteed benefits and imposing a lien on the plan sponsor's assets is the same in a forced termination as it is in a voluntary termination situation.

This brief discussion of the PBGC's ability to interact with the operation and termination of a defined benefit plan highlights the limitations that the PBGC can place on a plan sponsor's discretion with respect to plan funding and the termination of this type of benefit.

[L] Other Defined Benefit Plan Provisions Under the PPA

- In-service distributions (e.g., phased retirement) for participants age 62 or older who are still employed will be allowed starting in 2007.

- For calculating lump-sum payment amounts, plan sponsors must use segmented yield-curve rates, similar to the new funding interest rate (with a transition phase-in from 2008 to 2012). The previous law, with interest rates based on the 30-year Treasury interest rate, applied for 2006 and 2007.

- Beginning in 2008, all plans (regardless of funded status) must provide an annual funding notice to participants that includes the plan's funded status and asset allocation.

- Defined benefit plans with assets exceeding 120 percent of current liability will be allowed to use such excess assets to fund retiree health benefits.

- Plans may be required to add an additional joint-and-survivor (spouse) form of benefit to their current menu of optional annuity forms.

- Companies with underfunded pension plans may be prevented from setting aside assets to pay nonqualified plan benefits for some executives.

§ 8.06 DEFINED CONTRIBUTION PLANS

Under *defined contribution plans*, the amount of benefits an employee receives upon retirement is based upon contribution levels and is determined by the funds accumulated on the employee's behalf at the time of his or her retirement. Therefore, instead of the set benefit amount received under a defined benefit plan, the actual benefit payable at retirement under a defined contribution plan is based on the level of contribution allocations and investment experience of the participant's individual account.

The amount of retirement income an employee receives depends on many factors, including the length of time he or she was a plan participant, the level and frequency of contributions, and investment gains or losses. Because the plan provides for separate accounts representing each individual's accumulated value of contributions, earnings, and gains or losses, the employee bears the risk of loss.

A defined contribution plan provides for employer contributions for individual employees within certain dollar limits—generally, total contributions of not more than the lesser of 100 percent of pay or $49,000, whichever is less. The $49,000 2009 limit is indexed for future inflation. The aggregate *employer* contribution to all of the employer's defined contribution plans is 25 percent of pay. As with a defined benefit plan, if more than the deductible limit is contributed, not only is the excess not deductible, but a 10 percent excise tax is applied to the excess.

Under some defined contribution plans, only the employer contributes. The contribution may be fixed as in a money purchase pension plan, or the employer contribution may be totally variable and established each year on a discretionary basis, as in a profit-sharing plan.

Many defined contribution plans are contributory. In a contributory plan, contributions are provided jointly by the employer and employees or solely by employees. Thus the burden for retirement savings in these types of plans is shared with or placed on employees.

[A] Types of Defined Contribution Plans

Common forms of defined contribution plans include the following:

- *Money purchase pension plans.* Money purchase pension plans require employers to make contributions to each participant's individual account and have funding requirements that specify the minimum annual employer contributions to be made. If employers fail to make a minimum contribution, they may be subject to excise taxes.

- *Profit-sharing plans.* Previous IRS regulations define these plans as those established and maintained by an employer to provide for employee participation in employer profits, although profits are no longer required for an employer to make discretionary contributions to such a plan.

- *Cash or deferred compensation arrangements.* In general, a profit-sharing plan is a plan that allows employees to elect to defer a portion of their compensation in lieu of receiving cash (e.g., a 401(k) plan). The employee is not taxed currently on the deferred amount; however, any elective deferrals are subject to Federal Insurance Contribution Act (FICA) and Federal Unemployment Tax Act (FUTA) taxes. Participant deferrals are subject to limitations; in 2009, the maximum elective deferral is $16,500 for the year. Many employers provide a matching contribution to 401(k) plans. The most common employer matching formulas are 50 percent, 70 percent, or 100 percent of the first 3 to 6 percent of salary put in the plan by (eligible) employees. Employer contributions are also limited; for 2009, employer contributions added to employee contributions were limited to 100 percent of compensation up to $49,000 (this amount indexed for inflation for future years).

- In December 2004, the Treasury issued final regulations for cash or deferred compensation plans under Code Section 401(k). Most of the final regulations are not new; rather, they serve as a comprehensive update of the operating rules for these plan types. Most of the changes outlined in the regulations apply to the discrimination testing requirements, which are not detailed in this chapter. Where changes do apply, they are noted as the 2004 final regulations, which apply for plan years beginning after December 31, 2005.

- Under the 2004 final regulations, a cash or deferred compensation 401(k) plan must provide employees with an effective opportunity to make or change their deferral election at least once per plan year.

- *Safe harbor plans.* Since 1999, 401(k) plans can be designed to include "safe harbor" provisions that exempt the plan from the usual 401(k) plan nondiscrimination testing of employee deferrals and employer matching contributions. A safe harbor 401(k) plan generally will be deemed to satisfy these tests, regardless of the amounts that the company's HCEs defer under the plan. (Absent discrimination limitations and unless the percentage of pay limit of Code Section 415 applies, participants may defer up to $16,500 for 2009.) Essentially, the design and operation of a safe harbor plan must meet only two requirements: (1) provide a certain level of matching or nonelective employer contributions for all eligible NHCEs and (2) provide employees timely notice of their rights and obligations under the plan. Under the 2004 final regulations, the notice to employees must be in writing or in any other form proscribed by the Treasury. The notice must be given at least 30 days, but no more than 90 days before the beginning of each plan year. Some information required by the notice may be cross-referenced to the plan's summary plan description. However, effective for plan years beginning on or after January 1, 2007, a description of the plan's withdrawal and vesting provisions must be included in the notice and may not be cross referenced to a summary plan description. In addition, the safe harbor plan must:

- Be adopted prior to the beginning of a plan year;

- Be in effect for 12 months (although limited exceptions for "short" plan years are provided); and

- Specify in writing whether the safe harbor contribution will be a non-elective or matching contribution.

- *Simplified employee pensions.* A simplified employee pension (SEP) is an arrangement whereby an individual retirement account (IRA) or annuity is maintained for an employee to which an employer's annual contribution is limited to 15 percent of compensation, or $49,000, whichever is less (for 2009). All contributions to the employee's account vest immediately, and the employee controls the investment of the account. A SEP can be established by an employer merely by signing Form 5305-SEP and distributing a copy of the form to eligible employees. It is designed primarily for smaller employers because it is easy to administer.

  A salary reduction SEP (SARSEP), under which an employee may defer part of his or her pay into a SEP account, may continue to be maintained by employers with 25 or fewer employees, but no new SARSEPs may be established after 1996.

- *Savings incentive match plans for employees.* Since 1997, employers with fewer than 100 employees, each earning more than $5,000 annually, may establish a savings incentive match plan for employees (SIMPLE). A SIMPLE may be established either as an IRA for each employee or as part of a 401(k) plan.

  If established in IRA form, a SIMPLE is not subject to the nondiscrimination rules generally applicable to qualified plans (including the top-heavy rules) and simplified reporting requirements apply, but the employer may not maintain another qualified plan in the same year. A SIMPLE IRA must limit employee salary deferrals to $11,500 (for 2009) and requires a mandatory employer contribution that must be 100 percent vested immediately. Although the required employer contributions are defined in terms of percentages of an employee's compensation, neither the employer deferrals nor the employer contributions are restricted by limits on the employee's compensation. For example, an employee with $7,000 compensation could defer the full $7,000 under a SIMPLE IRA. A SIMPLE IRA may be established merely by completing and signing a Form 5304-SIMPLE or Form 5305-SIMPLE, or any other document that satisfies the statutory requirements.

  If adopted as part of a 401(k) plan, a SIMPLE does not have to satisfy the special nondiscrimination tests applicable to 401(k) plans and is not subject to the top-heavy rules (though other qualified plan rules continue to apply). An employer with a SIMPLE 401(k) may maintain other plans, unlike the case of the SIMPLE IRA, but participants in the SIMPLE 401(k) may not participate in any other qualified plan. Like SIMPLE IRAs, SIMPLE 401(k) plans must limit employee salary deferrals to $11,500 (for 2009) and require a mandatory employer contribution that must be 100 percent vested immediately. Unlike SIMPLE IRAs, however, SIMPLE 401(k) plans must apply the compensation restriction of qualified plans, which results in reducing the overall limits of what can be contributed to the plan for any one participant.

(See **Exhibit 8.5** for a comparison of SIMPLE IRAs, SIMPLE 401(k) plans, traditional 401(k) plans, SEPs, and profit sharing, money purchase, and defined benefit plans as salary deferral and other qualified plan options for employers.)

- *Employee stock ownership plans.* Employee stock ownership plans (ESOPs) provide each participant with an account, and participants invest primarily in employer securities. This type of plan is unique in that it is allowed to borrow money to purchase employer securities and may provide the employer and its owners with other special tax and financial advantages.

  Under some ESOPs, only the employer may contribute. The contribution may be fixed, as in a money purchase pension plan, or the employer contribution may be totally variable and established each year on a discretionary basis, as in a profit-sharing plan. Many other defined contribution plans are contributory, in which contributions are provided jointly by the employer and employees or solely by employees. The burden for retirement savings in these types of plans is shared with or placed on employees.

- *Roth contributions in a 401(k) or 403(b) plan.* Section 402A was added to the Code by Section 617 of EGTRRA to provide for the treatment of elective deferrals as designated Roth contributions, effective for taxable years beginning on or after January 1, 2006. Under Section 402A, participants may defer after-tax income to a Roth account within a 401(k) or 403(b) plan and the earnings on these contributions grow tax free. The deferral is subject to all applicable wage withholding requirements at the time of the deferral. Final regulations were published in the *Federal Register* on January 3, 2006 (29 C.F.R. Parts 1 and 602 [T.D. 9237] RIN 1545-BE05). Additional final regulations were published in the *Federal Register* on April 30, 2007 (T.D. 9324; 72 Fed. Reg. 21,103 (April 30, 2007)). The discussion that follows takes into account both sets of final regulations:

  — No income limits. The Roth 401(k) account is available to all employees included in the plan regardless of their income.

  — Matching. An employer can match a Roth 401(k) deferral. However, the employer contributions must be deposited into the participant's regular (pretax) 401(k) deferral account.

  — Contribution limits. The contribution limit in 2009 for a Roth 401(k) was $16,500 ($22,000 if eligible for the catch-up contribution). Note that this is the aggregate limit for all employee deferrals under the 401(k) plan; that is an employee may only defer a maximum total of $22,000 (if eligible for the catch-up contribution) for both the Roth and the pretax accounts in a 401(k).

  — Separate account required. The 401(k) plan must establish separate accounts for the Roth contributions. The regulations require that a plan allocate all investment gains and losses, expenses, etc. attributable to Roth 401(k) contributions on a reasonable and consistent basis. Separate accounting also applies to withdrawals and distributions. A 401(k) plan must allow pretax contributions if it allows Roth contributions.

  — Payroll system. The plan sponsor's payroll system must be able to separately identify and track each participant's pretax and Roth 401(k) deferrals. Roth contributions are wages, subject to all applicable payroll and employment taxes at the time the employee would have received the income.

— Qualified distributions. The final regulations define qualified distributions as those that are made from amounts that have been held in the Roth account for a minimum of five years and are made only upon a participant's death, disability, or attainment of age 59½ . The five-year period begins on the first day of the first taxable year in which the participant makes a designated Roth contribution under the plan. If a plan accepts a direct rollover from another Roth 401(k) account, the time in that account counts toward the five-year period. The five-year period ends when five consecutive taxable years have been completed. Plans are responsible for tracking the five-year period. Qualified distributions will be tax-free to the participant, including tax-free distribution of the interest earned on the participant's contributions. Distributions from Roth 401(k) accounts cannot be made without their corresponding earnings.

— Non-qualified distributions. If a distribution does not meet the requirements of a qualified distribution, the investment earnings, although not the deferrals themselves, will be taxed. The regulations indicate that the tax rules under Code Section 72 will determine the portion of the distribution that is not taxable.

— Hardship distributions are allowed if the plan is amended to allow for them. Plans may permit participants to designate from which account the hardship distribution should be withdrawn: the Roth account or the pretax deferral account.

— Conversion. Although regular IRAs are eligible for conversion to a Roth IRA, pretax 401(k) contributions are not eligible for conversion to the Roth 401(k) account. Also, once deferrals are elected to be Roth contributions, a participant may not convert those deferrals to pretax contributions.

— Nondiscrimination testing applies to Roth 401(k) accounts. Roth elective deferrals are subject to the ADP Test, in the same manner as the pretax elective deferrals.

— Rollovers are permitted. Rollovers from a Roth 410(k) account can be made to another Roth 401(k) account if it is a direct rollover and the receiving 401(k) plan accepts rollovers. Rollovers cannot be made to 403(b) plans (even though such plans are allowed to have a Roth feature). Rollovers to Roth IRAs are acceptable, even if the participant would not otherwise be eligible for a Roth IRA. If the rollover is made to a Roth IRA, the Roth IRA rules then apply to those amounts. Prototype Roth IRA plans must be amended to receive rollovers from Roth 401(k) accounts.

— Required minimum distribution rules apply. Once a participant reaches age 70½ and is no longer working for the plan sponsor, distribution of both the Roth and the pretax 401(k) accounts must begin.

— Roth 401(k) accounts can be added to safe harbor plans. Roth accounts can be added mid-year and the plan will not lose its safe harbor status merely because the Roth account was not included in the pre-year safe harbor notice.

— SIMPLE and SEP plans are not allowed to offer Roth accounts.

— Plan amendments. The plan must be amended to allow for Roth accounts. The plan amendment must be signed no later than the last day of the first plan year to which Roth 401(k) contributions are made. The IRS has developed a sample plan amendment that plan sponsors can use to amend their plan [IRS Notice 2006-44]. The amendment does not need to be adopted verbatim; it may be revised to conform to the operation of the plan. The sample amendment is available at: *http://www.irs.gov/pub/irs-drop/n-06-44.pdf.*

— Employee communication. Summary Plan Descriptions (SPDs) will have to be revised, employee communication materials developed, and enrollment forms modified to explain Roth accounts. These accounts can appear quite complex to employees, so care will need to be taken to properly communicate this new option.

In February 2007, the Profit Sharing/401(k) Council of America (PSCA) released its survey of 429 401(k) plan sponsors regarding their plans to adopt or not adopt Roth accounts. Among all survey participants, 22.4 percent offered a Roth account in 2006. Of those that did not offer a Roth account, 9 percent intend to add this option, 52.4 percent were considering it, and 34 percent were not intending to do so. Of those not planning to adopt Roth accounts, the primary reason was the additional participant education that would be necessary (cited by 59.5 percent of respondents). Additional reasons for not adopting Roth accounts included lack of participant demand (56.8 percent) and additional administrative burden (54.7 percent).

[B] Eligibility for Participation

The same rules apply here that apply to a defined benefit plan, except that, beginning in 1997, defined contribution plans are not required to cover at least 40 percent of eligible employees. The employer has some flexibility in determining when individuals become eligible and which individuals may enter the plan once they meet the eligibility standards.

[C] Automatic Enrollment

Automatic enrollment, also referred to as negative election or negative option, refers to a procedure through which employees are automatically enrolled in the 401(k) plan and the employer withholds contributions from the participant's pay unless he or she actively opts out of the program. Current IRS regulations allow for an automatic enrollment procedure; however, many employers had been reluctant to adopt automatic enrollment due to concerns over state garnishment laws and fiduciary liability. The PPA addresses these concerns and provides incentives for automatic enrollment:

- Employers using automatic enrollment are protected against state withholding laws (ERISA preemption)

- Plan sponsors receive fiduciary relief for the investment of participant account balances in certain default investments (see **Section 8.06[D][5]** below)

- Employees have a 90-day window from the initial payroll deduction to opt out and receive a penalty-free return of automatic elective contributions

- Eligible automatic contribution arrangements have 180 days after the end of the year to make corrective distributions

Plan sponsors can design their automatic enrollment program to take advantage of a nondiscrimination ADP/ACP safe harbor test that will be available to qualified automatic contribution arrangements. To have a qualified automatic contribution arrangement:

- Any eligible employee who has not made a written participation election or written non-participation election must be automatically enrolled in the arrangement.

- The required entry-level contribution is 3 percent, increasing in annual increments of 1 percent until reaching 6 percent of pay. Plans may provide for automatic increases in contributions up to 10 percent of pay.

- The plan must provide notice of the ability to opt out of contributions or automatic increases. Employees must have a reasonable period of time between receipt of this notice and when the first payroll deduction is taken to elect to opt out or to change the amount of the deferral.

- Automatic enrollment provisions do not have to be applied to employees who were eligible immediately before the plan added the automatic enrollment arrangement.

- The employer must match 100 percent of the first 1 percent of pay contributed by an eligible NHCE, plus 50 percent of the next 5 percent of pay, for a maximum match of 3½ percent of compensation to each NHCE. Alternatively, an employer may choose to make a non-elective contribution of 3 percent of pay for all eligible NHCEs. These employer contributions must be fully vested after two years of service.

The automatic enrollment enhancements are equally applicable to 403(b) plans.

Automatic enrollment is likely to be well received by employees. According to the 2006 Retirement Confidence Survey (Employee Benefit Research Institute, *EBRI Issue Brief No. 292*, April 2006), 69 percent of employed workers favor automatic enrollment. In addition, 65 percent favor automatically increasing the percentage of salary contributed when an increase in pay is received, and 59 percent approve of automatically investing the contributions on behalf of the employee.

Automatic enrollment provisions are generally effective for plan years beginning after December 31, 2007, except for the ERISA preemption rule, which was effective on the enactment date of the PPA.

[D] Employee Contributions

Again, the considerations applicable to a defined benefit pension plan apply equally to a defined contribution pension plan. However, since the availability of elective pretax employee contributions to 401(k) plans has become so popular and available, it is rare to see required employee contributions to a defined contribution pension plan.

The Code establishes limits to the amounts that can be contributed to a defined contribution plan. The maximum annual salary deferral limit for all salary deferrals made to 401(k) plans (pretax and Roth accounts), 403(b), and grandfathered SARSEP plans is $16,500 in 2009 (Code Section 402(g)(1), indexed for inflation). SIMPLE plans are limited to $11,500 in 2009 (also indexed for inflation). The maximum annual amount that can be contributed by both employer and employee, including forfeitures, into a defined contribution plan is $49,000 in 2009 (Code Section 415(c)(1)(A), indexed for inflation). (See **Exhibit 8.6** for IRS limits on retirement plan benefits and compensation for 2003 through 2009.)

[1] Timeliness of Depositing Employee Contributions

The DOL has been particularly active in recent years in policing the timeliness of the deposit of funds withheld from employees for ERISA plans. Most of this activity has focused upon 401(k) employee savings accounts. The same issues may arise, however, in the context of employee contributions to other retirement plans.

Employee contributions become "plan assets" as soon as the employer can reasonably segregate them from its general assets, even before they are deposited in the plan. Therefore, they should be deposited into the plan as soon as they can reasonably be segregated, but in no event later than the 15th business day of the month following the month in which they were withheld, as required by DOL regulations. The contributions need to be deposited into the plan; putting them into a separate employer's checking account or administrator's checking account does not qualify.

Essentially, a reasonable time period is as soon as possible after the amounts are withheld. This time period will vary from employer to employer. One way to determine a reasonable time period for depositing 401(k) contributions is by looking at the time period that an employer uses for depositing federal income taxes withheld from employees' pay. If an employer has a three-day period for depositing payroll taxes, perhaps a three-day period is also reasonable for depositing 401(k) contributions. In some cases, the DOL has applied a rebuttable seven-day period as reasonable and has assessed penalties for any deposit made after that time.

Early in 2008, the DOL issued a proposed regulation for employee benefit plans with fewer than 100 participants. [73 Fed. Reg. 11,072 (Feb. 29, 2008)] The regulation establishes a safe harbor period of seven business days during which amounts that an employer has received from employees or withheld from wages for contribution to employee benefit plans would not constitute "plan assets."

After a reasonable time period has expired and these amounts are considered plan assets but still held by the employer, all the risks of ERISA are applicable:

- *Prohibited Transaction.* If the employer holds the funds in its general assets for its own use for an unreasonable time, then a prohibited transaction may have occurred. For example, a prohibited transaction occurs if the employer maintains the funds in a general checking account and uses those funds to pay its other bills. This use of plan assets is subject to an excise tax of 15 percent of the amount involved. Another way of looking at it would be as if the plan made a loan to the employer. In that case, the excise tax would be based upon a reasonable cost of money associated with this loan.

- *Risk of Loss.* While those plan assets are held by the employer, they are subject to a risk of loss in the event of insolvency. If that occurred, the plan fiduciaries could be sued to recover the lost amounts and lost earnings.

- *Fiduciary Breach.* An ERISA fiduciary is required to operate the plan solely in the interest of the plan participants or beneficiaries. To the extent that the fiduciary has not done this by allowing the plan sponsor to retain funds that should be in the plan, the fiduciary could be liable to the plan for any losses, including lost earnings.

- *Negative Publicity.* On its public news page on the Internet, the DOL regularly lists the individual names of fiduciaries who have been penalized for violation of these rules on timely deposits of contributions.

- *Plan Qualification.* Though it is remote that this issue would be raised in anything but the most egregious of circumstances, it is a basic qualification principle for tax-qualified retirement plans that the plan be operated for the exclusive benefit of plan participants or beneficiaries. Thus, allowing the use of plan assets by the plan sponsor could be considered a violation of this rule and could lead to plan disqualification. Even if the late deposits are not considered under one of the IRS's self-correction programs, the interest amounts calculated for purposes of the prohibited transaction reporting and excise tax should also be deposited in the accounts of the affected participants.

In addition, the IRS will assess a 15 percent excise tax on the amount involved in the prohibited transaction.

The bottom line is to get the employee contributions into the plan as soon as possible and to make the employees whole if any unavoidable delay occurs.

[2] Investment Direction and Advice

ERISA Section 404(c) Fiduciary Relief. Many defined contribution plans that permit employee contributions also permit the employees to direct the investment of those contribution amounts or, in some cases, their entire account balance. If investment direction is permitted within the rules set forth in the plan and in compliance with ERISA Section 404(c), then some of the liability for investment decisions is shifted from the plan trustee to the employees, providing some "fiduciary relief."

ERISA Section 404(c) applies to individual account plans specifically: profit sharing plans, money purchase pension plans, and 401(k) plans. Although the Section 404(c) regulations are lengthy, they provide the basic guidelines to assist employers in transferring investment decision liability to the participants so employers can avail themselves of Section 404(c) relief. Note that plan participants will not be deemed fiduciaries because they exercise investment control. However, the plan fiduciaries will not be liable for losses on individual transactions when:

- The participants actually exercised control with respect to the transaction.

- The losses were directly and necessarily a result of investment instructions given by the participants.

The requirements can be met even if:

- Only certain participants may exercise control (assuming this is not discriminatory); and

- Participants may exercise control over only a portion of their account balance.

Participants also must be given a "broad range of investment alternatives." This requirement is met if investments are sufficient to permit participants a reasonable opportunity to materially affect the potential return and degree of risk on their investments. The participants must also have an opportunity to choose from at least three investments with the following characteristics:

- The investments are diversified.

- The investments have materially different risk and return characteristics.

- The investments, in the aggregate, enable the participant to achieve aggregate risk and return characteristics at any point within the range "normally appropriate for the participant."

- Each investment, when combined with the other alternatives, tends to minimize, through diversification, the overall risk of the portfolio.

Participants must be given the opportunity to diversify the investments to minimize the risk of large losses, taking into account the nature of the plan and the size of participant accounts.

In order for plan participants to exercise control under ERISA Section 404(c) requirements, the following elements must be met:

- Participants may give investment instructions by any means but must have the opportunity to receive written confirmation.

- The instructions must be given to an identified plan fiduciary who is obligated to comply.

- The plan fiduciary may be identified by position or function.

- The participants must receive specified information that is generally sufficient to enable the participant to make informed investment decisions.

- Some of the required information must be provided before an investment direction is given; some must be provided upon request.

The plan may impose a reasonable charge for carrying out investment instructions so long as it has a procedure to inform participants periodically of the actual expenses incurred with respect to their accounts. The fiduciary may decline to follow instructions that would result in a prohibited transaction or would generate income taxable to the plan. The fiduciary is not relieved of liability when a participant instruction, if implemented, would:

- Not be in accordance with the plan document;

- Cause the indicia of ownership of plan assets to be outside the United States;

- Jeopardize the plan's tax-qualified status;

- Plausibly result in a loss in excess of a participant's account balance; or

- Result in a prohibited transaction.

Since the fiduciary is not relieved of fiduciary responsibility in the above events, it can decline to carry out those investment instructions.

Participants must be given the opportunity to change their investments as often as the volatility of the investment requires (*general volatility rule*). They must be able to change core investment alternatives at least every three months, subject to the general volatility rule (*core investments* are those that constitute a broad range of investment alternatives).

If any investment alternative permits changes more frequently than once every three months, at least one core investment must permit the same frequency of change, and the investment into which participants can transfer must be income producing, low risk, and liquid. Non-core investments are not subject to the three-month requirement but are subject to the general volatility rule.

This is only a summary of the rules under ERISA Section 404(c). Any employer that is interested in exploring the advantages of Section 404(c) should contact its benefits advisor for details.

Investment Advice Under the PPA. Prior to the PPA, ERISA and the Code, in the absence of a statutory or administrative exemption, prohibited fiduciaries from rendering investment advice to plan participants that results in the payment of additional advisory and other fees to the fiduciaries or their affiliates. The PPA amended ERISA and the Code to add this statutory exemption that allows the provision of investment advice under an "eligible investment advice arrangement" to plan participants. An eligible investment advice arrangement is an arrangement that either:

- Provides that any fees (including any commission or other compensation) received by the investment advisor for investment advice or with respect to the investment of plan assets do not vary based on the investment option selected, or

- Uses a computer model under an investment advice program that:

  - applies generally accepted investment theories,

  - uses individualized participant information,

  - is not biased in favor of investments offered by the advisor or its affiliates,

  - takes into account all investment options available under the plan, and

  - has been certified by an independent third party.

Fiduciary investment advisors that may provide investment advice under this exemption include banks, insurance companies, broker dealers, and registered investment advisors and their employees and representatives.

Prior to the implementation of an investment advice arrangement, written or electronic notice must be provided to the participants. The notice must be written clearly and in a manner designed to be understood by the average plan participant. The notice must disclose at a minimum:

- The role of all parties involved in developing the advice arrangement or selecting investment options;

- The fiduciary status of the investment advisor;

- The past performance and rate of return of each investment option;

- The fees or other compensation received by the investment advisor;

- The contractual relationship or material affiliation the advisor has with any investment option;

- How participant and beneficiary information will be used; and

- The right of participants to obtain independent investment advice from their own advisors at their own expense.

Plan sponsors or fiduciaries are still responsible under ERISA for the prudent selection and periodic review of the selected investment advisor. Plan sponsors and fiduciaries do not have a duty under ERISA to monitor the specific advice given by an investment advisor to any particular recipient of the advice. In selecting investment advisors, plan sponsors and fiduciaries should engage in an objective process that is designed to elicit information necessary to assess the investment advisor's qualifications, quality of services offered, and reasonableness of fees charged for the service. The process also must avoid self-dealing, conflicts of interest and other improper influence. In monitoring investment advisors, plan sponsors and fiduciaries should periodically review the extent to which there have been any changes in the information that served as the basis for the initial selection of the investment advisor, including whether the advisor continues to meet applicable federal and state securities law requirements, and whether the advice being furnished to participants was based upon generally accepted investment theories. Plan sponsors should also take into account whether the investment advisor is complying with the contractual provisions of the engagement; utilization of the investment advice services by the participants in relation to the cost of the services to the plan; and participant comments and complaints about the quality of the furnished advice.

To ensure that plans are complying with all of the PPA's requirements, plans must undergo an annual audit by an independent auditor. This fiduciary advice exemption is available for plan years beginning after December 31, 2006.

[3] Catch-Up Contributions

Beginning in January 2002, EGTRRA allowed for additional employee contributions, called "catch-up contributions." This option allows participants who are age 50 or older (or who will attain age 50 during the plan year) to make additional deferrals beyond any plan or statutory limits. The maximum amount allowed as catch-up contributions increased each year, as follows:

2002	$1,000
2003	$2,000
2004	$3,000
2005	$4,000
2006	$5,000
2007	$5,000
2008	$5,000
2009	$5,500 and indexed thereafter in $500 increments.

Plan amendments to allow for the catch-up contributions were required to be drafted by the end of the plan year in which the additional deferrals are allowed. With the exception of Pennsylvania, all states have passed legislation allowing for deferral of state income taxes on catch-up contributions.

[4] Saver's Tax Credit

Beginning in 2002, some employees may have an added incentive to make contributions to a 401(k) plan or to other qualified retirement plans because their contributions make them eligible for a federal income tax credit known as the "Saver's Tax Credit." This credit reduces an individual's total income tax by an amount equal to a portion of the individual's contributions to an IRA, a 401(k) plan, a 403(b) plan, or a 457 plan. As a result, the total cost of saving for retirement may be reduced not only by a tax deduction for the contribution, but also by a credit applied directly against taxes owed.

The amount that an individual may claim as a saver's tax credit on his or her federal income tax return depends on the following factors:

- The individual's adjusted gross income for the year

- The amount contributed to a qualified retirement plan for the year, up to $2,000

- Whether the individual received distributions from an IRA or a qualified plan in the past three years

- The amount of income taxes the individual owes

Adjusted gross income (AGI) is total reported taxable income less certain deductions, such as alimony payments, moving expenses, payment of student loan interest, and contributions to an IRA or a medical savings account.

The percentage of total contributions, up to a maximum of $2,000, that an employee may take as a saver's tax credit is determined by his or her AGI, as follows:

Adjusted Gross Income Brackets For 2008

Joint return		Head of Household		All other filers		
Over	Not Over	Over	Not Over	Over	Not Over	Applicable Percentage
$0	$32,000	$0	$24,000	$0	$16,000	50%
$32,000	$34,500	$24,000	$25,875	$16,000	$17,250	20%
$34,500	$53,000	$25,875	$39,750	$17,250	$26,500	10%
$53,000	—	$39,750	—	$26,500	—	0%

This percentage is applied to the amount of contributions the employee made during the year, reduced by the amount of distributions, if any, received during the three years ending in the year for which the credit is being claimed. Note that the credit can be taken only up to the amount of taxes owed and cannot create a refund (if the credit takes the income tax liability below zero for the year).

Example 1. In 2008, Mary elects to reduce her taxable income by deferring $750 to her IRA and $1,750 to her 401(k) plan at work. Mary and her husband, Tom, have adjusted gross income (AGI) of $34,000 in 2008, and they file a joint return. Neither Mary nor Tom received distributions from an IRA or other retirement plan in 2006, 2007, or 2008. Mary's total contributions are $2,500. For purposes of the tax credit, that $2,500 amount is limited to the maximum of $2,000 for 2008. Because the couple's AGI is $34,000, Mary's credit percentage is 20 percent. Applying that percentage to her qualifying contributions of $2,000, Mary can take a tax credit of $400 for 2008. Mary and Tom can take an additional credit at the 20 percent rate for any qualifying contributions that Tom makes, up to the $2,000 maximum—for additional income tax savings and up to an additional $400 credit on their joint return.

Example 2. In 2008, Joe elects to reduce his taxable income by deferring $1,000 to his IRA and $1,800 to his 401(k) plan at work. Joe received a distribution of $900 from an IRA in 2005, but no distributions in either 2007 or 2008. Joe's total contributions of $2,800 for 2008, reduced by the $900 distribution he received, results in qualifying contributions of $1,900. Joe's AGI for 2008 was $22,000, and he files as head of household. Because his AGI was $22,000, his credit percentage is 50. Applying that percentage to his qualifying contributions of $1,900, Joe can take a tax credit of $950 for 2008. Adding the $950 tax credit to his tax savings for making the $1,900 net qualifying contributions at a 15 percent rate, Joe's total tax savings are $1,235.

The Saver's Tax Credit was designed to encourage greater participation in 401(k) plans by helping eligible employees maximize their retirement savings. An employer may want to formulate a program to educate its employees about this credit.

The PPA made makes the Saver's Tax Credit of up to $2,000 permanent. The law also indexes the income limits to increase with inflation.

[5] Default Investment Options

As discussed above, plan sponsors have some fiduciary protections where participants self-direct their accounts. The PPA extends similar fiduciary protections in situations where the participant does not make an investment choice, and the plan sponsor makes a default investment decision. The DOL released final regulations for default investment alternatives under participant directed individual account plans (72 Fed. Reg. 60,452 [29 C.F.R. Part 2550 RIN 1210-AB10 (October 24, 2007)]). The final regulation was effective on December 23, 2007 and extends fiduciary protection to a plan sponsor or fiduciary when, in the absence of investment direction from the participant, the plan invests the assets in a "qualified default investment alternative" (QDIA). In order to qualify, the following conditions must be met:

* Participants and beneficiaries must have been given an opportunity to provide investment direction, but failed to do so.

* A notice must be furnished to participants and beneficiaries 30 days before the first investment, and at least 30 days prior to each subsequent plan year.

* The notice must include: a description of the circumstances under which assets will be invested in a QDIA; an explanation of the right of participants and beneficiaries to direct the investment of assets in

their individual accounts; a description of the investment objectives of the QDIA; an explanation of the right of participants and beneficiaries to direct investment of the assets out of the QDIA; and an explanation of where the participants and beneficiaries can obtain investment information concerning the other investment alternatives available under the plan.

- All material, such as investment prospectuses and other notices, provided to the plan by the QDIA must be furnished to participants and beneficiaries.

- Participants must have the opportunity to direct investments out of a QDIA with the same frequency available for other plan investments, but no less frequently than quarterly, without financial penalty.

- The plan must offer a broad range of investment alternatives as defined by Section 404(c) of ERISA.

The QDIA must satisfy the following requirements:

- May not impose financial penalties or otherwise restrict the ability of a participant or beneficiary to transfer the investment from the QDIA to any other investment alternative available under the plan.

- Must be either managed by an investment manager or a registered investment company.

- Must be diversified so as to minimize the risk of large losses.

- May not invest participant contributions directly in employer securities.

- May be:

  - A life-cycle or targeted-retirement-date fund,

  - A balanced fund, or

  - A professionally managed account designed to achieve the same investment objectives as the life-cycle or targeted-retirement-date alternatives.

A life-cycle or targeted-retirement-date fund holds a diversified mix of stocks and bonds. Over time the fund reduces the amount of risky assets (e.g., equities) and increases more stable assets (e.g., bonds and cash). The roll down of the equities is targeted toward the participant's anticipated retirement date.

[6] Freedom to Divest Employer Securities

Effective for plan years that begin after December 31, 2006, the PPA has imposed a new rule regarding participants' rights to diversify out of publicly traded employer securities. If a plan offers employer securities (e.g., company stock or real estate) as an option in its participant-directed individual account plan, employees must be allowed to divest out of those employer securities. Employees must always be allowed to divest their own elective deferrals and after-tax contributions. After three years of vesting service, they must be allowed to divest that portion of their account attributable to employer matching or non-elective contributions. Plans must provide at least three materially different diversified investment options for the receipt of the divested assets. Plans cannot impose more onerous conditions or restrictions on the diversified assets than are imposed on any other assets in the plan.

The PPA provides for a three-year phase-in period for the diversification of employer matching and non-elective contributions. Approximately one-third of the assets held in employer securities must be available for diversification in each year of the three-year period (2007, 2008, and 2009). However, participants who are 55 years old and have at least three years of service (as of any plan year beginning after December 31, 2005) must be allowed to divest all employer securities upon the effective date of this rule.

Plans must provide notice to participants of any new divesture rights at least 30 days before such rights become available. The Treasury, in Notice 2006-107, provided a model notice. Treasury notes that the model should be customized to fit each plan sponsor's specific situation. The model notice is available on the IRS Web site: *http://www.irs.gov/pub/irs-irbs/irb06-51.pdf.*

On August 10, 2007, the DOL published its final regulation implementing civil penalties against plan sponsors who fail to give employees notice of the right to sell company stock in their accounts. [72 Fed. Reg. 44,970 (August 10, 2007)] Effective October 9, 2007, the existing procedures for assessing civil penalties for violations of ERISA's blackout notices are extended to violations of diversification notices. The penalty can be as much as $100 per day for each separate violation; each participant or beneficiary who does not receive the notice is treated as a separate violation.

[E]   Benefits Formula

As the term *defined contribution plan* indicates, this type of plan is required to have a clearly defined contribution allocation formula described in the plan document, not subject to the discretion of the employer sponsor and without regard to profits. Note the distinction—allocation, not contribution. This reflects the fact that contributions may be discretionary or defined and, in either case, forfeitures from terminated employees may be enough to cover the employer's current year commitment.

Contribution formulas may be used to determine how much the employer sponsor is obligated to contribute to the plan, and in some cases, these formulas will define both the amount of contribution and the manner in which it is allocated. Whether included in the contribution formula or not, however, the formula for allocating the contribution among the participants is common to all defined contribution plans and is important for determining the benefit of each individual participant in the plan.

[1]   Contribution Formula Parameters

Some defined contribution plans provide for contributions to be determined at the sole discretion of the plan sponsor. Others of these plans have formulas to determine how much is to be contributed and use the same parameters described under defined benefit plans—service, salary, and Social Security. In addition, the employee's current age can be used to determine the amount of the current contribution.

[2]   Types of Contribution Formulas

Defined contribution pension plans with contribution formulas fall into two basic categories—money purchase plans and target benefit plans.

   1. *Money purchase plan.* Money purchase plans are more common than target benefit plans. A money purchase plan may, but is not required to, have both contribution and allocation formulas. The simplest

money purchase plan requires a contribution or an allocation as a fixed dollar amount or percentage of pay. For example, a 10 percent of pay money purchase plan requires each employee to receive an allocation for the year that is equal to 10 percent of pay. That allocation could be just the employer contribution, with forfeitures creating additional benefits, or it could arrive at the 10 percent level by including both employer contributions and forfeitures. This type of formula can be combined with Social Security (discussed below). A second type of formula requires the plan sponsor to contribute a fixed percentage of all participants' pay to the plan but allocates that amount by using some other formula.

2. *Target benefit plan.* Target benefit plans use the same formula types as defined benefit plans with one exception: Each participant's cost for providing the projected benefit is determined separately rather than as a percentage of the aggregate cost for all plan participants. The maximum annual allocation that any one participant can receive is the lesser of 100 percent of pay, or $49,000, for 2009. This allocation includes any benefits that the participant might receive under another employer plan, such as a 401(k) plan. Thus, the cost of offering a target benefit plan is limited and easily predicted. Only the initial contribution is fixed by actuarial determinations. Subsequent gains or losses on the account are borne by the participant. An employee may not receive the described target benefit, but he or she will receive more or less of the benefit, depending on how the investments held in the account perform.

Although target benefit plans are cost-effective, they are complex and the terms are not easily understood. The benefit formula is similar to that of a defined benefit plan (e.g., 2 percent of pay per year of service), but there is no guarantee that the employee will ultimately collect the targeted benefit amount from the plan.

[3] Types of Allocation Formulas

Most defined contribution plans allocate contributions to participants in proportion to their share of total pay of all participants under the plan. As a result, all participants get a share of the contribution that is equal to the same percentage of pay as that for all other participants. Some other allocation formulas merely direct that each participant receive an allocation of the same dollar amount of contribution, regardless of his or her pay. Other formulas might be age-weighted, use a combination of compensation and service points, or take note of other factors. For example, an age-weighted formula would allocate more dollars to older participants, regardless of service, because older participants have less time to accumulate a retirement fund. Another example is a formula that awards points for pay, service or both. This type of formula might call for an employer contribution of 10 percent of eligible pay, which the administrator is to allocate on the basis of 10 points for every year of service and one point for every $100 of compensation. Another approach might group employees by some acceptable classification and allocate different percentages of pay to each grouping. Note, however, that this approach, often referred to as "new comparability" or "cross-testing," is very effective for targeting more benefits to specific groups, but is subject to complex nondiscrimination rules and exposed to potential regulatory or legislative changes. Another approach that is often used is similar to the proportionate pay approach mentioned above but is coordinated with Social Security within limits of permitted disparity.

A final contribution formula that doubles as an allocation formula is a matching contribution. Although a matching contribution may be discretionary, such a formula usually promises to make a contribution to the accounts of participants who elect to contribute to a 401(k) or thrift plan. The matching contribution is usually directly related to the amount contributed by the participant.

[4] Coordination with Social Security Benefits

Target benefit plans are coordinated with Social Security in the same manner as are defined benefit plans, discussed earlier in this chapter.

Money purchase plans and other defined contribution plans are coordinated with Social Security through the use of their allocation formulas, either alone or as part of their contribution formulas.

Defined contribution plans use a system similar to the step-rate formula described for defined benefit pension plans. A base rate of contribution is established for total pay. An excess rate is established for compensation in excess of some base. The amount of the difference between the base rate and the excess rate is set by law. In no event can the difference exceed the lesser of the base rate or 5.7 percent of pay.

The following table summarizes the spread allowed between the base rate and the excess rate. All of these methods refer back to the Social Security wage base, which is $102,000 for 2008.

Definition of Base Pay	Maximum Rate Spread Allowed
Lesser of $10,000 or 20 percent of the Social Security wage base	5.7%
Greater than $10,000 or 20 percent of the Social Security wage base, but less than 80 percent	4.3%
Greater than 80 percent of the Social Security wage base, but less than 100 percent	5.4%
100 percent of the Social Security wage base	5.7%

> **Example.** For 2008, a plan provides a benefit of 6 percent of pay on the first $85,000 of pay and 11 percent of pay on amounts over $85,000, which is 83.3 percent of the 2008 Social Security wage base. Thus, the maximum amount of disparity allowable would be 5.4 percent. The actual disparity provided is 5 percent (11 percent minus 6 percent), making it a permissible plan formula. An employer sponsoring this plan, however, might need to amend it shortly. As the Social Security wage base continues to increase, the plan could be confronted with a situation in which $85,000 is less than 80 percent of the wage base, and the maximum permitted disparity is only 4.3 percent.

[F] Pay for Pension Purposes

Target benefit plans face all the same issues in defining compensation that defined benefit plans do. Because of their character as defined contribution plans, most target benefit plans use the career average definition for projecting benefits.

Other defined contribution plans do not have to deal with the issues that arise with respect to career average or final average pay. They simply need to define the elements of compensation they are including for allocating plan contributions annually.

[G] Credited Service

Again, target benefit plans use all the same rules that defined benefit plans do. Other defined contribution plans that use years of service in the allocation formula also look at all three definitions of credited service, but plans that do not use years of service in their allocation formula need only consider eligibility and vesting years of service.

[H] Vesting

Defined contribution plans need to focus on vesting as part of their design. Vested interest is that portion of the employee's accrued benefits in which the employee has a nonforfeitable right. An employee's vested interest typically is expressed as a percentage of accrued benefit. Benefits based on employer contributions must be fully vested once the employee reaches normal retirement age, as defined by the plan. Before the normal retirement age, employers have a choice of two schedules for the vesting of their contributions: graduated or cliff.

All employer contributions (matching and non-elective) must vest under a six-year, graduated schedule (at least 20 percent vested after two years, with an additional 20 percent each year thereafter, ending with 100 percent vesting after six years), or a three-year cliff-vesting schedule (0 percent vesting for the first two years, and 100 percent vesting after three years).

If a plan's vesting schedule changes, employees with at least three years of service must be given the option of either the new or the old schedule.

[I] Other Typical Plan Provisions

The same features covered under a defined benefit plan can be included in a defined contribution plan. An early retirement feature does not affect the cost of a defined contribution plan in the same way that it might affect a defined benefit plan and is rarely used. Supplemental death benefits can be offered, but the limit on the amount of insurance offered is 25 percent of the contribution for term or universal life coverage (50 percent if whole life policies are used), rather than the 100 times benefit limit. The plan can offer postretirement health care coverage, but because a target benefit plan is primarily a defined contribution pension plan, it does so only rarely. The same forms of benefit payments would apply, but note that only target benefit and money purchase plans must provide the annuity provisions. Other defined contribution plans usually avoid the added complexity and administration of the joint and survivor annuity requirements by providing lump-sum or installment payments as their primary forms of distribution and not offering any annuity options.

[J] Funding

[1] General Concepts

Funding for a defined contribution plan is simpler than for a defined benefit plan, even for a target benefit plan. The funding commitment is simply the amount of the formula contribution or the amount annually determined at the discretion of the plan sponsor. For plans that define the contribution as a percentage of pay, funding is that percentage of pay. For plans that define the contribution as a percentage of pay less forfeitures, the required funding is only slightly less predictable. Target benefit plans require more work in defining the amount of the contribution, but since the amount is not subject to subsequent changes due to turnover or earnings variances, it is still very predictable.

[2] Funding Requirements

Defined contribution pension plans with fixed money purchase or target benefit contribution formulas are also subject to the funding standards and related excise taxes for missed contributions. However, they do not require quarterly deposits. In addition, these plans have a single required contribution number, not a range of allowable contributions. Defined contribution plans with discretionary contributions are not subject to the funding standards.

Note that the deductible limit for all defined contribution plans is 25 percent of covered compensation. This is a change from years prior to 2002, when the deductible limit for money purchase and target benefit plans was 25 percent, while the deductible limit for discretionary defined contribution plans was 15 percent of covered compensation. Employee salary deferrals do not count against this limit. As with the defined benefit plan, if more than the deductible limit is contributed, not only is the excess not deductible, but a 10 percent excise tax applies to the excess, as well.

[K] Accounting for Defined Contribution Plans

As long as the plan sponsor makes the current required contributions, the only impact that a defined contribution plan has on the balance sheet of the plan sponsor is the liability for any accrued but unpaid contribution for the year. If a funding waiver were requested, the balance sheet would reflect the five-year spread of the required contribution in current and long-term liabilities.

[L] Pension Benefit Guaranty Corporation

The PBGC does not regulate, or provide insurance for, defined contribution pension plans.

[M] Other Defined Contribution Plan Provisions Under the PPA

The PPA made additional changes to defined contribution plans. One such change regards the Economic Growth and Tax Relief Reconciliation Act of 2001 (EGTRRA). As originally enacted, many of the positive pension and tax law changes included in EGTRRA were originally scheduled to expire at the end of 2010.

The pension and individual retirement account provisions of EGTRRA listed below are made permanent by the PPA:

- Increased contribution limits for employees for 403(b) plans, 401(k) plans, 457(b) plans and individual retirement accounts (including SIMPLE-IRA and SAR-SEP plans)

- Ability to maintain deemed IRAs in a qualified plan

- Catch-up contributions for individuals age 50 and over

- Increased compensation limits

- Higher limits on contributions and benefits

- Simplified top-heavy plan determinations

- Provision for qualified plan loans to partners, sole proprietors, LLC members, and S Corporation shareholders

- Elective deferrals excluded from employer's deduction limits

- Increased deduction limits for profit-sharing plans (from 15 percent to 25 percent)

- Roth 401(k) and Roth 403(b) plan feature

- Repeal of the requirement to coordinate the 457(b) limit with the 403(b)/401(k) limits

- Tax credit for start-up pension plans

- The repeal of the same-desk rule

- Changes to the age 70½ minimum distribution rules for other than 5 percent owners

- Repeal of the multiple use test for 401(k) plans with matching contributions

In addition to the changes discussed earlier in this chapter, changes to defined contribution plans include:

- **The defined benefit 401(k) (DBK) plan.** Employers with 500 employees or fewer can now establish a combined defined benefit/401(k) plan. The plan is governed by one document and there are specific requirements respective to the defined benefit and defined contribution portions of the trust. In general, defined benefit rules apply to the defined benefit portions of the plan and defined contribution rules apply to the defined contribution portions of the plan. The defined benefit component has to satisfy minimum accrual requirements. If the defined benefit component is a cash balance plan (see **Section 8.05[D][2]** above on cash balance plans), the accrual must be in the form of minimum pay credits. The 401(k) component must have automatic enrollment and must meet minimum matching contribution requirements. This change is effective for plan years beginning after 2009.

- **Safest available annuity.** The PPA specifies that the DOL's "safest annuity available" standard does not apply to annuities paid as an optional distribution from a defined contribution plan. Effective for plan years beginning after December 31, 2006.

- **Expanded rollover rules.** The PPA permits the rollover of after-tax contributions from a qualified plan to a tax-sheltered annuity or vice versa. Effective for taxable years beginning after December 31, 2006.

Many of the newly added provisions will require additional guidance from the IRS and DOL. As regulatory guidance is provided, relevant sections of this chapter will be updated to provide appropriate support to the reader.

Exhibit 8.1
Worksheet for Testing Compliance with
Minimum Coverage and Participation Tests

*This test is only for a company with highly compensated employees (HCEs) in its plan.

	Highly Compensated Employees (HCEs)	Non-Highly Compensated Employees (NHCEs)
A. Total Employees Employed During Plan Year (Not Number of Employees at Year-end)	_____	_____
Exclusions:		
Collectively bargained employees	_____	_____
Employees who have not attained the plan entry age	_____	_____
Employees who have not satisfied the plan's waiting period	_____	_____
Nonresident aliens with no U.S. source income	_____	_____
Employees who have fewer than 500 hours of service and who are not employed on the last day of the plan year	_____	_____
Employees who are employed by other qualified separate lines of business (QSLOBs)	_____	_____
B. Total Exclusions		
C. Employees Eligible to Participate (A – B)	_____	_____
Ineligible employees:		
Leased employees	_____	_____
Employees who have more than 501 hours of service and are not employed on the last day of the plan year	_____	_____
Other (Describe)	_____	_____
	_____	_____
	_____	_____
D. Total Ineligible Employees	_____	_____
E. Total Eligible Employees (C – D)	_____	_____
	_____	_____
F. Covered Employees	_____	_____

Exhibit 8.1   Mandated Benefits: 2009 Compliance Guide

Exhibit 8.1 (cont'd)

G.   Covered Employees as a Percentage of Eligible   _____   _____
     Employees (F/E)

NHCE percentage must be at least 70 percent of HCE percentage. If not, other methods of testing may be available under which the plan will pass. These alternative methods of testing are complicated, and an employee benefit specialist should be consulted.

A covered employee in the case of elective and matching/employee contributions means one who is eligible to make or receive elective contributions, matching contributions, or employee contributions. With regard to nonelective contributions, a participant is covered if he or she receives allocation contributions, forfeitures, or both.

Participation Test

This test applies only to defined benefit plans.

A.   Total number of employees on test date   _____

B.   Number of excludable employees counted above   _____

   (An *excludable employee* is one who has not met minimum age or service
   requirements of the plan, one who is included in a collective bargaining unit,
   one who terminated employment with fewer than 501 hours of service and
   was not employed on the last day of the plan year, one who is employed by
   other qualified separate lines of businesses (QSLOBs), or one who is a
   nonresident alien. Do not count an employee more than once.)   _____

C.   Subtract line B from line A   _____

D.   Number of benefiting employees on test date   _____

E.   Enter the greater of 40 percent of line C or 2 (or if there is only one
     employee, one employee)   _____

F.   Enter the lesser of line E or 50   _____

G.   Is line D at least as great as line F? If yes, the plan passes the minium
     participation test of Code Section 401(a)(26).   _____

The answers to both the coverage test and the participation test must be ''yes'' for the plan to be guaranteed exempt status. If the coverage test is not met as of the last day of the plan year, go back and test on other dates during each quarter of operation for the year. Technically, this standard of Section 410(b) of the Code must be satisfied on at least one day of every quarter of the plan year. This standard was simplified with the proposed substantiation guidelines for nondiscrimination testing issued in Revenue Procedure 95-34, which permits a plan to determine who is an HCE on the basis of a ''snapshot day'' as well, if the document so provides. The participation test is to be satisified on every day of the plan year. However, final regulations provide a simplified testing method. Under the simplified method, a plan is treated as satisfying Section 401(a)(26) if the plan satisfies Section 401(a)(26) on a single day during the plan year as long as the day is reasonably representative of the employer's workforce and the plan's coverage. Therefore, if there is little margin for error on this test, the same test should be run on the plan's entry dates.

Exhibit 8.2
Worksheet for Determining Which Individuals
Are Highly Compensated Employees

1. Determination

year: _____

_____

2. Lookback

year: _____

_____

3. List the names of individuals who, at any time during the determination year (or the lookback year), owned (directly or indirectly) more than 5 percent of:

   a. The value of all classes of the employer's outstanding stock

   b. The outstanding voting stock issued by the employer

   c. The employer's capital (if the employer is a partnership or a proprietorship)

   d. The employer's income (if the employer is a partnership or a proprietorship)

The ownership interest given should be the largest held during the testing period.

Name   Highest Ownership Interest Held

_____

_____

_____

_____

(If more space is needed, attach additional sheets.)

4. By order of compensation, list the names of all individuals who, during the lookback year, received compensation from the employer greater than $105,000 for 2009, lookback to 2008; $100,000 for 2008 and 2007, lookback to 2007 and 2006; $95,000 for 2006, lookback to 2005. (This limit is adjusted for changes in the cost of living.) Also list the compensation of each of these employees for the lookback year. (*Note:* The employer may elect to measure compensation for this purpose over the calendar year beginning with or within the lookback year.)

Name   Highest Ownership Interest Held

_____

_____

_____

_____

(If more space is needed, attach additional sheets.)

Exhibit 8.2   Mandated Benefits: 2009 Compliance Guide

Exhibit 8.2 (cont'd)

5. Calculate the size of the top-paid group for the lookback year as follows:

   Insert total number of individuals employed during the lookback year: _____

   Subtract the number of employees who:

   a. Had not completed six months of service in the lookback year   _____

   b. Had not reached age 21 at the end of the lookback year   _____

   c. Usually work no more than six months each year   _____

   d. Usually work less than 17 and one-half hours weekly   _____

   e. Are nonresident aliens, with no earned income from sources with
       the United States   _____

   f. Are members of a collective bargaining unit (if more than 90 per-
       cent of all employees are members of a collective bargaining unit)

                                                            Subtotal: _____

   Multiply the subtotal by 20 percent: = _____
   This is the size of the top-paid group for the lookback year

6. List the names of all individuals listed in Item 3.

Name   Highest Ownership Interest Held

_____

_____

_____

_____

(If more space is needed, attach additional sheets.)

7. After eliminating all duplications, list the names of all individuals listed in Items 4 and 6. If the plan provisions limit those in Item 4 to the top-paid group, include in this list only the number of employees from that list, ordered by size of pay, equal to the number determined in Item 5. These are highly compensated active employees.

Name   Highest Ownership Interest Held

_____

_____

_____

_____

(If more space is needed, attach additional sheets.)

Note: The elections to use calendar-year data or to limit the top-paid group for purposes of compensation are included in the plan provisions or by amendments to the plan.

Exhibit 8.3
Sample Top-Heavy Test

Plan Name _____

Plan Year End _____

A key employee is an employee who, at any time during the plan year containing the determination date or any of the four preceding plan years, is (or was):

1. An officer receiving annual compensation in excess of $160,000 for 2009 (indexed for future years).

2. A 5 percent owner

3. A 1 percent owner whose annual compensation exceeds $150,000

Key Employee	PV Accrued Benefit and/or Account Balance
_____	_____
_____	_____
_____	_____
_____	_____
_____	_____
	_____
Add prior five years' in-service distributions to Key Employees	_____
Add the immediately prior year's distributions (other than in-service amounts) to Key Employees	_____
Subtract rollovers/transfers for Key Employees	_____
Total Accounts/Benefits for Key Employees	_____ (A)

Exhibit 8.3   Mandated Benefits: 2009 Compliance Guide

Exhibit 8.3 (cont'd)

Total for All
Participants _____ + _____ + _____ − _____

      All Accounts/   Prior   Prior In-Service   Rollovers/Transfers
        Benefits   Non-in-Service   Distributions for
                 Distributions for   5 years
                    1 year

                                      − _____ = _____ (B)

                                    Former Key
                                    Employees'
                             Accounts/Benefits

PV of Key Employee Accrued Benefits (A) _____

PV of All Employee Accrued Benefits (B) _____

                                  = _____ = _____

Is plan top heavy? (% > 60)   Yes   No

Exhibit 8.3 (cont'd)

In-Service Distribution Record for Top-Heavy Test

Plan Name _____

Plan Year End	In-Service Distributions Made		5-Year Cumulative Total	
	Key Employee	Non-key Employee	Key Employee	Non-key Employee
_____	_____	_____	_____	_____
_____	_____	_____	_____	_____
_____	_____	_____	_____	_____
_____	_____	_____	_____	_____
_____	_____	_____	_____	_____
_____	_____	_____	_____	_____
_____	_____	_____	_____	_____
_____	_____	_____	_____	_____
_____	_____	_____	_____	_____
_____	_____	_____	_____	_____
_____	_____	_____	_____	_____
_____	_____	_____	_____	_____
_____	_____	_____	_____	_____
_____	_____	_____	_____	_____
_____	_____	_____	_____	_____
_____	_____	_____	_____	_____
_____	_____	_____	_____	_____
_____	_____	_____	_____	_____
TOTALS	_____	_____	_____	_____

Exhibit 8.4   Mandated Benefits: 2009 Compliance Guide

Exhibit 8.4
Uniform Required Minimum Distribution Table
(For Account Balance Retirement Benefits)

Age of employee (on the birthday in the distribution year)	Distribution (in years)
70	27.4
71	26.5
72	25.6
73	24.7
74	23.8
75	22.9
76	22.0
77	21.2
78	20.3
79	19.5
80	18.7
81	17.9
82	17.1
83	16.3
84	15.5
85	14.8
86	14.1
87	13.4
88	12.7
89	12.0
90	11.4
91	10.8
92	10.2
93	9.6
94	9.1
95	8.6
96	8.1
97	7.6
98	7.1

Exhibit 8.4 (cont'd)
Uniform Required Minimum Distribution Table
(For Account Balance Retirement Benefits)

Age of employee (on the birthday in the distribution year)	Distribution (in years)
99	6.7
100	6.3
101	5.9
102	5.5
103	5.2
104	4.9
105	4.5
106	4.2
107	3.9
108	3.7
109	3.4
110	3.1
111	2.9
112	2.6
113	2.4
114	2.1
115 and older	1.9

Exhibit 8.5

Mandated Benefits: 2009 Compliance Guide

Exhibit 8.5
Salary Deferral Options for Small Employers
For Plan Years Beginning After December 31, 2001

Type of Plan	SEP IRA	SIMPLE IRA	SIMPLE 401(k)	Money Purchase	Profit Sharing	Traditional 401(k)	Defined Benefit
Plan Year	Calendar year (IRS model) or employer's fiscal year	Calendar year	Calendar year	Any fiscal year	Any fiscal year	Any fiscal year	Any fiscal year
Maximum Number of Employees	No maximum	100	100	No maximum	No maximum	No maximum	No maximum
Maximum Eligibility Requirements	Any employee who is age 21 and has worked in 3 of 5 years and earns more than $450 (indexed)	Any employee who has earned $5,000 in any 2 preceding years	1 year of service Age 21	1 year of service if not immediate vesting 2 years if 100% immediate vesting Age 21	1 year of service if not immediate vesting 2 years if 100% immediate vesting Age 21	1 year of service Age 21	1 year of service if not immediate vesting 2 years if 100% immediate vesting Age 21
Employee Deferral Limits[1]	None allowed	2004 = $9,000 2005 = $10,000 2006 = $10,000 2007 = $10,500 2008 = $10,500 2009 = $11,500	2004 = $9,000 2005 = $10,000 2006 = $10,000 2007 = $10,500 2008 = $10,500 2009 = $11,500	May allow for after-tax employee contributions	May allow for after-tax employee contributions	2004 = $13,000 2005 = $14,000 2006 = $15,000 2007 = $15,500 2008 = $15,500 2009 = $16,500	May allow for after-tax employee contributions
Employee Deferral Catch-up Contributions at Age 50	None allowed	2004 = $1,500 2005 = $2,000 2006 = $2,500 2007 = $2,500 2008 = $2,500 2009 = $2,500	2004 = $1,500 2005 = $2,000 2006 = $2,500 2007 = $2,500 2008 = $2,500 2009 = $2,500	None allowed	None allowed	2004 = $3,000 2005 = $4,000 2006 = $5,000 2007 = $5,000 2008 = $5,000 2009 = $5,500	None allowed

Type of Plan	SEP IRA	SIMPLE IRA	SIMPLE 401(k)	Money Purchase	Profit Sharing	Traditional 401(k)	Defined Benefit
Vesting Schedule Allowed on Employer Contributions	No	No	No	Yes. Maximum up to 5-year cliff or 7-year graded.	Yes. Maximum up to 5-year cliff or 7-year graded.	Yes. Maximum up to 3-year cliff or 6-year graded for matching contribution	Yes. Maximum up to 5-year cliff or 7-year graded
Mandatory Employer Contribution	None unless top-heavy	100% match deferrals up to 3% or flat 2% for all eligible employees (match may be as low as 1% in 2 out of 5 years). Must use full plan year compensation	100% match on deferrals up to 3% or 2% non-elective for all eligible employees. Must use full plan year compensation	Yes. Required contribution defined in plan document	None unless top-heavy, but contributions must be "recurring" and "substantial" so going 3–5 years without a contribution may cause plan to terminate automatically.	None unless top-heavy, but contributions must be "recurring" and "substantial" so going 3–5 years without a contribution may cause plan to terminate automatically.	Yes. Required minimum funding
Mandatory Contribution if Top-Heavy	Yes, up to 3%	No	No	Yes, up to 3%	Yes, up to 3%	Yes, up to 3%. No, if plan permits only ADP/ACP safe harbor contributions	Yes, 2% defined benefit accrual
Discretionary/ Employer Contributions Allowed	Yes, up to 25%	No	No	No	Yes, up to 25%	Yes, up to 25%	No
Last Day Rule or Hours Requirement Allowed	No	No	No	Yes	Yes	Yes	Only hours

Exhibit 8.5 (cont'd)
Salary Deferral Options for Small Employers

For Plan Years Beginning After December 31, 2001

Type of Plan	SEP IRA	SIMPLE IRA	SIMPLE 401(k)	Money Purchase	Profit Sharing	Traditional 401(k)	Defined Benefit
Employer Contribution Limit per Employee (§ 415 Limits) (§ 402(h) for SEPs)[2]	25% of individual pay or $49,000	None allowed	100% of individual pay or $49,000	100% of individual pay or $49,000	100% of individual pay or $49,000	100% of individual pay or $46,000	$195,000
Employer Allowed to Maintain Other Qualified Plans	Yes	No	Yes, if other plan is only for employees not covered in SIMPLE	Yes	Yes	Yes	Yes
Subject to § 401(a)(17) Compensation Limit	Yes (for employer deduction limit)	Only for 2% nonelective contribution	Yes	Yes	Yes	Yes	Yes
Subject to § 401(k) Non-discrimination Testing	No	No	No	No, but 401(m) if after-tax contributions allowed	No, but 401(m) if after-tax contributions allowed	Yes	No, but 401(m) if after-tax contributions allowed
Subject to § 401(a)(4) and § 410(b) Testing	No	No	Yes	Yes	Yes	Yes	Yes
Subject to "404" Limitations	Yes	No	Yes (greater of 25% or amount required by SIMPLE)	Yes	Yes	Yes	Yes

Type of Plan	SEP IRA	SIMPLE IRA	SIMPLE 401(k)	Money Purchase	Profit Sharing	Traditional 401(k)	Defined Benefit
Participant Loans	No	No	Yes, if plan allows	Yes, if plan allows	Yes, if plan allows	Yes, if plan allows	Yes, if plan allows
10-Year Averaging Grandfathered	No	No	Yes	Yes	Yes	Yes	Yes
Premature Distribution Penalty	10%	25% for first 2 years; 10% thereafter	10%	10%	10%	10%	10%
Minimum Distributions at Age 70	Yes	Yes	Only 5% owner or terminated employees	Only 5% owner or terminated employees	Only 5% owner or terminated employees	Only 5% owner or terminated employees	Only 5% owner or terminated employees
Form 5500 Required	No	No	Yes	Yes	Yes	Yes	Yes

[1] Limits indexed for inflation in $500 increments.

[2] $49,000 limits indexed for inflation in $1,000 increments, $195,000 limit is indexed for inflation in $5,000 increments. Amounts shown are 2009 limits.

Exhibit 8.6

Mandated Benefits: 2009 Compliance Guide

Exhibit 8.6
IRS Limits on Retirement Plan Benefits and Compensation

	2009	2008	2007	2006	2005	2004	2003
Defined Benefit Plan							
Maximum Annual Addition	$195,000	$185,000	$180,000	$175,000	$170,000	$165,000	$160,000
Defined Contribution Plan							
Maximum Annual Addition	$49,000	$46,000	$45,000	$44,000	$42,000	$41,000	$40,000
401(k) Plan							
Maximum Elective Deferral	$16,500	$15,500	$15,500	$15,000	$14,000	$13,000	$12,000
Maximum Catch-Up Contribution	$5,500	$5,000	$5,000	$5,000	$4,000	$3,000	$2,000
SIMPLE Deferral	$11,500	$10,500	$10,500	$10,000	$10,000	$9,000	$8,000
SIMPLE Catch-Up Contribution	$2,500	$2,500	$2,500	$2,500	$2,000	$1,500	$1,000
SEP Compensation Amount	$550	$500	$500	$450	$450	$450	$450
Qualified Plans							
Maximum Compensation Limits	$245,000	$230,000	$225,000	$220,000	$210,000	$205,000	$200,000
Highly Compensated Limits	$110,000	$105,000	$100,000	$100,000	$95,000	$90,000	$90,000
Officer Limits (Key Employee)	$160,000	$150,000	$145,000	$140,000	$135,000	$130,000	$130,000
PBGC Insured Maximum Per Month	TBA	$4,312.50	$4,125	$3,971.59	$3,801.14	$3,698.86	$3,644.77
Social Security/Medicare Salary, Tax, and Benefit Levels							
FICA Taxable Wage Base	$106,800	$102,000	$97,500	$94,200	$90,000	$87,900	$87,000
Employer and Employee Social Security Tax	6.20%	6.20%	6.20%	6.20%	6.20%	6.20%	6.20%
Employer and Employee Medicare Tax	$1.45%	1.45%	1.45%	1.45%	1.45%	1.45%	1.45%

Chapter 9
Life Insurance and Disability and Income Protection Benefits

§ 9.01 AUDIT QUESTIONS

1. Has the company determined whether its life insurance benefit passes the required nondiscrimination tests?

2. Does the company impute income for tax purposes for life insurance benefits over $50,000?

3. Has the company reviewed its short- and long-term disability benefits to ensure proper coordination for waiting periods and coverage periods?

4. If a disability benefit is available to employees, is pregnancy treated like any other disability?

5. Is a notice to employees of their right to workers' compensation benefits posted in a conspicuous place where it can be easily read by employees during the workday?

6. Is a record available of claims made by employees of injuries on the job that includes time, date, and location?

7. Is the Summary of Work-Related Injuries and Illnesses (OSHA Form 300A) posted in a conspicuous place, from February 1 through April 30, where it can be easily read by employees during the workday?

8. Does the company designate workers' compensation time off as leave under the Family and Medical Leave Act?

Note: Consistent "yes" answers to the above questions suggest that the organization is applying effective management practices and/or complying with federal regulations. "No" answers indicate that problem areas exist and should be addressed immediately.

§ 9.02 DEATH BENEFITS AND LIFE INSURANCE

Plans that provide payments and benefits to survivors are more diverse and less consistent than any other basic employer benefit plan. In many companies, a collection of largely independent plans has evolved gradually, primarily because of insufficient management planning and proactive marketing of new products by the insurance industry. The growth of these plans has been extensive. Many are complex to administer and designed for special executive compensation. Unless care is given in developing and implementing these plans, they may not be effective as an employee benefit or be cost-effective.

Despite this variety of plans, most companies offer the following basic survivor benefits:

- Group term life insurance with, in some cases, the opportunity for eligible employees to purchase supplementary coverage (at their own cost)

- Accidental death and dismemberment coverage

- Business travel accident insurance

- Survivor income benefit (SIB) insurance

- Employee death benefits

Statutory programs such as workers' compensation and Social Security pay survivor benefits, but they relate payments to marital status and survivor parental responsibilities. Most discretionary plans generally are not based on these need-related factors. Employers' discretionary survivor benefits, except SIB plans, are typically based on the cause of death and the deceased's final pay level. Unfortunately, overdependency on the cause-of-death and pay-level factors, without considering family or dependent needs, may result in the program's failing to adequately match the benefit level to the survivors' needs.

[A] Group Term Life Insurance

Employers often provide life insurance as a fringe benefit. According to the Society for Human Resource Management (SHRM) 2008 Benefits Survey Report, 92 percent of employers offer a life insurance benefit for their employees. Life insurance is designed to protect an employee's family financially in the event of the employee's death. Although employer-provided life insurance takes a variety of forms, the type offered most frequently is group term life insurance.

A group term policy pays benefits to the employee's designated beneficiary in the event of the employee's death. Policies usually cover a term of one year, for which premiums have been paid. In most cases, coverage ceases when the employee terminates employment. The policy has no cash value and cannot be paid up to avoid payment of future term premiums. A term life insurance policy at a group rate is usually less expensive per person than individual term policies for the same level of coverage.

[1] Legal and Tax Considerations

Although group term life insurance is not a federally mandated benefit, the company should follow certain laws and tax regulations if it chooses to offer this benefit. Group term life insurance is subject to the following laws and regulations:

- The Employee Retirement Income Security Act of 1974 (ERISA), specifically, the welfare plan reporting and disclosure requirements (see **Chapter 5**).

- Nondiscrimination rules under the Internal Revenue Code (Code) regarding both participation and benefits. A plan of group term insurance either must cover 70 percent of all employees or 85 percent of the participants in the plan must be non-key employees. Benefits are considered nondiscriminatory if all benefits available to key employees are available to other employees (taking into consideration the compensation of the employees). For purposes of determining nondiscrimination in benefits, each layer of coverage can be considered as a separate plan.

- The Equal Pay Act, which prohibits employers from providing different amounts of life insurance for male and female employees.

- The Age Discrimination in Employment Act (ADEA), which prohibits employment discrimination on the basis of age and prevents benefit plans from discriminating on the basis of age.

As a result, if an employer offers life insurance as an employee benefit, equally situated younger and older employees must receive equal benefit amounts, unless there is a cost justification for unequal benefits. Even if the life insurance amount available to older employees is reduced on this basis, it can be reduced only to the point at which the cost of the insurance is equal to the cost of insurance provided to younger workers. The employer's human resources (HR) manager should check with the insurance carrier, benefits agent, consultant, attorney, and/or broker before providing reduced life insurance benefit amounts to older employees.

Employers may provide up to $2,000 of group term life insurance for an employee's spouse or for each and every dependent and have that contribution considered a de minimis fringe benefit under Code Section 132. [IRS Notice 89-110, 1989-2 C.B. 447] The $2,000 contribution is excluded from the employee's gross income; if the amount is larger, it must be included in the employee's income.

Section 79 of the Code specifies that up to $50,000 of group term life insurance protection, including survivor income benefit insurance (see **Section 9.02[D]**), provided to an employee by an employer is generally excludable from the employee's gross income. As a result, many hourly and salaried nonexempt employees face no tax consequences from their company's group term life plan, even if the insurance is fully paid by the employer.

If the face value of an employee's coverage is greater than $50,000, the imputed premium cost for the excess coverage over $50,000 is taxable. Any taxable amount of group term life insurance must be reported on Form W-2 and is subject to employment taxes but not to income tax withholding. If the employee has contributed to the cost of the insurance, his or her entire contribution may be allocated to that portion in excess of $50,000. Thus, the employee may deduct the contribution from the amount that otherwise would be taxed.

Determination of an employee's taxable amount in these situations does not depend on whether the company has actually paid premiums during that taxable year or on the employer's cost of those premiums. Instead, the Internal Revenue Service (IRS) uses specific rates to determine the cost value for tax purposes. **Exhibit 9.1** indicates the rates used in calculating the taxable value of group term life insurance in excess of $50,000. **Exhibit 9.2** provides an example of how to calculate the tax liability on that insurance. **Exhibit 9.3** indicates how to calculate the tax liability when the level of coverage changes during the year. **Exhibit 9.4** illustrates typical schedules of basic group term life insurance coverage.

Group term life insurance is often the survivors' primary source of protection against loss of income. Whether a company can offer group term life insurance and the level of protection it can provide depend on the following factors:

- Insurance company underwriting rules and tax code considerations

- Cost considerations

- The degree of employee cost sharing

- Tax benefits and issues

- The overall employee benefits philosophy

Group term life insurance may be financed either on a noncontributory basis (i.e., the employer pays for the total amount of the insurance) or on a contributory basis (i.e., the employee shares the cost of the insurance with the employer). Many employers provide a base amount on a noncontributory basis and offer employees the option of purchasing additional insurance on a contributory basis. This additional, employee-paid coverage is referred to as supplemental life insurance. If the coverage is deemed to be a separate plan and the employee pays 100 percent of the cost of the supplemental coverage, there should be no imputed income. [PLRs 9227019, 9149033]

In designing a benefit plan, the HR manager should consider employees' and their families' financial needs, the company's available budget, and other death benefits that may be available, such as survivor benefits under the company's pension or disability program. Group term life insurance is a relatively inexpensive benefit that is generally understood and appreciated by employees.

[2] Underwriting Rules

Underwriting rules, which incorporate various legal requirements, are the guidelines insurers use to determine whether they are willing to assume the risk represented by an employee group and under what terms the risk should be assumed. The purpose of underwriting rules is to ensure that the risk involved is no greater than that assumed by the insurer when it sets its rate structure for a particular class of business. If the risk is excessive, the insurer may charge an additional premium or may decline to offer coverage. Some principal areas of underwriting concern are discussed in the following paragraphs.

[3] The Employee Group

Each business exposes employees to unique health risks, so carriers underwrite group term life insurance for companies using some variation of standard or usual risk level.

[4] Minimum Size Requirements

Most states and/or insurance carriers require that when employees pay part of the premium, at least 75 percent of eligible employees must enroll. The purpose of this 75 percent enrollment requirement is to protect against adverse selection, which results when only elderly workers or those in poor health enroll in the insurance program, thus increasing the insurer's risk. When no employee contribution is involved, the plan must generally cover all eligible employees to avoid discrimination and adverse selection.

From a tax perspective, Code Section 79 provides, in general, that to qualify as group term life insurance, a plan must cover at least 10 full-time employees. An employer with fewer than 10 employees can still take advantage of the tax benefits of Section 79 by meeting certain conditions.

[5] Classes of Eligible Employees

As required by law, employers must define classes of eligible employees based on conditions of employment. Definitions should be clear and well drafted to avoid administrative disputes and legal actions. Some definitions frequently used include:

- All salaried employees

- All corporate officers and all other employees

- All exempt and nonexempt employees

- All employees working more than 17.5 hours per week

Problematic definitions involve unclear classifications, such as clerical and administrative employees or management employees. Discriminatory definitions are based on sex and age, unless either of these factors is a legitimate condition of employment, which is rarely the case.

[6] The Individual Employee

Generally, no individual underwriting is involved for basic group term life coverage. The only requirement is that the individual be actively at work; otherwise, coverage is postponed until the employee returns to work. In many plans, if an employee declines coverage within 31 days of first becoming eligible, the plan may require evidence of insurability if the employee desires coverage at a later date.

[7] Amount of Insurance Coverage

The amount of insurance provided to each class of employee is probably the most important aspect of underwriting and the area of greatest variation among employers. As a general rule, the larger the group, the higher the maximum amount of coverage permitted by the carrier. In addition, groups with favorable claims experience can usually obtain higher coverage than groups with either no claims history or poor claims history.

To be considered group term life insurance under Code Section 79, the plan must compute the amount of insurance coverage provided to each employee under a formula that precludes individual selection. The formula must be based on such factors as age, years of service, and/or compensation. When a plan qualifies as group term life insurance under Section 79, it must not discriminate in favor of key employees regarding the level of benefit provided. Section 79 does provide that a plan is not considered discriminatory if the amount of life insurance provided under the plan bears a uniform relationship to compensation (e.g., one times pay) or if the plan provides a fixed level of insurance that is the same for all eligible employees. If a plan provides layers of coverage based on percentages of compensation, each layer of coverage will generally be tested separately.

Ideally, the amount of insurance will also bear some relation to the need for income replacement. Companies usually determine this relationship by basing the amount of insurance on job title or salary, usually providing a basic level of coverage equivalent to one or two times salary. **Exhibit 9.4** provides four examples of typical employer-provided group term life insurance coverage schedules.

[8] Plan Provisions

Most group term life insurance plans include the following provisions:

- *Beneficiary Designation.* An employee may name and change his or her beneficiary as desired. The only restriction is that the insurance must benefit someone other than the employer.

- *Settlement Options.* An employee's beneficiary may elect to receive the face amount of the group term life insurance on an installment basis rather than as a lump sum.

- *Assignment.* Group term life insurance usually can be assigned if the master policy and state law both permit it. Because tax laws allow unlimited estate tax marital deduction, this provision is seldom used.

- *Conversion Privilege.* If an employee terminates employment, terminates membership in an eligible classification, or retires, he or she may convert the group term life insurance to an individual permanent life insurance policy without medical evidence of insurability. Generally, under conversion, the employee must apply to the insurer in writing within 31 days of termination (and related loss of coverage) and must pay the premium. Failure to notify employees of the conversion privilege may result in the employer becoming the insurer of the benefit.

- *Thirty-One-Day Continuation of Protection.* This provision gives a terminated employee 31 days of protection while reviewing the conversion privilege or awaiting coverage under a group life insurance plan of another employer.

- *Premium Waiver.* Many insurance companies agree to a provision that continues coverage for individuals who are permanently and totally disabled and to waive premiums for such individuals. This provision ensures that disabled employees can maintain their life insurance protection.

- *Accelerated Death Benefits.* In response to requests from terminally ill employees, many insurance companies in recent years have added accelerated death benefit (ADB) riders to their group term life policies. Under this rider, terminally ill individuals, generally documented as having less than two years to live, can have access to life insurance benefits before death.

  For example, a 31-year-old female with terminal bone cancer has no dependents to whom to bequeath her life insurance benefits. Under the ADB rider, she can receive a percentage, generally ranging from 50 percent to 75 percent of the full face amount of the life insurance policy, before death, to spend as she pleases.

  The Health Insurance Portability and Accountability Act of 1996 (HIPAA) provides a reason for benefit plan administrators to reconsider adding ADB riders to employee life insurance policies. Beginning in 1997, HIPAA eliminated federal income tax on ADB benefits paid from life insurance policies to terminally ill policyholders. A *terminally ill policyholder* is an individual who has been certified by a physician as having an illness or physical condition that can reasonably be expected to result in death within 24 months following the certification. Insurance policies, however, generally anticipate a shorter period of life following the certification. Some insurance carriers automatically provide ADB riders for coverage above a certain amount.

A terminally ill policyholder whose life insurance does not include ADB paid directly by the insurer may sell his or her policy to a viatical settlement company at a discount. These viatical settlements are also tax-exempt beginning in 1997.

A chronically ill policyholder may also exclude from income a portion of any ADB benefit or viatical settlement paid under a long-term care (LTC) insurance contract, if the payment is for qualified LTC costs incurred by the payee, which are not otherwise compensated by insurance or Medicare.

- *Portability.* Although portability is similar to conversion, it provides an enhanced benefit to an employee who is terminating coverage. Portability allows the terminated individual to maintain the same group term insurance policy as he or she had previously, at the same group rates that existed at termination. This feature differs from conversion, which may offer a lesser term product or allow the eligible individual to apply only for whole life insurance. Because portability is a fairly new benefit feature, it is important to carefully review an insurance carrier's contract and state insurance law to understand the details of each specific, related rider. Because there may be additional cost to the employer for this benefit, it has not become a prevalent option.

[9] Cost Considerations

The cost of group term life insurance is determined principally by measuring the risk exposure of employees according to age and sex, although the number of employees covered is also a significant factor. In general, costs are higher for older male employees and lower for younger female employees. However, the average cost of group term life insurance remains stable as long as the employee group has a relatively stable age and sex distribution.

[10] Employee Cost Sharing

It is common practice today for employers to pay the entire cost of basic group term life insurance coverage: generally, either flat-dollar coverage of $15,000 to $25,000 or one times the employees' base, annualized salaries. The advantage of this basic arrangement is that it provides employees with low-cost protection paid with premiums that are tax deductible to the company, provided that the program qualifies as a group term life insurance program under Code Section 79. Offering a basic life insurance policy also simplifies plan administration.

Based on the plan design issues discussed in this section and on changing demographics in the U.S. workforce, many employers now also offer supplementary group term life insurance to employees. Employees are allowed to purchase additional term life insurance protection to meet their financial needs at preferred group rates without any company contributions. Generally, the employee pays the full cost of any supplemental life insurance, purchased through payroll deduction on an after-tax basis. The amount of coverage that employees are eligible for and any medical underwriting requirements are again determined by the size of the group, employees' average salaries, and the percentage of employees participating in the supplemental plan. Because group term life is an inexpensive product, supplementary life insurance allows employees to increase the value of the company's life insurance benefit without increasing the company's costs, except for administrative expenses. Some plans also allow employees to purchase additional supplemental protection for their spouses and other eligible dependents, as well.

[11] State Law

Almost all states regulate group life insurance policies offered to employees. Although a state law is preempted if it purports to regulate an employee benefit plan covered by ERISA, any state law that regulates the business of insurance is not preempted.

Although states do not require any minimum level of group life insurance coverage, the following provisions are common:

1. Most states provide that the insured individual may choose anyone to be the beneficiary. However, the employer is generally not permitted to be the beneficiary.

2. Many states set minimum limits on the number of employees, usually five to ten, who must be covered under a group policy.

3. Many state laws impose restrictions on who may pay premiums. Some states require employers to pay at least part of the premiums. Often, if employees pay part of the premiums, the state regulations require that a certain percentage (usually 75 percent) of employees must elect coverage. In some states, if the employer pays the entire premium, the group life insurance benefit must be made available to all employees.

4. Virtually all states require insurance companies to allow a one-month grace period if a premium payment is late.

5. Virtually all states provide for mandatory conversion; that is, insurers must allow individuals who are covered under a group policy to convert to an individual policy if they terminate employment.

A few states prohibit insurers from excluding or reducing benefits when AIDS is a cause of death. Generally, this type of exclusion is also prohibited by the Americans with Disabilities Act (ADA).

If the company purchases group term life insurance for its employees, the HR manager may wish to have an attorney or benefits expert review the policy to ensure compliance with applicable laws.

[B] Accidental Death and Dismemberment Insurance

Accidental death and dismemberment (AD&D) insurance provides special benefits in the event of an accidental death, or loss of sight or use of a limb. The cost of AD&D is minimal, often $0.04 to $0.07 per month per $1,000 of coverage, because of the fairly low incidence of claims. Plans may offer high levels of coverage, frequently up to as much as $300,000, but they may limit coverage to 10 or 15 times eligible employees' base, annualized salary. Dependent AD&D coverage is an attractive option, which is generally limited to 50 percent of the employee's coverage.

When providing AD&D insurance, companies may require that employees pay the full amount to supplement their basic level of term life insurance. Eligible employees are generally permitted to purchase coverage for their families at a very low cost. This approach is becoming popular, because it offers flexibility to employees without cost to the company. The company may also choose to furnish and pay for AD&D coverage equal to the amount of basic group term life insurance. This approach resembles a double indemnity provision in an ordinary life policy.

AD&D plans usually do not cover certain situations because of the difficulties involved in assessing whether those situations can be classified as accidents. AD&D plans often do not cover death or losses from some or all of the following situations:

- Disease or treatment for a disease

- Suicide or self-inflicted injury, while sane or insane

- Ptomaine poisoning or other infection or bacterial disease, except when contracted as a result of an accidental injury

- Drug overdose, sensitivity to a drug, or voluntary inhalation of fumes or gas

- War or any act of war

- An injury sustained while committing or attempting to commit an illegal act

- Participation in a riot

- Air travel in noncommercial flights

- Job-related accidents

The amount of benefits paid under an AD&D plan depends on the losses incurred. A typical schedule of benefits follows:

Nature of Loss	Amount Payable
Loss of life	100% of principal amount
Loss of one hand, one foot, or sight of one eye	50%
Loss of two or more such body members	100%

In general, an employer is entitled to a deduction for the cost of the company-paid insurance coverage, and the covered employee is not required to declare the cost of coverage as income. Supplemental AD&D rules are the same as those for supplemental life coverage. Because AD&D plans are considered *health* insurance coverage rather than life insurance coverage, the amount of coverage that can be provided tax free by the employer is unlimited.

[C] Business Travel Accident Insurance

Many companies have modified the concept of AD&D protection and arranged for business travel insurance. According to the SHRM 2008 Benefits Survey Report, 42 percent of employers provide business travel accident insurance. This insurance generally covers any accident that occurs while an employee is involved in travel on company business. Although commuting from home to workplace is rarely covered, business travel accident insurance does protect an employee traveling between a main office and branches or when traveling to clients or business-related training programs or seminars.

Underwriting rules for this insurance are based on the number of people covered and the frequency of business travel, rather than the age and sex of the individuals. In addition to usual AD&D restrictions, this insurance may exclude travel in war zones and may apply special provisions to travel in company owned (or leased) airplanes.

Coverage limits for business travel insurance are fairly substantial. In many plans, coverage is a multiple of four or five times base salary, with a $100,000 minimum and a $400,000 maximum benefit. Benefit payment schedules are usually similar to those of standard AD&D plans. The cost for this insurance is extremely low and is paid by the company, in most cases, as a company benefit.

The employer is generally entitled to a tax deduction for the cost of the insurance, and the employee is not required to declare the cost of coverage as income. In addition, in most situations, the employee or his or her beneficiaries may exclude any policy proceeds from gross income.

[D] Survivor Income Benefit Insurance

Group survivor income benefit (SIB) insurance is a fairly natural extension of need-related statutory survivor income programs and supplements basic group term insurance. SIB plans provide a regular monthly benefit only to specified surviving dependents, such as spouse and dependent children. A typical plan provides a spouse with an annual benefit of 25 percent of the insured employee's final pay, with an additional 5 percent for each dependent child under age 19 and a maximum benefit of 40 percent. Some plans establish a higher maximum benefit level but offset available benefits from the plan by Social Security and workers' compensation payments. Most plans continue the spouse's benefit payments until he or she remarries, dies, or reaches age 62, whichever occurs first. Employees with young children would be most attracted to an SIB plan.

In spite of the advantages, growth of employer-sponsored SIB plans has been relatively slow. The fairly high cost of funding continuing payments to younger survivors has contributed to this slow growth. Further, SIB plans are not designed to help employees build wealth. Companies offering SIB plans usually require the employee to pay the entire cost because of the benefit's high expense.

In general, policies issued after December 31, 1984, are taxed under the group term life insurance rules if the plan qualifies as group term life insurance. One federal district court has determined that, under certain circumstances, SIB plans are not life insurance plans and the death benefits are not eligible for tax-free treatment. Therefore, the HR manager should consult a tax specialist before implementing such a plan.

[E] Employee Death Benefits

As part of its overall survivor benefits package, a company can adopt an employee death policy. The employer can decide that, on the death of an employee, it will pay a certain sum to the beneficiary or the estate of the employee. Amounts distributed are generally taxable as compensation, unless it can be argued that the payment was a gift. Before enactment of the Small Business Job Protection Act of 1996, amounts up to $5,000 were excludable from gross income, but this exclusion has been repealed. The total payment of death benefits must be reported on Form 1099-R. The employer is generally entitled to a compensation deduction for the death benefits paid.

[F] Corporate Owned Life Insurance

Under corporate owned life insurance (COLI), the employer is both owner and beneficiary of permanent life insurance on the lives of participating executives. While the employer generally pays a death benefit to the executive's beneficiary upon his or her death, a COLI arrangement does not provide benefit security to the covered employee.

COLI is generally used to insure the employer's interest in executives' and key employees' lives. Some companies have purchased COLI for all their employees. In *Tillman v. Camelot Music Inc.* [408 F.3d 1300 (10th Cir. 2005)], the U.S. Court of Appeals for the Tenth Circuit ruled that employers cannot purchase COLI policies on all full-time employees because they do not have insurable interest in the lives of those employees. In order to have an insurable interest, the employer must have a substantial economic investment in the insured. According to this court, employers cannot have this substantial economic investment in all employees.

HIPAA prohibits employers' deduction of debt (e.g., interest on loans) against the value of COLI policies (capped at debt of up to $50,000 per individual). An exception applies to debt on life insurance policies covering up to 20 key persons. Phase-in rules vary. Interest rates are capped based on Moody's corporate bond monthly averages. Employers must determine, with counsel's assistance and advice, who may be a key person and the appropriate application of interest rates and phase-in rules.

§ 9.03 DISABILITY BENEFITS

[A] Short-Term Disability

Short-term disability (STD) is used to protect the income of employees who become ill or are unable to perform the duties of their present position, for limited periods of time, due to non-work-related circumstances. STD generally covers disabilities that occur after an employee's sick leave and/or salary continuation benefits have been exhausted. STD benefits are generally paid for periods of 13 to 26 weeks, although some employers provide coverage for more than 26 weeks, and up to two years.

STD provisions often include the following:

- Benefit duration of 13 or 26 weeks

- Waiting periods (i.e., the time between the day the disability begins and the first day that a covered individual is eligible for benefit payments) that range from first-day coverage (i.e., no waiting period before benefits start) to 30 days

- Waiting period for illness, but first-day coverage for accidents

- First-day payment of disability benefits if the employee is hospitalized (common among some older union plans)

STD benefits may be purchased from an insurance company or offered on a self-insured basis. Many companies, regardless of size, self-insure this benefit once they have several years of claims history to form a basis for their expected liability.

Benefits under STD insurance plans are generally expressed as a percentage of an employee's base pay and range from 50 percent to 70 percent of base pay. Some employers offer a flat dollar amount for all employees, such as $200 per week, or a schedule of flat benefits based on salary or job/position. Many insured programs provide benefit payment up to a weekly benefit maximum (e.g., $1,000 or $1,500 per week). Depending on the demographics of the group, typically 5 percent to 10 percent of employees file for STD benefits each year. STD benefit costs average between 2 percent and 5 percent of payroll.

STD plans generally cover only non-work-related illnesses and injuries. The work-related exclusion exists because work-related disabilities are covered by workers' compensation. If coverage is written on a 24-hour basis, meaning both work- and non-work-related disabilities are covered, the STD portion of any benefits will likely be reduced by any amount payable from workers' compensation.

The majority of STD benefits are 100 percent paid for by the employer. Most employers provide the STD benefit as a payroll practice, rather than through insurance. Because they are payroll practices, most employers have not calculated the true cost of providing this benefit. Of those employers who have quantified the cost of STD benefits, most estimate that they spend between 0 and 5 percent of payroll per year.

[B] Long-Term Disability

Long-term disability (LTD) programs are designed to provide financial protection to employees who become ill or are unable to perform the duties of their present position for extended periods of time. The benefit period generally begins when STD benefits have been exhausted. Therefore, LTD programs generally begin following the 13th or 26th week of disability, although waiting periods may be as long as one or two years. Benefit payment generally continues until the employee recovers and can return to active employment, until standard retirement age is reached or, in some cases, until the death of the employee (for lifetime benefits).

During the first two years of disability, an employee is typically considered disabled if he or she cannot perform the substantial and material duties of his or her own occupation (known as the "own occupation" provision). For example, if a warehouse worker who manually stocks shelves had a back injury and could no longer perform the lifting required, he or she would be considered totally disabled for his or her own occupation.

After two years of disability, the definition of disability normally becomes more stringent. The individual is then likely considered disabled only if he or she can no longer perform the substantial and material duties of any occupation for which he or she may be qualified based on education, training, or experience. This provision is referred to as an "any occupation" clause. If the warehouse worker, above, could transfer these skills to a sit-down position as a forklift driver who unloads shipments for the stockers, the worker would no longer be considered disabled and would stop receiving benefits after the two-year own occupation period.

As with STD, the amount of benefits paid under LTD plans is usually based on employees' base compensation. Benefits range from 50 percent to 67 percent of an employee's base pay and are subject to a monthly maximum. Unlike STD, there are generally no flat benefit amounts. However, because LTD benefits are calculated on base compensation, employees with substantial bonus or other variable compensation may find that the actual percentage of compensation replaced by LTD payments is significantly less than the stated percentage of replacement indicated in the summary plan description or other materials.

Because LTD benefits may be payable for an extended period of years, certain benefit options that are not available under STD are sometimes offered under LTD. A few examples are:

- A cost-of-living rider that increases the LTD benefit each year, based on a formula tied to the consumer price index

- Rehabilitation benefits that provide a financial incentive for employees to attempt a return to work

- Survivor benefits to surviving family members if an individual has been disabled under the program for a minimum defined benefit period

- The option for employees to convert their coverage to individual policies upon termination of employment

Only three to four employees per 1,000 receive LTD benefits each year. However, because salary payout can be up to age 65 or beyond, one LTD claim alone can cost a company close to $1 million. Because of the potential high-dollar payout, most employers that offer LTD benefits to their employees purchase LTD insurance.

Employers that choose to self-fund disability benefits must meet disclosure requirements under Financial Accounting Standards Board (FASB) Statement No. 112, which requires the recording of a liability for some types of benefits, including disability benefits, provided to former or inactive employees. The FASB takes the position that these benefits are part of compensation provided in exchange for services and that the cost should be recognized on an accrual basis.

Long-term disability policies generally cover both work-related and non-work-related conditions. Most employers reduce (i.e., integrate) LTD benefits by any workers' compensation benefits, Social Security disability income benefits, disability pensions, and any other type of group disability benefits received by the individual. Generally, LTD policies do not integrate with any type of retirement benefits, savings plan payouts, or any type of individual disability policy that may have been purchased.

Many employers provide sick leave and STD benefits only to their nonexempt employees and provide salary continuation and LTD benefits for their exempt and management-level employees. LTD usually costs an employer about 0.2 percent to 0.5 percent of annualized payroll.

[C] Laws Affecting Short- and Long-Term Disability Benefits

No federal laws mandate that STD or LTD coverage be provided to employees. However, if disability coverage is provided, federal law mandates that pregnancy-related disabilities must be treated like any other form of disability.

In addition, five states have mandatory short-term or temporary disability laws covering non-work-related disabilities. These state laws and laws that affect disability benefits are discussed in the following sections.

[1] State Laws

The five states with mandatory short-term or temporary disability laws covering non-work-related disabilities are California, Hawaii, New Jersey, New York, and Rhode Island. Puerto Rico has adopted similar legislation. Employers are required to provide a defined STD benefit. The benefit period ranges from 26 weeks (four of the states) to 52 weeks (California). These laws also define eligibility for coverage, the applicable benefit percentage, the maximum weekly benefit amount, and the state agency that regulates the program.

For example, New York's law is administered in conjunction with the state's workers' compensation law. Hawaii has a stand-alone law, and California, New Jersey, and Rhode Island administer their laws as adjuncts to their unemployment insurance laws. Each state benefit law also has specific withholding and reporting requirements, and employers are subject to state penalties for noncompliance. **Exhibit 9.5** provides a summary of the different plans, their requirements and benefits, and the regulating agency in each state.

Many states require certain levels or features of STD and/or LTD benefits, if benefits are offered through a fully insured plan. These provisions can vary significantly by state and include such items as minimum benefit levels, conversion rights, survivor benefits, and definition(s) of disability. The magnitude of specific provisions by state makes including that list in this text prohibitive.

If a company offers an insured STD or LTD plan, the HR manager should contact the state insurance department to determine applicable state insurance provisions and verify that the insurance carrier has included all these provisions in the company's insurance policy.

[2] Federal Laws

Federal law does not mandate that STD or LTD coverage be provided. However, some federal laws affect the administration of disability benefits, if employers choose to offer the benefit(s).

[3] The Internal Revenue Code

The IRC requires self-insured employers to withhold federal income, Federal Insurance Contribution Act (FICA), and Federal Unemployment Tax Act (FUTA) taxes from any payments made under an STD plan. If a third party (e.g., an insurer) is assuming the insurance risk, withholding is required only if an employee requests it. If benefits under an STD plan exceed six months, FICA and FUTA taxes are no longer applicable and are not withheld.

The amount of the benefit that is taxable is based on the relative contributions made by the employer and employee to the disability plan. If the employer pays the entire disability benefit or premium, the employee is taxed on the entire benefit amount. Similarly, if the employee pays disability premiums on a pretax basis, the benefit amount received is taxable. Therefore, including disability benefits in a Section 125 plan is often not recommended.

If an employee contributes all or a portion of disability premiums on an after-tax basis, the percentage of the benefit that is nontaxable to the employee is the same percentage of the premium that the employee contributes. For example, if an employee pays 40 percent of disability premiums on a post-tax basis, with the employer contributing 60 percent, 60 percent of the disability benefit (i.e., the employer contribution) is taxable and 40 percent is nontaxable. Because of this tax result, many employers "carve out" the disability benefit for key employees and provide the benefit to these employees on an after-tax basis.

Revenue Ruling 2004-55 [2004-26 I.R.B. 1081] indicates a permissible plan design that gives employees a choice as to whether to receive their long-term disability benefits as taxable or non-taxable income. To enable such a choice, the disability plan must provide for each eligible employee to irrevocably elect to have the employer-paid premiums for the long-term disability coverage taxed currently (i.e., the premiums paid by the employer will be reported on the employee's Form W-2 for that year). The employee's election must apply to the entire cost of the coverage that the employer pays to the insurance carrier, and must be made before the plan year to which the election applies.

Employees can change their election each year; however, it will be irrevocable for each plan year. Alternatively, the plan may state that the employee's prior election continues from year to year unless affirmatively changed before the beginning of the plan year. Another acceptable alternative is that the plan includes the premiums in the employee's income each year, unless the employee affirmatively elects otherwise.

Under the plan, as described above, disability benefits will not be taxed if received by an employee who had elected to have the premiums included in income. Under the same plan, if the employee did not elect to have the premiums taxed as income, disability benefits will be treated as taxable income.

[4] ERISA

Both STD and LTD plans are considered welfare benefit plans and are generally subject to ERISA (see **Chapter 5**). Therefore, they must meet the following reporting and disclosure requirements:

1. The plan must be in writing and must explain the claims and appeals procedures. (An insurance contract may be exempt from this requirement, especially with regard to the appeals procedures.)

2. If an employee's claim is denied, he or she must be given a written explanation for the denial.

3. The employer may be required to file an ERISA Form 5500 for its non–state-mandated disability plans each year.

Disability plans may be exempt from ERISA coverage under the "payroll practice" exemption. The DOL's regulations require that for a benefit to qualify under the payroll practice exemption, it must pay the employee's "normal compensation, out of the employer's general assets, on account of periods of time during which the employee is physically or mentally unable to perform his or her duties, or is otherwise absent for medical reasons." [29 C.F.R. § 2510.3-1] Even plans that pay less than full salary, as most disability benefits do, can qualify for the payroll practice exemption if the other requirements are met. If a disability benefit plan meets the requirements for a payroll practice exemption, it will not have to comply with ERISA's reporting and disclosure requirements noted above. However, it is still strongly recommended that the benefit plan be described in writing and that employees whose claims are denied are informed of the reason in clearly written form.

[5] ADEA

The ADEA makes it illegal for employers to deny LTD benefits on the basis of age. In addition, coverage for active employees cannot be terminated because of age. For example, denial of LTD benefits to an active employee who is over age 65 is illegal. However, the Equal Employment Opportunity Commission (EEOC) does permit employers to reduce either the level or the direction of benefits for some employees in the following ways:

1. If the disability occurs at age 60 or earlier, it is legal to cut off benefits at age 65.

2. If the disability occurs after age 60, it is legal to cut off benefits after five years.

[D]   Determining the Company's Short-Term and Long-Term Disability Policy

Issues to consider in designing your STD and/or LTD policy include:

1. How do STD and LTD tie in with existing sick leave and/or salary continuation policies? Which classes of employees receive which benefits? Should the policy include a service eligibility period before an employee is eligible for benefits? (Common service eligibility periods are 60 days to 90 days for STD and up to five years for LTD.)

2. What income replacement percentage does the company want to provide its employees? Does (or should) it vary by employee class? Does the objective vary regarding salary continuation, STD, and LTD benefits?

3. What is the waiting period before STD and LTD benefit payments begin? The waiting periods for all sickness and accident benefits should be coordinated to ensure there are neither unintended gaps nor overlaps in coverage.

4. What is the maximum duration for both STD and LTD benefits?

5. Are employee contributions required for either STD or LTD benefits? If so, how much?

6. Are employees able to contribute on a pretax basis?

7. What definition of salary is used to determine the benefits payable? Does it include or exclude overtime, bonuses, and commissions? What is the financial impact on the company under the different scenarios? What is the effect of these items on the percentage of income replacement for key and nonkey employees?

8. What other forms of income are offered in addition to STD and LTD benefits (e.g., workers' compensation, Social Security disability payments, or other pension payments)? Should these benefits be coordinated? If so, how?

9. What criteria does the company use to define disability to certify that someone is indeed disabled? Are partial or rehabilitation disability benefits offered if an employee attempts to return to work?

10. What benefits continue to accrue while the employee is out on disability? For how long?

11. Should the company provide supplemental disability benefits for executives or key employees who may not receive full coverage under an insured program?

§ 9.04 WORKERS' COMPENSATION

Workers' compensation is a required system of no-fault insurance for workers. In exchange for the ability to collect for any injury on the job, whether they were negligent or not, employees give up the right to sue employers for huge awards for pain, suffering, and punitive damages.

In the United States, the government first ventured into the business of offering employee benefits in 1912, when several states introduced workers' compensation laws in response to employee, union, and public dissatisfaction with employer efforts to prevent occupational injuries and accidents. Two basic objectives were established for workers' compensation: universal coverage and compensation to cover work-related injuries and diseases.

Workers' compensation does not seek to cover all worker health problems. To sort out the covered conditions, states have adopted fairly uniform statutory definitions and tests that generally limit compensation benefits to personal injury caused by accidents arising out of, and in the course of, employment. Today, each state specifies benefit levels and conditions for workers' compensation.

Most states permit an employer to pay benefits directly or through an insurance company. Administering claims and funding benefit payments through an insurance company is the customary practice, as many employers prefer not to be involved directly in these decisions. Benefits include temporary and permanent total disability pay, permanent partial disability awards, medical care benefits, rehabilitation, and survivor allowances. Numerous efforts have been made to bring workers' compensation under federal control, but to date no such legislation has been enacted. Over the past several years, workers' compensation benefits have increased dramatically, and because the benefits are more generous than most medical and disability plan payments, some experts believe that workers are abusing the system. For example, employers have seen an increase in claims by employees who maintain that accidents have happened at work when, in fact, the injuries are sustained at home.

A noticeable increase in a company's workers' compensation claims should be treated as a warning sign. If a plan administrator suspects that a particular claim is not based on a valid work-related injury, he or she should immediately communicate this suspicion to the insurance carrier or attorney. Under no circumstances, however, should the employer fail to process a workers' compensation claim, since this failure would automatically open the door for a lawsuit. Instead, the employer, with help from competent counsel, should conduct a thorough investigation. In addition, an aggressive follow-up program with the objective of returning the injured employee to work as soon as is practicable is an effective way of controlling costs and reducing insurance fraud.

The Taxpayer Relief Act of 1997 (TRA '97) included a provision that made it more advantageous from a tax standpoint for an employer to use structured settlements in workers' compensation cases, because it allows the employer to assign a structured settlement to a financial institution rather than maintain ownership of the settlement on behalf of an injured employee. The employer may immediately write off the entire value of the settlement rather than recognize the expense as payments are made to the employee—and it may pay the financial institution to administer the settlement for the injured worker. Plan administrators should consult with legal counsel to consider this alternative.

[A]   State Laws

Six states and two territories require that employers insure through monopolistic state funds. Five of these funds were created when the laws were newly enacted, between 1913 and 1915. Thirteen states permit employers to purchase insurance from either a state fund or private insurance companies. In all states but North Dakota and Wyoming—even states with monopolistic funds—some large companies are permitted to assume liability for workers' compensation benefits on a self-funded basis. Twenty-eight of those states permit small employers to self-fund through pooling of their workers' compensation risks.

[1]   Elective or Compulsory Coverage

All states have adopted workers' compensation laws that may require elective or compulsory coverage. Under an elective law, the employer may accept or reject the law. If the law is rejected, however, the employer loses the three common-law defenses that are generally available if the employer is challenged in a workers' compensation case: (1) contributory negligence, (2) assumption of risk, and (3) negligence of fellow employees. A compulsory law requires each employer within its scope to accept the provisions and provide for benefits specified. Coverage is elective in only two states: New Jersey and Texas.

[2]   Suits for Damages

Under workers' compensation laws, employers generally are exempted from damage suits. If an employee rejects remedies available under the Act and instead sues an employer that has accepted the Act, the employer usually retains the three common-law defenses outlined above. In a few states, however, courts have created exceptions to the exclusive-remedy rule under certain circumstances, leaving employers with potential additional exposure. The exceptions have mostly occurred within the manufacturing sector, where employees were knowingly exposed by their employer to hazardous chemicals or working conditions.

[3]   Insurance Requirements

Most jurisdictions require employers to obtain insurance, prove financial ability to carry their own risk (i.e., self-fund), or both. Penalties for failure to insure exist. States have different laws regarding whether self-insurance or group self-insurance (i.e., pooling of risk) is permitted. As noted earlier, some level of self-insurance is permitted in all states except North Dakota and Wyoming.

Self-insurance operates best when the employer's spread of risk (i.e., the total number of employees) is so large that the employer may benefit from the law of large numbers. The employer should establish protective services similar to those of insurance companies that would take care of such activities as claims adjustments and investigations. Also, the employer should consider retaining attorneys and/or doctors to handle problems arising from claims and medical and legal services.

Employers may set up a reserve fund for self-insurance to pay compensation and other benefits under the states' workers' compensation acts. Contrary to the treatment accorded in insurance premiums, amounts paid into this reserve fund are not always deductible from gross income as a business expense for income tax purposes. However, amounts paid out as cash or medical benefits are deductible. Competent tax advice should be sought when determining what might be deductible for income tax purposes.

[4] Required Records and Notices

A record must be made of each employee's claim that he or she has been injured on the job and must include the time, date, and location of the employee's illness or injury. Such records must be maintained for a minimum time period, as set by state regulations.

Employers are required to provide certain notices to employees of their rights to workers' compensation. The requirement includes posting the Workers' Compensation Notice on employee bulletin boards or in other conspicuous places, notifying employees of their rights once an alleged injury occurs, and clarifying whether the employee has a choice of doctor privileges. Failure to notify employees of their rights could lead to increased employer liability in the form of fines and lawsuits.

Employers are also required to post a Summary of Work-Related Injuries and Illnesses (OSHA Form 300A) for employee inspection. This log must be posted from February 1 through April 30 of each year.

[5] 24-Hour Coverage

In response to increasing costs for workers' compensation benefit claims and real and suspected fraud, many state governments and employer groups have considered the idea of 24-hour coverage, under which one plan combines health care benefits and workers' compensation medical coverage. Under such a plan, all claims for medical care, whether from work-related accidents and injuries or not, would be covered under a single, seamless medical plan, using the same physicians and programs.

A number of states (including Maine, Florida, Kentucky, Georgia, Louisiana, Oklahoma, Massachusetts, and California) have created 24-hour coverage (pilot) programs to test the concept in practice. Some of the key provisions of such programs are:

- Integrated management of a workers' compensation claim may not affect any benefits, rights, or coverage established under a workers' compensation insurance policy.

- Treatment of work-related conditions may not be made subject to either copayments or deductibles.

- Care by a number of providers must be delivered through an integrated or coordinated plan or through a single policy plan.

- Plans must be designed to eliminate or minimize differences in delivery of services.

- Purchase of a 24-hour health care policy does not exempt an employer from nonmedical workers' compensation insurance coverage provisions, but the premium for the nonmedical insurance must be reduced to reflect the absence of the medical component.

Among the concerns regarding potential implementation of a 24-hour coverage system are:

- Treatment for workers' compensation injuries requires the employer to pay the total bill. In return, employers receive the benefit of an exclusive-remedy provision. With potential employee contributions to 24-hour coverage, the exclusive-remedy provision may be eroded.

- Adding more bureaucratic layers to an already complex system will do nothing to effectively return an employee to work, but will instead increase the potential of losing more days of work, which increases cost.

- Employers expect and deserve to play an active role in both medical expenses and results (i.e., case or disability management) for workers' compensation claims. Control of the selection of medical providers is important. Providers must have knowledge of workplace demands and issues and must be aware of employer, as well as employee, roles.

- Timeliness of medical reporting (i.e., within hours, not weeks) is critical to determining treatment and internal handling of workers' compensation injuries.

Most proposals to date have not addressed the issue of "enough" medical attention. Employers who have developed exemplary safety records and competitive experience ratings for workers' compensation are concerned about maintaining these successes in an environment in which they become no more than a third-party payer of medical invoices. Will safety continue to be a number one priority?

Essentially, issues and opinions regarding the feasibility of 24-hour coverage depend largely on an employer's experience, information, and knowledge about its own systems and culture, as well as the real impact of proposed changes. To date no empirical data are available to assess the impact of 24-hour coverage and expected results under traditional (i.e., insured and managed care) programs.

[B] Disability Integration

As a progression from initial efforts toward 24-hour "medical" coverage, employers and health care providers have begun integrating all components of employee disability. Such programs seek to combine the claims, reporting, management, and return-to-work aspects of traditional workers' compensation group health, short-term disability, long-term disability, and "sick" pay/benefits.

An October 2000 survey report on integrated disability management (IDM) by consulting firm Watson Wyatt Worldwide found that disability-related expenses (including workers' compensation, sick pay, and short- and long-term disability payments) represented 6.3 percent of payroll, up slightly from 6.1 percent in the previous year. According to the report, of employers that have integrated at least two functions, 61 percent stated that workers' compensation costs were decreasing and 42 percent said short-term disability costs were decreasing. Forty-three percent of the survey participants had implemented IDM programs.

An analytical tool for assessing the impact of disability and medical management efforts on workers' compensation programs was created and released by the Workers' Compensation Research Institute (WCRI) of Cambridge, Massachusetts, at its annual conference in March 1998.

In the WCRI framework, the following six business processes are identified as important in integrated plan management:

1. Early notification of an injury or illness

2. Direction of the injured or ill worker to network providers

3. Case management directed at determining appropriate, individual treatment

4. Management of the case or claim

5. Network construction, maintenance, and management

6. Process integration

In addition, four outcomes were defined, two of which are seemingly new in employers' analyses of workers' compensation and related issues: participant satisfaction and worker functioning both at work and not at work.

Early studies that reviewed the issue of employee malingering in returning to work yielded recommendations for prevention—before injuries or illnesses occur. A supportive work environment and organizational culture, employee and supervisor education, and a safety-focused culture were seen to be critical in prevention. Secondarily, early active intervention in injury management and finding appropriate light-duty work assignments will also assist in encouraging return to work.

Related to the slow, yet apparent, trend toward disability benefits integration is a Washington state law that requires employers whose home base is not in Washington, but who employ workers to perform jobs in the state, to register with the Washington state department on workers' compensation. As growing numbers of multistate employers, including small employers, pool their workers' compensation risks, the result may be an increasing number of other, similar state requirements.

[C] Benefits-Related Legislation Interaction

In managing workers' compensation, employers are often confused about the interplay among workers' compensation, the Family and Medical Leave Act (FMLA), and the Americans with Disabilities Act (ADA). Many employers fail to understand that they have the right to designate workers' compensation time off as FMLA time, and they therefore miss the opportunity to start the clock and limit FMLA time-off exposure. The 12-week FMLA period provides an excellent opportunity to resolve any workers' compensation time-off issues, assess return-to-work or light-duty plans, and consider ADA implications. Even if an employee with an occupational injury has a disability as defined by workers' compensation law, the employee may not have a disability for ADA purposes. (For further information on coordinating workers' compensation with the FMLA and ADA, see **Chapter 15**.)

§ 9.05 UNEMPLOYMENT INSURANCE COMPENSATION

Both federal and state statutes exist to financially protect workers who lose their jobs. Each state has created some form of unemployment insurance tax to fund this mandated benefit. State provisions vary according to eligibility, amount of coverage, and duration of coverage.

The Federal Unemployment Tax Act (FUTA) imposes compulsory unemployment insurance at the expense of employers, or employers and employees jointly, through a tax assessed on the basis of payroll and determined, in part, by the amount of claims paid against the employer's account (i.e., the employer's experience rating) with the state. Along with these experience ratings, the tax rate is based partly on employee classification into appropriate jobs or job groups. Management should periodically review these classifications on unemployment insurance compensation payroll and notice registers.

On June 30, 2008, President Bush signed the Supplemental Appropriations Act of 2008 (H. 2642, Pub. L. No. 110-252), providing an additional 13 weeks of benefits to those workers who have exhausted their regular 26 weeks of unemployment benefits. The extended benefits will be effective through March, 2009.

On March 25, 2002, President George W. Bush signed Public Law 107-154 [116 Stat. 80], which extends unemployment insurance assistance from 26 weeks to 39 weeks for those individuals covered by the Robert T. Stafford disaster unemployment insurance program. This program, which is not funded by employers, covers the relatively few individuals who are not covered by regular unemployment insurance and who become unemployed as a result of a presidentially declared disaster.

[A]   State Differences

Each state has created some form of state unemployment insurance tax act to implement federal law. States' plans may differ on some of the following points:

- Requirements for employer coverage, including the length of time an employer must have employed at least one worker and the amount of an employer's quarterly payroll

- Required employer contributions, usually through payroll taxes, based upon factors such as taxable wage base, varying by state and providing maximum compensation level, per employee, to which the applicable rate is applied to determine the employer's liability, the standard tax rate, minimum and maximum tax rates, experience rating, and related specific provisions

- Individual benefit eligibility requirements

- Benefit determination

- Benefit disqualification requirements

Many employees incorrectly believe that they contribute to unemployment compensation and therefore are entitled automatically to benefits. Most states stipulate that an employee must work a minimum number of weeks at a specified average minimum wage or earn wages in a base period to be eligible for unemployment compensation. The base period varies by state and is defined as a series of consecutive months worked within a particular calendar year, not necessarily the current one.

[B]   Reasons for Ineligibility

There are four primary reasons employees are generally not eligible to collect unemployment compensation:

1. *Willful misconduct.* Employees who are discharged because of willful misconduct are not eligible for unemployment compensation if the employer can prove the charge. To prove a willful misconduct charge, an employer must show that it had a rule or past practice forbidding the act committed by the employee, that the employee had knowledge of the rule and violated it, and that the violation was the actual cause for the employee's discharge.

2. *Refusal to accept suitable employment.* The law requires that recipients of unemployment compensation look for jobs and accept any reasonable offer. If they do not, they may lose their benefits.

3. *Voluntary termination of employment.* Employees who leave work voluntarily are ineligible for unemployment compensation, with certain exceptions. For example, employees who leave after working conditions drastically deteriorate are often declared eligible. Also, employees who quit their jobs because their spouses are being relocated are usually eligible. Some states, e.g., Washington, allow employees who leave their job to protect themselves or their families from domestic violence or stalking to be eligible for unemployment insurance.

4. *Labor stoppage.* Striking employees are ineligible for benefits in most states. However, it is important to distinguish between being out on strike and being out of work because of a strike. In many states, employees who are laid off because their work is dependent on strikers' work are eligible for benefits, as long as their union is not participating in the work stoppage. Also, employees who are laid off before the strike are usually eligible, unless they directly participate in strike-related activities.

In some states (e.g., Virginia), an employee whose employment is terminated as a result of a drug test performed in accordance with applicable state law may be disqualified from receiving unemployment compensation.

Some states are attempting to minimize anticipated negative effects on employers of federal Welfare to Work legislation. For example, Arizona passed a bill directing that a person who has been on welfare for at least two quarters before being hired cannot be factored into an employer's unemployment compensation experience rating if that person's employment is terminated within six months of hire.

[C]   Cost Containment

The less unemployment an employer causes, the lower its tax rate. Because of this, employers should apply screening procedures carefully, particularly when hiring seasonal or temporary employees. Seasonal and temporary employees can quickly accumulate enough weeks of employment and earnings to be eligible for unemployment benefits. Other actions that can help employers control costs include keeping good termination records, responding promptly and accurately to all unemployment claims, and reviewing and appealing benefits determinations, as appropriate.

Employers should review the classification of their employees on periodic unemployment benefits determinations and payroll notice registers. Employers should also carefully review the annual statement of charges to the employer's unemployment account. The employees' classifications and the employer's experience are the primary determinants of their unemployment tax rate. Classification changes and errors found in the statement of charges should be brought to the attention of the appropriate agency.

§ 9.06   SOCIAL SECURITY

The most visible government plan is the federal Old Age, Survivors, and Disability Insurance (OASDI) program, more commonly known as Social Security. The original purpose of the program was to ensure continuing income for workers when their earnings either stopped or were reduced because of disability or retirement. In 1939, the law was expanded to pay certain dependents when a worker retires. Subsequently, benefits under the program have been extended to include disability income, payments to survivors after a worker dies, health insurance, and early retirement pensions.

Social Security originally covered workers only in industry and commerce. During the 1950s, coverage was extended to include self-employed individuals, state and local government employees, household and farm workers, members of the armed forces, and members of the clergy. In 1972 additional legislation was passed guaranteeing the automatic increase of Social Security benefits relative to the cost of living.

The cost of Social Security benefits is paid by both the employer and the employee in the form of a payroll tax applicable to a maximum earnings base. The current payroll tax for OASDI is 6.20 percent; the maximum taxable earnings on which it is applied changes annually. In 2009, the maximum taxable earnings amount is $106,800. The payroll tax is 1.45 percent on earnings for health insurance (Medicare), with no income limit. All payments an employee receives for working are subject to the payroll tax, including cash and, under certain circumstances, the cash value of clothing, lodging, and meals. Certain severance and other payments made to former employees affected by a workforce reduction will also be treated as taxable wages.

All monthly benefits are based on the *primary insurance amount*, which is the sum a worker would receive if he or she retired at the normal retirement age (age 65 if born before 1938, age 66 if born between 1938 and 1954, and age 67 if born after 1954). It is difficult to determine the primary insurance amount, which is a complicated calculation based on the employee's entire earnings history. Individuals can utilize an SSA on-line benefits estimator which uses current SSA records to automatically include an individual's earnings record without having to manually input the earnings data. However, individuals will need to enter earnings from the most recent year. The estimator is available at: *www.ssa.gov/planners/calculators.htm*. Employers and employees can find information about social security benefits on the SSA website: *http://www.socialsecurity.gov*.

Critical questions about the current and future status of the Social Security system have created concern over the system's financial integrity, internal inequities, increasing cost to employees, and the aging of the population. In recent years there have been political discussions concerning whether to allow individuals to direct the investment of some of their Social Security benefit dollars. Proposed reforms include the adoption of some form of private accounts, either voluntary or required. Other proposals include increasing the full retirement age from age 67 to age 68 for individuals born in 1963 or later. Regardless of the legitimacy of these concerns, Social Security remains the most important financial protection plan in the country. To address the uncertainty over future Social Security benefit levels, many companies have implemented employee pension plans or savings plans. (For further discussion of this issue, see **Chapter 8**.)

Exhibit 9.1
Rates Used in Calculating the Taxable Value
of Group Term Life Insurance in Excess of $50,000

Age Bracket[*]	Monthly Rate per $1,000[**]
Under 25	0.05
25–29	0.06
30–34	0.08
35–39	0.09
40–44	0.10
45–49	0.15
50–54	0.23
55–59	0.43
60–64	0.66
65–69	1.27
70 and over	2.06

* Employee's attained age on the last day of his or her taxable year.
** Rates shown were effective July 1, 1999, and will remain in effect until changed by the IRS.

Exhibit 9.2   Mandated Benefits: 2009 Compliance Guide

Exhibit 9.2
Calculation of Tax Liability on
Group Term Life Insurance in Excess of $50,000

John, who is 32 years old, is an employee of Euphoria State Bank, through which he has carried $200,000 of group term life insurance for the entire year. John has been contributing $10 per month toward the cost of this insurance on an after-tax basis. The beneficiary of the life insurance is John's wife, so the first $50,000 coverage is tax exempt. The amount that is taxable to John is calculated as follows:

The total amount of group term life insurance on the life of John in each calendar month of his taxable year	$200,000
Less allowable exclusion	−50,000
Remainder	150,000
Monthly cost of excess amount ($0.08 per $1,000)	12.00
Annual cost ($12 × 12 months)	144.00
Less John's annual contribution ($10 × 12 months)	−120.00
Amount taxable to John	$ 24.00

Exhibit 9.3
Calculation of Tax Liability on
Group Term Life Insurance in Excess of $50,000
When Level of Coverage Changes During Year

John, who is 32 years old, is an employee of Euphoria State Bank, through which he has carried $175,000 of group term life insurance for the period January 1 to April 30, 2007 (4 months) and $200,000 for the period May 1 to December 31, 2007 (8 months). John has been contributing $10 per month toward the cost of this insurance. The beneficiary of the life insurance is John's wife, so the first $50,000 coverage is tax exempt. The amount that is taxable to John is calculated as follows:

	January to April	May to December
Amount of coverage	$175,000	$200,000
Less allowable exclusion	− 50,000	− 50,000
Remainder	125,000	150,000
Monthly cost of excess amount ($0.08 per $1,000)	10.00	12.00
Number of months at level of coverage[*]	4	8
Cost of coverage for period	40.00	96.00
Annual cost of coverage		136.00
Less John's annual contribution ($10 × 12 months)		− 120.00
Amount taxable to John		$ 16.00

---

[*] If a change occurs during any month, coverage for that month is the average of the amount of coverage at the beginning and end of the month.

Exhibit 9.4

Mandated Benefits: 2009 Compliance Guide

Exhibit 9.4
Four Examples of Typical Schedules of Basic Group Term Life Insurance Coverage

Example 1	Corporate officers	$100,000
	All other exempt employees	50,000
	All other employees	10,000

Example 2   All exempt employees, 200% of annual base salary rounded to next highest $1,000, not to exceed $250,000

All other employees, 100% of annual base salary rounded to next highest $1,000

Example 3[*]

Annual Salary

At Least	But Less Than	Insurance
$ 9,000	$12,000	$10,000
12,000	15,000	12,000
15,000	20,000	15,000
20,000	30,000	20,000
30,000	50,000	40,000
50,000		75,000

Example 4   All employees' 100% of annual base salary with option to purchase additional coverage up to 200% of annual base salary, not to exceed $250,000

---

* This type of schedule can be inequitable because a $1 difference in salary can change the amount of insurance by thousands of dollars.

Note: Examples 1, 2, and 3 do not address the discrimination testing required by Section 79 of the tax code. The level of benefit provided to highly paid employees might be better than that provided to non-highly paid employees. Discrimination of this nature could cause highly paid employees to lose tax advantages afforded by Section 79.

Exhibit 9.5

Summary of State Temporary Disability Benefit Payment Laws

	Plan Type	Employers Covered	Employer Contribution	Employee Contribution	Minimum Qualifications for Coverage	Waiting Period	Weekly Benefit Amount	Duration of Benefit	Disqualifications	Administered by
CA	State-sponsored, private insured, self-insured.	One or more employees and payroll of $100 or more in a calendar quarter.	Voluntary.	0.08% of first $86,698 in wages.	Base period earnings of at least $300.	7 days.	$50 to $917.	Up to 52 weeks.	Receipt of unemployment insurance or workers' compensation, or in jail due to conviction.	Employment Development Department.
HI	Private insured, self-insured, or collectively bargained	One or more employees.	Required to cover at least half of plan costs.	Up to 50% of benefit cost, but not over 0.5% of weekly wage up to $4.21 per week.	Base period earnings of at least $400 and 20 or more hours worked in each of preceding 14 weeks.	7 days.	58% of average weekly wage up to $489.	Up to 26 weeks.	Eligible for workers' compensation or unemployment insurance, or unemployed due to labor dispute.	Department of Labor and Industrial Relations, Disability Compensation Division.

Exhibit 9.5　　　　　　　　　　　　　　　　　　　Mandated Benefits: 2008 Compliance Guide

Exhibit 9.5 (cont'd)
Summary of State Temporary Disability Benefit Payment Laws

	Plan Type	Employers Covered	Employer Contribution	Employee Contribution	Minimum Qualifications for Coverage	Waiting Period	Weekly Benefit Amount	Duration of Benefit	Disqualifications	Administered by
NJ	State-sponsored, private insured, or self-insured.	Employers subject to state unemployment laws.	Based on employer's experience, varies from 0.1% to 0.75% of first $28,900 in wages.	0.5% of first $28,900 in wages, plus 8.09% for Family Leave Insurance.	Earnings of at least $143 in each of 20 weeks in preceding year, or $7,200 in 52 weeks.	7 days, unless benefits paid for three weeks following the waiting period.	$66\frac{2}{3}\%$ of wages up to $546 weekly.	Up to 26 weeks.	Eligible for workers' compensation, unemployment compensation, benefits from any other disability law, or duration of labor disputes.	Department of Labor, Division of Temporary Disability Insurance.
NY	State-sponsored, private insured, or self-insured.	One or more employees on each of 30 days in a calendar year.	Additional costs over employee contributions.	0.5% of weekly taxable wage base up to $0.60 per week.	Four or more consecutive weeks fulltime work, or 25 days regular part-time work.	7 days.	50% of average weekly wage; maximum $170 per week.	Up to 26 weeks.	Eligible for workers' compensation, unemployment compensation, or any other disability benefit.	Workers' Compensation Board, Disability Benefits Bureau.
RI	State-sponsored.	One or more employees.	Not required.	1.3% of first $54,400 in wages.	Base period earnings of at least $8,880.	7 days, unless benefits paid for a disability that lasts 28 days or more.	$4.62% of wages paid in highest quarter of base period, from $69 to $671; additional benefits available to qualified dependents.	Up to 30 weeks.	Receipt of workers' compensation or unemployment insurance benefits.	Department of Labor and Training.

	Plan Type	Employers Covered	Employer Contribution	Employee Contribution	Minimum Qualifications for Coverage	Waiting Period	Weekly Benefit Amount	Duration of Benefit	Disqualifications	Administered by
PR	State-sponsored, private insured, or self-insured.	One or more employees.	0.3% of first $9,000 in wages.	0.3% of first $9,000 in wages.	Base period earnings of at least $150.	7 days or first day of hospital confinement, which, ever is sooner.	$12 to $113 (industrial); $12 to $55 (agricultural).	Up to 26 weeks.	Receipt of workers' compensation benefits, or unemployment compensation from any state or Puerto Rico, or if payments received from employer's fund plus disability benefits exceed regular wages.	Division of Labor and Human Services, Bureau of Employment Security.

Chapter 10
Supplemental Benefits

parameterization

§ 10.01   AUDIT QUESTIONS

1. Has the company prepared a plan document and summary plan description for supplemental benefit programs covered by the Employee Retirement Income Security Act of 1974?

2. Has the company measured the true costs of supplemental benefits on a regular basis and researched and implemented appropriate cost control measures?

3. Has the company implemented state-mandated benefits associated with its supplemental benefit programs?

4. Is there a written plan description of the company's educational assistance program under Section 127 of the Internal Revenue Code?

5. Has the company reviewed its wellness or health promotion program's incentives and disincentives for compliance with the Health Insurance Portability and Accountability Act of 1996, the Americans with Disabilities Act of 1990, and other federal and state regulations regarding nondiscrimination on the basis of health status?

Note: Consistent "yes" answers to the above questions suggest that the organization is applying effective management practices and/or complying with federal regulations. "No" answers indicate that problem areas exist and should be addressed immediately.

Employees today expect more from their jobs than fair wages and competitive benefits. Employers recognize that offering a variety of employee benefits, services, and activities can help improve employer-employee relations, increase motivation, improve employee retention, and stimulate productivity. They further understand that individuals who are weighing employment possibilities or considering a job change often base their decisions on extra services and activities offered by the organization—even if the individual may not personally participate in the program.

When considering which supplemental benefits to offer employees, it is important to evaluate employees' needs, the level of employee interest, the extent of anticipated use, projected effectiveness, and direct and indirect costs. It is also helpful to take a look at the benefits and services that competitors provide. Supplemental benefits may be paid for by the employer or the employee, or both. The growing number of voluntary benefits available (e.g., dental, vision, dependent care, wellness programs, and long-term care) may enhance a benefit package at minimal employer cost.

Many of the supplemental benefits are subject to certain federal and state laws or codes that must be followed if employers choose to offer them. A rule of thumb in reviewing each nonmandated benefit plan is to begin by answering the following questions:

- Is the program covered by the Employee Retirement Income Security Act of 1974 (ERISA)? If so, what are the ERISA reporting and disclosure requirements? Are there any other ERISA requirements (e.g., fiduciary responsibilities)?

- Do any sections of the Internal Revenue Code (Code) apply to the benefit being offered? If so, which tax sections apply, and what are the requirements to ensure that the plan is qualified?

- Does any other federal legislation apply to the benefits or policies, such as the Health Insurance Portability and Accountability Act of 1996 (HIPAA), the Family and Medical Leave Act of 1993 (FMLA), or the Americans with Disabilities Act of 1990 (ADA)?

- Does the state in which the company is located have specific requirements or regulations that affect this benefit?

- If the benefit is insured, does the state mandate any provisions that must be included in the benefit plan?

Depending on the benefit, the human resources (HR) manager may wish to consult with an independent benefits consultant or insurance agent, a tax specialist, or the state employment office or other state agency, and the HR staff may want to check state and federal employment laws, the tax code, and contact the state insurance commission.

To ensure that a company's benefits package is in compliance with benefits legislation, a standard benefits review procedure should be developed. The procedure should begin with HR's review of all existing benefit programs and the establishment of a regular (at least once a year) review for legal and other relevant changes affecting any benefits. In addition, the HR manager should identify benefits and tax specialists in whom he or she has confidence. These specialists should be relied upon to track recent legislative issues and changes and to provide tangible, proactive design and compliance recommendations.

§ 10.02 PRESCRIPTION DRUG BENEFITS

Prescription drug plans are nearly as popular as group health plans. The 2008 Benefits Survey Report by the Society for Human Resource Management (SHRM) reported that 96 percent of the responding employers offer some form of prescription benefits, up from 87 percent in 1998. Most employers cover prescription drug expenses in some way under their group hospital or major medical benefit plan. When prescription drugs are administered during hospital confinement, a plan often absorbs the full cost of the medicines as a part of covered inpatient hospital charges. In other situations, payment is often subject to deductible and coinsurance/copayment provisions of the plan.

Employees are strongly attracted to separate, or carved-out, prescription drug plans, because such plans typically do not require employees to pay the deductible or coinsurance that applies to expenses incurred within major medical plans. Employers should carefully evaluate the cost of these plans before implementing them only to meet employee desires.

One common type of carved-out prescription plan covers the full cost of individual prescription purchases, generally including insulin, after the employee pays an up-front prescription-only deductible or a per refill copayment. In most cases, limits are placed on the frequency of refills, but the number of prescriptions covered is typically not limited.

Drug plans may offer varying benefits, depending upon whether an order is filled by a participating or nonparticipating pharmacy. Participating pharmacies have contractually agreed to accept specific payment from the insurance plan or association. Under these plans, the participant often pays only a small amount out of pocket at the time of purchase, if the purchase is made from a participating pharmacy. Purchases from nonparticipating pharmacies typically must be paid in full by the participant, who then may submit the receipt for reimbursement from the plan, typically under the same conditions as other eligible expenses under the plan. Employees often respond favorably to such plans, with most participants willing to go to participating pharmacies to obtain the improved level of benefit.

Employers that have adopted carved-out prescription drug plans generally believe that such plans are at least as cost-effective as offering the same coverage under a major medical plan. Employers argue that the plans exert valuable leverage on pharmacy charges and that they encourage outpatient drug therapy as an alternative to more costly hospital confinement and employee absences. In addition, most employees use the plan and appreciate the fact that they are saving their own money. Some argue that low-paid employees are more likely to obtain necessary (i.e., maintenance) prescription medications when they must pay only a very small up-front cost.

At the same time, it remains important for plan sponsors to manage this benefit, including monitoring of costs over time. According to the Office of the Actuary at the Centers for Medicare and Medicaid Services, a division of the Department of Health and Human Services, costs of prescription drugs have been the fastest-growing segment of national health expenditures, increasing 66.2 percent between 2000 and 2005. In the same period, total national health expenditures grew by 46.9 percent.

One cost control technique that is common within carved-out prescription drug benefit plans is to periodically raise the level of copayments required from plan participants. The Kaiser Family Foundation and Health Research and Educational Trust (KFF/HRET) Employer Health Benefits 2007 Annual Survey found that copayments for non-preferred drugs (brand-name drugs not included on a formulary or preferred drug list) averaged $46.00 in 2008, more than two and one-half times the $29.00 in 2000, whereas copayments for generic drugs averaged $10.00 in 2008, up from $8.00 in 2000.

[A] Drug Cards

In response to market pressure, several prescription drug benefit programs are now available, including drug cards. Drug cards may be sponsored by a drug vendor (also known as a pharmacy benefit manager, or PBM), a particular pharmacy, a chain of pharmacies, or a particular drug manufacturer. An employee covered under such a plan presents a card to a pharmacist and is charged a flat fee for the prescription, usually based on whether a brand-name or generic drug is prescribed. Employees are often asked to pay a higher rate for brand-name drugs, to encourage them to use less expensive, equivalent generic drugs. The advantage of such a program to employers is a reduced cost for drugs, which are generally sold at the average wholesale price (AWP) or at a discount from AWP.

Another type of drug card is the prescription drug discount card. Rather than providing a prescription drug for a flat fee, this type of card offers a discount on the price of the prescription. Generally these types of programs charge an annual enrollment fee, which may be paid by the employer. Discounts are offered in a variety of ways, and employees must obtain the drug at participating pharmacies. Mail-order pharmacy service is generally also offered, with deeper discounts on certain drugs. Although no formulary is included, some programs have a preferred medication list, which provides deeper discounts for those drugs. Discounts are most often obtained from the participating pharmacies and, at lesser frequency, from manufacturer rebates. These programs are not group benefits. However, for employers who cannot afford prescription insurance coverage, the prescription drug discount card may offer some benefit to its employees.

As with other benefits included under a group health plan, plan administrators must monitor these costs over time. Although these benefits are received positively by employees, such programs actually end up costing—rather than saving—the employer money because of increased use.

[B] Mail-Order Pharmacy Service

Mail-order pharmacy services have generally proved effective in controlling prescription drug costs in group health plans. These plans are particularly desirable for purchasing drugs used for treating chronic medical conditions. They typically offer employees a 90-day supply of their medication per order, for a specified copayment, and save money by securing medication at deep volume discounts from the manufacturer. According to the 2008 Benefits Survey Report by SHRM, 87 percent of employers offer a mail-order discount plan for prescription drugs.

Copayments for mail-order drugs have increased over the years. The average copay for generic mail-order drugs was $14.61 in 2002 and rose to $17.58 in 2007, a 20 percent increase in five years (according to the Prescription Drug Benefit Cost and Plan Design Survey Report, 2007 Edition conducted by the Pharmacy Benefit Management Institute (PBMI)). The average copay in 2007 for mail-order brand name drugs on a formulary ("preferred drug") was $47.86, a 53 percent increase over the average copay of $31.21 in 2002. The average copay for a mail-order brand name drug not on a formulary was $80.80 in 2007, a 33 percent increase over the 2002 average copay of $60.61. Many benefit design experts recommend that, for cost-effectiveness, the copay for a 90-day supply of mail-order drugs be at least twice the copay for a retail 30-day supply.

Increasingly, large employers have integrated mail-order prescription drug programs into their existing drug plans, requiring employees to buy maintenance prescription drugs through the mail rather than through a local pharmacy. Generally, the programs require employees to order by mail prescriptions that need to be refilled more than twice. Medications taken for chronic conditions fall into this category; drugs such as antibiotics generally do not. According to the PBMI 2007 survey report, 95 percent of employers that offer prescription drug coverage offered a mail-order program in 2005 and 11 percent of all such employers mandated the use of the mail-order service for refilling maintenance prescriptions.

Often, an employer's decision to require employees to use a mail-order drug program is based on cost. Mail-order companies are able to provide a discounted rate because of low overhead and volume purchasing. Consumers benefit from the convenience, higher level of accuracy in orders (due to the high number of mail-order drug companies using automated ordering systems), and lower costs.

While mail-order drugs may reduce employees' out-of-pocket costs, as well as provide other benefits, recent research suggests that the health plan may incur higher total costs. As reported in *A Comparison of the Cost of Retail and Mail Order Pharmacy,* a study conducted by Norman V. Carroll, Ph.D., professor of pharmacy at Virginia Commonwealth University's Medical College of Virginia Campus, School of Pharmacy, and RxEOB, savings obtained by the reduced ingredient costs and dispensing fees for utilizing mail-order pharmacies were more than offset by the loss in copayments, when the copayment for a mail-order supply was less than the copayments for the same prescriptions filled at a retail pharmacy. Carroll's research revealed that the health plan spent 6.8 percent more on mail-order prescriptions than on retail prescriptions. Thus, copayments for mail-order drugs have increased faster than those for retail copayments. According to the 2007 PBMI survey report, the average mail-order copayment for a preferred drug increased 53.3 percent between 2002 and 2007. In the same period, the average retail copayment for preferred drugs increased only 30.8 percent.

Some states prohibit health plans that, by design, require employees to use mail order. Plan administrators should work closely with their carrier or benefits expert to determine application of the law in their state.

[C] Formulary Plans

Formulary plans may offer benefits under the group health plan but will cover only those drugs listed on the formulary. Formularies were developed in response to the variety of medications that physicians might prescribe for any given condition. They attempt to limit coverage to drugs that have been on the market for some time and have proved effective for certain medical conditions. The focus is on the most cost-effective clinically proven drug treatments for specific conditions. In 2007, according to the 2007 KFF/HRET survey, 91 percent of employees were covered by a drug plan with a formulary.

Participation of medical professionals is critical to the potential success of formulary type plans. Ideally, medical professionals should monitor any formulary and amend it as appropriate, based on currently accepted medical practice.

The pharmacy plan an employer offers should balance employee relations and cost control objectives. A well-managed drug card or mail order program integrated with formulary incentives may provide upfront coverage for employees while decreasing overall plan costs.

[D] Over-the-Counter Drugs

Over-the-counter (OTC) drugs do not require a prescription and typically are not covered under group health or prescription drug benefit plans. There is increasing pressure to cover OTC drugs, in part because of increasing costs. The Non-Prescription Drug Manufacturers Association (NDMA) has indicated that the typical cost of OTC medications is one-fourth the cost of a prescription drug. Because prescription medication generally involves a visit to the family physician, adding approximately $40 to the overall tab of a prescription, the potential savings of OTC medications is worth considering. The primary problem seen with adding coverage of OTC medications to pharmacy benefits is the nearly certain expansion of coverage (i.e., the plan would generally cover all OTCs, not just those in lieu of prescription drugs) and therefore of increased pharmacy costs in total.

In September 2003, the IRS issued Revenue Ruling 2003-102 [2003-I.R.B.], allowing OTC drugs to be paid for with pre-tax dollars through health care Flexible Spending Accounts and Health Reimbursement Arrangements (see **Chapter 12**). This is a significant change in IRS regulations. The guidance outlines that reimbursements for nonprescription drugs through a health Flexible Spending Account (FSA) or Health Reimbursement Arrangement (HRA) are excluded from income like other employer reimbursements of employee health expenses. The guidance specifically mentions allergy medicine, antacid, pain reliever and cold medicine as examples of OTC drugs that could be reimbursed by the health FSA or HRA and excluded from the participant's taxable income. However, the cost of OTC drugs continues to be non-deductible as an itemized medical expense deduction on individual tax returns. Also, reimbursements for OTC items, such as dietary supplements, that are "merely beneficial to the general health of an individual," are not excluded from income.

Prescription Solutions, a provider in Cypress, California, conducted a pilot program involving certain OTCs. Prescription Solutions did not add OTCs to its list of covered drugs but worked with a select group of patients, who were offered samples and coupons. Patients made their own decisions about the "value" of OTC medications in comparison with copayments for prescriptions within their respective benefit plans. In the end, including results of an expanded trial, Prescription Solutions realized savings of about 10 to 12 percent per member per month because of the OTC program. [*Business & Health,* Vol. 17, No. 4 (April 1999), pp. 33–35]

[E] Trends

Because pharmaceutical costs continue to receive scrutiny by employers, as well as governments and individuals, several innovative programs are appearing across the country.

One creative, and potentially effective, approach to prescription drug-related health care, is a program conducted by the city of Asheville, North Carolina. The program worked with local (not necessarily large chain providers) pharmacists to develop genuine, ongoing relationships between them and plan participants with targeted, chronic disease management concerns. Special plan benefits were offered to these individuals, who agreed to meet monthly with a trained pharmacist for disease management counseling. Results showed that individuals saw their physicians more frequently (i.e., sooner than they would have without counseling from the pharmacist) and improved their health. Overall plan costs for the city were reduced. [*Business & Health,* Vol. 17, No. 6 (June 1999), pp. 43–44]

After six years of experience with the program, known as the Asheville Project, the city found that while drug costs increased, total health care spending decreased. For example, spending on diabetes fell from

$7,042 per patient in 1996 (prior to the program's inception) to approximately $4,000 per patient for every year thereafter. Absenteeism rates for participants also decreased significantly—from 12.6 sick days per year to six. Initially, the Asheville Project targeted diabetes. It later added asthma, hypertension, and high cholesterol, all of which benefit, from both a monetary and a human standpoint, from early intervention. Other employers have adopted the Asheville Project, including Mission St. Joseph's Health Care System in Asheville and Blue Ridge Paper, a private employer with seven plants. [*Washington Post,* August 20, 2002, page A01]

Many employers are considering implementing more aggressive cost control methods. One such strategy is the three-, four-, or five-tier copayment structure. In 2008, the number of health plans with a three-tier structure increased to 70 percent, up from 27 percent in 2000. Seven percent of employees were covered by a four-tier structure, up from 3 percent in 2004 (2008 KFF/HRET Employer Health Benefits survey). In a three-tier structure, the lowest copayment is applied to generic drugs on the formulary. The second tier is applied to preferred drugs on the formulary or drugs without generic equivalents. The third tier (highest copayment) is used for nonformulary, nonpreferred brand-name drugs. In the four-tier structure, the fourth tier is used for certain specified drugs, such as "lifestyle" drugs—drugs that improve the patient's quality of life but are not medically necessary for treatment or prevention of disease. Fourth-tier drugs may also include high-priced specialty drugs or biotech drugs, and may be covered by the major medical portion of the health care coverage.

An alternative copayment plan requires the patient to pay the difference between the cost of the brand-name drug and that of the generic drug when both are available, in addition to the regular copayment. Mercer Health and Benefits 2005 survey revealed that 46 percent of the employers in its survey utilized this approach. An additional 26 percent utilized this penalty even if the physician requested the brand-name drug.

Some plans require a coinsurance percentage instead of a copayment for prescription drugs. Advocates of this methodology believe these strategies more strongly encourage patients to choose lower-cost generic drugs when available. Under a coinsurance arrangement, when the cost of the drug increases, the amount the employee must pay does so automatically. Employees understand that 20 percent of the cost of a generic drug that retails for $40.00 will be less than a similar brand name drug that retails for $100.00. Employees generally purchase the lower-cost generic drug, resulting in savings to them and their employers.

Coinsurance plans appear to be on the rise, especially among large employers. In 2006, according to Mercer Health and Benefits, 21 percent of large employers (those with 500 or more employees) used a coinsurance arrangement rather than a copayment arrangement for prescription drug coverage at retail pharmacies and 14 percent for mail-order services. Among the largest employers—those with 20,000 employees or more—the usage of coinsurance was 48 percent at retail and 35 percent for mail order.

Some plans institute minimums and maximums along with the coinsurance. For example, a plan may set the coinsurance rate at 20 percent for generics, with a minimum $5.00 charge, and 30 percent coinsurance for brand name drugs, with a $75.00 maximum charge. Tiers can also be combined with coinsurance plans, such as:

	Coinsurance	Minimum	Maximum
Generic	20%	$5.00	$25.00
Preferred (formulary)	30%	$15.00	$50.00
Non-preferred	40%	$25.00	$100.00

The downside to the coinsurance approach is the unpredictability of the drug costs at a pharmacy, and, for most employees, a higher out-of-pocket cost. Some employees may not take a medication they need, potentially resulting in higher non-drug medical costs due to, for example, an emergency room visit or hospitalization.

Another strategy provides higher coverage of prescription drugs for chronic illnesses, less for limited conditions, and even less (if any) for lifestyle drugs. For example, medicine for high blood pressure would be covered at 80 percent, antibiotics for an infection might be covered at 70 percent, and allergy medication might be covered at only 50 percent.

Employers considering adopting one or a hybrid of any of these cost containment strategies should also consider the effects on their employees. Multiple-copayment-tiered plans can be very confusing. And many employees might resent receiving less coverage for their children's antibiotics for life-threatening infections than they receive for chronic illnesses.

These approaches appear to be working. In 2007, 54.5 percent of all prescription drug claims filled at a retail setting were generic. Use of generic drugs reduces the overall cost of drugs. Various surveys in 2007 and 2008 indicated that the increase in drug costs is decreasing:

- The Segal Company surveyed more than 70 leading health care insurers to determine that the increase in prescription drug costs would be 10.7 percent in 2008, compared to 11.9 percent in 2007.

- Mercer, LLC reported that the prescription drug cost increase for large employers (500 or more employees) was 9.3 percent in 2007, continuing a downward trend over the previous three years: 9.9 percent in 2006, 11.5 percent in 2005 and 14.3 percent in 2004.

Reasons for the decrease in the prescription drug cost annual increases included:

- Reduced utilization

- Improved provider contracting

- Implementation of multi-tier plan designs

- More generic and over the counter drugs due to elimination of patent protection

- Use of consumer driven health plans (see **Chapter 12**) to educate employees to be more knowledgeable consumers

- Use of a variety of methods providing incentives to employees to purchase generic drugs

§ 10.03   VISION AND DENTAL CARE BENEFITS

An employer choosing to offer a group health plan is not required by any federal law to offer vision or dental coverage as a part of that plan. Many employers offer these benefits, however, because employees request them and incremental costs generally have not been significant. Recently, though, costs have risen, requiring careful plan management and monitoring. Many employers continue to offer vision and dental benefits because they are heavily used and valued by employees.

The costs and benefits of vision and dental plans are fairly easy to monitor if plan administrators secure appropriate management information. Providers should be required to send necessary summary information (e.g., premiums received, benefits in each plan category paid out, and administration costs) on a periodic (at least quarterly) basis. Plan administrators can use this information to determine how much of their premium costs are being returned to their employees in the form of benefits and how much of their premium dollars are being retained by the provider as administrative and profit expenses. Administrators then need to determine whether the cost-to-benefit ratio is reasonable.

Vision and dental care benefit plans are following the lead of group health care in several respects. Employers are reviewing funding options, preferred agreements with providers, per capita fee arrangements, limitations on benefit design, and other issues.

[A]   Vision Plans

Vision plans are generally stand-alone plans, although some medical plans (usually health maintenance organizations) include vision coverage. Vision plans typically cover eye examinations, corrective lenses, and frames. Because many vision care choices involve cosmetic and fashion considerations, employers should build several different forms of cost controls into their plans. Some of these cost control features include:

- Scheduled cash allowances (e.g., set amounts reimbursed per visit or per lens)

- Coinsurance percentages

- Deductibles

- Frequency of reimbursement limitations (e.g., full or partial reimbursement once every 24 months for lenses or frames)

- Maximum (e.g., annual, lifetime, or both) plan benefits

Standards for medically required contact lenses are often related to postcataract surgery or to restoration of 20/70 visual acuity, and these benefits may be offered either within the group health plan or within the vision care benefit plan. Group vision plan coverage generally excludes extra costs for tinted lenses, photosensitive lenses, and oversized or designer label frames.

Another vision plan option is the discount plan. Discount plans have contracted with selected providers to provide vision services at a discounted rate to plan participants. In general these plans are the least costly to employers and may be the first type of vision plan offered. According to the 2000 Spotlight on Benefits survey by William M. Mercer, Inc., 4 percent of the survey participants offered a discount vision plan.

The number of employers offering vision care benefits increased in the late 1990s and early 2000s. In the SHRM 2008 Benefits Survey Report, 79 percent of the respondents said they offer vision benefits to their employees, compared with 63 percent in 2000. Generally, employers indicated that the most common reasons for offering vision plans are employee interest, low cost, and advantages in recruiting and retaining employees. Approximately half of the U.S. population wears corrective lenses of some type, and the overall population is aging, resulting in continuing interest in this benefit by employees.

But employers may have more reason than ever to offer vision benefits. A study published in *Optometry: Journal of the American Optometric Association (AOA)* (January 2004) indicated that improvements in vision could improve the productivity of workers who use computers. The researchers were interested in determining whether there was a link between computer eyestrain and worker productivity. Study participants performed various tasks on computers. Slight miscorrections in an individual's eyesight could reduce his or her productivity by 10 percent and accuracy by as much as 40 percent. The study concluded that providing vision care benefits could have a significant impact on an employer's profitability. For example, if an employee earning $25,000 per year could improve his productivity by 10 percent, the result would be a productivity improvement of $2,500. According to the AOA, the cost of a typical eye doctor visit and new pair of glasses averages $300 (at the time of the study). In this example, the employer could show an $8.33 gain for every $1.00 invested in vision care benefits.

[B] Dental Plans

Dental plans have become a standard benefit among companies. In the SHRM 2008 Benefits Survey Report, 94 percent of employers offered dental benefits to their employees.

Dental benefit plan structures typically differ from those of traditional medical plans, even though both are a form of health care. Traditional medical plans are oriented toward treatment, covering expenses incurred as a result of accidents and illnesses. In contrast, dental care is generally elective in nature and focused on preventive care. Because neglect can lead to serious dental and medical problems requiring long-term care and costs, most dental plans emphasize prevention and hygiene. They do so by providing such incentives as covering all or most of the costs related to diagnostic and preventive services.

[1] Choosing a Dental Plan Provider

The four principal sources for group dental plans are as follows:

1. Private insurance carriers;

2. Dental services corporations;

3. Blue Cross/Blue Shield organizations; and

4. Dental maintenance organizations (DMOs).

Of these four sources, insurance companies are the dominant providers of group dental benefits, largely because of their firmly established role in providing other medical benefits. In fact, many employers that use an insurance company for dental benefits use the same carrier that handles their major medical coverage. The two types of coverage usually operate separately, although a few companies may integrate them.

Dental service corporations, coordinated through the nonprofit Delta Dental Plans, which are similar in concept to Blue Cross/Blue Shield plans, are sponsored by state dental societies. Participating dentists agree to provide service under specified terms and conditions and to receive payment directly from the plan. The plans generally cover services provided by nonparticipating dentists at a reduced benefit level.

All the Blue Cross/Blue Shield organizations also offer dental benefits, some of which are in conjunction with a Delta Dental plan.

DMO plans operate like medical HMO plans. An employee selects a primary care dentist who directs all care. Because dental care costs are predictable, such plans are generally less expensive than medical plans. However, DMO plans are decreasing in number. According to the Radford Benefits Survey (Aon Consulting, Inc.), only 19 percent of technology and life science employers offered a DMO plan in 2008, down from a high of 25 percent in 2003.

Since the mid-1990s, PPO dental plans have become available. PPO plans borrow elements from both fee-for-service plans and DMOs. This design results in plans with reduced premiums, reduced frequency of procedures, and other cost-containment features—including the elimination of deductibles, preauthorization of procedures, payment of dentists on a reduced fee-for-service basis, and requirement for copayments on all procedures. PPO plans require enrollees to receive dental care from "participating" dentists. According to the Radford survey, the number of PPO plans is increasing: 94 percent of employers offered such plans in 2008, compared to only 78 percent in 2003.

When selecting an insurance company or other provider for a group dental plan, an employer should ask the following critical questions:

- Will a "managed" dental care plan meet employees' needs for dental care and the company's need for cost containment?

- Is the dental plan provider accredited by a nationally recognized dental agency?

- Does the underwriter have sufficient profile information to adequately process claims on a reasonable and customary basis?

- For how long would the underwriter be willing to guarantee rates?

- Where would the plan's claims be processed, and what is the current turnaround time in claims processing?

- Must the company accept the underwriter's plans, or can it design a specific plan with its own exclusions and limitations?

Many employers have considered self-funding dental benefits to avoid paying greater premiums than employees receive in benefits. Alternatively, employers design their cafeteria plans to include a flexible spending account, which allows employees the opportunity to pay all qualified dental expenses on a pretax basis. In many cases, hybrid approaches to dental benefits may meet employee needs more cost-effectively than offering an insured dental benefit plan.

[2] Benefits Structure

As described earlier, the benefits structure of dental plans differs significantly from that of traditional medical plans. Following are some of the service classifications and coverage levels commonly found in group dental plans:

- *Diagnostic services.* Routine oral examinations and X-rays are usually not subject to deductibles, coinsurance payments, or copayments under DMOs, but are subject to frequency limits.

- *Preventive services.* Services such as cleaning, scaling, fluoride treatment (often restricted to dependents under a certain age), and providing space maintainers are typically covered on the same basis as diagnostic services.

- *Basic restorative services.* Services such as fillings, inlays, crowns, and removal of dental decay can be subject to specific limits on payment for use of precious metals; otherwise, these services are typically covered on a reasonable and customary basis and may be subject to a small annual deductible (e.g., $25 per person) or copayments.

- *Oral surgery.* Dental plans generally exclude surgery necessary as the result of an accident because such surgery ordinarily would be covered under a major medical plan. Any other oral surgery is generally subject to a deductible and reasonable and customary charge limitations, as well as copayments.

- *Endodontics.* Procedures used for prevention and treatment of diseases of the dental pulp, such as root canal work, are subject to a deductible and copayments.

- *Periodontics.* The treatment of gums and other supporting structures of the teeth is generally subject to a deductible and copayments.

- *Prosthodontics.* Many plans cover only 50 percent of reasonable and customary charges for these major and costly procedures, which include construction, replacement, and repair of dentures and bridgework.

- *Orthodontics.* Most plans do not offer coverage for the correction of malocclusion and abnormal tooth position. When coverage is provided, it is frequently restricted to dependent children. The benefit level is similar to that for prosthodontics, and there is often a lifetime maximum benefit, such as $1,000 per person.

[3] Cost Control Techniques

Employers that adopted dental plans in the early and mid-1970s generally did not require employee contributions to the cost of coverage because of the fear of adverse selection. Adverse selection occurs when employees are asked to contribute to a dental plan, and those who have neglected to care for their teeth join quickly to make maximum use of the plan. Conversely, those employees with good teeth do not join the plan because of the contribution requirement. Adverse selection thus distorts the risk base of a group plan and places increased pressure on plan costs.

Although some dental plans still do not require employee contributions, more employers are taking a closer look at employee participation in an effort to contain expenses. As reported in the Aon 2006 National

Employee Benefits Trends Survey Findings, only 15 percent of employers pay the entire dental plan premium. In addition to expense sharing, employers use other dental benefit cost control techniques, such as:

- *Payment of deductibles.* Deductibles usually range from $25 to $100 per individual per plan year with $50 per individual and $150 for a family being most common; deductibles seldom apply to diagnostic and preventive services.

- *Payment of coinsurance.* Plans may require employees to pay a specified percentage of reasonable and customary costs for various services. The coinsurance rate is generally 80/20 for restorative services, endodontics, and oral surgery, and 50/50 for major restorative services, such as periodontics and prosthodontics.

- *Copayments.* Managed care dental plans may require payment of predetermined amounts for services. Generally, the amount varies with the type of service provided.

- *Payment of annual maximum amounts.* Annual maximums place a ceiling on a plan's liability on behalf of any one person in one year. The most common annual maximum amounts are $1,000 and $1,500 per person.

- *Payment of lifetime maximum amounts.* Lifetime maximums are usually imposed on payments for certain costly services, such as orthodontics and periodontics, and generally match the annual maximum dollar amount (e.g., a lifetime maximum of $1,000 or $1,500).

- *Predetermination of benefits.* Predetermination is a fairly common requirement when dental fee quotations exceed a certain amount (e.g., $200). In these cases, the patient and dentist are advised in advance of treatment regarding what portion of the quoted fee the plan will cover. Predetermination sometimes encourages employees to choose a less expensive treatment plan.

- *Instituting a waiting period.* Although a less common practice than it once was, some employers institute waiting periods before an employee is eligible for dental coverage and benefits to protect themselves against workers who take early and full advantage of benefits and then leave. Although this practice may be a prudent defense in some industries, it deters recruiting efforts and detracts from the value of the benefit. Some companies are considering introducing waiting periods for certain costly dental plan services, particularly for employees who elect coverage after their initial eligibility.

The structure of self-funded dental plans typically matches these common insured plan features. There is no reason for employers to believe that the rapid growth and popularity of dental health insurance will diminish in the near future. Dental health insurance is clearly popular with employees and their families because dental expenses, even for routine care, can be burdensome.

[4] Trends in Dental Benefits

A recent trend is for the employer to contract directly with a dental practitioner or practice to provide benefits to its employees. The company self-funds the dental benefits, generally using a third-party administrator to process payments claims. The popularity of direct contracting is expected to increase as a result of the growing number of dental groups and the emergence of dental centers where DMOs have combined practices and groups. The benefits of size include expanded treatment hours and the availability of specialists on site.

Direct contracting may offer savings to employers by providing a set schedule of payments for dental procedures, an overall discount, and participation in prepaid plans that pay a uniform amount per participant. The downside for employees is that they must receive dental care from a given dental group or dental center.

Because there are as yet no national (or even large regional) dental networks, direct contracting may work best for companies located in one or two specific geographic areas.

§ 10.04 GROUP LONG-TERM CARE BENEFITS

Long-term care (LTC) insurance continues to develop as an employee benefit. The diversity of today's workforce means employees commonly have both child care responsibilities and, at some point in their careers, responsibility for long-term care for themselves, their spouses, or elder members of their families. In many cases, the burden of long-term care responsibility can limit an employee's ability to be effective on the job. A 1999 study by John Hancock and the National Council on the Aging indicated that 65 percent of employees want their employers to offer LTC coverage. Of that number, 76 percent say they would be likely to purchase such coverage. Accordingly, employers should consider adding LTC coverage as a benefit to attract and retain employees as well as to help employees handle the high costs often associated with long-term care.

Survey results regarding the prevalence of LTC insurance vary widely. For example, the SHRM 2008 Benefits Survey reported that 45 percent of employers offer LTC insurance to their employees. However, the United States Bureau of Labor Statistics, a division of the Department of Labor (DOL), reported that in March 2007 only 12 percent of all employees had access to LTC insurance. Access to LTC varied by type of employer; for example, in firms with 100 or more employees, 21 percent of all employees had access to LTC insurance, whereas only 4 percent of employees in firms with less than 100 employees had such access. In June 2004, America's Health Insurance Plan (AHIP) (formerly the Health Insurance Association of America (HIAA)), released its study of LTC insurance ("Long-Term Care Insurance in 2002"), which indicated that 9.16 million individual policies had been sold in the United States as of the end of 2002. More than 5,600 employers offer LTC insurance to their employees. By 2007, according to the American Association of Long-Term Care Insurance, nearly 10,000 employers offered LTC insurance to employees.

LTC policies reimburse medical and personal costs to individuals who are, for an extended period, unable to care for themselves. Under a traditional policy, the insured person becomes eligible for benefits when he or she cannot engage in some or all of the activities of daily living (ADLs)—dressing, bathing, walking, and eating. Reimbursements are made to cover a variety of services, such as meal preparation, housekeeping, and transportation. Most health and disability plans do not provide this type of benefit.

[A] Choosing the Right Plan

The LTC product is an evolving plan in today's insurance market. Plan administrators should review policy features carefully. Common features include:

- *Eligibility.* The most common insured is between the ages of 45 and 84. Most insurers allow those between the ages of 18 and 99 to purchase LTC insurance. An employee can generally insure himself or herself, a spouse, parents, or parents-in-law.

- *Plan Features.* Plans generally cover nursing homes, assisted living facilities, home health care, hospice care, respite care, and alternate care services. In addition, plan features may include case management or care coordination services, homemaker services, medical equipment coverage, home-delivered meals, meal preparation at home, home modification, survivorship benefits, and caregiver training.

- *Benefit levels.* Daily benefit rates for nursing home care, in-home care, or adult day care range from $75 to $200 per day. However, with rising costs of health care, rates are generally increasing to keep pace with the average cost of nursing home care. The two models for providing benefits are (1) the reimbursement model and (2) the disability model. The reimbursement model reimburses actual expenses up to a daily maximum amount, while the disability model provides the daily amount regardless of the actual cost of service. Some feel that the disability model may run out benefits faster than the reimbursement model, whereas others believe that the disability model provides additional needed funds to the insured.

- *Maximum benefit.* This varies. Some plans provide a one-time benefit period for the insured, but others allow multiple uses, up to a five-year maximum. All of the top insurers (the 13 companies that sold about 80 percent of all the individual and group association policies in 2002, as reported by AHIP) offered policies that provided unlimited or lifetime nursing home maximum periods.

- *Preexisting conditions.* Most policies do not cover expenses incurred as a result of preexisting medical conditions that began within six months of the issue date of the policy. However, most of the top insurers offer a plan that waives the preexisting condition limitation as long as medical conditions are disclosed during the application process.

- *Inflation adjustment.* This option ensures that benefits keep up with inflation of medical costs. Adding this option can increase premium costs by as much as 20 to 40 percent. All of the top insurers' plans offered an inflation protection benefit whereby the policy benefits increased at an annual 5 percent compounded rate. An alternative inflation adjustment approach provides the insured with opportunities to purchase additional coverage without proof of insurability. The cost of the original coverage remains the same; however, the cost of the additional coverage is determined by the insured's age at the time of purchase of the additional coverage.

- *Waiting period.* Generally, employees desire plans with 30- or 60-day waiting periods.

- *Waiver of premium.* This option allows the insured to waive the premium when the insured is receiving benefits under the policy.

- *Options.* Employees may be interested in programs that offer coverage options for various LTC levels, such as facility-only, facility and professional, or facility, professional, and home care.

- *Proof of insurability.* Employees are most attracted to policies that offer some level of benefits without proof of insurability.

Premiums vary widely based mostly on plan features and benefits and the health history and age at which the employee first elects coverage. In 2008 the American Association for Long-Term Care Insurance reported average annual costs for LTC policies: for a married 55-year old who qualifies for preferred health coverage, the average cost is $709 per year for a 3-year policy with $100 daily benefits. For a married

65-year old in average health the cost is $1,342 for a 3-year policy with $100 per day benefits. As shown by these statistics, LTC premiums are more affordable at younger ages and if in good health.

To find the best LTC insurance available in the employer's market, experts make the following recommendations:

- Compare plan features and benefits carefully.

- Ensure the financial health of the insurance company offering the policy.

- Examine plan language carefully, especially those sections that affect when and how payments are made.

- Determine the average (median or mean) price of LTC insurance policies in the employer's local market area.

- Ask about transfer provisions in case the employer wishes to move the coverage to another carrier.

- Ask about limits and exclusions.

- Determine how much service the carrier will provide (e.g., education, materials, knowledgeable advisors, and so on).

- Determine what the insurance companies' history of rate increases has been.

- Determine whether state tax incentives exist (see below for federal tax information).

[B]   Tax Consequences

Before the enactment of HIPAA, rules were not clear as to tax treatment of LTC insurance contracts or services. HIPAA provides that, beginning in 1997, an employer-sponsored LTC insurance plan is generally treated as an accident and health insurance contract and therefore receives favorable tax treatment. That is, benefit amounts received under a qualified long-term care insurance contract are excludable from income, subject to a cap of $280 per day, or $102,200 annually (for 2009; adjusted for the cost of living index; see *www.irs.gov* for current amounts), on per diem contracts, or the actual cost of long-term care services, if greater. However, if the coverage is provided through a pretax cafeteria plan, the benefits are not excludable from an employee's income. Similarly, expenses for long-term care services cannot be reimbursed under a flexible spending account.

An LTC insurance contract is defined as any insurance contract that provides coverage of qualified LTC services and that meets other specific requirements. These requirements are determined by the long-term care insurance model act and model regulations promulgated by the National Association of Insurance Commissioners (NAIC) (as adopted in January 1993). The Internal Revenue Service describes these requirements as follows:

- Guaranteed renewable

- Does not provide for a cash surrender value or other money that can be paid, assigned, pledged or borrowed

- Provides that refunds, other than refunds on the death of the insured or complete surrender or cancellation of the contract, and dividends under the contract may be used only to reduce future premiums or increase future benefits, and

- Generally does not pay or reimburse expenses incurred for services or items that would be reimbursed under Medicare, except where Medicare is a secondary payer or the contract makes per diem or other periodic payments without regard to expenses.

Qualified LTC services include necessary diagnostic, preventive, therapeutic, curing, treating, mitigating, and rehabilitative services, and maintenance or personal care services that are required by a chronically ill individual and that are provided pursuant to a plan of care prescribed by a licensed health care practitioner.

Maintenance and personal care will be defined in Department of Treasury regulations still under development. These forms of care include meal preparation, household cleaning, and other similar services that the chronically ill individual is unable to perform.

The Pension Protection Act (PPA) allows qualified LTC to be purchased from certain life insurance or annuity contracts on a tax-free basis. Although regulations have not been published, experts believe that these new rules will allow a qualified LTC rider to be added to life insurance or annuity contract that is funded from a partial cash surrender of the life insurance or annuity contract. Prior to the PPA, this would have been a taxable event. Also, exchanges between an annuity or life insurance contract and qualified LTC insurance or between an existing LTC contract and another qualified LTC contract will now be allowed tax-free. However, annuities from a qualified plan (e.g. 401(k) or 403(b) plan) and qualified LTC contracts are not allowed on a tax-free basis. These tax-free exchanges will first be allowed in taxable years beginning after December 31, 2009.

Rules under the Consolidated Omnibus Budget Reconciliation Act of 1985 (COBRA) do not apply to coverage under an LTC insurance contract. Unreimbursed amounts paid for qualified LTC services provided to a taxpayer (or to his or her spouse or dependent) are treated as medical care for purposes of the medical expense itemized deduction. Eligible LTC insurance premiums that exceed 7.5 percent of adjusted gross income (AGI) are also treated as medical expenses for purposes of the medical expense deduction (see **Exhibit 10.1**). The maximum deductible portion is capped incrementally, depending on an individual's age. Only eligible long-term care premiums, as described earlier, are deductible by self-employed individuals, and the deductions limit applies. [I.R.C. § 162(1)]

Currently, most employers that offer LTC insurance require employees to pay the full cost of the premium. Employer-sponsored plans generally spread the risk and have lower premiums and better benefits than individual policies that employees could buy on their own.

In situations in which employers have expressed interest in paying some portion of LTC benefit costs, employers have generally offered to contribute between $100 and $125 per year per employee, with the employee picking up the remaining cost for basic coverage (which varies widely according to the employee's age). A 2007 study conducted by Unum, Landscape of Long Term Care, revealed that more than 90 percent of Unum's employer clients paid for some portion of the LTC cost.

Employees often have the option to upgrade to a more comprehensive plan. Further, LTC benefits are fully portable—employees may take the coverage with them when they leave the company.

Some employers are exploring the option of paying 50 percent; of the premiums for LTC. The employers' cost of doing so is a deductible business expense, while providing a non-taxable benefit to the employee. Such a benefit might be provided only to longer-term employees by applying a one-year (or greater) waiting period before providing the benefit. Although more employees may enroll in an LTC benefit if the employer pays one-half of the premium, requiring a one or more year waiting period helps to ensure that only those most likely to stay with the employer will receive this valuable benefit.

§ 10.05   EDUCATIONAL ASSISTANCE PROGRAMS

Educational assistance programs help employees to gain the skills to improve their current positions and keep employees current in their fields. Educational assistance programs also aid in recruiting and retaining employees, increasing employee morale, and supplementing internal training efforts. Collectively, American businesses spend billions of dollars annually to help employees earn a college education.

In a study released in June 2006, the International Foundation of Employee Benefit Plans (IFEBP) reported that 94 percent of respondents offer education assistance to their employees. Almost all (99 percent) make their benefits available to full-time salaried employees, and 86 percent to full-time hourly employees. In an earlier study released in February 2005, Hewitt Associates reported that 78 percent of the nearly 1,000 respondents offered education assistance options to their workforce. Of these, nearly 75 percent provided educational reimbursement, with an average reimbursement amount of $5,000 per year.

If an employer pays job-related educational expenses, it can exclude them from the employee's gross income as a working-condition fringe benefit under Code Section 132. There is no limit on the amount of excludable assistance if the education is directly related to an employee's current job.

[A]   Policy Considerations

Job-related and non-job-related educational assistance programs exist primarily in the form of tuition aid and scholarship grants. Employer policies often:

- Require prior approval and authorization by an employee's supervisor.

- Limit tuition reimbursement to a specified dollar amount per semester or year.

- Allow direct payment of expenses, reimburse employees for their expenses, or provide reimbursement only upon achieving a specific grade (e.g., achieving a C or better). In the IFEBP survey, 73 percent of the respondents reimburse expenses based on completion of the course and 69 percent reimburse based on the grade received.

- Decide what expenses will be paid: tuition, books, fees and/or supplies. In the IFEBP survey, in addition to tuition (100 percent), 64 percent of the respondents paid for books, 63 percent paid for fees and 21 percent paid for supplies.

- Require employees to remain at the company for a specified time following tuition reimbursement or pay the employer back for educational assistance; in the IFEBP survey, 43 percent required that employees pay back all or part of the money reimbursed for education if they leave employment. The most common time period that employees must continue working after receiving the reimbursement is one year.

- Require employees to provide written verification of successful completion of the approved class or program.

- Set minimum service requirements (although a growing number of employers offer immediate eligibility to new employees).

- Determine what types and levels of course work will be reimbursed. In the IFEBP study, 93 percent provided reimbursement for both undergraduate- and graduate-level courses, 69 percent covered online and distance-learning courses, and 56 percent included vocational and technical course work.

- Determine whether only full-time employees will be eligible for the benefit (more employers are now offering prorated benefits to part-time employees). In the IFEBP 2006 survey, 37 percent of the companies responding to the survey indicated they provided benefits to part-time salaried employees and 33 percent offer benefits to part-time hourly employees.

[B] Tax Treatment

If amounts paid by an employer for employee educational benefits are not directly related to an employee's current job, those amounts may still receive favorable tax treatment under Code Section 127 if the following specific guidelines regarding educational assistance programs are followed:

- Payments of up to $5,250 per year received under an employer's Section 127 educational assistance program may be excluded from an employee's gross income. Any excess is to be included in the employee's gross income and is subject to income tax withholding. The exclusion applies whether the employee is reimbursed for expenses or the employer pays expenses directly. In addition to tuition, the program may cover books and other expenses (e.g., supplies and equipment). Meals, lodging, and transportation are not covered.

- For the period between July 1, 1996, and December 31, 2001, graduate-level courses could not be included in a Section 127 educational assistance program. With the passage of the Economic Growth and Tax Relief Reconciliation Act of 2001 (EGTRRA), graduate-level courses that begin on or after January 1, 2002, may once again be included in the Section 127 program.

- The program must be a separate written plan of the employer established for the exclusive benefit of employees of the company. Employees must be given reasonable notification of the availability and terms of the program.

- The program may not provide eligible employees with a choice between educational assistance benefits and additional cash compensation.

- The program may not discriminate in favor of certain classes of employees (i.e., officers, owners, highly compensated employees, or their spouses or dependents who are employees).

- The program may not provide more than 5 percent of amounts paid or incurred for the class of individuals who are shareholders or owners (or their spouses or dependents), each of whom (on any day of a year) owns more than 5 percent of the stock or the capital or profits interest in the employer.

The applicable prohibited discrimination rule is the same as that used for qualified pension, profit-sharing, and stock bonus plans. The program may be part of a more comprehensive plan providing a choice of nontaxable benefits to employees; however, it cannot offer employees a choice between educational assistance and other compensation included in gross income.

The exclusion from employees' gross income for educational assistance received from an employer under Code Section 127, which was originally approved only temporarily by Congress, expired several times in the 1990s and was retroactively reinstated. However, EGTRRA also made the Section 127 exclusion a permanent feature of the tax code effective for courses that began after December 31, 2001. Although this benefit will now not expire every year or two, the tax impact of educational assistance programs continues to be complicated, and employers should consult their accountants or tax attorneys regarding the provisions of Code Section 127.

[C] Laws and Regulations

An educational assistance plan that is unfunded and paid out of a company's general assets is generally exempt from ERISA requirements. If a company sponsors such programs, it does not have to apply to the Internal Revenue Service (IRS) for a determination that the plan is qualified. However, the company must maintain applicable tax records for years in which the plan paid benefits and the costs were excluded from employees' gross income. Section 127 plans are not subject to ERISA's welfare plan reporting requirements.

§ 10.06 ADOPTION ASSISTANCE BENEFITS

A provision of the Small Business Job Protection Act of 1996 (SBJPA) created Code Section 137, which allows a tax exclusion for employer-provided adoption assistance benefits. This provision also permits individuals to claim tax credits for adoption expenses instead of excluding employer-provided benefits. Adoption assistance benefits were a growing trend. According to the SHRM 2008 Benefits Survey Report, 16 percent of employers provide adoption benefits to their employees, compared to 20 percent of employers in 2007 and 16 percent of employers in 2001. However, even when offered, utilization is very low. According to the National Adoption Center in Philadelphia, it is estimated that only 0.5 percent of eligible employees use adoption benefits each year.

The maximum amount of tax-free reimbursement is $12,150 for tax years beginning after December 31, 2008. Although some employers do provide a lump-sum amount for each adoption, the amount that is tax-free is based on the qualified adoption expenses incurred by the employee. For adopted children with special needs, a $12,150 tax-free exclusion is provided, less any previous credit or exclusion taken for that child, regardless of the amount of adoption expenses, for tax years beginning after December 31, 2008. Special-needs children are those who, at the states' determination, cannot be returned to a parent's home or who cannot easily be placed with adoptive parents because of such factors as ethnic background, age, membership in a minority or sibling group, or such specific conditions as a physical, mental, or emotional handicap. The excludable amount decreases proportionately for employees with adjusted gross incomes between $182,180 and $222,180 (for 2009, adjusted annually). Employees earning more than $222,180 are ineligible for this benefit.

In addition to providing a tax exclusion, Section 137 plans must meet certain requirements:

- They must operate like Section 127 educational assistance plans, including a written plan, notification to eligible participants, similar nondiscrimination testing, and limited benefits to 5 percent or more stockholders.

- The exclusion will apply to foreign adoptions only if the adoption is finalized (a restriction that does not apply to domestic adoptions).

- Qualified plan participants, if married, must file joint federal income tax returns. Qualified plans must reimburse only qualified expenses (e.g., reasonable and necessary court costs, attorneys' fees, and other related expenses).

- Qualified expenses can occur, and the reimbursements may be excluded, over more than one year.

- Reimbursements of expenses incurred before the effective date (January 1, 1997) cannot be reimbursed. Expenses incurred before a written plan was adopted or before employees were notified of the plan cannot be reimbursed. Tax-free benefits for expenses incurred before January 1, 2002, will be limited to $5,000 ($6,000 for a special-needs child).

- Expenses for surrogate parenting or adoption of a stepchild will not qualify for reimbursement.

- An employee who receives and excludes Section 137 benefits cannot also claim a tax credit for reimbursed adoption expenses, but he or she can claim a credit for unreimbursed adoption expenses.

- Participants must report the names, ages, and Social Security numbers of their adopted children on their federal income tax returns.

Section 137 amends the Social Security Act to generally prohibit states and other organizations from denying an adoption petition on the basis of the race, color, or national origin of the adopting parent or child. Denial of an adoption petition on the basis of race, color, or national origin could constitute prohibited conduct under Title VI of the Civil Rights Act of 1964. Provisions of the Indian Child Welfare Act of 1978 are not altered by Code Section 137.

§ 10.07 DEPENDENT CARE ASSISTANCE PLANS

Dependent care assistance plans (DCAPs) are an increasingly popular employee benefit because more women with children have entered the workplace, and the need for affordable, quality child care is growing. According to the Employment Policy Foundation's analysis of data from the Bureau of Labor Statistics, 37 percent of the 141 million workers in the U.S. labor force are parents with children under the age of 18. Many employers are offering DCAPs not only in response to employee requests for help in meeting work-family responsibilities, but also to reduce absenteeism and tardiness and improve employee retention, morale, loyalty, and productivity. The SHRM 2008 Benefits Survey Report indicates that 75 percent of all respondents offer dependent care flexible spending accounts, 18 percent offer child care referral services, 6 percent provide a subsidized child care center and 4 percent provide a non-subsidized child care center. Another growing benefit is emergency/sick child care; according to the SHRM survey, 31 percent of employers allow employees to bring a child to work in an emergency and 4 percent offer access to backup child care due to an unforeseen event.

It is estimated that one in four workers in the United States has some elder care responsibility. This is not always recognized by either the employer or employee. Employees will say they are helping their parents, for example, by balancing their checkbooks or taking them to the doctor, but do not recognize that this is a form of providing elder care. However, employers may be catching on; according to the SHRM 2008

Benefits Survey Report, 20 percent of responding employers offer elder care referral services, compared to 19 percent in 2001. As employees grow older, elder care responsibilities will increase.

Dependent care assistance, including elder care, can take many forms, including referral assistance, on-site day care facilities, off-site facilities, voucher programs, alternative work schedules, flexible spending accounts, and direct subsidies. Under Code Section 129, employees in a qualified employer-sponsored DCAP may receive a federal tax exclusion of up to $5,000 per year for dependent care expenses.

Section 129 covers the following types of DCAPs:

- Flexible spending accounts (FSAs) allow employees to set aside pretax income, receive employer-provided funds, or both, for the purpose of paying qualified dependent care expenses. Employers may also reimburse employees in pretax dollars for receipted expenses after they have occurred. Dependent care FSAs are subject to Code Section 125, including the use-it-or-lose-it provisions (see **Chapter 12**).

- Voucher systems allow employees to submit monthly vouchers to the employer with a copy of their canceled checks or receipts, certifying that expenses were incurred and requesting reimbursement. Under some voucher systems, the employer pays the day care provider directly.

- Vendor programs generally involve the employer's purchasing slots at one or more local day care center and reselling them, often at subsidized rates, to employees.

- Day care centers sponsored by employers on-site or near-site allow employees the convenience of placing their children or dependent parents in a facility near work, with the quality of the center assured by the company. The fair market value of the services provided is excludable from the employee's gross income, up to the statutory limit.

Under EGTRRA, employers receive significant tax credits for providing on-site child care facilities or referral services to their employees. The tax credit for an on-site child care facility is equal to 25 percent of the expenses for establishment and maintenance of the center. A tax credit for 10 percent of the costs of providing referral services to employees is also included in EGTRRA. A cap of $150,000 in these tax credits per taxable year has been established. This tax benefit has been available for tax years after 2001.

Employees who qualify for assistance under an employer-sponsored DCAP generally must decide to forgo a federal tax credit that would otherwise be available to them under Code Section 21. The available tax credit amount is generally reduced dollar for dollar by the amount excluded from income under the DCAP. Employers generally may deduct amounts paid or incurred under a DCAP as an ordinary and necessary business expense under Code Section 162. The plan need not be funded.

The DCAP must pass a special nondiscrimination test and, for qualification under Code Section 129, must meet numerous requirements, including the following:

- The DCAP plan must be in writing.

- Employees' rights under the plan must be enforceable.

- Employees must be given reasonable notification of the benefits under the plan.

- The plan must be maintained for the exclusive benefit of its participants.

- Employees must receive a written record, such as a W-2 statement, of the amounts the employer paid each year for tax purposes.

Section 129 also defines qualified dependent and qualified expenses and discusses the earned-income limitation. Code Section 6039D contains reporting and recordkeeping requirements. IRS Notice 90-24 [1990-1 C.B. 335] delayed the effective date of the provision for DCAP reporting until further notice.

[A] Developing a Dependent Care Assistance Policy

An employer that is contemplating developing a DCAP should consider the following questions:

- What percentage of employees would use a DCAP? Should the current and potential future needs of employees for elder care as well as child care be considered?

- Should the DCAP be included as part of a cafeteria plan to allow freedom of choice between dependent care and other benefits?

- What are the costs for establishing a written plan and the costs for setting up administrative procedures?

- How active does the company intend to be in providing the benefit? Should it make the benefit available on a tax-advantaged basis, play a proactive role in providing the service, or play a role in identifying quality providers in the area (for employee referral purposes)?

- Does the company want to direct employees to specific day care providers or provide them complete freedom of choice?

- Will the company assist employees in determining whether they would benefit more from the DCAP or a tax credit, or will the decision be totally at employees' discretion?

- Will the company provide additional benefit options to employees without dependents if this benefit is added?

[B] Recent Trends and Results

Many dependent care programs have been introduced to meet employer concerns for women's issues. Inevitably, business interests have turned to examining the bottom-line results of such programs. Those results consistently show value added to the bottom line. Millions of business dollars in the form of reduced absenteeism, turnover, and medical costs are being saved.

Employers include DCAPs within a broad range of *work-life benefits*. Work-life programs provide a wide variety of assistance to employees to help them achieve balance between their personal and work lives. Flexible scheduling arrangements, wellness programs, and personal and concierge services are examples of programs that fall under the work-life umbrella.

Specific companies' reported results to date from work-life programs include:

- Saving $800,000 in one year by providing backup child care for employees' children

- Reducing absenteeism 30 percent by allowing work schedules other than 9:00 A.M. to 5:00 P.M., five days a week

- Cutting attrition of high-potential women who took leave for childbirth by more than 50 percent and experiencing a 90 percent retention rate for leave takers after five years—resulting in annual savings of more than $1 million

- Realizing a 50 percent longer retention rate of employees whose bosses are "supportive"—saving more than $1 million in turnover costs over three years

In the 2003 survey, "Work/Life—A Delicate Balance," conducted by Mellon Financial Corporation's Human Resources & Investor Solutions (HR&IS), 73 percent of the respondents indicated that their primary reason for implementing work-life initiatives was employee recruitment. Other reasons cited by the respondents included employee morale (74 percent) and to remain competitive (72 percent). The general consensus is that if an employer wants to be the employer of choice, it must create a supportive environment.

The key to success in all work-life programs, including those directed at dependent care, is to understand the company and how it profits. A plan administrator should look for what his or her organization reaps from a program, have realistic expectations, introduce programs that make sense, and communicate them continually.

§ 10.08   COUNSELING PROGRAMS

Many employers provide various types of counseling services to their employees to help employees address issues that may be hampering their productivity both on and off the job. Work-related counseling may include career-development counseling to encourage and assist employees in pursuing work opportunities. Outplacement counseling is often used to assist employees who have lost their jobs to find new positions and careers. The most common types of non-work-related counseling programs include counseling for family problems, drug and alcohol abuse, and financial or legal issues. Broad-based counseling programs that address these issues may also include employee assistance programs, legal services plans, and relocation counseling and services programs.

[A]   Employee Assistance Programs

Employee assistance programs (EAPs) are employer-sponsored programs designed to help employees address problems at work and personal difficulties that may impair job performance. They reduce absenteeism, improve employee morale, increase productivity, and help to control overall health care benefit costs. The services offered by EAPs include assessment, counseling, and referrals to professional services for career and personal issues, such as:

- Drug and alcohol abuse

- Psychological symptoms or mental health disorders

- Marital or family-related difficulties (including child care or elder care)

- Domestic violence

- Divorce

- Legal and financial concerns

- Compulsive or addictive behavior (e.g., gambling)

- Catastrophic medical conditions

- Career/family life conflicts (e.g., relocations)

Because of the diversity of problems encountered, a broadbrush EAP ordinarily cannot provide intensive in-depth counseling; however, an employee or family member can obtain knowledgeable assessment, short-term counseling, referral, and follow-up service.

Institutions that provide EAPs as an employee benefit believe that the expense is justified by reduced absenteeism, improved employee morale, increased productivity, and control of overall health care benefit costs. The 2008 SHRM Benefits Survey Report stated that 75 percent of employers offer their employees an EAP. According to a 4-year study conducted by The Hartford Financial Services Group, Inc. (released in 2007), employees on disability leaves returned to work sooner if they worked for employers who sponsored EAPs than if they worked for companies without EAPs.

[1] Legal Issues

Two major legal issues concern EAPs: liability and confidentiality. Employees who use the program have a right to treatment that is not harmful, is provided in confidence, and is kept confidential thereafter. Managers may ask employees to seek help from an EAP whenever work behavior leads to concerns that personal problems may be adversely affecting job performance. Employees will use an EAP only if they feel sure that by revealing problems they are not jeopardizing their jobs, and that word of their problems will not leak out. Individuals and companies that provide EAP services are governed by many of the same laws and rules that govern other health and social service professionals.

In an important Ninth Circuit Court decision (that the Supreme Court declined to review), the therapist/client confidentiality privilege was extended to unlicensed EAP counselors and employees. [Oleszko v. State Compensation Ins. Fund, No. 99-15207 (9th Cir. 2002)] Based on this case, employers do not have the right, even though they may sponsor the EAP, to obtain confidential medical or other information from the EAP about their employees.

EAPs may be considered ERISA plans if they provide services for the treatment of mental health problems (e.g., depression, anxiety, stress, etc.) or drug and alcohol abuse. The DOL has issued advisory opinion letters indicating that such services constitute benefits "in the event of sickness, accident, or disability" as defined by Section 3(1) of ERISA. If the EAP provides only referrals to such services, and the EAP employs coordinators who make referrals to publicly available services, it is likely the DOL will find such plans not to be employee welfare plans as defined by ERISA.

If the EAP is an ERISA plan, it will have all of the reporting requirements otherwise required of ERISA plans (see **Chapter 5**). The reporting requirements include the preparation of a summary plan description and, as necessary, a summary of material modifications, and the preparation and filing of Form 5500 (if the plan otherwise meets the requirements for this filing). EAPs that meet the ERISA definition of a welfare plan are also subject to COBRA's requirements (see **Chapter 7**).

[2] Establishing an EAP

To ensure that an EAP provides high-quality, confidential and cost-effective services, HR should carefully evaluate outside vendors, seek referrals from satisfied customers, and review the types of problems reported to the EAP. The HR manager should also have monitoring and follow-up procedures in place. For example, the HR manager should review the credentials and number of telephone and short-term counselors available to employees, as well as the waiting times for hotline calls and counseling sessions. Individuals involved in providing services through the EAP should have good familiarity with the company's health plan and other benefits to help refer employees to outside resources.

An effective telephone-counseling EAP can be implemented for approximately $1 to $2 per employee per month, whereas other programs that provide managed mental health or a predetermined number of on-site counseling sessions may cost substantially more. The HR manager should carefully consider the employer's corporate culture and general business philosophy when establishing an EAP and must develop an effective communication plan to introduce the program to employees. Preparation of a written EAP policy statement should be one of the first steps in the process.

[3] Plan Structure

EAPs vary significantly in form from company to company. Some companies offer formal or informal in-house programs that are developed and run on site by an in-house physician, nurse, or counselor. An in-house EAP is often part of, or closely allied with, an employee health department. Other companies contract with an outside firm that specializes in EAP services on a fee basis. A third option is to contract with an EAP through the company's health or disability insurance carrier, in effect carving out EAP-related concerns and costs (as pharmacy or maternity benefits may be carved out). A combination of in-house and external resources may also be offered.

The objective of an EAP is to help troubled employees identify and solve problems that may be interfering with their work and personal lives. To achieve this objective, an EAP may provide one or more of the following services:

- *Problem identification and assessment.* Generally, a counselor interviews the employee or family member over a 24-hour telephone hotline to determine the nature and extent of a problem. The counselor then helps the individual resolve the problem or refers the individual to appropriate plan or community resources.

- *Short-term counseling.* Some EAPs provide a defined number of counseling visits to resolve minor problems that do not require extensive use of outside resources or extended counseling. In many cases, short-term counseling visits covered under the EAP are limited to a set number per year.

- *Long-term counseling or treatment.* Some EAPs coordinate with a managed mental health and/or substance abuse program and make referrals to these vendors to manage the employee's or dependent's care while controlling the care, setting, and cost on behalf of the employer.

- *Follow-up.* EAP counselors monitor an employee's progress during and after treatment. The employee's needs determine the length and type of follow-up.

- *General orientation and training.* Some EAPs develop training sessions for managers and supervisors on how to identify and approach employees whose work behavior or performance is cause for concern.

- *Employee communications.* Many EAPs provide newsletters and other employee communications to identify self-help methods as well as the services the EAP can provide.

- *On-line services.* Some EAPs now offer services over the Internet. Such services may include child and elder care referrals, self-assessment tools, health and wellness educational materials, links to community resources, profiles of EAP counselors (including credentials, experience, and training), and frequently asked questions. Research conducted by the University of Maryland at Baltimore School of Social Work in 2002 reported that employees find on-line EAPs helpful to obtain specific information quickly, to make appointments for face-to-face visits with a counselor, and to obtain information anonymously.

Since January 1, 1998, the effective date of the federal Mental Health Parity Act (MHPA), stand-alone EAPs have become more popular. Stand-alone EAPs provide employees access to quality mental health care, permit employers to monitor their value and effectiveness, and help to avoid increasing related costs in the employer group health or medical plan.

Because employees may see an EAP as an integral part of their health care benefits, some EAPs have linked up with providers of wellness programs to offer more complete behavioral health benefits. For example, one national EAP features smoking-cessation and weight-loss telephone support programs. Another national EAP offers an option to employers that provides wellness and alternative medicine such as acupuncture, massage therapy, and chiropractic care. Proponents of these integrated wellness/EAPs suggest that the combination helps employees with complex problems more thoroughly while reducing expenses of running both plans and eliminating administrative duplication. Examples of the reduced administrative burden include one invoice instead of two, one set of integrated reports, and one contact at the provider. Before signing on for these additional benefits, it is essential to determine whether they are worth the additional cost in terms of expected reduced care costs, reduced absenteeism, and/or potential prevention of costly employee problems.

[B] Legal Services Plans

Group legal services plans are a form of employee benefit that has grown in popularity. Experts estimate that seven of ten employees will face personal legal issues and will need to deal with them while at work. In 1998, according to the National Resource Center for Consumers of Legal Services, the number of Americans covered by group legal services plan grew by 7.1 percent. In the SHRM 2008 Benefits Survey Report, 24 percent of the respondents offered legal service plans to their employees. Legal services plans range from the informal use of a company's legal counsel to structured, formal plans with a specific set of scheduled benefits.

The following three major types of legal services plans are prevalent:

1. The ad hoc reimbursement program, which requires no formal structure or plan and reimburses employees on an ad hoc basis for personal or business-related legal expenses;

2. The qualified legal services plan, which allows employers to exclude legal benefits from employees' gross income, so long as the employer establishes a formal, written plan and complies with IRS requirements; and

3. The cafeteria plan, which can be designed to include a qualified legal services plan.

Some services offered within typical group legal services plans include assistance with the following matters:

- Real estate transactions

- Divorce

- Adoption

- Simple wills and trusts

- Bankruptcy proceedings

- Defense in traffic cases that could result in loss or suspension of a driver's license

- Defense in civil or criminal cases

- Tax and financial planning

Legal services that are usually excluded from group plan coverage include:

- Class actions

- Routine tax matters

- Actions relating to an outside business or profession

- Actions involving the employer

A qualified legal plan generally provides a toll-free number (and sometimes online access) for a panel of attorneys who have contracted with the legal services plan provider. Often, an employee's problem can be resolved by talking with an attorney over the phone. If it cannot, the employee is referred to an attorney located close to the employee. Either the employer or the employee pays the monthly legal plan fee. In most plans the monthly fee covers the services listed above. If the cost of a service (e.g., services in a criminal defense case) is not completely covered by the plan, the employee generally pays a reduced hourly fee for the attorney's services.

Recently, legal plans have begun offering on-line services. Such services may include access to an online library of legal information or an expert to answer questions, ratings of attorneys by plan participants, and plan service information. Employers may be able to find out more about the legal services plan and sign up on-line. Employees may also be able to enroll in the plan on-line.

Under Code Section 120, employer contributions for legal services plans and the value of legal services actually received under these plans are excludable, within limits, from employee gross income. At various times, however, employee exclusion from gross income may have expired and not been continued. The plan administrator should consult a tax expert on the current tax status of such plans. Prepaid legal services plans provided to employees on a group basis are subject to ERISA reporting and disclosure requirements for welfare plans.

[C] Relocation Counseling and Services Plans

Relocation services are provided by many employers for transfers, promotions, or relocations. Employers provide these services so relocations are less stressful for the employee and his or her family, allowing the employee to focus on the new job. In addition, these services tend to help the family members feel they have not lost financially from the relocation. In the SHRM 2008 Benefits Survey Report, 40 percent of the responding employers offer temporary relocation benefits to their employees. Other benefits may include:

- Helping employees find living quarters

- Paying travel and moving expenses

- Protecting employees from losses in the sale or purchase of their home

An employer may also provide family counseling for a relocating family to help the family adjust to its new surroundings, especially if the employer does not otherwise provide an EAP. For the dual-career family, the employee's spouse may be given assistance with finding a job in the new location. Of the employers responding to the SHRM 2008 Benefits Survey Report, 19 percent offered this assistance.

Note: Code Section 82 provides that any payment received by an employee, directly or indirectly, as a payment for or reimbursement of moving expenses is considered gross income for the employee and subject to taxation.

[D] Financial and Retirement Planning Education

Survey data suggest that employees would welcome workplace-based financial and retirement planning advice and education. For example, the 6th annual MetLife Study of Employee Benefits Trends reported that 49 percent of employees are interested in receiving financial education at work and 44 percent would like access to general financial-planning advice at work. In 2008, the International Foundation of Employee Benefit Plans reported in Retirement and Financial Planning Programs that 77 percent of the respondents to their survey offer retirement planning to employees, 60 percent provide investment education, and 28 percent provide investment advice.

Financial and retirement planning programs can provide many benefits to employers and employees. Employees who understand the rewards of an employer's retirement benefit program are more likely to participate in that plan, boosting overall participation and contributions to the plan. Employees who understand the need to save for retirement and how savings can compound over time are also more likely not to invest in the lowest-return option in the plan. Employees also appreciate the employer's efforts and are more likely to retain a positive perception about their employer, and that may lead to longer retention.

Employer-provided education can be as simple as offering financial education literature at work and via the company's intranet. Programs can be one-hour workshops or "brown-bag" lunches where experts are brought in to discuss financial topics. Or an entire educational program can be designed to provide meaningful education at the worksite and after work hours. Some employers provide sessions that spouses can attend to ensure the family is working together to reach its financial goals.

Potential topics for financial education include:

- How to effectively manage credit

- Personal budgeting

- Investment diversification

- Basics of stocks and bonds

- Providing and using financial calculators

- How to set and achieve financial goals

- Wealth accumulation

- Basics of taxation

- How to structure an investment portfolio

- Estate planning

- How to get out of debt

- Protecting your financial assets

- Planning for retirement

The cost of such programs is generally paid for by the employer, although a small percentage of employers require employees to pay some or all of the cost. Employers can consider using their retirement plan vendors as educators, but should be sure that program facilitators are experts in the topic and are skilled in providing education to adults. In addition, most employers prefer that no selling of stocks, bonds, insurance or other financial vehicles takes place during the education sessions. [See **Section 8.06[D][2]** for information on providing investment advice to retirement plan participants] Many employers find that their vendors provide excellent education on certain topics, but supplement them with other subject matter experts. Utilizing on-line or other technology-based approaches to financial education can offer a more personalized educational experience for employees.

§ 10.09 WELLNESS PROGRAMS

One important benefit program that many employers add to their health plans to help control overall health benefit costs is a wellness or health-promotion program. For employers, a wellness program functions under one basic assumption: the cost of preventing or mitigating an illness or injury is significantly less than the cost of treating someone after the event occurs.

Studies have found that healthy, motivated employees have increased productivity, miss fewer days of work, and are less likely to be involved in both on-the-job and off-the-job accidents. Therefore, wellness programs not only control medical costs but also may improve bottom-line profits through reduced absenteeism, disability, and workers' compensation expenses.

Although smaller companies, which are affected most by rising insurance costs, seldom have the resources to institute an extensive wellness program, in many ways such a program is more desirable for a smaller organization than a larger one. This is true simply because a small operation emphasizes the health and condition of each employee; the sickness or absence of one or two people can greatly influence the workload of all the others, in addition to having an impact on the organization's ability to service customers.

Statistics show that wellness is a worthwhile effort, regardless of a company's size. Not only are benefits reflected in the bottom line, but the lives of employees are enriched as well. Wellness programs provide management with a means of saying to employees, "We really care," and the programs can also serve as a valuable recruiting and retention tool in tight labor markets.

Many tactics encourage employee fitness, from a broad program including health club membership, to simply distributing informational brochures. To determine what may be best for the company, a constructive way to begin is with a survey to identify employee preferences. Questions about specific activities and time frames should be included in the survey. For example, attendance at after-work exercise classes will be nominal if the majority of employees are parents who must rush from work to pick up their children at day care centers. Similarly, costs for smoking-cessation classes are typically wasted on people who either do not smoke or do not want to quit.

According to the SHRM 2008 Benefits Survey Report, 72 percent of responding employers offer their employees wellness resources, and information, 58 percent offer a wellness program, and 40 percent provide a wellness newsletter or column in their employee newsletter.

[A] Results of Wellness Programs

Implementing a wellness program may lead to decreased health care costs, absenteeism, and short-term disability absences and costs. By improving the health of the wellness program participants, those participants are likely to use fewer health care services, driving down utilization. In November 2004, "Health Improvement: A Comprehensive Guide to Designing, Implementing and Evaluating Worksite Programs" (Center for Prevention and Health Services, National Business Group on Health) reported on a review of more than 120 studies of wellness programs. In this review, for every $1.00 invested in wellness programs, employers realized $3.48 in reduced health care costs and $5.82 in lower absenteeism costs. Within five years of beginning the wellness program, employers realized a return on investment (ROI) of $3 to $8 per dollar invested. In 2002, the Johnson and Johnson companies released to the public results of a four-year study of its wellness program. In 1995, employees completed health risk assessments. Those identified to be at high risk for a health problem, such as high blood pressure, were invited to participate in the wellness program. Each employee received a tailored program focused on changing behaviors over time by using a multidelivery approach. The study compared the four years of the program to the immediately preceding five-year period. Johnson and Johnson found that they saved $225 per employee per year in medical care costs alone. These costs included hospital admissions and medical outpatient and mental health treatment. In addition, the study found that employee health risks were significantly reduced in 8 of 13 risk categories.

Focusing wellness efforts on particular types of health care usage can pay off in terms of reduced expenditures in the health plan. Blue Cross/Blue Shield of Massachusetts found that providing individuals with a medical self-care guide for the most common medical conditions reduced the use of emergency room care. The guides were distributed to over 330,000 members. Prior to receiving the guide, 30 percent of members visited the emergency room. After they received the guide, visits decreased to 26.8 percent, while visits to the emergency room by those who did not receive the guide remained the same. In addition, emergency room visits for the conditions covered by the guide were reviewed. The data showed that there was a 3.2 percent drop in emergency room visits because of those conditions.

Wellness programs are often associated with a drop in absenteeism and workplace injuries. The University of Michigan Health Management Research Center conducted a four-year study of Xerox Corp.'s wellness program. It found that only 5.6 percent of the employees participating in the wellness program submitted a workers compensation claim, while 8.9 percent of the nonparticipating employees submitted such claims.

[B] Recent Wellness Trends

One survey of 106 wellness professionals concluded that wellness programs have many positive effects in the workplace. Seven out of 10 survey respondents said that wellness programs had improved employee morale; half said the programs increased productivity; and nearly half indicated the programs helped reduce absenteeism. Other respondents credit wellness programs, attention to fitness, and reducing health risks for reductions in overall health care costs. Health screenings, a relatively simple and inexpensive wellness benefit, are the most often cited wellness feature related to reduced health care costs.

Hewitt Associates has conducted a survey that reveals that employers are continuing to encourage participation in wellness activities. Of more than 1,000 companies responding to the survey, 42 percent provide some sort of incentive or disincentive to employees in an attempt to increase participation in such activities or programs. Common incentives include monetary gifts or awards for participation in health screenings.

The most common disincentive cited in the survey is adding surcharges to health care and life insurance premiums of workers who smoke. Other disincentives designed to target and reduce specific employee behaviors include adding extra deductible charges for employees who demonstrate risky behavior (e.g., being injured while not wearing a helmet or seat belt). Any disincentive should be carefully reviewed by legal counsel before implementation, in light of applicable federal regulations (e.g., the ADA) as well as applicable state statutes (e.g., Right to Privacy or Fair Employment Practices).

Other survey findings revealed that 72 percent of large employers offer some type of health promotion education or training. These programs might include classes, workshops, or individual counseling related to lifestyle habits and compliance with treatment protocols for chronic conditions, such as asthma or diabetes. Many of these employers are offering training that utilizes newer technology; only 37 percent offer classroom-based training.

An additional wellness benefit offered by a significant percentage of employers (75 percent) in the Hewitt survey was health risk appraisals. These screenings include medical tests such as blood pressure checks or cholesterol testing administered by the company medical provider, the health plan, or, frequently, at health fairs that are open to all members of the employees' families. In many areas of the country, such assessments are available at no or low cost through public health agencies or community not-for-profit organizations. Many employers (28 percent) administer health risk questionnaires to employees; these questionnaires are designed to help employees detect preventable health conditions sooner rather than later.

[C] Setting Up Wellness Programs

Wellness programs can range from creative low-cost or no-cost strategies, such as removing cigarette and candy machines from the work premises, to extensive efforts, such as installing an on-site health club. Ideas, and their success, depend on the demographics of the individual workplace, budget limitations, and related company goals.

By analyzing high medical claim cost areas, absenteeism trends, and workplace accidents, the plan administrator can identify which types of wellness benefits would be most beneficial for the company. The focus should be on corporate objectives and available budget, to start. The administrator may even want to contact an independent consultant to conduct a health risk appraisal. This confidential questionnaire, completed by employees, can further identify lifestyle patterns and high-risk behaviors to help in targeting high-cost areas that the wellness program could affect. Many employers have created successful wellness programs by working with their medical and EAP providers. Small rewards or other financial incentives may be necessary to encourage high-risk individuals to participate in the program.

The idea of giving employees incentives to participate in wellness options is catching on. Incentives may include cash bonuses, discounts, free merchandise, or company recognition of individually achieved goals. Regardless of the means (and there is no consensus about the "best" one), incentives work only if they fit the employees' lifestyles and interests.

Incentives must be flexible enough to meet the needs of different employees. For example, cash incentives or discounts at health and fitness centers may be appropriate for some people, but employees with young children may be more interested in reimbursements to offset the cost of buying exercise equipment for their homes. Some organizations believe traditional incentives are not enough and that employees are truly motivated only by creative and unique programs, such as earning points toward health or sports related items, vacations, and more. Some common features of wellness programs include the following:

- *Weight management, fitness, or exercise programs.*

- *Alternative programs.* Some companies offer an alternative to on-site classes, allowing employees to attend local community sessions during lunch hours. The company may absorb the cost of the classes, offer an outside organization a room at the company to hold classes, or allow employees the necessary time off from work to attend the programs. Simply offering the program on the premises, without lost work time, is often enough to inspire those who would not otherwise participate in the program.

- *On- or off-site smoking cessation classes.* In June 1999, the IRS issued Revenue Ruling 99-28 [1999-1 C.B. 1269], which qualified smoking cessation programs (including prescription drugs to alleviate nicotine withdrawal) as deductible medical expenses under Code Section 213. Therefore, employers may now pay for these expenses on a tax-favored basis, and employees may receive reimbursement under a Section 125 FSA.

- *Other on-site screening programs.* Some employers believe so strongly in the positive impact of health promotions that they work with local providers to offer on-site health screening, such as mammograms, bone-mass density testing (for osteoporosis), and health fairs that are available to employees' family members (whether or not they are covered as dependents under the group health plan).

- *Prenatal or managed maternity programs.* These programs are designed to ensure adequate prenatal care and counseling for all pregnant employees and dependents and to identify high-risk pregnancy factors. These programs may be offered by the group health plan.

Alternatively, organizations such as the March of Dimes offer free or low-cost programs to employers willing to provide the meeting facility and make the time commitment to implement these (or similar) programs. Some programs provide expectant mothers with $100 toward pregnancy-related medical expenses to encourage program participation.

Suggestions for offering inexpensive programs include the following:

- Organizing group activities, such as softball and volleyball tournaments, or arranging for an aerobics instructor to teach a class two or three times a week in a conference room after work

- Providing education in the form of informational material stuffed in pay envelopes

- Permitting local nonprofit groups to assist with classes on such subjects as nutrition, stress management, chemical dependency, cancer, and diabetes

- Organizing self-help groups (e.g., weight reduction classes), for which members share the cost

- Holding special events such as promoting the Great American Smoke-Out day or designating a monthly wellness day

In addition to adding new preventive programs, wellness benefits can be built into an existing group medical insurance program. Insurance carriers often let an employer add coverage for important medical preventive services if they are not offered as standard practices. Add-on services may include one or more of the following:

- Well-child care

- Childhood immunizations

- Routine physical examinations

- Annual Pap smears for women and prostatic specific antigen (PSA) screenings for men

- Mammograms

Self-funding the cost of preventive care benefits is possible, by giving employees pretax dollars in a flexible spending account (FSA) (see **Chapter 12**). Employer funding of preventive benefits supports wellness initiatives and provides employees with an additional nontaxable benefit.

Ongoing employee communication is essential to a successful wellness effort. Effective means of communication may include a monthly or quarterly wellness newsletter, which can be produced internally or purchased from an outside service; promotion of important employee activities and successes, such as running in a local event; or using an outside service to provide materials for company bulletin boards.

[D] Laws and Tax Regulations

Although no federal legislation addresses wellness benefits as a broad category, the following federal and state laws may apply:

- The ADA states that benefits may not discriminate against individuals classified as having a disability, unless such benefit distinction can be actuarially justified. Therefore, if a company offers wellness benefits, it must ensure that access is provided to all individuals. For example, any classes or testing offered by the program, such as blood pressure screening or a stress-management class, must be accessible to employees with disabilities. Further, the ADA requires confidentiality of an employee's medical information resulting from testing. Results of any wellness screening tests may not be used to terminate an employee or to discriminate against a person with a disability.

- If any of the benefits offered are part of a cafeteria plan, they are subject to provisions under Code Section 125.

- HIPAA requires confidentiality of employees' medical information. An employer may incur significant penalties for not keeping results of wellness program testing and other medical information confidential. In addition, HIPAA does not allow employers to discriminate against employees on the basis of health. A company cannot charge a higher premium for an employee who smokes than for one who does not. However, an employee who participates in a bona fide wellness program (e.g., aerobic exercise classes) may receive an incentive (e.g., lower premiums) than an employee who does not participate in the program.

In 2001, the federal government issued proposed regulations for reward-based wellness programs. On December 13, 2006, the Departments of Labor, Treasury, and Health and Human Services jointly issued final rules on nondiscrimination and wellness programs in health coverage in the group market (71 Fed. Reg. 75,014 (December 13, 2006)). While in general the final rules are similar to the proposed rules, some important differences and clarifications were made. The final regulations are effective for plan years beginning on or after July 1, 2007.

Under HIPAA's nondiscrimination rules, a health benefit plan is not required to provide coverage for any particular benefit to any group of similarly situated individuals. If benefits are provided, they must be uniformly available to all similarly situated individuals. Likewise, any restriction on a benefit or benefits must apply uniformly to all similarly situated individuals and must not be directed at individual participants or beneficiaries based on any health factor of the participants or beneficiaries. While the HIPAA nondiscrimination provisions do not prevent a plan or health insurance issuer from establishing discounts or rebates or modifying otherwise applicable copayments or deductibles in return for adherence to programs of health promotion and disease prevention, they do generally prohibit a plan or issuer from doing so if the arrangement is based on a health factor. Generally, those plans that will provide financial incentives will be subject to additional standards in order to comply with HIPAA's nondiscrimination requirements.

Under the final rule, there are two types of wellness programs: programs not subject to additional standards, and programs that are. Programs that provide a reward that is not based on an individual satisfying a standard related to a health factor and programs that provide no reward at all will not need to meet the additional requirements. These programs will be required to make participation available to all similarly situated individuals. Examples of these kinds of wellness programs include:

- A program that reimburses all or part of the cost for memberships in a fitness center

- A diagnostic testing program that provides a reward for participation and does not base any part of the reward on outcomes

- A program that encourages preventive care through the waiver of the copayment or deductible required under a group health plan; for example, the costs of prenatal care or well baby visits

- A program that provides a reward to employees for attending a monthly health education seminar.

Programs under which any of the conditions for obtaining a reward is based on an individual satisfying a standard related to a health factor must meet these 5 additional requirements:

- Limit on the reward. The reward may be in the form of a discount or rebate of a premium or contribution, a waiver of all or part of a cost-sharing mechanism (such as deductibles, copayments, or coinsurance), avoidance of a surcharge, or the value of a benefit that would otherwise not be provided under the plan. The total of all of these rewards may not exceed 20 percent of the cost of employee-only coverage under the plan (if the wellness program is available only to employees). The cost of employee-only coverage is based on the total amount of employer and employee contributions for the benefit package under which the employee is receiving coverage.

- Reasonable design. The program should have a reasonable chance of improving the health of participants, not be a subterfuge for discriminating based on a health factor, and not be highly suspect in the method chosen to promote health or prevent disease. There does not need to be a scientific record that the method promotes wellness. The standard of reasonableness is meant to prohibit bizarre, extreme, illegal, or immoral requirements in a wellness program.

- Annual opportunity to qualify. The program must allow eligible individuals to qualify for the reward at least once per year.

- Uniform availability. The wellness program must provide a reasonable alternative to the usual standard for obtaining the reward for those individuals for whom, for that period, it is unreasonably difficult due to a medical condition to satisfy the usual standard, or for whom for that period, it is medically inadvisable to attempt to satisfy the usual standard. A program does not need to establish the specific reasonable alternative standard before the program commences. It is sufficient to determine a reasonable alternative standard once a participant informs the plan that it is unreasonably difficult for the participant due to a medical condition to satisfy the usual standard (or that it is medically inadvisable for the participant to attempt to achieve the usual standard) under the program. Examples of reasonable alternative standards include: lowering the threshold of the existing health-factor-related standard, substituting a different standard, or waiving the standard. For the alternative standard to be reasonable, the individual must be able to satisfy it without regard to any health factor. A reasonable alternative standard could include following the recommendations of an individual's physician regarding the health factor at issue. The program may seek verification, such as a statement from a physician, that a health factor makes it unreasonably difficult or medically inadvisable for an individual to meet a standard.

- Disclosure of reasonable alternative standards. All plan materials describing the terms of the program must disclose the availability of a reasonable alternative standard. The final regulations provides the following model language:

  > If it is unreasonably difficult due to a medical condition for you to achieve the standards for the reward under this program, or if it is medically inadvisable for you to attempt to achieve the standards for the reward under this program, call us at [insert telephone number] and we will work with you to develop another way to qualify for the reward.

- In addition, the final regulation provides three examples with substantially similar language to this model that would satisfy the disclosure requirement. The preamble to the rule notes that if the program is merely mentioned and does not describe the usual standard, disclosure of the availability of a reasonable alternative standard is not required.

On February 14, 2008, the DOL released Field Assistance Bulletin (FAB) 2008-02 (available at *http://www.dol.gov/ebsa/regs/fab2008-2.html*) which contains a "Wellness Program Checklist" designed to help employers determine if their wellness program complies with the final regulations. The FAB is done in a question and answer format, making it easy for employers to understand the regulation's requirements.

If a company that has a wellness program plans to offer incentives or disincentives based on an individual meeting a health-factor based standard, it should seek legal counsel.

Employers that offer Health Savings Accounts (HSAs) may want to design the wellness program so that it will not interfere with employees' eligibility for the HSA. To be eligible for an HSA (see **Chapter 5**), an employee must not be covered by any health plan other than a high deductible health plan (HDHP). If a wellness program does not provide significant benefits in the nature of medical care or treatment, it will not be considered a "health plan" for purposes of HSA-eligibility. When determining whether significant medical care or treatment is provided, certain screening and other services can be disregarded. These disregarded services include smoking cessation programs, weight-loss programs, adult immunizations, screening for heart and infectious diseases, cancer screening, and periodic health evaluations. The IRS's guidance for HSAs provides an example of a wellness program that is not a health plan and would therefore not interfere with an employee's HSA-eligibility. In addition to the screening services listed above, the IRS's wellness program example includes health and wellness education, fitness activities, and stress management. The program's costs, if any, are separate from the employees' costs for coverage under the HDHP plan, and all employees, whether they participated in the HDHP plan or not, are eligible to participate in the wellness program.

As discussed in **Chapter 5**, some states mandate wellness-type benefits within group health plans under their insurance laws. A plan administrator should discuss state-mandated health benefit provisions with the insurance consultant or agent and the group insurance carrier.

For wellness programs to succeed, commitment must come from top management and be evident throughout the organization. Employees will generally participate if all levels of management are setting a positive example by their participation. One major drawback to wellness programs is that the people who need them most are often the ones who refuse to participate. Even so, the numbers are clearly in favor of work site wellness and fitness.

§ 10.10 TRANSPORTATION AND PARKING BENEFITS

Under IRS final regulations on qualified transportation fringe benefits, effective January 11, 2001, and applicable for tax years beginning after December 31, 2001 [66 Fed. Reg. 2,241 (Jan. 11, 2001)], employees may use pretax dollars to pay for parking and commuting. The complete final regulations can be downloaded at *www.access.gpo.gov*. Although similar in structure to flexible spending accounts, these transportation benefits must be offered in a distinct plan separate from a cafeteria plan. According to the SHRM 2008 Benefits Survey Report, 15 percent of responding employers offer their employees a qualified transportation spending account.

Since January 1, 1992, under Code Section 132(a)(5), employers have been allowed to pay for employees' commuting, transit fares, and parking. If the amounts paid do not exceed set limits, they are not included in employees' taxable income.

These limits, which will be adjusted for inflation, state that an employee may set aside up to $120 a month in 2008 for transit fares, van pools, and so forth, and up to $330 per month for parking. If an employee drives and rides (e.g., drives to the transit parking lot and takes a train to the office from there), the amounts may be combined, up to a maximum of $350 per month.

The amount the employee sets aside in a transportation spending account is exempt from federal income tax and Social Security (FICA) tax. Employers might also save FICA expenses on these amounts if an employee's total annual income is less than the FICA taxable wage base. Some states might also allow the amounts an employee sets aside in a transportation spending account to be excluded from taxable income. The employer should check with its tax advisor.

Although the regulations allow employers to set up and operate programs without a written plan (usually required of other benefits under ERISA), there are administrative requirements. Employees must elect to defer the income before they earn their salary or wages and before the transportation benefit is provided. The election must be in writing or other permanent and verifiable form (such as an electronic ballot). To be reimbursed, employees must submit their receipts or a written declaration that they incurred the transportation costs. The unused portion of the monthly allotment from a transportation spending account, unlike the flexible spending account, may be carried forward to a future year for employees, but cannot be refunded to terminated employees. Only transportation expenses that were incurred and paid while an individual is employed may be reimbursed by the plan.

In November 2006, the IRS released a Revenue Ruling outlining the qualified use of debit cards to provide qualified transportation benefits (Rev. Rul. 2006-47, Nov. 20, 2006). "Smart cards" (plastic cards with an embedded memory chip) and "terminal restricted" debit cards purchased by an employer from either a transit company or a third-party debit card provider for use by its employees qualify as a transit system voucher because the cards could only be used to purchase transit fares. The terminal restricted debit card can only be "loaded" with a maximum of the monthly transit fare limit in effect for that month (e.g., no more than $120 per month in 2009). If a debit card can be used to purchase other than transit fares even though it is restricted to use at merchants that sell transit fares, the cards do not qualify as transit system vouchers. However, as explained in example 3 of the revenue ruling, because no other types of vouchers were available, the debit card could be used to provide qualified transportation fringe benefits under a bona fide reimbursement arrangement by implementing reasonable substantiation procedures. It is not sufficient under the IRS requirements for an employee to merely certify that the card was only used to purchase transit passes; substantiation of actual purchases of transit fares or passes in the form of monthly statements provided by the debit card company that included the identity of the merchants, the date of the transaction, and the amount of the fare purchased, in addition to the employee certification that the debit card was used only to purchase transit fares or passes, is required. The requirements were originally set to become effective on January 1, 2008. However the IRS delayed the ruling until January 1, 2009 in order to give transit systems enough time to modify their technology to comply with the ruling.

Regarding parking benefits, the IRS, in October 2004, addressed an employment tax arrangement that it found to be abusive. Revenue Ruling 2004-98 [2004-42 I.R.B. 664] described the following benefit arrangement:

> Employer X provides parking for its employees near or on its premises. It reduces its employees' cash compensation in exchange for providing this parking. Employer X then reimburses its employees the amount that was deducted from their pay, such that the employees' net after-tax pay would be the same, if there had been no reduction or reimbursement from their pay in the first place.

> Employer X believes that both the initial compensation reduction and the reimbursement are excludable from employees' income and no federal income tax nor FICA and FUTA taxes are withheld.

The IRS stated the following in its ruling:

> X's position with respect to the transaction described in this ruling is meritless. An employee may exclude from gross income employer reimbursements for qualified parking expenses, but only if those expenses were actually incurred by the employee.

> In this case, the cost of the parking is incurred by Employer X, not by the employees, and the value of that benefit is excludable from the employees' income because it meets the requirements of Code Section 132(a)(5). Because the employee did not pay for the benefit, there are no expenses to reimburse. In this situation, the reimbursements are treated as income and are taxable.

The IRS went on to say that any such arrangement for employee benefits would be similarly treated:

> In addition, this ruling applies to arrangements with respect to benefits other than parking where: (1) an employee's salary (and gross income) is reduced in return for a non-taxable benefit, and (2) the employer "reimburses" the employee for some or all of the cost of the non-taxable benefit and excludes the reimbursement from the employee's salary (and gross income) even though that cost was paid by the employer and not the employee.

§ 10.11 CREDIT UNIONS

Credit unions are nonprofit entities set up to assist members with various financial needs. Usually, a credit union allows its members to conduct personal checking, secure credit cards, make savings deposits, use automatic teller services, and process loan applications at a rate generally more favorable than those at other commercial financial institutions.

Credit unions are organized and supervised under both federal and state laws. Membership is limited to groups with a common occupation or association, or groups within well-defined geographic areas.

Many employers make credit union membership available to their employees because it assists employees with their financial needs, thereby reducing management's involvement with employees' financial problems, and it may minimize employees' time off from work for banking activities. According to the SHRM 2008 Benefits Survey Report, 43 percent of responding employers offer their employees credit union membership.

Any group of seven or more employees may apply for permission to set up a credit union. Credit unions may be chartered and supervised under either a federal or a state agency. The first step in establishing a credit union is to contact the National Credit Union Administration (for a federal-chartered credit union) or the state regulatory agency (for a state-chartered credit union). Information on starting credit unions is also available from the Credit Union National Association (CUNA), an association of individual credit unions in Madison, Wisconsin.

§ 10.12 EMPLOYEE DISCOUNTS

Many companies offer employees discounts on goods and services produced or provided by the company. This type of discretionary benefit is generally viewed favorably by employees and instills goodwill and loyalty. Code Section 132 excludes from gross income qualified employee discounts in the form of reduced sales prices of goods and services sold by the employer to the employee. A qualified employee discount is given to employees on the price of qualified property or services offered by the employer to customers. To be qualified, the property or services must be offered for sale to the employer's customers in the ordinary course of the business where the employee is working. Real or personal property held for investment is not qualified property. For property, the discount may not exceed the gross profit percentage of the price at which the property is offered for sale to customers. For services, the discount may not exceed 20 percent of the price at which the services are offered to customers.

A number of states have mandated provisions that relate to employee discounts. Most relate to employee reimbursement of an open account. For example, Montana does not allow an employer to deduct more than 40 percent of an employee's gross pay to pay off an employer account. Nebraska and Wyoming, on the other hand, address reimbursement by terminated employees. In addition, Nebraska does not allow an employer to take the balance due on an account from the employee's last paycheck unless there was a prior written agreement. Wyoming does allow an employer to take legitimate offsets to the account from the final paycheck, as long as gross wages do not go below minimum wage. Because of the changing nature of state legislation, employers should verify current state legislative requirements with their state employment office.

§ 10.13 AUTOMOBILE AND HOMEOWNER'S INSURANCE

Company-sponsored insurance coverages are offered by a limited number of carriers and have been rather slow in gaining acceptance as an employee benefit. (According to the SHRM 2008 Benefits Survey Report, 15 percent of the respondents offer automobile insurance to their employees.) Although company-sponsored coverage can save some employees a sizable amount of money, for others there may be no savings at all, or costs may be more than they might pay if obtaining their own coverage. The principal advantage of these coverages for employees is the opportunity they provide to spread a relatively large expense over a longer period of time than usually permitted under standard forms of coverage. This benefit frequently appeals to younger employees, who typically have high automobile insurance premiums. These coverages are attractive to employers because they are completely employee-funded.

A new related product is a home warranty plan sponsored by the employer. Such plans may cover repairs and replacements of appliances, air conditioning and heating systems, electrical systems, plumbing, and water heaters. A deductible usually applies. Such plans can be offered as fully employee paid, or the employer may wish to provide a subsidy.

An organization offering these insurance benefits usually commits to promoting the program on an ongoing basis, collecting the premiums through payroll deductions, and remitting the collected premiums to the carrier. Under some carrier programs, payroll deductions by the employer are unnecessary; the carrier simply issues a draft on the employee's checking account, thus collecting the premium directly. From the employer's standpoint, this is certainly the better approach, because it reduces the amount of administrative time and expense involved.

Employees generally fill out an application form on which, in the case of automobile insurance, they indicate the desired level(s) of coverage and information concerning their driving record(s.) The completed application is then sent to the carrier, which determines, from its underwriting standards, the premium to be charged and notifies applicants of that expense. At this point, employees have the choice of accepting or declining the coverage and then notifying the carrier of their decisions. The carrier, in turn, advises the employer to begin the payroll deduction or initiates the draft process.

Employee expense for automobile and home insurance programs varies according to individual coverage needs and the ability to meet the carrier's underwriting standards for that coverage. If employment is terminated, employees usually can continue coverage by converting to direct premium payment.

§ 10.14   CONCIERGE AND PERSONAL BUSINESS BENEFITS

Businesses are springing up across the country to offer employees personal business benefits, with the employer's cooperation as sponsor.

Innovative employers are acting on their belief that time is money and that employees free from personal worries are more productive than others (and likely to remain working). Employers are sponsoring such benefits as:

- Dry cleaning pick-up and drop-off service

- Washing and servicing the car

- Providing access to pet health insurance, veterinary services, and pet products

- Standing in line (e.g., for tickets)

- Making appointments

- Arranging for housecleaning and other services

- Having the mail room handle employees' packages (for the price of postage)

- Buying event tickets in blocks (at a discount)

- Packing hot meals from the company cafeteria for employees to take home or serving complimentary dinners (to entice employees to work late)

- Having employees' prescriptions filled at local pharmacies

- Having a sitter at an employee's home to await repair service, deliveries, and so forth

- Sponsoring group participation and rates for oil changes and other routine car maintenance or detailing (e.g., in the parking lot)

- Arranging for and picking up birthday cakes, gifts, cards, and flowers

Whether offered through direct relationships with local businesses or through national concierge services, these benefits meet employee needs while supporting corporate objectives. In fact, concierge and personal business benefits are often offered as an employee-pay-all service because of their perceived high value.

Exhibit 10.1
Dollar Limits for Deductibility of Long-Term Care Premiums
Under the Health Insurance Portability and Accountability Act of 1996

Age Before Close of Tax Year	Dollar Limit
40 or less	$ 320
More than 40 but less than 50	600
More than 50 but less than 60	1,190
More than 60 but less than 70	3,180
More than 70	3,980

Long-term care premiums, up to the limits noted, are treated as medical expenses for purposes of the itemized deduction for medical expenses. The amounts are per person. The provisions of HIPAA are generally effective for taxable years after December 31, 1996. For the years after 1997, the amounts increase to reflect increases in the medical care component of the Consumer Price Index. The amounts shown are those in effect for 2009.

Chapter 11
Time Away from Work

§ 11.01   AUDIT QUESTIONS

1. Is the company's vacation policy in compliance with the state's requirements on vacation pay, if any?

2. Are exempt employees' salaries paid in full when they take partial day absences?

3. Are the company's time-off policies coordinated so that time away from work is minimized while still meeting legislated requirements?

4. Has the company implemented policies or practices to minimize abuse of its sick pay and/or salary continuation programs?

5. Are the company's time-away-from-work policies in writing and consistently applied?

6. Does the company's military leave policy comply with the Uniformed Services Employment and Reemployment Rights Act?

Note: Consistent "yes" answers to the above questions suggest that the organization is applying effective management practices and/or complying with federal regulations. "No" answers indicate that problem areas exist and should be addressed immediately.

Most employers recognize the importance of providing some form of time off from work in order to attract and retain a qualified and productive workforce. This chapter examines discretionary time-off benefits offered and the state statutes governing such benefits.

This chapter does not address time-off requirements under the 1993 Family and Medical Leave Act (FMLA). For an in-depth review of FMLA and sample policy statements regarding leave under FMLA, see **Chapter 14.**

§ 11.02 ABSENCE OF FEDERAL MANDATE

The federal government does not mandate any time off for employees other than that available under the FMLA and the Uniformed Services Employment and Reemployment Rights Act of 1994 (USERRA). The federal government, through the Department of Labor, enforces the Fair Labor Standards Act (FLSA). Under the FLSA, an employer may work employees 24 hours per day, 365 days per year, as long as the employer compensates the nonexempt employee at minimum wage and pays overtime at a rate of one and one-half times regular rate of pay for time worked totaling more than 40 hours in a workweek.

However, it is not practical, or even legal in some states, to take advantage of the absence of federal legislation concerning time off from work. Time-off-from-work benefits that are generally governed by state laws include:

- Voting

- Serving as an election official

- Serving as a juror or witness

- Attending annual town meetings

- Serving in the state National Guard

- Taking maternity leave

- Taking military family leave

- Attending a meeting at the school of a suspended child or taking time off for other school-related activities

- Taking meal or rest breaks

- Providing paid breaks to nursing mothers

- Taking a day of rest or working maximum hours in the workweek

§ 11.03 PAYMENT FOR TIME NOT WORKED

As a result of the number of disputes that may arise relating to employee time off from work, the human resources (HR) manager should examine the company policy to ensure that it reflects time-off legislation.

Company policy should also take into account how such legislation can affect the time-off benefits it voluntarily provides.

Payment for time not worked may include vacation, paid holidays, and sick pay. Each of these employee benefits is discussed below.

[A]   Vacation Policy

Although employers are not obligated to offer paid or unpaid vacations to their employees, most employers have a policy providing for some type of paid vacations. Federal law does not require employers to pay their employees for accrued or unused vacation time when an employee terminates. States may have legal provisions requiring payment of accrued vacation upon termination.

Regardless of whether a company is in a state that requires payment of accrued or unused vacation time to an employee upon termination of employment, it is wise to have a consistent, written policy that covers how accrued vacation is handled and how consistent compliance with the policy will be enforced.

Vacation policies vary, depending on the nature of the company and its employees. For white-collar employees, a typical vacation policy grants employees two weeks off with pay after one complete year of service. For blue-collar employees, employers generally offer one or two weeks' vacation after one year of service. After the first year of employment, paid vacation time usually increases with an employee's length of service. For example, many companies establish vacation schedules similar to the following:

Service to Company	Vacation Benefit
One complete year of service	2 weeks, following completion of the first year
2–5 years of service	2 weeks
6–10 years of service	3 weeks
11 or more years of service	4 weeks

A few companies provide vacation schedules based on an employee's job classification or level within the company. For example, managers may immediately be eligible for three weeks of vacation, and officers may be immediately eligible for four weeks of vacation, regardless of their years of service. In recent years, as a result of tight labor markets and employees' desires for flexibility, employers have used enhanced vacation schedules as prime recruiting and retention tools—often creating individualized vacation schedules. Some companies even give an employee credit for years of directly related prior experience in determining his or her vacation benefit. Such vacation schedules are possible because there are no rules relating to discrimination in vacation pay or benefits.

A company's vacation policy should consider such factors as scheduling and approval, accrual and carryover, pay in lieu of vacation, and holidays during vacation time. A company may require advance supervisory approval of vacations, a minimum vacation period, or both. Many companies require that employees take at least one week (five consecutive days) of vacation per year so they may rest and have the opportunity to return to work refreshed and rejuvenated.

A vacation policy should indicate whether employees must take their vacations at a set time each year or whether vacation days are accrued over the course of a year. In addition, the policy should state whether unused vacation days may be carried over from year to year. Allowing carryover of all or some portion of vacation time is a practice that cultivates positive employee relations. Employees feel they have earned their vacation time and want the opportunity to use the time, whether they use all of it in the year it was accrued or in a subsequent year. According to Benefits USA's 2007 annual survey, 55 percent of employers allow employees to carry over their accrued vacation. To minimize long vacation leaves, some companies put a cap on the number of days that can be carried over annually. In the Benefits USA survey, 85.3 percent of employers that allowed carryover of vacation placed a cap on the amount of vacation time an employee could accrue. This policy provision must be written carefully to conform to state law in states mandating payment of accrued unused vacation.

A company's vacation policy should indicate whether employees are permitted to exchange vacation time for pay. For example, the policy might have a provision that allows employees to buy or sell one or two weeks of vacation per year, separately or as part of a cafeteria benefits program. It should also indicate whether employees are granted an extra day's pay—or an extra paid day off—when a holiday falls during a scheduled vacation.

Maintaining exempt employees' salaried status when using vacation time for partial days off can be a challenge to employers. Under FLSA rules, an exempt employee must be paid on a "salary basis" defined as regularly receiving "a predetermined amount constituting all or part of the employee's compensation, which amount is not subject to reduction because of variations in the quality or quantity of the work performed." One exception to this "no deduction" rule is that deductions may be made when an exempt employee is absent from work for one or more full days for personal reasons, other than sickness or disability. If an exempt employee is absent from work for one and one-half days on vacation or other personal business, the employer may deduct one day's pay, but not one and one-half day's pay. However, if the employer has a bona fide vacation (or other personal time-off) plan, the employer may deduct the hours of the partial day absence from the accrued vacation time, as long as the exempt employee's actual paid salary remains the same. When an employee is absent for a partial day, payment of the employee's guaranteed salary must be made even if an employee has no accrued benefits, has used up his or her benefits, or has a negative balance in the vacation plan.

What can be considered a partial-day absence? Some experts believe that if exempt employees call their office while on vacation or check their e-mail or voice mail, they will have performed "work" and are therefore due their full day's pay, with only part of that day charged to vacation (or none, if they have no vacation time accumulated). Some employers want employees to stay connected, and will work out the vacation usage/pay issues. Others want their employees to take a complete break from the office and have specifically (and often in writing) indicated that they should not call in or check voice or email. Employers who are serious about ensuring employees get a complete break can assist by:

- Cross-training employees so they can fill-in for absent colleagues

- Hiring temporary employees during the vacation

- Helping employees complete projects prior to leaving for vacation

[B] Paid Holidays and Personal Days

There is no federal law governing holiday pay. However, almost universally, employers provide time off and compensation for at least a few of the major holidays. It is a common practice, however, for employers to award holiday pay only to full-time employees and require employees to work the day before and the day after the holiday to receive holiday pay. (See **Chapter 3** for further discussion of mandated pay practices regarding holidays and overtime if an employee is required to work on a holiday.)

Changing workforce demographics have influenced the way some companies offer holiday pay and decide which days to close. The six most common paid holidays are New Year's Day, Memorial Day, Independence Day, Labor Day, Thanksgiving, and Christmas. The second group of commonly paid holidays include Martin Luther King, Jr.'s Birthday, Presidents' Day (honoring Lincoln's Birthday and Washington's Birthday), Good Friday, the day after Thanksgiving, Christmas Eve, and New Year's Eve. Some companies include Columbus Day and Veterans' Day.

Then there are local holidays observed by certain states and municipalities. For example, Massachusetts celebrates Patriot's Day, and Illinois observes Kasimir Pulaski Day. A company's choice of which local holidays to observe depends on accepted community norms, the significance of the holiday to the majority of the company's employees, and related business needs.

A company's industry and the market it serves are among the factors determining when a company will close. Banks, for example, are required to close on certain federal holidays. Manufacturers usually try to avoid closing a plant or disrupting a specific shift on holidays, and restaurants and department stores stay open on weekends and major holidays to do as much business as they can get.

Many larger companies now offer fewer defined holidays and provide more floating holidays or personal days (paid days off that may be taken at the employee's discretion), but they may require that the floating holidays be taken in the year they are accrued or earned and not carried over. In determining a policy for floating holidays, paid personal days, and other paid time off, a company should regard all time-off policies as a part of its overall compensation and benefits package. For example, a company may allow six major holidays, two personal days, and three additional floating days. This approach gives employees flexibility for observing religious holidays or spending time with their children. It also provides a standard approach for individual flexibility regarding time off.

A company's policy regarding floating holidays, paid personal days, and other forms of paid time off should be articulated as part of its overall compensation and benefits package and should address the following issues:

- *Amount of pay received for holiday work.* Nonexempt employees who are asked to work on an observed holiday customarily receive straight time pay for all hours worked (unless they work more than 40 hours for that week or the hours worked exceed the state's overtime requirement), plus holiday pay, or the employees may be granted a floating holiday to be used within a given period following the actual holiday. Exempt employees who are required to work on a designated holiday may receive compensatory time off.

- *Absence on the day before and/or the day after a paid holiday.* To deter absenteeism, particularly on days surrounding a midweek holiday, it is common practice for employers to require employees to work the day before and the day after the holiday to be eligible for holiday pay. This rule is waived for illness and certain personal reasons (such as pre-approval to use a floating holiday or personal day).

- *Relationship of vacations to holidays.* When a holiday occurs during an employee's vacation, employers generally provide holiday pay instead of vacation pay for the observed holiday. The holiday may be added to the employee's vacation period, or the employee may take the holiday at a later date. Such a policy may encourage employees to schedule their vacations around holidays.

- *Sickness or disability and various forms of leave relative to holidays.* Most companies do not grant additional time off or pay for a holiday that falls during an unpaid leave of absence.

- *Holidays that fall on a Saturday or a Sunday.* Holidays that fall on a Saturday are frequently observed on Friday, and those that fall on a Sunday are often observed on the following Monday. For companies that operate on weekends, the practice is to observe the holiday on the day it actually falls and decide how administrative employees (who generally do not work on weekends) will receive the holiday benefit.

[C] Paid Time Off for Illness, Injury, or Disability

Employers are not obligated by federal law to provide employees paid time off for illness or injury, unless the illness or injury is work-related. Although paid time off is not required by the FMLA, covered employers are required under the FMLA to continue providing employee health benefits and vesting for other benefit programs during an approved FMLA leave, including a leave for an employee's own covered disability (i.e., serious health condition).

The HR manager should coordinate the company's sick pay and disability policies to ensure that employees have effective financial protection from illness or disability and that the program meets company cost considerations. Coordination of paid time off policies will also help keep time off at a minimum. For example, requiring that employees use available paid sick days or vacation days as part of their total available 12 weeks of FMLA leave deters employees from taking off from work for more than 12 weeks in a 12-month period, yet it provides for the full 12-week FMLA leave. (See **Chapter 14** for further discussion of the FMLA.)

No federal laws relate to sick pay, and state regulatory codes generally refer to sick pay only as a component of salary subject to withholding. However, some states do specify whether accrued or earned sick pay is due upon the employee's termination. The HR manager should refer to state regulations to ensure compliance.

Companies whose employees work under union contracts tend not to include specific provisions for employee sick pay. Most employers require that employees work for a specific period (e.g., a minimum of three months) before becoming eligible for sick pay or days off from work.

Most companies have adopted some type of plan to provide employees with income protection during periods of short-term illnesses or injuries. These sick-pay plans are designed to fill the gap in coverage for absences of generally up to one week. In addition, these plans often recognize and reward length of service by granting better benefits to employees who have been with the company the longest.

Beyond a set number of sick days, some employers provide a salary continuation program for accidents and illnesses that last longer than the number of available sick days. Under these salary continuation plans, employers continue to pay a full or partial percentage of base pay to the ill or injured employee. Generally, a physician's note is required to verify that the employee's condition warrants additional time off from work before the employee is eligible for salary continuation.

Employers who provide salary continuation often do so based on criteria such as the employee's job classification and years of service. For example, a program based on job classification might provide for the following:

- Company officers—26 weeks at full pay

- Directors—20 weeks at full pay and 6 weeks at 60 percent pay

- Managers—13 weeks at full pay and 13 weeks at 60 percent pay

- Administrative or clerical workers—13 weeks at full pay and 13 weeks at 50 percent pay

- Plant workers—6 weeks at full pay and 20 weeks at 50 percent pay

A plan based on years of service might look very similar to an employee classification program, substituting years of service (e.g., one to five years) for the employee classifications. Employee classification programs may favor highly compensated employees (HCEs) without triggering tax penalties related to discrimination.

To control costs and absences, some sick-pay plans are designed to do the following:

- Eliminate coverage for the first one to three days of absence

- Permit carryover of unused days up to a maximum number

- Pay a bonus for unused days each year

- Apply sick days on a sliding 12-month scale instead of a calendar year

To minimize the abuse of sick-pay plans, employers may require that:

- Employees personally call in their absences within 20 minutes of the time they usually start work

- Employees report absences only to their immediate supervisor

- Supervisors tactfully determine a sick employee's expected return-to-work date and point out when an employee's absence requires rescheduling work

- Supervisors or the HR department maintain formal attendance records that monitor frequency and patterns of absence

- Employees submit a signed physician's statement of ability to return to work, designed by the company, for any absence of more than three days

Sick pay is generally includible in the employee's income and is fully taxable regardless of whether the employer pays it directly or an insurance company pays it from employer-paid premiums. In most situations, the employer is responsible for income tax and payroll tax withholding on the payments.

Sick pay and salary continuation programs are generally not subject to discrimination testing under the Employee Retirement Income Security Act of 1974 (ERISA). Consequently, such programs may favor HCEs. All programs—even self-funded, pay-as-you-go programs—should be considered formal plans and should be in writing. Consistent application of a sick pay and/or salary continuation policy is a strong defense against possible lawsuits by disgruntled employees. Companies must ensure that the sick leave and/or salary continuation policies are consistent with requirements of both the Americans with Disabilities Act of 1990 (ADA) and the FMLA, as well as any specific business needs, regarding definitions of disability, vesting privileges, and coverage of group health benefits during periods when employees are not actively at work. Policies should also explore reasonable accommodations to return a qualified, disabled individual to work.

In addition to the previously mentioned issues, the following issues should be considered when a company drafts its sick-pay or salary continuation policy:

- Are there any waiting period requirements? If so, what are the requirements? Will the requirements be different for illness versus injuries? For hospitalization versus nonhospitalization?

- Are there requirements for documenting eligibility and/or need for salary continuation and sick pay?

- How many sick leave days and salary continuation days are awarded annually?

- Does the number of days depend on an employee's length of service, employment status, employee classification, or other criteria?

- Does the benefit level vary based on employee classification, years of service, or both? If so, what should the schedule of benefits look like?

- Are employees required to present a physician's statement about the need for sick leave? If so, after how many days of absence? Will a physician's statement of the employee's ability to return to work be required? How will these confidential records be handled—being mindful of varying responsibilities and prohibitions under federal laws that may apply (e.g., FMLA, ADA)?

- Can unused sick days be accumulated, and if so, for how long? Will an employee be paid for unused sick leave at the end of a year and/or upon termination of employment? If so, will the employee be paid full salary or a percentage of salary for each unused sick day?

- Will sick leave time be counted as hours worked for overtime purposes?

- Do any other benefits continue to accrue while an employee is on sick leave (e.g., vesting for pension and profit-sharing plans)? (FMLA requirements are important to remember in this situation.)

- What happens if an employee is sick before or after a vacation or holiday? Does the employee still receive holiday pay?

- Are part-time employees eligible for paid sick leave and/or salary continuation? If so, are they eligible for the full amount? Or what percentage of benefits or days are they entitled to, as compared with full-time employees?

- How do sick leave and salary continuation plans coordinate with short- or long-term disability programs provided by the company?

Because current language of the FMLA prohibits employers from considering an employee's use of FMLA leave as a negative factor in making any employment decisions (e.g., discipline), the employer must not treat any absence protected as FMLA leave as counting against any total number of absences in a ''no fault'' type of attendance policy or limitation.

Exempt employees' pay can only be docked when they are out due to illness or injury if (i) the employer provides a bona fide sick leave plan and (ii) the employees have no sick leave accrued, either because they do not yet qualify for the plan or because they have used up all benefits provided by the plan. According to the DOL, in order for a plan to be bona fide under FLSA regulations, it must be:

- Communicated to eligible employees

- Impartially administered

- Operated as described

- Not designed to evade the requirement that exempt employees be paid on a salary basis

- The type that provides a reasonable number of absences for sickness without loss in pay to exempt employees

The DOL does not provide a "safe harbor" number of absences that will meet the last requirement. In various opinion letters, it has indicated that the actual design of and practices applicable under the plan will determine whether the plan is bona fide.

Although no national mandate for paid time off for illness or injury currently exists, that could change in the future. Such changes often start at the local or state level and mandatory paid sick time off is no exception. On November 7, 2006, voters in San Francisco approved the first law in the United States to require that private employers provide their employees with paid sick leave due to the illness or injury of the employee or his or her extended family members. The "Sick Leave Ordinance" applies to all employers who have employees within the boundaries of the City and County of San Francisco, not just those employers who have contracts with the city or county. Under the Sick Leave Ordinance, employees earn one hour of paid sick leave for every 30 hours worked, up to a maximum of 72 hours. Employees in small businesses (fewer than 10 employees including full-time, part-time and temporary employees) will accrue up to a maximum of 40 hours. The law went into effect on February 5, 2007.

Several states are looking into establishing their own paid sick leave laws. California, Connecticut, Maine, Massachusetts, Michigan, Montana, Ohio, Vermont, and Wisconsin are considering the issue. Maryland passed the Flexible Leave Act into law on May 22, 2008, and it will take effect October 1, 2008. The District of Columbia passed the Accrued Sick and Safe Leave Act, which will become effective on November 13, 2008. According to a Wall Street Journal Online/Harris Interactive Healthcare Poll conducted in March 2007, 80 percent of adults are in favor of requiring employers to provide paid sick time to employees.

In February 2007, Senator Edward M. Kennedy (D-MA) and Representative Rosa L. DeLauro (D-CT) introduced the Healthy Families Act to both houses of Congress (H.R. 1542 and S. 910). This legislation would require employers with 15 or more employees to provide at least seven paid sick leave days per year. The sick days could be used for the employee's own or a family member's illness or injury. As of this writing, the bills have been heard in the Health, Education, Labor and Pension (HELP) Committees, but no further action has been taken. Other proposed legislation, the Volunteer Firefighter and EMS Personnel Job Protection Act (HR 1643), would provide up to 14 days per year of job-protected time off to emergency service personnel who respond to federal or state-declared emergencies or disasters.

§ 11.04   LEAVES OF ABSENCE

Companies grant time off with pay for a variety of personal reasons, the most common of which are personal leaves of absence, jury duty, time off to vote, death in the family, and short-term military leave. Often, unpaid leaves are limited to 30 calendar days, but may be more or less depending on the employer's business needs.

Because employers have a fair amount of discretion in granting personal leaves, they usually approve or deny requests based on the facts and circumstances of the situation. Factors to consider include the requested length of the absence, the requesting employee's position, the impact of that employee's absence, and the disruption to the business. Employers may also want to consider the requesting employee's performance record and length of employment and the reason for the request.

To ensure as much consistency as possible, it is recommended that a company put its personal leave policy in writing. The policy should include the following:

- *Eligibility requirements.* Consider service requirements (e.g., employment of at least one year) and employee classification (e.g., exempt employees only).

- *Maximum duration of leave.* Although most companies limit the duration to 30 calendar days, some allow an extension, if appropriate, for an additional 30 days. Still others allow a maximum of 15 days.

- *Effect on benefits during the leave.* Will vacation and other earned time-off benefits continue to accrue? Will medical coverage continue during the personal leave of absence? If so, will employees pay only their share of the benefit cost, or will they be responsible for the entire cost? How will this be implemented? What will happen if they do not pay (their share of) the benefit cost? Will holidays be paid during the leave? Will employees be required to use all accrued vacation, personal days, or other paid time off before unpaid leave begins?

- *Effect on seniority, performance review dates, and similar employment-related dates.* Will these dates be adjusted by the length of the personal leave? Will they be adjusted only if the leave is longer than 30 days?

- *Method of requesting leave.* Will a written request be required? If so, the request should indicate the timing of the leave (when it would begin and when the employee would return) as well as reason(s) for the leave.

- *Review and approval of the leave.* Who will have responsibility for approving or denying the request? Some companies, in order to ensure more consistent treatment, require the employee's direct supervisor to recommend approval or denial of the leave, but leave the final decision up to the HR department.

- *Reinstatement.* Will the employee's pre-leave job be available, or will a similar job be offered? Will any guarantee of job restoration be made, or will the employee be offered the next available job for which he or she is reasonably qualified?

- *Effect on other regulated leaves.* Employers need to consider how the administration of personal leaves of absence may affect other leaves. For example, the procedure and benefits for pregnancy leaves can be no less than those for any other type of leave offered by the employer. Thus, if the employer grants more benefits or better reinstatement privileges to employees on personal leaves than to those on medical leaves, the company must offer the same benefits of personal leaves to those on pregnancy leaves, even if that was not its original intent.

Although no law or regulation specifically regulates personal leaves of absence, employers must administer this benefit in a nondiscriminatory manner. Because companies have faced charges of unlawful discrimination in the denial of personal leaves, it is recommended that employers carefully consider all precedents when evaluating an employee's request for a personal leave of absence. Employers should carefully document all factors leading to a denial of that request, especially the differences in the circumstances that led to a denial of one request that appears similar to other request(s) that were not denied.

[A]   Jury Duty

Employees at all levels in the organization may be called on to fulfill this civic responsibility as often as once every year. A jury duty assignment usually lasts two weeks. A juror is paid a small per diem allowance, which the employer may deduct from the employee's usual salary. Some companies elect not to deduct the per diem amount, however, because of the resulting administrative payroll problems and the extra expenses employees often incur as a result of serving on jury duty. In many cases, companies give employees their regular paychecks, and the employees then remit the jury duty stipend checks to the employer (typically less mileage and expenses).

Jurors are often excused for a portion of a day or even a full day. Employers should provide clear instructions that employees on jury duty are expected to report to work whenever they are excused for a reasonable portion of a workday.

[B]   Time Off to Vote

Most states now require employers to give workers a maximum of two hours off to vote, and many of those states specify that such time off must also be with pay. Every company should become familiar with the appropriate laws in its state.

[C]   Death in Family

Most employers understand that an employee who sustains a death in the family needs some time off for mourning and making various arrangements. Companies typically grant three days with pay in the case of the death of an immediate family member, although they may extend the time off if major travel is required. To ensure administrative consistency, the HR department should prepare a written policy defining the composition of the immediate family and describing pay practices in the event of a death in that group or of other relatives, coworkers, and friends.

[D]   Military Leave

The Uniformed Services Employment and Reemployment Rights Act (USERRA), enacted December 12, 1994, substantially improved reemployment rights of employed veterans. USERRA prohibits employment discrimination due to an individual being "a member of, applies to be a member of, performs, has performed, applies to perform, or has an obligation to perform, service in a uniformed service."

The "uniformed services" include the Army, Navy, Marine Corps, Air Force, Coast Guard, Army National Guard, Air National Guard, the Commissioned Corps of the Public Health Service, and the reserves of the Army, Navy, Marine Corps, Air Force and Coast Guard, as well as training for or activation for intermittent disaster response to the National Disaster Medical System. Employees must be given a leave of absence with reemployment to the same or similar position for up to five years of military service.

On September 20, 2004, the DOL published the first ever set of regulations on USERRA, which were developed to explain and clarify the law's requirements. After considering 80 comments from a wide variety of interested parties, including employer organizations, employee organizations and individuals, the DOL issued final regulations to implement the law. They were published in the *Federal Register* on December 19, 2005 and became effective on January 18, 2006. Any changes made by the regulations have been incorporated into the following paragraphs, without utilizing such phrases as "the final regulations state" or "the regulations provide," etc.

Nearly all employers and employer-like organizations are covered by USERRA. If an organization pays salary or wages to an individual to perform work, or if it has control over an individual's employment opportunities, it is a covered employer under USERRA. Thus, professional employer organizations (PEOs) and "hiring halls" are covered employers. But entities that only perform administrative functions, such as maintenance of personnel files or the preparation of forms for submission to a government agency are not covered employers. A successor employer (after a merger or acquisition, for example) is a covered employer. Foreign employers with employees in the United States and American employers with employees in foreign countries are covered employers. Note that there are no size limits; an organization with only one employee is a covered employer under USERRA.

If an employee serves for 30 days or less (e.g., for summer encampment, which is required of members of the military reserve and the National Guard) or for a period of any length for the purpose of a fitness for service examination, the employee must report back to the employer for reemployment no later than the beginning of the first full regularly scheduled work period on the first full calendar day following the completion of the period of service, and expiration of eight hours after a period allowing for safe transportation from the place of that service to the employee's residence. For leaves of 31 to 180 days, an employee must submit an oral or written application for reemployment to the company within 14 days after release, and the deadline is 90 days for service of more than 180 days. If the employee is hospitalized for, or recuperating from, an illness or injury incurred in, or aggravated during the period of service, he or she must report or submit an application for reemployment to the employer at the end of the period necessary for recovering from the illness or injury. This period of hospitalization and/or recuperation extends by up to two years the time period an employee has to report back to his or her employer. In all cases, in order for an employee to retain his or her reemployment rights, he or she must give prior oral and, if requested by the company, written notice of the absence, unless precluded by military necessity. This notice must be as far in advance as is reasonable under the circumstances. The Department of Defense (DOD) recommends that advance notice be given at least 30 days prior to departure when it is feasible to do so.

Employees returning from military leave must be promptly reinstated to the position he or she held prior to the commencement of the leave. "Promptly" means within two weeks of the employee reapplying for employment. If an employee would have received any promotions during the leave period, the returning employee must be reinstated into the promoted position. If needed, an employer must provide training to the employee to enable him or her to perform that job. If an employee is disabled while on military leave, the employer must offer reasonable accommodations to allow the employee to perform the functions of the job. If the employee is not able to perform the job he or she would have had had he or she not been on a military leave (with accommodations, if appropriate), the employer must place the employee in an available position with comparable pay, benefits, duties and opportunities for advancement.

An employee will lose his or her USERRA protection if he or she is dishonorably discharged, discharged for bad conduct, discharged under other than honorable conditions, a commissioned officer who receives a court martial, is absent from service for three months or longer, or is sentenced to confinement in a federal or state correctional institution. Employers also do not need to reinstate a returning employee, if:

- Assisting the employee in becoming qualified for reemployment would impose an undue hardship on the employer;

- The employer's circumstances have changed such that it makes reemployment impossible or unreasonable (e.g., if the employee's unit was laid off during the time the employee was in military service and he or she would have been laid off had he or she not been in service, provided that the employee would not have been rehired during a subsequent period while the employee was in service); or

- The employee's employment with the employer prior to the military leave was short-term, temporary and with no reasonable expectation of continuation.

Employers must consider the "escalator" principle when reemploying and paying returning service members. This principle requires employers to determine what position and at what amount of pay an employee would have had, had he or she not taken military leave, if the employer can determine this with reasonable certainty. For example, if it is reasonably certain that an employee would have been promoted to a new position during the period of the military leave, then the employee should be placed in that new position upon return from leave. The employer should take into consideration the employee's previous job performance and work record in determining to what position the employee is reasonably likely to have been promoted and at what pay level. If a promotion would have required a skills test or other examination, the employee should be placed in an appropriate reemployment position, given time to adjust and then given an opportunity to take the missed test or exam. Pay and benefits of the promotion should be retroactively applied to the date the employee would have received the promotion to the extent that such date can be reasonably ascertained. Reasonable certainty is defined as a high probability that the employee would have received the promotion (or other seniority-based right or benefit) if there had been no military leave.

Although the law does not require employers to pay for this time off, many employers pay the difference between the employee's usual salary and the base military pay for short-term leaves of 15 days or less. If the base military pay exceeds the employee's usual salary, no adjustment is made, and the employee is simply on unpaid leave.

Employers often apply this same pay practice in cases of brief emergency duty call-ups. Because emergency call-ups can last for a number of months, however, the HR department should be sure to define time limits for salary continuation in the employer's short-term military leave policy. Employees must be allowed to use any accrued vacation or other similar paid time off, but cannot be required to do so. Employees are not allowed to use accrued sick leave or similar paid time off unless the employer allows employees to do so on other non-medical leaves of absence.

A company must offer its employees on military leave the option to continue health benefits. If such leave is for 30 consecutive days (or less), the employee may be required to pay the employee's share (if any) of the cost of the individual and family coverage. For leaves of more than 30 days, health benefits may be continued for the length of the leave or 24 months, whichever is shorter, and the employee is responsible for 102 percent of the applicable premium. The USERRA continuation coverage period begins on the date the military leave of absence begins. It ends on the day the employee reapplies for work, the day after the employee fails to apply for reemployment, or when 24 months have past, whichever is shorter. Further information on USERRA's effects on medical benefits can be found in **Chapter 5**.

Employers are given flexibility to develop notification and election procedures for employees to elect USERRA continuation coverage. They may elect to use the same procedures and time limits they use for COBRA continuation coverage (see **Chapter 7**) or develop other procedures, time limits, etc. The procedures and time limits must be reasonable however. (It should be noted that even employers who are not required to provide COBRA continuation coverage must provide USERRA continuation coverage.) If an employer does not develop USERRA continuation coverage procedures, employees on service leave have the option of electing USERRA continuation coverage anytime during the 24-month period when the continuation coverage must be offered. Such coverage must be retroactive to the date the employee first lost their health care coverage. Unlike COBRA, USERRA continuation coverage may only be elected by the employee (dependents do not have an independent right to elect USERRA continuation coverage as they do for COBRA). In addition to USERRA continuation coverage, COBRA may also apply to employees (and/or their dependents) on military leave; if so, for each right and responsibility included under both laws, those which provide the service member the greater benefit must be applied.

Other non-seniority and welfare benefits, such as life insurance, must be treated the same for employees on a military leave as for those on nonmilitary leaves. If the benefits employees receive vary based on the type of (non-military, but comparable) leave, employees on military leave must receive the benefits provided by the most favorable leave. The DOL considers vacation to be a non-seniority based benefit. If other comparable non-military (non-FMLA) leaves of absence do not provide for the accrual of vacation benefits during the leave, then the military leave policy does not need to provide for vacation accrual, either. Employees returning from military leave do not need to receive vacation accrued during the leave period, unless employees on non-military leaves receive accrued vacation. Note, however, that the escalator clause does apply. For example, an employee in his fourth year of employment is called to military service and otherwise meets all of the law's and the employer's requirements for approved military leave. After two years of service the employee returns and is reemployed by the same employer. If the employer's vacation accrual policy called for an increase in the amount of vacation when an employee has completed five years of service, the employee returning from military leave must receive the same accrual rate provided to employees who have completed five years of service. In determining what is a comparable leave, the Department of Justice and courts primarily look at other leaves of similar length. Thus, jury duty or bereavement leave are unlikely to be comparable, whereas a long-term disability leave may be.

In addition, an employee returning from military leave must be reinstated to employment without loss of his or her retirement plan benefits, including any accruals and allocations that would have been made during the leave period. If accruals or allocations depend on an employee's contributions, the employee must be allowed to make up the missed contributions. He or she must be given up to three times the length of the leave, or five years, whichever is longer, to make up the missed contributions. In addition, the employee must be employed with the employer on the date of repayment. Employees on military leave may not be charged with a break in service for purposes of plan participation, vesting, or accrual of benefits.

Employers have 90 days to make up any missed contributions. The 90-day tolling begins on the date the employee makes his repayments, if required, or on the reemployment date.

For specific periods of time, employees returning from military service may not be terminated unless it is for cause. If an employee's military leave was for less than 181 days, he or she may not be terminated for six months; if the leave was for 181 days or more, he or she may not be terminated for twelve months. Cause is defined as discharge based on conduct where the employer must prove that the discharge is reasonable for the conduct and that the employee had received notice that the conduct would result in discharge. Job elimination or layoff may also be allowed within these time limits if the employer can show that the job elimination or layoff would have occurred even if there had been no military service.

The Veterans Benefits Improvement Act (VBIA) [Pub. L. No. 108-454, 118 Stat. 3598] mandates that employers provide notice to employees of their rights and benefits under USERRA. On March 10, 2005, the Department of Labor (DOL) released a poster that can be used by employers to satisfy this requirement. Coincident with the publishing of the final USERRA regulations, the DOL published its final rule on the Notice of Rights and Duties under USERRA including a revised poster. The poster must be displayed in the place where employees typically look for such information. The poster for non-government employers can be obtained on the DOL's Web site: *www.dol.gov/vets/programs/userra/USERRA_private.pdf*.

Many states also have reinstatement requirements for employees on military leave, especially if the leave is to serve in the state's militia. States may also extend unpaid leave rights to employees whose family member has been called to service or was injured or killed while serving. HR personnel should ensure that their policies also comply with state laws.

§ 11.05   MISCELLANEOUS REQUESTS FOR TIME OFF

Miscellaneous requests for time off can cover every legitimate reason. Some of the most common reasons include:

- Medical and dental appointments

- Graduation ceremonies

- Weather emergencies

- Court appearances

- Household disasters

- Traffic accidents

- School-related meetings and events

To avoid having to decide whether a reason is legitimate, many companies establish a pool of two to five personal days for each employee. It is then up to the employee to determine whether a particular situation is serious enough to warrant the use of a personal day. There are, of course, employees who view taking the maximum number of personal days as a full entitlement. After the pool is depleted, any further absences are without pay. Administering the absence days on the basis of a 12-month period diminishes the temptation by some employees to rush and use them at the end of the calendar year.

§ 11.06 PAID REST BREAKS

As of January 1, 2007, seven states require paid rest breaks for employees: California, Colorado, Kentucky, Minnesota, Nevada, Oregon, and Washington. Illinois also requires paid rest breaks but only for hotel room attendants. Generally, these states require that employees be given one 10-minute paid rest break for every four hours worked, or a major portion thereof. Because these rest breaks are paid, they are often not recorded on the employer's time-keeping system or on written time sheets. Some employers in these states have begun requiring employees to keep written records of their rest breaks; others schedule mandatory rest breaks into employees' daily schedules. Most states require that employers provide the opportunity for employees to take their rest breaks, and employees may elect not to take the break. However, an employee may claim that he or she was not provided the opportunity to take a break. Employers in these states may want to consider adding a statement to employees' time cards or time sheets, which employees must sign, indicating that they have been provided the opportunity to take their rest breaks. This can be critical, as the penalty for missed rest breaks can be significant. In California, employers must pay one additional hour of pay when the rest break is not provided.

In states where paid rest breaks are not mandated, paid rest breaks may be subject to time limits set by the employer. The observance of those limits depends both on management monitoring and employee respect and cooperation. Employees do not recognize that the costs of extended coffee and rest breaks are meaningful. However, these costs can be significant in terms of uncompleted work or extra staff required to absorb lost productivity. The best way to prevent the abuse of break time is through firm and tactful management.

§ 11.07 TRENDS AND PRACTICES

Paid time off (as well as unpaid time off) from work has become a critical element of employers' total compensation packages. Employees in today's labor market are aware of their responsibilities in both work and personal/family arenas, and they seek employers whose total compensation practices offer flexibility and choices (to support both of these personal priorities).

[A] Paid Time Off Programs

A Paid Time Off (PTO) Program bank is a tool used by employers to accommodate both employee and company objectives. PTO Programs provide employees with a "bank" of hours to use as they please instead of separate accounts for sick days, vacation days, and personal time. In 2006, the Alexander Hamilton Institute reported on its survey of 800 employers in "AHI's 2006 Survey of Traditional Time Off and PTO Program Practices." Forty-six percent of the respondents offered a PTO program.

PTO Programs have been implemented in a variety of organizations, generally to control unscheduled employee absences and the workplace/productivity problems that absences create. Over half of the respondents with PTO programs in the AHI survey (56.1 percent) reported that their PTO program has reduced unscheduled absences. Related objectives often include:

- Promoting individual employee responsibility to plan ahead for possible year-end situations and to schedule absences necessary to address work and life balance issues

- Reducing administrative complexity (e.g., in tracking maximum allowances and categories of employee time off from work)

- Reducing supervisor/manager discomfort regarding any need to know why an employee is absent, to record time in an appropriate category

- Increasing consistency in handling employee absences so that decisions (regarding staffing, discipline, overtime) may be made on the basis of business need, without consideration of who is absent or why

In the AHI survey, 78.6 percent of employers with PTO programs reported that their expectations for the PTO program were met, and 9.5 percent indicated that their expectations were exceeded.

Because individual employees must take responsibility for managing their absences from work in a PTO environment, employers should be aware that current abusers may resist a PTO bank, as abuses will quickly create problems for these individuals.

As a basis for making important decisions regarding implementing a PTO Program, the employer should analyze certain historical and current data, such as:

- Absence rate among the employee group or groups (e.g., nonexempt and exempt)

- Planned absence rate (for vacations or holidays)

- Unscheduled absence rate

Average age of the employee group or groups and percentages of males and females in the workplace may also be useful data, particularly if that information is related to absence rates.

The *2007 CCH Unscheduled Absence Survey* (CCH, Inc.) reported that the rate of unscheduled absentee-ism was 2.3 percent, down from 2.5 percent in 2006, which was the highest rate since 1999, when it was 2.7 percent. (The rate of unscheduled absenteeism is calculated by dividing the total paid unscheduled hours of absence by the total paid productive hours.) While this percentage can be useful as a benchmark, each company should establish its own benchmark and measure actual results against that benchmark over time. It is particularly important to measure and monitor unscheduled absences, because staffing and work needs cannot be planned in advance for these absences; they create costs of pay for nonproductive time, as well as for temporary help, training, overtime, and so forth.

The *2007 CCH Unscheduled Absence Survey* found that the primary reasons provided for unscheduled time off from work were:

- Personal illness

- Family issues

- Personal reasons

- Entitlement mentality

- Stress

Additional PTO planning decisions relate to the types of absences to be included in the program. Federal and state laws may affect these decisions. Consideration should be given to:

- State holidays

- State pregnancy/maternity and/or disability leave requirements

- State requirements regarding payment of vacation (or other accrued time-off-from-work benefits) as compensation

Once the data are analyzed to provide useful management information, several specific PTO Program design decisions must be made, including:

- What categories of absences will be rolled into the PTO Program? Will the PTO Program replace all forms of absence pay, or will more traditional leave policies remain in place for unanticipated absences such as bereavement leave or jury duty?

- How will the initial balance of PTO time be determined for each employee?

- How will "excess" balances be handled (e.g., during the first 12 to 18 months of the PTO Program)?

- What will be the minimum increment of PTO time permitted to be scheduled?

- What will be the maximum amount of time that can be accumulated in a PTO Program?

- Will any unused PTO time be carried over at year-end?

- At what rate will employees earn/accrue PTO, and will that rate change over time (based on years of service or job level)?

- Will employees, under any circumstances, be permitted to take PTO before it is earned/accrued?

- How much advance notice will employees be required to give to permit the supervisor to evaluate staffing and other needs before approving (or refusing) requests for PTO?

- Will employees who do not use all available PTO be eligible for payout of some portion of PTO at year-end (assuming carryover is not permitted)? Will payout be based upon employees' current base rate of pay, rate at the beginning of the year, or base plus routine enhancements (such as shift differentials)?

- If an employee leaves the organization, will PTO time be paid to the terminating employee (including consideration of state requirements)?

- Who will be responsible for monitoring of the program, coordinating it with payroll, etc.? Will the program be reviewed periodically? If so, by whom, and how often?

- Will some portion of unused PTO be rolled into a catastrophic time-off bank at year-end? If such a bank is created, what maximum will be permitted, and what other conditions or limits will apply to the use of that time? Will employees be permitted to share cat time with other employees, and, if so, according to what procedures? (Catastrophic banks and sharing of time are addressed in **Section 11.07 [C]**.)

A company must exercise caution if a PTO Program includes allowing partial days of absence or if negative PTO Program balances are prohibited regarding application of these limitations to exempt employees (see **Section 11.03**). Language of the policy and its consistent application must not provide that exempt employees may be (or will be) subject to reduction of salary for partial-day absences, except for partial-day absences approved under the FMLA.

[B] Sabbaticals

In the last 20 years, sabbaticals have gained attention particularly in firms where competition for talented employees has been especially tight.

The Society for Human Resources Management (SHRM) 2008 Benefits Survey indicated that 13 percent of all respondents provided unpaid sabbatical programs (a significant decrease from 22 percent in 2006), and 22 percent of government employers, and 19 percent of not-for-profit service employers offered such programs. Five (5) percent of all employers offered paid sabbatical programs.

Generally, sabbatical programs are designed to allow workers with a minimum number of years of service (often at least seven) time off for community service (e.g., holding public office), teaching, traveling, or pursuing other long-term interests. Typically, benefits and status related to employment are "suspended" during a sabbatical, and employees return to work in the "same position" as prior to the leave.

When a company institutes a sabbatical program, several issues must be considered, including the following:

- What will the maximum leave period be? Will leave be renewable and, if so, under what terms?

- Which employees will be eligible—all employees with a minimum number of years of service or only those employees in certain classifications or jobs, with certain years of service?

- How will sabbaticals be requested and approved?

- Will sabbaticals be paid or unpaid? (Most companies offer only unpaid sabbaticals, but may allow employees to use all accrued vacation days, sick time, and paid time off.)

- How will benefits be handled during a sabbatical? (Note: Some benefits issues will need to be addressed in contract language or in plan documents.)

- What administrative process will be required (e.g., projecting and monitoring costs; preventing "discrimination" issues in selection/award of the benefit; separating company from employee interests during the leave)?

[C] Leave Sharing

Another recent trend in addressing the variety of employee work/life issues that arise is that of permitting employees to share their paid leave time. These programs are designed to permit employees with large accruals of time to transfer portions of their own leave time to other employees who are experiencing medical or family crises. The SHRM 2008 Benefits Survey found that 21 percent of the respondents had a vacation leave sharing program (up from 18 percent in 2005) and 13 percent offered a sick leave sharing program (down from 14 percent in 2005).

Programs can be designed to permit direct transfer of time from one employee to another or to permit employees to direct portions of their own time into a catastrophic leave bank, from which employees in need may request time through an administrative process. In a leave banking program, employees are typically eligible to request time from the bank only if they have, in fact, contributed time to the bank.

Historically, government, not-for-profit and university employers have been most likely to offer leave sharing. However, private employers are looking at creative solutions for addressing employee relations and retention concerns, and leave sharing is a program worth considering. Employers who cannot afford to offer short-term disability to their employees could establish a leave sharing program to help employees during crises, without the company's incurring the expense of providing salary continuation program for short-term disabilities. Companies with a leave sharing program in place generally report that employee morale increases whenever it is used, and describe it as a win-win situation.

Issues to consider when developing this type of program include:

- What types of paid time off may be donated? Some companies allow the donation of only sick time into a leave sharing program; others allow donations of vacation time only; still others allow both. It is important to consider how paid time off hours are viewed under state law (e.g., some states require payment for all accrued vacation, but not sick time, at employment termination).

- Will the program be administered on a voluntary basis only? Generally, a leave sharing program should be designed as a voluntary program, and solicitation of employees by their fellow employees to donate leave time should not be permitted. Passing around a sign-up sheet to enlist employees to donate time to the bank could be construed as a concerted activity by employees and become a mandatory issue for bargaining. Some organizations do not promote leave sharing programs, or include them in employee handbooks, to avoid the appearance of solicitation.

- What will be the eligibility criteria? Some companies allow employees to receive donated time only for their own emergencies. Other programs are designed to provide assistance to employee's family members when there is a crisis. Yet other programs have no restrictions. When designing a program, consider the company's sick leave and disability policies, as well as the general culture of the organization.

- What will be the value of the time be when it is donated? Transferring paid time off hours from one employee to another can become an administrative burden. Companies can face situations in which lower-paid employees want to donate time that will be used by higher-paid employees, or vice versa. Before that happens, an organization must decide whether it will implement the program on an hour-for-hour basis or on a wage basis. If the program is administered on a wage basis, an employee who donates 10 hours of time off at $10 an hour will have donated $100. An employee who earns $20 an hour can withdraw five hours (equal to $100) from the bank because of the difference in wages. A program designed on an hour-for-hour basis would state time off donated and transferred in the bank in hours only. A dollar value would not be attached to hours until they are used by the employee.

- Can employees convert the time to a cash benefit? A program that is designed with an option permitting employees to draw hours from the bank and convert them into cash, rather than taking the time off, may result in "constructive receipt" of the value of the time, which an employee could have elected to receive in cash. Constructive receipt may result when employees have the option to select between receiving a taxable benefit (generally cash) now and deferring receipt of that taxable benefit to another tax year.

If a program is designed to allow employees to draw hours from the bank to be converted into cash, the program may have to treat hours converted into cash differently from hours used as time off to avoid constructive receipt. Some organizations place a lower value on hours converted into cash than on hours taken as time off (e.g., they treat cashed out hours at 75 percent of their value) to avoid constructive receipt. Employers should consult an attorney to ensure that their leave sharing program avoids constructive receipt of taxable benefits by employees drawing on the bank.

Administrative issues to consider include:

- Who will authorize the use of donated time?

- What procedures will employees use to request hours from the bank?

- Will there be a cap on the amount of time an employee may donate and receive?

When designing a program, an organization should consider how the use of paid time off is treated under its FMLA policy. Are employees required to use available paid time off before using unpaid leave during approved leaves under the FMLA? If so, does the company want to allow an employee to receive more leave time under the leave sharing program than the organization allows under the FMLA?

There are also accounting considerations when designing a leave sharing policy. Organizations must determine what the process will be for reporting donated and transferred income. Most companies have a process in which the person donating the time simply does not earn the money the time represents, and the person receiving it does. Wages and taxes would appear on the employees' W-2 forms to reflect the transfer of those earnings. However, employers should also consult IRS regulations relating to the taxation of donated leave. Generally, paid leave donated under a leave sharing program is included in the donor employee's gross income and treated as his or her wages for employment tax purposes. Two exceptions apply: if the leave sharing program is for medical emergencies (see IRS Revenue Ruling 90-29) or if it is for major disasters (see IRS Notice 2006-59). If a pool of time accumulates, a company may put it on its ledger as a liability.

A company should consult an attorney when designing a leave sharing program to ensure that it is in compliance with federal and state requirements.

§ 11.08   TIME-OFF-FROM-WORK POLICY FOR EMPLOYEES

A company's HR manager should formulate policies and introduce them to the company's employees. Formal policy development allows the company to showcase its time-off-from-work benefits, to ensure compliance with the law, to keep employees informed of the company's expectations, and to provide invaluable support in defending termination and discipline decisions.

Because paid time-off benefits are included in base pay, employees tend to take them for granted. The employer, however, must view the employee's paid absence as an expense and a loss of productivity. Although not a direct out-of-pocket cost, paid absences may very well cause extra expense in the form of replacement workers, additional staff, or overtime payments. To have a better idea of the cost implications of paid time off, consider an employee who has a total of 34 paid days off per year (25 vacation days plus nine floating and observed holidays). Dividing 34 by 260 possible workdays reveals that 13 percent of this employee's work time consists of time off with pay for only vacation and holidays.

A logical vehicle for communicating the company's policies is an employee handbook. The handbook should avoid careless or ambiguous language that carves away the company's rights by possibly granting unintended contractual benefits. This is an important precaution, because the employee handbook's usefulness can be undermined by mistakes in drafting or implementation. The HR manager should insist on uniform application of policies to promote nondiscriminatory treatment of employees. (See **Exhibit 11.1** for sample leave of absence policies from an employee handbook.)

Time off from work is a constantly changing area, so the HR manager should consult experts. The benefits provided by a review from the company's legal counsel far outweigh the costs.

Exhibit 11.1   Mandated Benefits: 2009 Compliance Guide

Exhibit 11.1
Sample Leave of Absence Policies

Sample Military Leave and Annual Training Policy

If an employee enters active military service, his or her leave will extend for the period the law provides.

Members of the National Guard or any Armed Forces Reserve component may use leave for annually scheduled training duty for the length of time the law provides. If an employee is eligible, he or she may elect to be paid for this time by using his or her vacation benefit.

Sample Jury or Witness Duty Policy

If an employee is notified to serve on jury or witness duty, that employee shall be granted leave of absence upon presentation of subpoena from the court. For hourly or salaried nonexempt employees, jury duty shall be unpaid. For salaried exempt employees, jury duty shall be unpaid only for complete weeks of absence.

Sample Returning from (Non-FMLA) Leave of Absence Policy

When an employee is placed on a leave of absence, every effort will be made to hold his or her position open for the period of the approved leave. However, due to business needs, it is not possible to guarantee reinstatement, except where required by law. Every effort will be made to place the employee in a comparable position for which he or she is qualified. If one is available and the employee does not accept the position offered, he or she will be considered to have voluntarily terminated employment, effective the day such refusal is made. If no comparable position becomes available within 30 calendar days after the employee is ready to return, it will be treated as an involuntary termination.

A doctor's release may be required for the employee to return to work if the employee is absent for medical reasons for five consecutive days or more. The employee should give the note to his or her supervisor immediately upon returning to work.

Acceptance of outside employment while on leave of absence without prior approval will be considered a voluntary termination. Falsification of the reasons for going on leave will result in the employee's termination.

Sample Request for Additional Leave Policy

If the employee is unable to return from a leave of absence within the time required, the employee must contact his or her supervisor at least five days before the return date to determine if the policy permits granting the employee additional leave. Failure to contact the company before the end of the employee's scheduled leave may result in termination. This will be considered a voluntary resignation.

Chapter 12
Managing the Benefits Package

§ 12.01 AUDIT QUESTIONS

1. Are employees given access to the full contribution to their medical spending accounts at the beginning of the plan year, regardless of whether the contribution has actually been taken from their pay?

2. Does the cafeteria plan or medical spending account allow for midyear election changes that are consistent with Internal Revenue Service regulations?

3. Has the self-funded employee group health plan been assessed to ensure that the plan does not discriminate in favor of highly compensated employees?

4. Does the cafeteria plan have a written plan document that complies with Section 125's requirements?

5. If the employer contributes to employees' health savings accounts, does it do so on a comparable basis, either by dollars or as a percentage of the health plan's deductible?

6. If retiree health benefits are offered as part of the benefit package, is there compliance with all appropriate financial accounting standards?

Note: Consistent "yes" answers to the above questions suggest that the organization is applying effective management practices and/or complying with federal regulations. "No" answers indicate that problem areas exist and should be addressed immediately.

This chapter reviews the key aspects of managing a benefits package. Specifically, it reviews compliance issues relating to employee contribution plans (i.e., cafeteria benefits programs), managing the health care benefits plan, and evaluating and communicating the entire benefits package. This chapter also discusses the provision of benefits for domestic partners and retirees.

Employers not only have the responsibility for keeping abreast of ever-changing regulations, but also are charged with maximizing benefits dollars to support organizational goals and employee interests. To help employers with this balancing act, this chapter covers the following topics:

- Section 125 of the Internal Revenue Code (Code) and administrative plan design options

- Managing group health plans (planning, funding, administration, and design) within the guidelines of federal and state regulations

- Clarifying plan objectives, available options, costs, employee relations, and long-term business implications

- Promoting the value and parameters of the benefits program

§ 12.02   EMPLOYEE CONTRIBUTION PLANS: CAFETERIA BENEFITS PROGRAMS

Cafeteria plans, also known as flexible benefits plans or Section 125 plans, evolved as employers recognized that different employees value different benefits. For example, a single employee may be less interested in life insurance than a married employee with young children. On the other hand, employees over 40 may be very interested in maximizing their contributions to a 401(k) plan.

The Internal Revenue Service (IRS) first began issuing guidance on Section 125 plans in 1984. Many of those regulations were only "proposed" and never became final. On August 1, 2007, the IRS removed temporary regulations issued in 1986, and on August 6, 2007, issued new proposed regulations. Generally, the new proposed regulations consolidate and clarify the guidance provided in earlier regulations, but significant new and expanded guidance is also proposed. In the sections that follow, we will highlight where these new proposed regulations change or significantly update the information. As of this writing, no final regulations have been published. However, plan sponsors may still rely on the proposed regulations, which originally planned to be effective for plan years that begin on or after January 1, 2009.

[A]   Premium-Only Plans

A cafeteria plan can be either simple or sophisticated, depending on the size and needs of the employer. The most basic type of cafeteria plan is sometimes referred to as a premium-only plan (POP). A POP allows an employee to pay his or her share of the group health plan's premiums on a pretax basis. Because these contributions are not subject to certain payroll taxes, both the employee and the employer benefit from tax savings. In many cases, savings to the employer outweigh the costs of implementing and administering the plan. Accordingly, unless the company pays 100 percent of all medical plan premiums, a POP should be considered.

A POP, as with any plan under Code Section 125, must be created as a formal benefits plan and requires a written plan document. Employees elect to participate in the plan by indicating in writing that they have chosen to participate in the underlying plan(s) and to have their pay reduced, before taxes, for the necessary amounts. The following example demonstrates the effect of pretax and after-tax premium payments and the cost of each plan to employees and employers.

> **Example.** Jane receives a salary of $1,000 per pay period and pays $100 per period for her share of group health plan premiums. If Jane's premium payments are deducted from after-tax dollars and her tax rate is 35 percent, she will have $550 of her salary left to spend each pay period ($1,000 salary − $350 taxes − $100 premium = $550). If Jane's employer sponsors a POP cafeteria plan, the same $100 Jane pays for group health plan premiums may be paid with pretax dollars. Thus, the 35 percent that goes toward taxes is applied to only $900 of salary, resulting in paid taxes of $315. Jane now has $585 of her salary to spend each pay period ($1,000 salary − $100 premium − $315 taxes = $585), gaining a take-home income benefit of $35 per pay period.

	Premiums Paid After Tax	Premiums Paid Before Tax
Jane's salary	$1,000	$1,000
Pretax premium	—	100
Taxable amount	1,000	900
Taxes @ 35%	350	315
After-tax premium	100	—
Jane's net take-home pay	550	585

Some employees resist participation in a POP because they see it as a potential reduction in their Social Security benefits when they reach retirement age. True, employees' income taxes are reduced during the time they participate in the POP, and thus their Social Security taxes and benefits are calculated on a reduced income level. However, most employees do not see this as a detriment, preferring the ongoing benefit of reduced income taxes, which need not be repaid to the government at any time in the future.

A POP can be created to allow employees to pay their share of group health plan premiums, as well as their share of other specified welfare benefit costs that the employer sponsors and to which they contribute.

One benefit frequently omitted from a POP arrangement (and other cafeteria plans) is disability insurance. If employees are not taxed on the premium cost of a disability benefit, as in a POP, the full amount of that benefit becomes taxable to the employee, should the employee receive benefits under the plan. Unless this potential tax issue is understood by employees, offering disability plans under a POP arrangement can lead to negative employee relations, because employees might receive less take-home income than expected while receiving benefits under the disability plan.

The 2007 proposed regulations allow for pretax premium payment of employees' individual accident and health insurance premiums and COBRA premiums. Thus, POP plans can reimburse employees for their payment of such premiums with appropriate documentation. The 2007 proposed regulations do not discuss whether the reimbursement of premiums for spouse's or dependents' policies is allowed.

Section 125 plans are generally prohibited from utilizing deductions from one tax year to pay for expenses in a future tax year. Under this current rule, deductions from employees' December paychecks cannot pay for January premiums. The 2007 proposed regulations will allow December deductions for January premiums.

Section 125 pre-tax benefits may only be provided for the employee and his/her dependents who meet the IRS definition of dependent (IRC Section 152). These generally include the employee's spouse and children, but there has been some confusion about the status of children of divorced and separated parents. On August 18, 2008, the IRS issued Revenue Procedure 2008-48 which applies to parents who are (i) divorced; (ii) legally separated under a decree of divorce or separate maintenance, or a written separation agreement; or (iii) have been living apart for the last six months of the calendar year. Under this ruling, both parents may claim the child as a tax dependent for employee benefit plan purposes, if the child: (i) receives over one-half of his or her support from the parents during the calendar year; (ii) is in the custody of one or both parents for more than half the calendar year; and (iii) is a qualifying child or qualifying relative of one of the child's parents.

[B] Flexible Spending Accounts

To mitigate the rising cost of health care, many employers have established plans that allow employees to pay their share of the group health plan deductible, out-of-pocket expenses, and other noncovered expenses (e.g., certain prescriptions, eye examinations) on a pretax basis. These plans and similar plans established to accommodate dependent care expenses are known as flexible spending accounts (FSAs). They are frequently incorporated into a benefits package.

FSAs provide tax savings benefits for both employers and employees. Employees save because they are receiving reimbursement of eligible expenses with pretax dollars, which reduces their taxable income. Employers save because their share of FICA (Social Security) taxes is reduced on amounts employees set aside in FSAs. The following example demonstrates the value of an FSA.

> **Example.** Sally and John are married and have a combined earned income of $40,000, itemized deductions of $8,000, two small children in day care at a cost of $5,000 per year, and uninsured medical expenses of $1,500 (the maximum out-of-pocket level in John's group health plan). Neither Sally nor John has an FSA. They pay state and federal income and FICA taxes totaling approximately $6,500. If either Sally's employer or John's employer offers health and dependent care FSAs, Sally and John and the employer offering the FSA plan would significantly reduce their tax bills, as follows:

FSA Contributions	
Dependent care contributions	$5,000
Health care contributions	+1,500
Total FSA contributions	$6,500
Employee Tax Savings	
Federal income tax savings in 15% marginal tax bracket	$ 975
State income tax savings in 5% marginal tax bracket	+ 325
FICA tax savings @ 7.65%	+ 497
Total employee tax savings	$1,797
Employer Tax Savings	
FICA tax savings @ 7.65%	$ 497
Combined (Employee and Employer) FSA Tax Savings	$2,294

Only medical care expenses under Internal Revenue Code (IRC) Section 213 may be reimbursed by a health FSA. Medical care expenses include "amounts paid for the diagnosis, cure, mitigation, treatment or prevention of disease, or for the purpose of affecting any structure or function of the body." Occasionally, tuition at special schools may be considered a medical care expense. In Private Letter Ruling 200729019 (April 10, 2007), the IRS ruled that the tuition for a program that was designed primarily to enable the employee's daughter to compensate for and overcome her diagnosed medical conditions was a medical care expense under IRC Section 213. In Revenue Ruling 2007-72, the IRS indicated that an annual physical exam, a full-body electronic scan and a pregnancy test are all medical care expenses under Section 213 as they are all medically diagnostic. The cost of weight-loss programs may be reimbursable for employees who are diagnosed with weight-related medical conditions (for example, obesity, heart disease, and high blood pressure).

In September 2003, the IRS issued Revenue Ruling 2003-102 [2003-38 I.R.B. 559], allowing over the counter (OTC) non-prescription drugs and medical treatments to be paid for with pre-tax dollars through health care FSAs. The guidance specifically lists allergy medicine, antacid, pain reliever and cold medicine as examples of OTC drugs that could be reimbursed by the health FSA. Generally reimbursements for OTC items such as dietary supplements that are "merely beneficial to the general health of an individual" cannot be reimbursed by the FSA. Dietary supplements recommended by a medical provider to treat a medical condition may be medical care under Section 213. Proper substantiation including written recommendation or prescription from a medical provider would be required for reimbursement.

Code Section 213 does not include "cosmetic surgery or other similar procedures, unless the surgery or procedure is necessary to ameliorate a deformity arising from, or directly related to, a congenital abnormality, a personal injury resulting from an accident or trauma, or disfiguring disease." Cosmetic surgery is defined as a procedure "directed at improving the patient's appearance and does not meaningfully promote the proper function of the body or prevent or treat illness or disease." Generally facelifts would be a cosmetic surgery and not eligible for reimbursement from the FSA, but orthodontia and eye surgery to correct vision problems, even though they may effect appearance, are designed to promote the proper function of the body and would be eligible for FSA reimbursement.

[1] Maximum Contributions and Uniform Coverage

A critical consideration in establishing an FSA in a company is determining the maximum dollar amount employees may contribute to their individual accounts. In conjunction with this determination, plan administrators must consider risks to the employer and employees.

From the employer's standpoint, one of the risks to be considered and planned for is that a medical reimbursement account must exhibit the risk-shifting and risk characteristics of insurance. Within an FSA, to some degree, the employer acts as an insurance company, accepting some potential risk. For example, if an employee elects at the beginning of the plan year to contribute $2,000 to his or her medical FSA, he or she is entitled to use the $2,000 in benefits as soon as that plan year begins, regardless of whether the contribution has been taken from his or her pay. Therefore, the employer assumes some financial risk. This is known as the uniform coverage rule.

The worst-case scenario is that the employee incurs, and is reimbursed for, FSA-eligible medical charges early in the plan year and then leaves the company. In this case, the employer must reimburse the employee up to the full amount of his or her elected annual FSA contribution for all FSA-eligible expenses incurred before the employee's termination date. The employer is prohibited from requiring that terminated employee to repay the company for "excess" reimbursements made on his or her behalf.

[2] Use It or Lose It

Employees are also at risk under FSA arrangements. If the same employee incurs only $1,500 in eligible expenses during the plan year, the remaining $500 of his or her $2,000 annual contribution is forfeited under the "use it or lose it" provision. The employer will retain any forfeited benefits and may use them to pay plan expenses.

In May 2005, the IRS and the Treasury Department issued Notice 2005-42 [2005-23 I.R.B. 1204], which allows employees to use their FSA contributions for an additional two and one-half months beyond the end of the plan year. If an employer wishes to make this "grace period" available to its employees, it will need to modify the plan document. Notice 2005-42 contains the following regarding the grace period:

- The grace period must apply to all participants in the cafeteria plan.

- The grace period must not extend beyond the fifteenth day of the third calendar month after the end of the immediately preceding plan year (i.e., the 2-month rule); however, it can be shorter than 2 months.

- Participants can incur expenses during the grace period and receive reimbursement from the contributions made during the plan year that precedes the grace period; the expenses incurred in the grace period are treated "as if the expenses had been incurred in the immediately preceding plan year."

- During the grace period, a cafeteria plan may not permit unused benefits or contributions to be cashed-out or converted to any other taxable or nontaxable benefit.

- Unused amounts in a medical FSA cannot be used to pay dependent care expenses, and unused amounts in a dependent care FSA cannot be used to pay medical expenses.

- Plans may still have a run out period after the end of the grace period, allowing participants time to submit claims which were incurred during the plan year and the grace period.

- At the end of the grace period, all unused funds are forfeited under the use it or lose it rule.

Plans that wish to provide the grace period for the current plan year can do so by amending the plan document before the end of the current plan year. The grace period does not extend the plan year (e.g., a plan year of January 1, 2009 through December 31, 2009, is not changed to a plan year of January 1, 2009 through March 15, 2010 by the addition of a grace period).

A summary of an example provided in Notice 2005-42 is as follows:

> Employer X amends its health FSA plan to adopt a 2-month grace period. Employee A elects a $1,000 contribution for the 2005 plan year (January 1 through December 31, 2005) and then elects a $1,500 contribution for the 2006 plan year.

> As of December 31, 2005, A has $200 remaining unused in his health FSA. In February, he incurs $300 of qualified unreimbursed medical expenses. The unused $200 from the plan year ending December 31, 2005 is applied to reimburse $200 of A's $300 medical expenses incurred during the grace period. Therefore, there are no unused funds remaining in the health FSA for the plan year ending December 31, 2005. The remaining $100 of medical expenses incurred in February 2006 is paid or reimbursed from A's health FSA for the plan year ending December 31, 2006, which will result in a balance of $1,400 for that plan year.

Effects on COBRA and HIPAA are not addressed in Notice 2005-42. However, IRS Notice 2005-86 does provide some clarification on the effects of the grace period on COBRA continuation coverage. This notice provides that any grace period that applies to a health FSA would also apply to participants who are receiving COBRA continuation coverage for their health FSA at the end of the year. The notice also clarifies that the grace period remains in effect for employees who terminate during the grace period. Thus, employees who terminate employment during a health FSA grace period do not need to be offered COBRA continuation coverage for the grace period. However, depending on the participant's health FSA status for the plan year in effect when the employee terminates, COBRA coverage may need to be offered for the current plan year (see **Chapter 7** for further information on COBRA and health FSAs). The notice does not address the effect on or to grace periods for COBRA qualifying events other than termination of employment. The Treasury and IRS noted that further guidance would be provided in the future.

The Heroes Earnings Assistance and Relief Tax Act of 2008 (HEART Act) provides an exception to the use-it-or-lose-it rule: health FSAs (but not dependent care FSAs) may distribute all or a portion of the account balance to employees who are called to active military duty for at least 180 days or for an indefinite period. The distribution must be made between the date the employee was called to active duty and the last day of the FSA coverage period that includes the date of the call to active duty. The FSA coverage period is the FSA plan year plus the grace period, if any. This exception became effective on June 17, 2008, the date the HEART Act was enacted.

Under earlier regulations, amounts that are forfeited were considered to be plan assets that must be used exclusively to benefit plan participants or to pay reasonable plan administrative expenses. However, the 2007 proposed regulations specifically indicate that the employer sponsoring the cafeteria plan may retain such forfeitures. The plan document must state exactly how forfeitures will be applied and the plan must comply with these requirements. Many plans use forfeitures to offset plan losses. Plan losses occur when the plan reimburses a participant's expenses prior to the participant's contributions being equal to the amount of the expense, and the participant leaves the plan sponsor's employment. If the forfeitures are greater than the plan losses, the excess amounts can be used to pay plan administrative expenses (such as fees for outside administration). Alternatively, the forfeitures may be allocated among the participants on a reasonable and uniform basis. The allocation must not be based on employees' claims.

[C]   Additional Cafeteria Plan Choices

Employees have different benefit needs and different family situations. As a consequence, the idea that one plan fits all employees no longer seems to make financial or employee-relations sense. Cafeteria plans can be designed to let employees choose different benefits, over time, as their life situations change.

> **Example.** Linda, age 20, has worked for Hi-Tech Company for over three years. Linda does not perceive value in Hi-Tech's generous, low-deductible health plan or in its long-term savings or pension plan. Instead, she opts for a high-deductible (catastrophic) health plan and more vacation time during the year. Subsequently, Linda marries Bob, and they have two children, Ginny and Gus. Linda still works for Hi-Tech. Now she finds the company's low-deductible health plan an attractive and valuable benefit, even if it means giving up those extra vacation days. As time goes by, however, Linda may see even greater value in contributing the maximum allowable amount to a long-term savings or pension plan. Then, the catastrophic health plan may become more attractive again.

A cafeteria plan allows employees to allocate benefit dollars among a menu of benefits choices; this is commonly referred to as flex-credits. The benefit to the employer includes positive employee relations and an expectation of increased productivity, as employees see that flexible benefits meet their needs. Flex-credits are not included in non-exempt employees' regular rate of pay for purposes of determining overtime pay.

Cafeteria plans provide employees with choices between taxable and qualified non-taxable benefits. Taxable benefits include cash, payment for paid time off (e.g., vacation, sick leave, PTO), severance pay, property and certain other after-tax contributions. Qualified non-taxable benefits include medical coverage, dental coverage, group-term life insurance, accidental death and dismemberment insurance, health and dependent FSAs, adoption assistance, 401(k) plan contributions, health savings account contributions (see **Section 12.04[D][2]**), and disability coverage. Benefits that cannot be offered through a Section 125 cafeteria plan include scholarships, employer-provided meals and lodging, employer-provided educational assistance, long-term care insurance and long-term care services. These benefits cannot be provided through the cafeteria plan, even if they are provided on an after tax basis. However, the 2007 regulations do allow for the after-tax reimbursement of non-spouse and non-dependent health coverage. So, for example, an employee could elect to pay for a former spouse or a domestic partner's health care coverage through the cafeteria plan on an after-tax basis.

[D]   Midyear Election Changes

Generally employees elect health and related benefit plan options once a year, during the period known as open enrollment. These elections include the plan or plans under which the employee wishes to be covered and who is covered (the employee only; the employee and his or her spouse; the employee and his or her dependents; or the employee, the employee's spouse, and their dependents). Often insurance carriers do not allow employees to make changes more often than once per year. In addition, the HR or benefits department does not want to deal with all the paperwork associated with employee changes to benefits.

Because a cafeteria plan reduces taxable income, the Internal Revenue Service (IRS) originally did not allow changes to benefit elections at any time other than at the open enrollment period. Since 1989, however, the IRS has promulgated regulations that allow midyear election changes. The IRS issued regulations in January 2001 that were effective for all plans for plan years beginning on or after January 1, 2002.

The new IRS regulations allow midyear election changes to cafeteria plans when a change in a participant's status occurs, and the change in election *is consistent with the change in status*. A consistent election change is one that is "on account of and corresponds to" the change in status, such as the following:

- Change in marital status—marriage, death of spouse, divorce, legal separation, or annulment. If the change in status were the employee's divorce from his or her spouse, the election to remove the spouse from coverage under the cafeteria plan is consistent with the change in status.

   — The plan may also allow for a mid-year change to add a child in accordance with a Qualified Medical Child Support Order (QMCSO – see **Section 5.07A**) and to pay for the coverage with salary reductions if the child qualifies as a tax dependent.

- Change in number of dependents—birth, death, or adoption of a child, or placement of a child for adoption. If the employee and his or her spouse adopt a child, providing coverage for the child would be consistent with the change in status.

- Change in employment status—commencement or termination of employment, strike or lockout, commencement or return from an unpaid leave of absence, change in worksite, or any of these events that may apply to the employee, the employee's spouse, or the employee's dependent(s). If the change in status is the change in the spouse's employment, a consistent election change would be either to remove the spouse from coverage under the employee's plan or to drop coverage altogether on account of the employee's coverage under the spouse's plan, if it provides better coverage or provides similar coverage at lower cost. (Note: IRS regulations specify that an employee must actually obtain coverage under the spouse's or dependent's plan for the election change to be consistent. The employee's certification that he or she either has or will obtain the coverage is sufficient proof for the employer.)

  — The 2007 proposed regulations specifically allow cafeteria plans to reimburse COBRA premiums for a medical plan sponsored by the same employer that sponsors the cafeteria plan. So, for example, if an employee changes from full-time to part-time and loses coverage under the employer's health plan, a COBRA-qualifying event, and is still eligible to participate in the cafeteria plan, the employee can pay the COBRA premiums through the cafeteria plan.

- Dependent's fulfillment or nonfulfillment of eligibility requirements—dependent reaches age at which he or she is no longer eligible for coverage under the plan or loses his or her student status. If an employee's child reaches the age at which he or she can no longer be covered under the employer's health plan, the removal of the child from coverage would be consistent with this change in status.

- Change of residence—change in the place of residence of the employee or the employee's spouse or dependent. If, for example, an employee and/or the employee's family moves to another town, changing their coverage to a plan that provides coverage in the new location would be consistent with the change of status.

- Significant cost increase or coverage reduction—a significant cost increase (e.g., the salary reduction amount used to pay for the employee's share of the coverage is significantly increased) or reduction in coverage. For this reason, however, only the election for plan coverage may be changed at midyear; medical flexible spending accounts (FSAs) may not be changed at midyear on account of changes in cost or coverage.

  — A substantial loss of providers available in a network option plan may be considered a coverage decrease; however, the loss of a single physician from a network where there are other physicians available in the network and in the geographic area covered by the plan would not be considered a coverage decrease.

  — If there is a significant cost decrease for a specific plan, an employee may be allowed to make a change to participate in that plan if he or she is not a current participant. Similarly, if there are significant improvements in the plan, employees may be allowed to make an election to participate.

  — Changes are not allowed if employees experience a reduction in compensation. For example, an employer's institution of a 5 percent pay cut for all employees does not constitute a cost increase under the midyear election rules. The same is true if the employee accepts a demotion or transfer that results in a pay cut. In these cases, employees will have to wait until the next open enrollment before making a change to their plan coverage.

One major rule is that changes must always be prospective; that is, they must apply to the future. There is one exception, however: Both the IRS cafeteria plan regulations and the Health Insurance Portability and Accountability Act of 1996 (HIPAA) special enrollment provision require employers to allow the retroactive enrollment of newborns, adopted children, and children placed for adoption.

Marriages do not receive this special treatment. An employee's spouse can be covered and salary reduction for that coverage can begin only after the employee notifies the plan administrator. Most health plans allow for a new spouse to be covered retroactively to the date of the marriage if the health plan is notified within 30 days of the marriage. According to the IRS regulations, however, retroactive coverage for a new spouse must be provided outside the cafeteria plan and the additional costs, if any, must be post-tax until the plan notification date.

Although not included in the IRS's midyear election change regulations, a military leave protected under USERRA (see **Chapter 11**) may also provide an acceptable reason for a midyear election change. In the preamble to the final USERRA regulations issued in December 2005, the DOL indicates that the IRS and Treasury have taken the position that the Section 125 rules will not be violated if a plan "provides for a new [health FSA] election either upon leaving employment for military service or subsequent reemployment."

A change in status allows the employee to make a corresponding change in coverage and a corresponding change in the amount of his or her FSA. The employee's FSA can also be changed if the HIPAA special enrollment provision is the cause of the change in status. As noted above, changes in cost or coverage do not allow for an employee to make a change in the FSA.

The IRS regulations merely indicate which changes in status, cost, and coverage may result in the participant's being allowed to make a corresponding change in the cafeteria plan elections; they do not require the employer to allow such changes. Employers should carefully consider which changes they wish to allow their employees to make.

The regulations for midyear election changes are complex and not always entirely logical. The IRS's final regulations provide several examples to help guide employers. (See the Government Printing Office Web site at *www.access.gpo.gov.*)

[E]   Dependent Care Flexible Spending Accounts

Dependent care assistance programs governed by IRC Section 129 can also be offered through a cafeteria plan as an FSA. Dependent care FSAs allow employees to deduct up to $5,000 per year from their pay on a pre-tax basis to reimburse dependent care services necessary for gainful employment. If the employee is married but files taxes separately, the maximum annual amount is $2,500. If married, both spouses must be employed or the non-employee spouse must be a full-time student or incapable of caring for him/her-self. Only expenses necessary for the care of a "qualifying individual" can be reimbursed. Although there are detailed rules regarding who is a qualifying individual, generally an employee's child under the age of 13 would be a qualifying individual. In order to receive reimbursement from the FSA, all expenses must be substantiated by information from a third party that is independent of the employee, employee's spouse or employee's dependents. The substantiation must include the name, address and taxpayer identification number of the individual or organization that is providing the dependent care services (a not-for-profit organization is not required to provide a taxpayer identification number). To receive reimbursement by a dependent care FSA, the dependent care service provider may not be an employee's child under the age of 19 or an individual claimed as a dependent on the employee's tax return.

In 2006, the IRS issued proposed regulations (26 CFR Parts 1 and 602 [REG 139059-02], May 24, 2006) that revise and clarify the dependent care services that are necessary for gainful employment. The proposed regulations:

- Permit expenses for specialty day camps, such as computer camp and soccer camp;

- Do not allow kindergarten expenses to be reimbursed as they are primarily educational;

- Clarify that expenses are only eligible in the later of the year in which the services are provided or the expenses are paid;

- Allow for the reimbursement of certain transportation expenses which enable a dependent to receive services (e.g., transportation to a day camp or to an after-school program);

- Provide that certain indirect expenses (e.g., application or agency fees that are necessary to obtain the dependent care service) may be reimbursable;

- Provide that dependent care expenses incurred while the employee is absent from work are not reimbursable, except that short, temporary absences (e.g., vacation or sick leave) may be disregarded if the expenses must be paid on a weekly, monthly or longer basis.

If the dependent care FSA utilizes the definition of expenses under IRC Section 21, the proposed rules can be relied upon until final rules are published (which have not been published as of this writing).

The uniform coverage rule does not apply to dependent care FSAs. Plan sponsors need only reimburse expenses up to the amount available in the employee's account at the time of request for reimbursement. The plan cannot reimburse for services provided prior to or after the end of a plan year. The new proposed regulations allow for one exception to this general rule: the plan may allow a terminated employee to use up the funds in his/her account with services provided after the date of termination, if all other requirements of IRC Section 129 are met.

All other requirements of IRC Section 125 are required for dependent care FSAs, including the use-it-or-lose-it rule, mid-year change rules, the applicability of the grace period and the requirement for a written plan document.

Under USERRA, dependent care FSAs are non-health, non-seniority-based benefits. As such, whether these benefits may continue during a military leave is based on the employer's policies for other non-health, non-seniority-based benefits during other unpaid leaves of absence. USERRA requires employers to provide the same non-seniority-based rights and benefits that are provided by the employer to employees with similar seniority, status and pay on other unpaid leaves. If these benefits vary, the "most favorable treatment accorded to any comparable form of leave" must be provided to employees on military leave.

[F] Other Section 125 Requirements

Cafeteria plans provide employees with a choice between taxable and nontaxable benefits. IRS Section 125 provides the only tax framework that allows for this choice without triggering taxable income. If the cafeteria plan does not satisfy all of the requirements of Section 125, all plan participants' choices between taxable and nontaxable benefits will result in taxable income.

Section 125 plans must have a written plan document. A cafeteria plan document must be adopted and the plan must be effective on the first day of the cafeteria plan year to which it relates. Most cafeteria plans use the calendar year as their plan year; under a calendar year plan the adoption of the plan document and the effective date of the plan must be January 1. The terms of the plan must be uniformly applied to all participants. In the 2007 proposed regulations, 10 specific requirements of the plan document are outlined, as follows:

1. A specific description of each of the benefits available through the plan, including the periods of coverage;

2. The plan's rules governing participation, and specifically requiring that all participants in the plan be employees (self-employed individuals and 2 percent shareholders of an S corporation are not employees under the Section 125 regulations and cannot participate in a cafeteria plan);

3. The procedures governing employees' elections under the plan, including:

   • the period when elections may be made,

   • the periods when such elections will be effective, and

   • a statement providing that the elections are irrevocable, except to the extent that the plan has adopted any change in status rules allowing for midyear election changes

4. The manner in which employer contributions may be made under the plan (for example, through an employee's salary reduction election or by non-elective employer contributions (i.e., flex-credits));

5. The maximum amount of employer contributions available to any employee through the plan, by stating:

   • the maximum amount of elective contributions (i.e., salary reductions) available to any employee through the plan, expressed as (i) a maximum dollar amount, (ii) a maximum percentage of compensation, or (iii) the method for determining the maximum dollar amount; and

   • for contributions to Section 401(k) plans, the maximum amount of elective contributions available to any employee through the plan, expressed as a maximum dollar amount or maximum percentage of compensation that may be contributed as elective contributions through the plan by employees;

6. The plan year (Note: generally, a plan year must be 12 months, but a limited exception for short plan years is available if the reason for the short plan year is for a legitimate business purpose);

7. If the plan offers paid time off, the plan must state that non-elective paid time off must be used before elective paid time off is used (the "required ordering rule");

8. If the plan includes flexible spending accounts, the plan's provisions complying with any additional requirements (for example, the uniform coverage rule and the use-it-or-lose-it rule);

9. If the plan includes a grace period, the plan's provisions for complying with the regulations for grace periods; and

10. If the plan includes distributions from a health FSA to the employees' HSAs, the plan provisions complying with the regulations for such distributions.

If the cafeteria plan also provides for a self-insured medical reimbursement plan (Section 105(h) plan), a dependent care assistance program (Section 129 plan) or an adoption assistance program (Section 137(c) plan), the requirements for a written plan document for those plans may be satisfied by either including the description of those plans (as required by their various Code Sections) in the cafeteria plan document or through a separate written document. In addition, if the cafeteria plan includes deferrals into a Section 401(k) plan, the requirements under Section 401(k) must also be met, which include a requirement for a written plan document.

In describing the benefits available through the cafeteria plan, the written plan document may incorporate by reference the benefits offered by separate plan documents.

The 2007 proposed regulations make it clear that if there is no written document, if the written plan fails to satisfy the requirements for a written plan, or if the plan does not operate according to its written plan, then the plan is not a cafeteria plan and an employee's election between taxable and nontaxable benefits will result in taxable gross income to the employee.

These "operational failures" include paying or reimbursing expenses that are incurred before the date the cafeteria plan is adopted or becomes effective; failure to comply with the FSA's uniform coverage or use-it-or-lose-it rules; allowing employees to make changes to their elections without following the IRS' mid-year change rules; reimbursing employees' expenses without appropriate substantiation; reimbursing disallowed FSA expenses; improper use of FSA plan forfeitures; and not complying with the grace period rules, if included in the plan.

The 2007 proposed regulations expand on Section 125's nondiscrimination requirements. Cafeteria plans must not discriminate in favor of highly compensated individuals as to contributions and benefits during the plan year. The regulations provide definitions of "highly compensated individual" and "key employee" to be used to conduct the nondiscrimination testing. A safe harbor test is provided for plan sponsors to conduct annual nondiscrimination testing on the cafeteria plan.

The 2007 proposed regulations also provide lengthy guidance on making and revoking elections. Much of this information consolidates previous regulations on this topic, including the midyear election changes described above.

[G] IRS and ERISA Form 5500 Requirements

For years, Section 125 cafeteria plans were required to file Form 5500, Annual Return/Report of Employee Benefit Plan. In April 2002, the IRS issued Notice 2002-24 [2002-16 I.R.B. 785], which suspended indefinitely the requirement for cafeteria plans, as well as for educational and adoption assistance plans, to file Form 5500. For such plans:

- Form 5500 need not be filed for the 2001 plan year.

- Forms 5500 need not be filed for years prior to 2001 (if the reports should have been filed but were not).

- Forms 5500 need not be filed for 2002 or future years (until further notice from IRS, which indicated that it would give employers ample notice).

However, Form 5500 is still required of Section 125 plans with more than 100 participants that offer medical FSAs and of plans (with any number of participants) that are funded through a trust. In addition, plans subject to the Employee Retirement Income Security Act of 1974 (ERISA) must continue to file Form 5500. ERISA requires most employers (with the exception of governmental entities and certain religious organizations) to file Form 5500 if their plans offer health, sickness and accident, death, unemployment, and disability insurance, employer-provided day care centers, scholarship funds, or prepaid legal services plans (see **Chapter 5**).

§ 12.03 MANAGING THE HEALTH CARE BENEFITS PLAN

Effective management of group health and related benefits plans centers around four issues: planning, funding, administration, and design.

[A] Planning

As part of the overall strategic and HR planning process, management and, if applicable, the board of directors should develop a long-range benefits plan to guide future benefits decision making. As part of this plan, the company's purpose in providing employee benefits should be articulated. Generally, in considering the purpose of the organization's employee benefits, plan administrators evaluate assumptions regarding the workforce: productivity, employee wants and needs, expected turnover, and homogeneity or lack thereof (e.g., the numbers of single and married employees and those with and without dependents). Following development of an overall purpose statement and identification of underlying assumptions, the company is in a position to define its goals for the overall employee benefits program. Strategies for implementing these goals follow, leading toward achievement of the long-term plan for employee benefits. Strategies should include techniques for measuring the ongoing performance of the benefits programs in terms of the company's goals.

[B] Funding

Funding is based on a number of factors, including:

- The size and composition of the employee group

- The external market

- The company's willingness to accept financial risk

Plan administrators may choose from a variety of funding mechanisms for their group health plans, such as insured plans, self-funded plans, and hybrids of these two types.

[1] Insured Plans

Insured plans are just what the name implies. In an insured arrangement, the company selects a provider (most often an insurance company) and arranges to pay a premium each month for coverage. Premiums are established by the provider to cover the cost of claims, as well as premium taxes, insurance company profits, overhead, and administrative costs, such as printing of booklets and broker or agent insurance commissions.

Over time, insured plan premiums may be determined based on the company's own group claims experience and benefit usage, which is known as experience-rated premium rates. If the group's experience is not sufficient to stand on its own, premiums are typically determined based on the overall experience of a more broadly defined group, which is known as community pooling or community rating.

Experience-based premium rates are calculated by the insurance company's underwriting staff and are based on the claims and benefit utilization of employees in the company's group, projected health care inflation, and expected future health care usage.

Community or pooled ratings may be based on a group of companies of similar size or in similar industries, called the "book of business." The community premium rating is generally based on groups in a defined geographic area.

[2] Self-Funded Plans

Many employers with employee groups large enough to take advantage of the so-called law of large numbers choose to self-fund their employee group health benefits. Under these arrangements, the company accepts risk for payment of eligible employees' health plan claims and pays those claims from general assets. Some employers and multiple employer groups choose to create trusts from which to pay claims, but a trust is not a requirement for handling these benefit funds.

Despite the increased potential financial risk, self-funding is attractive because it allows the plan administrator to design a plan that meets the requirements of ERISA, which are generally less burdensome than state insurance requirements. If a group self-funds, ERISA preemption exempts the group from having to offer state-mandated benefits. In many states, premium taxes are also avoided, and the company saves the profit and risk charges of the insurance company.

Amounts received by non-highly compensated employees (NHCEs) through a self-insured health plan are excludable from gross income. Amounts received by highly compensated employees (HCEs) are excludable from gross income if the plan does not discriminate in favor of highly compensated individuals as to eligibility or benefits. Amounts received for reimbursement of insurance premiums or medical diagnostic procedures are not covered by these rules. For this purpose, an HCE is an individual who is one of the company's five highest paid officers, is a greater than 10 percent shareholder, or is among the 25 percent highest paid employees. These HCE criteria are different from those that apply to qualified retirement plans.

A self-funded plan is considered discriminatory unless it meets the following requirements:

- *Eligibility.* At least 70 percent of all employees must benefit under the plan, or the plan must benefit at least 80 percent of all employees who are eligible under the plan, as long as at least 70 percent of all employees are eligible. Alternatively, the plan must benefit a group of employees who qualify under a classification test found by the IRS not to discriminate in favor of HCEs, as described in Code Section 410(b).

- *Benefits.* Plan benefits provided to HCEs and their dependents must be equally available to all other employees and their dependents who are similarly situated. Benefit reimbursements that are measured or determined in proportion to compensation may be considered discriminatory. A plan can generally establish a maximum limit for the amount of reimbursement an employee can receive. Such a limit must be uniform for all employees and not based on employee age, years of service, or compensation.

If a plan is discriminatory, the HCEs would have to include in income any excess reimbursements.

[3] Hybrid Funding Plans

Several variations of partial self-funding, including split-premium or shared-risk arrangements, are available in most health care markets. Such hybrid arrangements attempt to provide some benefits of self-funding (e.g., cash flow) with some level of insured risk protection. If a company has a large number of employees and is willing to consider potential financial risk greater than that for an insured plan, the plan administrators should ask the broker, agent, or consultant to solicit these alternative funding proposals. In most jurisdictions, hybrid funding is considered a fully insured arrangement, subjecting the plan to state insurance department requirements. A benefits specialist (or the state's insurance department) should be consulted for confirmation of this issue before designing a benefits plan.

[C] Administration

Administration of the group health plan involves three essential functions: paying employees' claims on a timely basis, providing quality service to employees regarding questions and referrals, and reviewing management reports from the insurance company or claims administrator and making informed decisions based on that information.

Under an insured plan, claims are generally paid by the insurance company as part of the premium cost. In a self-funded or partially self-funded arrangement, however, the plan sponsor may choose to pay claims in-house or may make a separate agreement with a third-party administrator (TPA) or insurance company for processing or payment of employees' medical claims.

TPAs typically charge a monthly per capita fee for providing claims service to employees. They have authority to produce checks to health care providers (e.g., physicians and hospitals) from one of the company's accounts. Because TPAs have this payment authority, plan sponsors should conduct periodic performance reviews to ensure that employees are, in fact, receiving benefits outlined in their group health plan.

The company's insurance carrier or claims administrator should provide management reports that indicate how benefit dollars are being spent. At a minimum, the company should receive reports summarizing, by employee and dependents, major categories of benefits covered in the plan. Items on a typical report would include:

- Inpatient (hospital) charges

    — Room and board

    — Psychiatric care

    — Intensive care unit

    — Drugs

    — Emergency room

    — Surgeon

    — Anesthesiologist

    — Physician

- Outpatient charges

    — Physician office visits

    — Physician and psychiatric services

    — X-rays or laboratory tests

    — Chiropractic

    — Drugs

    — Ambulance services

In addition, the company should receive reports indicating how benefit dollars are allocated between actual benefit expenses and administration costs. One such report would include loss ratio information, which shows how much of the company's benefit dollars are applied directly to employee benefits received. Another report should analyze administration fees, including, for example, installation fees, participant booklets, network access, reporting, reinsurance, and broker fees.

External regulations, including those under the Consolidated Omnibus Budget Reconciliation Act of 1985 (COBRA) and HIPAA, impose additional requirements on employers to handle benefits administration. (See **Chapter 7** for a discussion of administrative requirements under COBRA and **Chapter 6** for a discussion of HIPAA requirements.)

[D] Design

The first step in designing the group health plan is determining what types of benefits will be provided, including:

- What charges will be covered

- What charges will be excluded

- What types of benefits will be limited and how

- What the individual and family deductibles will be and what other cost-sharing features are available

- What types of cost containment or managed care features will be included

The continued effectiveness of the design decisions should be monitored over time through administrative management reports. The plan design will likely change over time to reflect differences in employee benefits usage. For example, if the plan offers coverage at a 100 percent benefit level for emergency room treatment, with no exceptions, employees may use emergency rooms too often, choosing to use them rather than finding a primary care physician to deal with health concerns that are not truly medical emergencies. Employees simply find it easier to use the emergency room instead.

Under those circumstances, revising the plan design is a cost-effective and beneficial (to employees) measure. Options are to pay only the same level of benefit for emergency room treatments as for other benefits (e.g., 80 percent after the deductible) or to implement a per-visit deductible for each use of an emergency room that is not a medical emergency, as determined by the treating physician.

At the same time, the human resources (HR) department should encourage and assist employees in finding their primary care physicians. This design change reduces short-term costs, because emergency rooms are generally much more expensive than physician office visits. In addition, long-term costs are reduced, as employees become better health care consumers.

§ 12.04   COST CONTAINMENT STRATEGIES

According to the U.S. Chamber of Commerce, employers paid on average $21,527 per employee for benefits in 2006 (the latest data available), for a total benefit cost equal to 42.7 percent of payroll. The dollars spent on benefits increased 16.4 percent from 2005, when employers paid an average $18,489 per employee. However, the percentage of payroll was higher in 2006 than 2005, when it was only 40.2 percent of payroll. Also in 2006, the employers' share of total medical and medically related payments averaged 12.1 percent of payroll, the largest share of employer benefit costs. The Bureau of Labor Statistics reported a 2.8 percent increase in the cost of employee benefits from June 2007 to June 2008. According to the Centers for Medicare & Medicaid Services (CMS), spending in the United States on health care in 2006 rose 6.6 percent. This indicates a slight increase from 2005 (6.5 percent), but a reduction from previous years' increases, in 2004 it was 7.2 percent, in 2003 it was 8.2 percent and was 9.1 percent in 2002. Insurance cost trends have generally been higher with a 10 or more percent growth in 2002, 2003, and 2004. According to several studies, the average increase in medical insurance costs fell below 10 percent in 2005, 2006, and 2007 and is expected to fall in the 8 to 10 percent range for 2008.

Because of the significant cost of health benefits, an increasing number of organizations are now willing to implement substantial changes in health coverage programs, including changes they would have be deemed "too radical" only a few years ago.

A sure but dramatic way to reduce employee health benefit plan costs is simply to cut back on the benefits. For example, an organization can eliminate mental health benefits, impose large front-end deductibles, raise the stop-loss levels, and require employees to pay a higher percentage of the premiums. These measures certainly lower the employer's expense, obviously to the potential detriment of employees. This choice may be necessary if the organization is under severe financial pressure, but it is contrary to the general philosophic commitment of most employers to this highly valued employee benefit.

Most organizations focus on cost containment through better plan design, better incentives, and better plan management. However, a prudent strategy for a particular institution might very well include cutting back on an expensive benefit of doubtful value or of questionable insurability.

Following are a number of approaches that organizations can use to help contain the costs of employee health plans:

- Cost sharing, including:

    — Deductibles

    — Coinsurance

    — Premium expense sharing

- Utilization review, including:

    — Preadmission certification of hospital benefits

    — Concurrent review of extended hospitalization

    — Discharge planning for hospitalized patients

    — Catastrophic care assistance

    — Second surgical opinions

- Preferred provider plans

- Defined contribution health plans

[A] Cost Sharing

Organizations can use four devices to share medical benefit costs with employees: deductibles, coinsurance, premium sharing, and pricing options.

[1] Deductibles

The purpose of deductibles is to discourage marginal demands for covered services and to promote price consciousness on the part of patients. Inflationary trends over recent years have sharply reduced the effect of fixed deductibles, however. Further, there is growing controversy over whether deductibles actually serve as deterrents at all, unless they are very large. This controversy notwithstanding, high deductibles do reduce premiums by shifting expenses to the employee. According to findings of the Employer Health Benefits 2008 Annual Survey, conducted by Kaiser Family Foundation and Health Research and Educational Trust (KFF/HRET), the average annual deductible for in-network services under a PPO plan is $560 for single coverage and $1,344 for family coverage. HMOs have recently begun requiring deductibles for hospitalization. Nineteen percent of all HMO plans have deductibles; the average single deductible in a plan offered by a large firm (200 or more employees) is $307 and $626 for family coverage.

Organizations usually apply deductibles on a calendar-year basis. This approach is logical and easy to communicate; it also coincides with the employee's tax year. Other approaches that are rarely used apply the deductible on a fiscal- or contract-year basis or on a per-cause basis.

The use of the fourth-quarter carryover is a common liberalization of the per-year deductible. Under the standard deductible rules, an employee with no prior claims in a calendar year who incurs expenses during the fourth quarter is subject to the deductible for those expenses. The fourth-quarter carryover feature credits those expenses toward the next year's deductible. Under this approach, employees who experience additional expenses early in the next year would not be subject to the deductible twice in a short period of time.

Another common deductible feature is a prior-carrier carryover that occurs when an organization changes from one medical program carrier to another. In this situation, the new carrier agrees to credit unreimbursed expense incurred in the last 90 days of the prior program toward the new deductible.

The use of a family deductible is fairly common in health plans. This feature normally applies two or three deductibles per family per year, without regard to family size. For example, if a program has a $400 deductible per person per year, applying two deductibles for a covered family would not mean that the family has a $800 maximum deductible. Instead, it would mean that at least two members of the family must each meet the $400 deductible before deductibles are no longer applied to the remaining family members. Thus, if six covered family members each incur $150 of medical expenses, there would be no plan payment for any of the claims because two members have not each met the $400 deductible.

[2] Coinsurance

Coinsurance, the sharing of covered expenses between the carrier and the insured patient, is applied after an individual or a family has met the deductible. The most common form of coinsurance covers 80 percent of medical expenses, leaving the employee responsible for the remaining 20 percent. Because coinsurance transfers a sizable portion of the medical expense to the insured person, it effectively lowers the premiums for a given set of benefits or allows a given premium level to purchase a wider range of benefits. Managed or preferred care agreements often provide an incentive for plan participants to take advantage of services provided by the preferred provider(s). This incentive generally provides a "better" level of plan coinsurance to the preferred providers (e.g., 90 percent, rather than the typical 80 percent payment).

Many organizations support coinsurance with an individual out-of-pocket limit. Coinsurance with an out-of-pocket limit means that the plan will pay all covered expenses in full once the employee has met the deductible and paid 20 percent of all covered expenses up to a certain dollar amount. For example, a calendar-year health plan might cover 80 percent of the first $5,200 of covered expenses in a calendar year and then provide 100 percent coverage for the remainder of the year. With a $200 deductible and $1,000 coinsurance for the next $5,000, the employee would bear a maximum of $1,200 in out-of-pocket costs.

Under the pressure of escalating health care costs, employers and insurers are considering additional coinsurance strategies. One such strategy is the use of tiered coinsurance for prescription drug benefits (e.g., one tier for generic drugs, a second for preferred brand-name drugs, and a third for nonpreferred brand-name drugs). In one such plan, the coinsurance for generic drugs is 10 percent, for preferred drugs, 30 percent, and for nonpreferred drugs, 50 percent. (See **Chapter 10** for further discussion of prescription drug benefits.)

Another strategy is the use of coinsurance tiers for hospitals. Under such a plan, participants pay a higher coinsurance for costlier hospitals, including hospitals that do not contract for lower reimbursements from the insurer and hospitals that provide premium and/or hard-to-obtain services. Advocates of tiered hospital coinsurance believe that this strategy lowers the out-of-pocket costs for employees who are willing to restrict their choice of hospitals while providing more options to participants who are willing to pay higher costs. Employers generally favor tiered hospital coinsurance plans because the less frequent use of expensive hospitals by employees may slow the increase in insurance premiums.

[3] Sharing Premium Expense

Cost sharing can also involve dividing the premium expense between employer and employee. There are two common approaches to sharing premium expense:

1. *The employer fully pays employee coverage but asks the employee either to share or to fully pay the cost of dependent coverage.* One issue with providing cost-free employee coverage is that because nobody is likely to refuse a free benefit, the employer may bear an expense and assume a risk to the plan that can be avoided if the employee had to make a choice based on economics and opted to be covered as a dependent under a spouse's plan. Some employers counter by saying that the expense is negligible, and they want the assurance that all employees have coverage.

2. *The employer and the employee share the premium cost for both employee and dependent coverage.* Many employers believe that this approach helps the employee to become a wiser purchaser of services and to better understand the economic forces in the benefit marketplace. In this type of cost sharing arrangement, the employer usually pays from 66 to 75 percent of the premium cost for employee coverage and from 50 to 75 percent of the cost for dependent coverage.

According to findings of the KFF/HRET Employer Health Benefits 2008 Annual Survey, employers typically pay 84 percent of the employee-only insurance premium and 73 percent of the family coverage premium. The percentages have remained relatively stable since 2000. However, the actual dollar amounts have increased: for individual coverage, employers paid on average $2,064 in 2000 and $3,983 in 2008; for family coverage, employers paid on average of $4,608 in 2000 and $9,325 in 2008.

When premiums are deducted from employees' pay they become plan assets. These contributions must be forwarded to the welfare benefit plan as soon as they can be reasonably separated from the general assets of the employer, but in no case later than 90 days from the date the premiums are deducted from employees' pay. Once deducted from employees' pay, the contributions must not be used as general assets of the company. If the contributions are used by the employer or are not paid to the plan within the 90-day period, plan fiduciaries can be held personally liable. Liability may include civil penalties and criminal sanctions. In February 2008, the DOL proposed a safe harbor rule for employee contributions to small welfare and pension plans (those plans with fewer than 100 participants (73 Fed. Reg., 11072, February 29, 2008)). The safe harbor rule would provide that participant contributions to the plan will be deemed to be in compliance with the law if those amounts are deposited into the plan within 7 business days of payroll withholding. Although the rule won't be final until published in the Federal Register (not done as of this writing), employers may rely on the safe harbor rule in the interim.

[4] Pricing Options

To meet the needs of employees who want to play a greater role in choosing their benefit plans, some organizations offer two different levels of medical benefits, priced accordingly, in their standard plan. **Table 12-1** provides an example of a two-level program.

Table 12-1

Two-Level Medical Benefits Program

Plan Feature	High-Level Plan	Low-Level Plan
Annual deductible per person	$200	$500
Annual deductible per family (maximum)	$400	$1,000
Coinsurance	80/20	70/30
Copayment out-of-pocket limit (per year with two-person maximum both levels and excluding the deductibles)	$1,000	$2,000

The pricing of health coverage has reached the level of a fine art. In recognition of the demographics of today's workforce, employers have begun offering many levels of premiums—single, single adult with dependents (may be children or dependent parents), two adults without dependents, and so on. In addition, employers must be conscious of the need to coordinate coverage when there are two or more insured members in an employee's household. For example, both spouses may work, and a college-age dependent may have coverage through a job or through the college. Benefits under these programs need to be integrated and coordinated to keep costs under control and to avoid duplication of benefits.

Cost coordination is not limited to making sure that only one provider pays for a specific treatment. In addition, coverage needs to be coordinated so that everyone knows which provider is responsible for which dependent and for which charges or benefits.

[B]   Utilization Review

Utilization review is based on the concept of a physician peer review process. By reviewing the manner in which services are delivered, the carrier or plan administrator can improve the quality of the decision-making process and pass on to the bank the benefits of a corresponding reduction in waste, inefficiency, and inappropriate services.

Complex computer analysis of hospital stays according to the patient's age, sex, and diagnosis is now commonplace. Utilization analysis focuses not only on how long patients stay hospitalized but also on their use of ancillary services such as X-ray studies, laboratory tests, operating rooms, prescription drugs, and special therapies. The result of all this analysis is increasingly detailed standards and norms citing the medical appropriateness of specific methods of treating specific injuries and illnesses.

An organization should ensure that its carrier or plan administrator has a strong utilization review program to keep costs down and that the carrier or administrator has access to the utilization review activities of the hospitals serving the employees and their dependents. Insurance carriers normally charge a fee for this service, which may be itemized separately or included in the retention fee.

These programs generally include one or more of the following mechanisms: preadmission certification of hospital benefits, concurrent review of extended hospitalization, discharge planning for hospitalized patients, catastrophic care assistance, and second surgery opinions.

[1]   Preadmission Certification of Hospital Benefits

This strategy is designed to control hospitalization costs, which represent a large percentage of medical benefit expenses. A preadmission certification program requires that a patient scheduled for nonemergency hospital admission contact the carrier's managed care center, either personally or via the doctor or hospital, to obtain prior approval of the benefits for admission and for a fixed number of days in the hospital. If the patient calls, the center typically talks to the admitting physician to obtain the necessary information to either certify the benefits or deny the certification. If the attending physician later decides that a longer stay is necessary, the patient, the physician, or the hospital must again contact the managed care center to set a new target discharge date.

Benefits are usually certified according to simple clinical criteria that reflect generally accepted medical standards. For example, a proposed inpatient admission of an adult for arthroscopic knee surgery would prompt preprogrammed questions about whether the patient had some underlying medical condition that would make ambulatory surgery unsafe.

Emergency admissions obviously do not require preadmission certification. However, most programs do require certification within two or three days of an emergency admission. If a patient is admitted to a hospital without preadmission certification, the carrier decides whether the situation was an emergency. If the situation was not an emergency, the patient's benefits are reduced according to a predetermined schedule. If the situation was an emergency, any penalties are waived.

[2] Concurrent Review of Extended Hospitalization

This procedure, which frequently is used in conjunction with preadmission certification programs, focuses on patients who have to stay in the hospital beyond the initial target discharge date or who are likely to remain hospitalized longer than some predetermined maximum time period, such as 14 or 21 days. In these cases, the managed care center typically telephones the hospital to check on the patient's progress. The center's nurses again apply professionally accepted criteria to establish a new target discharge date or the next review date, certifying that the carrier will pay benefits through this period. If the patient stays longer, he or she may be penalized after the carrier investigates the circumstances.

[3] Discharge Planning for Hospitalized Patients

Another expense for medical benefits programs results when patients who no longer need hospital services remain hospitalized because they require nursing or other services that the family cannot readily furnish at home. To address this problem, many large hospitals assign nurses or social workers to discharge planning. Responsibilities include arranging home nursing, transfers to an extended care facility, or other support services that the patient needs to leave the hospital, as soon as it is medically feasible.

When a health care program offers discharge planning, the managed care center's nurses are responsible for communicating and working with the hospital to help arrange the necessary services.

[4] Catastrophic Care Assistance

Catastrophic care assistance comes into play when an employee or family member experiences a serious illness or major injury that involves costly and intensive medical services. In these cases, the managed care center directly intervenes to help the patient find the most effective care. Because these situations are extremely infrequent, each case is unique and must be judged on an individual basis. For example, in some cases organizations may agree to cover services that are not ordinarily insured benefits because they are less costly and more effective for a particular patient.

[5] Second Surgical Opinions

Second surgical opinions (SSOs) provide employees and their dependents with incentives to obtain second opinions prior to certain surgical procedures. For example, patients who fail to obtain an SSO when required may have to pay 50 percent rather than 20 percent of the cost of the surgery, anesthesia, and other hospital bills. On the other hand, if the patient obtains an SSO before the surgery, the plan might waive, for example, the typical 20 percent coinsurance payment provision.

The list of surgical procedures requiring SSOs varies among programs. Generally, the SSO procedures focus on elective operations rarely done on an emergency basis, which frequently generate differences of opinion among physicians as to their appropriateness in particular situations. The list typically includes operations such as tonsillectomies, hysterectomies, knee surgery, spinal disk surgery, and podiatric surgery for bunions and hammertoes.

Recently, group health plans have implemented similar second-opinion requirements before an individual undergoes certain (expensive) testing or treatment procedures, such as magnetic resonance imaging (MRIs), positron emission tomography (PET) scans, pain control center programs, and psychiatric or substance abuse care. The key to the success of SSO incentive programs is an effective and ongoing communication campaign to ensure that employees and their families are aware of the program requirements and penalties. Many employers distribute detailed brochures and other educational materials explaining how to obtain SSOs and describing the monetary incentives that employees should consider when a surgeon proposes performing one of the operations on the SSO incentive procedure list. In addition, it is helpful for employers to notify area hospitals, clinics, and surgeons that patients covered by a particular plan are subject to special SSO requirements for certain procedures.

[C] Preferred Provider Plans

Preferred provider plans provide cost savings to the plan and plan participants when participants utilize the in-network services. These plans take two basic forms:

1. *Preferred provider organizations.* Preferred provider organizations (PPOs) are organizations established by physicians and hospitals, sometimes as joint ventures with insurance carriers, to provide services to health plan members at favorable prices in return for receiving preferential consideration from the plan. For example, a physician PPO may offer its services to a particular plan at a 15 percent discount in return for the plan's waiving half of its usual 20 percent cost sharing whenever an employee uses one of the preferred physicians. In addition to the fee discount, the PPO usually promises to implement its own utilization controls, which may include some managed care techniques.

    Although PPOs are growing in popularity, enrolling more employees nationally than any other health plan type, critics have suggested that the discounts offered by some groups are applied, at least in part, to artificially inflated fees and that their utilization controls may be inadequate.

2. *Preferred provider arrangements.* Preferred provider arrangements (PPAs) are initiated by third-party payment plans, which invite the providers to participate on a preferred basis. If they decide to join, hospitals must accept a lower than usual reimbursement level and agree to operate under a set of utilization controls. Physicians must accept similar conditions and may also be required to refer patients to participating specialist physicians and to preferred hospitals.

    When deciding whether to adopt a preferred provider plan, organizations must analyze whether they will actually save money if some employees shift to the preferred providers. Although the shift may result in better utilization controls and lower payment rates, some employees would have used the preferred providers anyway. The important question is whether the gross savings are greater than the net costs of the insurance incentives in the program.

[D]   Defined Contribution Health Plans

In the mid- to late 1990s, cost increases in employee health plans were relatively low. Beginning in 2000, this trend changed drastically as annual double-digit percent increases once again became the norm. Annual increases in premiums for HMO plans reached the same level as those for PPO and traditional indemnity plans. Many experts asserted that managed care had done all that it could to contain costs.

Some theorized that the reason for the huge cost increases was patients' insulation from the true cost of care. Most patients had some form of medical insurance and did not pay the actual cost; therefore medical care decisions were not based on any economic rationale. Employers, the prime payers of medical care costs, paid ever-increasing premiums, and, especially at a time when recruiting and retention were difficult, were reluctant to pass on the increased costs to employees. Employers were faced with a dilemma: how to maintain (or even improve) employee health benefits in the face of rapidly increasing costs and a slowing of the economy.

A proposed solution was the defined contribution (DC) health plan. Analogous to a defined contribution retirement plan, a DC health plan would quickly educate the employee about health care costs. In its purest form, the DC health plan would provide employees a fixed amount of dollars (from the employer) and require the employee to find and pay for an appropriate plan for his or her needs.

Most employers realized that a pure DC health plan would not be well received by employees; employers still needed to find and negotiate group benefit plans that fit the circumstances of their employees and provided cost efficiencies by spreading the insurance risk through a group of individuals and families. Some form of plan that combined employee education and choice with fixed employer cost was needed.

Consumer-directed health plans (CDHPs) generally combine these aspects. The plans come in several forms, the most typical of which are:

- *Benefit design plans.* This type of plan allows employees to make selections in several health care cost categories, such as hospital, provider (or provider network), prescription drugs, vision care, and alternative care. Premiums and copayments in each category vary according to the employee's choice. Choice of higher copayments, for example, results in lower premiums; any savings can be used to "buy" a higher level of service in one of the other categories.

- *Health plan catalog plans.* Similar to the "pure" form of DC plan described above, this type of plan provides employees with benefit dollars and a catalog of health plans. Employees select the plan that best meets their needs. If the plan costs less than the employer's contribution, the excess is placed in a fund for qualified medical expenses. If the plan costs more than the employer's contribution, the employee pays the difference with pretax dollars.

- *High deductible/spending account plans (HD/SA plans).* Employers deposit a significant amount (usually $1,000 for single coverage, $2,000 for family coverage) into one or more forms of a financial account to be used for medical care. A catastrophic plan, with a deductible higher than the annual funding of the health account is also provided. Funds not spent from the health account may be rolled over to be used for future years' medical care with no maximum accumulation. An incentive for employees to use their medical funds wisely is built into the design: if an employee receives medical care that costs more than what is available in the account, the cost must be paid directly by the employee with out-of-pocket dollars. The premise is that employees will educate themselves to find the most cost-effective medical care combined with the quality of care they desire.

DC plans are not without their critics. One criticism is that employees will forgo preventive care in favor of not spending their health account funds. Plans have countered this criticism either by providing all preventive care at no cost to the employee (essentially including it in the catastrophic plan but without requiring the meeting of the deductible) or by requiring that some portion of the employee's health account funds be used only for preventive care and making that portion ineligible for rollover into future years.

A second criticism is that employees do not know, nor can they find information, about specific health conditions or detailed information about the cost, performance, and quality of doctors, hospitals, and other medical providers. Without such information, employees cannot make informed decisions. DC plans attempt to provide educational material for employees about providers, costs of care, and quality of care. The information is often available through the insurance carriers' or plan administrator's Web site and allows employees to make direct provider-to-provider comparisons.

The Employee Benefit Research Institute (EBRI) and the Commonwealth Fund released the 2007 Consumerism in Health Survey of privately insured adults. Their findings revealed HDHP participants (with and without spending account plans) report lower overall satisfaction with their health plan compared to participants in traditional health plans. The survey also found that participants in HDHP and HD/SA plans were more likely to skip needed medical care or prescriptions due to the higher cost than in traditional plans. The survey's respondents also reported that there have been no significant gains in the provision of provider cost and health plan quality information by the HDHP and HD/SA plans during the three years this survey has been conducted.

Interest and enrollment in DC plans is growing. In March 2008, Watson Wyatt and the National Business Group on Health reported that 47 percent of large companies had implemented a CDHP compared to 33 percent in 2006. Fifteen percent of all employees in these companies were enrolled in a CDHP compared to 8 percent in 2006 (most companies offer a CDHP as one of several options for employee health coverage). The KFF/HRET 2008 Employer Health Benefits Annual Survey indicated that about 13 percent of all firms offered an HD/SA plan in 2008 (a significant increase from 7 percent in 2006). Larger firms (those with 1,000 or more employees) offered an HD/SA plan more often than smaller firms (3 to 199 employees): 22 percent vs. 13 percent. In this survey, 8 percent of employees were enrolled a HD/SA plan. In December 2006, the Center for Studying Health System Change reported that 19 percent of employees choose a CDHP when it was offered with other types of health plans. Of the estimated 2.7 million workers enrolled in employer-sponsored CDHPs in 2006, 39 percent had no choice of another plan. And, according to the Employee Benefit Research Institute and the Commonwealth Fund, only 2 percent of the privately insured population ages 21–64 are currently enrolled in CDHPs.

Insurance carriers report that medical care costs are lower for CDHPs than they are for HMO, PPO or traditional medical plans. HealthPartners noted that the cost of care for members in their CDHP plans was 4.4 percent lower than the cost for those in non-CDHP plans. CIGNA's CDHP members' costs were more than 12 percent lower in the first year of coverage and 5 percent lower in the second year. Milliman reported that CDHP costs were an average of 4.8 percent lower than the costs in their traditional health care options. Milliman further reported that the lower cost was due to reduced utilization in the plan, as well as that healthier employees enrolled in the CDHP. Watson Wyatt and the National Business Group on Health reported that if an employer had at least half of their employees enrolled in a CDHP, the medical cost increases were 3.6 percent per year (over a two-year period), compared to a 7 percent per year increase trend among companies without a CDHP. All companies with a CDHP (regardless of enrollment) had a two-year increase trend of 5.5 percent per year.

[1] Health Reimbursement Arrangements (HRA)

On June 26, 2002, the IRS issued Notice 2002-45 [2002-28 I.R.B. 93] and Revenue Ruling 2002-41 [2002-28 I.R.B. 75], providing guidance to employers on establishing HRA plans. According to the IRS, an HRA:

- Must be funded solely by the employer (no direct or indirect salary reduction is allowed)

- May reimburse only the medical expenses incurred by the employee, the employee's spouse or dependent (but not domestic partner), for which no other reimbursement has been made or will be made

- May allow employees to carry forward unused funds to future plan years

- Allows reimbursements to be excludable from employees' gross income, and allows employers to deduct reimbursements as a business expense

- Cannot cover self-employed individuals or their partners or independent contractors

- May reimburse only substantiated (e.g., documented) medical expenses defined under Code Section 213(d), including premiums for other health insurance coverage, such as COBRA and retiree coverage, and long-term care insurance premiums

  Note: In September 2003, the IRS issued Revenue Ruling 2003-102 [2003-38 I.R.B. 559], which allows HRAs to reimburse employees for over-the-counter, nonprescription medicine (see **Chapter 10**).

- May not reimburse costs of long-term care services

- Is a plan feature covered by COBRA and must be offered for the full COBRA period

- Cannot be converted to cash upon termination or retirement but, if the plan allows, may be used by the ex-employee or retiree for qualified medical expenses in years following termination or retirement

An HRA is not a cafeteria plan and cannot be included as part of a cafeteria plan. Therefore, it is not subject to the "use it or lose it" rule. Nor does the maximum amount of reimbursement have to be available at all times during the plan year—employers are free to fund the HRA on a gradual basis throughout the year. The HRA is not required to reimburse a claim if there are insufficient funds to pay the entire claim.

HRAs may be used with medical FSAs. However, employers must heed IRS regulations that no salary deduction, direct or indirect, can be used to fund the HRA (although salary reduction can be used to fund the FSA). Employers may determine the order in which funds are used (that is, require that the HRA be used first, or that the FSA be used first). In addition, the plan may require that certain expenses may be paid only out of the HRA or only out of the FSA. The HRA and the FSA cannot both reimburse the same expense.

The IRS has determined that an HRA is a self-insured medical plan, and therefore it must meet nondiscrimination requirements—that is, it cannot discriminate in favor of highly compensated employees. However, IRS Notice 2002-45 did not provide guidance on how to apply discrimination testing. Most experts suggest that employers offer the same health plan with the same HRA amounts to all their employees.

In 2005, the IRS issued new guidance on tax-free employer contributions of accrued but unused vacation and sick leave to HRAs for retirees. Revenue Ruling 2005-24 [2005-16 I.R.B. 892] includes four possible scenarios for such contributions; however, only one of them would be qualified under IRS regulations. In the qualified scenario, when an employee retires, the employer contributes the dollar value of the amount of accumulated vacation and sick leave to the HRA on a mandatory basis. The contribution to the HRA is allowed because the contribution is mandatory, and the employee/retiree has no opportunity to obtain the funds in cash or in any other form of benefit. Thus, the IRS considers these contributions to be qualified employer contributions.

This new guidance ignores potential conflicts with state laws and with nondiscrimination rules. For example, in states that mandate the payment of unused leave upon termination of employment, including retirement, the qualified scenario presented in the revenue ruling would violate state law. Also, the revenue ruling assumes that the scenario is nondiscriminatory. However, if the leave accumulates on the basis of seniority, it is possible that highly compensated employees will have accumulated more leave than non-highly compensated employees, resulting in a potentially discriminatory arrangement. HRAs with carry-over features will not violate HIPAA's nondiscrimination rules if the maximum reimbursable amount for employees with the same coverage period would be the same, except for amounts already reimbursed. For example, Jim and Mary both work for the same company, which provides them an HRA reimbursement of $2,000 per year. Both have been covered for two years. Jim has been reimbursed $800 out of his HRA for qualified expenses and Mary has been reimbursed $500. Even though Jim and Mary's account balances are different ($3,200 for Jim and $3,500 for Mary), because the maximum reimbursement available during the same coverage period (two years) is $4,000, the HRA will meet the requirements of HIPAA's nondiscrimination rules.

Employers are not required to offer a health plan with an HRA. A stand-alone HRA may be all that some employers (especially small employers) can offer their employees.

HRAs will not work for all employers. Significant management support and employee education and communication will be needed, especially in the first few years of the plan. Further, the guidelines provided by the IRS for HRAs, while helpful, can be confusing and it is recommended that employers work with knowledgeable benefits experts (including legal review of all plan documents) to establish and implement HRAs. HRAs that do not comply with the regulations can result in all plan reimbursements becoming taxable income to all participants in the plan. In Revenue Ruling 2006-36 (August 14, 2006), the IRS ruled that if an HRA allowed reimbursements to be made to nonemployees, nonspouses and nondependents, then all reimbursements paid from the HRA would be taxable. This situation may occur when an employee dies and designates a beneficiary who is neither the spouse nor a tax-dependent. The IRS gave plans that permitted this practice before August 14, 2006 until January 1, 2009 to remove this provision from the plan. However, new plans and plans that never had this provision should not include this practice at all.

[2] Health Savings Accounts (HSAs)

The latest entrant into the defined contribution plan marketplace is the health savings account (HSA) coupled with a high-deductible health plan (HDHP). HSAs became a legal entity when the Medicare Prescription Drug Improvement and Modernization Act (see **Chapter 5**) was enacted in December 2003. HSAs combine many of the positive features of Archer Medical Savings Accounts (MSAs), health reimbursement accounts (HRAs), and health flexible spending accounts (FSAs).

HSAs are becoming more popular benefit offerings. As reported by America's Health Insurance Plans (AHIP), by the end of March 2005, there were 1.03 million HSA compatible HDHPs in the United States—556,000 individual plans and 397,000 group plans. As of January 2006, there were 3,168,000 accounts. Of these, 855,000 were individual plans, and 1,436,000 were in group plans. By 2007, there were 4.532 million health savings accounts, with 1.1 million individual plans and 3.4 million in group plans. In January 2008, the number of these accounts had grown to 6.1 million, and 1.5 million individual plans and over 4.6 million group plans.

HSAs allow employees (as well as the self-employed) to set aside dollars to pay for future medical expenses. HSAs can be set up by employees of both small and large employers (unlike MSAs, which can be set up only by employees of small employers). However, only individuals who are covered by an HDHP can have HSAs, and individuals with HSAs may not have any coverage other than an HDHP, with the exception of "permitted coverage" (limited benefit e.g., dental or vision), "permitted insurance" or preventive care. Permitted insurance includes (i) insurance paying a fixed amount per day (or other period) of hospitalization; or (ii) insurance for a specified disease or illness. There are two other eligibility rules for HSAs: individuals must not be entitled to Medicare and must not be a tax-dependent of any other taxpayer. Employee contributions to HSAs are tax-deductible (or employer contributions are not included in income). Distributions from HSAs used to pay for qualified medical expenses for the employee and the employee's dependents are tax-free. Qualified medical expenses for HSAs include qualified long-term care services. Earnings in the HSA accrue tax-free. One of the major benefits of the HSA is that, like an MSA, and unlike an FSA, unused funds in the account may be rolled over from one year to the next and transferred from one employer to another. Although retirees cannot set up HSAs, they may use the funds previously contributed to pay for medical expenses, tax-free, after retirement.

There are legal and regulatory requirements to setting up HSAs. As noted above, the account holder must be covered by an HDHP that meets certain requirements. The limits imposed on the HDHP for 2009 are as follows:

	Individual Coverage	Family Coverage
Minimum Deductible	$1,150	$2,300
Out-of-pocket Limit	$5,800	$11,600

Health plans that apply no deductibles to preventative care will still qualify as HDHPs, as will plans that have annual deductibles and out-of-pocket limits that are higher than the aforementioned limits for out-of-network providers.

Similarly, an HSA has contribution limits. For 2009, an individual (or an employer on behalf of an individual) may contribute up to $3,000 for single coverage or $5,950 for family coverage. Individuals age 50 and above may also contribute an additional "catch-up" amount of $1,000 for 2009 and beyond.

Note: Prior to the passage of the Tax Relief and Health Care Act of 2006 (TRHCA) (signed into law on December 20, 2006, Pub. L. No. 109-432), the contribution was limited to the lesser of the HDHP's applicable deductible amount, or the annual limits. The TRHCA removed this limitation. These dollar limits apply to all contributions in one year, whether they are made by the employee, by the employer, or by a third party.

Amounts contributed by an employer to its employees' HSAs must be comparable for all similarly situated HSA-participating employees (see below for IRS guidance).

HSAs must be set up and maintained by a bank, insurance company, or other IRS-approved IRA or MSA trustee or custodian. The IRS has provided model HSA trust and custodial account forms. Trustees and custodians of HSA accounts must report contributions to and the fair market value of these accounts to the IRS annually.

Table 12-2 compares the features of HSAs, FSAs, and HRAs.

Table 12-2

Comparison of Plan Features: HSAs, HRAs, and FSAs

This table summarizes—from an employer's perspective—the key elements of HSAs and compares them to those of HRAs, which are funded through employer contributions, and health FSAs, which are funded through employee pretax contributions.

	Health Savings Accounts	Health Reimbursement Accounts	Health Flexible Spending Accounts
Carry over unused funds to future years	Yes	Yes, if desired	No
Employee tax savings[*]	Contributions are tax free	Claim reimbursements are tax free	Contributions are tax free
Employer tax savings[*]	Business expense deduction for contributions plus 7.65% of employee contribution	Business expense deduction for claims reimbursements	Business expense deduction for contributions plus 7.65% of employee contribution
Contributions subject to annual dollar limits	Yes	Employer decides how much to provide	Employer decides limits

Must have high-deductible coverage, no other health coverage	Yes	Employers often require high-deductible coverage, but it is not mandatory	No
Funds must be nonforfeitable, held in trust account	Yes	No	No
Account prefunded by employer (all amounts available during plan year)	No	No	Yes
Insurance premiums reimbursable tax free	Limited cases[**]	Yes	No[***]
Other medical expenses reimbursable tax free	Yes	Yes	Yes
Account is fully portable	Yes	No	No
Distributions permitted for non-medical reasons (but are taxable)	Yes	No	No
Plan Document required	No	Yes	Yes
Summary Plan Description (SPD) required	No	Yes	Yes
Annual IRS-DOL Form 5500	No	Yes, if over 100 participants	Yes, if over 100 participants
COBRA applies	No	Yes	Yes
HIPAA Certification rules apply	No	Yes	Generally, no
HIPAA privacy and security rules apply	Yes, if claims are substantiated	Yes	Yes

*Federal taxation; state taxation may differ.

**Can reimburse for COBRA and USERRA coverage, long-term care insurance, and premiums for coverage that is not Medicare supplemental insurance for account holders who are at least 65 years old or who are receiving unemployment compensation.

***Except that the 2007 proposed regulations specifically allow cafeteria plans to reimburse COBRA premiums for a medical plan sponsored by the same employer that sponsors the cafeteria plan.

Employees who elect coverage under a "general purpose" health FSA will not be eligible for the HDHP/ HSA option. This is because the health FSA is an impermissible "other coverage" under the HSA rules. However, a health FSA which only pays for limited purposes (e.g., dental and vision expenses) or which only covers expenses once the mandated HDHP deductible limit has been met ("post-deductible FSA"), will not violate the HSA "other coverage" rule. Employers may want to consider offering a health FSA with options (full coverage, limited-purpose, post-deductible coverage, or both limited-purpose and post-deductible) if they will also be offering an HDHP/HSA option to their employees.

If the employer elects to extend the 2-month grace period to its full coverage health FSA (as described in **Section 12.02[B][2]**), many employees who are participants under that health FSA will not be eligible for HSA coverage during the grace period. Under the TRHCA, participants with a $0 balance in their health FSAs at the end of the plan year (before the grace period begins) will have the grace period disregarded for the purposes of HSA eligibility. Alternatively, the health FSA may be converted into a limited-purpose or post-deductible health FSA during the grace period to allow employees to have coverage under the HDHP/ HSA during the grace period. If the employer wishes to do so, the plan document and SPD for the health FSA must indicate this and employees must receive communication that this change will be made. Note that the change in the type of health FSA during the grace period must be effective for all employees, not just those that are participating in the HDHP/HSA. Further information about how to effect this change can be found in IRS Notice 2005-86 (Nov. 22, 2005).

HSA Regulations and Guidance

In general, HSA accounts are exempt from ERISA, even though employers may establish and contribute to their employees' HSAs. On October 27, 2006, the DOL released Field Assistance Bulletin No. 1006-02 providing that the following employer actions will not result in coverage by ERISA: (i) establish HSAs for its employees without their consent (presumably to make contributions on their behalf); (ii) determine which providers may market their products to employees, even if such marketing is limited to a single HSA provider; (iii) pay the administration and management fees for the HSA account; and (iv) limit the number of providers to which it will forward contributions. The Field Assistance Bulletin also informs employers that they must remit employee HSAs contributions (e.g., payroll deductions) as soon as such funds can be reasonably segregated from the employer's general assets.

Contributions to HSAs are free from federal income tax, but each state determines whether contributions are free from state income tax. As of this writing, Alabama, California, New Jersey and Wisconsin have not conformed their laws regarding HSAs to federal laws, and therefore HSA contributions in these states will be subject to state income tax. New Hampshire and Tennessee do not tax the amounts contributed to HSAs, but do tax dividends and interest. Pennsylvania does not tax amounts that employers contribute, nor do they tax employees' contributions through a Section 125 plan, but will otherwise tax employees' contributions.

In August 2005, the IRS issued proposed regulations and on July 31, 2006 issued final regulations on the HIPAA comparability requirements for employer contributions to HSAs and the exception to these requirements for contributions made through a Section 125 (cafeteria) plan. [26 C.F.R. Part 54 [T.D. 9277] RIN 1545-BE30, 43056 (July 31, 2006)] The regulations define "comparable participating employees" as HSA-eligible individuals who are in the same category of employment and who have same type of HDHP coverage. The "same category of employment" refers to current full-time, current part-time or former employees. The "same type of HDHP coverage" refers to self-only, self plus one, self plus two, self plus three or more or family. These are the only acceptable categories for comparability testing. Employer contributions are comparable if they are either the same dollar amount or the same percentage of the HDHP deductible. Each category of comparable employees must receive comparable contributions. Contributions to the self plus two category must be equal to or more than contributions to the self plus one category, and contributions to the self plus three or more category must be equal to or more than contributions to the self plus two category. Employers do not need to make contributions to all categories of employees. The TRHCA amended these rules by allowing employers to make larger contributions (on either a dollar or percentage basis) to non-highly compensated individuals' HSAs than they make to HCEs' accounts. Employers may fund the contributions on either a pay-as-you-go, lookback or prefunded basis. Generally, the same funding method must be used for all comparable employees. If an employer fails to satisfy the comparability rules, it will have until April 15 of the following year to remedy the failure by making additional contributions, but it cannot take back contributions already made. Failure to correct the violation will result in the imposition of a 35 percent excise tax on all HSA contributions made by the employer for the calendar year.

The regulations allow for one exception: if the employer contributions are made through a cafeteria (Section 125) plan, the employer contributions will be subject to the Code Section 125 nondiscrimination rules rather than the comparability rules. In order to be eligible for this exception, the cafeteria/Section 125 plan must allow employees to make an election to either receive the employer HSAs contribution, a taxable benefit, a qualified benefit or receive taxable cash.

On April 17, 2008 the IRS published final regulations regarding the comparability of contributions for employees who were eligible to establish HSAs, but did not, and those who establish HSAs, but do not inform their employers. [26 C.F.R. Part 54 [T.D. 9393] RIN 1545-BF97, 20794 (April 17, 2008)] Under the final rules, in order to comply with HSA comparability requirements, employers must notify employees by January 15 of the availability of comparable contributions from the employer. The notice must indicate that if the employee establishes an HSA and notifies the employer of that establishment by the end of February, the employer will make the comparable contribution by April 15.

The final regulation provides a model notice for employers. This final regulation also allows employers to accelerate all or part of their contributions to employees who have incurred medical expenses that exceed the amount available in the HSA. Under the comparability requirement, however, an employer must accelerate contributions to all eligible employees on an equal and uniform basis, if it wants to accelerate contributions to one employee. The final rule is effective for calendar years on or after January 1, 2009, but employers may rely on the rule during the interim.

The THRCA made additional changes to HSAs including:

- Permits an employee who becomes covered by an HDHP in any month other than January to make the full annual contribution to his/her HSA. However, if the employee who became HSA-eligible after January becomes non-eligible at any time during the 13-month period beginning with the last month of the year in which he/she became eligible, the contributions attributable to the months preceding the month in which the individual became HSA-eligible will be includible in income and subject to an additional 10 percent tax.

- Provides for a one-time, tax-free transfer of the balance remaining in an FSA or HRA account as of September 21, 2006 (or, if less, the balance on the date of the transfer) to an HSA, but no later than

January 1, 2012. The amount transferred will not apply to the annual contribution limit, and the employee must remain HSA eligible for the 12 months following the date of the transfer.

- Allows an employer to make higher contributions to the HSAs of non-highly compensated employees than to highly compensated employees. Such contributions may be in the form of higher dollar amounts or higher percentages of deductibles. The employer must still satisfy the comparability rules for the contributions made to the non-highly compensated employees.

Following passage of the law, the IRS issued proposed regulations on the above changes. [73 Fed. Reg. 40793 (July 16, 2008)] Although compliance with the regulations will not be required until after publication of the final rule, employers may rely on them for contributions made on or after January 1, 2007. In addition, the IRS issued Notice 2007-22 (February 15, 2007) providing guidance on the rollover of balances in an FSA or HRA to an HSA. On June 4, 2008, the IRS published additional guidance implementing some of the changes noted above, as well as additional HSA-related topics in IRS Notice 2008-52. The final guidance published as of this writing is IRS Notice 2008-59 in the form of questions and answers. This guidance covers eligible individuals, high-deductible health plans, contribution limits, distribution methods, prohibited transactions, establishing HSA dates, and HSA administration.

Because HSAs are so new, this is a developing area of tax regulation. Employers interested in this option should obtain assistance from competent legal, accounting, and benefit advisors. Regulatory updates are available from the IRS and Treasury Web sites: *www.irs.gov* and *www.treas.gov*.

[E] Disease Management

Often, the most expensive medical conditions to treat are those that are chronic with occasional, but serious, acute episodes. Conditions such as asthma, diabetes, heart disease, and high blood pressure respond well to disease management programs. Costs are reduced due to fewer hospital admissions, reduced disability claims, and, ultimately, reduced insurance premiums.

Disease management takes a proactive approach to managing chronic illnesses to reduce costs over the long term. Utilizing best practices, multiple disciplines work with the patient to improve self-care and self-management with the goal of reducing acute episodes and, typically, the accompanying hospitalizations. Physicians, nurses, and pharmacists work together with the patient in a personalized disease management program. Disease management incorporates a range of resources to help the individual manage the illness, including education on the disease, self-help materials, diagnostic testing, regular physician services, nurse help-line, and consistent use of maintenance medication.

Disease management results in healthier, more productive employees. Disease management often significantly reduces employees' out-of-pocket costs, and can lead to lower health care costs in the long term for both the employee and the employer. Many employers provide financial incentives to employees with chronic conditions to encourage their participation in disease management programs; often, these incentives take the form of reduced premiums, as well as reduced copayments and coinsurance for the chronic condition.

As reported in *HR Focus*, April 2005, a study by the American Association of Health and Health Insurance Association of America indicates that disease management programs provide health care cost savings. Asthma management programs were shown to result in a savings of between $1.25 and $1.40 for every $1.00 spent, and diabetes programs returned $1.75 to $2.00 for every dollar invested. According to findings of the KFF/HRET Employer Health Benefits 2006 Annual Survey, 26 percent of all firms offer at least one disease management program. Notably, as the size of the firm grows, so does the percentage offering a disease management program:

Size of firm (Number of employees)	Percentage of firms that offer disease management
5,000 or more	75
1,000–4,999	63
200–999	50
25–199	32
3–24	23

Most commonly, disease management programs cover diabetes, heart disease/hypertension, and asthma/ respiratory disease. Other common conditions covered by disease management programs include cancer, depression, and low-back pain.

§ 12.05 DOMESTIC PARTNER BENEFITS

Domestic partner (DP) benefits are employee benefits provided to unmarried partners of the same sex or opposite sex. Such benefits may include coverage for medical, dental, and vision care and prescription drugs; life insurance for the domestic partner; and leave benefits such as bereavement leave.

In 1990, fewer than 25 U.S. employers offered DP benefits. According to the Human Rights Campaign Web site (*www.hrc.org*) as of August 1, 2007, more than 9,370 U.S. employers—and over 50 percent of Fortune 500 companies (267)—offer DP benefits. In general, larger companies are more likely to offer DP benefits. According to the Society for Human Resource Management (SHRM) 2008 Benefits Survey, 43 percent of respondents with over 500 employees offer DP benefits to same-sex partners, and 40 percent of large employers offer DP benefits to opposite-sex partners. However, only 28 percent of respondents with less than 100 employees offer DP benefits to same-sex partners, and 35 percent offer them to opposite-sex partners. The survey also found that employers in the services (not-for-profit) and finance sectors were more likely to offer DP benefits to both same-sex and opposite sex partners. As of January 1, 2008, 10 states (California, Connecticut, Hawaii, Maine, Massachusetts, New Hampshire, New Jersey, Oregon, Vermont, and Washington) and the District of Columbia provide legal recognition for same-sex partners and their dependents. Such laws will affect the provision of benefits to DPs.

The reasons most often given for the growing popularity of DP benefits include improved recruitment efforts, employers' commitments to equality and diversity, benefit competitiveness, and improved employee retention. Many employees feel that an employer that offers DP benefits is progressive and, even if they have no need for DP benefits, appreciate the forward thinking of their employer.

Shifting demographics have also played a role. According to 2000 U.S. census data, only 24 percent (down from 25 percent in 1998) of households nationwide include a married heterosexual couple with children, while the number of unmarried-partner households increased more than 35 percent from 1996 to 2000.

When DP benefits were first considered, it was difficult, if not impossible, to obtain insured health coverage for a domestic partner. Currently, medical benefits for DPs are generally available, although many employers offering such benefits do so through a self-insured plan. In addition to local insurance carriers, four national insurance companies have indicated that they are interested in offering DP coverage in all states.

There are a variety of issues to be considered when an employer is considering adding DP benefits. As with the addition of any benefit, the principal issue is: Does this benefit fit the company's benefits philosophy? Additional considerations include:

- Definition of domestic partner

- Regulatory and legal issues

- Costs of adding benefits

- Tax implications

[A]   Defining "Domestic Partner"

Before adding DP benefits, an employer must establish the definition of a domestic partner. Most employers will incorporate one or more of the following criteria:

- Both partners must be at least 18 years old.

- The partners must not be related by blood.

- The partners must be in a "committed" exclusive relationship.

- The partners must be financially interdependent.

The employer must further decide whether domestic partner means a partner of the opposite sex, the same sex, or both. Some employers may also require that the partners have a preexisting relationship of a specified period of time—for example, the partners must be in a committed relationship for one year before they are eligible for coverage.

After formulating a definition, the employer must determine what proof it will require to ensure that the employee's partner meets that definition. Proof could be anything from a signed statement by the employee to a financial document, such as a bank statement, attesting to the partner's financial interdependence. The employer must be careful to require documents solely for the purpose of proving the relationship so as not to give rise to claims of invasion of privacy. Finally, the employer must also determine what proof or notification is required in the event of the dissolution of a domestic partner relationship.

Some states and municipalities now provide for registration or certification of domestic partners (see **Section 12.05[C]**). Employers may wish to require that if domestic partner benefits are sought, the partners must register or certify with the local or state agency before such benefits are provided. Often these registries also provide for the dissolution of the partnership. In such an instance, employers may consider requiring the submission of dissolution certifications before dropping the domestic partner from coverage under the benefit. Employers may also consider whether such registrations or certifications will be accepted if they are from a governmental body outside of the employer or employee's location.

[B] Regulatory and Legal Issues

Effective May 17, 2004, Massachusetts became the first state to legalize same-sex marriages. This is a result of the Massachusetts Supreme Judicial Court's ruling that prohibitions against same-sex marriages violate the state's constitution. [Goodridge v. Department of Public Health, 440 Mass. 309 (2003)] The state legislature did not uphold an amendment to the state's constitution to overturn the Court's ruling. Until an amendment to the state's constitution is approved by the voters, same-sex marriages are legal in Massachusetts.

On May 15, 2008, the California Supreme Court ruled that same-sex couples have the same right to marry as opposite sex couples in California. They ruled that the state constitution requires that same-sex couples cannot be denied the legal benefits of marriage, and that the state's legal recognition of domestic partnerships does not satisfy the state constitution.

In New York, according to a recent decision by a New York appeals court, public and private employers must recognize same-sex marriages that have been lawfully created in other states or nations.

However, the federal Defense of Marriage Act will preclude couples in same-sex marriages from being treated as spouses under federal laws including ERISA and the IRC.

The city of San Francisco was one of three government entities in 1990 to offer DP benefits to its employees. It was the first to adopt an ordinance requiring that all contractors doing business with the city or county of San Francisco offer the same benefits to domestic partners of their employees as they offered to spouses of employees. The requirement affects the contractor's employees who are working in San Francisco or are working on the contract even if the location of the work is outside San Francisco. Many employers did not want to be told how to run their businesses, including what benefits would be offered to whom, and two of them filed suit. In *S.D. Myers, Inc. v. City & County of San Francisco* [253 F.3d 461, 466 (9th Cir. 2001)], the Ninth Circuit ruled in favor of San Francisco and upheld the ordinance. In this case, however, the court did not address whether ERISA preempted the local ordinance.

That issue may have been determined in *Air Transport Association of America v. City & County of San Francisco* [992 F. Supp. 1149, 1156-57 (N.D. Cal. 1998)]. The Ninth Circuit agreed with the district court that, because ERISA governs health benefits, those portions of the San Francisco ordinance that relate to ERISA plans must be stricken from the ordinance.

Although *Air Transport* may have wide impact, the *Myers* case still has significance. It is the first time a court has upheld the DP benefit regulations, and it encouraged other municipalities (such as New Orleans and Cleveland Heights) to offer DP benefits.

A more recent case addressed whether ERISA preempts government requirements for domestic partner benefits. New York City enacted the Equal Benefits Law in 2004 over the mayor's veto. The law required city agencies to contract only with organizations that provided benefits to domestic partners of employees equal to those provided to spouses of employees. The mayor refused to implement the law and sued the City Council, and the City Council commenced its proceedings to compel the mayor to implement the law. At issue was whether ERISA (and the City's General Municipal Law) preempted the Equal Benefits Law. On February 14, 2006, the Court of Appeals, agreeing with the lower court, ruled that the Equal Benefits Law, insofar as it applied to ERISA plans, was preempted by ERISA. The City Council's argument was that the City was not compelling any firm to offer domestic partner benefits, but was only acting as a "market participant" (a purchaser of goods and services) by choosing the organizations it would do business with based on the benefits those organizations provided to their employees. The court utilized the Supreme Court's definition of the "marketplace participant exception" in reaching its conclusion. The Supreme Court had previously clarified that the "marketplace participant exception" could only be used when the government has no interest in setting policy. The court in this case concluded that the Equal Benefits Law was, in fact, enacted to set policy, and therefore the exception did not apply and the law was preempted by ERISA. [Council of the City of N.Y. v. Bloomberg, 6 N.Y.3d 380, 846 N.E.2d 433, 813 N.Y.S.2d 3 (2006)]

On April 26, 2000, Vermont's domestic partnership bill was signed into law. The law establishes a system for couples to form state-recognized *civil unions*. A couple applies for a civil union license from a town clerk. The certificate of civil union entitles the couple to all the benefits of a legal marriage, and dissolution of the union would be handled by the family court system. It is still unknown how other states will respond to the civil unions of same-sex couples. More than half the states have passed "defense of marriage" laws that prohibit state recognition of same-sex marriages performed in other states. Vermont's law, however, specifically avoids the term *marriage*, reserving it for heterosexual couples. Hawaii and Oregon also allow civil unions.

Since then, Maine has passed a law that requires state health insurers and HMOs to offer coverage to DPs. Maine defines a DP as a mentally competent adult "legally domiciled" with the employee who is a health plan member for a minimum of one year. The DP must not be married to or legally separated from anyone else and must be the sole partner of the health plan member. Insurers and HMOs may require documentation that both the partner and the member meet these requirements. Eligible partners can obtain health coverage under the same terms and conditions as apply to spouses of married health plan members. The law became effective on January 1, 2002.

The Human Rights Campaign reports that, as of August 2007, 13 states, the District of Columbia and 145 local governments provide domestic partner benefits to their employees. Twelve states and the District of Columbia have laws that ban discrimination based on sexual orientation and gender identity. Twenty states and the District of Columbia have laws that ban discrimination based on sexual orientation. Twelve cities and the State of California have enacted laws that require government contractors to provide benefits to their employees' same-sex domestic partners. Human Resource staff should determine whether such laws cover their employees and benefit programs.

On June 6, 2007, the Tax Equity for Domestic Partner and Health Plan Beneficiaries Act (S. 1556) was introduced into the Senate. The bill would amend the Internal Revenue Code to extend the exclusion from gross income for employer-provided health care coverage to domestic partners and their dependent children. Previously, on March 29, 2007, a companion bill was introduced into the House (H.R. 1820). Both bills have been forwarded to their respective committees, but no other action has been taken as of this writing.

[C]   Employer Cost and Tax Considerations

Most employers find that actual enrollment in DP benefits is relatively low; estimates put the enrollment rate at 1 to 2 percent of employees. Generally, both partners in a relationship are working, whether they are in a same-sex or opposite-sex relationship, and therefore they do not need the benefits offered by their partner's employer. The cost of offering DP benefits is therefore also low, with the largest cost arising from the initial plan setup (including changing the employee handbook, printing benefits booklets, and communicating with employees). Claims costs rise in proportion to the number of additional participants.

Many employers begin a DP benefit program with relatively low-cost benefits, such as including DPs among those for whom an employee may take a paid bereavement leave. When DP health benefits are offered, the employee is often required to pay the entire premium cost of the partner's coverage.

Employers may deduct premiums paid for employees' health and welfare coverage for tax purposes. Although it is not likely that the deduction will be eliminated or reduced because employees can choose to cover DPs, it is recommended that employers consult with their legal or tax advisor on this issue. In general, the tax code allows deduction of premiums paid for health coverage if there is a business reason for offering the coverage. The business reasons for offering DP coverage should be sufficient justification for employers to offer this benefit and thus to maintain the deductibility of the premiums.

The implication for FSAs is not quite as simple. ERISA preempts state laws and is subject to the Defense of Marriage Act (DOMA), signed by President Clinton in 1996. DOMA states, "In determining the meaning of any Act of Congress, or of any ruling, regulation, or interpretation of the various administrative bureaus and agencies of the United States, the word 'marriage' means only a legal union between one man and one woman as husband and wife, and the word 'spouse' refers only to a person of the opposite sex who is a husband or wife." Therefore, domestic partners and same sex spouses are not "spouses" under ERISA and the Code. FSAs may not reimburse employees for medical care or dependent care expenses of their domestic partners or same-sex spouses. However, if the domestic partner or same sex spouse meets the definition of a tax-dependent under the Code (see **Section 12.05[D]**), the FSA may be able to or be required to provide reimbursement for their expenses. In these cases, it is recommended that competent legal and tax advisors be consulted.

For all non-ERISA plans, the plan documents should be revised to reflect the changes in benefits. In states where domestic partner benefits are required, ensure that the insurance and other plan documents reflect the state laws, as well as the company's desires, where there is flexibility in the implementation of those laws. The definitions of domestic partnership should be carefully described. It is recommended that terminology be developed to refer to employees who have successfully documented their status as part of a domestic partnership and to differentiate them from married employees.

[D] Employee Tax Considerations

Offering health coverage and other welfare benefits to the unmarried partners of employees, whether same-sex or opposite-sex, raises a number of tax issues for companies and their employees. Employees will generally be taxed on the fair market value of the benefit provided, less the amount paid by the employee for the coverage. There are two exceptions: (1) if the DP qualifies as a dependent and (2) for state income tax, if the partner is recognized under state law as the employee's spouse.

To qualify as a dependent, the following basic requirements of Code Section 152(a)(9) must be met:

- The employee must have provided more than half of the partner's support for the calendar year;

- The partner's place of residence must be the employee's home; and

- The partner must be a member of the employee's household.

A caveat in Code Section 152 (b)(5) states that an "individual is not a member of a taxpayer's household if at any time during the taxable year of the taxpayer the relationship between such individual and the taxpayer is in violation of local law." In most locations, this caveat would prohibit any DP from qualifying as a dependent of an employee. However, as discussed in the preceding section, many localities have passed laws or ordinances that have legalized same-sex relationships.

Unless the partner can qualify as the dependent of the employee, the value of the benefits provided on behalf of the partner will be included as taxable income, less the amount paid by the employee for the benefit. The benefits received under the plan will not be taxable to either the employee or the partner.

Similarly, unless the partner qualifies as a dependent, the employer will also be required to pay Federal Insurance Contributions Act (FICA) and Federal Unemployment Tax Act (FUTA) taxes on the amount taxed to the employee for income tax purposes. Both the employer and the employee will be assessed FICA taxes, and if applicable, the company will pay FUTA taxes. Generally, because the FUTA tax base is low ($7,000 in 2009) the employer will not owe any FUTA tax beyond what would already be due on wages. FICA taxes, however, are distributed between Old-Age, Survivors, and Disability Insurance (OASDI), which funds Social Security, and Hospital Insurance (HI), which funds Medicare. OASDI is taxed only up to a maximum, whereas the HI tax is applied on all income. Employers will have to pay OASDI tax (e.g., 6.2 percent for 2009) on the imputed income for the coverage of the DP only if the employee's wages are less than the statutory limit (e.g., $106,800 for 2009). The HI tax (1.45 percent for 2009) is due on all income received by or imputed to the employee.

States laws that recognize same-sex relationships may also provide for state-income-tax-free DP benefits. At least four of these states, California, Connecticut, Massachusetts, and Vermont, provide that no state income taxes will apply to DP benefits.

§ 12.06   RETIREE HEALTH FUNDING AND PLAN DESIGN

While still in the minority, the number of organizations continuing health benefits for retirees, both under and over age 65, was increasing until the late 1980s, at which point the growth rate slowed because of the passage of less favorable tax legislation. Also, organizations are more concerned about the huge unfunded liabilities that retiree health benefits now represent. Other postretirement welfare benefits, such as life insurance, also present significant, but less difficult, problems. The Financial Accounting Standards Board (FASB) has highlighted the retiree health benefits issues with its accounting standard, adopted in December 1990: Statement of Financial Accounting Standards No. 106 (FAS 106), Employer's Accounting for Postretirement Benefits Other Than Pensions.

Affected employers generally must have complied with FAS 106 for fiscal years beginning after December 15, 1992. For small nonpublic employers, the effective date was fiscal years beginning after December 15, 1994. A small employer is an employer that has no more than 500 participants earning retiree benefits under all plans.

Generally, the FASB has forced employers to recognize the cost of retiree health benefits much earlier on their financial statements by requiring accrual instead of cash (pay-as-you-go) accounting. As a result, many employers now recognize considerably more in current annual expenses. Because tax incentives for funding retiree health benefits are limited, employers accrue large liabilities on their balance sheets.

The accounting and funding issues are only part of the problem. An employer's attempt to reduce retiree health costs by redesigning the plan would very likely lead to employee relations problems. Furthermore, plan design changes could result in lawsuits if the employer has not reserved the right to amend the plans and communicated this right to its employees. Such lawsuits may take the approach used in *Erie County Retirees Association v. County of Erie, Pennsylvania* [220 F.3d 193 (3d Cir. 2000), *cert. denied*, 532 U.S. 913 (2001)]. In this case (generally referred to as the *Erie County* case), the Third Circuit Court of Appeals ruled that it was discriminatory under the Age Discrimination in Employment Act (ADEA) to provide Medicare-eligible retirees with benefits different from those provided to retirees who are ineligible for Medicare because they have not yet attained retirement age. The court further ruled that the employer either had to provide equal benefits to all retirees or spend the same amount of money on each plan.

The Equal Employment Opportunity Commission (EEOC) subsequently incorporated the *Erie County* decision into its compliance manual and applied it in reviews of employer-sponsored health plans. Many employer, employee, industry, and labor groups opposed the EEOC's position, fearing that it would jeopardize retiree health plans that are currently in place and would alter, reduce, or eliminate the level of employer-sponsored retiree health benefits when retirees attain age 65 and become eligible for Medicare. In response to these concerns, the EEOC rescinded its policy and removed from its compliance manual the provision derived from *Erie County*. In its rescission, the EEOC stated, "[T]hough it is clear that 'Medicare carve-out' plans that simply deduct from the benefits provided to Medicare eligible retirees those benefits that Medicare provides do not violate the ADEA, additional review is needed to assess other types of retiree health plan practices."[EEOC Directives Transmittal, No. 915.003, Aug. 20, 2001]

The EEOC published a proposed regulation in July 2003 on the coordination of retiree health benefits with Medicare. This proposed regulation would

- Provide a narrow exemption from all prohibitions of the ADEA for coordination of employer-provided retiree health coverage with eligibility for Medicare or a state-sponsored retiree health benefits program;

- Make it lawful for employers and plan sponsors to provide retired participants with altered or reduced health benefits, or eliminate health benefits, when such participants become eligible for Medicare or for health benefits under a state-sponsored retiree health benefits program; and

- Allow employers to offer the Medicare carve-out plans referred to in the EEOC's rescission in 2001.

As proposed, the exemption applies only to retiree coverage; no such reduction in benefits is allowed under the ADEA for employees.

In April 2004, the EEOC approved a proposed final rule essentially similar to the July 2003 proposed regulation. The proposed final rule must be reviewed by several federal agencies and the Office of Management and Budget (OMB), and published in the *Federal Register* before it will become final. The United States Senate Special Committee on Aging held hearings on this subject in May 2004, and the final rule was originally scheduled to be published in the summer of 2004.

On February 4, 2005, the American Association of Retired Persons (AARP) filed a lawsuit requesting an injunction against the proposed final rule. On March 30, 2005, the Federal District Court for the Eastern District of Pennsylvania found in favor of AARP and issued a permanent injunction against the EEOC from publishing the rule. On June 30, 2005, the EEOC filed an appeal and motion for relief from the March 30, 2005 judgment [AARP v. EEOC 2:05-cv-00509-AB]. While the appeal in this case was being considered, the Supreme Court ruled in a different case that a government agency is not bound by a court's interpretation of a statute, unless the court determined that its interpretation was the only permissible meaning of the statute [National Cable and Telecommunications Association v. Brand X Internet Services, 125 S. Ct. 2688 (2005)]. Going even further, Justice Clarence Thomas stated that judges in most cases should defer to the expertise of federal agencies. Based on this ruling, the judge in *AARP v. EEOC* determined that she was not bound by the *Erie County* ruling, and reversed her March 30, 2005 decision. Although she vacated the permanent injunction against the EEOC's publication of the final rules, she maintained a temporary injunction until the appeals court can rule.

On June 4, 2007, the Third Circuit Court filed its ruling on this case [AARP v. EEOC, 2007 U.S. App. LEXIS 12869 (3d Cir. 2007)]. The court ruled in favor of the EEOC, vacating the March 30, 2005 injunction against the EEOC and lifting the temporary injunction of the implementation of the proposed regulation. The Court believed that the EEOC acted within the authority of Section 9 of the ADEA, which allows the EEOC to establish reasonable exclusions from the ADEA, if those exclusions are "necessary and proper in the public interest." The EEOC is now cleared to issue final regulations on this issue, and employers can feel reasonably secure in coordinating their retiree benefits with Medicare.

Following the court's ruling, the EEOC issued its final regulation allowing for the coordination of retiree health benefits with Medicare (or comparable state health program). This final regulation, issued on December 26, 2007, and effective immediately, emphasizes that it is to be narrowly construed. It applies only to: (i) retirees over the age of 65 (and their spouses and dependents) and not current employees even if they are Medicare-eligible; (ii) health benefits, not life insurance or disability coverage; and (iii) coordination with Medicare and comparable state plans, but not any other type of governmental program (e.g., Medicaid).

Coordination with Medicare benefits is not the only retiree health benefit issue under the ADEA. Some employers provide better benefits to older retirees than to younger ones. Originally, the EEOC believed that this was a form of discrimination prohibited by the ADEA. However, based on the Supreme Court's ruling in *General Dynamics Land System, Inc. v. Cline* [540 U.S. 581 (2004)], the EEOC published a final rule allowing employers to provide better benefits to relatively older workers (for example, providing retirees over the age of 60 with retiree health benefits, but none to those under 60).

[A] Funding Techniques

Funding will reduce an employer's balance sheet liabilities and provide increased benefit security for retirees. Unfortunately, Congress at this point has not provided enough options to encourage most employers to fund retiree health benefits. Three basic options are currently available:

1. *Voluntary Employee Beneficiary Associations (VEBAs).* Authorized under IRC Section 501(c)(9), such associations may be used to provide tax-deductible current funding for postemployment health coverage. However, the amount of funding allowable is fairly limited, unless the VEBA has been established through collective bargaining. The funding is based on actuarial assumptions that recognize the expected return on plan assets, the projected number of employees who will be eligible for benefits, and the cost of benefits. The major shortfall is that the assumption about the cost of benefits does not include any adjustment for inflation or technological advances. Since these are responsible for a significant amount of the projected future benefit cost, funding through a VEBA simply will not meet the need.

2. *401(h) Accounts.* Code Section 401(h) allows qualified pension plans to place funds specifically used for providing postemployment medical care in a separate account. However, funding of this account is limited to 25 percent of the amount contributed to the pension plan. Thus, for most employers, the amount of assets that can be set aside under a 401(h) account is also severely limited.

Some employers are presented with defined benefit plans that are overfunded (i.e., they have more assets than benefit obligations). Because it is difficult to recover this excess, many employers consider using the assets to fund 401(h) accounts. Employers should use caution in making this decision, as it is fraught with the following hazards:

a. Asset transfers can be used only to pay retiree health benefits for the year of transfer.

b. All plan participants must be vested in the accrued pension benefits associated with the excess transferred.

c. Per capita health expenses may not be decreased for five years after the transfer.

3. *Offset Plans.* An offset plan is an indirect method of funding retiree health benefits. The employer establishes another qualified retirement plan, which may be a money purchase pension plan, an employee stock ownership plan (ESOP), a profit-sharing plan, an incremental matching contribution to a 401(k) plan, or some other plan. The amounts accumulated under these arrangements serve to reduce the employer's obligation for providing postemployment health benefits. In other words, health care costs are first paid out of withdrawals from the offset plans. The employer's obligation extends only to costs incurred in excess of the benefits accumulated under the offset arrangements.

Employees find offset arrangements less attractive because any withdrawals are currently taxable. However, even if employees do not incur any medical expenses, they still realize a benefit. Employers are aware of this. In some cases, offset arrangements cease to be offset plans: the employer simply funds an additional retirement plan arrangement and terminates all other obligations for postemployment benefits.

[B] Plan Design

When confronted with the financial implications of providing retiree health benefits, many employers have resorted to traditional cost shifting, including:

- Increasing retiree employee contributions, deductibles, coinsurance, and out-of-pocket maximums

- Indexing these cost sharing provisions with inflation

- Decreasing lifetime maximums

- Coordinating with Medicare through a carve-out approach

In December 2006, the Kaiser Family Foundation and Hewitt Associates released the 2006 Survey on Retiree Health Benefits. The survey reports on responses from over 300 large private sector firms (those with 1,000 or more employees) that provide retiree health benefits. The survey found that as the cost of providing retiree medical benefits increased, retiree's share of those costs also increased. Seventy-four percent of employers participating in the survey reported that they had increased their retirees' contributions for premiums in 2006; 34 percent increased the retirees' cost sharing requirements in 2006 (e.g., deductibles and copayments). Prescription drug copayments or coinsurance amounts were increased by 32 percent of participants. Twenty-five percent of participants raised the maximum out-of-pocket amount in 2006.

Some employers are changing their eligibility rules. Simply retiring under a retirement plan is no longer enough to receive full postretirement health coverage (except as required by law by certain public employers). Eligibility is now a function of independent age and service requirements, and early retiree coverage can be different from normal retiree coverage. Service-based contribution schedules are being used to charge short-service retirees more for than long-service retirees for their coverage.

Some employers are making employees pay the entire cost of their retiree health plans. At the same time, they are contributing amounts that previously went to retiree health plans to existing or new qualified defined contribution plans, including ESOPs. Retirees can then use their defined contribution accounts to pay for retiree health coverage. The longer an employee works, the larger the employee's account balance. One disadvantage to this approach is that retiree health plan contributions are made with after-tax dollars.

Under the defined dollar approach, an employer promises to pay not more than a specified amount toward the annual cost of a retiree's health coverage. As with defined contribution plans, the defined dollar approach eliminates an employer's commitment to pay for future inflated medical costs. The employer need not fund its defined dollar obligation with current contributions. An employer can also vary its defined dollar commitment on the basis of a retiree's length of service.

The defined dollar approach provides greater tax benefits to retirees than the defined contribution plan approach because health plan contributions are not taxable to retirees. The defined dollar approach also is more efficient because benefits are used only to meet retiree health needs. It also is more flexible; for example, if the employer wants to provide more assistance to retirees with dependents, it can easily increase the defined dollar amount for those retirees only. Unlike the defined contribution plan approach, however, the defined dollar approach does not prevent large liabilities from accruing on the employer's balance sheet under FAS 106.

More and more employers are using managed care for active and retired employees. Some employers are also exploring managed health care designed specifically for retirees.

§ 12.07   EVALUATING THE BENEFITS PACKAGE

A company's benefits package is not developed or introduced to employees in a vacuum. Its design and purpose are components of business and HR objectives within a total compensation framework (i.e., in coordination with cash, paid time off (PTO), and long-term incentive programs).

Because the benefits package itself is a significant portion of the total compensation program, it is important to routinely monitor and evaluate the package, in comparison with benefits objectives and benchmarks.

Employee opinions regarding the benefits package may be one measure of its effectiveness. Another important component is the quality of care provided (i.e., made accessible) to participants in the plans.

[A] Monitoring Quality

The Health Plan Employer Data and Information Set (HEDIS) has been gathered and analyzed over time by the National Committee for Quality Assurance, based in Washington, D.C. The committee's focus has been on evaluation of HMOs, but it began reviewing PPOs in 1999. HEDIS, through voluntary collection of health plan data, proposes to measure how well managed care networks adhere to procedural standards of excellence and whether they are achieving good patient outcomes.

Independent consulting firms are in the market to prepare variations on the HEDIS quality data and are adding their own unique measurements to their databases. Some of this supplemental data includes:

- 24-hour availability (measures) of primary care physicians in addition to the geographic accessibility measures typically provided by networks

- Turnover and time on the job information for clinical and nonclinical (management) staff

- Claims processing/turnaround time as one measure of employee/customer service

Most benefits experts agree that data analysis for meaningful management and evaluation purposes is in its infancy, although having some measures seems better than having none. One recurring issue continues to make data analysis challenging: Employers and employees value (and want to see) different information.

It is critical when using such quality measurements to be aware of potential pitfalls in data design and analysis. Probably more important, particularly to small employers, is the ability to obtain benefit utilization data for the company plan that is meaningful in supporting the plan management and design decisions.

[B] Considering New Plans and Carve-Outs

When evaluating a benefits package in terms of its impact on the total compensation program offered to employees, individual plans may be added to the package. Based on a clear, long-range benefits plan, these considerations can be made rather easily in terms of their "fit" with the company's organizational and HR goals.

Benefits plans that are increasing in employer use (and in employee value) include:

- Stock purchase plans

- Stock options

- Long-term care insurance

- Legal insurance

- Financial planning benefits

- Adoption assistance benefits

Many of these benefits programs have been described in other chapters of this book. Carving out coverage features of existing group health benefits plans is also a consideration in evaluating a benefits package.

Over time, the market has developed specialists to handle employee health concerns. Carving out prescription coverage has been popular for several years (see **Chapter 10**), and "centers of excellence" programs for organ transplants are a part of many employer plans.

Coverage features such as mental health treatment, severe burn and trauma care, neonatal (and prenatal) care, and specialized cardiology or oncology care can now be carved out of a health plan in some markets. Providers of critical disease carve-out benefits often offer employers significant cost reductions along with higher quality of medical care and customer/patient care.

The potential drawback—the inability to obtain aggregate claims risk protection (because a health plan is no longer comprehensive in and of itself)—bears consideration, however. It is important to clearly define the plan objectives and to then work closely with benefits experts and potential carriers/providers in the market to understand available options and the impact of these decisions on costs, employee relations, and long-term business and HR goals.

The area of mental health coverage has a lengthy market history, including specialized providers who focus solely on the many aspects of this area of health care. Because the quality of this coverage is critical to those individuals who need it, and because it is different in many respects from physical health and illness, carving out of mental health coverage probably bears consideration. The Mental Health Parity Act of 1996, which prohibits annual or lifetime dollar limitations on mental health treatment unless the same dollar limits also apply to medical and surgical benefits under the employer's health plan, may also be a trigger for carving out mental health benefits from the group health plan.

In evaluating carving out any coverage feature of the health plan, including mental health coverage, the following questions are significant:

- How effective is the current plan design?

- What alternatives are available in the market?

- What cost containment or control mechanisms are appropriate?

- Are there creative methods for providing coverage and maintaining flexibility in plan design?

- What impact will a new design have on overall plan costs and value to employees?

§ 12.08 COMMUNICATING THE BENEFITS PACKAGE

Many employers have developed comprehensive statements to communicate the value of the benefits package to employees. These statements often begin with an individual's base pay and then provide some level of detail regarding the additional monetary value of both mandatory (e.g., payroll taxes) and discretionary (e.g., group health, qualified plan contributions) benefits provided to employees, paid by the company. When these statements are well planned and designed—and, particularly, when they reflect a more-than-competitive package—employees appreciate their usefulness, as well as the information they convey.

In today's electronic, global environment where more and more employees are not bound to any single location, communication methods must keep pace. Print media and face-to-face meetings with employees (permitting them to address unique, individual issues) will always be critical, but interim electronic communication is important as well.

Providers are entering the benefit communication market in a variety of ways with a variety of products and services, and large employers are implementing creative communication techniques within their intranet environments.

Regardless of the communication techniques (e.g., paper forms, employee meetings, telephone attendant systems, kiosks from which employees can obtain information, software programs that permit employees to run "what if" retirement planning scenarios, online enrollment and change), the overriding consideration is to provide employees complete, accurate information without overburdening them with confusing details.

Chapter 13
The Americans with Disabilities Act

§ 13.01 AUDIT QUESTIONS

1. Do all job descriptions include stated job qualifications (education, skills, experience, etc.), and is each qualification job-related and consistent with business necessity?

2. If medical examinations, including testing for drugs, are required before employment, are they required only after the job offer and are they job-related and consistent with business necessity?

3. Are supervisors informed about an employee's disability if the disability might require emergency treatment while at work?

4. Is the reasonable accommodation process conducted as an interactive discussion between the employee with a disability and the employer?

5. Are employee benefits offered to all employees without regard to disability status?

Note: Consistent ''yes'' answers to the above questions suggest that the organization is applying effective management practices and/or complying with federal regulations. ''No'' answers indicate that problem areas exist and should be addressed immediately.

When Congress enacted the Americans with Disabilities Act (ADA) in 1990, it estimated that more than 43 million Americans had one or more physical or mental disabilities, and that this number would increase as the population aged. The ADA was initiated to protect people with physical and mental disabilities from discrimination in employment, public services, public accommodations, private services, and telecommunications. ADA sponsors promoted it because, historically, society has segregated people with disabilities, and the sponsors viewed this as a serious and pervasive social problem.

The ADA's underlying purpose is to send a message to businesses across the country that Americans with disabilities are being overlooked both as employees and as customers, and American industry needs to correct this situation. Generally, sponsors and proponents of this legislation hope that by increasing exposure to people with disabilities in the workplace, worker and management attitudes can be changed. Over 253,000 complaints have been filed under the ADA with the Equal Employment Opportunity Commission (EEOC) between 1992 and September 30, 2007.

This chapter outlines ADA requirements and provides some assistance with compliance. It does not address state and local disability discrimination laws, which, when applicable, also require employer compliance.

§ 13.02   MAJOR PARTS OF THE LAW

The ADA is patterned after the Rehabilitation Act of 1973 and contains five major sections: Title I, Employment; Title II, Public Services; Title III, Public Accommodations Operated by Private Entities; Title IV, Telecommunications; and Title V, Miscellaneous Provisions.

The following overviews of each title in the ADA will provide a better understanding of the scope of the statute.

[A]   Title I: Employment

Title I deals with the hiring, treatment, and accommodation of applicants and employees with disabilities. (See **Appendix 13-A.**)

[1]   General Purpose

This title provides protection against discrimination for people with disabilities in employment-related matters, such as job-application procedures, hiring, advancement, discharge, compensation, training, and other terms, conditions, and privileges of employment (including benefits).

[2]   Effective Dates

The ADA became effective July 26, 1992, for employers with 25 or more employees, and July 26, 1994, for employers with 15 or more employees. An EEOC representative estimated the second provision extended ADA requirements to an additional 400,000 employers.

[3]   Covered Entities

Covered are private employers, employment agencies, labor organizations, joint labor management committees, and state and local governments.

[4] Protected Individuals

Protection extends to qualified people with a physical or mental impairment that substantially limits one or more major life activities and to those with a record of such impairment, who are regarded as having such impairment, and who are able to perform the essential functions of a job with or without reasonable accommodation. Section 1630.8 of the ADA was amended to clarify that harassment or any other form of discrimination against a qualified individual because of the known disability of a person with whom the individual has a relationship or an association is also a prohibited form of discrimination.

[5] Hidden Disabilities

Handling hidden disabilities under the ADA has proved particularly difficult. To address some of these unique challenges, specifically focusing on issues of "impairment" and "disability," the EEOC issued Notice 915.002 (Mar. 25, 1997), "EEOC Enforcement Guidance on the Americans with Disabilities Act and Psychiatric Disabilities," which presents the EEOC's position on Title I application to individuals with psychiatric disabilities.

The guidance offers sample questions and answers for a variety of situations: definition of impairments and disabilities, when or how employers can ask about a psychiatric disability, and how employers might treat an individual with a psychiatric disability for disciplinary purposes. None of this is entirely new information, however. It should sound familiar, in light of an employer's routine employment policies and practices for all qualified individuals, including those with disabilities.

According to the guidance, the first question in evaluating whether an individual is substantially limited and potentially disabled is whether an individual is substantially limited in a major life activity other than working (e.g., sleeping, concentrating, or caring for self). Working should be analyzed only if no other major life activity is substantially limited by an impairment. The guidance reinforces the fact that evaluation of substantial limitation must be done without regard to medications and other issues. That is, if an individual has an ADA disability that is substantially limiting if left untreated, that individual remains disabled under the ADA when he or she is receiving treatment.

The following cases are representative of other situations involving "hidden disabilities":

- *Kotlowski v. Eastman Kodak Co.* [922 F. Supp. 790 (W.D.N.Y. 1996)]. A federal judge in Rochester, New York, ruled that a person taking an antidepressant medication that might cause grogginess in the mornings does not have a disability that substantially limits the ability to work, within the meaning of the ADA. The judge concluded that, although the individual might have been diagnosed and treated for depression for several years, her ability to work was not impaired, and she was not disabled. He also found that, even if the plaintiff were disabled, she was not otherwise qualified for her job with the company, in light of her attendance and tardiness problems. The ADA does not require an employer to accommodate an employee who cannot get to work, the court found. The judge further stated: "Kotlowski's inability to get to work on time, if at all, made her unqualified to perform the functions of her job."

- *Soileau v. Guilford of Maine* [105 F.3d 12 (1st Cir. 1997)]. The First Circuit found that the ability to get along with others does not generally constitute a "major life activity" under the ADA. Although the "ability to get along with others" might be considered a major life activity in some circumstances, the employee did not show that he had difficulty in interacting with anyone other than his supervisor, the court reasoned, and therefore he was not substantially impaired in a major life activity. In that finding, the court concluded that "the ability to get along with others . . . is remarkably elastic and is often a matter of subjective judgment and to impose legally enforceable duties on an employer based on such a concept would be problematic."

(For assistance with accommodating psychiatric disabilities, review the Job Accommodation Network's pamphlet, "Accommodation and Compliance Series: Employees with Psychiatric Impairments," which can be found at *www.jan.wvu.edu/media/Psychiatric.html.*)

Three Supreme Court cases have held that the analysis of whether an individual is disabled under the ADA should include consideration of measures that mitigate the impairment, such as medication or eyeglasses. These decisions reinforce not broadening the original ADA's mandate reference to 43 million Americans with physical or mental disabilities to include those with correctable conditions—in these cases, those who can function normally when they wear their glasses or take their medicine. These decisions may cause a new wave of litigation but are generally viewed as favorable to employers for the time being.

[6] ADA Amendments Act of 2008

On September 25, 2008, President Bush signed into law the ADA Amendments Act of 2008 (ADAAA). This legislation, intended to "reinstate a broad scope of protection to be available under the ADA," includes a number of significant changes to the ADA, and expressly overturns several key Supreme Court decisions.

In the most significant changes, the ADAAA: (1) broadens the definition of "Disability," including impairments that are "episodic or in remission"; (2) expands the definition of "Major Life Activity" to include a non-exhaustive list of activities such as "performing manual tasks, seeing, hearing, eating, sleeping, walking, standing, lifting, bending. . ."; (3) charges the courts not to consider mitigating measures in determining whether an individual is disabled, and includes a non-exhaustive list of measures such as medication, medical supplies, equipment or appliances, hearing aids and cochlear devices (the Act specifically excludes from these measures regular eye glasses and contacts); and (4) clarifies the definition of "regarded as disabled" in include someone who can establish that he or she has been discriminated against because of an actual or perceived physical or mental impairment; however, an individual so "regarded" is not entitled to "reasonable accommodation."

[7] Enforcement and Remedies

The EEOC is the primary enforcing agency. Remedies available to people with disabilities that have been discriminated against include compensatory and punitive damages, back pay, front pay, restored benefits, attorneys' fees, reasonable accommodation, reinstatement, and job offers. (See **Appendix 13-D**.) In an early 2004 case, the Seventh Circuit Court of Appeals ruled that the ADA does not allow plaintiffs to seek compensatory and punitive damages in retaliation discharge cases. [Kramer v. Banc of Am. Sec. LLC, 355 F.3d 961 (N.D. Ill.), *aff'd,* 2004 U.S. App. LEXIS 760 (7th Cir. Jan. 20, 2004), *cert. denied,* 124 S. Ct. 2876 (2004)]

[B] Title II: Public Services

Title II provides that services available to the general public, especially public transportation, must also be made available to and usable by people with disabilities.

[1] General Purpose

Public services must be provided to qualified individuals with disabilities with or without reasonable modifications to rules, policies, or practices of the entity. Such services include public bus systems, public rail systems, paratransit, and other transportation services.

[2] Effective Date

For all activities of state and local governments, the effective date was January 26, 1992. Physical modifications to various transportation systems have varying deadlines.

[3] Covered Entities

Covered entities include public entities such as state and local governments and any department, agency, special-purpose district, or other entity of a state or local government.

[4] Enforcement and Remedies

The U.S. Attorney General is responsible for issuing regulations to implement this title. Remedies available to people who have been discriminated against under Title II follow the procedures and rights set forth in Section 505 of the Rehabilitation Act of 1973 and include reasonable accommodation and limited compensatory and punitive damages.

[C] Title III: Public Accommodations and Services Operated by Private Entities

Title III covers public accommodations that are privately owned or operated (e.g., banks and movie theaters).

[1] General Purpose

The title's intent is to provide full and equal enjoyment of the goods, services, facilities, privileges, advantages, or accommodations of any place of public accommodation to people with disabilities.

[2] Effective Dates

Services must have been made accessible to people with disabilities by January 26, 1992, for businesses with 26 or more employees, by July 26, 1992, for businesses with between 11 and 25 employees, and by January 26, 1993, for businesses with 10 or fewer employees. Alterations to existing facilities that began after January 26, 1992, must be made in accordance with specific technical requirements. New buildings designed and constructed for first occupancy after January 26, 1993, must be made fully accessible and usable in accordance with specific technical requirements.

[3] Covered Entities

Title III covers all private entities that affect commerce, including places of lodging, establishments serving food or drink, places of exhibition or entertainment, places of public gathering, sales or rental establishments, service establishments, stations used for public transportation, places of public display, places of recreation, places of education, social service centers, and places of exercise.

[4] Enforcement and Remedies

The U.S. Attorney General is the enforcing entity for Title III. Remedies available to people who have been discriminated against under this title follow the procedures and rights set forth in Section 204(a) of the Civil Rights Act of 1964 and include reasonable accommodation and limited compensatory and punitive damages.

(See **Exhibit 13.1** for an outline of the ADA accessibility guidelines.)

[D] Title IV: Telecommunications

Title IV of the ADA covers various aspects of telecommunications.

[1] General Purpose

Title IV provides telephone relay services to people using telecommunication devices for the deaf (TDDs) or similar devices.

[2] Effective Dates

As of July 26, 1993, telecommunication relay services must operate 24 hours a day.

[3] Covered Entities

Included are any common carrier engaged in interstate communication, intrastate communication, or both, by wire or radio.

[4] Enforcement and Remedies

The Federal Communications Commission (FCC) is the enforcing agency. Remedies for violations of this title are the same as remedies, penalties, and procedures that apply to other FCC regulation violations.''

[E] Title V: Miscellaneous Provisions

The general purposes of Title V are (1) to provide regulations regarding the ADA's relationship to other laws and implementation responsibilities for each title, (2) to explain insurance issues, (3) to prohibit state immunity, including that for Congress, and (4) to set parameters for regulations to be issued by the Architectural and Transportation Barriers Compliance Board.

§ 13.03 THE ONGOING RESPONSIBILITIES OF COMPLIANCE

Since the implementation of the ADA, employers often ask what specific actions they should take to comply with the many ADA employment and facility requirements. The congressional sponsors, however, never intended the legislation to provide a precise answer to how much is enough of a compliance effort. Nor, for that matter, did they feel that Washington could provide one answer that would work for every employer.

Questions and charges that have been raised with various enforcement agencies indicate that Title I employment issues remain employers' primary compliance concerns. Title I requirements encompass recruiting, testing, and selecting candidates for employment. They also affect an employer's ongoing relationship with its employees and the administration of many employee benefits programs.

In response to some of these concerns and in an attempt to clarify some requirements, the EEOC issued specific guidance regarding the ADA and employer-sponsored health benefits plans, preemployment inquiries, and medical examinations. The following sections discuss each of these employment-related compliance areas. In addition, **Appendix 13-A** outlines the steps to ensure success in implementing an effective ADA program, and **Appendix 13-B** serves as a checklist for addressing general compliance issues. **Appendix 13-C** summarizes ADA Do's and Don'ts.

§ 13.04 PREEMPLOYMENT RESPONSIBILITIES

[A] Job Description Development: Establishing Job Qualification Standards

The ADA allows employers discretion in establishing necessary job qualifications (education, skills, experience, physical and mental abilities, health and safety requirements, interpersonal skills, and so on). Stated qualifications must be job-related and consistent with business necessity, and they must apply consistently to all applicants for a given job at the company.

Even if a qualification or selection standard at an organization is job-related and consistent with business necessity, it cannot be used to exclude someone with a disability if that person could satisfy the criterion with a reasonable accommodation. An employer need not consider accommodation in establishing the standard. Accommodation comes into play only when an otherwise qualified person with a disability requests it.

For example, a company might find it necessary and job-related for a secretary to be able to produce letters and other documents on a word processor. But it would be discriminatory to reject a person whose disability prevented manual keyboard operation but who could meet the qualification standard by using a computer assistive device. Thus, providing this device would be a reasonable accommodation.

Any discussion about hiring practices under the ADA requires the employer to identify essential job functions. In practice, essential functions address the distinction between what the individual must do and how he or she accomplishes it.

The ADA outlines three factors to consider in determining whether a job function is essential (rather than marginal) to a job. The function is essential if:

1. The reason the position exists is to perform that function.

2. There are a limited number of employees available within the company among whom the performance of that function may be distributed.

3. The function is so highly specialized that the incumbent is hired for his or her expertise or ability to perform that particular function.

Evidence of whether a particular function is essential may include, but is not limited to, the following:

1. The employer's judgment

2. Written job descriptions prepared before advertising or interviewing applicants for the job at the company

3. The amount of time spent performing the function

4. The consequences of not requiring the person to perform the function

5. The terms of a collective bargaining agreement

6. The work experiences of people who are performing or who have performed similar jobs at the company

This list is not exhaustive; other types of available evidence may also be relevant to the determination of essential job functions. Recent claims point to the need for the employer to identify both physical and psychological elements. The important task is to define all functions of each job in the company that are essential before advertising or interviewing candidates for the job.

Marginal functions are those that could be delegated to someone else or are peripheral to the job (e.g., taking the mail to the post office may be marginal if assigned to the receptionist).

[B]   Recruitment of New Employees

Job announcements, advertisements, and other recruitment notices employers use should include information about essential job functions as well as qualification standards to attract qualified applicants, including people with disabilities. Job information should be accessible to people with disabilities. Written information should be made available in alternative, accessible formats on request. Such alternative formats include the following:

- A TTD number

- Large print for written job information

- Audiotapes that detail job information

Employment agencies are also required to comply with the ADA. If an employer uses the services of employment agencies to recruit, screen, and refer potential employees, it must be certain that the agency complies with ADA employment requirements. Otherwise, both the employer and the agency, as its agent, may be held liable for any violation. The employer should provide the agency with information about ADA requirements regarding qualification standards, preemployment inquiries, and reasonable accommodation.

Although the ADA does not require employers to make special efforts to recruit people with disabilities, it is consistent with the ADA's purpose for employers to expand recruiting efforts to sources of qualified candidates with disabilities. Many organizations can provide this employment service.

Assistance is available for employers that would like to recruit and hire employees with disabilities. A video, released by the Department of Labor's Office of Disability Employment Policy (ODEP), promotes the benefits of hiring employees with disabilities. The ODEP has a variety of resources, including publications, fact sheets, and interviewing and hiring tips. All of these resources are available on their Web site at *www.dol.gov/odep*.

[C]   Application Forms

Employers should review job application forms to eliminate any questions related to the existence, nature, or severity of a disability. Questions that may not be asked on an application form or in a job interview include:

- Have you ever had or been treated for any of the following conditions or diseases? (This question is generally followed by a checklist of conditions or diseases for which the applicant has been treated in the past four years.)

- Have you ever been hospitalized? If so, for what condition?

- Have you ever been treated for any mental condition?

- Is there a health-related reason you may not be able to perform the job for which you are applying?

- How many days were you absent from work because of illness or injury last year? (The employer may, however, describe attendance requirements or provide a written policy and ask if an applicant is able to meet those requirements.)

- Do you have any physical defects that prevent you from performing certain kinds of work? If so, describe them. (This question is prohibited even if the applicant is later asked to identify an accommodation that would enable him or her to do the job. Rather, the applicant may be asked about his or her ability to perform specific job functions with or without a reasonable accommodation.)

- Have you ever been treated for drug addiction or alcoholism?

- What prescribed medication(s) are you currently taking?

- Have you ever filed for workers' compensation insurance benefits?

[1]   Affirmative Action

Many organizations are required to meet federal affirmative action guidelines. The EEOC guidance addresses some concerns regarding the relationship between affirmative action objectives and ADA objectives.

At the pre-offer stage, an employer may invite applicants to volunteer disability-related information necessary to comply with affirmative action if the employer is either (1) undertaking affirmative action pursuant to Section 503 of the Rehabilitation Act of 1973, or any federal, state, or local law, including relevant veterans' preference laws, that requires affirmative action for individuals with disabilities; or (2) voluntarily undertaking affirmative action for individuals with disabilities. Alternatively, the employer may invite voluntary self-identification at the pre-offer stage when a law permits or encourages, rather than requires the employer to gather such information or requires the employer to collect data without requiring affirmative action. In these cases, the employer may gather the information only if it uses the data to actually provide affirmative action for individuals with disabilities.

[D] Preemployment Inquiries and Medical Examinations

The EEOC has issued two enforcement guidances concerning preemployment inquiries. These two documents serve as the current interpretative resource for EEOC investigators. Both documents also provide detailed information useful to employers covered by the ADA.

The first document, issued on May 19, 1994, is titled "EEOC's Enforcement Guidance on Preemployment Disability-Related Inquiries and Medical Examinations Under the Americans with Disabilities Act of 1990." It provides investigators with detailed information and instructions for determining whether an inquiry is disability-related or whether an examination is medical, and it provides guidance on the use of such inquiries and examinations at both the pre- and post-offer stages.

The May 1994 guidance defines the following important terms:

- *Preemployment*—The period before an individual starts to work for the employer

- *Pre-offer stage*—The preemployment period before the employer has made an applicant a conditional job offer, which is the primary focus of the guidance

- *Post-offer stage*—The preemployment period after the employer extends a conditional job offer but before an individual starts work

- *Disability-related inquiries*—Inquiries or a series of inquiries that are likely to gather information about a disability, as opposed to an individual's ability to perform job functions

The guidance provides detailed examples to help employers address situations that may arise infrequently and raise some concern regarding acceptability. Permissible inquiries focus on the principle that the employer may ask applicants about their ability to perform job functions. The employer may not ask about the existence, nature, or severity of their disabilities at the pre-offer stage. Requests to demonstrate or describe performance of job-related functions are generally permissible, if they are not likely to gather information about a disability. For example:

- In interviewing a word processing candidate, the interviewer may ask, "How did you break your arm?" The interviewer may not, however, follow up the question or the applicant's response with questions regarding when the arm is expected to heal or whether he or she will have full use of the arm in the future, even if the applicant offers disability-related information.

- The employer may ask applicants to demonstrate their ability to distinguish color-coded paper or retrieve packages from shelves that are four feet high, if these are specific job functions. If in response an applicant indicates that a reasonable accommodation is necessary, the employer must either provide, without creating undue hardship, a reasonable accommodation to allow the applicant to demonstrate job performance or allow the applicant to simply describe how he or she would perform the specific job function.

- The employer may ask whether an applicant has 20/20 corrected vision. If the applicant answers no, the employer may not follow the question with prohibited questions such as "What is your corrected vision?" or "What is your uncorrected vision?" These prohibited questions may lead an applicant to provide information about a disability (in this case, severe vision impairment) rather than his or her ability to perform job functions.

- An employer may ask job-related questions about handling stress, such as "How well do you perform under stress?" or "Do you work better or worse under pressure?" An employer may make a statement such as "This job requires an employee to prepare written reports containing detailed factual summaries and analyses; these reports frequently must be prepared within tight time frames." The employer may ask: "Can you perform this function with or without reasonable accommodation?" The employer may not, however, ask a follow-up question such as "Have you sought treatment for your inability to handle stress?" because it may lead an applicant to divulge information about a disability (e.g., a substantially limiting psychological impairment).

The EEOC reasons that responses to such follow-up questions can be expected to solicit information about a potential disability, rather than the ability to perform job functions.

The employer may ask performance-related questions about either essential or marginal job functions, but may not reject an applicant because of an inability to perform a marginal function due to a disability. Requesting applicants to describe or demonstrate performance of job functions may, on an individual basis, be risky. The employer should instead determine which job categories will consistently include requests for demonstration of performance as a part of pre-offer inquiries.

On October 10, 1995, the EEOC issued "ADA Enforcement Guidance: Preemployment Disability-Related Questions and Medical Examinations" (3 EEOC No. 205). This document is written in a question-and-answer format to address specific situations that may arise in an employer's preemployment screening and selection process. It is intended to accompany and broaden information provided in the earlier EEOC notice.

In general, the October 1995 guidance clarifies that employers may not ask disability-related questions or require a medical examination at the pre-offer stage, even if the employer intends to look at the answers or results only at the post-offer stage. Despite this broad prohibition, employers may ask a wide variety of questions to evaluate whether an applicant is qualified for a particular job, including:

- Asking about applicant's ability to perform specific job functions (e.g., telling an applicant that the job requires the ability to routinely lift a 40-pound box of paper and then asking if he or she can satisfy this requirement).

- Asking about nonmedical qualifications and skills (e.g., education, required licenses, and work history).

- Asking the applicant to demonstrate or describe how he or she would perform certain job tasks (e.g., lifting that box of paper). In this situation, if the applicant indicates that he or she would require an accommodation to perform the requested task, the employer must either provide a reasonable accommodation that does not create an undue hardship or allow the applicant to simply describe how he or she would perform the job function in question.

General guidelines provided in the ADA enforcement guidance remind all employers that under no circumstances is it permissible to ask a third party (e.g., workers' compensation services, a state agency, or the applicant's friends, references, or former employers) questions that cannot be asked directly of a potential applicant.

[1] Prior Attendance Records

Most employers are concerned about potential applicants' attendance. The guidance offers several examples of permitted and prohibited pre-offer inquiries about prior attendance records.

Permissible inquiries include:

- How many days were you absent from work last year?

- Did you have any unauthorized absences from your job last year?

- How many Mondays or Fridays were you on leave last year, other than on approved vacation leave?

Prohibited inquiries include:

- Were you sick? How many days were you sick? How many separate episodes of sickness did you have?

- How often will you require leave for treatment of your disability?

[2] *Medical Examination* Defined

EEOC's guidance provides a detailed definition of medical examinations. Generally, any procedure or test that seeks information about an individual's physical or mental impairments or health is a medical examination under the ADA. The guidance provides factors to consider, as well as some examples. It also provides employers with practical advice regarding certain preemployment inquiries. For example:

- Evaluating an applicant's ability to read business labels or distinguish objects as part of a demonstration of the applicant's ability to do a job is not a "medical examination." An ophthalmologist's or optometrist's analysis of vision is medical, however, as is requiring an individual to read an eye chart.

- Testing applicants to determine whether or how much alcohol (versus illegal drugs) an applicant has consumed is a medical examination, and there is no permitted exception.

Employers should be aware of a 2005 Seventh Circuit ruling that defined some "personality tests" as "medical examinations," which, in the preemployment context, would be prohibited under the ADA. The Seventh Circuit, in its determination, relied on the EEOC's guidelines that define a medical examination as a "procedure or test that seeks information about an individual's physical or mental impairments or health," and "psychological tests that are designed to identify a mental disorder or impairment qualify as medical examinations, while psychological tests that measure personality traits such as honesty, preference, and habits do not."

In the case of *Karraker v. Rent-A-Center* [No. 04-2881, 2005 WL 1389443 (7th Cir., June 14, 2005)], the Minnesota Multiphasic Personality Inventory (MMPI) was used as part of larger test Rent-A-Center (RAC) used to determine "promotability." In this case, three brothers were denied the opportunity for promotion due to low test scores. RAC stated that the test was used only to determine an applicant's "state of mood."

The court found that, despite the fact that RAC did not use a psychologist to interpret the results, the test was designed to reveal mental illness, and certain responses could be used to measure traits such as depression and paranoia. As such, the court determined that MMPI was in fact a medical examination and, in the preemployment context, was prohibited by the ADA.

[3]   Intellectual Disability

The EEOC estimates that approximately 2.5 million Americans have an "intellectual disability." An individual is considered to have an intellectual disability if:

- The individual's IQ is less than 70 to 75;

- The individual has significant limitations in adaptive skill areas as expressed in conceptual, social, and practical adaptive skills; and

- The individual's disability originated before the age of 18.

"Adaptive skill areas" refers to basic skills needed for everyday life. They include communication, self-care, home living, social skills, leisure, health and safety, self-direction, functional academics (reading, writing, basic math), and work.

As with any area of disability, the employer is prohibited from asking an applicant questions about the disability, such as current or past treatments, medications, and so on. The employer may ask job-related questions, such as the applicant's ability to file, spell, drive, and lift. If and when the applicant reveals his or her disability, it is permissible only to ask questions about reasonable accommodation. In the post-offer stage, the employer may require a medical assessment that is job related, provided that this assessment is required of all applicants for that particular job.

The EEOC has issued a fact sheet, "Questions & Answers About Persons with Intellectual Disabilities in the Workplace and the Americans with Disabilities Act" that provides guidance on working with applicants and employees with intellectual disabilities, which is available on its Web site: *www.eeoc.gov./types/ada.html.*

[4]   EEOC Guidelines on Certain Medical Conditions

The EEOC has issued fact sheets to help employers understand how to work with applicants and employees with certain disabilities. In addition to the fact sheet covering intellectual abilities noted above, the following resources are available at *www.eeoc.gov/types/ada.html*:

- Questions and Answers about Deafness and Hearing Impairment in the Workplace and the Americans with Disabilities Act

- Cancer in the Workplace and the ADA

- Epilepsy in the Workplace and the ADA

- Diabetes in the Workplace and the ADA

- Blindness and Vision Impairments in the Workplace and the ADA

- Health Care Workers and the ADA

- The ADA's Association Provision

[E]   Candidate Testing

The ADA imposes two major requirements on employers regarding the use of employment tests:

1. Tests that screen out or tend to screen out individuals on the basis of disability are not allowed, unless the test is shown to be job-related for the position in question and is consistent with business necessity.

2. Tests must be administered in the most effective manner to ensure that results accurately reflect the skills, aptitude, or other factors the test purports to measure, rather than the impaired sensory, manual, or speaking skills of a disabled individual, except if these skills are the factors the test purports to measure.

Even if a test is job-related and consistent with business necessity, the employer must provide specific reasonable accommodation for taking the test if the candidate needs and requests it. The disabled applicant has the responsibility of notifying the employer of the need for accommodation for testing; the employer has the responsibility of providing the reasonable accommodation.

Providing information about application procedures early in the hiring process may help applicants meet their responsibility. This practice also helps the employer comply with the ADA's intent. For example, the employer may attach information regarding all steps in the application process to its application forms, to inform candidates of upcoming procedures and to allow them the opportunity to request needed accommodation.

[F]   Checking References

An employer may not ask a job applicant's previous employers or other sources about the applicant's disability, illness, or workers' compensation history before making a conditional offer of employment. Previous employers may, however, be asked about the following:

- Job functions and tasks the candidate performed and how they were performed

- The quality and quantity of work the candidate performed

- The candidate's attendance record

- Other job-related issues not related to disability

If an applicant has a known disability and has indicated that he or she can do the job with reasonable accommodation, a previous employer may be asked about accommodations made.

§ 13.05   POST-OFFER TESTING FOR DRUG AND ALCOHOL USE

Employees who are recovering alcoholics and drug addicts have limited protection from discrimination under the ADA. However, the ADA explicitly requires employers to maintain workplaces that are free of illegal drugs and alcohol, and it does not prohibit employers from being in compliance with other federal laws on drug or alcohol testing.

Recovering is the key word in understanding whether a person is classified as having a disability. People who continue to use illegal drugs or alcohol are not classified as disabled when the employer takes such use into consideration, and testing for the illegal use of drugs is not an ADA violation. Employers may refuse to hire users of illegal drugs and may terminate current employees who use illegal drugs. If a person has a history of illegal drug use but is not currently using drugs, employers may not discriminate on the basis of past history.

Although it is clear that urinalysis for illegal drugs does not constitute a medical examination under the ADA, the EEOC's Technical Assistance Manual provides that a blood alcohol test cannot be performed until after a conditional offer of employment has been extended.

Some experts warn that once an independent medical review officer (MRO) is involved with the review of any drug test results, the test may become a prohibited pre-offer medical examination. The employer should review its drug testing procedures with legal counsel and be certain that approved procedures are applied consistently.

§ 13.06 POST-OFFER PREEMPLOYMENT INQUIRIES AND MEDICAL EXAMINATIONS

After making an applicant a conditional job offer, and before employment has begun, an employer may ask the applicant certain disability-related questions and perform medical examinations. Such inquiries may concern the existence, nature, or severity of a disability and may involve the applicant's prior sick leave, illness, diseases, or impairments, general physical and mental health, and workers' compensation history. (Because certain states have laws and regulations regarding workers' compensation, disability, discrimination, and privacy laws that may restrict an employer's questions about an applicant's workers' compensation history, employers should check their state and local laws before asking job applicants about their workers' compensation history.)

The employer may condition the job offer on the results of a medical examination or inquiry so long as the following apply:

- All entering employees in the same job category are subjected to the same examination or inquiry, regardless of disability.

- The examination results are kept confidential, and only individuals involved in the hiring process who need the information have access to it.

A job applicant's medical information must remain confidential after a hiring decision is made, unless the applicant voluntarily discloses such information. Confidential medical information should always be maintained in files separate from the human resources (HR) department's employee files; individuals who are responsible for checking and evaluating job references have no need for medical information.

If, after a conditional job offer, the successful applicant undergoes a medical examination and is rejected by the employer for medical or disability reasons, EEOC investigators may closely scrutinize that decision. Under the ADA, just as under other discrimination regulations and restrictions, such a decision must be supported by the employer's demonstration that the reason for rejecting an applicant is "job-related and consistent with business necessity." For example, assume that an employer makes a conditional job offer to an applicant and an essential function of the job is that the incumbent be available to work every day for the next three months. A subsequent medical examination reveals that the applicant has a disabling impairment that, according to reasonable medical judgment based on the most current medical knowledge, will require treatment that will render the applicant unable to work for a portion of the three-month period. Under these circumstances, the employer is allowed to withdraw the job offer without violating the ADA.

A 2005 court case highlights the need for care in the post-offer preemployment arena. In *Leonel v. American Airlines* [400 F.3d 702 (9th Cir. 2005)], the company made a "conditional" offer to three individuals contingent on a drug test, medical examination, and background check. American Airlines sent the individuals to the clinic prior to the completion of the background checks. During the medical exam, the applicants failed to disclose that they were HIV positive. When the facts came out after the exam, American Airlines rescinded the employment offer because the applicants failed to provide "full and correct information." The applicants claimed the medical exam was conducted "pre-offer" and therefore unlawful. The Ninth Circuit Court agreed, stating that medical examinations are prohibited under ADA until all non-medical contingencies (e.g., background checks) have been cleared.

[A]   Refusal to Hire Because of Direct Threat to Health and Safety

The ADA allows employers to refuse to hire an applicant who, because of a disability, poses a direct threat to the health or safety of other workers. The EEOC's regulations include permission for employers to deny employment to a disabled applicant if employment in the position sought would pose a direct threat to the individual's own health.

In *Echazabal v. Chevron U.S.A., Inc.* [226 F.3d 1063 (9th Cir. 2000)], the plaintiff Mario Echazabal had worked for an independent contractor at a Chevron, U.S.A. oil refinery. He applied for two positions at the refinery and both times was offered employment contingent on passing a medical examination. When the examinations revealed that Echazabal had chronic Hepatitis C—a condition that Chevron's doctors indicated would be aggravated by exposure to the chemicals in the refinery and would put Echazabal at risk of further illness or death—Chevron rescinded the offers.

Echazabal filed suit, claiming that Chevron's refusal to hire him and asking the independent contractor to take him off the job discriminated against him because of a disability, his liver condition, and was in violation of the ADA. Chevron defended under a regulation of the EEOC permitting the defense that a worker's disability on the job would pose a "direct threat" to his health. The district court granted summary judgment for Chevron. It held that Echazabal raised no genuine issue of material fact as to whether Chevron had acted reasonably in relying on its own doctors' medical advice, regardless of its accuracy.

The Ninth Circuit Court of Appeals ruled in favor of Echazabal, rejecting the employer's direct-threat-to-self defense. This ruling, however, conflicted with rulings in similar cases in the Seventh and Eleventh Circuits.

The Supreme Court overturned the Ninth Circuit's ruling in *Chevron U.S.A. Inc. v. Echazabal* [536 U.S. 73 (2002)], rejecting its argument that Congress intended employers to ignore the possibility of injury to self if a disabled employee were permitted to work in a position that posed serious health risks for the employee. The Court ruled that the EEOC's "direct threat" regulation was reasonable and not contradicted by the ADA. The Court further indicated that employers must conduct "individualized assessment" of an employee's current ability to perform the essential functions of a current or sought-after job in a safe and healthy manner. Such assessments, the Court said, must be based on an "objective medical judgment," not on paternalistic stereotypes that individuals with disabilities need protection.

Another case that revolved around the issue of "direct threat to self or others" is *McKenzie v. Benton.* [388 F.3d 1342 (10th Cir. 2004), *cert. denied*, 544 U.S. 1048, 125 S. Ct. 2294, 161 L. Ed. 2d 1088 (2005)] Lorraine "Jade" McKenzie, a sergeant in a Wyoming County Sheriff's Department, had developed post-traumatic stress syndrome. After being hospitalized for self-inflicted wounds and drug overdoses, she voluntarily resigned when her psychiatrist told the Department she might be hazardous to herself or others. She later re-applied for employment and was not hired, based on the fact that she might be a "direct threat." McKenzie sued under the ADA. The lower court found for the employer, because McKenzie failed to show she did not pose a direct threat. The Tenth Circuit Court of Appeals agreed, and the U.S. Supreme Court denied review of the decision. The importance of this case is that generally the burden of proof is with the employer; but the Appeals Court stated that there is an exception when the essential duties of the job involve safety or health. Under these conditions, the burden of proof falls to the employee.

§ 13.07   COMPLIANCE WITH THE ADA DURING EMPLOYMENT

[A]   Disability-Related Inquiries and Medical Examinations

After employment begins, employers may make disability-related inquiries and require medical examinations only if they are related to the individual's specific job and are consistent with business necessity.

The EEOC has published enforcement guidance, "Disability-Related Inquiries and Medical Examinations for Employees Under the Americans with Disabilities Act (ADA)" (July 2000). This document provides useful definitions and examples, including:

- Definitions of "disability-related inquiries," "medical examinations," and "employees";

- A discussion of "job related and consistent with business necessity";

- Information on leaves of absence as they relate to disabilities;

- Documentation requirements; and

- A discussion of testing and monitoring.

This guidance is available at *www.eeoc.gov/policy/guidance.html.*

[B]   Performance Management Development: Standards for Evaluations, Disciplinary Action, and Terminations

All discipline and performance evaluation policies and procedures should be developed in accordance with the ADA. Supervisors and managers should be trained to adhere to consistent practices when evaluating and managing employee performance.

Specifically, this means:

- A company may hold employees with disabilities to the same performance or production standards as other, similarly situated employees without disabilities in performing essential job functions (with or without reasonable accommodation).

- Disabled employees who need reasonable accommodation should not be evaluated on their ability to perform job functions without the accommodation, nor should they be downgraded because they need the accommodation.

- A company should not give employees with disabilities special treatment. Equal employment opportunity is not served by providing for evaluation on a lower standard and/or discipline less severe than that given to other employees.

- A company may take the same disciplinary action against employees with disabilities that it takes against other, similarly situated employees if the illegal use of drugs or alcohol affects job performance and/or attendance.

- A company should consider providing (and, if applicable under other federal, state or local laws, may be required to provide) accommodation to employees who "self-identify" a substance abuse problem. Employees self-identify when they seek help independently of a drug or alcohol test, disciplinary action, or investigation of improper conduct.

- A company may not discipline or terminate an employee with a disability if the employer has refused to provide a requested reasonable accommodation and the reason for unsatisfactory performance was the lack of accommodation.

- A company may not terminate an employee with a disability based on previous disciplinary action that was itself due to the employee's disability, even if at the time of the original disciplinary action it was unknown to the company that the employee had a disability.

[C]   Drug and Alcohol Use and Testing

As indicated earlier, employees who use drugs and consume alcohol are not classified as disabled under the ADA. If alcohol use causes an employee to be frequently absent from work or unable to carry out his or her job responsibilities, the employee may be disciplined or terminated, but he or she does not qualify as disabled. When alcohol use causes an employee's performance to fall below an established acceptable level for all workers, the employer may not discipline the employee in a manner more severe than that used to discipline other employees for similar misconduct or poor performance.

In *Shafer v. Preston Memorial Hospital* [107 F.3d 274 (4th Cir. 1997)], at least one court gave its definition of "current" drug use. The Fourth Circuit held that the ADA protects "only persons who have refrained from using drugs for some time." In this case, a nurse was said to be "currently engaging in the illegal use of drugs" at the time of her discharge, even though she did not use drugs on the day of discharge. The court said that the word *current* when applied to an activity means activity that is periodic or ongoing and has not permanently ended. The court concluded that the plain meaning of the ADA excludes from statutory protection an employee who illegally uses drugs during the weeks and months before discharge, even if that employee is participating in a drug rehabilitation program and is drug-free on the day she is fired.

In *City of Sioux Falls v. Miller* [1996 S.D. 132 (1996)], South Dakota's Supreme Court decided a case that addressed some tough questions, particularly on the issue of alcohol abuse. In this case, a civil service employee had a history of spotty attendance and poor work performance. After an incident at work, he admitted he had a drinking problem and underwent a physical to determine if he was fit to perform his job. He returned to work under the condition that he undergoes periodic testing for alcohol and drug use during a 90-day probationary period. He was told upon returning to work that continued poor performance or failure to comply with testing might result in termination.

Following a positive drug test indicating the presence of cocaine, the employee was terminated. In a subsequent hearing before the civil service board, the board concluded that because the violation of the conditions of employment, which the employee admitted were clear to him at the time, was caused by the disability, there was no just cause for termination. The employer appealed.

On appeal, the court found there was no question that the employee failed to remain drug- and alcohol-free during the probationary period, and this failure was misconduct. Employers must be able to terminate their employees for misconduct regardless of whether the employee has a disability. The court held that entering a rehabilitation program does not immediately convert a current user into an individual with a disability protected under the ADA. The term *reasonable accommodation* does not mean protracted accommodation that enables an addicted employee to continue abusing a controlled substance.

In another test of the ADA safe harbor for drug- and alcohol-addicted employees (those participating in a supervised rehabilitation program and no longer engaging in the use of alcohol or drugs), the Ninth Circuit Court of Appeals found in favor of an employer who terminated an alcoholic employee. In *Brown v. Lucky Stores, Inc.* [246 F.3d 1182 (9th Cir. 2001)], Brown was arrested for driving drunk and possession of methamphetamines on November 10, 1996. Brown's sister-in-law called Brown's supervisor to inform him Brown was in jail and would not be at work. Brown missed work on November 10 and 11. After conviction, she was ordered to participate in a 90-day drug- and alcohol-rehabilitation program beginning on November 15, and as a result missed her scheduled work shift on November 16. She was fired for missing three consecutive shifts without an authorized reason ("job abandonment"). Brown sued under the ADA, claiming discrimination based on alcoholism.

In district court, Brown's employer was granted summary judgment; that court relied on a previous Ninth Circuit Court decision that an employer may terminate an alcoholic employee even if the misconduct is related to the employee's alcoholism. On appeal, Brown argued that the ADA safe harbor protected her because she was enrolled in a rehabilitation program on the date of her third unexcused absence.

In reaching its decision, the Ninth Circuit observed that "the 'safe harbor' provision applies only to employees who have refrained from using drugs for a significant period of time." Brown had been under the influence of alcohol as late as six days before the date she missed her third shift. "Because she had not refrained from the use of drugs and alcohol for a sufficient length of time, [Brown] was not entitled to the protections of the ADA's safe-harbor provision," according to the court. Employers may reasonably believe that drug involvement is an ongoing problem if an employee has recently used alcohol or illegal drugs. The determination of recent use and ongoing problem is made on a case-by-case basis.

In another Ninth Circuit case, *Hernandez v. Hughes Missile Systems Co.* [362 F.3d 564 (9th Cir. 2004)], the court examined what appeared to be a neutral employment policy against rehiring former employees who violated company rules of conduct. Hughes Missile Systems had a policy of not rehiring former employees who had been discharged, including employees who had "resigned in lieu of termination." Hernandez, an employee of Hughes Missile Systems, had quit in lieu of discharge after he failed a drug test at work and was given the option of resigning or being terminated. Two years later, when Hernandez re-applied for employment at Hughes, he submitted two reference letters with his application giving evidence of his rehabilitation from drug and alcohol abuse. Hughes rejected his application based on its policy of not rehiring former employees who were terminated, or who resigned in lieu of discharge.

Hernandez sued, claiming discrimination because of his disability. The trial court judge dismissed the case, but the Ninth Circuit ruled that Hernandez should have a chance at trial to prove that Hughes' policy was a violation of the ADA because it refused to hire anyone who had been previously fired for a drug related reason. Hughes argued that its decision not to rehire Hernandez was based only on the employee separation sheet, that it was unaware of his record of drug addiction. Hughes also asserted that its policy was not discriminatory because it applied to all former employees whose employment ended because of termination or resignation in lieu of termination, and it did not single out employees with a record of a drug addiction. The Ninth Circuit rejected Hughes' argument. The court concluded that although the no rehire policy did not look discriminatory on its face, it potentially violated the ADA as applied to former drug addicts. If Hernandez was, in fact, no longer using drugs and had been successfully rehabilitated, then he could not be denied reemployment simply because of his past record of drug addiction, which would be considered a "disability" under state and federal law.

HR or other personnel selection staff should keep in mind the ADA's narrow exceptions for disclosing specific, limited medical information. Applicable language in the ADA [29 C.F.R. Part 1630.14(b)(1) (i-iii)] specifies that information obtained regarding an applicant's medical condition or history must be collected and maintained on separate forms placed in separate medical files and be treated as a confidential medical record, except that:

- Supervisors and managers may be informed regarding necessary restrictions on the work or duties of an employee and necessary accommodations.

- First aid and safety personnel may be informed, when appropriate, if the disability might require emergency treatment.

- Government officials investigating compliance with the ADA must be given relevant information on request.

The Appendix to 29 C.F.R. Part 1630.14(b) further specifies that confidential medical information obtained as a result of preemployment medical inquiries may be given to state workers' compensation offices or second injury funds, in accordance with state workers' compensation laws, without violating this part of the regulation.

[D]   Association or Relationship with an Individual with a Disability

In October 2005, the EEOC issued a fact sheet regarding the "association" provision of the ADA. This provision prohibits employers from discriminating against applicants or employees based on their relationship or association with an individual with a disability. As with other causes of action, employers cannot terminate, refuse to hire, make any adverse employment action, or deny benefits or privileges of employment based on association. Some examples included in the EEOC fact sheet:

1. The president of a small company learns that his administrative assistant, Sandra, has a son with an intellectual disability. The president is uncomfortable around people with this type of disability and

decides to transfer Sandra to a position in which he will have less contact with her to avoid any discussions about, or interactions with, Sandra's son. He transfers her to a vacant entry-level position in the mailroom which pays less than Sandra's present position, but will allow him to avoid interacting with her. This is a violation of the ADA's association provision.

2. An employer is interviewing applicants for a computer programmer position. The employer determines that one of the applicants, Arnold, is the best qualified, but is reluctant to offer him the position because Arnold disclosed during the interview that he has a child with a disability. The employer violates the ADA if it refuses to hire Arnold based on its belief that his need to care for his child will have a negative impact on his work attendance or performance.

"Questions and Answers About the Association Provision of the Americans with Disabilities Act" can be found online at *www.eeoc.gov/types/ada.html*.

[E] "Regarded As" Disabled

The ADA from the beginning has prohibited discrimination against an individual who is "regarded as" disabled. However, there were differing court opinions about whether or not an employer must provide reasonable accommodation to one who is regarded as disabled. The passage of the ADAAA resolves this dilemma by affirming that an individual who is regarded as disabled does not need to be provided with reasonable accommodation.

[F] Emergency Evacuation Procedures

Following the terrorist attacks on the World Trade Center and the Pentagon on September 11, 2001, many employers became acutely aware that emergency evacuation procedures needed to be revised or developed to assist those employees who may needed assistance in the event of an emergency evacuation.

To help employers abide by the guidelines of the ADA, the EEOC developed a fact sheet on obtaining and using employees' medical information as part of emergency evacuation procedures. According to the fact sheet (available at *www.eeoc.gov*), employers may ask employees and potential employees whether they would need assistance in the event of an evacuation. However, they may ask for that information in one of only three ways:

1. After a job offer has been made but prior to the actual start of employment, a potential employee may be asked whether he or she will need assistance during an emergency.

2. After starting on the job, an employee may be surveyed on a periodic basis to determine whether he or she will need assistance in an emergency evacuation, provided the employer explains the reason for asking the question and makes clear that such identification is voluntary.

3. An employee with a known disability may be asked whether he or she will require assistance in the event of an emergency, regardless of whether a periodic survey of all employees is conducted.

Employers should not assume that all employees with known disabilities will need assistance. When requesting such information, employers should make it clear that any information provided by its employees will be kept confidential and shared only with individuals who need to know in order to implement the emergency evacuation plan. Individuals who need to know may include safety personnel, medical professionals, emergency coordinators, floor captains, coworkers who have volunteered to act as "buddies," and building security officers.

Employees who have indicated that they will need assistance during an emergency evacuation may be asked to specify the type of assistance that will be needed. The employer may request that the information be provided in writing on a form or solicit the information in a meeting with the employee to determine the type of assistance that will be needed and whether special medication, equipment, or devices will be needed.

Employers should remember that they need only the minimum information necessary to be able to provide the required assistance. An employer generally will not need to know the details of an employee's medical condition.

§ 13.08   REASONABLE ACCOMMODATION

Reasonable accommodation is a key nondiscrimination requirement of ADA and is unique to the ADA.

People with disabilities are restricted in employment opportunities by various barriers. Some face physical barriers that make it difficult to move into or about a job location or to use necessary equipment. Some are limited by the way people communicate with one another. Others may be excluded because of inflexible work schedules. Many are prohibited from working at certain jobs by the misconceptions of those around them. Other people in the workplace might develop fears, stereotypes, and presumptions about job performance, safety, absenteeism, cost, or acceptance by coworkers or customers.

The ADA recognizes that such barriers may discriminate against qualified people with disabilities. For this reason, the ADA requires reasonable accommodation as a means of overcoming unnecessary barriers that would prevent or impede employment opportunities for otherwise qualified people with disabilities.

The ADA considers an accommodation to be any change to a job function, employment practice, or work environment that would allow someone with a disability to enjoy an equal employment opportunity. The obligation to provide reasonable accommodation is ongoing and may change as the job changes or as a person's disability changes. The only time reasonable accommodation may be denied is if the accommodation creates an undue hardship. In that case, the person with the disability should be given the opportunity to provide the accommodation or pay that portion of the cost that presents the hardship.

The ADA requires the company to provide reasonable accommodation in three aspects of employment: (1) in applying for work, (2) in performing essential functions of a job, and (3) in enjoying equal benefits and privileges of employment.

The choice of "reasonable" accommodation is very important. An employee does not have a right to force an employer into an unreasonable accommodation. If the employer cannot handle the employee's suggested accommodations, the cost and inconvenience to the organization and fellow employees should be documented. The employer may *not* be required to grant the employee's choice of accommodation.

The four steps to consider when identifying a process for reasonable accommodation are as follows:

1. Reexamine the jobs at the company and determine the purpose and essential functions of each job. Identify potential accommodations for each essential function.

2. Ask current employees with disabilities or qualified applicants with disabilities what they need to do the job. Ask them what barriers they perceive and how they feel the barriers can be removed.

3. When consulting with people with disabilities, explore various accommodation options and assess the overall effectiveness of each one. The reasonable accommodation selected need not be the best accommodation available, as long as it enables the individual to perform the essential functions of the job and allows those with disabilities to enjoy equal benefits and privileges.

4. If there are several alternatives, consider the preference of the employee, but select the one that best serves the needs of both the company and the employee.

Examples of reasonable accommodations include the following:

-   Making facilities accessible by

    — Installing ramps for access to property

    — Creating parking spaces to allow employees with disabilities clear access without having to reenter traffic patterns

    — Creating accessible rest rooms, including modifying toilet stalls, sinks, and soap and towel dispensers and lowering mirror heights

    — Rearranging desks and chairs to allow for wider internal traffic patterns

-   Modifying work schedules by

    — Allowing for longer lunch breaks because of the time it might take to move from a work area to a lunchroom or restaurant. Have employees arrive earlier or stay later to make up the time.

    — Allowing employees who need specific medical treatment during the week to have weekdays off and to work on Saturdays.

-   Providing flexible leave policies for employees who may require time off because of their disabilities. The policies need not be in the form of additional paid leave. Employees may receive unpaid leave, use accrued leave, or even request advance use of leave time for

    — Medical treatment

    — Repair of prosthesis or other equipment

    — Temporary loss of heat or air-conditioning, which may cause undue discomfort

-   Allowing telecommuting/work at home on a part-time or full-time basis

-   Reassigning employees to vacant positions

A recent study indicates that employers are very willing to make accommodations to their seriously ill workers. In the fall of 2005, the International Foundation of Employee Benefit Plans conducted a poll of benefit managers and human resources professionals. The study found that half of the respondents made accommodations for seriously ill employees whenever the requests were made. The other half made the accommodations most of the time. Employers' accommodations included a variety of work schedule accommodations. Eighty-four percent allowed reduced work hours. Other accommodations included telecommuting, flexible schedules, and additional work breaks.

[A] Representative Court Cases on Reasonable Accommodation

Two court cases decided in 2003 address the issue of retaining employees with violent behavior who have been diagnosed with medical conditions that contribute to that behavior.

The first case, *Koshko v. General Electric Company* [14 Am. Disabilities Cas. (BNA) 208 (N.D. Ill. 2003)], was dismissed by the judge because the defense could not support the claim that the condition "substantially limited in a major life activity." More importantly, the judge held that even if the employee had a disability under the ADA, he was not a "qualified individual with a disability" because he posed a "direct threat" to the health and safety of others.

The second case, *Calef v. Gillette Company* [322 F.3d 75 (1st Cir. 2003)], concerned an employee who had been diagnosed with a disease that contributed to his argumentative and threatening behavior. Fred Calef, Jr. had been involved in a number of altercations with his co-workers. Following a series of incidents, Calef was issued a final warning, indicating that any further infraction would result in termination. Shortly thereafter, Calef was diagnosed with attention deficit hyperactivity disorder (ADHD) and prescribed Ritalin. When Calef began acting in an "irrational and increasingly erratic" behavior following an argument with his supervisor, he was terminated. The First Circuit, on appeal, upheld the trial judge's dismissal based on the determination that Calef was not covered under ADA. Similar to *Koshko*, Calef failed to show that he was "substantially limited in a major life activity." And, like Koshko, the court wrote that "the ADA does not require that an employee whose unacceptable behavior threatens the safety of others be retained, even if the behavior stems from a mental disability."

In *Buckles v. First Data Resources* [176 F.3d 1098 (8th Cir. 1999)], the Eighth Circuit reversed a previous 1994 court decision awarding damages to an employee who had acute recurrent rhinosinusitis triggered by irritants such as perfume, nail polish, glue, adhesives, tar, and smoke. The employer had accommodated the employee by moving him to a room with better ventilation and issued memorandums dealing with other employees' use of irritants (e.g., nail polish). The employee claimed that the employer was not reasonable because it did not provide for "total avoidance," and that when the employee began suffering from an irritant he should be allowed to go home. The Eighth Circuit stated: "Unfettered ability to leave work at any time is certainly not a reasonable accommodation here." The court added that though the employer's adjustments proved unsuccessful, the burden was on the employee to propose a reasonable accommodation. Going home was not reasonable and would impose an undue financial and administrative burden on the employer.

Reasonable accommodation is a process, not a one-time event. In *Humphrey v. Memorial Hospital Association* [239 F.3d 1128 (9th Cir. 2001)], the Ninth Circuit held that an employer must continue to engage in the interactive accommodation process with an employee with a disability until either the accommodation works or the only accommodations left are those that would place an undue hardship on the employer. In *Humphrey*, the employer, a hospital, refused to permit the employee, who had been diagnosed with obsessive compulsive disorder (OCD), to work at home, an accommodation the employee had requested when her previous accommodation, flexible work hours, did not accommodate her disability. Humphrey had been disciplined for attendance problems, which resulted directly from her OCD. The hospital rejected the work-at-home accommodation, relying on its policy that only employees who had no prior disciplinary action were allowed to work at home.

The court found the employer liable for not continuing the accommodation process by (1) terminating the employee instead of discussing possible accommodations, including the work-at-home option, and (2) relying on past disciplinary actions as the reason for denying the accommodation, when the reason for the disciplinary actions was the disability.

The ruling in a 2003 case highlights the fact that the employee shares in the responsibility to engage in the interactive process. In *Allen v. Pacific Bell* [348 F.3d 1113 (9th Cir. 2003)], the employer, Pacific Bell, made efforts to work with the employee to find a reasonable accommodation in light of his disability. The employee failed to provide evidence of his improved physical condition, which would allow him to return to his original position, and subsequently failed to appear for a keyboarding test that might qualify him for an alternate position. The court held that the employee failed to cooperate with the job search process and that Pacific Bell had fulfilled its obligation to engage in the interactive process.

These cases remind employers to create and follow policies that require an interactive, ongoing process for arriving at reasonable accommodation(s) for an employee with a disability. Employers should document all efforts at reasonable accommodation. These include recording any costs associated with the accommodation (actual or estimated) and maintaining any written correspondence (including e-mails). After a plan has been established, employers need to monitor it and determine whether it is actually helping the employee perform the job's essential functions. If the initial plan does not help, the dialogue with the employee should be continued to arrive at a workable accommodation, if possible.

Employers must also remember that they should not take any disciplinary action against an employee when the reason for that action is the employee's disability. If the employer did not know (or have reason to know) that the reason for the employee's performance or behavior problem was a disability, it can conduct appropriate disciplinary action. However, as soon as the employer is aware of the disability and its influence on or cause of the disciplinary action, no further action of that kind should be taken, and the record should not be used against the employee in any future, unrelated, disciplinary actions.

In general, it is the responsibility of the employee with a disability to request an accommodation. However, under the following conditions, the employer must grant an accommodation even if an employee fails to request one:

- The employer knows the employee has a disability;

- The employer knows or has reason to know that the employee is experiencing workplace problems because of the disability; and

- The employer knows or has reason to know that the disability prevents the employee from requesting a reasonable accommodation.

[B] Sources of Information on Reasonable Accommodation

The number of potential accommodations is unlimited. The cost of providing accommodations is usually minor. The Job Accommodation Network (JAN) is a service of the President's Committee on Employment of People with Disabilities that provides free information on many job accommodations to employers at its toll-free number: (800) JAN-7234, or on its Web site: *www.jan.wvu.edu.*

In 2007, a study was conducted by the University of Iowa's Law, Health Policy and Disability Center to assess the costs and benefits of accommodation. They interviewed 1,182 employers between January 2004 and December 2006 who had contacted JAN for assistance. Of those employers who gave cost information, 46 percent reported that the accommodations they made had no cost at all. Another 45 percent experienced a one-time cost averaging $500. The employers in this study reported the following benefits:

- Allowed the company to retain a valued employee (86 percent)

- Eliminated the cost of training a new employee (56 percent)

- Saved workers' compensation and/or other insurance costs (39 percent)

- Increased employee productivity (71 percent)

- Increased profitability (32 percent)

JAN continues to recommend that employers seek out leaders in their local labor or disability community to provide effective, minimal-cost accommodations.

In October 2002, the EEOC issued a revision to its publication, *Enforcement Guidance: Reasonable Accommodation and Undue Hardship Under the ADA.* This guidance clarifies the rights and responsibilities of employers and individuals with disabilities regarding reasonable accommodation and undue hardship. To view this document, go to *www.eeoc.gov/policy/docs/accommodation.html.*

§ 13.09   THE ADA AND EMPLOYEE BENEFITS

[A]   Employer-Sponsored Group Health Benefits Plans

Following the release of the EEOC's guidance regarding the ADA and employer-sponsored health benefits plans [EEOC Interim Enforcement Guidance on the Application of the ADA to Disability-Based Distinctions in Employer-Provided Health Insurance, dated June 8, 1993], experts have discussed significant concerns. One concern is that because actual damages may be substantial when a group health policy does not cover a claim, more ADA claims will likely have a benefits component. Another concern is that nothing in the law or the guidance permits employers to engage in a practice considered a "subterfuge" to evade the purposes of the law. However, such prohibited practices are not defined or described.

It is not clear what the subterfuge rule means. The guidance indicates that a disability-based distinction may be justified when the condition or treatment may cause significant costs. In such cases, the EEOC will review whether similar limitations are imposed on other high-cost treatments. If other such limitations do not exist, the EEOC may determine the cost argument is, in fact, a subterfuge.

The guidance also states that a disparate impact challenge probably could not be brought regarding an employer health plan. However, an EEOC official has indicated uncertainty that disparate impact is unavailable. It is not clear if the EEOC will change its position.

The EEOC has entered at least one case as a party to enforce "the public interest" in eliminating disability discrimination in health benefits. Settlement of that case required the employer to remove a cap on AIDS related claims retroactive to the effective date of the ADA. The employer sponsored a self-funded health benefits plan. The employer's argument—that subterfuge was clearly not intended because the cap was instituted in 1987, before the ADA was effective, and because similar caps were not imposed on other catastrophic illnesses that could result in even greater costs to the plan—was denied.

The guidance issued in June 1993 is not the EEOC's final word on benefits plans or health insurance. Employers may expect to hear more about this critical ADA issue. (See **Exhibit 13.3** for a list of medical insurance do's and don'ts.)

The following court findings outline the current employer environment:

In *Anderson v. Gus Mayer Boston Store* [924 F. Supp. 763 (E.D. Tex. 1996)], the court held that an employer violated the ADA because it did not provide equal access to a group health insurance benefit. The employer had changed health insurance carriers after the employee, Anderson, contracted AIDS, and the new carrier would not consider covering the HIV-positive employee. Although it was the insurer that denied coverage, the court reasoned that the employer was liable because it selected the insurer. The court indicated the employer was obliged to make provisions for the excluded employee to receive comparable coverage in some other way. The employer could, however, attempt to prove that providing such coverage would create an "undue hardship" under the ADA. (Such a decision under the Health Insurance Portability and Accountability Act of 1996 (HIPAA) would likely be similar, as HIPAA also prohibits discrimination based on health status; see **Chapter 5**.)

In *Krauel v. Iowa Methodist Medical Center* [95 F.3d 674 (8th Cir. 1996)], the Eighth Circuit Court of Appeals ruled that employers may exclude coverage for infertility treatment from their health care insurance without violating the ADA. Since 1990, the employer's health plan had excluded coverage for male or female infertility problems. An employee underwent and paid for three procedures before giving birth to a baby girl. The employer's health plan reimbursed expenses for the pregnancy and delivery but excluded coverage for the infertility treatments, as outlined in the plan.

The employee filed suit, claiming that denial of the infertility coverage violated the ADA. The trial court determined that the employee was not a person with a disability, because she did not have an impairment that substantially limits a major life activity (e.g., caring for oneself, performing manual tasks, walking, seeing, hearing, speaking, breathing, learning, and working). Treating reproduction as a major life activity would be inconsistent with the regulations, the Eighth Circuit said, "and a considerable stretch of federal law."

The court also ruled that the plan's exclusion for infertility treatment was not "a subterfuge to evade the purposes of the ADA." Since she suffered no discrimination on the job, the plan was not a subterfuge.

[B] Implications for Employees

Although employees may complain if a health plan provides different coverage for different disabilities, recent court decisions have sided with employers so long as coverage variations apply equally to all participants. At a minimum, employers should analyze their plan limitations to be sure they are targeted at particular benefits or treatments and do not limit overall coverage and that they are not stated in terms of participants with particular conditions. The ADA clearly prohibits exclusion of people with disabilities from eligibility and participation in a plan, charging them higher premiums or otherwise discouraging them from employment.

[C] Wellness Programs

Employers offering wellness programs must comply with the ADA. As participation in and costs of these programs increase, so does the risk an employer faces. Of particular concern are wellness programs tied into group health plans, through the use of incentives, penalties, or both. Persons targeted to benefit from wellness programs (e.g., people with high blood pressure or obesity) may well assert that they should also be classified as disabled and protected from discrimination under the ADA. Although guidance for employers regarding compliance requirements for wellness programs within the ADA is limited, employers cannot afford to take a wait-and-see approach. Programs should be reviewed carefully.

[D] Leaves of Absence

Leaves of absence are a benefit established by employers. Any established leave of absence policy must be administered equally to all employees, regardless of disability. However, in some cases, more flexibility or additional unpaid time off might constitute "reasonable accommodation" to some employees. Unless a leave creates an "undue hardship," reasonable accommodation could allow a person with a disability to receive medical attention if he or she has a need to use more time off than the standard sick time policy might provide for. Under the ADA, employers do not have to provide a reasonable accommodation leave for an employee to care for a disabled person with whom the employee has a relationship.

[E] Company-Sponsored Activities and Company Lounges and Cafeterias

The employer has the responsibility to reasonably accommodate employees with disabilities so they may attend all sponsored social or diversionary activities. Included are access to transportation and any or all other benefits provided. This means all employees have equal access to the following benefits, among others:

- Company-sponsored parties, picnics, or meetings, which must be held in accessible locations, with interpreters and other accommodations provided for, as necessary

- Rooms used for employee breaks, lounges, cafeterias, and other nonwork areas

- An in-house health club or exercise facility, at the discretion of the disabled employees

- Company-sponsored teams, activities, or leagues

Note that a company cannot simply construct lounges or lunchrooms exclusively for the disabled. Under the ADA, separate is not equal. Thus, if the employee cafeteria is on the second floor and access is limited, the construction of a separate first-floor lunchroom does not solve the problem. Either access to the second-floor location should be provided or everyone should be allowed to use the new first-floor location.

§ 13.10 EEOC GUIDANCE ON TEMPORARY AGENCIES AND OTHER STAFFING FIRMS

The EEOC has published two guidance documents on how some ADA requirements apply to staffing firms and their clients. Specifically, the guidance issued in December 2000 addresses reasonable accommodation, disability-related inquiries, and medical examinations.

The timing of the job offer and EEOC's definitions are critical to understanding this guidance. The EEOC defines an offer of employment as occurring when a specific assignment to a specific client is made, not when the staffing firm places an individual on its roster for potential assignments. Therefore, all disability-related inquiries and medical examinations can be made only after a specific assignment is offered to the staffing firm's employee. During this "pre-offer" stage of employment, only the staffing firm is responsible for accommodating applicants. However, if an employer asks applicants to apply for work through a staffing firm, the employer and the firm will both be responsible for accommodating the applicant.

Once an offer has been made, "undue hardship" may be claimed if either the staffing firm or the employer cannot provide the accommodation quickly enough to meet the scheduling requirements of the assignment. However, the 2000 EEOC guidance indicates that firms and their clients should be prepared to provide common accommodations, such as sign language interpreters or readers.

If it is not imperative to quickly fill the assignment, both the staffing firm and the employer will be required to engage in the informal interactive process to reach a reasonable accommodation. Even if a contract between the two entities specifies the entity responsible for accommodation, the ADA holds both responsible.

As in situations without a staffing firm's involvement, accommodations do not have to be made if they would result in undue hardship for the employer. When both the staffing firm and the employer can show undue hardship (e.g., if the cost of the accommodation would exceed the combined resources of the staffing firm and the employer), no accommodation need be made. If the accommodation can be made only by pooling their resources, either entity may show undue hardship if it can prove that:

- Alone, its resources are insufficient to provide the accommodation, and

- It has made good-faith but unsuccessful attempts to obtain the contribution from the other entity.

However, if either entity can provide the accommodation on its own, it must do so. If a client does not provide the accommodation or the resources that could help provide for the accommodation, and it has the resources to do so, the staffing firm must refrain from providing any other employees to that entity until it agrees to abide by its ADA obligations. In addition, the staffing firm must offer the employee with the disability the next available position for which that person is qualified.

If the staffing firm refuses to help pay for the accommodation, and it otherwise could do so, it may then be liable. If the employer continues to use that staffing firm, it may also be liable for violations of the ADA.

The EEOC's 2000 guidance also indicates that both the staffing firm and the employer may be liable for discrimination under the ADA if one entity discriminates and the other knew or should have known about the discrimination and did nothing about it.

§ 13.11 WHAT IS NOT REQUIRED BY THE ADA

Employers hoped that when the ADA became effective, case law would begin to form a consistent basis for related decision making. Instead, over time, courts have made narrowly applicable decisions, not unlike the original intent of the law, supporting individual rights.

Various court decisions suggest what measures are not as yet required under the ADA, though it is important to keep in mind that each decision applies only in that court's jurisdiction. Following is a summary description of what is not required:

- *Condoning alcohol or illegal drug use on the job or reporting to work inebriated.* However, some courts have held that alcoholism and former drug addiction are disabilities and may require reasonable accommodation.

- *Indefinite leaves of absence as a form of accommodation.* Employers are not required to hold a job open indefinitely, until an employee's "serious health condition" is corrected. Of course, applicable requirements of the Family and Medical Leave Act of 1993 (FMLA) must be considered (see **Chapter 14**).

- *Lowering or ignoring production standards.* Reasonable accommodation does not include excluding disabled employees from meeting production standards or lowering those standards. The employer may be called on to demonstrate that such standards are applied to all employees in the same position or are related to business requirements.

- *Creating new jobs.* Several courts have heard cases on this issue. Generally, to date, courts have repeated that creating new positions, including light duty, for disabled employees is not a requirement of the ADA, provided the job functions in question are essential, as opposed to marginal.

- *Reassignment to another job.* Although a reasonable accommodation may include transferring nonessential or marginal functions of the position to other employees, the ADA does not require any employer to restructure a job to eliminate the essential functions. An employer might violate the ADA if it refused to assign a disabled employee to an available duty position when it has accommodated other employees in the past.

- *Accommodating or retaining a potentially violent employee.* Even though behavior may stem from a disability, ADA does not require employers to retain employees that threaten the safety of others.

- *Assistance from another employee.* Hiring another worker to perform a disabled employee's essential job functions is not required if the assistance would amount to a job restructuring by eliminating the essential functions of the disabled employee's job.

Note: This summary of findings is not intended as a definition of absolute trends in case law.

§ 13.12 REQUIRED RECORDKEEPING AND POSTING

To comply with the law [29 C.F.R. Part 1602, Recordkeeping and Reporting Requirements under Title VII and the ADA (amended)], employers should be aware of the following:

- The date for annual filing of the standard EEOC Form 100 is September 30. Information should be reported from the three months preceding September 30. [29 C.F.R. Part 1602.7]

- Employers must preserve personnel or employment records for a period of one year from the date of the making of the record or of the personnel action involved, whichever is later. [29 C.F.R. Part 1602.14]

- The EEOC requires employers to retain records on all employees, regular, temporary, and seasonal, for one year. [29 C.F.R. Part 1602.14(b)]

In addition, the EEOC requires employers to post notices concerning ADA provisions. The notices must be accessible to employees, including, as needed, those with visual or other reading disabilities. A poster containing ADA and other federal employment nondiscrimination provisions may be obtained free of charge from the EEOC by calling (800) 669-EEOC, visiting the Department of Labor's EEO Poster Web site at *www.dol.gov/esa/regs/compliance/posters/eeo.htm* or writing to:

U.S. Equal Employment Opportunity Commission Clearinghouse
P.O. Box 541
Annapolis Junction, MD 20701

§ 13.13 RESOURCES AVAILABLE

To promote awareness and enforcement efforts, regular quarterly status reports about the ADA are prepared by the Disability Rights Section of the Justice Department's Civil Rights Division. Typically, these reports outline cases surrounding the ADA in which the Department of Justice has participated in some way. The department also routinely makes a variety of printed materials available to entities covered by the ADA. Among such materials are:

- Numerous EEOC Enforcement Guidance outlining interpretive bases regarding definitions and ADA implementation issues (available as public information at Federal Depository libraries, from the EEOC Web site (*www.eeoc.gov*), or by calling (202) 663-4900)

- Various Question and Answer (Q&A) sheets providing information to employers regarding the practical applications of the ADA compliance process, available at *www.eeoc.gov*; for example, the EEOC published a Q&A in February 2008 titled "Veterans with Service-Connected Disabilities and the ADA: A Guide for Employers"

- Handbooks and pamphlets addressing specific compliance issues (e.g., Title III highlights regarding accessibility in new or existing buildings)

- Marketing information pamphlets, such as a pamphlet titled "The Americans with Disabilities Act Can Bring You New Customers"

- Fact sheets (e.g., Fact Sheet 4, "Tax Incentives for Improving Accessibility")

- Checklists (e.g., "Checklist for Readily Achievable Barrier Removal")

- Targeted informational booklets (e.g., "Americans with Disabilities Act: Questions and Answers for Persons Who Are HIV-Positive or Living with AIDS")

- Reprints of the text of the ADA or portions thereof

All this information is intended to keep the ADA and its intent immediately at the forefront of public and employers' attention. The Justice Department makes ADA information available in 15,000 libraries across the country and posts other sources of information (publications, technical assistance programs, new and proposed regulations) on the ADA home page at *www.usdoj.gov/crt/ada.*

§ 13.14   ENFORCEMENT

Following the form of a national enforcement plan approved by the EEOC in February 1996, EEOC district offices have developed similar local enforcement plans. As with the national plan, local plans combine public outreach and education efforts with voluntary resolution of disputes and litigation when necessary. At the same time, local plans vary because they are tailored to communities' specific legal issues and resources. A three-pronged approach to eliminating employment discrimination is shared by both the national and local plans.

In one example, the EEOC's Chicago district office sponsored seminars, with sessions on disability and age discrimination, for employers, community groups, and advocacy groups. An EEOC spokesperson indicated that the intent was to teach people to investigate charges and to be proactive in terms of providing public education. The plans include an alternative dispute resolution (ADR) program and a provision that if the first two steps fail and if issues cannot be resolved through ADR, the EEOC will remain committed to enforcement through litigation.

Other priorities explored under the national enforcement plan are problems in the area of the development of law, including issues on which courts have made conflicting decisions. The number to call with questions or concerns regarding local EEOC Guidelines is (800) 669-4000.

§ 13.15   THE IMPACT OF EEOC CHARGES AND SELECTED CASE FINDINGS

Several significant ADA suits have been filed and concluded. Suits range from allegations regarding discriminatory discharge to those for refusal to hire, failure to provide reasonable accommodation, and disability-specific restrictions in benefits or compensation/wages.

In fiscal 2007, 8.3 percent of charges filed involved allegations of back impairment and another 6.8 percent of charges filed were for depression. Both types of impairments involve "hidden" disabilities (e.g., emotional/psychological impairments), which are difficult for employers to handle in the workplace. Another 17.7 percent of the charges raised the issue of being regarded as disabled, and 16.4 percent was for "all other" types of disability.

In more recent years, many charges have been filed by individuals who were injured on the job, a trend that is likely to continue. It should lead to a variety of issues concerning the coordination of ADA and workers' compensation requirements (and often the FMLA), which sometimes are in conflict.

[A]   Hostile Work Environment

In 2001, two federal circuit courts ruled that employees could sue for disability-based harassment under the ADA. Both courts relied on the similarity between Title VII of the Civil Rights Act of 1964 and the ADA to determine their rulings.

In *Flowers v. Southern Regional Physician Services* [247 F.3d 229 (5th Cir. 2001)], the employee, Flowers, contracted human immunodeficiency virus (HIV). On learning of this, her supervisor began avoiding her and eavesdropping on her conversations. In addition, Flowers was required to undergo four "random" drug tests within a one-week period, received at least three written reprimands, and was twice placed on 90-day probationary periods, despite having received excellent job evaluations before the discovery of her HIV status. Flowers sued, partly on the basis of the hostile work conditions, and the jury in the original trial held in her favor, awarding her $100,000. The Fifth Circuit ruled that the behavior of the plaintiff employee's supervisors was harassment and that Flowers was entitled to recover damages from her employer.

The Fifth Circuit upheld the jury's findings, indicating that "both Title VII and the ADA are aimed at the same evil—employment discrimination against individuals of certain classes" and that both "are also alike in their purposes and remedial structures." Therefore, the court concluded, "the ADA provides a cause of action for disability-based harassment."

The Fourth Circuit came to the same basic conclusion. In *Fox v. General Motors Corp.* [2001 U.S. App. LEXIS 6256 (4th Cir. 2001)] the plaintiff employee injured his back and was placed on a disability leave of absence. On his return, he injured his back again and was restricted to light duty. His supervisor verbally harassed him and instructed his coworkers not to talk to him and other disabled employees, who were labeled "911 hospital people." At the jury trial, Fox was awarded $200,000 because of the hostile work environment; on appeal the Fourth Circuit upheld the award, finding that "Fox presented evidence of objectively severe and pervasive workplace harassment."

Employers should ensure that their policies specifically prohibit disability-based harassment, and disability-based harassment should be included in employee and management training. All complaints of disability-based harassment should be promptly and thoroughly investigated. Immediate corrective action should be taken when warranted.

[B] Essential Job Function

In a 2007 Eighth Circuit case, a rotating shift schedule was deemed to be an essential function of the job [Rehrs v. The Iams Company, No. 06-1609 (8th Cir., May 15, 2007)]. A warehouse worker in Tennessee with diabetes suffered a heart attack. When he returned to work, his doctor restricted him to working an 8-hour day shift, rather than the normal 12-hour shift that rotated every two weeks. The company allowed the accommodation for 60 days. However, the company could not make the accommodation permanent, stating that the rotating shift was an essential function of the job. The rotating shift allowed the workers exposure to "more resources, suppliers and other customers," thereby making them more productive and allowing for more development opportunities leading to promotions. Allowing one worker to have a permanent 8-hour day shift would put more burdens on the other workers in that group. The court agreed that making this accommodation would have caused other employees to "work harder, longer, or be deprived of opportunities."

It is interesting to note the court's position that "the term essential function encompasses more than core job requirements; indeed, it also may include scheduling flexibility."

[C] Knowledge of Disability

In *Hedberg v. Indiana Bell Telephone Co.* [47 F.3d 928 (7th Cir. 1995)], the Seventh Circuit Court of Appeals addressed the issue of whether an employer is liable under the ADA for firing a disabled employee when the company had no knowledge of the disability. The court of appeals affirmed a district court ruling of summary judgment in favor of the employer. Generally, the court rejected the employees' argument and stated that "tardiness and laziness have many causes—few of them based in illness." The ADA does not require employers to retain an employee on the chance that he or she may have a disability causing unacceptable behavior—in this case, tardiness and perceived laziness—if the employer has not been informed of and has no reason to know of a disability. Specifically, although deliberate ignorance cannot shield an employer from liability, the ADA "does not require clairvoyance."

In a related case, *Miller v. National Casualty Co.* [61 F.3d 627 (8th Cir. 1995)], the Eighth Circuit found that when an employee's disability is not obvious or if there are no symptoms, an employer is not obligated to make any accommodations under the ADA. In this case, the court ruled the employer acted within its rights when it fired an employee for excessive absenteeism, even though a mental condition prevented her from working. One week after the firing, the employee notified the employer of the related diagnosis. Before that time, the employee had concealed her condition and had revealed no symptoms over several years of employment.

[D] Regarded as Having a Disability

A significant number of ADA cases are being filed because an individual was "regarded as having a disability." According to EEOC statistics, 17.7 percent of ADA cases in 2007 were filed for this reason. In a case that highlights this issue, *Fitzmaurice v. Great Lakes Computer Corp.* [803 N.E.2d 854 (Ohio 2004)], an employee announced that she had been diagnosed with multiple sclerosis (MS). A month later, she was transferred to another job. Her boss told her, "The number one thing you don't need is stress. I'm doing this for your own good." When the employee later requested that she return to her old job, she was told the job had changed and that she was no longer qualified. She was subsequently fired. The court ruled that the manager's decisions to transfer and fire her were the result of his perception that her ability to work was substantially limited due to the MS.

[E] Total Disability

In one unusual case, a district court judge in Galveston ruled that an employee who received a $305,000 jury award for an allegedly career-ending back injury—and then sought reinstatement eight days later— could not sue his former employer under the ADA. Looking solely at the facts, the court was "astonished by the audacity of the plaintiff in asserting that he was 'rehabilitated' from a permanent disability within eight days."

In several cases, employees and former employees have attempted to simultaneously obtain both disability benefits by claiming they are totally unable to work and ADA protection when denied employment. In the following cases, the courts ruled against the employee. In *Cleveland v. Policy Management Systems Corp.* [119 S. Ct. 1597 (1999)], the plaintiff obtained Social Security Disability Insurance (SSDI) benefits by swearing that he was totally and completely disabled and therefore unable to work. He filed suit under the ADA, which requires that the plaintiff be able to work. The U.S. Supreme Court ruled that in order to survive summary judgment, the plaintiff must provide an explanation "sufficient to warrant a reasonable juror's concluding that, assuming the truth of, or the employee's good faith belief in, the earlier statement, the employee could nonetheless 'perform the essential functions' of [his] job, with or without 'reasonable accommodation.'" The court's analysis suggests that an employee cannot merely disavow the previous statement.

In *Holtzclaw v. DSC Communications Corp.* [255 F.3d 254 (5th Cir. 2001)], the Fifth Circuit upheld the district court's grant of summary judgment. Although Holtzclaw obtained benefits from a private long-term disability insurer rather than from SSDI, the facts in this case were similar to those in *Cleveland* in that Holtzclaw asserted that he was "unable to work at all" and was "too sick" to consider retraining.

[F] AIDS and the ADA

In an important decision on June 25, 1998, the U.S. Supreme Court ruled that HIV is a disability under the ADA, even if an individual has no symptoms of acquired immune deficiency syndrome (AIDS). As research on AIDS progresses, more individuals are living longer, healthier lives. Many HIV-positive individuals are well enough to make return-to-work issues critical for their employers.

Although accommodating these individuals is, in theory, no different from accommodating individuals with any other disabling condition, the realities—including coworkers' misunderstanding and fears—complicate the matter altogether.

Employers must now consider accommodation for individuals taking available "cocktails" of antiviral drugs and protease inhibitors, who must follow a very strict regimen of taking numerous pills at very precise times. Employers must be sure that people returning to work after an episode with HIV/AIDS are reentering a workplace that is supportive of this need.

Ongoing training and education that emphasize the medical realities of this disease and address coworkers' misunderstanding and fears are critical components of an employer's ADA compliance efforts. Employers with a genuine desire to work things out are looking for ways to address a combination of both legal obligations and ethical and employee relations issues when dealing with AIDS-affected employees returning to work.

[G] EEOC Informal Discussion Letters

The decisions of the courts provide useful guidance to employers as they seek to comply with the ADA. Employers should be aware that additional assistance in ADA legal interpretation can be found in the EEOC's informal discussion letters. These letters, published on the EEOC Web site, are responses to individual employers that have requested clarification based on a specific set of circumstances. While they do not have the weight of legal precedent, they do provide insight into the thought process of the EEOC. These informal discussion letters are available at *www.eeoc.gov/foia/letters*.

§ 13.16 CONCLUSION

The ADA continues to challenge the courts, the EEOC, HR professionals, employers, and employees. Even the EEOC's publication *Guidance on Reasonable Job Accommodations for Individuals with Disabilities* (available at the EEOC Web site: *www.eeoc.gov*) raises many questions regarding the lengths to which employers must go to provide accommodation.

Generally, in cases regarding reasonable accommodation, courts are finding that employers are not required to provide specific accommodations requested by an individual or even the "best" accommodation, only one that effectively permits an individual to perform essential job functions. The lesson for employers is that they should carefully scrutinize medically based discharges. Whereas the ADA does not protect individuals with disabilities who cannot perform a job, the employer's responsibility is to ensure that employees' ability to perform essential job functions is accurately assessed.

Employers must consistently document any deficiencies in attendance, performance, and work conduct for all employees. In addition, they should consider reasonable accommodations when they are requested by a person who indicates that he or she has a disability.

Employers should also make the best determination and establish a good-faith defense against potential claims or damages by consulting the individual with the disability about the accommodations, and carefully review and revise any disability-specific restrictive policy or benefit.

Employers should stay current with new case law as it evolves and remember the original intent of the act. Good-faith efforts by employers and a focus on people's abilities rather than their disabilities will allow organizations to utilize the skills of all workers.

(See **Chapter 15** for a discussion of the ADA's interaction with other federal, state, and local laws.)

Exhibit 13.1
ADA Accessibility Guidelines

All new construction and alterations made by the company must be accessible in compliance with the ADA Accessibility Guidelines (ADAAG).

The guidelines contain general design standards for building and site elements, such as parking, accessible routes, ramps, stairs, elevators, doors, entrances, drinking fountains, bathrooms, controls and operating mechanisms, storage areas, alarms, signs, telephones, fixed seating and tables, assembly areas, and dressing rooms. The guidelines also contain scoping requirements for various elements. For example, they specify how many elements and under what circumstances accessibility features must be incorporated.

Some requirements for new construction are as follows:

- *Entrances.* At least 50 percent of public entrances must be accessible. At least one public entrance must be a ground floor entrance. The entrances from enclosed parking garages, pedestrian tunnels, and elevated walkways also must be accessible.

- *Routes to public transportation.* An accessible route must connect accessible public transportation stops, parking spaces, passenger loading zones, and public streets or sidewalks to all accessible features and spaces within a building.

- *Rest rooms.* Every public and common rest room must be accessible. Only one stall must be accessible, unless there are six or more stalls, in which case two stalls must be accessible.

- *Areas of rescue assistance.* Each floor in a building without a supervised sprinkler system must contain an area of rescue assistance where people unable to use the stairs may wait for help during an emergency evacuation.

- *Telecommunication devices for the deaf (TDD).* One TDD must be provided inside any building that has four or more public pay phones, counting both interior and exterior phones. In addition, one TDD must be provided whenever there is an interior public pay phone in a stadium or arena, convention center, hotel with a convention center, covered shopping mall, or hospital emergency, recovery, or waiting room.

- *Public telephone.* One accessible public phone must be provided for each floor, unless the floor has two or more banks of phones, in which case there must be one accessible phone for each bank.

- *Assistive listening devices.* Fixed-seating assembly areas that accommodate 50 or more people or that have audio-amplification systems must have a permanently installed assistive listening system.

- *Wheelchair seating.* Dispersal of wheelchair seating in theaters is required where there are more than 300 seats. In addition, at least 1 percent of all fixed seats must be aisle seats without armrests or with movable armrests. Fixed seating for companions must be located adjacent to each wheelchair location.

- *Accessible parking.* Accessible parking spaces serving a particular building must be located on the shortest accessible route of travel from adjacent parking to an accessible building entrance. Standard

Exhibit 13.1   Mandated Benefits: 2009 Compliance Guide

accessible spaces must have a parking space width of 96 inches, access aisle width of 60 inches, and vertical clearance of 80 inches. Van-accessible building entrance spaces must have a parking space width of 96 inches, access aisle clearance of 96 inches, and vertical clearance of 98 inches. Accessible parking spaces are to be designated as reserved by a sign showing the international symbol of accessibility. The number of parking spaces required is as follows:

Total Spaces Required	Accessible Spaces
1 to 25	1.00
26 to 50	2.00
51 to 75	3.00
76 to 100	4.00
101 to 150	5.00
151 to 200	6.00
201 to 300	7.00
301 to 400	8.00
401 to 500	9.00
501 to 1,000	2% of total
1,001 and more	20, plus 1 for each 100 over 1,000

Exhibit 13.2
Medical Insurance Plan Do's and Don'ts

Do:

- Continue to offer health insurance policies that contain preexisting clauses, even if they adversely affect individuals with disabilities, as long as the clauses are applied consistently and are not used as a subterfuge to evade the purpose of the ADA. Ensure that preexisting clauses are applied in compliance with the Health Insurance Portability and Accountability Act (HIPAA).

- Place limits (to individuals with and without disabilities equally) through the insurance policy on reimbursements for certain procedures or on the types of drugs or procedures covered (e.g., limits on the number of permitted X-rays, or noncoverage of experimental drugs or procedures)

- Conduct voluntary medical examinations, including voluntary medical histories, as part of employee wellness programs (e.g., medical screening for high blood pressure, weight control counseling, and cancer detection) (Medical records developed in the course of such activities must be maintained in a confidential manner and must not be used to limit health insurance eligibility.)

Don't:

- Make an employment decision or justify disparate treatment of an individual with a disability based on speculation that the individual may cause increased health insurance costs

- Refuse to make reasonable accommodations that enable employees with disabilities to enjoy the same benefits and privileges of employment as those enjoyed by other similarly situated employees without disabilities

- Reduce the level of health insurance benefits offered simply because a dependent of an employee has a disability

- Use voluntary medical examinations, including voluntary medical histories, that are part of an employee wellness program for the purpose of limiting health insurance eligibility

- Use any of the accepted principles of risk assessment or current insurance industry underwriting practices as a subterfuge to evade the purpose of the ADA

Appendix 13-A
Implementing Title I of the ADA:
Sample Policies and Procedural Issues to Consider

To help identify possible ADA-related problems in the company's employment policies and procedures, the company could use a self-audit checklist (see **Appendix 13-B**). A number of procedural issues must be addressed, however. Essentially, all management personnel must be involved in communicating, training, and conducting the policy review and, as a result, there are a number of preliminary issues and actions to consider. Managers should:

- *Obtain support from top management.* Even if top management consists of one person, that person must demonstrate commitment to the principles of the ADA.

- *Designate someone in the company to coordinate ADA compliance efforts.* This is likely to be either an officer or the HR director.

- *Solicit comments of employees with disabilities, if any, by having them participate in the policy review process.* This will give the broadest range of participation possible.

- *Write a policy of nondiscrimination to be included in all written information about the company that you distribute to the public and prospective and current employees.*

- *Contact all groups that represent segments of the company's workforce, such as unions and employment services, to tell them of the company's nondiscrimination policies.*

- *Through employee communication or open-door policies, encourage employees or applicants to share complaints or observations about the company's efforts to comply with the ADA.* If negative observations are presented, managers should establish methods to deal with problems promptly and with equality.

- *As people in the company conduct the parts of the self-audit in which they have particular expertise, assign specific responsibility and a date for completion for each area in which a deficiency exists.*

The company should document its ADA compliance efforts and retain a written record of the review process. Having this information on file will serve as evidence of the company's desire to achieve compliance.

Appendixes 13-C and **13-D** provide a breakdown of compliance do's and don'ts and enforcement powers and penalties under Title I.

Appendix 13-B
ADA Self-Audit Checklist

The following checklist has been designed to address ADA-related compliance issues concerning current employees and candidates for employment. Employers should:

- Make compliance issues specific and unambiguous.

- Restructure position descriptions to determine both the physical and the psychological essential functions of each job, making sure the standards that have been developed do not discriminate against anyone, unless the company can prove that the standards are necessary and specifically related to the position.

- Develop a written policy concerning reasonable accommodation.

- Develop a procedure for evaluating whether reasonable accommodation causes undue hardship.

- Determine whether all company events and activities are accessible to all employees.

- Review job advertisements (which should not refer to nonessential or marginal requirements).

- Review all company benefits, including life insurance, health and hospitalization coverage, and retirement packages, to be sure that disabled employees are not treated in a discriminatory manner.

- Post EEO notices so they can be read and provide access to these notices in braille, large print, and audiocassette or CD.

- Review policies and practices to ensure that any known employee who is a recovering alcoholic or drug abuser (who is not presently using alcohol or drugs) is not discriminated against under the law (candidates for employment who are recovering from alcohol or drug abuse are also included).

- Review all administrative procedures to determine if job standards or criteria have the effect of discriminating against those with disabilities and whether common administrative controls create discrimination against others.

- Determine if the company has contracts or other arrangements that subject employees and applicants with a disability to discrimination.

- Review relationships with labor unions, employment agencies, benefits providers, apprenticeship programs, and agencies that provide training.

- Assess whether employees or employment candidates are limited, classified, or segregated in ways that would not allow for promotion or other positive changes in status due to disability.

- Review procedures to be sure employees and applicants are not being discriminated against because they have friends or family who are disabled.

- Edit current job applications to remove any prohibited questions or inquiries about whether a candidate has a disability.

- Make not only the area where applications are accepted and interviews are given accessible, but also the processes (e.g., providing readers for a person with a visual impairment).

- If employment tests are used, give them in a way that relates the skill or ability to the position. (Readers, sign language, interpreters, and assistance for people with manual disabilities may be necessary. Tests may need to be made available in braille or audiocassette.)

- Make no medical judgments; consult a doctor or other experts to determine whether a disabled applicant can perform essential functions.

- Review employment policies to be sure all applicants and employees are treated in a nondiscrimina-tory fashion. Specific policies to review include:

    — Recruiting procedures for new employees

    — Tests and testing formats

    — Actual hiring decisions

    — Factors on which to base promotions

    — Factors on which to base demotions

    — Layoffs

    — Terminations

    — Calls back to work from layoffs

    — Rehires

- Review the company's application processes, clearly defining when applications will and will not be accepted and how long they will be retained for future consideration.

Appendix 13-C
Title I Compliance Do's and Don'ts

Do:

- Make sure that any person with a disability can access any of the company's facilities and the human resources department

- Review all employment applications, and interviewing and selection forms, to ensure that no unlawful inquiries are made by the HR department or by others involved in the selection process

- Carefully review all the company's job descriptions and selection criteria to ensure that selection criteria are job-related

- Identify essential job functions for all positions and the physical and mental demands of each job

- Train employees and managers on how to communicate appropriately with persons who have disabilities

- Train employees who interview on what can and cannot be asked in job interviews

- Identify accommodations for specific jobs and functions

- Describe or demonstrate the job functions to applicants and ask them whether they can perform the functions with or without reasonable accommodation

Don't:

- Make any inquiries regarding a person's physical characteristics, health, disability, or workers' compensation history either on the employment application or during the interview process

- Make employment decisions based on a perception or belief about the individual's physical or mental abilities or disabilities

- Limit an employee's duties on the basis of a presumption of what is best for that person

- Deny a person access to the company building or personnel office on the basis of a disability

- Segregate employees with disabilities

- Establish selection criteria for positions that are not clearly required of or related to the job

- Require medical examinations or physicals on a preemployment basis

- Refuse to provide a reasonable accommodation to an individual at any point in the employment or preemployment process

Appendix 13-D
Enforcement Powers and Penalties Under Title I

Charges of discrimination can be filed against employers with 25 or more employees beginning July 26, 1992. The alleged act of discrimination by a company must have occurred on or after July 26, 1992.

Charges can be filed against employers with 15 or more employees beginning July 26, 1994. The alleged discrimination must have occurred on or after July 26, 1994, if the charge is against an employer with 15 to 24 employees.

Charges may be filed in person, by phone, or by mail by an applicant or employee who feels that he or she has been discriminated against in employment on the basis of a disability.

The Equal Employment Opportunity Commission (EEOC) is the agency primarily responsible for enforcing the ADA. Some charges, however, may be sent to a state or local agency for investigation, depending on the work-sharing agreements the EEOC has with many state and local fair-employment agencies.

An individual also may file a lawsuit against a company, but the charge must be filed first with the EEOC. The charging party can request a "right to sue" letter from the EEOC 180 days after the charge was first filed with the EEOC. A charging party will then have 90 days to file suit after receiving notice of the right to sue. If the charging party files suit, the EEOC will ordinarily dismiss the original charges filed with the commission. Right-to-sue letters also are issued when the EEOC does not believe discrimination occurred, or when conciliation attempts fail and the EEOC decides not to sue on the charging party's behalf.

The relief or remedies available for employment discrimination, whether caused by intentional acts or by practices that have a discriminatory effect, may include hiring, reinstatement, promotion, back pay, front pay, reasonable accommodation, or other actions. Remedies also may include payment of attorneys' fees, expert witness fees, and court costs.

Compensatory and punitive damages may be available when intentional discrimination by the company is found. Damages may be available to compensate for actual monetary losses, for mental anguish, and for inconvenience. Punitive damages may be awarded if the company acted with malice or reckless indifference. The total amount of punitive damages and compensatory damages for future monetary loss and emotional injury for each individual is limited, based on the size of the employer, using the following schedule:

Number of Employees	Damages Cannot Exceed
15 to 100	$ 50,000
101 to 200	100,000
201 to 500	200,000
501 or more	300,000

In cases concerning reasonable accommodation, compensatory or punitive damages may not be awarded to the charging party if the company can demonstrate that good faith efforts were made to provide reasonable accommodation.

Chapter 14
Family and Medical Leave

§ 14.01   AUDIT QUESTIONS

1. Has the company posted a notice explaining rights and responsibilities under the Family and Medical Leave Act of 1993 (FMLA), including the new Military Family Leave Notice?

2. Has the company provided written notice to employees who have requested a family or medical leave, providing them with the required information?

3. Has the company determined whether the state(s) in which it operates has/have FMLA regulations, and has it written its leave policies to comply with both state and federal requirements?

4. Has the company devised a uniform method of determining the 12-month period in which FMLA leave entitlements occur?

5. Has the company developed a procedure for collecting the employee's share of the health plan premium while the employee is on an FMLA leave?

Note: Consistent "yes" answers to the above questions suggest that the organization is applying effective management practices and/or complying with federal requirements. "No" answers indicate that problem areas exist and should be addressed immediately.

This chapter summarizes the provisions of the Family and Medical Leave Act of 1993 (FMLA). The chapter also provides definitions of related key terms and interpretations.

Medical leave requirements typically deal with an employee's inability to work due to a medical condition. Family leaves permit employees to be absent from work for reasons other than their own health, usually to assist an immediate family member. The FMLA covers both types of leave. Employers should be aware that many states have their own family and medical leave laws. They should check the family and medical leave laws in the states where their companies do business in order to properly integrate those laws into their companies' leave policies.

§ 14.02   EVOLUTION OF THE LAW

Before the enactment of the federal FMLA, U.S. employers were not required by law to provide either paid or unpaid leave, but did so voluntarily. As more women, especially single mothers, entered the U.S. workforce from the 1960s through the 1980s, attention began to focus on all employees, both male and female, who need to balance work and family responsibilities. As a result, by 1993, 30 states had passed laws providing some type of job-protected family or medical leave.

Legislation on family and medical leave had been an issue at the national level since the mid-1980s. Congress passed several family and medical leave bills in the late 1980s; all, however, were vetoed by then President George H. Bush.

The FMLA was introduced in the House of Representatives in January 1993 and was passed by the Senate on February 4. It was the first law signed by President Bill Clinton on February 5, 1993. The Department of Labor (DOL) issued final regulations that became effective on April 6, 1995. In 2001, the DOL released a survey of employers and employees regarding the use of family and medical leave. The survey estimated that the FMLA's provisions cover more than half of all employees in the private sector (58.3 percent) and 10.8 percent of all U.S. businesses. The survey estimated that between 83 million and 94 million employees were eligible to take FMLA leave.

In the first major update since the passage of the law, the DOL issued notice of new regulations in February 2008. A summary of proposed regulations is found in **Section 14.20**. As of this writing, final regulations have not been published.

Another significant new law was passed in 2008, the National Defense Authorization Act for Fiscal Year 2008 (NDAA). This "Military Family Leave" law is an amendment to the FMLA. A description of the new law is found in **Section 14.11**.

The FMLA has six titles, five of which refer to family and medical leave:

- Title I, General Requirements for Leave, covers most private employers. It describes the reasons allowed for leave, duration of leaves and reinstatements, and obligations of employers and employees, and it provides definitions of the key terms of the FMLA.

- Title II, Leave for Civil Service Employees, provides the same type of information as Title I but covers civil service employees.

- Title III, Commission on Leave, established a bipartisan commission to investigate and prepare a report regarding the impact of this legislation on employers and employees, to review the state laws, and to investigate potential legislation to provide leave benefits for employees not covered under the FMLA. The commission, which was chaired by Senator Christopher Dodd (D-CT), disbanded in 1996 following completion of its investigation and report.

- Title IV, Miscellaneous Provisions, includes provisions for integrating with state laws, a statement of nondiscrimination, and establishment of regulations that had to be provided by the DOL within 120 days of the signing of the FMLA.

- Title V, Coverage of Congressional Employees, provides for similar coverage for Senate and House employees and describes a few areas of distinction from Titles I and II.

- Title VI, Sense of Congress, is a rider that requires the Secretary of the Department of Defense to review its policies with respect to the service of homosexuals in the armed forces.

§ 14.03 BASIC PARAMETERS OF THE LAW

The federal FMLA provides that an eligible employee must be allowed up to 12 workweeks of unpaid, job-protected leave within a 12-month period for any of the following reasons:

- Birth or adoption of a child, placement of a child for adoption, foster care for children under age 18, or adoption of a child age 18 or older if the child is incapable of self-care because of physical or mental disability.

- Caring for a child, spouse, or parent with a serious health condition.

- The employee's own serious health condition.

The law also provides that heath care benefits, if offered, must be continued during the employee's absence, but not other benefits.

§ 14.04 DEFINITIONS

The FMLA defines a number of terms, which will be discussed in the following sections.

[A] Eligible Employee

To be eligible for FMLA leave, an employee must meet all the following requirements:

- Be an employee who has been employed for a total of at least 12 months by the employer on the date on which any FMLA leave is to commence.

- Have been employed, on the date on which any FMLA leave is to commence, for at least 1,250 hours with the employer granting the leave during the previous 12-month period.

- Be employed in any state, the District of Columbia, or any U.S. territory or possession.

The following individuals are not eligible employees and therefore are not entitled to FMLA leave:

- Any federal officer or employee covered under U.S.C. Title V, chapter 63, subchapter V.

- Any employee of the Senate or the House of Representatives covered under Title V of the FMLA.

- Any individual who is employed at a work site at which the employer employs fewer than 50 employees, if the total number of employees within 75 miles, measured by the shortest route using surface transportation, is also fewer than 50.

- Any individual employed anywhere other than in the United States, a U.S. territory, or a U.S. possession

The 12 months the employee must have been employed need not be consecutive months. If the employee is maintained on the payroll for any part of a week, including any periods of paid or unpaid leave (e.g., sick or vacation leave) during which other benefits are provided by the employer (e.g., workers' compensation), the week counts as a week of employment. To determine when intermittent, casual, or occasional employment equates to at least 12 months, 52 weeks is considered to equal 12 months. Throughout the regulations, calendar days are intended when a number of days is prescribed, unless the regulation explicitly states business days.

According to a First Circuit ruling, employees with a break in service can count prior service as part of the 12-month eligibility requirement. [Rucker v. Lee Holding Co., dba Lee Auto Malls, 471 F.3d 6 (1st Cir. 2006)] In this case, the employee had a five-year break in service, and had been reemployed for less than one year. However, counting his employment prior to the break in service, he had 12 months of employment. Note that an employee must also meet the requirement to have worked at least 1,250 hours in the last 12 months to be covered by FMLA.

Any accurate method of accounting for the hours worked is acceptable under the FMLA. If the employer cannot account for the time worked, including the time worked for exempt employees, such as executive, administrative, or professional employees, the burden of proof is on the employer to show that an employee has not met the hours test to be eligible for leave. The method of recording time worked for all employees should be reviewed to ensure that company records are sufficient for this purpose.

The term *work site* is equivalent to the term *single site of employment* under the Worker Adjustment and Retraining Notification Act of 1988 (WARN Act) regulations. For employees with no fixed work site (e.g., construction workers), the work site is the single site of employment to which they are assigned as their home base. For salespersons and other employees who work out of their homes, the site of employment is the site from which their work is assigned or to which they report; their homes are not their site of employment.

Under the FMLA's definition of *employee*, persons who are partners in a business are not counted as employees even if their names appear on the payroll. However, equity owners (e.g., stockholders) may be considered employees in the corporation and, as such, if their names appear on the payroll, they are included in the count of employees and may be eligible for leave.

[1] Employees of Local Education Agencies

The FMLA contains special rules for employees of private and public elementary and secondary schools (i.e., those involved in instruction). The rules' stated intention in addressing those who teach is to balance the education needs of children with the family leave needs of teachers. Full-time teachers of an elementary or secondary school or institution of higher education or other educational establishment or institution are automatically assumed to have met the 1,250-hour eligibility test. If the employer wishes to deny leave, the burden of proof is on the employer to show that an employee has not met the hours test.

The term *teacher* applies to any employee employed principally in an instructional capacity by an educational agency or school whose principal function is to teach and instruct students in a class, a small group, or an individual setting, and it includes athletic coaches, driving instructors, and special education assistants (e.g., signers for the hearing impaired).

The FMLA rules do not apply to the following employees:

- Teacher assistants or aides who do not have as their principal function actual teaching or instructing

- Auxiliary personnel such as counselors, psychologists, curriculum specialists, cafeteria workers, maintenance workers, school bus drivers, or other primarily noninstructional employees

One of the key provisions regarding teachers is in the area of intermittent and reduced leave requests. If a teacher requests leave for his or her own illness or to care for a spouse, child, or parent, and the intermittent leave means that the teacher will be out of the classroom for more than 20 percent of the time, the school may require that the teacher either take a complete leave for the necessary period or transfer to a similar position that better accommodates intermittent or reduced leave.

The other key provision has to do with the timing of a teacher's return from leave. If the return would fall within the last few weeks of an academic term, the following regulations apply:

- If a teacher requests three or more weeks of leave more than five weeks before the end of the academic term, the employer may require the teacher to continue taking leave until the end of the term, as long as leave would otherwise end within three weeks of the end of that term;

- If a teacher requests leave for purposes other than the teacher's own serious health condition less than five weeks before the end of an academic term, and leave is to be of at least two weeks in duration, the employer may require the teacher to continue taking leave until the end of the term, as long as the leave would otherwise end within two weeks of the term; or

- If a teacher requests to begin leave for purposes other than the teacher's own serious health condition less than three weeks before the end of an academic term, and leave is to be more than five working days in length, the employer may require the teacher to continue taking leave until the end of the term.

[2] Civil Service Employees

The provisions for civil service employees are basically the same as those for private industry employees. The regulations for such employees are issued by the Office of Personnel Management, which makes every effort to keep the regulations consistent with those issued by the Secretary of Labor. Unless agreed to before the performance of work, public employers may not use their employees' compensatory time as a form of accrued paid leave to be used as FMLA leave.

In April 1997, President Clinton expanded leave for federal employees by granting up to 24 hours of unpaid leave each year for emergencies and family matters, allowing the time to be used for such reasons as attendance at a child's school conference or for family medical appointments.

On May 27, 2003, the Supreme Court affirmed that the FMLA covers state employees by ruling that they may sue their employers in federal court for alleged violations of the FMLA. The main issue in *Nevada Department of Human Resources v. Hibbs* [123 S. Ct. 1972 (2003)] was whether Congress could apply the FMLA to state employers and authorize employees to sue the states if they failed to provide the required leave. In its 6-3 decision, the Court indicated that state employees may sue their employers, providing them the same rights as private sector employees.

[3] Coverage of Congress

Senate and House employees are covered basically in the same manner as private industry employees.

[B] Covered Employer

The term *employer* applies to any entity engaged in interstate commerce or in an industry or activity affecting commerce that employs 50 or more employees for each working day during each of 20 or more calendar workweeks in the current or preceding year. The term also applies to any person who acts directly or indirectly in the interest of an employer, any employee of an employer, any successor in interest of an employer, and any public agency.

The FMLA covers all federal, state, and local government agencies, public schools, and private employers with 50 or more employees at a work site or within a 75-mile radius, as measured by accessible roads. The company must have employed 50 or more people—either part time, full time, or temporary—for 20 weeks or more in the current or previous year. Those weeks do not have to be consecutive, but there must be a cumulative total of 20 weeks. The total number of employees maintained on the payroll, not just the eligible employees, must be counted.

> **Example.** Fancy Fashions, a department store, has two sites 100 miles apart. Site A has 30 employees; Site B, 40. Fancy Fashions is a covered employer under the FMLA, even though it may have no eligible employees at either site. Drake's Hardware has a different situation. Drake's has two sites located 100 miles apart. Site A has 30 employees; Site B has 50 employees. Drake's Hardware is a covered employer under the FMLA. Eligible employees are at Site B. From an employee-relations standpoint, Drake may have a difficult time offering leave to employees at Site B but not to those at Site A. Treating similarly situated employees differently may be prohibited by state law as well.

If an eligible employee of a covered predecessor employer begins FMLA leave before the business is sold, that employee is entitled to be returned to employment by the successor employer without restriction.

[C] Integrated Employers

The FMLA covers leased employees, franchises, and other similar business arrangements by adopting an integrated employer test that is parallel to the test used under Title VII of the Civil Rights Act of 1964. The individual determinations of whether to treat separate entities as a single entity are highly fact-specific and are based on (1) common management, (2) the interrelation between operations, (3) centralized control of labor relations, and (4) the degree of common ownership, financial control, or both.

Not all factors have to be present. The relationship is viewed as a whole, not judged on a single criterion. Because each case rests on a specific set of facts, the regulations do not provide detailed guidance. One case, *Hukill v. Auto Care, Inc.* [192 F.3d 437 (4th Cir. 1999)], has analyzed whether distinct corporate entities would be viewed as an integrated employer. In finding that the entities involved were not an integrated employer, the court relied on the fact that each entity at issue controlled its own labor relations on a day-to-day basis. In light of this ruling, the court refused to address whether the regulation adopting the integrated employer analysis into the FMLA is valid.

[D] Joint Employers

Joint employment relationships present unique compliance concerns for temporary help and leased employees. At issue is the legal right guaranteed to the eligible employee on leave to be returned to the previous position or an equivalent position. Under the regulations, the primary employer (i.e., the temporary placement or leasing agency) is responsible for providing FMLA information, maintenance of health benefits, providing leave, and restoring the employee to the job. Because of the joint nature of the employment relationship, however, the secondary employer (i.e., the employer at whose site the employee works) is responsible for accepting an employee returning from leave in place of any replacement employee.

The secondary employer is prohibited by statute from interfering with, restraining, or denying the employee his or her full rights under the FMLA, nor may the secondary employer interfere with, restrain, or deny efforts by the primary employer to restore the employee to his or her prior position, provided that the primary employer is still providing the same services to the secondary employer. Because the secondary employer is acting in the interest of the primary employer, the secondary employer assumes this responsibility regardless of the number of employees employed by the secondary employer. In other words, if the primary employer meets the requirements for coverage under the FMLA, whether the secondary employer meets the requirements is irrelevant.

Thus, an individual employee's right to take leave is determined by counting the number of employees employed by that employee's primary employer. The count excludes any permanent employees primarily employed by the secondary employer, thereby preventing the same employee from being counted twice. The employee's primary employer at the time the employee requests FMLA leave is responsible for counting hours to determine when an employee has worked the required 1,250 hours of work.

In limited situations, temporary employees who find their spots filled upon return from leave go to the head of the list for placement by the temporary help company. If, for legitimate business reasons unrelated to the taking of FMLA leave, the client of a temporary help company discontinues the services of the temporary help company (i.e., the contract under which the employee who took FMLA leave was working has ended) or discontinues the services formerly performed by the employee who took FMLA leave, and no equivalent temporary help jobs are available at the same client of the temporary help company, the obligation of the temporary help employer is to find an equivalent temporary help job to which to restore the returning employee at another client company. If no other equivalent positions are available with other clients, and if the returning employee typically experienced waits between jobs in the ordinary course of his or her employment with the temporary help placement company, the employee is entitled to priority consideration for the next suitable placement with other customers.

On the other hand, if the client is still using agency employees in the same or equivalent positions, the agency is required to reinstate the employee immediately, even if it would be required to remove another employee.

The factors that are considered in meeting a joint employer test include:

- The nature and degree of control of workers

- The degree of supervision of work

- The power to determine pay rates or methods

- The right to make employment decisions

- The payment of wages

While many joint employer issues involve a hiring company and an agency, joint employers could also involve two separate organizations with common ownership or joint venture projects. In a recent case, the 7th Circuit addressed the issue of joint employment between the City of Pekin and the County of Tazewell, Illinois. The two organizations created a non-profit corporation to provide 911 emergency communication. The created entity was called Tazcom.

An employee diagnosed with chronic pancreatitis requested FMLA leave, and was denied the leave because Tazcom was under 50 employees. She was subsequently fired for excessive absenteeism. She filled suit in federal court against Tazcom, the City of Pekin and the County of Tazewell, claiming she was fired in violation of her FMLA rights. The district court granted summary judgment to the defendants, affirming that Pekin and Tazewell were not joint employers. Although Tazcom rented office space from Pekin and contracted for health care benefits from Pekin, Tazcom was run independently by their executive director, and the other entities had no control over the hiring or firing of employees or the way work was performed. [Moldenhauer v. Tazewell-Perkin Consolidated Communications Center, No. 07-1118, 2008 U.S. App. LEXIS 16230 (7th Cir., July 31, 2008)]

[E] Public Agencies

All public agencies are covered employers under the FMLA, regardless of the number of employees. Public agencies include the U.S. government, state governments or a political subdivision thereof, any U.S. agency (including the U.S. Postal Service and the Postal Rate Commission), a state or a political subdivision of a state, and any interstate governmental agency.

[F] Indian Tribes

As of 2002, no court decisions regarding the applicability of the FMLA to Indian (Native American) tribes existed. However, the Secretary of Labor at the time took the position that the FMLA applies to tribes. In 2004, the Second Circuit Court of Appeals affirmed that Native American tribes are not subject to the FMLA. [Chayoon v. Chao, 355 F.3d 141 (2d Cir. 2004)] The court stated that only Congress could extend FMLA application to Indian tribes.

Tribes should be aware that the Second Circuit covers only New York, Connecticut, and Vermont, and should consult counsel regarding the latest court decisions in their respective areas.

[G] Child and Parent

The law is intended to be flexible here. The term *child* is defined as "biological, adopted, or foster child, legal ward, or a child of a person standing in loco parentis." This chapter uses the phrase "birth or adoption of a child" to include all circumstances that fall under this definition.

The term "parent" may also be subject to some flexibility. In a 2005 Maryland case, the court stated that a grandparent could qualify as "immediate family" if he or she acted "in loco parentis." [Dillon v. Maryland-Nat'l Capital Park & Planning Commission, 382 F. Supp. 777 (D. Md. 2005)]

Employers should note that, with respect to family leave following the birth of a child, the FMLA does not include a requirement that the parent requesting leave be married to the child's other parent. The child must be under 18 years of age or incapable of self-care because of mental or physical disability. "Incapable of self-care" means that the person requires active assistance or supervision to provide daily self-care in several of the activities of daily living (ADLs) or instrumental activities of daily living (IADLs). ADLs include caring for one's grooming and hygiene, bathing, dressing, and eating. IADLs include cooking, cleaning, and shopping.

[H] Health Care Provider

A *health care provider* is defined as one of the following:

- A doctor of medicine or osteopathy who is authorized to practice medicine or surgery by the state in which the doctor practices

- A podiatrist, dentist, clinical psychologist, optometrist, or chiropractor (limited to treatment consisting of manual manipulation of the spine to correct a subluxation identified by X-ray) authorized to practice in the state and performing within the scope of his or her practice as defined under state law

- A nurse practitioner, nurse-midwife, or clinical social worker who is authorized to practice under state law and who is performing within the scope of his or her practice as defined under state law

- Any Christian Science practitioner listed with the First Church of Christ, Scientist, in Boston, Massachusetts

- Any health care provider from whom an employer or a group health plan's benefits manager accepts certification of the existence of a serious health condition to substantiate a claim for benefits

- A health care provider (as defined above) who practices in a country other than the United States and is licensed to practice in accordance with the laws and regulations of that country

The FMLA provides that the Secretary of Labor may determine that additional health care providers are eligible under the FMLA.

[I] Serious Health Condition

Serious health condition is defined as an illness, injury, impairment, or physical or mental condition that involves inpatient care in a hospital, hospice, or residential medical care facility or continuing treatment by a health care provider.

Continuing treatment is defined as a serious health condition involving continuing treatment by a health care provider in one or more of the following:

- A period of incapacity (i.e., inability to work, attend school, or perform other regular daily activities owing to a serious health condition, treatment, or recovery) of more than three consecutive calendar days and any subsequent treatment or period of incapacity relating to the same condition that also involve:

  — Treatment two or more times by a health care provider, by a nurse or physician's assistant under direct supervision of a health care provider, or by a provider of health care services (e.g., a physical therapist) under orders of, or on referral by, a health care provider.

  — Treatment by a health care provider on at least one occasion that results in a regimen of continuing treatment under the supervision of the health care provider.

- Any period of incapacity due to pregnancy or for prenatal care

- Any period of incapacity or treatment for such incapacity due to a chronic serious health condition that:

  — Requires periodic visits for treatment by a health care provider, or by a nurse or physician's assistant under direct supervision of a health care provider.

  — Continues over an extended period of time, including recurring episodes of a single underlying condition.

  — May cause episodic rather than a continuing period of incapacity (e.g., asthma, diabetes, or epilepsy).

- A period of incapacity that is permanent or long term due to a condition for which treatment may not be effective; a period under the continuing supervision of, but not necessarily requiring active treatment by, a health care provider (e.g., Alzheimer's disease, a severe stroke, or the terminal stages of a disease).

- Any period of absence to receive multiple treatments, including any recovery period, by a health care provider or by a provider of health care services under orders of, or on referral by, a health care provider, either for restorative surgery after an accident or other injury or for a condition that would likely result in a period of incapacity of more than three consecutive calendar days in the absence of medical intervention or treatment, such as cancer (e.g., chemotherapy or radiation), severe arthritis (e.g., physical therapy), or kidney disease dialysis.

Additional visits to a health care provider are not necessary in conjunction with each absence.

The FMLA is not intended to cover short-term conditions for which treatment and recovery are brief, such as illnesses that last only a few days or surgical procedures that do not involve hospitalization and require only a brief recovery period. Conditions for which cosmetic treatments are administered, such as most treatments for acne or plastic surgery, are not serious health conditions unless inpatient hospital care is required or unless complications develop. Ordinarily, unless complications arise, the common cold, the flu, earaches, upset stomach, ulcers, headaches other than migraine, routine dental or orthodontia procedures, and periodontal disease are examples of conditions that do not meet the definition of a serious health condition and do not qualify for FMLA leave. However, the courts have routinely noted that this list does not take the place of the application of the regulations defining serious health conditions and that each case must be judged on a case-by-case basis. The courts have made it clear that the nature of the underlying condition has no bearing on the issue of whether or not it constitutes a serious health condition. The only question is whether the condition meets the technical requirements of the statute. One example is *Miller v. AT&T Corp.* [60 F. Supp. 2d 574 (S.D. W. Va. 1999)], a case in which the court granted the employee summary judgment, concluding that the employee's flu met the definition of serious health condition despite its exclusion by the regulation.

Companies should be aware that in 1997, the DOL issued an opinion letter stating that any medical condition lasting for three consecutive calendar days or more and requiring continuing treatment by a health care provider qualifies under the FMLA. They should also be aware that in a related court case in which an employee with a routine stomach disorder who was fired for missing work was found to be covered under FMLA, the court determined that even though the cause for missing several weeks of work was not severe, the employee was receiving continuing treatment by a health care provider.

Even working a second job may not negate a finding of a serious health condition. In *Stekloff v. St. John's Mercy Health Systems* [218 F.3d 858 (8th Cir. 2000)], an employee continued to work a second job after taking a leave of absence due to emotional distress in her primary job. In the second job, she performed essentially the same job functions as in her primary job. The primary employer fired her for "job abandonment" contending that if she could work an essentially similar job, she could not have a serious health condition. The court ruled that the employee's leave was protected under the FMLA—she proved she could not work in the primary employer's environment due to the emotional distress it created. The court further ruled that she did not need to prove that she could not work in any environment in order to prove she had a serious health condition.

The FMLA final regulations of 1995 expand the definition of treatment to include "examinations to determine if a serious health condition exists." Presumably, treatment includes a physical examination during which the patient reports some symptom. Routine physical, eye, and dental examinations are excluded from coverage. Similarly, taking prescription medications is a qualifying regimen of treatment, but taking over-the-counter medications, bed rest, ingestion of fluids, and exercise are not.

Restorative dental or plastic surgery after an injury and removal of cancerous growths are serious health conditions, provided all the other conditions are met. Allergies and mental illness resulting from stress may be serious health conditions, but only if all other conditions are met.

The term *incapacity* includes injuries or illnesses that are work related and inpatient care or continuing treatment or supervision by a health care provider. Pregnancy is given as an example of continuing care. Incapacity because of pregnancy and prenatal care is now considered a serious health condition, so companies must recognize that such incapacity triggers leave rights for the pregnant woman's husband, parents, and presumably even her children, if and when they are needed to care for her.

The 1995 regulations make it clear that absences occasioned by pregnancy-related incapacity qualify for FMLA leave even though the employee or the immediate family member does not receive treatment from a health care provider during the absence. The example cited involved an employee who was unable to report to work because of "severe morning sickness." In this case, it seems clear that leave is now available to the employee who must stay home to care for a similarly incapacitated wife, daughter, or mother.

In a related court case, *Gudenkauf v. Stauffer Communications, Inc.* [158 F.3d 1074 (10th Cir. 1998)], the employee claimed her employer violated the FMLA when it discharged her following her request to work a reduced schedule on account of complications she suffered during her pregnancy. The court recognized that a period of incapacity caused by complications from pregnancy is specifically recognized as a serious health condition by the regulations. However, the employee was not able to provide sufficient evidence of her inability to work. As a result, the court concluded that her pregnancy was not a serious health condition and she was not protected by the FMLA.

Congress has listed a number of examples of "serious health conditions." They include, but are not limited to, "heart attacks, heart conditions requiring heart bypass of valve operations, most cancers, back conditions requiring extensive therapy or surgical procedures, strokes, severe respiratory conditions, spinal injuries, appendicitis, pneumonia, emphysema, severe arthritis, severe nervous disorders, injuries caused by serious accidents on or off the job, ongoing pregnancy, miscarriages, complications or illnesses related to pregnancy, such as severe morning sickness, the need for prenatal care, childbirth, and recovery from childbirth." Chronic and long-term conditions, such as asthma, requiring multiple treatments and brief, episodic absences, are also covered.

The regulations deal with chronic conditions much more broadly than the interim regulations, which state that a condition involving continuing treatment or supervision by a health care provider is considered a serious health condition, even though the individual does not suffer more than three days of incapacity, so long as the condition is "incurable or so serious that, if not treated, would likely result in a period of incapacity of more than three calendar days." The final regulations contain additional provisions defining chronic serious health conditions without reference to any minimum periods of actual or potential incapacity.

The regulations also indicate that even though a chronic serious health condition must, by definition, require periodic treatments over an extended period, an absence due to incapacity caused by a chronic serious health condition may qualify for FMLA leave even if the employee or family member does not receive any treatment. The example cited was that of an employee unable to report to work because of an asthma attack "or because the employee's health care provider has advised the employee to stay home when the pollen count exceeds a certain level."

Under the regulations, the health care provider may be required to certify that an employee is either unable to perform his or her functions or is needed to care for the family member. To be unable to perform the job, the employee must be unable to perform any one or more of the essential functions of the job he or she held at the time the need for leave arose.

The regulations clearly indicate that absence to obtain treatment for substance abuse qualifies for FMLA leave. However, FMLA leave may be taken only for treatment for substance abuse by a health care provider or by a provider of health care services referred by a health care provider. Such treatment need not interfere with an employer's taking disciplinary action against an employee, provided an established written policy is applied consistently. In *Jeremy v. Northwest Ohio Development Center* [33 F. Supp. 2d 635 (N.D. Ohio 1999)], the employee requested FMLA leave for the length of his DUI (driving while under the influence) jail term on grounds that he needed the leave to be treated for alcoholism. His employer denied the request. The court upheld the employer's denial of FMLA leave, stating that although alcoholism may qualify as a serious health condition, FMLA leave may be taken only for the treatment of substance abuse.

In *Domnick v. Ver Halen, Inc.* [No. 02-C-375-X, 2003 U.S. Dist. LEXIS 11694 (W.D. Wis. Mar. 10, 2003)], an employee hospitalized with alcoholic pancreatitis was fired for unexcused absences. The employer argued that because the hospitalization was the result of alcohol abuse, the employee was not covered by the FMLA. The court held that the employee's condition met the definition of serious health condition, and that the cause was not relevant.

The final version of the law specifically states that absence because of the "employee's use of the substance, rather than for treatment" does not qualify for FMLA leave. Given this language, it is possible to contend that an alcoholic employee's absence while on a drinking binge may not be FMLA-protected, but his or her absence during a severe hangover may well be, as long as the employee has sought treatment for alcoholism.

By specifically limiting the use disqualification to employees, the regulations seem to support the claim that an employee's absence caused by a child's, spouse's, or parent's drug- or alcohol-induced incapacity may be protected by the FMLA. Either the health condition or its treatment must require that the employee be incapacitated and absent from work on a recurring basis or for more than three calendar days for treatment or recovery.

[J] To Care For

The term *to care for* is intended to include either physical or psychological care and comfort to family members. The regulations specifically refer to situations in which the family member is receiving inpatient or home care. Employers are permitted to require reasonable documentation of a family relationship for purposes of FMLA leave.

One case highlights the courts' interpretation of the "intent" of the law. In *Briones v. Genuine Parts Co.* [No. 01-1792, U.S. Dist. LEXIS 17552 (E.D. La. Sept. 17, 2002)], an employee's child had a serious health condition. Because his wife needed to be at the hospital with the child, the employee took time off to stay at home with the other three children. The employer fired him, stating that the FMLA did not cover "caring for" healthy children. The court held that the employee was covered by the FMLA: had the employee been the parent who went to the hospital to care for the child with the serious health condition, he would have been covered. The court noted that "a literal reading of the FMLA makes it clear that Congress passed it to aid families when faced with a crisis, such as the one faced by this family."

[K] Spouse

Spouse is defined as "husband or wife, as the case may be" according to the laws of the state in which the employee, not the employer, resides. For example, some states recognize common-law marriage, while others do not.

[L] Intermittent and Reduced Leave

Intermittent leave is leave that is taken in separate blocks of time for a single qualifying reason, rather than during a continuous period. Such leave may be taken for a period of hours or a period of days. *Reduced leave* is defined as reduced work hours in a day or reduced workdays in a week.

[M] Employment Benefits

Employment benefits are all the benefits provided or made available by an employer to its employees, including group life insurance, health and disability insurance, sick leave, annual leave, educational benefits, and pensions, regardless of whether such benefits are provided by practice or by written policy, or through an employee benefits plan, as defined in Section 3(3) of the Employment Retirement Income Security Act of 1974 (ERISA). [29 U.S.C. § 1002(3)] Employment benefits do not include nonemploymentrelated obligations paid by employees voluntarily through deductions, such as supplemental insurance coverage.

[N] Group Health Plan

A *group health plan* is any plan including self-insured plans of, or contributed to by, an employer to provide health care, directly or otherwise, to the employer's employees, former employees, or the families of such employees or former employees.

For purposes of the FMLA, a group health plan does not include an insurance program providing health coverage under which employees purchase individual policies from insurers if:

- No contributions are made by the employer.

- Participation in the program is completely voluntary for employees.

- The sole functions of the employer with respect to the program are, without endorsing the program, to permit the insurer to publicize the program to employees, to collect premiums through payroll deductions, and to remit them to the insurer.

- The employer receives no consideration in the form of cash or otherwise in connection with the program, other than reasonable compensation, excluding any profit, for administrative services actually rendered in connection with payroll deduction.

- The premium charged with respect to such coverage does not increase if the employment relationship terminates.

§ 14.05 LEAVE APPROVAL

The regulations stress that, in all circumstances, the employer's responsibility is to designate whether the leave is regarded as FMLA leave. This designation must be promptly communicated in writing to the employee, generally within two business days after the company has acquired knowledge of the underlying reason for the leave (i.e., oral notification from the employer with written follow-up by the employer no later than the next payday is permitted).

Changes in the business situation of the employer that would normally exclude an employer from FMLA coverage (i.e., dropping below 50 employees within 75 miles) do not rescind an employee's approval for leave if the approval was before the business change.

Only in one of the two following situations may the employer designate leave that has already been taken as FMLA leave after the employee returns to work:

1. An employee is out for an FMLA-qualifying reason, and the employer does not learn of the reason for the leave until the employee returns to work. In this case, the employer may designate the leave as FMLA leave promptly (i.e., within two business days) after the employee's return to work, including a

provisional designation based on information from the employee, subject to confirmation, upon the employer's receipt of medical certification if it requires certification and has previously notified the employee of the requirement.

2. The employer has provisionally designated the leave as FMLA leave and is awaiting receipt from the employee of medical certification or other reasonable documentation to confirm that the leave was FMLA qualifying, or the employer and employee are in the process of obtaining second or third medical opinions. When in doubt, the employer should designate the leave as FMLA. The designation can be changed if the leave later turns out not to qualify. If it does qualify, but the employer did not designate it within two days, the employer cannot make it FMLA leave after the fact.

If an absence that begins as other than FMLA leave later develops into an FMLA-qualifying absence (e.g., an employee takes a two-week vacation for a ski trip and suffers a severe accident requiring hospitalization beginning the second week), the entire portion of the leave period that qualifies under the FMLA may be counted as FMLA leave (e.g., the second week). Employers must still base their designations of FMLA leave on information obtained directly from the employee or the employee's spokesperson, in the event the employee is incapacitated or otherwise designates a point of contact, such as an immediate family member. If an employee does not provide the required information certifying the necessity for the leave, leave may be denied.

Likewise, if an absence begins as FMLA leave in the case of an employee who is caring for a spouse, parent, or child, and the family member passes away during an approved leave, the employee is no longer protected under the FMLA upon the death of that individual. The employee may be recertified under the FMLA if any of the 12 weeks of leave remain and there is some other eligible reason to take the leave. The employee may be eligible for other coverage under state law. In addition, the employer may provide leave under the company's own bereavement or personal leave policy. The employer and employee are required to resolve disputes through mutual discussions at the beginning, rather than at the end, of leave.

§ 14.06 LEAVE PROVISIONS

[A] Amount of Leave

The FMLA states that an eligible employee is entitled to "a total of 12 workweeks of leave" during the 12 month period selected and identified in policies by the employer. Thus an employee's normal "workweek" before the start of FMLA leave is the controlling factor for determining how much leave an employee uses when switching to a reduced-leave schedule. If an employee's normal workweek exceeds 40 hours, the calculation of total FMLA leave available for a pro rata reduction of total-leave entitlement during intermittent leave or reduced leave schedules should be based on the employee's normal workweek, even if it exceeds 40 hours.

If an employee with a disability has already switched to a permanently reduced work schedule for reasons other than the FMLA and needs leave on an intermittent basis, the hours worked under the current schedule would be used for making the calculation.

Periods during which employees do not normally report to work (e.g., summer vacation for teachers) or weeks when an entire establishment shuts down for a vacation or maintenance cannot be considered FMLA leave.

An employee's FMLA leave entitlement may be reduced only for time in which the employee would otherwise be required to report for duty, except for the taking of the leave. If the employee is not scheduled to report for work, the time period involved may not be counted as FMLA leave.

[B] Unpaid Leave

The FMLA provides that the leave may be unpaid unless the employer's own family leave plan provides paid leave covering the particular circumstance for which the employee is seeking FMLA leave. However, it may be coordinated with other paid-time-off (PTO) plans in existence.

The employer may require use of unused PTO benefits or allow employees to elect to use PTO, such as vacation. By allowing the use of PTO, the employer does not add to the total length of the leave, but rather substitutes the paid time for the unpaid time. For example, an employee who has two weeks of PTO would have 10 weeks of unpaid time off, for a total leave of 12 weeks.

In a case filed in the Seventh Circuit, the court held that an employer may not require the use of paid leave such as PTO or vacation if the employee is already receiving employer-provided disability benefits. [*Repa v. Roadway Express*, 477 F.3d 938 (7th Cir. 2007)] In addition, employers may not require use of paid leave if an employee is receiving workers' compensation benefits.

Although the FMLA allows employers to require that employees use PTO benefits in some cases, some states prohibit it. Also, an employer may not override an employee's initial election to substitute appropriate paid leave for FMLA leave or place any other limitations on its use (e.g., minimum of full days or weeks at a time). At the same time, in the absence of other limiting factors (e.g., state law or an applicable collective bargaining agreement), when an employee does not elect substitution of appropriate paid leave, he or she must accept the employer's decision to require paid leave, even when the employee would have desired a different result.

If paid leave is substituted for all or part of the FMLA leave, and if the employer's paid leave rules are less stringent than the FMLA requirements, the employer may impose only the less stringent rules. For example, an employer's paid sick leave policy does not require medical certification; the substitution of paid sick leave for FMLA leave disallows the employer from requiring medical certification during the period when paid sick leave is substituted for FMLA leave.

If the employer requires use of paid sick leave to run concurrently with FMLA, it need only allow an employee to use the sick pay benefit in the same manner as the employee would under the employer's existing leave policy (e.g., no paid sick leave to care for an ill child or ill parent if the company policy does not normally allow pay for those purposes).

[C] Methods for Determining the 12-Month Period

Unless the employer is in a state that dictates the method, it must select a uniform method from among four options for determining the 12-month period in which FMLA leave entitlement occurs. The four methods are as follows:

1. *The calendar year.* The statute provides no authority to limit the employee to leave on a per-event basis. For example, if an employee has a heart attack in December, she or he will still be eligible for FMLA leave for the same condition in the new year. The only exception to this is for leave to care

for a newborn or newly adopted child. The eligibility for that leave expires 12 months after the date of birth or placement, however it falls within or between years.

2. *Any fixed 12-month leave year.* This method includes, for example, the fiscal year, the year required by state law, or the year beginning on employee's anniversary date.

3. *Twelve months measured forward.* The leave would be measured from the date an employee's first FMLA leave begins.

4. *A rolling 12-month period.* The 12-month period is measured backward from the date an employee uses any FMLA leave. Each time the employee takes FMLA leave, the amount of leave available would equal the difference between any leave already used in the immediately preceding 12 months and the full allotment of 12 weeks. For example, if an employee used four weeks starting February 1, 1996, four weeks starting June 1, 1996, and four weeks starting December 1, 1996, the employee would not be eligible for any additional leave until February 1, 1997. Beginning on February 1, 1997, the employee would have eligibility for four weeks of leave. On June 1, he or she could use another four weeks, and so on.

Under the first two methods, an employee could take 12 weeks at the end of one fixed year and 12 weeks at the beginning of the following year.

Whichever method is chosen must be applied consistently and uniformly to all employees. If the employer wishes to change methods, it must provide all employees with at least 60 days' notice. The transition must allow employees to retain the full benefit of 12 weeks of leave under whatever method affords the greatest employee benefit. The provisions provide multistate employers an exemption allowing them to comply with each state's law, provided they have a uniform methodology for determining the 12-month period elsewhere. Employers may not use different methods of calculating the 12-month period at their different facilities; all sites must use the same method.

If an employer does not select a method and include a definition in its written FMLA policy, eligible employees are provided FMLA leave under the most generous definition available. Many states have family leave statutes that require a certain method.

[D] Expiration of Leave Entitlement for Birth or Adoption

The FMLA provides that eligibility for leave taken upon the birth or adoption of a child expires 12 months after the event. This means that the leave must be completed by the one-year anniversary of the event. Leave may begin before birth or adoption, as circumstances dictate.

[E] Intermittent or Reduced Leave

Provisions exist for taking leave intermittently (i.e., not all at one time), or on a reduced schedule. No provision exists, however, for limiting the time period over which an employee may take intermittent or reduced leave. The law differs, depending on the reason for the leave.

In the case of a serious health condition, either the employee's or the family member's leave may be intermittent or reduced if medically necessary. When the leave is for adoption or birth of a child, leave may be intermittent or reduced only with the approval of the employer. Intermittent or reduced leave is limited to times that are scheduled for treatment, recovery from treatment, or recovery from illness. This includes both periods of disability due to a chronic serious health condition and time taken to provide care or comfort when such psychological care would prove beneficial to the patient.

If the employee requests intermittent or reduced-leave status, the employer may temporarily transfer the employee to another position of equivalent pay and benefits to better accommodate the leave. Documentation is important as to why the transferred position better accommodates the employee's intermittent or reduced schedule. Employees transferred to another position must receive the same pay and benefits and work under the same conditions as if they had not been transferred, regardless of the employer's benefits policies regarding employees who work less than full time. An employer may only proportionately reduce the kinds of benefits that are calculated based on hours worked, such as vacation or sick leave, or insurance or other benefits based on the amount of earnings.

Once an employee's need for a reduced-leave schedule under the FMLA has ended, the employer must restore that employee to his or her original position or to a position that is equivalent to the original position (i.e., with equivalent benefits and pay). An employer may not transfer an employee to an alternative position to discourage the employee from taking the leave or otherwise create a hardship for the employee (e.g., a transfer to the graveyard shift, assigning an administrative employee to perform laborer's work, or reassigning a headquarters staff employee to a remote branch site).

No provisions exist for how short a time may be taken, or how often. Only the time actually taken for leave should be charged against the employee's leave entitlement. It is appropriate for an employer to account for FMLA leave in the same way as it accounts for other leaves of absence and to use established time-keeping systems to track increments of leave of less than one hour in the same manner as is done for other leaves. For example, if an employer's payroll system accounts for time-keeping allocation in as little as 10-minute or 5-minute increments, intermittent time off must be allowed in those increments as well. An employer may not require FMLA leave to be taken in increments of more than one hour; otherwise, the employee may be required to take more leave than is necessary, thereby unnecessarily eroding the 12-week leave entitlement.

Leave taken on an intermittent or reduced leave basis is calculated according to the following examples:

- A full-time employee, who normally works 8-hour days, works 4-hour days on reduced leave. The employee uses one half week of FMLA leave each week.

- An employee who normally works 30 hours per week works only 20 hours on a reduced leave. The employee's 10 hours is one-third of a week of FMLA leave each week.

If an employee's schedule varies weekly, an average of hours worked over the 12 weeks before the beginning of the leave should be used to calculate a normal workweek.

The ultimate resolution of the leave schedule always remains subject to the approval of the health care provider and the schedule established for the planned medical treatments. Once the health care provider has established the medical necessity for the intermittent leave schedule, denial of the leave is out of the question. Even delay of the leave is inappropriate unless the health care provider agreed to reschedule the medical treatments.

What would be a reasonable effort by the employee and an undue disruption of the employer's operations is fact-specific in each case. For example, requesting that an employee attempt to schedule planned medical treatments outside normal work hours when scheduling them during work hours would not unduly disrupt the employer's operations is not reasonable or consistent with the FMLA's requirements.

[F] Flexible Work Schedules

As the company assesses its leave policies, it should consider flexible work schedules as one means of reducing the need for employees to take FMLA leave. When flexible work schedules are available, employees can often manage their need for leave around the schedule without taking FMLA leave.

[G] Protection of Exempt Status

In the past, the DOL had successfully challenged an employee's exempt status under the Fair Labor Standards Act of 1938 (FLSA) because the employee's pay was docked for partial-day absences. The regulations from the DOL clarify that FMLA-covered employers are able to dock an FMLA-eligible exempt employee's pay for qualifying absences of less than one day without affecting his or her exempt status if leave is required under the FMLA. Such deductions are not permitted for any leave that does not qualify as FMLA leave (i.e., leave to care for a grandparent or leave that is more generous than that provided under the FMLA).

[H] Provisions for Spouses Working for the Same Employer

The law differs according to the reason for taking leave. In the case of adoption or birth, the maximum leave for both spouses combined is 12 weeks. When a husband and wife each take a portion of the total 12-week leave for the birth or placement of a child, each is entitled to take the remaining portion of the 12-week leave for his or her own serious illness or to care for a sick child. For example, if each spouse takes four weeks of leave for the birth of a child, each could later use an additional eight weeks of FMLA leave to recuperate from a serious health condition.

Several states have nondiscrimination regulations that prohibit discrimination based on marital status. In those states, use of the above "aggregation" rule may be prohibited.

[I] Integration with the ADA

Congress intended the Americans with Disabilities Act of 1990 (ADA) and the FMLA to be applied simultaneously. The employer must comply with whichever statutory provision provides the greater rights to employees. Employees are not required to choose between the two acts. Thus, if an employee has a serious health condition covered under the FMLA and is also a qualified individual with a disability under the ADA, the more generous provisions of each act apply. However, providing the more generous provisions of each act does not relieve the employer's obligation to follow the requirements of both acts. For example, satisfying any or all of the FMLA's requirements, including providing the employee with 12 weeks of leave, does not relieve the employer of its obligations under the ADA. When FMLA leave ends, the employer will need to review whether accommodation under ADA can be granted to the disabled employee.

(See **Chapter 15** for further discussion of the integration of the ADA and the FMLA.)

[J] Outside Employment While on FMLA Leave

The FMLA is silent on this issue. The employer's established policy regarding outside employment determines whether an employee may engage in outside employment and earn W-2 wages while on

FMLA leave. For example, if the employer has a policy that all outside employment requires preapproval from the employer, outside work performed during an employee's FMLA leave falls under the same policy.

The need for employers to have policies in this area was emphasized in *Pharakhone v. Nissan North America, Inc.* [324 F.3d 405 (6th Cir. 2003)]. In this case, the employee informed his supervisor that he would need time off after his wife gave birth, and would be helping manage a restaurant his wife recently purchased. The employee handbook indicated that employees were prohibited from working without authorization while on leave. When his child was born, his supervisor reminded him that working while on leave was prohibited. The employee continued to work at his wife's restaurant while on leave from Nissan, and was subsequently fired from employment. The court held that the right to reinstatement was not absolute, and that if an employee would have been fired for violation of a company policy while on any leave, it was legal to fire him for that violation even while on FMLA leave. The existence of a written policy that was uniformly applied was critical in the court's decision.

§ 14.07 RETURN FROM LEAVE

If an employee requests a leave and once on leave asks to return to work earlier than originally planned, the employer is obligated to promptly restore the employee, generally within two working days. Employees may not be required to take more leave than is necessary to take care of the FMLA-qualifying need. Employees are expected to give reasonable advance notice of their intent to return, defined in the FMLA as a minimum of two working days.

If an employee requests leave beyond the length of time protected by the FMLA, the employer has an obligation to inform the employee of the potential effects (e.g., loss of guaranteed reinstatement). In one case the court ruled that not informing an employee of the consequences of staying on leave beyond the time allowed for FMLA leave deprives the employee of his or her opportunity to maintain FMLA rights and protection.

[A] Restoration to Position

Employers must restore employees returning to work from leave to "an equivalent position with equivalent benefits, pay, and other terms and conditions of employment." [FMLA § 104(a)(13)] The language in the FMLA is purposely stringent; it is intended to have more teeth than the "similar or comparable" language found in other legislation.

The standard of equivalence requires that the duties and all other terms, conditions, and privileges of an employee's new position correspond to those of the old position. The regulations stipulate that the employee's right to reinstatement to the same or equivalent position is contingent upon the employee's ability to perform all the essential functions of the job. This point is important for employers that choose to accommodate individuals who are not protected by the ADA. The employer reinstating an employee to a less than equivalent position runs the risk of litigation, even if that position is all the employee can perform.

The regulations confirm that individuals on FMLA leave due to a work-related injury or illness may not be forced to return to work under a light-duty program if they cannot perform the essential functions of their own jobs. Even though this may result in a discontinuation of workers' compensation benefits, the decision to return to work remains with the employee. State laws may have an additional impact in this area, and employers should be aware of their state's regulations.

The DOL lacks authority to require the employer to place an employee in the same position he or she held when the leave began, and there is no compelling reason to control this decision. If the position offered is equivalent, the employee has no right to obtain the original job back. However, the employer may wish to return employees to their original positions as often as possible, to avoid lengthy disputes with the employee over the equivalence standards.

Several court cases have interpreted *equivalent position*. In *Land v. Sheraton Tunica Corp.* [No. 2:96CV109, 1997 U.S. Dist. LEXIS 9884 (N.D. Miss. May 20, 1997)], the employee returned to her same job with the same wages and benefits. However, the shift she had worked before her FMLA leave was no longer available. The court held that changing the employee's shift did not violate the obligation to restore the employee to an equivalent position. In another case, *Lobster v. Sierra Power Co.* [12 F. Supp. 2d 1105 (D. Nev. 1998)], the court concluded that the job offered to the employee upon her return from FMLA leave was not equivalent because it paid a lower salary than the job she held when she went on leave.

Employers are prohibited from refusing to place an employee in the same position because the employee had taken FMLA leave. In the same vein, an employer that eliminates the employee's job by, for example, redistributing the work to other employees bears the burden of establishing that the employee's job would have been eliminated if the employee had not been on leave.

For example, in one case, a Washington, D.C., jury awarded $212,135 to a former insurance association employee in an FMLA lawsuit. The employee's position was eliminated during the course of a reorganization while she was on maternity leave. The company defended its decision to eliminate the position on the grounds that it was part of an overall reduction in force and that the employee was offered the opportunity to interview for other positions. They argued that the position would have been eliminated anyway. The jury, however, found that the employee was entitled to her job back.

In another case, the Eighth Circuit Court of Appeals found for the employer who had terminated an employee while on FMLA leave. When the employee, a nurse in a hospital, took leave, her employer found she had made a number of costly errors in her work. They terminated her on that basis, stating that they would have made the same decision to terminate had she not been on leave. [Throneberry v. McGehee Desha County Hospital, 403 F.3d 972 (8th Cir. 2005)]

For union-affiliated employers, eligible employees who request leave may be replaced from a hiring hall. In this situation, the employer may believe that it has no authority to recall a worker to his or her original position at the end of the leave. Under the FMLA, the rights of an employee on leave may not be diminished by any collective bargaining agreement or employee benefit program or plan. Under the circumstances described, the employer is still required to restore the employee to the same or equivalent position.

[B] Effect on Benefits

Employee benefits are defined under the FMLA as meaning all benefits provided or made available to employees by an employer, including group life insurance, health insurance, disability insurance, sick leave, annual leave, educational benefits, and pensions, regardless of whether such benefits are provided by a practice or written policy of an employer or through an "employee benefit plan," as defined in Section 3(3) of ERISA. [29 U.S.C. §§ 101(5), 1002(3)]

Employment benefits do not include non-employment-related obligations paid by employees through voluntary deductions, such as supplemental insurance coverage.

Upon return from FMLA leave, an employee cannot be required to requalify for any benefits he or she enjoyed before the leave. An employee may not be required to meet any qualification requirements, including any new preexisting condition waiting period, waiting for open enrollment, or passing a medical examination. These restrictions apply even if coverage lapses during an FMLA leave as a result of the employee's failure to make required premium payments.

The FMLA permits employees to withdraw voluntarily from their group health plan coverage during FMLA leave and request reinstatement at a desired future date, if their decisions are truly voluntary and future reinstatement on the requested date is not barred by the terms of the plan or the employer.

The employer may find it necessary to amend benefit plans to restore these equivalent benefits, arrange for continued payment for such benefits by the employee during the leave, or pay these costs during the leave subject to recovery from the employee upon return from leave.

For pension and other retirement plans, periods of FMLA leave must be treated as continued service for eligibility and vesting purposes.

[C] Fitness for Duty Certification

If the company requires employees to provide medical certification of fitness to return to work following a leave, it must apply this requirement consistently to all employees in this situation, and it must meet ADA requirements stating that any return-to-work physical be specifically job-related. Such medical certifications should be maintained in confidential employee files, separate from personnel files.

§ 14.08 THE KEY EMPLOYEE EXEMPTION

A *key employee* is an employee whose salary is among the top 10 percent of salaries paid to employees of the company and works within 75 miles of his or her work site. The earnings used for the computation include:

- Wages (e.g., salaries)

- Premium pay (e.g., overtime premium pay)

- Incentive pay (e.g., commissions)

- Nondiscretionary and discretionary bonuses

An employer does not have to guarantee key employees the same position when they return. The key employee rule is intended as a narrow, limited exemption. The procedural requirements set forth in the rule ensure that the standards for the exemption have been properly met. That is, based on facts existing at the time an employee seeks restoration to employment, the employer must establish that denial of restoration at that time is necessary to prevent substantial and grievous economic injury to the employer's operations. Substantial and grievous economic injury under the FMLA is different from undue hardship under the ADA. The FMLA creates a narrow exception to the reinstatement rights of a key employee, whereas the ADA's standard provides a measure of the reasonableness of any accommodation based on significant difficulty or expense. The FMLA rules define substantial and grievous economic injury to include substantial long-term injury. Accordingly, the FMLA's standard is more stringent than the ADA's standard. Further regulatory guidelines, however, in the form of a more precise test cannot be established because of the fact-specific circumstances that must be evaluated on a case-by-case basis.

The circumstances under which an employer can deny key employee restoration are as follows:

- When bringing the employee back would create "substantial and grievous economic injury to the operations of the employer."

- When the employer advises the employee that he or she will not be restored, as soon as that determination is made.

- When leave has already begun, and the employee elects not to return.

An employee who continues leave after receiving notice from the employer is still entitled to request reinstatement at the conclusion of the leave period, and the employer must again determine if substantial and grievous economic injury will result from reinstatement based on the facts existing at that time.

The determination of whether a salaried employee is among the top 10 percent is made at the time of a request for leave, and the employer must inform a key employee in response to a request for leave that he or she is a key employee. The employer must also inform the employee that he or she may be denied restoration following the leave.

If an employer believes reinstatement may be denied, such written notice must be provided to the employee at the time of the leave request, or when the FMLA leave commences, whichever is earlier. Failure to provide timely notice that the employee is a key employee and restoration may be denied causes the employer to lose its right to deny restoration, even when substantial and grievous economic injury results from restoring the employee.

A key employee's rights under the FMLA continue until the employee either gives notice that he or she no longer wishes to return to work or is actually denied reinstatement by the employer at the conclusion of the FMLA leave period.

The designers of the FMLA acknowledge that key positions do exist that cannot reasonably be held open during a leave. However, the FMLA clearly provides that key employees receive benefit coverage during any period of leave. One court case that analyzed this issue relied on a number of factors in concluding that the employee was in fact a key employee. In *Kephart v. Cherokee County* [52 F. Supp. 2d 607 (W.D.N.C. 1999)], the employee, a tax assessor, requested leave under the FMLA during a time when the tax department was scheduled to send out the tax bills for the year. The county, because of civil service rules, could not hire an interim replacement. If the tax bills did not go out, the county would be severely strapped for money. Under the circumstances, the court concluded that granting the leave would cause grievous economic injury to the county.

§ 14.09   EMPLOYEE OBLIGATIONS

Two areas in which employees have distinct obligations are notification and certification.

[A]   Notification

Employees are obligated to notify the employer of their need for a leave, which may be given by the employee's spokesperson, such as his or her spouse, adult relative, attorney, or doctor. Notice must be given to the same person the employee ordinarily contacts to request other forms of leave, usually the employee's supervisor. The supervisor's responsibility is either to refer the employee who needs FMLA leave to the appropriate person or to alert that person to the employee's notice.

Once the employee has provided notice to the supervisor or other appropriate person in the usual manner, the employee's obligation to provide notice of the need for FMLA leave has been fulfilled. However, although the FMLA requires an employee only to give oral notice of the need for leave, the regulations allow an employer to require that an employee comply with its usual and customary notice requirements, including a requirement of written notice when the need for leave can be foreseen. If an employee fails to give written notice in these circumstances, an employer may not deny or delay leave but may take appropriate disciplinary action. When the need for leave was unforeseeable, the employer may not deny or delay FMLA-qualifying leave if the employee provides verbal notice as soon as practicable.

Having a hard-and-fast rule that the employee must give written notice or confirm the verbal notification within one or two working days would create an unnecessary hardship for many employees who have taken leave for a medical emergency and are not in a position to provide written notice because of either their own serious health condition or that of an immediate family member.

Determining whether the employee has given enough information to the company to determine whether the leave being requested may fall under the FMLA will depend on the facts and circumstances of each situation. Several court cases attest to this. In a 1998 case, an employee notified his employer of a "pain in his side." The court concluded this was not enough information to put the employer on notice to obtain additional information. In another 1998 case, an employee missed work repeatedly for migraine headaches; the employer was aware of this fact even though it was after the employee returned to work. In this case, the court concluded that the employer did have enough information to be put on inquiry notice.

In a significant case, *Byrne v. Avon Products, Inc.* [328 F.3d 379 (7th Cir. 2003)], an employee with a good work history was seen sleeping on the job. Before his employer could confront him, the employee called in sick. He was diagnosed with depression. When the employee was ready to return to work after two months, the employer would not reinstate him. The employer's position was that the employee had not given notice; the court held that sudden and unusual change of behavior should have been sufficient notice. If an employee has a mental or physical condition that prevents him or her from giving notice, he or she may nonetheless be entitled to FMLA leave. This case has given rise to the term "Byrne exception," which is still used by courts to support the concept that unusual behavior alone can be enough to notify a reasonable employer that an employee suffers from a valid FMLA illness. Even if verbal and written notice is not given by an employee, unusual behavior may be deemed "constructive notice" and the obligation is on the employer to obtain additional information about a possible FMLA need.

The current regulations make it clear that if an employer fails to provide the required information, it may not take action against an employee for failure to comply with the employee's notice obligations. The FMLA states 30 days' notice, or, if that is not possible, whatever is "practicable." Practicable is defined as one or two business days, unless that is not feasible. The employer may delay, not deny, leave when required notice has not been given. Employees may retroactively claim that paid or unpaid leave was for an FMLA purpose if they notify the employer within two business days of their return from leave.

The employer may require the employee to report periodically, though in general not more often than 30-day periods, on his or her status during the leave period. Employers may not require status reports from an employee on leave in a manner that is burdensome or disruptive to the employee. The requests for status updates from the employee need to be reasonable based on the circumstances. The employer may not impose stricter notice requirements upon an employee taking FMLA leave than are required for another type of leave being substituted.

In a federal court case, the court rejected the FMLA claim of an employee who was terminated for taking time off for a serious health condition because the employee failed to tell the employer the nature of her condition or specifically request FMLA leave. The court held that even if she had given the employer adequate notice of her condition, her failure to periodically update the company on her condition was independent grounds for terminating her under FMLA.

The employee had what the court assumed was a protected "health condition" under FMLA. Her leave would have been covered under FMLA, except that she failed to give her employer notice of her condition "as soon as practicable" as required and failed to give the company periodic updates on her condition. Although she informed her employer that she had chickenpox in her second trimester of pregnancy, she failed to explain that she was hospitalized for her condition or to describe the scope of her medical treatment. The failure to communicate the gravity of her illness meant that the company was not on notice of a possible FMLA condition. The court therefore concluded that despite the fact that the employee had a serious health condition, her failure to advise the employer of her need for FMLA leave meant that the company was within its rights under FMLA to terminate her.

[B] Certification

A company policy regarding documentation necessary to verify the legitimate need for leave should be communicated in advance to employees and should be applied consistently to all cases. The company may require certification of illness, injury, or whatever the reason for a requested leave, from the employee or family member. A simple signed statement by the employee could be considered reasonable documentation of a qualifying reason for FMLA.

Employers are permitted to require reasonable documentation from the employee to confirm family relationships. Some employers include a broader definition of family in their family leave policies than that given in the FMLA and include domestic partners or in-laws. This is considered a greater benefit within the context of the FMLA.

The employer may count leave taken for such reasons under its own leave policy but may not count leave taken to care for persons out of the scope of the FMLA toward an employee's FMLA leave entitlement. If the employee never provides the required certification, the leave is not considered FMLA leave. Therefore, because the leave is not protected under the FMLA, the employee does not enjoy FMLA protections.

Ordinarily, when leave is foreseeable and at least 30 days' notice has been provided, the employee should provide the medical certification before the commencement of leave. If the need for leave does not allow for this, the employee should provide the certification within the time frames established by the employer for submission of the certification, which must allow at least 15 days after the employer's request.

A company may request an employee to provide the following information from the employee's medical provider:

- The date the serious health condition began.

- The duration of the condition.

- Applicable medical facts, to verify the actual existence of an employee's serious health condition and the likely periods of absence, but no more, such as the health care provider's "diagnosis" of the serious health condition.

- A statement that the employee cannot perform the job functions.

- Additional medical information, only to the extent required for the employee to obtain payments from the employer's benefits plan, or if applicable, the state workers' compensation statute.

- A definition of the serious health condition for the provider's use and a brief statement about how the medical facts meet the criteria for a serious health condition.

- Clarifying information, with the employee's consent, but no more once an employee has provided a completed medical certification form.

- If the leave is for taking care of a family member, a statement of the need for the employee to care for the ill person and an estimate of how long.

- Medical reasons for the intermittent or reduced leave request, such as schedule of treatments.

The regulations confirm that an employer cannot require the health care provider to provide a "diagnosis"; rather, the physician or other provider may only describe the "medical facts" that give rise to the need for leave. In addition, if an employee provides its employer a complete certification form signed by the provider, the employer may not request additional information from the employee's provider. The company may request its own provider, however, to clarify the document with the employee's provider. The DOL revised their sample certification form, WH-380, in 2007. It is available on its Web site: *www. dol.gov.*

The employer may require a new medical certification at the beginning of a new "FMLA year," not just a recertification. This is supported by a 2005 DOL opinion letter. [FMLA 2005-2-A]

If the medical opinion provided by the employee's physician is disputed, the employer can require a second opinion by a physician not employed by the company, at the employer's expense. If a third opinion is necessary, the company must pay for it, the company and the employee must agree on the doctor, and the company may not employ the doctor on a regular basis. This third medical opinion is binding.

Employees on unpaid FMLA leave do not need to be paid for time spent obtaining a second or third medical opinion. Employers may not ordinarily require an employee to travel outside normal commuting distances to obtain the additional certifications. However, the employer is responsible for reimbursing the employee or family members for any reasonable out-of-pocket travel expenses incurred in obtaining the required second or third medical opinions. Upon request, employees are entitled to copies of the second or third medical opinions within two business days.

If the employer is dealing with a health care provider in a foreign country and a second or third medical opinion is required, the employer must make arrangements to obtain the opinions from health care providers in that country.

Pending ultimate resolution of the employee's entitlement to leave, the employee is provisionally entitled to FMLA benefits, including maintenance of group health benefits. If the certifications do not ultimately establish that the employee is eligible for leave, the leave is not counted as FMLA leave, and the time off may be treated as paid or unpaid leave under the employer's established leave policies.

If the FMLA leave is running concurrently with a workers' compensation absence under state provisions that permit the employer or employer's representative to have direct contact with the health care provider treating the workers' compensation injury or illness, such authorized direct contact with the health care provider is not prohibited under FMLA, unless the employee chooses to forgo the workers' compensation claim. This contact may be made only by a health care provider representing the employer, as most employers are not medically qualified to pose clarifying questions to the employee's health care provider.

[C] Recertification

If a certification provides a minimum duration of more than 30 days, the employer may not obtain recertification until that minimum period has passed, unless the circumstances specified in the regulations are present. For chronic conditions, recertification ordinarily is permitted every 30 days, but only in connection with an absence. Exceptions are provided only if circumstances have changed significantly or the employer has reason to believe the employee was not absent for the reason indicated. Because the statute does not provide for second or third opinions for recertifications, no such opinions can be requested.

The recertification must be obtained at the employee's expense, unless the employer voluntarily chooses to pay for the recertification itself. If the employee fails to provide the recertification within 15 days when it was practicable to do so, the employer may delay further FMLA leave until the recertification is provided.

In a recent DOL opinion letter (FMLA 2005-2-A), the agency confirmed that an employer may request a new medical certification, not just a recertification, for an employee's first FMLA absence in a new leave year.

§ 14.10 EMPLOYER OBLIGATIONS: THE COMPANY'S RESPONSE

[A] General Requirements

When an employee requests leave under the FMLA, the employer must provide detailed information about the requirements and availability of the leave at the time the employee provides notice of his or her need for leave.

The final regulations issued in 1995 indicate that the notice must be given within a "reasonable time— within one or two business days if feasible" after the employee gives notice of the need for a leave or if the employer's notice is to be mailed to the employee's last address of record, or both. This notice should include the following information, as appropriate:

- The fact that the leave will be counted against the employee's annual FMLA leave entitlement (The regulations specify that an employer may designate a leave as FMLA after the employee returns to work, if the employer is waiting for medical certification or if the reason for absence is not known until the employee returns.).

- Any requirements that the employee furnish medical certification of a serious health condition and the consequences of failing to do so.

- The employee's right to substitute paid leave, whether the employer will require the substitution of paid leave, and the conditions related to any substitution.

- Any requirements that the employee make premium payments to maintain health benefits, and the arrangements for making such payments (The regulations require that the company provide an employee written notice 15 days before discontinuing group health plan coverage following his or her failure to pay his or her share of a premium throughout an FMLA leave.).

- Any requirement that the employee present a fitness-for-duty certificate to be restored to employment (Fitness-for-duty certifications are uniformly applicable only to those employees in similar circumstances, that is, in the same occupation or suffering from the same serious health condition. A standard "one size fits all" certification is not consistent with ADA requirements.).

- The employee's status as a key employee and the potential consequence that restoration may be denied following FMLA leave, explaining the conditions required for such denial.

- The employee's right to restoration to the same or an equivalent job upon return from leave.

- The employee's potential liability for payment of health insurance premiums paid by the employer during the employee's unpaid FMLA leave if the employee fails to return to work after taking FMLA leave.

The intent of the notice requirement is to ensure that employees receive the information they need to enable them to take FMLA leave and comply with company policies regarding payment of insurance premiums and medical certifications. Employers may mail the notice to the employee's address of record if the leave has already begun.

When an employee is taking leave intermittently, notice does not have to be provided each time. If an employee takes multiple leaves within a six-month period, notice does not have to be given every time but must be provided "no less often than the first time in each six-month period that [the] employee gives notice of the need for FMLA leave." In most circumstances, notice need be given only once in each six-month period, starting on the occasion of the first employee notice of the need for leave. However, if the specific information required to be furnished in the notice changes, notice of the changed information must be provided in response to a subsequent notice of need for leave.

An employer is required to give notice of a requirement for medical certification, or for a fitness-for-duty report, upon the employee's return to work, each time the employer receives notice of a need for FMLAqualifying leave. However, this requirement does not apply if both the notice given at the beginning of the six-month period and any employee handbooks or other written documents regarding the employer's leave policies make it clear that medical certification or a fitness-for-duty report will be required under the circumstances of the employee's leave.

The company is also expected to answer the employees' questions regarding their rights and responsibilities under the FMLA.

[B] Failure to Provide Notice

The regulations specifically address the result of an employer's failure to provide requisite notices: "The employer may not take action against an employee for failure to comply with any provision required to be set forth in the notice."

There are several court cases that support an employer's obligation to provide notice to employees. In *Cline v. Wal-Mart Stores, Inc.* [144 F.3d 294 (4th Cir. 1998)], the employee was demoted when he returned from a 13-week leave of absence. His employer argued this action did not violate the FMLA because the employee was no longer under FMLA leave when he returned. The court disagreed, finding that because Wal-Mart had not designated the week of vacation the employee had at the time he began the leave, the employee had a right to a full 13 weeks of leave (12 weeks of FMLA leave plus one week of vacation).

In a very similar case, *McGregor v. Autozone* [180 F.3d 1305 (11th Cir. 1999)], the court found the notice requirements of the regulations invalid. The court's position was that the statute provides for only 12 weeks of leave and "where an employer exceeds the baseline 12 weeks by providing not only more leave than FMLA but also paid leave, the employer should not find itself sued for violating FMLA."

Even though some of the results of court cases have conflicted with the regulations, in practical terms, any employer that fails to give timely required notice to an employee may not, among other things, count the absence against the employee's available FMLA leave time, require that the employee obtain medical certification of the need for the leave, require that the employee obtain medical certification of his or her fitness to return to work, compel the employee to substitute accrued vacation or paid sick days for the leave, or even request reimbursement for payment of health insurance premiums during the employee's absence if the employee decides not to return to work. The message to employers is to provide notice as required.

In *Ragsdale v. Wolverine World Wide, Inc.* [122 S. Ct. 1155 (2002)], the Supreme Court's first ruling on the FMLA, Ragsdale, an employee of Wolverine World Wide, Inc. (Wolverine), took seven months of unpaid sick leave, then requested additional leave or part-time work. Wolverine did not grant either request and terminated her employment. Ragsdale sued on the basis that Wolverine had not provided her with the individual notice informing her that her unpaid sick leave would be counted under the FMLA. The Court found that the employer's failure to provide notice that the employee's unpaid sick leave would be counted as leave under the FMLA did not cause the employee any harm, and therefore she was not entitled to an additional 12 weeks of FMLA leave. In its decision, the Court indicated that Ragsdale could not show that she was harmed by the lack of notice or that she would have acted any differently had she received the notice. The Court ruled that the regulation requiring employers to give employees individual notice of their FMLA rights still stands; only the penalty (of requiring 12 weeks of additional FMLA leave) was invalid.

[C] Approval of a Request for Leave

The FMLA encourages employees to provide employers with as much advance notice of the need for leave as possible. To encourage this to happen, and to allow both parties to plan for the leave effectively, the determination of an employee's eligibility for leave is made within two business days from the time the request is made. Following approval of leave, no subsequent change in the business situation of the employer (e.g., the employer drops below 50 employees within 75 miles of the work site) can rescind the prior approval for leave.

[D] Discipline or Termination for Cause

The FMLA cannot be used by an employee as a shield to avoid legitimate discipline. Unless laws, regulations, or collective bargaining agreements to the contrary exist, such sanctions as discharge for misconduct may continue to be applied to an employee on FMLA leave for actions that would have resulted in the employee's discharge if she or he had continued to work.

In the first case ever tried under the FMLA, on December 11, 1995, a federal jury in Rhode Island ruled that Citizens Savings Bank had the right to terminate an employee following an FMLA leave for unsatisfactory work performance. The employee in this instance, a manager at Citizens, filed suit against the bank alleging that she was harassed and demoted because she took a 13-week maternity leave. The FMLA guarantees the right of an employee to return to the same or an equivalent position after taking leave for medical or family care reasons. Although conceding that the employee's duties were reduced upon her return to work, the bank argued that this was warranted because of her unsatisfactory work performance. The jury accepted the bank's argument and found that Citizens Savings Bank had not terminated an employee in violation of the FMLA following her return from pregnancy leave. Following the verdict, the bank spokesman said that the bank strongly believed in the letter, intent, and spirit of the FMLA and was pleased that the jury confirmed that the bank had not violated the law.

§ 14.11 MILITARY FAMILY LEAVE

On February 28, 2008, President George W. Bush signed into law the National Defense Authorization Act for Fiscal Year 2008 (NDAA), which amends the FMLA. This law provides two important additions to the FMLA.

[A] Caregiver Leave

This portion of the new law allows the spouse, son, daughter, parent or next of kin of a covered service member to take up to 26 weeks of leave within a 12-month period to care for a seriously injured or ill service member. Some important definitions are:

Next of kin—defined as the closest blood relative of the covered service member.

Covered service member—a member of the Armed Forces, including members of the National Guard or Reserves, who is undergoing medical treatment, recuperation, or therapy, is otherwise in outpatient status, or is otherwise on the temporary disability retired list.

Serious injury or illness—incurred in the line of active duty which may render the member medically unfit to perform the duties of the member's office, grade, rank, or rating.

[B] Active Duty Leave

The new law provides leave for qualified employees of up to 12 weeks in a 12-month period due to a "qualifying exigency" because the employee's spouse, child, or parent is on active duty, or has been notified of a call to active duty, in the Armed Forces (including National Guard and Reserves) in support of a "contingency operation." Contingency operation is a military operation that "is designated by the Secretary of Defense as an operation in which members of the armed forces are or may become involved in military actions, operations, or hostilities against an enemy of the United States or against an opposing military force" (Section 101(a)(13) of Title 10, United States Code).

The term "qualifying exigency" has not yet been defined by the Department of Labor as of this writing, but may include events such as:

- Making financial and legal arrangements

- Making child care arrangements

- Attending pre-deployment or welcome home activities

- Attending counseling or orientation sessions related to deployment

Technically, the Active Duty Leave portion of the law is not effective until the DOL issues its definition of "qualifying exigency." It has stipulated that there must be "some sort of connection between" the employee's need for leave and the family member's military service. The DOL is encouraging employers (rather than requiring them) to make good faith efforts to provide FMLA leave to family members of service members who have a relevant need.

[C] Provisions of the New Law

In general, the new law does not change the basic provisions of the FMLA. For example, nothing in the NDAA changes the existing definitions contained in the FMLA regulations. The employee may take leave all at once or intermittently. Employers may allow or require substitution of paid leave for military family leave. Benefits must be maintained in the same manner as other FMLA leaves. The new law does not make any changes to the job restoration language of the FMLA.

The NDAA does add new wording to the FMLA regarding notice employees must give when taking Active Duty Leave. Where leave is foreseeable, the employee is required to provide notice to the employer that is "reasonable and practicable." The employer may also require certification from the employee to support the request for leave.

For Caregiver Leave, employers may require certification from the medical provider of the injured service member.

The unpaid time off provided by the NDAA is not intended to be in addition to the time provided under the FMLA. For example, if someone has taken 12 weeks of family leave within a 12 month period, they are only eligible for 14 additional weeks to care for an injured service member, not the full 26 weeks.

Employers are required to post a notice advising employees of their rights under this new law. The poster is available at *www.dol.gov/esa/whd/fmla/NDAAAmndmnts.pdf*.

The DOL plans to issue additional definitions and regulations in the near future to further clarify the administration of the NDAA. For the most recent information available, refer to the DOL's Web site at *www.dol.gov/esa/whd/fmla*.

§ 14.12   ENFORCEMENT PROVISIONS

Employees may file charges of violations of the FMLA with the Secretary of Labor, usually through the nearest office of the Wage and Hour Division (WHD), or in federal or state court under a private suit. If the Secretary has filed on behalf of the employee, the employee cannot also do so. The DOL has the right to investigate claims and requires employers to maintain records demonstrating compliance. In addition to creating an appropriate policy, the employer should document each employee's request for leave, whether it was granted, and reasons for denial, if applicable. In the event an employee falsifies the need for leave, the fraud should be treated as any other fraud in connection with leave.

Section 105 of the FMLA prohibits an employer from interfering with, restraining, or denying the exercise of any right provided by the Act. It also prohibits an employer from discharging or in any other manner discriminating against any individual for opposing any practice made unlawful by the FMLA. The FMLA provides the same sorts of protections to workers who oppose, protest, or attempt to correct alleged violations of the FMLA as are provided to workers under Title VII of the Civil Rights Act of 1964. Interfering with the exercise of rights includes not only denying authorization for or discouraging FMLA leave, but also manipulation by the employer to avoid responsibilities, such as unnecessarily transferring employees among work sites to avoid the 50-employee threshold for employees' eligibility.

The statute does not permit an employer to replace an employee who takes FMLA leave or restructure a position and then refuse to reinstate the returning employee on the ground that no position exists. Further, an employee's acceptance of a different but allegedly equivalent job does not extinguish an employee's statutory rights to be restored to a truly equivalent job or to challenge an employer's placement decision.

An employer is prohibited from requiring more of an employee who took FMLA leave than the employer requires of employees who take other forms of paid or unpaid leave (e.g., requirements to furnish written notice or certification for use of leave). In addition, employers are prohibited from considering an employee's use of FMLA leave as a negative factor in any employment actions (e.g., promotions or discipline).

The rules specifically indicate that FMLA leave may not be counted under no-fault attendance policies. Actions may be brought within two years after the date of the last event constituting the alleged violation, unless the violation is willful, in which case a three-year statute of limitations applies. Given the complexities involved, it may well be advantageous for employers to restore returning employees to their same positions, but it is not a requirement of compliance in the regulations. Finally, employees may not waive their rights under the FMLA, nor can employers induce employees to waive their rights.

[A] Damages

The employer may be liable for monetary damages and equitable relief, such as employment, back wages, reinstatement, promotions, attorneys' fees, and expert witness fees. In the case of monetary damages, the employer may be liable for an additional amount equal to the actual damages as liquidated damages. The employer may avoid liquidated damages if it can show to the satisfaction of the court that a violation was in good faith and the employer had reasonable grounds to believe that it was not in violation of the statute. The regulations do not limit the employer's liability for violations of the statute, because no such limit is provided under the law.

Although the FMLA does not expressly permit awards for compensatory damages, in 2002 the Eighth Circuit Court of Appeals allowed the jury to award damages for pain and suffering. The court stated that the jury could consider damages for mental anguish as well as actual damages such as lost wages. [Duty v. Norton-Alcoa Proppants, 293 F.3d 481 (8th Cir. 2002)]

Employees are under no obligation to exhaust administrative remedies before they can bring private suit.

[B] Statute of Limitations

Normally, charges must be filed within two years of the alleged violation. If the violation is determined to be willful, the DOL accepts a claim that is three years old. The DOL has accepted complaints from employees as well as other persons with knowledge of circumstances, such as a relative of the employee or a competitor.

[C] Waiver of Rights

There are two conflicting Circuit Court decisions regarding the ability of employees to waive their rights under FMLA. In *Taylor v. Progress Energy Inc.*, 415 F.3d 364 (4th Cir. 2005), an employee was laid off due to poor productivity ratings. In exchange for extended benefits, the employee signed a general release and severance agreement. She later sued under FMLA. The lower court ruled that she had waived her FMLA claim when she signed the release, but the Fourth Circuit disagreed stating that an employee cannot legally waive their FMLA rights without court or DOL supervision. In June 2006, the court vacated its opinion and granted a rehearing. A year later, the court reaffirmed its decision that FMLA rights could not be waived [2007 U.S. LEXIS 15846 (4th Cir., July 3, 2007).

In an earlier case, *Faris v. Williams WPC-I Inc.*, 332 F.3d 316 (5th Cir. 2003), the Fifth Circuit allowed a signed release to preclude the employee from filing an FMLA claim.

[D] The Department of Labor Report

According to the DOL's "2007 Statistics Fact Sheet," the WHD received 1,983 complaints in fiscal year 2007 for alleged failures to comply with the FMLA, 8.2 percent less than the prior year. Fifty-five percent were valid complaints for which apparent violations of the FMLA existed. Forty-five percent of the complaints were about situations that were not covered by, or were found not to violate, the FMLA.

A breakdown to the nature of the valid complaints follows:

- Termination: 39 percent

- Employer refusal to reinstate employee to same or equivalent position: 12 percent

- Employer refusal to grant FMLA leave: 23 percent

- Employer interference with or discrimination against an employee using FMLA leave: 25 percent

- Employer refusal to maintain employee's group health benefits: 1 percent

The WHD offers the Family and Medical Leave Act Advisor on its Web site: *www.dol.gov/elaws,* which addresses employers' commonly asked questions about the FMLA, including eligibility, reasons for leave, notification and certification responsibilities, and employee rights and benefits.

§ 14.13 RECORDS AND POSTING

Employers are required to post a notice that summarizes the FMLA. The DOL provides the notice, which can be duplicated, free of charge (available at *www.dol.gov*). Employers are required to post this information with other employment-related posters in a format large enough to be read (e.g., 8½-by-11 inches). There is a penalty of up to $100 for failure to post the notice. The notice must be placed in a conspicuous place where other notices to employees and applicants are usually posted. A contractor with employees working at multiple sites should ensure that the notice is posted on the work site in a conspicuous place to which employees have access.

There is a new poster designed to inform employees of their new rights for Military Family Leave. It is available at *www.dol.gov/esa/whd/fmla/NDAAAmndmnts.pdf*.

The company's employee handbook or manual of company policies must include information about FMLA entitlements and employee obligations. There is no need, however, to include information about filing complaints or private rights of action. If a company does not have an employee handbook, it must still provide written information about the FMLA to employees. An FMLA fact sheet, which may be duplicated and provided to employees, is available from the nearest WHD office.

The records required to demonstrate compliance with the FMLA include those required to meet the FLSA guidelines. Specifically, the employer must maintain for at least three years and make available to the DOL for inspection, upon request, the following information:

- Basic payroll and identifying employee data (e.g., name, address, occupation, rate or basis of pay, terms of compensation, daily and weekly hours worked per pay period, additions to or deductions from wages, and total compensation paid) (A covered secondary employer in a joint employment situation need keep only basic payroll records on its secondary employees; other records are not necessary.).

- Dates FMLA leave is taken (available from time records, requests for leave), designated in records as FMLA leave (which may not include leave provided under state law or an employer plan that is not covered by the FMLA).

- If FMLA leave is taken in increments of less than one full day, a record of the hours of the leave.

- Copies of employee notices of leaves furnished to the employer under the FMLA, if in writing, and copies of all general and specific notices given to employees as required under the FMLA (which may be maintained in employee personnel files).

- Any documents, including written and electronic records, describing employee benefits or employer policies and practices regarding the taking of paid and unpaid leaves.

- Premium payments of employee benefits.

- Records of any dispute between the employer and an employee regarding designation of leave as FMLA leave, including any written statement from the employer or employee of the reasons for the designation and for the disagreement.

If employees are not subject to the FLSA's recordkeeping regulations for purposes of minimum wage or overtime compliance (i.e., not covered by or exempt from the FLSA), the company does not have to keep a record of actual hours worked, as otherwise required under the FLSA, provided that:

- Eligibility for FMLA leave is presumed for any employee who has been employed for at least 12 months.

- With respect to employees who take FMLA leave intermittently or on a reduced-leave schedule, the employer and employee agree on the employee's normal schedule or average hours worked each week and put the agreement into a written record.

Records and documents relating to medical certifications, recertifications, or medical histories of employees or employees' family members should be maintained in separate files or records and be treated as confidential medical records, in accordance with the ADA's confidentiality rules on medical information.

§ 14.14   IMPLEMENTING FMLA REQUIREMENTS

Before implementing FMLA requirements, the employer should consider the following questions:

- How does the FMLA compare with state and local law?

- How does the FMLA compare with company policy and/or preferences?

- What are the implications for benefit plans?

- What are the implications for health and COBRA benefits?

This section discusses how these factors affect FMLA implementation and how the manager should proceed in integrating these requirements into the company's current environment.

[A]   State and Local Law

To ensure that the company has covered all contingencies, the employer should compare and contrast the FMLA, state laws, and company practice in a chart, as shown in **Exhibit 14.1**.

When state and federal laws differ, the company must provide the benefit that is most favorable to the employee. The company cannot determine which law in aggregate is most beneficial and then follow those provisions. For example, federal law provides a maximum of 12 weeks' leave per year. If state law provides 16 weeks per year, the company must provide 16 weeks.

Unless a union contract is in force or other contracts exist that specify the terms and conditions of employment for an individual employee or group of employees, the company may change policies as it deems appropriate. Certain policy provisions can be decreased, as long as they do not fall below state or federal requirements. In making a final determination of policy, the employer needs to consider four things:

1. The minimum obligations by law

2. The level of benefits the company wants to provide

3. The cost of providing benefits beyond legal minimums

4. The ease of administration

> **Example.** Company X formerly granted up to 16 weeks for pregnancy but only 8 weeks for medical leave. The FMLA requires that a company allow an employee 12 weeks' leave for a serious illness. Company X must decide whether to grant 16 weeks for pregnancy, 12 weeks to care for an adopted child, and 8 weeks for a "nonserious" illness, or grant 16 weeks for any leave. To make this decision, Company X's HR manager weighs the cost of providing additional time off against the difficulties of having different parameters for each of several different leaves. The manager should consider what benefits, if any, the company wishes to provide employees with less than 12 months' service. For example, if those employees are granted medical leave, who will pay the company's portion of the health insurance premium? The law provides 12 weeks as a maximum leave, but not every employee who takes a leave will automatically require all 12 weeks. Employees with less than 12 months' service may also have leave rights under state law.

[B] Review of Employee Benefits Plan Documents and Practices

The employee benefits plan documents, communication literature, employee handbook, and other policy material should be reviewed thoroughly for compliance with the FMLA. Benefits plan administration should also be reviewed. Written benefit materials must be clear to employees, must support management discretion, and must ensure that related practices are always consistently applied. The DOL may rely on these documents and practices as evidence of the company's compliance with the FMLA.

Some items to review in the company's plan documents and policies follow:

- Policies for vacation, sick, and other PTO benefits should indicate that employees taking leave under some FMLA provisions may be required to use all available paid time off under these benefit programs before taking unpaid leave for the remainder of the required leave, up to the 12-week maximum. [FMLA § 102(d)(2)]

- Because leave for an employee's own "serious illness" is covered under the FMLA and related policies, the company may revise current policies for employee medical or maternity leave benefits, or both.

- Personal-leave benefit policies may also be affected, if they include provisions regarding taking care of family members, a benefit not provided under the FMLA.

- Because disability benefits plans (i.e., long-term, short-term, and weekly) typically provide benefits only for an employee's own illness, these benefits plans may not be affected by provisions of the FMLA.

- Employees taking leave under the FMLA may not lose any employment benefit accrued before the date the leave started, but they are not entitled to accrue any employment benefits while on leave.

[1] Benefit Accruals

Under the FMLA, unpaid leave does not constitute service credit—except for purposes of "break in service" rules because the taking of FMLA leave cannot "result in the loss of any employment benefit accrued prior to the date on which the leave commenced." Thus, employees are not deemed to accrue hours of service during periods of unpaid FMLA leave; paid leave is counted as service credit. However, if any FMLA leave is also covered by special maternity and paternity leave plan pension break in service rules under ERISA, the more generous rule applies.

The company should revise its benefit accrual, HR, or payroll systems (manual or automated), or all three, to discontinue accrual of benefits for an employee on leave under the FMLA. The company also must ensure that these systems reflect the employee's existing benefit accruals before such a leave.

§ 14.15 HEALTH BENEFITS: THE GROUP HEALTH PLAN

The term *group health plan* does not include non-employment-related health benefits paid directly by the employee through voluntary payroll deduction, such as individual insurance policies. The company is not responsible for maintaining or restoring such benefits for employees who take FMLA leave unless it maintains coverage for such benefits plans for workers on other forms of paid or unpaid leave. It does include employer-provided group dental plans, as was affirmed in a 2006 DOL opinion letter (FMLA 2006-6-A, October 5, 2006).

As group health plan has been defined within the FMLA, maintenance of non-employment-related health benefits are solely the responsibility of the employee, who should make arrangements directly with the insurer or employer for payment of premiums during periods of unpaid FMLA leave. If an employee on unpaid FMLA leave allows coverage to lapse on "nonmandatory" benefits (e.g., life and disability insurance) and a situation occurs that would have been covered had the insurance not been allowed to lapse, the company would not have to incur expenses or pay for the resulting condition. For example, if disability coverage is discontinued by an employee while on unpaid leave to care for a family member with a serious health condition and that employee becomes disabled while on leave, the employer would not be responsible for providing coverage for that incident of disability. However, because of the requirement to restore the employee fully to all benefits after return from FMLA leave, that employee cannot be denied disability coverage because of any disability that arose while on leave and the corresponding lapse of coverage. This requirement remains even if the employee voluntarily opts to stop paying the premiums until he or she returns to work.

The company may therefore elect to pay premiums for nonhealth benefits to avoid a lapse of coverage or for other reasons. If the company makes such payments and the employee returns to work, the company is entitled to recover only the costs incurred for paying for the employee's share of the premiums, regardless of an employee's argument that he or she did not want coverage during the leave. If the employee does not return to work, the company may recover only the employee's share of any nonhealth benefit costs it incurs.

If the employer chooses to make health or welfare premium payments, as required to comply with the FMLA, on behalf of an employee on FMLA leave who participates in a non-ERISA plan, the plan may be inadvertently converted to ERISA status. The DOL has no comment on this result due to underlying statutory provisions over which it has no control. The company should consult an ERISA benefits/tax specialist for assistance on this issue.

[A]   Maintenance

An employer must maintain an employee's group health plan coverage for the duration of any leave under the FMLA, at the level and under the conditions that would have been provided if the employee had continued employment.

Company premiums must be maintained at the level they held before the leave. Employee contributions existing before the leave may continue during the leave. If general premium increases occur, they may be passed on to the employee on leave.

[B]   No Requirement to Create a Plan

Nothing in the FMLA requires employers to create a health benefit plan if one did not exist before the FMLA effective date. In addition, compliance does not require the employer to alter an existing group health plan's eligibility requirements or employer and employee premium contributions.

[C]   Entitlement to New or Revised Benefits

If an employer should create a new group health benefits plan or revise an existing one during an employee's leave under the FMLA, that employee's entitlement to the group health benefits must start at the same point during the leave that the employee would have become entitled to those benefits had he or she remained on the job. If the employer fails to maintain group health coverage and in so doing drops the employee's coverage, in effect the employer becomes self-insured and assumes liability for any medical expenses incurred by the employee that would have been covered by the group health plan.

[D] Key Employees

Key employees who are not provided reinstatement to employment following leave are entitled to group health benefits during the leave, as are other employees. The employer may not recover a premium if the key employee chooses to take leave under the FMLA with the knowledge that his or her employment will not be reinstated following the leave.

[E] COBRA Implications

There is no intention for leave under the FMLA to trigger a qualifying event for purposes of COBRA. When it becomes known that an employee will not return to employment after leave under the FMLA, or on the last day of FMLA leave, that event constitutes a COBRA qualifying event. The employer's obligation to continue to provide group health benefits, except under COBRA, ceases at the time the employer learns from an employee on FMLA leave that he or she will not be returning to work.

If an employee has not paid the required premium to the company during FMLA leave and loses coverage during the leave, the employer is still obligated to offer COBRA coverage at the end of the leave. The FMLA employee would have the same rights as any other active employee in terms of the company reinstating the same health coverage he or she had before nonpayment, for a COBRA period of 18 months.

[F] Cafeteria Plan Implications

In 1995, the Internal Revenue Service (IRS) released proposed regulations addressing the interaction between Section 125 of the Internal Revenue Code (Code) and the FMLA. In October 2001, the IRS issued final regulations regarding Section 125 cafeteria plans. [Treas. Reg. § 1.125-3, 66 Fed. Reg. 52,675 (Oct. 17, 2001)] The final regulations, which became effective for plan years beginning after January 1, 2002, made limited but significant changes to the earlier proposed regulations.

Cafeteria plans under Code Section 125 allow employees to pay their health care premiums on a pretax basis and may also allow employees to set up pretax health care flexible spending accounts (FSAs).

An employer may continue to permit an employee on FMLA leave to pay health coverage premiums, and/ or contributions to a health care FSA on a pretax basis. This may be handled by the employee's either prepaying the full amount prior to the leave, or paying on a catch-up basis after returning from leave. The employee may also pay for coverage in after-tax dollars during the term of the unpaid leave ("pay-as-you-go").

No matter what the method of payment, the full amount of the employee's FSA balance must be available to him or her during the time the employee is on FMLA leave, if the employee elected to continue the FSA during FMLA leave.

If the employee elected not to continue coverage under the health plan and/or FSA during FMLA leave, the employer must allow the employee, upon his or her return from leave, the following options:

- Resume coverage at the original health plan/FSA level and make up the missed payments, or

- Resume coverage at a prorated level (with no coverage during the leave) and make payments at the original level.

Under the latter option, proration is based on the length of the FMLA leave. For example, assume an employee elects a $1,000 FSA, takes three months of unpaid FMLA leave, then revokes the FSA coverage during the leave. Upon her return from leave, the employee elects the proration option. She will not be eligible to receive more than $750 from her FSA for the year (12 months less 3 months of FMLA leave = 9 months; $9 \div 12 \times \$1,000 = \$750$).

Note, however, that if the FSA plan has already made disbursements to the employee that exceed the amount available after the proration, the employee may not be required to pay any more than the remaining amounts due.

An employee may not make prepayments of premiums or payments to the health plan or FSA if the prepayments are for the following plan year. For example, if an employee wants to prepay cafeteria plan payments for the two months that he or she will be on leave, where the first month of the leave falls in the current plan year, and the second month of the leave falls in the next plan year, the employee could make a pretax payment for the first month of the FMLA leave but would not be permitted to make a make a pretax payment for the second month. The employee could either wait until he or she returns from leave and "catch up" the payment, in which case the payment would qualify for pretax treatment, or make a *non*-pretax payment prior to or during the FMLA leave.

If an employer continues an employee's coverage during the employee's FMLA leave and pays the employee's share of the premiums or FSA contributions during that leave, the employer may recover the employee's premiums or contributions even if the employee has not previously agreed to the recovery.

An employer may require an employee returning from an FMLA leave during which he or she revoked health plan coverage to reinstate such coverage if the employer also requires all employees who return from unpaid *non*-FMLA leave to resume participation upon return.

Note that the issues discussed in this section apply only to health care plan premiums collected under a Section 125 plan. FMLA issues regarding post-tax premiums are discussed in the subsection below titled "Contributions."

In January 2006, the DOL released an opinion letter (FMLA 2006-3-A) that interpreted the application of the FMLA health care continuation rules under a "cafeteria plan." The employer, who was the subject of the Opinion Letter, allocated a set amount of dollars to each employee per month under the cafeteria plan. Out of this amount, employees paid the premium for one of the employer's group health plans and the balance was used, at the employee's option, to pay for dental, disability or life insurance, or it could be taken as cash compensation. The employer had a policy of requiring all employees on unpaid leave of any kind to make their own group health coverage payments. The employer paid the group health insurance premium during a period of unpaid leave and required returning employees to repay the employer upon return to work. During unpaid leaves, including unpaid FMLA leave, no cafeteria plan allotment is provided.

The DOL opined that employees taking unpaid FMLA leave must have that portion of their cafeteria plan allotment allocated to group health insurance (including dental) premiums paid by the employer in the same amount as paid prior to the start of FMLA leave. [See 29 U.S.C. § 2614(c)(1); 29 C.F.R. § 825.209(a); 29 C.F.R. § 825.209(b)] The DOL also took the position that because the employer provides the money for the group health insurance coverage when employees are working, it may not recover such payments for periods of FMLA leave. [See 29 U.S.C. § 2614(c)(1)]

[G] Plan Documents

Group health plan documents should describe COBRA qualifying events and timing of these events as they relate to the FMLA. These documents also should include information about such subjects as layoffs and workers' compensation absences. Plan provisions regarding payment of employee premium contributions and employees' return to work also should be outlined in plan documents and any communication directed to employees.

To document compliance and prepare required records, a company may wish to create and distribute employee benefits communication materials that outline the impact of the FMLA on the company's benefits programs. This communication should include a statement that employees returning from leave under the FMLA will not be subject to any preexisting condition or other benefit eligibility limitation that may apply to extended absences for other reasons (e.g., layoff). A copy of the written communication provided to all employees should be retained with plan documents and incorporated into any later plan revision or restatement. Such communication should also be maintained as part of the records required under the FMLA.

[H] Administrative Issues

Two administrative issues of importance are how to handle employee premium contributions during an employee's leave and how to recover premiums if the employee does not return to work.

[1] Contributions

Employee premium contributions required as a part of an employer's group health plan that is not part of a cafeteria or Section 125 plan may continue to be required of employees on leave under the FMLA. The employer must develop a procedure for collecting employee contributions directly from employees on leave, preferably before the effective date.

To drop group health plan coverage for an employee whose premium payment is late, the employer must provide written notice to the employee 15 days before coverage will cease that the payment has not been received. If the employer has established policies regarding other forms of unpaid leave that permit the employer to cease coverage retroactively to the first date of the period to which the unpaid premium relates, the employer may cease the employee's coverage retroactively in accordance with that policy, provided the 15-day notice was given. In the absence of such a policy applicable to other forms of unpaid leave, coverage for the employee ceases at the end of the 30-day grace period after the payment was due, again only if the required 15-day notice has been provided. The same rules apply to payment of claims under self-insurance plans.

The employer may collect health plan contributions that were collected before taxes via payroll deduction directly from employees on leave under the FMLA, after taxes, without affecting the plan itself.

[2] Recovery of Premiums

If an employee on leave under the FMLA fails to return to work for reasons other than the two that follow, the employer may recover premiums paid for maintaining coverage for the employee under a group health plan that is not part of a cafeteria or Section 125 plan during any period of unpaid leave. That employee must return to work for at least 30 calendar days to be considered to have "returned to work" for the purposes of this provision. The only acceptable reasons for failing to return to work are:

1. Continuation, recurrence, or onset of a serious health condition that entitles the employee to leave

2. Other circumstances beyond the control of the employee

[FMLA § 104(c)(2)(A)]

The employer may request medical certification to verify the existence of the qualifying serious health condition. Employers must provide written notice of the terms of payment during FMLA leave and may not apply more stringent requirements to an employee on FMLA leave than those applied to employees on other forms of leave. Nor can the employee's share of the premium be raised because an employee is on FMLA leave.

Employers need to create payroll and other administrative procedures for recovering premiums under appropriate circumstances.

§ 14.16   OTHER BENEFITS

The company's time-off policies and practices should be reviewed to ensure that they reflect FMLA requirements; these policies encompass sick leave, attendance, vacation and holiday accruals, bereavement leave, workers' compensation according to state law, and long-term disability coverage.

[A]   Employment Benefits Employers Are Not Required to Pay

The FMLA does not require employers to provide paid sick leave or paid medical leave in any situation that would not normally create such paid time off (PTO) for an employee. [FMLA § 102(d)(2(B)] Specifically, the law provides that:

- If the company did not provide PTO benefits before the effective date of the FMLA, there is no requirement for creating such a benefit to comply with the FMLA.

- If the company provides PTO benefits to particular groups or classes of employees, nothing in the FMLA requires the company to alter eligibility for these benefits.

The FMLA provides no greater right or benefit to eligible employees than they would have received if they had worked continuously during FMLA leave. Consistent with this provision, if employers have "use it or lose it" policies for various benefits, the simple fact of an employee's being on leave does not extend the use-it-or-lose-it date for his or her benefits.

[B]   Attendance

It appears that just about any illness or injury that lasts for more than a few days (generally, three) can be classified as a serious illness. If that is the case, an employee could accumulate up to 12 weeks of leave under the FMLA and be protected from termination due to excessive absence. Many states have allowed companies to establish a maximum-days-absent policy. These policies say that if an employee is absent for more than x days, for any reason, the organization can discharge him or her. The theory is that even though there may be good reasons for the absences, at some point it is not economically feasible for the organization to carry that employee. According to the final rules, days absent under the FMLA leave may not be counted under any maximum-days-absent policy.

If someone is on intermittent leave, the employer must set a schedule based on medical necessity. An employee should be committed and held accountable to the leave schedule as if he or she were on a regular work schedule.

For example, suppose an employee is scheduled to leave one hour before the end of his or her shift on Mondays and Wednesdays to take an ailing parent to the doctor. What happens if he or she comes in late twice in one week? Can he or she be disciplined? The way to handle this is to discuss the cause of the tardiness with the employee. If it is due to the medical situation, the employee's manager might suggest a further reduced schedule. If the reason is not medical, the case should be handled as for any other tardy employee.

[C] Vacation and Holiday Accrual and Bereavement Leave

The FMLA does not require that an employee on unpaid leave continue to accrue vacation or holiday time while on leave.

The company's policy decision on how or if to pay holidays or funeral leave during unpaid FMLA leave should be in accordance with the manner in which the company pays for holiday and funeral leave during other leaves of absence.

[D] Workers' Compensation

The FMLA covers work-related injuries and illnesses, so long as the employee gives proper notice. The employer must carefully review the state workers' compensation laws. Key issues to review include eligibility of the employee to use his or her own doctor and the timing and reason of leaves.

When an employee is injured on the job and the injury also results in a serious health condition that causes the employee to be unable to perform one of the essential functions of the job (within the meaning of the FMLA), the employee qualifies for both workers' compensation benefits and FMLA job-protected leave. Therefore, the employee is eligible to receive workers' compensation replacement wages, and the employer is required to maintain the employee's preexisting health benefits coverage, as if the employee were still at work, until the employee's FMLA leave entitlement is exhausted.

An employee who incurs a work-related illness or injury elects whether to receive paid leave from the employer or workers' compensation benefits. An employee cannot receive both. Therefore, if a work-related illness or injury also causes a serious health condition that is covered by the FMLA and the employee has elected to receive workers' compensation benefits, the employer cannot require the employee to substitute, under FMLA, any paid vacation or other leave during the absence that is covered by payments from the state workers' compensation fund. Similarly, an employee cannot elect to receive both workers' compensation and paid leave benefits.

The absence can count, however, against an employee's FMLA leave entitlement if it is properly designated at the beginning of the absence as required by these regulations. Neither the statute nor its legislative history suggests that time absent from work for work-related accidents should not run concurrently for purposes of FMLA and the state workers' compensation laws, provided the illness or injury also meets the FMLA's definition of "serious health condition."

Whereas time absent from work can simultaneously count under workers' compensation benefits and the FMLA, state workers' compensation funds are not to be considered "accrued paid medical or sick leave" within the meaning of the FMLA. Also during this time the employee may not elect, nor may the employer require, the employee to exhaust any form of accrued paid time off during any part of the time off during which the employee is receiving workers' compensation funds.

If an injured employee is offered a light-duty assignment as part of a workers' compensation return-to-work program, the employee may decline the assignment and choose instead to begin or continue FMLA leave until the employee's FMLA leave entitlement is exhausted. If the employee chooses to accept the light-duty assignment in lieu of leave or returns to work with unused leave remaining, he or she retains the right to return to the original or equivalent position until 12 weeks have passed, including all leave that year. After 12 weeks have passed, including all leave that year, if the employee is still not able to perform the essential functions of the job, his or her right to job restoration ceases under the FMLA. However, the employee's job restoration rights may be protected under the ADA (see **Chapters 13** and **15**).

[E]   Long-Term Disability

The employer should review policies and, when applicable, the plan documents for long-term disability provisions. In light of the maximum leave required under FMLA, the manager should explore such issues as the waiting period and required employment status for eligibility.

[F]   Incentive Pay Plans and Bonuses

Bonuses for perfect attendance and safety do not require performance by the employee but rather contemplate the absence of occurrences. To the extent an employee who takes FMLA leave meets all the qualifications to receive these types of bonuses up to the point that FMLA leave begins, the employee must continue to qualify for this entitlement upon returning from FMLA leave. In other words, the employee may not be disqualified from perfect attendance, safety, or similar bonuses because of the taking of FMLA leave. A monthly production bonus, on the other hand, does require performance by the employee. If the employee is on FMLA leave during the period for which the bonus is computed, the employee is not entitled to any greater consideration for the bonus than other employees receive while on paid or unpaid leave during the period.

Because restored employees are not entitled to accrue seniority during FMLA leave, pay increases based on performance reviews conducted after 12 months of completed service with the employer may be delayed by the amount of unpaid FMLA leave an employee takes during the 12-month period, in the absence of policies that treat other forms of unpaid leave differently. In contrast, a pay increase based on annual performance reviews geared to an employee's "entry on board" anniversary date without regard to any unpaid leave taken during the period may not be denied or delayed, once the employee returns from FMLA leave.

[G]   Other Benefits During Leave

The employer needs to decide the status of other company-provided benefits during FMLA leave and give appropriate notice to the employee at the time FMLA leave begins. The employer needs to determine if it will, for example, continue paying for life insurance premiums while the employee is on FMLA leave and also to communicate that policy to the employee at the time FMLA leave begins.

When an employee returns to work, an employee must be restored immediately to the same level of benefits, including any changes in benefit levels that occurred during the leave. The employee must be reinstated upon return from FMLA leave without a waiting period.

The employer should make a decision on how to administer premium payment or payment to the employee for non-health benefits and should include a review of:

- Long-term disability plans

- Short-term disability plan eligibility for a purpose other than the employee's own serious health condition

- Life insurance

- Holidays and funeral leave occurring during FMLA leave

§ 14.17 THE FMLA'S IMPACT

As Congress intended, the FMLA became a first national step in the effort to establish a balance between work and family issues for the U.S. worker. But, as the law matures and is affected by court rulings and additional legislative activity—and interactions with other federal employment legislation such as the ADA—efforts of the employer to maneuver around the administrative complexities of the FMLA can be costly in terms of both time and money. There are numerous FMLA issues remaining to be clarified.

Currently available survey results demonstrate mixed reviews of the impact of the FMLA on employers and employees. Depending on who is sponsoring the survey, and when the survey was conducted, compliance with FMLA can be considered burdensome to the employer or not. Some surveys show that the FMLA is viewed as a great benefit to employees who no longer need fear losing their jobs if their own illness or that of a family member may require them to take time off from work. On the other hand, research shows that many employees do not seek FMLA leave because they cannot afford to take time off work without pay.

The sections below describe the most recent surveys of employers and employees conducted since the implementation of the FMLA.

[A] The SHRM FMLA Surveys

The Society for Human Resources Management (SHRM) first surveyed employers about their experiences with the FMLA in 2000. Subsequent surveys were conducted in 2003, 2005, and 2007. The SHRM 2007 survey results were based on the responses of 521 HR professionals throughout the United States. SHRM released the following survey findings:

- Eighty percent of respondents had difficulties tracking and administering intermittent FMLA leave.

- Fifty-seven percent had difficulty determining a "serious health condition."

- HR professionals expressed concerns about employees' abuse of FMLA rights. They noted conditions that are difficult to prove medically or do not require a doctor's visit; suspicious timing of leaves (e.g., around weekends or when the weather is nice); and questionable documentation. Thirty-nine percent of respondents said they had to grant FMLA requests that they thought were not legitimate.

- The top three types of leaves reported were: employee's serious health condition as a result of an episodic condition; maternity, birth, or adoption of a child; and care for a parent with a serious health condition.

- Forty-four percent of organizations provide job-protected leave beyond FMLA requirements; this is down from 59 percent reported in the SHRM 2003 survey.

- More than half of respondents said that the FMLA can have a negative impact on employee absences (63 percent) and employee productivity (55 percent).

[B] Other FMLA Surveys

Several other surveys have looked at the impact of FMLA legislation on the workplace.

- "Employers' Time-Off and Disability Programs," conducted by Mercer Human Resources Consulting, 2005.

  Fifty-three percent of employers reported an increase in FMLA usage in 2004 over the prior year. Most organizations (84 percent) reported challenges with FMLA administration. The most difficult issues: managing intermittent leave (64 percent), recordkeeping/tracking use of leave (57 percent), coordination with other time-off plans (31 percent), timely notification of employee rights (26 percent), and clinical management (23 percent).

- "FMLA Perspectives and Practices," World at Work, 2005.

  This survey focused on the impact to the employer of FMLA administration. World at Work reported that, on average, employers are spending between thirty minutes and two hours of administrative time per FMLA leave to provide notice, determine eligibility, request and review documentation and request a second and/or third opinion.

  Employers in this survey expressed a desire for clarification and reformation of certain provisions. Specifically, they indicated need for clarification on the intermittent leave provision. Fifty-five percent believe that FMLA should allow adult children to qualify as an "immediate family member."

- "The Cost and Characteristics of Family and Medical Leave," Employment Policy Foundation, 2005.

  In a study conducted by the Employment Policy Foundation (EPF), 500,000 employers were surveyed about FMLA utilization, intermittent leave, and advance notice. EPF reported that compliance with FMLA cost employers $21 billion in 2004.

  The study reported that 14.5 percent of employees took FMLA leave in 2004; of those, 35 percent took leave more than once during the year. The number of employees that took leave more than once during 2004 is up almost 50 percent over 2000. Thirty percent of FMLA leave is intermittent leave comprising shorter periods of leave sporadically throughout the year and without prior notice to employers. In fact, almost 50 percent of employees notified their employer of FMLA leave either the day of the leave or after.

[C] Implications of the Research

All of these surveys provide information as to the impact of the law on employers and employees. There are those who say that the FMLA currently poses significant administration and legal headaches for employers and should be tightened, especially in the areas of redefining intermittent leave and a serious health condition, and perhaps limiting leave to full-time employees. On the other hand, there are those who believe work and family benefits should be expanded to include additional leave and paid time off for family and medical reasons.

[D]   Impact on Supervisory and HR Personnel

Court cases have held that a supervisor or an HR professional can be held personally liable under the FMLA.

In 1997, a court in Illinois determined that a supervisor was responsible as an agent of the employer after he fired a subordinate for missing too much work following surgery. Although the supervisor asked the judge to dismiss the case because he was not actually the employer but acting on behalf of the employer, the court refused. The judge ruled that the FMLA is like the FLSA. Under the FLSA, a person acting directly or indirectly in the interest of the company can be considered the employer.

Likewise, under the FMLA, a supervisor, HR manager, or company representative may not retaliate in any manner against an employee who is asserting rights under the FMLA. In order to reduce the risk to supervisors and HR professionals, companies should implement:

- Established guidelines,

- Management training, and

- A designated central source for the employee and supervisor to obtain information about leaves of absence.

§ 14.18   STATE FAMILY LEAVE LAWS

Across the country, many states have acted on the belief that the societal costs of forcing employees to choose between job security and caregiving are more than we as a society want to bear. In response to this, a large number of states have enacted their own family medical and parental leave laws. Until recently, most of these laws have provided for unpaid leave, similar to the FMLA. However, more and more states are proposing legislation that would provide employees with paid leave for certain purposes. Hawaii, for example, requires certain employers to offer four weeks of caregiving leave, and employees may receive partial wage replacement through the state's Temporary Disability Program. California allows employees to take up to six weeks paid leave to care for a seriously ill relative or to bond with a new child. The program is funded through increased payroll deductions paid to the State Disability Insurance Program. Both Washington and New Jersey have recently enacted legislation to provide paid family leave, effective in 2009.

Exhibits 14.2, 14.3, and **14.4** describe the provisions of states' family and medical leave laws.

The FMLA specifically states that it does not supersede any state or local provision that provides a greater level of rights or benefits than those afforded in the FMLA. This position is meant to include any state or local laws already in existence or any enacted in the future. Thus, the FMLA represents the minimum or basic package of rights and obligations. States are free to exceed any specific provision of the federal law, but no provision of state law can provide less than is mandated by the FMLA. Leave taken for a reason specified under both state and federal law may be simultaneously counted against the employee's entitlement under both laws.

[A]   Integrating State and Federal Law

The company's challenge is to integrate any state-mandated family medical leave, parental leave, pregnancy leave, and other disability leave with the FMLA. First, it is critical to recognize the differences between state and local laws and the federal FMLA. The key areas of possible differences are employer coverage, length of leave, employee eligibility, and certification requirements.

[1]   Employer Coverage

Each law specifies how many employees the company must have before the law applies. The minimum number for the state may be less than that for the FMLA.

For example, the FMLA specifies 50 or more employees within a 75-mile radius of the work site regarding employee eligibility. Minnesota law, on the other hand, specifies 21 employees, and Vermont specifies 10 employees, and neither state law contains a reference to geographic distribution. The employee distribution issue can also complicate legal compliance. The FMLA designated a radius around a work site as a method of "counting up" employees to determine eligibility for employees. California law, for example, does not allow for this type of aggregation. It simply specifies a total number of employees working for an employer in the state, without regard for their proximity to one another.

[2]   Length of Leave

Under the FMLA, every eligible employee is entitled to 12 workweeks of leave within any 12-month period. Two critical numbers are the total length of leave and the leave window. The interaction between the FMLA and state law determines the actual effective length of the leave allowed in any particular length of time.

For example, the California Pregnancy Disability Act provides for up to four months of leave to a female employee as a result of pregnancy or childbirth. Because this is a qualifying reason for the FMLA, the employer may count the employee's pregnancy disability leave (PDL) against her FMLA entitlement. Thus, the first 12 weeks of leave would run concurrently with FMLA leave. If, at the end of that time, the employee is still disabled by her pregnancy, she is entitled to an additional month of PDL. At the end of her pregnancy disability, or four months, whichever occurs first, the woman, if eligible, is also entitled to take up to 12 additional weeks of birth and bonding leave under the California Family Rights Act. Thus, her total length of leave is actually four months and 12 workweeks. Rather than listing her leave as seven months, this awkward phrasing provides a more accurate definition of her maximum entitlement to leave.

[3]   Employee Eligibility

The FMLA requires that an employee work at least 1,250 hours during the 12-month period before the leave is requested, and the work does not have to be done in consecutive workweeks. In Oregon, 90 days of employment is necessary, and in Utah, a public employee must have worked only two complete pay periods before being eligible for leave under the FMLA. State law that grants employers the right to deny the taking of leave to high-level key executives cannot be applied to any FMLA-eligible employees, because FMLA extends to all eligible employees the entitlement to leave for qualifying reasons. (Under the FMLA, key employees are not the same as eligible employees.) If the same state law contained a provision mandating that all employees who take leave be restored to employment when the leave ends, the FMLA's key employee exemption could not be applied to deny an employee reinstatement (i.e., the federal law would not apply at the time of reinstatement).

[4]   Certification Requirements

The FMLA leaves it up to the employer whether to require employee certification of the need for leave in the event of a serious health condition of that employee or a family member. However, the regulations prevent an employer from requiring a diagnosis, but the FMLA does allow the medical professional to "describe the medical facts." California law also does not permit an employer to require that the medical certification specify the underlying diagnosis of serious health condition that led to the leave request. If the provisions of the state statute are more beneficial to the employee or more restrictive in terms of the rights of the employer, such as by prohibiting a requirement that more medical information be required, the employer must comply with that state statute.

[B]   Definitions in State Laws

A number of states have expanded the definitions of key terms in fairly unique ways. The employer must consider these definitions when comparing state laws with the FMLA. **Sections 14.17[B][1] through 14.17[B][7]** provide a sampling of how some state laws define terms and conditions as well as several interesting approaches worth reviewing.

[1]   The Equivalent Job Requirement

Almost all states require restoration to the same or a similar position, without loss of pay, benefits, or seniority. The framers of the FMLA were adamant that an employee on leave should be returned to a "genuinely equivalent" job. Thus, if *equivalent job* is not clearly defined in state law, the manager must be very careful when framing the company's job-restoration policies.

In Oregon, employees are entitled to reinstatement in the same or an equivalent position without loss of pay, benefits, or seniority at the same job site; an equivalent job differs only in job title. If an equivalent job is not found at the same work site, the employee may be placed at an equivalent job site within 20 miles of the former work location. The state also notes that if the employer's business conditions have dramatically changed, reinstatement may be to any available and suitable position. The employer is not obligated to terminate other employees to reinstate the returning employee unless required to do so by contract, agreement, or policy. What makes the wording in this law different is the reference to work site location and the reference to an equivalent job's being different from the original position only in job title.

[2]   Serious Health Conditions

The FMLA lists many examples of an employee's serious health condition, also called serious illness, and notes that the list is not exhaustive. The ailments range from heart attacks to serious back conditions. It includes strokes, severe respiratory conditions, spinal injuries, and appendicitis. Even injuries and illnesses on the job are included, as well as the need for prenatal care, childbirth, and recovery from childbirth.

Few state laws include a list this specific. Under the FMLA, serious health condition is interpreted very liberally. Any medical condition is considered serious if the doctor allows an employee more than three calendar days off. An all-encompassing definition of serious illness for a family member is absent from the FMLA and all state laws.

[3]   Health Care Provider or Treating Physician

The FMLA broadly defines health care provider, including many professionals who are authorized to practice medicine or surgery in their respective state or country and any other person determined by the secretary of DOL to be capable of providing health care services.

States may want to be fairly broad in their definition of health care provider. Several states have expanded their definition to recognize various cultural or religious tenets regarding health care. For example, Wisconsin law stipulates that certification of a serious health condition may be required from a health care provider or Christian Science practitioner. In Maine, a credentialed spiritual healer may verify an employee's request for leave.

Under California law, employers may not obtain second or third opinions except in the case of an employee's own serious health condition. Thus, provided that the family member's certification met the employer's requirements, the employer must accept the certification as sufficient. California employers are also unable to obtain second or third medical opinions in connection with the serious health condition of a spouse, child, or parent.

[4] Immediate Family Member

The FMLA includes broad definitions of family member. The term *spouse* is defined as a husband or wife, as the case may be; no other definition is given.

Most states define *family member* as the employee's child, spouse, or parent without any further elaboration. A few states have expanded the definition slightly to account for a stepchild, foster child, legal ward, or child who lives with the employee. Many states include parents-in-law in the definition.

Two states, however, have broadened the definition, apparently to recognize the complexity of contemporary family relationships. In the District of Columbia, a family member is a person to whom the employee is related by blood, legal custody, or marriage, a child living with the employee for whom she or he permanently assumes and discharges parental responsibility, or a person with whom the employee shares or has shared a residence within the last year and with whom the employee has maintained a committed relationship for at least one year.

West Virginia law includes in its definition of *family member* a child, a spouse who is legally married to an employee, a parent, or other person with a serious health condition who is living with or dependent on the financial support of an employee, whether related by blood or not. The law further defines a *child* to mean a son or a daughter who is either under age 18 or over age 18 but mentally or physically incapable of self-care.

The company may want to be reasonably liberal in its interpretation of family member in the granting of leave. The approved leave relationships should be carefully documented to help ensure that company policy is applied consistently and that the risk of discrimination is minimized.

[5] Denial of Job Restoration Rights

The FMLA prohibits employers from denying leave to any eligible employee. However, it does not prohibit denying job restoration to certain key personnel.

This is one area in which many states' laws differ from the FMLA. Many states now limit the length of leave or denied job restoration to some number or percentage of the highest paid employees in the employer's workforce. A few states do not allow the employer to deny job restoration to any employees, especially public employees.

The FMLA directs employers to determine pay level according to year-to-date earnings so that they may decide who is highly paid. Such personnel certainly should not be selected on the basis of age or sex to avoid compliance with the law. It also may be difficult to defend naming an employee "key" after he or she makes known his or her intent to take family leave. Employers should document in advance what is included in the calculation to determine who is in the group of key personnel. Under the rules, earnings means wages, premium pay, incentive pay, and discretionary and nondiscretionary bonuses.

[6]   Restoration to Former Position in Relation to Layoff

State laws are very consistent in this area. In almost all states with laws affecting both public and private employers, the employee on leave is to be reinstated to the same position held before the leave or to an equivalent position with equivalent benefits, pay, and other terms and conditions of employment. A few states with laws covering only public employees require restoration to the same job.

Several states address the possibility of a general layoff that affects the employee while the employee is on leave. Under the rules, an employee returning from FMLA leave "has no greater right to reinstatement or to other benefits and conditions of employment than if he or she had been continuously employed during the FMLA period."

The employer must be able to show that an employee would not otherwise have been employed at the time of reinstatement (i.e., because of layoff, elimination of shift, termination of a discrete project) to deny restoration of employment. New Jersey law also stipulates that if there is an employment layoff or workforce reduction while an employee is on leave, and the employee would have been laid off had he or she not been on leave, the employee is not entitled to restoration to the former or comparable position, assuming that the layoff was handled in good faith, and subject to any applicable recall system under a collective bargaining agreement.

In this circumstance, the employee has the same rights under the layoff and recall system, and any relevant collective bargaining agreement, as if the employee had not taken the leave. Further, several states' laws include the clause that employers are not obligated to terminate another employee simply to restore the job of an employee returning from leave, unless obligated to do so by contract, policy, or agreement. The employer is advised to seek local legal counsel if an employee on leave is subject to layoff.

[7]   Certification Dispute Resolution

The FMLA defines resolution procedures, and the states that define the process are generally consistent with the FMLA. If there is a certification dispute, the employer, at its expense, may require a second opinion from an approved health care provider. If necessary to resolve a dispute, the employer may, at its expense, obtain a third opinion from a health care provider that it approved. The third opinion is final and binding. The second and third opinions may not be rendered by a health care provider who has an established relationship with the employer.

This process should be carefully communicated to employees to reduce the chance that exercise of this employer right will be confused with an attempt to deny the employee his or her rights under the law.

§ 14.19 DEVELOPING POLICIES AND PROCEDURES

A sample family and medical leave of absence employee handbook policy (**Exhibit 14.5**) incorporates the provisions of the FMLA. Employers should keep in mind that, in addition to the FMLA, the laws of their state must also be incorporated into their company policies. The FMLA does not supersede any state or local provisions that provide a greater level of rights or benefits than those provided by FMLA. A sample family and medical leave of absence procedural manual policy (**Exhibit 14.6**) shows how a company may tailor its policy to reflect state laws and organizational objectives.

Four other sample forms are found in this chapter:

1. Request for Family and Medical Leave of Absence Form (**Exhibit 14.7**)

2. Combined Leave Policy Form (**Exhibit 14.8**)

3. Insurance Premium Recovery Authorization Form (**Exhibit 14.9**)

4. Leave Certification Requirements (**Exhibit 14.10**)

Employers may contact the nearest office of the WHD for additional information. The FMLA notice is available in both English and Spanish. The DOL has published state and federal comparisons of family and medical leave statutes, a Fact Sheet, and a Guide to Compliance with the FMLA.

§ 14.20 REGULATORY AND LEGISLATIVE UPDATES

In June 2005, the Senate Health, Education, Labor and Pensions (HELP) Committee conducted a "Roundtable Discussion: The Family and Medical Leave Act: A Dozen Years of Experience." Representatives from a number of associations met with the Committee to provide input, including SHRM, World at Work, and the National Association of Manufacturers. Panelists representing women's groups were among the participants in this Roundtable. CEOs and others from various employers also presented testimony. Among the areas of concern raised were the following:

- Definition of "serious health condition"

- Intermittent leave

- Notice requirements

- Compliance time to comply with FMLA requirements

In December 2006, the DOL asked for public comments on the FMLA. In June 2007, the agency released its review of the 15,000 comments received: Family and Medical Leave Act Regulations: A Report on the Department of Labor's Request for Information. Comments came from both workers and employers. According to the report, FMLA is generally working well—at least with regard to leaves for the employee's own serious health condition and for the birth or adoption of a child. Many comments were from employees who expressed gratitude for the ability to take leave and balance work and family issues. The primary frustration expressed by employers was dealing with unscheduled intermittent leave by employees with chronic health conditions. In particular, they cited the difficulty in determining or monitoring employees' incapacity when a chronic condition does not involve any active, direct treatment or care by a health care provider, and difficulty in verifying that an unscheduled absence is caused by a chronic serious health condition, in part due to the inability to seek additional medical verification. An Executive Summary can be found on the DOL's Web site: *www.dol.gov.*

On February 11, 2008, the DOL proposed a number of changes to the FMLA regulations. Comments were requested through April 11, 2008. As of this writing, the final regulations have not been issued. Until then, employers should continue to operate under the regulations issued in 1995. However, the following are highlights from the proposed regulations:

Eligible employee—Currently, one requirement for eligibility is for an employee to be employed for 12 months, and the 12 months do not have to be continuous. The proposed regulations specify that employment prior to a continuous break in service of five years or more need not be counted. There would be two exceptions: one for breaks due to military obligations, and the other when the break is approved in a written agreement or collective bargaining agreement.

Eligibility of a "joint" employee—In most cases currently, if an employee is jointly employed by a leasing or placement agency and an employer, where the employee works on the employer's work site, the eligibility provision of "50 employees employed within 75 miles" was with the agency. Under the proposed regulations, after the employee has been on a work site for one year, the "50 employees..." provision would be with the entity where the employee physically works.

Serious health condition—Under the current regulations, for a condition to be classified as a "serious health condition," an individual must be incapacitated for three consecutive days, and visit a health care provider twice. The proposed regulations clarify that the two visits must be within 30 days of incapacity, barring extenuating circumstances.

Medical certification requirements—The proposed regulations would allow the employer to contact the employee's medical provider directly to clarify or authenticate documentation. The proposal also provides more specific guidance on employer and employee responsibilities when medical certifications are incomplete. The medical certification form (WH-380) is being revised to conform to the proposed regulations.

Employer notification—Currently, the employer has two days to notify the employee that the leave taken is designated as FMLA. The proposed regulations extend that to five days. The proposed regulations also provide that one identical document can be used as notice both for posting and distribution to employees. If the notice is not in the employer's handbook, it would need to be distributed annually.

Employee notification—The proposed regulations clarify the information that the employee needs to provide in order for the employer to recognize it as a potential FMLA leave. The employee, currently allowed two days to notify an employer, would be required to follow the employer's call-in policies when absent from work.

Holidays during leave—The regulations clarify that when an employee takes less than a full week of FMLA, and a holiday falls within that week, the holiday hours not worked cannot be counted as FMLA leave. If the employee does take a full week of FMLA, the holiday hours can be counted as FMLA leave.

Perfect attendance awards—Employees out on FMLA leave are not entitled to perfect attendance awards if employees on other unpaid leaves are also ineligible.

To review the entire body of proposed regulations, go to *www.dol.gov/esa/whd/fmla.*

Exhibit 14.1   Mandated Benefits: 2009 Compliance Guide

Exhibit 14.1
Guidelines for Coordinating FMLA and State Laws and Company Policy*

	FMLA	State Law	Company Policy
Covered Employer	An employer employing 50 or more employees within 75 miles of a work site.	Check state's leave laws' definition of *employer (e.g., one state requires leave privileges for companies employing as few as 10 employees).*	If a company has operations in several states, it may want to implement one policy that will meet federal and state requirements.
Eligible Employee	An individual who has worked for the employer for at least one year and worked at least 1,250 hours in the 12-month period preceding leave.	State laws will vary, with some states covering employees after as few as 90 days worked.	The organization's minimum service requirements for leave can exceed FMLA or state leave laws if it so chooses.
When Leave Can Be Taken	The birth or adoption of a child; the employee's own serious health condition; the serious health condition of a spouse, parent, or minor or incompetent child; a "qualifying exigency" due to the active duty status of a spouse, child, or parent; to care for an ill or injured covered service member.	A state may allow broader reasons for leave, such as to care for ill in-laws or grandparents; or, a state may mandate time off for bone marrow donations.	An employer can determine reasons for leave to extend beyond FMLA or state leave laws, such as to care for ill grandparents. Leave taken beyond FMLA regulations cannot be charged to FMLA leave.
Length of Leave	Up to a total of 12 weeks per year. In the case of adoption or birth of a child, leave must be taken within 12 months of the birth or placement. In the case of a serious health condition, the leave may be available on an intermittent basis. In the case of an ill or injured service member, up to 26 weeks in a 12-month period.	A state may require longer periods of leave for pregnancy, birth, or adoption.	Regardless of which leave mandate the organization must follow, situations involving leaves of absence should be administered in a consistent manner. Supervisors should be knowledgeable of leave laws and be able to advise employees to contact a central department such as human resources.
Paid or Unpaid Leave	An employer may require the employee to use accrued paid vacation, medical or sick leave, or personal leave as part of the 12-week leave period.	Parental leave is generally unpaid. However, each state may have specific criteria for an employer to require use of accrued sick or vacation pay.	Employers must decide if disability leave taken due to the employee's serious medical condition is a paid or unpaid benefit; if paid time off can be substituted or if its use is mandatory by the organization. How will a company handle holiday or funeral leave pay during FMLA? Vacation and holiday accruals? Long-term disability and workers' compensation?

*The information in this exhibit does not cover all FMLA and state requirements that need to be considered when formulating company policy; it is intended only as a guide.

Exhibit 14.1 (cont'd)

	FMLA	State Law	Company Policy
Certification Requirements	An employer may require medical certification outlining the "medical facts" and cannot require a diagnosis.	Where only one medical certification is required by state law, no additional certification may be required by the employer, unless the employee is requesting, or the employer has already provided more leave than required under state law.	The use of the DOL certification form is not mandatory. A company can create its own form as long as it does not overstep the limitation of information that can be requested.
Impact on Benefits	The employer must pay its normal portion of the employer's group insurance premium during leave. The employee may be required to pay the employee's portion.	The company will need to verify a state's continuation of group health coverage rules to determine if coverage is available at an employee's own expense, or if the employee's normal contribution to the premium is required.	The company needs to decide how it will handle continuation of insurance coverages other than medical if the employee does not make payment. Check plan documents to ensure reinstatement upon return to work.
Return to Work	Employees must be returned to former or equivalent positions, except if the employee would otherwise have been laid off during the leave. Certain exceptions exist for highly compensated "key employees."	During the leave, employers in many states are required to hold open the employee's former position or return the employee to an equivalent job.	FMLA can run concurrently with state workers' compensation benefits. If light duty work is offered by the organization and denied by the employee, workers' compensation benefits cease, but FMLA can continue for the remainder of FMLA eligibility.
Posting Required of Employers	Employers who are subject to FMLA must display a poster prepared by the federal Wage and Hour Division, which includes the Military Family Leave Notice.	In some states, posting of state leave rights is optional; in others, posting is required.	If a company has an established handbook, information about FMLA is required to be included. Check for state leave information requirements to be included in the handbook.
Notices Required of Employers	Employers have extensive notification requirements to employees.	Check the state leave laws to determine the time period in which to respond to an employee either orally or in writing.	Good communication and employee relations policies with workers always pay off.

Exhibit 14.1   Mandated Benefits: 2009 Compliance Guide

Exhibit 14.1 (cont'd)

	FMLA	State Law	Company Policy
Notices Required of Employees	Employees are required to give 30 days' notice, or as much notice as is practicable. If leave is due to a serious health condition, employees are required to make reasonable efforts to obtain treatment so that employer operations are not unduly disrupted.	An employer must allow a shorter notice period than the FMLA if state law requires it.	Ask employees to stay in touch with the company by establishing a written policy to require calling in to a supervisor or HR department at certain intervals.

Exhibit 14.2
State Family and Medical Leave Laws: Eligibility and Coverage

(States not listed have no statutory requirements.)

	Employers Subject to Leave Laws	Criteria for Eligibility	Maximum Length of Leave	Paid Leave	Citations to Authority
AL	State employers.	State employees.	Employees accrue leave at the rate of 4 hours per biweekly period worked and may take up to 150 days for sick leave. For serious illness, employees may be advanced up to 24 additional days. Certain education employees earn 1 day per month and may accumulate an unlimited number of days.	Leave may be paid for state employees and is paid for certain education employees.	Ala. Code § 16-1-18.1; Ala. Admin. Code r. 670-X-14-.01, 670-X-14-.02.
AK	Public employers with at least 21 employees; state employers.	Employee must be employed for at least 35 hours per week for at least 6 consecutive months or for at least 17.5 hours per week for at least 12 consecutive months.	For health leave, 18 weeks in any 24-month period. For pregnancy or birth/adoption of child, 18 weeks in any 12-month period.	Employees must use accrued paid leave until only 5 days paid leave remain, at which point they may use the 5 days paid leave or switch to unpaid leave.	Alaska Stat. §§ 39.20.500–39.20.550.
AZ	State employers.	State employees.	8 hours of sick leave accrue monthly and may be accumulated without limit. For parental or serious health condition leave, generally up to 12 weeks. Medical leave without pay, up to 180 days. Sick leave for illness, injury, examination, or treatment of a spouse, dependent child, or parent shall not exceed 40 hours per calendar year.	Leave may be paid or unpaid, depending on the availability of paid sick and/or annual leave.	Ariz. Admin. Code 2-5-404, 2-5-411–2-5-413.

Exhibit 14.2   Mandated Benefits: 2009 Compliance Guide

Exhibit 14.2 (cont'd)

State Family and Medical Leave Laws: Eligibility and Coverage

(States not listed have no statutory requirements.)

	Employers Subject to Leave Laws	Criteria for Eligibility	Maximum Length of Leave	Paid Leave	Citations to Authority
AR	Public employers.	Employee must be a permanent or probationary employee of a state agency. Sick leave for employee illness accrues at the rate of 1 day per month, including the probationary period.	6 months. For school leave, 8 hours per calendar year.	State does not require paid leave for illness of immediate family member; paid leave is given for employee illness.	Ark. Code Ann. §§ 21-4-209, 21-4-210; 21-4-216; Act 2235, L. 2005.
CA	Public and private employers with 50 or more employees for family and medical leave. For leave to visit school of a suspended child, all employers. For leave to visit school or day care for any other reason, employers with 25 or more employees. For family military leave, employers with 25 or more employees.	For family and medical leave, employee must be employed for at least 1 continuous year, for a minimum of 1,250 hours per year. For school or day-care visit leave, all employees. For family military leave, employee must average 20 or more hours per week.	For family and medical leave, 12 weeks in a 12-month period; for state employees, pregnancy and childbirth leave for either parent may be up to 4 months, as determined by employer. For leave to visit school or day care for reasons other than suspension, up to 40 hours per year, not exceeding 8 hours per calendar month. For family military leave, up to 10 days of unpaid leave.	Cal FRA does not require paid leave unless paid time-off benefits (e.g., vacation) are used. The state disability program provides paid leave for employees to care for a new child or a sick family member effective 7/1/04. Employees receive about 55% of their salaries for up to 6 weeks. For family military leave, leave is unpaid.	Cal. Gov't Code §§ 12945, 12945.2, 19991.6; Cal. Lab. Code §§ 230.7, 230.8; Cal. Unemp. Ins. Code §§ 2613, 3301 et seq.; Cal. Military & Vet. Code, § 395.10.
CO*	Employers with full- or part-time classified employees in the Colorado state personnel system.	Employee must be employed for more than 1 year. Temporary employees must have worked 1,250 hours in the year before the leave.	520 hours in a fiscal year for full-time employees; prorated for part-time employees.	State does not require paid family leave unless paid time off benefits (e.g., vacation) are used.	Colo. Rev. Stat. Ann. § 19-5-211; 4 Colo. Code Regs. § 801-2, ch. 5 P-5-5, P-5-11, P-5-23–P-5-38.

* Note: Colorado also has a law that requires any employer that permits time off for the birth of a child to allow time off on the same basis for the adoption of a child.

	Employers Subject to Leave Laws	Criteria for Eligibility	Maximum Length of Leave	Paid Leave	Citations to Authority
CT	All state agencies and private employers with 75 or more employees.	Public employee must have permanent status; private employee must have at least 1 year of service and 1,000 hours of work. Employees of municipalities who are a party to a civil union and have been employed for at least 12 months and 1,250 hours during the previous 12-month period.	24 weeks in a 2-year period for public employees; 16 weeks in a 2-year period for private employees. Employees of municipalities must receive the same family and medical leave benefits under the federal FMLA.	State does not require paid leave for public or private employees.	Conn. Gen. Stat. Ann. §§ 5-248a, 5-248b, 31-51kk–31-51nn, 31-51rr, 46a-60.
DE	State employers.	Any employee who has been continuously employed on a full-time basis for at least 1 year.	6 weeks.	State does not require paid leave.	Del. Code Ann. tit. 29, § 5116.
DC	All employers with 20 or more employees (family leave); all employers (school leave).	Employee must have at least 1 year of continuous service and 1,000 hours of work in a 12-month period. For school related leave, all employees.	16 weeks in a 24-month period for family and medical leave; 24 hours per year for school-related leave.	District does not require paid leave, but employee may substitute available paid leave.	D.C. Code Ann. §§ 32-501–32-505, 32-516, 32-1202; *Harrison v. Children's National Medical Center*, 678 A.2d 572 (D.C. 1996).
FL*	All state agencies.	Employee must have career service status.	Up to 6 months (no other specification is given).	State does not require paid leave.	Fla. Stat. Ann. § 110.221.

* Note: Dade County has a family and medical leave ordinance that covers some private employees as well as public employees.

	Employers Subject to Leave Laws	Criteria for Eligibility	Maximum Length of Leave	Paid Leave	Citations to Authority
HI	Public and private employers with 100 or more employees. For parent-teacher conference leave, public employees.	Employee must be employed for 6 consecutive months. For school-related leave, all employees.	4 weeks per calendar year for family and medical leave; 4 hours per year school-related leave.	Employer must permit employees to use any accrued and available paid leave above the amount required under the temporary disability insurance law for family leave purposes. School-related leave is paid.	Haw. Rev. Stat. §§ 78-31, 398-1–398-10.
ID*	State employers.	State employees.	12 weeks in a 12-month period.	Paid leave not required, but employees may elect to use available paid leave.	Idaho Admin. Code § 15:04:01:243.

*Note: Idaho essentially follows the federal FMLA, applied only to state employers and without the 50-employee requirement.

Exhibit 14.2　　　　　　　　　　　　　　　　　　　　　Mandated Benefits: 2009 Compliance Guide

Exhibit 14.2 (cont'd)
State Family and Medical Leave Laws: Eligibility and Coverage

(States not listed have no statutory requirements.)

	Employers Subject to Leave Laws	Criteria for Eligibility	Maximum Length of Leave	Paid Leave	Citations to Authority
IL	For parental leave, employers with at least 50 employees.	For parental leave, employee must be employed for at least 6 months and work an average number of hours per week equal to at least half of the full-time equivalent position.	8 hours of school conference and activity leave during any school year (maximum of 4 hours on any given day).	For parental leave, paid leave is not required.	820 Ill. Comp. Stat. Ann. 147/10, 147/15, 147/30, 147/40; 5 Ill. Comp. Stat. Ann. § 327/20.
IN	For family and medical leave, public employers. For family military leave, employers with 50 or more employees for each working day during at least 20 calendar weeks per year.	For family and medical leave, state employees, except hourly, per diem, temporary, intermittent, or contractual employees or those working less than half-time.	Sick leave generally accrues at the rate of 7.5 hours for every 2 full months of employment, plus 7.5 additional hours for every 4 months of full-time employment. Personal leave generally accrues at the rate of 7.5 hours for every 4 months of full-time employment. Accrued personal leave that would cause balance to exceed 22.5 hours is credited to accrued sick leave. Leave without pay, when granted, may not exceed 2 years. For family and medical leave, up to 10 days.	State does not require paid leave.	Ind. Code Ann. §§ 22-2-13-1 – 22-2-13-16; Ind. Admin. Code tit. 31, r. 2-11-4, 2-11-4.5, 2-11-9.
IA	Employers with at least 4 employees.	State has no minimum employment requirements.	8 weeks or the period of disability, whichever is less.	State does not require paid leave.	Iowa Code Ann. § 216.6.
KS	All employers with 2 or more employees.	State has no minimum employment requirements.	Reasonable period of time.	State does not require paid leave.	Kan. Stat. Ann. §§ 44-1009 (a), 44-1030(a)(1); Kan. Admin. Regs. 1-9-5, 1-9-6.

	Employers Subject to Leave Laws	Criteria for Eligibility	Maximum Length of Leave	Paid Leave	Citations to Authority
KY*	All employers (adoption leave); state employers (family and medical leave).	State has no minimum employment requirements for adoption leave. For family and medical leave, same as federal FMLA.	6 weeks for adoption of child under age 7; for family and medical leave, same as federal FMLA.	State does not require paid leave.	Ky. Rev. Stat. Ann. § 337.015; 101Ky. Admin. Regs. § 2:102, 3:015.
*Note: State employers in Kentucky must essentially follow federal FMLA.					
LA	For pregnancy-related leave, employers with more than 25 employees; for school leave, all employers.	State has no minimum employment requirements for pregnancy-related leave, but provision covers only female employees. State has no minimum employment requirements for school leave.	Reasonable period of time during disability; 6 weeks for disability arising from normal pregnancy or childbirth; pregnancy leave not to exceed 4 months. For school leave, 16 hours in 12 months.	Paid leave not required.	La. Rev. Stat. Ann. §§ 23:341, 23:342, 23:1015.2, 40:1299.124.
ME	For family and medical leave, state employers; city, town or municipal employers with 25 or more employees; employers with 15 or more employees. For family military leave, employers with 15 or more employees.	For family and medical leave, employee must be employed for more than 12 consecutive months.	For family and medical leave, 10 weeks in a 2-year period. For employers with 25 or more employees, if paid leave is provided, employees must be able to use at least 40 hours of paid leave for care of a family member. For family military leave, up to 15 days leave per deployment.	Employer has discretion.	Me. Rev. Stat. Ann. tit. 26, §§ 843–848.
MD	State employers. (Note: Although private employers are not required to provide leave under state law, private employers that provide paid leave to an employee following the birth of the employee's child must provide the same leave with pay to an employee when a child is placed with the employee for adoption.)	For sick leave, employee must be a service employee in the state personnel management system; for family leave, employee must be in the executive branch of state government.	Varies. Sick leave accrues at the rate of 15 days per year, not to exceed 120 hours, and may be used anytime. Up to 12 weeks in a 12-month period may be taken for family leave.	Sick leave must be paid; family leave is without pay.	Md. Code Ann., State Pers. & Pens. §§ 9-501-9-508, 9-1001–9-1105; Lab. & Empl. § 3-802.

Exhibit 14.2   Mandated Benefits: 2009 Compliance Guide

Exhibit 14.2 (cont'd)

State Family and Medical Leave Laws: Eligibility and Coverage

(States not listed have no statutory requirements.)

	Employers Subject to Leave Laws	Criteria for Eligibility	Maximum Length of Leave	Paid Leave	Citations to Authority
MA	Public employers; private employers, of 50 or more employees. For maternity leave, public employers and private employers with at least 6 employees.	For small necessities leave, employee must have worked for at least 12 months, which need not be consecutive, or at least 1,250 hours during 12 months preceding leave. For maternity leave, female employee must have been employed full time for at least 3 consecutive months or have completed any initial probationary period set by employer.	For small necessities leave, up to 24 hours in a 12-month period. For maternity leave, up to 8 weeks.	Employer has discretion.	Mass. Gen. Laws Ann. ch. 149, §§ 52D, 105D.
MN	For birth/adoption of child and illness, public and private employers with 21 or more employees; for school leave, employers with 1 employee; for leave for family members of military personnel, all employers.	Employee must work an average number of hours per week equal to at least half of the full-time equivalent position for at least 1 year.	6 weeks for birth/adoption of child or illness; an employer that has fewer than 21 employees and allows maternity leave must allow 4 weeks for the adoption of a child. 16 hours per year for school leave. Up to 10 days leave for family members of military personnel who are killed or injured. Up to 1 day per year to attend a send-off or homecoming ceremony for immediate family members in active service.	State does not require paid leave unless paid time-off benefits (e.g., vacation) are used.	Minn. Stat. Ann. §§ 181.940-181.948.
MS	State employers.	—	Available medical leave.	Paid medical leave may be used after employee uses one day of accrued personal leave or leave without pay (for care of family member).	Miss. Code Ann. § 25-3-95.
MO	State employers.	State employee adoptive parents who are primarily responsible for furnishing care of a child.	Same length as that granted to biological parents.	Leave may be with or without pay.	Mo. Rev. Stat. § 105.271.

	Employers Subject to Leave Laws	Criteria for Eligibility	Maximum Length of Leave	Paid Leave	Citations to Authority
MT	All employers.	State has no minimum employment requirements.	Reasonable leave; no more than 15 working days if employee is birth father or if employee is adopting.	State does not require paid leave.	Mont. Code Ann. §§ 2-18-606, 49-2-310, 49-2-311.
NE	For adoption leave, all employers. For family military leave, employers with 15 or more employees.	For family military leave, employee must have been employed for at least 12 months with the same employer and have worked at least 1,250 hours during the 12-month period preceding the leave request.	For employers with 15 – 50 employees, up to 15 days family military leave. For employers with more than 50 employees, up to 30 days family military leave.	Paid leave is not required.	Neb. Rev. Stat. Ann. § 48-234; L.B. 497, L. 2007.
NV	All employers for pregnancy leave. State employers are also subject to an adoption/childbirth requirement.	For pregnancy leave, if employer offers leave benefits to employees for sickness or disability, it must offer leave benefits to female employees for pregnancy and related conditions; there are no minimum employment requirements.	For pregnancy leave, the state has no requirements except that if employers offer leave benefits for sickness and disability, they must also offer the same benefits for pregnancy and related conditions. For adoption/childbirth leave, 12 weeks.	For pregnancy leave, the state has no requirements except that if employers offer leave benefits for sickness and disability, they must also offer the same benefits for pregnancy and related conditions. For adoption/childbirth leave, paid leave is not required.	Nev. Rev. Stat. Ann. §§ 284.360, 613.335.
NH	All employers with 6 or more employees.	—	—	Paid leave is not required.	N.H. Rev. Stat. Ann. §§ 354-A:2, 354-A:7.
NJ	Employers with 50 or more employees with a minimum of one employee in New Jersey.	Employee must be employed for 1,000 hours for at least 1 year.	12 weeks in a 24-month period.	Employer may provide paid, unpaid, or a combination of paid and unpaid leave.	N.J. Stat. Ann. §§ 34:11B-3-34:11B-13; 39 N.J.R. 781(c).
NM	—	—	—	—	—
NY	For birth/adoption leave, all employers. For breast or prostate cancer screening, public employers, including school districts. For family military leave, *(continued)*	If employer allows employees leave benefits for the birth of a child, it must offer the same leave benefits to adoptive parents. No minimum employment requirements. For family military leave, *(continued)*	Leave benefits for adoptive parents must be the same as those extended to biological parents, except that there is no entitlement to leave for adoption of a child after the child reaches the minimum age for *(continued)*	Leave benefits for adoptive parents must be the same as those extended to birth parents. Family military leave may be unpaid.	N.Y. Lab. Law § 201-c; 202-i; 202-:; N.Y. Civil Serv. Law §§ 5.2, 22.1, 29.1, 159-b, 159-c.

Exhibit 14.2　　　　　　　　　　　　　　　　Mandated Benefits: 2009 Compliance Guide

Exhibit 14.2 (cont'd)

State Family and Medical Leave Laws: Eligibility and Coverage

(States not listed have no statutory requirements.)

	Employers Subject to Leave Laws	Criteria for Eligibility	Maximum Length of Leave	Paid Leave	Citations to Authority
NY *(continued)*					
NY	all employers with 20 or more employees at (at least) one site.	employee must work at least 20 hours per week.	attendance in public school unless the child is handicapped or otherwise considered difficult to place for adoption. Public employees may also entitled (at the discretion of the employer) to up to 2 years maternity leave without pay. For breast or prostate cancer screening leave, up to 4 hours per year. For family military leave, up to 10 days.		
NC	For parental leave, all employers.	For parental leave, any employee who is a parent/guardian or standing *in loco parentis* to a school-age child.	For parental leave, 4 hours per year.	State does not require paid leave for parental leave.	N.C. Gen. Stat. § 95-28.3; N.C. Reg. title 25, ch. 1E § 1607.
ND	State employers.	Any employee who has been employed by the state for at least 1 year, working at least 1,250 hours in the past 12 months.	For a part-time (20 hours per week) employee, 2 months; for a full-time (40 hours per week) employee, 12 weeks.	Leave is without pay, unless employer or employee policy specifies otherwise.	N.D. Cent. Code §§ 54-52.4–01-54-52.4-10; S. 2298, L, 2005.
OH	State employers.	Must work 30 or more hours per week.	6 weeks.	First 2 weeks unpaid, next 4 weeks (or 160 hours) paid at 70% of regular pay for full-time employees. Part-time employees receive prorated number of hours of paid leave. Employees may opt to receive $2,000 for adoption expenses in lieu of paid leave.	Ohio Rev. Code Ann. § 124.13.6.
OK	State employers. Employees participate in a shared leave program by which hours may be donated.	Employee must be employed for at least 6 months.	12 weeks in any 12-month period.	—	Okla. Stat. Ann. tit. 74, §§ 840-2.22, 840-2.23, and accompanying regulations.

	Employers Subject to Leave Laws	Criteria for Eligibility	Maximum Length of Leave	Paid Leave	Citations to Authority
OR	Employers with 25 or more employees.	Employee must be employed for 180 days for parental leave; employee must be employed for 180 days and average 25 hours of work per week for family leave.	12 weeks in a 12-month period. A woman who takes leave because of a pregnancy-related purpose may take an additional 12 weeks for an other purpose. An employee who takes 12 weeks of parental leave may take an additional 12 weeks of sick-child leave.	—	Or. Rev. Stat. § 659A.150–659A.186.
RI*	Private employers with at least 50 employees; all state employers; cities/towns/municipal agencies with at least 30 employees.	Employee must be employed for at least 30 hours per week for at least 12 consecutive months with the same employer.	For family leave, 13 weeks in any 2 calendar years. For school leave, 10 hours per 12-month period.	For family leave, if employer provides paid leave for less than the required 13 weeks, the balance of the required leave may be unpaid. For school leave, paid leave is not required.	R.I. Gen. Laws §§ 28-48-1–28-48-4, 28-48-12.
SC	State employers.	State employee with accrued sick leave. Leave accrues at the rate of 15 days per year, and up to 180 days may be carried over to the next year.	Statutory limits of 8 days to care for family member, 6 weeks for adoption of child.	State requires paid leave.	S.C. Code Ann. §§ 8-11-40, 8-11-155.
SD	State employers.	For paid sick leave, state employees, excluding temporary and emergency employees and patient, inmate, and student employees.	Up to 14 days paid sick leave, up to 5 of which may be used for personal emergency reasons per year. Additional unpaid sick leave may be granted on a discretionary basis.	Up to 14 days paid sick leave may be taken, as many as 5 of which may be used annually for personal emergency reasons. After regular and continuous state employment for at least one year, up to 28 days of sick leave may be advanced to employees.	S.D. Codified Laws §§ 3-6-7, 3-6-8, 3-6-10.

* Note: Rhode Island also has a statute that provides that an employer that allows sick leave to be taken after the birth of a child must allow the same leave after the adoption of a child who is age 16 or younger. R.I. Gen. Laws § 28-48-11.

Exhibit 14.2 (cont'd)
State Family and Medical Leave Laws: Eligibility and Coverage

(States not listed have no statutory requirements.)

	Employers Subject to Leave Laws	Criteria for Eligibility	Maximum Length of Leave	Paid Leave	Citations to Authority
TN	Employers with 100 or more employees; state employers.	Mothers of newborn or adopted children who have been employed full-time for 12 consecutive months; adoptive parents.	4 months; can be extended with use of accrued paid time off. 30 days for state employees who adopt; may be extended at discretion of employer. For school-related leave, 1 day per month.	Employer may provide paid or unpaid leave, or a combination, at its discretion.	Tenn. Code Ann. §§ 4-21-408, 8-50-806, 49-6-7001.
TX	State employers.	State employees.	12 weeks for parental leave; amount accrued for sick leave (sick leave accrues at the rate of 8 hours per month). 8 hours of sick leave for parent-teacher conferences; leave without pay for death in family and for foster-care meetings; leave without pay to train with an assistance dog (10 days per year).	Sick leave is paid; other types of leave are unpaid.	Tex. Gov't Code Ann. §§ 661.001–661.008, 661.206, 661.902, 661.906 *et seq.*
UT	All state agencies.	Full-time employee must be employed for at least 12 months and have worked at least 1,250 hours in the previous 12 months.	Half-time status up to 6 weeks; temporary disability up to 12 months.	Paid leave is required for half-time leave; paid leave is not required for long-term leave.	Utah Admin. Code 477-8-7, 477-8-9.
VT	For parental leave, employers with 10 or more employees; for family leave, employers with 15 or more employees.	Employee must be employed an average of 30 hours per week for at least 12 months.	12 weeks of leave in any 12-month period for parental and family leave. For short-term leave, 24 hours per year, not to exceed 4 hours per 30 days.	State does not require paid leave.	Vt. Stat. Ann. tit. 21, §§ 470–472a.
VA	State employees.	State employees.	Employees with less than 120 months of state service receive 32 hours per year; employees with more than 120 months of state service receive 40 hours per year.	Leave is paid.	Va. Code Ann. §§ 51.1-1107, 51.1-1108.

	Employers Subject to Leave Laws	Criteria for Eligibility	Maximum Length of Leave	Paid Leave	Citations to Authority
WA	For family and medical leave, private employers with 50 or more employees. For parental and sick leave, all employers.	Employee must have worked at least 1,250 hours in the previous 12 months.	12 weeks of leave in a 24-month period.	State does not require paid leave. Beginning October 1, 2009, the state will provide paid family leave for the birth and care of an employee's child or the placement of a child with an employee for adoption. Benefits are payable up to $250 per week for up to five weeks following a one-week waiting period.	Wash. Rev. Code Ann. §§ 49.78.010–49.78.100, 49.78.110, 48.78.130, 49.78.140, 49.78.180–49.78.200.
WV	State agencies and county boards, divisions, and any units of the state and county boards of education.	Employee must have permanent status working for pay at least 12 consecutive weeks.	12 weeks of leave in any 12-month period.	State does not require paid leave.	W. Va. Code §§ 21-5D-2–21-5D-7; S. 240, L. 2005, *Hudok v. Board of Education of Randolph County*, 415 S.E.2d 897 (W. Va. 1992).
WI	Employers with 50 or more employees.	Employee must be employed for more than 1 year and must have worked 1,000 hours in 52 weeks prior to leave.	8 weeks of leave in a 12-month period; exact length depends on reason for leave. Up to 6 weeks of leave for birth/adoption of child or care of foster child; up to 2 weeks for care of a child, spouse, or parent; and up to 2 weeks for employee illness.	State does not require paid leave.	Wis. Stat. Ann. § 103.10.
WY*	State employees.	State employees.	Same as federal FMLA.	Paid leave is not required.	Wyo. Admin. Code ch.10, § 15.

*Note: Wyoming essentially follows the federal FMLA.

Source: John F. Buckley & Ronald M. Green, *2008 State by State Guide to Human Resources Law* (New York: Aspen Publishers, Inc. 2008).

Exhibit 14.3　　　　　　　　　　　　　　　　　　　Mandated Benefits: 2009 Compliance Guide

Exhibit 14.3

State Family and Medical Leave Laws: Administration of Leave

(States not listed have no statutory requirements.)

	Acceptable Reasons for Leave	Employment Guarantees After Leave	Use of Vacation or Other Time-Off Benefits	Certification Required	Effect of Leave on Other Benefits	Citations to Authority
AL	Illness of employee or of family member. Leave may be used in lieu of maternity leave for days employee is actually disabled. Leave may also be used for death of family member, or for death, injury, or sickness of a person to whom one has unusually strong ties.	—	—	Certification may be required.	—	Ala. Code § 16-1-18.1; Ala. Admin. Code r. 670-X-14.-01. 670-X-14.-02.
AK	Birth/adoption of child; serious health condition of employee, child, spouse, or parent.	Employee is entitled to reinstatement in the position held prior to the leave or an equivalent position.	Employee may use any accrued paid leave.	—	Group health coverage continues, but employer may require employee to pay all or part of the cost of coverage during the leave.	Alaska Stat. §§ 39.20.500–39.20.550.
AZ	For sick leave, illness or injury that renders the employee unable to perform the duties of the position; disability caused by pregnancy, childbirth, miscarriage, or abortion; examination or treatment by a *(continued)*	Employee returning to work from unpaid leave taken as part of parental leave shall return to the position occupied at the start of the parental leave. If the position no longer exists, the agency *(continued)*	Paid sick, annual, or compensatory leave may be used. Sick and annual leave must be used for serious health conditions. All leave balances, including donated leave, must be exhausted before *(continued)*	Submission of evidence or examination by a designated physician may be required. For medical leave without pay, employee's physician must document the seriousness and extensiveness of the *(continued)*	Participation in health benefit plan continues. Employees on FMLA leave without pay continue to participate in the Basic Life and Accidental Death and Dismemberment Insurance Plan, and *(continued)*	Ariz. Admin. Code 2-5-404, 2-5-411–2-5-413.

	Acceptable Reasons for Leave	Employment Guarantees After Leave	Use of Vacation or Other Time-Off Benefits	Certification Required	Effect of Leave on Other Benefits	Citations to Authority
AZ *(continued)*						
	physician; or illness, injury, examination, or treatment of spouse, dependent child, or parent. For parental leave, pregnancy, childbirth, miscarriage, abortion, or adoption of children. For serious health condition leave, same as FMLA for both employees and family members. For medical leave without pay, non-jobrelated, seriously incapacitating, and extended illness or injury rendering employee unable to work.	shall conduct a reduction in force.	medical leave without pay (but not parental leave) may be taken.	incapacitating illness or injury, subject to confirmation by an agency-selected physician, at the expense of the agency, whose opinion is used to determine whether a medical leave without pay should be granted.	may continue to participate in the supplemental life and dependent life insurance coverage by paying the full premium.	
AR	Employee illness; care for immediate family member; school-related events for employee's child.	Employee is entitled to reinstatement without loss of any rights unless the position is no longer available because of reduction of staff for budgetary reasons. Whenever an employee is laid off because of budgetary reasons and is reinstated within 6 months, accumulated sick leave may be restored to the employee's credit.	Employee must first use all other accumulated leave.	Certification may be required for more than 5 consecutive days of leave.	Employee must pay to participate in group insurance programs while on leave.	Ark. Code Ann. §§ 21-4-207, 21-4-209, 21-4-210; 2005 Ark. Acts 2235.

Exhibit 14.3   Mandated Benefits: 2009 Compliance Guide

Exhibit 14.3 (cont'd)
State Family and Medical Leave Laws: Administration of Leave

(States not listed have no statutory requirements.)

	Acceptable Reasons for Leave	Employment Guarantees After Leave	Use of Vacation or Other Time-Off Benefits	Certification Required	Effect of Leave on Other Benefits	Citations to Authority
CA	Birth/adoption of child or care of foster child; illness of employee, child, spouse, domestic partner, or parent; need to visit school or day care of employee's child. For family military leave, spouse of employee is a qualified member of the Armed Forces, National Guard or Reserves and is on leave from deployment during a period of military conflict.	Employee is entitled to reinstatement in the same or an equivalent position and at the level of seniority held prior to the leave.	Employer may require employee to use vacation or other time-off benefits first before receiving the leave benefits (e.g., using sick leave before requesting employee health leave). For school or day-care visit, employee may choose to use any available paid or unpaid leave. Employees may use up to half of paid sick leave to care for sick child, spouse, or parent.	Employer may require certification of illness if leave is taken to care for an ill child, spouse, or parent, as well as require a second or third opinion at employer's expense. Employer may also require documentation of visit to child's school or day care. For family military leave, employee must submit written documentation certifying the spouse will be on leave from deployment during the requested leave time.	All benefits continue while employee is on leave, the same as for other unpaid leave.	Cal. Gov't Code §§ 12945, 12945.2, 19991.6; Cal. Lab. Code §§ 230.7, 230.8, 233; Cal. Military & Vet. Code § 395.10.
CO	Birth/adoption of child or placement of foster child; illness of employee; or care for family member.	Employee is entitled to the same or equivalent position, including the same pay, benefits, location, work schedule, and other working conditions. If the employee is no longer qualified (e.g., unable to renew an expired license), the employee must be given an opportunity to fulfill the requirement.	Generally, paid leave must be exhausted before an employee is placed on unpaid leave. The employee must use all accrued personal leave, subject to any conditions for use, before being placed on unpaid leave for the remainder of family and medical leave, except for workers' *(continued)*	Employee is required to provide proper medical certification within 15 calendar days, absent extenuating circumstances, for any absence of more than 3 consecutive full working days, and may be required for shorter absences at the employer's discretion. Additional certification *(continued)*	Employees pay their share for health benefits for any unpaid portion of leave.	Colo. Rev. Stat. Ann. § 19-5-211; 4 Colo. Code Regs. § 801-2, ch. 5 P-5-5, P-5-6, P-5-8, P-5-9, P-5-11, P-5-23-P-5-38.

	Acceptable Reasons for Leave	Employment Guarantees After Leave	Use of Vacation or Other Time-Off Benefits	Certification Required	Effect of Leave on Other Benefits	Citations to Authority
CO *(continued)*			compensation and compensatory time. Temporary reductions in schedule are not allowed until all paid personal leave is exhausted.	may be required every 30 days or the time period established in the original certificate, whichever is longer. A second or third opinion may also be required at employer's expense. If an absence is over 30 days for an employee illness, a fitness-to-return certification is required, and may be required for shorter absences in case of business necessity.		
CT	Birth/adoption of child; illness of employee, child, parent, spouse, or spouse's parent. A definition of "spouse" includes partners in a civil union.	Employee is entitled to reinstatement in the position held prior to the leave or an equivalent position (private employee), unless employee is disabled (public employee).	When there are other benefits that cover the same conditions as family leave, the length of family leave benefits is reduced (private employee).	Employer may require certification of illness if leave is taken to care for an ill child, parent, or spouse, or for employee illness.	Fringe benefits accrued prior to leave are restored at the end of leave. Health benefits continue for public employees.	Conn. Gen. Stat. Ann. §§ 5-248a, 5-248b, 31-51kk-31-51nn, 46a-60, § 15, 5.963, L 2005.
DE	Adoption of a child.	Employee is entitled to reinstatement in position held at time of leave.	Employee is entitled to use accumulated sick leave for birth of a child or adoption of a pre-kindergarten-age child (for employees with one year of employment, this includes travel for a foreign adoption)	—	Vacation and sick leave do not accumulate.	Del. Code Ann. tit. 29, § 5116; 2005 Del. Laws 198.

Exhibit 14.3   Mandated Benefits: 2009 Compliance Guide

Exhibit 14.3 (cont'd)
State Family and Medical Leave Laws: Administration of Leave

(States not listed have no statutory requirements.)

	Acceptable Reasons for Leave	Employment Guarantees After Leave	Use of Vacation or Other Time-Off Benefits	Certification Required	Effect of Leave on Other Benefits	Citations to Authority
DC	Birth/adoption of child or foster child; care for family member; employee illness; school-related events for employee's child. Family members include domestic partners.	Employee is entitled to reinstatement in the position held prior to the leave or an equivalent position, unless employee is a key employee under statutory guidelines.	Employee may elect to use paid sick, vacation, or personal benefits before receiving the leave benefits.	Employer may require certification of illness if leave is taken to care for a family member or for employee illness, as well as require a second or third opinion at employer's expense.	Health benefits continue while employee is on leave; all other fringe benefits accrued prior to leave are restored at end of leave. For school-related leave, employee shall not lose accrued benefits.	D.C. Code Ann. §§ 32-501–32-505, 32-516, 32-701, 32-705, 32-1202.
FL*	Birth/adoption of child; serious family illness ("family" includes child, parent, or spouse).	Employee is entitled to reinstatement in the position held prior to the leave or an equivalent position.	Employee may use accrued sick leave or annual leave to extend the leave benefits.	Employer may require certification of illness if leave is taken to care for ill family member or for employee illness.	All benefits continue while employee is on paid leave; fringe benefits accrued prior to unpaid leave are restored at the end of the leave.	Fla. Stat. Ann. § 110.221.
* Note: Dade County has a family and medical leave ordinance that covers some private employees as well as public employees.						
HI	Birth/adoption of child; illness of child, spouse, reciprocal beneficiary, or parent, parent-in-law, grandparent, or grandparent-in-law; parent-teacher conference.	Employee is entitled to reinstatement in the position held prior to the leave or an equivalent position.	Employee may elect to substitute any of the employee's accrued paid leaves, including but not limited to vacation, personal, or family leave for any part of the four-week period *(continued)*	Employer may require certification of birth/ adoption of a child or of a serious health condition.	All benefits continue to accrue while employee is on leave and are restored at the end of leave.	Haw. Rev. Stat. §§ 398-1–398-10; 2003 Haw. Sess. Laws 389, H. 1318.

	Acceptable Reasons for Leave	Employment Guarantees After Leave	Use of Vacation or Other Time-Off Benefits	Certification Required	Effect of Leave on Other Benefits	Citations to Authority
HI (*continued*)			provided, however, that employer permits employee to use any accrued and available sick leave above the amount required under the temporary disability insurance law for family leave purposes.			
ID	Birth/adoption of child; illness of employee, child, spouse, or parent.	Employee is entitled to reinstatement in the position held prior to the leave or an equivalent position.	Accrued paid leave may be used by employee or required by employer.	Employer may require certification of employee or family member's serious health condition and may require second or third opinion at employer's expense.	Health benefits continue during leave on same conditions as before leave, including any employee contribution to insurance.	Idaho Admin. Code § 15:04:01:243.
IL	Child's school conferences and school activities.	None.	For parental leave, employee must first use other leave benefits (e.g., vacation, personal leave), except sick and disability leave benefits.	Employer may require documentation of school activity or conference.	Employee may not lose benefits for exercising right to take leave.	5 Ill. Comp. Stat. Ann. 327/20, 820 Ill. Comp. Stat. Ann. 147/10, 147/15, 147/30, 147/40.
IN	For family and medical leave, personal illness, injury, or legal quarantine; illness or injury of spouse, child, or parent who resides with and is dependent upon the employee for care and support and whose (*continued*)	Upon expiration of a regularly approved leave without pay, the employee shall be returned to a position in the same class as the position held at the time leave was granted.	Personal leave may be used; unpaid leave may be used. The appointing authority, with the approval of the Director of State Personnel, may grant an employee leave without pay whenever such leave (*continued*)	For sick leave, a medical certificate from the attending physician or a designated physician, documenting the nature and extent of the disability or fitness to return to duty. The cost of certification by a (*continued*)	—	Ind. Code Ann. §§ 22-2-13-1–22-2-13-16; Ind. Admin. Code tit. 31, r. 2-11-4, 2-11-4.5, 2-11-9.

Exhibit 14.3   Mandated Benefits: 2009 Compliance Guide

Exhibit 14.3 (cont'd)
State Family and Medical Leave Laws: Administration of Leave

(States not listed have no statutory requirements.)

	Acceptable Reasons for Leave	Employment Guarantees After Leave	Use of Vacation or Other Time-Off Benefits	Certification Required	Effect of Leave on Other Benefits	Citations to Authority
IN (*continued*)	illness or injury requires employee's absence from work. For family and medical leave, deployment to active military duty of spouse, parent, grandparent, or sibling.		is considered to be in the best interests of the service. For family and medical leave, employer may require use of available vacation or personal leave, except for sick leave or medical leave.	designated physician is paid by the appointing authority. Employees on leave without pay due to personal illness, injury, or legal quarantine may be required to submit medical proof from a designated physician of fitness to return to work. For family military leave, employer may require certification.		
IA	Birth of child; disability related to pregnancy.	—	Employer may require employee to use other disability benefits prior to leave.	Employer may require certification of condition of disability.	—	Iowa Code Ann. § 216.6.
KS	Birth of child, illness or disability related to pregnancy or childbirth.*	Employee is entitled to reinstatement in the position held prior to the leave or an equivalent position if employee expresses an intention to return to work within a reasonable period of time after childbirth.	—		No loss of other benefits.	Kan. Stat. Ann. §§ 44-1009(a), 44-1030(a)(1); Kan. Admin. Regs. 1-9-5, 1-9-6, 21-32-6.

* Note: Kansas law also provides that state employees may use sick leave (which accrues at the rate of 8 hours per month) for illness of a family member or the adoption of a child.

	Acceptable Reasons for Leave	Employment Guarantees After Leave	Use of Vacation or Other Time-Off Benefits	Certification Required	Effect of Leave on Other Benefits	Citations to Authority
KY	Reception of an adopted child under age 7. All reasons for leave as in federal FMLA.	For family and medical leave, same as federal FMLA.	For family and medical leave, same as federal FMLA.	For family and medical leave, same as federal FMLA.	Health and life insurance must be paid while on leave.	Ky. Rev. Stat. Ann. § 337.015. 101 Ky. Admin. Regs. 2:102, 3:015.
LA	Birth of child or pregnancy and/or disability due to pregnancy, or related medical condition; school-related activities for employee's children.	Employee is entitled to the same benefits and privileges as other employees who are similarly situated in employment.	Employee may use any accrued vacation leave.	—	Employee may use accrued vacation leave.	La. Rev. Stat. Ann. §§ 23:341, 23:342, 23:1015, 40:1299.124.
ME	Birth/adoption or serious illness of child, domestic partner's child, parent, spouse, or domestic partner; employee illness; death or serious health condition of employee's spouse, domestic partner, parent, or child who is a member of the military; deployment to active military duty for period longer than 180 days of employee's spouse, domestic partner, or parent. If employee's spouse, *(continued)*	Employee is entitled to reinstatement in the same position held prior to the leave or an equivalent position.	—	Employer may require certification of illness if leave is taken to care for an ill child, parent, or spouse, or for employee illness.	Benefits may continue at employee expense.	Me. Rev. Stat. Ann. tit. 26, §§ 843-848, 850.

Exhibit 14.3   Mandated Benefits: 2009 Compliance Guide

Exhibit 14.3 (cont'd)
State Family and Medical Leave Laws: Administration of Leave

(States not listed have no statutory requirements.)

	Acceptable Reasons for Leave	Employment Guarantees After Leave	Use of Vacation or Other Time-Off Benefits	Certification Required	Effect of Leave on Other Benefits	Citations to Authority
ME (continued)	child, or parent is the victim of violence or stalking, then for preparing for and attending court proceedings, receiving medical treatment or attending to medical treatment, or obtaining necessary services to remedy a crisis, related to the violence or stalking.					
MD	For sick leave, illness/ disability of employee; death, illness, or disability of a member of employee's immediate family; or birth or placement of a child with employee for adoption; and medical appointment of employee or member of employee's immediate family. For family leave, birth/adoption of child; adoption of foster child; illness or disability in employee's immediate family; or care for employee's school-age child under 14 during school vacations.	For sick leave, state has no statutory requirements; guarantee of reinstatement in the same job for family leave.	For sick leave, state has no statutory requirements; for family leave, employer may require employee to use other leave benefits first.	Certification is required for employee illness of more than 4 days in a 30-day period for personal illness or disability of immediate family member. Certification regarding employee's illness or disability must include prognosis on ability to work.	For sick leave, state has no statutory requirements; for family leave, suspension of benefits except for health benefits.	Md. Code Ann., State Pers. & Pens. §§ 9-501–9-508, 9-1001-9-1105; Lab. & Empl. § 3-802.

	Acceptable Reasons for Leave	Employment Guarantees After Leave	Use of Vacation or Other Time-Off Benefits	Certification Required	Effect of Leave on Other Benefits	Citations to Authority
MA	Birth/adoption of child (adoption of child under 18, or under 23 if child is mentally/physically disabled); child's medical appointments or education- related school activities; appointments related to care of elderly relative.	For maternity leave, employee is entitled to reinstatement in the position held prior to the leave or an equivalent position, unless a layoff during the leave would have applied to the employee.	For maternity leave, employee may use accrued vacation and sick leave benefits to extend family leave.	May be required for small necessities leave.	All benefits to which employee was entitled prior to maternity leave continue in effect; however, employer is not obligated to pay for the cost of benefits unless it does so for all employees on leave.	Mass. Gen. Laws Ann. ch. 149, §§ 52D, 105D.
MN	Birth/adoption or serious illness of child; child's school conferences and activities; death or injury while in active service of an immediate family member who is in the armed services; send-off or homecoming ceremony for an immediate family member in active service in the armed forces.	Employee is entitled to reinstatement in the position held prior to the leave or an equivalent position.	Employer may require that employee use sick leave to care for a sick child.	—	All benefits are restored at the end of leave.	Minn. Stat. Ann. §§ 181.940–181.948.
MS	Illness of employee or family member.	—	Employee must first use 1 day of accrued personal leave per incident.	—	—	Miss. Code Ann. § 25-3-95.
MO	Adoption of child.	Employer may not penalize employee for exercising right to take leave.	Employee may first use sick leave, annual leave, and leave without pay.	—	—	Mo. Rev. Stat. § 105.271.

Exhibit 14.3

Mandated Benefits: 2009 Compliance Guide

Exhibit 14.3 (cont'd)
State Family and Medical Leave Laws: Administration of Leave

(States not listed have no statutory requirements.)

	Acceptable Reasons for Leave	Employment Guarantees After Leave	Use of Vacation or Other Time-Off Benefits	Certification Required	Effect of Leave on Other Benefits	Citations to Authority
MT	Pregnancy; birth or adoption of child.	Employee is entitled to reinstatement in the position held prior to the leave or an equivalent position, unless a change in circumstances makes it impossible or unreasonable for employer to do so.	Employee may use sick leave up to 15 days after adoption of child, or after birth if employee is the father.	Employer may require certification of disabling condition due to pregnancy.	Fringe benefits that employee had prior to the leave are restored when employee returns to work, unless a change in circumstances makes it impossible or unreasonable for employer to do so.	Mont. Code Ann. §§ 2-18-606, 49-2-310, 49-2-311.
NE	Family military leave for spouse or parent of an individual called to active military duty for at least 179 days. If employer gives leave for birth of a child, leave must also be given to employees who adopt, subject to statutory criteria (adopted child must be under age 8 or if older, be a special needs child).	Employee must be reinstated.	—	For family military leave, employer may require verification from the military.	—	Neb. Rev. Stat. § 48-234; L.B. 497, L. 2007.

	Acceptable Reasons for Leave	Employment Guarantees After Leave	Use of Vacation or Other Time-Off Benefits	Certification Required	Effect of Leave on Other Benefits	Citations to Authority
NV	Childbirth, miscarriage, or other natural resolution to pregnancy. For state employees, adoption or childbirth.	—	—	—	—	Nev. Rev. Stat. Ann. §§ 284.360, 613.335.
NH	Disability related to pregnancy, childbirth, or related medical conditions.	Employee must be reinstated to original job or comparable position, unless business necessity makes it impossible or unreasonable.	—	—	Employee must be treated in the same manner as other employees with temporary disabilities.	N.H. Rev. Stat. Ann. § 354-A:7.
NJ	Birth/adoption of child; serious health condition of child, spouse, parent, or parent-in-law. Family leave benefits will apply to civil union couples in the same manner as they apply to spouses.	Employee is entitled to reinstatement in the position held prior to the leave or an equivalent position, unless a layoff during the leave would have applied to the employee.	—	Employer may require certification of illness if leave is taken to care for ill child, parent, or spouse; certification of birth or adoption may also be required. Employer may obtain second or third opinion at employer's expense.	All benefits continue in effect while employee is on leave.	N.J. Stat. Ann. §§ 34:11B-3–34:11B-13.
NY	Birth/adoption of child; breast or prostate cancer screening; leave during a period when a spouse is on leave from military service during a posting to a combat zone during a military conflict.	—	—	—	—	N.Y. Lab. Law § 201-c, 202-i; Civil Serv. Law §§ 5.2, 22.1, 29.1.

Exhibit 14.3　　　　　　　　　　　　　　　Mandated Benefits: 2009 Compliance Guide

Exhibit 14.3 (cont'd)
State Family and Medical Leave Laws: Administration of Leave

(States not listed have no statutory requirements.)

	Acceptable Reasons for Leave	Employment Guarantees After Leave	Use of Vacation or Other Time-Off Benefits	Certification Required	Effect of Leave on Other Benefits	Citations to Authority
NC	Involvement in child's school.	Employer may not discharge, demote, or take any adverse action against an employee taking leave.	—	—	Not applicable.	N.C. Gen. Stat. § 95-28.3; N.C. Reg. tit. 25, Ch. 1 E § 1607.
ND	Newborn or adopted child; care for child, spouse, or parent with serious health condition; employee illness or disability.	Employee is entitled to reinstatement in the position held prior to the leave or an equivalent position.	Employee may use up to 1 week of medical leave, if provided by employer, to care for a family member with a serious health condition. For leave due to pregnancy, employee may first use sick leave.	Employer may request certification of a serious health condition.	Health benefits continue, but employee may have to pay premiums.	N.D. Cent. Code §§ 54-52.4-01–54-52.4-10; S. 2298, L. 2005.
OH	Birth/adoption of child.	No provision, but reinstatement implied.	Employee may use available sick, personal, or vacation leave or compensatory time for unpaid portion of parental leave.	—	Employee will not receive holiday pay during leave; otherwise no effect.	Ohio Rev. Code Ann. § 124.13.6.
OK	Birth/adoption of child or to care for family member.	Employee is entitled to reinstatement in the same position held prior to the leave.	Employee must first use any other benefits (e.g., sick leave, vacation) before receiving the leave.	Employer may require certification of illness if leave is taken to care for ill family member.	Employee pays premium for continued health and life insurance benefits.	Okla. Stat. Ann. tit. 74, §§ 840-2.22, 840-2.23, and accompanying regulations.

	Acceptable Reasons for Leave	Employment Guarantees After Leave	Use of Vacation or Other Time-Off Benefits	Certification Required	Effect of Leave on Other Benefits	Citations to Authority
OR	For family leave, care for serious condition of spouse, child, parent, parent-in-law, grandparent or grandchild; for parental leave, birth/adoption of child or for a child requiring home health care.	Employee is entitled to reinstatement in the position held prior to the leave or an equivalent position.	Employer may require employee to use accrued benefits (e.g., sick leave, vacation) during parental leave. Employee may opt to use any accrued benefits during family leave.	Employer may require certification of illness if leave is taken to care for ill child, spouse, parent, or in-law.	Benefits cease during leave unless employer is obligated to continue benefits under a separate contract.	Or. Rev. Stat. §§ 659A.150–659A.186.
RI	For family leave, birth/adoption of child, serious illness of child, parent, spouse, parents-in-law, or employee. For school leave, school conferences or other school-related activities. For state employees, domestic partners are considered to be family members.	Employee is entitled to reinstatement in the position held prior to the leave or an equivalent position.	For school leave, employee may use paid vacation leave or other appropriate accrued paid leave.	Employer may require certification of illness.	Health benefits continue in effect during leave; no loss of benefits accrued during leave.	R.I. Gen. Laws §§ 28-48-1-28-48-4, 28-48-12.
SC	Sickness of employee or family member; adoption of child, provided employee is primarily responsible for the child.	—	—	—	—	S.C. Code Ann. §§ 8-11-40, 8-11-155.

Exhibit 14.3   Mandated Benefits: 2009 Compliance Guide

Exhibit 14.3 (cont'd)
State Family and Medical Leave Laws: Administration of Leave

(States not listed have no statutory requirements.)

	Acceptable Reasons for Leave	Employment Guarantees After Leave	Use of Vacation or Other Time-Off Benefits	Certification Required	Effect of Leave on Other Benefits	Citations to Authority
SD	For personal leave, death or illness of immediate family member; temporary care of members of immediate family. For family and medical leave, birth; adoption; care of newborn; serious health condition of spouse, child, parent, or employee.	No provision, but reinstatement implied.	Employee must use accrued sick leave for personal leave. For family and medical leave, employee may choose to use sick leave, vacation leave, personal leave, leave without pay, or any combination thereof.	Certification of employee's or family member's serious health condition may be required.	—	S.D. Reg. 55:01:22:02, 55:01:22:02:04, 55:01:22:08:02.
TN	Birth/adoption of child; pregnancy; school visitation leave.	Employee is entitled to reinstatement in the position held prior to the leave or an equivalent position if employee gives 3 months' notice, unless medical emergency prevents employee from giving notice. Failure to reinstate is acceptable if employee held a unique job position.	State employees may use a maximum of 30 sick days toward adoption leave. Employer may request certification for school-related leave.	For adoption leave, state employee must submit to employer statement from licensed child placement agency. Employer may request certification for school related leave	Employer's obligation to pay for benefits ceases during leave, unless other on-leave employees receive benefits.	Tenn. Code Ann. §§ 4-21-408, 8-50-806, 49-6-7001.
TX	Parental leave for birth/ adoption of a child and foster child meetings; sick leave for illness of employee or family member, disability due to pregnancy, and parent-teacher conference.	—	Employees must use vacation and sick leave first.	—	—	Tex. Gov't Code Ann. §§ 661.001–661.008, 661.910 et seq.

	Acceptable Reasons for Leave	Employment Guarantees After Leave	Use of Vacation or Other Time-Off Benefits	Certification Required	Effect of Leave on Other Benefits	Citations to Authority
UT	Maternity/adoption/ placement for foster care of child, illness, or to care for spouse, dependents or parents.	Employee is entitled to reinstatement in a position with the same pay and seniority as the position held prior to the leave.	Employees may use sick leave or other annual benefits (annual leave, converted leave, excess hours, compensatory leave) to offset or extend the leave benefits.	Employer may require certification of illness if leave is taken to care for children or spouse.	Sick leave accrues at 4 hours per pay period without limit. Employee may pay premiums for continued health benefits.	Utah Admin. Code 477-8-7, 477-8-9.
VT	For family leave, illness of employee or to care for ill child, parent, parent-in-law, or spouse; for parental leave, birth/adoption of child under age 16; for short-term family leave, visits to child's school or physician, or to employee's parent's care provider.	Employee is entitled to reinstatement in the position held prior to the leave or an equivalent position, unless a layoff occurring during the leave would have affected the employee or economic circumstances required hiring of permanent replacement because the job position was unique.	Employer may require employee to use up to 6 weeks of accrued sick leave or vacation time as part of the leave. For short-term leave, employee may use any accrued paid leave.	Employer may require certification if leave is taken for employee illness or to care for seriously ill family member.	All benefits continue while employee is on leave, but employee may be required to pay premiums for benefits.	Vt. Stat. Ann. tit. 21, §§ 470–472a.
VA	Short-term incident, illness, or death of a family member, or other personal need.	—	State employees may also use up to 33% of accrued sick leave or 100% of other accrued leave when taking time off that qualifies as federal FMLA.	—	—	Va. Code Ann. §§ 2.2-1201, 51.1-1108.

Exhibit 14.3　　　　　　　　　　　　　　　　　　Mandated Benefits: 2009 Compliance Guide

Exhibit 14.3 (cont'd)
State Family and Medical Leave Laws: Administration of Leave

(States not listed have no statutory requirements.)

	Acceptable Reasons for Leave	Employment Guarantees After Leave	Use of Vacation or Other Time-Off Benefits	Certification Required	Effect of Leave on Other Benefits	Citations to Authority
WA	Birth/adoption of child or care of foster child; care for child, spouse, or parent with serious health condition; serious health condition that makes employee unable to perform functions of his or her position. Employees entitled to sick leave or other paid time off must be permitted to use any or all of their choice of such leave to care for a child, spouse, parent, parent-in-law, or grandparent.	Employee is entitled to reinstatement in the position held prior to the leave or an equivalent position, unless employer's business conditions have significantly changed.	Employee may use sick leave for own illness and may use accrued vacation and sick benefits to extend the leave.	Employer may require certification.	All benefits continue while employee is on leave, but employee may be required to pay premiums for medical and dental benefits.	Wash. Rev. Code Ann. §§ 49.12.265, 49.12.630, 49.78.010–49.78.100, 49.78.110, 48.78.130, 49.78.140, 49.78.180–49.78.200.
WV	Birth/adoption of child; illness of spouse, child, parent, or other dependent.	Employee is entitled to reinstatement in the same position held prior to leave. Employer may hire a temporary replacement during leave.	Employer may require that employee use all other accrued annual and personal benefits prior to receiving the leave benefits. Employee may also choose to use other accrued leaves first.	Employer may require certification of illness if leave is taken to care for ill family member or dependent.	Health benefits continue during leave, but employee must pay premiums.	W. Va. Code Ann. §§ 21-5D-2-21-5D-7; S. 240, L. 2005; *Hudok v. Board of Education of Randolph County*, 415 S.E.2d 897 (W. Va. 1992).

	Acceptable Reasons for Leave	Employment Guarantees After Leave	Use of Vacation or Other Time-Off Benefits	Certification Required	Effect of Leave on Other Benefits	Citations to Authority
WI	Birth or adoption of child or care of foster child; care for child, spouse, parent or parent-in-law with serious health condition; employee's own serious health condition.	Employee is entitled to reinstatement in the position held prior to the leave or an equivalent position.	Sick leave must be used first for employee illness; employee may substitute other benefits (e.g., vacation, sick leave) for the leave, but this will not extend the leave benefits.	Employer may require certification if leave is taken for employee illness or to care for ill family member.	Health care benefits continue during leave.	Wis. Stat. Ann. § 103.10. Chap. ER 18, Section 18.17.
WY	Same as federal FMLA. State employees are also permitted to take any accrued leave or leave without pay for adoption or birth of child.	Same as federal FMLA.	Same as federal FMLA.	Same as federal FMLA.	Same as federal FMLA.	Wyo. Admin. Code ch. 10 §§ 10, 15.

Source: John F. Buckley & Ronald M. Green, *2008 State by State Guide to Human Resources Law* (New York: Aspen Publishers, Inc. 2008).

Exhibit 14.4

State Family and Medical Leave Laws: Required Notice, Denial, and Other Provisions

(States not listed have no statutory requirements.)

	Relationship of Family and Medical Leave Requirements to Pregnancy Disability Leave	Effect on Seniority Accrual During Leave	Minimum Requirements for Notification to Employer	Conditions for Denial of a Request for Leave	Citations to Authority
AL	No separate provisions exist for pregnancy disability leave.	—	—	—	Ala. Admin. Code r. 670-X-14-.01, 670-X-14-.02.
AK	No separate provisions exist for pregnancy disability leave.	—	Reasonable notice is required where leave is foreseeable.	If both spouses are employed at the same location and both request time off at the same time to care for a child or parent, employer may deny the request of one spouse.	Alaska Stat. §§ 39.20.500–39.20.550.
AZ	Sick leave may be used for disability caused by pregnancy. Annual leave, compensatory leave, or leave without pay may also be used as "parental leave" by an employee due to pregnancy.	—	—	Sick leave must be approved by agency head, but approval of parental leave is mandatory. Minor, nondisabling injuries and illnesses do not qualify for sick leave. Submission of evidence may be required for sick leave; if the agency head determines the evidence is inadequate, the absence shall be charged to another category of leave or considered absence without leave.	Ariz. Admin. Code 2-5-404, 2-5-411.
AR	Employee may use leave without pay for pregnancy after sick leave and annual leave are used.	—	Notification in advance, if possible, is required.	—	Ark. Code Ann. §§ 21-4-209, 21-4-210.

	Relationship of Family and Medical Leave Requirements to Pregnancy Disability Leave	Effect on Seniority Accrual During Leave	Minimum Requirements for Notification to Employer	Conditions for Denial of a Request for Leave	Citations to Authority
CA	Pregnancy leave is stated separately; full pregnancy leave is 4 months.	Seniority continues while employee is on leave.	Reasonable advance notice for planned leave is required; no notice for unforeseeable leave is required. For family military leave, employee must provide employer with notice of intent to take leave within two business days of receiving official notice that the spouse will be on leave from deployment.	Employer may deny request if leave exceeds 12 weeks in a 12-month period, if child's other parent is on leave or unemployed, if employee requesting leave is among the top 10% of highest-paid employees, or if leave will create undue hardship for employer.	Cal. Gov't Code §§ 12945, 12945.2, 19991.6; Cal. Lab. Code §§ 230.7, 230.8; Cal. Military & Vet. Code § 395.10
CO	No separate provisions exist for pregnancy disability leave.	No service credit during unpaid leave. Service date is adjusted 1 month forward for every 173 hours of unpaid leave during a 12-month period.	For family leave, employee must provide advance written notice within 30 days, or as soon as practical. "As soon as practical" means within 2 business days, if feasible, after the employee requests the leave. Notice may be verbal followed by written confirmation. Advance notice is not required in case of medical emergency. In such cases, notice may be given by any means and by an adult family member or other responsible party if the employee is unable to do so personally.	Leave may be denied if no certification is given.	Colo. Rev. Stat. Ann. § 19-5-211; 4 Colo. Code Regs. § 801-2, ch. 5 P-5-5, P-5-11, P-5-23–P-5-38.
CT	Pregnancy leave is treated separately; employer must grant female employees a leave of reasonable length for pregnancy disability leave.	Seniority benefits do not accrue while employee is on leave.	At least 2 weeks' notice is required for medical leave if possible; reasonable notice of birth or adoption is required; 2 weeks' notice of expected date of return to work is required.	When husband and wife are working for the same employer, leave may not exceed the total length of leave for a single eligible person in any 2-year period (except to care for sick child).	Conn. Gen. Stat. Ann. §§ 5-248a, 5-248b, 31-51kk–31-51nn, 46a-60.

Exhibit 14.4 (cont'd)

State Family and Medical Leave Laws: Required Notice, Denial, and Other Provisions

(States not listed have no statutory requirements.)

	Relationship of Family and Medical Leave Requirements to Pregnancy Disability Leave	Effect on Seniority Accrual During Leave	Minimum Requirements for Notification to Employer	Conditions for Denial of a Request for Leave	Citations to Authority
DE	No separate provisions exist for pregnancy disability leave, except for teachers of specified school districts, who may use accumulated sick leave for birth (or adoption) of a child.	—	—	—	Del. Code Ann. tit. 14, § 1333, tit. 29, § 5116.
DC	No separate provisions exist for pregnancy disability leave.	Seniority benefits do not accrue while employee is on leave, except for employees who take school-related leave.	Reasonable notice, if possible, is required. For school-related leave, 10 days' notice, unless not reasonably foreseeable.	When husband and wife are working for the same employer, leave may be limited to a combined total leave of 16 weeks in any 24-month period, and simultaneous leave may be restricted to a maximum of 4 weeks if harmful to employer. School leave may be denied if it would disrupt business and make production or service delivery unusually difficult.	D.C. Code Ann. §§ 32-501–32-505, 32-516, 32-1202.
FL*	No separate provisions exist for pregnancy disability leave.	Seniority benefits do not accrue while employee is on leave.	Notice is required.	—	Fla. Stat. Ann. § 110.221.
* Note: Dade County has a family and medical leave ordinance that covers some private employees as well as public employees.					
HI	Pregnancy leave is treated separately; employer must give a female employee who is disabled because of pregnancy and related conditions a leave of reasonable length.	Seniority benefits accrue while employee is on leave.	Reasonable notice, if possible, is required.	State has no conditions for denial of leave.	Haw. Rev. Stat. Ann. §§ 398-1–398-10.

	Relationship of Family and Medical Leave Requirements to Pregnancy Disability Leave	Effect on Seniority Accrual During Leave	Minimum Requirements for Notification to Employer	Conditions for Denial of a Request for Leave	Citations to Authority
ID	Pregnancy disability is covered under sick leave.	—	Reasonable notice may be required.	If husband and wife work for same employer, leave may be limited to combined total of 12 weeks.	Idaho Admin. Code § 15:04:01:243.
IL	Not applicable.	Not applicable.	Written notification at least 7 days in advance is required, except for emergencies.	Request may be denied if the leave would result in 75% of the employer's workforce or a shift taking leave at the same time.	820 Ill. Comp. Stat. Ann. 147/10, 147/15, 147/30, 147/40.
IN	—	—	—	Sick leave may be denied for failure to provide certification. Leave without pay may be denied for failure to request in writing, for lack of written approval by the appointing authority and/or the Director of State Personnel, or because leave is not considered to be in the best interests of the service.	Ind. Admin. Code tit. 31, 2-11-4, 2-11-4.5, 2-11-9.
IA	No separate provisions exist for pregnancy disability leave.	—	Timely notice is required.	Leave may be denied for failure to provide notice and/or certification.	Iowa Code Ann. § 216.6.
KS	Employer must grant female employees a leave of reasonable length for pregnancy disability leave.	—	—	—	Kan. Stat. Ann. §§ 44-1009(a), 44-1030(a)(1). Kan. Admin. Regs. 21-32-6.
KY	Not applicable.	—	Written notice is required.	—	Ky. Rev. Stat. Ann. § 337.015.

Exhibit 14.4

Mandated Benefits: 2009 Compliance Guide

Exhibit 14.4 (cont'd)

State Family and Medical Leave Laws: Required Notice, Denial, and Other Provisions

(States not listed have no statutory requirements.)

	Relationship of Family and Medical Leave Requirements to Pregnancy Disability Leave	Effect on Seniority Accrual During Leave	Minimum Requirements for Notification to Employer	Conditions for Denial of a Request for Leave	Citations to Authority
LA	No separate provisions exist for pregnancy disability leave.	—	Reasonable notice may be required by employer.	—	La. Rev. Stat. Ann. §§ 23:341, 23:342, 40:1299.124.
ME	No separate provisions exist for pregnancy disability leave.	Seniority benefits do not accrue while employee is on leave.	30 days' notice for nonemergencies is required.	—	Me. Rev. Stat. Ann. tit. 26, §§ 844–848.
MD	No separate provisions exist for pregnancy disability leave.	—	For sick leave, state has no statutory requirements; for family leave, prior approval is required.	For sick leave, no statutory requirements exist. A request for family leave may be denied, depending on the disruption to the work unit.	Md. Code Ann., State Pers. & Pens. §§ 9-501–9-508, 9-1001–9-1105; Lab. & Empl. § 3-802.
MA	No separate provisions exist for pregnancy disability leave.	Seniority benefits do not accrue during leave.	For maternity leave at least 2 weeks' notice of anticipated absence is required. For small necessities leave, 7 days' notice is required.	—	Mass. Gen. Laws Ann. ch. 149, § 105D.
MN	No separate provisions exist for pregnancy disability leave.	Seniority benefits do not accrue while employee is on leave.	Prior notice may be required; notice of return date is required if leave is over 4 weeks.	State has no conditions for denial of leave.	Minn. Stat. Ann. §§ 181.940–181.945.
MS	No separate provisions exist for pregnancy disability leave.	—	—	—	Miss Code Ann. § 25-3-95.
MO	No separate provisions exist for pregnancy disability leave.	—	—	—	Mo. Rev. Stat. § 105.271.
MT	No separate provisions exist for pregnancy disability leave.	Seniority benefits accrue during leave.	—	—	Mont. Code Ann. §§ 49-2-310, 49-2-311.

	Relationship of Family and Medical Leave Requirements to Pregnancy Disability Leave	Effect on Seniority Accrual During Leave	Minimum Requirements for Notification to Employer	Conditions for Denial of a Request for Leave	Citations to Authority
NE	No separate provisions exist for pregnancy disability leave.	—	For leave requests of 5 or more consecutive days, employee must give 14 days' notice to employer.	—	Neb. Rev. Stat. § 48-234; L.B. 497, L. 2007.
NV	No separate provisions exist for pregnancy disability leave.	If employer offers protection against loss of seniority to employees for sickness or disability, it must offer the same protection to female employees for pregnancy and related conditions.		—	Nev. Rev. Stat. Ann. § 613.335.
NH	—	Employee must be treated as any other employee on temporary disability.	—	—	N.H. Rev. Stat. Ann. § 354-A:7.
NJ	Family leave provisions supplement the state's temporary disability laws.	Seniority benefits do not accrue while employee is on leave.	For leave for serious health condition of a family member, 30 days' notice is required, except in emergencies where shorter notice is acceptable. For other leaves, prior notice, if possible, is required.	Leave may be denied if employee is among the highest paid 5% of employees and is salaried; leave may also be denied if it will cause substantial economic injury to employer.	N.J. Stat. Ann. §§ 34: 11B-3–34:11B-13; 39 N.J. R. 781(c).
NY	No separate provisions exist for pregnancy disability leave.	—		—	N.Y. Lab. Law § 201-c.
NC	No separate provisions exist for pregnancy disability leave.	Not applicable.	Leave is to be taken at a mutually agreed-upon time; employer may request 48 hours' written notice.	—	N.C. Gen. Stat. § 95-28.3.
ND	No separate provisions exist for pregnancy disability leave.	Seniority benefits do not accrue.	Advance notice is required for birth/adoption of a child; notice is required, if possible, for other leaves.	When husband and wife have the same employer, total leave for the couple may be limited to 4 months.	N.D. Cent. Code §§ 54-52.4-01–54-52.4-10.

Exhibit 14.4   Mandated Benefits: 2009 Compliance Guide

Exhibit 14.4 (cont'd)
State Family and Medical Leave Laws: Required Notice, Denial, and Other Provisions

(States not listed have no statutory requirements.)

	Relationship of Family and Medical Leave Requirements to Pregnancy Disability Leave	Effect on Seniority Accrual During Leave	Minimum Requirements for Notification to Employer	Conditions for Denial of a Request for Leave	Citations to Authority
OH	No separate provisions exist for pregnancy disability leave.	—	—	—	Ohio Rev. Code Ann. § 124.13.6.
OK	Family leave includes any pregnancy leave already taken by employee.	—	Reasonable notice, if possible, is required.	State has no conditions for denial of leave.	Okla. Stat. Ann. tit. 74, §§ 840-2.22, 840-2.23, and accompanying regulations.
OR	Pregnancy leave is treated separately; the same reinstatement rights to employment under family and medical leave provisions are afforded for pregnancy leave.	Seniority benefits do not accrue while employee is on leave.	30 days' written notice is required. In emergency situations, verbal or written notice within 24 hours of commencement of leave is required.	For family leave, when family member's health condition is not life-threatening or terminal, request for leave may be denied if another family member is available to provide care; for parental leave, when husband and wife are working for same employer and their combined leave would exceed 12 weeks, employer may refuse request for both to take leave at the same time.	Or. Rev. Stat. §§ 659A. 150–659A.186.
RI	No separate provisions exist for pregnancy disability leave.	Seniority benefits accrue during leave.	For family leave, at least 30 days' notice is required, except for emergencies. For school leave, 24 hours notice is required.	—	R.I. Gen. Laws §§ 28-48-1–28-48-4, 28-48-12.
SC	No separate provisions exist for pregnancy disability leave.	—	—	—	S.C. Code Ann. §§ 8-11-40, 8-11-155.

	Relationship of Family and Medical Leave Requirements to Pregnancy Disability Leave	Effect on Seniority Accrual During Leave	Minimum Requirements for Notification to Employer	Conditions for Denial of a Request for Leave	Citations to Authority
SD	Accrued sick leave may be used for pregnancy disability.	—	—	—	S.D. Reg. 55:01:22:02, 55:01:22:02:04, 55:01:22:08:02.
TN	No separate provisions exist for pregnancy disability leave.	Seniority benefits do not accrue during leave.	Except in an emergency, 3 months' notice is required, plus declaration of intent to return to work.	State has no conditions for denial of leave.	Tenn. Code Ann. § 4-21-408.
TX	No separate provisions exist for pregnancy disability leave.	—	—	—	Tex. Gov't Code Ann. §§ 661.001–661.008.
UT	Pregnancy leave is treated separately; length of maternity leave should be consistent with leave allowed for other temporary disability.	Seniority benefits do not accrue during leave.	Employee must apply for leave in writing.	Employee must plan to return to work to get leave approved; leave must be beneficial to both the employee and the state.	Utah Admin. Code 468-8-5.3, 468-8-5.9.
VT	No separate provisions exist for pregnancy disability leave.	Seniority benefits do not accrue during leave.	Reasonable notice of departure and duration of leave is required. For short-term leave, earliest possible notice, in no case later than 7 days, except in case of emergency.	State has no conditions for denial of leave.	Vt. Stat. Ann. tit. 21, §§ 470–472a.
VA	—	—	Reasonable notice is required.	—	Va. Code Ann. § 51.1-1108.
WA	Family leave under FMLA and state law is in addition to any leave allowed for sickness or temporary disability due to pregnancy.	Seniority benefits do not accrue during leave.	30 days' notice, if possible, prior to birth/adoption of child is required; 14 days' prior notice for child care is required.	Leave may be denied or limited for up to 10% of the workforce or for key personnel. If both spouses work for the same employer, total leave time for the couple may be limited to 12 weeks in a 24-month period.	Wash. Rev. Code Ann. §§ 49.78.010–49.78.100, 49.78.110, 49.78.130, 49.78.140, 49.78.180–49.78.200.

Exhibit 14.4 (cont'd)

State Family and Medical Leave Laws: Required Notice, Denial, and Other Provisions

(States not listed have no statutory requirements.)

	Relationship of Family and Medical Leave Requirements to Pregnancy Disability Leave	Effect on Seniority Accrual During Leave	Minimum Requirements for Notification to Employer	Conditions for Denial of a Request for Leave	Citations to Authority
WV	No separate provisions exist for pregnancy disability leave.	Seniority does not accrue during leave.	2 weeks' written notice, if possible, is required.	—	W. Va. Code Ann. §§ 21-5D-2–21-5D-7; *Hudok v. Board of Education of Randolph County*, 415 S.E.2d 897 (W. Va. 1992).
WI	No separate provisions exist for pregnancy disability leave.	Seniority does not accrue during leave.	Prior notice is required for expected birth of child or placement of child in foster care; if possible, reasonable notice is required for medical leave.	Leave may be denied if employee fails to notify properly or to provide requested certification (except when leave involves emergency health care).	Wis. Stat. Ann. § 103.10.
WY	No separate provisions exist for pregnancy disability leave.	Same as federal FMLA.	Same as federal FMLA.	Same as federal FMLA.	Wyo. Admin. Code ch. 10 § 15.

Source: John F. Buckley & Ronald M. Green, *2008 State by State Guide to Human Resources Law* (New York: Aspen Publishers, Inc. 2008).

Exhibit 14.5
Sample Family and Medical Leave of Absence Policy
for Inclusion in Employee Handbook

This sample policy description summarizes the company's complete family and medical leave policy and is suitable for inclusion in the company's employee handbook. The human resources manager must check the laws of his or her state that cover this area, to integrate them with the FMLA provisions. PLEASE NOTE THAT WHILE THE MILITARY FAMILY LEAVE IS REQUIRED BY LAW, AS OF THIS WRITING THE DOL HAS YET TO ISSUE FINAL REGULATIONS AND DEFINITIONS FOR THIS LEAVE. PLEASE REVIEW THIS POLICY WITH A LABOR ATTORNEY PRIOR TO IMPLEMENTATION.

FAMILY AND MEDICAL LEAVE OF ABSENCE

If you have worked for the company for a minimum of one year and have worked 1,250 hours or more during the 12 months before requesting leave, you are eligible for family and medical leave.

If you are eligible, you will be allowed up to 12 weeks of unpaid leave within any 12-month period for the birth or adoption of a child, to provide either physical or psychological care for a child, spouse (i.e., husband or wife), or parent with a serious health condition, to care for your own serious health condition, or for a "qualified exigency" due to the active duty status of a spouse, parent or child. If you are eligible, you will be allowed up to 26 weeks of unpaid leave within any 12-month period to care for a child, parent, spouse or next of kin to care for a spouse, parent or child who has been injured during active duty military action.

You must conclude leave for the birth or placement of a child for adoption or foster care within 12 months after the event. Leave may begin before birth or placement, as circumstances dictate.

To qualify for medical leave, the health condition or treatment must be such that it requires you to be absent from work on a recurring basis or for more than a few days for treatment or recovery.

INTERMITTENT OR REDUCED LEAVE

In the case of your own serious health condition or that of a family member, you may take leave intermittently or on a reduced work schedule, if medically necessary. You may also take intermittent leave or work a reduced work schedule for military family leave. When the leave is for adoption or birth of a child, you may take leave intermittently or on a reduced work schedule only with the joint approval of you and the company. If you request intermittent or reduced leave status, the company may temporarily transfer you to another position of equivalent pay and benefits to better accommodate your leave.

USE OF PAID-TIME-OFF BENEFITS

You may elect to substitute paid-time-off benefits, such as accrued vacation or sick pay, for the unpaid time off. Using paid-time-off benefits does not add to the total length of the leave.

Unless you substitute paid-time-off benefits, your pay will be reduced for all full days of unpaid leave taken or for all partial days of leave taken. If you are an exempt employee, reducing your pay for partial days off will not affect your exempt status under the Fair Labor Standards Act.

Exhibit 14.5   Mandated Benefits: 2009 Compliance Guide

Exhibit 14.5 (cont'd)

LEAVE PROVISIONS FOR SPOUSES BOTH WORKING FOR THE COMPANY

If leave is taken for the adoption or birth of a healthy child, or to care for a parent with a serious health condition, the maximum combined leave for both spouses is 12 weeks. If the leave is to care for an ill or injured military family member, the maximum combined leave for both spouses is 26 weeks. If leave is taken to care for an ill child or spouse, each spouse is entitled to 12 total weeks of leave.

JOB RESTORATION

Most employees granted leave will be returned to the same position held before the leave or a position that is equivalent in pay, benefits, and other terms and conditions of employment.

Certain highly compensated salaried employees are eligible for leave but are not guaranteed restoration to their position if they choose to take leave.

EMPLOYEE BENEFITS

Your health care benefits will continue during your leave. Both you and the company will continue to pay your customary portions of the monthly premium. The human resources department will advise you of the payment due dates. If you choose not to return from leave, you may be required under certain circumstances to repay the company's portion of the premium payment.

NOTIFICATION

You must provide the company with 30 days' written notice of your need for leave or, if emergency conditions prevent such notice, you must notify the company as soon as is practicable. You may need to report periodically on your status during the leave period.

CERTIFICATION

Certification of the need for leave to care for your illness or injury or that of a family member is required. You must obtain the following information from a responsible health care provider and make it available to the company:

- The date on which the serious health condition began

- The duration of the condition

- A statement that you need to care for the ill person and the estimated length of the leave or a statement that you cannot perform the functions of your job

- If applicable, the appropriate medical facts within the knowledge of the health care provider verifying the need for intermittent leave or a reduced work schedule, such as scheduled dates for treatments (some states limit employers' ability to require medical diagnosis)

Exhibit 14.5 (cont'd)

DISPUTE RESOLUTION

If the medical opinion provided by your physician is disputed, the company may require a second opinion by a physician of its choice, at its expense. If a third opinion is necessary, a third doctor may be selected, also at company expense. The doctor must be agreed on by both you and the company, and the doctor may not be employed on a regular basis by the company.

RELEASE TO RETURN TO WORK

A doctor's release is required if you are returning from a medical leave of one week or longer.

PROBLEM RESOLUTION

It is the policy of the company not to discharge or discriminate against any employee exercising his or her rights under the Family and Medical Leave Act. If you think you have been treated unfairly, contact the human resources manager. If for any reason the problem cannot be resolved at that level, contact the vice-president of human resources or the company president. The president's decision will be final and binding.

FOR MORE INFORMATION

For more information about family and medical leaves of absence, contact the employee benefits coordinator in the human resources department.

Exhibit 14.6   Mandated Benefits: 2009 Compliance Guide

Exhibit 14.6
Sample Family and Medical Leave of Absence Policy
for Inclusion in Procedural Manual

This sample policy could be included in the company's procedural manual to provide more specific direction to human resources and other department managers about how the FMLA is actually to be implemented. This sample family and medical leave policy reflects the FMLA; however, it does not reflect state variations that the human resources manager needs to consider. PLEASE NOTE THAT WHILE THE MILITARY FAMILY LEAVE IS REQUIRED BY LAW, AS OF THIS WRITING THE DOL HAS YET TO ISSUE FINAL REGULATIONS AND DEFINITIONS FOR THIS LEAVE. PLEASE REVIEW THIS POLICY WITH A LABOR ATTORNEY PRIOR TO IMPLEMENTATION.

TITLE

Family and Medical Leaves of Absence

PURPOSE

To outline the conditions under which an employee may request time off without pay for medical reasons or to provide family care

DEFINITION

A family and medical leave of absence is defined as an approved absence available to eligible employees for up to 12 weeks of unpaid leave in any 12-month period under certain circumstances that are critical to the employee's health or the health of the employee's family, or to take care of certain issues that arise out of the deployment of a military family member. Approved absences up to 26 weeks in any 12-month period may be granted to care for an ill or injured military family member.

Family Care Leave

A family care leave is a leave for reason of:

- The birth of a child of the employee

- The placement of a child with an employee in connection with the adoption or state-approved foster care of the child by the employee

- The serious health condition of a child, parent, or spouse

For purposes of this policy, *child* means a biological, adopted, or foster child, a stepchild, a legal ward, or a child of a person standing in loco parentis, who is either under 18 years old or a dependent adult. *Parent* means a biological, foster, or adoptive parent, a stepparent, a legal guardian, or a person standing *in loco parentis*. *Parent* does not include a parent-in-law.

Serious health condition means an illness, injury, impairment, or physical or mental condition of a child, parent, or spouse that warrants the participation of a family member to provide care during a period of treatment or supervision of the child, parent, or spouse and also involves either an inpatient facility or continuing treatment or continuing supervision by a health care provider.

Exhibit 14.6 (cont'd)

Medical Care Leave

A medical care leave is a leave taken when the employee is unable to perform the functions of his or her job because of a serious health condition.

Military Family "Caregiver" Leave

"Caregiver" leave allows the employee to care for a spouse, son, daughter, parent or next of kin who has sustained a "serious injury or illness" while on active duty in the U.S. Armed Forces, including National Guard and Reserves.

For purposes of this policy, "serious injury or illness" is defined as "rendering the member medically unfit to perform the duties of the member's office, grade, rank or rating."

Military Family "Active Duty" Leave

"Active Duty" leave is given when the employee has a "qualifying exigency"; that is, the employee needs to take care of certain family matters relating to active duty (or call to active duty) status of a spouse, son, daughter, or parent.

SUBSTITUTION OF OTHER PAID LEAVE

An eligible employee may elect to substitute any accrued paid vacation leave, personal leave, family leave, or other paid employment benefit plans or policies for any part of the 12 weeks of leave to which the employee may be entitled under this policy.

Note: *Under the FMLA, an employer may require an employee to substitute such paid leave for any part of the 12-week period.*

ELIGIBILITY

To be eligible for leave, an employee must have been working for the organization for at least 12 months in total and must have worked at least 1,250 hours during the 12-month period before the request for leave.

Note: *The policy statement should indicate the method chosen to determine the 12-month period. Some states have specified a method of calculation.*

EMPLOYMENT RESTORATION

Any eligible employee who takes a leave for a purpose intended by the law will be entitled upon return from such leave to be restored to the same position of employment as held when the leave began, or to be restored to an equivalent position with equivalent employment benefits, pay, and other terms and conditions of employment. Restoration to the same or equivalent position is contingent upon the employee's ability to perform all of the essential functions of the job.

An exception to the employment-restoration provisions of this policy is made if the employee on leave is a salaried employee and is among the highest-paid 10 percent of the company's employees within 75 miles

Exhibit 14.6   Mandated Benefits: 2009 Compliance Guide

Exhibit 14.6 (cont'd)

and if restoring employment of the employee would result in substantial economic injury to the company. In this situation, however, the employee will be notified of the company's intent to deny restoration and will be given an opportunity to return to work.

A doctor's release may be required if the employee is returning from a medical leave of three or more days.

Note: *Employers may want to consult legal counsel to determine the restoration rights of an employee on leave in the event of a general layoff affecting the employee.*

BASIC CONDITIONS OF LEAVE

The company will require medical certification from the health care provider to support a request for leave for an employee's own serious health condition or to care for a seriously ill child, spouse, parent, or seriously ill or injured child, spouse, parent, or next of kin serving active duty in the military. For the employee's personal medical leave, the certification must state that the employee is unable to perform the functions of his or her position because of a serious health condition. For leave to care for a seriously ill child, spouse, parent, or next of kin (Caregiver leave only), the certification must state that the employee is needed to provide care. The company will require certification of the need for "Active Duty" leave. The company may also require documentation from the employee to confirm family relationships.

At its discretion, the company may require a second medical opinion and periodic recertification at its own expense. If the first and second medical opinions differ, the company, at its own expense, may require the opinion of a third health care provider, approved by both the company and the employee. This third opinion is binding.

If medically necessary for a serious health condition of the employee or his or her spouse, child, parent, or next of kin, leave may be taken on an intermittent or reduced leave schedule. If leave is required on this basis, however, the company may require the employee to transfer temporarily to an alternative position that better accommodates recurring periods of absence or a part-time schedule, provided the position has equivalent pay and benefits.

If both spouses are employed by the company, they are entitled together to a total of 12 weeks of leave, rather than 12 weeks each, for the birth or placement of a child. Both spouses are entitled, together, to a total of 26 weeks for "Caregiver" leave. Leave for the birth or placement of a child must take place within 12 months after the event. Leave may begin before birth or adoption, as circumstances dictate.

NOTIFICATION AND REPORTING REQUIREMENTS

When the need for leave can be planned, such as the birth or placement of a child or scheduled medical treatment, the employee must, if possible, provide 30 days' advance notice and make efforts to schedule the leave to minimize disruption to company operations. In cases of illness, the employee will be required to report periodically on his or her leave status and intention to return to work.

STATUS OF EMPLOYEE BENEFITS DURING LEAVE OF ABSENCE

Any employee who is granted an approved leave of absence under this policy may continue his or her group insurance coverage by arranging to pay his or her portion of the premium contributions during the period of

Exhibit 14.6 (cont'd)

unpaid absence. Employees will be required to continue to pay their share of group health benefits costs during a period of leave under the law.

If an employee elects not to return to work upon completion of an approved unpaid leave of absence, the company may recover from the employee the cost of any premiums paid to maintain the employee's coverage even if it was not the employee's choice to continue coverage, unless the failure to return to work was for reasons beyond the employee's control. Benefit entitlements based on length of service will be calculated as of the last paid workday before the start of the unpaid leave of absence.

An employee on leave will not lose any employment benefits accrued before the leave, unless a benefit, such as accrued paid vacation, is used by the employee during the leave. An employee on leave accrues no additional seniority or employment benefits during any period of unpaid leave.

PROCEDURES

Employees must follow specific procedures to request a family or medical leave. These procedures are as follows:

- The employee must complete the Request for Family and Medical Leave of Absence form, sign it, make a copy of it, and return it to the human resources department. If possible, the form should be submitted 30 days in advance of the effective date of the leave.

- A Combined Leave Policy form is to be completed by any employee who is requesting leave and whose spouse also works for the company.

- All employees must complete an Insurance Premium Recovery Authorization form. This form certifies that an employee acknowledges the company's legal right to recover the cost of any premium paid by it to maintain his or her coverage in group health benefits during any period of unpaid leave except under the following conditions:

    — The continuation, recurrence, or onset of a serious health condition that entitles the employee to leave to care for a child, parent, or spouse with a serious health condition or if the employee is unable to perform the functions of the position due to his or her own serious health condition

    — Other conditions beyond the employee's control that prevent him or her from returning to work

Note: *Employers are advised to consult legal counsel to ensure compliance with state or local laws regarding employee debt collection.*

- Employees requesting family and medical leaves of absence due to illness must complete a Leave Certification Requirements form.

- The employee must submit a completed Request for Family and Medical Leave of Absence and a Combined Leave Policy form, if applicable.

Exhibit 14.6   Mandated Benefits: 2009 Compliance Guide

Exhibit 14.6 (cont'd)

- To request leave for the care of a child, parent, spouse or next of kin ("Caregiver" leave only) with a serious health condition, the employee must provide certification from the health care provider who is treating the child, parent, spouse, or next of kin, including the following information:

  — The date on which the condition began

  — The probable duration of the condition

  — The appropriate medical facts regarding the condition

  — An estimate of the time needed to care for the individual involved, including any recurring medical treatment

  — A statement that the condition warrants the health care provider's involvement

- To request leave due to an employee's serious health condition, the employee must provide certification from the health care provider who is treating his or her own serious health condition regarding the following information:

  — The date on which the condition began

  — The probable duration of the condition

  — The appropriate medical facts regarding the condition

  — A statement that the employee is unable to perform the functions of his or her position due to his or her condition

- To request intermittent leave or leave on a reduced leave schedule, the employee must provide the following additional information from the health care provider:

  — For leave for the employee, the employee must provide a statement of medical necessity for his or her intermittent leave or reduced leave schedule, and the expected duration of the schedule, and a listing of the dates of his or her planned medical treatment and the duration of the treatment

  — For leave to care for a son, daughter, spouse, parent, or next of kin, the employee must provide a statement attesting to the necessity of intermittent leave or reduced leave for the employee to provide care or to assist in the person's recovery, and an estimate of the expected duration and schedule of his or her intermittent or reduced leave

EMPLOYEE RECOURSE

The FMLA provides additional relief to employees through complaints filed with the secretary of the DOL or a private lawsuit.

EFFECT OF LABOR AGREEMENT

All provisions of this policy will prevail, except as modified by any applicable labor agreement.

Exhibit 14.7
Request for Family and Medical Leave of Absence Form

Confidential
Company XXX

REQUEST FOR FAMILY AND MEDICAL LEAVE OF ABSENCE

Employees who have worked for at least 1,250 hours during the 12-month period immediately before the request for leave are eligible for leave.

Name: _____   Employee Number: _____

Department: _____   Hire Date: _____

THE TYPE OF LEAVE REQUESTED

(Check one box)

☐ Employee Medical Leave of Absence
☐ Extension of Employee Medical Leave of Absence. Dates of prior approved medical leave are: _____ to _____
☐ Family Medical Leave of Absence
☐ Extension of Family Medical Leave of Absence. Dates of prior approved family medical leave are: _____ to _____
☐ Leave to care for newborn or adopted child or a child placed for foster care by state procedures
☐ Military "Caregiver" Leave
☐ Military "Active Duty" Leave

The leave or extension requested will begin on _____ and end on _____.
If the request is for multiple days off for recurring medical treatments of a child, parent, spouse, or next of kin ("Caregiver" leave only), or for your own medical treatments, specify the dates requested: _____

THE REASON FOR LEAVE

I request a family leave of absence for the following reason:

(Check one box)
☐ My personal serious health condition
☐ Birth of my child
☐ Adoption of a child by me
☐ Placement by the state of a child with me for foster care
☐ Serious health condition of my child
☐ Serious health condition of my parent
☐ Serious health condition of my spouse

Exhibit 14.7   Mandated Benefits: 2009 Compliance Guide

- ☐ Serious illness or injury of my child
- ☐ Serious illness or injury of my parent
- ☐ Serious illness or injury of my spouse
- ☐ Serious illness or injury of my next of kin
- ☐ "Qualifying exigency" of my child serving in U.S. military service
- ☐ "Qualifying exigency" of my parent serving in U.S. military service
- ☐ "Qualifying exigency" of my spouse serving in U.S. military service

File: one copy to employee; the original in personnel file

Exhibit 14.8
Combined Leave Policy Form

This form is to be completed by any employee who is requesting leave and whose spouse also works for Company XXX.

Check the leave being requested:

_____ Family leave to care for a newly arrived child

_____ Family medical leave to care for a parent with a serious health condition

_____ Military "Caregiver" leave to care for a child, parent, spouse or next of kin with a serious illness or injury

Circle Yes or No:

I have a spouse employed at Company XXX   Yes   No

Spouse's Name: _____   Employee Number: _____

Department: _____   Hire Date: _____

I certify by my signature that I have read the following policy and agree to abide by it:

In any case in which a husband and wife are both employed by company XXX and both entitled to leave, if the leave is taken for the birth or adoption of a child, the aggregate number of workweeks of leave to which both may be entitled may be limited to 12 workweeks during any 12-month period. In the case of a "Caregiver" leave, the aggregate number of workweeks of leave to which both may be entitled may be limited to 26 workweeks during any 12-month period.

If there is a change in circumstances with respect to the above, I will notify the Company immediately.

Date: _____   Name (Print): _____

Employee Number: _____   Name (Sign): _____

File: one copy to employee; the original in personnel file

Exhibit 14.9

Mandated Benefits: 2009 Compliance Guide

Exhibit 14.9
Insurance Premium Recovery Authorization Form

To: _____ (the appropriate company officer)

I certify by my signature that I have read and understand the following policy:

I acknowledge the Company's legal right to recover the cost of any premium paid by it to maintain my coverage in group health benefits during any period of unpaid leave under the following conditions:

- I fail to return from leave at the expiration of the leave to which I am entitled and

- The reason I fail to return to work is not one of the following:

  — The continuation, recurrence, or onset of a serious health condition that entitles me to leave to care for a child, parent, or spouse with a serious health condition, or if I am unable to perform the functions of my position due to my own serious health condition.

  — Other conditions beyond my control prevent me from returning.

Date: _____   Name (Print): _____

Employee Number: _____   Name (Sign): _____

INSURANCE PREMIUM REIMBURSEMENT AGREEMENT

I certify by my signature that I have read and agree to do the following:

If I fail to return from leave for any reason other than excepted above, I agree to coordinate with the Company to develop a mutually acceptable schedule to reimburse the Company for any premium it paid to maintain my coverage in group health benefits during any period of unpaid leave I took.

Date: _____   Name (Print): _____

Employee Number: _____   Name (Sign): _____

(Employers are advised to seek legal counsel to determine whether state or local laws affect the collection of employee debt.)

File: one copy to employee; the original in personnel file

Exhibit 14.10
Leave Certification Requirements

Note: Some states restrict the amount or type of medical information a health care provider may release to an employer (or other third party). Employers are advised to consult legal counsel to ensure compliance with state or local laws.

PLEASE NOTE THAT WHILE THE MILITARY FAMILY LEAVE IS REQUIRED BY LAW, AS OF THIS WRITING THE DOL HAS YET TO ISSUE FINAL REGULATIONS AND DEFINITIONS FOR THIS LEAVE. PLEASE REVIEW THESE REQUIREMENTS AS THEY RELATE TO MILITARY FAMILY LEAVE WITH A LABOR ATTORNEY PRIOR TO IMPLEMENTATION.

SECTION I

To request leave for the care of a child, parent, or spouse with a serious health condition, or the care of a child, parent, spouse or next of kin with a serious illness or injury as the result of active duty military action

I have attached a certification from the health care provider who is treating my child, parent, spouse, or next of kin ("Caregiver" leave only). The certification includes the following:

- The date on which the condition began

- The probable duration of the condition

- The appropriate medical facts within the knowledge of the health care provider regarding the condition

- An estimate of the time needed to care for the individual involved, including any recurring medical treatment

- A statement that the condition warrants my participation to provide care

SECTION II

To request leave for the care of any employee's personal serious health condition

I have attached certification from the health care provider who is treating my own serious health condition. The certification includes the following:

- The date on which my condition began

- The probable duration of my condition

- The appropriate medical facts within the knowledge of the health care provider regarding my condition

- A statement that I am unable to perform the functions of my position due to my condition

Exhibit 14.10   Mandated Benefits: 2009 Compliance Guide

Exhibit 14.10 (cont'd)

SECTION III

Additional certification requirements for intermittent leave or for leave on a reduced leave schedule

In addition to the foregoing certifications from the health care provider involved, I have attached additional information from the health care provider as stipulated:

- Leave for the employee

  — A statement of medical necessity for my intermittent leave or reduced leave schedule and the expected duration of the schedule

  — A listing of the dates of my planned medical treatment and the duration of the treatment

- Leave to care for a son, daughter, spouse, parent, or next of kin ("Caregiver" leave only)

  — A statement attesting to the necessity of intermittent leave or reduced leave for me to provide care or to assist in his or her recovery

  — An estimate of the expected duration and schedule of my intermittent or reduced leave

I certify by my signature that I have read and understand the Company's certification policy.

Date: _____   Name (Print): _____

Employee Number: _____   Name (Sign): _____

File: one copy to employee; the original in personnel file

Chapter 15
Integrating ADA, FMLA, Workers' Compensation, and Related Requirements

§ 15.01 AUDIT QUESTIONS

1. When an employee files a claim under workers' compensation law, does the employer have a procedure in place to also determine whether the employee is disabled under the Americans with Disabilities Act (ADA) and, if necessary, to provide reasonable accommodation?

2. If an employee files a claim under workers' compensation law that requires a leave of absence, does the employer have a procedure in place to also determine the employee's eligibility for leave under the Family and Medical Leave Act (FMLA) as well as to provide adequate notice to the employee regarding designation of the leave as FMLA leave?

3. If an employee requests leave under either the ADA or the FMLA, does the employer have a procedure in place to also review the employee's request under the other law, to ensure compliance with both laws?

Note: Consistent ''yes'' answers to the above questions suggest that the organization is applying effective management practices and/or complying with federal regulations. ''No'' answers indicate that problem areas exist and should be addressed immediately.

This chapter focuses on the interplay between the Americans with Disabilities Act (ADA), the Family and Medical Leave Act (FMLA), and workers' compensation law. It does not discuss in detail the provisions of the ADA (see **Chapter 13**), the FMLA (see **Chapter 14**), or workers' compensation (see **Chapter 9**).

The chapter briefly discusses a number of related federal and state laws that govern the employment of individuals with disabilities and employers' responsibilities toward disabled employees, including:

- Title VII of the Civil Rights Act of 1964

- The Vocational Rehabilitation Act of 1973

- The Vietnam Era Veterans' Readjustment Assistance Act of 1974

- The National Labor Relations Act

- The Fair Labor Standards Act

- State Fair Employment Practice and Right to Privacy Statutes

- State Anti-Smoking Statutes

- The Architectural Barriers Act

§ 15.02 INTERACTIONS BETWEEN THE ADA, THE FMLA, AND WORKERS' COMPENSATION

The major area of interplay between these laws occurs when a leave of absence is taken due to an employee's own health condition. Each law establishes requirements for qualification and provisions for administration, and it is critical that human resource (HR) professionals understand these requirements.

The HR professional, when faced with an employee requesting a leave of absence (or one who is placed on leave by a medical professional), must ask: is the employee eligible for FMLA? Is the leave a reasonable accommodation for a person covered by the ADA? Is the injury or illness work-related? If the answer to any of these questions is "yes," the provisions for each law must be followed.

Following are key provisions associated with leaves of absence, and the considerations to be taken under each law. The discussion of workers' compensation is general, because this is an area of state law and each state may establish its specific provisions and guidelines.

[A] Triggering Event

Triggering events for the FMLA, the ADA, and workers' compensation are as follows:

- FMLA—Employee's own "serious health condition"; serious health condition of a child, a spouse, or a parent; the birth, placement, or adoption of a child ; "serious injury or illness" of a covered military service member; "qualifying exigency" of a child, parent, or spouse because of active military duty or the call to active military duty

- ADA—"Disability," record of disability, or being perceived as having a disability

- Workers' compensation—Work-related injury or illness

With any FMLA leave for medical reasons, it is necessary to determine whether the "serious health condition" could also be considered a disability triggering the reasonable accommodation obligations of the ADA. Similarly, with a work-related injury, the FMLA and/or the ADA may also be triggered.

The terms *serious health condition* and *disability* are not equivalent under the FMLA and the ADA. The FMLA recognizes serious health conditions (e.g., cancers and serious strokes) that the ADA regards as disabilities. Pregnancy and "routine" broken bones, which the FMLA considers "serious health conditions," are likely not considered disabilities under the ADA.

When an employee is faced with a serious health condition that may be a disability, the employer must determine whether the leave requested is a reasonable accommodation of the disability. Under the ADA, EEOC regulations suggest an unpaid leave of absence can be a reasonable accommodation when there is no other accommodation that would allow the employee to perform the essential functions of the job. In addition, the courts have consistently held a temporary finite leave of absence that will allow the employee to return to the job in the near future is required. On the other hand, courts have also made it clear that an employer is not obligated to provide an employee with an indefinite leave of absence, as this would be considered an undue hardship on the employer.

When faced with a request for a medical leave not required by the FMLA, an employer should consider the following:

- Whether the leave of absence is the result of an impairment that may be an ADA disability

- What the employer's policies are regarding leaves of absences, both medical and nonmedical

- What information is currently available to evaluate the request

- What information is still needed in order to evaluate the request (i.e., prognosis, anticipated date of return)

- How the employee's absence will affect the company's operations

- Whether the leave of absence will create an undue hardship for the employer

The employer's determinations regarding these considerations should help the employer decide whether the requested leave is a reasonable accommodation. The difficulty of handling a leave of absence does not automatically result in an undue hardship.

A key distinction between the ADA and workers' compensation is that a work-related injury is not a disability under the ADA unless it substantially limits one or more major life activities. As a result, many injuries and illnesses frequently encountered in the workers' compensation system do not rise to the level of a disability under the ADA. An example of this can be found in *Snow v. Ridgeview Medical Center* [128 F.3d 1201 (8th Cir. 1997)]. In this case, the court found an employee who had a work-related injury with a general lifting restriction was not disabled within the meaning of the ADA. The facts of the case showed the employee was not precluded from performing a class or a broad range of jobs as compared with the average person in the general population.

Injured or ill employees who are entitled to workers' compensation may or may not have rights under the ADA or the FMLA. Many injured employees do not have disabilities within the meaning of the ADA, although many states use the term *disability ratings* in classifying injured workers. Similarly, an entitlement to workers' compensation benefits does not automatically lead to the conclusion that the employee has a serious health condition under the FMLA, although that is likely when injuries cause multiple-day absences.

[B] Length of Leave

The lengths of leave allowable under the FMLA, ADA, and workers' compensation are as follows:

- FMLA—Maximum 12 weeks (for employee's own "serious health condition")

- ADA—No clear guidelines; whatever is "reasonable" and not an "undue hardship"

- Workers' compensation—Generally no established minimum or maximum

An employee who has coverage under both the ADA and the FMLA may need to be granted leave of longer than 12 weeks if the leave represents a reasonable accommodation to the employee's disability. The EEOC's "ADA Enforcement Guidelines," issued in March 1999, provides the following example:

> **Example.** Amy has a disability. She needs 13 weeks of leave for treatment related to the disability. The employee is eligible under the FMLA for 12 weeks of leave (the maximum available), so this period of leave constitutes both FMLA leave and a reasonable accommodation. Under the FMLA, the employer could deny the employee the 13th week of leave. But, because the employee is also covered under the ADA, the employer cannot deny the request for the 13th week of leave unless it can show undue hardship. The employer may consider the impact on its operations caused by the initial 12-week absence, along with other undue hardship factors.

[C] Continuation of Medical Coverage

The requirements for the continuation of medical coverage under the FMLA, the ADA, and workers' compensation are as follows:

- FMLA—Must be continued as if employee were still actively at work

- ADA—No requirement

- Workers' compensation—Generally must follow provisions for other employees with medical leave status

During leaves covered by the FMLA, the ADA, or workers' compensation, the employer need only continue the employee's health insurance coverage during the FMLA leave period, provided it does not continue health insurance for other, nondisabled employees on non-FMLA leaves.

[D] Requests for Medical Information

The guidelines for requests for medical information under the FMLA, the ADA, and workers' compensation are as follows:

- FMLA—Employer may require employee to provide medical certification for serious health condition before and during the leave

- ADA—Exams or medical inquiries must be strictly job-related and must relate to the employee's ability to perform the functions of the job

- Workers' compensation—Exams or inquiries must be job-related; few restrictions on availability of medical information related to specific injury

The FMLA places some restrictions on an employer's ability to obtain information regarding an employee's physical condition when the employee returns to work (see **Chapter 14**). The employer is limited to receipt of a statement from the employee's physician that the employee is capable of returning to work; it is not permitted to have direct contact with the employee's health care provider.

The ADA allows an employer greater freedom in obtaining information about an employee's physical condition as it relates to the employee's ability to perform the essential functions of the job. Under the final regulations of the ADA, "a covered entity may require a medical examination (and/or inquiry) of an employee that is job-related and consistent with business necessity. A covered entity may make inquiries into the ability of an employee to perform job-related functions." [29 C.F.R. § 1630.14(c)] Inquiries may involve seeking information from the employee's health care provider related to the employee's ability to perform essential job functions. Despite the clear restriction on information available under the FMLA, its regulations also consider the availability of an ADA physical examination.

The Fourth Circuit was the first court to address the difference between ADA and FMLA standards in *Porter v. United States Alumoweld Co.* [125 F.3d 243, 245-46 (4th Cir. 1997)]. Porter, the employee, had a history of back injuries. His employer terminated him when he refused to undergo a functional capacity evaluation. Porter sued his employer, alleging his employer's request was in violation of both the ADA and the FMLA. The court rejected both claims. With regard to the ADA claim, the court found the examination was clearly job-related and a business necessity. The court went on to note the FMLA limitation on return-to-work certificates was not violated because the examination was consistent with the requirements of the ADA.

A district court in Massachusetts reached a different conclusion when it evaluated a U.S. Postal Service's request that an employee who had gone on FMLA leave for depression take a psychiatric exam before being allowed to return to work. [Albert v. Marvin T. Runyon, Jr., Postmaster General of the United States Postal Service, 6 F. Supp. 2d 57, 1998 U.S. Dist. LEXIS 7505] The employee's physician provided the postal service with a return-to-work slip stating the employee was fit to return. The postal service refused the employee's request to return to work on the basis that the note was vague, that the postal service's regulations allow it to conduct fitness-for-duty exams at any time, and the ADA's less restrictive statements regarding return-to-work physicals. The court rejected the employer's theories. Regarding the relationship between the ADA and the FMLA, the court stressed that the FMLA places the determination of the employee's ability to return to work exclusively in the hands of the employee's physician, not the employer. This provision is in direct contrast to the EEOC's guidance on the employer's duty to evaluate an employee's ability to return to work under the ADA. While not concluding that the FMLA and ADA rights were in conflict, the court appeared to presume that in the event of a conflict, the FMLA's restriction would override what the ADA allowed.

Medical information regarding an applicant's or employee's occupational injury or workers' compensation claim must be collected and maintained on separate forms and kept in a separate, confidential medical file, along with other information required to be kept confidential under the ADA. Generally, all documents in which the reason for an absence is listed in more descriptive language than merely "sick" should be considered medical records under the ADA. The ADA allows disclosure of such information only in specific circumstances. In addition, any medical certification of a serious health condition for FMLA leave would also be considered confidential medical information and should be maintained in the separate, confidential medical file.

[E]   Substitution of Paid Leave

The requirements for substitution of paid leave under the FMLA, the ADA, and workers' compensation are as follows:

- FMLA—Employer may require substitution of paid leave such as vacation or sick pay

- ADA—No restriction

- Workers' compensation—Generally a paid (by insurance company) leave, although the pay typically does not equal the employee's fulltime pay. The ability to provide additional compensation through the use of vacation or sick leave benefits is somewhat ambiguous. The Department of Labor Regulation 29 C.F.R. 825.207 Section (d) (1) states: "Because the leave pursuant to a temporary disability benefit plan is not unpaid, the provision for substitution of paid leave is inapplicable." Later in the regulation, Section (e) states: "Paid vacation or personal leave, including leave earned or accrued under plans allowing 'paid time off,' may be substituted, at either the employee's or the employer's option, for any qualified FMLA leave." Employers should contact their labor attorney to review the federal regulations as well as any applicable state regulations before deciding on a substitution of paid leave policy.

Employers should keep in mind that, whether a leave is paid or unpaid, any combination of the three leaves can run concurrently.

[F]   Attendance Policies

Attendance policies under the FMLA, the ADA, and workers' compensation are as follows:

- FMLA—Cannot count FMLA leave, including intermittent leave, as absences for disciplinary purposes

- ADA—Certain absences may be considered "reasonable accommodation," and therefore not subject to disciplinary action; for certain positions, attendance level may be considered an "essential function"

- Workers' compensation—Generally no prohibition against considering absences for disciplinary purposes (although employers should consider whether state "anti-retaliation" laws may apply)

Another significant aspect of the interaction of the FMLA, the ADA, and workers' compensation is in the way employers handle the attendance records of employees who may miss work as a result of a serious health condition, disability, or work-related injury. Where a serious health condition is involved and the other conditions for eligibility are met, the FMLA requires employers to grant up to 12 weeks of leave per year, regardless of any hardship this entails for the employer. Under the ADA, employers may have a duty to allow even longer absences because of work-related disabilities where time off would not impose an undue hardship. Termination or discipline for excessive absenteeism caused by work-related injuries is not prohibited by most workers' compensation laws.

Darby v. Bratch [287 F.3d 678 (8th Cir. 2002)] provides an excellent example of these issues. Darby, a dispatcher for the Kansas City Police Department, was diagnosed with Graves' disease (a form of hyperthyroidism), which caused her to miss work. Eventually, Darby's serious health condition resulted in her taking FMLA leave. While on FMLA leave, she was disciplined for her absences from work and the use of unpaid leave. Upon her return to work, Darby was informed by her supervisor she would not be considered eligible for promotion. The court ruled this was sufficient evidence of an adverse employment action to sustain her claim of retaliation in violation of the FMLA. In addition, the court found Darby had been disciplined for engaging in activity protected by FMLA—the taking of unpaid leave.

[G] Return from Leave

The requirements regarding return from leave under the FMLA, the ADA, and workers' compensation are as follows:

- FMLA—Must reinstate to former position or substantially similar position; cannot require employee to return to "light duty"

- ADA—Must reinstate to former position if able to perform essential functions with or without reasonable accommodation, if no undue hardship; "light duty" may be a temporary reasonable accommodation

- Workers' compensation—Generally no guarantee of former position; employer cannot retaliate against employee who exercises rights under workers' compensation; can provide and require "light duty"

The EEOC contends that the ADA (federal) standard for return to work prevails over any conflicting state or local workers' compensation law. However, definitive information about the relationship between the the ADA and state workers' compensation regulations are still lacking.

The EEOC's "ADA Enforcement Guidelines" offers this example for integrating the ADA and FMLA with regard to a returning employee:

Example. An employee with an ADA disability has taken 10 weeks of FMLA leave and is preparing to return to work. The employer wants to put her in an equivalent position other than her original one. Although this is permissible under the FMLA, the ADA requires that the employer return the employee to her original position. Unless the employer can show that this would cause an undue hardship, or that the employee is no longer qualified for her original position (with or without reasonable accommodation), the employer must reinstate the employee to her original position.

Employers must be careful to correctly determine which laws apply to each case when applying its return-to-work policies. In *Cooper v. Olin Corporation* [24 F.3d 1083, 1088 (8th Cir. 2001)], the court found an employee who was suffering from depression was not protected by the ADA because the employee failed to prove that she was substantially limited in her ability to care for herself, which would establish a disability under the ADA. However, the court found in favor of the employee's claim that she had not been reinstated to an equivalent position under the FMLA. As a result, even though the employer considered the employee disabled, the court found her not disabled and required the employer to reinstate the employee to an equivalent position. The court further defined the term *equivalent* by ruling that "the employer may take into account the employee's physical capabilities in determining the equivalent work and compensation involved."

It is possible for an employee to lose his or her protection under the various laws. For example, under the ADA, an employee who refuses an accommodation that would allow him or her to perform the job may lose protection of the ADA. Such an employee, if he or she had been medically released to return to work, might also lose his or her workers' compensation benefits.

[H] The FMLA's Discussions on Its Interaction with the ADA and Workers' Compensation

The following excerpt from the Code of Federal Regulations describes various circumstances that highlight how the FMLA, the ADA, and workers' compensation interact:

Section 825.702(a)-(e) of the FMLA [29 C.F.R. § 825] provides:

(a) The FMLA's legislative history explains that FMLA is not intended to modify or affect the ... Americans with Disabilities Act of 1990, or the regulations issued under that act. Thus, the leave provisions of the FMLA are wholly distinct from the reasonable accommodation obligations of employers covered under the ADA. ... The purpose of the FMLA is to make leave available to eligible employees and employers within its coverage, and not to limit already existing rights and protection. ... An employer must therefore provide leave under whichever statutory provision provides the greater rights to employees.

(b) If an employee is a qualified individual with a disability within the meaning of the ... ADA, the employer must make reasonable accommodations, etc., barring undue hardship, in accordance with the ADA. At the same time, the employer must afford an employee his or her FMLA rights. ADA's "disability" and FMLA's "serious health condition" are different concepts, and must be analyzed separately.

(c) FMLA entitles eligible employees to 12 weeks of leave in any 12-month period, whereas the ADA allows an indeterminate amount of leave, barring undue hardship, as a reasonable accommodation. FMLA requires employers to maintain employees' group health plan coverage during FMLA leave on the same conditions as coverage would have been provided if the employee had been continuously employed during the leave period, whereas ADA does not require maintenance of health insurance unless other employees receive health insurance during leave under the same circumstances. Examples in the following paragraphs of this section demonstrate how the two laws would interact with respect to a qualified individual with a disability.

(1) A reasonable accommodation under the ADA might be accomplished by providing a qualified individual with a disability a part-time job with no health benefits, assuming you did not ordinarily provide health insurance for part-time employees. However, the FMLA would permit this employee to work a reduced leave schedule until the equivalent of 12 work weeks of FMLA leave were used, with his or her (full-time) group health benefits maintained during this period. The FMLA permits an employer to temporarily transfer an employee who is taking leave intermittently or on a reduced leave schedule to an alternative position, whereas the ADA allows an accommodation of reassignment to an equivalent, vacant position only if the employee cannot perform the essential functions of the employee's present position and an accommodation is not possible in the employee's present position, or an accommodation in the employee's present position would cause an undue hardship.

(2) A qualified individual with a disability who is also an "eligible employee" entitled to FMLA leave requests 10 weeks of medical leave as a reasonable accommodation, which the employer grants because it is not an undue hardship. The employer advises the employee that the 10 weeks of leave is also being designated as FMLA leave and will count towards the employee's FMLA leave entitlement. This designation

does not prevent the parties from also treating the leave as a reasonable accommodation and reinstating the employee in the same job, as required by the ADA, rather than an equivalent position under FMLA, if that is the greater right available to the employee. At the same time, the employee would be entitled under the FMLA to have the employer maintain group health plan coverage during the concurrently running leave period, as that requirement provides the greater right to the employee.

(3) If the same employee needed to work part-time (a reduced leave schedule) after returning to his or her same job, the employee would still be entitled under the FMLA to have group health plan coverage maintained for the remainder of the two-week equivalent of FMLA leave entitlement, notwithstanding an employer policy that part-time employees do not receive health insurance. This employee would be entitled under the ADA to reasonable accommodations to enable the employee to perform the essential functions of the part-time position. In addition, because the employee is working a part-time schedule as a reasonable accommodation, the employee would be shielded from FMLA's provision for temporary assignment to a different alternative position. Once the employee has exhausted his or her remaining FMLA leave entitle-ment while working the reduced (part-time) schedule, if the employee is a qualified individual with a disability, and if the employee is unable to return to the same full-time position at that time, the employee might continue to work part-time as a reasonable accommodation, barring undue hardship; the employee would then be entitled to only those employment benefits ordinarily provided by the employer to part-time employees.

(4) At the end of FMLA leave entitlement, an employer is required under FMLA to reinstate the employee in the same or an equivalent position, with equivalent pay and benefits, to that which the employee held when leave commenced. The employer's FMLA obligations would be satisfied if the employer offered the employee an equivalent full-time position. If the employee were unable to perform the essential functions of that equivalent position even with reasonable accommodation, because of a disability, the ADA might require the employer to make a reasonable accommodation at that time, by allowing the employee to work part-time or by reassigning the employee to a vacant position, barring undue hardship.

* * * * *

(d)(1) If FMLA entitles an employee to leave, an employer may not, in lieu of FMLA leave entitlement, require an employee to take a job with a reasonable accommodation. However, ADA may require that an employer offer an employee the opportunity to take such a position. An employer may not change the essential functions of the job in order to deny FMLA leave. See Section 825.220(b).

(d)(2) An employee may be on a workers' compensation absence due to an on-the-job injury or illness which also qualifies as a serious health condition under FMLA. The workers' compensation absence and FMLA leave may run concurrently (subject to proper notice and designation by the employer). At some point, the health care provider providing medical care pursuant to the workers' compensation injury may certify the employee is able to return to work in a "light duty" position. If the employer offers such a position, the employee is permitted but not required to accept the position (see Section 825.220(d)) as long as FMLA leave is not exhausted. As a result, the employee may no longer qualify for payments from the workers' compensation benefit plan, but the employee is entitled to continue on unpaid FMLA leave either until the employee is able to return to the same or equivalent job the employee left or until the 12-week FMLA leave entitlement is exhausted. See Section 825.207(d)(1). If the employee returning from the workers' compensation injury is a qualified individual with a disability, he or she will retain rights under the ADA.

(e) If an employer requires certifications of an employee's fitness for duty to return to work, as permitted by FMLA under a uniform policy, it must comply with the ADA requirement that a fitness-for-duty physical be job-related and consistent with business necessity.

[I] Selected Court Cases

The courts continue to clarify distinctions between the various laws.

In *Praigrod v. St. Mary's Medical Center* [No. 3:05-cv-0166-JDT-WGH, 2007 U.S. Dist. LEXIS 4505 (S.D. Ind. Jan. 19, 2007)], the court dealt with a discrimination lawsuit under the ADA. The plaintiff, a nurse, took intermittent leave under an approved FMLA leave for her own "serious health condition." She also missed time to care for her ill mother. In 2003, she was absent for more than 25 percent of her scheduled workdays. In 2004, she missed over half of her scheduled workdays up to the time of her termination. She filed for discrimination under the ADA. The hospital claimed that she was not covered under the ADA, as she could not meet one of the essential functions for all nursing positions—attendance. The plaintiff claimed that the hospital could not count her time off under FMLA as part of the attendance requirement. The court found for the hospital, stating that FMLA absences can be used to show the employee's inability to meet the attendance requirement.

The Tenth Circuit addressed a case where the plaintiff was given FMLA leave at her request because of her own serious health condition, namely, multiple sclerosis. When the plaintiff was fired for poor performance, she claimed, in part, that she was discriminated against under the ADA because she was "regarded as having a disability." The court held that the FMLA's "serious health condition" and the ADA's "disability" definitions are different concepts, and therefore approving an FMLA leave did not indicate that the company regarded her as disabled. [Berry v. T-Mobile USA, 2007 U.S. App. LEXIS 15258 (10th Cir. June 27, 2007)].

§ 15.03 RELATED FEDERAL AND STATE LAWS

[A] Title VII

Under Title VII of the Civil Rights Act of 1964, as amended by the Pregnancy Discrimination Act, an employer is required to provide the same benefits for pregnant women as it provides to other employees with short-term disabilities. Because Title VII does not require employees to be employed for a certain period of time before they are protected, an individual employed for fewer than 12 months by the employer (and, therefore, not an "eligible" employee under the FMLA) may not be denied maternity leave if the employer normally provides short-term disability benefits to employees with the same tenure who are experiencing other short-term disabilities. Additionally, a "neutral" policy that prohibits all employees from taking sick leave or short-term disability leave during the first year of employment may have a disparate impact on women and thus violate Title VII.

To help employers cope with the requirements of multiple employment laws, the EEOC has issued a fact sheet on the ADA, the FMLA, and Title VII. The fact sheet, which is available on the EEOC's Web site (*www.eeoc.gov*) addresses employers' concerns in question-and-answer format, focusing particularly on differences between the FMLA's "serious health condition" and the ADA's "disability," as well as issues related to conditions of pregnancy and childbirth.

Before starting down this path of potential confusion, an employer should determine whether the FMLA and the ADA apply to its situation. Essentially, only private employers with 50 or more employees are covered concurrently by the ADA, the FMLA, and Title VII. Of course, issues related to the ADA and Title VII (but not the FMLA) apply to employers with 15 or more employees. State and local governmental employers are covered by the ADA and FMLA, regardless of the number of employees, but are covered by Title VII only if they have 15 or more employees.

[B] Health Insurance Portability and Accountability Act

The Health Insurance Portability and Accountability Act (HIPAA) restricts the use or disclosure of protected health information (PHI). Employers trying to comply with FMLA, ADA, and workers' compensation laws need to understand how HIPAA affects this compliance.

Employees who request leave for their own serious health condition generally need to provide the employer with certification from their health care provider. The completed form is considered an employee record, rather than PHI, and so in this case, the employer is not covered under HIPAA. However, the health care provider who must release the information is covered by HIPAA, and cannot release it without proper authorization from the employee. Employers need to ensure their FMLA Certification form has the proper employee authorization section.

Similarly, employers often need medical information from the health care provider to determine reasonable accommodation under the ADA. Again, it is the provider who cannot release the information without proper authorization. Employers should review their ADA forms to make sure the proper authorization is included. Alternately, the health care provider is in compliance if he or she can give the information directly to the employee, who then gives it to the employer.

HIPAA specifically addresses workers' compensation, allowing a health care provider to release PHI if needed to "comply with" workers' compensation laws. Employers must make sure that the information needed complies with the workers' compensation laws. If not, the employer should get a medical information release authorization from the employee.

[C] Uniformed Services and Reemployment Rights Act

The Uniformed Services and Reemployment Rights Act (USERRA) (see **Chapter 11, Section 11.04[D]**) provides employment rights to certain members of the "uniformed services" who take a leave of absence to serve. The Act requires that covered service members, upon reemployment with a company, receive the rights and benefits of employment they would have received had they not served their tour of duty. When calculating time worked for purposes of FMLA eligibility, employers need to count the time the employee would have worked had he or she not been on military leave. The Department of Labor has issued a memorandum to this effect, which can be found at *www.dol.gov/vets/media/fmlarights.pdf*.

For those service employees returning with disabilities, the provisions under USERRA are more generous than the ADA. Under the ADA, employees with disabilities must be able to perform the essential job functions, with or without reasonable accommodation. USERRA requires training or retraining of covered individuals who are not currently qualified for the position so they may become qualified.

[D] The Vocational Rehabilitation Act

Section 503 of the Vocational Rehabilitation Act of 1973 requires employers with federal contracts of more than $2,500 to take affirmative action for the employment of qualified people with disabilities. If the contract is for $50,000 or more and the employer has 50 or more employees, the employer is required to prepare a written affirmative action program. Section 504 forbids discrimination against people with disabilities by employers receiving federal financial assistance, and Section 501 requires federal agencies to take affirmative action in hiring and promoting qualified people with disabilities.

In October 1992, proposed rules were issued by the Office of Federal Contract Compliance Programs (OFCCP), a branch of the DOL that administers Section 503 of the Vocational Rehabilitation Act. The rules were meant to harmonize with requirements of the ADA. The rules were finalized in 1993, issued on May 1, 1996, and took effect on August 29, 1996. The basic revisions to Section 503 of the Vocational Rehabilitation Act generally covered the following changes:

1. Government contractors and subcontractors are required to take affirmative action to employ and advance in employment qualified individuals with disabilities.

2. Government contractors and subcontractors are prohibited from discriminating against individuals on the basis of disability.

Significantly, the revisions specifically include conformance with the nondiscrimination provisions of the ADA. [29 U.S.C. § 793; 41 C.F.R. § 60-741.4]

[E] The Vietnam Era Veterans' Readjustment Assistance Act

The Vietnam Era Veterans' Readjustment Assistance Act of 1974 protects special veterans with disabilities from being discriminated against because of a disability incurred or aggravated in the line of duty. Section 2012 requires employers holding federal contracts in the amount of $10,000 or more to take affirmative action to employ and advance in employment qualified special disabled veterans. Depending on the disability, reasonable accommodations might be required. Section 2013 indicates the eligibility requirements for special disabled veterans under federal employment and training programs. Section 2014 stipulates federal government agency responsibility in employing and advancing in employment special disabled veterans.

A *special disabled veteran* is an individual who is entitled to compensation under laws administered by the Department of Veterans Affairs for a disability rated at 30 percent or more, or, if the individual has a serious employment disability, rated at 10 or 20 percent, or a person who was discharged or released from active duty because of a service-related disability.

[F] The National Labor Relations Act

The EEOC has a formal agreement (memorandum of understanding) with the National Labor Relations Board (NLRB) to coordinate enforcement of Title I of the ADA and Section 8 of the National Labor Relations Act (NLRA). This memorandum of understanding states that unfair labor practice charges involving the ADA will be investigated by the NLRB general counsel, who will consult with the EEOC's Office of Legal Counsel regarding the applicability of the ADA. In turn, a discrimination charge that may involve the NLRA will be investigated by the EEOC, followed by a consultation with the NLRB Associate General Counsel.

According to the memorandum of understanding, the EEOC and the NLRB share information about an employer's or union's employment policies and practices that might assist in complying with the memorandum. Shared information includes complaints, charges, and investigative files. The agencies comply with each other's requirements for confidentiality of information.

[G]   The Fair Labor Standards Act

Provisions of the ADA prohibiting discrimination in employment practices (e.g., compensation) do not require employers to pay individuals employed under Section 14(c) of the FLSA at the same rate as other "qualified" individuals. Section 14(c) is directed at mainstreaming individuals with severe disabilities into the workforce. If it can be demonstrated that individuals employed under Section 14(c) are disabled and that the disabilities cause the individuals to be less productive than other workers in the job, even with accommodation, the employer may follow applicable FLSA wage guidelines. (For a detailed discussion of the FLSA, see **Chapter 3**.)

[H]   State Fair Employment Practice Statutes

Almost every state has a statute prohibiting discrimination against a person because of a disability, whether in employment or in access to public facilities. Some states may have a separate disability law covering physical and mental disabilities, whereas other states include discrimination against people with disabilities in a broader human rights statute that includes protection for groups on the basis of race, color, religion, sex, national origin, age, and marital status.

The common purpose of all state fair employment practices (FEP) statutes is, as public policy, to give qualified people with disabilities the same opportunity and treatment, under the same conditions and privileges, as people who have no disability. Each state is different. Therefore, the HR department must review specific state laws to make sure personnel practices and policies do not conflict with these requirements.

[I]   State Anti-Smoking Statutes

The ADA does not require employers to accommodate smokers. The statute also does not preclude employers from prohibiting or restricting smoking in the workplace. However, under right-to-privacy statutes, a number of states have implemented regulations that prohibit employers from discriminating against job applicants or employees who use legal substances (i.e., alcohol or tobacco) outside work hours. HR managers should consult state laws when considering imposing restrictions on smoking.

[J]   The Architectural Barriers Act

The Architectural Barriers Act, enacted in 1968, requires federally owned, leased, or funded buildings and facilities to be accessible to persons with disabilities. As a result, uniform federal accessibility standards have been developed that present uniform standards for the design, construction, and alteration of buildings. Even though these standards apply to federally supported facilities, states have either adopted them or developed their own standards and have included them in FEP statutes or building codes, or both. When a change in the physical layout of a facility is indicated or new construction is warranted, employers must heed the accessibility requirements under federal or state statutes.

§ 15.04 RESOURCES FOR EMPLOYERS

The EEOC Guidance on Workers' Compensation and ADA (Notice No. 915.002), available on-line at *www. eeoc.gov/policy/docs/workcomp.html,* sets forth the EEOC's position on the interaction between Title I of the ADA and state workers' compensation laws concerning the following:

- Whether a person with an occupational injury has a disability as defined by the ADA

- Disability-related questions and medical examinations relating to occupational injury and workers' compensation claims

- Hiring of persons with a history of occupational injury, return to work of persons with occupational injuries, and application of the direct threat standard

- Reasonable accommodation for persons with disability-related occupational injuries

- Light duty

- Exclusive remedy provisions in workers' compensation laws

The following agencies can provide resources to assist employers in complying with the overlapping laws and regulations governing employees with disabilities:

- The Human Rights Commission of the employer's state

- The Governor's Committee on Employment of People with Disabilities for the employer's state

- The Office of Federal Contract Compliance Programs in the employer's region

- The U.S. Department of Labor

- The Equal Employment Opportunity Commission

- The National Council on Disabilities

These agencies can help employers understand their obligations under federal and state laws and regulations. Many of the agencies maintain offices in major metropolitan areas, where they can be reached by telephone or via the Internet.

Chapter 16
The Interview and Selection Process

§ 16.01 AUDIT QUESTIONS

1. Is the company minimizing the potential for discrimination claims by having a clearly written and widely communicated recruitment policy?

2. Has the company adjusted its technical recruiting strategy to attract the hard-to-find qualified candidates?

3. Does the company require an applicant to provide a signed, written release before it conducts background checks?

4. Does the company conduct background checks and drug testing post-offer and pre-hire?

5. Does the company protect itself from negligent hiring and negative referral liability by conducting reference checks on all new hires?

6. Does the company understand its liability as a joint employer under the Equal Employment Opportunity Commission when using a temporary staffing agency?

Note: Consistent "yes" answers to the above questions suggest that the organization is applying effective management practices and/or complying with federal regulations. "No" answers indicate that problem areas exist and should be addressed immediately.

This chapter discusses essential activities involving applicant recruiting and interviewing and employee selection. It also discusses activities that make up the on-boarding process—integrating new employees in the organization. All organizations, even those with relatively low turnover, are on the lookout for individuals who might function as competent and motivated team members. As job vacancies occur, those individuals who meet the company's requirements for successful job performance must be recruited and screened and, if subsequently hired, must be given an orientation to the company's culture, procedures, and methods of operation.

The typical hiring process encompasses initial recruitment (sourcing), selection (interviewing, testing, and background checking), placement (job offer), processing of new-hire documentation, and orientation to the company. However, the hiring process is most effective if both a job analysis and an organization-needs analysis are performed *before* recruitment begins. The job analysis provides basic information for the employer's use throughout the entire recruitment and selection process. The needs analysis is an assessment of the organization's departmental mission and procedures, the HR plan, relevant technological advances, and recent work distribution and productivity trends. If a company has an overall business strategic plan, the recruiting objectives will flow from its HR portion. Even without a strategic plan, it is important to establish a recruiting strategy.

This chapter also addresses liabilities associated with negligent hiring (and the related phenomenon of negligent referral), which place increased importance on the practices of effective applicant reference and background checking. The general use of arbitration agreements and clauses, which directly relate to litigation avoidance, is described.

Finally, current trends in executive search, outsourcing, contingent—or temporary—staffing, and professional employer organizations (PEOs) (formerly employee leasing) will be discussed in relation to today's challenges in human resources (HR) management. Employers will be given situations under which these resources are best utilized. Any one or more approaches may potentially complement an organization's recruitment and selection program, with careful review and analysis performed beforehand.

Recordkeeping requirements relative to both applicant tracking and employees are discussed in **Chapter 24**.

§ 16.02   RECRUITING AND INTERVIEWING EMPLOYEES

Effective employee recruitment and selection is one of the most critical of all management functions. Intuitively, employers know that hiring the right people will help to drive the company to greater success. However, a recent study by Watson Wyatt provided statistical evidence to support that understanding. The study found that organizations with superior recruiting practices performed better financially (as reflected in Total Shareholder Return, or TSR) than those with less effective practices. For example, companies that hired more employees on the first offer had average TSR of 44 percent, while companies that made two or three offers before hiring had an average TSR of 32 percent. Organizations that were able to fill positions within two weeks had a TSR of 59 percent, compared to a TSR of 11 percent for organizations that took seven weeks or more to fill positions.

Conversely, hiring the wrong person has significant negative impact on an organization. It will:

— Consume valuable management time in coaching, disciplining, and possibly terminating the employee;

— Increase the risk of legal liability, with potential charges brought by the problem employee;

— Cost the employer up to two times the annual salary of the employee, in lost time, inefficient operations of the poor employee, and replacement costs.

To maximize the chances for an effective hire, and to minimize the potential for claims of discrimination or other legal problems, uniformity in the recruitment process is important. Therefore, a clearly written and widely communicated recruitment policy should be developed. All individuals who will be involved in the selection process must have a clear understanding of the essential functions of the job, the qualifications required to successfully perform it, as well as the knowledge and training to conduct interviews that are both productive and legally sound.

When selecting a company recruitment strategy, the following factors should be considered:

- Organizational goals

- Business strategy

- Labor market conditions

- Pay and benefits

- The specific position within the company

- Company location

- Company promotion policies

- Time and budget constraints

- Affirmative action goals (if any)

- Labor union obligations (if any)

Because of the extra efforts in supervising a poor hiring choice and the high cost of replacement, it is cost-effective to design and implement systematic and professional recruiting, interviewing, and selection procedures, regardless of the organization's size, location, mission, or line of business. The following sections describe the main components of a complete employee selection program.

[A] Preparation for Candidate Selection

Preparation is one of the most important aspects of the selection process; it is also frequently one of the most neglected. Managers often spend little time and energy determining the required qualifications for the position. Consequently, during the selection process, they find it difficult to determine whether candidates meet the essential qualifications of the job.

When defining a position, managers should consider the following factors:

- Tasks performed on the job

- Abilities needed to learn and perform the job

- Knowledge and skills used on the job

- Behaviors demonstrated at work

- Relevant training and work experience

- Upcoming technological changes

- The hiring department's and the organization's strategic direction

- Policies on promotion from within (if any)

- The relevance of downgrading or upgrading for the position

- The organization's recent work distribution, productivity trends, and expectations

Preparation begins with an analysis of the job to be filled. The purpose of the analysis is to determine (1) the overall purpose of the position, as well as the duties, responsibilities and requirements of the position, and (2) the type of employment relationship: regular employee, temporary employee, or outsource agent.

[1] Duties and Responsibilities

The most efficient way to obtain sufficient job information is to establish standard procedures and tools for data collection (e.g., questionnaires and interview checklists). Information should be secured from appropriate sources, such as incumbents, supervisors, coworkers, trainers, work documents, and instructions, and through direct observation of incumbents doing the job.

Once the duties and responsibilities are established, they should be properly documented. The employer is free to choose a job description and/or other means of documentation.

As the employer documents the job duties, it will be important to indicate which duties are essential for Americans with Disabilities Act (ADA) purposes. (See **Chapter 13** for a detailed discussion of the ADA.)

[2] Type of Relationship

The current availability of contingent, or temporary, workers provides other solutions to an open position besides that of a company employee. Many organizations utilize these workers to maximize staffing, offset cyclical workloads, and improve their bottom line. The needs evaluation will determine whether the position is best filled by a regular employee, a temporary employee, an agency employee, or a consultant.

It is interesting to note that, according to a recent survey by Staffing Industry Analysts, the contingent workforce is expected to grow to 10 percent of the total U.S. workforce. Employers may choose to hire contingent workers because they cannot find qualified "regular" employees to fill a job.

[3] Different Types of Contingent Workers

Contingent workers may be temporary workers hired from a staffing agency, temporary workers hired directly on the employer's payroll, or independent contractors. Each group has potential for employer liability, so it is important to clearly define the role of the contingent worker.

For the company's protection, the definition of a temporary employee who is a direct hire (not an employee of an outside staffing agency) should be clearly covered in the employee handbook, specifying the period of time a person may be employed as a temporary (usually a maximum of one year). The employee handbook should also contain a definition of a regular employee. Typically, regular employees are eligible for benefits whereas (nonagency) temporary employees are not. As the agency temporary employee receives benefits, the lack of the same treatment for the nonagency temporary has been under scrutiny; therefore, clearly written definitions can eliminate confusion.

Employers should be careful not to create a "co-employment" relationship when hiring a temporary worker through a staffing agency. Co-employment is a legal doctrine that applies when two organizations have control over an employee's work, thereby creating two organizations with legal liability. Co-employment may add liability in the areas of the Family and Medical Leave Act (see **Chapter 14, Section 14.04(D)**), wage and hour laws, and other employment arenas. Employers may avoid this additional liability by:

- Conducting business through the staffing agency rather than directly with the worker, including pay issues, discipline, and establishing work hours;

- Limiting the length of time that a contingent worker is utilized;

- Providing policy information to the worker that applies only to the contingent worker (for example, do not provide an employee handbook that covers all employees)

The importance of properly classifying employees is illustrated in *Vizcaino v. Microsoft Corp.* [97 F.3d 1006 (9th Cir. 1996)]. Microsoft had hired workers for special projects and classified them as independent contractors (ICs) or temporary employees. The ICs received cash compensation but no benefits. In all other ways, however, the ICs appeared to be treated as regular employees: they often worked on teams along with regular employees, reported to the same supervisors, performed the same functions, worked the same core hours, and received card keys for admission to company facilities. The ICs were also required to work on site.

After the Internal Revenue Service (IRS) reclassified the ICs as employees and contended that they were eligible for benefits under Microsoft's 401(k) and employee stock purchase plans, Microsoft denied the ICs' request for benefits and the workers sued. Microsoft lost at the district court level and appealed the decision. The Ninth Circuit presented its final decision on May 12, 1999, reaffirming the district court decision. [Vizcaino v. Microsoft Corp., 120 F.3d 1006 (9th Cir. 1999)] The U.S. Supreme Court refused to hear Microsoft's appeal, thereby letting the district court's decision stand. In May 2001, the court affirmed a settlement agreement requiring Microsoft to pay out $96.9 million in benefits to approximately 10,000 ICs, and administrative and legal costs.

[B] Finding the Best Candidates

[1] Sourcing Candidates

Sourcing is defined as the process of generating a pool of qualified applicants for organizational jobs. Sourcing candidates begins with identifying the places from which to attract qualified candidates to apply for the open positions. Sourcing methods fall into two categories: internal and external.

Internal sourcing often relies on job postings and job-bidding procedures within the organization to identify candidates from among current employees. Organizations that promote from within generally find it easier to attract and retain ambitious employees. A consistent job-posting program can minimize employee complaints of unfair treatment, unlawful discrimination, or favoritism, which often arise when promotion candidates are hand-selected, without prior posting of job openings. Both current and former employees may also serve as effective recruitment sources through the process of word-of-mouth advertising.

Some organizations provide referral rewards to employees who refer applicants ultimately selected for job openings. However, caution should be taken to ensure that the referral program does not result in discriminatory hiring practices. Referral programs are most effective when standard screening processes are in place for all applicants.

External sourcing takes place on several levels. Active sourcing includes word of mouth, targeting companies that meet desired criteria, and direct discussions with career centers or employment offices at educational institutions, public employment agencies, public interest groups, private employment agencies, executive search firms, job fairs, and trade and professional institutions. More passive recruiting options include advertising through print and electronic media, manual and electronic bulletin boards, call waiting, messages, job banks, statement stuffers, radio spots, and marquees.

Recruiters are increasingly using the Internet to advertise job openings and solicit qualified candidates. There has been tremendous growth in the number of online recruiting venues for employers. These include local newspapers (which post job listings), news groups, the company's Web site, industry-related Web sites, and online job and resume banks that reach millions of people. Many posting services can be found by logging on to a search engine and typing in "job postings."

No advertisement for employment should disclose a preference for hiring based on a discriminatory classification, such as age, sex, race, religion, or other protected classes. The company should avoid such phrases as "recent college graduate" (implies a preference for younger applicants) or "front-office appearance" (implies a preference for an attractive young person, generally female). In a recent informal discussion letter published by the EEOC on April 8, 2008, the EEOC allows that it is lawful to encourage applicants from protected groups, but not lawful to "seek" them. Therefore, a lawful phrase would be "women and minorities are encouraged to apply."

[2] Recruiting and Sourcing Strategies for the Shrinking Workforce

As we moved into the 21st century, HR professionals talked about "hot jobs"—those that were especially difficult to fill due to high demand and low supply of personnel. One obvious example was the Information Technology field at the turn of the century. With a booming economy, the proliferation of the dot.coms, and Y2K approaching, there simply were not enough qualified professionals to go around. Halfway into the first decade, the talk was about the "shrinking workforce." A survey published by Manpower, Inc. during those years indicated that 41 percent of employers around the world were struggling to find qualified candidates. Particularly tough to find were sales representatives, technicians, and skilled manual trades people. And in 2008, even with a struggling economy, there is still a concern that our workforce will not be able to supply all of the talented workers needed in the future. With the imminent retirement (or move to part-time) of hundreds of thousands of baby boomers, and fewer people in the subsequent generations, experts predict there is a coming shortage of qualified workers in many fields. (For an interesting list of facts relevant to this topic, visit *http://www.perfectlaborstorm.com/facts.html*.)

Recruiting job candidates has become one of the most critical functions of the HR professional. In a highly competitive market, employers have become more creative in their recruitment strategies and employment practices.

In recruiting for high demand positions, the job applicant has become the key customer. Applicants know their worth and negotiate everything.

It is important to understand how people in different types of jobs look for new positions. For example, the majority of technical professionals prefer to explore the Web sites and job postings of their target employers and then send their resumes to a select number. Clearly, this means every employer needing technical support should create and maintain an attractive and informative Web site and ensure that it is linked to hot "career" or "employment" sites on the Web.

Because no one source can generate the flow of applicants needed to satisfy the demand for talent, employers need to develop more creative and comprehensive sourcing strategies. Enhanced employee referral programs can provide both higher visibility and better focus. Many firms find that frequent, high-quality communications bring a higher response. Therefore, they have developed the following approaches:

- In the hottest markets, use direct mail, billboards, and other highly visible media to make passive job seekers aware of the opportunities.

- Link open houses with radio and TV advertising and online accessibility to produce rapid hires.

- Expand college relations programs to provide for earlier and wider visibility at colleges that produce graduates in needed disciplines.

- Develop co-op and intern programs and send speakers to classrooms to create interest in a particular company.

- Actively participate in professional associations, career fairs, and users groups as an aid to recruitment.

- Use outplacement firms, state employment services, military transition services, and government downsizing programs as no-cost sources.

The recruiter must play the role of a marketeer. Not only must sourcing strategies be comprehensive, but they must also be highly visible, accessible, and interesting to all job applicants. The marketing message must clearly communicate what makes working for your organization different and better than most others. The total compensation package must be competitive, as verified through continuous market research. Finally, employers must treat applicants as customers and sell to their individual needs and expectations.

[3] Creative Sourcing

Employers need to make every effort to develop and maintain strong relationships with a variety of recruiting sources, even when there is no immediate need for job applicants. The wider the scope of the recruiting effort and the greater the number of sources used, the more likely it is that the company will generate a large and diverse pool of applicants to fill a variety of position openings.

Following the successful introduction of a voice-mail response system to handle customer calls, the HR department of a New York savings bank formulated the idea of using the system to convey information about its job opportunities. This method is particularly useful for the regional offices. Candidates using a touch-tone telephone receive a recorded greeting and are instructed to access a menu with options to receive information about jobs. The bank also uses other methods to publicize job openings, including advertising in newspapers in its regional areas, mailing postcards to former applicants, enclosing fliers with bank statements, and printing tent cards to place in branch offices. Effective, creative recruiting techniques are limited only by the imagination.

A small number of hospitals are allowing nurses to bid on vacant shifts for extra work and pay as a result of the eBay.com and Priceline.com craze. For example, St. Peter's Health Care Services in Albany, New York, previously used an outside agency to fulfill vacant shifts. St. Peter's found, however, that the agency was not familiar with its procedures and practices and it cost more money to use the agency. Thus, St. Peter's Jobs Online was created. Nurse managers post vacant shifts on the Web site, and nurses (employees of St. Peter's or approved by St. Peter's to work) log on to the site and bid on shifts at a certain rate per hour. The nurse managers approve or reject each bid. If a bid is rejected, the nurse can bid again. This initiative allows for shifts to be covered without violating the hospital's policy against overtime. The objective was to reduce turnover and increase retention. By 2003, St. Peter's had reduced its nurse vacancy rate to less than 5 percent.

As mentioned previously, employee referral programs have proven effective in increasing the number of quality applicants. Some company referral programs offer either a fixed amount of cash for any position filled, or an amount that varies with the position or job category for which the referral was received. For example, a company may offer employees who refer successful candidates for positions $300 for nonexempt positions, $1,500 for exempt positions, and $5,000 for highly skilled and/or hard-to-fill positions.

Keeping track of recruiting results also helps in identifying the sources that have produced the types of employees sought and that are cost-effective.

[C] Application Form

Employment applications should ask only questions that are job-related and that can be used to make a hiring decision. In addition, although it is not illegal to ask some questions, it may be ill-advised. The information elicited could be used later to support a discrimination charge.

Commonly acceptable inquiries on a job application include:

- Name

- Current and previous address

- Current and previous employer(s)

- References (professional references have more relevance to evaluating job qualifications than personal references and are less likely to elicit information unrelated to work)

- Social Security Number (for purposes of conducting a background check)

- Telephone number

- Educational background

- Emergency contact

- Legal ability to work in the United States

Other questions are acceptable if they are related to a specific job: for example, can the applicant be bonded, or does the applicant have a valid driver's license? Questions on the application form or in an oral interview about the following matters should be avoided:

- Personal life, including sexual orientation

- Work and family arrangements

- Health, accident history, or disability

- History of workers' compensation and unemployment claims

- Economic status

- Arrest or police record

- Military discharge

- Maiden name or marital status (the interviewer may ask for other names used by the candidate in other employment for the purpose of conducting a reference and a background check)

- Dates of attendance or completion of education

- Place of birth

- Citizenship

- Nationality, lineage, ancestry, national origin, or descent

- Names of an applicant's spouse or children

- Age

- A photograph (before the hire date)

All disclaimers and notices on the application and associated forms should be as direct and explicit as possible. Statements made should describe policies regarding drug testing, employment at will, and other conditions of employment. It is critical that the statements made in writing are actually and consistently carried out in practice. The applicant should be asked to give the company permission to verify credentials and check references by signing an authorization.

[D] Interviewing

The employment interview remains the most common selection procedure; when well planned, it is also one of the most useful. It is important to remember that interviewing skills are not innate; they are developed through training. Pre-interview planning is essential to a well-conducted comprehensive selection interview. Sufficient time should be allotted so that neither the interviewer nor the interviewee feels rushed, and a private location should be arranged to allow both to concentrate on the interview content. The interviewer should review the application form for completeness (i.e., no gaps in dates of employment) and accuracy before beginning the interview, then make notes to question the applicant about specific areas during the interview. The interviewer should be careful not to put personal notes on the application form unrelated to job requirements (e.g., race, appearance), since this could result in future employer liability. It is important to have the candidate complete an application form even if he or she provides a resume, as current application forms contain language that protects the employer, such as acknowledgment that any falsification is cause for dismissal, an at-will clause, an arbitration clause, and release of liability/authorization to check references.

Control is an important aspect of the interview. If the interviewer does not control the interview, the applicant usually will. Control includes knowing in advance what information must be obtained, systematically collecting it, and stopping when that information has been collected. The interviewer should talk no more than about 10 percent of the time in an in-depth interview.

Successful interviews are structured to cover a representative sampling of job-related topics and aspects of the applicant's background that relate to the job. Topics and resulting questions should be based on the job requirements as determined by information in the position definition. A structured interview guides the interviewer through a series of meaningful questions and provides clear, consistent direction for evaluating each applicant's qualifications.

An important component of an employment interview is the need to record key responses and evaluations. This is important because after an interviewer has interviewed several candidates, the details of their individual responses and qualifications are not always easy to recall. During the interview, the interviewer should take notes, unobtrusively, which will help later in recalling the candidate's responses and the interviewer's evaluation. It can also be useful to provide numerical rating scales with defined scale categories. Rating scales can be used for individual performance dimensions, as well as for an overall evaluation. One helpful technique involves the use of applicant interview scoring forms that contain relevant interview questions, space to record key elements of applicant responses, and rating scales for the evaluation of each candidate.

Conducting an interview is not a mechanical or routine procedure. Interviewing requires a great deal of awareness, sensitivity, and understanding of the candidate's feelings and needs for information, as well as a sharp focus on the data-gathering task at hand.

For interviewers to gain as much information as possible from the applicant, they should create an atmosphere that allows the applicant to speak freely. The following are suggestions for establishing a fostering atmosphere:

- Put the applicant at ease at the beginning of the interview.

- If the applicant freezes on a certain question, go to the next one until the applicant relaxes; don't be uncomfortable with silence while the applicant formulates his or her answer, and recognize the difference between thinking and freezing.

- Ask open-ended questions that facilitate discussion; avoid those that require a "yes" or "no" answer.

- Ask questions that focus on the applicant's specific job experience, which gives insight into the individual's behavior under certain circumstances.

- Ask only job-related questions.

- Listen carefully; let the applicant speak without interruption to ensure that you gain as much information as possible.

- To gain additional insight about applicants, watch their body language and facial expressions while they are speaking to you.

[1]   Types of Interviews

Several types of interviews may be conducted with a candidate during the hiring process. Usually, they include a telephone screen, an in-person screening, and the selection interview. The goals of each type of interview are to assess the candidate's knowledge, skills and abilities and to form realistic expectations about the possible fit of the candidate into the job and work environment.

Telephone Screening

A telephone screening interview is conducted first to save time. Candidates judged to be a poor fit are eliminated on the basis of some basic criteria such as salary, employment objective, location, and key required skills. A telephone screening interview helps both parties clarify the major aspects of the position. At this point, either party or both parties may decide not to pursue the discussion further—a decision reached with the speed and cost benefit of a telephone conversation.

In-Person Screening

The in-person screening interview is conducted by the recruiter to verify the candidate's qualifications for the position, and to establish a preliminary impression of the candidate's attitude, interest, and professional style. At this stage, the interviewer's objective is to identify candidates who are qualified for further consideration by the decision maker.

The Selection Interview

The selection interview is conducted by the decision maker, usually the manager to whom the position reports. The purpose of this interview is for the manager to probe more deeply into the candidate's qualifications and to assess the ease with which the candidate might establish a comfortable working relationship in the work group and with the manager. For parties with significant responsibility or multi-department impact, it is wise to consider involving other key managers in the interview process. Hence, there could be several interviews at this stage.

Many factors affect the accuracy of the interview, from stereotypes held by interviewers to the order of seeing the interviewees. An accurate interview is one in which an interviewer has drawn the correct conclusions about a candidate's potential. Whether the interview is a valid selection tool depends on whether its results are related to the individual's job performance following the selection decision. The validity of the interview depends on the type of interview and the capabilities of the individual interviewers.

There are six types of selection interviews: structured, behavioral description, situational, nondirective, stress, and panel. Research on interviews has found the structured interview to be more reliable and valid than other approaches. It uses a set of standardized questions that are asked of all applicants. This type of interview allows an interviewer to prepare advance job-related questions and then complete a standardized interviewee evaluation form. This form provides documentation if anyone, including an equal employment opportunity (EEO) enforcement body, should question why one applicant was selected over another.

The structured interview is especially useful in the initial screening because of the large number of applicants in this step of the selection process. It is less flexible than more traditional interview formats and thus may be less appropriate for second or later interviews.

Behavioral description interviewing and situational interviewing are productive styles that are designed to elicit information from the candidate about his or her ability to respond to typical work situations with appropriate work behaviors. In behavioral description interviewing, the candidate is asked to report actual behavior from prior work experience. It is based on the premise that job candidates who previously demonstrated a particular behavior to address a situation will repeat that behavior when confronted with a similar set of problems in the future. For example, applicants might be asked the following:

- How did you handle an employee discipline situation (give a specific example) when there were no rules or guidelines?

- What led you to that approach?

- How was the situation finally resolved?

The situational interview is a structured interview composed of questions about how applicants might handle specific job situations. With experienced applicants, the format is essentially one of job-knowledge or work-sample test. There are three types of questions:

1. Hypothetical—in which an applicant is asked what he or she might do in a certain job situation

2. Knowledge-related—which might entail explaining a method or demonstrating a skill

3. Requirements-related—in which areas such as willingness to work the hours required and meet travel demands are explored

The nondirective interview uses general questions from which other questions are developed. It should be used mainly in psychological counseling, but it is also used in selection. Difficulties include keeping it job related and obtaining comparable data on various applicants.

In a stress interview, the interviewer(s) may assume an aggressive posture or deliberately ask challenging questions for occupations where proper response under pressure is desired, such as law enforcement. Done inappropriately, this style can generate a poor image of the employer.

In a panel interview, several interviewers interview the candidate at the same time, and all the interviewers hear the same responses. The object is to be time efficient if the applicant must meet with a number of people; however, applicants are frequently uncomfortable with the group interview format.

[2] Sample Interview Topics

An interviewer might ask questions to determine if the candidate:

- Has the ability to plan and form goals and allocate resources to meet them

- Recognizes and responds successfully to crisis situations

- Maintains accurate records and documents actions

- Manages time and organizes daily tasks

- Communicates effectively, thoroughly, and accurately

- Develops and maintains acceptable standards for products, services, and equipment

- Applies knowledge to solve job-related problems for timely corrective action

- Persists with special efforts to complete assignments

- Anticipates and responds to change by innovative problem solving

- Demonstrates a professional approach with customers

- Develops employees through performance feedback and job coaching

- Keeps up to date technically

- Motivates employees through work challenges and by example

- Negotiates and cooperates with others to accomplish use of all organizational resources

- Displays good interpersonal skills and maintains smooth working relations with people inside and outside the department

- Estimates and monitors expenses to achieve cost-effectiveness

Employers are not permitted by law to discriminate against protected classes in selecting new employees. To avoid any appearance of discrimination, employers should not ask prospective candidates questions that are not job-related. This caution applies to both a formal interview session and the more informal process of "getting to know the candidate." For example, this restriction extends to the informal conversation, or "small talk," that often takes place when an interviewer takes a candidate to lunch during the interview process. A good point of reference is to stick to questions based on the information contained in the job definition; the general practice is, if it's not job-related, don't ask it.

Exhibit 16.1 contains a representative list of acceptable and unacceptable questions to ask applicants, based on the Equal Employment Opportunity Commission's (EEOC's) Pre-Employment Inquiry Guidelines in 1981 and Enforcement Guidance: Pre-Employment Disability-Related Questions and Medical Examinations in 1995. Although federal EEO laws do not specifically prohibit any preemployment questions, the EEOC does look with "extreme disfavor" on questions about age, color, disability, national origin, race, religion, gender, or veteran status. State law may prohibit discrimination against additional groups and therefore discourage or prohibit other preemployment inquiries, such as questions about a candidate's medical condition or marital status.

§ 16.03 EMPLOYMENT TESTING

Employment testing can be a valuable tool for evaluating the qualifications of job candidates. Properly developed employment tests can be of great help in identifying persons not likely to perform successfully on the job and those likely to perform more successfully than others. It is important, for effective selection, to develop tests carefully by a professional method including job analysis, test design, and analysis of test results.

There are legal requirements that apply to the use of employment tests and to employee selection by any method, including interviews. If a test or any selection procedure results in adverse impact against a group protected by discrimination law (a lower acceptance rate for persons in the protected group), the selection procedure can be legally challenged with a charge of discrimination. The employer can defend against a discrimination charge by showing that the selection procedure in question is job-related. Therefore, it is important to document the selection procedure development process, demonstrating the job-relatedness. Following the descriptions of different types of test are sections that discuss adverse impact and test validation, the process of demonstrating that a test or selection procedure is job-related.

[A] Types of Tests

A wide variety of tests have been used successfully for employee selection, and this section describes the most common types of tests. The advantages of tests are that they are standardized and objectively scored. Also, they can be used to measure qualifications that are very difficult to evaluate in a subjective manner. Tests are particularly suitable for evaluating certain abilities, skills, and knowledge of applicants.

[1] Ability Tests

Ability tests measure underlying abilities and basic skills that are fundamental to the specific skill requirements of most jobs. Examples of useful abilities and basic skills are:

- Reading comprehension

- Reasoning ability

- Computational ability

- Writing skills

- Mechanical comprehension

- Reading diagrams and drawings

Ability tests are usually general in nature, which means that a particular test can often be useful for different occupations. These tests provide a measure of a candidate's potential for learning specialized skills and applying them successfully to the job. As stressed earlier, the specific abilities to be measured for a particular job are determined by conducting a job analysis. The job analysis reveals the significant job requirements, which in turn define the critical abilities.

[2] Knowledge and Skills Tests

These measure practical knowledge and skills that have been acquired through training or work experience and are more specialized than ability tests. Knowledge and skill tests often apply only to a small number of similar jobs or occupations. Some of the most common knowledge and skills tests are designed to measure the following:

- Knowledge of operational procedures for a process or system

- Operating skills for using equipment (e.g., typing or keyboarding skills)

- Knowledge of equipment functions and maintenance

- Knowledge of instructions, policies, and regulations

Knowledge and skills tests are used to measure a person's readiness to perform in a particular job or function. They can also be used to evaluate the effectiveness of training and to determine specific training needs.

[3] Assessment Exercises

These consist of work simulations, such as performance exercises, but they involve the measurement of more complex, global, or interpersonally related work behaviors. Some of the work behaviors that are measured with assessment exercises are leadership, teamwork, planning, and decision making. Such test exercises are particularly suitable for measuring interactive dimensions, such as cooperation, persuasion, and communication. They are often used to evaluate candidates for positions in management, sales, or service.

Assessment exercises are used to simulate a wide variety of work situations, and they can be designed to be very realistic. Some of the most frequently used forms of assessment exercises are the following:

- Role-playing interactions

- In-basket exercises

- Group discussions

- Verbal presentations

Assessment exercises are used for the following purposes in selection programs:

- Obtaining direct, firsthand observation of a candidate's behavior

- Evaluating a candidate's total response to a situation

- Observing a candidate's performance in settings involving interaction

- Evaluating the application of knowledge and ability to practical requirements

Assessment exercises allow the measurement of a wide variety of personal characteristics that are difficult to measure with tests or interviews but that can be very important in relation to job requirements.

[4] Honesty or Integrity Tests

These tests are gaining in popularity, especially among organizations that have employees who are unsupervised and have responsibility for products or cash. So far, the validity studies have been favorable to this type of test. In fact, some studies have shown that organizations that use these tests in the hiring process have experienced a decrease in inventory losses over time. However, employers need to be cognizant of the legal implications of these and any type of test they wish to conduct.

[B] Legal Requirements

There are important legal implications for employment testing and selection, under the Civil Rights Act, the Age Discrimination in Employment Act (ADEA), and the ADA. Also, many states have enacted laws parallel to these federal laws. All of these laws prohibit discrimination in employment against various groups, based on race, sex, age, disability, and other protected classes. Through the course of a number of Supreme Court decisions, a process has evolved for bringing charges of discrimination against an employer and for defending against those charges. This process has been embodied in the Uniform Guidelines on Employee Selection Procedures, regulations published by the EEOC, and other federal government agencies. These guidelines do not have the force of law, but the Supreme Court has stated that they are entitled to "great deference."

According to the Uniform Guidelines, adverse impact exists where there is a substantially different rate of selection in hiring or other employment decisions that works to the disadvantage of members of a race, sex, ethnic group, or other protected class. If a selection procedure has an adverse impact against a protected group, a discrimination charge may be brought against the employer. The employer may defend itself against the discrimination charge by showing that the selection procedure is job-related and measures qualifications that are related to job performance. If job-relatedness cannot be demonstrated, then the use of the selection procedure in question constitutes discrimination. None of these laws or regulations prohibit employment testing. However, if a test or any other selection procedure results in adverse impact, it is necessary for the employer to clearly demonstrate the job-relatedness of the selection procedure.

Sections 16.06[C] and 16.06[D] discuss in greater detail what constitutes adverse impact and selection procedure validation, which is the process of demonstrating job-relatedness.

On December 3, 2007, the EEOC issued a fact sheet on the application of federal anti-discrimination laws to employer tests and other selection procedures. The fact sheet describes common types of employer administered tests and selection procedures, including cognitive tests, personality tests, medical examinations, credit checks, and criminal background checks. The fact sheet is available on the agency's Web site at *www.eeoc.gov/policy/docs/factemployment_procedures.html*.

[C] Adverse Impact

Adverse impact is defined in terms of relative hiring rates. If the hiring rate for a protected group is less than 80 percent of the highest group hiring rate, there is adverse impact for the protected group. For example, if the highest hiring rate is for Caucasian, and it is 20 percent, and the hiring rate for Hispanics is 15 percent, there is adverse impact for Hispanics. The Hispanic hiring rate is only 75 percent of the Caucasian hiring rate, and that is less than 80 percent.

[D]   Test and Selection Procedure Validation

Validation is an analytical process for demonstrating that a test or other selection procedure is job-related. Successful test validation will establish the legitimacy of a selection procedure, even though it may have adverse impact for a protected group. There are two types of process for practical validation of a selection procedure: content validation and criterion-related validation.

Content validation is a process whereby a candidate demonstrates the particular work behavior required on the job, as indicated in the job description. The process involves identifying the specific elements of work behavior or job requirement that are used in each item or exercise of the selection procedure. Content validation may be accomplished successfully for job knowledge and skill tests, work samples, performance exercises, structured interviews, and assessment exercises if the selection procedure content is based directly on job content and requirements.

Criterion-related validation is used for selection procedures that do not directly measure work behaviors, such as aptitude tests and personality inventories. Criterion-related validation involves a statistical analysis to calculate the correlation coefficient between the selection procedure and a suitable measure of job performance for a sample of employees in the job of interest. The size of the correlation coefficient will indicate whether the selection procedure can be considered valid for the job.

Any validation study should be based on a review of information about the job for which the selection procedure is to be used. The process should include a job analysis showing what tasks or work behaviors are required for successful performance of the job.

Amendments made to Title VII by the 1991 Civil Rights Act prohibit adjusting test scores to make up for a disparate impact on a protected group. Tests must be administered in such a way that an equal employment opportunity is afforded to applicants with disabilities. For example, employers may be required to provide readers for blind applicants to accommodate them reasonably in taking written tests.

Interpretation of test results often involves the establishment of *cutting scores* for determining selection decisions. The cutting scores separate groups of candidates with different levels of potential for performing successfully on the job. The reasons for setting particular cutting scores should be stated in terms of factors that are related to job performance.

Clear, appropriate procedures should be written for the administration of selection procedures and to ensure proper interpretation of results. Validation procedures and other relevant information should be carefully documented to provide evidence that the use of the selection procedure is in compliance with all legal requirements.

[E]   Drug Testing

If a company is in an industry that requires preemployment drug testing, or if a company chooses to require it, there are many issues it must address. (See **Chapter 23** for further discussion.)

§ 16.04   REFERENCE CHECKING

No specific law requires employers to check an applicant's references. However, employers may be held liable for negligent hiring for an act of the employee the employer should have foreseen. (See **Section 16.08**.) Therefore, most prospective employers find it good practice to seek information from the applicants' former employers. In fact, reference checking continues to be the leading method of obtaining information on prospective employees before putting forth the employment offer.

Reference checking can provide critical information. In a study conducted by the Society for Human Resources Management in 2004, HR professionals reported on inconsistencies they found between the records and what the applicant reported. For example, 55 percent of HR professionals said they "sometimes" found discrepancies in dates of previous employment, and 3 percent said they "always" found errors. Only 6 percent of HR professionals reported that they "never" saw discrepancies in employment dates. Among those HR professionals that conduct criminal background checks, 48 percent said they sometimes found errors, and 6 percent said they "always" found errors. Employers should validate to the fullest degree possible the job experiences, employment history, and specific qualifications candidates have listed on resumes and employment applications. It is important to note that various local, state, and federal laws now affect a prospective employer's ability to secure and use information for screening and hiring purposes. Most noteworthy is the Privacy Act of 1974, requiring government entities to have a signed, written release before providing any information to prospective employers. In recent years additional bills have been introduced in Congress to enforce similar restrictions upon employers within the private sector. It is important to be thoroughly familiar with all laws and regulations pertaining to background investigations and preemployment inquiries in the employer's state. For a more thorough discussion of reference checking, see the sections in this chapter on negligent hiring and negligent referral. (For further discussion on the subject of privacy in the workplace, see **Chapter 20**.)

[A]   Obtaining a Reference

Employers who attempt to check the references of candidates prior to hiring them are often confronted with previous employers' reluctance to provide information. Previous employers are uncertain about what to say when providing information about former employees. They do not want to discuss negative experiences for fear of incurring potential defamation claims and liability. These concerns have led many employers to initiate policies prohibiting meaningful reference comments. It is not unusual for a former employer to release only information regarding dates of employment and position(s) held and, possibly, verifying final compensation. Numerous states have passed job reference immunity statutes designed to shield employers from lawsuits brought by an employee as a result of providing information about him or her to a prospective employer. As a general rule, even without a specific state statute an employer is immune from liability for providing inaccurate job reference information if the employer disclosed the information in good faith (i.e., without "malice"). However, because the majority of new statutes do not grant a "guarantee" of immunity, providing a job reference critical of an employee will still expose the employer to some level of litigation risk. Therefore, wise employers ask candidates to sign a reference release form authorizing them to conduct a reference check and holding them harmless from any negative information that may result. Under the common law, an employee's consent to the release of information may provide stronger protection to employers than statutory immunity. Specifically, some courts recognize an absolute privilege where the employee has "consented" to the reference by authorizing a prospective employer to obtain background information from prior employers. A sample reference release is provided in **Exhibit 16.2**. In any event, employers should still proceed to make every effort to verify information provided by the applicant and to thoroughly check the references and prior employers listed by the applicant. HR officers should document every contact made, whether the attempt at data gathering was successful or unsuccessful.

[1] Candidate Checks on the Internet

With easy Internet access, employers may be tempted to enter a candidate's name in a search engine to see what information might be available. Information on the Internet is in the public domain, so there should not be an issue of invasion of privacy. Although this type of search is not illegal, employers are cautioned about using Internet sites as a resource for candidate information. Potential problems include (1) information posted about a candidate may not be true (you cannot be sure of the source of the posting); (2) the site may reveal information that could be used to discriminate, such as race or medical condition; and (3) you may inadvertently obtain information about a different person with the same name.

[B] Background Checks

There are several types of employee background checks, such as credit checks, criminal record checks, driving records checks, educational and/or certification verification, and past-employer checks. By conducting proper background checks, employers can minimize potential liability and employment-related litigation by screening out applicants who are not qualified for a job or who may become problem employees. Before conducting a background check, the employer should obtain the applicant's written consent to investigate the applicant's employment and educational and personal references, as well as to conduct a criminal background check and a credit report. Most outside firms will provide their forms for this purpose.

A cottage industry of background check firms has sprung up in recent years. For relatively little cost, typically under $200, employers can outsource the background checking process. Employers can also conduct the reference checking process themselves. Publications are available to assist employers by providing listings of public record sources. These directories and guides are available in hard copy, CD-ROM, and on-line.

The Social Security Administration (SSA), through the Social Security Number Verification Service (SSNVS), offers a free service to employers for checking new hires' or employees' names and Social Security numbers. This service is now available via the Internet. Employers can check up to 10 names at one time and get immediate results, or upload large numbers for next day results. This service is intended to be used to verify W-2 forms. Employers may also call (800) 772-6270 (toll free) to verify up to five Social Security numbers. To verify up to 50 numbers, an employer may submit a paper listing containing the necessary data to its local SSA office. For information, see the SSA's Web site: *www.ssa.gov/employer/ ssnv.htm*. To use any of these services, the employer must provide the applicant's or employee's name exactly as it appears on his or her Social Security card (last name, first name and middle initial, if applicable), Social Security number, date of birth, and gender.

Employers need to be aware that if a background check turns up reports of a candidate's arrest or conviction record, or financial or credit problems, this information cannot be used to arbitrarily reject the applicant unless the employer can show a business necessity for disqualification on that basis. Similarly, employers cannot obtain credit reports on a job applicant's spouse. Seeking such reports violates the FCRA, as amended, and exposes the employer to civil liability.

The disposal rule of the Fair and Accurate Credit Transactions (FACT) Act requires that employers take appropriate measures to dispose of sensitive information derived from consumer reports in order to protect against unauthorized use and identity theft. (See **Chapter 20** for further discussion.)

[1] The Fair Credit Reporting Act

An employer who uses an outside resource to obtain consumer reports, such as criminal background reports, motor vehicle records, or credit reports as part of a background check on applicants or current employees must comply with the Fair Credit Reporting Act of 1970 (FCRA). This outside resource is termed a *consumer reporting agency* by the FCRA. The FCRA protects applicants by preventing employers from obtaining information that they have no right or need to know. The requirements are part of a major modification of the Fair Credit Reporting Act of 1970, which governs the use of consumer reports in all employment decisions. [15 U.S.C. §§ 1681 *et seq.*] The amendments, known as the Consumer Credit Reporting Reform Act of 1996 (Reform Act), [Pub. L. No. 104-208, 110 Stat. 3009 (Sept. 30, 1996)] became effective September 30, 1997.

A consumer report, which may be either oral or written, covers a consumer's creditworthiness, credit standing, credit capacity, character, general reputation, personal characteristics, and mode of living. Employers who use consumer reports should do the following to comply with the FCRA:

- Before requesting the report, (1) provide written disclosure to the individual that a consumer report may be obtained for employment purposes and (2) obtain written authorization from the individual.

- Before obtaining the report, provide certification of compliance with the FCRA to the agency, indicating that the above steps have been followed and that the information being obtained will not be used in violation of any federal or state equal employment opportunity law, and that, if any adverse action is going to be taken based on the report, a copy of the report and a summary of rights promulgated by the Federal Trade Commission (Summary of Rights) will be provided to the applicant or employee.

- Before using the report to exclude the applicant, provide written information to the individual, to include a copy of the report and a copy of the Summary of Rights.

- After using the report to exclude the applicant, provide a written explanation to the individual, to include (1) notice of the adverse action; (2) the name, address, and telephone number of the agency that provided the report; (3) a statement that the agency did not take the adverse action and is not able to explain why the decision was made; (4) a statement setting forth the applicant's or employee's rights to obtain free disclosure of his or her file from the agency if the individual requests the report within 60 days; and (5) a statement setting forth the applicant's or employee's right to dispute directly with the agency the accuracy or completeness of any information provided by the agency.

An investigative consumer report frequently contains more detailed information about an applicant's character, general reputation, personal characteristics, and mode of living than has been secured through personal interviews with friends, neighbors, and other associates. Employers who use investigative consumer reports should do the following:

- Before requesting an applicant's investigative consumer report, provide written disclosure and infor-mation to the applicant, including (1) a statement that such a report as well as a consumer report may be obtained by the employer, (2) a statement informing the applicant of the right to request additional disclosures about the nature and scope of the investigation, and (3) a copy of the Summary of Rights (this disclosure is required to be mailed or otherwise delivered to the applicant no later than three days after the date on which the report was first requested, providing the disclosure before requesting the report ensures compliance with the FCRA).

- Obtain written authorization from the applicant to obtain the investigative consumer report.

- Before obtaining an investigative consumer report, provide certification of compliance with the FCRA to the agency. If the applicant makes a written request for a complete disclosure of the nature and scope of the investigation that was requested, the employer should provide written disclosures of the nature and scope of the investigation to the applicant. The disclosure must be mailed or otherwise delivered to the applicant no later than five days after the date on which the employer received the applicant's request, or five days after the report was first requested from the agency, whichever is later.

- Before using an investigative consumer report to make an adverse employment decision, provide the following written information to the applicant: (1) a copy of the report and (2) a copy of the Summary of Rights.

- After using the investigative consumer report to exclude the applicant, provide a detailed written explanation to the applicant, including (1) notice of the adverse action; (2) the name, address, and telephone number of the agency that provided the report; (3) a statement that the agency did not take the adverse action and is not able to explain why the decision was made; (4) a statement setting forth the applicant's rights to obtain free disclosure of his or her file from the agency if he or she requests the report within 60 days; and (5) a statement setting forth the applicant's right to dispute directly with the agency the accuracy or completeness of any information provided by the agency.

A commercial consumer reporting agency, when asked and supplied with proper identification, must disclose the following information:

- The nature and details of all information in the applicant's files, except medical information, at the time the report was made

- The source or sources of the commercial agency's information

- The reports that the employer has furnished in the past two years on the applicant if they were made for employment purposes

- Reports made during the past six-month period for any purposes other than employment (unless a report covers a job paying more than $20,000 per year, the report must provide notice that it has excluded adverse information seven years old and older, except bankruptcies, which may be included up to 10 years, and arrests or convictions, which may be included for seven years after release or parole)

It is generally advisable that a prospective employer seek only enough information through consumer credit reports as is reasonably required for the purposes of making an employment decision, even if more information is available to the employer. These records should be retained for two years.

Willful noncompliance with the FCRA may result in a recovery by an appellant of actual damages suffered, punitive damages as allowed by the courts, court costs, and reasonable attorneys' fees as determined by the court. If negligent noncompliance is found, the penalty can be actual damages suffered, court costs, and reasonable attorneys' fees as determined by the court.

[2] Credit Checks

Credit checks are often performed for positions that involve financial responsibilities, especially if the position involves handling large sums of money or exercising financial discretion. It is a good practice to limit the use of credit reports to situations where business necessity demands good references. Employers should know the EEOC has found that credit checks may have an adverse impact on minorities. (Note: If an investigation is requested but never performed, the duties and obligations of the FCRA do not apply.)

Provisions of the Bankruptcy Act must be followed if the employer finds that the applicant has declared bankruptcy. These provisions ensure that the applicant's bankruptcy does not prohibit him or her from finding employment.

[3] Criminal Record Checks

Employers may want to consider doing a criminal record check for positions that involve close, unsupervised contact with the public. An example of such a position would be a security guard or hotel personnel with access to guest room keys.

Access to federal criminal records is not generally available to private employers, with the exception of banks. However, private employers are more likely to secure criminal conviction records from the state if the employer is able to show a real need for the information. Another situation that would warrant the release of this information is if the incumbent's position could jeopardize the financial security or the public image of the company. Some states have laws prohibiting discrimination against people who have a criminal record. Therefore, it is advisable to check with the state department of labor before securing criminal record information.

[4] Driving Records

Employers should check driving records of applicants who will be using a company vehicle before the applicant is hired and periodically throughout employment. The employer could be held liable for negligent hiring if it knew or should have known about the record and the employee had an accident in a company vehicle. Employers should also check to see if the applicant has a valid driver's license.

[5] Chemical Workers

The Department of Homeland Security has issued interim final rules that require certain chemical facilities to conduct background checks on some of their workers. For details on these requirements, visit the DHS Web site (*www.dhs.gov*) or contact an employment attorney with expertise in this area.

§ 16.05 REFERENCE LIABILITY

There are two avenues for liability in hiring, each related to an applicant's references. These are negligent hiring and negligent referral.

[A] Negligent Hiring

An increasingly common cause of action in employment litigation is that of negligent hiring. Typically, this cause of action arises when an employee causes injury to another employee or third party (e.g., assault, theft, sexual harassment, or some other form of discrimination) while acting in the scope of his or her employment. The injured party brings suit against the organization for the misconduct of the employee and for not having learned of the potential problems and avoided the hire in the first place.

There are no foolproof methods to fully ensure against the hiring of an unfit or dangerous person, but exposure to negligent hiring claims can be minimized by taking the following steps:

1. Tailor the background investigation to the job sought.

2. Request that applicants sign a release for job-related information from former employers.

3. Obtain and check as many employment and personal references as feasible before hiring, and do not hire an applicant before completing all such inquiries.

4. Document the comprehensiveness of the pre-hire investigation, noting even those reference requests that produced no information. For high-risk positions (e.g., security jobs), try to verify former residences.

5. Carefully examine employment applications, and then interview applicants thoroughly, making a careful record of what was asked and how each question was answered. Ask for more information about gaps in employment history or between school and jobs. Try to confirm any adverse information from a former supervisor by asking what he or she thinks the former boss might say.

6. Consider retaining a commercial service if the company has insufficient trained staff to conduct a thorough pre-hire investigation. However, select background investigation agencies with great care, as employers can be held liable for unlawful inquiries or other misconduct by these investigative companies if they are considered agents of the employer.

Some relief from this liability may be forthcoming, however. The courts are beginning to define limits to employer responsibility for negligent hiring.

[B] Negligent Referral

Negligent referral arises out of the obligation created for employers to disclose negative information regarding former employees when the information has a bearing on the job in question. An employer's failure to provide a requesting company with key information about a former employee could create a liability for the employer under certain circumstances—for example, if something negative happens in the employee's new position that could have been prevented if the former employer had disclosed the information to the hiring company. An example might be a situation in which an individual applies for a position with a bank and the bank calls the previous employer for a reference, but the previous employer does not tell the bank that the individual was terminated for stealing money. If the employee were to steal money from the bank, the bank could potentially sue the previous employer for failing to disclose this pertinent piece of information.

As was affirmed in the case of *Randi W. v. Muroc Joint Unified School District* [929 P.2d 582 (Cal. 1997)], an employer may be held liable for negligent misrepresentation and fraud if it provides a reference or letter of recommendation containing "unreserved and unconditional praise" for a former employee known to present a "foreseeable and substantial risk of physical injury" to a prospective employer or third person. In such a case, the state's supreme court held, the recommending employer, which ordinarily "should not be held accountable for failing to disclose negative information," nonetheless has a duty to not misrepresent the qualifications and character of a former employee if doing so could result in serious risk of harm to others. Alternatives to avoid tort liability are available to employers; these alternatives include writing a "full disclosure" letter that reveals "all relevant facts" about an individual's background or writing a "no comment" or "neutral" letter of reference, "merely verifying basic employment dates and details."

[C] Limiting Exposure to Liability

Some states are taking the initiative to protect employers from liability when they provide factual references, both positive and negative. In 1991 Georgia became the first state to pass a reference checking law that protected employers in the health care industry. To date, at least 35 additional states have passed similar legislation. Virtually every state, whether by statute or case law, provides (1) an allowance for employers to make truthful statements about former employees, or (2) a conditional privilege that protects the employer from liability for false negative references if the employer acted in good faith.

Regardless of specific state laws, the general rules in reference checking are as follows:

- Handle reference requests consistently.

- Ask only job-related questions when requesting information.

- Ask the applicant's previous employer to be as objective, honest, and unbiased as possible and stick to the facts. Ascertain that the information received is factual and can be substantiated. Resist the temptation to discuss conjecture with the former employer or to participate in any discussion in which malice is detected, no matter what the circumstances of the employee's departure from the company.

[D] Past-Employed Protection from Retaliation

One case, *Robinson v. Shell Oil Co.* [519 U.S. 337 (1997)], demonstrates the application of Title VII protection from retaliation to past employees who suffered as a result of a former employer's providing false information and bad references to a possible future employer. A former employee of Shell Oil, who had filed an EEOC charge against the company after being terminated, sued the company for retaliation after it gave him a negative reference. The U.S. Supreme Court found that the retaliation suit, which had been dismissed by the trial court, was properly brought by the former employee. The Court stated that excluding former employees from protection against retaliation would undermine the effectiveness of Title VII by deterring employees from complaining about discrimination. The Court's decision in *Robinson* suggests that employers should carefully consider potential liability when giving a negative reference, especially if the former employee made any complaints of unlawful conduct before leaving the job.

In general, a full disclosure should be made to applicants about the kinds of information to be gathered in a reference or background check and the purposes for which information is requested. The company should have applicants attest, in writing, to having been informed of the reference check or background check and should secure the applicant's written consent to conduct a specified records search. The company should institute and follow procedures consistently to maintain the confidentiality of all information obtained.

§ 16.06 COMMON SELECTION ERRORS

The final step in the selection process is extending an employment offer to the top candidate. (See **Exhibit 16.3** for a sample job offer letter.) If the organization has done a thorough job in applicant recruitment and sourcing, interviewing, testing, and reference/background checking, it is much more likely to have the necessary information to make a good decision. The following are some common errors to keep in mind that may affect the quality of the selection process:

- Poorly defined or undefined qualifications for the position

- Unfocused interviews conducted with candidates

- Little or no documentation from the interviews

- Decisions made primarily on subjective "gut" factors

- Decisions made on the verbal "selling skills" of the candidate

- Interpersonal and cultural factors not weighed properly

To help ensure that the company avoids these traps, it is important to analyze, compare, and rank the candidates interviewed in each factor identified as critical for success in the position. This comparison should be in writing, to uncover any missing data about a candidate that should be explored before making the final decision. The manager should not rely too heavily on any one component when making the selection, because each is important to the decision.

§ 16.07 HIRING EMPLOYEES WITH THE LEGAL RIGHT TO WORK IN THE UNITED STATES

Employers must take care to verify that new employees have the legal right to work in the United States. Significant fines and penalties are associated with hiring unauthorized foreign workers.

The DHS announced in April, 2006 that they were increasing their efforts to enforce existing laws prohibiting employment of unauthorized foreign workers. One of the most significant laws is the Illegal Immigration and Immigrant Responsibility Act of 1996 (IIIRA), signed by President Clinton on September 30, 1996, which contains significant enforcement provisions.

[A] Form I-9

Each new employee must complete a Form I-9, the method by which employees verify their identity and eligibility to work in the United States. Section 1 of the I-9 must be completed by the employee within three days of hire. He or she must present an original of either one of the documents on List A (which verifies eligibility and identity) or one each from List B (identity) and List C (eligibility). Employers must complete Section 2.

A new I-9 was issued by the U.S. Citizenship and Immigration Services (USCIS) in November 2007. The revision date, found on the lower right corner of the form, is June 5, 2007. As of December 27, 2007, this is the only valid form to be completed by new hires. It must also be used when recertifying existing employees. Use of older versions will be considered a violation and could result in a penalty to the company.

The most significant revision on the new I-9 is the change in the List A acceptable documents. Acceptable documents are:

- U.S. Passport

- Permanent Resident Card or Alien Registration Receipt Card (Form I-551)

- Unexpired foreign passport with a temporary I-551 stamp

- Unexpired Employment Authorization Document that contains a photograph (Form I-766, I-688, I-688A or I-688B)

- Unexpired foreign passport with an unexpired "Arrival-Departure Record," Form I-94, for nonimmigrant aliens authorized to work for a specific employer

The following five documents are no longer acceptable:

1. Certificate of U.S. Citizenship (Form N-560 or N-561)

2. Certificate of Naturalization (Form N-550 or N-570)

3. Alien Registration Receipt Card (I-151)

4. Unexpired Reentry Permit (I-327)

5. Unexpired Refugee Travel Document (Form I-571)

The new form also indicates that the new employee is not required to provide a Social Security Number in Section 1 unless the employer participates in the E-Verify program (see **Section 16.07.B**).

To obtain a current copy of Form I-9, and for detailed information on completing the form, employers can log on to *http://www.uscis.gov/portal/site/uscis*, then click on the link "For Employers."

The Department of Homeland Security (DHS) has created an interim rule that allows employers to sign and retain the Form I-9 electronically. The employer may use one of a number of electronic systems as long as it complies with current IRS guidelines. Details can be found in a Fact Sheet on the U.S. Immigration and Customs Enforcement Web site: *http://www.ice.gov/pi/news/factsheets/i-9employment.htm*.

Completed I-9 forms must be maintained by the employer for three years after the date of hire or one year after the date of termination, whichever is longer.

[1] Technical Form I-9 Violations

When an employer has made a good-faith effort to comply with the Form I-9 completion requirements, it is possible that paperwork fines for "technical and procedural failures" may not be imposed. The USCIS is required to provide an employer with a notice of deficiency and a 10-day window of opportunity to fix the technical and procedural deficiencies.

This provision, however, appears to apply only to failures occurring on or after September 30, 1996. It does not go back over the prior 10 years. It is also unclear how the USCIS will interpret the meaning of a "minor, technical" violation. It appears from comments made by high-ranking USCIS officials that such events as failing to sign the Form I-9, failing to date the document, or leaving significant data off would not be considered a minor, technical violation.

On October 7, 1996, the USCIS promulgated employer sanction regulations, which provide that a warning notice be given to employers if minor I-9 verification violations have occurred, but future compliance is expected. Unlike the IIIRA signed by President Clinton, the regulations provide that giving a warning notice is discretionary, but not mandatory. However, this regulation would cover I-9 problems that have occurred over the previous 10 years, not just those since September 30, 1996.

Failure to comply with the I-9 process can result in penalties that range from $375 to $16,000.

[2] Document Fraud

Document fraud in connection with completion of a Form I-9 is prohibited under the provisions of Section 274C of the Illegal Immigration Reform and Immigrant Responsibility Act of 1996. Document fraud may result in both civil and criminal penalties. Examples of such fraud are backdating Form I-9, knowingly accepting fraudulent documents, and making misleading statements about their authenticity under penalty of perjury. Penalties start at $375 and may go up to $6,500.

[3] "Overdocumentation" Liability Provision Revised

The strict liability provision in Section 274B of the Immigration and Naturalization Act of 1990 has been revised. This provision imposed fines on employers who "overdocumented" the I-9 and insisted on reviewing too many documents. The revision included a specific-intent requirement.

[4] Limiting Exposure to Liability

To limit the employer's exposure to liability and ensure proper compliance, it is recommended that:

- Employees complete the Form I-9 no later than their first day of employment. The form can be completed after an offer of employment is accepted; however, the timing of completing the form should be consistent for all similarly situated employees.

- Employers verify an employee's documents of eligibility to work in the United States no later than the third day of employment.

- Employees without the required documents must obtain and present to the employer a receipt for replacement document(s) within the first three days of employment.

- Employers terminate any employees who cannot produce the required documents or a receipt for replacement document(s) within the first three days of employment. Employees without the required documents or receipts may not work until they produce the required information.

- Employers receive the actual document from the employee within 90 days of the date employment begins, if an employee presents a receipt for a replacement document within the first three days of employment. If the actual documents are not presented, the employer may terminate the employee, so long as all employees in the same situation receive consistent treatment.

- Employers ensure that all employees receive a list of the appropriate documents for proof of work eligibility, without a requirement that specific documents (e.g., a driver's license and/or Social Security card) be produced.

- If employers make copies of eligibility documents, employers consistently process copies of documents submitted as proof of eligibility to work.

- Employers ensure that all necessary fields on the Form I-9 are completed.

- Employers ensure that all I-9 documentation is updated (in other words, do not let document renewal dates lapse).

Employers should maintain all I-9 documentation separate from other employee files. Following the signing of bill H.R. 4306 by President Bush on October 30, 2004, I-9 files may now be saved electronically. H.R. 4306 requires that the U.S. Department of Homeland Security allow electronic completion and storage of I-9 employment verification forms.

[B] E-Verify

E-Verify, formerly known as the Basic Pilot/Employment Eligibility Verification Program, is an Internet-based system operated by the USCIS in partnership with the SSA. E-Verify is currently free to employers and is available in all 50 states. It provides an automated link to federal databases to help employers determine employment eligibility of new hires and the validity of their Social Security numbers. According to the USCIS Web site, the EEV "virtually eliminates Social Security mismatch letters, improves the accuracy of wage and tax reporting, protects jobs for authorized U.S. workers, and helps U.S. employers maintain a legal workforce."

E-Verify is currently a voluntary program for most employers, although in June, 2008, President Bush amended Executive Order 12989 to require federal contractors to use E-Verify. Various states have enacted legislation that would require employers to participate in this system, although there are legal challenges to these laws. There are also states, such as Illinois, seeking to prohibit employers from participating in E-Verify. There is concern that the accuracy of the database, most recently reported at 94 percent, is too low, and that some individuals with the legal right to work in the United States may be denied employment because of inaccurate records.

The program was originally set to expire in November 2008. However, on July 31, 2008, the house passed the Employee Verification Amendment Act, which would extend the E-Verify program for five years. As of this writing, the bill has been sent to the Senate, but not ratified. Additionally, there are two Senate bills pending that would reauthorize E-Verify.

For further information about this program, log on to its Web site at *http://www.uscis.gov/portal/site/uscis.*

[C] Increased Governmental Agency Cooperation

The USCIS (formerly the Immigration and Naturalization Service (INS)) is increasing its effort to hire investigators to step up the apprehension of undocumented workers. To facilitate this process, the IIIRA mandated increased exchange of information between the USCIS and the SSA. As of January 1, 1997, the SSA is required to provide to the USCIS the names and addresses of employers who report earnings on fraudulent Social Security account numbers. Further, wiretapping and undercover operations are authorized for investigating document fraud and alien smuggling.

Although a company may not be engaging in this activity as a matter of policy, management may not always be aware of the activities of supervisors who have been given hiring authority. If a supervisor recruits relatives and friends for employment and facilitates or directly assists them in obtaining fraudulent documents, he or she is placing the company at risk. The IIIRA states that any person who knowingly hires 10 or more unauthorized aliens who have been smuggled into the United States may be imprisoned for up to five years.

§ 16.08   THE ON-BOARDING PROCESS

On-boarding is a term used to describe the process of orienting and integrating a new employee into the organization. This is critical to the success of the employee, and is the step that must follow the selection process. Employers spend a great deal of time and money to find and hire the right person—there is a risk of wasting it all when they don't properly integrate the new hire into the organization.

On-boarding takes the concept of "orientation" to a new level. Orientation has traditionally been a one- to three-day process of completing paperwork and learning about the policies, procedures, structure and culture of the new employer. Many companies now are looking at opportunities to fully integrate new employees into their organizations over a much longer period of time—in some companies, up to two years. The goals of on-boarding are to:

- Provide an understanding and appreciation of the "greatness" of the company

- Inspire pride, excitement, enthusiasm

- Provide an atmosphere of openness

- Allow the employee to ask for help

- Provide an understanding of how the new employee can contribute to the greatness of the company

- Build relationships between the new hire and other employees

On-boarding involves a variety of innovative programs and processes designed to work together to meet these goals. Some ideas and approaches that have contributed to successful on-boarding:

Technology

Organizations are using technology to add to the efficiency of on-boarding. New hires can "pre-board" by accessing the company's Web site before their first day. They can fill out required forms, learn about the company through videos or virtual tours, and get introduced to the people in their department or work unit.

Mentors

Companies may assign a mentor or buddy to the new hire. The mentor takes a proactive approach to assisting the new hire to become acclimated. He or she makes introductions, answers questions, provides education about the history and future of the company, and helps the new hire understand the culture of the organization. Some mentors will meet with their new hire on a regular basis for six or 12 months or longer.

Training and Development

Companies are working with the new hire from the beginning of her or his employment to create a plan for learning and career development. Plans are typically in writing, extend over one to three years, and begin within a short time of the hiring date.

Access to Key Executives

Some organizations have developed "shadowing" programs for new hires, allowing them to spend organized time with one or more executives in their department, work unit or company.

Responsible Managers

A successful on-boarding program will ensure that managers play an integral role in the program. Through formal and informal processes, the managers create an environment where the new employee feels welcome, able to ask questions, and part of an exciting team.

Employers are encouraged to be imaginative in creating their on-boarding program. While it is helpful to get ideas from other organizations, it is equally important that the program fit the individual organization's culture.

§ 16.09   OTHER LEGAL CONCERNS

So often today, seemingly routine decisions affecting employees provide cause for employment litigation. It is important to review the entire hiring process for objectivity and consistency. Outlined in the following sections are a number of potential liability issues to be aware of during the employment process.

[A]   Job Reassignment

In a 1996 case, the Seventh Circuit Court of Appeals ruled that an employee who is reassigned to a prior position after "resigning" because of disability cannot sue the employer years later to restore lost seniority. The court determined that reasonable accommodation "cannot be stretched to the point of requiring the provision of superseniority." [Kennedy v. Chemical Waste Mgmt., Inc., 79 F.3d 49 (7th Cir. 1996)]

Richard Kennedy was a unionized truck driver for Chemical Waste Management. After 20 years with the company, Kennedy was diagnosed with multiple sclerosis. His doctor recommended that he be removed from his position of driving trucks carrying volatile chemicals and be reassigned to a nonunion janitorial position. Four years later, Kennedy's doctor reevaluated the situation and decided that he could return to his job as a truck driver with minor alterations to the work routine. The company returned Kennedy to a position as a truck driver and treated him as a new hire. Kennedy knew at that time that his seniority had not been restored.

Two years passed, and Kennedy lost his job as part of a workforce reduction. He sued under the ADA, claiming that he would not have been laid off if the company had restored his seniority from his previous employment.

Although Kennedy had filed in a timely manner under the ADA, the court dismissed the suit as untimely. The court found that any injuries suffered by Kennedy had occurred at the time that the employer had restored him to his truck driver position without seniority. At that time, Kennedy did not object. The court noted that there are cases in which a person may not realize that an injury has occurred until the effect of the employer's actions becomes clear, but the court found no latent discrimination based on disability in this case. The company followed the doctor's recommendations when it first removed Kennedy as a truck driver, a job move that caused him to resign from the union. In that company, union seniority did not vest. Therefore, the company did not discriminate by treating him as a new employee when he returned to driving a truck.

This case demonstrates the importance of defining how changes in employment status will be treated when an employee changes jobs and the new job has different benefits and rights. The company must clearly define how it will handle seniority and vesting if job conditions change.

[B] The Arbitration Clause

[1] Job Application Provision

The U.S. Court of Appeals for the Fourth Circuit ruled that a provision in a job application that required applicants to agree to arbitrate any disputes in the application process or arising in employment is enforceable, reversing a district court ruling that the agreement was invalid because the employer provided no consideration. The consideration provided by the employer for requiring applicants to sign the agreement was that the employer also would be bound by the same arbitration requirement. [Johnson v. Circuit City Stores, 148 F.3d 373, 77 FEP Cases 139 (4th Cir. 1998)]

[2] Arbitration Agreements

As an additional aspect to the employee selection process, one option being considered by some employers is to prepare and have employees sign, as a condition of employment, arbitration agreements, requiring any resulting dispute between the employee and the employer to be resolved through the arbitration process rather than traditional litigation.

The Fifth Circuit Court of Appeals has joined the ranks of federal appeals courts that have ruled that employees are bound by arbitration clauses contained in employment contracts.

The Fifth Circuit case involved a disc jockey named Rojas who alleged that she was subjected to sexual harassment by her supervisor and that the station owners did nothing to resolve the situation. [Rojas v. TK Communications, 87 F.3d 745 (5th Cir. 1996)] Rojas claimed that she was terminated for reporting the problem. Rojas signed an employment contract while she was working at the station that included an arbitration clause covering "the validity of [the contract of employment], the enforcement of its financial terms, or other disputes." When Rojas filed suit, the employer moved to compel arbitration per the employment agreement.

The employee contested the arbitration clause. The Federal Arbitration Act (FAA) includes a clause that excludes arbitration from the "contracts of employment of seamen, railroad employees, or other class of workers engaged in foreign or interstate commerce." Rojas claimed that in her job as a disc jockey she was involved in "commerce," which would invalidate the arbitration clause.

Prior to *Rojas,* the Supreme Court avoided interpreting the FAA exclusion clause. In *Rojas,* the Fifth Circuit noted that Congress could have excluded "any contracts of employment" under the FAA clause.

Instead, the court used seamen and railroad employees as examples of the types of employees who were engaged in "foreign or interstate commerce."

With the *Rojas* decision, the Fifth Circuit joins the First, Second, Third, Sixth, and Seventh Circuits in narrowly interpreting the FAA exclusion clause. The only federal appellate court decision that applied this exclusion to all employment contracts was made by the Fourth Circuit, in 1954. The other federal circuit courts have yet to consider this issue.

The Supreme Court has ruled in agreement with the majority of federal appellate courts. In the case of *Circuit City Stores, Inc. v. Adams,* [121 S. Ct. 1302 (2001)] the Court reversed a decision by the Ninth Circuit Court of Appeals and narrowly interpreted an exemption in the FAA, excluding from its coverage "contracts of employment of seamen, railroad employees, or any other class of workers engaged in foreign or interstate commerce." That exemption, read in tandem with the FAA's provision limiting its application to "any maritime transaction or contract evidencing a transaction involving commerce" indicates that the exemption applies only to certain transportation workers, the Court said.

Even though the Supreme Court has upheld the narrow reading of the FAA exclusion, any company considering adoption of an arbitration clause is advised to seek legal counsel.

§ 16.10   TRENDS

[A]   Executive Search

Rapid societal change, constant pressure from increasing competition, and the cost of training new people are forcing hiring authorities to go outside their own organizations to attract special talent, especially in executive leadership. Executive leadership is provided by key individuals in organizations within the positions of chief executive officer, chief operating officer, chief financial officer, and so forth. Smaller companies that do not have many employees to choose from are becoming primary users of the advanced technology and skills of established executive search professionals who work directly with such companies in the sourcing, recruiting, and employment of executive talent.

The executive search profession is a $6.8 billion industry world-wide that contacts millions of candidates each year and places thousands of executives and technical personnel. Fees range from 20 percent to 35 percent of starting annual salaries plus expenses.

If a company is considering the services of a search firm, it should select a professional search consultant who demonstrates personal maturity, has previous management experience, and can show a track record of success in recruiting key employees, particularly in the company's industry. A consultant with knowledge of the job market and compensation expectations can help focus on what it will take to attract someone to the company. For this selection, it is recommended that the consultant:

- Personally visit the organization, become familiar with the company culture, and be capable of helping the hiring authority define the parameters of the specific position

- Demonstrate high ethics in relation to how he or she identifies which organizations can be sourced for talent

- Possess an extensive database of outside contacts, as well as a broad knowledge of existing employment laws and regulations

- Consider all persons in protected classifications (i.e., women, minorities, and disabled candidates) to the benefit of the organization and the customers they will serve

- Make a commitment to complete the project in a timely manner and guarantee the performance of the new employee for a reasonable period of time

Regardless of whether a company conducts the search in-house or with the help of a consultant, the following are steps to help ensure that the executive search experience is both positive and successful:

- Writing a complete job description for the position

- Defining work style characteristics that are realistic for the "ideal candidate"

- Determining a timetable for the search (ordinarily including a description of how the search will be conducted)

- Determining whether the company will solicit resumes or rely on direct solicitation

- Developing job-related interview questions

- Screening resumes, conducting telephone interviews, or both, before scheduling personal interviews

- Conducting personal interviews with the top and final candidates

- Remaining flexible, within reason, when negotiating compensation packages

- Proceeding at a prudent pace, to avoid making a hasty decision

[B] Outside HR Services

Outside HR services are available from outsourcing firms, professional employer organizations (PEOs), and contingency—or temporary—staffing firms. These services can involve outsourcing the whole department to a service provider, establishing coemployment with a PEO through an employee leasing program, or outsourcing tasks as needed, such as to an HR consulting firm for a compensation study. Each of the following arrangements presents different possibilities for time and cost savings.

1. *Outsourcing*. Using employees of the outsourcing firm to handle the administration of a function, such as payroll processing and insurance claims administration, externally when it is cost-effective to do so.

2. *PEOs*. Using employees leased to the company long term. This arrangement is best suited for firms with five to 500 employees. The PEO can offer rich benefits packages to smaller businesses, which helps with employee retention. Employees performing a certain function are terminated by the client, then hired by the PEO, which leases them to the client to perform the same function at the client location.

3. *Temporary Staffing.* Using temporary employees provided by an outside firm to perform skilled, often highly specialized labor on short notice. Positions may include office help as well as professionals and tend to be provided on a short-term basis. These are employees of the staffing firm, and work is performed at the client location. Human resources contract services are included under this definition.

4. *Consulting.* Consultants generally perform work on a project basis, although retainer or hourly arrangements are also available. They are employees of an outside firm, and much of the work is performed at their offices.

[C]   Outsourcing

Outsourcing involves contracting with an outside firm to administer one or more functions previously handled in-house, such as payroll processing and claims administration. In some cases, entire HR functions, such as benefits administration, are outsourced. A number of tasks within most HR departments are well suited for outsourcing. HR can lend itself well to outsourcing because the tasks in many areas are well defined, are fairly consistent from company to company, and use a common language among most people in the field to describe major tasks.

[1]   Benefits of Outsourcing

Factors such as company size and location and vendor accessibility and specialization influence the decision to outsource.

Any HR department looking to outsource successfully should first analyze current processes and procedures and streamline them as much as possible, then centralize and consolidate services to facilitate comparisons of the cost and efficiency of internal and external alternatives.

Employers that outsource say they do so because outsourcing can:

- Eliminate the need to add permanent staff to fulfill a short-term need;

- Provide access to technical expertise or experience that may be lacking or difficult to develop in-house;

- Avoid the cost of acquiring, updating, and maintaining in-house systems;

- Provide access to new technology;

- Improve HR's capability to fulfill staffing or other needs more quickly;

- Reduce or eliminate overhead, thus reducing operating costs;

- Preserve capital through immediate cost reductions by paying only for services that are needed;

- Help HR maintain or improve service levels without sacrificing efficiency or quality;

- Ease the burdens of or improve legal compliance; and

- Allow HR to shift its focus to support of customer-oriented activities and strategic initiatives.

[2] Risks of Outsourcing

Among the risks associated with outsourcing are loss of control over such things as price, quantity, and quality of service; different interpretations of the service to be provided between the company and the service provider; and reliance on a sole-source provider.

[3] Pre-Outsourcing Audit

The decision to outsource an HR activity or other business function is specific to each company's needs and should not be made hastily. Outsourcing's potential effects on the organization need to be considered and balanced against considerations of cost, efficiency, and quality, as well as HR's strategic goals and long-range objectives.

Conducting a pre-outsourcing audit—to identify strengths and weaknesses by evaluating critical tasks and workflows and determining how service processes might be streamlined or otherwise consolidated, integrated, or changed via outsourcing—is a recommended first step that should lead to more informed decision making.

Two especially important sets of questions to ask during a pre-outsourcing audit are:

1. What are HR's strategic goals and objectives? What does HR contribute to other departments?

2. Who performs the various HR functions? Where are the activities conducted? How often? At what cost?

[4] Future of Outsourcing

Outsourcing many of the core HR functions will continue to grow, according to the 2006-2007 Society of Human Resources Management Workplace Forecast. This is due in part to the shift in the HR function from operational to strategic. HR executives are participating more in their companies' overall strategic planning and cost reduction decisions, and utilizing outsourcing companies to handle functions such as background checks, benefits administration, and temporary staffing. There will be a high demand for those that can provide efficiencies to the HR function without sacrificing appropriate service.

[D] Professional Employer Organizations

Professional employer organizations (PEOs) are an upgraded version of employee leasing. The emphasis, however, is on a long-term rather than temporary relationship. The PEO industry regards itself and its client companies as "co-employers." Employee leasing is neither a temporary help nor an outsourcing arrangement. Leased employees perform work for only one client of the leasing company on a routine basis. The leased relationship often originates when a client terminates all employees in a specific department (e.g., information technology) and a leasing company hires the terminated employees. The individuals are then leased back to the client and perform functions identical to the functions they performed as employees of the client company. The responsibilities of direction and control are usually shared by the employee leasing company and the client company.

PEOs are not all alike. Some offer minimal services, such as health care benefits and payroll processing, while others provide more extensive services, which might include recruitment and screening and a variety of training (leadership, safety). In terms of size, PEOs are best suited for companies with about five to 500 employees. PEOs can afford to offer rich benefits packages to smaller businesses because of their economies of scale. According to the National Association of Professional Employer Organizations, two to three million Americans are currently co-employed with a PEO, and the industry is growing 20 to 30 percent per year.

The following states require PEOs to be licensed: Arkansas, Florida, Illinois, Kentucky, Maine, Montana, New Hampshire, New Mexico, Nevada, Oregon, South Carolina, Tennessee, Texas, Utah, and Vermont. Rhode Island requires registration of PEOs.

There are some potential downsides to using a PEO because PEO costs may creep up over time. In fact, with any type of outsourcing arrangement, you must proactively manage the relationship. To determine if you need a PEO—if HR issues such as recruitment, training, and bookkeeping now get little attention because you don't have time for them, or if you cannot afford an adequate benefits package—a PEO is worth considering. Be sure it is financially strong and offers the services you need.

[E] Contingency (Temporary) Staffing

To fill labor gaps, more organizations are using temporary employees rather than hiring new people to join their "regular" staff. According to the American Staffing Association, the average number of individuals employed daily in temporary help jobs was 2.96 million. Temporary employment represents about 2.2 percent of the average daily employment in this country.

There are advantages to temporary employment, not the least of which is the access, often at a moment's notice, to skilled, often highly specialized labor for which the company has assumed no long-term commitment. While temporary employees are mainly thought of as office help, about 21 percent work in professional capacities—such as accountants, attorneys, sales and marketing professionals, as well as those in middle and senior management—and 35.1 percent are in production, laborer, craft, and service positions. The most persistent myth of temporary employment is that such employees can be terminated without thought or consequence. Employers who believe this are placing their company at risk, in the form of liability arising out of an illegal employment action, such as a termination in violation of Title VII of the Civil Rights Act of 1964, the ADA, or the ADEA.

The determination of liability is dependent upon the relationship between the employee, the placement agency, and the hiring employer. The amount of responsibility the hiring employer has depends on the amount of control it assumes over day-to-day management of the temporary employee. Included in the realm of control are such activities as negotiating wages and benefits, evaluating performance, and rewarding, promoting, disciplining, and discharging employees. Typically, when a temporary employee sues, the employment agency and the hiring employer are named as codefendants. The extent to which the hiring employer has acted to control the employment relationship before the suit makes all the difference in establishing joint liability.

To establish liability, the hiring employer must at least be considered a joint employer. This does not appear to be especially difficult to prove. For example, the FMLA specifically defines the joint employer relationship as "where two or more businesses exercise some control over the work or working conditions of the employee." The FMLA regulations also specifically state that "joint employment will ordinarily be found to exist when a temporary or leasing agency supplies employees to a second employer."

Even though a temporary employee performing the job is employed by a temporary staffing agency, the client company where temporary employees work can be a "joint employer." In December 1997, the EEOC issued its enforcement guidance titled "Application of EEO Laws to Contingent Workers Placed by Temporary Employment Agencies and Other Staffing Firms." The enforcement guidance concludes that "both staffing firms and their clients share EEO responsibilities toward these workers." The EEOC enforcement guidance is merely persuasive authority and not binding on the courts; however, the courts often defer to EEOC guidance. Laws covered within the EEOC enforcement of Title VII are the ADEA, the ADA, and the Equal Pay Act. Under these laws, client companies and temporary staffing agencies are joint employers.

The EEOC enforcement guidance is clear that there is no defense if a temporary staffing agency participates in a discriminatory staffing request from the client company. If both the client company and the temporary staffing agency discriminated against a temporary employee, the temporary employee may seek relief from both joint employers.

The employment relationship between the company and any temporary employees needs to be defined carefully at the beginning of the hire so that it is well defined in advance who is responsible for defending any litigation that may arise.

Exhibit 16.1   Mandated Benefits: 2009 Compliance Guide

Exhibit 16.1
Acceptable and Unacceptable Questions to Ask Applicants

Acceptable	Subject	Unacceptable
Name "Have you ever used another name?" or "Is any additional information relative to change of name, or nickname necessary to enable a check on your work and education record? If yes, please explain."	**Name**	Maiden name
Place of residence	**Residence**	"Do you own or rent your home?"
Statement that photograph may be required after employment	**Physical Description Photograph**	Questions as to applicant's height and weight Require applicant to affix a photograph to application Request applicant, at his or her option, to submit a photograph Require a photograph after interview but before employment Videotaping interviews
Statement by employer that offer may be made contingent on applicant's passing a job related physical examination "Can you perform (*specific task*)?"	**Physical or Mental Disability**	Questions regarding applicant's general medical condition, state of health, or illnesses Questions regarding receipt of workers' compensation "Do you have any physical or mental disabilities or handicaps?"
Statement by employer of regular days, hours, or shifts to be worked	**Religion**	Questions regarding applicant's religion Religious days observed or "Does your religion prevent you from working weekends or holidays?"
Job-related questions about convictions, except those that have been sealed, expunged, or statutorily eradicated	**Arrest, Criminal Record**	Arrest record or "Have you ever been arrested?"
Questions regarding relevant skills acquired during applicant's U.S. military service	**Military Service**	General questions regarding military services, such as dates and type of discharge Questions regarding service in a foreign military

Exhibit 16.1 (cont'd)

Acceptable	Subject	Unacceptable
"Please list job-related organizations, clubs, professional societies, or other associations to which you belong. You may omit those that indicate your race, religious creed, color, disability, marital status, national origin, ancestry, sex, or age." Be sure to include any class protected by state statute.	**Organizations, Activities**	"List all organizations, clubs, societies, and lodges to which you belong."
"By whom were you referred for a position here?" Names of persons willing to provide professional and character references for applicant	**References**	Questions regarding the applicant's former employers or acquaintances that elicit information specifying the applicant's race, religious creed, color, disability, marital status, national origin, ancestry, sex, age, or any class protected by state statute.
Name and address of person to be notified in case of accident or emergency	**Notice in Case of Emergency**	Name, address, and relationship of relative to be notified in case of accident or emergency
Statement that hire is subject to verification that applicant meets legal age requirements "If hired, can you show proof of age?" "Are you over 18 years of age?" "If under 18, can you, after employment, submit a work permit?"	**Age**	Age Birth date Dates of attendance or completion of elementary or high school Questions that tend to identify applicants over age 40
"Can you, after employment, submit verification of your legal right to work in the United States?" or a statement that such proof may be required after a decision is made to hire the candidate	**Birthplace and Citizenship**	Birthplace of applicant, applicant's parents, spouse, or other relatives "Are you a U.S. citizen?" or citizenship of applicant, applicant's parents, spouse, or other relatives Requirements that applicant produce naturalization, first papers, or alien card before a decision to hire
Languages applicant reads, speaks, or writes, if use of a language other than English is relevant to the job for which applicant is applying	**National Origin**	Nationality, lineage, ancestry, national origin, descent, or parentage of applicant, applicant's parents, or spouse "What is your mother tongue?" Language commonly used by applicant How applicant acquired the ability to read, write, or speak a foreign language

Exhibit 16.1　　　　　　　　　　　　　　　　　　Mandated Benefits: 2009 Compliance Guide

Exhibit 16.1 (cont'd)

Acceptable	Subject	Unacceptable
Name and address of parent or guardian if applicant is a minor Statement of company policy regarding work assignment of employees who are related	**Sex, Marital Status, Family**	Applicant's sex Applicant's marital status Number, ages, or both, of children or dependents Provisions for child care Questions regarding pregnancy, child bearing, or birth control Name and address of relative, spouse, or children of an adult applicant "With whom do you reside?" or "Do you live with your parents?"
	Race, Color	Applicant's race or color Applicant's complexion or color of skin, eyes, or hair
	Investigative Report	Any report that would indicate information that is otherwise illegal to ask (e.g., marital status, age, or residency)

Exhibit 16.2
Applicant's Authorization to Release Information

I hereby authorize all past employers and educational institutions to release the information listed below to ABC Co., its employees, representatives, and agents for use in determining my qualifications for employment.

Please release and verify the following information:

Past Employers
Salary history
Dates of employment
Positions held
Responsibilities and duties performed
Reason for leaving
Eligibility for rehire
Performance

Educational Institutions
Years of attendance
Degree obtained
Transcript

In addition to authorizing the release of the information above, I hereby fully waive any rights or claims I have or may have against ABC Co., all past employers and educational institutions, and their employees, representatives, and agents and release ABC Co., all past employers and educational institutions, and their employees, representatives, and agents from any and all liability, claims, or damages that may directly or indirectly result from the use, disclosure, or release of any information by any person or party, whether such information is favorable or unfavorable to me.

I acknowledge that I have read this authorization and release, fully understand it, and voluntarily agree to its provisions.

_____   _____

Signature   Date

Name: _____

Social Security Number: _____

Exhibit 16.3
Sample Job Offer Letter—Exempt

[Date]

CONFIDENTIAL

[Name]

[Address]

Dear _____:

We are delighted to extend to you this offer of employment with [Company name] as [Title], effective [Date], or such other date as may be mutually agreed upon. This offer is contingent upon our completion of a satisfactory [background investigation and a] preemployment physical, including drug and alcohol testing. The purpose of this letter is to confirm the terms of this employment offer, including reporting relationships, compensation, and employee benefits.

As [Title], you will be located in our [Location] office, reporting to [Position].

Compensation

Your entry compensation will comprise a base salary of $[Annual amount], payable in [Frequency] increments. In addition, you will be eligible for an annual salary review, which generally takes place on or around your anniversary date each year.

Employee Benefits

As [Title], you will be entitled to [number] holidays, [number] days of vacation, and [number] days of sick leave per year.

You will also be enrolled in the Company's group insurance program, which includes life, accidental death and dismemberment, and health benefits. Basic life insurance coverage will be equal to one time your base salary up to a maximum of $[Amount]. You may also enroll for supplemental, employee paid life insurance coverage, for yourself and/or your dependent(s). If you elect the supplemental and/or dependent coverage, you will pay the premium cost through payroll deduction.

You may also participate in the Company's health benefits plan. A variety of plans are offered, and the cost will vary with the plan you select. The cost is partially paid by the Company, and the remainder is paid by you through payroll deduction. Your plan coverage begins on the first day of the month following the month you begin work, or on the first day of the month if you start work on the first day of the month.

You may participate in the [Company name] 401(k) plan. Tax-deferred employee contributions can begin immediately upon the start of your employment with us.

You will receive a complete benefits package with enrollment forms and plan descriptions during your first week of employment. [Company name] reserves the right to change, add to, modify, or eliminate any or all of these employment benefits.

Preemployment Requirements

[Company name] requires all applicants to pass a preemployment physical, including drug and alcohol testing. The physical is conducted at [Name and address of medical facility]. Our [Title], [Name], will contact you to set up a mutually convenient appointment and will provide all necessary information and forms.

Pursuant to the Immigration Reform and Control Act, our company is required to verify the identity and employment eligibility of all new hires. In order to comply with this legal obligation, you must complete an Employment Eligibility Verification Form I-9 within three days of hire. We have enclosed a Form I-9 for your review. Please note that you will need to provide either (i) one document from "List A" *or* (ii) one document from "List B" *and* one document from "List C" of the form (see page two of the enclosed I-9 Form). If you anticipate having difficulty completing the Form I-9 or producing the required documents, please contact me.

Employment Conditions

Employment with [Company name] is "at will," meaning that either [Company name] or you may terminate your employment at any time for any reason whatsoever or for no reason, with or without notice.

Acceptance of Employment

Upon your acceptance of this offer of employment, please acknowledge your agreement with the terms set forth in this letter by signing in the designated space below and returning the original to us. A copy of this letter is enclosed for your records.

We look forward to your joining us and to your success with [Company Name]. If you have any questions, please do not hesitate to contact me.

Sincerely,

Signature

Director, Human Resources

ACCEPTED:

_____   _____

Employee Name   Date

Chapter 17
Layoffs and Termination

§ 17.01 AUDIT QUESTIONS

1. When layoffs are necessary, is close attention paid to the demographic patterns of any protected class (e.g., race, sex, age) that are created when selecting employees for termination?

2. Is care taken to ensure that the workforce is properly notified well in advance of the termination date if a layoff will affect large numbers of employees or a significant percentage of them?

3. When terminations are necessary, are severance pay and outplacement assistance considered as a means of demonstrating goodwill and providing assistance to those affected?

4. Has the severance pay plan been amended to comply with Internal Revenue Code Section 409A?

5. Is care taken to avoid language used in corporate documents and conversations with employees that would suggest guarantees of continued employment or progressive discipline?

6. When terminations occur, is paperwork provided that informs employees of their rights under the Consolidated Omnibus Budget Reconciliation Act of 1985?

Note: Consistent "yes" answers to the above questions suggest that the organization is applying effective management policies and/or complying with federal regulations. "No" answers indicate that problem areas exist and should be addressed immediately.

Employers today are faced with considerable risk when making layoff and termination decisions. Ways to reduce employer risk without limiting management discretion do exist, but they require careful analysis of the situation not only from the employer's perspective but also from the employee's perspective. Employees are becoming increasingly knowledgeable and assertive about their rights. For a company to reduce its exposure to lawsuits, it should be able to document objective reasons for termination and objective selection criteria for identifying employees to be terminated. This chapter discusses employer responsibilities and employees' rights with regard to layoffs and terminations.

§ 17.02   LAYOFFS

Layoffs are reductions in force, either temporary or permanent. Companies use layoffs to respond to a variety of situations, including downturns in business, mergers and acquisitions, cancellations of orders or contracts, and natural disasters that cause damage to a facility. When facing any of these situations, the company may choose to offer its employees other options; for example, the company may want to offer workers unpaid leave of absence, extend a shutdown, or shorten workweeks to relieve the need for a formal layoff.

[A]   Layoff Policy

Any layoff should be designed carefully. To protect the company from possible legal challenges, a layoff policy should be considered before implementing a downsizing. There are two schools of thought on layoff policies. A layoff policy can provide guidelines for decision making around layoffs that are consistent throughout an organization. However, some feel that layoff policies lock organizations into certain obligations for every layoff. Whether or not a written policy exists, efforts should be made to follow a relatively consistent approach to executing layoffs to ensure the process is not perceived to be discriminatory. If there is any reason to believe that the company will be subject to litigation, human resources (HR) directors can discuss their layoff policy with qualified counsel before implementation.

Criteria used to determine which employees are selected for layoff should be written, understood by supervisors and employees, and consistently followed. Every layoff decision should be documented. Supervisors must be able to explain and justify how the decisions were made. Companies should be sensitive to possible discrimination issues arising from the layoff. If a particular group—women, minorities, or older workers, for example—seems disproportionately affected by a layoff, the company should review the criteria to be sure they are not inadvertently discriminatory or creating a situation of adverse impact.

Many employers use seniority as a critical factor in determining who is to be laid off, possibly because it is easy to administer. Title VII of the Civil Rights Act of 1964 has a specific exemption from discrimination for a seniority system, because that criterion is not a discrimination issue; everyone has a start date, regardless of who he or she is. However, there are drawbacks to using a straight seniority system. A straight seniority system restricts management's right to consider other factors, such as overall performance, and useful job skills. Because there are usually long-term ramifications to a layoff, management is advised to consider many factors in the choice of selection criteria in addition to ease of administration. Other factors that may be considered should be as objective as possible. Objective criteria can lessen employee's suspicion of bias, and may also lessen the risk of unlawful discrimination. An example of an objective performance criteria is attendance. Criteria may also be specific to a department or work group, such as the number of accidents or traffic violations as criteria for driver positions.

The policy should also include a statement about whether or how individuals will be rehired. Committing to rehire can severely limit the company's future options, so it should consider this policy carefully. Such a policy also requires ongoing administration.

In 1996, one court held that an employer's failure to rehire a protected-age former employee, who had been discharged pursuant to a reduction in force, for positions that existed at the time of discharge and for which she was qualified, when coupled with the employer's hiring of younger workers to fill those positions, gave rise to a rebuttable inference that the employer intended to discriminate against the employee on the basis of age. The court held that the employers must consider protected-age employees who apply for jobs for which they are qualified and which are available at the time they were discharged along with all other candidates and cannot deny the protected-age employees positions on the basis of their age. The court held that this applies even though the Age Discrimination in Employment Act of 1967 (ADEA) does not mandate that employers establish an interdepartmental transfer program during the course of a reduction in force, does not require discharge of younger employees so that protected-age employees can be hired, and does not impose any added burden on employers to transfer or rehire laid-off protected-age workers as a matter of course.

[B] Worker Adjustment and Retraining Notification Act

If an employer with 100 or more employees has to close a plant or work site or terminate a significant number of employees within the organization, it must comply with specific notification requirements under the Worker Adjustment and Retraining Notification Act of 1988 (WARN Act). Under the WARN Act, notice is required when 50 or more employees at one site will lose their jobs within a 30-day period and those employees make up at least one-third of the site's workforce. This is known as the "33 percent rule." For layoffs of 500 or more employees (considered a mass layoff), notification is also required, but the 33 percent rule does not apply. Notice includes:

- Providing employees with *written* notification of a plant closing or layoff;

- Providing written notice to each affected employee or union, if unionized; and

- Notifying the state's dislocated worker unit and the chief elected official of the local government where the plant or site is located.

In determining whether it meets the minimum size requirement for the purposes of the WARN Act, a company may count only those individuals who have worked for six months or longer within the last 12 months and for 20 or more hours per week at the time of the layoff. An employer will also be covered by the WARN Act if it has 100 employees (full- and part-time) who in the aggregate, work at least 4,000 hours per week. In determining whether the minimum required number of employees will lose their jobs, a company need not count part-time employees (those who work less than 20 hours per week), retirees, employees who resigned or were terminated for cause, and certain employees who are offered transfers with the employer.

These requirements apply to planned layoffs or shutdowns that result in a loss of work for more than six months, reductions in work hours, and terminations. The WARN Act defines a reduction in hours of work of more than 50 percent during each month of any six-month period as an "employment loss." In the context of WARN, an employment termination, other than a discharge for cause, voluntary departure, or retirement, is also considered an "employment loss."

A plant closing will also trigger the notice requirement. The WARN Act defines a plant closing as the temporary or permanent shutdown of either (1) a single employment site, or (2) one or more work units within a single employment site, if the employment loss at the single employment site during any 30-day period results in the termination of employment for 50 or more employees.

Failure to comply with the WARN Act can result in significant penalties. The Act provides for a civil penalty of up to $500 per day for each day of failure to provide notice to the local government unit. Employers will also have to provide back pay to each affected employee equal to the amount of pay and benefits for the period of the violation. The length of the back pay penalty period will not exceed one-half the number of days the employee was actually employed by the company. In the case of a lawsuit, attorney fees may also be awarded to the prevailing party. In at least one case, an employer who failed to give employees 60 days' advance notice, but paid them their full compensation and benefits for 60 days after the plant shutdown, did not violate the WARN Act. [Long v Dunlop Sports Group Americas, Inc, 506 F.3d 299 (4th Cir. October 29, 2007)]

[1]   Providing Notice

Employers must provide employees with appropriate notice of plant closings or layoffs before the scheduled date of the closing or mass layoff. All affected employees, full-time and part-time, must be notified. Generally, the company must give employees 60 days' advance written notice. In certain situations, employers cannot follow through on the plant closing or layoff until the 60-day notification period has expired. The notices must be in writing, and must be sent to all employees, whether unionized or not. Additional requirements exist for notifying union employees. The notice for nonunion and union employees must include the following information:

- The name and address of the employment site where the layoff or plant closing is occurring.

- A statement indicating whether the planned closing or mass layoff is expected to be temporary or permanent.

- A statement that the entire facility is closing, if that is the case.

- The expected date of closing or mass layoff and the date on which the employee will be separated from the company (or, if a specific date is not known, the anticipated schedule of layoffs).

- A statement indicating whether bumping rights exist.

  Note. Usually, when seniority is the primary selection criterion for layoff decisions, employees with the least amount of seniority are laid off, and those with the longest service are retained. However, when senior employees are targeted for layoff because their jobs are nonessential, bumping policies would permit a targeted senior employee to displace a junior worker from an essential job.

- The name and telephone number of a company designee who can provide additional information.

The employer may include additional information that would be useful to the employee if it so chooses.

In unionized workplaces, the notice to the representative of affected employees must include the following additional information:

- The job titles or positions affected by the planned closing or layoff and the names of workers holding these positions.

Employers must provide separate written notices to the state's dislocated worker unit and to the chief elected official of the local government. These notices must contain the following information:

- The name and address of the site where the planned closing or mass layoff is expected to occur.

- A statement indicating whether the mass layoff is expected to be temporary or permanent.

- Information regarding the facility closing, if appropriate.

- The job titles of positions affected and the number of employees in each job classification.

- The expected date of the first separation and the expected schedule for separations.

- Whether bumping rights exist.

- The name, address, and chief elected officer of each union, if any, as well as the name of the union representing affected employees.

- The name and telephone number of a company official who can provide additional information.

Some states have specific notification laws in addition to the WARN Act's requirements. (See **Exhibit 17.1** for a list of specific state requirements.)

[2]   Serving Notice

Employers are required to use reasonable methods for providing notice of mass layoff or plant closing to employees. Some of these acceptable methods include first-class mail, personal delivery with optional signed receipt, and if the employees are notified directly by the employer, insertion of a notice into each pay envelope. These notices should be prepared by the appropriate employer designee, such as the human resources (HR) director or the plant manager.

[3]   Exceptions to the Notice Requirements

Specific work situations trigger exceptions to the notice requirements.

[a]   Temporary Facilities

Sixty-day advance notices are not required for closings of temporary facilities, if employees were hired with the understanding that their employment was only temporary and meant to last as long as the facility was planned to remain open.

[b]   Agricultural and Construction Work

Employers hiring temporary seasonal workers are not required to give notice, provided that employees understand at the time of hire that their employment is only temporary. Notice must be provided, however, to employees who work on tasks continuously throughout most of the calendar year and who are not considered temporary.

[c]   Contract-Related Work

Certain contractual jobs may be exempt from notification, depending on whether the contract or order is part of a long-term relationship.

[d]   Strikes and Lockouts

Written notice is not required when a closing or mass layoff brings about a lockout or strike that is not intended to evade the law's requirements. Written notice is not necessary when a person is being permanently replaced because he or she is an economic striker. As defined by the National Labor Relations Act, an *economic striker* is a worker who refuses to work in order to put pressure on an employer after the parties have failed to reach agreement during collective bargaining.

In the event of strikes or lockouts, notice must be given to the following employees:

- Nonstrikers who are at the same site

- Members of nonstriking bargaining units

- Employees who are not striking but will be affected by a closing or mass layoff as an indirect or direct result of the strike or lockout

[e]   A Reduction of the Notice Period

In some situations, employers may order a plant closing or mass layoff before the end of the required 60-day notification period. Such employers must prove that they have met the requirements for the exception, must provide as much notice as possible, and must explain in a statement the reasons for reducing the notification period. Considered an exception to the requirements, this reduction applies to two exceptions:

1. *The faltering-company exception.* Applies to plant closings only. To qualify for this exception, the company must have been actively seeking capital through loans, issuance of stock or bonds, or business at the time the 60-day notice would have been required. The company must have realistically pursued the opportunity to obtain the financing or business necessary to avoid closing or layoff and must have reasonably and in good faith believed that giving notice would have prevented the company from gaining the finances or new business.

2. *The unforeseeable-business-circumstance exception.* Applies to both mass layoffs and plant closings that were caused by business situations not reasonably foreseeable at the time the 60-day notice would have been required. The WARN Act does not fully define "not reasonably foreseeable." It lists only limited meanings, such as a sudden, dramatic, and unexpected action or condition outside the employer's control. Examples are the unexpected termination of a contract, a strike at a major supplier, or an important aspect of a business situation whose outcome is not reasonably foreseeable. Some examples of an important aspect of a business situation are an unanticipated and dramatic major economic downturn or a government-ordered closing of an employment site that occurs without prior notice. The employer is not required to predict accurately general economic conditions that may also affect demand for its products or services. However, the employer must exercise commercially reasonable business judgment.

The unforeseeable-business-circumstance exception requires that each claim of unforeseeable business circumstance be examined separately and meet the employer's business judgment. The rule implies that the employer, in predicting the demands of its particular market, must have exercised such business judgment as would a similarly situated employer.

[f]   Natural Disasters

This exception applies to both mass layoffs and plant closings. Natural disasters include events such as floods, earthquakes, hurricanes, tornadoes, droughts, storms, tidal waves, or similar effects of nature. To use this as an exception, the employer must be able to show how the natural disaster contributed to the resulting mass layoff or plant closing.

[g]   Other Exceptions

If the posted notice provided to employees about plant closing or layoffs is changed and the event is postponed, the employer must provide the following additional notification:

- If the postponement is for less than 60 days, additional notice should be given as soon as possible, referring to the date given in the original notice, the new, postponed date of the action, and reasons for the postponement.

- If the postponement is for 60 days or more, the notice should be treated as a new notice, and the company should comply with all the specified requirements again.

- A rolling notice (i.e., periodic notice about impending layoff or plant closure) is unacceptable and is considered an evasion of the law. Time extensions for mass layoffs lasting more than six months require 60 days' advance notice. An employer is eligible for this exception only if the employer could not reasonably foresee at the time of the layoff that business conditions would require an extension or if the employer gave written notice as soon as it was reasonably foreseeable that the layoff would extend beyond six months.

The Department of Labor, which regulates the WARN Act, has posted a "Guide to Advance Notice of Closing and Layoffs" on its Web site: *www.dol.gov*.

[C]   Options in Lieu of Layoffs

If a company believes the layoffs are only temporary, it can consider the following to minimize or avoid the layoff:

- *Work sharing.* An arrangement that allows remaining employees to divide up and share the work to be done after some jobs are lost and some employees are laid off. Employees' hourly pay remains the same but reflects the reduced hours. Some state unemployment compensation laws allow employees to collect partial unemployment benefits during a work-sharing period.

- *Reduced workweek.* Some hourly employees may want to work part time or reduce the number of days they work, and the total number of hours and pay are reduced. In this case, work may be consolidated or shifted to others.

- *Reduced schedule.* Also known as "skip week," a reduced schedule allows employees to work only every other week. Some states allow employees to collect unemployment during skip weeks.

- *Leave of absence without pay.* A voluntary leave of absence without pay may be offered to help reduce the workforce. Some employees may choose to take some extended time off, for example, over the summer or during the holidays, if the employee knows he or she is entitled to return to work at the end of the leave.

- *Mandatory vacation.* Requiring employees to use accrued vacation or paid time off banks.

- *Reduced pay.* A reduction in pay is most effective if it is shared by all employees, including management. This alternative may be acceptable to employees, particularly if their unemployment benefits during a layoff would be less than their reduced pay.

- *Eliminate overtime.* Mandate the elimination of overtime in the affected units. If necessary, temporarily reassign staff to cover work previously done by overtime.

- *Early retirement.* To reduce staff, a company may want to consider developing attractive retirement incentives for employees who are about to reach retirement age. The advantage is that employers can cut costs without requiring employees to leave their jobs involuntarily. These packages, however, cannot be offered selectively, or the company faces issues of age discrimination. The risk is that the company may lose some employees it would prefer to keep. Early retirement benefits are legitimate options, but the HR director must be cautious about how these programs are designed. If this option is exercised, HR directors should seek professional assistance with the program design.

The impact of salary reductions on exempt staff is an important consideration. While reducing pay is an acceptable cost-cutting measure, the employer needs to be careful not to correlate cut hours with cut pay, as the exempt employees may lose their exempt-from-overtime status.

Benefits continuation is important to remember. In some cases of layoff or for all terminations except a termination for gross misconduct, the company must offer continuation of group health insurance benefits under COBRA. (See **Chapter 7** for further discussion of COBRA.)

[D]   Severance Pay

Although severance pay is not required in most states, many employers provide it to ensure some level of financial security, at least temporarily, to employees who are involuntarily separated from the company. This not only eases the transition for the employee, but it also generates goodwill for the employer. According to the 2005 Severance Survey published by Compensation Resources, Inc., over 70 percent of employers provide severance pay in some circumstances; 56 percent of companies have a formal severance policy.

[1]   Employee Retirement Income Security Act of 1974

Even a limited, one-time severance payment would generally be considered a benefit plan under the Employee Retirement Income Security Act of 1974 (ERISA). Consequently, there are certain plan characteristics that may minimize ERISA's impact. In addition, depending upon design choices, these plans may require current cash expenditures but may not generate current tax deductions. To minimize ERISA's impact, the program should meet the following general criteria.

First, if the payments are provided as part of a limited program of terminations of a number, percentage, or class of employees specified in advance, the payout requirement should be extended to 24 months from the later of termination or normal retirement age. A written plan document is required and the terminations must be completed by a scheduled date or event, but the group of employees would not need to be limited to key, highly compensated, or management employees. For example, the program could specify a division or operating unit as eligible. The program could also specify a particular age group of employees. Note, however, that if a fairly large number of involuntary layoffs occur, a "public relations" problem could result if some employees receive a severance package and others do not.

Second, the funding, vesting, participation, and more detailed reporting requirements of pension plans do not apply to severance pay plans that meet the criteria outlined above. Because they are not pension benefit plans, severance pay plans are considered welfare benefit plans for ERISA purposes. Therefore, employers could be required to provide summary plan descriptions and file annual Form 5500s. However, the reporting requirements do not apply at all if the plans are unfunded (which severance plans generally are) and they have fewer than 100 participants.

Recently a court case was decided based on whether severance plans are vested or not. In *Gonzales v. Phelps Dodge Miami, Inc.*, [2008 U.S. App. LEXIS 9960 (9th Cir. May 1, 2008] the employees claimed that their employer could not terminate the severance plan because the benefits were described in the employee handbook and were therefore vested. The court disagreed because the handbook, severance plan document, and SPD did not expressly vest the severance benefit. In fact, the documents clearly reserved the right for the employer to amend or terminate the plan.

[2] Taxation of Severance Benefits

The fact that severance pay plans are considered welfare benefit plans for ERISA purposes does not automatically mean they will be considered welfare plans for tax purposes. Some courts have held that a welfare plan that contains any elements of a deferred compensation program will be treated as a deferred compensation plan subject to the deduction rules of Section 404 of the Internal Revenue Code (Code), not Section 162 or Section 419. Therefore, for severance pay plans that are not qualified under Section 401(a), the deduction may not be taken by the employer until the employee realizes income for the benefit received. This does not make the severance pay plan a pension benefit subject to ERISA, but it does change the deductibility of its funding under the Code.

The probable form of any proposed severance pay plan for early retirees will be payments based on pay and service, rather than a flat benefit amount. For that reason, it is possible that, for deduction purposes, funding such a plan may be viewed by the Internal Revenue Service as contributions to a nonqualified deferred compensation plan. Therefore, in these cases, deductions to the employer for any severance payments will be delayed until payments are actually received and taken as taxable income by the former employee.

As a result, there may be timing differences between any liability recorded for financial reporting purposes when the severance pay commitment is made and a deduction being taken for actual payment. By definition, however, the difference would not exceed more than a three-year period that might be spanned by the maximum 24-month payout period dictated to minimize ERISA, unless the company decides to extend the payout past normal retirement age. Whether the employer chooses to set aside a fund for these payments will depend upon a comparison of cash-flow needs and financial statement needs during the intervening period.

[3] Determining the Amount of Severance Benefits

Aside from the regulatory issues, the benefit to be paid must be determined. For top executives, the level rarely exceeds the twice annual compensation limit to avoid becoming an ERISA pension plan.

For other executives, nine months to one year of annual pay is a common limit. For most employees, one week of pay per year of service is common. The employer's situation may dictate some other benefit amount or formula. Within the twice-annual-compensation limit, no regulatory requirements restrict how much may be awarded, except in the case of Chapter 11 bankruptcy filings (see below). Many employers set minimum severance amounts as follows: four weeks for executives and officers, two weeks for all other employees.

Some employers opt to provide continuation of current employer-paid health coverage following employee termination. Typically, this coverage extends to the earlier of Medicare eligibility (age 65), length of severance payout, or whenever coverage is available from a subsequent employer.

Other program design decisions include whether to pay a lump sum or make periodic payments (and how such "extended payroll" amounts will affect other benefits); whether to pay a guaranteed amount or period, or to stop or offset payments if the employees are employed elsewhere; and whether to limit the existence of the plan by reserving the right to unilaterally amend or terminate the plan at any time, or to set the lifespan of the plan from its beginning. Once these issues are decided, employers must consider how the rules regarding income and FICA (Social Security) tax withholding will be applied to payments. The rules and limitations of the plan should be fully but carefully disclosed to employees to avoid mistaken expectations or unanticipated claims in the future.

[4] Bankruptcy Abuse Prevention and Consumer Protection Act of 2005

On April 20, 2005, President Bush signed the Bankruptcy Abuse Prevention and Consumer Protection Act of 2005 (BAPCPA; Pub. L. No. 109-8, 119 Stat. 23). As a result, after October 17, 2005, the ability of companies that file for a Chapter 11 bankruptcy to pay severance benefits to insiders will be severely limited. Under the 2005 Bankruptcy Law, insiders are those who "control" the company, including officers and directors. After a company files for Chapter 11 bankruptcy, the court may only approve severance payments to insiders if the payment is part of a program that generally applies to all full-time employees. Payments to insiders are capped at 10 times the amount of the average (arithmetic mean) payment to nonmanagement employees during the calendar year in which the insider's payment is made. The BAPCPA practically eliminates executive-only severance plans for companies in bankruptcy.

[5] Internal Revenue Code Section 409A

The American Jobs Creation Act of 2004 [Pub. L. No. 108-357, 118 Stat. 1418], signed into law on October 22, 2004, added Section 409A to the Code. The major substance of Code Section 409A is that nonqualified deferred compensation is taxable at the earliest time the deferred compensation is not subject to a substantial risk of forfeiture (i.e., at the time it becomes "vested") unless the deferred compensation plan satisfies precise requirements. (For further information on nonqualified deferred compensation plans, see **Chapter 27**.) Failure to comply with Code Section 409A can result in immediate taxation of deferred amounts, excise taxes, and other penalties.

Severance pay plans were not specifically excluded from Code Section 409A. The final regulations for Code Section 409A provide that some separation pay will be treated as nonqualified deferred compensation and some will not. If the separation pay and severance pay plan fall under the exemptions of the final 409A regulations, the severance pay will escape the Code Section 409A requirements. However, if the severance plan is merely a replacement or substitute for amounts deferred under a separate nonqualified deferred compensation plan, the purported severance plan will be deemed to be a plan providing for the deferral of compensation, and thus be required to comply with all of 409A's requirements. Note that Code Section 409A refers to "service recipient" and "service provider"; for purposes of this description of severance pay plans, we will utilize the terms *employer* and *employee* (or *former employee*) instead.

One way to avoid application of Code Section 409A to severance plans is through the use of the short-term deferral rule. Many severance pay plans provide for the payment of severance immediately upon termination or shortly thereafter. The short-term deferral rule requires that the payment of the severance amounts be completed within 2½ months after the end of the year in which the severance benefits "cease to be subject to a substantial risk of forfeiture." For most severance plan purposes, severance pay is provided upon an involuntary termination of employment; this becomes the date on which the benefits "cease to be subject to a substantial risk of forfeiture." Note that if there are other requirements for obtaining severance pay, for example, the signing of a waiver or release, the benefits will not cease to be subject to a substantial risk of forfeiture until the waiver is signed (or other requirement is fulfilled). If the severance pay plan specifies a payment date or event that is longer than the 2½ month grace period, the plan will automatically be subject to Code Section 409A, even if the payment is actually made within the 2½ month grace period.

However, if the short-term deferral rule cannot be used, employers need to be aware of the grace period under 409A. If the severance pay plan does not specify a date for payment (e.g., payment will be made as soon as possible after termination), the employer must make the payment no later than 90 days after the employment termination date (or date when the benefits "cease to be subject to substantial risk of forfeiture") or the payment will violate the grace period under Code Section 409A. However, if the severance pay plan states that payment will be made on the 90th day following the date of termination, then the employer actually has until December 31 of the year of termination to make the payment and remain within the 409A grace period.

In addition, the regulations provide that certain "separation pay arrangements" (the term used in the regulations to describe severance pay plans) will not be deemed nonqualified deferred compensation plans if they meet one or more of the following exemptions:

1. Collectively bargained separation pay arrangements or window plan benefits provided to bargaining unit employees;

2. Plans that provide for separation pay upon an actual involuntary separation from service or pursuant to a window program established by the employer, provided the amount of separation pay does not exceed two times the lesser of (i) the annual compensation for the calendar year preceding the calendar year of separation, or (ii) the amount of compensation that can be taken into account for qualified pension plans under Code Section 401(a)(17) (which for 2008 is $230,000) and, further provided, that the separation pay is paid no later than December 31 of the second calendar year following the calendar year in which the separation from service occurred (the regulations also define "actual separation" to mean that no further services will be performed after the separation date, or the level of services will permanently decline to 20 percent or less of the average level of services the employee performed during the immediately preceding 36-month period);

3. "Limited time reimbursements" that are otherwise excludable from gross income, including (i) certain reimbursements for expenses that the employee can deduct as ordinary and necessary business expenses under Code Sections 162 or 167, or (ii) reasonable outplacement and moving expenses

actually incurred by the employee and directly related to the termination of service. "Limited time reimbursements" are defined as reimbursements that do not extend beyond December 31 of the second calendar year following the calendar year in which the separation from service occurred;

4. Reimbursement for a limited time of payments of medical expenses (as defined in Code Section 213) incurred and paid by the employee that are not otherwise reimbursed; the right to reimbursement applies during the time the former employee would be entitled to COBRA continuation coverage under the employer's group health plan, but COBRA election is not required (see **Chapter 7** for more information on COBRA); and

5. Pay and benefits that do not exceed the 402(g) limit (which is $15,500 for 2008).

These exemptions apply in combination, such that former employees may receive any or all of the above exempt benefits and avoid the application of Code Section 409A.

Finally, separation pay provided to employees who quit based on a "good reason" may also be exempt from the Code Section 409A regulations. A good reason to quit will be treated as an involuntary termination if the reason the employee quits is due to an employer action that results in a material negative change to the employment relationship. Under the regulations' safe harbor definition of "good reason," employer actions include significant or material decrease in base salary; decrease in employee's job duties, authority, or responsibilities; decrease in budget over which employee has authority; decrease in the duties, authority, or responsibilities of the employees' supervisor; or change in the geographic location of the employee's work. The safe harbor definition also requires the employee to provide notice to the employer of the good reason condition (within 90 days of the condition's initial existence) and allow for the employer to have at least 30 days to fix the condition before the employee quits. The severance pay package that an employee receives under a good reason to quit situation must be the same as he or she would have received if there had been an involuntary termination.

If a severance pay plan (i) does not meet the exemptions noted above, (ii) is paid to one of the employer's key employees, and (iii) the employer is a publicly traded company, then the severance pay must be delayed six months from the date of termination. A key employee is one of the employer's top 50 paid employees in the preceding year. The final regulations provide further definitions and rules for identifying key employees.

Under the final regulations, all written severance pay plans, separation agreements, and individual employment agreements that provide for severance pay must be revised, as necessary, no later than December 31, 2009 to comply with the above exemption requirements or to meet code Section 409A's requirements.

[E]   Supplemental Unemployment

Laid-off employees are normally eligible for unemployment benefits under state regulations. Supplemental unemployment benefit plans were intended to supplement state unemployment insurance benefits. Many plans now include severance pay, education and training, hospitalization, and health coverage during unemployment and relocation. Financing is normally through employee contributions for a supplemental unemployment fund.

[F]   Outplacement

Many employers provide outplacement services to workers affected by layoffs. This has become a sensible business practice for the following reasons:

- They help employees make the transition and find new positions more quickly.

- They improve the morale of the remaining workforce by reducing "survivor guilt."

- They reduce the likelihood of litigation.

- They reduce the expense of unemployment benefits by shortening the length of unemployment.

- They create goodwill and a positive company image within a community.

Outplacement assistance typically includes the following services:

- Counseling

- Résumé preparation

- Instruction in interviewing skills, including use of videos and role play

- Personal marketing plan

- Career workshops

Outplacement assistance may also include the following:

- Job fairs

- Placement assistance, including temporary volunteer positions

- Job opportunity listings

- Retraining

- Office support, which may include an office space, a telephone, word processing, photocopying, fax, answering services, and supplies

Some companies set up their own outplacement programs if large numbers of employees are affected. Others refer former employees to the state employment service office or hire professional outplacement consultants or companies providing this service.

§ 17.03   TERMINATIONS

HR directors must know their responsibilities and the employees' rights when handling terminations. They should understand the concept of employment at will and how to preserve that right, if applicable within the state. Care should be taken to achieve compliance with state laws that may require action different from or in addition to federal requirements.

[A]   Terminations Because of a Disability

Employers are justifiably cautious about terminating employees who are disabled or who have gone out on disability leave and are unable to return. Employers should:

- Review their benefit plans for specific language about continued disability payments if the employee is taken off the payroll.

- Understand the Pregnancy Discrimination Act (PDA), which in 1978 amended Title VII of the Civil Rights Act of 1964. (The PDA specifically prohibits discrimination on the basis of pregnancy, childbirth, or related medical conditions. It does not require employers to provide pregnancy leave, but if an employer does have a short-term disability plan, it must be available to pregnant women just as it is to employees with other temporary disabilities.)

In *Turic v. Holland Hospitality, Inc.* [85 F.3d 1211, 1216 (6th Cir. 1996)], the Sixth Circuit held that under the federal PDA, an employer cannot discriminate against a woman for having an abortion. The court also said that having an abortion includes contemplating whether to have an abortion. In this case, a hotel employee told her employer that she was pregnant and could not afford the baby, would not consider giving up the child for adoption, and had not ruled out abortion. Her decision became a topic of debate among fellow employees. Her manager met with her, told her that abortion was not to be discussed at work, gave her a written warning, and told her if she discussed the issue again she would be fired. Six days later, she was terminated for poor performance. In the termination interview, the issue of abortion was discussed. The court found that had it not been for her consideration of having an abortion, she would not have been terminated.

The Equal Employment Opportunity Commission (EEOC) regulation provides that abortion is a childbirth-related condition under the federal PDA. Other courts have assumed that a woman who has had an abortion is protected by the PDA.

- Review retirement and vesting language in the plans.

- Review policies and procedures under the Family and Medical Leave Act of 1993 (FMLA) and the Americans with Disabilities Act of 1990 (ADA), to ensure full compliance with the requirements, including making accommodations if the employee is qualified (and protected) under the ADA.

- Review the workers' compensation policy (if the disability is work-related).

- Provide managers with guidelines for hiring temporary staff and determining at what point a vacancy can be posted (even if the disabled employee is still on leave or on the payroll and not terminated).

- Contact legal counsel.

[B] Employment at Will

Employment is considered "at will" in almost all states. Employment at will means that an employer and an employee have an equal right to sever the employment relationship at will, with or without cause, with or without notice. However, there are many exceptions to this consideration. In fact, many states have adopted specific legislation that restricts this concept of at-will employment.

[1] Exceptions

Employers that elect the literal exercise of this right to terminate at will open themselves up to considerable potential liability. As with many employment laws, the basic law has exceptions. Employers are restricted in discharging employees for exercising protected rights that include:

- Taking military leave

- Taking leave for jury service

- Right of association

- Filing workers' compensation claims

- Whistle blowing

- Filing a complaint under the Occupational Safety and Health (OSH) Act

- Paying garnishments through wage reductions

The right to at-will employment is also eroded by any of the following:

- *An implied contract.* An implied contract is an agreement, not directly expressed, between two or more persons that creates an obligation to perform or not to perform a specific act. In some cases, personnel policies and manuals have been construed as implied, enforceable contracts. A statement about "permanent" employment could also be construed as an implied contract.

- *A covenant of good faith and fair dealing.* When a contract implied by law exists, each contracting party has an obligation to honor the contract's provisions and not to interfere with or impede the other party's ability to perform the contract. A written or oral agreement that would cause a reasonable person to conclude that something is true (e.g., "We always use a system of progressive disciplinary action so everyone is treated fairly.") is an example of a covenant of good faith and fair dealing.

- *A tort.* A private or civil wrong for which the court provides a remedy. A tort requires the existence of three factors: (1) the wrongdoer must have a legal duty to the plaintiff, (2) the wrongdoer must have breached his or her duty to the plaintiff, and (3) the plaintiff must have suffered damage.

- *A promissory estoppel.* A promise by one party to another that causes the second party to substantially alter his or her life circumstances. Such a promise prevents the first party from contradicting his or her assertions. For example, a promise by an employer to a prospective employee that causes the latter to substantially alter his or her life circumstances (e.g., "You are hired; sell your house and move out here.") erodes an employer's at-will rights.

Inducing a candidate to accept an employment offer that is false is fraud, and fraud can be quite costly to an employer. A promise to do something necessarily implies the intention to perform; hence, when a promise of employment is made without such intention, it is an implied misrepresentation of fact that may be actionable fraud.

If fraud is found, in some circumstances employees are not limited strictly to contract damages arising out of a termination but may also recover tort damages arising from fraud. Tort damages may include costs of relocation, damages arising from loss of security and income, emotional distress damages, punitive damages, and any other damages caused by the wrongful conduct of the employer.

Some courts have indicated that any action must be considered in the context of the total employment relationship. Even simple references, when combined with oral statements made during an employment interview, for example, can imply a contract and erode employment at will. **Exhibit 17.2** provides a state-by-state list of statutory restrictions on discharging employees.

[2]   Effect of Employment Policies on Employment at Will

Two common employment policies, requiring a notice of termination from employees and probationary periods, can also affect the employer's right to employment at will:

- *Requiring Notice.* Employers in at-will employment states may request but not require advance notice of employee resignations. The requirement for advance notice of resignation is in direct violation of the employees' right to employment at will. Further, employers are prohibited from punishing an employee for exercising this right by, for example, placing the employee on no-rehire status for lack of notice.

  Many employers not in at-will states require a two-week notice of termination from the employee. A conservative approach to avoiding wrongful discharge (discussed in the next section) in these states is to require employees to give notice of termination equal to the number of days or weeks that the company generally gives to employees when announcing a layoff, or when the company gives severance pay.

- *Probationary Period.* The existence of a probationary period per se may also jeopardize an employer's right to employment at will. The probationary period or initial employment period is generally assumed to be the time employers take to evaluate a newly hired employee's performance or the performance of a promoted or transferred employee. Many companies select 90 days for their probationary period. Some employers reserve the right to extend the probationary period if they deem it necessary. At the end of the period, many policies reclassify the employee as a ''regular'' employee who now has access to the same rights and benefits as longer-tenured employees.

  However, the focus on time (e.g., a 90-day period) and on evaluations carried on during this time for continued employment, and the importance placed on controlling the length of the period (e.g., reserving the right to extend the probationary period) can send the wrong message. That is, taken together, the employee's employment may appear somehow more protected on day 91 of the probationary period than it is on day 89.

  The employer may also be implying that because the employee becomes a regular employee and has access to the same rights and benefits as longer-tenured employees after the probationary period, the employee is covered under the terms of the progressive disciplinary system (discussed in a following section) and is therefore protected from the threat of immediate termination implied in the probationary period. This is absolutely the opposite of employment at will. To minimize the risk of jeopardizing the employer's right to employment at will brought about by a probationary period policy, HR directors might think about eliminating the probation policy. Under employment at will, the employer has the right at any time to evaluate an employee's performance and determine whether he or she should continue to be an employee. If the employer considers the entire initial hiring period to be "a new-employee orientation period," it can eliminate the focus on time frames, evaluation, and retention.

  As an alternative, employers might identify a specified period at the beginning of an employee's career and place the employee in a separate classification. If the employee's benefits do not start until after the end of the period, employers might consider calling this time the "benefits-eligibility period." This also shifts the focus away from evaluation and retention.

[3] Preserving the Right to Employment at Will

To strengthen the right to at-will employment, employers should add at-will terms and language to all agreements (e.g., job offer letters, promotion letters, employee handbooks, employment applications, and relocation agreements). All forms, documents, and agreements should be reviewed to ensure that the language does not contradict the right to at-will employment.

Employee handbooks are especially important. Employee handbooks should contain a disclaimer that emphasizes the non-contractual nature of employment. This should be written clearly so employees understand that their employment is at-will. Employees should be required to sign an authorization of receipt of the employee handbook and the at-will nature of employment should be repeated in that acknowledgement. **Exhibits 17.3 and 17.4** present sample handbook acknowledgement and disclaimer documents. See **Section 17.06 [G]** for further information on employee handbooks.

When investigating an employee action or behavior that may lead to an involuntary termination decision, be sure to get all sides of the story. Obtain the employee's statements about the situation, as well as the statements of supervisors and any other witnesses or interested parties. Do not draw a conclusion before conducting a reasonable investigation. (See **Section 17.06[K]** for further information about conducting investigations.)

§ 17.04 WRONGFUL DEMOTION

Another source of potential litigation can be a wrongful demotion. One California court held that an employee may assert a breach of contract claim for wrongful demotion. In 1995 a case was filed by two long-term senior managers employed by Pacific Gas and Electric Company (PGE) who were also operating an outside engineering consulting service. PGE demoted them, claiming they had negligently supervised their own department and had a conflict of interest with PGE because of their outside business activities. The employees' cause of action for wrongful demotion relied heavily on PGE's personnel policies, which included a specific progressive discipline policy that the company allegedly failed to follow. Their activities were well known and had gone on for quite some time.

PGE had adopted a system of progressive discipline, applicable to all employees, that was well publicized. The court concluded that no rational reason explained why an employer's policy that stipulated that employees would not be demoted except for sufficient cause could not become an implied term on an employment contract, as in policies restricting termination. Employees thus had a reasonable expectation that the company would follow its own human resources policy, which had as its basic premise the discipline of employees only for good cause. The court held that the evidence in the case was compelling to support an implied agreement not to demote without good cause.

California employers must now exercise greater caution to ensure that written policies and procedures as well as oral communications do not create an implied-in-fact contract contrary to their best intentions. This caution should focus not only on hiring and firing procedures, but also on all procedures for employee evaluation and discipline. Accordingly, employers across the country with polices or practices involving disciplinary action may wish to review these policies, to evaluate whether unintended promises or guarantees are being made.

§ 17.05   WRONGFUL DISCHARGE

At the center of many termination cases is the issue of wrongful discharge, which is discharge from employment for reasons that are not legal. Many states now recognize exceptions to employment at will and permit employees to sue former employers for wrongful discharge. State courts have upheld wrongful-discharge cases when a clear expression of public policy has been violated by the employee's discharge and the termination is a breach of the good faith and fair dealing implied in the employment contract.

Employers must follow the nondiscrimination requirements for employment contained within Title VII of the Civil Rights Act of 1964, which is enforced by the EEOC. In general, Title VII prohibits an employer from terminating an employee on the basis of race, color, sex, religion, pregnancy, or national origin. In addition, persons with disabilities and older employees are protected classes under the Americans with Disabilities Act (ADA) and the Age Discrimination in Employment Act (ADEA).

The EEOC stresses the need for employers to set forth policies to protect employees from all forms of harassment, including sexual harassment. Consequently, the employer is prohibited from terminating an employee who files a sexual harassment complaint. HR managers must understand the scope of these requirements and take measures to act responsibly and comply with the law.

[A]   Avoiding Wrongful Discharge Claims

Companies commonly have documents and policies that define standards of performance and thus employee termination for failing to meet those standards. These policies, if applied consistently and understood by supervisors administering the policies, help in addressing a charge of wrongful discharge.

[B]   Constructive Discharge

Constructive discharge occurs when an employer makes working conditions difficult or unpleasant in order to force an employee to resign. In one case an employer transferred an employee to a more difficult job on the day after she discussed wages with management on behalf of other employees. The work was harder and the employee lost her position as line leader and a chance for promotion. By requiring the employee to either resign or accept the transfer, the employer had constructively discharged the employee.

In another case an employer refused to transfer an employee to the night shift because the employee had been a "troublemaker" and had played a prominent role in filing a grievance against a night shift supervisor. The employee requested the transfer so that she could take care of her children during the day. The employer said there were no vacancies on the night shift; however, four new employees were hired for the night shift after she made her request. Denying the transfer request was constructive discharge. The employer should have reasonably foreseen that the denial would force the employee to quit, since she could no longer work the day shift.

§ 17.06   OTHER EMPLOYMENT POLICIES AFFECTING TERMINATION

[A]   Vacation Accruals

Employers frequently ask if they have to pay out accrued unused vacation balances when an employee resigns or is terminated. Many states require that the balance of vacation pay be paid unless the company has a policy that states otherwise. (See **Chapter 4** for more information on vacation payout.)

If it is allowed in the state in which the company is operating, the employer might consider a policy like the following:

> The balance of accrued but unused vacation will be paid upon resignation if two weeks' notice of resignation is given. If two weeks' notice is not given, the balance of vacation owed will be forfeited.

Another approach is to indicate that vacation pay will be provided upon resignation, but if the employee is fired (involuntarily terminated), no vacation pay will be provided.

Employers who give vacation allowance at the beginning of each year should have a policy that addresses payout on a prorated basis if the employee leaves before using all of the vacation. Again, some states require payment in any event. For example, if an employee has 12 vacation days at the beginning of the calendar year and resigns April 1, only three days (one-third of 12 days) of the vacation would be paid out. If the employee had already taken more than three days of vacation at that time, the company should also have a policy that "advanced" vacation will be repaid out of the final paycheck.

[B] Advanced Pay or Vacation Time

If employees have been allowed advanced pay or vacation time and they resign or are terminated, the employer can garnish the last check only if they signed an agreement to pay time back. A sample policy might read:

> The earned vacation time will be paid upon termination. This means that only the vacation actually accrued will be paid out. As an example, if an employee terminates March 1, she/he will have accrued only two-twelfths of the vacation for the year. Also, note that if the employee has taken more vacation than actually earned prior to termination, the "advanced" vacation pay will be deducted from her/his last paycheck.

Regardless of the policy used, be sure to clearly define the vesting policy, so employees know exactly how and when they accrue vacation benefits and how much vacation they have accrued at any given time.

[C] Sick Time

Many companies pay accrued vacation upon termination but not accrued sick time, a reflection of the theory that sick time is not an entitlement but a type of insurance against the eventuality that employees need to be away from work for reasons beyond their control.

An employer's policy on sick time payout upon termination, like its vacation payout policy, must be spelled out clearly. Some states require employers to pay accrued sick time upon termination. Others do not require sick time payout unless there is a stipulated policy.

[D] Resigning in Lieu of Being Involuntarily Terminated for Cause

If employees are being terminated for poor performance, and especially in cases of termination for misconduct, they should not be allowed to resign. Although this may help the employee to "save face," it does not send the appropriate message to other employees or to prospective new employers. In some instances, the terminating employer might be liable if the employee were hired somewhere else and during a reference check the new employer did not discover the actual circumstances of termination.

HR directors may find it appropriate to develop, with the assistance of legal counsel, a policy for handling employee terminations for cause.

[E] Waivers

Employers have used waivers or releases (i.e., a document the terminated or laid-off employee signs) to minimize liability. These may be used with an individual termination or with group terminations. Legal counsel can help an employer determine if and when such an approach is appropriate, especially because recent rulings have strongly suggested that waivers may not be effective.

Releases should not include statements requiring employees to waive their right to sue under laws that do not themselves allow employees to waive claims. These laws include the Fair Labor Standards Act, the Family and Medical Leave Act (FMLA), the Uniformed Services Employment and Reemployment Rights Act, and workers' compensation. (Some jurisdictions may allow for waiver of claims under the FMLA, but most do not.) In addition, the EEOC has taken the position that a release that bars the employee from cooperating with EEOC investigations or filing EEOC charges is illegal. [EEOC v. Lockheed Martin Corp., No. 05cv0287 RWT, 2006 WL 2294540 (D. Md. Aug. 8, 2006)] According to the EEOC, employers that ask employees to waive their right to file discrimination charges with the EEOC are retaliating against those employees. Although other court cases have not agreed with the EEOC on this tenet, all court cases looking at this issue have found that this aspect of a waiver is not enforceable.

The Older Workers Benefit Protection Act (OWBPA), which amended the ADEA, places further restrictions on waivers and releases. If employees who are protected under ADEA (over age 40) are being terminated or laid off, HR directors should work with legal counsel to determine whether it is appropriate to secure waivers. Under OWBPA, an employee may waive his or her rights under the ADEA only if the waiver is "knowing and voluntary." The provisions of OWBPA require that such a waiver (1) be part of a written agreement between the employer and the employee, (2) reference ADEA rights and claims, (3) not waive rights or claims that may arise after the agreement is signed, (4) be executed in exchange for additional consideration (i.e., something of value to which the employee is not already entitled), and (5) advise the employee to consult with an attorney before signing. In addition, if the agreement is between the employer and a single employee, the employee must be given at least 21 days to consider the waiver. If the waiver would affect a group of employees, (referred to as a reduction in force, or RIF), the affected employees must be given at least 45 days to consider it. If the terminations are part of a RIF, employees that the waiver would affect must also be given specific written information, including (1) a description of the class, unit or group of individuals covered by the RIF, any eligibility factors for inclusion in the RIF, and any time limits applicable to the RIF; and (2) the ages, job titles, and organizational units of those employees who are eligible or are selected for the layoff or termination and those who are not. This group is referred to as the "decisional unit." The EEOC has suggested that decisional units may be a division, department, facility, reporting group or job category, or other similar grouping. Once the agreement is signed, an employee must have at least 7 days in which to revoke it.

One recent case highlights the need to be in strict compliance with OWBPA. In *Kruchowski v. Weyerhaeuser Co.* (No. 04-7118, 10th Cir. May 2, 2006), the courts invalidated the ADEA waivers signed by a group of employees because the waivers did not comply with OWBPA. As noted above, OWBPA requires that certain information be given to employees listing who is eligible to sign a waiver and who is not. This information must be for all employees in the "decisional unit" to which the terminating employees belong. OWBPA defines the "decisional unit" as "that portion of the employer's organizational structure from which the employer chose the persons who would be offered consideration for the signing of a waiver and those who would not be offered consideration for the signing of a waiver." 29 C.F.R. § 1625.22(f)(3)(i)(B).

In the release given to the affected employees, Weyerhaeuser identified the "decisional unit" as all salaried employees employed at the mill. However, during the course of the case, Weyerhaeuser identified the "decisional unit" as only those salaried employees who reported to the mill manager. The court held that because Weyerhaeuser misidentified the "decisional unit" in the release, the release was invalid as a matter of law. The ruling meant that the employees did not waive their rights under ADEA, and were therefore able to bring an age discrimination suit against their former employer.

In another case, the Eighth Circuit Court of Appeals held that IBM did not use "language that could be understood by the average person" as required by OWBPA. The terminating employee asked for clarification on some of the wording used in the release he was asked to sign, and his supervisor suggested he consult with his attorney. After doing so, the employee determined that the release did not prohibit him from filing an ADEA claim. The employee signed the agreement, then sued for age discrimination. The trial court found for IBM, but the Eighth Circuit reversed the decision on the basis that the agreement was unclear. [Thomforde v. International Business Machines Corporation, 406 F.3d 500 (8th Cir. 2005)] In a similar case against IBM, the court ruled that the waiver of all employment-related claims drafted by IBM was confusing for employees and that it could not overcome this confusion by directing employees to consult an attorney. The court held that the ADEA requires the agreement to explain, *in a manner that the average employee can understand* (italics added for emphasis) how a release of claims and a covenant not to sue work with respect to the ADEA. [Syverson v. International Business Machines Corporation, No. 04-16449, 2006 WL 2506421 (9th Cir. Aug. 31, 2006)]

[F] References

An employer should have a reference policy that describes who is authorized to provide references and what information will be provided when a reference is requested. Each employee or ex-employee requesting a reference should sign a form agreeing to have the information released. (See **Exhibit 16.2**.)

A reference that provides more information than position held, date of hire, and date of termination, should be documented. Although some states have enacted reference protection laws, and truth is always a defense, the documentation of the reference is always recommended. (See **Chapter 16** for more information about giving and obtaining employment references.)

Companies must be aware of a liability arising out of providing incomplete, potentially misleading references for former employees. The California Supreme Court held that an employer could be held liable for fraud or negligent misrepresentation for providing a positive letter of recommendation for a former employee while omitting the negative information. In *Randi W. v. Muroc Joint Unified School District* [14 Cal. 4th 1066 (1997)], the court stated that "ordinarily a recommending employer should not be held accountable for failing to disclose negative information regarding a former employee; nonetheless, liability may be imposed if, as alleged here, the recommendation letter amounts to an affirmative misrepresentation presenting a foreseeable and substantial risk of physical harm to a prospective employer or third person."

Therefore, following the court's reasoning in *Randi W.*, employers that choose to provide references should not make unqualified recommendations of employment if they possess facts that reveal that the employee may present a risk of harm to someone in the future. In practical terms, this means that any oral comments or any letter that highlights a former employee's strengths and leaves out any negative comments should be provided only if it is not in fact a misrepresentation about the employee that could conceivably create potential liability to future employers or third parties.

[G]   The Employee Handbook

An employee handbook generally contains a series of policy statements that provide a general summary of the terms and conditions of employment pertaining to all employees. The handbook describes to employees what is expected of them. Employees must be able to rely on the handbook as a true representation of company policy. In some states, the courts consider the employee handbook to be the same as a contract. Frequently, when discharges are challenged, the EEOC, an arbitrator, or an attorney reviews the handbook policies on standards of performance, discipline, and termination. Therefore, the handbook needs to be accurate, up-to-date, and realistic and should describe actual company employment practices.

Use of the word "may," instead of "will" or "should," in the handbook can provide employers with flexibility in employment matters. Ensure that disciplinary policies provide for flexibility and allow immediate termination based on the facts and circumstances.

As additional protection, a competent expert or legal counsel should review the employee handbook at least annually for consistency, appropriateness, and statutory compliance. One easy way to keep a handbook current is to use a looseleaf format, which allows for easy revision.

[H]   Rules of Conduct

Employers often define the types of conduct that may lead to disciplinary action or discharge. Because establishing expectations of employee performance is important, a list of company rules is an acceptable way to accomplish this, especially when notification of health or safety rules is critical. A list of company rules, however, can lead to a challenge of wrongful discharge. For example, an employee may claim he or she did not realize he or she could be terminated because the infraction was not on the list. To minimize this occurrence, every list should begin and end with the statement that the list is merely representative and is not all-inclusive of prohibited activities and that the company reserves the right to administer disciplinary action up to and including immediate termination, as it sees fit.

Some examples of conduct leading to disciplinary action under company rules are:

- Insubordination (refusal to perform assigned work)

- Fighting or disorderly conduct

- Possession of weapons, ammunition, explosives, or firearms while on company property

- Falsification of company documents (e.g., time cards, expense reports, or employment application)

- Possession, sale, or use of controlled substances or alcohol on company property

- Misappropriation of company property or removal of company property without permission from the premises

- Failure to comply with attendance requirements

- Safety violations

[I]   Progressive Disciplinary Action

Many employers follow a system of progressive disciplinary action to manage employee performance. Common steps include:

1. Issuance of a verbal warning for the first occurrence of a lesser offense (e.g., abusing personal telephone call privileges, tardiness, absenteeism, or personal appearance)

2. Issuance of a written disciplinary warning that outlines performance expectations and consequences

3. Final written warning and/or suspension

4. Discharge

Any written reprimand given to the employee should contain the following:

- A description of the specific behavior that resulted in the reprimand

- A chronology of past disciplinary action for the same activity

- The penalty assessed for the employee's behavior

- Specific actions required of the employee to improve behavior, including a timeline for improvement

- The consequences of continued disciplinary problems

The supervisor should follow up in a timely manner to determine whether the employee is satisfying the conditions of the reprimand. If the requisite changes are not made within the established time frame, the supervisor should promptly initiate the next step in the disciplinary action process. Without consistent follow-up by supervisors, disciplinary action becomes meaningless and loses its value to the employer in defending termination decisions.

The aim of disciplinary action should be to correct poor employee performance and retain the employee; such discipline is not meant as punishment. One advantage of this system is the documentation that is created, which can be used later to defend a decision to discharge. On the other hand, publishing and committing to this policy may imply that employees will be given a chance to redeem themselves for all but the most egregious acts. The challenge in this case is for the employer to retain the right to manage as it sees fit, including maintaining the right to immediate termination for issues for which an employee may not have received prior warnings. If company policy includes progressive disciplinary action, the handbook should state that the company reserves the right to bypass any disciplinary step as it deems necessary, depending on management's review of specific circumstances. This helps ensure that employees do not assume they are entitled to all steps in the process before they can be terminated. In at-will states, some attorneys advise against any description of a progressive disciplinary action policy. In these states, employers are advised to seek legal counsel to review the wording in their handbooks prior to publication.

[1]   Effects of Rules and Progressive Discipline on Employment at Will

In employment-at-will states, a list of rules and a specified "progressive" disciplinary action process can have a negative impact on a company's right to employment at will. Employers should repeat the provisions of at-will employment in the sections of the handbook dealing with company rules and disciplinary action. In employment-at-will states, employers should also include at the front of the employee handbook a clearly worded at-will policy. The following is a sample at-will employment provision:

> It must be remembered that the employment relationship is based on the mutual consent of the employee and the Company. Accordingly, at any time, either the employee or the Company can terminate the employment relationship at will, with or without cause or advance notice. There is no implied promise that employment

will continue for a set period or that employment will be terminated only under particular circumstances. No one, other than the President or Chief Executive Officer (CEO), has the authority to make representations, either express or implied, that are inconsistent with this policy. The President or CEO may amend the policy in a written statement, at any time. This policy supersedes all written and oral representations to the contrary.

Employees should be required to sign a separate document that repeats this clause, attesting to the fact that they understand that their employment relationship with the company is at will. That document should be witnessed and filed in HR's employee file, and it should be revised and re-signed at least every other year.

[J] Supervisory Training

Correct execution of the disciplinary action policy is a critical step in minimizing the liability risk inherent in termination. Supervisory training is key to minimizing an employer's risk of wrongful discharge, because the supervisors are responsible for implementing the company's policy.

When implementing progressive discipline and/or employee termination supervisors must:

- Understand how to handle the interaction with employees

- Understand how to prepare complete, accurate documentation for the file

- Understand when to take action and know the appropriate steps outlined in the policy if further disciplinary action becomes necessary

- Be notified promptly whenever there is a new policy or policy change

- Understand appropriate, consistent application of the policy

Many sources of risk arise from the relationship between supervisors and employees in light of the wrongful-termination issue. In addition to training in how to handle work rule violations using progressive discipline, supervisors need to understand the laws against harassment and the statutory protections discussed at the beginning of the section on termination. Annual reviews of the supervisor's role in the application of progressive discipline in the company should be conducted.

[K] Termination Review

Companies often require an HR department review before an employee is terminated. This review ensures consistent application of company policy and determines whether there are precedents that will modify the decision or whether undesirable precedents will be set.

The key to demonstrating that disciplinary action is fair, consistent, and lawful is written documentation. It is critical that supervisors recognize that any form of misconduct or performance problem that warrants disciplinary action also warrants written documentation. To be useful in defending company actions, the documentation should include specific, objective information about each incident, such as the names of witnesses, the date and time of the event, the location, statements made by the employee, the order of events, and actions taken by the supervisor.

Sometimes employers are tempted to tell employees "little white lies" to soften the blow of involuntary termination. In *Reeves v. Sanderson Plumbing Products, Inc.* [197 F.3d 688 (5th Cir.), *rev'd,* 530 U.S. 133 (2000)], the U.S. Supreme Court decided in favor of Reeves (the employee in the case), who alleged he was really fired because of age when the company said he was fired for failure to maintain proper time records. The issue before the Court was what "proof" a plaintiff must present in order to go to trial. The Court held that in this case, and similar cases, the employee need only establish certain basic facts that support the theory of discrimination and demonstrate that the employer gave a false reason for the discharge. The Court therefore determined that a jury could infer that the employer was covering up a discriminatory termination. The Supreme Court's ruling reversed the Fifth Circuit Court's reversal of the jury verdict, thereby allowing Reeves's jury trial win to stand.

Employers can minimize their liability and help the employee save face by processing the termination in an honest and caring way. Treating a terminated employee with respect lessens the risk of the employee's filing a lawsuit. In addition, supervisors should take the following basic steps to minimize the risk of litigation and help ensure a successful termination:

Step 1. Use progressive discipline so employees are given an opportunity to correct their poor work performance. Discuss unacceptable behavior with employees and let them know that their performance must improve or more serious consequences will follow. Prepare and retain complete documentation.

Step 2. Never use immediate termination no matter what the circumstances; no reason is sufficient to risk summarily terminating any employee without thorough investigation. If an infraction is serious consider suspending an employee without pay to gain the time necessary to investigate the incident. Make sure the investigation is thorough, complete, and well documented to minimize the chance of error and possibly save thousands of dollars in back pay and damage awards, legal fees, and other related legal costs.

Step 3. Be consistent. Do not let emotion cloud judgment. Carefully review the employee's entire personnel history and compare discipline given before to other employees or to the same employee for similar misconduct, unacceptable behavior or poor performance.

Step 4. If an investigation is warranted, it should be conducted as soon as possible. Delay causes facts to be forgotten or distorted. Avoid accusatory or adversarial comments or actions. Remember, the purpose of the investigation is to gather facts, not to make the decision.

Step 5. Conduct a final review of all data collected. Analyze the overall findings for completeness and accuracy. Determine whether further investigation is needed before making a final decision.

Whenever the proposed termination involves possible allegations of disparate treatment of protected employees or significant legal issues, secure legal assistance before finalizing any termination decision.

Step 6. Identify the specific rule or policy that the misconduct violated or the performance standard that was not met. Generally, the more specific this point, the better the employer can make its case. For instance, if an employee is to be terminated for absenteeism, spell out the specific provision of the absentee policy that was violated.

Step 7. Make the decision to terminate when the facts of the case are clear and support the decision to terminate.

Step 8. In the case of an investigation following a specific incident, inform the employee in person, if possible, within 24 to 48 hours after completion of the investigation. Have two management officials present when the employee is told about the decision to terminate his or her employment.

Step 9. When employees collect their final paychecks, provide a complete written explanation of COBRA rights, severance pay, accrued vacation or sick leave, or other fringe benefits to which the employee may be entitled. (See **Chapter 7** for a complete discussion of COBRA rights.)

A termination checklist (see **Exhibit 17.5**) is particularly useful to help organize the termination process.

[L] Exit Interviews

A well-conducted exit interview is an excellent way to gather and provide valuable information, as well as limit legal liability. Generally, employees are willing to share more openly when they are leaving the organization. Among the many benefits:

- *Learn more about the department and the organization.* This is an opportunity to hear about supervisory concerns, potential discrimination or harassment issues, and operational concerns. Of course, it is important to validate any issues uncovered, rather than accepting what is said as "the whole truth."

- *Identify the full reason for leaving (if voluntary).* An employee may check a box or tell a supervisor "better job" or "more money," but an exit interview provides an opportunity to hear about misunderstandings among employees, lack of proper tools, a desire for more responsibility, etc. All information gathered will prove useful in an organization's ongoing efforts to hire and retain good people.

- *Give the employee an opportunity to "vent."* Sometimes issues that could escalate to a lawsuit can be eliminated when the employee has a chance to talk to someone who is willing to listen.

- *Assess potential legal risks.* An employer may be able to learn of potential litigation, such as discrimination lawsuits or workers compensation filings.

- *Provide a clear understanding of termination issues.* Employers can make sure proper information is provided regarding pay, ongoing benefits, property to be returned, etc.

Most employers find that a face-to-face interview is most effective. When conducted face-to-face, exit interviews should be well documented. The interview may be followed by a written questionnaire sent to the employee's home. Sample exit interview questions are found in **Exhibit 17.6**.

As information is collected from exit interviews, it is recommended that the HR Department prepare periodic summaries for distribution to top management. This allows the company to identify and correct potential impediments to successful attraction and retention of employees.

[M] Reinstatement of Service

Many companies have a policy concerning employees who resign and then choose to return to work. Such policies discuss the effect on employee benefits if their service is reinstated within a given time period. A typical policy might be as follows:

> Employees with two or more years of service who voluntarily terminate employment and who are rehired within one year of their termination date may have their previous seniority reinstated after one year of continuous service following rehire. This policy does not establish an obligation to rehire terminated employees. Vested benefits, such as 401(k), pension, or employee stock option plans, may be eligible for reinstatement upon a former employee's return to employment. For specific information, refer to the Plan Document for each program. Time-off benefits, such as sick leave pay and vacation time, do not accrue during the period of absence. However, when seniority is reinstated, vacation will then accrue at the rate associated with the employee's amount of seniority.

Exhibit 17.1
State Notification Laws for Layoffs and Plant Closings*

California	Applies to employers with 75 or more employees (full and part-time) who have been employed for at least 6 of the last 12 months, including employees who are not employed at the time of the layoff. Precludes employers from ordering a mass layoff, relocation, or termination, as defined, of an industrial or commercial facility meeting the minimum number of employees test above, without first giving 60 days' notice to affected employees and specified government agencies. Provides for civil penalties against an employer who fails to provide the required notices. Provides employers would not be required to comply with the 60-day notice requirement if the employer is actively seeking capital or business that would enable the employer to avoid or postpone a relocation or termination, and the employer reasonably and in good faith believed that giving the 60 days' notice would preclude the employer from obtaining the capital or business.
Colorado	Applicable to state employees only. The only reasons for layoff of classified state personnel are lack of work, lack of funds, or reorganization. In the case of a reorganization not caused by lack of work or lack of funds, a written plan must be prepared that addresses the effect of the changes on employees. The plan must be posted in a conspicuous place in the workplace for at least 45 days from the first date of layoff. Written layoff notices are required to be given to affected employees. Any certified employee to be laid off must receive notice at least 45 days before the date of the action; any certified employee displaced because another employee exercises his or her retention rights must be given notice at least ten workdays prior to the date of displacement. If a certified employee is terminated because another employee exercises his or her retention rights, the separated employee must be paid for a minimum of 22 workdays after receiving a notice that retention rights have been exercised. A probationary, provisional, or noncertified employee whose position is abolished or who is displaced must be given notice at least 10 workdays before the effective date of the action.
Connecticut	Private employers with 100 or more employees in the 12 months preceding a facility closing or relocation are required to pay the full premium of an affected employee's and dependent's existing group health insurance policy for 120 days following the closing or relocation, or until the employee becomes eligible for other group coverage, whichever is less. Companies that close because of bankruptcy or natural disasters and those that relocate within the state are not covered by this law.
Georgia	Applicable to state employees only. Employees who are to be laid off or demoted by a reduction in force must be notified in accordance with a plan approved by the commissioner of personnel administration.
Hawaii	Private employers with 50 or more employees must provide 45 days' advance written notice of a plant closing, partial closing, divestiture, or relocation. This notification of closure, divestiture, or relocation must be given to each employee and the state Department of Labor and Industrial Relations at least 60 days prior to its occurrence. Companies must pay a four-week dislocated workers allowance, which is equal to the difference between a worker's average weekly wages before the closing and the weekly unemployment compensation benefits. Penalties for noncompliance are significant. Employees have the right to sue employers for noncompliance and are eligible for injunctive relief in some circumstances
Illinois	Any business enterprise that employs 75 or more full-time employees must provide notice to the affected employees, representatives of affected employees, the Illinois Department of Commerce and Economic Opportunity, and the chief elected official of each municipal and county government where a mass layoff is to occur. Mass layoff is defined as a reduction in force that results in an employment loss of a minimum of 33 percent of the employees and at least 25 full-time employees, or at least 250 full-time employees. Employers must also provide 60 days' written notice of relocation of the business unit. Full-time employees are those who work 20 or more hours per week, or who have worked six or more of the 12 months prior to the date notice is given.

* Only states that have notification laws are included.

Exhibit 17.1   Mandated Benefits: 2009 Compliance Guide

Exhibit 17.1 (cont'd)

Kansas	Under the Compulsory Arbitration and Mediation Act, employers in clothing, food products, manufacturers, fuel mining, transporter of food products or clothing, or public utilities are required to apply to the state Department of Human Resources for authority to limit or cease operations. State employees must be given at least 30 calendar days before the effective date of the proposed layoff.
Maine	Employers with at least 100 employees are required to pay severance pay, equal to one week's pay for each year of employment, to each employee with at least three years of service. Employers that intend to close or relocate a facility must give 60 days' advance written notice to the director of the Bureau of Labor, the employees affected by the closing or relocation, and local officials. Employees and labor organizations may pursue legal action in state or federal court to recover unpaid severance benefits. If an employer fails to provide 60 days' advance written notification to both employees and officials of a relocation of an establishment outside the state or the termination of the business, it is subject to a $500 fine.
Maryland	There are voluntary state guidelines for notification for private employers of 50 or more employees that have been in business for at least one year. The guidelines do not apply if the reduction results solely from labor disputes; occurs in a commercial, industrial, or agricultural enterprise operated by Maryland or its political subdivisions; occurs at construction sites or other temporary workplaces; results from seasonal factors that are customary in the industry, as determined by the Economic Development Department; or results when an employer files for bankruptcy under federal bankruptcy laws. The guidelines advise employers to give 90 days' advance notice in writing when they plan to relocate a facility or lay off at least 25 percent or 15 employees over any three-month period. The guidelines recommend that the employer provide "appropriate" continuation of benefits, such as health, severance, and pension benefits, to employees who will be terminated because of a reduction in operations. To minimize the effects of a relocation or layoff, the law establishes a "quick response program" designed to assist employers and employees.
Massachusetts	Employers of 12 or more employees that relocate an operation within the state must report the action to a designated state official. Violations are subject to fines of up to $100 and imprisonment of up to two months. Companies with 50 or more employees that close or partially close must report the action to affected employees, their collective bargaining representative (if any), and the director of the state Department of Labor and Workforce Division. The employer must provide enough information to enable the director to determine whether the employees are eligible for certain state reemployment assistance benefits. Employers must make a good faith effort to provide each affected employee with "the longest practical advance notice" when notice is possible and appropriate. Covered employers are expected to continue group health insurance for 90 days following a closing, whenever possible.
Michigan	The state's Employee-Owned Corporation Act encourages businesses that are considering closing or relocating operations to give notice as early as possible to the state Labor Department, employees, any employee organizations representing the employees, and the communities in which their establishments are located.
Minnesota	Any employer providing notice under the WARN Act must report the names, addresses, and occupations of employees who will be or have been terminated to the Commissioner of Jobs and Training. A plant closing is defined as a permanent or temporary shutdown of a workplace during any 30-day period, for 50 or more employees, excluding those employed for fewer than 20 hours per week, or 500 or more employees who work a total of at least 20,000 hours per week, excluding overtime hours. A "substantial layoff" is defined as any reduction in the workforce affecting the same numbers of employees as defined by a plant closing.

Exhibit 17.1 (cont'd)

Montana	Applicable to state employees only. The state must provide employees adequate notification when it plans the closure or retrenchment of a governmental facility in a local area. A governmental facility includes any institution, department, agency, bureau, or office operated by the state and employing more than 25 persons. Upon making a decision to close or retrench (i.e., lay off at least 250 employees over a two-year period) at a governmental facility, the employer should immediately notify the employees, the affected employee organizations, the affected local governments, and a newspaper of general circulation in the county where the facility is subject to closure. Within 90 days, the employer must provide employees, the affected employee organizations, and the affected local governments with a written impact statement including information about the number of employees affected, the amount of affected employees' payroll, the potential tax losses to local government and school districts, the expected effect on other businesses, and the reasons for the closure or retrenchment.
Nevada	Applicable to state employees only. All permanent state employees who are to be laid off must be given written notice at least 30 calendar days before the effective date of the layoff.
New Hampshire	Applicable to state employees only. The appointing authority is required to give written notice of the proposed layoff and reasons for the action to the affected employees and to the HR director at least 14 calendar days before the layoff can take place.
New Jersey	In addition to complying with the WARN Act, employers must provide the same notice of a plant closing or mass layoff to the state Dislocated Worker Unit. Within 10 working days, employers are sent confirmation of the date the unit received the notification. Employers must notify the state Division of Unemployment Insurance 48 hours prior to a mass layoff (50 or more employees for 7 days or more). If a mass separation is to occur and the employer has no advance knowledge, the notice must be filed within 24 hours after the mass separation occurs. The Millville Dallas Airmotive Plant Job Loss Notification Act (NJ Act) became effective on December 20, 2007, and requires advance notification of terminations or transfers of operations that result in the termination of employment of 50 or more full-time employees during any 30-day period (facilities that have been operated by the employer for less than 3 years are exempt). The NJ Act does not include the exceptions for notices due to a faltering business or unforeseeable business circumstances. The NJ Act requires additional information to be provided in the notice including the reasons for the transfer or termination of operations or mass layoffs and information regarding employment available at the employer's other establishments, if any. The NJ Act also provides for additional penalties to employers who fail to provide the required notices: one week of pay for each full year of employment. This penalty would be in addition to any severance already provided by the employer, but would be offset by the amount of penalty due under the federal WARN Act. The penalty applies even if the employer is in partial compliance with the requirements; that is even if the notice is only one day late.
New York	Effective February 1, 2009, employers with 50 or more employees must give at least 90 days advance written notice of a "mass layoff," "relocation," "employment loss," or "plant closing" to affected employees, representatives of affected employees, local workforce boards and the New York State Department of Labor. A "mass layoff" is defined as a reduction in force that results in employment loss at a single site of (i) at least 33 percent of the employees at that site and 25 or more employees, or (ii) a minimum of 250 employees (excluding part-time employees in both situations). A "relocation" is a move of "all or substantially all of the industrial or commercial operations" of an employer to a location 50 or more miles from its current location. A "plant closing" is the permanent or temporary shutdown of a single site of employment (or the shutdown of one or more facilities or operating units at one work site) if the shutdown results in employment loss of 25 or more employees within a 30-day period (excluding part-time employees). Notice is not required if the triggering event results from a natural disaster or an act of terrorism or war.

Exhibit 17.1   Mandated Benefits: 2009 Compliance Guide

Exhibit 17.1 (cont'd)

Oregon	The Business Resources Division of the state Economic Development Department must be notified if an employer is required to provide written notice of a plant closing or mass layoff under the WARN Act.
South Carolina	Any employer that requires employees to give notice before quitting a job must itself give notice. This must happen at least two weeks in advance of the shutdown, or for the same amount of time required of employees who resign their positions, and must include the date of shutdown and approximate duration. Notices must be posted in each room of a company's plant. Fines are up to $5,000 for employers that do not comply, in addition to damages to employees. Notice posting is not required when a shutdown is caused by an unforeseen accident to machinery, some act of God, or of the public enemy.
South Dakota	Applicable to state employees only. Under the state's Bureau of Personnel rules pertaining to nondisciplinary separations, an approved departmental layoff procedure must be in place before a state career service system employee can be laid off. An employee must be notified at least 14 days before the effective date of a reduction in force or a reduction in hours and must be given written notice of the reasons for the layoff or reduction. The appointing authority must notify the state labor commissioner within five days after making a layoff or reduction decision. The same provisions apply to nondisciplinary separations involving incumbents in law enforcement civil service positions.
Tennessee	Companies with at least 50 employees that are planning a reduction in operations that will permanently or indefinitely reduce the workforce by 50 or more during any three-month period must give notice to the state government as well as affected employees.
Wisconsin	Employers of 50 or more employees are required to give 60 days' advance written notice of a business closing or mass layoff. The notice must go to any affected employees and their collective bargaining representatives, the state labor department, and the highest city official where the affected employment site is located. ''Business closing'' is defined as a permanent or temporary shutdown of an employment site or one or more facilities or operating units at a site or within a single municipality affecting 25 or more workers, excluding ''new employees'' (i.e., persons employed for fewer than six of the 12 months preceding the date on which notice must be given) and ''low hour'' employees (persons averaging fewer than 20 hours of work per week). ''Mass layoff'' is defined as a reduction in a workforce at an employment site or within a single municipality that is not the result of a business closing, that affects at least 25 percent of the workforce, or 25 workers, whichever is greater, or at least 500 employees. Employers must provide to the state labor department written information about their payroll, affected employees and their wages, and any remuneration due employees. Employers are also required to post a notice at the establishment informing workers of these rights. Failing to post can result in a $100 fine. Failure to notify local governments can result in fines of $500 per day, which may run from the date the notice is first required and end on either the date notice is given or when the layoff or closing actually occur, whichever is earlier. Failure to notify employees can result in payment of back pay and benefits for a specified ''recovery'' period, beginning on the day notice was first required and ending on either the day notice is actually given or the day the closing or layoff occurs.
Wyoming	Applicable to state employees only. The state Personnel Management Division requires that each state agency designate which divisions within the agency will be subject to a reduction in force (RIF). No layoffs from a RIF can occur within 60 days of the designation of a division. Layoffs due to a RIF can occur only within affected designated divisions. No employee affected by a RIF can displace any other employee outside the designated divisions. No employee affected by a RIF can displace any other employee outside the designated division. Designation within agencies must be made by the agency director and is not effective until approved by the governor. Such designations are not subject to contested case procedures or judicial proceedings.

Exhibit 17.2
Statutory Restrictions on Discharging Employees

NOTE: A "—" means that no specific statutory authority exists; other authority, including case law, may apply.

	Are Employers Prohibited from Discharging Employees for Taking Military Leave?	Are Employers Restricted from Discharging Employees for Taking Leave for Jury Service?	Is There a Restriction on Using Employment Consequences to Influence Employee Vote?	Are Employers Restricted from Discharging Employees Whose Wages Are Subject to Garnishment?	Are Employers Restricted from Making Labor Organization Membership or Nonmembership a Condition of Employment?	Are Employers Restricted from Discharging an Employee for Filing a Workers' Compensation Claim?	Are Employers Restricted from Discharging an Employee for Filing an OSHA Complaint?	Are Employers Restricted from Discharging Employees for Whistleblowing?
AL	Yes.	Yes.	Yes.	Yes. Applies to garnishments for child or spousal support and crime restitution. Applicants for employment are also protected.	Yes.	Yes.	Yes.	Yes.
AK	Yes.	Yes.	—	Yes.	Yes, if public employee objects to collective bargaining settlement based on religious convictions. Employee must pay amount equivalent to union dues, which will be distributed to charitable organization.	Yes.	Yes.	Yes.
AZ	Yes.	Yes.	Yes.	Yes. Applies to garnishments for child support or spousal maintenance.	Yes.	—	Yes.	Yes.

(continued)

Exhibit 17.2　　　　　　　　　　　　　　　　　　Mandated Benefits: 2009 Compliance Guide

Exhibit 17.2 (cont'd)
Statutory Restrictions on Discharging Employees

NOTE: A "—" means that no specific statutory authority exists; other authority, including case law, may apply.

	Are Employers Prohibited from Discharging Employees for Taking Military Leave?	Are Employers Restricted from Discharging Employees for Taking Leave for Jury Service?	Is There a Restriction on Using Employment Consequences to Influence Employee Vote?	Are Employers Restricted from Discharging Employees Whose Wages Are Subject to Garnishment?	Are Employers Restricted from Making Labor Organization Membership or Nonmembership a Condition of Employment?	Are Employers Restricted from Discharging an Employee for Filing a Workers' Compensation Claim?	Are Employers Restricted from Discharging an Employee for Filing an OSHA Complaint?	Are Employers Restricted from Discharging Employees for Whistleblowing?
AZ (*continued*)				Applicants for employment are also protected.				
AR	Yes.	Yes.	Yes.	—	Yes.	Yes.	Yes. Applies to public employees' reports concerning hazardous substances.	Yes, if employer employs 9 or more persons.
CA	Yes.	Yes.	Yes.	Yes.	Yes.	Yes.	Yes.	Yes.
CO	Yes.	Yes.	Yes.	Yes. Also, employers may not discharge employees as a result of service of the national medical support notice.	Yes.	—	—	Yes.
CT	Yes. Includes leave to attend drills, parades, and encampments.	Yes.	Yes.	Yes. Applicants for employment are also protected.	Yes.	Yes.	Yes.	Yes.

	Are Employers Prohibited from Discharging Employees for Taking Military Leave?	Are Employers Restricted from Discharging Employees for Taking Leave for Jury Service?	Is There a Restriction on Using Employment Consequences to Influence Employee Vote?	Are Employers Restricted from Discharging Employees Whose Wages Are Subject to Garnishment?	Are Employers Restricted from Making Labor Organization Membership or Nonmembership a Condition of Employment?	Are Employers Restricted from Discharging an Employee for Filing a Workers' Compensation Claim?	Are Employers Restricted from Discharging an Employee for Filing an OSHA Complaint?	Are Employers Restricted from Discharging Employees for Whistleblowing?
DE	Yes. Leave must be allowed for reserve members on temporary active duty and for employees entering the armed forces or the National Guard.	Yes.	Yes.	Yes.	Yes. Applies to public employers and employees.	Yes.	Yes. Applies to complaints concerning hazardous chemicals.	Yes.
DC	Yes. Includes drills, parades, and encampments.	Yes.	Yes.	Yes.	Yes.	Yes.	Yes.	No specific statutory prohibition exists, but statute provides that public employees are encouraged to report violations of law and misuse of government resources.
FL	Yes.	Yes.	Yes.	—	Yes.	Yes.	Yes. Applies to public employees only.	Yes.
GA	Yes.	Yes.	Yes.	Yes.	Yes.	—	Yes. Applies to public employees' reports concerning hazardous chemicals.	Yes.

Exhibit 17.2

Mandated Benefits: 2009 Compliance Guide

Exhibit 17.2 (cont'd)
Statutory Restrictions on Discharging Employees

NOTE: A "—" means that no specific statutory authority exists; other authority, including case law, may apply.

	Are Employers Prohibited from Discharging Employees for Taking Military Leave?	Are Employers Restricted from Discharging Employees for Taking Leave for Jury Service?	Is There a Restriction on Using Employment Consequences to Influence Employee Vote?	Are Employers Restricted from Discharging Employees Whose Wages Are Subject to Garnishment?	Are Employers Restricted from Making Labor Organization Membership or Nonmembership a Condition of Employment?	Are Employers Restricted from Discharging an Employee for Filing a Workers' Compensation Claim?	Are Employers Restricted from Discharging an Employee for Filing an OSHA Complaint?	Are Employers Restricted from Discharging Employees for Whistleblowing?
HI	Yes.	Yes.	Yes.	Yes.	Yes, except that employer may enter an all-union agreement with employees' bargaining representative unless a majority of employees have voted to revoke their bargaining representative's authority to enter such an agreement within 1 year before the agreement is made.	Yes, unless employee is no longer able to perform duties because of the work injury and employer has no other available work the employee is capable of performing. Applies to employers with three or more employees at the time of the work injury or employers who are not parties to collective bargaining agreements that prevent the continued employment of injured employees.	Yes.	Yes.
ID	Yes.	Yes.	Yes.	Yes. Additional protection of garnishments for child support.	Yes.	—	—	Yes.
IL	Yes. Full-time employee other than an independent contractor shall be granted leave.	Yes.	Yes.	Yes.	Yes. Applies to public employers and employees.	Yes.	Yes.	Yes.

	Are Employers Prohibited from Discharging Employees for Taking Military Leave?	Are Employers Restricted from Discharging Employees for Taking Leave for Jury Service?	Is There a Restriction on Using Employment Consequences to Influence Employee Vote?	Are Employers Restricted from Discharging Employees Whose Wages Are Subject to Garnishment?	Are Employers Restricted from Making Labor Organization Membership or Nonmembership a Condition of Employment?	Are Employers Restricted from Discharging an Employee for Filing a Workers' Compensation Claim?	Are Employers Restricted from Discharging an Employee for Filing an OSHA Complaint?	Are Employers Restricted from Discharging Employees for Whistleblowing?
IN	Yes. Employee must provide employer with evidence of dates of departure and return as soon as practicable before departure, Upon return, employee must furnish employer with evidence of satisfactory completion of training.	Yes.	Yes.	Yes.	Yes.	—	Yes.	Yes.
IA	Yes.	Yes.	Yes.	Yes.	Yes.	Yes.	Yes.	Yes.
KS	Yes, for the National Guard of Kansas.	Yes. Applies only to permanent employees.	Yes.	Yes.	Yes.	—	Yes.	Yes.
KY	Yes.	Yes.	Yes.	Yes.	Yes.	Yes.	Yes.	Yes.
LA	Yes.	Yes.	Yes.	Yes. Applicants for employment are also protected.	Yes.	Yes.	—	Yes.

Exhibit 17.2 (cont'd)
Statutory Restrictions on Discharging Employees

NOTE: A "—" means that no specific statutory authority exists; other authority, including case law, may apply.

	Are Employers Prohibited from Discharging Employees for Taking Military Leave?	Are Employers Restricted from Discharging Employees for Taking Leave for Jury Service?	Is There a Restriction on Using Employment Consequences to Influence Employee Vote?	Are Employers Restricted from Discharging Employees Whose Wages Are Subject to Garnishment?	Are Employers Restricted from Making Labor Organization Membership or Nonmembership a Condition of Employment?	Are Employers Restricted from Discharging an Employee for Filing a Workers' Compensation Claim?	Are Employers Restricted from Discharging an Employee for Filing an OSHA Complaint?	Are Employers Restricted from Discharging Employees for Whistleblowing?
ME	Yes.	Yes.	Yes.	Yes. Also employers may not discharge or take disciplinary action against employees as a result of the existence of a health insurance withholding order.	No.	Yes.	Yes.	Yes.
MD	Yes.	Yes.	Yes.	Yes.	—	Yes.		Yes.
MA	Yes.	Yes.	Yes.	Yes. Applies only to garnishments for child support.	Yes.	Yes.	Yes. Applies to complaints concerning hazardous substances.	Yes.
MI	Yes.	Yes.	Yes.	Yes.	Yes.	Yes.	Yes.	Yes.
MN	Yes.	Yes.	Yes.	Yes.	Yes, except by means of provisions of collective bargaining agreements entered into voluntarily by employer and employees or labor organization representing the employees.	Yes.	Yes.	Yes.
MS	Yes.	Yes.	Yes.	Yes. Applies only to	Yes, except this provision does not apply to	Yes. Applies to corporate employers.	Yes.	Yes.

	Are Employers Prohibited from Discharging Employees for Taking Military Leave?	Are Employers Restricted from Discharging Employees for Taking Leave for Jury Service?	Is There a Restriction on Using Employment Consequences to Influence Employee Vote?	Are Employers Restricted from Discharging Employees Whose Wages Are Subject to Garnishment?	Are Employers Restricted from Making Labor Organization Membership or Nonmembership a Condition of Employment?	Are Employers Restricted from Discharging an Employee for Filing a Workers' Compensation Claim?	Are Employers Restricted from Discharging an Employee for Filing an OSHA Complaint?	Are Employers Restricted from Discharging Employees for Whistleblowing?
				garnishments for child support.	employers and employees under the jurisdiction of the Federal Railway Labor Act.			
MO	Yes.	Yes.	Yes.	Yes.	The state constitution gives employees right to organize collectively, but there exists no specific statutory authority prohibiting employers from making labor organization membership or nonmembership a condition of employment.	Yes.	—	Yes.
MT	Yes.	Yes.	Yes.	Yes.	—	Yes.	—	Yes. Statute also includes constructive discharge.
NE	Yes.	Yes.	Yes.	Yes.	Yes.	—	Yes.	Yes.
NV	Yes.	Yes.	Yes.	Yes.	Yes.	—	Yes.	Yes.

Exhibit 17.2   Mandated Benefits: 2009 Compliance Guide

Exhibit 17.2 (cont'd)
Statutory Restrictions on Discharging Employees

NOTE: A "—" means that no specific statutory authority exists; other authority, including case law, may apply.

	Are Employers Prohibited from Discharging Employees for Taking Military Leave?	Are Employers Restricted from Discharging Employees for Taking Leave for Jury Service?	Is There a Restriction on Using Employment Consequences to Influence Employee Vote?	Are Employers Restricted from Discharging Employees Whose Wages Are Subject to Garnishment?	Are Employers Restricted from Making Labor Organization Membership or Nonmembership a Condition of Employment?	Are Employers Restricted from Discharging an Employee for Filing a Workers' Compensation Claim?	Are Employers Restricted from Discharging an Employee for Filing an OSHA Complaint?	Are Employers Restricted from Discharging Employees for Whistleblowing?
NH	Yes.	Yes.	Yes.	—	Yes.	—	Yes.	Yes.
NJ	Yes.	Yes.	Yes.	Yes.	Yes.	Yes.	Yes.	Yes.
NM	Yes.	Yes.	Yes.	—	Yes.	Yes.	Yes.	—
NY	Yes.	Yes.	Yes.	Yes.	Yes.	Yes.	Yes.	Yes.
NC	Yes.	Yes.	Yes.	Yes. Applies only if 1 of any garnishments is for a debt owed to a public hospital.	Yes.	Yes.	Yes.	Yes.
ND	Yes.	Yes.	Yes.	Yes.	Yes.	Yes.	—	Yes.
OH	Yes.	Yes. Applies only to permanent employees.	Yes.	Yes. Applies only to garnishments that are for orders of support.	Yes.	Yes.	Yes.	Yes.
OK	Yes.	Yes.	Yes.	Yes. Applies to judgments arising from consumer credit sale, consumer lease, or consumer loan.	Yes.	Yes.	Yes. Applies only to public employees.	Yes.

	Are Employers Prohibited from Discharging Employees for Taking Military Leave?	Are Employers Restricted from Discharging Employees for Taking Leave for Jury Service?	Is There a Restriction on Using Employment Consequences to Influence Employee Vote?	Are Employers Restricted from Discharging Employees Whose Wages Are Subject to Garnishment?	Are Employers Restricted from Making Labor Organization Membership or Nonmembership a Condition of Employment?	Are Employers Restricted from Discharging an Employee for Filing a Workers' Compensation Claim?	Are Employers Restricted from Discharging an Employee for Filing an OSHA Complaint?	Are Employers Restricted from Discharging Employees for Whistleblowing?
OR	Yes.	Yes.	Yes.	Yes.	Yes. Applies to public employees.	Yes.	Yes.	Yes.
PA	Yes.	Yes, but statute does not apply to an employer in a retail or service industry employing fewer than 15 persons or to a manufacturing employer with fewer than 40 employees.	Yes.	Yes. Applies only to garnishments that are orders of support. Employee must give employer notice of the garnishment.	Yes.	—	—	Yes.
RI	Yes.	Yes.	Yes.	Yes. Applies only to garnishments for child support.	Yes.	—	Yes.	Yes.
SC	Yes.	Yes.	Yes.	Yes, if the garnishment is for the purpose of paying a judgment arising from a consumer credit sale, consumer lease, consumer loan, or consumer rental purchase agreement.	Yes.	Yes.	Yes.	Yes.

Exhibit 17.2

Exhibit 17.2 (cont'd)
Statutory Restrictions on Discharging Employees

NOTE: A "—" means that no specific statutory authority exists; other authority, including case law, may apply.

	Are Employers Prohibited from Discharging Employees for Taking Military Leave?	Are Employers Restricted from Discharging Employees for Taking Leave for Jury Service?	Is There a Restriction on Using Employment Consequences to Influence Employee Vote?	Are Employers Restricted from Discharging Employees Whose Wages Are Subject to Garnishment?	Are Employers Restricted from Making Labor Organization Membership or Nonmembership a Condition of Employment?	Are Employers Restricted from Discharging an Employee for Filing a Workers' Compensation Claim?	Are Employers Restricted from Discharging an Employee for Filing an OSHA Complaint?	Are Employers Restricted from Discharging Employees for Whistleblowing?
SD	Yes.	Yes.	Yes.	—	Yes. State attorney is responsible for enforcement.	—	—	Yes.
TN	Yes.	Statute exempts an employer with fewer than 5 employees and any temporary employee who has worked for less than 6 months. Employee is excused from work if jury service exceeds 3 hours of the day.	Yes.	—	Yes.	—	Yes.	Yes.
TX	Yes.	Yes. Applies to private employers.	Yes.	—	Yes.	Yes.	Yes.	Yes.
UT	Yes.	Yes.	Yes.	Yes. Additional protection for garnishments to pay child support.	Yes.	—	Yes.	Yes.
VT	Yes.	Yes.	Yes.	Yes.	Yes.	Yes. Also applies to applicants.	Yes.	Yes.

	Are Employers Prohibited from Discharging Employees for Taking Military Leave?	Are Employers Restricted from Discharging Employees for Taking Leave for Jury Service?	Is There a Restriction on Using Employment Consequences to Influence Employee Vote?	Are Employers Restricted from Discharging Employees Whose Wages Are Subject to Garnishment?	Are Employers Restricted from Making Labor Organization Membership or Nonmembership a Condition of Employment?	Are Employers Restricted from Discharging an Employee for Filing a Workers' Compensation Claim?	Are Employers Restricted from Discharging an Employee for Filing an OSHA Complaint?	Are Employers Restricted from Discharging Employees for Whistleblowing?
VA	Yes.	Yes.	Yes.	Yes.	Yes.	Yes.	Yes.	—
WA	Yes.	Yes.	Yes.	Yes.	Yes.	Yes.	Yes.	Yes.
WV	Yes.	Yes.	Yes.	Yes. Applies to judgments arising from consumer credit sales or consumer loans.	Yes.	Yes.	Yes. Applies only to public employees.	Yes.
WI	Yes.	Yes.	Yes.	Yes.	Yes, except that employer may enter into an all-union agreement with the voluntarily recognized representative of the employees in a collective bargaining unit if a majority of employees have voted by secret ballot in favor of such an *(continued)*	Yes.	Yes. Applies to employee requests for information concerning toxic substances, infectious agents, and pesticides with which employee works; applies to employee complaints and participation in proceedings concerning such substances.	—

Exhibit 17.2   Mandated Benefits: 2009 Compliance Guide

Exhibit 17.2 (cont'd)
Statutory Restrictions on Discharging Employees

NOTE: A "—" means that no specific statutory authority exists; other authority, including case law, may apply.

	Are Employers Prohibited from Discharging Employees for Taking Military Leave?	Are Employers Restricted from Discharging Employees for Taking Leave for Jury Service?	Is There a Restriction on Using Employment Consequences to Influence Employee Vote?	Are Employers Restricted from Discharging Employees Whose Wages Are Subject to Garnishment?	Are Employers Restricted from Making Labor Organization Membership or Nonmembership a Condition of Employment?	Are Employers Restricted from Discharging an Employee for Filing a Workers' Compensation Claim?	Are Employers Restricted from Discharging an Employee for Filing an OSHA Complaint?	Are Employers Restricted from Discharging Employees for Whistleblowing?
WI (continued)					agreement. Employers engaged in the building and con- struction industry or the motor freight industry or an employer who is an orchestra or band leader may enter into an all- union agreement without an employee vote.			
WY	Yes.	Yes.	Yes.	Yes.	Yes.	—	Yes.	Yes. Applies only to employees of health care facilities.

Source: John F. Buckley & Ronald M. Green, *2008 State by State Guide to Human Resources Law* (New York: Aspen Publishers, Inc. 2008).

Exhibit 17.3
Employee Handbook Acknowledgment of Receipt

The statements contained in the Handbook are intended to provide only general information about the current policies and practices of employment. Nothing contained herein is intended to create, or shall be construed as creating, an express or implied contract or guarantee of employment for a definite or indefinite term.

I recognize, understand, and agree that such employment will be "at will" employment and that, at any time, I or [*name of company*] may, with or without cause, terminate such employment.

[*Name of company*] retains the right at any time, in its own discretion, to delete, add to, alter, and amend any and all information, statements, employee benefits, or terms and conditions of employment contained herein with or without advance notice to me.

Upon termination I agree to return all property including this Handbook to the company. Any money owed to [*name of company*] will be deducted from my last paycheck (if legal in the state).

My signature below represents that I have received, read, and understand the information outlined in this Handbook.

Full name (print): _____

Signature: _____

Date: _____

Supervisor: _____

Exhibit 17.4   Mandated Benefits: 2009 Compliance Guide

Exhibit 17.4
Employee Handbook Disclaimer Statement

The statements and policies in this Handbook are intended to provide only general information about the policies and procedures at [*name of company*]. Nothing contained herein is intended to create, or shall be construed as creating, an expressed or implied contract or guarantee of employment for a definite or indefinite term. Employees shall retain the right to terminate their employment and [*name of company*] retains the right to terminate the employment of any employee for any reason with or without cause or notice.

[*Name of company*] also retains the right to delete, add to, and amend any information, statements, employee benefits, or terms and conditions of employment contained in this Handbook at its own discretion, in accordance with state and federal requirements with or without advance notice to employees.

Exhibit 17.5
Termination Checklist

_____   _____   _____
Employee name   Date   Social Security Number

HR SECTION

* ☐   Final paycheck

* ☐   COBRA notification (Companies with 20+ employees)

* ☐   Certification of group health plan coverage (Companies with 2+ employees covered on their health plan)

**☐   Notice to employee as to change in relationship (Only needed for a layoff, discharge, or leave)

**☐   401(k) benefit choices form, if applicable

☐   Clean out locker

☐   Clean out desk

☐   Notify security, if applicable

☐   Computer access deleted, if applicable

☐   Voice mail access deleted, if applicable

☐   Final time/expense report, if applicable

COMPANY PROPERTY: (If applicable)

☐   Keys

☐   Company handbook

☐   Equipment: computer, telephone, fax machine, printer, modem, etc.

☐   Manuals (computer manuals, standard operating procedures)

☐   Uniforms

☐   Company credit card

☐   Parking and building access card

☐   Telephone directories

☐   Log books

_____   _____
Human Resources Representative   Date
_____

* Required

** Required under certain circumstances

Exhibit 17.6   Mandated Benefits: 2009 Compliance Guide

Exhibit 17.6
Sample Exit Interview Questions

These are sample questions that might be asked in a face-to-face interview and/or on a written question-naire. They should be adapted to fit the needs of the organization and the circumstances of the termination.

What was the most beneficial/enjoyable/satisfying part of your job?

What was the least beneficial/enjoyable/satisfying part of your job?

Did you receive the proper support to be able to do your job well? If not, what was lacking?

How would you evaluate the training you received? Was it adequate to enable you to perform your job?

Were there any obstacles or conditions that made your job more difficult? If yes, what were they?

Were your job expectations clear?

What improvements would you make to your current position?

If going to a new job, what does that job/company offer that we do not?

Please tell me the reasons you are leaving our company.

Would you consider working at our company in the future?

Would you recommend working for this company to others?

Did your supervisor treat employees fairly and consistently?

What was the quality of the supervision you received?

Do you have any suggestions for making this company a better place to work?

Are there any issues that you would like to bring to our attention at this time?

Please rate the following on a scale of 1 to 5 (5 highest):

    Opportunity for advancement
    Training (internal as well as opportunities for external)
    Working environment
    Quality of supervision
    Company communications
    Salary
    Benefits

Chapter 18
Equal Employment Opportunity and Affirmative Action Plan

§ 18.01   AUDIT QUESTIONS

1. Does the company have a written effective equal employment opportunity policy that is in compliance with the law?

2. Has management been trained in effective, nondiscriminatory human resources practices, such as interviewing, making promotion decisions, and handling employee complaints?

3. Does the company have a formal and well-defined procedure for receiving and responding to employee complaints, including complaints about potential discriminatory actions?

4. Has the company determined if it is required to comply with federal mandatory affirmative action regulations? If the company is required to comply:

    a. Does it have current affirmative action plans for minorities, women, veterans, and individuals with disabilities that comply with the regulations?

    b. Has it made a reasonable attempt to create all required statistical analyses in a manner that is consistent with Office of Federal Contract Compliance Programs (OFCCP) regulations and current compliance evaluations investigative processes?

    c. Does it retain all records that comply with OFCCP regulations, including data on employment transactions such as hires, promotions, transfers, and terminations?

    d. Is it prepared for an OFCCP compliance evaluation, including a compliance check in which it may receive only three days' notice from the agency?

5. Is the company filing appropriate Employer Identification Reports (e.g., EEO-1 and VETS-100) each year?

Note: Consistent "yes" answers to the above questions suggest that the organization is applying effective management practices and/or complying with federal regulations. "No" answers indicate that problem areas exist and should be addressed immediately.

The diversity found in the workforce today and the ever-increasing need for talent have made human resource (HR) issues a top business priority. Successful employers must learn how to harness the strength of a diverse labor force to support and achieve their business objectives. Nonetheless, complaints of employment discrimination are at an all-time high and costing employers millions annually. Inequities in pay, hiring, promotion, training, and termination continue to persist for individuals in legally protected groups, who often lag behind their white male counterparts in most benefits and privileges of employment.

This chapter summarizes, in two separate sections, the basic concepts, legal requirements, and practices related to federal equal employment opportunity and mandatory affirmative action. Although mandatory affirmative action is grounded on the principles of equal employment opportunity, obligations for employers who are covered by these laws and regulations are more defined and extensive. In addition, separate statutes and regulations govern equal employment opportunity and affirmative action, and different federal organizations are charged with monitoring employer compliance.

§ 18.02   EQUAL EMPLOYMENT OPPORTUNITY

Employment discrimination, intentional or inadvertent, subtle or direct, is illegal in the United States. There are few rights more deeply embedded in the consciousness of employees than the right to be treated fairly and not to be discriminated against because of, for example, the color of their skin or the place where they were born.

The practice of discrimination in any aspect of employment is a significant risk to a company's reputation and financial security, as the Chuck E. Cheese pizza chain (a subsidiary of Showbiz Pizza Time, Inc.) found out in November 1999. A jury awarded a former employee of the pizza chain over $13 million in damages for being fired because of his disability, which was mental retardation. This verdict represents the largest monetary relief awarded by a jury in a case brought by the Equal Employment Opportunity Commission (EEOC) under the Americans with Disabilities Act of 1990 (ADA). The employee was awarded $10,000 in back pay, $70,000 in compensatory damages, and $13 million in punitive damages.

[A]   Definitions

Congress originated the principle of equal employment opportunity, as we know it today, with the passage of Title VII of the Civil Rights Act of 1964. This statute and subsequent legislation gave rise to the following terms and concepts commonly associated with this area of employment law.

Discriminate means "to make a choice." However, the term *discrimination* has a broader meaning when used in employment laws and regulations. Discrimination in an employment context means to treat job applicants or employees who are members of legally protected groups (e.g., those based on race, color, national origin, religion, sex, age, and disability) less favorably than other applicants or employees. (Many states and local municipalities include among legally protected groups individuals in other categories, such as marital status, sexual preference, and status with regard to public assistance.)

Discrimination occurs when an employer intentionally takes actions that are disadvantageous for members of a protected group (commonly known as disparate treatment discrimination) or when an apparently neutral or nondiscriminatory employment practice has an unjustified exclusionary effect on members of a protected group (commonly known as disparate impact discrimination). Both forms of discrimination are illegal in any and all aspects of employment, including:

- Hiring and firing

- Compensation, assignment, or classification of employees

- Transfer, promotion, layoff, or recall

- Job advertisements

- Recruitment

- Testing

- Use of company facilities

- Training and apprenticeship programs

- Fringe benefits

- Pay, retirement, and disability leave

- Other terms and conditions of employment

Equal employment opportunity (EEO) means the absence of discrimination against job applicants or employees, either intentionally or unintentionally, based on their protected group status or other non-job-related criteria in any term, condition, or privilege of employment. Under EEO regulations, discrimination encompasses:

- Harassment on the basis of race, color, national origin, religion, sex, age, or disability;

- Retaliation against an individual for filing a charge of discrimination, participating in an investigation, or opposing discriminatory practices;

- Employment decisions based on stereotypes or assumptions about the abilities, traits, or performance of individuals of a certain race, color, national origin, religion, sex, age, or disability; and

- Denial of employment opportunities to individuals because of their marriage to, or association with, an individual of a particular race, national origin, religion, or disability, or because of their participation in schools or places of worship associated with a particular racial, ethnic, or religious group.

Protected group status refers to those applicants or employees that federal job bias laws protect from discrimination on the basis of race, color, national origin, religion, sex, age, and disability.

[B] Equal Employment Opportunity Commission

The Equal Employment Opportunity Commission (EEOC) is an independent regulatory agency established through Title VII of the Civil Rights Act of 1964. The commission's five members are appointed by the President of the United States, confirmed by the Senate, and serve staggered five-year terms. The President appoints a General Counsel for a four-year term, who is also confirmed by the Senate. Its mission, as set forth in its strategic plan, is to promote equal opportunity through administrative and judicial enforcement of the federal civil rights laws and through education and technical assistance. The EEOC enforces the six principal federal statutes prohibiting employment discrimination:

Title VII of the Civil Rights Act of 1964, as amended; the Equal Pay Act of 1963; the Age Discrimination in Employment Act of 1967 (ADEA), as amended; Title I of the Americans with Disabilities Act of 1990 (ADA); the Civil Rights Act of 1991; and Section 503 of the Rehabilitation Act of 1973, as amended.

The EEOC provides assistance to employers through initiatives, written guidance, training, and outreach. Employers can find this assistance on the EEOC Web site: *www.eeoc.gov*.

[C] Key Equal Employment Opportunity Laws

The EEOC monitors six key statutes passed by Congress that define an employer's legal obligations regarding equal employment opportunity. Employers are required to post notices to all applicants and employees advising them of their rights under those laws and their right to be free from retaliation. Such notices must be accessible, as needed, to persons with visual or other disabilities that affect reading ability.

[1] Title VII of the Civil Rights Act of 1964

Title VII of the Civil Rights Act of 1964, as amended, prohibits employment discrimination based on race, color, religion, sex, or national origin. Title VII prohibits not only intentional discrimination but also practices that have the effect of discriminating against individuals because of their race, color, religion, sex, or national origin. Examples of actions or practices that are defined as illegal under Title VII include:

- Discriminating against an individual because of birthplace, ancestry, culture, or linguistic characteristics common to a specific ethnic group

- Requiring that employees speak only English on the job unless the employer can show that the requirement is necessary for conducting business

- Failing to provide reasonable accommodation for the religious beliefs of an employee or prospective employee, unless doing so would impose an undue hardship on the employer

- Requiring employees who wear certain attire for religious reasons, such as a Sikh turban or a Muslim hijab (headscarf), to remove such attire while at work

- Tolerating the sexual harassment of an employee or prospective employee, ranging from direct requests for sexual favors to workplace conditions that create a hostile environment for persons of either gender, including same sex harassment

- Failing to treat pregnancy, childbirth, and related medical conditions like other temporary illnesses or conditions

- Retaliating against an employee because he or she engages in a protected activity, such as filing a charge; testifying, assisting, or participating in an investigation of the employer; or opposing a discriminatory practice

Title VII covers private employers, state and local governments, and education institutions that employ 15 or more individuals. It also covers private and public employment agencies, labor organizations, and joint labor-management committees controlling apprenticeship and training. Title VII also applies to the federal government, but different procedures are used for processing complaints of federal discrimination. Many states and local municipalities have passed equal employment opportunity statutes, regulations, or ordinances that list other categories in their definition of legally protected groups, including marital status, sexual preference, and status with regard to public assistance. Companies should contact local civil or human rights agencies to determine whether there is a need to comply with additional local and state regulations.

[2] Equal Pay Act of 1963

The Equal Pay Act of 1963 prohibits discrimination on the basis of sex in the payment of wages or benefits, where men and women perform work of similar skill, effort, or responsibility for the same employer under similar working conditions. Under this Act, it is important that an employer be aware of the following:

- The wages of either sex may not be reduced to equalize pay differences between men and women.

- A violation may occur when a different wage is paid to a person who works in the same job before or after an employee of the opposite sex.

- A violation may also occur when a labor organization causes the employer to discriminate against an employee in violation of the law.

The Equal Pay Act covers all employees who are covered by the Fair Labor Standards Act of 1938; thus, it covers virtually all employees.

[3] Age Discrimination in Employment Act of 1967

The ADEA, as amended, prohibits employment discrimination against individuals who are age 40 or older. The ADEA's broad ban against discrimination specifically prohibits:

- Statements or specifications in job notices or advertisements of age preference and limitations (an age limit may be specified only in the rare circumstances where age has been proven to be a bona fide occupational qualification)

- Discrimination on the basis of age in apprenticeship programs, including joint labor-management apprenticeship programs

- Denial of benefits to older employers (an employer may reduce benefits based on age only if the cost of providing the reduced benefits to older workers is the same as the cost of providing similar benefits to younger workers)

The ADEA covers private employers with 20 or more employees, state and local governments (including school districts), employment agencies, and labor organizations.

[4] Title I of the Americans with Disabilities Act of 1990

Title I of the ADA covers private employers, state and local governments, and educational institutions that employ 15 or more individuals. It also covers private and public employment agencies, labor organizations, and joint labor-management committees controlling apprenticeship and training programs. Title I prohibits discrimination in all employment practices against qualified individuals with disabilities. It is necessary to understand several important definitions to know what persons are protected by this law and what constitutes illegal discrimination. (For further discussion of the ADA, see **Chapter 13**.)

[5]   The Civil Rights Act of 1991

The Civil Rights Act of 1991 made major changes in the federal laws against employment discrimination enforced by the EEOC. Enacted in part to reverse several Supreme Court decisions that limited the rights of persons protected by these laws, the Act also provides additional protections. It authorizes compensatory and punitive damages in cases of intentional discrimination based on sex, religion, or disability, and provides for obtaining attorneys' fees and the possibility of jury trials. It also directs the EEOC to expand its technical assistance and outreach activities.

[6]   Section 503 of the Rehabilitation Act of 1973

Section 503 of the Rehabilitation Act of 1973, as amended, prohibits employment discrimination against qualified individuals with disabilities who are employed by a federal contractor or subcontractor with contract(s) in excess of $10,000. It incorporates the requirement of the ADA.

[7]   Uniformed Services Employment and Reemployment Rights Act

The Uniformed Services Employment and Reemployment Rights Act (USERRA), enacted December 12, 1994, substantially improved employment and reemployment rights of employed veterans. USERRA prohibits employment discrimination due to an individual being "a member of, applies to be a member of, performs, has performed, applies to perform, or has an obligation to perform, service in a uniformed service." The "uniformed services" include the Army, Navy, Marine Corps, Air Force, Coast Guard, Army National Guard, Air National Guard, the Commissioned Corps of the Public Health Service, and the reserves of the Army, Navy, Marine Corps, Air Force, and Coast Guard, as well as training for or activation for intermittent disaster response to the National Disaster Medical System. Employers cannot refuse to hire an otherwise qualified applicant due to his or her military status or obligation to perform service. For example, an employer cannot refuse to hire an applicant because he or she was called to duty and cannot begin work immediately.

Information on employee benefits under USERRA can be found in **Chapter 5** (see **Section 5.12**). For information on how USERRA affects leaves of absence, see **Chapter 11, Section 11.04[D]**.

[8]   Genetic Information Nondiscrimination Act of 2008

The Genetic Information Nondiscrimination Act of 2008 (GINA) prohibits employers, employment agencies, labor unions, and insurance providers from discriminating on the basis of genetic information. GINA amends ERISA, the Public Health Service Act and the Code, as well as Title VII of the Civil Rights Act. The provisions that effect employers will go into effect 18 months after enactment on November 21, 2009. Genetic information is defined as (1) the individual's genetic tests; (2) the individual's family members' genetic tests; and (3) the manifestation of a disease or disorder in family members of an individual. Gender and age are not genetic information. GINA defines family member as: (1) the individual's spouse; (2) a dependent child of the individual, including children placed for adoption; or (3) parents, grandparents or great-grandparents.

Employers, labor unions, and employment agencies may not use genetic information to discriminate against employees in hiring, promotion, job assignment, firing, training, retraining, and all other privileges and conditions of employment. Employers may not use genetic information to limit, segregate, or classify employees to deprive them of employment opportunities or otherwise adversely affect their employment. In general GINA prevents an employer from requiring, requesting or purchasing genetic information about an employee or a family member. There are exceptions: (1) inadvertent requests for such information; (2) genetic services provided by the employer, including wellness programs; (3) when required to correctly administer leaves under FMLA; and (4) when obtained through the purchase of commercially available documents. Employers must maintain the confidentiality of all genetic information in the same manner as medical information is protected under the Americans with Disabilities Act, including maintaining the information on separate forms and in separate medical files. Genetic information can only be disclosed under certain circumstances, including, for example (1) at the employee's written request, (2) for approved occupational and health research, (3) in response to a court order, and (4) to comply with the FMLA's requirements. Employers may not retaliate against an employee for exercising rights under GINA.

If an employee feels that their rights under GINA have been violated, they may seek relief under Title VII of the Civil Rights Act. The individual must file a complaint with the EEOC or with their state agency. If a violation is found, the agency will bring suit on behalf of the employee; if the agency decides not to bring suit, the employee may sue ("right to sue"). However, GINA does not provide for disparate discrimination claims.

Information on GINA's health care nondiscrimination requirements can be found in **Chapter 5**.

[D] Types of Discrimination

Since 1964, the courts have defined two types of discrimination under Title VII:

1. *Disparate treatment discrimination* (*unequal treatment*). Refers to practices in which an employer treats similarly situated members of protected groups less favorably than others, either openly or covertly. Under this definition, an employment practice is unlawful if it applies different standards to different employees—for example, establishing a standard based on performance for women but one based on seniority for men. Under disparate treatment discrimination, intent to discriminate must be shown. Discriminatory intent can be shown by direct evidence or inferentially by comparative or statistical evidence. Unequal treatment of individuals in different groups may be taken as evidence of an employer's intention to discriminate.

2. *Disparate impact discrimination* (*unequal impact*). Addresses employment practices that appear to be neutral but result in disadvantageous treatment of members of protected groups at a substantially higher rate than such treatment for others. Disparate impact discrimination is unlawfully discriminatory if an employer fails to demonstrate that the practice is job-related and consistent with business necessity. Under disparate impact discrimination, the burden of proof lies with the employer with respect to defending employment actions that result in underrepresentation of protected class members.

   This interpretation of Title VII was established by the landmark case of *Griggs v. Duke Power Co.* [401 U.S. 424 (1971)], in which the court struck down employment tests and educational requirements that screened out a greater proportion of blacks than whites. Even though the practices were applied equally and both blacks and whites had to pass the tests, they were prohibited because:

a. The result was to exclude a protected group (blacks) disproportionately, and

b. The tests were not related to the jobs in question.

Disparate impact discrimination has applied to Title VII cases since 1971; until recently, it had not been applied to age discrimination under the ADEA. This changed with the Supreme Court's ruling in 2005 on *Smith v. City of Jackson, Miss.* [125 S. Ct. 1536 (2005)]. The court held that, due to the similarity of language in both the ADEA and Title VII, similar remedies should be available under both statutes. In *Smith*, the City of Jackson, Mississippi, raised the pay of its police officers, giving those with less than five years of service proportionally larger increases than those (older officers) with more than five years of service. The older officers, claiming age discrimination, sued the city.

The Supreme Court found that disparate impact cases can be brought under the ADEA, even though it ruled against Smith in this case. Citing *Atonio v. Wards Cove Packing Co.* [275 F.3d 797 (9th Cir. 2001)], the Court found that plaintiffs are "responsible for isolating and identifying the specific employment practices that are allegedly responsible for any observed statistical disparities." In this case, the Court did not find that Smith identified any such specific test, requirement or practice within the pay plan that adversely impacted older workers. In addition, the Supreme Court also indicated that "the scope of disparate impact liability under ADEA is narrower" than under Title VII. Under the ADEA, the employer need only show that the business policy or practice is reasonable, not that it is the best or fairest approach.

These two types of discrimination have been well established in employment or access discrimination issues, but they have been somewhat more difficult to apply to pay issues, since different pay may be legal for dissimilar work. Court decisions imply that pay differentials between dissimilar jobs are prohibited under Title VII if the employer can show that the differences are based on the content of the work, its value to the organization's objectives, and the employer's ability to attract and retain employees in competitive external labor markets. The courts appear to recognize that the value of a particular job to an employer is only one of several factors that influence the rate of compensation for a job. But under Title VII, courts are authorized to order such corrective action as may be appropriate. Under this provision, the court may:

- Require reinstatement and restoration of seniority to an improperly fired employee

- Require hiring an improperly rejected job applicant

- Grant tenure

- Order promotions

- Freeze promotions

- Expunge adverse material from personnel files

- Order transfers or reassignments

- Permanently enjoin specific practices, such as height or weight requirements

Employment discrimination disputes are frequently resolved by court-approved agreements between the parties that are enforced by the courts. An example of such an agreement is a case in which a company entered into a consent decree with the Department of Labor (DOL), thereby ending 14 years of litigation over charges that the company discriminated against women. Under this decree, the company was ordered to pay $14 million in back pay to several thousand current and former employees.

[E] Complying with Equal Opportunity Laws

Equal opportunity laws require the special attention of companies for a number of reasons. First, these laws regulate the design and administration of all employment-related processes and systems. Second, the definition of discrimination under these laws continues to evolve on a case-by-case basis according to the interpretation of the courts.

Many provisions of discrimination laws simply require high-quality, sensible HR management practices. Sound HR practices have three basic features:

1. They are work-related;

2. They are related to the company's mission; and

3. They include an appeals process for employees who disagree with the results of an employment decision.

The responsibility for complying with equal opportunity laws rests on the shoulders of all managers and supervisors, who, ideally, are supported by trained HR professionals. Management must avoid stereotyping or dealing with employees and candidates in any manner perceived as biased. Planned, systematic processes must replace intuitive, undocumented HR actions. The principal job of the HR manager is to ensure that the overall personnel system is properly designed and managed.

[1] The Employment Interview

Federal, state, and local antidiscrimination laws should be considered by a manager when interviewing potential employees. Interviews are a key component of most selection processes for hiring, transferring, training, and promoting individuals. The selection process is a major employment area and one that can leave companies vulnerable to charges of discrimination. (For further discussion of employment interviews, see **Chapter 16**.)

With the increased government attention on compensatory and punitive damages, companies should go to great lengths to prevent discrimination charges from arising in the course of employment interviews. One way to do so is to ensure that every manager has a good understanding of the pitfalls of employment interviews. Managers must be aware that even apparently innocent questions asked in good faith of job applicants can leave a company open to costly and time-consuming discrimination charges.

The EEOC regards preemployment questions on the following subjects as potential evidence of discrimination, unless the employer can present a convincing case based on some nondiscriminatory business need:

- Marital status

- Child care arrangements (e.g., questions such as "Do you have someone dependable to look after your children every day?" and "If your child is ill, would you have to stay home from work?" can be considered discriminatory.)

- Contraceptive practices

- Plans to have children

- Age

- Height and weight unless they are a bona fide occupational qualification

- Arrest and some conviction records (An arrest is not evidence that an individual has committed a crime. Further, arrest inquiries are considered discriminatory since minorities have a higher percentage of arrests than nonminorities. Questions concerning convictions may be appropriate if the convictions are job-related and recent.)

- Garnishment (Such inquiries are considered discriminatory for some of the same reasons as are inquiries about arrests and conviction records.)

- Credit history

- Education (e.g., asking if the candidate has a high school diploma or a college degree) (Questions concerning educational history are not in themselves discriminatory, provided the job actually requires such educational qualifications. EEOC guidelines, which have been upheld in the courts, prohibit requiring a high school education when this requirement discriminates significantly against some protected groups and there is no real evidence that it is highly predictive of job success. As a result, managers may want to reconsider existing requirements for a high school diploma or a college degree for many jobs if they cannot prove that these requirements are directly job-related.)

When faced with myriad statutes and regulations concerning interviewing, many managers become confused about what they can and cannot ask when interviewing job candidates. An applicant's job-related skills and abilities for a particular position are the most relevant selection criteria. Previous directly related work experience should also be explored. The key to a good placement is to select the candidate whose skills and abilities, often demonstrated through prior work experience and performance, most closely match the requirements of the job.

[2]   Assessing Employee Performance and Potential

Once an employee has been hired, a manager has two primary responsibilities: to evaluate the employee's performance and assess the employee's potential for advancement against the requirements of the job. Both are complex functions involving personal judgment, which is subject to an individual manager's biases and perceptions. Organizational norms and biases may also influence performance assessment and identification of employees eligible for promotion.

Most progressive companies are striving to overcome norms and biases originally based unconsciously on white males' behavior and characteristics and to ensure that irrelevant factors are recognized and treated as such. It is particularly important to ensure that members of protected groups are treated fairly and that all employees are evaluated and promoted on the basis of their skills, ability, and performance. In fact, appropriate job placement and increased work performance benefit the company as well as the employee.

[3] The EEO-1 Report

The EEO-1 report, Standard Form 100, was developed by the EEOC and the Office of Federal Contract Compliance Programs (OFCCP) as a single form, which meets the statistical needs of both agencies. The EEO-1 report collects race, ethnicity, and gender data in broad occupational categories. The EEOC uses this data to support its enforcement of Title VII of the Civil Rights Act of 1964, as amended.

The following employers must complete the EEO-1 report:

- Private employers with 100 or more employees, except for state and local governments, primary and secondary school systems, institutions of higher education, Native American tribes and tax-exempt private membership clubs other than labor organizations; or

- Federal contractors (private employers) who have 50 or more employees and (1) are prime contractors or first-tier subcontractors, and have contracts, subcontracts, or purchase orders amounting to $50,000 or more; (2) serve as a depository of government funds in any amount; or (3) that are financial institutions that serve as issuing and paying agents for U.S. savings bonds and notes.

The EEO-1 report is generally completed and filed online and is due by September 30 each year. Employers must use employment figures from any one pay period between July and September of the survey year in question. Links to the EEO-1 form and specific information about how to complete and file it can be found on the EEOC's Web site: *http://www.eeoc.gov/eeo1survey/index.html*.

On November 28, 2005, the EEOC published the final rule changing the job categories and race and ethnic categories on the EEO-1 report. The "Hispanic" race category has been reclassified to ethnicity, and has been renamed "Hispanic or Latino." Employees who self-identify as Hispanic or Latino ethnicity are not counted in any of the race categories. The phrase "not Hispanic or Latino" has been added to all race categories. A new category, "two or more races," has been added to the race categories. The category "Asian or Pacific Islander" has been divided into two separate categories, "Asian" and "Native Hawaiian or other Pacific Islander."

In addition, the number of job categories has been increased as a result of dividing the Officials and Managers category into two groups: "Executives/Senior Level" and "First/Mid Level" Officials. The "Executive/Senior Level" Officials category includes those who set strategy and provide overall direction for the organization. The "First/Mid Level" Officials category includes those who manage implementation of the strategy. Finally, individuals in business and financial occupations should be moved from the Officials and Managers category to the Professional category. Examples of positions that should be in the Professionals category include accountants, auditors, and computer programmers.

The EEOC strongly encourages employers to use employee self-identification for ethnicity or race categorization. Employment records or visual observation should be used only if the employee refuses to self-identify. Self-identification forms should be voluntary and the EEOC has published the following statement for use on self-identification forms:

> The employer is subject to certain governmental recordkeeping and reporting requirements for the administration of civil rights laws and regulations. In order to comply with these laws, the employer invites employees to voluntarily self-identify their race or ethnicity. Submission of this information is voluntary and refusal to provide it will not subject you to any adverse treatment. The information will be kept confidential and may only be used in accordance with the provisions of applicable laws, executive orders

and regulations, including those that require the information to be summarized and reported to the federal government for civil rights enforcement. When reported, data will not identify any specific individual.

The self-identification forms are confidential employment records. They should be maintained separately from other personnel files and records.

The revised EEO-1 report was to be filed for the first time in calendar year 2007 by September 30, 2007. Employers were not required to resurvey current employees using the new ethnicity and race categories in 2007, but were encouraged to do so. Employers are required to have resurveyed their entire workforce by September 30, 2008.

In October 2007, the OFCCP submitted a proposal to the Office of Management and Budget to revise the race and ethnicity categories for AAPs to correspond to the revised EEO-1 categories. However, by August 2008, the OFCCP had not published any revisions. The OFCCP published interim guidance in 2007, updated in 2008, indicating that until final rules and guidance are published, the agency will not, as a matter of enforcement discretion, cite a contractor for noncompliance solely because the contractor uses the race and ethnic categories required by the revised EEO-1 report to prepare its AAP. Alternatively, a contractor may continue to use the race categories utilized by the previous edition of the EEO-1 report. If a contractor chooses to use the "old" race categories, data collected separately for Asians and Native Hawaiian or other Pacific Islanders will be combined to be counted as Asian or Pacific Islander. Under current regulations, AAPs do not include a "two or more races" category. Contractors will need to identify (through self-identification, visual observation, or other employment records) the primary race of those employees who identify themselves as two or more races. An example of a self-identification form that can be used by an employer with both AAP, EEO-1, Vets-100 and Vets-100A requirements can be found in **Exhibit 18.1**.

[F]   Case Studies

Many discrimination charges are the result of procedures, practices, and actions that were not intended to be discriminatory. The following cases of potential discriminatory situations could occur at your company.

Case 1: Age Discrimination. Deanna, a female applicant with excellent references, applies for a position as a receptionist. In the course of the interview, Deanna reveals that she is 43 years old. The interviewer says, "I was afraid of that. Please don't misunderstand me. I think you're a capable and attractive woman. It's just that management is trying to maintain a more youthful image for our customers and prefers to hire women in their twenties and early thirties as receptionists. Besides, there is a lot of pressure in the job, and most older women cannot handle it."

Although more managers are now becoming attuned to the issue of age discrimination, age stereotyping in employment is still fairly common. This is an obvious case of age discrimination, but more often than not, age discrimination takes a subtler form.

Case 2: Race and Gender Discrimination. Conscious of its equal employment responsibilities, ABC Company wants to promote Melanie, a black female employee, into a business development position involving outside customer contact. Previously, white males have always held this position. In the course of the conversation with Melanie, the hiring manager indicates the resistance that she might encounter in the business community because she is a black female. He explains that he is simply trying to make Melanie aware of all aspects of the position and that this could be a problem for her if she assumes such a position. He promises her the next business development position that becomes available. A month later ABC Company receives notification from the EEOC that Melanie has filed a charge of race discrimination.

The situation described in Case 2 is not uncommon. A charge of discrimination is sometimes the result of an explanation like the one the hiring manager gave Melanie. Melanie alleged that the manager was merely going through the motions of offering her a promotion. In reality, he was encouraging her to turn down the position because of the hostility she could expect.

In a similar type of situation, a manager says to a female candidate, "You have excellent qualifications, but there is one problem. This is a small department with all men who have worked together for a long time. The atmosphere is casual, to say the least, and the men have made it plain that they don't want to have to mind their manners because of a woman in the department. Keeping the other employees in the department happy is good for you and the company." At issue is the fact that the preferences of customers and coworkers do not justify race and gender discrimination.

> **Case 3: Child Care Concerns.** The hiring manager at Blake & Co. has an ideal candidate for a clerical position. During the candidate's interview, the manager learns that the candidate has school-age children and asks about her child care plans. The manager explains, "I'm sensitive about this area because my last secretary had small children, and it became a problem. She often came in late because she had trouble getting them to school and stayed home when they were sick. It was very disruptive to the routine of the whole office." The candidate charges the manager with discrimination.

Companies should be aware that the courts have found discussions of the type described in Case 3 discriminatory. Concerns that are not work-related should not enter the employee selection process.

[G] Discrimination Complaints and Charges

A *discrimination complaint* is an allegation by an employee that the employer has violated his or her equal employment opportunity rights. The complaint is filed with the employer and may be made informally or in writing, depending on the employer's policy and procedures. A *discrimination charge*, on the other hand, is an employee's written allegation of a violation of his or her equal employment opportunity rights that is formally filed with the EEOC or with state or local human rights agencies.

Until the early 1960s, employers almost always resolved discrimination complaints, often in their favor and in an abrupt and final manner. Because the resolution of these complaints was frequently disadvantageous to employees, Congress took notice and passed the Civil Rights Act of 1964 and other equal employment opportunity legislation designed to give employees a fair hearing of their complaints. The Civil Rights Act of 1964 elevated the importance of discrimination complaints in the workplace and offered employees an external avenue for resolving discrimination issues.

Discrimination complaints filed directly with an employer are often best remedied or resolved between an employee and an employer. Formal discrimination charges, as they are defined, involve the intervention of a third party, usually a civil or human rights agency, to resolve them. The role of the third party is to objectively gather facts and investigate the issue by talking to both the employee filing the charge and the employer. A third party is often important in dealing with discrimination charges because the issues may impact other individuals in addition to the employee who filed the charge. For example, a charge filed by a minority female employee that she should have been given a promotion cannot be resolved without taking into consideration the interests of other employees, both minority and nonminority, male and female, who may have deserved or should have received the promotion in question.

Resolving discrimination complaints or charges related to selection decisions is rarely as simple and clear-cut as determining whether the complainant had the minimum education or training for a specific job. More often, it is a complicated situation in which the relative qualifications of multiple candidates are compared (i.e., are the complainant's qualifications less than, equal to, or better than the qualifications of other candidates?).

In general, if HR actions and decisions appear to be arbitrary or based on favoritism, discrimination complaints and charges are much more likely to occur. It is not uncommon for an employer to have disgruntled employees who perceive that discrimination has occurred or is occurring but who have not yet registered a complaint or filed a charge. Often these individuals are letting their grievances fester, waiting for an opportune time to take action on them. Symptoms of employee discrimination problems and issues include low morale, poor work attitudes, increased turnover, and low productivity.

When a formal established employee complaint process is available, employees know that there are procedures for airing their complaints and having them reviewed by management. The complaint process should be well communicated, and carefully and consistently followed, regardless of whether it is very simple or entails several formal steps. Further, an effective internal complaint process can help a company avoid formal agency discrimination charges and the intervention of a third party. If all efforts fail and a charge is filed with a government human rights agency, a company can show that, at a minimum, it had an effective complaint process and was open to addressing and resolving the issue internally.

[H]   EEOC Charge-Processing Procedures

As noted above, EEOC discrimination proceedings begin when an employee, former employee, or, in some cases, a rejected job applicant files a formal charge with the agency. Normally, a charge under Title VII, the ADEA, or the ADA must be filed with the EEOC within 180 days from the date of the alleged violation for the charging party to protect his or her rights. The 180-day deadline is extended to 300 days if a state or local antidiscrimination law also covers the charge and the charge must first be presented to a state or local agency. In those jurisdictions, the charge must be filed with the EEOC within 300 days of the alleged violation or 30 days after receiving notice that the state or local agency has terminated its processing of the charge, whichever is earlier. In July 2005, the EEOC revised its compliance manual to base the determination as to timeliness on whether the complaint involves a "discrete act" or a hostile work environment. If the claim is about a discrete act—such as a failure to hire, termination, or denial of a transfer request—the filing of the claim must occur within 180 (or 300) days of the act. However, if the claim regards a hostile work environment, the claim will be considered timely if at least one incident that makes up the hostile work environment claim is within the time limit.

These time limits do not apply to persons filing claims under the Equal Pay Act (EPA) because they do not have to first file a charge with EEOC in order to have the right to go to court. EPA claims must be filed within two years of the alleged violation, or within three years if the violation is considered a "willful" act.

After investigating the circumstances behind the charge, the EEOC determines whether there is reasonable cause to believe that there was a violation of the law and whether discrimination has occurred. If the EEOC finds reasonable cause, it will attempt to conciliate with the employer to develop a remedy for the discrimination. If the case is successfully conciliated, or if the case has been successfully mediated or settled earlier, neither the EEOC nor the charging party may get to court unless the conciliation, mediation, or settlement agreement is not honored. If the evidence obtained in the investigation does not establish that discrimination has occurred, the EEOC will notify the charging party of its decision and close the case. After receiving a notice of dismissal and a "right to sue" notice, the charging party has 90 days to file a lawsuit on his or her own behalf. Under the ADEA, a lawsuit may be filed at any time 60 days after filing a charge with the EEOC, but not later than 90 days after the EEOC gives notice that it has completed action on the charge. Under the Equal Pay Act, a lawsuit must be filed within two years (three years for willful violations) of the discriminatory act, which in most cases is payment of a discriminatory lower wage.

The purpose of judicial relief in employment discrimination cases is to reimburse or make whole the individual or class affected by the discrimination. Moreover, this relief is meant to prevent employers from engaging in such illegal actions in the future. Full corrective and preventive remedies for violations are contained in the various employment discrimination laws.

Depending on the statute involved, monetary relief may include back pay, front pay, attorneys' fees, expert witness fees, court costs, and compensatory and punitive damages. Other remedies may include hiring, promotion, reinstatement, or reasonable accommodation.

If discrimination has affected an entire class or group of protected individuals, the court may impose hiring or promotional goals or take other steps to implement equal employment opportunity. In addition, it may require periodic reports to confirm the employer's progress in implementing the court order.

Although relatively stable over time, the number of discrimination charges filed each year has varied over the last 10 years from a low of 75,428 in fiscal year 2005 to a high of 84,442 in 2002. For the most recent year for which charge statistics are available (2007), 82,792 charges were filed. In 2007, the most common charges by type of discrimination were: race (30,510), retaliation (26,663), sex (24,826), age (19,103), and disability (17,734). In the future, employers can expect to see more class action charges, more complex charges alleging multiple types of discrimination, and more policy guidance from the EEOC and the courts.

[I] Retaliation

Title VII of the Civil Rights Act prohibits retaliation, making it unlawful for an employer to discriminate against an employee because he or she has filed a charge of discrimination (or otherwise participated in a proceeding under the Act) or opposed any practice made unlawful by Title VII. Until June 22, 2006, the Circuit Courts had been split as to what adverse actions are sufficient to create a charge of retaliation. On that date, the Supreme Court ruled on *Burlington Northern & Santa Fe Railway Co. v. White* (No. 05-529) and resolved the split.

Sheila White was hired by Burlington Northern & Santa Fe Railway Co to perform the job of "track laborer." Shortly after her hire, she was assigned forklift duties which, although "cleaner" and less difficult than the typical track laborer duties, were included in the written job description of track laborer. White complained to company officials that her supervisor made discriminatory and harassing remarks and actions. The railroad conducted an investigation and suspended the supervisor and ordered him to attend sexual harassment training. At that same time, the railroad removed White from the forklift duties, claiming that a coworker complained that a "more senior man" should have that job. There were no changes to White's salary or benefits. White filed a discrimination and retaliation complaint with the EEOC. She filed a second complaint that the supervisor had placed her under surveillance and was monitoring her daily activities. Thereafter, upon a disagreement with another supervisor, White was suspended for insubordination. After she filed an internal grievance, the railroad investigated and determined that she had not been insubordinate. She was reinstated and provided back pay for her entire suspension. White filed a third claim of retaliation with the EEOC.

After completing the EEOC's administrative process, she filed a lawsuit against Burlington in federal court alleging unlawful retaliation under Title VII. At trial, the jury agreed with White and awarded her $43,500 in compensatory damages and $54,295 in attorney's fees. Although a divided partial Sixth Circuit Court of Appeals reversed the trial court's findings, the full panel of the Sixth Circuit affirmed the first decision for White on her retaliation claims.

On appeal, the Supreme Court agreed with the full Sixth Circuit decision. The Supreme Court reviewed the language of Title VII and found that the language describing retaliation was broader than the language describing discrimination. The language describing discrimination references adverse employment actions (e.g., firing, demotions, reductions in pay, etc.). However, the language describing retaliation does not reference employment actions at all. The Court reasoned that an employer can effectively retaliate against an employee by taking actions not directly related to employment, but which will be reasonably likely to deter the employee or others from engaging in protected activity. In this case, the Court found that a reasonable employee would find the employer's actions materially adverse, and therefore illegal under the anti-retaliation provision of Title VII.

The Court cautioned that not all actions will rise to this level: "normally, petty slights, minor annoyances and simple lack of good manners will not create such deterrence." The determination of "material" will be objective, and "context matters"; for example, a transfer to a night shift might be trivial to some employees, but be highly significant to a single mother with school-age children. Thus, non-adverse employment actions that are "materially adverse" and significant may be considered retaliatory actions under this Supreme Court ruling.

§ 18.03   MANDATORY AFFIRMATIVE ACTION

Employers commonly confuse the concepts of equal employment opportunity and affirmative action and assume they are the same. Affirmative action is more than a commitment not to discriminate and to ensure equal opportunity in all areas of employment; it is a commitment to take specific results-oriented actions that are designed to correct the effects of past discrimination for individuals in protected groups. Its goal is to take positive steps to recruit, hire, train, and promote individuals in protected groups who have traditionally been discriminated against.

Employers need to pay special attention to affirmative action because for many it is a mandatory requirement. Affirmative action regulations prescribe specific activities and action that employers are required to take, such as the development of a written affirmative action plan document, the calculation and analysis of specific workforce data, and compliance with specialized recordkeeping and reporting requirements. A sample affirmative action program (AAP) for an organization with fewer than 150 employees, prepared by the OFCCP, is available online at *www.dol.gov/esa/ofccp/index.htm*.

[A]   Definitions

To understand affirmative action and its many requirements, it is important to define some of the key terms and concepts associated with this area of law. The following list is not exhaustive (see federal statutes and regulations that define contractors' legal obligations for a more extensive listing of important affirmative action terms and definitions):

- *Affirmative action.* Encompasses policies, procedures, and results-oriented actions that employers take to ensure that traditional victims of discrimination (i.e., racial and ethnic minorities, women, individuals with disabilities, Vietnam veterans, special disabled veterans, and other covered veterans) are afforded equal opportunity in employment. Under affirmative action, an employer will positively and proactively recruit, hire, train, and promote members of protected groups to ensure that they are represented appropriately at all levels throughout the organization.

- *Voluntary affirmative action.* Permitted under Title VII of the Civil Rights Act of 1964 and governed by the EEOC. Unlike government contractors and subcontractors, who must comply with mandatory affirmative action requirements, other private employers may voluntarily elect to adopt affirmative action polices, procedures, or plans. However, organizations establishing a voluntary affirmative action plan must also comply with all federal affirmative action program (AAP) requirements. They cannot pick and choose only some portions of the plan and not others.

- *Mandatory affirmative action.* A set of government-imposed requirements that apply to employers who do business with government agencies. Mandatory affirmative action applies to any contractor or subcontractor with a federal executive branch agency as well as contractors or subcontractors with any number of state and local government agencies. (It is important that companies check with their state and local governments to identify any mandatory affirmative action requirement that might apply to them.)

The Office of Federal Contract Compliance Programs (OFCCP), the federal agency charged with monitoring federal mandatory affirmative action, states:

> [Mandatory] [a]ffirmative action is not preferential treatment. Nor does it mean that unqualified persons should be hired or promoted over other people. What affirmative action does mean is that positive steps must be taken to provide equal opportunity for those who have been discriminated against in the past and who continue to suffer the effects of that discrimination. For OFCCP, affirmative action is the tool; equal employment opportunity is the goal.

Recent actions by government human rights agencies suggest that mandatory affirmative action requirements for governmental contractors and subcontracts will not disappear anytime soon. Since 1996, there have been numerous changes in federal affirmative action regulations, and in December 2000 a number of significant federal regulatory changes became effective.

- *Affirmative action program.* Defined by Executive Order 11246, as "a set of specific and result-oriented procedures to which a contractor commits itself to apply every good faith effort . . . to achieve prompt and full utilization of minorities and women, at all levels and in all segments of its work force where deficiencies exist."

- *Protected group* or *protected status.* Applicants or employees that federal job bias laws protect from discrimination on the basis of race, color, religion, sex, national origin, age, disability, or veteran status.

- *Minorities.* A designation for men and women who belong to the minority groups for whom EEO-1 reporting is required: Black, Hispanic, Asian or Pacific Islander, American Indian or Alaskan native.

- *Availability.* A "theoretical" estimate of the number of minorities and women in an employer's internal workforce and the external labor market that have the skills required for each employer job group. Availability is stated in the form of a percentage of the population.

- *Underutilization.* Having fewer minorities or women in a particular job group than would reasonably be expected from the availability estimate.

[B]   The Office of Federal Contract Compliance Programs

The OFCCP, under the direction of the DOL, is responsible for monitoring contractor compliance with federal affirmative action obligations set out in Executive Order 11246, Section 503 of the Rehabilitation Act of 1973, as amended, and Section 402 of the Vietnam Era Veterans' Readjustment Assistance Act of 1974 (VEVRAA), as amended. The OFCCP's primary responsibility is to evaluate contractor AAPs through compliance evaluations and complaint investigations initiated by the agency.

[C]   Federal Mandatory Affirmative Action Laws

An Executive Order and two statutes passed by Congress created the requirement for mandatory affirmative action for contractors and subcontractors.

[1]   Executive Order 11246

Executive Order 11246 was issued by President Lyndon B. Johnson in 1965 to prohibit race discrimination by federal contractors and subcontractors and to require them to take affirmative action in the employment of racial and ethnic minorities. It was amended in 1967 to include women as well as minorities.

Executive Order 11246 has two coverage thresholds. The first, known as basic coverage, applies to any federal contractor or subcontractor having a contract or contracts with an executive branch agency or department exceeding $10,000 in any 12-month period. Contractors that meet this threshold must comply with the requirements defined in the Equal Opportunity Clause of the regulations but are not required to create a written AAP.

The second threshold applies to any supply and service contractor and subcontractor that has 50 or more employees and one or more contracts totaling $50,000 or more within one year. Contractors who meet this threshold are required to create and maintain a written AAP.

[2]   Section 503 of the Rehabilitation Act of 1973

Section 503, as amended, requires covered federal contractors to "take affirmative action to employ and advance in employment, qualified individuals with disabilities." Section 503 has the same coverage thresholds as does Executive Order 11246.

[3]   Vietnam Era Veterans' Readjustment Assistance Act of 1974

VEVRAA, as amended, requires federal contractors to take affirmative action to "employ and advance in employment" two classes of veterans: veterans of the Vietnam War and special disabled veterans. These classes were expanded in 1998 with the enactment of the Veterans Employment Opportunities Act of 1998 (VEOA) and expanded again in 2000 with the enactment of the Veterans Benefits and Health Care Improvement Act of 2000 (VBHCIA). The VEOA added to those veterans already covered "any other veterans who served in active duty during a war or in a campaign or expedition for which a campaign badge has been authorized" as a covered class. The VBHCIA added the class of "recently separated veterans"—defined as "any veteran during the one-year period beginning on the date of such veteran's discharge or release from active duty."

The two coverage thresholds for VEVRAA are the same as those set out by Executive Order 11246 and Section 503 of the Rehabilitation Act of 1973. However, the VEOA raised the dollar amount for mandatory affirmative action coverage from $10,000 to $25,000. Final regulations implementing the affirmative action provisions of the VEOA and the VBHCIA were published in the *Federal Register* on December 1, 2005 (41 C.F.R. Part 60-250 RIN 1215-AB24).

In November 2002, President Bush signed the Jobs for Veterans Act (JVA) [Pub. L. No. 107-288, 116 Stat. 2033 (Nov. 7, 2002)]. The changes under the JVA include:

- The coverage threshold for mandatory affirmative action plans is raised from a government contract of $25,000 or more to a contract of $100,000 or more.

- The term "Vietnam-era Veteran" has been eliminated.

- The definition of "recently separated" changes from one year to three years.

- For the Vets-100 report, in addition to reporting number of covered veterans employed and hired by job category, employers must also report total number of employees in each category.

- Modification of the mandatory job-listing requirement for covered contractors. The previous requirement allowed contractors to list employment openings with either the appropriate local employment service office or with America's Job Bank. Under the JVA, employment openings must be listed with the appropriate employment service delivery system, defined as a nationwide system of public employment offices established under the Wagner-Peyser Act. In addition, contractors can list openings with "one-stop career centers under the Workforce Investment Act of 1998, other appropriate service delivery points, or America's Job Bank."

  As of July 1, 2007, America's Job Bank ceased to be operational. Noting that transition to new job listing mechanisms may cause difficulties for contractors, the OFCCP has indicated that it will not cite a contractor for non-compliance solely because it has failed to list all of its employment openings with the appropriate employment service delivery system, as long as the contractor has made good-faith efforts to recruit and employ qualified covered veterans. As of this writing, additional guidance from the OFCCP is anticipated, but still pending. In the interim, the OFCCP has created a Web site contractors can use to find state job banks: *http://careeronestop.org/ajbprsjbl/*.

The final rule for regulations implementing the JVA were published in the *Federal Register* on August 8, 2007 (41 C.F.R. Part 60-300 RIN 1215-AB46). The final rule was effective on September 7, 2007, although federal contractors were given one year from the effective date to comply with the changes to the Vets-100 report. See **Section 18.03[F][1]** for more information on the Vets-100 and Vets-100A reports.

For further information on the latest requirements, refer to the Web site *www.dol.gov/vets*.

[D] Components of Federal Affirmative Action Programs or Plans

For each of the three federal laws described in the preceding section, accompanying regulations have been developed by the OFCCP. These regulations have been codified at 41 C.F.R. Section 60-1. (It is important that every contractor or subcontractor covered by these legal requirements have a copy of these regulations.) Each regulation contains a set of guidelines for the creation of a written AAP. Although, theoretically, each contractor could end up with three separate plans, in practice, most contractors create one AAP to comply with Executive Order 11246, Section 503 of the Rehabilitation Act of 1973, and VEVRAA. There is no guidance from the OFCCP regarding combining affirmative action programs. However, if an organization is required to have a written plan for minorities and women, it also must have plans for the disabled and veterans. Therefore, the plans can be combined with shared sections that apply to all three laws.

Effective December 13, 2000, 41 C.F.R. Section 60-2 was revised. The OFCCP deleted several previously required narrative sections and made revisions to the statistical analysis portion of the AAP. The changes are summarized in **Table 18-1**.

Table 18-1
Changes to Executive Order 11246

Previous AAP Requirements	New AAP Requirements*
Reaffirmation of policy	Not required for minorities and women, but is still required for disabled and veterans
Internal and external dissemination of policy	Not required
Guidelines on sex, religion, and national origin discrimination	Not required
Consideration of women and minorities not in the workforce	Not required
Support of community action programs	Not required
Workforce analysis	Contractors may use either the traditional workforce analysis or an organizational profile. The profile can be depicted graphically, in charts, spreadsheets, or texts to display the required information.
Job group analysis	Contractors with a total workforce of less than 150 employees (company-wide, not just in one location) may use EEO-1 categories instead of company-specific job categories.
Availability analysis	The previous eight-factor analysis has been reduced to two: one external and one internal factor.
Utilization analysis	Now referred to as "Comparing Incumbency to Availability." The new regulations recognize a wide variety of methods for this analysis including the one-person rule, the 80 percent test, and the two-standard deviation test.
Placement goals	The contractor sets annual percentage goals for females and minorities for each job group. There are no numerical goals and no timetables.

* All plans that begin on or after December 13, 2001, must conform to the new regulations.

[1] Inclusion of All Employees in the AAP

Each employee in the contractor's workforce must be included in the AAP. Employees should be included in the AAP for the establishment where they work except in special circumstances. For example, employees who work at a different location than their manager must be included in the AAP of their manager. If there are fewer than 50 employees at the location, the contractor has three options:

1. The location, though small, may maintain its own AAP.

2. The employees can be placed in the AAP where their HR function is.

3. The employees can be placed in the AAP where their manager is.

If employees are placed in a different establishment's AAP, the OFCCP requires notation of the organizational profile (workforce analysis) and the job group analysis to identify the location of those employees.

[2] Functional AAPs

In March 2002, the OFCCP issued an Administrative Notice outlining the procedures for development of an AAP that is organized around the employer's business function or line(s) of business. Functional AAPs do not need to take into account the geographic location of the businesses. They must be authorized by the OFCCP and, until authorized, employers must maintain separate AAPs for each physical location.

The Notice defines a functional or business unit as a component of a company that operates somewhat autonomously. The unit may have its own managing official or be listed separately on the company's organization chart. The unit also may conduct personnel transactional activities (such as hiring) that are distinguishable from activities conducted by other parts of the company.

An employer must write to the OFCCP requesting approval for a functional AAP at least 120 days before the current AAP expires. The OFCCP will provide written acknowledgment of the request within two weeks of the receipt of the employer's written request. The OFCCP then has 120 days to approve or deny the request. If no approval or denial is received within the 120-day period, the request is deemed approved.

The OFCCP may schedule an initial meeting or conference call for the purpose of obtaining information it may need to determine whether to approve or deny the employer's request.

A functional AAP must include the employer's entire workforce; it must also include all required components of federal AAPs (as described below).

In general, once an employer's request for a functional AAP is approved, that approval will remain in effect for five years. Either the employer or the OFCCP can terminate the agreement with 90 calendar days' written notice. An employer with a functional AAP must notify the OFCCP if its structure changes significantly—for example, if a merger or acquisition results in the elimination of functions that were included in the original functional AAP agreement. Upon the expiration of an approved five-year agreement, the employer may request renewal for an additional five-year period. The renewal request must be received by the OFCCP at least 120 days before the original agreement's expiration.

[3] Applicant Definition

To help employers comply with EEO and AAP requirements, the "Uniform Guidelines on Employee Selection Procedures" released in 1979 defines the term *applicant* as follows:

> The precise definition of the term "applicant" depends upon the user's recruitment and selection procedures. The concept of an applicant is that of a person who has indicated an interest in being considered for hiring, promotion, or other employment opportunities. This interest might be expressed by completing an application form, or might be expressed orally, depending on the employer's practice.

The new AAP regulations do not provide contractors with a revised definition of the term *applicant* to be used for analysis of hiring data. Contractors must maintain records of the "race, gender, and ethnicity" of each employee and, "where possible," of each applicant. The OFCCP does offer nonregulatory guidance to contractors, stating the burden is on the contractor to demonstrate that "every reasonable effort" has been made to identify the gender, race, and ethnicity of applicants. The guidance also states that "self-identification" is the most reliable method and encourages contractors to adopt measures such as electronic or hard copy tear-off sheets for this purpose.

In today's world of recruiting on the Internet and other electronic recruiting, the definition supplied in 1979 is not adequate to assist employers in meeting their EEO and AAP requirements. Therefore, on March 4, 2004, a proposed revised definition of "applicant" for Internet and related technologies was published by the EEOC, the DOL, the Department of Justice, and the Office of Personnel Management. That definition states:

> In order for an individual to be an applicant in the context of the Internet and related electronic data processing technologies, the following must have occurred:
>
> • The employer has acted to fill a particular position;
>
> • The individual has followed the employer's standard procedures for submitting applications; and
>
> • The individual has indicated an interest in the particular position.

In the Questions and Answers published with the new definition, the agencies indicated that the "Internet and related electronic technologies" included e-mail, Web sites (such as third-party job or résumé banks and employment Web pages), electronic scanning technology, applicant tracking systems, and internal databases of job seekers. The agencies emphasize that this definition applies only to an applicant in the context of the Internet and related electronic technologies.

On March 29, 2004, the OFCCP published its proposed definition of an Internet applicant. On October 7, 2005, the OFCCP published its final regulations on this definition and related issues. [Obligation to Solicit Race and Gender Date for Agency Enforcement Purposes, 70 Fed. Reg. 58,946 (Oct. 7, 2005) (to be codified at 41 C.F.R. Part 60-1)] Although similar to the proposed definition, the final regulation states the following:

> Internet Applicant means any individual as to whom the following four criteria are satisfied:
>
> (i) The individual submits an expression of interest in employment through the Internet or related electronic data technologies;
>
> (ii) The contractor considers the individual for employment in a particular position;

(iii) The individual's expression of interest indicates the individual possesses the basic qualifications for the position; and

(iv) The individual at no point in the contractor's selection process prior to receiving an offer of employment from the contractor removes himself or herself from further consideration or otherwise indicates that he or she is no longer interested in the position.

This final definition further defines "advertised, basic qualifications" as qualifications that the employer advertises (e.g., posts a job description and necessary qualifications on its Web site) to potential applicants that they must possess in order to be considered for the position. Alternatively, if the contractor does not advertise for the position, but uses an alternative device to find candidates (e.g., an external resume database), the contractor must establish the qualifications in advance of any consideration of candidates and record and maintain the record of such qualifications. In either case, the qualifications must meet the following three conditions: (1) the qualifications must be noncomparative (i.e., they cannot state that the qualification is that the applicant possesses one of the top five years of experience among all applicants for the position); (2) they must be objective; and (3) they must be relevant to the performance of the specific position and enable the contractor to meet its business-related goals.

Because employers must gather race, gender, and ethnicity data from all job applicants—Internet or traditional—it is critical to determine who qualifies as "job applicants" under the Internet Applicant definition. The Frequently Asked Questions (FAQs) for the Internet Applicant Recordkeeping Rule (as posted on the OFCCP's Web site, *http://www.dol.gov/esa/regs/compliance/ofccp/faqs/iappfaqs.htm*) provides a "real life" example of how the basic qualifications would work to determine who the Internet Applicants are:

> A contractor initially searches an external job database with 50,000 job seekers for 3 basic qualifications for a bi-lingual emergency room nursing supervisor job (a 4-year nursing degree, state certification as an RN, and fluency in English and Spanish). The initial screen for the first three basic qualifications narrows the pool to 10,000. The contractor then adds a fourth, pre-established, basic qualification, 3 years of emergency room nursing experience, and narrows the pool to 1,000. Finally, the contractor adds a fifth, pre-established, basic qualification, 2 years of supervisory experience, which results in a pool of 75 job seekers. Under the Internet Applicant rule, only the 75 job seekers meeting all five basic qualifications would be Internet Applicants, assuming the other three prongs of the "Internet Applicant" definition were met.

The second of the four prongs of the Internet Applicant definition requires the contractor to "consider" the applicant for employment in a particular position. For this criteria, a contractor does not consider an applicant if it merely attempts to determine whether a potential applicant has the basic qualifications for the position. Consideration will occur when the contractor reviews applications/résumés, for example, to compare applicants to each other in order to determine "the most qualified." In the OFCCP's FAQs, the definition of consideration is further explained. Often, when external résumé banks are searched by key words, the job bank will forward short résumé summaries to the contractor. Review of these summaries to determine whether the applicant has the basic qualifications is not "consideration" for the purpose of the Internet Applicant Recordkeeping Rule. This explanation will help reduce the contractor's recordkeeping burden, because the contractor will not have to maintain the applications of those who do not have the basic qualifications.

Contractors may establish procedures to refrain from considering "expressions of interest" from individuals that are not submitted in accordance with the contractor's standard procedures. Similarly, the contractor can establish a policy or procedure that it will not consider expressions of interest that are not submitted with respect to a specific position (e.g., unsolicited résumés). Note that if the contractor wishes to refrain from considering such applicants, it must apply the relevant policies and procedures consistently.

Individuals may remove themselves from the selection process by either active or passive demonstrations of disinterest. An applicant who expressly states he no longer wishes to be considered for the position is demonstrating an active disinterest in the position. Passive disinterest may be shown by repeatedly failing to respond to a contractor's telephone inquiries or e-mails asking about his or her interest in a job. The OFCCP has defined "repeatedly" to mean two or more times. In addition, if an individual, in his or her original expression of interest, states a desire for a specific position or type of position, specific location, or salary requirements which do not match the contractor's job opening, these may also be considered passive disinterest in the job. Employers must retain expressions of interest from those who qualify as Internet Applicants, even if the Internet Applicant later withdraws from consideration. In addition employers must keep any statement of withdrawal, demographic data previously solicited from the individual and test results. However, the contractor is not obligated to solicit demographic data from the individual if it has not already done so.

The final rule emphasizes that if an employer considers applications via both the Internet or related electronic technologies ("electronic applications") and paper applications, the Internet Applicant standard applies to the solicitation of demographic information from all applicants for that position. If the employer does not consider any electronic applications, then the definition of applicant under the "Uniform Guidelines" should be used. In addition to the types of Internet and related electronic technologies cited in the proposed rules, the final rule indicates that transmission of a résumé by fax constitutes transmission by a related electronic data technology, and would fall under the definition of an electronic application.

To obtain the demographic data, the OFCCP lets employers decide how and when. The OFCCP states that the preferred method is self-identification. An employer may ask a job applicant for the data, but must indicate that disclosure is voluntary. If a job seeker declines to self-identify, an employer's visual observation is acceptable, but employers should not try to guess race, ethnicity, or gender. The requirement is for the contractor to solicit demographic information about applicants or Internet Applicants where possible. Although request for this information does not need to be made immediately upon determining that an individual is an Internet Applicant, it should not be delayed so long that it is no longer feasible to request the information.

The record retention period is the same for all applicants and is based on the contractor's size and contract(s). For companies with fewer than 150 employees or a contract of less than $150,000 (annually), the record retention period is one year. If the company has 150 employees or more, or a contract of $150,000 or more, the record retention period is two years. The time period is measured from the time the record was created or from the time of the personnel action associated with that record, whichever is later.

The Internet Applicant rule requires contractors to maintain all electronic applications that the contractor considered for a specific position, except for searches of external résumé databases discussed below. Contractors must also retain records identifying job seekers contacted regarding their interest in a specific position. For internal résumé databases, the contractor must maintain a record of each résumé added to the database, a record of the date each résumé was added, the position for which each search of the database was made, and for each search, the date of the search and the substantive search criteria used. For external résumé databases, the contractor must retain a record of the position for which each search of the database was made, and for each search, the substantive search criteria used, the date of the search and the résumés of any job seekers who met the basic qualifications for the specific position who are considered by the contractor. These records must be maintained regardless of whether the individual meets the definition of an "Internet Applicant."

Use of an external recruiting agency does not eliminate the contractor's recordkeeping requirements. Although contractors can require that recruiting agencies obtain the same data and keep the same records as if the contractor had conducted the search itself, it will be the contractor who will be held accountable if such data and records are not produced during an OFCCP compliance evaluation.

The final Internet Applicant rule emphasizes that OFCCP will compare the proportion of women and minorities in the employer's Internet Applicant pool with labor force statistics or other data on the percentage of women and minorities in the relevant labor force in order to evaluate the impact of basic qualifications. If there is a significant difference between these figures, the OFCCP will investigate further as to whether the contractor's recruitment and hiring practices conform to affirmative action standards.

The OFCCP's final regulations are available on the Web site of the *Federal Register*: *http://www.dol.gov/ esa/regs/fedreg/final/2005020176.htm.*

[E]   Affirmative Action Plan for Minorities and Women—Executive Order 11246

The AAP required under Executive Order 11246 has two major components: a narrative document and statistical data and analyses.

[1]   Required Narrative Sections

The following narrative sections are required by revised regulations effective December 13, 2000:

- *Responsibility for implementation.* This section designates the individuals that are responsible for the AAP and its implementation. It should include an itemized description or list of each individual's primary responsibilities.

- *Identification of problem areas.* This section discusses the potential problem areas a contractor must evaluate, including (1) its workforce by organizational unit and job group to determine if there is utilization (presence in the unit or group) or distribution (placement in jobs within the unit or group) problems; (2) its personnel activity, including applicant flow, hires, terminations, promotions, and other personnel activity, to determine whether there are disparities (adverse impact); (3) its compensation system to determine whether there are disparities; (4) its selection, recruitment, referral, and other personnel procedures to determine whether there are disparities in hiring or promotion; and (5) any other areas that might impact the success of the affirmative action program. (This is a difficult and sensitive section, and it is advisable that a company seek legal guidance when drafting the narrative. Speaking with legal counsel might allow the company to place any detailed analysis of discrimination under attorney-client privilege.)

- *Placement goals.* The contractor sets annual percentage goals for females and minorities for each job group. There are no numerical goals and no timetables. The OFCCP confirms that setting a single goal for all minorities will be the norm for most contractors except where separate goals may be required by the OFCCP where there is substantial disparity in the utilization of a particular minority group.

- *Development and execution of action-oriented programs.* This section should describe the specific affirmative action activities that the contractor will develop and implement to eliminate deficiencies and problem areas and help to attain its statistical goals.

- *Internal audit and reporting systems.* This section should include a description of the internal auditing and reporting systems that exist or will be designed to monitor the effectiveness of the AAP.

While the revised regulations make no specific reference to the narrative section on accomplishment of prior-year placement goal, it is recommended that this section be included in the AAP.

- *Accomplishment of prior-year placement goals.* This section should report on the results of the contractor's affirmative action goals for the prior AAP year and include:

  — The job group representation at the start of the AAP year in each job group for which a goal was established

  — The percentage placement rate goal established

  — The actual number of placements made into each job group where there are goals

When writing the narrative sections for a federal AAP, it is important to not overcommit what the organization will do in a particular year. Remember, a contractor is obligated to carry out all of its AAP commitments, so it should not list those it cannot or does not want to be obligated for.

[2] Required Statistical Analyses

The statistical analyses that are required elements of an AAP are (1) an organizational profile or workforce analysis, (2) a job group analysis, (3) an availability analysis, (4) a comparison of incumbency to availability, and (5) placement goals.

Organizational Profile. An organizational profile is a detailed graphical or tabular chart, text, spreadsheet, or similar presentation of the contractor's organizational structure. The profile must identify each organizational unit and show the relationship of each unit to the other units in the establishment. An organizational unit is any component that is part of the structure of the company. It may be a department, section, division, branch, or other similar group. In a less traditional organization, it could be a project team, job family, or other similar structure. For each unit, the profile must include (1) the name of the unit; (2) the job title, gender, race, and ethnicity of the unit supervisor (if applicable); (3) the total number of male and female incumbents; and (4) the total number of male and female incumbents by ethnicity.

Workforce Analysis. Alternatively, contractors may use a workforce analysis rather than an organizational profile. A *workforce analysis* is a vertical array of the jobs within each department or organizational unit. Such an analysis provides the OFCCP with a static snapshot of a company's current employee population on a payroll date just prior to the beginning of the AAP year. To create the workforce analysis, a contractor selects a payroll date within 45 days of the AAP year start date. From the data, a listing or chart is created for each department or similar organizational unit, which lists all the different job titles, arranged in ascending or descending order by pay. For each job title, the total number of minorities and women and the total number of minorities in each racial and ethnic group are listed along with the wage rate or salary range. If there are formal lines of progression or usual promotional sequences in specific departments, these must be denoted along with the order in which employees move through the jobs in each line.

Job Group Analysis. A *job group* is the fundamental unit for determining whether there is underutilization of minorities and women in a contractor's workforce and for setting affirmative action placement goals. By evaluating the minority and gender makeup of each job group, the OFCCP may discern patterns of minority and female hiring and promotion in similar jobs. Each job group is a cluster of jobs that have similar content, wage rates, and promotional opportunities, regardless of departmental structure or progression lines. While a workforce analysis is a vertical array of the organization's jobs, the job group analysis is a horizontal array of jobs grouped according to their similarity. Forming job groups is not an exact science. The OFCCP usually recommends that contractors start with the nine EEO-1 Report categories (i.e., officials and managers, professionals, technicians, sales workers, office and clerical workers, skilled workers, operatives, laborers, and service workers) when creating job groups. These categories should be further subdivided according to the nature and character of a contractor's workforce. Examples of customized job groups include administrative managers, production supervisors, engineering professionals, secretaries and administrative assistants, mechanics, machine operators, materials handlers, and janitors. Under the revised regulations, if a contractor has a total workforce of fewer than 150 employees company-wide, the contractor may prepare a job group analysis that utilizes the EEO-1 categories as job groups.

Because underutilization and placement goals depend on how group jobs are structured, a thoughtful and realistic approach for creating job groups at the outset will eliminate the need to revise these analyses in the event of a compliance evaluation. When establishing major job groups, a commonsense, practical approach should be used. Entry-level and non-entry-level jobs should not be combined in the same job group, nor should technical and administrative jobs or jobs that have clearly different qualifications and advancement opportunities.

It is important not to create too many or too few job groups. Developing too many job groups risks having groups that are statistically insignificant and makes it difficult to set meaningful goals. A contractor that does not create enough job groups may end up combining very dissimilar jobs, often with very different minority and female availability rates in the labor market. Some experts recommend a rule of thumb of 30 to 50 total job incumbents as the minimum size for a job group. Generally, 7 to 15 groups should be sufficient for establishments with fewer than 1,000 employees.

Finally, in creating job groups, contractors should consider the accessibility of labor force availability statistics. If they are not able to find adequate availability information from state human rights departments or the DOL for the jobs in a particular group, they will have to revise the groups.

Availability analysis. The *availability analysis* (previously referred to as the eight-factor analysis) has been reduced to a two-factor analysis under the revised regulations. It is designed to estimate the percentages of minorities and women available for placement into each job group. Contractors must estimate total minority and female availability by considering the following two factors:

1. The percentage of minorities and women having requisite skills in an area in which the contractor can reasonably recruit, where reasonable recruitment area refers to the geographical area from which the contractor usually seeks or reasonably could seek workers to fill the positions in question; and

2. The percentage of promotable, transferable, and trainable minorities and women in the contractor's organization where trainable employees refers to employees who could, with appropriate training that the contractor is reasonably able to provide, become promotable or transferable within the AAP year.

The two factors are to be considered for both total minorities and women for each job group. For each factor, a contractor should:

- *Determine the geographic area.* The geographic area will be the same for both minorities and women. According to the definition of the factor, a contractor needs to determine the parameters of the area, which is usually a single county, metropolitan statistical area, or state or a combination of these, or the entire United States. In defining the geographic area, contractors are limited by the availability and format of the data obtainable from state human rights departments or the DOL.

- *Calculate the raw statistic for both minorities and women.* This step may be as simple as looking up a percentage on a table or chart or it may require the calculation of a weighted average from multiple counties or states. In December 2003, the Census Bureau released the EEO Special File, which contains most of the data used to calculate these statistics. The release is based on the 2000 census. The EEO Special File may be viewed on the EEOC's Web site: *http://www.eeoc.gov/stats/census/index.html.* All AAPs with plan years that begin on or after January 1, 2005, must use the 2000 census data.

- *Determine the appropriate value (percentage) weight of the factor according to its importance as a source of candidates for the job group.* The weight will be the same for both minorities and women. In setting the weight for a factor, it is important to remember that the weights of all factors that are viable sources of candidates for a job group must total 100 percent.

- *Multiply the raw statistic by the value weight for both minorities and women.* Add the totals for each factor together to calculate the final availability percentage for the job group for both minorities and women.

The regulations state that both factors must be considered in calculating the final availability for each job group. This does not mean that a value weight must be assigned to a factor if it is not a viable source of candidates. If a factor is not applicable to a particular job group, a contractor must be prepared to justify its exclusion from the analysis.

Comparing Incumbency to Availability/Underutilization Analysis. After completing the job group and availability analyses, a federal contractor is required to compare the percentage of minorities and women in each of its job groups with the availability estimates or percentages. The comparison determines whether all minorities or women are underutilized and whether statistical placement goals need to be established for some job groups.

In determining whether underutilization exists in a job group, the OFCCP allows contractors to measure the difference between availability and the actual number of minorities and women employed by using a statistically appropriate technique designed to measure deviation from an expected norm. The following are recommended methods:

Rule	Underutilization Occurs If
The Any Difference Rule	There is any numerical difference between availability estimates and their current representation.
The 80 Percent Standard (also known as the Four-Fifths Rule)	The employment percentage is less than 80 percent of their estimated availability.
The Two-Standard-Deviation Rule	The difference between availability estimates and current representation is greater than two standard deviations.

Often, contractors may have job groups in which one protected group is underutilized but not others. For example, underutilization may exist for minorities but not for women. It is important to remember that a determination of underutilization for either minorities or women for a job group is not a finding or admission of discrimination. It is often advised that contractors include a disclaimer in their underutilization analysis or at the beginning of their AAP to the effect that by declaring underutilization in some job groups, they are simply complying with OFCCP guidelines and not identifying or admitting discrimination.

Placement Goals. OFCCP regulations require that contractors establish statistical placement goals for total minorities and/or women in job groups in which they are underutilized. Goals should be considered statements of desired results of good faith efforts to correct underutilization, not fixed quotas. A placement goal is the percentage at which a contractor will place minorities or women in a job group if underutilization exits. It should be equal to the final availability estimate for minorities or women for the job group. Numeric goals (i.e., an absolute number of minorities or women that must be placed in a job group in order to achieve full utilization based on availability) are not required and, in most cases, are not desirable.

[3] Compensation Analyses

Executive Order 11246 prohibits compensation discrimination on the basis of sex, race, color, national origin, and religion. Prior to 2004, there had been no standards or regulations to assist contractors in this area. In November 2004, the OFCCP published two notices: (1) a notice that proposed standards on systemic discrimination under Executive Order 11246 (changing the OFCCP's processes used to evaluate compensation discrimination in compliance evaluations); and (2) a notice proposing guidelines for contractors' self-evaluation of their compensation practices. On June 16, 2006, the OFCCP published its final notices on these topics in the *Federal Register* (71 Fed. Reg. 35114-35122 & 35124-35141). The final notices were effective immediately upon publication.

As part of its compliance programs, the OFCCP reviews contractors to determine whether they have engaged in systemic compensation discrimination on the basis of sex, race, color, religion, or national origin. Under the final standards, the agency will find systemic discrimination when there are statistically significant compensation disparities between similarly situated employees that cannot be accounted for by legitimate factors that influence compensation (e.g., education, experience, performance, productivity, location).

The final standards define similarly situated employees as those who perform similar work, have similar responsibility levels, and are in positions that have similar skills and qualifications. Determining whether employees are similarly situated will depend on the actual facts of each situation, and will be obtained by reviewing job descriptions and interviewing employees. The final notices indicate that the OFCCP, in determining whether employees are similarly situated, will investigate other workplace factors such as the functional unit of the employer (e.g., department or division), employment status (full-time or part-time), union status, and compensation type (e.g., hourly, salaried, commissioned, etc.).

The multiple regression analysis will be used to determine whether a disparity in compensation is statistically significant. The Discussion of the Final Interpretive Standards describes the multiple regression technique as follows:

> Multiple regression analysis is a statistical tool for understanding the relationship between two or more variables. Multiple regression involves a variable to be explained—called the dependent variable— and additional explanatory variables that are thought to produce or be associated with changes in

the dependent variable. For example, a multiple regression analysis might estimate the effect of the number of years of work on salary. Salary would be the dependent variable to be explained; years of experience would be the explanatory variable. Multiple regression analysis is sometimes well suited to the analysis of data about competing theories in which there are several possible explanations for the relationship among a number of explanatory variables. Multiple regression typically uses a single dependent variable and several explanatory variables to assess the statistical data pertinent to these theories.

The final standards also indicate that before a finding of discrimination is made, generally, some anecdotal evidence of compensation discrimination must be provided. Anecdotal evidence includes testimony of employees, comments made by management, and individual examples of pay disparities between similarly situated employees.

The notice for contractors' voluntary guidelines for self-evaluation of their compensation practices provides guidelines for meeting the self-evaluation requirements under Executive Order 11246 (Voluntary Guidelines). Contractors are not required to follow the guidelines. However, if a contractor complies with the proposed self-evaluation guidelines, the OFCCP will coordinate its compliance monitoring activities with the contractor's approach and will deem the contractor to be in compliance with the compensation analysis section of Executive Order 11246. The OFCCP has stated that a contractor's decision not to implement a self-evaluation program under the Voluntary Guidelines will not be taken into consideration when it is assessing whether that contractor has complied with Executive Order 11246.

The following general standards are adopted in the final notice:

1. *Perform the evaluation on groupings of employees that are similarly situated.* As indicated in the first notice, to establish similarly situated employee groupings (SSEGs), the *actual* (emphasis added) work performed, responsibility level and required skill and qualifications must be similar, regardless of any employer-created designation, such as job title, job classification, pay grade or range, etc. Other relevant factors should also be considered, such as the functional unit of the employer (e.g., department or division), employment status (full-time or part-time), union status, and compensation type (e.g., hourly, salaried, commissioned, etc.).

2. *Make a reasonable attempt to produce SSEGs that are large enough for meaningful statistical analysis.* Generally, SSEGs should contain at least 30 employees overall, and contain five or more incumbents who are members of either of the following pairs: male/female or minority/non-minority. If there are SSEGs that are smaller than these guidelines, they may be removed from the statistical evaluation process; the contractor must however use non-statistical techniques to evaluate the pay decisions related to these employees. Further, it is expected that the statistical analyses will cover at least 70 percent of the contractor's workforce. However, under no circumstances should a contractor attempt to group employees into an SSEG who do not meet the standards for similarly situated employees. Contractors may also develop self-evaluation programs that include more than the employees covered under one AAP or establishment.

3. *Perform the statistical analysis at least annually.* This analysis must account for factors that legitimately affect the compensation of each SSEG, such as experience, education, performance, productivity, location, etc. In order to receive the OFCCP's coordinated compliance benefit (that is, the incentive noted above), employers with 500 or more employees must use multiple regression analyses for the annual statistical analysis. The final notice does not address what statistical technique is required (to obtain the OFCCP's coordinated compliance benefit) for

employers with fewer than 500 employees. However, the proposed regulations indicated that small employers could use either the multiple regression analysis or any other analysis, which includes tests of statistical significance that are generally recognized as appropriate in the statistics profession.

4. *Investigate any statistically significant compensation disparities produced by the self-evaluation analyses.* A statistically significant compensation disparity occurs if the significance level of the disparity is two or more standard deviations from the zero disparity level. This criterion means that a two standard deviation disparity in the pay between (for example) males and females would have a less than one in 20 chance of occurrence unrelated to potential discrimination. If such a disparity exists, the employer must adequately determine whether such statistical disparities are explained by legitimate factors or are otherwise not the product of unlawful discrimination. If the disparities cannot be explained, the employer must remedy the disparity. For the initial self-evaluation period, remedies must correct the current disparity, and any previous disparity. Contractors should investigate when the disparity began to determine how far back to go to correct the previous disparity. The Voluntary Guidelines infer that back pay should be provided for up to a two-year period. For other than the first self-evaluation period, remedies should be provided for the current disparity.

5. *Create and retain documents and data.* Such documents and data include: (1) documents relating to the creation of SSEGs, exclusion of employees from SSEGs, factors included in the statistical analyses, and the form of the statistical analyses; (2) data used in the statistical analyses and the results of those analyses; (3) data and documentation of the non-statistical analyses performed on the employees eliminated from SSEGs; and (4) documentation of the follow-up investigations on statistically significant pay disparities and pay adjustments made to remedy any disparities.

6. *Provide all documents and data to the OFCCP during a compliance review.* The OFCCP may also review any personnel records and conduct any employee interviews necessary to determine the accuracy of any representation made by the contractor in the documentation or data. The OFCCP will generally use a three-tier process for investigating compensation practices during a compliance review. In the first tier, the OFCCP will compare the average compensation data provided by the contractor. Comparisons will be made generally by pay grade, title, or other similar groups. If this comparison reveals significant disparities (females or minorities paid significantly less than males or non-minorities), it will result in the next level evaluation. In the second tier, the OFCCP will conduct a "cluster" regression analysis. This analysis compares employee groups created by clustering job titles with the closest average compensation values until the group contains at least 30 employees and at least 5 employees from each comparator group (minority/non-minority and male/female). If significant disparities result from this evaluation tier, the OFCCP will move to the third tier, which is a comprehensive evaluation of the contractor's compensation practices, including the multiple regression analysis outlined in the OFCCP's final notice (and described above).

The proposed guidelines also provide an alternative method for compliance certification (Alternative Compliance Certification or ACC). The OFCCP understands that some contractors, on the advice of legal counsel, may take the position that their compensation self-evaluation is subject to protection from disclosure under the attorney-client privilege or attorney work privilege. If the contractor disclosed its self-evaluation to the OFCCP, it would result in a waiver of these protections. The OFCCP will permit the contractor to certify its compliance with the compensation non-discrimination requirements of Executive Order 11246 in lieu of producing the methodology or results of its compensation self-evaluation analyses. The certification must be in writing, signed by an officer of the contractor under penalty of perjury, and must state:

> that the contractor has performed a compensation self-evaluation with respect to the affirmative action program or workplace at issue, at the direction of counsel, and that counsel has advised the contractor that the compensation self-evaluation analyses and results are subject to the attorney-client privilege and/or the attorney work product doctrine.

Employers who choose to follow the Voluntary Guidelines and who receive an OFCCP Scheduling Letter should respond to Item 11 by noting that it "seeks compliance coordination under the OFCCP Voluntary compensation self-evaluation guidelines." These employers should not submit the requested compensation data. An OFCCP Scheduling Letter is sent to contractors selected for a compliance review. The Scheduling Letter contains an itemized listing of documents and information that the contractor must submit to OFCCP. Item 11 of the itemized listing requests "annualized compensation data (wages, salaries, commissions and bonuses) by either salary range, rate, grade, or level showing total number of employees by race and gender and total compensation by race and gender."

A contractor that opts for the ACC will not receive the benefit of the OFCCP coordinating its compliance monitoring activities with the contractor's compensation self-evaluation methodology. Rather, the OFCCP will evaluate the contractor's compensation practices without regard to the analysis or results of the employer's self-evaluation system. Employers who elect the ACC and who receive an OFCCP Scheduling Letter should submit all data requested in Item 11.

In both notices, the OFCCP made a point of informing the contractor community that it intends to keep compensation and personnel information confidential "to the maximum extent the information is exempt from public disclosure under the Freedom of Information Act. [5 U.S.C. § 552] It is the practice of OFCCP not to release data where the contractor is still in business, and the contractor indicates, and through the Department of Labor review process it is determined, that the data are confidential and sensitive and that the release of data would subject the contractor to commercial harm."

[F] Affirmative Action Plan for Individuals with Disabilities and Special Disabled and Other Covered Veterans

The regulations defining affirmative action under Section 503 of the Rehabilitation Act of 1973 and VEVRAA have been revised in the past few years. As noted earlier, the AAP requirements under these statutes are nearly identical, which enables contractors to draft one AAP document for both. Unlike an AAP under Executive Order 11246, an AAP drafted under these statutes is required to develop only a narrative document. No statistical analyses are required for an AAP under Section 503 of the Rehabilitation Act 1973 or VEVRAA. An AAP drafted under these statutes must be updated annually. A brief description of each component that should be included in this AAP follows.

Under VEVRAA as amended, there are two thresholds when an AAP is required:

1. If an employer has a federal contract (or subcontract) of $50,000 or more in one year that was entered into before December 1, 2003, that employer is required to comply with the earlier VEVRAA

requirements found at 41 C.F.R. Part 60-250 (available at the OFCCP's Web site: *http://www.dol. gov/dol/allcfr/ESA/Title_41/Part_60-250/toc.htm*).

2. If the contract was entered into on or after December 1, 2003, and the contract is for $100,000 or more, the employer must comply with the regulations of 40 C.F.R. Part 60-300, (available at the DOL's Web site: *http://www.dol.gov/esa/regs/fedreg/final/ofcfinal.htm*). These regulations will also apply if the contract was originally entered into before December 1, 2003, but was modified after that date to an amount of $100,000 or more.

If the employer has contracts entered into both before and after December 1, 2003 that are at or above the amounts specified above, the contractor must develop an AAP that meets both sets of regulations.

Affirmative action plans under threshold 1 above must include the following veterans:

- *Special disabled veterans*: veterans who (i) are entitled to compensation (or who, but for the receipt of military retired pay, would be entitled to compensation) under laws administered by the Department of Veterans Affairs for a disability: (a) rated at 30 percent or more; or (b) rated at 10 or 20 percent in the case of a veteran who has been determined under 38 U.S.C. Section 3106 to have a serious employment handicap; or (ii) were discharged or released from active duty because of a service-connected disability. (In this usage, a serious employment handicap means a significant impairment of a veteran's ability to prepare for, obtain, or retain employment consistent with such veteran's abilities, aptitudes and interests.)

- *Veterans of the Vietnam era*: veterans who (i) served on active duty for a period of more than 180 days, and were discharged or released therefrom with other than a dishonorable discharge, if any part of such active duty occurred: (a) in the Republic of Vietnam between February 28, 1961 and May 7, 1975; or (b) between August 5, 1964 and May 7, 1975 in all other cases; or (ii) was discharged or released from active duty for a service-connected disability if any part of such active duty was performed: (i) in the Republic of Vietnam between February 28, 1961 and May 7, 1975; or (b) between August 5, 1964 and May 7, 1975 in all other cases.

- *Other protected veterans*: veterans who served on active duty during a war or in a campaign or expedition for which a campaign badge has been authorized, under laws administered by the Department of Defense.

- *Recently separated veterans*: veterans during the one-year period beginning on the date of such veterans' discharge or release from active duty.

AAPs under threshold, above, must include the following covered individuals:

- *Disabled veterans:* veterans who are entitled to compensation (or who, but for the receipt of military retiree pay, would be entitled to compensation) under laws administered by the Secretary of Veterans' Affairs, or a person who was discharged or released from active duty because of a service-connected disability;

- *Other protected veterans:* veterans who served on active duty in the Armed Forces during a war or in a campaign or expedition for which a campaign badge has been authorized under laws administered by the Department of Defense;

- *Armed Forces Service Medal Veterans:* veterans who, while serving on active duty in the Armed Forces, participated in a United States military operation for which an Armed Forces service medal was awarded pursuant to Executive Order No. 12985; and

- *Recently separated veterans:* that is, veterans during the three-year period beginning on the date of such veterans' discharge or release from active duty in the U.S. Military, ground, naval or air service.

The narrative sections required by VEVRAA as amended (under both thresholds) and Section 503 of the Rehabilitation Act of 1973, are the same or similar to those in the AAP for minorities and women and can be written in a like manner.

- *Equal employment opportunity policy.* The contractor's EEO Policy Statement covering individuals with disabilities and veterans should be included here.

- *Review of human resource processes.* A discussion of how the contractor will ensure that its HR processes provide for the proper consideration of the qualifications of veterans, and individuals with disabilities. This section should include a statement that its processes do not stereotype these individuals, which limits their access to jobs. Also included here should be a description of the procedures the contractor will follow to periodically review its HR processes.

- *Physical and mental qualifications.* A description of the review of all physical and mental job qualifications to ensure that, to the extent qualification standards tend to screen out qualified individuals with disabilities, they are job-related and consistent with business necessity.

- *Reasonable accommodation to physical and mental limitations.* A discussion of the contractor's commitment to make reasonable accommodation for the known physical and mental impairments of qualified veterans and individuals with disabilities in compliance with the regulations.

- *Harassment prevention.* A statement that the contractor has developed procedures to prevent the harassment of employees on the basis of their disabled or veteran status. This section should include the contractor's anti-harassment policy covering veterans and individuals with disabilities.

- *External dissemination of policy, outreach, and positive recruitment.* A description of the actions that the contractor will take to ensure its EEO Policy Statement is known externally to customers and vendors. A description of the outreach and recruitment actions that the contractor will take to identify and attract qualified veterans and individuals with disabilities should also be included.

- *Internal dissemination of policy.* A description of the actions that the contractor will take to ensure its EEO Policy Statement is known to applicants and employees should be included in this section.

- *Audit and reporting systems.* A discussion of the contractor's audit and reporting systems which should be designed to measure the effectiveness of the AAP/EEO program, document personnel activities, identify problem areas where remedial action is needed, and determine the degree to which the contractor's AAP goals and objectives have been met.

- *Responsibility for implementation.* A list of the individuals responsible for the AAP and its implementation, including an itemized description of each of their primary responsibilities.

- *Training.* A statement that all of the contractor's personnel involved in employment processes will be trained to ensure that its AAP commitments for veterans and individuals with disabilities are implemented.

- *Invitation to self-identify.* The invitation to self-identify as a qualified veteran, disabled veteran and/ or individual with a disability should be included in the AAP. A sample invitation to self-identify can be found in the regulations implementing VEVRAA, which are available on the DOL's Web site. The current final rule (*http://www.dol.gov/esa/regs/fedreg/final/2005023403.htm*) will be in effect until a final rule implementing the JVA is published. The proposed rule for the JVA, available at: *http://www.dol.gov/esa/regs/fedreg/proposed/2006000440.htm,* also includes a sample invitation to self-identify.

[1] Vets-100 and Vets-100A Reports

Federal contractors meeting the threshold requirements must also prepare annual reports describing the number of covered veterans and total employees hired by the contractor. Private employers who have a contract or subcontract with any department or agency of the federal government for the furnishing of supplies and services or the use of real or personal property and who meet the threshold amounts described below must prepare the report. Services include, but are not limited to, utility, construction, transportation, research, insurance and fund depository, irrespective of whether the federal government is the purchaser or seller.

1. Vets-100 Report is required for employers with a federal contract (or subcontract) of $25,000 or more in one year that was entered into before December 1, 2003.

2. Vets-100A Report is required for employers with a federal contract (or subcontract) of $100,000 or more in one year and was entered into on or after December 1, 2003. The Vets-100A will be required if the contract was originally entered into before December 1, 2003, but was modified after that date to an amount of $100,000 or more.

3. Both reports will be required if the federal contractor has contracts before and after December 1, 2003 meeting both threshold amounts.

Although the Vets-100A is "effective" June 18, 2008, the Veterans Administration is allowing contractors one year to implement the new report's tracking requirements. The Vets-100A will first be required for the 2009 reporting cycle.

The Vets-100 and Vets-100A reports are due on or before September 30 each year. Contractors may begin submitting the reports on August 1 of each year. Contractors are urged to submit the reports electronically, but mailed hard copies and submitted on a properly formatted disc are also accepted. The reports are no longer mailed out to contractors; they must visit the Veterans Administration's Web site to obtain the report and further information about how to complete the report. The Web site is: *http://vets100.vets.dol.gov/.*

[G] AAP Recordkeeping Requirements

Developing an AAP is only the first step that contractors must take to fully comply with federal mandatory affirmative action requirements. In fact, it is often thought that program or plan development and maintenance constitute only about half of what a contractor must do in order to be in compliance.

Implementation of the commitments and the actions described in a contractor's AAP is as important as—and sometimes more important than—the development of the plan. When monitoring contractor compliance, the OFCCP concentrates on what actions and good-faith efforts the contractor has taken to try to achieve its affirmative action goals.

Recordkeeping and documentation are also a critical part of complying with affirmative action regulations. The OFCCP has stated that the most frequently cited violation in compliance reviews involves recordkeeping. The OFCCP has formally defined for contractors their recordkeeping requirements. Under Executive Order 11246, Section 503 of the Rehabilitation Act of 1973, and VEVRAA, the OFCCP states:

> Contractors with 150 or more employees and a contract of $150,000 or more must maintain employment records for *two years*. . . . Contractors below these thresholds must retain employment records for *one year*.

All relevant records must be kept according to these time frames from the date the employment action occurs, (e.g., all records related to filling a position must be kept for one or two years from the date the new employee starts, not from the date the position become available). For many employment actions this will result in a retention period longer than one or two years. In addition, when an evaluation is scheduled, a complaint is filed, a compliance review initiated, or an enforcement action commenced, the contractor must keep all relevant records until final disposition of the action.

Personnel or employment records that are required to be kept under these regulations include:

- Records relating to requests for reasonable accommodations

- Results of physical examinations

- Job advertisements and postings

- Applications and resumes

- Tests and test results

- Interview notes

- Other records having to do with hiring, assignment, promotion, demotion, transfer, layoff, termination, rates of pay, or other terms of compensation, and selection for training or apprenticeship

The employer should create and maintain employment records as the events resulting in records take place. For example, applicant flow logs should be created as each application is received, applicants are interviewed, and decisions made. The OFCCP considers the term record very broadly. E-mails are records if they are relevant to an employment decision, as are other electronic communications and even "Post-It" notes. Contractors might want to consider auditing their applicant records to ensure that applications and/or résumés match their applicant flow logs. Missing documents should be investigated, and the reasons for their omission documented.

Currently, contractors are not required to submit their AAP to the OFCCP annually for review or approval, but they must have the document available in the event of a compliance evaluation or if an applicant or employee requests a document review (applicant and employee access to the AAP is required only for AAPs under Section 503 of the Rehabilitation Act of 1973 and VEVRAA). Contractors should retain, at a minimum, their current and prior year's AAP in the event of a compliance review or discrimination complaint. When contractors do not maintain accurate records, the OFCCP may, by regulation, infer discrimination.

In May 2008, the OFCCP issued a directive allowing for the electronic maintenance of required records. While the OFCCP allows contractors to maintain required records via an electronic recordkeeping system, the system must comply with the following requirements:

- The integrity, accuracy, authenticity and reliability of the records must be ensured;

- The OFCCP must be able to inspect and/or copy the records;

- If the paper originals are stored in electronic format, they must be readily converted to legible and readable paper copy;

- Adequate records management practices are developed and implemented; and

- Original paper records may be destroyed after being transferred to electronic format, but only if those electronic records accurately reproduce the original record.

[H] AAP Maintenance

Mandatory federal AAPs must be updated on an annual basis. According to the regulations, they should be completed and in force by the first day of the plan year. Newly covered contractors have 120 days from the time they are covered by the regulations to develop and implement an AAP.

It is important for a company to stay abreast of AAP requirements. Many states and municipalities have separate and distinctly different AAP requirements that may vary from the federal AAP requirements. Although it is not required, some employers feel these differences force them to develop a separate AAP for each municipality or level of government.

[I] Compliance Evaluations

Each year, the OFCCP conducts approximately 6,000 compliance evaluations of employer affirmative action efforts. The purpose of the evaluations is "to determine whether a contractor maintains nondiscriminatory hiring and employment practices and is taking affirmative actions to ensure that applicants are employed and that employees are placed, trained, upgraded, promoted and otherwise treated during employment without regard to race, color, religion, sex, or national origin [or veterans or disabled status]."

In 1997, the OFCCP adopted a multitiered compliance evaluation process, which consists of any one or a combination of the following investigative procedures:

- *Compliance review.* A comprehensive analysis and evaluation of the hiring and employment practices of the contractor, the written affirmative action plan or program and the results of the affirmative action efforts taken by the contractor.

- *Off-site review of records.* An analysis and evaluation of the AAP (or any part) and supporting documentation, and other documents related to the contractor's personnel policies and employment actions that may be relevant to a determination of the contractor's compliance.

- *Compliance check.* A review of a contractor's documentation of job advertisements, including listings with the state employment services, and examples of accommodations made to persons with disabilities to ascertain whether the contractor has maintained records consistent with the regulations. The contractor can have the review conducted during an on-site visit, or can mail the requested information to the OFCCP.

- *Focused review.* An on-site review restricted to one or more components of the contractor's organization or one or more aspects of the contractor's employment practices.

In 2004, the OFCCP implemented a new system for selecting contractors for compliance evaluations—the Federal Contractor Selection System (FCSS), which replaces the former Equal Employment Data System (EEDS). It is the belief of OFCCP that the FCSS, based on a thorough and external analysis of 10 years of OFCCP compliance reviews, improves the accuracy of the selection process. Data was used to identify and characterize relationships between information from EEO-1 reports and historical OFCCP findings of discrimination. The new model, utilizing 17 factors, compares the workforce profile of contractors to other companies in the same industry and to the profile of the local labor market supply as obtained from 2000 Census data. The OFCCP uses the FCSS system to rank contractors on their likelihood of discrimination, and selects those contractors highest on the list for compliance evaluation. In 2004–2005, the OFCCP selected 3,600 establishments for compliance evaluations using this new system. In 2007–2008, 5,000 facilities were selected for compliance evaluations. In addition, the OFCCP may schedule compliance evaluations based on other factors, such as contract award notices, monitoring complaints as a result of a conciliation agreement, or when it receives what it believes to be a credible report of alleged violations. In late 2007, the OFCCP announced that it would focus more of its compliance evaluations on contractors with functional AAPs. The OFCCP schedules its compliance reviews in two rounds per year. Corporate contractors selected for evaluation received a "Corporate Scheduling Announcement Letter," which advised the headquarters and any subsidiary companies of their selection for evaluation.

Some of the deficiencies that are commonly found in compliance evaluations include:

- Lack of recordkeeping and AAP support data

- Lack of a written EEO policy

- Inadequate results of prior year's goal attainment

- Inadequate utilization analysis

- Failure to develop written AAP

- Inadequate workforce analysis

- Inadequate goal establishment

In August 2004, the OFCCP informed federal contractors that it would "give serious consideration" to any voluntary remedial action undertaken by a contractor prior to an OFCCP compliance evaluation. The extent to which the remedial action taken by the contractor corrects the deficiency found in the OFCCP's evaluation may completely mitigate any remedial action sought by the OFCCP.

A contractor selected by the OFCCP for a compliance evaluation of any type should immediately review the regulations and seek the guidance of an expert or attorney knowledgeable in current OFCCP compliance practices. The demands of a compliance evaluation can be extensive and, in some cases, the contractor may have only three days to prepare for an agency visit.

[J]   Affirmative Action and the Glass Ceiling

Although federal mandatory affirmative action requirements have been in place for over 30 years, employers covered by them are still grappling with a number of important issues. Recent debate on affirmative action has shifted attention from hiring guidelines to the process of removing employment inequities and obstacles that block minorities and women from achieving high-level positions.

In 1998, the federal Glass Ceiling Commission submitted recommendations for eliminating these barriers. The findings from the 53 corporate management reviews conducted by the commission fully supported the premise that a glass ceiling exists in U.S. corporations. The commission recommended that the OFCCP continue to carry out its mandate under the Corporate Management Initiative to eliminate barriers encountered by minority men and women of all races. Corporate leaders must recognize that women and minorities will make up 62 percent of the workforce by 2005, and the sooner they tap into this enormous pool of talent, the better their competitive advantage will be.

Today, businesses must increasingly focus on managing a diverse workforce. Employee diversity per se is not just an HR issue; it is a core business issue impacting all aspects of corporate growth, strategy, business objectives, productivity, and competitiveness. Diversity management focuses on maximizing the strength of today's far-from-homogeneous workforce. The blend of cultures, races, and religions in the current workforce virtually forces employers to effectively manage all employees if they hope to achieve their business objectives.

Exhibit 18.1   Mandated Benefits: 2009 Compliance Guide

Exhibit 18.1
Employee Self-Identification Form

This form is to be used by those employers which are required to complete a federal Affirmative Action Plan and comply with the EEO-1, Vets-100 and Vets-100A reporting requirements to collect gender, ethnicity, race, dis - ability and veteran status information.

[NOTE: For employees and all candidates for employment, after an offer of employment is made, but before the candidate actually begins work.]

This employer is subject to certain governmental recordkeeping and reporting requirements for the administration of civil rights laws and regulations. In order to comply with these laws, the employer invites employees to voluntarily self-identify their race and ethnicity. Submission of this information is voluntary and refusal to provide it will not subject you to any adverse treatment. The information will be kept confidential and will only be used in accordance with the provisions of applicable laws, executive orders and regulations, including those that require the information to be summarized and reported to the federal government for civil rights enforcement. When reported on the EEO-1, Vets-100 and Vets-100A Reports, data will not identify any specific individual. Employees are treated during employment without regard to race, color, religion, sex, age, national origin, disability or veteran status. This data is for periodic government reporting and will be kept in a confidential file separate from the employment file.

(PLEASE PRINT)

Name _____ Position _____

      Last,   First   Middle

Check one: ☐ **Male**   ☐ **Female**

I.   Please answer the following question(s) regarding ethnicity/race:

Are you Hispanic or Latino (a person of Cuban, Mexican, Puerto Rican, South or Central American, or other Spanish culture or origin regardless of race)?

    Check one: ☐ **Yes**   ☐ **No**

If you answered "Yes" to the above question, go to question II, you do not need to answer the next question.

If you answered "No" to the above question, please identify your race:

☐ **American Indian or Alaskan Native** (Not Hispanic or Latino) – A person having origins in any of the original peoples of North America and South America (including Central America), and who maintains tribal affiliation or community attachment.

☐ **Asian** (Not Hispanic or Latino) – A person having origins in any of the original peoples of the Far East, Southeast Asia, or the Indian subcontinent including, for example, Cambodia, China, India, Japan, Korea, Malaysia, Pakistan, the Philippine Islands, Thailand, and Vietnam.

☐ **Black or African American** (Not Hispanic or Latino) – A person having origins in any of the Black racial groups of Africa.

☐ **Native Hawaiian or Other Pacific Islander** (Not Hispanic or Latino) – A person having origins in any of the original peoples of Hawaii, Guam, Samoa, or other Pacific Islands.

☐ **White** (Not Hispanic or Latino) – A person having origins in any of the original peoples of Europe, the Middle East, or North Africa.

☐ **Two or More Races** (Not Hispanic or Latino) – All persons who identify with more than one of the above five races. Please list the **one race** above with which you most strongly identify:
_____

II.   After reviewing the "Invitations to Self-Identify" on the back of this form, please check all that apply:

United States Military Only: All Employees:
☐ **Vietnam Era Veteran**   ☐ **Individual with a Disability**
☐ **Disabled Veteran**
☐ **Special Disabled Veteran**
☐ **Armed Forces Service Medal Veteran**
☐ **Recently Separated Veteran**
☐ **Other Protected Veteran**

1

Invitation to Employees to Self-Identify as an Individual with a Disability

1. This employer is a Government contractor subject to section 503 of the Rehabilitation Act of 1973, as amended, which requires Government contractors to take affirmative action to employ and advance in employment qualified individuals with disabilities. If you have a disability and would like to be considered under the affirmative action program, please tell us.

2. You may inform us of your desire to benefit under the program at this time and/or at any time in the future. This information will assist us in placing you in an appropriate position and in making accommodations for your disability. Submission of this information is voluntary and refusal to provide it will not subject you to any adverse treatment. The information provided will be used only in ways that are not inconsistent with section 503 of the Rehabilitation Act of 1973, as amended.

3. Information you submit will be kept confidential, except that (i) supervisors and managers may be informed regarding restrictions on the work or duties of individuals with disabilities, and regarding necessary accommodations; (ii) first aid and safety personnel may be informed, when and to the extent appropriate, if the condition might require emergency treatment; and (iii) Government officials engaged in enforcing laws administered by OFCCP or the Americans with Disabilities Act, may be informed.

4. If you are an individual with a disability, we would like to include you under the affirmative action program. It would assist us if you tell us about (i) any special methods, skills and procedures which qualify you for positions that you might not otherwise be able to do because of your disability so that you will be considered for any positions of that kind, and (ii) the accommodations which we could make which would enable you to perform the job properly and safely, including special equipment, changes in the physical layout of the job, elimination of certain duties relating to the job, provision of personal assistance services or other accommodations.

Invitation to Employees to Self-Identify as a Disabled Veteran, Special Disabled Veteran, Veteran of the Vietnam Era, Recently Separated Veteran, Armed Forces Service Medal Veteran, or Other Protected Veteran

1. This employer is a Government contractor subject to the Vietnam Era Veterans' Readjustment Assistance Act of 1974, as amended, which requires Government contractors to take affirmative action to employ and advance in employment qualified disabled veterans, special disabled veterans, veterans of the Vietnam era, recently separated veterans, Armed Forces service medal veterans and other protected veterans.

2. If you are a disabled veteran, special disabled veterans, veterans of the Vietnam era, recently separated veteran, Armed Forces service medal veteran or other protected veteran, we would like to include you under our affirmative action program. If you would like to be included under the affirmative action program, please tell us.

   a. The term "disabled veteran" refers to a veteran who is entitled to compensation (or who, but for the receipt of military retired pay, would be entitled to compensation) under laws administered by the Secretary, or was discharged or released from active duty because of a service-connected disability.

   b. The term "special disabled veteran" refers to a veteran who is entitled to compensation (or who, but for the receipt of military retired pay, would be entitled to compensation) under laws administered by the Department of Veterans Affairs for a disability rated at 30 percent or more, or rated at 10 or 20 percent in the case of a veteran who has been determined by the Department of Veterans Affairs to have a serious employment handicap. The term also refers to a person who was discharged or released from active duty because of a service-connected disability.

   c. The term "veteran of the Vietnam era" refers to a person who served on active duty for a period of more than 180 days, and was discharged or released therefrom with other than a dishonorable discharge, if any part of such active duty occurred in the Republic of Vietnam between February 28, 1961 and May 7, 1975, or between August 5, 1964 and May 7, 1975 in all other cases. The term also refers to a person who was discharged or released from active duty for a service connected disability if any part of such active duty was performed in the Republic of Vietnam between February 28, 1961 and May 7, 1975, or between August 5, 1964 and May 7, 1975 in all other cases.

   d. The term "recently separated veteran" refers to any veteran during the three-year period beginning on the date of such veteran's discharge or release from active duty.

   e. The term "Armed Forces service medal veteran" refers to a person who, while serving on active duty in the Armed Forces, participated in a United States military operation for which an Armed Forces service medal was awarded pursuant to Executive Order 12985 (62 FR 1209).

   f. The term "other protected veteran," refers to a person who served on active duty during a war or in a campaign or expedition for which a campaign badge has been authorized, under laws administered by the Department of Defense.

3. You may inform us of your desire to benefit under the program at this time and/or at any time in the future. Submission of this information is voluntary and refusal to provide it will not subject you to any adverse treatment. The information provided will be used only in ways that are not inconsistent with the Vietnam Era Veterans' Readjustment Assistance Act of 1974, as amended.

4. The information you submit will be kept confidential, except that (i) supervisors and managers may be informed regarding restrictions on the work or duties of disabled veterans and special disabled veterans, and regarding necessary accommodations; (ii) first aid and safety personnel may be informed, when and to the extent appropriate, if

Exhibit 18.1   Mandated Benefits: 2009 Compliance Guide

you have a condition that might require emergency treatment; and (iii) Government officials engaged in enforcing laws administered by OFCCP or the Americans with Disabilities Act, may be informed.

5. If you are a disabled veteran or a special disabled veteran, it would assist us if you tell us about (i) any special methods, skills and procedures which qualify you for positions that you might not otherwise be able to do because of your disability so that you will be considered for any positions of that kind, and (ii) the accommodations which we could make which would enable you to perform the job properly and safely, including special equipment, changes in the physical layout of the job, elimination of certain duties relating to the job, provision of personal assistance services or other accommodations. This information will assist us in placing you in an appropriate position and in making accommodations for your disability.

Chapter 19
Alternative Work Schedules

§ 19.01   AUDIT QUESTIONS

1. If the company is subject to the Clean Air Act or its amendments, have alternative work schedules and telecommuting been considered?

2. Has the company developed safety and liability policies specifically for home-based telecommuting?

3. Does the company have a telecommuting agreement, covering such things as company-owned equipment, working hours, confidentiality, and so forth?

4. Have managers and supervisors been trained to manage telecommuters and others on alternative work schedules?

Note: Consistent "yes" answers to the above questions suggest that the organization is applying effective management practices and/or complying with federal regulations. "No" answers indicate that problem areas exist and should be addressed immediately.

Organizations in a variety of industries use alternative work schedules or flexible work options to better meet organizational and employee needs. This form of job design, which allows employees more flexibility in where, when, and how they do their work, has resulted in a larger measure of job satisfaction, increased productivity, and reduced absenteeism.

According to the Society for Human Resources Management (SHRM), about 37 percent of companies offer telecommuting or similar arrangements, and these programs are increasing at an annual rate of 11 percent. This was reinforced by WorldAtWork who reported that 28 million Americans work at least one day per month from home. This is expected to increase to an estimated 100 million by 2010 (Legal Workplace.com, July 1, 2008).

The *2008 National Study of Employers* by Families and Work Institute reported that in the ten years since it has been conducting its study, there has been surprising stability in practices, policies, programs, and benefits provided by U.S. employers with 50 or more employees. The exception is that currently 79 percent (versus 68 percent ten years ago) of employers now allow employees to periodically change their arrival and departure time, and 47 percent (versus 57 percent ten years ago) allow some employees to move from full-time to part-time and back again.

The *2007 CCH Unscheduled Absence Survey* found that 66 percent of people who call in sick to work at the last minute are really taking time off to deal with personal and family issues. Alternative work schedules help employees deal with these issues. They give organizations a way to partner with employees to be more successful.

There are several key fundamentals (or ground rules) that any organization using alternative work schedules needs to consider in developing programs. They vary from organization to organization, but generally include the following:

- Alternative work schedules (AWS) should support the work of the organization

- Supervisors need to understand and accept that presence is not performance

- AWS are not right for everyone

- AWS are a shared responsibility

- Flexibility requires give and take

- Job performance makes a difference

- AWS are not an entitlement

- Time reductions should be proportional

§ 19.02 USE OF ALTERNATIVE WORK SCHEDULES

The forces that have propelled companies to implement alternative work scheduling include:

- *Globalization.* Companies are doing business around the world (in many different time zones), which necessitates nontraditional work schedules to meet customer expectations.

- *Challenging job market.* Companies are competing to attract and retain qualified personnel. Employers want to reduce the cost of recruiting and replacing valuable employees.

- *Growing sensitivity to work and family issues.* More and more workers want to achieve a better balance between their work and their personal lives.

- *Technological advances.* Computers, modems, fax machines, and personal digital assistants are increasingly affordable, making it possible for employees to confer with colleagues and work from remote locations across different time zones.

- *Government regulation.* The Clean Air Act Amendments of 1990 required employers in certain high density areas to provide their employees with alternatives to commuting to work by automobile five days a week. Statutory and regulatory provisions vary among states, but the methods of achieving compliance are reasonably uniform and include alternative work schedules (e.g., four-day workweeks, staggered work schedules) and telecommuting (i.e., working at home or at satellite work centers near the employee's home).

The SHRM 2008 Benefits Survey reported on the use of various forms of alternative work schedules. Fifty-eight percent of respondents in 2008 offered flextime, 47 percent offered telecommuting on an ad hoc basis, 35 percent offered telecommuting on a part-time basis, and 37 percent offered compressed workweeks. Job sharing, one form of alternative work schedule, has been decreasing in use—18 percent of respondents in 2008 reported offering this form of work schedule; this is compared to 2006 (18 percent), 2003 (22 percent), 2002 (24 percent), and 2001 (26 percent).

In the Kenexa Research Institute (KRI) 2007 survey of over 10,000 worker opinions, KRI found that men are playing a larger role in out-of-work responsibilities and, therefore, are feeling the pressures of balancing work and family demands. The study showed that 21 percent of men have unfavorable views of the company's support for work/life balance while 55 percent had favorable views. The men who had unfavorable views also reported having unfavorable pride in their company, being less likely to recommend their company as a place to work and being likely to leave their company.

In the 2007 CCH Survey described above, it was found that 79 percent of employers do not anticipate that changing workforce demographics will affect the work-life or absence control programs they have in place. However, most experts believe that the demographics of the working population are beginning to change dramatically as the Baby Boomers begin to retire and the millennials enter the workforce. Employers need to look at this shift with new expectations and new programs to stay competitive.

§ 19.03   TYPES OF ALTERNATIVE WORK SCHEDULES

Alternative work arrangements include a number of options, such as regular part-time work, temporary work, flextime, and job sharing. Each of the options is described in this section.

[A]   Regular Part-Time Work

Regular part-time work provides both employee and employer with flexibility to meet individual and customer needs. It has traditionally saved employee group benefit costs, although not in all companies. According to the 2006 Employee Benefits Study published by the U.S. Chamber of Commerce, over one in three employers offer benefits to part-time staff; 38 percent paid for holidays; 36 percent offered vacations; and 33 percent provided retirement benefits. Many organizations prorate benefits for their part-time workers on the basis of the minimum or average number of hours worked per week or on the amount of time a worker has been employed.

[B] Temporary Work

The temporary work industry has existed for many years but has recently experienced a "boom" as employers seek to maximize workforce flexibility. Temporary staffing was traditionally used to meet employer needs when employees were on vacation or on leave or to staff for peak hours or seasons. (See **Chapter 16** for further discussion of contingency/temporary staffing.)

[C] Flextime

Flextime (also known as flexitime, gliding time, moving schedules, dynamic schedules, and flexible working hours) allows workers to arrange their schedules to fit their needs. For example, an employee may work late on Wednesdays and Thursdays in order to leave early on Fridays. Although it may not be appropriate for employees in certain positions, in most situations flextime allows employees to choose work hours within limits established by the employer, such as a band of time during which employees may start and finish work and a core time when all employees are required to work. Flextime is a common practice in large cities in which commuting is an issue and in companies that must meet customer needs in a variety of time zones.

V-time or FlexYear, a variation of flextime, allows employees to meet personal needs by voluntarily taking a portion of the year off or changing to a part-time schedule (and accepting less pay). Unlike regular part-time work, V-time scheduling anticipates the employee's return to a full-time work plan. V-time is a common practice in the public sector and is often used as a way of minimizing layoffs.

Degrees of flexibility in V-time may vary from program to program. For example, some employers may require employees on V-time to stay on a selected schedule for six months or longer, whereas others may allow such employees to vary their hours from day to day. Some flextime programs may only provide for extended lunch periods at the employee's choice. Lastly, there are some programs that allow an exempt employee to work full-time for part of a year and part-time the rest of the year while he or she maintains a consistent, but prorated paycheck and benefits throughout the year.

Usually, the determining factor when considering a flextime program is the type of work operation, not the type of worker, to be covered. Employers have found that most employees in operations that are suitable for flextime can be trusted to use flextime privileges appropriately.

[D] Job Sharing

Two or more employees share the responsibilities and prorated salary and benefits of a single full-time position by splitting a shift, a workday, or a workweek. This form of alternative work schedule requires a great deal of coordination and communication. A transition day may be scheduled so both employees work at the same time to improve communication and coordination of assignments.

[E]   Compressed Workweek

Reducing a five-day (40-hour) workweek to something less (e.g., 4.5 days, four 10-hour days, or three 12-hour days) by extending hours worked in the workday allows an employer greater flexibility in staffing and offers the advantage of more hours of job coverage. The most common compressed workweek schedule involves four days of 10 hours each (a 4/40 plan). This practice is most common in the production/ manufacturing environment, where companies often schedule approximately half of the workforce Monday through Thursday and the other half Tuesday through Friday.

Another common compressed workweek schedule is referred to as the 9/80. Employees on this schedule work eight 9-hour days and one 8-hour day, working the typical 80 hours (over two weeks) in 9 days. This schedule gives employees one normal workday off every other week. While employees often prefer to be off either Monday or Friday, the day off can be scheduled to accommodate the employer's business needs. For example, the day off could be scheduled to coincide with the company's lightest workday.

[F]   Compressed Summer Schedule

The compressed summer schedule gives employees extra time off in the summer (e.g., Friday afternoons) if they work longer hours on four of the five days in the typical workweek. Compressed work schedules better accommodate leisure activities and facilitate the scheduling of employees' medical, dental, and personal appointments.

[G]   Phased Partial Retirement

This alternative allows workers to gradually shift from full-time to retired status by reducing their hours.

[H]   Leaves of Absence

Employers are realizing the benefits of allowing employees authorized periods of time away from work without loss of employment rights. Leaves may be paid or unpaid and are usually extended for family, health care, education, or leisure purposes.

[I]   Hoteling

Some employers have implemented a unique arrangement that is termed *hoteling*. Instead of having individual work spaces assigned to them on any sort of "permanent" basis, employees who plan to work in the office on a particular day call ahead to arrange/reserve office space and necessary telephone and computer links and services for that day. Ideally, when employees have reserved office space, they come in to find their office-for-the-day equipped with personal items (e.g., family photographs, art) that have been pulled from personal inventories maintained for that purpose. Despite not having permanent space, employees in a hoteling arrangement have said that they feel comfortable and are ready to work when they arrive at their space.

[J]   Telecommuting

Technology makes it possible to link employees anywhere in the world to the office electronically via e-mail, voice mail, fax machines, and various other modes of communication. With telecommunications, an employee may work from home, the beach, or some other location and still manage to fulfill his or her responsibilities to an employer, shop for groceries, and care for dependent children or parents.

More recently, the costs of fuel and other vehicle expenses has heightened the desire for telecommuting arrangements. According to "The Impact of Commuting on Employees Survey" released in 2008 by the BusinessWeek Research Services in partnership with TransitCenter, Inc., 92 percent of employees are concerned with the high cost of fuel, and 65 percent feel employers should take the lead in helping ease employees' commuting difficulties. Additionally, this survey reported that 72 percent of employees view telecommuting as an important benefit when looking for a new job and 26 percent would leave their current job for another job due to commuting difficulties (Legal Workplace.com, July 1, 2008).

Most telecommuters periodically come into the office to attend meetings and maintain contact with colleagues. Some employers allow employees to telecommute on an occasional or as-needed basis. The U.S. Government Accountability Office (formerly the U.S. General Accounting Office) report "Tele-commuting: Overview of Potential Barriers Facing Employers" estimated that 16.5 million employees telecommute at least once per month, and 9.3 million do so once per week. According to the World at Work 2006 Telework Trendlines commissioned from the Dieringer Research Group, 45 million Americans worked remotely at least one day during all of 2006, and 12.4 million worked at home during business hours at least one day per month. The survey further reported that the total number of U.S. once-per-month teleworkers has increased by roughly 39 percent since 2002.

Studies have shown that telecommuting can significantly enhance quality of life for employees by enabling them to better balance their work and family obligations. Telecommuting also benefits employers in terms of improved employee morale and loyalty to the company.

In the Kenexa Research Institute (KRI) 2007 survey of over 10,000 worker opinions, KRI found that telecommuter outscored their bricks and mortar colleagues in the areas of pride in their organization, confidence in the future, willingness to recommend their organization as a place to work, and overall satisfaction. The study did find that the highest percentages of employees who work remotely come from larger organizations and are professionals, managers, and technical and sales positions. The industries with the highest percentage of telecommuting employees are non-profits, business services, financial services (real estate and insurance), and healthcare services.

Employees who are good candidates for telecommuting generally have the following attributes:

- Able to work autonomously

- Self-motivated

- Able to remain focused even with distractions

- Do not require constant reinforcement

- Solid performer

- Strong communication skills

Jobs that are good candidates for telecommuting generally have the following attributes:

- Do not require a lot of face-to-face interaction with colleagues

- Do not require use of special equipment, facilities, or security

Some employers located in big cities have joined together to locate their employees in suburban facilities where rent is cheaper. Arrangements can be made between employers for sharing equipment and reception areas, and the employees do not feel as isolated as they might feel if they were telecommuting from home. Companies have reported that employees are saving on real estate costs as they can live further from expensive work locations.

Employers must establish an effective process to record and track hours worked by telecommuters. The Fair Labor Standards Act, as well as many state laws, has significant requirements for recording hours worked and time subject to overtime (see **Chapter 3**). As the popularity of telecommuting has increased, so have the lawsuits related to nonexempt employees—many of which are class action lawsuits. In addition to recording time, employers need to carefully consider waiting time, travel time and principal workplace issues as they relate to hours worked by telecommuters. Finally, employers need to ensure telecommuters are complying with meal and rest laws and policies.

Successful telecommuting requires special management attention in structuring the program, identifying likely successful employees and jobs for telecommuting, reviewing/monitoring employees' performance, and establishing policies and procedures (e.g., safety).

Protecting confidential information is a new concern for companies with telecommuters. There have been well-publicized occurrences where employees transfer confidential data to their home workplace where it is stolen. Many companies are encrypting data drives and/or restricting where certain data can be worked on to prevent this from happening.

Organizations are encouraged to develop guidelines for telecommuting safety because employers are required by law to maintain a safe workplace for employees, even if the workplace is the employee's home. The Occupational Safety and Health Administration is concerned with workplace conditions, such as proper ventilation, exposure to hazardous chemicals, cleanliness, good lighting, properly guarded tools or machinery, smoke detection equipment, and the like. Some employers reserve the right to perform home office safety inspections to ensure that telecommuting employees comply with established safety procedures. Employers should be aware of employee concerns when developing home inspection policies.

Repetitive stress injuries are equally as likely to occur in a telecommuting program as in an office. Developing effective ergonomics policies and ensuring that employees are trained on the appropriate setup of their home offices will help prevent these types of potential injuries.

Another employer risk in telecommuting is exposure to fraudulent workers' compensation claims. Workers' compensation coverage is not as straightforward when workers are not on site. It may be difficult to differentiate when an accident is work related (e.g., did employee trip and break an arm while on the job or on the way to the refrigerator to fetch a snack?). Basically an employee is covered for injuries incurred when performing a specific task at home at the request of the employer during the ordinary course of employment. Some experts suggest that the phrase "ordinary course of employment" should be defined as the time during which duties are performed in a telecommuter's home office, thus confining workers' compensation liability to injuries or accidents that occur while the telecommuter is working. Some employers have even gone as far as designating the specific work site (e.g., office area of home only), to limit where incidents can occur. Because the telecommuter will often be the only witness to the injury, employers should develop a process for reporting incidents that employees must follow.

Employers who have telecommuting employees also risk insurance carrier conflicts regarding responsibility of claims. For instance, is it the responsibility of the employee through a personal insurance policy or is it the employer's responsibility to cover equipment losses? Homeowners' policies typically do not cover liabilities for business equipment and office supplies.

Other difficulties that an employer with telecommuting employees may encounter include the following:

- Policing employee behavior, particularly substance and alcohol abuse, when there is no supervisor on the premises

- Ensuring the safety of telecommuting employees who do not live in safe neighborhoods

- Ensuring business confidentiality, which may be jeopardized when telecommuting employees maintain sensitive information on their home computer hard drives

- Helping telecommuting employees avoid burnout or problems separating work and family life

Most of these risks are manageable. A good way to manage exposure and prevent claims is to develop a telecommuting agreement, in advance of a telecommuting arrangement, addressing the issues noted above (e.g., what is covered and what is not, prescribed work hours, securing company-owned equipment, and clarifying whether the employee is working or engaged in other activities).

Companies have found that workers' compensation claims filed by telecommuters are not very common. Reasons supporting this finding include high employee morale among telecommuters, lack of knowledge regarding the right to file a claim, lack of knowledge that the injury might be work-related, and concern that filing a claim will terminate the telecommuting privilege. This trend may change as telecommuting becomes more common. Telecommuting is ultimately expected to reduce work-related injuries, especially those caused by stress.

Telecommuting is also used to retain high-potential employees. Employers have begun to include these arrangements in their management succession plans. It allows the company to hold on to top talent who increasingly are unable or unwilling to relocate for new job assignments. According to Salveson Stetson Group as published on their Web site (ssgsearch.com) on June 4, 2008, the days of executives having to move five times in ten years are over. Companies need to budget extra travel and logistics expense. Employers may not always like this arrangement, but they are beginning to realize it is a good alternative to losing their top performers.

Special effort may be required to develop a successful telecommuting program, but the payoff may be worth it. Studies indicate that telecommuters often put in longer hours and are more productive than their counterparts at the office because they are in no rush to go home: they are home. Studies also have shown that turnover for telecommuters tends to be minimal.

§ 19.04 BENEFITS AND POTENTIAL DRAWBACKS OF IMPLEMENTING ALTERNATIVE WORK SCHEDULES

Companies that have implemented alternative work schedules commonly reap the following benefits:

- Improvement of employees' attitude toward work: more engaged, resilient, and focused

- Increased employee retention, loyalty, and morale

- Improved ability to attract and recruit employees

- Reduced employee turnover

- Decreased occurrences of employee tardiness and unscheduled absences

- Savings on overtime payments

- Ability to employ persons who may otherwise be unavailable for regular full-time work (e.g., students, parents with young children, individuals with disabilities, and retirees)

- Reduced commuter congestion in large urban areas

- Less need for office space

- Expanded hours of service to customers

- Maximum use of equipment and technology

- Increased productivity through employees' ability to work during their individual "peak" working hours and with fewer distractions

- Increased opportunity to cross-train teams

- An opportunity to control compensation by offering AWS in lieu of higher pay

One employer found that implementing several different alternative work schedules resulted in a significant decrease in its turnover. As reported in the June 15, 2001, issue of *Employee Benefit News,* the National Association of Insurance Commissioners (NAIC), a 320-employee not-for-profit organization in Kansas City, Missouri, implemented flexible schedules and compressed workweeks in 1997. About 70 percent of its employees have adopted one of these alternative schedules. A formal but limited telecommuting program was also adopted to increase job satisfaction and retain highly skilled technology employees. The NAIC allows up to 20 employees to participate in the telecommuting program at one time, but generally only 15 employees participate at any given time. As a result of these alternative work schedules, turnover went from 30 percent just prior to implementing the first of the programs to less than 15 percent four years later, a reduction of more than 50 percent.

As reported in HR Magazine, June 2007, Best Buy implemented a new program, ROWE, which allows those employees participating in the program an opportunity to do their work wherever and whenever they wish. Early results (six to nine months after implementation) in the participating departments have been encouraging: productivity increased 35 percent and voluntary turnover dropped between 52 and 90 percent.

On the other hand, companies that provide for alternative work schedules must be prepared for a number of drawbacks, including the following:

- Difficulty developing and implementing a program that works for both the company and its employees, as well as the cost of establishing and maintaining the appropriate work environment

- Difficulty maintaining strong communications between the organization and its employees, as well as communications among employees who may be working as a team

- Difficulty training supervisors and managers regarding how to handle employee relations issues (e.g., training, work monitoring, and performance evaluation)

- Difficulty operating alternative schedules in a culture where management equates putting in time—being visibly at work, often for long hours—as a sign of commitment, loyalty, competence, and high potential

- Difficulty in accurately tracking all hours worked by nonexempt employees

- Difficulty maintaining attendance records

- Higher utility costs because flextime may mean longer operating hours

- Difficulty handling employees whose jobs may not meet the criteria for successful alternative scheduling but who want an alternative schedule anyway

- Possible zoning, union, and other issues to be resolved when employees work at home, depending on the type of work the company does

The results of a study released by Rensselaer's Lally School of Management and Technology in January 2008 suggest that the prevalence of telecommuters in an office adversely impacts coworkers who do not telecommute, in terms of their job satisfaction and likelihood that they will leave the company. While the results of this study were not scientifically measurable, it does raise concerns that employers must be careful when implementing telecommuting programs and monitor the satisfaction of all employees.

§ 19.05 IMPACT OF ALTERNATIVE WORK SCHEDULES ON UNSCHEDULED EMPLOYEE ABSENCES

Alternative work schedules are proving to be an effective means for controlling the costs and headaches associated with unscheduled absences. The national 2007 Unscheduled Absence Survey compiled by CCH, Inc. reported the following reasons for unscheduled absenteeism:

- Personal illness (34 percent of all unplanned time off)

- Family concerns (22 percent)

- Stress (13 percent)

- Personal needs (18 percent)

- Employee entitlement mentality (13 percent)

The CCH survey of 317 organizations randomly selected across industry segments and company sizes indicated that absenteeism cost the nation's largest employers more than $760,000 per year in direct payroll costs. The costs would be more if lower productivity, lost revenue and effects on poor morale were considered. To combat the impact of unscheduled absenteeism and address these concerns, employers are still instituting a variety of programs, the goals of which are to improve productivity through reduced unscheduled absences. This survey also reports that telecommuting programs are being used by 30 percent of employers to help deter the problems experienced with presenteeism. According to CCH, presenteeism occurs when employees come to work even though they are ill. While employees are well-meaning, their good intentions may have ill effects as they deliver low productivity and pose contagion risks to other employees and customers.

According to the survey, the three programs rated most effective for reducing unscheduled absenteeism were alternative work arrangements, flu shot programs, and leave to attend child's school functions. Other programs rated most effective by the survey respondents were on-site child care, telecommuting, and compressed workweeks.

§ 19.06   CONSIDERATIONS IN DESIGN AND IMPLEMENTATION OF ALTERNATIVE WORK SCHEDULES

Successful alternative work schedules are a shared responsibility between the employee and management. They must have the following:

- Clear identification of the organization's goals and needs (e.g., whether there are core service hours and needs that must be covered)

- Clear, written plan for each employee participating in the AWS including their schedule, description of job duties and types of assignments, when they must come into the office, equipment needed to perform their job, and how their performance and progress will be tracked.

- Implementation of administrative process to track all aspects of the plans

- Support of top management

- Involvement of both management and employees

- Lack of unlawful discrimination in the administration of the program (i.e., avoid denying alternative work schedules only to employees in protected classifications)

- A management philosophy that workers who take advantage of alternative work arrangements are afforded the same opportunity as other employees to receive raises, promotions, and bonuses

- A schedule for supervisor and employee communications (e.g., weekly or daily status reports or teleconferences)

- Development of a consistent plan structure that meets requirements of applicable wage and hour laws, unemployment insurance compensation criteria, bargaining unit agreements, and commitments

- Training of employees who will be involved in the program and their supervisors or managers

- Clear communication to employees of performance expectations, evaluation, pay, hours of work, and recordkeeping

- Safety and ergonomics guidelines for those working at home

- Identification of potential income tax issues (computers, other equipment, and furniture given by employers to employees for their use at home may be considered taxable fringe benefits by the Internal Revenue Service; to avoid this, employers should retain title to all equipment and furniture and maintain documentation that the employee is not the owner)

- Implementation of ongoing follow-up and monitoring practices to identify when the program is working and how it can or should be revised over time

Alternative work scheduling is different in each organization. Determining which, if any, alternative work schedules will work for a given organization depends on job responsibilities, work environment, management philosophy, and organizational culture. Often, the flexibility of alternative scheduling is used when an organization undergoes reengineering, or "right sizing," to meet changing economic market needs.

Viewed as part of a business strategy, it is clear that companies that are considering alternative work schedules will need to become more formal in their approach, more strategic in their use of flexibility, more inclusive in terms of which employees may use flexible work arrangements, and more global in their perspective. Companies who incorporate flexible work arrangements need to be careful as they are very difficult to change and/or rescind. With the proliferation of the Internet and media like "You Tube," employers can quickly find themselves with negative press, which could hurt the company's reputation.

One additional benefit to workplace flexibility was revealed in a study released by Wake Forest University Baptist Medical Center in December 2007. The lead author of the study, Joseph G. Grzywacz Ph.D. of the Wake Forest University School of Medicine, "found that people who believe they have flexibility in their work lives have healthier lifestyles. Individuals who perceive an increase in flexibility are likely to start some positive lifestyles. This study is important because it reinforces the idea that workplace flexibility is important to workplace health."

Flexible work options provide new ways to do business in a changing business environment. They should have a positive or neutral effect on business results. Well-managed programs should be beneficial to the organization, its employees, and its customers.

Chapter 20
Privacy in the Workplace

Exhibit 20.1: A Sample Policy on Reference Checks on Job Applicants
Exhibit 20.2: A Sample Policy on Searches
Exhibit 20.3: A Sample Policy on Electronic and Telephonic Communication Monitoring
Exhibit 20.4: A Sample Policy on Internet Acceptable Use
Exhibit 20.5: A Sample Policy on Medical Records and Serious Health Conditions
Exhibit 20.6: AIDS Testing in the Workplace: Statutes and Policies
Exhibit 20.7: A Sample Policy on Access to Employee Personnel Files
Exhibit 20.8: A Sample Policy on Providing Employment References

§ 20.01   AUDIT QUESTIONS

1. If the company conducts drug testing, does it ensure that all results are kept confidential?

2. Does the company have a written policy regarding the use of company computers, Internet access, and the company e-mail system?

3. Does the company require that hard copy files containing employee personal information be kept in locked file cabinets?

4. Does the company have a policy preserving the right to search employees' work areas and any belongings employees bring onto company property?

5. Is employee medical information maintained in a file separate from other employee information files?

6. Are company practices regarding medical information consistent with privacy requirements of the Americans with Disabilities Act of 1990 and the Family and Medical Leave Act of 1993?

7. Does the company have a written policy on who has access to employee information?

Note: Consistent "yes" answers to the above questions suggest that the organization is applying effective management practices and/or complying with federal regulations. "No" answers indicate that problem areas exist and should be addressed immediately.

This chapter provides private sector employers with information and guidelines related to employees' right to privacy in the workplace. The right to privacy falls within three general time periods: before employment, during employment, and after employment. Areas covered in this chapter include the extent of employer control and access in a cross-section of federal and state legislation and current workplace practices.

The chapter also provides an assessment of legal implications and specific laws, with case law provided when available. Because state laws vary widely, readers are urged to refer to the *2008 State by State Guide to Human Resources Law* (Aspen Publishers, New York) for detailed discussion of laws in their respective states.

In the past decade, the right of privacy in the workplace has become a key issue for companies and their employees because laws protecting employee privacy rights have not kept pace with the rate of technological advancement in electronic, computer, and video surveillance methods. Labor and government interest groups have expressed concern regarding privacy violations related to employer access and abuse of employee work activity records and personnel records. Employees maintain that privacy in the workplace often is denied and that new methods for employee testing procedures herald a further invasion of privacy.

Historically, public sector employees have a right to privacy based on the Constitution. However, there is no comprehensive federal law that guarantees private-sector workplace privacy. The Fourth Amendment provides some protection in that it protects all U.S. citizens from unreasonable searches and seizures. Nevertheless, it is statutory law that provides the primary privacy protection available to private sector employees, and those laws are generally weak. In fact, the statutes often assume that the employer owns everything in the workplace and, therefore, has the right to set rules for supervision and employee conduct.

Often, employers and employees alike are unaware of the legal issues and even the nature of the many privacy violations in the workplace. Improved technology increases the need for companies and individuals to assess and self-monitor the information they share, how they share it, and with whom.

§ 20.02   PREEMPLOYMENT PRACTICES

New issues related to personal privacy during the preemployment stage continue to surface due to the employer's ability to directly access personal data about potential employees via electronic methods. The enhanced access to personal data creates a greater potential for "blacklisting" job applicants for illegal reasons. To guard against potential abuse, companies need to develop policies and practices to control their use of personal data stored on electronic media, especially when the law in this area is still in an evolutionary stage.

This section discusses specific areas of candidate privacy that present risk to the employer and some of the laws related to preemployment practices.

[A]   Reference Checks

Various local, state, and federal laws affect a prospective employer's right to secure and use information for screening and hiring purposes. Employers are encouraged to become thoroughly familiar with all state laws and regulations pertaining to background investigations and preemployment inquiries within their states.

No specific law requires employers to check an applicant's employment references. Nonetheless, employers may be held liable for negligent hiring for acts committed by their employees that the employers should have known might occur if they had performed the due diligence of preemployment reference checking. Employers should validate applicants' job experiences, explore gaps in employment history, and validate claims to educational and other qualifications that candidates have listed on resumes and employment applications.

Unfortunately, employers who attempt to check the references of candidates for employment are often unsuccessful. Former employers are uncertain about what to say when providing information about former employees. They do not want to discuss negative experiences for fear of incurring potential defamation claims and liability. These concerns have led many employers to initiate policies prohibiting meaningful reference comments. It is common for a former employer to release only information regarding dates of employment, position(s) held, and possibly verification of final compensation. To counter this trend, many employers are asking candidates to sign a reference release form before releasing further information.

Many states have passed legislation providing immunity to managers and HR professionals who provide good-faith job references on former employees. For example, in the state of Washington, H.R. 1625 was signed into law and became effective on July 24, 2005. H.R. 1625 states that an employer that discloses information about a former or current employee to a prospective employer or employment agency at the request of that employer or agency is presumed to be acting in good faith and is immune from civil liability for the disclosure of that information. An employer can lose the presumption of good faith when there is clear and convincing evidence of knowingly presenting false information, deliberately misleading the prospective employer or agency, or making disclosures with reckless disregard for the truth. Pennsylvania passed a similar statute in 2005, as did West Virginia in 2006.

Regardless of the outcome, prudent employers make an effort to verify information provided by the applicant, contact prior employers listed by the applicant, and thoroughly check references. Hiring managers should document every contact made, whether the attempt at data gathering was successful or unsuccessful.

[B] Criminal Background Checks

The Equal Employment Opportunity Commission (EEOC) and some state agencies contend that certain conviction records are irrelevant to some jobs. The EEOC takes the position that the use of conviction records as an automatic bar to employment may have a disproportionate impact on protected classes and thus may be unlawful. Accordingly, an employer inquiry about conviction records, either on the employment application form or in an interview, should be accompanied by a statement that the existence of a criminal record is not an absolute bar to employment.

When conducting a background check for criminal records, care must be taken to distinguish between information about arrests and convictions. Many states prohibit an employer from asking a job applicant to provide information regarding arrests or detentions that did not result in conviction or from seeking this information from any source. Moreover, some states prohibit employers from using arrest records as a factor in making hiring decisions.

In some industries a criminal check is absolutely critical. Thorough criminal checks are especially applicable to firms that provide services for vulnerable persons such as children, persons with disabilities, and the elderly. For example, nursing homes must ask certain job applicants whether they have been disciplined or convicted for offenses relating to the elderly. In Alaska, employers are permitted to request records on convictions for sex crimes or for contributing to the delinquency of a minor, provided the job being sought involves supervisory or disciplinary power over a minor. Louisiana passed a law in 2006 which requires that the Louisiana Bureau of Criminal Identification and Information provide information about all criminal convictions for a period of ten years prior to the request, to potential employers of persons applying for a position of supervisory or disciplinary authority over children. (See **Exhibit 20.1** for a sample policy on reference checks on job applicants.)

Some states are making it more difficult for employers to obtain information on applicants' criminal behavior. In West Virginia, for example, individuals can clear their criminal records of charges for which they were acquitted or that were dismissed. Charges cannot be removed if they resulted in a felony conviction or were plea-bargained. In 2003, the Rhode Island legislature considered a bill (H.R. 5771) that would have prohibited employers from accessing background information before hiring prospective employees. These actions place companies in a tough position. If the employer's state has enacted regulations such as those listed above, the employer will need to comply but should take every legal action it can to obtain background information. If criminal background information is not available, interviewing carefully about gaps in the applicant's employment history may reveal such information, if applicable.

[C] Credit Reports

The Fair Credit Reporting Act of 1970 (FCRA), as amended September 1997, defines two types of credit reports: consumer reports and investigative consumer reports.

A consumer report is any written, oral, or other form of information provided by a consumer reporting agency that addresses creditworthiness, credit standing, credit capacity, character, general reputation, personal characteristics, or mode of living. These reports are informally called credit checks and can be provided through a number of consumer reporting agencies.

An investigative consumer report is a consumer report in which information on a consumer's character, general reputation, personal characteristics, or mode of living is obtained through personal interviews with neighbors, friends, or associates of the consumer. In other words, the data are not obtained from a creditor of the consumer or a consumer reporting agency.

The FCRA requires an employer who wishes to obtain either type of credit report to provide a job applicant with an appropriate disclosure form with a written statement disclosing that a report may be obtained for employment purposes and to obtain the applicant's written authorization and release.

Some employers request credit reports when conducting background checks on prospective employees. If credit reports are conducted, the FCRA, as well as many states, require employers to provide applicants with written notice of any adverse action taken by the employer against the applicant because of information contained in a credit report. The notice must state that the adverse action against the applicant was based in whole or in part upon the information contained in the credit report. In addition, the notice must include the name, address, and telephone number of the consumer credit agency that furnished the report to the employer and must inform the applicant that he or she has a right to obtain a free copy of the credit report from the agency and may dispute its accuracy.

Employers need to be aware that if a credit report indicates financial or credit problems, this information cannot be used to reject the applicant unless the employer can show a business necessity for disqualification on that basis. In addition, employers need to be aware that credit reports can be inaccurate.

Any information that reflects negatively on the applicant should be carefully verified before using the information to make an employment decision.

Practical considerations and recommendations for employers conducting credit or criminal history information include the following:

- Use care when hiring a third party or credit reporting agency to collect credit information.

- Ensure that the person collecting the information is properly bonded and licensed; the employer is not protected from liability because it used a third party to conduct the investigation.

- Provide the applicant with an opportunity to explain or correct any negative information.

- Include on the application form language whereby the applicant explicitly authorizes the employer to conduct appropriate consumer reports and language identifying the methods used by the employer.

- Limit the information collected to information the employer has a legitimate business-related reason to collect. The type of information collected may vary according to the duties and responsibilities of the job involved. Generally, an employer should not ask about the job applicant's assets, liabilities, charge accounts, bank accounts, credit ratings, prior garnishments, or home ownership.

- Ensure consistency and confidentiality. The employer should have a clear, written policy regarding the situations in which preemployment information will be gathered and how that information will be used and stored. Information gathered should be disseminated only to those with a legitimate need to know. The information gathered should not be maintained in the employee's personnel file, but rather should be kept in a separate employment file with access generally limited to those involved in the hiring decision.

- Implement the Fair and Accurate Credit Transactions (FACT) Act Disposal Rule. Effective June 1, 2005, all consumer reports and information derived from a consumer report must be appropriately disposed of when the employer no longer requires the information. Reasonable methods of disposal will depend on the format of the information (paper or electronic) and the employer's means. For example, paper documents may be burned, pulverized, or shredded; electronic documents may be wiped, overwritten, or the discs might be destroyed. Alternatively, an employer may hire a document destruction contractor. The disposal rule does not address the timing of destruction, only that the objective of the disposal of personal and financial information should be to protect against "unauthorized use of the information."

[D] Genetic Testing

Medical research has reached the point where the predisposition for some diseases may be detected through genetic testing. Genetic testing, therefore, has the potential to help identify persons at risk for serious health problems or for early diagnosis of disease.

According to a study conducted by the National Center for Genome Resources, 73 percent of the respondents stated that it is a good rather than a bad thing for a healthy person to receive advance warning that he or she is predisposed to a serious health condition. However, there is a fear that negative genetic results will be used against an individual in employment decisions and in determining benefit eligibility. Hence, the widespread concern about the privacy of genetic testing and test results and reluctance to have testing at all if there is any chance the results could be revealed inappropriately.

The Genetic Information Nondiscrimination Act of 2008 (GINA) prohibits employers, employment agencies, labor unions, and insurance providers from discriminating against applicants and employees on the basis of genetic information. GINA amends ERISA, the Public Health Service Act and the Code, as well as Title VII of the Civil Rights Act. The provisions that effect employers will go into effect on November 21, 2009, 18 months after enactment. Genetic information is defined as (1) the individual's genetic tests; (2) the individual's family members' genetic tests; and (3) the manifestation of a disease or disorder in family members of an individual. Gender and age are not genetic information. GINA defines family member as: (1) the individual's spouse; (2) a dependent child of the individual, including children placed for adoption; or (3) parents, grandparents, or great-grandparents.

Employers, labor unions, and employment agencies may not use genetic information to discriminate against employees in hiring, promotion, job assignment, firing, training, retraining, and all other privileges and conditions of employment. Employers may not use genetic information to limit, segregate or classify employees to deprive them of employment opportunities or otherwise adversely affect their employment.

If an employee feels that their rights under GINA have been violated, they may seek relief under Title VII of the Civil Rights Act. The individual must file a complaint with the EEOC or with their state agency. If a violation is found, the agency will bring suit on behalf of the employee; if the agency decides not to bring suit, the employee may sue ("right to sue"). However, GINA does not provide for disparate discrimination claims.

Information on GINA's health care nondiscrimination requirements can be found in **Chapter 5.**

In one case decided before the enactment of GINA, the court ruled that testing employees for sensitive medical and genetic information, without their consent, as part of a mandatory pre-placement medical examination may violate the employees' federal and state constitutional rights to privacy. Seven clerical and administrative employees had objected to tests for syphilis, sickle cell trait, and pregnancy conducted without their knowledge or consent.

The tests were part of a pre-placement medical exam required by the Lawrence Berkeley Laboratory, operated by the University of California under contract with the Department of Energy. The court held that testing for sickle cell trait and pregnancy may violate Title VII prohibitions against race and sex discrimination. In addition, the court said: "The mere fact that an employee has given a blood or urine sample does not provide notice that an employer will perform any and all tests on that specimen that it desires—no matter how invasive—particularly where the employer has yet to offer a valid reason for the testing." The court stressed that there would be no violation if the testing were authorized or if the employees "reasonably should have known that the blood and urine samples they provided would be used for the disputed testing and failed to object."

[E]   Drug Testing

Many employers administer drug tests to job applicants. In some industries, such as transportation and construction, there are specific legal requirements to conduct drug testing on job applicants for certain jobs. Ten years ago, there were concerns that drug testing invaded employees' privacy. In recent years, however, drug testing is generally not considered an invasion of privacy, provided applicants are informed in advance that they will be tested. Drug testing can work to the employer's benefit if the process is carefully planned and controlled.

At the federal level the EEOC has issued guidelines, based on the Americans with Disabilities Act of 1990 (ADA), regarding drug testing for both applicants and employees. In addition, more and more states have passed laws regulating drug testing (see **Exhibit 23.4**).

A 1997 California case provided a set of guidelines for employers to review when considering applicant drug testing. In *Loder v. City of Glendale* [14 Cal. 4th 846 (1997)], the California Supreme Court held that employers may conduct preemployment drug tests as a condition for hiring. The court set forth the following steps for employers that test for drugs:

1. *State in the job application form that the employment is conditioned on satisfactorily passing a drug test.* (Although the ADA permits pre-offer drug tests, to minimize risk, employers should administer a drug test after a conditional offer of employment has been made but before actual on-the-job service begins.)

2. *Require the test of all similarly situated applicants who receive conditional offers of employment and give the test to all applicants under the same circumstances.*

3. *Have the test conducted by a reputable laboratory that follows consistent procedures that ensure the individuals' privacy.* (The lab should obtain written consent from the applicant and provide the applicant with an opportunity to explain why the test may read positive for any illegal substances. Test results should be provided to the employer in writing. Samples should be retained for possible retesting.)

4. *Treat test results (and ensure that the laboratory treat test results) as highly confidential.*

5. *If an applicant's test result is positive, notify him or her and provide an opportunity to have the same sample retested, if requested.*

In a significant California case, *Wilkensen v. Times Mirror Corp.* [264 Cal. Rptr. 194 (Cal. App. 1989)], the court upheld that the employer did not unlawfully invade the privacy of job candidates by testing them for drug use as part of a routine preemployment medical examination. In this case, the court found that the employer had taken steps to minimize the intrusiveness of the testing and to protect the confidentiality of the persons involved.

[F] Medical Examination

Under the ADA, an employer may describe the essential visual, mental, and physical requirements of a position and inquire if the candidate is able to perform the essential requirements of the job, with or without accommodation. The employer may not ask general questions about an applicant's physical or mental limitations before making an offer of employment to the applicant. The employer may, however, condition an offer of employment on the results of a medical examination to be conducted before beginning work to determine the applicant's fitness to perform the essential requirements of the job as described.

An employer's right to require applicants to undergo a medical examination is subject to the following restrictions:

- All final candidates for the same or similar positions must take the medical examination.

- If certain job standards are used during the examination to disqualify applicants with disabilities from employment, the exclusionary standards must be job-related and consistent with business necessity.

(In addition, the employer must be able to demonstrate that reasonable accommodations would not enable the disabled applicant to perform the essential functions of the job.)

- When the results of the medical examination would result in disqualification, an applicant may submit independent medical opinions for consideration before a final determination on disqualification is made.

- Candidates' medical examination results must be maintained separately from the personnel file and kept confidential.

§ 20.03 PRIVACY ISSUES DURING EMPLOYMENT

Employers must be aware of numerous issues regarding their employees' privacy in the workplace. The issues include workplace searches, surveillance and monitoring of employee work activity, confidentiality of employee information, AIDS/HIV privacy issues, e-mail and voice mail privacy, and testing for drugs.

[A] Workplace Searches

Employers at times may face workplace issues that cause them to consider searching employees' work areas, lockers, or cars, or consider conducting a personal search of an employee. Usually, these situations arise out of concerns about suspected theft, sale of illegal drugs, and other security issues. The employer must be aware of the legal limitations regarding workplace searches and the need for legal counsel regarding these situations.

The Fourth Amendment protects individuals from unreasonable searches and seizures. Regardless of whether the employer operates in the public or private sector, constitutional issues may arise from a search. Employer intrusions and searches of an employee's area where the employee has a reasonable expectation of privacy may give rise to an independent tort of invasion of privacy. The tort, or civil wrong, causes of action most frequently alleged as a result of an employer search include assault, battery, slander, false imprisonment, and invasion of privacy.

Many arbitrators agree, however, that Fourth Amendment protection against illegal searches may not be applicable to the workplace, particularly if an employer conducting a search has experienced serious problems with theft or has other reasonable or probable cause to conduct a search because a theft has occurred. In such situations, the employer may be entitled to tighten its security rules and begin inspecting the packages of employees as they leave the plant. Regardless of whether an employee contends that a search is an affront to his or her dignity, an arbiter would conclude that management has a paramount right to search packages because they might contain stolen property. Regardless of the reason for conducting such a search, an employer should seek legal counsel before implementing it.

A number of legal issues involved in conducting workplace searches are illustrated by the following instances:

- *Desk Searches.* Search of an employee's personal property must be conducted in a discreet manner and in such a way that personal matters unrelated to the workplace are not revealed. [Borse v. Piece Goods Shop, Inc., 963 F.2d 611, 614 (3d Cir. 1992)]

- *Locker Searches.* A jury awarded $108,000 to an employee whose locker was searched without her consent. The employee had a reasonable expectation that the locker and its contents would be free from intrusion and interference because she used her own lock and was never informed that the locker might be subject to search. [KMart v. Trotti, 677 S.W.2d 632 (Tex. Ct. App. 1984), *writ refused,* 686 S.W.2d 593 (Tex. 1985)]

- *Car Searches.* An employer did not invade an employee's privacy by attempting to search the employee's car in accordance with a published policy of periodic and random searches of vehicles leaving company property. [Gretencord v. Ford Motor Co., 538 F. Supp. 331 (D. Kan. 1982)]

- *Body Searches and Detainment.* Body searches and detainment are not actions that private employers should undertake for any reason. An employer runs substantial risk of liability if it conducts a physical search of any employee. Because the greatest danger of litigation exists when performing body searches, individuals with the responsibility for conducting searches should be instructed not to touch any employee. If an employer believes a body search is required (e.g., if the employer believes an employee has secreted an item on his or her person), the employer is advised to contact the proper legal authorities. A body search should be conducted away from other employees and during company time.

Note: Physical searches of employees can result in a variety of legal accusations, including constitutional violations, invasion of privacy, false imprisonment, intentional infliction of emotional distress, and breach of contract. Unreasonable searches and seizures are prohibited by the Fourth Amendment. If employees are detained for various purposes, the tort of false imprisonment may be used. The employee may claim that the employer's search violated employer policies, a collective bargaining agreement, or a binding provision in the company's employee handbook.

Examples of poorly handled searches are:

— A cafeteria cashier was strip-searched when her cash register was $100 short. She was awarded $300,000. [Taylor v. Rush-Presbyterian St. Luke's Med. Ctr. (Ill. 1987)]

— A female retail store employee was ordered to disrobe down to her underwear in front of a female assistant manager and a customer who had accused her of taking $20. The court held that a jury could find that this was so degrading and humiliating as to constitute an invasion of privacy. [Bodewig v. KMart, Inc., 635 P.2d 657 (Or. 1981)]

- *Trash Searches.* A search by police of an individual's garbage bags placed at the curb for collection did not violate any "reasonable expectation of privacy." [California v. Greenwood, 108 S. Ct. 1625 (1988)]

[B] Search Policies and Practices

An employer should have a search policy to minimize its exposure to search-related liability. Employers who are considering drafting a policy on workplace searches should do the following:

- Draft the policy to cover all types of searches the company intends to conduct, and include a statement that the request to search any employee does not imply an accusation of theft.

- Form an employee committee to discuss the investigative techniques to ensure employees understand the policy. Employees can help to provide a balance between the organization's needs and employees' privacy. Ensure that the selected employee committee does not purport to speak for the rest of the employees; it is important not to create a de facto union.

- Publicize the policy widely.

- Provide employees with adequate notice of when the policy will be implemented.

- Distribute a copy of the policy to each employee and obtain the employee's signature on a copy, kept in the personnel files, indicating the employee has read and understood the policy.

- Have all policies reviewed by legal counsel.

Employers that are considering whether or not to conduct a search should observe the following guidelines:

- A search must be justified by a compelling business reason—one that is likely to withstand judicial scrutiny.

- It is generally legal to randomly search lockers and desks used by employees, given proper cause and published policy.

- Specific information that could be gathered during a search and that may become important later on should be documented in advance of the search.

- Choose the least intrusive methods for gathering information.

- If an employee refuses to submit to a search, take disciplinary action only if the search request was justified.

- The search policy must apply to everyone and be applied evenly.

(See **Exhibit 20.2** for a sample policy on searches.)

[C]   Electronic Surveillance for Productivity Purposes

Employers in pursuit of greater productivity have found ways to take advantage of the latest technological advances in office computers, electronic mail (e-mail), and telephone tracking systems to track employee work output. Employers contend that surveillance accomplishes the following:

- Tracks attendance

- Reviews punctuality of employees

- Determines employee activity and charts work flow

- Determines exact employee whereabouts during the workday

- Generates statistics on individual and department accomplishments

- Determines future workloads

- Provides employee feedback on productivity and allows the supervisor more time for coaching and giving attention to other important employee needs and concerns

- Increases employee safety and adherence to company rules (e.g., on-board trucking monitors record speed, engine idling time, and length of stops, all meant to ensure that truckers drive safely and take necessary rest breaks)

- Is a good tool when reasonable evidence of wrongdoing comes to light (e.g., theft or negligence)

Monitoring employees' keystrokes and e-mail was the subject of a review by the Department of Justice (DOJ) in *PC Week* [June 23, 1993, p. 2041]. The DOJ warned that employers conducting keystroke monitoring should inform both authorized and unauthorized users that such monitoring is taking place. It said that a written notice is insufficient; administrators must add to users' log-ins a clear statement that, by using the system, employees are consenting to have their keystrokes monitored.

Privacy is best protected and employee morale is most effectively maintained when monitoring is visible, minimally intrusive, and directly relevant to job performance.

[D] Telephone Monitoring for Service Quality Control

Many states have adopted laws that regulate the monitoring of employees' phone conversations. In Illinois, for example, employers engaged in marketing, opinion research, or telephone solicitation are allowed to monitor employees' conversations for the purpose of service quality control, *provided* employers obtain the consent of at least one of the parties to the conversations being monitored. The law also includes several controls designed to protect employees' rights. For example, employers must immediately stop listening and destroy the tape upon determining that the telephone conversation does not fall within one of three categories: (1) market research, (2) opinion research, or (3) telephone solicitation. In addition, employers must post a prominent notice at work stating that telephone conversations will be monitored or recorded, and must provide employees with access to unmonitored telephone lines or pay phones for personal use.

There are other legal restrictions on employers when monitoring employees' telephone conversations or other electronic communications. The Federal Omnibus Crime Control and Safe Streets Act of 1968 prohibits intentionally intercepting any wire, oral, or electronic communication without the consent of a party involved in the communication. Connecticut law prohibits employers from monitoring personal calls, whether authorized or not, and prohibits anyone from "intentionally overhearing" or recording a conversation pertaining to employment contract negotiations, unless all parties to the conversation give their consent. [Conn. Gen. Stat. Ann. § 31-48b] Otherwise, employers may generally monitor calls on an extension telephone in the "ordinary course of business."

A prime example of the problem of general call monitoring in the "ordinary course of business" is the case of *Griffin v. City of Milwaukee* [74 F.3d 824 (7th Cir. 1996)], in which a former telecommunicator for the Milwaukee Police Department alleged that her former employer had illegally intercepted her personal communications in violation of the federal wiretapping statues. Because the communicators handled all incoming emergency calls, they had been previously informed that their calls could be monitored for supervisory, evaluation, and training purposes. Further, the telecommunicators had been told that they should use an unmonitored lunchroom telephone rather their workstation telephones for any personal phone calls. The plaintiff argued that documents indicating 950 uses of the silent monitoring function in the department led to the "inescapable and reasonable inference" that the department had illegally intercepted her phone calls.

The Seventh Circuit summarily rejected the plaintiff's inference, finding that the plaintiff could not actually demonstrate how many times the telecommunicators' calls had been silently monitored. The court went on to note that plaintiff's testimony that she heard beeps and breathing sounds while using the lunchroom telephone did not demonstrate that the department illegally monitored her phone calls.

[E]   Surveillance Cameras

The general rule is that an employer can conduct surveillance in any area of its facility where an employee would not expect privacy. Surveillance cameras in a lobby or waiting area, for example, are likely permissible, whereas a camera in employee rest rooms, shower areas, or locker room areas would probably not be permissible. What is permissible or not must be decided on a case-by-case basis. However, an employer can reduce employees' reasonable expectations of privacy by clearly indicating by means of appropriate signs, written notices, or information in employee handbooks that the physical facility at which the employees work will be subject to monitoring in every area except, for example, rest rooms. Employers are reminded that engaging in surveillance beyond that which is described in the written notices may constitute a violation of employees' rights to privacy.

The State of New York enacted a law in 2006 that prohibits employers from video recording employees in a restroom, locker room or any other room where, as designated by the employer, employees change their clothes. Exceptions are allowed if authorized by court order. The law does not apply to law enforcement personnel engaged in their authorized duties. [New York Labor Law section 203-c, enacted by A.B. 10548, L. 2006, and amended by S.B. 8289, L. 2006, effective July 5, 2006]

According to the 2007 Electronic Monitoring & Surveillance Survey conducted by the American Management Association and The ePolicy Institute, 48 percent of employers use video monitoring in the workplace.

[F]   Electronic Mail and Voice Mail

E-mail and voice mail are important business communication tools. They have also become sources of liability and concern for employers. Employers find it useful to engage in electronic monitoring of computer data and computerized communications for the purposes of checking on the status of projects, assessing employee productivity or performance evaluations, and investigating problems in the workplace. Employers are realizing, however, that such monitoring is not without potential problems: Surreptitious monitoring can create stress and low morale among employees, which can result in higher health care costs and increased turnover.

Monitoring of e-mail and voice mail has opened a new area of litigation involving the right to privacy. In *Smyth v. Pillsbury Co.* [914 F. Supp. 97 (E.D. Pa. 1996)], the court held that the plaintiff's termination for transmitting inappropriate and unprofessional comments over his employer's e-mail system did not violate public policy. The court said employees do not have a reasonable expectation of privacy in the contents of their e-mail communications over their employer's e-mail system. Even if they did, the court held, a reasonable person would not consider an employer's interception of e-mail communications to be a substantial and highly offensive invasion of privacy. Users should expect little privacy on most UNIX or e-mail system accounts for two reasons:

1. Every keystroke has the potential to be intercepted by someone else.

2. Extensive backups, invisible to the user, are made by system administrators and may cover several weeks' worth of communications.

The Electronic Communications Privacy Act of 1986 (ECPA) generally protects electronic communications from illegal interception, recording, and disclosure. Originally designed to prevent unauthorized access by outside intruders of electronic communications sent over large systems used by the public, the ECPA addresses concerns in two key areas:

1. Protecting all electronic communications systems, including internal e-mail systems and public systems, from outside intruders.

2. Protecting messages sent over public service e-mail systems and calls over public system telephones.

Purely internal systems are generally not subject to the ECPA's privacy provisions. The ECPA states: "The person or entity providing a wire or communications service" is not liable for offenses regarding stored communications (i.e., e-mail).

While there are a number of exceptions to the ECPA's prohibition of interception of electronic communications, the three exceptions most relevant to the workplace are (1) where one party consents, (2) where the provider of the communication service can monitor communications, and (3) where the monitoring is performed in the ordinary course of business.

Regarding the first exception, the employer should ensure actual (rather than implied) consent by writing a carefully worded e-mail policy that explains the scope of employer monitoring and having employees sign the statement.

Regarding the second exception, the ECPA exempts from liability the person or entity providing the communication service. If the service is provided by the employer, the ECPA has been interpreted as permitting employers broad discretion to read and disclose the contents of e-mail communications without the employees' consent. The exception may not apply, however, to incoming (as opposed to internal) e-mail if e-mail service is provided by a common carrier (e.g., America Online or MCI mail) rather than the employer.

Regarding the third exception, the courts will analyze whether the content of the intercepted communication is business or personal.

According to the 2007 Electronic Monitoring & Surveillance Survey, 28 percent of employers have fired workers for misusing e-mail. The top 3 reasons for these terminations were: violation of company policy (64 percent), inappropriate or offensive language (62 percent) and excessive personal use (26 percent). Forty-three percent of the respondents in this survey monitor e-mail; of those that do, 73 percent use technological tools to perform automatic monitoring and 40 percent assign an individual to manually read the e-mails.

[G] Policies and Practices for Monitoring and Surveillance

To develop effective policies and practices for monitoring and surveillance, employers must be aware of the following realities:

- Employees are entitled to reasonable expectations of personal privacy on the job. They should know what electronic surveillance tools are used in the workplace and how management uses the collected data.

- Employers are not permitted to practice continuous electronic monitoring and searches of data. Employees should participate in decisions about how and when management conducts electronic monitoring or searches.

- Employers should gather and use data for clearly defined, work-related purposes only.

- Employers should not engage in secret monitoring or searches, except when credible evidence of criminal activity or other serious wrongdoing comes to light.

- Employers should not make data obtained through monitoring the sole factor in evaluating employee performance.

- Employees may inspect, challenge, and correct electronic records of their activities or files captured through electronic means.

- Employers should destroy records that are irrelevant to the purposes for which they were collected.

- Employers should not release monitoring data that identify individual employees to any third party, except to comply with legal requirements.

- Employees or prospective employees cannot waive privacy rights.

- Employees should be informed that if they violate the privacy policies, they may be subject to discipline or termination.

When an employer decides to monitor its e-mail and voice mail systems, it must notify its employees in writing, post the notice in the workplace, and include such notification in the employee handbook. The notice should explain that employees have no legitimate expectation of privacy regarding voice mail, e-mail, or telephone conversations and require employees to sign acknowledgment forms indicating their understanding of the notice. The notice should also explain that the employer reserves the right to monitor personal internet and e-mail accounts accessed using the company's equipment. E-mails transmitted through personal, Internet-based accounts that are stored on an employee's hard drive as temporary Internet files can be monitored, if employees receive prior notice. Employers should also ensure that all monitoring is done during the course of business and for business purposes only.

A Ninth Circuit Court of Appeals ruling in 2007 underscores the importance of employer Internet and computer privacy policies. In *United States v. Ziegler* [no. 05-30177 July 30, 2007] Ziegler appealed his conviction of child pornography charges on the basis that his employer did not have the right to provide the FBI with access to his computer. In 2001, his employer notified the FBI this employee had used his workplace computer to access Web sites containing child pornography. The employer voluntarily turned over the computer to the FBI, and therefore the FBI never obtained a search warrant for the computer. The FBI found that the computer did, indeed, contain many images of child pornography, and thus Ziegler was convicted. On appeal, the court determined that the employer did have the right to turn over the computer to the FBI without a search warrant because it was the owner of the computer and it is the owner of property that has the right to voluntarily provide the consent to the search. The court made its decision based on the following:

- The employer installed a firewall program to monitor its employees' access to the Internet and routinely, sometimes daily, reviewed the information collected by the firewall;

- The employer's system administrators had complete administrative access to all employees' computers; and

- Through training and the employment manual, employees were informed of the firewall and its monitoring, as well as the employer's policy that computers were company-owned and not to be used for personal activities.

(See **Exhibit 20.3** for a sample company policy on electronic and telephonic communication monitoring.)

[1] Company E-Mail Policies

Employers should develop and distribute to employees a clear e-mail policy with regard to the access, use, and disclosure of e-mail. (See **Exhibit 20.3** for a sample e-mail consent form.)

Because of its flexibility, e-mail substitutes for a range of workplace communications; no single workplace analogy provides a simple answer to the question of the level of privacy protection that companies should afford employees' use of e-mail systems. In formulating a privacy policy, a company must consider not only its interest and the interest of its employees, but also the interest of third parties that may have a legal right to or interest in accessing company records, including e-mail. The key to handling the issues successfully is to reach a balanced judgment based on all applicable circumstances.

[2] Internet Use Policies

Business use of the Internet has experienced extraordinary growth. It is commonplace for employees to have access to the Internet to perform their jobs effectively. Although the business uses of the Internet are many, much of the information available to employees on the Internet is not related to performance of the worker's job. Thus, many employers have recognized that unrestricted use of the Internet by employees has the potential to drain, rather than enhance, productivity. One solution may be to implement a policy outlining the permissible parameters of employee Internet use, or an Internet Acceptable Use Policy (IAUP).

An IAUP is a written agreement, signed by each employee, that sets out the permissible workplace uses of the Internet. In addition to describing permissible uses, an IAUP should specifically set out prohibited uses, rules of online behavior, and access privileges. Penalties for violations of the policy, including security violations and vandalism of the systems, should also be covered. Anyone using a company's Internet connection should be required to sign an IAUP and know that it will be kept on file as a legal, binding document.

An IAUP can inform employees about the use of storage space and bandwidth on the system to maximize its utility to all employees. Restrictions that serve this interest include directives against downloading games or other non-work-related files; directives against downloading large files that can be obtained off-line; and instructions to move old or seldom-used files, programs, or e-mail to alternative storage. Employers who have sensitive data on their computer systems (e.g., company plans, customer demographic data, or product designs) may want to include a clause concerning trade secrets in the IAUP. Employers should make it clear to employees that under no circumstances should proprietary company information be accessed through the Internet or that, if transmitted over the Internet, such material should be encrypted.

An employer may want to institute an IAUP for many reasons. The chief reason, not surprisingly, is that an IAUP helps to prevent loss of productivity. Another reason to institute an IAUP is to shield the employer from possible sexual harassment suits. As in most communications media, some of the pictures, video, sound, and text on the Internet is sexually oriented. If such material is brought into the workplace, it has the potential to create a hostile work environment, thereby exposing the employer to liability under federal or state prohibitions against sex discrimination.

Inappropriate Internet usage may also lead to employers' liability to third parties. As a result of a New Jersey court case, employers may want to strengthen their IAUPs and ensure that the policy is being enforced. In *Doe v. XYC Corp.*, 382 N.J. Super. 122, 887 A.2d 1156 (N.J. Super. Ct. App. Div. 2005), an accountant at the XYC Corp. allegedly viewed numerous pornographic Web sites while at work, including child pornography. More than a few company employees, including the network administrator and several members of management, knew or had reason to know that the employee was visiting pornographic Web sites. Despite a company policy providing for disciplinary action if the Internet was used for non-work reasons, the employee was not disciplined and only told to refrain from visiting those Web sites at work. Thereafter, the employee allegedly uploaded nude pictures of his step-daughter to a child pornography Web site while at work. During a police search of the employee's work computer pursuant to a warrant, they found child pornography materials. The company terminated the employee, but the employee's wife sued the company on her and her child's behalf, claiming the company's failure to act when it had knowledge of the employee's actions caused harm to the child. The appellate court held that once the company had reason to believe the employee was using its property to view pornography, the employer had the duty to investigate and may be required, at least in the case of child pornography, to report the activity to the appropriate authorities. This duty arose out of the public policy against child pornography and the duty to prevent harm. The appellate court remanded the case back to the trial court for jury trial.

Technological reasons for supporting the implementation of an IAUP include restricting use of the Internet to work-related matters to prevent a drain on limited computer resources. Access to the Internet costs money, either in fees to Internet service providers or in hardware costs necessary to accommodate increased network traffic and data storage. An employee's inappropriate use of Internet services may negatively affect other employees' speed of access or storage space for work product.

Employers should also institute guidelines that prohibit illegal use of the Internet in general. A directive that employees take care not to violate copyright laws should be included in every IAUP. Gambling on the Internet is also a concern, and an IAUP should contain a prohibition against such activity not only because of its potentially adverse effect on productivity, but also because the activity may be illegal. (See **Exhibit 20.4** for a sample company policy on acceptable Internet use.)

According to the 2007 Electronic Monitoring & Surveillance Survey, 30 percent of employers have fired workers for misusing the Internet. The top 3 reasons for these terminations were: viewing, downloading or uploading inappropriate or offensive content (84 percent), violation of company policy (48 percent), and excessive personal use (34 percent).

[3] Text Messaging and Other Electronic Communications

New communication methods are being developed and will continue to be developed. One such method is text messaging, available on cellular phones and pagers. When employers develop their communication monitoring policies, they should ensure that all forms of electronic communications are included.

Such was not the case in *Quon v. Arch Wireless Operating Company, Inc.* [529 F.3d 892 (9th Cir. 2008)] The City of Ontario, California issued pagers to certain employees which included text messaging capabilities. When the City was charged for text messages above the limit set by its carrier (Arch Wireless Operating Company), it reviewed the employees' text messaging. Although the employer had a general computer usage, Internet and e-mail policy, it did not have a specific written policy on text messages or pagers. The City's policy did indicate that it might monitor all network activity and the computer systems were not confidential. One employee, Quon, sued the City for invasion of privacy. The Ninth Circuit Court of Appeals concluded that Quon had a reasonable expectation of privacy for his text messages, because the employees were informed that if they went over the limit on their text messages they would have to pay the overage charges. The court reasoned that because the penalty imposed (charging the employees) was for going over the limit, and not for message content, there was a reasonable expectation that the messages would not be reviewed. In addition to the lack of notice that the actual messages might be read, the City did not request the employees' consent to have their messages read.

Although this case deals with a governmental employer, the following recommendations apply to all employers:

- Ensure that general computer usage policies include all forms of electronic communication provided by the employer.

- Ensure that even if the policy allows for some personal use (e.g., in the case of an emergency) that employees should have no expectation of privacy in their messages and the employer retains the right to search all messages.

- Train all supervisors and managers not to make oral representations contrary to the written policy.

- In the Quon case, the employer used a third-party pager service provider. To ensure that the employer may still search and monitor electronic communications provided by or stored by a third-party provider, the employer can require employees to sign a written consent allowing disclosure by the third-party provider for all messages sent or received by the employee before providing the device to the employee.

[H] Dissemination of Employee Medical Information

Owing to their sensitive nature, employee medical records are handled with intense scrutiny and regulation on both the federal and state level. In addition to the requirement that medical records be stored separate from the general personnel file, all relevant federal and state statutes contain a provision mandating strict confidentiality of employee medical records. The Health Insurance Portability and Accountability Act of 1996 (HIPAA) specifically mandates privacy of medical information (see **Chapter 6**). Two other federal laws—the Americans with Disabilities Act (ADA) and the Family and Medical Leave Act (FMLA)—also address the issue of confidentiality of medical information, as described below.

[1] Americans with Disabilities Act

An employer may not require a medical examination and may not make inquiries of an employee about any disability he or she may possess or the nature or severity of the disability, unless the request for a medical exam or inquiry for medical information is shown to be job-related and consistent with business necessity. [42 U.S.C. § 12112(d)(4)(A)] Inquiries and exams are allowed in three circumstances:

1. Where there is a need to determine whether an employee is able to perform the essential function of his or her job.

2. To determine the extent reasonable accommodation is needed for the employee to continue to perform his or her essential job functions.

3. Where certain physical or medical standards or requirements exist at the federal, state, or local level.

The ADA expressly prohibits an employer from disclosing confidential medical information to anyone, including coworkers, except as provided by law. The ADA allows disclosure of medical information only in the following circumstances:

- Supervisors and managers may be informed regarding necessary restrictions on the work or duties of the employee and necessary accommodations.

- First aid and safety personnel may be informed, when appropriate, if the disability might require emergency treatment.

- Government officials investigating compliance with the ADA shall be provided relevant information on request.

- Employers may submit information to state workers' compensation offices, state second-injury funds, or workers' compensation insurance carriers in accordance with state workers' compensation laws.

- Employers may use the information for insurance purposes.

(See **Chapter 13** for additional information on the ADA.)

[2] Family and Medical Leave Act

Under the FMLA, an employer may adopt a uniformly applied policy or practice that requires an employee who takes FMLA leave because of his or her own serious health condition to obtain and present certification from the employee's health care provider specifying when the employee is fit to return to work.

The employee must be informed at the commencement of leave that a certification of fitness for duty is required. There is an important limitation regarding fitness for duty certifications; no information other than a simple statement of an employee's ability to return to work can be requested. In addition, an employer covered under FMLA may also require recertification after a reasonable time and a return-to-work examination to ensure that the employee can perform his or her essential job functions. [29 U.S.C. § 2613(a), (b)] (See **Chapter 14** for additional information on FMLA.)

[3] Guidelines for Return to Work

When an employee returns to work following absence or leave for medical reasons, employers should do the following:

- Review the provisions of the ADA and the FMLA to determine if the employee returning to work is covered under either of these laws.

- Ensure that company forms requesting medical information are asking for information allowable under the ADA and the FMLA.

- Ensure that all employee medical information is stored in files separate from the personnel file and only those with a "need to know" have access to these records.

- Refrain from communicating or otherwise disseminating employee medical information to anyone who does not have a "need to know."

Employers should also be aware that many states have laws that mandate confidentiality of employee medical information.

[I] Employees with AIDS/HIV

The need for privacy with regard to personnel and medical records is underscored by human immunodeficiency virus (HIV) and acquired immune deficiency syndrome (AIDS), probably the most controversial and fear-laden workplace issues since the 1990s. Instances exist of managers illegally terminating employees with AIDS from jobs because of the demands or the threats of other employees.

Illnesses that are transmitted through direct blood and bodily fluid contact (such as some forms of hepatitis and AIDS) provoke feelings akin to panic. Many employees worry about exposure to such illnesses in the workplace. In fact, it would be very difficult and unusual for these diseases to be transmitted in the normal course of work. The exceptions are health care facilities, where care providers and laboratory technicians are exposed to bodily fluids or materials that may be contaminated with blood-borne pathogens.

In response to employee pressure, employers often feel constrained to release information about a sick employee to those who work with that employee. However, employers must remain firm in their commitment and maintain confidentiality for all employee health information, even information concerning HIV status and AIDS. The employer, and all employees who come to possess private individual employee medical information, must keep the information confidential.

The ADA and the FMLA provide powerful protection for employee medical information; they require the maintenance of separate files and a limited need-to-know circle and provide severe sanctions for breach of confidentiality. Most states have strengthened their protection of employee medical information, but this protection varies from state to state.

Special issues arise with regard to health care workers. Lawmakers are struggling with the legal issues surrounding AIDS. The issues of personal rights to privacy conflict with the issues of workplace safety for health care workers. HR professionals in health care organizations should consider the rationale for educating medical staff about the importance of confidentiality as well as the use of appropriate precautions when working with blood-borne pathogens. The case of a San Francisco nurse who contracted the AIDS virus raised troubling questions about how to deal with AIDS in the workplace. The case laid the foundation for the fight to secure medical benefits without sacrificing privacy.

[1] Life-Threatening Illness Policy

Some companies have developed policies specifically for dealing with AIDS in the workplace. However, there is a trend toward developing polices that include all life-threatening illnesses such as heart disease, cancer, and AIDS. It is perhaps safer for employers to adopt this broader and more inclusive approach rather than to single out a particular group of protected employees (i.e., those with AIDS). A comprehensive approach to life-threatening illnesses includes the following five-point strategy:

1. Allow employees with life-threatening illnesses to work as long as they pose no health threat to themselves or others and are able to perform their jobs.

2. Provide reasonable accommodations according to legal requirements.

3. Alert managers to take precautions to guard against disclosure of private and confidential information about an employee's health.

4. Maintain a list of internal and external contacts (e.g., an occupational nurse, community support groups, or an employee assistance program) for an employee needing assistance in dealing with a life-threatening illness.

5. Make available disability leaves of absence to the employee with a life-threatening illness.

(See **Exhibit 20.5** for a sample company policy on medical records and serious health conditions.)

[2]   State and Local Laws Regarding AIDS

Depending on the size and nature of the company and where it operates, the employer's obligations to employees who contract AIDS may be subject to regulation by local, city or municipal ordinance, general state antidiscrimination statutes, and federal regulation. Federal and state laws prohibiting discrimination in employment on the basis of disability have been held to prohibit discrimination in employment based on AIDS. However, routine AIDS testing of city firefighters and paramedics was upheld in a 1992 case decided by a district court in Ohio. Concern about the privacy issues gave rise to that lawsuit against the city. [Nursing Management, December 1992]

Employers should realize that some state restrictions on testing are relaxed if a bona fide occupational qualification is involved. Employers should also remember that legal authorities remain divided on the circumstances in which freedom from infection may be deemed an occupational qualification. (See **Exhibit 20.6** for a state-by-state summary of provisions dealing with AIDS discrimination, testing, and other requirements.)

[J]   Confidentiality of Employee Personal Information

Throughout an employee's history with an organization, the employer obtains information about the employee either intentionally or inadvertently. Some of this information needs to remain confidential in order to comply with existing privacy laws. Information that may be considered private includes information about the employee's medical/health status, personal lifestyle, and illicit conduct outside of the workplace. Some of this information may be documented in employee files and other information may simply be known by the employer. The extent to which an employer shares any of this information is governed by several existing privacy and other employment laws. The employer must be knowledgeable of these restrictions to ensure compliance with these laws.

There are a variety of documents that may contain sensitive and confidential employee information such as benefit enrollment and claim forms, W-4 forms, child support documents, and wage garnishment documents. Documents that contain sensitive or personal information should be maintained in confidential files with access limited to those who have a legitimate need to know. Such documents include those containing information such as age, race, religion, marital or parental status, Social Security number, home address or phone number, some investigative reports, and credit reports. (See **Chapter 24** for additional information on the retention of documents containing employee information.)

[1] Personal Relationships on the Job

Employer regulation of personal relationships is an important privacy-related issue. It has become more common because of the increasing number of women in the workplace and increasing objections by employees to perceived relationship interference with employment decisions such as promotions or salary determination.

The absence of a written policy unfortunately leaves managers as judges and jury when dealing with an office romance. Private employers have a potential liability for discharging an employee because of personal involvement with a coworker or competitor. The employer could face charges of breach of contract and intentional infliction of emotional distress. The situation is made more difficult because even when a relationship appears to be mutual, it could in actuality be coercive, and therefore the basis of sexual harassment.

Many employers have adopted a ''no-spouse'' policy. This has been upheld when employers could establish that it was designed to avoid aggregation of family members and was applied in an evenhanded manner. However, in some states, such as California, Illinois, and Minnesota, marital status is a protected classification. In these states, employers are generally prohibited from implementing ''no-spouse'' policies.

[2] Lifestyle Outside of Work

Off-the-job privacy issues range from an employee's political and recreational activities to whether an employee smokes, drinks, or uses drugs when away from the job. The difficulty arises when a employee is engaged in behavior off the job that company officials may not condone but that is perfectly legal. Employer concerns may be justifiable in some cases, but they raise questions about the employee's right to privacy away from the workplace. Employers should proceed with caution before disciplining an employee for legal after-hours behavior.

As a general rule, an employer may not discipline a worker for off-duty activities, as the discipline could be seen as an employer's invasion of the employee's personal life. Although existing civil rights laws do not generally protect against lifestyle discrimination, privacy rights advocates fear that once employers start questioning one type of employee behavior, the list of ''unsuitable habits'' will grow.

States are currently enacting three types of ''lifestyle'' statutes to protect employees from discrimination for off-duty activities: smokers' rights, the right to use lawful substances, and the right to engage in lawful activities. Lifestyle-related issues have been addressed in some states under right-to-privacy legislation. In Illinois, for example, employers are prohibited from discriminating on the basis of use of lawful products (e.g., tobacco or alcohol) off premises, during nonworking hours. Illinois employers may not charge differential premium rates under health insurance (or related) policies unless the rates reflect differential costs to the specific employer. [820 ILCS § 55/5]

[3] Illicit Conduct

Management may have to make a tough decision if an employee is convicted of criminal conduct that is regarded as immoral or repugnant by society. Even though agreeing that the private life of an employee is beyond the reach of his employer, some arbitrators have pointed out that the effect of the conduct on a worker's job relationship may prevail over considerations of privacy. Therefore, management may be entitled to discipline workers for off-duty misconduct when there is a direct and demonstrable relationship between illicit conduct and the performance of the employee's job.

On the one hand is the threat to employee relations, customer relations, or both, if the employee is returned. On the other hand, an argument may be made that punishment of the employee should be left to the courts and that the employee should not be placed in double jeopardy by loss of employment as well. In resolving this dilemma, arbitrators tend to weigh the employee's past record against the threat of a recurrence of the misconduct.

For example, when an airline purser was arrested once in an altercation arising from his taking pictures of nude males in a hotel room, an arbitrator converted a discharge to a 90-day suspension. However, when the employee subsequently pled guilty to criminal charges involving the photographing of a nude minor, a discharge penalty was upheld. The cumulative effect of these incidents exposed the airline employer to potential damage, the arbiter said, noting that "some people may be given to pause" in riding planes under the control of persons who are so "inept at managing their own affairs."

Certain cases labeled as "misconduct" involve no criminal activity but rather represent transgressions of societal taboos. Two classic examples are the unwed pregnant worker and the two married coworkers conducting an extramarital affair. In such cases, arbiters generally require that management conclusively demonstrate how the employee's private affairs can have a negative affect on the employment relationship.

In *New York v. Wal-Mart Stores, Inc.* [621 N.Y.S.2d 158 (1995)], the New York Court of Appeals upheld the firing of two Wal-Mart employees who violated the store's fraternization policy, which prohibited dating between a married employee and another employee who was not his or her spouse. The state challenged the termination under a state labor law that prohibits employer discrimination for "legal recreational activities" that occur off duty. The court held that dating was "entirely distinct" from the statutory definition of "legal recreational activity," examples of which were "sports, games, hobbies, exercise, reading, and the viewing of television, movies and similar material." The court also stated that its holding did not infringe on the right of employees who were not dating to engage in recreational activities together, because the employer had the burden of proving "mutual romantic interest."

Under New York's recently enacted Legal Activities Law [N.Y. Labor Law § 201-d], public and private employers are prohibited from discriminating against job applicants and employees who engage in "lawful" activities (e.g., legal political activities, use of consumable products, such as alcohol and cigarettes, recreational activities, or union membership) during nonworking hours.

During the next few years, more efforts will likely be seen to enact or expand workplace and off-the-job privacy laws because today's workers are less likely than their predecessors to agree with the presumption that employing someone entitles an employer to determine what an employee may or may not do off duty.

[4] Drug Testing

Private employers holding federal contracts must comply with both the Drug-Free Workplace Act of 1988 and the Department of Defense Drug-Free Workforce Policy. Certain industries that fall under the federal jurisdiction of the Department of Defense or the Department of Transportation have very specific drug testing policies and procedures imposed upon them.

Drug testing can be an effective weapon against substance abuse in the workplace. However, employers who test for drugs can also be sued for invasion of privacy, based on the allegation that the company, without reasonable suspicion, threatened, coerced, or forced an employee to submit urine samples for testing.

In 1989, the U.S. Supreme Court decided two cases involving challenges to drug testing programs that were based on whether drug testing violated the Fourth Amendment's guarantee against unreasonable searches and seizures. These decisions indicate that a compelling social or government interest may well override the right to privacy vis-à-vis drug testing when health and safety or law enforcement is involved.

Poorly drafted, implemented, or applied drug testing policies invite significant legal reprisal. In the absence of federal or state guidance, case law becomes very informative for employers seeking assistance in formulating policy.

In *Hennessey v. Coastal Eagle Point Oil Co.* [129 N.J. 81, 92-93 (1992)], the New Jersey Supreme Court found that an oil refinery worker who was fired after failing a mandatory random urine test for drugs was wrongfully dismissed. *Hennessey* was important as a privacy case because the court made the following recommendation to employers in its ruling:

> Employers should formulate and implement measures designed to minimize the intrusiveness of the testing process. Those measures should include a testing procedure that allows as much privacy and dignity as possible. They should also include a notice, close in time to the beginning of testing program but sufficient to provide adequate advance warning, that:

> - Announces the program and details of the method for selecting employees to be tested

> - Warns employees of the lingering effects of certain drugs in the system

> - Explains how the sample will be analyzed

> - Notifies the employees of the consequences of testing positive or refusing to take the test.

> Furthermore, employers may conduct only those tests necessary to determine the presence of drugs in the urine, and employers are under an obligation not to disclose information obtained as a result of testing.

Although this was a victory for privacy, the court ruled against Hennessey when it held that the competing public interest (here, public safety) was greater than his individual privacy interests because of the "safety sensitive" nature of his job. The court ruled:

> If the employee's duties are so fraught with hazard that his or her attempts to perform while in a state of drug impairment would pose a threat to coworkers, to the workplace, or to the public at large, then the employer must prevail.

Although testing is presumed to be lawful unless there is a specific restriction in state or federal law, legal issues concerning employee privacy and related issues continue to be raised. Any drug testing program that is not explicitly authorized by law may be considered open to legal challenge. Employers, especially those that must deal with labor-management relations, should seek counsel on employee drug testing. (See **Chapter 23** for further discussion of substance abuse in the workplace.)

[5] Genetic Information

As described above (see **20.02[D]**) the Genetic Information Nondiscrimination Act of 2008 (GINA) prohibits employers, employment agencies, labor unions, and insurance providers from discriminating against employees on the basis of genetic information. In general GINA prevents an employer from requiring, requesting or purchasing genetic information about an employee or a family member. There are exceptions: (1) inadvertent requests for such information; (2) genetic services provided by the employer, including wellness programs; (3) when required to correctly administer leaves under FMLA; and (4) when obtained through the purchase of commercially available documents. Employers must maintain the confidentiality of all genetic information in the same manner as medical information is protected under the Americans with Disabilities Act, including maintaining the information on separate forms and in separate medical files. Genetic information can only be disclosed under certain circumstances, including, for example (1) at the employee's written request, (2) for approved occupational and health research, (3) in response to a court order, and (4) to comply with the FMLA's requirements. Employers may not retaliate against an employee for exercising rights under GINA.

[6] Smokers' Rights

From a legal perspective, smokers are protected by constitutional rights in the due process clause of the Fifth and Fourteenth Amendments. However, the rights of nonsmokers must be weighed against those of smokers. According to an analysis by the Action on Smoking and Health non-profit organization, at least 46 states and the District of Columbia have enacted laws restricting smoking in public workplaces. However, these laws generally provide that employers may not discriminate against individuals who use tobacco products outside the workplace.

Smoking in the workplace is causing considerable concern and conflict for employers and employees. Social pressure may make nonsmoking policies acceptable, but the business reasons for their implementation are court decisions, state and federal legislation, and cost effectiveness.

Many employers have adopted some kind of policy regarding smoking in the workplace, but there is no consensus. Unless otherwise specified by state statute, the policies range from simply asking employees who smoke to "be considerate" to those who do not smoke to a total prohibition of smoking in the workplace. Smoking policies protect the employer against health, economic, and legal liability exposure. In addition to the conclusions issued by the Surgeon General regarding the effects of passive smoke on nonsmokers, employers should consider the economic factors involved in implementation of a smoking policy in the workplace, such as health care costs, property damage, and lawsuits. The differences in policies allowed under federal, state, or local laws also may be related to the feelings or philosophy of individual company management with regard to smoking.

Conflicts between smokers and nonsmokers have escalated in recent years because of growing public awareness of the potential danger of exposure to secondhand smoke (i.e., passive smoking). The widower of a nurse who died from lung cancer won benefits in what is believed to be the first workers' compensation claim tied to secondhand smoke on the work site. In that case, nurse Mildred Wiley worked for 18 years in a Veterans Administration psychiatric ward in Indiana, where patients smoked heavily. The Department of Labor ruled that Wiley's death in 1991 was partly due to secondhand smoke and awarded her husband $21,500 a year.

The State of Maryland fined five employers up to $1,350 for violating the state's strict workplace smoking ban. State officials were investigating other complaints from employees and customers. The Maryland law bans most workplace smoking, except for bars and adjacent seating areas in restaurants and in enclosed, separately ventilated rooms. In 2007, at least nine states enacted or amended their laws banning smoking in enclosed spaces, including work locations (i.e., Colorado, Idaho, Illinois, Maine, Maryland, Mississippi, North Carolina, Oklahoma, and Tennessee).

A written policy on workplace smoking protects an employer against health, economic, and legal liability exposure. In addition to the conclusions issued by the Surgeon General regarding the effects of passive smoke on nonsmokers, employers should consider the economic factors involved in implementation of a smoking policy in the workplace, such as health care costs, property damage, and lawsuits. Legal risks can include everything from discrimination against employees who are hypersensitive to smoke to charges of battery.

Separating smokers from nonsmokers is one solution, as long as such a policy does not cause smokers to feel stigmatized and ostracized. Such an indignity might contribute to both mental and physical problems. Clearly, the more extensive policies that create a total ban on smoking and an enforcement procedure that pries into a worker's privacy outside of work invite invasion-of-privacy lawsuits. For example, the federal district court in Massachusetts ruled that a plaintiff could proceed with his invasion of privacy claim against an employer who prohibited any of its employees from smoking at any time. In *Rodrigues v. The Scotts Co., LLC,* 2008 U.S. Dist. LEXIS 6682 (D. Mass., January 30, 2008), the recently hired employee tested positive for nicotine and was fired by the company. The court ruled that to assert an invasion of privacy claim, the employee only had to express a plausible privacy interest that outweighed the employer's interest; in this case, the employee's assertion that what he did outside of work was protected privacy met that standard.

[7] Moonlighting

Moonlighting, or holding more than one job at a time, is a common lifestyle for many American workers. Just how far can the company delve into the private life of an employee and restrict such behavior? An important consideration in any attempt to restrict moonlighting is whether the management rule or policy forbidding outside employment or business ventures is "reasonable."

A company is not required to establish beyond doubt that the employee's moonlighting has damaged its business or led to financial loss. In matters of loyalty and security, employers may lawfully discharge an employee who moonlights for a competitor. Outside employment may be a cause for disciplinary action, if the issue of dishonesty is raised, such as when an employee fraudulently takes sick leave to work at the outside job. Disciplinary action may also be appropriate if an employee's second job negatively affects such factors as performance and attendance on the job. The employer can also take action when it reasonably can infer that the outside employment might lead to disclosure of company information. Some states (e.g., Illinois) have considered moonlighting an issue serious enough issue to require legislation. Typically, such legislation prohibits employers from implementing strict no-moonlighting policies because of the prevalence of workers who must hold two or more jobs for economic reasons.

[8]   Nepotism

Each organization must determine what makes sense for its culture and try to understand how its policies will affect the employees' right to privacy and other statutory rights. Some employers welcome family members into their companies, and others have policies that prohibit or restrict employing relatives. There are arguments both for and against anti-nepotism policies.

On the positive side, hiring related employees can be an efficient way of bringing readily available and presumably dedicated candidates to staff the business. On the other hand, nepotism can give rise to a variety of concerns. Internally, the company could receive claims of unfair treatment or create awkward supervisory or disciplinary situations. From a legal perspective, nepotism could make the company vulnerable to issues of discrimination based on gender or marital status. Anti-nepotism policies can also be challenged as being discriminatory, as well as being viewed as invasion of an employee's privacy.

In a case in Georgia, the Eleventh Circuit upheld a city police department's policy that if two employees marry, the individual with less seniority must resign from the department. The policy was implemented to avoid conflicts of interest, reduce favoritism or the appearance of favoritism, prevent family conflicts, and decrease the likelihood of sexual harassment in the workplace. An engaged couple sued the city, claiming that the anti-nepotism policy unlawfully interfered with their fundamental right to marry. The court stated that the city's anti-nepotism policy did not create a direct legal obstacle that would prevent marriage between a class of people. The mere fact that the policy "increased economic burdens on certain city employees who wish to marry one another" was insufficient to find that the policy directly interfered with the couple's right to marry. The Eleventh Circuit held that the right to marry is protected by the Constitution. However, reasonable regulation may be imposed, provided that the regulation does not significantly interfere with the decision to enter into marriage. Regulation must directly and substantially interfere with such rights before it will be found in violation of the Constitution. The court also found that the city's policy did not interfere with the rights of individuals to "associate," in part, because the employees could always transfer to different departments. The fact that more women than men might actually be "forced" to transfer was not sufficient evidence to prove an intent to discriminate against women.

[9]   Polygraph Testing

The Employee Polygraph Protection Act of 1988 (EPPA; Pub. L. No. 100-347, 102 Stat. 646) restricts testing of current employees, unless the employer has reason to suspect that the employee has been involved in workplace theft or other incidents causing economic loss to the employer. An employer may request that an employee submit to a polygraph examination in specific loss situations, but employers cannot discharge, discipline, or discriminate in any manner on the basis of polygraph test results or because of a refusal to take a lie-detector test. Limited exemptions are provided for security firms and drug manufacturers. The law is applicable only to employers that are engaged in or are affecting commerce or that are involved in the production of goods for commerce. All public sector employees are exempt from the EPPA, as are certain defense, security, and Federal Bureau of Investigation contractors.

[10]   Social Security Numbers

Social Security numbers are needed for payroll and Form I-9 purposes, but they need to be kept confidential. Incidents of identity theft are increasing, and the availability of Social Security numbers in the workplace may be contributing to the problem. Employee records are a major source of information for identity thieves. An employer should ensure that all sensitive information is protected and that employees who legitimately have access to these data understand the need for their confidentiality. The employer should consider using forms of identification other than Social Security numbers for badges, computer files, and other electronic links to employee data. It must make sure that hard copies of W-4s, I-9s, and other documents with employees' Social Security numbers are kept under lock and key and that paperwork is not left on desks or in mailrooms unattended. Employees who handle confidential information should be required to turn off their computers when they leave their desks and use a password to log back in.

Legislation has been introduced that would limit the use of Social Security numbers. The Social Security Number Privacy and Identity Theft Prevention Act of 2007 (H.R. 3046) prohibits the sale, purchase, and display to the public of Social Security numbers. The bill also would require that "no person that is an employer, and no other person offering benefits in connection with an employee benefit plan maintained by such employer or acting as an agent of such employer, may display a social security account number on any card or tag that is commonly provided to employees of such employer (or to their family members) for purposes of identification or include on such card or tag a magnetic strip, bar code, or other means of communication which conveys such number." The bill has 50 cosponsors and has been referred out of committee. As of the date of this writing, no further action has been taken.

Several states have passed laws that protect employers' use of Social Security numbers. The most significant may be Michigan's, which requires companies that obtain Social Security numbers to create, and publish in their employee handbook, a privacy policy that prohibits unlawful disclosure, ensures confidentiality, limits access, mandates procedures for disposal, and establishes penalties for violations. California, Arizona, Arkansas, Colorado, Connecticut, Michigan, Nebraska, New York, Oklahoma, Texas, and Maryland have also passed laws restricting the use of Social Security numbers.

Employees may decide that their Social Security number is too private to share with an employer. However, employers need that information for payroll and payroll tax processing and payment. In one case, when the employee refused to give her Social Security number to her employer, the employer fired her. She sued for discrimination under the Civil Rights Act and for violations of her privacy rights under the Fourth and Fourteenth Amendments to the U.S. Constitution. Both the district court and the appeals court held that requiring Social Security number was not discriminatory because it applied equally to all employees. The courts also ruled that the Constitution does not provide a privacy right with regard to Social Security numbers.

[11]   Breaches of Personal Information

Most employers and HR departments have policies and procedures in place to secure employees' personal information. Security of such data includes written documentation as well as electronic measures. Identity theft can happen in any workplace. Even if a security breach does not result in identity theft, employees do not want other employees, customers, or clients having access to their personal information. Although thousands of dollars can be spent on sophisticated electronic security measures, many procedures cost very little, but require the application of good common sense. Measures that should be taken by all HR departments to help ensure the security of their employees' personal information include:

- Lock all file cabinets that contain personal information at all times.

- Do not leave files with personal information unattended on a desk, even if the door is closed.

- Limit access to personal data; determine who *really* has a need to know and ensure that only those individuals have access to personal data. Determine whether building security needs a key to the offices that contain personnel files.

- Do not allow non-employees unsupervised access to the workplace.

- Do not allow employees to remove files with personal information from the workplace. This includes electronic and hard copy files. Work with the IT department to set up systems that allow employees to securely log in to the company's computer system so they can work remotely without taking hard drives or memory sticks with them.

- Encrypt all electronic data, using several layers of protection as necessary.

- Require that employees create complex passwords to log in to their computers and to the system. Complex passwords are those that require use of upper- and lower-case letters, numbers, and/or special characters. Require that passwords be changed routinely, creating brand new passwords, not just altering a few characters.

- Utilize password-protected screen savers. These programs require employees to log in to their computers if the screen saver is activated. Require the use of short periods of computer inactivity before the screen saver activates.

- Keep personal and other sensitive data off public servers and drives.

- Use combination locks whenever possible because these are harder to pick.

- Place outgoing mail in a locked box. Internal mail with confidential information should be sealed in an envelope.

- Use a shredder regularly. Individual shredders for each HR employee may be useful.

- Train all employees on the requirements for confidentiality and security of sensitive data, including employee information as well as company data.

- Consistently discipline employees who violate the company's confidentiality and security policies.

Although HR departments and employers may do as much as possible to ensure the security and confidentiality of personal identifying information, it is still possible for security breaches to occur. Many states have enacted notification laws, regulating how companies must notify the affected employees. The basic requirement in these laws is that if an unauthorized person or persons acquire or access personally identifying information, the employer must notify the affected employees. During the last five years, at least 35 states, the District of Columbia and Puerto Rico have enacted these statutes.

The majority of these laws apply only to electronic data that include employees' names and at least one other type of identifying information, such as a Social Security number, driver's license number, or checking or other financial account number. At least one state, Hawaii, also includes paper records in its definition of protected employee information.

Notification of the breach must be given to employees. Some states also require that state government agencies and consumer protection agencies be notified. While most states only require that employees who live in that state be notified, some of the newer laws, e.g., Wisconsin and New Hampshire, require that all employees affected by the breach be notified, regardless of where they live.

State laws also vary as to when the notification must occur. New York, for example, requires that notification occur immediately upon the employer learning of the breach rather than waiting for an investigation to determine the extent of the breach.

Penalties for failure to notify affected employees vary. Some are as high as $10,000 per day. New York's law provides for a civil penalty for up to $150,000 if a court finds that an employer knowingly or recklessly failed to provide notice.

HR departments should develop written policies on how to deal with security breaches before there is the need for it. In addition to taking into account all state laws that might apply (consider the state laws of employees who work in states other than the state in which the company is based), the policy could include the following:

- Notify legal counsel

- Develop an investigation team—appropriate representatives from IT, HR, Legal, Executive office, etc.)

- Conduct an investigation

- Prepare appropriate notification (e.g., e-mail, personal letter, personal call, etc.)

- Notify affected employees

- Notify appropriate agencies, credit organizations and law enforcement, as appropriate

- Prepare document outlining the scope of the investigation and its findings

- Determine what assistance will be provided to affected employees (e.g., help employees deal with credit agencies, reimbursement if funds stolen from bank accounts, etc.)

Although the states were the first to enact notification legislation, in 2007, the Personal Data Privacy and Security Act of 2007 (S. 495) was introduced in the Senate. This bill would require institutions to notify consumers when a breach in the security of their personal information has occurred. The Senate Judiciary Committee has approved S. 495, but as of this writing, no further action has been taken.

§ 20.04 POSTEMPLOYMENT PRIVACY ISSUES

A company's obligation to protect an employee's privacy extends beyond the worker's active employment period. Employers must retain personnel files for at least one year after termination (two years if the employer is subject to Executive Order 11246; see **Chapter 18**). Access to personnel files should be limited to those in the company who have a need to know. Upon written request, former employees are entitled to inspect their personnel files. (See **Exhibit 20.7** for a sample policy on access to employee personnel files.)

[A]   Postemployment References

Employers may receive requests for information about former employees. Most requests will be from other employers seeking employment references about a former employee. Employers must have current knowledge of state and federal laws with regard to what information they may or may not share to avoid violating confidentiality and privacy laws. (See **Exhibit 20.8** for a sample policy on providing employment references.) (See **Section 16.08** for additional information on providing references on former employees.)

[B]   Confidentiality of Employee Records

Medical and personal information of former employees should remain confidential, and access to this information should be limited to only those with a legitimate need to know. Medical information can include, but is not limited to:

- Preemployment medical or drug screening results

- Benefit forms that may include information about an employee's health status

- Information retained by an employer regarding occupational injuries or illnesses or exposure to a blood-borne pathogen

- Return-to-work forms completed by a health care provider

- Workers' compensation claim forms and other related information

A variety of documents may contain sensitive and confidential information about former employees (e.g., benefit enrollment and claim forms, W-4 forms, child support documents, and wage garnishment documents).

Any of the following types of information should be kept in confidential files with access restricted to only those with a legitimate need to know:

- Age and date of birth

- Race

- Religion

- Marital status

- Parental status

- Social Security number

- Immigration and Naturalization Service Forms (I-9s)

- Home address and personal telephone number

- Preemployment aptitude or other employer-administered preemployment test results

- Records of wage garnishments

- Credit reports or negative financial information

- Some investigative reports such as sexual harassment investigation reports or polygraph test results

Maintaining the privacy of employee data includes the proper disposal of such data. The Fair and Accurate Credit Transactions Act mandates the appropriate disposal of all information that is a consumer report or derived from a consumer report (see **Section 20.02**). In addition, numerous states have enacted legislation regulating the disposal of personal identifying information, including employee data. The State of New York's legislation, "Disposal of Personal Records Law," became effective on December 6, 2006. It covers almost all types of records, including reports, statements, examinations, memoranda, files, forms, papers, microfilms, and computer tapes/discs. The type of information to be properly disposed of includes "any information concerning a natural person which, because of name, number, personal mark or other identifier, can be used to identify such natural person." Such personal identifying information includes Social Security number, driver's license number, mother's maiden name, electronic serial number, or personal identification number. Employers are covered by this law and may not dispose of a record containing personal identifying information unless it does one of the following: makes the personal identifying information unreadable, shreds the document, destroys the personal identifying information, or takes an action consistent with commonly accepted industry practices to safeguard personal information.

Other states have also passed similar, but not identical, laws. These states include California, Georgia, New Jersey, Texas and at least 13 other states. It is important to know what state law may apply to your business and what that state law requires.

§ 20.05 CONCLUSION

Privacy in the workplace continues to evolve. In the months and years ahead, technical advances in communication and surveillance techniques will continue to challenge employers to balance their desire for increased information and improved productivity with employees' needs and rights to privacy. As case law continues to define accepted practice, employers must adopt a philosophy to assist in defining corporate privacy policies.

Understanding the legal parameters of privacy in the workplace is a first step for employers. How employers choose to protect privacy in the workplace significantly affects employee morale and employees' perceptions of the workplace environment. Management's perceptions must be supported by well-drafted procedures and day-to-day practices that both incorporate the legal requirements and strive for a balance between employer and employees needs.

Exhibit 20.1   Mandated Benefits: 2009 Compliance Guide

Exhibit 20.1
A Sample Policy on Reference Checks on Job Applicants

STATEMENT OF POLICY

ABC COMPANY

Purpose: To protect ABC in its selection of new employees

Applies to: All ABC departments and divisions

It is the policy of ABC to check references of all potential new hires. ABC will attempt to obtain at least three references on each candidate and prepare written notes for the applicant's file. If possible, these references should be obtained from prior supervisors or peers of the candidate.

This policy also applies to applicants who have been submitted through recruiters. Reference checks must be provided by the recruiters from the last three employers listed on the employee's resume or application form if the companies are still in existence. The company also reserves the right to obtain its own references for employees referred through recruiting agencies.

An exception to this policy is provided if an applicant is currently employed and a reference check would violate the confidential nature of the applicant's job search. In this case, the current employer would not be contacted until possibly after hire, at the discretion of ABC.

Procedures

All applicants for employment must sign a release for verifying previous employment, obtaining personal references, conducting a background check, and validating educational degrees and/or professional certifications.

Following are the guidelines for conducting a telephone reference check:

- Have the hiring criteria or position description for the relevant position available.

- Ask open-ended questions, then wait for the respondent to answer.

- Listen carefully, then ask follow-up questions based on answers received.

- Ask the reference for additional names to call.

No one is to be hired until reference checks are completed and reviewed by the appropriate department head or human resources.

Exhibit 20.2
A Sample Policy on Searches

STATEMENT OF POLICY

ABC COMPANY

Purpose: To state the Company's position regarding safeguarding of employees' property at work and to notify employees of the Company's right to search Company and employee's property to prevent theft, detect the presence of alcohol, drugs, or other prohibited items, or recover stolen property.

ABC Company, at its expense, provides lockers or storage areas for the convenience and use by employees for safekeeping of clothing and a few small personal effects during working hours. Employees are responsible for maintaining their lockers in a clean and sanitary manner, and lockers must be kept locked at all times. The company at its expense will supply locks and keys and will retain a pass key to all locks. Employees should not place any other lock on a locker or storage area. The Company is not responsible for any items placed or left in a locker or storage area that are lost, damaged, stolen, or destroyed.

All locks, lockers, and storage areas remain the sole property of ABC Company. The Company reserves the right to open and inspect lockers, desks, personal computer hard drives, network files, external electronic storage media, and storage areas, as well as any contents or articles found within them. ABC Company may inspect any item brought onto Company property or placed in Company vehicles, such as briefcases, purses, or lunch boxes. Private or Company autos and other vehicles brought onto Company property may also be inspected.

An inspection may occur at any time, with or without advance notice or consent. An inspection may be conducted before, during, or after working hours, by any supervisor, manager, or security personnel designated by the Company.

ABC Company may remove all Company property found in lockers, desks, storage areas, personal computer hard drives, network files, or external electronic storage media, vehicles, or personal effects. Alcohol, nonprescribed medications, illegal drugs, weapons, explosives, or any other item prohibited by law or company policy may not be placed in a locker or storage area. Any such item found in a locker or storage area may be removed. Illegal substances may be turned over to the appropriate legal authorities.

Employees may be requested to cooperate with the inspection of a locker or storage area. Employees who fail to comply with this policy may be subject to disciplinary action, up to and including termination.

Exhibit 20.3   Mandated Benefits: 2009 Compliance Guide

Exhibit 20.3
A Sample Policy on Electronic and Telephonic Communication Monitoring

STATEMENT OF POLICY

ABC COMPANY

Purpose: To describe the ABC Company's policy on the use and monitoring of its electronic and telephonic communications systems, including e-mail, voice mail, text messages, and all other electronic and telephonic communications that may be developed in the future.

Applies to: All ABC employees

All electronic and telephonic communication systems and all communications and stored information transmitted, received, or contained in the company's information system are the property of the Company and, as such, are to be used solely for job-related purposes.

The use of any software and business equipment for private purposes is strictly prohibited, including but not limited to cell phones, pagers, facsimiles, telecopiers, computers, and copy machines. Employees using this equipment for personal purposes do so at their own risk. Further, employees shall not use a code, access a file, or retrieve any stored communication, other than where authorized, unless there has been prior clearance by an authorized Company representative. All pass codes are the property of the Company. No employee may refuse to disclose a pass code or intentionally substitute a pass code which is unknown to the Company.

Violations of this policy are subject to disciplinary action, up to and including discharge from employment. To ensure that the use of electronic and telephonic communications systems and business equipment is consistent with the Company's legitimate business interests, authorized representatives of the Company may monitor the use of such equipment at any time.

Procedure

As a condition of employment and continued employment, employees will be required to sign the acknowledgment form that is attached to this policy. Applicants will be required to sign this form upon acceptance of an employment offer by the Company.

Exhibit 20.3 (cont'd)

E-MAIL CONSENT FORM

I understand that all electronic communication systems as well as all information transmitted, received, or stored in these systems is the property of the ABC Company. I also understand that such systems are to be used solely for job-related and not for personal purposes and that I have no expectation of privacy in connection with the use of this equipment or the transmission, receipt, or information stored in such equipment. I further understand the Company reserves the right to monitor any personal e-mail accounts that I may have when accessed using the Company's equipment or that may be stored on the Company's equipment (such as my computer's hard drive) as temporary Internet files.

I further understand and agree not to use a code, access a file, or retrieve any stored communication unless authorized; and I acknowledge and consent to the Company's monitoring my use of this equipment at any time at its discretion. Such monitoring may include printing up and reading all e-mail entering, leaving, or stored in these systems.

I understand and agree that this policy can only be modified in writing and only if signed by the Company's Chief Executive Officer.

Name of Employee _____

(Print name)

Signature of Employee _____

Date _____

Name of Management Witness _____

(Print name)

Signature of Witness _____

Date _____

Exhibit 20.4   Mandated Benefits: 2009 Compliance Guide

Exhibit 20.4
A Sample Policy on Internet Acceptable Use

STATEMENT OF POLICY

ABC COMPANY

Purpose: To describe the ABC Company's policy on the acceptable use of the Internet.

Applies to: All ABC employees

As a condition of providing Internet access to its employees, the ABC Company places certain restrictions on workplace use of the Internet. ABC Company encourages employee use of the Internet as follows:

- To communicate with fellow employees and clients regarding matters within an employee's assigned duties

- To acquire information related to, or designed to facilitate the performance of, regular assigned duties

- To facilitate performance of any task or project in a manner approved by an employee's supervisor

Please be advised that your use of the Internet access provided by ABC Company expressly prohibits the following:

- Disseminating or printing copyrighted materials (including articles and software) in violation of copyright laws

- Sending, receiving, printing, or otherwise disseminating proprietary data, trade secrets, or other confidential information of ABC Company in violation of company policy or proprietary agreements

- Accessing, sending, or receiving offensive or harassing statements or language including disparagement of others based on their race, national origin, sex, sexual orientation, age, disability, religious or political beliefs, or other protected characteristics

- Sending or soliciting sexually oriented messages or images

- Operating a business, usurping business opportunities, soliciting money for personal gain, or searching for jobs outside ABC Company

- Sending chain letters, gambling, or engaging in any other activity in violation of local, state, or federal law

Disciplinary action for violation of ABC Company's Internet Acceptable Use Policy may include, but is not limited to, termination, suspension, or transfer of the offending employee. In cases involving less serious violations, disciplinary action may consist of a warning or reprimand. Remedial action may also include counseling, changes in work assignments, or other measures designed to prevent future misconduct. The measure of discipline will correspond to the potential effect of the offense on the Company and fellow employees, up to and including involvement of local law enforcement.

Exhibit 20.5
A Sample Policy on Medical Records and Serious Health Conditions

STATEMENT OF POLICY

ABC COMPANY

Purpose: To delineate procedures to be used for employees with serious health conditions.

Applies to: All ABC departments and divisions

It is the policy of ABC Company that employees with infectious, long-term, life-threatening, or other serious health conditions may work as long as they are physically and mentally able to perform the duties of their job without undue risk to their own health or that of other employees or customers. Such serious diseases may include cancer, heart disease, multiple sclerosis, hepatitis, tuberculosis, and acquired immune deficiency syndrome (AIDS).

If an employee has a serious health condition that affects his/her ability to perform his/her assigned duties, such employees are to be treated like other employees who have disabilities that limit their job performance.

Employees who are diagnosed as having a serious health condition that will affect their performance are to communicate with the Human Resources (HR) Department as soon as possible. The HR professional should respond with compassion and understanding and review with the employee the Company policy on such issues as employee assistance, leaves and disability, infection control, and available benefits. The HR professional will advise the employee exactly what his/her rights and obligations are under the law.

Employees who have a serious disease are to provide HR with information needed to make decisions regarding job assignments, ability to continue working, or ability to return to work. ABC Company may require a doctor's certification of an employee's ability to perform his/her duties safely. HR will provide the employee with specific information regarding ABC's right to know about the employee's medical condition.

ABC Company will attempt to maintain the confidentiality of the diagnosis and medical records of employees with serious health conditions, unless required otherwise by law. This includes cooperating fully with law enforcement and government agencies that have legitimate need for information relating to certain investigations, as required by law. Information relating to an employee's serious health condition will not be disclosed to other employees unless the information is, in the opinion of the Company, necessary to protect the health or safety of the employee, coworkers, or others. The desire to know is not sufficient reason to divulge health information. Information will be released only to those with a legitimate need to know.

Employees concerned about being infected with a serious disease by a coworker, customer, or other person should convey this concern to their supervisor or the Human Resources Department. Employees who refuse to work with or perform services for a person known or suspected to have a serious health condition without first discussing their concern with a supervisor will be subject to discipline, up to and including termination.

If an employee transfers to another facility, the medical file goes to the new facility. Only [*insert names or titles*] have access to all medical files. Employees are not entitled to copy all or part of their medical files, unless required by law. In this case, ABC Company will charge per copy.

Exhibit 20.6

Exhibit 20.6
AIDS Testing in the Workplace: Statutes and Policies

KEY: **Bona fide occupational qualification.** A limited defense to charge of discrimination. (See Glossary.)

Person with AIDS. Encompasses both persons with AIDS and persons who have tested positive for the human immunodeficiency virus (HIV) that causes AIDS. Although state statute may not specifically classify AIDS as a handicap or disability, state courts may follow federal law, under which a person with AIDS may be considered to be a person with a disability.

NOTE: States not listed have passed no legislation governing AIDS testing in the workplace. The following states have enacted statutes that protect the confidentiality of HIV test results: AL, AZ, CO, CT, DE, GA, HI, ID, IL, IN, IA, KS, LA, ME, MD, MI, MO, MT, NV, NH, NJ, NY, ND, OH, OK, OR, PA, TX, VA, WV, and WI.

*With respect to whether AIDS is classified as a handicap, the Supreme Court in *Bragdon v. Abbott*, 54 U.S. 624 (1998), held that the ability to reproduce and to bear children constitutes a major life activity within the meaning of the Americans with Disabilities Act (ADA). The court found that HIV status is a physical impairment that interferes with the ability to have children and that individuals infected with HIV are covered by the ADA. The court stated that HIV infection satisfies the statutory and regulatory definition of *physical impairment*. Most state courts are likely to follow the Supreme Court ruling in construing state fair employment practice statutes.

	AIDS Classified as a Handicap*	Mandatory Testing Prohibited	Prohibition Against Use of Positive AIDS Test to Discriminate	Other Requirements	Citations to Authority
AL	State has no statutory requirements.	Yes. Must obtain informed consent of person to be tested.	State has no statutory requirements.	Testing facility shall maintain confidentiality regarding HIV test results.	Ala. Code §§ 22-11A-50–22-11A-54.
AZ	Yes. Op. Ariz. Att'y Gen. No. R86-005 (1987).	Yes. Must obtain written informed consent of person to be tested. Consent may be withdrawn at any time before drawing the sample.	State has no statutory requirements.	Civil Rights Act governs whether employment decision can be made based on AIDS test result (Op. Ariz. Att'y Gen. No. R86-005 (1987)). State law protects confidentiality of HIV/AIDS test results.	Ariz. Rev. Stat. Ann. § 36-663.
AR	State has no statutory requirements.	Informed consent not required for HIV test for health care provider or employee of health care facility who has direct skin or mucous membrane contact with blood of patient.	State has no statutory requirements.	None.	Ark. Code Ann. § 20-15-905.

	AIDS Classified as a Handicap*	Mandatory Testing Prohibited	Prohibition Against Use of Positive AIDS Test to Discriminate	Other Requirements	Citations to Authority
CA	Yes. California Fair Employment and Housing Act.	Must obtain written informed consent of person to be tested.	Yes.	None.	Cal. Gov't Code § 12940; Cal. Health & Safety Code §§ 121132, 121135; *Chalk v. United States Dist. Court*, 840 F.2d 701 (9th Cir. 1988); *Raytheon Co. v. California Fair Employ. & Hous. Comm'n*, 212 Cal. App. 3d 1242, 261 Cal. Rptr. 197 (1989).
CO	Yes. Colorado Civil Rights Commission ruling.	Must obtain written informed consent of person to be tested.	State has no statutory requirements.	State law protects confidentiality of HIV/AIDS test results.	Colo. Rev. Stat. Ann. § 10-3-1104.5.
CT	Yes. Connecticut Commission on Human Rights and Opportunities.	Yes. No employer shall order HIV-related test without first receiving written informed consent or oral informed consent. Whenever practical, written consent shall be obtained. Informed consent shall be obtained without undue inducement or any element of compulsion, fraud, deceit, duress, or other form of constraint or coercion.	State has no statutory requirements.	No person who obtains HIV-related information may disclose or be compelled to disclose such information except to the classes of persons to whom disclosure of such information may be required, authorized, or permitted by law. Explanation of confidentiality protections afforded confidential HIV-related information, including the circumstances under which it is given, must also be provided. When communicating the test result, the person ordering the test must provide counseling or referrals for counseling.	Conn. Gen. Stat. Ann. §§ 19a-581 *et seq.*; Conn. Agencies Regs. §§ 46a-54-41 *et seq.*
DE	Yes. Delaware Attorney General's Office.	Must obtain consent of person to be tested. Exception to consent exists if the health of a health care worker has been threatened during the course of duties as a result of exposure to blood or other bodily fluids.	State has no statutory requirements.	State law protects confidentiality of HIV/AIDS test results. Infected teachers and school employees may continue working (State Board of Education and Department of Public Instruction Guidelines).	Del. Code Ann. tit. 16, §§ 1201–1205.

Exhibit 20.6

Mandated Benefits: 2009 Compliance Guide

Exhibit 20.6 (cont'd)
AIDS Testing in the Workplace: Statutes and Policies

KEY: **Bona fide occupational qualification.** A limited defense to charge of discrimination. (See Glossary.)

Person with AIDS. Encompasses both persons with AIDS and persons who have tested positive for the human immunodeficiency virus (HIV) that causes AIDS. Although state statute may not specifically classify AIDS as a handicap or disability, state courts may follow federal law, under which a person with AIDS may be considered to be a person with a disability.

NOTE: States not listed have passed no legislation governing AIDS testing in the workplace. The following states have enacted statutes that protect the confidentiality of HIV test results: AL, AZ, CO, CT, DE, GA, HI, ID, IL, IN, IA, KS, LA, ME, MD, MI, MO, MT, NV, NH, NJ, NY, ND, OH, OK, OR, PA, TX, VA, WV, and WI.

*With respect to whether AIDS is classified as a handicap, the Supreme Court in *Bragdon v. Abbott*, 54 U.S. 624 (1998), held that the ability to reproduce and to bear children constitutes a major life activity within the meaning of the Americans with Disabilities Act (ADA). The court found that HIV status is a physical impairment that interferes with the ability to have children and that individuals infected with HIV are covered by the ADA. The court stated that HIV infection satisfies the statutory and regulatory definition of *physical impairment*. Most state courts are likely to follow the Supreme Court ruling in construing state fair employment practice statutes.

	AIDS Classified as a Handicap*	Mandatory Testing Prohibited	Prohibition Against Use of Positive AIDS Test to Discriminate	Other Requirements	Citations to Authority
DC	Yes. D.C. Office of Human Rights.	District has no statutory requirements.	Yes. Statute incorporates business necessity test.	None.	D.C. Code Ann. §§ 1-2502, 1-2503.
FL	Yes. By statute.	Yes. Must obtain informed consent of person to be tested unless absence of HIV is a bona fide occupational qualification.	Yes. State law authorizes state to administer voluntary tests to identify persons with AIDS, but test results may not be used to discriminate against prospective or current employees.	Violation of nondiscrimination law permits recovery of larger of $1,000 or actual damages; if violation is willful, recovery is larger of $5,000 or actual damages, plus attorneys' fees and other costs.	Fla. Stat. Ann. §§ 381.004, 760.50; Florida Commission on Human Rights No. 85-0624, 2 Empl. Prac. Guide (CCH) ¶ 5014 (1985).
GA	State has no statutory requirements.	State has no statutory requirements.	State has no statutory requirements.	State law protects confidentiality of HIV/AIDS test results. A person can be ordered to submit to an HIV test if the state has evidence that the person is reasonably likely to be infected.	Ga. Code Ann. §§ 24-9-40.1, 24-9-47, 31-17A-3.
HI	State has no statutory requirements.	Employer may test employee with consent, but may not compel test.	State has no statutory requirements.	State law protects confidentiality of HIV/AIDS test results. Results may be released to schools, preschools, and day care centers.	Haw. Rev. Stat. §§ 325-101(a), 325-101(c).
ID	State has no statutory requirements.	State has no statutory requirements.	State has no statutory requirements.	State law protects confidentiality of test results.	Idaho Code § 39-610.

	AIDS Classified as a Handicap*	Mandatory Testing Prohibited	Prohibition Against Use of Positive AIDS Test to Discriminate	Other Requirements	Citations to Authority
IL	Yes. Illinois Human Rights Commission.	Yes, except for emergency medical workers, firefighters, and law enforcement officers exposed to HIV.	State has no statutory requirements.	State law protects confidentiality of test results and patient identity.	410 Ill. Comp. Stat. Ann. §§ 305/1 *et seq.*
IN	State has no statutory requirements.	Yes, except for certain medical diagnoses and emergencies. Can test with informed consent. Consent may be withdrawn at any time.	State has no statutory requirements.	State law protects confidentiality of medical information, including AIDS tests.	Ind. Code Ann. §§ 16-41-6-1 *et seq.*
IA	Yes. Iowa Civil Rights Act.	Yes, but may test only with consent.	Yes.	State law protects confidentiality of HIV/AIDS test results.	Iowa Code Ann. §§ 141A.1 *et seq.*
KS	Yes. By statute.	Yes. Must obtain consent of person to be tested.	Yes.	State law protects confidentiality of test results.	Kan. Stat. Ann. §§ 65-6001 *et seq.*
KY	Yes. By statute.	Yes, unless absence of HIV is bona fide occupational qualification.	Yes, unless absence of HIV is bona fide occupational qualification; burden of proof on employer.	Duty of accommodation applies. Nothing prevents the employer from making preemployment inquiries as to the handicap.	Ky. Rev. Stat. Ann. §§ 207.130 *et seq.*
LA	Yes. Louisiana Civil Rights for the Handicapped.	Yes. Informed consent of person to be tested required.	State has no statutory requirements.	State protects confidentiality of test results.	La. Rev. Stat. Ann. §§ 40:1300.11 *et seq.*
ME	Yes. Maine Human Rights Commission ruling.	Yes. Exception: Employee of health care facility may be tested if testing is related to a bona fide occupational qualification.	Employment status may not be affected because of HIV test results or refusal to be tested.	State law protects confidentiality of test results and patient identity. Violation of law permits recovery of actual damages, civil penalty of $1,000 (up to $5,000, if violation deemed willful), plus attorneys' fees and costs.	Me. Rev. Stat. Ann. tit. 5, §§ 19203, 19204A, 19204-B.
MD	Yes. Maryland Handicap Guidelines.	Yes. Informed consent required of person to be tested.	State has no statutory requirements.	State protects confidentiality of test results and patient identity.	Md. Code Ann. Health-Gen. I § 18-336.

Exhibit 20.6   Mandated Benefits: 2009 Compliance Guide

Exhibit 20.6 (cont'd)

AIDS Testing in the Workplace: Statutes and Policies

KEY: **Bona fide occupational qualification.** A limited defense to charge of discrimination. (See Glossary.)

          Person with AIDS. Encompasses both persons with AIDS and persons who have tested positive for the human immunodeficiency virus (HIV) that causes AIDS. Although state statute may not specifically classify AIDS as a handicap or disability, state courts may follow federal law, under which a person with AIDS may be considered to be a person with a disability.

NOTE: States not listed have passed no legislation governing AIDS testing in the workplace. The following states have enacted statutes that protect the confidentiality of HIV test results: AL, AZ, CO, CT, DE, GA, HI, ID, IL, IN, IA, KS, LA, ME, MD, MI, MO, MT, NV, NH, NJ, NY, ND, OH, OK, OR, PA, TX, VA, WV, and WI.

*With respect to whether AIDS is classified as a handicap, the Supreme Court in *Bragdon v. Abbott*, 54 U.S. 624 (1998), held that the ability to reproduce and to bear children constitutes a major life activity within the meaning of the Americans with Disabilities Act (ADA). The court found that HIV status is a physical impairment that interferes with the ability to have children and that individuals infected with HIV are covered by the ADA. The court stated that HIV infection satisfies the statutory and regulatory definition of *physical impairment*. Most state courts are likely to follow the Supreme Court ruling in construing state fair employment practice statutes.

	AIDS Classified as a Handicap*	Mandatory Testing Prohibited	Prohibition Against Use of Positive AIDS Test to Discriminate	Other Requirements	Citations to Authority
MA	Yes. Massachusetts Commission Against Discrimination ruling.	Yes. Must obtain written informed consent of person to be tested.	Yes.	Employees with AIDS may remain on the job; employer must protect confidentiality of employees with AIDS; AIDS testing will not be routinely conducted among state workers (state policy).	Mass. Gen. Laws Ann. ch. 111, § 70F; *Estate of McKinley v. Boston Harbor Hotel*, No. 90-B-EM-1263 (Mass. Comm'n Against Discrimination, Aug. 10, 1992).
MI	Yes. Michigan Civil Rights Commission and Michigan Civil Rights Act.	Yes. Must obtain informed consent of person to be tested. Ann Arbor city regulation covering present and prospective city employees prohibits mandatory testing.	Yes. Detroit law covers all employers; Ann Arbor city regulation covers present and prospective city employees.	State law protects confidentiality of HIV test results and patient identity.	Mich. Comp. Laws Ann. §§ 37.1103, 333.5131, 333.5133; *Sanchez v. Lagoudakis*, 486 N.W.2d 657 (Mich. 1992).
MN	Yes. Minnesota Human Rights Commission.	Yes. St. Paul city policy covering present and prospective city employees prohibits mandatory testing.	Yes. State court ruling applies to all employers; Minnesota Department of Employee Relations policy covers state employees; governor's executive order covers present and prospective state employees.	State law requires reasonable accommodation.	Minn. Stat. Ann. §§ 363.01 *et seq.*

	AIDS Classified as a Handicap*	Mandatory Testing Prohibited	Prohibition Against Use of Positive AIDS Test to Discriminate	Other Requirements	Citations to Authority
MO	Yes. By statute.	State has no statutory requirements.	Yes. State fair employment law prohibits discrimination against persons with AIDS unless such persons present a danger to coworkers or others.	State law protects confidentiality of HIV test results. Routine screening for positive antibody test not recommended under employment guidelines. Employment policies applicable on same basis as for persons with other conditions affecting job performance (Missouri Department of Health 1986 Guidelines).	Mo. Rev. Stat. §§ 191.650-191.695; *Rose City Oil Co. v. Missouri Comm'n on Human Rights*, 832 S.W.2d 314 (Mo. Ct. App. 1992).
MT	Yes. Montana Commission for Human Rights.	Yes. Must obtain written, informed consent of person to be tested.	State has no statutory requirements.	State law prohibits disclosure of identity of subjects of AIDS tests.	Mont. Code Ann. §§ 50-16-1007, 50-16-1009.
NE	Yes. By statute.	No.	Yes, unless person with AIDS cannot perform requirements of job or poses threat to health and safety of others.	No specific statutory provision dealing with AIDS. Topic is covered under fair employment practice laws for physical disabilities.	Neb. Rev. Stat. §§ 48-1101–48-1125.
NH	State has no statutory requirements.	Yes. Must obtain informed consent of person to be tested with certain exceptions.	State has no statutory requirements.	State law protects confidentiality of test results and identity of patient.	N.H. Rev. Stat. Ann. § 141-F.
NJ	Yes. By statute.	Yes.	Yes.	State law protects confidentiality of HIV test information.	N.J. Stat. Ann. §§ 10:5-1, 26:5C *et seq.*
NM	Yes. New Mexico Attorney General's Office.	No.	Yes, bar to requiring disclosure of HIV test results as condition of employment unless bona fide occupational qualification; burden of proof on employer.	None.	N.M. Stat. Ann. § 28-10A-1.

Exhibit 20.6

Mandated Benefits: 2009 Compliance Guide

Exhibit 20.6 (cont'd)

AIDS Testing in the Workplace: Statutes and Policies

KEY: **Bona fide occupational qualification.** A limited defense to charge of discrimination. (See Glossary.)
Person with AIDS. Encompasses both persons with AIDS and persons who have tested positive for the human immunodeficiency virus (HIV) that causes AIDS. Although state statute may not specifically classify AIDS as a handicap or disability, state courts may follow federal law, under which a person with AIDS may be considered to be a person with a disability.

NOTE: States not listed have passed no legislation governing AIDS testing in the workplace. The following states have enacted statutes that protect the confidentiality of HIV test results: AL, AZ, CO, CT, DE, GA, HI, ID, IL, IN, IA, KS, LA, ME, MD, MI, MO, MT, NV, NH, NJ, NY, ND, OH, OK, OR, PA, TX, VA, WV, and WI.

*With respect to whether AIDS is classified as a handicap, the Supreme Court in *Bragdon v. Abbott*, 54 U.S. 624 (1998), held that the ability to reproduce and to bear children constitutes a major life activity within the meaning of the Americans with Disabilities Act (ADA). The court found that HIV status is a physical impairment that interferes with the ability to have children and that individuals infected with HIV are covered by the ADA. The court stated that HIV infection satisfies the statutory and regulatory definition of *physical impairment*. Most state courts are likely to follow the Supreme Court ruling in construing state fair employment practice statutes.

	AIDS Classified as a Handicap*	Mandatory Testing Prohibited	Prohibition Against Use of Positive AIDS Test to Discriminate	Other Requirements	Citations to Authority
NY	Yes. By statute.	Yes. Must obtain informed, written consent of person to be tested. Consent may be withdrawn at any time.	Yes.	State law protects confidentiality of test results.	N.Y. Pub. Health Laws §§ 2780–2787; N.Y. Comp. Codes R. & Regs, tit. 9, § 367.3; tit. 18, § 303.7; *Barton v. N.Y. City Comm'n on Human Rights*, 140 Misc. 2d 554, 531 N.Y.S.2d 979 (N.Y. Sup. Ct. 1988).
NC	State has no statutory requirements. Under judicial interpretation, person who tests positive for HIV, but who is otherwise asymptomatic, is not a "handicapped person" within meaning of North Carolina Handicapped Persons Protection Act.	Yes, for employees, except as part of annual medical examination.	Yes, unless continued employment poses risks to person with AIDS or others. Job applicants can be denied employment solely on the basis of a confirmed positive test for the AIDS virus.	Statute may be enforced by civil action; back pay and attorneys' fees available for violation of statute.	N.C. Gen. Stat. § 130A-148; *Burgess v. Your House of Raleigh, Inc.,* 326 N.C. 205, 388 S.E.2d 134 (1990).
ND	Yes. North Dakota Department of Health ruling.	Yes. Must obtain written consent of person to be tested.	State has no statutory requirements.	State law protects confidentiality of test results.	N.D. Cent. Code §§ 23-07.5-01, 23-07.5-02, 23-07.5-05.

	AIDS Classified as a Handicap*	Mandatory Testing Prohibited	Prohibition Against Use of Positive AIDS Test to Discriminate	Other Requirements	Citations to Authority
OH	Yes. Ohio Civil Rights Commission.	Yes. Must obtain informed consent of person to be tested. Cincinnati Board of Health regulation covering private and government employees prohibits mandatory testing.	Yes. Cincinnati Board of Health regulation covers private and government employees.	State law protects confidentiality of HIV test results. Employers immune from liability to employees for workplace transmission of HIV unless employers act recklessly.	Ohio Rev. Code Ann., §§ 3701.24.2, 3701.24.3, 3701.24.9.
OK	State has no statutory requirements.	Yes. Must obtain written consent of person to be tested.	State has no statutory requirements.	State protects confidentiality of test results.	Okla. Stat. Ann. tit. 63 §§ 1-502.2, 1-502.3.
OR	Yes. Oregon Attorney General's ruling.	In general, yes. Informed consent or court order must be obtained to mandate testing.	State has no statutory requirements.	State law protects confidentiality of HIV/AIDS test results.	Or. Rev. Stat. § 433.045.
PA	Yes. Pennsylvania Human Relations Act.	Yes. Must obtain written informed consent from person to be tested. State executive order applies to state employees; Philadelphia mayoral executive order covers city employees and clients.	Yes. State executive order applies to state employees; Philadelphia mayoral executive order covers city employees and clients.	State law protects confidentiality of test results.	35 Pa. Cons. Stat. §§ 7601 et seq.
RI	Yes. Rhode Island Human Rights Commission.	Yes. Must obtain informed consent of person to be tested.	Yes, unless the person with AIDS poses clear and present danger to others.	State law protects confidentiality of HIV test results.	R.I. Gen. Laws §§ 23-6-13, 23-6-17, 23-6-22.
SC	Yes. South Carolina Human Affairs Commission.	Yes. South Carolina Department of Health and Environmental Control policy prohibits testing of present and prospective state employees without prior consent.	Yes. South Carolina Department of Health and Environmental Control policy covers present and prospective state employees.	Testing of a person without consent is allowed if health care worker is exposed to blood during treatment and reasonable medical judgment indicates significant risk of HIV exposure.	S.C. Code Ann. § 44-29-230; see S.C. Dep't of Health & Envt'l Control Regs., chs. 61, 65.

Exhibit 20.6

Exhibit 20.6 (cont'd)

AIDS Testing in the Workplace: Statutes and Policies

KEY: **Bona fide occupational qualification.** A limited defense to charge of discrimination. (See Glossary.)

Person with AIDS. Encompasses both persons with AIDS and persons who have tested positive for the human immunodeficiency virus (HIV) that causes AIDS. Although state statute may not specifically classify AIDS as a handicap or disability, state courts may follow federal law, under which a person with AIDS may be considered to be a person with a disability.

NOTE: States not listed have passed no legislation governing AIDS testing in the workplace. The following states have enacted statutes that protect the confidentiality of HIV test results: AL, AZ, CO, CT, DE, GA, HI, ID, IL, IN, IA, KS, LA, ME, MD, MI, MO, MT, NV, NH, NJ, NY, ND, OH, OK, OR, PA, TX, VA, WV, and WI.

*With respect to whether AIDS is classified as a handicap, the Supreme Court in *Bragdon v. Abbott*, 54 U.S. 624 (1998), held that the ability to reproduce and to bear children constitutes a major life activity within the meaning of the Americans with Disabilities Act (ADA). The court found that HIV status is a physical impairment that interferes with the ability to have children and that individuals infected with HIV are covered by the ADA. The court stated that HIV infection satisfies the statutory and regulatory definition of *physical impairment*. Most state courts are likely to follow the Supreme Court ruling in construing state fair employment practice statutes.

	AIDS Classified as a Handicap*	Mandatory Testing Prohibited	Prohibition Against Use of Positive AIDS Test to Discriminate	Other Requirements	Citations to Authority
TX	Yes. Texas Attorney General's opinion.	Yes. State statute prohibits testing by employers unless bona fide occupational qualification can be shown; burden of proof on employer.	Yes. State court ruling. Austin city ordinance covers employers with 16 or more workers, employment agencies, and labor unions.	State law protects confidentiality of HIV test results. Violation of law permits recovery of actual damages, civil penalty of up to $5,000 (between $5,000 and $10,000 if violation is deemed willful), attorneys' fees, and costs.	Tex. Health & Safety Code Ann. §§ 81.102–81.104.
VT	Yes. Vermont Fair Employment Practices Act.	Yes.	Yes. Requiring HIV test as condition of job is unlawful employment practice, as is discriminating against persons with AIDS.	None.	Vt. Stat. Ann. tit. 21, § 495.
VA	State has no statutory requirements.	Yes. Informed consent required except in specified cases involving health care employees.	State has no statutory requirements.	State law protects confidentiality of test results. Unauthorized disclosure is punishable by a civil penalty of up to $5,000.	Va. Code Ann. §§ 32.1-36.1, 32.1-37.2, 32.1-45.1.
WA	Yes. Washington State Human Rights Commission.	Yes, absent bona fide occupational qualification.	Yes. Discrimination barred absent bona fide occupational qualification; burden of proof on employer.	Employers immune from liability for HIV transmission in workplace unless grossly negligent.	Wash. Rev. Code Ann. § 49.60.172.

	AIDS Classified as a Handicap*	Mandatory Testing Prohibited	Prohibition Against Use of Positive AIDS Test to Discriminate	Other Requirements	Citations to Authority
WV	Yes. West Virginia Human Rights Act.	Yes. Must obtain consent from person to be tested. Certain exceptions apply. Testing can be required by the courts for persons convicted of prostitution, sexual abuse, sexual assault, incest, or sexual molestation.	No.	State law protects confidentiality of HIV test results.	W. Va. Code §§ 5-11-3(m), 16-3C-1-16-3C-9; *Benjamin R. V. Orkin Exterminating Co.*, 182 W. Va. 615, 390 S.E.2d 814 (1990).
WI	Yes. Wisconsin Attorney General's ruling.	Yes. Wisconsin Attorney General's ruling.	Yes. State law prohibits use of test results by employers to discriminate unless state health officials find substantial risk of transmission through employment.	State law protects confidentiality of HIV test results.	Wis. Stat. Ann. § 103.15; *Racine Unified Sch. Dist. v. Labor & Indus. Review Comm'n*, 476 N.W.2d 707 (Wis. Ct. App. 1991).

Source: John F. Buckley & Ronald M. Green, *2008 State by State Guide to Human Resources Law* (New York: Aspen Publishers, Inc. 2008).

Exhibit 20.7

Mandated Benefits: 2009 Compliance Guide

Exhibit 20.7
A Sample Policy on Access to Employee Personnel Files

STATEMENT OF POLICY

ABC COMPANY

Purpose: To establish a policy for information contained in employee personnel files, to conform to applicable federal and state laws, and to establish procedure for employee access.

Applies to: All ABC employees

It is the policy of the Company to maintain personnel records and information for each applicant, employee, and past employee. The Company tries to balance each individual's right to privacy with the Company's need to obtain, use, and retain employment information.

Personnel Files

Personnel files for each employee are maintained in the Human Resources (HR) Department. These contain documents that have been used to determine employment, promotion, compensation, transfer, disciplinary action, or termination.

Employee personnel files reside in local offices within the HR Department. If there is no HR Department, they reside in the office of the Managing Director. If an employee transfers to another office, the personnel file goes to the new office.

Access

Personnel files may not be removed from the HR Department. Only [*insert names or titles*] have access to employee personnel files.

Department heads have access to the complete personnel files of their respective groups only. Department heads have access to the personnel files of those not in their group only when the HR Director or HR Manager has been informed. The HR Director or the HR Manager must be present when the file is reviewed.

Employees have the right to access their personnel files, subject to the following limitations:

- Employees are permitted, within a reasonable time after their written request, to inspect their personnel files during business hours and in the presence of an HR Department staff member.

- If the employee disagrees with information in his/her personnel file, the employee may submit a written statement explaining his/her position. Such employee documents must remain part of the personnel file.

- The employee is entitled to copy those documents contained within the HR file that he/she has signed. The employee has no right to review reference notes or supervisor notes to file. The employer may charge a reasonable fee for the copies.

Exhibit 20.7 (cont'd)

- Information contained in a personnel file will be released to a party other than the employee, only under the following circumstances: pursuant to a lawfully issued administrative summons of judicial order including a search warrant or subpoena; in response to a government audit in the investigation or defense of personnel-related complaints against the employer; in response to a request by a law enforcement agency for the employee's address and dates of attendance at work; or to comply with federal, state, or local laws or regulations.

Exhibit 20.8   Mandated Benefits: 2009 Compliance Guide

Exhibit 20.8
A Sample Policy on Providing Employment References

STATEMENT OF POLICY

ABC COMPANY

Purpose: To establish policy regarding employment verification of current and past employees.

Applies to: All ABC employees

Under the Federal Privacy Act, the Company is obliged to preserve the privacy of an employee, past or present.

It is the policy of ABC Company that any inquiries received either by telephone or in writing regarding a present or past employee are to be referred to the Human Resources (HR) Department.

ABC's policy regarding providing employment references is that the Company will state only that a person was employed with the Company, the dates of employment, and the employee's title or position. Only if an employee submits a reference release request in writing will additional information be released. This pertains to both present and past employees.

Notwithstanding the paragraph above, ABC Company will cooperate fully with law enforcement and government agencies that have a legitimate need for information relating to certain investigations, as required by law.

Chapter 21
Sexual and Other Prohibited Harassment

§ 21.01 AUDIT QUESTIONS

1. Does the organization have a clearly written policy prohibiting sexual harassment and other forms of harassment?

2. Has the organization's harassment/sexual harassment policy been widely communicated to all employees and managers/supervisors?

3. Has training on harassment and sexual harassment in the workplace been provided to all managers/supervisors and employees?

4. Do all managers/supervisors and employees understand the process for bringing forth and dealing with complaints regarding harassment/sexual harassment?

Note: Consistent "yes" answers to the above questions suggest that the organization is applying effective management practices and/or complying with federal regulations. "No" answers indicate that problem areas exist and should be addressed immediately.

This chapter examines sexual harassment and other prohibited forms of workplace harassment. The objective of this chapter is to give employers the information they need to identify the problem of harassment, deal with harassment effectively and legally, and develop an aware, educated workforce.

Several key messages underlie the legal issues related to sexual harassment. For the employer, the message is that considerable legal exposure—and cost—is associated with inappropriate or inadequate measures to prevent and respond to sexual harassment. For the victims, the message is that they have legal remedies when confronted with sexual harassment, including the possibility of being awarded substantial damages. For the harasser, the message is to stop the harassment or run the risk of discipline, including termination, costs associated with personal liability, and even criminal charges.

Sexual harassment exposes an organization to more costs than generally realized. In addition to direct litigation, costs are generated by:

- Replacing employees who left their jobs because of sexual harassment

- Paying medical insurance claims for services to harassed employees who sought professional help because of physical or emotional stress

- Paying sick leave to employees who missed work, and losses created by decreasing productivity

The effectiveness of any organization is diminished to some extent by the problems that sexual harassment can cause, including the following:

- Employee dissatisfaction, unrest, and absenteeism

- Disruption of the work environment within the organization

- Problematic employee relations and potential union difficulties

- Decreased individual and organizational productivity

- Reduced goodwill, reputation, and image of the organization

Although sexual harassment does not typically cause all these problems in every company, it certainly causes some, and the possibility of encountering many of them is not unusual.

Appropriate behavior in the workplace has long been an issue of concern for employers and workers alike. However, while harassing behaviors have always existed in the workplace, legal guidelines and laws regarding harassment date from no earlier than 1975. The buildup of legal guidelines coincides with the fact that the workforce today is more diverse than ever before. The increasing diversity in the workplace introduces new values and perceptions that continually redefine "appropriate behavior."

The definition of harassment has evolved over time and continues to change. It is important for employers to understand the most current legal definition of sexual and other prohibited harassment to ensure the workplace is free of these liability-laden behaviors.

There are similarities in how employers treat incidents of sexual harassment and other prohibited forms of harassment. However, to maintain clarity for each issue, sexual harassment is discussed separately in the chapter from the other prohibited forms of harassment.

(See **Exhibit 21.1** for a means whereby companies may gauge how current their attitudes are regarding harassment in the workplace and **Exhibit 21.2** for a summary of the evolution of the definition of sexual harassment.)

§ 21.02 DEFINITION OF SEXUAL HARASSMENT

Sexual harassment is a violation of Section 703 of Title VII of the Civil Rights Act of 1964 [42 U.S.C. § 2000e-2(a)(1)] as amended. The Equal Employment Opportunity Commission (EEOC) reaffirmed its position that sexual harassment is an unlawful employment practice. The guidelines specifically stipulate that unwanted sexual advances, requests for sexual favors, and other verbal or physical conduct of a sexual nature constitute sexual harassment when any of the following conditions exist:

- *When submission to such conduct is a term or condition of employment.* An employee's rights are violated when submitting to sexual harassment is an implicit or explicit provision of attaining or maintaining employment.

- *When submitting to or rejecting such conduct is a basis for employment decisions affecting the individual.* To the extent that submission to or rejection of sexually harassing behavior affects an employee's promotions, transfers, job assignments, and performance appraisals, it constitutes a violation of Title VII.

- *When the harassment unreasonably interferes with the employee's work or creates an intimidating, hostile, or offensive working environment.* The employee's perception of the sexual harassment as unreasonably interfering with work or creating a problematic or stressful environment is enough to constitute a violation of Title VII under these guidelines. The EEOC looks at the "totality of circumstances" surrounding allegations of sexual harassment, and it determines the legality of a particular action on a case-by-case basis. Nonetheless, the general principles of Title VII apply and, as in the broad range of other possible violations under Title VII, the employer is responsible for the acts of its agents and supervisors.

In fact, the employer is responsible for acts of sexual harassment by supervisors, regardless of whether the acts were authorized or forbidden by the employer, and whether the employer knew or should have known about them. However, in its advisory brief to the U.S. Supreme Court in *Meritor Savings Bank FSB v. Vinson* [477 U.S. 57 (1996)], a brief noted to be "in tension" with the guidelines, the EEOC differentiated between hostile environment and quid pro quo sexual harassment.

[A] Hostile Environment Harassment

A hostile environment is created when regular or repeated actions or objects of a sexual nature unreasonably interfere with an employee's job performance. These actions or objects have the effect of creating an intimidating, hostile, or offensive work environment. The actions can be either a single occurrence or ongoing behaviors in combination with other forms of environmental harassment that occur over time.

The EEOC considers the following factors in determining whether a hostile environment has been created:

- Was the conduct verbal or physical, or both?

- Was the conduct a one-time occurrence or repeated?

- Was the conduct hostile and patently offensive?

- Is the alleged harasser a coworker or a supervisor?

- Did others participate in perpetrating the harassment?

- Was the harassment directed at more than one individual?

No one factor controls. An assessment of the work environment is made based on the totality of circumstances.

The scope of a hostile work environment can be broad. In *Biddle v. Department of Treasury* [63 M.S.P.R. 521 (1994)], an employee's surveillance of a coworker's apartment created a hostile working environment even though the coworker was not physically touched or pressured for sexual favors. The court held that the harasser's behavior went beyond what was reasonable.

However, in *Saxton v. American Telephone & Telegraph Co.* [10 F.3d 526 (7th Cir. 1993)], the court found that two incidents of unwelcome touching and a supervisor's subsequent coldness toward an employee did not constitute sexual harassment. The Seventh Circuit held that although the behavior might have made the employee's workplace unpleasant, it did not meet the standards articulated in *Harris v. Forklift Systems, Inc.* [510 U.S. 17 (1993)] that establish a hostile work environment, including frequency of the conduct, its severity, whether it is physically humiliating or threatening, and whether it interferes with the employee's ability to work.

A 1998 U.S. Supreme Court ruling further clarified the employer's liability for a hostile work environment. In *Faragher v. City of Boca Raton* [524 U.S. 775 (1998)], Beth Faragher was employed as a lifeguard by the city of Boca Raton, Florida. The court found that during their employment Faragher and another woman were subjected to uninvited and offensive conduct by two male supervisors, which included touching the women's buttocks, rubbing against them, and making demeaning and offensive comments to all the female lifeguards. Neither of the women complained to management about their supervisors' conduct while they were employed or when they resigned. Faragher later sued the city and the two supervisors for sexual harassment based on a hostile work environment. Reversing earlier court decisions, the Supreme Court ruled that a former employee could sue her employer even though she had never complained to senior management of harassing behaviors.

In 2001, the Supreme Court ruled that an isolated sexual remark does not constitute sexual harassment. In *Clark County School District v. Breeden* [533 U.S. 912 (2001)], Breeden was employed as a school administrator. In one discussion with her supervisor and her subordinate, both male, a sexual remark was made in regard to an applicant for employment, and both men laughed. Breeden later complained to her supervisor that the men's behavior had offended her. She then claimed that her supervisor began treating her more harshly, transferred her first to a position with less authority and then, after she filed sexual harassment and retaliation claims with the school district, to a clerical position several miles away from the main office. Her salary and benefits remained the same. At the original trial, her lawsuit was dismissed, but on appeal it was reinstated. The Supreme Court reversed the court of appeals, finding that "no reasonable person could have believed that the single incident recounted [by the plaintiff] violated Title VII's standard."

In a recent ruling by the Seventh Circuit, the court held that a hostile work environment may be created by comments that were sexist, as opposed to sexual, in nature. In *Boumehdi v. Plastag Holdings, LLC*, No.

06-4061 (7th Cir. June 4, 2007), a female press operator was allegedly subject to multiple sexist comments by her supervisor. Following her complaints to her employer, she allegedly experienced a number of retaliatory actions (a negative performance review and frequent payroll shortages). The frequency of the comments, subsequent actions, and failure of the employer to intervene were enough to support the hostile environment claim.

[B] Quid Pro Quo Harassment

The other type of harassment the courts have recognized is quid pro quo harassment. This may be the most commonly understood type of harassment, in which unwanted conduct affects or may be perceived to affect the terms or conditions of a person's employment (e.g., exchanging a promotion or job benefit for sexual favors). The nature of this type of harassment requires that the harasser be a supervisor or another person in the organizational structure in a position to provide or deny a benefit, change the conditions of employment, or otherwise have the power to affect the victim's job.

For example, in *Dirksen v. City of Springfield* [842 F. Supp. 1117 (C.D. Ill. 1994)], the plaintiff sued her former supervisor, the chief of police, for quid pro quo and hostile work environment sexual harassment. In addition to these more "traditional" forms of harassment, the plaintiff claimed that her boss discriminated against her when he demoted her in favor of another female employee who did submit to his sexual advances. Although the employer argued that these actions were not illegal discrimination, the court held that the plaintiff's demotion was a result of refusing her boss's sexual demands.

In November 1994, the Ninth Circuit Court of Appeals held that a supervisor who discussed employment-related topics, like performance appraisal or sick leave, with an employee shortly before asking her to perform oral sex had engaged in quid pro quo sexual harassment, which is prohibited by Title VII of the Civil Rights Act. Further, the court held that the employer, the U.S. Postal Service, was strictly liable for the supervisor's conduct. In legal analysis, the court found that although the supervisor made no explicit demand for sexual activity for the employee to keep her job, in this case, the "discussion of work related matters and his requests for oral sex were so close [in time] that there can be no doubt that a reasonable person in [the employee's] position would have understood that [the supervisor] was conditioning the granting of job benefits on the performance of oral sex."

[C] Forms of Actionable Conduct

Under the EEOC's definition, for alleged conduct to constitute sexual harassment, it must be sexual in nature and unwelcome. The following verbal and physical behaviors have been interpreted by the courts to be sexual harassment:

- Improper questions about a worker's private life (e.g., sexual life)

- Discriminatory ridicule or insults

- Undesired, intentional touching (e.g., embracing, patting, or pinching)

- Attempted or actual sexual assault or threat of rape

- Offensive gestures

- Repeated sexual comments or obscene and suggestive remarks that are objectionable to the recipient

- Offers of employment conditions in exchange for sexual favors or threats of reprisals for refusing sexual advances

- Offensive sexual jokes and posters in the workplace (Telling sexual jokes does not necessarily constitute sexual harassment. However, if other employees complain that the jokes are offensive, the jokes may be said to contribute to a hostile or offensive work environment and should be stopped. Similarly, pornographic or sexually explicit photographs, posters, graffiti, or calendars should be removed from the workplace.)

- Requiring employees to wear revealing or suggestive uniforms or costumes

When any of the above behavior occurs off-site at work-related social events, courts may also consider it sexual harassment.

§ 21.03   THE LAW AND SEXUAL HARASSMENT

Understanding the legal issues involved in sexual harassment gives employers and employees a better sense of their obligations as well as their rights. The principal legislation on the subject is the Civil Rights Act of 1964.

[A]   The Civil Rights Act of 1964

Sexual harassment was declared illegal on the basis of language in the Civil Rights Act of 1964, as amended by the Equal Employment Opportunity Act of 1972. Although it prohibits discrimination in employment on the basis of race, color, religion, national origin, and sex, the Civil Rights Act of 1964 says nothing about sexual harassment. Section 703(a) of Title VII of the act deals with sex discrimination:

It shall be an unlawful employment practice for an employer:

(1) To fail or refuse to hire or to discharge any individual, or otherwise to discriminate against any individual with respect to his compensation, terms, conditions, or privileges of employment, because of such individual's race, color, religion, sex, or national origin; or

(2) To limit, segregate, or classify employees in any way which would deprive or tend to deprive any individual of employment opportunities or otherwise adversely affect his status as an employee because of such individual's race, color, religion, sex, or national origin.

On the basis of Section 703(a), the argument can be made that sexual harassment is, in fact, sex discrimination: were it not for the sex of the victim, the conduct in question would not have taken place. This is partly why a female victim's male coworkers may be interrogated in court to determine whether they have been sexually harassed. If they have, the case does not fall under Title VII because the victim's sex was not the cause of the differential treatment: males and females were treated the same. In such a case, other claims could be filed, but not under Title VII.

Although the federal courts have recently been finding that sexual harassment is a form of sex discrimination, and the Supreme Court did so in 1986, historically the courts tended to do so only in cases that were examples of flagrant sexual harassment. In fact, the earliest cases that asserted that sexual harassment was a form of sex discrimination were lost.

[B] Legal Evolution of Sexual Harassment

Some of the early sexual harassment cases show the varying interpretations of the law, as well as the gradual yet pronounced change in the direction and impact of the legal rulings over a relatively short period of time.

Tomkins v. Public Service Electric & Gas Co. [568 F.2d 1044 (3d Cir. 1977)] was based on the female plaintiff's complaint that she was sexually assaulted by her male supervisor and was threatened with demotion and even layoff when she tried to stop the behavior in question. In this case, the court referenced Title VII and ruled: "It is not intended to provide a federal tort remedy for what amounts to physical attacks motivated by sexual desire on the part of the supervisor and which happens to occur in a corporate corridor rather than in a back alley."

At the time, the courts typically found that sexually oriented behavior was motivated by individual needs and predilections and, as a result, was not covered under Title VII.

By 1977, the orientation of the courts was starting to change. When the *Tomkins* case was appealed, the original ruling was reversed. The appeals court found that the lower court failed to consider adequately the fact that Tomkins's employer had tolerated the supervisor's sexual behavior so that acquiescence to the supervisor's demands became a prerequisite for continued employment and advancement within the organization. In essence, the court indicated that Title VII did pertain in this case because a condition of employment was imposed on a basis that discriminated by sex. The court even added that once an employer becomes aware of such sexual harassment in the organization, the employer must take "prompt and appropriate remedial action after acquiring such knowledge or be held liable."

By 1978, the courts were generally finding that sexual harassment was a form of sex discrimination and therefore fell within the coverage of Title VII; the appeals courts were reversing many earlier decisions by lower courts, which had determined that such harassment was not sex discrimination. However, no court had interpreted the phrase "terms, conditions, or privileges of employment" to include intangible job injuries, such as the extent to which the harassment made the work environment more hostile, threatening, or stressful.

In the early 1980s a new concept was introduced: work environment harassment. This concept expanded the legal definition of sexual harassment to include intangible terms and conditions of employment, such as making the work environment more stressful, intimidating, or offensive.

The landmark case dealing with this issue is *Bundy v. Jackson* [205 U.S. App. D.C. 444 (1981)]. In this case, the U.S. Court of Appeals reversed the district court, which had found that making unwanted sexual advances toward females was essentially a normal condition of employment. The appeals court held that a plaintiff need not demonstrate the loss of a tangible employment benefit resulting from sexual harassment in order to have Title VII protection. This court indicated that the conditions of employment include the "psychological and emotional work environment." The court extended the coverage of Title VII to include sexual harassment situations in which no tangible employment injury existed.

Then, in June 1986, the Supreme Court confirmed in *Meritor Savings Bank, FSB v. Vinson* [477 U.S. 57, 72 (1996)] that sexual harassment is a cause of action under Title VII, regardless of whether it is quid pro quo or hostile environment harassment. In terms of hostile environment, the Court ruled that the victim need not suffer an economic loss, but the harassment must be pervasive enough to alter working conditions and create an abusive environment. In addition, the Court ruled that even if an individual voluntarily engages in sexual relations with a supervisor, there can be actionable harassment if the conduct of the alleged harasser was unwelcome.

In June 1988, in *Broderick v. Ruder* [685 F. Supp. 1269 (D.D.C. 1998)], the U.S. District Court for the District of Columbia went a step further in the definition of hostile environment sexual harassment by holding that an employee need not be the direct target of sexual harassment in a claim of hostile environment harassment. Ms. Broderick, an attorney with the Securities and Exchange Commission (SEC), claimed that the prevalence of sexual harassment in her office created offensive and inhospitable working conditions for her. The work environment at the SEC was described as being like a brothel, with preferential treatment for employees who submitted to the sexual demands of some of the senior attorneys. The court awarded Ms. Broderick three promotions, retroactive pay plus interest, and the removal of all negative evaluations from her file. In addition, the SEC was ordered to put an end to the sexually hostile work environment.

[C]   Same-Sex Harassment

In March 1998, the U.S. Supreme Court ruled in *Oncale v. Sundowner Offshore Services* [523 U.S. 75, 82 (1998)] that same-sex harassment is covered under Title VII prohibiting discrimination based on sex. The case involved Joseph Oncale, employed by Sundowner Offshore Services as a roustabout on an eight-man crew stationed on an oil platform in the Gulf of Mexico. On several occasions, Oncale was forcibly subjected by two men with supervisory authority over him to sex-related, humiliating actions against him in the presence of the rest of the crew. The two supervisors also physically assaulted Oncale in a sexual manner, and one of the supervisors threatened him with rape. Oncale's complaints to supervisory personnel produced no remedial action, and Oncale eventually quit, stating that he was leaving because of sexual harassment and verbal abuse. In his deposition he stated that he feared if he did not leave, he would be raped or forced to have sex.

The Supreme Court contended in this case that while the original intent of Title VII was to cover sexual harassment between males and females, the same protection should be extended to cases of same-sex harassment where the case meets the statutory requirements. Behavior that meets statutory requirements includes:

> Behavior so objectively offensive as to alter the "conditions" of the victim's employment. Conduct that is severe or pervasive enough to create an objectively hostile or abusive work environment—an environment that a reasonable person would find hostile or abusive.

In other words, one should not mistake ordinary socializing in the workplace such as male-on-male horseplay or intersexual flirtation for discriminatory "conditions of employment."

The Seventh Circuit relied on *Oncale* in *Spearman v. Ford Motor Co.* [231 F.3d 1080 (7th Cir. 2000)]. Spearman, a gay African-American autoworker, was harassed and subjected to animosity in the workplace. He was taunted with racist comments, which continued after he filed a complaint. He sued Ford Motor Company for sexual harassment and sex discrimination. The U.S. Court of Appeals for the Seventh Circuit held the employee could not sue because "Congress intended the term 'sex' to mean 'biological male or biological female,' and not one's sexuality or sexual orientation."

In rejecting the employee's claims, the appeals court relied on the *Oncale* case, stating, "Title VII is not a general civility code for the workplace." Inasmuch as the civil rights law prohibits harassment because of an employee's sex, same-sex harassment is actionable only when it occurs because of the plaintiff's sex. In this case, those requirements were not met. The employee's harassers used sexually explicit, vulgar insults to express their anger at him over work-related conflicts. However, the harassment did not arise because the employee was a man.

[D] State Provisions

A number of states have laws that address sexual harassment. These laws vary from state to state. Employers must be familiar with the laws in their states and the implications of these laws.

In many states, sexual harassment victims may also use the state court system, claiming a violation of state fair employment laws. Depending on the state, the sexual harassment victim may be awarded back pay and other make-whole relief, legal fees, and compensatory and punitive damages. There is no jury in suits heard under Title VII, but plaintiffs are entitled to a jury trial under statutes in a number of states.

The victim of sexual harassment may also file a lawsuit directly against the harasser or employer, or both. The suit may be based on breach of contract or on tort law. (A tort is a wrongful act on which the victim can take civil action.) The outcomes in these suits can include not only actual damages but also compensatory damages for pain and suffering as well as economic loss. In addition, tort remedies may include punitive damages that can amount to far more than actual or compensatory damages. Depending on the specific harassment and its impact, victims may sue for such torts as intentional infliction of emotional distress and wrongful termination.

[E] Criminal Suits

Extreme forms of sexual harassment may result in the harasser's being charged with a criminal offense. The kinds of harassment that fall under the criminal statutes include assault and battery, rape, and attempted rape. In most cases, employers have no direct liability under the criminal statutes, but the employer may still be exposed to civil liability through failure to provide a safe work environment.

§ 21.04 HOW COMMON IS SEXUAL HARASSMENT?

All kinds of myths surround the causes of sexual harassment. Perhaps the most damaging is that it is somehow caused by the victims, particularly in terms of male harassment of females. The mythologists contend that something about the potential victim's actions, behavior, or general appearance causes males to sexually harass her. In their scenario, it is the victim's fault. To the contrary, no evidence proves that victims cause the harassment.

Another myth is that the victims tend to be young, attractive, and single. On the contrary, studies show that there is no relationship between sexual harassment and the victim's appearance, age, race, ethnic background, occupation, job level, marital status, or any other factor.

The EEOC has maintained statistics on sexual harassment charges since 1992. There was a large increase in charges filed between 1992, when 10,532 charges were filed, and 1995, when 15,549 charges were filed. Over the next six years, the number remained fairly consistent—between 15,222 and 15,889. Since 2002, the number of charges has dropped almost every year. In 2007, 12,510 charges were filed. Complaints filed by males have increased steadily since 1992. In 2007, 16.0 percent of all sexual harassment charges were filed by males, compared to 9.1 percent in 1992. Monetary benefits have remained close to $50 million each year since 1999, with the exception of 2004, when they dipped to $37.1 million. Benefits paid in 2007 were $49.9 million. These amounts are for settlements only—they do *not* include benefits obtained through litigation.

It may be that teenagers are at particular risk. A study conducted by Susan Fineran of the University of South Maine in 2002 indicated that 35 percent of part-time high school workers had been sexually harassed on the job. Further research by Susan Fineran and James Gruber of the University of Michigan-Dearborn in 2006 showed that 46.8 percent of female working students had been sexually harassed during the previous year.

There are a number of factors that may contribute to the high numbers of teens who have experienced harassment. They are new to the workforce, and may not know what "normal" behavior should be at work. They may not have received proper training in recognizing harassment when it occurs or what avenues of reporting or relief are available to them. Employers should make sure that all their workers, even part-time temporary workers, are well informed of their rights and obligations regarding sexual harassment.

§ 21.05   SOURCES OF EMPLOYER LIABILITY

Under Title VII, an employer, employment agency, joint apprenticeship committee, or labor organization (hereinafter collectively referred to as "employer") is responsible for its acts and those of its agents and supervisory employees with respect to sexual harassment. The employer is responsible, regardless of whether the specific acts were authorized or even forbidden by the employer and regardless of whether the employer knew or should have known of their occurrence. The courts examine the circumstances of the particular employment relationship and the job functions performed by the individual in determining whether an individual acts in either a supervisory or agency capacity.

In cases of sexual harassment, the courts compare the severity of the sexual harassment to the timeliness and thoroughness of the employer's investigation and appropriateness of its response. This standard can be used as a guide in responding to the complaint and taking appropriate action. The primary factors to consider in taking "appropriate action" will probably be the severity and frequency of the conduct and its effect on the harassed employee.

When employment opportunities or benefits are granted because of an individual's submission to the employer's sexual advances or requests for sexual favors, the employer may be held liable for unlawful sex discrimination against other persons who were qualified for but were denied that employment opportunity or benefit.

In *Burlington Industries Inc. v. Ellerth* [524 U.S. 742 (1998)] and *Faragher v. City of Boca Raton* [524 U.S. 775 (1998)], the U.S. Supreme Court decided that employers can be held liable for their supervisors' harassment of subordinates. Before the *Ellerth* and *Faragher* decisions, courts around the country differed as to whether an employer would be liable where there had not been any adverse employment action taken against the person claiming harassment. Now, the law specifically states that when the supervisor's harassment results in a "tangible employment action" against the subordinate (e.g., discharge, demotion, or undesirable reassignment), the employer's liability is absolute, and the employer will not have the opportunity to raise affirmative defenses. If the harassment has not resulted in negative employment action against the subordinate, then the employer may defend itself as to liability or damages.

In both *Ellerth* and *Faragher,* the Supreme Court held that when a tangible employment action is taken against the person claiming harassment, the employer will be held liable for the supervisor's actions, even if the alleged victim had not made anyone aware of his or her complaints. In *Ellerth,* the plaintiff's claim involved only unfulfilled threats—the plaintiff refused the unwelcome sexual advances of her supervisor, yet she did not suffer any adverse employment action as the result of her refusals. The Supreme Court held that where the plaintiff-employee has not suffered any tangible employment action, the defendant-employer may raise an affirmative defense to liability or damages.

In 2004, the Supreme Court expanded on the *Ellerth* and *Faragher* decisions by allowing the employers to raise an affirmative defense in the case of a constructive discharge. In *Pennsylvania State Police v. Nancy Drew Suders* [124 S. Ct. 2342 (2004)], the lower courts held that a constructive discharge—where the employee quits because the workplace environment is so intolerable—constituted a "tangible employment action." As such, the employer is strictly liable for the actions of the supervisor. The Supreme Court disagreed with this decision and held that the constructive discharge "may or may not" be a tangible action, depending on whether the hostile environment that caused the employee to quit was a result of the employer's official actions as opposed to the result of coworkers' or unofficial supervisory conduct.

In general, the courts have held that an employer will not be strictly liable when the employee does not suffer a tangible employment action, as long as (1) the employer has exercised reasonable care to prevent and correct the harassment, and (2) the employee unreasonably failed to take advantage of corrective opportunities. A 2007 case highlights the fact that both factors must be in place to avoid strict liability. In *Craig v. M&O Agencies*, [496 F.3d 1047 (9th Cir. 2007)] Ms. Craig was subject to repeated inappropriate and unwelcome sexual comments by her supervisor, Mr. Byrd, the Branch Manager and interim President of the company. At one point he followed her into the women's restroom, grabbed and kissed her. She reported the incident 19 days later, following the company's proper complaint procedure. Ms. Craig was reassigned to another supervisor, and Mr. Byrd was reprimanded and provided with sexual harassment training. One month later, with his training completed, Ms. Craig was again put under the authority of Mr. Byrd. Ms. Craig claimed that he retaliated against her by keeping work-related information from her. Eventually, Ms. Craig resigned and filed a sexual harassment claim. The company moved for summary judgment, claiming that they had responded immediately to correct the harassment, and the employee had "unreasonably failed to take advantage of corrective opportunities" by waiting 19 days to report the bathroom incident. The 9th Circuit determined that the company could not avoid liability at the summary judgment stage, as Ms. Craig's action of waiting 19 days was not unreasonable.

When sexual harassment is so pervasive that a hostile work environment exists, an employer is liable even if no economic harm results, if it knew or should have known about the harassment. A hostile environment can be created by supervisors, coworkers, or even nonemployees, such as customers.

Failure to investigate claims promptly and thoroughly and to take sufficient remedial action to eliminate the harassment can amount to constructive discharge if the harassed employee quits—leading to higher damage awards for victims not only under federal law but under state statutes as well. In addition, employers must ensure that there is no retaliation against the complainant, even if the claim does not prove actionable under Title VII.

[A] Harassment by Nonemployees

An employee may be sexually harassed by a nonemployee of the company. This form of harassment, known as third-party sexual harassment, may come from customers, vendors, consultants, or others who do business with the company.

Employer liability is created when the employer, or its agents or supervisory employees, knows or should have known of the conduct and fails to take immediate and appropriate corrective action. In reviewing these cases, the court considers the extent of the employer's control and any other legal responsibility that the employer may have with respect to the conduct of such nonemployees.

The EEOC regulations list three key factors to evaluate when determining employer liability for harassment by a nonemployee: (1) whether the employer knew or should have known about the conduct, (2) whether the employer took immediate and appropriate corrective action, and (3) the extent of the employer's control and legal responsibility for the nonemployee harasser.

Although the courts must apply and further define these factors in the context of sexual harassment by nonemployees, past decisions on sexual harassment among employees provide some basis for predicting sexual harassment by nonemployees and raise questions that have yet to be answered by either the courts or the EEOC.

[B] The Judge's Instructions to the Jury

Employers and those who choose to harass should understand how, in gender discrimination or sexual harassment cases, the judge instructs the jury. A plaintiff has alleged that he or she has been forced to work in a hostile work environment because of sexual harassment. To prevail on such a theory, the plaintiff must prove that sexual harassment in the workplace was so severe or pervasive as to alter the conditions of employment and create an abusive working environment, and that he or she was subjectively offended by the harassing conduct. Conduct that merely involves offensive utterances, or conduct that may be harassing but not sexual in nature or based on gender, does not constitute sexual harassment.

In evaluating hostile environment sexual harassment claims, the employer must consider the following factors:

- The total physical environment of the plaintiff's work area

- The degree and type of sexual conduct in the workplace, both before and after the plaintiff arrived

- The reasonable expectations of the plaintiff upon entering the environment

- The nature of the unwelcome sexual acts or words

- The frequency of the offensive encounters

- The severity of the conduct

- The context in which the sexual harassment occurred

- Whether the conduct was unwelcome (i.e., whether the plaintiff was an instigator or willing participant in the conduct)

- The effect of the conduct on the plaintiff's psychological well-being

- Whether the conduct was physically threatening

- Whether the conduct unreasonably interfered with the plaintiff's work performance

- Whether the plaintiff was subjectively offended by the conduct

[C] The Reasonable Person Standard

In determining whether a hostile work environment exists as a result of sexual harassment, the employer must consider the evidence from the perspective of a reasonable person's reaction to a similar environment under similar circumstances, not from the perspective of an overly sensitive person.

The court has grappled with defining the standard by which sexual harassment is judged. Three cases have established the definition thus far.

In the first case, a female employee stated a prima facie case of hostile environment sexual harassment when she alleged conduct that a ''reasonable woman'' would consider sufficiently severe or pervasive to alter the conditions of employment and create an abusive work environment. [Ellison v. Brady, 924 F.2d 8712 (9th Cir. 1991)]

In the second case, the court looked to the ''totality of the circumstances'' in its determination. [Fisher v. San Pedro Peninsula Hosp., 214 Cal. App. 3d 590 (1989)] The totality of the circumstances includes the nature of the acts, the frequency, the total time period, and the context.

The above analysis has been somewhat undercut, however, by a subsequent Supreme Court case that relies on a ''reasonable person'' standard. [Harris v. Forklift Sys., Inc., 510 U.S. 17 (1993)]

[D] The ''Reasonableness'' of Complaint Procedures

A recent case highlights the importance of making the company's complaint procedure clear to all employees. A 16-year-old female employee of a fast-food restaurant who was harassed by her 35-year-old male supervisor complained a number of times to other supervisors and managers in the store. She asked for a company phone number so she could make a complaint, and the number she was given was an incorrect number. Shortly after she refused the advances of her supervisor, he fired her. The company claimed they were not liable for sexual harassment because the female employee had not used the proper complaint procedure, and the district court agreed. However, the 7th Circuit reversed the district court's decision, stating that the company had an obligation to make the procedure understandable to the employees. Because the chain had a large number of teenage employees, the company was ''obligated to suit its procedures to the understanding of the average teenager.'' [EEOC v. V & J Foods, Inc., 507 F.3d 575 (7th Cir. 2007)]

§ 21.06   DAMAGES AND AWARDS

The term *employer liability* is often used loosely in discussions of sexual harassment. Most people have only an abstract notion of its meaning until a price tag is put on it. Over the past few years, judges, juries, state agencies, and out-of-court settlements have done just that, and the price has not been cheap. Additionally, turnover, insurance claims, sick leave, and lost productivity directly associated with sexual harassment cost employers millions each year.

Under Title VII, the harassment victim is entitled to actual damages—that is, to be made whole by receiving any promotions, back pay, or benefits that were lost as a result of the harassment. The victim can also receive injunctive relief ordering the employer to stop the harassment in question and to take specific steps to prevent it in the future. Attorneys' fees are also typically granted in these cases. However, when victimized by sexual harassment, employees have a number of legal options other than filing a claim under Title VII. The outcomes associated with these options can vary greatly.

Substantial amounts of money have also been awarded to employees who have been sexually harassed at work. In *Kimzey v. Wal-Mart Stores, Inc.* [107 F.3d 568 (8th Cir. 1997)], the court awarded the plaintiff $350,000 in punitive damages related to a hostile work environment claim. In this case, the plaintiff's supervisor and assistant store manager repeatedly made sexual remarks to the plaintiff and kicked, screamed at, and swore at her and other women. Although the plaintiff complained to Wal-Mart management several times, no action was taken. Finally, the plaintiff quit, citing the harassment conduct and management's indifference as her reasons for leaving. The jury awarded the plaintiff $50 million in damages, but the court eventually reduced the amount to $350,000, finding the penalty excessive because the harassment was not egregious, Wal-Mart Stores did have a policy against sexual harassment, and no one outside the plaintiff's store was aware of the harassment.

Although the amounts awarded in sexual harassment cases can vary widely, a number of recent cases have resulted in million dollar plus awards to plaintiffs. In *EEOC v. Rio Bravo International, Inc.* [No. 99-1371-CIV-T-17A (M.D. Fla. 2003)], an assistant manager created a hostile work environment by both physically touching and making offensive sexual remarks to female employees. Even after hearing complaints, the company failed to take corrective action. The court awarded five female employees $1.55 million. In *Pollard v. E.I. DuPont de Nemours & Co.* [No. 95-3010 Mlv, 2004 U.S. Dist. LEXIS 6345 (W.D. Tenn. Feb. 24, 2004)], the plaintiff, Sharon Pollard, was awarded almost $2 million after having endured eight years in a hostile work environment created by coworkers during which time her complaints were ignored by her employer.

These cases clearly demonstrate that an employer's potential dollar liability from sexual harassment claims can be considerable. Monetary liability, moreover, extends beyond the direct cost of judgments and settlements into hidden costs such as loss of goodwill, employee dissatisfaction, absenteeism, and potential loss of customers.

[A]   Litigation and Agency Proceedings

Substantial costs can result when an organization is named as a defendant in a sexual harassment suit, regardless of any ultimate rulings. These include such direct costs as legal fees, reproduction of documents, and possibly overtime for employees who carry out work related to the case or complete assignments that were delayed because of it. Indirect costs include the decline in productivity when employees cannot complete their regular assignments because they are working on various aspects of the lawsuit or claim.

[B] Employee Dissatisfaction and Unrest

A decline in job satisfaction can extend well beyond the victim; other employees can also experience job dissatisfaction as a result of the harasser's actions. For example, coworkers may be afraid that they, too, will be victims, may fear retaliation if they try to help the victim, and may suffer stress and anxiety if they perceive that they cannot help. All of this undermines coworker satisfaction on the job and may also become the basis for additional claims of sexual harassment because of the hostile and offensive work environment.

Many employees are distressed that sexual harassment is allowed to exist in the organization in the first place. For them, intentional or inadvertent tolerance of sexual harassment sends several messages: the rights of the employees do not mean a great deal to the organization; the law can be selectively interpreted and discarded at will; individual feelings, needs, emotions, and even careers are of secondary importance; employees are viewed as expendable rather than as significant resources within the organization; and, if employees can be sexually harassed, other kinds of harassment and discrimination may also be tolerated within the organization.

[1] Absenteeism

Sexual harassment can raise the level of job dissatisfaction to the point that staying away from work becomes more satisfying than going to work, regardless of the economic consequences. Sexual harassment can also contribute significantly to the probability of a victim's becoming physically ill or having an accident, both of which result in increased absenteeism. When this occurs, those employees who do come to work often become increasingly dissatisfied because of the additional workload and pressures placed on them. As these employees' dissatisfaction grows, absenteeism may increase even more.

[2] Turnover

A second result of job dissatisfaction is turnover. When the level of dissatisfaction becomes too great, employees withdraw and find more satisfying jobs.

[C] Disruption of the Workplace

Sexual harassment can have a negative impact on the overall atmosphere within an organization. Certainly the nature and extent of the harassment and the size and configuration of the organization may be initial limiting factors. Sexual harassment, however, can adversely affect the atmosphere and working conditions of the department in which it occurs, and it does not take many incidents of sexual harassment for the negative impact to spread beyond a given work area or department.

A common employee reaction to such working conditions is to lose respect for the organization and perceive that it is harmful, dangerous, untrustworthy, and even destructive. These feelings can elicit a broad range of additional negative responses from the employees such as significant decreases in employee motivation, commitment, loyalty, concern for the work per se, willingness to put forth the required effort (let alone any extra effort), and less adherence to the basic standards and policies of the organization.

[D] Pressure to Unionize

If harassment occurs in a nonunion environment and employees feel that they cannot do anything about it, employee interest in a union may increase. Union organizers can easily contend that employees need a strong and powerful voice to be heard by management and that the union can get results when the employees have previously failed. Sexual harassment will not always lead to a union organizing effort, but it can play a definite role, particularly if the lack of response to harassment fits into an overall pattern of management's lack of communication, interest, concern, and responsiveness to employees and their other concerns.

[E] Insurance Issues

Actions taken by the victims of sexual harassment can also adversely affect the organization's insurance rating and lead to increased premiums. Employees in a number of states are eligible for unemployment benefits if they quit because of sexual harassment. Such a claim, once verified by the appropriate state agency, typically causes an increase in the unemployment insurance premiums that an organization must pay.

In addition, sexual harassment can contribute to illness and even accidents. As a result, it can increase the number of hospital and medical insurance claims, thereby increasing the company's health care insurance premiums.

[F] Decreased Productivity

Sexual harassment interferes with individual and organizational productivity in a broad way. Productivity is simply the ratio between the amount of output, such as goods and services produced, and the amount of input, such as the hours allocated to produce such goods and services. To the extent that sexual harassment interferes with this input or output, productivity suffers.

Many sexual harassment victims lose time from work, partly because of illness and partly because of a conscious attempt to avoid the problems associated with harassment on the job. As a result, the victim puts fewer hours into his or her job assignments, with the resultant decline in output or productivity.

A victim's productivity is further diminished when he or she must rely upon the harasser to fulfill job responsibilities. If the harasser is in a position to control access to information, resources, or people that the victim needs, the victim may be reluctant to approach the harasser when such resources should be used.

Time is also wasted in harassment itself. Productivity further declines when the victim fails to complete job assignments or provide needed information. The quality of the final product is likely to suffer.

As with any system, problems in one part of an organization have an impact on many other parts. In light of this, if a harassed employee misses a good deal of work, misses deadlines, or produces substandard work, employees or departments that rely on such work can encounter a wide range of problems, including delays, missed deadlines of their own, confusion, and difficulties with the departments with which they deal. All of this leads to decreased organizational productivity.

One incident of sexual harassment will not bring an organization to a grinding halt, but the productivity problems associated with sexual harassment can extend far beyond the direct victims. There is no automatic way to increase productivity, but sexual harassment can certainly decrease it.

[G] Loss of Goodwill

Goodwill is an abstract and intangible aspect of an organization's worth, reflecting such factors as reputation, image, code of ethics, and overall mode of operating. It tends to be the result of an organization's past practices and history and the track record established in relation to employees, customers, suppliers, and the public at large. Although the value of an organization's goodwill can be debated, one point is clear: goodwill can decrease as a result of sexual harassment. When an organization has sexual harassment problems, any number of undesirable outcomes are possible:

- The employees may discuss it in public.

- Publicity may be associated with any hearings, trials, judgments, or settlements.

- The victim may take steps to publicize the case.

- Various equal rights groups may become involved.

- There may be considerable media attention.

These developments, whether occurring singly or in combination, tend to bring an organization negative publicity.

§ 21.07 STRATEGIES TO PREVENT OR ELIMINATE SEXUAL HARASSMENT

Prevention is the best tool. An employer should take all steps necessary to prevent sexual harassment from occurring, such as affirmatively raising the subject, expressing strong disapproval, developing appropriate sanctions, informing employees of their right to raise and how to raise the issue of harassment under Title VII, and developing methods to sensitize all concerned.

In a 1986 decision, the U.S. Supreme Court indicated that employers should have a specific policy addressing sexual harassment, not just an antidiscrimination policy. Some states have legislated similar provisions.

The EEOC clearly views sexual harassment as a form of sex discrimination and therefore places an obligation on employers to maintain an environment free of it, not only on a reactive basis but on a preventive basis as well. Whether liability can be reduced often depends on the employer's actions once it becomes aware of the harassment. Claims should be investigated promptly and thoroughly, and sufficient remedial action should be taken to eliminate the harassment. The rights of the accused harasser must also be protected.

Employers are expected to implement proactively a wide range of policies, procedures, sanctions, and training to provide employees at all levels with a thorough understanding of the issue and the steps to take to address harassment. Fear of reprisal often deters women from reporting incidents of sexual harassment, so managers must promote an atmosphere that allows employees to "feel safe" in reporting incidents. This is best accomplished through strict enforcement of company policies regarding inappropriate behaviors and by providing ample communication options and opportunities.

It is true that if a supervisor's harassment results in a "tangible employment action" against a subordinate, the employer's liability is absolute. However, if the harassment has not resulted in negative employment action against the subordinate, then the employer may defend itself as to liability or damages. The employer's defense can include the following:

- The employer exercised reasonable care to prevent and promptly correct any sexually harassing behavior.

- The plaintiff-employee unreasonably failed to take advantage of any preventive or corrective opportunities provided by the employer or failed to avoid harm otherwise.

It follows that it is prudent for employers to take preventive actions to build a legal defense should it be necessary.

In cases involving harassment by a nonemployee, some situations seem easier to deal with than others. For example, if a photocopier repair person harasses one of your employees, management can call the vendor and tell it to remove the person from the company's account.

Other situations may be less comfortable to deal with. It is very possible for third-party liability to be created by a customer's acting inappropriately. For example, it is not difficult to imagine a situation where a female employee is being harassed in a sexually explicit way by a male customer. This situation must be dealt with as seriously as if the customer were employed by the company.

Customer harassment must not be minimized. Nor should any employee be instructed to "just ignore it" based on the source of the harassment. Either response—in fact, any response other than prompt and deliberate action to investigate and stop the offensive behavior—creates a serious potential liability for the employer.

Following the proper steps to prevent, investigate, and promptly deal with any harassment can provide an affirmative defense for employers. In *Hardage v. CBS Broadcasting, Inc.* [03-35906, 9th Cir. (Nov. 1, 2005)], the employee reported harassment by his supervisor to the employer. The human resources representative followed up with him twice, offering to talk to the supervisor and keep his identity anonymous. Both times the employee asked human resources not to do anything. Five months later, the employee quit the company and filed a claim of hostile work environment. The trial court found that the employer had exercised reasonable care to prevent harassment by adopting a policy and promoted awareness of that policy. In addition, the employee had unreasonably failed to utilize the corrective measures available to him. It should be noted that in a dissenting opinion, Judge Paez argued that the employer had an obligation to investigate, despite the employee's request not to intervene. Future cases will undoubtedly explore the employer's responsibility under Title VII to "adequately investigate and take prompt corrective action reasonably calculated to end the harassing behavior."

[A] Establishing a Program

For an organization establishing a harassment awareness and prevention program, the most logical place to begin is the EEOC's "Guidelines on Discrimination Because of Sex," issued in 1980. These guidelines provide a framework for dealing with sexual harassment. The EEOC's five strategic steps are:

1. Obtain top-management support.

2. Clearly define and enforce policies and procedures.

3. Establish multiple channels of communication.

4. Institute broad-based formalized training.

5. Practice continuous evaluation and updating.

The advantages of implementing a program include the following:

- The incidence of sexual harassment will very likely be reduced.

- The employer will be well positioned to take prompt and appropriate corrective action, as has been called for not only in the EEOC guidelines but also in various court rulings and state laws.

- Sexual harassment victims will be far more inclined to have their claims handled within the organization than to go immediately to an attorney or outside agency.

- If a claim does go to court or to an outside agency, there is a good chance the organization will not be found liable.

- The costs of sexual harassment are much more likely to be reduced, if not eliminated, for all parties (the victim as well as the organization).

- The organization may be perceived as a caring and safe place to work.

Although EEOC guidelines are not laws, courts often rely on them for clarification and have adopted some of the definitions and standards from the guidelines in their decisions on sexual harassment. Because the guidelines suggest what to do but not how to do it, many employers have questions about creating a workable sexual harassment prevention program. These questions may best be answered by reviewing the five strategic steps.

[B] Strategic Step 1: Top-Management Support and Commitment

As a first step in creating a program to prevent sexual harassment, employers are often advised to develop appropriate policies and sanctions. However, this may create a false sense of security. Almost all organizations have formal documented policies that are ignored, overlooked, or forgotten. The risk is that even if specific policies prohibit sexual harassment, the employer can still be held liable if they are not enforced.

The mere existence of written policies and procedures in no way guarantees that they will be followed. Policies and procedures must be functional, publicized, respected, and enforced at all levels of the organization. The extent to which any policy is followed depends on a number of basic factors:

- The history of practices related to the policy

- The extent that employees view it as fair or necessary

- Employee experiences with the policy's sanctions

- The clarity of the policy itself

A more critical factor in determining the extent to which a given policy is followed is top-management support. This does not mean merely introducing a new policy. Rather, it means a bona fide commitment on the part of top management to actively focus on the issues that necessitated the policy in the first place, a willingness to employ sanctions to enforce the policy, and a willingness to apply such sanctions to individuals at all levels of the organization.

For a sexual harassment prevention program to work, top management must be willing not only to enforce the policy, but also to personally adhere to it. If top management violates a given policy, employees receive a clear message that the policy means nothing.

HR managers can help ensure top-management support for sexual harassment policies by taking the following steps:

1. Review with members of top management the entire range of problems caused by sexual harassment, as is done with other situations that expose the organization to substantial liability.

2. Review the wide range of benefits associated with a work environment free of sexual harassment.

3. Have top management participate in developing the policy on sexual harassment.

[C] Strategic Step 2: Documented Policies and Procedures

Develop, distribute, and post a "zero tolerance" policy statement against sexual harassment. All employees should be informed of the company's policy, their rights under Title VII, and the remedies available to them.

Although the specific language of the sexual harassment policy statement must be tailored to the particular organization, certain key areas should be covered. Specifically, it should contain a definition of sexual harassment and the organization's philosophy. A useful definition of sexual harassment should be concise, easily understood, and broad enough to cover the full range of the issue. The policy on sexual harassment should contain at least a brief statement of the organization's philosophy and orientation toward the issue itself, particularly in terms of the employee's personal and legal rights. Such a statement provides a context and rationale for the policy and gives employees insight into the values, standards, and expectations of the organization.

Policy statements vary from one organization to another; they may be only a few lines long or may be considerably detailed.

A brief version of a statement might be: "It is the policy of our company to provide and maintain a work environment that is free of all forms of illegal discrimination, including sexual harassment."

A policy statement should be included in the company policy manual, and a similar statement should be included in the employee handbook. (See **Exhibit 21.3** for a sample policy on sexual harassment.) Many employers also post their policy on all company bulletin boards (electronic and physical); some states mandate this requirement.

[1] Steps for the Victim to Take

The policies describing the steps a victim should take to report harassment vary considerably from one organization to another, partly because work situations and methods of resolving conflict differ considerably. Whatever the method, it should be spelled out clearly. The victim should know exactly what to do if he or she wishes to file a complaint of sexual harassment. The policy should provide information describing how to file a complaint, with whom, under what time constraints, and in what form.

The policy should also provide information on possible outcomes, the time it will take to investigate, the means of appeal, and alternatives available to the employee. Any policy on sexual harassment should also contain a clear statement that reprisal or retaliation against potential victims who attempt to use any of the mechanisms for dealing with sexual harassment will not be tolerated. Allegations of reprisals should be processed through the same mechanisms used to handle original claims of sexual harassment because such retaliatory acts fall within the context of sexual harassment.

The following options will be helpful in developing this aspect of the policy.

[2]   The Reporting Procedure

Establish procedures for reporting sexual harassment and for seeking remedial actions. The procedure should be in writing and should be well communicated throughout the organization; it should also ensure confidentiality, include alternate methods of reporting incidents, and explain the investigative procedure.

[3]   Reporting to a Specific Individual or Alternate

Many sexual harassment policies indicate that the first step for a victim to take is to inform his or her supervisor. Unfortunately, some policies stop here. Such policies do not take into account that the supervisor may be the sexual harasser. All policies should address this possibility.

The best approach is to indicate that in such a case the employee should appeal to the supervisor's boss, the HR manager, or, in smaller organizations, directly to a vice president, the president, or general manager.

[4]   Using the Complaint Procedure

Many organizations that have complaint procedures advise employees to use them for sexual harassment complaints. An in-place complaint procedure can be useful in resolving sexual harassment complaints because employees are familiar with the procedure and believe that the proceedings are impartial.

A complaint procedure is a multistep process through which employee complaints are heard at increasingly higher levels within the organization until the problem is resolved. The first step of the complaint procedure is usually a meeting with the employee's supervisor, while the final step of most complaint procedures is arbitration or a formal hearing. Cases in which the supervisor is accused of being a harasser should enter the procedure at the second step, usually involving a more senior supervisor or a representative of the human resources department.

Some organizations have actually established an entirely separate complaint procedure for sexual harassment complaints. It functions in much the same way as a traditional complaint procedure but may be less threatening to the employee, because sexual harassment is already well understood by the individuals involved in the process. As a result, more time can be spent on the issues constituting the specific complaint, rather than dealing with the concept of sexual harassment per se.

In fact, the Supreme Court has indicated that an employer's claim of immunity from liability would be strengthened if the employer's policy and practices encouraged use of an internal complaint procedure and the allegedly harassed employee failed to use the procedure. A separate complaint procedure for sexual harassment claims does just that.

[5] Conducting an Investigation

Take all sexual harassment complaints seriously and treat complainants with dignity and respect, investigating allegations immediately, thoroughly, and fairly, while consistently applying disciplinary sanctions to offending employees. Sanctions may include warning, suspension, demotion, transfer, or termination. Prompt action can considerably reduce the employer's liability.

[6] Who Should Investigate

The size and structure of an organization typically determine who will conduct the investigation (e.g., a manager, supervisor, HR specialist, or outside investigator). In some organizations, the HR department plays the central role in handling claims of sexual harassment. This department should have a well-defined system for processing the complaints from start to finish. The employee should be well aware of the steps to be taken. This implies that the department is clearly functioning in a professional capacity and is not perceived by members of the organization as being relegated to paper pushing and routine administrative work. If the HR department does play a central role in the organization and is respected by the employees, it may be in a unique position to effectively function as an impartial body to hear, review, and decide on claims of sexual harassment.

Some organizations designate an employee as an equal employment opportunity (EEO) advisor. This person's responsibilities include overseeing the organization's programs dealing with fair employment. The position itself may well be a focal point of an organization's policy on sexual harassment. In fact, the policy may indicate that the victim must review his or her allegation with the EEO advisor before turning to any of the other procedures available. (Again, allow for the possibility that the EEO advisor may be the harasser and include an alternative.) The policy may stipulate that the EEO advisor also function as a facilitator to settle the case, or, if necessary, as a hearing officer to adjudicate it. In light of the costs and liabilities associated with illegal discrimination, organizations of all sizes are charging one key employee with EEO duties, if not creating a full-time EEO advisor position.

[7] Investigation Process

The process of investigating sexual harassment should be spelled out in specific steps:

1. *Interview the complainant and obtain specific information about exactly what occurred (i.e., the alleged perpetrator, the behavior or actions in question, and the date, time, location, and circumstances surrounding the actions).*

2. *Obtain from the complainant the names of any witnesses, as well as any related evidence, including letters or records.* Detailed notes should be taken during the interview, and copies should be made of all related evidence. In fact, keep thorough records, document all incidents of sexual harassment in writing, and keep them in a separate file to establish a defense against future liability. The interviewer should ask the following specific questions:

   a. Who harassed you?

   b. What did he or she do? (The specifics should be gathered; generalities are not sufficient.)

    c. When did he or she do it? (The interviewer should find out if there have been repeated offenses.)

    d. Where did it happen? (On or off company property is a key fact.)

    e. What did you do and say in response? (Again, generalities are not sufficient.)

    f. Were there any witnesses? (The interviewer should try to corroborate the employee's story and be careful not to lead the witnesses.)

    g. Who else did you tell? (The EEOC asks who else knew about the alleged harassment.)

    h. Who else has been harassed? (The interviewer should find out if the employee knows of anyone else who has suffered similar harassment.)

    i. What do you want done? (The interviewer should document the answer in the event that the victim later claims that he or she requested a different action.)

    j. Would you like to see a counselor? (If the company health insurance covers counseling, or if the employer has an employee assistance program, specifically recommend that the employee use the service. If the employee refuses, document the refusal in writing.)

3. *Review any evidence that the complainant can provide, such as letters, performance records, photographs, changes in work assignments, transfers, and wage and salary data.*

4. *Interview all the witnesses using the same line of questioning used with the complainant—namely, the who, what, where, when, why, and how of the matter.*

5. *Interview other employees in the department or work area to obtain a more accurate picture of the range of the harassment and the extent to which the overall work atmosphere has been affected.*

6. *Interview the harasser and provide him or her with an opportunity to explain or defend the actions in question, as well as present any evidence.* Essentially two defense options are available to the accused harasser: either the incidents never occurred, or the actions in question were neither sexual harassment nor sex discrimination.

7. *Review all the evidence in light of the information presented by the complainant and the accused.*

8. *Determine the validity of the complainant's charges.* Again, depending on the size and structure of the organization, this can be a final determination by the individual who conducted the investigation or a preliminary determination with final judgment to be made by the HR director, a special panel, or top management.

If the claims are judged to be valid, immediate steps should also be taken to make the complainant "whole"—that is, to provide him or her with any promotions, job reinstatement, monetary increases, accurate ratings, or benefits that might have been lost as a result of the harassment.

Employees must be advised of their right to appeal the decision. The policy should name a specific individual, such as a member of top management, an outside consultant, or a senior management panel, to review all the evidence and rule on an appeal. As with the investigatory process itself, the appeal should be carried out as expeditiously as possible.

[8]   Sanctions Associated with Sexual Harassment

The policies and procedures should specify the sanctions associated with sexual harassment. Knowledge of these sanctions gives the victim some sense of security, confidence, and power in making the harassment claim in the first place. Knowledge of the sanctions is important to the supervisor or manager as well, particularly in assessing the harassing behavior and relating it to some established consequences. Since sexual harassment presents itself in many forms, the guidelines for sanctions should clearly reflect this. However, even if a "guideline" is established, management should carefully reserve the right to apply any sanction it feels is appropriate in any specific situation.

Although some organizations have policies indicating that sexual harassment may result in immediate termination, this kind of a sanction introduces the potential for liability without any knowledge of the severity of the harassment. Some forms of harassment may warrant immediate termination, whereas others may deserve only a written warning. Management needs to allow for greater flexibility in its response.

In employment-at-will states, seek legal counsel prior to issuing a defined set of sanctions.

[D]   Strategic Step 3: Two-Way Communication

The company should make its position on sexual harassment clear to all managers, supervisors, employees, suppliers, and contractors. Effective two-way communication is the cornerstone of any successful program to prevent and eliminate sexual harassment. For the program to meet its objectives, regular two-way communication is necessary from inception through implementation and ongoing administration.

Without adequate communication, employees may be unaware that their own organization even has a sexual harassment program.

Effective communication of the organization's harassment policy may include:

- *Meetings.* The issue of sexual harassment should be discussed, in part, through employee meetings. Whether sexual harassment should be the only item or one of several items discussed depends primarily on the availability of other communication channels, as well as on the extent of the sexual harassment problem within the particular organization.

- *Manuals and handbooks.* Employee manuals, if available, should thoroughly cover information and procedures related to sexual harassment. Whether in a personnel manual, administrative manual, or general policy and procedures manual, all employees in supervisory positions should be provided with descriptions of the step-by-step procedures for handling sexual harassment issues. At the same time, the general employee handbook should clearly inform employees about the specific reporting steps to take if sexual harassment occurs.

- *Posted notices.* Commonly posted notices include a statement on sexual harassment from the company president, a summary of procedures to follow if victimized by sexual harassment, printed materials from the government or appropriate agencies that describe the laws pertaining to this employee rights issue, as well as articles from newspapers or magazines.

- *The company paper or newsletter.* If the company sends regular publications to employees, these can be used to provide information on the organization's program for dealing with sexual harassment.

- *Memos.* The issue of sexual harassment can be further addressed and communicated through memos to employees. Memos can advise or update the employees on such issues as increases in cases reported, changes in the organization's policy, adjustments in the procedures, actions taken in given instances of sexual harassment, and any other new developments.

- *One-on-one communication.* In addition to the methods above, some employees may benefit from face-to-face communication. Whether done formally through counseling, disciplinary sessions, or coaching, or informally through a reminder or general discussion, this approach may help some employees to better understand the issue and adjust their own behavior accordingly.

- *Employee goal setting and performance appraisal.* The performance of employees in supervisory positions can be evaluated in part on adherence to the organization's policy on sexual harassment, orienting subordinates in this area, taking appropriate action to prevent or address sexual harassment, and taking steps to reduce the incidence of harassment in their departments. Including prevention of sexual harassment in formal supervisory objectives not only serves as an additional means of communicating the issue to supervisors, and from them to their subordinates, but can also motivate the supervisors to take direct preventive action.

- *Ad hoc communication measures.* Management can take several ad hoc measures to further improve communication on this issue. These measures are designed to remind employees of the issue itself as well as keep them up to date on the policies and procedures for dealing with it. Leaflets, pamphlets, and paycheck inserts are but a few examples. The key issue is that management should not feel limited to formal channels for communicating information regarding sexual harassment prevention policies. Rather, organizational leadership is well advised to be flexible and open to using less formal and even less conventional communication techniques.

[E]   Strategic Step 4: Formal Training

Train all supervisors and employees about the legal and other ramifications of sexual harassment, as well as their rights and responsibilities. Training should increase awareness of the issues, cover liability and responsibilities, and explain procedures for handling and resolving complaints.

Many states now mandate harassment training prevention for governmental and/or private employers, including California, Connecticut, Illinois, Maine, Pennsylvania, and Texas. Other states "encourage" such training, including Colorado, Florida, Massachusetts, Michigan, Oklahoma, Rhode Island, Tennessee, Utah, and Vermont.

Before any training on the prevention of sexual harassment is implemented, whether conducted by outside specialists or internal trainers, the following points should be reviewed.

[1]   Training Objectives

For a training program to succeed, it must have clear, realistic, and measurable objectives that meet the needs of the organization. Many programs focus simply on informing the employees about sexual harassment, but this is too limited. Employees need to learn more than a string of facts. Training objectives should be expressed in terms of:

- Decreasing sexual harassment within the organization

- Reducing the number of sexual harassment complaints

- Motivating employees to change their behavior

- Creating and maintaining a respectful work environment

If these objectives are met, an even broader goal may be reached: improved productivity. An additional advantage of these types of objectives is that they can be measured before and after training, thus providing useful information about the effectiveness of the training itself.

[2]   Training Techniques

Training techniques should be appropriate for the material being presented. Training in sexual harassment prevention lends itself to many techniques, and programs that incorporate a number of them are more likely to keep people interested and have a real impact on their behavior. Techniques that work well include role playing, modeling, group discussions, films or videos, and case studies.

[3]   Review of Content

The content of the program should be reviewed in terms of its approach to sexual harassment. Programs that dwell on the legal aspects of sexual harassment really can be quite boring to participants. There should be a basic focus on legal matters, but the program should present a broad view of the nature of sexual harassment, its impact on the victims as well as on the organization, individual and organizational liability, and the steps to take in handling and preventing sexual harassment.

To be effective, a training program must be more than just a session or two in a meeting room. The program should provide for such training to continue beyond the classroom. It should provide participants at all levels with some basic tools and skills that enable them to act as quasi coaches with their coworkers when sexual harassment problems arise. If employees are trained in preventing sexual harassment and are trained to be coaches to a certain extent, the program will likely be more than just another in-class exercise.

[4]   Training Evaluation

The training program should include some means of evaluating how well it meets its objectives. The most practical approach is to use a combination of evaluation techniques, applied before and after the actual training. This can include surveying employee needs and knowledge of sexual harassment, analysis of performance review data, analysis of sexual harassment claims, observation, and group discussions. These techniques provide some basic information about the effectiveness of the training and about the parts of the training program that need improvement.

[F]   Strategic Step 5: Evaluation and Updating Mechanisms

The final step in a sexual harassment prevention program is to develop an ongoing system for evaluating and updating the total program. The follow-up and review system should include the following:

- Analysis of performance reviews

- Review of the frequency and nature of sexual harassment complaints and their final dispositions

- Structured observations of on-the-job situations

From the standpoint of keeping the program current, the individual or individuals who oversee its evaluation and updating should also be responsible for monitoring any laws, rulings, and studies related to sexual harassment. This is an important function in revising company policy and procedures in light of new developments.

§ 21.08 THE FUTURE OF SEXUAL HARASSMENT

Although not all modern management concepts are the same, they share one common theme: a clear focus on the employee as the most important resource in the organization. The trend is toward far more interest in the skills, objectives, input, and ideas of employees. This calls for a work environment that can foster and encourage employee growth, involvement, commitment, achievement, and advancement—an environment that truly invests in its human resources. Sexual harassment conflicts with virtually every aspect of this management philosophy. There is simply no place for it in modern organizations.

A 1999 SHRM survey found that 84 percent of companies believed that employees are making a greater effort to avoid behavior that could be perceived as sexual harassment. Through numerous organization-sponsored programs, public and university seminars, and media exposure, employees are becoming increasingly aware of their rights in relation to sexual harassment. Clear signs indicate that employees are more willing to exert these rights when necessary. Further, the number of support groups and organizations created to help and guide sexual harassment victims has grown. These groups provide assistance in dealing not only with the pain and suffering of sexual harassment, but also with the actual processing of claims against harassers and employers.

Seminars and media exposure are also steadily increasing the number of employers that are aware of sexual harassment, particularly in terms of the costs, liabilities, and exposure associated with it. As employees become more willing to exert their rights on this issue, employers are showing increased willingness to incorporate bona fide programs to reduce sexual harassment, as well as provide numerous internal systems to deal with these problems. Some employers are acting out of humanitarian concern for employees; others believe they are making a business decision to manage a clear business risk. Either way, the trend is toward an increased number of employers taking formal steps to deal with sexual harassment.

§ 21.09 OTHER FORMS OF PROHIBITED WORKPLACE HARASSMENT

Harassment on the basis of gender—sexual harassment—is not the only form of harassment that can create a hostile work environment. Often, at the crux of harassment complaints is a lack of appreciation and respect for diversity (e.g., religion, ethnicity, race, age, and disabilities) in the workplace.

The changing demographics of our workforce create challenges as well as opportunities for employers. Company management can leverage these differences to create new and better ways of working. The challenge is to develop an environment that is respectful of the differences. Employers should consider providing training or awareness sessions that highlight the positive side of diversity and communicate the company's intention to create and maintain a positive work environment for all employees.

[A] Statutory Authority

Federal statutory authority for workplace harassment claims includes Title VII, the Americans with Disabilities Act (ADA), and the Age Discrimination in Employment Act (ADEA). These federal laws prohibit discrimination based on protected factors other than sex: race, color, national origin, disability, religion, and age.

Many states and localities have laws that prohibit discrimination based on other protected classes such as sexual orientation, ethnicity, and marital status. Employers must be aware of the various state and local laws to ensure they understand the full scope of protected classes covered by these laws.

[B] Harassment Based on Hostile Environment

Employees' claims alleging a hostile work environment based on race, religion, disability, age, or other forms of workplace harassment are actionable under a number of federal statutes and comparable state statutes. The analysis of such claims generally is the same as that used for hostile work environment sexual harassment claims. Key issues include the pervasiveness of the harassing conduct, whether the harassment is so egregious so as to alter the conditions of the plaintiff's employment, to what extent the employer knew of the conduct, and, if it did, what the employer did about it.

To establish a harassment claim based on a hostile work environment, a plaintiff must show that (1) he or she suffered intentional discrimination; (2) the discrimination was pervasive and ongoing; (3) the discrimination detrimentally affected him or her; (4) the discrimination would detrimentally affect a reasonable person of the same race, religion, or disability in that position; and (5) the existence of *respondeat superior* liability. [Aman v. Cort Furniture Rental Corp., 85 F.3d at 1081 (3d Cir. 1996)]

To state a claim for relief under a theory of hostile work environment, a plaintiff must show that (1) he or she belongs to a protected class; (2) he or she was subject to unwelcome harassment; (3) the harassment was based on race, religion, disability, or other protected class; and (4) the harassment affected a term, condition, or privilege of employment. [Waymire v. Harris County, 86 F.3d 424, 428 (5th Cir. 1996)]

"The existence of a hostile work environment cannot be predicated on isolated acts."[Porter v. City of Little Rock, 941 F. Supp. 804, 806 (E.D. Ark. 1995)] In other words, an isolated expression of an ethnic or racial epithet that creates offensive feelings in an employee does not necessarily qualify as a hostile work environment as described in the law. The intent of Title VII was only to bar conduct that is so severe and pervasive that it destroys a protected class member's opportunity to succeed in the workplace, and thus conduct that only offends but does not hinder an employee's performance is not actionable.

Some examples of behavior or actions that could be perceived by others to be harassing include but are not limited to:

- Repeated racial or ethnic epithets

- Discriminatory verbal intimidation, ridicule, and insults

- Denying salary increases, promotions, and assignments to more desirable work that is motivated by race, religion, or other protected class status

- Yelling by a supervisor that is directed at a person in a protected class but not at others

- Frequent jokes directed at race, disability, ethnicity, age, religion, and so forth

Members of management must be observant of the working environment and, when these behaviors or actions are noted, take appropriate action to ensure that a harassing environment is not tolerated or continued.

[C] Scope of Employers' Liability

An employer may be held liable for events of harassment about which it knows or should have known, either directly or constructively, and with respect to which it fails to take corrective action. Actual notice of the alleged harassment to the employer may be found if the employee complained of the harassment to the company's HR department or other management personnel. Knowledge of the alleged harassment to the employer may also be imputed if the harassment is so severe or pervasive that a reasonable employer would be inspired to investigate and discover facts.

In today's litigious society, employers are now purchasing employment practices insurance as a means to offset costs associated with potential employment litigation, including claims of harassment.

[D] Investigation of Harassment Allegations

An employer's response to claims of harassment based on a hostile work environment should be similar to that described in the section "Conducting an Investigation."

When allegations of harassment based on a protected class (e.g., disability, age, or race) are brought to the attention of management, the company must respond by promptly investigating the claim and, if sufficient facts support the allegation, taking the appropriate action(s) to resolve the issue. The Fourth Circuit has joined the Fifth, Sixth, and Tenth Circuits in ruling that a harassment claim can go to trial because the employer did not attempt to remedy the situation. [Spriggs v. Diamond Auto Glass, 165 F.3d 1015, 1018–19 (4th Cir. 1999)] Just as in sexual harassment claims, employers can raise affirmative defenses (outlined in *Faragher* and *Ellerth*) to limit their liability; one of the most important is prompt and thorough investigation when they become aware of harassment in the workplace.

[E] Prevention of Other Prohibited Forms of Harassment

The same strategies described previously (see section "Strategies to Prevent or Eliminate Sexual Harassment") also apply to harassment based on other protected classes:

- Make sure that management provides models for the behavior expected from employees regarding sensitivity and respect for others.

- Develop, distribute, and communicate a strongly worded policy statement against any form of harassment.

- Establish and widely communicate procedures for reporting harassment complaints.

- Take all harassment complaints seriously and investigate promptly and thoroughly.

- Document all complaints and subsequent investigations.

- Consistently apply disciplinary sanctions to offending employees.

- Train all supervisors and employees about harassment, their rights, and responsibilities.

Exhibit 21.1
The Sexual Harassment Quiz

For each incident that appears to be a case of sexual harassment, place an X in the box under the word *Yes*. For each incident that does not appear to be sexual harassment, place an X in the box under the word *No*.

Incident	Yes	No
1. A female truck driver is offended and upset by the frequent whistles, catcalls, and ogling some of the male drivers have directed toward her.	☐	☐
2. A female job applicant is advised that part of her job responsibilities would include engaging in sexual relations with her boss.	☐	☐
3. A female secretary is offended by the daily sexually oriented "pranks" indulged in by some of the men in her office—such as the sex manual and sexually explicit statue left on her desk.	☐	☐
4. A male researcher is bothered by his female supervisor who gives him an occasional pinch and keeps insisting that they get together after work.	☐	☐
5. A male office manager often walks around the office and gives the female secretaries neck and shoulder massages. One of the secretaries has frequently asked him to stop, but the massages continue. She has found it difficult to concentrate on her work as a result.	☐	☐
6. A female account executive who wears stylish clothing is upset by the barrage of sexually oriented comments made by her coworkers and manager.	☐	☐
7. A female nurse is annoyed with one of the male doctors, who keeps "accidentally" touching her.	☐	☐
8. A female receptionist for a manufacturing facility is upset with a male customer who keeps putting his arms around her, hugging her, and asking her to go away with him for a weekend. Her supervisor insists that he is just joking and she should try to be more friendly to him—after all, he is an important customer.	☐	☐
9. A female accountant is upset with one of her male coworkers who keeps pressuring her to go out with him. Although she is not interested in having any kind of a social relationship with him, he has recently started to call her at home.	☐	☐
10. A female data entry clerk was told that she would be promoted if she would have sex with her male supervisor.	☐	☐
11. The female waitresses are dissatisfied with management's insistence that they wear more revealing outfits. The change has resulted in more sexually oriented comments from their male coworkers and from customers as well.	☐	☐

Exhibit 21.1   Mandated Benefits: 2009 Compliance Guide

Exhibit 21.1 (cont'd)

Incident	Yes	No
12. A male engineer put his arm around one of his female assistants. She immediately backed off and told him that such behavior was not appreciated. He apologized, but over the next few months gave her tedious assignments and ultimately gave her an extremely poor performance evaluation.	☐	☐
13. Although not singled out for unwanted sexual attention, a female office employee finds that the widespread sexual demands placed on many of her female coworkers, along with the preferential treatment for those who comply, have created a work environment that, to her, is offensive and hostile.	☐	☐
14. A female employee engages in sexual relations with her male supervisor but later claims that her supervisor's advances were unwelcome and she complied only out of fear of losing her job.	☐	☐
15. A female executive is offended by the constant sexual references, comments, and propositions made to her and about her by her male supervisors.	☐	☐
16. A male employee is offended by repetitive, sexually explicit comments made by his male boss.	☐	☐

SCORING THE QUIZ

Scoring the quiz is simple: All 16 incidents are examples of sexual harassment. One point is given for each question answered in the *Yes* column. A score of less than 16 means the possibility of exposure to charges of sexual harassment.

Sexual harassment is not an issue that can be partly understood. If it is not entirely understood, all parties involved could suffer potentially great damages.

Most people are surprised to learn that all of the incidents in the quiz are examples of sexual harassment, because most people define sexual harassment solely as supervisory demands for sexual favors, backed by the promises of rewards, such as a promotion or salary increase, or the threat of retaliation, such as poor appraisals or termination. The image of the casting couch prevails in this notion. Various court rulings have concurred, holding that sexual harassment exists only if the harasser's demands for sexual favors are linked in some demonstrable way to a specific term or condition of employment. Today, this quid pro quo behavior is still recognized as one form, but recent court decisions and government guidelines have significantly expanded the meaning of sexual harassment.

At present, sexually oriented behavior or demands for sexual favors no longer need to be linked to any terms, economic benefits, or promises related to one's employment to be considered harassing. Sexual harassment now includes any sexually oriented behavior, such as ogling, teasing, or touching, that is unwelcome by the recipient and creates a hostile work environment. Sexual harassment now includes the sexually oriented actions and behavior not only of supervisors but of coworkers and nonemployees as well.

Exhibit 21.2
The Evolving Definition of Sexual Harassment

Sexual harassment has undergone a good deal of redefining in recent years. In fact, the definition of sexual harassment has evolved through six distinct stages in the eyes of the law:

- *Stage One.* Stone Age to early 1970s: The term *sexual harassment* was not acknowledged.

- *Stage Two.* The mid-1970s: Sexual harassment as an outcome of the interaction between males and females working together started to gain attention, but it was not considered an area for the courts to enter, particularly as a form of sex discrimination under Title VII of the Civil Rights Act of 1964.

- *Stage Three.* The late 1970s: Sexual harassment was defined as any behavior that makes demands for sexual favors a term or condition of employment. As such, it falls under the statutes dealing with sex discrimination.

- *Stage Four.* 1980 to mid-1986: As defined by the Equal Employment Opportunity Commission (EEOC) in its 1980 guidelines, sexual harassment means any unwelcome sexual advances, requests for sexual favors, or verbal or physical conduct of a sexual nature when these act as a term or condition of employment, are a criterion for employment decisions, interfere with the recipient's performance, or have the effect of creating an intimidating, hostile, or offensive working environment.

- *Stage Five.* Mid-1986 through 1996: In June 1986, the U.S. Supreme Court, in *Meritor Savings Bank, FSB v. Vinson* [477 U.S. 57 (1996)], affirmed that sexual harassment is indeed a cause of action under Title VII. The Court also ruled that the victim need not suffer an economic loss, although the harassment must be severe enough to alter the working conditions and create an abusive or hostile environment. In addition, the Court ruled that even if an individual voluntarily engaged in sexual relations with a supervisor, there can be actionable harassment if the conduct itself was unwelcome. At the same time, in ruling that the "totality of circumstances" will be used to determine the presence of sexual harassment, it stated that testimony about a plaintiff's dress and even personal fantasies is admissible. In addition, the Court concluded that employers are not always liable for acts of sexual harassment by supervisory personnel. On the other hand, the lack of notice from a complainant will not always insulate employers from liability, and they will not be automatically insulated if they have a policy or procedure that the complainant does not use.

- *Stage Six.* 1998 to Present: In *Burlington Industries Inc. v. Ellerth* [524 U.S. 742 (1988)] and *Faragher v. City of Boca Raton* [524 U.S. 775 (1998)], the Supreme Court decided that employers can be held liable for their supervisors' harassment of subordinates even if company officers were not aware of the problem and the victim did not report it. The law specifically states that when the supervisor's harassment results in a "tangible employment action" against the subordinate (e.g., discharge, demotion, or undesirable reassignment), the employer's liability is absolute, and the employer will not have the opportunity to raise affirmative defenses. Further, in *Ellerth,* the plaintiff's claim involved only unfulfilled threats. That is, the plaintiff refused the unwelcome sexual advances of her supervisor, and yet she did not suffer any adverse employment action as the result of her refusals. The Supreme Court held that where the plaintiff-employee has not suffered any tangible employment action, the defendant-employer may raise an affirmative defense to liability or damages.

Exhibit 21.2   Mandated Benefits: 2009 Compliance Guide

In the past, the courts have had difficulty applying the traditional sexual harassment standards to cases of same-sex harassment. However, in March 1998, the U.S. Supreme Court ruled on a case, *Oncale v. Sundowner Offshore Services* [523 U.S. 75 (1998)], involving same-sex harassment, finding that samesex harassment is covered under Title VII prohibiting discrimination based on sex.

Exhibit 21.3
Sample Policy on Sexual Harassment

Sexual harassment of any kind will not be tolerated and is grounds for disciplinary action, up to and including termination of employment. Sexual harassment is a continuing pattern of unwelcome sexual advances, requests, or demands for sexual favors, physical contact of a sexual nature, and verbal abuse or threats of a sexual nature under any of these conditions:

- When submission to the conduct involves a condition of the individual's employment, either stated or suggested

- When the individual's submission or refusal is used, or creates a condition where it might be used, as the basis of an employment decision that affects the individual

- When the conduct unreasonably interferes with the individual's job performance and ability to get the job done or creates a work environment that is intimidating, hostile, or offensive

Employees are directed to take a complaint of sexual harassment to the HR manager immediately or to the vice president of their division or department, or any officer of the company. This includes any incident of harassment that they have personally witnessed or experienced, or that has been reported to them.

The HR manager is responsible for investigating all charges fully and completely, regardless of the manner in which they are made and who is involved. All complaints and the investigation thereof will be kept as confidential as reasonably possible in the course of the investigation. All complaints will be investigated fully without bias and prejudgment. Such an investigation may include interviews with both parties to the complaint, and coworkers and former employees who may have knowledge of the situation. An investigator will be appointed by the HR manager, and the investigator will have access to all personnel files and will be granted all necessary access to information. No employee will be subject to retaliation of any type for reporting an incident of harassment. Any person who retaliates against any employee for reporting harassment will be subject to disciplinary action, up to and including termination of employment.

Chapter 22
Workplace Health and Safety

§ 22.01   AUDIT QUESTIONS

1. Does the company have an emergency plan, in compliance with the employee training and awareness component of the Occupational Safety and Health Act?

2. Does the company post Occupational Safety and Health Administration (OSHA) citations of violations at or near the site where violations have occurred to warn employees of potential hazards in the workplace?

3. Does the company comply with all applicable recordkeeping and posting requirements, including, but not limited to, injury and illness data, emergency phone numbers, emergency response/evacuation plan, fire prevention, general environmental controls, forklift/lift truck safe operating procedures (if used in workplace), physician's approval letter for first aid kits, posted phone number of nearest OSHA office, proof of workers' compensation insurance, phone number and location of nearest industrial clinic or emergency room, and other signage according to site-specific hazards?

4. Does the company have a comprehensive, written program describing how the Hazard Communication Standard will be implemented in the workplace?

5. Does the company have safety standards for the control of hazardous energy sources through lockout/tagout/tryout procedures?

6. Does the company provide mandated Personal Protective Equipment (PPE) that is appropriate to protect employees from site-specific workplace hazards?

7. Does the company monitor the safe work environment of its home-based manufacturing operations, if any?

8. Does the company have an employee training program to comply with the safety requirements of OSHA? Does the company have a system or method to ensure that employee safety training is effective (i.e., testing for comprehension, verification of understanding, and competence)?

9. Does the company have a comprehensive, written program (e.g., "safety manual") that communicates organization-specific safety requirements, including disciplinary actions that may occur for employee non-compliance with company standards?

Note: Consistent "yes" answers to the above questions suggest that the organization is applying effective management practices and/or complying with federal regulations. "No" answers indicate that problem areas exist and should be addressed immediately.

§ 22.02   THE OCCUPATIONAL SAFETY AND HEALTH ACT

Congress enacted the Occupational Safety and Health Act of 1970 (OSH Act) on December 29, 1970, to guarantee every worker safe and healthful working conditions and to preserve human resources. The OSH Act created its own agency, the Occupational Safety and Health Administration (OSHA), within the Department of Labor (DOL). OSHA is responsible for setting legally enforceable standards.

Employers must comply with all OSHA rules and regulations that apply to their businesses and workplaces. Where OSHA has not set specific standards, employers are required to follow the Act's General Duty Clause, which states that each employer "shall furnish ... a place of employment which is free from recognized hazards that are causing or are likely to cause death or serious physical harm to his [or her] employees."

[A]   General Requirements

Under the OSH Act, *recognized hazards* are defined as flagrantly dangerous conditions that are known to the employer and that are considered hazards in the employer's business or industry.

Employers are expected to take the initiative in identifying and eliminating recognized hazards and have a legal duty to inform employees of OSHA safety and health standards that apply to their workplace. OSHA coverage extends to all employers in the 50 states, the District of Columbia, Puerto Rico, the Canal Zone, and all other territories under U.S. jurisdiction. Under OSHA, *employer* is defined as any person engaged in a business affecting commerce who has employees, but it does not include the U.S. government or any state or political subdivision of a state. Other federal agencies, such as the departments of transportation and defense, are authorized to regulate job safety and health conditions in particular industries; however, if an agency does not address a specific area, then OSHA regulations apply.

Section 18 of the OSH Act encourages states to develop and operate their own job safety and health programs. State programs, however, must be approved by OSHA. To obtain OSHA's approval, a state must establish an occupational safety and health program with standards that are at least as stringent as the federal standards. Many states' plans thus adopt standards identical to the federal ones.

The following table lists states that have approved state plans. Information about state OSH plans may be found at *www.osha.gov/dcsp/osp/index.html*, which provides hyperlinks to the states' Web sites.

Alaska	Michigan	South Carolina
Arizona	Minnesota	Tennessee
California	Nevada	Utah
Connecticut*	New Jersey*	Vermont
Hawaii	New Mexico	Virgin Islands*
Indiana	New York*	Virginia
Iowa	North Carolina	Washington
Kentucky	Oregon	Wyoming
Maryland	Puerto Rico	

*Plans cover public sector (state and local government) employment only.

[B]   Exemptions to the Regulations

Not covered under the OSH Act are self-employed persons, family-owned-and-operated farms, and workplaces already protected under other federal statutes and enforced by other federal agencies.

[C]   Employee Training

The employee training and awareness component of the OSH Act requires that the employer:

1. Prepare an overview of mandatory OSH Act standards.

2. Provide employees with a copy of the OSH Act standards upon request.

3. Inform all employees about their rights and duties under the OSH Act.

4. Instruct all employees as to how to recognize and report workplace hazards.

5. Ensure that employees have and use safe tools and equipment, including appropriate personal protective equipment, and that employees are trained in the proper use and maintenance of such equipment.

6. Instruct employees in proper operating procedures or work rules, enforce and revise work rules as necessary, and retrain employees when work rules are revised.

Employee communications are an integral part of OSHA's training and awareness program. A company must ensure that it meets the following requirements:

- Have an emergency plan that has been reviewed with affected employees and include escape procedures and routes, critical plant operations, employee accounting after an emergency evacuation, rescue and medical duties, means of reporting emergencies, and persons to be contacted for information or clarification.

- Affix in a prominent position in each workplace the most current OSHA poster informing employees of their rights and responsibilities under the OSH Act. Some of the more important changes to OSHA posting requirements are those associated with "whistle blower" protection. The required posters are available free at local OSHA offices, can be downloaded for free (*www.osha.gov*), or can be secured from third-party publishers for a fee.

- Post OSHA citations of violations at or near the site where violations have occurred to warn employees of possible danger.

OSHA has developed a new publication to make employers aware of the agency's requirements for emergency action plans. "Principal Emergency Response and Preparedness" provides an overview of the applicable OSHA standards and procedures for developing a workplace emergency action plan. (See OSHA's Web site: *www.osha.gov.*)

OSHA also provides employers with training assistance. In December 2002, the DOL announced the selection of 20 Training Institute Education Centers, nearly doubling the then current number of centers (12) offering training courses on OSHA standards and workplace safety. As of this writing, there are 31 OSHA training centers throughout the United States. The OSHA Training Institute located in Illinois is the primary training center. For addresses of all OSHA training centers, the national office, and regional offices, go to *www.osha.gov.*

On its Web site, OSHA provides a number of helpful fact sheets, press releases, forms and regulatory assistance. For example, in April 2003, OSHA published a fact sheet on workplace exit routes in the event of an emergency. Employers can also sign up for Quick Takes, a bi-weekly e-newsletter published by the Department of Labor. The e-mailed news update provides information on safety and health, compliance assistance, ergonomics, training, and notices of proposed and final rulemaking.

[D] Workplace Health and Safety Recordkeeping Requirements

Workplace injuries and illnesses are to be tracked on OSHA Form 300, Log of Work-Related Injuries and Illnesses, throughout the year. Work-related injuries and illnesses that must be recorded include those that result in death, loss of consciousness, days away from work, restricted work activity, job transfer, or medical treatment beyond first aid. The following conditions also must be recorded if they are work-related:

- Needle pricks or cuts by sharp objects that are contaminated or potentially contaminated with another person's blood or other potentially infectious material;

- Any case in which a worker must be medically removed under requirements of an OSHA health standard;

- Tuberculosis infection after exposure to a known case of active tuberculosis; or

- An employee's hearing test reveals that the worker has experienced a Standard Threshold Shift.

An injury or illness that existed prior to a work-related event may be considered a workplace injury or illness if an event or exposure in the work environment contributed to or significantly aggravated the preexisting condition. For example, an employee who has a preexisting asthma condition suffers an asthma attack that was triggered by exposure to dust in the work environment and seeks medical treatment. Under OSHA regulations, the asthma attack must be recorded in the Log of Work-Related Injuries and Illnesses. Other examples include preexisting spinal disk injuries that are made worse by working conditions or tasks performed at work and for which medical treatment is sought.

At the conclusion of each calendar year, the numbers of injuries and illnesses should be totaled and all required information (e.g., calendar year covered, average number of employees at the company) filled in. The form must be certified by a company executive, who must be one of the following persons: (1) an owner of the company (if the company is a sole proprietorship or partnership); (2) an officer of the corporation; (3) the highest ranking company official working at the establishment; or (4) the immediate supervisor of the highest ranking company official working at the establishment. The OSHA Form 300A, Summary of Work-Related Injuries and Illnesses, must be posted in a conspicuous place in the establishment or in the place where all other required work-related documents are posted, beginning no later than February 1 of each year and must remain posted until April 30 of each year. A company that did not experience any recordable injuries or illnesses the previous year is required to post the form indicating the same. OSHA Forms 300 and 300A are available on OSHA's Web site: *www.osha.gov*.

An employer that has 10 or fewer employees during a calendar year is not required to maintain OSHA Form 300, unless it is asked in writing to do so by OSHA or the Bureau of Labor Statistics (BLS), or a state agency operating under the authority of OSHA or the BLS. Employers in certain low-hazard industries (such as finance, insurance, and real estate) are also exempt from the requirement to maintain OSHA Form 300. See the list of exempt establishments classified by industry description and Standard Industrial

Classification (SIC) code posted on OSHA's Web site: *www.osha.gov/recordkeeping/index.html*. All employers, including those partially exempted by reason of company size or industry classification, must report to OSHA any workplace incident that results in a death or the hospitalization of three or more employees.

On July 1, 2002, OSHA issued its final rule for recording work-related hearing loss, which became effective January 1, 2004. Employers may seek assistance from physicians to determine whether an employee's loss of hearing is work-related, to make adjustments for hearing loss due to aging, and to perform additional tests to determine whether the hearing loss is "persistent." Under the new rule, employers must record Standard Threshold Shifts (STSs) of 10 decibels or more from the employee's initial hearing test only when they result in an overall hearing level of at least 25 decibels from audiometric zero averaged over 2000, 3000, and 4000 Hertz. These recordkeeping requirements apply only to employers who are required to conduct hearing tests by OSHA's occupational noise standard and employers who conduct such tests voluntarily. If any employee is found to have sustained a level of hearing loss equal to one STS, the employer must take protective measures, including requiring the employee to use hearing protectors to prevent further loss of hearing.

On July 1, 2002, OSHA proposed to delay until January 1, 2004, the application of its proposed definition of musculoskeletal disorder (MSD). On June 30, 2003, OSHA announced that it would not revise OSHA Form 300 to include a separate column for MSDs. Employers should continue to record MSDs as either injuries or "all other illnesses" as appropriate.

[E] The Hazard Communication Standard

The federal right-to-know law, known as the Hazard Communication Standard (HCS)—more commonly referred to as the "Haz-Com Standard"—is intended to give employees access to certain information about the physical and health hazards of chemical substances produced, imported, or used in the workplace. The HCS applies to all employers in all industries and requires employers to:

- Establish a written hazard communication program to inform employees of the potential dangers of hazardous substances used or encountered in the workplace.

- Train workers in safe handling, emergency, and first aid procedures.

- Place a warning label on all containers of potentially dangerous materials.

The federal standard is enforced by OSHA in all states that do not operate their own OSHA-approved workplace safety and health programs. States that have plans are required to adopt regulatory provisions that are at least as stringent as the federal regulation. State agencies have primary enforcement responsibility in their respective jurisdictions.

Employers also must comply with requirements under the Emergency Planning and Community Right-to-Know Act of 1986, known as Title III. Under Title III, both manufacturers and nonmanufacturers must provide chemical hazard information not only to their employees but also to state and local governments.

Although the HCS gives workers the right of access to information about hazardous substances to which they are or may be exposed, it does not require employers to control exposures. Nor does it give employees the right to refuse to work.

[1] Employee Safety Training Under the HCS

The scope and application of the HCS are very broad. The HCS applies to all employers. Any chemical "known to be present in the workplace in such a manner that employees may be exposed under normal conditions of use or in a foreseeable emergency" is covered under the standard. Every workplace must have a comprehensive, written program that describes how the HCS will be implemented. Employees and their representatives have a right to a copy of the plan. Companies with multiple work sites must maintain a written hazard communication program at each site.

Material safety data sheets (MSDSs) must be maintained for each hazardous substance in the workplace and must be readily accessible to employees and their representatives, on all work shifts, at all work sites. The MSDS must identify a product's manufacturer, any hazardous chemical, and the percentage of such chemical contained therein. It must also identify the chemical's known safety and health hazards, its exposure limitations, proper handling procedures, first aid measures in the event an overexposure occurs, and information regarding proper disposal of the hazardous chemical. The specific chemical identity of each hazardous substance present in the workplace must appear on the relevant MSDS, unless that chemical identity is a trade secret. Employers, including chemical manufacturers, bear the burden of demonstrating the validity of trade secret claims.

Employees must be informed about the specific components of the written hazard communication program, including which operations in the work areas have hazardous substances present; the locations of any written hazard evaluation procedures; copies of communications programs; and a listing of hazardous chemicals and required MSDS for each hazardous chemical. In multiemployer workplaces where exposures to another company's employees may occur, hazard information must be exchanged to ensure that workers have sufficient information to protect themselves, regardless of which employer uses the hazardous chemical. Employee training must include instruction in:

- How to read and interpret warning labels and MSDSs in order to understand the physical and health hazards of the chemicals in the work area; how to obtain and use the appropriate hazard information, including the details of the hazard communication program developed by the employer

- How to recognize and detect the presence of chemical hazards, including methods and observations (e.g., monitoring conducted by the employer, continuous monitoring devices, or monitoring the visual appearance or odor of hazardous chemicals when being released) that may be used to detect the presence or release of a hazardous chemical in the work area

- How to obtain hazard information

- How to respond to workplace accidents involving hazardous materials

With training, employees can take specific measures to protect themselves from hazards, such as appropriate work practices, emergency procedures, and personal protective equipment.

[2] Exemptions from the Standard

Certain companies are exempt from the HCS labeling requirement. Except for chemical manufacturers and importers, companies do not have to evaluate chemicals to determine whether the substances are hazardous unless they choose not to rely on the evaluation performed by the chemical's manufacturer or importer.

Chemical laboratories in manufacturing are exempt from the labeling provisions of the standard but are covered by all other HCS provisions.

Labeling is not required for the following products:

- Medical and veterinary devices already labeled in accordance with Food and Drug Administration (FDA) regulations

- Foods, food or color additives, drugs, or cosmetics labeled as required by FDA regulations

- Distilled spirits that meet the labeling requirements of the Federal Alcohol Administration Act

- Consumer products labeled in accordance with requirements of the Consumer Product Safety Commission

- Pesticides either labeled as required by the federal Insecticide, Fungicide, and Rodenticide Act or subject to regulations issued under this Act by the Environmental Protection Agency

The following products are completely exempt from the standard:

- Operations that are wholly regulated by the Mine Safety and Health Administration (MSHA), which now has its own HCS.

- Hazardous wastes regulated under the Resource Conservation and Recovery Act

- Wood (but not wood dust), tobacco, and tobacco products

- Articles (i.e., products) that are formed to a specific shape or design and that do not release or produce exposure to hazardous substances under normal use (e.g., metal file cabinets or plastic beach chairs)

- Potentially hazardous substances, such as drugs, food, and cosmetics brought into the workplace for personal use

[3]   Compliance Enforcement

Exhibit 22.1 contains a listing of the right-to-know laws by state. It lists which states have regulations in addition to the requirements of the HCS and highlights certain state requirements as they relate to training requirements. If a state has not adopted an approved OSHA plan, the federal HCS preempts the state law if the state law is not as stringent as the federal regulation. Employers should consult legal counsel or a specialty consultant about the state's right-to-know plan. **Exhibit 22.1** also includes state agencies and their respective phone numbers.

[F]   The Lockout/Tagout (LOTO) Requirement of the OSH Act

The lockout/tagout requirements issued by OSHA require employers to adopt safety standards for the control of hazardous energy sources by means of lockout or tagout procedures. Hazardous energy is defined as stored energy that is unexpectedly released (1) at start-up of machines or equipment or (2) during service, repair, maintenance, operation, and associated activities. The rule states that during maintenance or service activities, energy sources for industrial equipment must be turned off or disconnected, and the activating switch must be locked in the off position (i.e., the lockout method). If this is not possible, the activating switch must be labeled with a warning tag (i.e., the tagout method). The lockout method is preferred.

Although many employers may recognize electrical energy as being the primary concern of the rule, they need to understand that *stored energy* can also refer to pneumatic, gravitational, and fluid energy.

The rule applies to general industry employers and does not cover the construction, agriculture, or maritime industries. The rule supplements other general industry rules that require lockout procedures.

[1] Energy Control Program

Companies required to follow the OSHA lockout or tagout provision must establish a hazardous energy control program that includes written procedures for employees engaged in maintenance or servicing activities, unexpected energizing or start-up of machines or equipment, service, repair, maintenance, operation, and associated activities. Employee training must be included in the program to ensure that employees understand the purpose and function of the energy control program and have the knowledge and skills required for the safe application, usage, and removal of energy controls.

The program procedures must clearly outline the scope, purpose, authorization, rules, and techniques to be used for the control of potentially dangerous energy sources and the methods of compliance. Specifically, procedures should include:

- A statement of the intended use of the procedures

- Steps for shutting down, isolating, blocking, and securing machines or equipment to control hazardous energy

- Steps for the placement, removal, and transfer of lockout or tagout devices and a designation of who is responsible for these steps

- Requirements for testing (often referred to as "tryout") a machine or equipment to determine and verify the effectiveness of lockout or tagout devices and other energy control measures

Employers must have records in the form of a certification that employee training has been accomplished and is being kept up to date. The certification must show each employee's name and dates of training participation.

[2] Employee Training

The employees who actually lock out or tag out machines or equipment to perform the servicing or maintenance on that machine or equipment must be authorized to do so. These employees must be trained to recognize hazardous energy sources, the type and magnitude of the energy present in the workplace, and the methods and means necessary for energy isolation and control. Employees who use the machines or equipment on which servicing or maintenance is performed under lockout or tagout, or whose jobs require them to work in an area where servicing or maintenance is performed, must be trained in the purpose and use of the energy control procedures. Any other employees who perform work operations in an area where energy control procedures may be used must be instructed about the energy control procedure. Training should emphasize that any attempts to restart or reenergize machines or equipment that are locked or tagged out is prohibited.

Employers must provide retraining for all authorized and affected employees whenever there is a change in their job assignments; a change in machines, equipment, or processes that presents a new hazard; or a change in energy control procedures. If an inspection uncovers deviations from required practice or inadequacies in employees' knowledge or use of energy control procedures, employees must be retrained.

[G]   Occupational Exposure to Blood-Borne Pathogens Under the OSH Act

Few health problems have generated as much controversy or have presented employers with as many thorny issues as the need for employees to work with potentially hazardous materials, especially those containing blood-borne pathogens, such as the human immunodeficiency virus (HIV) and hepatitis B. OSHA issued the Blood-Borne Pathogens Standard and the Hazardous Waste Operations Emergency Response Standard to deal with occupational exposure to blood-borne pathogens. Both standards apply to workplaces where hazardous (i.e., bodily fluid) waste and infectious materials are used. If a conflict or overlap occurs between the two standards, the provision that is more protective of employee health and safety applies.

The Blood-Borne Pathogens Standard applies to any employer that is regulated by OSHA and has at least one employee who may be exposed to potentially infectious materials in the course of the employee's duties. This rule applies to all operations where there is occupational exposure to blood or other potentially infectious materials. If employees are faced with the risk of acquiring HIV in the workplace, the standard requires that adequate warning about the occupational hazards of blood-borne pathogens be communicated to them through use of labels, signs, information, and training. (See **Chapter 20** for a discussion of right-to-privacy issues regarding HIV and the acquired immunodeficiency syndrome in the workplace.)

It is important that even those employers who do not in the course of regular business handle or encounter potentially infectious materials consider the impact of the Blood-Borne Pathogens Standard. If the employer has provided first aid training to the workforce and anticipates that those trained individuals will be called upon to provide emergency treatment in the event of an accident at the workplace, the standard applies. However, the nature and scope of the control plan and employee training need only be appropriate to the hazards that might be encountered by those providing emergency treatment. This training is best conducted as a part of regular first aid training.

[1]   Work Practice Control Plan

The Blood-Borne Pathogens Standard requires employers to institute and monitor adherence to establish effective and safe work practice controls in various areas, including:

- *Engineering*—Use of machines and or devices that reduce or eliminate hazards, such as self-contained sharps disposal boxes, retractable hypodermic needle covers, properly located eye wash stations, and first-aid/bodily fluid cleanup kits

- *Administration*—Procedures and practices established by management that are designed to reduce or eliminate hazards, such as establishing quarantine areas or zones, assigning only trained personnel to handle or dispose of infectious materials, and posting warnings of hazardous conditions

- *Protective equipment*—Use by all affected personnel of equipment that will reduce or eliminate exposure to hazardous conditions, such as latex gloves, face shields, safety goggles, aprons, and disposable coveralls.

A written work practice control plan must be developed by every employer of an employee with a type of occupational exposure listed above. The plan must be designed to eliminate or minimize employee exposure to blood-borne pathogens. Once the plan is established, it must be:

- Accessible to employees at any time

- Reviewed and updated at least annually or whenever necessary to reflect new or modified tasks and procedures and new or revised employee positions with occupational exposure

- Made available upon request to OSHA for inspection and copying

[2] Employee Training

Employers that fall under the Blood-Borne Pathogens Standard's provisions are mandated to provide all employees with training about the hazards associated with blood handling and other potentially infectious materials and the protective measures to be taken to minimize exposure to risks. OSHA views training as the critical element of any exposure control program.

Employers must provide training at no cost to employees and at a reasonable location, during work hours. Training must be provided at the time of initial assignment to tasks where occupational exposure may take place and at least annually thereafter. Retraining for all workers is required within one year of employees' previous training, and annually thereafter. Employers must provide additional training when changes (e.g., modification of tasks or procedures or institution of new tasks or procedures) are made that affect employees' occupational exposure risks. Additional training may be limited to addressing the new exposures created.

A grandfather clause is included among the standard's training provisions to allow employers the option of supplementing rather than repeating prior employee training. Specifically, for employees who have received training on blood-borne pathogens in the year preceding the standard's effective date, employers need to provide training on only those provisions of the standard that were not covered. Retraining for these employees is required within one year of their original training.

[3] Content of Training

The Blood-Borne Pathogens Standard allows some flexibility to tailor the training to employees' backgrounds and responsibilities. In other words, training material must be appropriate in content and vocabulary to employees' educational level, literacy level, and primary language. At a minimum, the training program should provide the following:

- A copy of OSHA's Blood-Borne Pathogens Standard, the text of the OSH Act, and an explanation of its contents

- A general explanation of the epidemiology and symptoms of blood-borne diseases

- An explanation of the modes of transmission of blood-borne pathogens

- An explanation of the employer's exposure control plan and how employees can obtain a copy of the written plan

- An explanation of the appropriate methods for recognizing tasks and other activities that may involve exposure to blood and other potentially infectious materials

- An explanation of the use and limitations of methods that prevent or reduce exposure, including appropriate engineering controls, work practices, and personal protective equipment

- Information on the types, proper use, location, removal, handling, decontamination, and disposal of personal protective equipment

- An explanation of the basis for selecting personal protective equipment

- Information, offered free of charge to employees, on the hepatitis B vaccine and the benefits of being vaccinated, including information on vaccine efficacy, safety, and method of administration

- Information on the appropriate actions to take and persons to contact in an emergency involving blood or other potentially infectious materials

- An explanation of the procedures to follow if exposure occurs, including how to report the incident and the medical follow-up that is available

- Information on the postexposure evaluation and follow-up that the employer is required to provide following an exposure incident

- An explanation of the signs, labels, and color coding required by the HCS

Employees should be given an opportunity for interactive questions and answers with the person conducting the training session. The person conducting the training must understand the application of the training to the specific workplace.

Additional training is required for employees of research laboratories and production facilities that handle concentrated preparations of HIV and hepatitis B virus and may be at especially high risk of infection following exposure.

[4] Recordkeeping

Employers are required to establish and maintain an accurate record for each employee with occupational exposure. The HCS does not require employers to maintain possession of the records; however, employers bear the responsibility for the records' creation, maintenance, and confidentiality, regardless of where the records are kept. Two types of records must be maintained: medical records and training records.

1. *Medical records.* Employers are required to establish and maintain medical records to aid in the collection of information on the causes of occupational illnesses and injuries involving blood-borne pathogens. This requirement is considered essential because documentation is necessary to ensure proper evaluation of employees' immune status and for proper health care management following exposure incidents. The medical records should include:

a. The employee's name and Social Security number

b. A copy of the employee's hepatitis B vaccination status, including the dates of all hepatitis B vaccinations and any medical records relative to the employee's ability to receive the vaccination

c. A copy of all results of examinations, medical testing, and follow-up procedures

d. A copy of the health care professional's written opinion for hepatitis B vaccination or postexposure evaluation, or both, and the follow-up

e. A copy of the information provided to the evaluating health care professional following an exposure incident, including a description of the exposed employee's duties as they relate to the exposure incident, documentation of the routes of exposure and circumstances under which exposure occurred, and results of the source individual's blood test

Employers are required to keep medical records on each employee occupationally exposed to potential infectious materials in the workplace for 30 years after the employee's last date of employment. The records must contain the employee's name and Social Security number, vaccination status, and records of medical evaluations and follow-up visits. The employer must keep such records confidential, and cannot disclose or report on them, without the employee's written consent, to any person within or outside the workplace.

2. *Training records.* Employers must maintain training records to verify that employees receive appropriate information on blood-borne pathogen hazards and effective prevention and treatment measures. In fact, training records are a critical component of any training assessment program because they allow trainers to closely monitor the content and completeness of the program, thus ensuring that employees receive the training required.

Employee training records should contain training session dates, contents or summary of the sessions, names and qualifications of persons conducting the training, and the names and job titles of all persons attending the training sessions. Such records must be retained for three years from the date on which the training occurred. The records, however, are not considered confidential and may be maintained in any file (e.g., in the employee's individual training or personnel file or in a single collective file). Upon request, employers are required to make training records available for examination and copying by OSHA employees and employees' representatives. Employers may also be required, upon request, to make these same records available for review and copying by the National Institute for Occupational Safety and Health (NIOSH), an agency that works with OSHA in an advisory capacity to help determine the existence of a safety issue. NIOSH has impact on OSHA decisions, but it does not have regulatory powers.

[H] Compliance and Accident Prevention Assistance

Federal and State OSHA agencies have increased the number and scope of compliance assistance and accident prevention programs available to businesses. These programs include:

- Interactive accident prevention/hazard recognition "eTools" on the OSHA Web site;

- Free to low-cost publications from applicable industry groups and trade associations;

- Video and CD-ROM training materials; and

- Online and telephone consultation.

For small businesses, free on-site workplace consultations are available to assist business owners establish safety and health programs and identify and correct workplace hazards.

[I] OSHA Enforcement

OSHA's mission is to "assure the safety and health of America's workers by setting and enforcing standards; providing training, outreach, and education; establishing partnerships; and encouraging continual improvement in workplace safety and health."

To fulfill this mission, OSHA enforcement officers are charged with conducting inspections in workplaces. When regulatory violations are discovered, citations may be issued. Inspections generally occur under the following circumstances:

- Serious injury accidents

- Fatalities or catastrophes

- Complaints and/or referrals

- Programmed inspections

- Follow-up inspections

Citations can result in penalty assessments and can vary according to the degree of non-compliance, seriousness of any associated injuries, level of negligence and other factors. Obviously, the more serious the citation, the higher the penalty will be. In many cases, OSHA may issue an information notification which is not a citation per se and which does not carry penalty assessment. In these instances, there is an understanding that a repeat of the violation will result in a higher penalty assessment because the employer had been put on notice of the violative condition or practice and should have taken steps to eliminate recurrence.

It should be noted that employers can be held liable for the actions of subcontractors if the primary employer has some level of control over that work. Common examples include a construction project in which a wide variety of subcontractors are utilized by a primary contractor. Employers have a duty to ensure that subcontractors perform their work in a safe manner, especially when the subcontractor's work can affect the safety of others at a workplace. It is advised that when selecting subcontractors, a pre-qualification process is utilized to determine if the subcontractor has a good safety record and an established safety program.

In general, a single citation is issued to cover multiple violations of the same standard, especially when the conditions can be corrected with a single "fix." However, in a recent legal decision, employers were cited for multiple violations of the same standard. For example, a company was cited for each violation of the personal protective equipment (PPE) standards. For each employee that was not wearing proper PPE, a separate citation was issued.

Employers are afforded certain rights and responsibilities following an inspection and/or the issuance of a citation. Guidance is available on the OSHA Web site: *www.osha.gov/Publications/osha3000.html*. Except for the most serious citations, employers may elect to discuss the citation by requesting an informal conference and settlement with an OSHA Area Director. The request for an informal conference must take place within 15 days of the receipt of a citation. The request can be performed telephonically, but it is suggested that the request also be done in writing as a record of the request. The request for an informal conference does not extend the time period for the filing of a formal contest, which is also 15 days from the date of the citation. It is not uncommon for employers to request an informal conference and file a formal contest in the event that the informal conference does not result in a satisfactory outcome.

The best defense for any employer to avoid (and contest) OSHA citations is to establish and sustain a pro-active health and safety program. The elements of such a program, many of which are mentioned in other sections of this chapter, should include:

- Understanding of all health and safety regulatory agency requirements

- Well defined company health and safety standards

- Effective two-way health and safety communications

- Consistent and fair enforcement of company standards

- Recognition of positive behaviors and performance

- Effective health and safety training

- Programmed audits of health and safety conditions and practices

[J] Changing Regulations

OSHA is continually reviewing existing regulations and adding new regulations aimed at maintaining safe work environments. Twice a year the Department of Labor publishes its Semi-Annual Regulatory Agenda, listing the status of regulations under development or review. Employers are encouraged to review this agenda to see if any current regulatory activity may have an impact on their workplaces. The agenda is available on the DOL's Web site: *www.dol.gov/asp*.

§ 22.03 THE HAZARDOUS WASTE OPERATIONS EMERGENCY RESPONSE

The HCS, or right-to-know law, applies to work sites where hazardous wastes and infectious materials are used. To deal with the unique issues facing these employment sites, OSHA issued an additional standard, the Hazardous Waste Operations Emergency Response (HAZWOPER) Standard. If this standard conflicts or overlaps with the Blood-Borne Pathogens Standard, the provision that is more protective of employee health and safety applies. Employers must comply with both the HAZWOPER Standard and the Blood-Borne Pathogens Standard if their employees are:

- Engaged in cleanup operations at hazardous waste sites involving regulated waste

- Working at incinerators permitted by the Resource Conservation Recovery Act to burn infectious waste

- Responding to emergencies caused by the uncontrolled release of regulated waste (e.g., a transportation accident)

Questions about compliance with the blood-borne pathogens requirements should be directed to the Office of Health Enforcement, Department of Labor/OSHA, by calling (202) 693-2190 or by writing to:

Office of Health Enforcement
Department of Labor/OSHA
Directorate of Health Enforcement Programs
Room N-3119
200 Constitution Ave., N.W.
Washington, DC 20210

Copies of the requirements can be obtained from OSHA's Web site (*http://www.osha.gov/pls/publications/ pubindex.list*), by calling (202) 693-1888, or by writing to:

U.S. Department of Labor/OSHA
OSHA Publications
P.O. Box 37535
Washington, DC 20013-7535

§ 22.04 HOME-BASED WORK SITES

In early 2000 a great deal of controversy surrounded an OSHA directive that, in essence, indicated that employers are responsible for ensuring a safe work environment of employees who work from their homes. After a great deal of public and congressional outcry, OSHA rescinded the original directive with Directive Number CPL 2-0.125. The directive superseded all previous "statements and guidance on the subject."

In the new directive, the agency states that it "will not conduct inspections of employees' home offices," that "OSHA will not hold employers liable for home offices," and that it does not "expect employers to inspect the home offices of their employees." In addition, if the agency receives any complaints about a home office, "the complainant will be advised of OSHA's policy" but may "informally let employers know of complaints" regarding the alleged conditions.

OSHA, however, reserved the right to conduct inspections of home-based manufacturing operations when the agency receives a complaint or other indication that a violation of a safety or health standard exists. The criterion for such an inspection is an allegation that a threat of physical harm or imminent danger exists, or any indication that there has been a work-related fatality.

OSHA also reiterates that the employer is responsible for any hazards that are caused by materials, equipment, or work processes that the employer provides or requires to be used in an employee's home.

In this regard it is advised that the human resources (HR) professional provide guidance and support to those workers who perform duties in home-based offices to create a comfortable and safe work environment. However, it is important that home-based manufacturing operations be viewed as an extension of the employer's operations and that they be more closely monitored for safety and be subject to all the company's work and safety rules, regardless of location.

§ 22.05 WORKPLACE VIOLENCE PREVENTION

In recent case law, workplace violence prevention has generally been accepted as falling under the auspices of the OSH Act "General Duty Clause," mandating a workplace free from hazards, when the hazards:

- Create a "significant risk" to employees in other than "a freakish or utterly implausible concurrence of circumstances";

- Are known to the employer and are considered hazards in the employer's business or industry; and

- Are hazards that the employer can reasonably be expected to prevent.

(See *Secretary of Labor v. Megawest Financial, Inc.* [OSHRC Docket No. 93-2879 (May 19, 1995)] for more detailed information on this subject.)

[A] Penalties for Lack of Compliance

OSHA has issued citations to employers for gross violations of the General Duty Clause or when serious incidents have occurred that could have been prevented with a reasonable amount of due diligence. In Crisis Management International, Inc.'s Fall 1999 "Crisis Management Report," it was noted that negligence suits filed by victims or families of victims cost employers an average of $2 million per incident.

[B] Perpetrators of Workplace Violence

Generally, incidents of workplace violence are committed by a single individual. Typical perpetrator profiles are grouped into one of the following categories:

- An individual who has no legitimate relationship with an employee or the employer

- An employee or ex-employee

- An individual who is or has been a client, customer, contractor, or vendor or has another legitimate relationship with the employer

- An individual who has an intimate, family, or other relationship with an employee

[C] Who Is Affected

Unfortunately, workplace violence can occur in virtually any business or industry that employs people or provides services and products. According to the Department of Justice, 1.7 million employees report being victims of non-fatal violent crime on the job each year.

The positions within a company that have the greatest exposure to workplace homicide are the ones that involve handling cash or other valuables and that deal directly with customers or other people in providing a service. In a February 2001 report titled "Workplace Violence: A Report to the Nation," the Injury Prevention Research Center at the University of Iowa noted that this category accounts for 85 percent of all workplace homicides.

Employee-on-employee violence accounts for 7 percent of all workplace homicides, violence in the workplace arising from domestic disputes accounts for 5 percent, and customer violence accounts for 3 percent. In addition, approximately 2 million nonfatal incidents of workplace violence are reported annually, with the most heavily affected industries being late-night retail or convenience stores, law enforcement/security, education, health services, and transportation.

The most recent data available comes from the Bureau of Labor Statistics (BLS), which reports on its Web site (*www.bls.gov*) that workplace homicides in 2007 were up significantly over 2006—from 540 to 610. Workplace homicides in 2006 were the lowest number since the BLS started tracking these statistics in 1992. The numbers in recent years are significantly lower than those in the early to mid-1990s. Workplace homicides from 1992 to 1995 were over 1,000 per year. From 1996 to 1999, the numbers dropped from 927 to 651. Excluding the deaths in the World Trade Center Towers in 2001, the numbers since 1999 have been between 677 and 516.

[D] Combating Workplace Violence

There are two key interrelated steps that employers can take to detect and, if not prevent, minimize potential workplace violence:

1. *Risk assessment.* Aims to identify physical weaknesses and possible vulnerabilities that exist in the firm's physical facilities that could lead to, or give rise to, significant risk. It includes assessing such features as the firm's physical structure, office layout, window locations, key control, parking areas, and lighting.

2. *Organizational violence assessment.* Involves review of management practices that can influence the potential for violence and circumstances that may contribute to underlying causes of violence and identification of cultural norms that create stress and conflict in an organization. This assessment can identify any incongruence between HR and security policies, as well as obtain information on an organization's prior history of violent incidents or close calls to determine trends and patterns. For example, an organizational violence assessment will review termination policies that are a potential source of violence-inducing procedures. Poor termination practices such as walking a terminated employee through a facility to the door in front of other employees or terminating an employee via e-mail can give rise to violence because they can be perceived as unfair treatment or injustice. Company policies should ensure that employees are treated with dignity and professionalism throughout the separation process.

Only personnel who are professionally trained in physical security and risk management, whether internal or external to the company, should conduct organizational violence assessments. In practice, the two types of assessment are often combined.

[1] Managing Workplace Violence Prevention

Responsibility for workplace violence prevention should be assigned to one person, generally a member of senior management. This person would have responsibility for implementing and overseeing the firm's efforts to reduce hazards in the work environment. He or she may or may not be the HR manager. If he or she is not the HR manager, the designated workplace violence reduction "point person" should work very closely with the HR department.

The nature of workplace violence demands a multidisciplinary approach to ensure that the many aspects of the issue are defined and considered in building the company's prevention effort. Accordingly, it is recommended that the person assigned this responsibility establish a workplace violence prevention committee (or a threat management committee). The committee should be composed of representatives from various departments, including security, HR, occupational health and safety, legal, risk management, public relations or corporate communications, and operational management.

One of the key responsibilities of the workplace violence prevention committee is to formulate a policy that focuses on creating a violence-free work environment and on eliminating "at risk" behavior both at the individual level and at the organizational level.

A second key responsibility of the committee is to diligently research, evaluate, quantify, and report the nature of the risks to the company that are associated with the business of the firm, its industry, and the geographic locations of its facilities. If there are known hazards in a particular type of business, industry, or area, specific actions should be taken to mitigate the potential problems.

[2] Typical Violence Prevention Interventions

Various types of interventions that employers use to help prevent workplace violence include:

- Establishing a workplace violence prevention policy that includes addressing and acting on all incidents of violence and potential violence

- Establishing a no-weapons-on-company-premises policy that encompasses firearms, knives, potentially explosive devices and/or materials, unless such items are necessary or required by the workers' specific job duties (e.g., security personnel)

- Performing workplace violence audits that incorporate confidentiality considerations and necessary follow-up actions

- Establishing an incident response team whose members have been trained in appropriate emergency and trauma response

- Using an employee assistance program that includes counseling services

- Performing professional assessments of an employee's likelihood of becoming violent

- Requiring background and reference checks for job candidates and verification of identity

- Establishing emergency protocol with local law enforcement to ensure that local police know the facility layout

- Reducing crime potential through environment design and work procedures (e.g., security doors, entry intercoms, regular "money drops" in safes, and so forth)

- Training managers and employees in workplace violence prevention

Although workplace violence cannot be prevented entirely, it can be significantly mitigated. Employers must be prepared to contend with the inevitable impact of violence on employee morale, productivity, absenteeism, the company's public image, and customers. Employers who are prepared and can respond quickly and properly to incidents are much more likely to preserve their corporate reputation and goodwill and protect their revenue stream. The National Institute for Occupational Safety and Health (NIOSH) has developed a 27-minute video on workplace violence prevention called "Violence on the Job," which offers practical measures for identifying risk factors and recommendations to protect employees from workplace violence. The video is available in DVD format and can be obtained through the organization's Web site: *www.cdc.gov/niosh.*

§ 22.06 ERGONOMICS

OSHA has developed a four-pronged approach to reduce ergonomically related injuries in the workplace that includes: (1) industry-specific voluntary ergonomic guidelines; (2) enforcement; (3) compliance assistance; and (4) the National Advisory Committee on Ergonomics (NACE). Many OSHA Regions working in partnership with specific industries have developed voluntary guidelines to reduce musculo-skeletal disorders and injuries. The first set of voluntary guidelines, developed for the nursing home industry, was published in March 2003. Other industries with guidelines include, but are not limited to:

- Retail Grocery Stores

- Poultry Processing

- Furniture Manufacturing

- Apparel and Footwear Manufacturing

In addition, OSHA has developed online "eTools" for several industries. An eTool is an interactive training tool specializing in occupational safety and health topics. The tools are available at: *www.osha. gov/SLTC/ergonomics/outreach.html#etools*.

The primary purpose of these guidelines is to provide solutions for preventing and reducing work-related injuries. Each set of guidelines will comprise three sections:

1. *Management practices*—training, management of injuries, and evaluation of ergonomics programs;

2. *Worksite analysis*—assessment of work activities geared to the specific operations that are inherent in the industry and tasks; and

3. *Control methods*—illustrations of ways to control common ergonomic stressors.

OSHA announced the initial 15 members of NACE in December 2002. This committee was chartered for two years, until November 2004, and met two to four times per year. NACE's purpose was to provide advice on a comprehensive approach to ergonomics, including industry or task-specific guidelines, identification of gaps in existing research and application to the workplace, ways to provide outreach and assistance to employers, and increased communication among all stakeholders.

In 2002, OSHA began issuing Ergonomic Hazard Alert Letters (EHALs) to employers with identified deficiencies. On April 2, 2007, OSHA issued the Ergonomic Hazard Alert Follow-Up Policy. This policy instructs the regional and area offices to follow up with employers who previously received an EHAL. Their intent is to determine what, if any, corrections have been made. Based on the employer's response, OSHA may determine that an inspection of the worksite is necessary to "determine if the ergonomic hazards are being addressed."

Some states have attempted to enact their own ergonomics standards without much success. For example, in 2000, Washington State adopted an ergonomics rule that required employers to implement preventive measures. It was struck down by voters in 2003. California, since 1996, has had an ergonomics standard that requires employers to take action after two injuries based on the same task occur within a 12-month period and is the only state that currently has mandated ergonomic requirements. Other states have only voluntary or advisory programs due to the difficult nature of creating and then enforcing ergonomic standards. There has been a growing consensus among rule-makers that ergonomic issues are often task-specific and even worker-specific, which oftentimes makes it impractical to apply a general, "wide brush" approach to the problem.

Even in states that have no defined ergonomics standard, OSHA and state safety enforcement agencies are utilizing the General Duty Clause standards against employers for creating or permitting alleged ergonomically unsafe conditions or practices.

Despite the lack of federal standards for all industries and relevant state requirements, HR managers are advised to review a company's workers compensation and industrial injury records to determine if there is a history of musculoskeletal claims. If musculoskeletal injuries are found, a proactive ergonomics program may be in the best interest of the employees and the employer. Information on and assistance for development of ergonomics programs and technical expertise are available on the OSHA Web site (*www.osha.gov*), which also provides links to other sources of information and publications.

§ 22.07 REQUIREMENTS FOR GOVERNMENT EMPLOYERS

The Congressional Accountability Act, signed by President Clinton on January 23, 1995, extends to the 35,000 employees of Congress coverage of the federal employment laws (including OSHA) that apply to private industry. Implementing regulations are issued by the Office of Compliance, headed by a five-member board appointed by congressional leaders.

[A] Provisions for Federal Employees

Under OSHA, federal agency heads, rather than OSHA, are responsible for providing safe and healthful working conditions for their employees. However, these conditions must conform to standards issued by OSHA for private sectors. Under the provision for federal employees, one federal agency cannot propose monetary penalties against another for failure to comply with OSHA standards.

[B] Provisions for State and Local Governments

OSHA provisions do not apply to state and local governments. However, the Act requires that any state wanting OSHA approval for a private sector occupational safety and health program must provide a program for its state and local government workers that is at least as effective as its program for private employees. Alternatively, state plans may cover only public sector employees. Private sector employers automatically fall under the jurisdiction of the Act in this situation.

§ 22.08 SAFETY TRAINING

Compliance with the safety requirements of all aspects of the OSH Act is most effectively done through employee training. As the pace of regulatory change continues, employee training becomes more critical to a company's success and survival.

[A] Establishing Safety Training Programs

The single most important thing an employer can do to ensure the success of the training department or programs is to understand the company's business goals and priorities and design and implement training to directly support them. For some companies, it may mean limiting training to compliance and risk-management activities; for others, it may mean using training as one of several tools to achieve more strategic or proactive goals.

Corporate trainers should keep key management aware of the focus of training activities and the role of training in achieving corporate objectives and specific management needs. Training results (i.e., changes in employee work practices or behaviors) should be routinely reported to key executives and managers.

[B] Timing of Training

Safety training should be conducted when new employees are hired and as new regulations are enacted or changes to existing regulations are made. Refresher courses should be scheduled periodically to keep skills and information in employees' current frames of reference and perspective.

[C] In-House Versus Third-Party Training

Employers have two basic options for delivering training: in-house instructors or third-party experts. The goal is to deliver effective training in the most cost-effective and efficient manner possible. In addition, companies have a choice of methods for obtaining training materials, including developing the material in-house, purchasing or leasing a program, or hiring a third party who brings the material with him or her. Most programs developed outside the company, however, usually need some customization to fit the company's needs. If a company leases or purchases a program, it should be sure to inquire about the amount of customization allowed.

The following factors should be considered when selecting the optimum combination of trainer and training program:

- *Experience.* Does the company have the experience and expertise to produce an in-house program? Does the third-party vendor have the content or industry experience and expertise required?

- *Development time.* How much time will it take to develop a quality program in-house? Does the individual or department have the time to invest?

- *Resources.* Does the company have the content experts and production capabilities to produce a quality training program?

- *Money.* Does the company have the money available to spend on purchasing or leasing a training package or contracting with a third party?

- *Quality.* Are the training products on the market of the quality the company needs? Are they current? Can an in-house program achieve the level of quality desired?

- *Specificity.* Are any of the training products on the market specific enough to meet the company's current training need, or are they too general? Do the third-party trainers have programs that are specifically targeted to the company's issues, or can programs be customized to meet the company's business needs?

- *Credibility.* Does an in-house program have the same credibility with line personnel and management as a third-party expert or a purchased product?

- *Effectiveness:* Does the training work? Is there a means to verify that the training resulted in understanding of the material, created a positive change in worker behavior or otherwise helped to sustain existing positive behaviors?

[D] Program Design

Successful safety training meets the identified needs of the organization. Therefore, the first step in the design of a quality safety training program is to conduct a needs analysis. For technical, compliance-related training, the needs-assessment process is somewhat simplified because of the highly specific nature of many regulations. Setting up the first training class to introduce a new procedure is fairly straightforward. The challenge comes in monitoring actual compliance and assessing ongoing needs.

The first step in assessing training needs is to seek input from the safety or compliance officer. Assuming the company has well-established safety policies, the results of compliance audits should reveal where targeted training would be useful. Trainers must collect three types of data in a needs analysis:

1. Pre-training behavior, or the knowledge that the trainees already possess

2. Post-training behavior, or the expectations that the organization has of the trainees once the training is complete

3. Workplace reinforcers and constraints, or the factors on the job that help or hinder trainees in applying what they learn

Most training needs to be documented in the form of written policies and reference guides. Such materials need to be aligned with recommendations flowing from training.

A variety of different formats may be used for delivering training. The most appropriate format to choose is the one that creates a setting most conducive to learning any particular topic, so trainers should be flexible. Informal training formats include one-on-one tutoring, user groups, discussion groups, and newsletters. Formal training formats include classroom training (e.g., lectures, demonstrations, and hands-on work), videos, audiotapes, computer-based training, satellite conferencing, teleconferencing, manuals, and on-the-job training.

[E] Training Course Documentation

To maintain appropriate records of training and resources, employers should keep written records of course offerings, including a description of each course, the audience, estimated time, media, and the trainer's name. In many instances, regulations require that a trainer be used because he or she has been identified as a "competent person" or a person who, by reason of experience, specialized knowledge, or specific "train-the-trainer" instruction, is qualified to conduct safety training. In lieu of identifying individual trainers, training records may indicate vendors or organizations that are recognized as being competent in the safety training. Typical organizations include the Red Cross for first aid training and safety supply vendors for personal protection equipment training. Records allow training officers, other employees, management, and, if necessary, government regulators to see at a glance what courses are available.

[F] The Americans with Disabilities Act and Training Considerations

The Americans with Disabilities Act of 1990 (ADA) prohibits discrimination against qualified persons with disabilities in all aspects of employment, including training. Under the law, training opportunities cannot be denied because of the need to make reasonable accommodation for a qualified employee's disability. Accommodations may include:

- Accessible training sites and facilities

- Training materials in alternate formats (e.g., large print, audiotapes) to accommodate a disability

- Modifications in the ways training is provided

- Note-takers, interpreters, or readers

- Captions in audiovisual materials

Under the federal HCS and similar state regulations, employers are mandated to provide certain types of comprehensive training, which have already been addressed in this chapter.

Exhibit 22.1   Mandated Benefits: 2009 Compliance Guide

Exhibit 22.1
State Hazard Communication Standards

State	Summary	State Right-to-Know Contact	OSHA Office
Alabama	Employees are covered under federal law.	Dept. of Labor (334) 242-3460	Department of Labor P.O. Box 303500 Montgomery, AL 36130-3500 (334) 242-3460
Alaska*	State law covers all employers, including the state and its political subdivisions, with one or more employees working in a place not used primarily as a personal residence. It covers approximately 7,000 substances. Employers must conduct a safety education program for workers before they perform a new work assignment that could result in exposure to a toxic or hazardous substance. Where workers are or may be exposed to hazardous materials, employers must display either a safety poster, an OSHA form 20 or equivalent information on each substance, a list of the chemical and product names of each substance, and identification of an accessible location where workers may review the information on the listed substances.	Dept. of Labor (907) 465-4855	Department of Labor & Workforce Development P.O. Box 111149 Juneau, AK 99811-1149 (907) 465-4855
Arizona*	The state adopted the federal law.	Division of Occupational Safety and Health (520) 628-5478	Industrial Commission of Arizona 800 West Washington St. Phoenix, AZ 85007-2922 (602) 542-4411
Arkansas	The state law covers public employees. Private employees are covered under federal law.	Dept. of Labor (501) 682-4500	Department of Labor 10421 West Markham Little Rock, AR 72205 (501) 682-4500

State	Summary	State Right-to-Know Contact	OSHA Office
California*	The state law is more stringent than federal HCS. All employers that use, sell, or manufacture hazardous substances and suppliers that manufacture, package, import, or distribute chemicals are covered by the state law. The state law covers many other substances besides those regulated under the federal HCS. The state requires employers to inform their employees about toxic chemicals in their workplace and to train them to work safely with those substances. Employers must develop a written hazard communication program that describes how hazard communication requirements are being met, explains how workers are informed of the hazards of nonroutine tasks, and states how contractor personnel working in the employer's location are informed of hazards, when necessary. Employee training must cover the requirements of hazard communication regulations, the identity of hazardous substances and associated operations in the workplace, and the location, availability, and contents of the written hazard communication program. Records must be maintained for at least 30 years.	Division of Occupational Safety and Health (800) 963-9424	CalOSHA 455 Golden Gate Ave. 10th floor San Francisco, CA 94102 (415) 703-5050
Colorado	Employees are covered under federal law.	Dept. of Labor & Employment (303) 318-8000	Department of Labor and Employment 633 17th Street, Suite 201 Denver, CO 80202-3660 (303) 318-8000
Connecticut** (continued)	The private sector is covered under federal law; state law covers the public sector. A list of carcinogenic substances must be provided to prospective employees and to each current employee, annually, on January 1. During the first month of new workers' employment, employers must conduct an education and training program that describes the dangers inherent in the exposure to, and the methods for avoiding, harmful effects of carcinogenic substances. Information on toxic substances also must be provided to new employees during the first month of employment and within one month of the transfer of a worker who is exposed to additional toxic substances in the new job. Information must be posted in the workplace informing employees of their right to this information. Employees cannot be required to work with the hazardous substance if the information is not provided within five days of an employee's request to review.	Dept. of Labor (860) 263-6900	Occupational Safety and Health Labor Department 38 Wolcott Hill Rd. Wethersfield, CT 06109 (860) 263-6900

Exhibit 22.1 (cont'd)
State Hazard Communication Standards

State	Summary	State Right-to-Know Contact	OSHA Office
	Prospective and current employees also must be informed of any chemical toxic substances, radioactive materials, or any other substances that are used or produced in the workplace that could be hazardous to a worker's reproductive system or to a fetus.		
Delaware	The state law covers all non-manufacturing employers and any chemical manufacturer, importer, or distributor doing business in the state, as well as the state and its political subdivision. It provides emergency personnel access to information. The states' right-to-know rules are preempted by the federal HCS, with exceptions

Delaware law requires employers to maintain a workplace chemical list along with a MSDS for each hazardous chemical on the workplace chemical list. Emergency information must be relayed to the local fire chief. Employers must compile and maintain for 30 years a workplace chemical list. New or newly assigned workers must be informed of the existence of the list before those employees begin to work with or in an area containing hazardous chemicals.

The law requires an education and training program to be provided at least annually for workers using or handling hazardous chemicals | Dept. of Health and Social Services (302) 255-9040 | Division of Industrial Affairs Dept. of Labor 4425 Market St. Wilmington, DE 19802 (302) 761-8200 |
District of Columbia	Employees are covered under federal law.	Office of Occupational Safety and Health (202) 671-1800	Department of Employment Services Office of Occupational Safety and Health 64 New York Avenue, N.E., 2nd Floor Washington, DC 20002 (202) 671-1800
Florida	Employees are covered under federal law.	Regional OSHA Office (404) 562-2300	Regional OSHA Office 61 Forsyth St., S.W. Atlanta, GA 30303 (404) 562-2300
Georgia	The private sector is covered under federal law; state law covers the public sector.	Dept. of Labor Safety Engineering (404) 679-0687	Department of Labor 148 International Blvd., NE Atlanta, GA 30303 (404) 232-3685

State	Summary	State Right-to-Know Contact	OSHA Office
Hawaii[*]	The state adopted the federal law.	Dept. of Labor & Industrial Relations (808) 586-9100	Occupational Safety and Health Division Department of Labor and Industrial Relations 830 Punchbowl St. Honolulu, HI 96813 (808) 586-9100
Idaho	Employees are covered under federal law.	Department of Labor (208) 332-3570	Department of Labor 317 W. Main Boise, ID 83735-0001 (208) 332-3570
Illinois	The state law covers the public sector. The Illinois Act is preempted in the private sector by the federal HCS. However, all employers, public and private, must obtain MSDSs for each toxic substance and provide a written chemical safety contingency plan and arrangements with local fire departments. Posters advising employees of their right to know must be on display in work areas, and employees must be trained about toxic substances in the workplace. MSDSs must be maintained for at least 10 years after the substances are no longer used, produced, or stored. An employee may refuse to work with a toxic substance only if the employer has failed to make a "good faith effort" to provide information on the MSDS within 10 days of the request. Before an employee's work assignment, and annually thereafter, each employer must provide education and training. Many industrial firms must have written education and training programs that are documented and repeated annually.	Dept. of Labor (312) 793-2800	Department. of Labor 160 N. LaSalle St. 13th Floor, Suite C-1300 Chicago, IL 60601-3150 (312) 793-2800
Indiana[*]	The state adopted the federal law.	Industrial Compliance Division (317) 232-2655	OSHA Dept. of Labor 402 West Washington St. Room W. 195 Indianapolis, IN 46204-2751 (317) 232-2378

Exhibit 22.1

Mandated Benefits: 2009 Compliance Guide

Exhibit 22.1 (cont'd)
State Hazard Communication Standards

State	Summary	State Right-to-Know Contact	OSHA Office
Iowa*	The state law is similar to federal law; state law includes community right-to-know and fire department inspections provisions. It covers all employers, as well as manufacturers, distributors, and importers of hazardous substances. Employers must make information available to their employees and provide special training whenever they assign an employee to a special function or task involving hazardous substances.	Bureau of Labor (515) 281-5870	OSHA Workforce Development Division of Labor Services 1000 East Grand Ave. Des Moines, IA 50319-0209 (515) 281-8067
Kansas	Employees are covered under federal law.	Industrial Safety and Health (785) 296-4386	Kansas Department of Labor Industrial Safety and Health Section 800 SW Jackson Suite 1500 Topeka, KS 66612-1227 (785) 296-4386
Kentucky*	The state adopted the federal law.	Dept. of Labor (502) 564-3070	Labor Cabinet 1047 US Hwy 127 South Suite 4 Frankfort, KY 40601 (502) 564-3070
Louisiana	Employees are covered under federal law.	Dept. of Labor (225) 342-3111	Office of Workers' Compensation P.O. Box 94094 Baton Rouge, LA 70802-9094 (225) 342-3111
Maine	The law covers all employers except agricultural employers. Employers must provide employees with extensive information about hazardous substances, employee education and training, and access to written records. Instruction on hazardous chemicals must be given before employees' initial assignment, with additional training provided whenever new information is obtained.	Dept. of Labor (207) 623-7900	Department of Labor P.O. Box 259 45 Commerce Drive Augusta, ME 04333 (207) 623-7900

State	Summary	State Right-to-Know Contact	OSHA Office
Maryland*	The law applies to most employers, including construction. Fire department and independent contractor provisions are included. Under the state law, employers also are required to submit to the Department of Environment a list of hazardous chemicals in the workplace and train employees to properly handle these substances. Employers must compile and continually update a list of hazardous chemicals used and maintain it for at least 40 years. The chemical list and an MSDS must be made available to the employees upon request. If the employer refuses to comply, the employee may refuse to work with the hazardous chemical. An employee training and education program also must be provided to inform workers of any chemical hazards to which they may be exposed. The program must be offered to each new employee before initial work assignment and to all other employees when additional information is available.	Division of Labor and Industry (410) 767-2241	Division of Labor and Industry Department of Labor, Licensing and Regulation 1100 N. Eutaw St. Rm. 613 Baltimore, MD 21201-2206 (410) 767-2241
Massachusetts	The state law covers the public sector; the private sector is covered under federal law, although private employers still must submit MSDSs to the state environmental protection department. Employers must provide and post in the workplace an MSDS for each product present and retain the MSDS for 30 years. If an employee requests an MSDS and the employer does not comply within four days, the employee may refuse to work with the substances until the MSDS is provided. Employees must receive annual instruction on the nature and effects of all hazardous substances present in the workplace. For new employees, instruction must be furnished within the first month of employment.	Dept. of Occupational Safety (617) 969-7177	Department of Labor and Industries 19 Staniford Street, 2nd Floor Boston, MA 02114 (617) 626-6975
Michigan*	The state law covers most manufacturing employers with SIC codes 20–39, nonmanufacturing and public employers, and service industries. The Michigan right-to-know law incorporates the federal HCS and goes beyond it to include the public sector. Information must be provided to fire departments. The state law requires employers to develop a communication program designed to protect employees who handle hazardous chemicals.	Dept. of Labor and Economic Growth (517) 373-1820	Bureau of Safety and Regulation Occupational Safety & Health Admin. P.O. Box 30643 Lansing, MI 48909-8143 (517) 322-1814
Minnesota* (continued)	The Minnesota OSHA covers most employers. Training on infectious agents is required for hospital/clinic workers. Employers must evaluate	Occupational Safety & Health Division,	OSHA Department of Labor and

Exhibit 22.1 (cont'd)
State Hazard Communication Standards

State	Summary	State Right-to-Know Contact	OSHA Office
	their workplaces for the presence of hazardous substances, and employees must be trained concerning those substances or agents to which they may be exposed. Training to update the required information must be repeated at least annually. Every employer must maintain current information both for training and for requests by employees who wish to have access to required data. An employee acting in good faith has the right to refuse to work under conditions that the worker "reasonably believes" present "imminent danger of death or serious physical harm."	Dept. of Labor and Industry (651) 284-5060	Industry 443 Lafayette Rd. North St. Paul, MN 55155-4307 (651) 284-5050
Mississippi	Employees are covered under federal law.	Employment Security Commission (601) 321-6000	Employment Security Commission P.O. Box 1699 Jackson, MS 39215-1699 (601) 321-6000
Missouri	Employees are covered under federal law.	Dept. of Labor & Industrial Relations, Labor Standards Division (573) 751-2461	Division of Labor Standards Department of Labor and Industrial Relations 3315 West Truman Blvd. Rm. 214, PO Box 599 Jefferson City, MO 65102-0599 (573) 751-2461
Montana	Law is administered at local level; it covers manufacturing and non-manufacturing employers. Fire department inspections and public access provisions are included in the law. An employer that fails to provide an employee with information on a hazardous chemical within five work-days of a request for such information may not require the employee to work with the chemical until the information is made available. Employers must conduct, at least annually, an education and training program on the use and handling of hazardous substances. New hires and newly assigned employees must be informed of the existence of the chemical list and receive training before they begin to work with or in areas containing a hazardous chemical. A record of the dates of employees' training sessions and the names of employees attending those sessions must be kept by every employer.	Dept. of Labor and Industry (406) 444-1605	Dept. of Labor and Industry, Safety and Health Bureau, P.O. Box 1728 Helena, MT 59624-1728 (406) 444-1605

State	Summary	State Right-to-Know Contact	OSHA Office
Nebraska	Employees are covered under federal law.	Dept. of Labor (402) 471-2239	Department of Labor, Labor and Safety Standards 301 Centennial Mall South P.O. Box 95024 Lincoln, NE 68509-5024 (402) 471-2239
Nevada *	The state adopted the federal law.	Division of Industrial Relations, Occupational Safety & Health Administration (702) 486-9044	Occupational Safety and Health Administration, Division of Industrial Relations 1301 N. Green Valley Parkway, Suite 200 Henderson, NV 89074 (702) 486-9044
New Hampshire	State law is preempted by federal law, but public sector employees are covered by state law. Information must be posted about hazardous substances in the workplace. An employee may request an MSDS on a substance. If the information is not received within 72 hours, an employee may refuse to work with the substance until such information is provided. Employers must conduct an education and training program for all employees routinely exposed to toxic substances. The program must be conducted within the first month of hire.	Dept. of Labor (603) 271-6850	Department of Labor, Safety and Training Division, P.O. Box 2076 Concord, NH 03302-2076 (603) 271-6850
New Jersey **	The state law is preempted by federal HCS, except for labeling provisions. Every employer is required to complete, and retain for 30 years, both a workplace survey and an environmental survey containing information on each hazardous or environmental hazardous substance in the workplace. Notices must be posted in Spanish wherever Spanish-speaking workers are employed. An employee may refuse to work with a hazardous substance if information has not been provided to the employee within five days of a written request. An education and training program must be conducted annually to inform employees of the potential health risks of exposure to hazardous substances and appropriate safety procedures. New hires must receive training within the first month and, when requested, the training must be in Spanish.	Dept. of Labor, Division of Public Safety and Occupational Safety and Health (609) 292-7036	Office of Public Employees' Occupational Safety and Health, 1 John Fitch Plaza P.O. Box 386 Trenton, NJ 08625-0386 (609) 292-2975

Exhibit 22.1 (cont'd)
State Hazard Communication Standards

State	Summary	State Right-to-Know Contact	OSHA Office
New Mexico*	The state law covers manufacturing and nonmanufacturing sectors. Employers must keep inventories of all incoming containers of hazardous chemicals or substances and check for labels, obtain and maintain MSDSs for those substances, prepare a written hazard communication program, and provide training and information to employees.	Occupational Health & Safety Bureau (505) 476-8700	Occupational Health and Safety Bureau Environment Department 525 Camino de Los Marquez, Suite 3 Santa Fe, NM 87505 (505) 476-8700
New York**	The state law covers all employers doing business in the state. Employers must keep and retain for 40 years records of any employee exposure to any substance listed in OSHA regulations. Employees have the right to access employee exposure records and information on the identity and hazardous effect of toxic substances. Employees may refuse to work with a toxic substance if the employer fails to respond to a request for information within 72 hours.	Dept. of Labor (518) 457-2238	Department of Labor State Office Campus Bldg. 12 Rm. 158 Albany, NY 12240 (518) 457-3518
North Carolina*	The law covers both private and public employers.	Division of Occupational Safety & Health, Dept. of Labor (800) 625-2267	Department of Labor 1101 Mail Service Cent. Raleigh, NC 27699-1101 (919) 807-2796
North Dakota	The state law is preempted in the private sector; the law applies to state, city, and county government employers. Instruction in the proper use and handling of hazardous substances must be provided to all supervisors and employees. Training efforts must be documented using a form signed by each employee who receives instruction. All employees covered, including part-time and seasonal workers and temporary transfers, must be given initial training; thereafter, workers should receive remedial or refresher training at least once a year.	Department of Labor (701) 328-2660	Department of Labor 600 East Boulevard Avenue #406 Bismarck, ND 58501 (701) 328-2660
Ohio	Employees are covered under federal law.	Division of Labor and Worker Safety (614) 644-2239	Division of Labor and Worker Safety 77 South High Street, 22nd Floor

State	Summary	State Right-to-Know Contact	OSHA Office
Oklahoma	The law covers only public employers; the private sector is covered under federal law.	Dept. of Labor (405) 528-1500	Columbus, OH 43215 (614) 644-2239 Department of Labor Occupational Safety and Health Administration 4001 N. Lincoln Blvd. Oklahoma City, OK 73105 (405) 528-1500
Oregon*	The state law includes labeling requirements for all employers, including agricultural and construction employers. Public access to information is required. Employers must develop and implement a written hazard communication program that describes how they plan to comply with requirements for labels and other forms of warning, MSDSs, and employee information and training. Information and training on hazardous chemicals must be provided to employees in their work areas at the time of initial assignment and whenever a new hazard is introduced. Records on the identity of a substance, where it was used, and when it was used must be kept for 30 years.	Oregon OSHA (503) 378-3272	OSHA 350 Winter St., NE Room 430 P.O. Box 14480 Salem, OR 97309-0405 (503) 378-3272
Pennsylvania	Private sector coverage is preempted by federal law but must complete surveys. Public sector is covered by state law. Employees have the right to request from the employer an MSDS, list, or survey. Employers must comply with a written request for such information within five days or employees may refuse to work, without penalty, with hazardous substances until the requested information is provided. Nonmanufacturing employers must conduct annual employee health and safety training programs.	Bureau of PENNSAFE, Dept. of Labor & Industry (717) 783-2071	Department of Labor and Industry 1700 Labor and Industry Bldg. 7th and Forster Sts. Harrisburg, PA 17120 (717) 787-5279
Rhode Island (continued)	Community right-to-know provisions are included. Employers must maintain the chemical identification list for 30 years and make it available upon request to any affected employee within three workdays or the employee may refuse to work with the designated substance or mixture. Before an employee's initial work assignment and annually thereafter, employers must provide training and education about hazardous substances in the workplace.	Division of Occupational Safety Dept. of Labor and Training (401) 462-8570	Division of Occupational Safety Department of Labor and Training Center General Complex Building 70-2 1511 Pontiac Avenue

Exhibit 22.1

Exhibit 22.1 (cont'd)
State Hazard Communication Standards

State	Summary	State Right-to-Know Contact	OSHA Office
			Cranston, RI 02920 (401) 462-8570
South Carolina*	The state adopted the federal law; the law is enforced by the state OSHA office.	Dept. of Labor (803) 896-7665	Department of Labor Kingstree Bldg. 110 Centerview Dr. Columbia, SC 29210 (803) 896-7665
South Dakota	Employees are covered under federal law.	Dept. of Labor (605) 773-3101	Department of Labor 700 Governors Dr. Pierre, SD 57501-2291 (605) 773-3101
Tennessee*	The state law covers all employers; fire department and community access provisions are included. A written request to examine an MSDS must be honored within three business days or, under certain conditions, an employee may refuse to work with the hazardous chemical until furnished. Nonmanufacturing employers must provide an education and training program annually for employees who use or handle hazardous substances. New or newly assigned employees must receive training before they begin working in an area containing hazardous chemicals. Employers are required to keep a record of the dates of employee training sessions. Manufacturing employers shall provide employees with a written copy of the workplace chemical list to be signed by each employee upon their review and maintained by the employer for the period of employee's term of employment.	Occupational Safety & Health Administration, Dept. of Labor (615) 741-2793	Department of Labor 220 French Landing Drive Nashville, TN 37243-0659 (615) 741-2793
Texas	The law only covers public employees of the state and local governments and political subdivisions; the private sector is preempted by the federal communication standard. Employers are required to maintain a list of hazardous chemicals, update it annually, and maintain the list for a minimum of 30 years. Every employer must provide, at least annually, an education and training program for those employees who use or handle hazardous substances. New or newly assigned employees must receive training before they begin working with or in an area containing hazardous chemicals.	Division of Workers Compensation (800) 687-7080	Texas Department of Insurance, Division of Workers' Compensation 333 Guadalupe Austin, TX 78701 (800) 687-7080
Utah*	The state adopted the federal law.		OSH Division Utah Labor Commission

State	Summary	State Right-to-Know Contact	OSHA Office
		Utah Labor Commission (801) 530-7606	160 East 300 South, 3rd Floor PO Box 146650 Salt Lake City, UT 84114-6650 (801) 530-7606
Vermont*	The state adopted the federal law for private and public sectors for worker right-to-know. The state law covers community and fire department inspection provisions.	Occupational Safety & Health Administration, Dept. of Labor (802) 828-2765	Division of OSH Department of Labor 5 Green Mountain Drive P.O. Box 488 Montpelier, VT 05601-0488 (802) 828-2765
Virginia*	The state adopted the federal law. The state law covers public employees of state, county, and local governments and political subdivisions.	Bureau of Occupational Health Compliance (804) 371-2327	Department of Labor and Industry Powers-Taylor Bldg. 13 South 13th St. Richmond, VA 23219-4101 (804) 371-2327
Washington*	The state law covers manufacturing and nonmanufacturing employers and state government offices and its political subdivisions that use chemicals or produce chemicals for use or distribution. Employees may request in writing a copy of a workplace survey or MSDS for their respective work areas. The employee has the right to refuse to work with the particular hazardous substance for which the request was made if not provided within three working days. Employers must provide employees with information and training on hazardous chemicals in the workplace. The information and training must be provided at the time of the employees' initial assignment to the workplace.	Dept. of Labor and Industries (306) 902-9166	Department of Labor and Industries P.O. Box 44600 Olympia, WA 98504-4600 (360) 902-9166

Exhibit 22.1   Mandated Benefits: 2009 Compliance Guide

Exhibit 22.1 (cont'd)
State Hazard Communication Standards

State	Summary	State Right-to-Know Contact	OSHA Office
West Virginia	The private sector is covered under the federal standard. A separate worker right-to-know law covers public employees. The community right-to-know law has firefighter and community provisions. Employers must report exposure incidents within 10 days.	Division of Labor (304) 558-7890	Division of Labor Bldg. 6, Room B749 Capitol Complex Charleston, WV 25305 (304) 558-7890
Wisconsin	The law covers all employers, including the state and its political subdivisions, engaging the services of an employee in a workplace, and using, studying, or producing toxic substances, infectious agents, or pesticides. Employers must post information in every workplace informing the employees of the right-to-know information about toxic substances. Within 30 workdays of a written request, employers must provide employees with a copy of hazardous substances list. Employees may refuse to work with or be exposed to the toxic substance, infectious agent, or pesticide until the required information is provided by the employer. Prior to employees' initial assignment to a workplace, education and training must be provided.	Dept. of Commerce (608) 266-2780	Workers' Compensation Division Department of Workforce Development 201 East Washington Madison, WI 53702 (608) 266-3131
Wyoming*	The state adopted the federal law. Every employer must develop and make available to workers, upon request, a written hazards communication program. Employers must provide employees with information and training at the time of initial assignment and whenever a new chemical is introduced.	Dept. of Occupational Health & Safety (309) 777-7786	Division of OSH, Department of Employment Cheyenne Business Center 1510 E. Pershing Blvd. West Wing, Cheyenne, WY 82002 (307) 777-7700

*OSHA-approved state plan.
**OSHA-approved state plan for public sector (state and local government) employment only.

Chapter 23
Substance Abuse in the Workplace

§ 23.01   AUDIT QUESTIONS

1. If the company is a federal contractor meeting the requirements of the Drug-Free Workplace Act of 1988, has it established and implemented the policies and procedures to certify that it has a drugfree workplace?

2. If there is even one employee who is required to have a commercial driver's license to perform his or her duties, have policies and procedures been established that comply with the United States Department of Transportation's regulations, including random drug testing?

3. Has a written drug-free workplace policy been given to all employees (including new employees as they are hired), and have all employees signed a written statement indicating they will comply with the policy?

4. Are employees educated about the dangers of drug use and alcohol abuse?

5. Are supervisors trained to recognize the signs of drug use and alcohol abuse?

6. Is the drug testing policy and procedure in writing, and has it been distributed to every employee covered by the program?

7. Is the drug-free workplace program evaluated each year and modifications made to make it as effective as possible?

Note: Consistent "yes" answers to the above questions suggest that the organization is applying effective management practices and/or complying with federal regulations. "No" answers indicate that problems areas exist and should be addressed immediately.

This chapter discusses the impact of substance abuse in the workplace, the federal laws that require certain organizations to implement policies and procedures to deal with substance abuse, and the programs and policies employers can use to bring about a drug-free workplace.

§ 23.02 THE IMPACT OF SUBSTANCE ABUSE IN THE WORKPLACE

Drug and alcohol abuse—collectively known as *substance abuse*—saddles employers with millions of dollars in direct and indirect costs every year. One estimate places the average costs of employee substance abuse to a company at $7,000 per user in lost productivity, accidents, absenteeism, and replacing fired and suspended employees.

In 2007, the Office of Applied Studies (OAS) of the Substance Abuse and Mental Health Services Administration (SAMHSA) released its latest annual report on substance abuse and dependence in the United States. The 2006 National Survey on Drug Use and Health (NSDUH) (formerly the National Household Survey on Drug Abuse (NHSDA)) surveyed approximately 67,500 persons, including full- and part-time employees. The report indicates that an estimated 8.8 percent of America's full-time workforce age 18 and older use illicit drugs—an increase from the 2005 survey, which estimated that 8.2 percent of full-time workers used illicit drugs, and the 2004 survey, which estimated that 8.0 percent of full-time workers age 18 and older used illicit drugs. The report also indicated that 8.9 percent of full-time workers admitted to heavy alcohol use (defined as having five or more drinks on five or more occasions in the past 30 days), an approximate 0.5 percent increase from 2005.

A previous survey, released in 1999, titled "Worker Drug Use and Workplace Policies and Programs: Results from the 1994 and 1997 National Household Survey on Drug Abuse," found that 44 percent of employees who abuse illegal drugs work in small businesses with fewer than 25 employees, whereas 43 percent work in medium-sized businesses with 26 to 499 employees. That survey found that large businesses (500 or more employees) were more likely to have drug- and alcohol-free workplace policies, to implement drug testing, and to offer employee assistance programs (EAPs) than do small businesses. Not surprisingly, perhaps, the percentage of workers in large businesses that admit to illegal drug use and heavy alcohol use (5.8 percent) is lower than that of workers in small businesses (8.6 percent) and mediumsized businesses (7.6 percent).

The 2000 NHSDA found that 11.6 percent of illicit drug users and 8.4 percent of heavy alcohol users missed two or more workdays in the month before the survey due to illness or injury, compared with 6.5 percent of employees who do not use illicit drugs and 6.8 percent of employees who are not heavy alcohol users. Further, the survey found that 4.4 percent of illicit drug users and 3.9 percent of heavy alcohol users skipped one or more days of work in the month before the survey, whereas only 1.7 percent of workers who were nonusers missed work voluntarily in the same period.

The Quest Diagnostics' Drug Testing Index reported that 3.8 percent of all drug tests conducted in the workplace in 2007 were positive—equal to the rate in 2006 and the lowest level since Quest Diagnostics began publishing the Drug Testing Index in 1988. Of the positive tests, 13.2 percent were positive for cocaine, 9.6 percent were positive for amphetamines, 7.6 percent were positive for opiates, and 48.4 percent were positive for marijuana.

In federally mandated tests administered to workers in safety-sensitive positions, positive results were obtained in 11.1 percent of for-cause tests (administered upon suspicion of drug use), 3.3 percent of return-to-duty tests (administered upon return to work following leave for treatment and/or rehabilitation), 2.0 percent of preemployment tests, 2.6 percent of postaccident tests, 1.5 percent of random tests, and 0.75 percent of periodic tests. For all tests conducted in the workplace, the positive testing rates for all positions were higher: 19.2 percent (for-cause tests), 5.6 percent (return-to-duty tests), 3.9 percent (preemployment tests), 5.8 percent (postaccident tests), 5.7 percent (random tests), and 1.4 percent (periodic tests). From these statistics, it would appear that federally mandated testing has contributed to decreased drug use in safety-sensitive positions.

Other studies have estimated that substance abusers have absenteeism rates three to eight times higher than those of other employees and incur medical costs three times the average of other employees' costs. Substance abusers are two to three times more likely to be injured on the job and five times more likely to file a workers' compensation claim. Up to 40 percent of industrial fatalities and 47 percent of industrial injuries can be linked to substance use.

Other studies have estimated that drug-using employees are only 65 to 75 percent as productive as nonusers. Problems related to substance abuse are one of the four top reasons for the rise in workplace violence. A study conducted by the Institute for Health Policy, Brandeis University, as reported by the Department of Labor (DOL), found substance abuse to be the number-one health problem in the country, resulting in more deaths, illnesses, and disabilities than any other preventable health condition.

Clearly, the costs of substance abuse in the workplace are high for both the employee and the employer. Progress in ameliorating the problems is possible, however, and the returns on investing in a comprehensive substance-free workplace program can be significant. Studies have estimated that for every $1 spent on treatment, employers can save between $2 and $10. For example, General Motors Corporation's EAP saves the company $37 million per year. United Airlines estimated that it receives a return of $16.95 on every dollar it spends on its EAP. In Ohio, a study of the economic impact of treatment for substance abuse found significant improvements (e.g., a 91 percent decrease in absenteeism and a 97 percent decrease in workplace injuries). These studies suggest that employees who are pressured into treatment by their employers are slightly more likely to recover from their alcoholism and improve their performance than those who are not so pressured.

§ 23.03   DRUG-FREE WORKPLACE LEGISLATION

To combat the effects of drugs in the workplace, Congress passed two major pieces of legislation that require employers to deal with drug-related problems: the Drug-Free Workplace Act of 1988 (DFWA) and the Omnibus Transportation Employee Testing Act of 1991 (OTETA).

[A]   The Drug-Free Workplace Act of 1988

The DFWA requires covered employers to certify that they will provide drug-free workplaces.

[1]   Covered Employers

Employers that are subject to the DFWA's requirements include:

- Employers with a contract or seeking a contract from any federal agency for the procurement of any property or services of $25,000 or more

- Individuals with a contract or seeking a contract of any dollar amount from any federal agency

- Recipients of grants of any amount from any federal agency

- Contractors and grantees who perform work in federal facilities

Interim guidelines prepared by the Office of Management and Budget (OMB) indicate that hospitals are not subject to the DFWA merely because they receive Medicare reimbursements. Similarly, financial institutions are not covered by the DFWA merely because they sell U.S. treasury bonds.

[2] Requirements

The DFWA requires covered employers to certify that they will satisfy the following seven standards:

1. Prepare a written policy or statement that (a) notifies employees that the unlawful manufacture, distribution, dispensation, possession, or use of a controlled substance is prohibited in the workplace and (b) specifies the actions that will be taken for violations of this prohibition.

2. Develop and implement a drug-free awareness program that informs employees about:

   a. The dangers of drug use in the workplace;

   b. The employer's policy of maintaining a drug-free workplace;

   c. Any *available* counseling, employee assistance, or rehabilitation programs; and

   d. The penalties that will be taken if violations of the policy occur.

3. Give employees who perform the work on the contract or grant a copy of the drug-free workplace policy described in item 1 above.

4. State in the drug-free workplace policy that, as a condition of employment on the government contract or grant, employees must (a) agree to abide by the terms of the policy and (b) notify the employer of any conviction for a drug violation that occurs in the workplace within five days of that conviction.

5. If an employee notifies the employer of a conviction, as described in item 4 above, the employer must notify the contracting federal agency of that conviction within 10 days of receiving such notice.

6. Employers must take disciplinary action (or impose other appropriate punishment) on any employee who is convicted of a drug offense that occurs in the workplace, or require the employee to satisfactorily complete a counseling or rehabilitation program.

7. Employers must make a good-faith effort to continue to maintain a drug-free workplace through implementation of the above requirements.

[3] Sanctions

The DFWA imposes significant sanctions against contractors and grantees who fail to comply with the requirements of the law. These sanctions include suspension of payments, termination of the contract, and debarment from future government contracts.

[B] The Omnibus Transportation Employee Testing Act of 1991

OTETA came out of the realization that alcohol and other drugs are involved in a significant number of motor vehicle and other transportation-related accidents. It requires employers who have employees in transportation-related "safety-sensitive" positions to have drug-free workplace programs that include both alcohol and drug testing.

The U.S. Department of Transportation (DOT) is responsible for implementing and enforcing OTETA's regulations. OTETA covers five modes of transportation, which are represented by five agencies within the DOT: (1) aviation (Federal Aviation Administration), (2) motor carriers and highways (Federal Motor Carrier Safety Administration), (3) mass transit (Federal Transit Administration), (4) railroads (Federal Railroad Administration), and (5) maritime (U.S. Coast Guard). In addition, the Research and Special Programs Administration of the DOT covers the pipeline industry.

The DOT has created a handbook for employers to assist in their compliance with the DOT drug and alcohol testing regulations. "What Employers Need to Know About DOT Drug and Alcohol Testing [Guidance and Best Practices]" is available on the DOT's Web site: *http://www.dot.gov/ost/dapc/test-ingpubs/what_employers_need_to_know.pdf.*

[1] Covered Employers

OTETA covers interstate and intrastate truck and motor coach operations, including those operated by federal, state, and local governments; church and civic organizations; Indian tribes; farmers; custom harvesters; and for-hire and private businesses.

The requirements of OTETA went into effect on January 1, 1995, for employers with 50 or more covered employees and one year later for all employers.

[2] Covered Employees

A covered employee under OTETA is an employee who has a commercial driver's license and who operates a commercial vehicle as defined by the Federal Motor Carrier Safety Administration (FMCSA). A commercial motor vehicle means a motor vehicle (or combination of motor vehicles) used in commerce to transport passengers or property, if the motor vehicle fits one of the following descriptions:

1. Has a gross combination weight rating of 11,794 or more kilograms (26,001 or more pounds) inclusive of a towed unit with a gross vehicle weight rating of more than 4.536 kilograms (10,000 pounds); or

2. Has a gross vehicle weight rating of 11,794 or more kilograms (26,001 or more pounds); or

3. Is designed to transport 16 or more passengers, including the driver; or

4. Is of any size and is used in the transportation of hazardous materials (as defined by the Hazardous Materials Transportation Act), which requires the motor vehicle to be placarded under the Hazardous Materials Regulations.

[Title 49, C.F.R. Part 172, subpart F]

Some states have expanded the requirements for a commercial driver's license (CDL). If the business operates in a state that requires a CDL but the driver does not operate a vehicle fitting the descriptions above, the driver is exempt from the federal DOT's regulations. Active-duty military personnel are also exempt from the regulations.

The safety-sensitive function refers to the on-duty time of drivers and other personnel. It includes the following times:

1. All time at a carrier or shipper plant, terminal, facility, or other property, or on any public property, waiting to be dispatched, unless the driver has been relieved from duty by the motor carrier

2. All time inspecting equipment as required by Sections 392.7 and 392.8 of 49 C.F.R. or otherwise inspecting, servicing, or conditioning any commercial motor vehicle at any time

3. All driving time as the term *driving time* is defined by the Hazardous Materials Transportation Act

4. All time, other than driving time, in or upon any commercial motor vehicle except time spent resting in a *sleeper berth* as defined by the Hazardous Materials Transportation Act

5. All time loading or unloading a vehicle, supervising or assisting in the loading or unloading, attending a vehicle being loaded or unloaded, remaining in readiness to operate the vehicle, or giving or receiving receipts for shipments loaded or unloaded

6. All time repairing, obtaining assistance, or remaining in attendance upon a disabled vehicle

[3] Employer Requirements

The DOT's regulations require employers to develop a program that contains, at a minimum, the following components: a written policy, prohibition of alcohol and drug use, a description of the consequences of violating the regulations, two hours of annual supervisor training on the effects of drugs and alcohol and on the supervisory responsibilities of DOT-covered workers, employee drug and alcohol education, drug testing, and alcohol testing, each of which is described as follows:

1. *Written policy.* The DOT regulations mandate that the following specific items are to be included in every covered employer's written policy:

   a. The identity of the person designated by the employer to answer covered employees' questions about the policy, procedures, and materials

   b. The categories of covered employees subject to the testing requirements

   c. Clear information about the safety-sensitive functions performed by these employees such that they will understand during what period of their workday they will be required to be in compliance

   d. The conduct that is specifically prohibited

   e. The circumstances under which the covered employee will be tested for drugs and/or alcohol

   f. Specifics on the drug testing program, including the procedures that will be used to test and verify for drugs and/or alcohol, protect the covered employee and the integrity of the testing processes, safeguard the severity of the test results, and ensure that the results are attributed to the correct covered employee

g. The requirement that covered employees must submit to the drug and alcohol testing required by the regulations

h. A description of what actions establish a refusal to submit to drug and/or alcohol testing, providing adulterated or substituted samples, and the consequences of those actions

i. The consequences for covered employees who have violated the prohibitions of the policy, which include the requirement that they be removed immediately from safety-sensitive functions

j. The consequences for covered employees who have been found to have a blood alcohol concentration of at least 0.02 but less than 0.04

k. Drug and alcohol use education, including at a minimum

— The effects of alcohol use on an individual's health, work, and personal life

— The signs and symptoms of drug and/or alcohol abuse, and

— The available assistance for intervening when an abuse problem is suspected, such as confrontation, referral to an EAP (if available), and/or referral to management

As noted above, the written policy must describe the prohibited conduct. The DOT regulations discuss alcohol and drug prohibitions separately.

2. *Alcohol prohibitions.* Any alcohol misuse that could affect performance of a safety-sensitive function is prohibited, including:

a. Alcohol use while performing safety-sensitive functions

b. Use during the four hours immediately preceding the performance of safety-sensitive functions

c. Reporting for duty or remaining on duty with an alcohol concentration of 0.04 or greater

d. Possession of alcohol, including possession of medicines containing alcohol, unless the packaging seal is unbroken (possession of alcohol that is manifest and being transported as part of a shipment is excluded from these prohibitions)

e. Alcohol use during the eight hours following an accident, or until the covered employee is administered a postaccident test

f. Refusal to take a required test

A covered employee found to have an alcohol concentration of at least 0.02 but less than 0.04 shall not be allowed to perform safety-sensitive functions for at least 24 hours.

3. *Drug prohibitions.* Any drug misuse that could affect performance of a safety-sensitive function is prohibited, including:

a. Use of any drug, unless prescribed by a licensed medical practitioner, provided that the medical practitioner has advised the covered employee that the drug will not adversely affect the driver's ability to perform safety-sensitive functions

b. Verifiably testing positive for drugs

c. Refusing to take a required test or providing an adulterated or substituted sample

4. *Consequences.* The employer's policy must also describe the consequences associated with violations of the regulations. They include the following:

a. The employer may prevent the covered employee from performing any safety-sensitive function if any of the prohibitions are violated.

b. The employer may advise the covered employee of resources available to evaluate and resolve the problem, including names, addresses, and telephone numbers of substance abuse professionals and treatment programs.

c. The employer may have the covered employee evaluated by a substance abuse professional (SAP), who shall determine what assistance, if any, he or she needs to resolve the problems.

d. Before returning for duty, the covered employee must undergo a return-to-duty test for alcohol (if the prohibited conduct involved alcohol) with a test result of less than 0.02 or drugs (if the prohibited conduct involved drugs) with a verified negative result.

e. If the SAP determined that the covered employee needed assistance in resolving the problem, then he or she must be reevaluated by the SAP to determine whether he or she properly participated in the prescribed rehabilitation program. The covered employee will also be subject to unannounced follow-up testing, as discussed below.

Note: DOT regulations do not require employers to provide or pay for any rehabilitation or counseling services or to hold covered employees' jobs for them while they undergo treatment. However, other federal, state, or local laws may apply (e.g., the Family and Medical Leave Act of 1993 or the Americans with Disabilities Act of 1990). Also, employers do not have to comply with the referral, evaluation, or treatment requirements for applicants who provide adulterated or substituted samples or refuse to submit to or fail a preemployment drug test. They need not hire such applicants for safety-sensitive positions.

A written policy on substance abuse must also take into consideration all other potentially applicable laws, such as state drug testing laws and regulations, state privacy and discrimination laws and regulations, state leave laws and regulations, Title VII of the Civil Rights Act, and union laws and contract requirements (e.g., grievances and arbitration requirements).

5. *Training and education.* The DOT regulations stipulate one hour of training each for alcohol and drugs (separately) for supervisors and other employees who have the responsibility of determining when an employee should have a reasonable-suspicion test. The training in each area must include education on the physical, behavioral, speech, and performance indicators of probable misuse. Training for supervisors (and the documentation of such training) is critical in case an employee challenges a supervisor who is requiring a reasonable-suspicion test. In addition, the training for supervisors must include the legal and regulatory aspects of testing and the employer's policies and procedures to comply with the DOT's testing and related requirements.

Education for employees must include information on the dangers of drug use and alcohol abuse, addictive potential, and destructive consequences to a person's physical, emotional, family, and social life. It also must include the requirements of the DOT's regulations and the employer's policies and procedures for compliance with the regulations.

6. *Drug testing.* The DOT regulations separate drug testing from alcohol testing. The drugs for which testing is mandated are marijuana (THC metabolite), cocaine, opiates (including heroin), phencyclidine (PCP), and amphetamines (including methamphetamines). Employers must use urine specimen collection and testing by a laboratory certified by the Department of Health and Human Services.

The following types of testing are required by the DOT regulations:

a. Preemployment testing is required for all new covered employees. Some limited exceptions are allowed (e.g., a covered employee who has participated in a DOT-regulated drug testing program within the last 30 days). (The requirements for meeting the exceptions are significant, and discussion of them is beyond the scope of this book.)

b. Postaccident testing is required as soon as practicable following an accident when either the accident involved a fatality or the covered employee receives a citation for a moving traffic violation arising from the accident. The term *accident* is defined in 49 C.F.R. § 390.5, and testing is required by the regulations only when the incident meets those definitions, even if a moving traffic violation citation is received for an accident not defined by the regulations. The drug test should be administered within 32 hours of the accident. If it is not, the employer should cease attempts to test and should prepare and maintain a record of the reasons why the test was not administered. In some cases, employers may substitute a test administered by on-site law enforcement officials. If they do, the employers must obtain a copy of the test results.

c. Random testing is required under the DOT regulations. Although there have been many court challenges to random drug testing, in the major cases involving the DOT regulations (e.g., the U.S. Supreme Court in *Skinner v. Railway Labor Executives Association* [489 U.S. 602 (1989)] and the Ninth Circuit in *Teamsters v. Department of Transportation*), the courts have found that the public's interest in safe transportation (e.g., highways, railways) outweighs employees' privacy interests.

Random drug testing is to be administered at a minimum annual rate set by the DOT of each agency within its jurisdiction. The testing rate is expressed as a percentage of the average number of covered employee positions. This rate of testing may be lowered or raised) if the industrywide positive testing rate is less (or more) than 1 percent for two calendar years. For 2006, the minimum annual testing rate for commercial motor vehicle operations is 50 percent. (See **Exhibit 23.1** for the random drug and alcohol testing rates for all DOT agencies.) Selection of which covered employees will be tested must be made by a scientifically valid method that is matched with an employee identification number, such as Social Security number or payroll number. Random drug tests must be unannounced and spread reasonably throughout the year. Once the covered employees are selected and notified, the employer must ensure that they proceed immediately to the testing site.

It is recommended that small employers (those who have 10 or fewer covered employees) join a consortium of other employers to conduct random testing. Employers with only one covered employee must join a consortium for random testing purposes.

d. Reasonable-suspicion testing is required when specific observations about the covered employee's appearance, behavior, speech, or body odor lead a trained observer to believe that the covered employee is under the influence of drugs. A written documentation of the covered employee's conduct or appearance must be prepared and signed by the witness within 24 hours of the observation, or before the results of the drug test are released, whichever is earlier.

e. Return-to-duty testing is required when a covered employee has engaged in prohibited conduct (e.g., has tested positive for drugs) and before the employee can return to his or her safety-sensitive functions. In this situation, a covered employee must be evaluated by the SAP and must participate in any assistance program prescribed before returning to work.

f. Follow-up testing is required whenever the SAP determines that the covered employee needs assistance in resolving a drug problem. Follow-up tests are unannounced and given following the covered employee's return to duty. Although the number and frequency of such tests are to be determined by the SAP, the regulations mandate at least six tests during the first 12 months following the employee's return to work.

7. *Alcohol testing.* Employers must conduct two separate tests to determine if a person has a prohibited alcohol concentration. A screening test is conducted first. This consists of a breath test using either a nonevidential breath alcohol screening device (ASD) or an evidential breath testing device (EBT). The National Highway Traffic Safety Administration (NHTSA) has also approved saliva ASDs. Any result less than 0.02 alcohol concentration is considered a "negative" test. If the alcohol concentration is 0.02 or greater, a second or confirmation test must be conducted.

The confirmation test, if required, must be conducted using an EBT that prints out the results, date and time, a sequential test number, and the name and serial number of the EBT to ensure the reliability of the results. The result of the confirmation test determines any actions taken.

This testing can be done on the employer's site by the employer (after appropriate training) or off-site by a contractor trained in this type of testing.

a. Preemployment alcohol testing was suspended as of May 1, 1995.

b. Postaccident alcohol testing must be administered as soon as is practicable after the accident (see the preceding section on drug testing for determining when testing must be administered after an accident). If the covered employee has not submitted to an alcohol test within two hours after the accident, the employer must prepare and maintain documentation as to the reasons why the test was not administered. After eight hours, the employer should stop the attempts to administer the test and prepare and maintain documentation as to the reasons why the test was not administered. As with drug tests, the employer may substitute an appropriate (blood or breath) alcohol test administered by local law enforcement after an accident. The employer must obtain a copy of the test results.

c. Random testing for alcohol use is required by the DOT regulations. Random alcohol testing, like random drug testing, is to be administered at a minimum annual rate of the average number of covered employee positions, as determined by the DOT. The minimum annual percent testing rate may be decreased or increased by the FMCSA based on the industry-wide violation rates. For 2006, the minimum annual testing rate is 10 percent for commercial motor vehicle operations.

A covered employee may be tested only while he or she is performing safety-sensitive functions, immediately before or immediately thereafter. The employer must use the requirements for selection and notification described above in drug testing for random alcohol testing. (See **Exhibit 23.1** for the random drug and alcohol testing rates for all DOT agencies.)

d. Reasonable-suspicion testing for alcohol use is authorized only if the observations are made during, just before, or just after the covered employee performs safety-sensitive functions. The individual who observes the behavior, appearance, speech, or body odor that leads to the reasonable-suspicion testing shall not conduct the actual alcohol test. As with postaccident testing, if the test is not conducted within two hours of the observation, the employer shall prepare and maintain documentation of the reasons why the test was not administered promptly. If the test is not conducted within eight hours of the observation, all attempts to administer the test shall cease and the documentation shall be prepared and maintained.

e. Return-to-duty testing is required of covered employees who have engaged in prohibited conduct (alcohol use) before the employees begin performing any safety-sensitive function. The test result must indicate a breath alcohol concentration of less than 0.02.

f. Follow-up testing is similar to that required of follow-up testing for drug use. However, the actual testing for alcohol shall be performed only when the covered employee is performing safety-sensitive functions, just before or just after.

The testing procedures in the DOT regulations are detailed and extensive, covering both alcohol breath testing and urine drug testing. On June 25, 2008 the DOT issued a new Part 40 Final Rule [73 Fed. Reg., 35961 (June 25, 2008)] amending certain provisions of the drug and alcohol testing procedures. These amendments change instructions to collectors, laboratories, medical review officers, and employers regarding adulterated, substituted, diluted, and invalid urine specimen results. These changes are intended to create consistency with specimen validity requirements established by the U.S. Department of Health and Human Services. The final rule makes specimen validity testing mandatory within the regulated transportation industries. It is imperative that employers covered by the DOT requirements receive appropriate training in conducting these tests in a manner consistent with these regulations and other applicable laws.

[4] Recordkeeping

The DOT regulations require that employers prepare and maintain records related to their drug and alcohol programs. Necessary records include:

- Records related to the drug and alcohol test collection process

- Test results records

- Documentation of other violations of the employer's policy

- Evaluation records

- Education and training records

- Drug testing documentation

Most of the records noted above must be kept for a minimum of five years. Exceptions include records related to the collection process and training, which must be kept for two years, negative and canceled test results, and alcohol test results of less than 0.02, which must be kept only one year.

The records must be kept in a secure, confidential location with controlled access, which may be on the employer's premises or off site. If records are maintained off site, the employer must make them available at its principal place of business within two days of an FMCSA request.

If required by the FMCSA or upon request of an official with proper authority, an employer must prepare and maintain an annual calendar year summary of its alcohol and drug testing programs. A select number of employers will be notified each year in January that they must submit the calendar year summary to the FMCSA by March 15 of that year. The information and the form of the summary are prescribed by the FMCSA.

Employers who need further information may call the DOT's Anti-Drug Information Center at (800) 225-DRUG.

§ 23.04 ANTI-SUBSTANCE ABUSE PROGRAMS

This section and the following sections are specifically written for employers who are not covered by either the DOT regulations or the DFWA. The requirements of those laws are not addressed in the discussion that follows.

There are many good reasons for companies to have anti-substance abuse programs even if they are not required by law to do so. It has been demonstrated that impressive change in employees' drug and alcohol abuse can be achieved through the use of effective anti-substance abuse programs. Employer education, prevention, and assistance programs can make a difference.

Start by gathering data. Talk to supervisors and employees. Listen to their ideas. Stress the positive aspects of an alcohol- and drug-free workplace, such as decreases in accidents and missed work days. Conduct research. There are many free or low-cost resources available to employers who want to develop an alcohol- and drug-free workplace, including those listed in **Exhibit 23.2**.

In 2006, the DOL initiated Drug-Free Work Week to highlight the fact that being drug free is key to protecting workplace safety and health and to encourage workers with alcohol and drug problems to seek help. In 2008, Drug-Free Work Week was held October 20-26, and will be held annually in the fall. Individual employers and employees are encouraged to conduct workplace activities and education. Employers can obtain ideas, information, and resources for implementing their own Drug-Free Work Week activities on the DOL's Web site: *http://www.dol.gov/asp/programs/drugs/workingpartners/wpdrug-free.asp*.

The six steps in developing and implementing an alcohol- and drug-free workplace program are as follows:

1. Develop and distribute a substance abuse policy.

2. Train supervisors.

3. Educate employees.

4. Provide employee assistance.

5. Consider drug and alcohol testing.

6. Evaluate and revise program periodically.

[A]   Developing a Substance Abuse Policy

An official written company policy is one of the best ways to let employees know that the employer is committed to an alcohol- and drug-free workplace. Although policies must be written in compliance with federal and state laws and regulations, they should also be sensitive to the company's goals, culture, employee relations, and benefit plan provisions. It is recommended that a competent lawyer review the written policy prior to its implementation and distribution.

A written substance abuse policy should contain at least the following elements: an explanation of why the program is being implemented, a clear description of the behaviors that are prohibited, and a description of the consequences for policy violations. If applicable, the policy should also describe the testing program and the assistance that will be given to employees with substance abuse problems.

The specific areas to be covered in a substance abuse policy include the following:

- Definition of *substance*

- Use of illegal drugs or controlled substances

- Sale or distribution of illegal drugs or controlled substances

- The use, sale, or distribution of nonprescribed drugs

- Misuse, sale, or distribution of prescribed drugs

- Any of the above types of conduct while on the premises, whether on duty or not

- Any of the above types of conduct while on duty, but off employer premises

- Any of the above types of conduct while operating a vehicle or equipment owned or leased by the employer

- Off-duty conduct as it could affect the employee's job, such as behavior at a company-sponsored function where alcohol is served

- Whether the company adheres to zero tolerance for alcohol or whether it has an allowable limit. If there is an allowable limit, state that limit in the policy. (It is recommended that the term *under the influence* not be used for determining the testing limit.)

Employers must be careful not to overreach their authority by trying to regulate the mere use of alcohol by employees on their own time. For example, under California Labor Code Section 96, employers are not permitted to discipline employees for lawful off-duty conduct—including the consumption of alcohol by adults over 21 years of age. All employers should review their policies to ensure they have not "over-stepped" their reach into employees' personal off-work lifestyle choices.

The consequences of prohibited behavior must be addressed in the substance abuse policy. Will the result be immediate termination or suspension? Or will the employee be allowed or required to enter a treatment program? Various federal and state laws may also affect the consequences of violations of the company's policy. Some employers have decided that if an employee voluntarily requests assistance for a substance abuse problem, no disciplinary action will result; but if an employee is determined to be working with alcohol or controlled substances in his system (e.g., as a result of reasonable-suspicion testing), disciplinary action will result.

However, the ADA considers self-disclosed alcohol abuse a disability that requires reasonable accommodation. One of the more frequent accommodations is the decision to "roll back" to zero those performance problems that are specifically related to alcohol abuse and occurred before the self-disclosure. In this case, employees who complete a formal rehabilitation program are given a clean slate for certain discipline problems and presumed to be starting over free of alcohol addiction. Consult the company's employment attorney for guidance on identifying which types of incidents are normally presumed to be related to drug and alcohol abuse, and which are generally not.

If an employer decides to implement a testing program, the substance abuse policy must address the consequences of a positive result of the test and also what will happen if an employee refuses to be tested. It is also recommended that an alcohol- and drug-free policy include information (or refer to a separate policy) on the company's right to conduct searches of the workplace, including all employee belongings brought onto the premises. (See **Chapter 20** for a discussion of privacy in the workplace.)

Each employee should receive a copy of the company's substance abuse policy. Many employers ask employees to sign a formal statement acknowledging that they have read and understood the policy, and keep the signed statement in the employee's personnel file.

(See **Exhibit 23.3** for a sample policy on drug testing and substance abuse.)

Employers may also want to consider whether alcohol will be served at workplace events as part of its overall substance abuse policy. Questions that may be addressed include: if alcohol is served, will there be a limit? Will employees be provided with transportation home, if needed? Will prior education about drinking and driving be provided? Online resources to assist employers with planning safe workplace celebrations are available at: *http://www.dol.gov/asp/programs/drugs/workingpartners/sp_iss/idhome.asp*.

[B] Training Supervisors

Supervisors and managers may be a company's most effective resource in eliminating alcohol and drug use on the job if they are committed to the company's anti-substance abuse program and trained to recognize and handle job performance problems, including knowing when and how to refer employees to outside assistance.

An effective training program will cover at least the following:

- The company's policies and procedures

- Behavior and conduct that might be indicative of alcohol and drug use

- How to determine whether an employee is fit for duty

- Observation and documentation of unsatisfactory job performance

- Discussion of unsatisfactory job performance and applying appropriate consequences

- If testing is part of the company's program, the procedures associated with the testing process

- How to refer an employee to outside assistance

[C] Educating Employees

The education of employees on the dangers of substance abuse is a critical component of an effective alcohol- and drug-free workplace program. Such education has a workplace benefit of assisting in the reduction of absenteeism and improving the safety of the workplace. In addition, employees benefit from the knowledge and potentially can use the information with their families and communities.

The basics of employee education should include:

- A detailed description of the company's policies and procedures

- The health, social, and familial risks associated with alcohol and drug abuse

- A description of the effect of alcohol and drug use on the company's productivity, quality, absenteeism, health care costs, and so forth

- Ways that employees can determine whether they or others may have a problem with drugs or alcohol

- Where to go for help, including information on the company's employee assistance program (EAP), if available

- The consequences of violating the company's policies, including the testing program, if any, and disciplinary action that might be taken

Employee education is not a one-time effort. As new employees are hired, they must also receive this education. Moreover, policies and procedures may change. It may be helpful for a company to hold periodic meetings on the program and policies to ensure that all employees are aware of the latest information.

[D] Providing Employee Assistance

A determination must be made about whether to provide employee assistance and, if so, what kind. An EAP is generally defined as a source of job-based services intended to assist workers whose job performance is negatively affected by personal problems. EAPs can be formal and provide significant counseling and mental health services, including rehabilitation from alcohol and drug addiction. Often, this type of EAP is included in the employer's overall health care benefits program and is paid for entirely or significantly by the employer. EAPs can also provide referrals to community-based programs offering services that are paid for by the employee. (See **Chapter 10** for more information on EAPs.)

Employers that are selecting an EAP should do the following:

1. Contact other companies in the area and inquire into their programs: what they offer, how the service is provided, what the costs are, and how results are measured.

2. Determine whether there is an EAP consortium in the community that local businesses can join. (A consortium may provide services to smaller employers at prices usually available only to large companies.)

3. Interview several EAP providers to determine the number and education of the counselors, exactly what services will be provided (e.g., education, assessment, fixed number of counseling sessions, referral only) and their cost (to the company and/or to the employee), under what circumstances the employee and his or her family can use the services, what information the EAP will release to the employer (much of the information is confidential, but management reports that do not associate individual names with diagnosis and treatment should be available), and how success will be measured.

[E] Drug and Alcohol Testing

Deciding to set up and implement a drug and alcohol testing program (when not required to do so by law) is not an easy decision. While a drug testing program can be a successful deterrent to substance abuse, there are serious issues to consider before implementing a testing program.

The legal risks of implementing a drug testing program are significant. Private employers may be sued on such grounds as invasion of privacy, defamation, and intentional infliction of emotional distress by employees who refuse to submit to a drug test and by those who are disciplined due to the results of a drug test. Additional substantive issues concerning drug tests include reliability of drug tests and the use of test results that may have no bearing on job performance. (See **Chapter 20** for a discussion of drug testing and workplace privacy concerns.) Despite two significant cases decided by the Supreme Court, which concluded that a compelling social or government health and safety interest may override the right to privacy, the issue is not completely clear for private employers. Therefore, many employers limit the circumstances of testing to preemployment, reasonable suspicion, postaccident, and follow-up after rehabilitation.

Preemployment drug testing is generally an accepted practice if the tests are "reasonable." The "reasonableness" of the test generally involves balancing the applicant's privacy interests against the employer's need for the test. Defamation cases arise if employees believe that complete confidentiality of test results is not maintained. Information such as whether an employee refused to submit to a drug test and the results of such a drug test should never be communicated to anyone without a clear need to know. Those who might have a real need to know include supervisors and managers and first aid and safety personnel in emergency situations.

When probable cause exists, arbitrators will likely rule that failure to submit to testing is a dischargeable offense. The burden of proof in drug-related discharge cases is the "clear and convincing evidence" standard. Arbitrators generally hold that discharge because of off-duty drug use requires a showing that such use affects job performance.

One way to help avoid legal problems is to develop written policy and procedures and follow them consistently. Either prepare a separate drug testing policy or include it as part of the overall drug-free workplace policy. All employees who will be included in the drug testing program should receive a written copy of the policy before the program is implemented. If drug testing is included as part of the preemployment (or any other employment-related) medical examination, it is recommended that the applicants and employees be explicitly informed of this.

Other steps to take when establishing a drug testing program include the following:

- Determine what type of test (begin with the least intrusive method) will be used (e.g., urine, blood).

- Ensure that positive results are confirmed by a licensed laboratory using gas chromatography/mass spectrometry (GC/MS) or equivalent.

- Determine which drugs will be tested and establish cut-off levels for each (work with drug and/or medical experts).

- Decide what laboratory and/or medical clinic will be used (experts recommend a lab certified by the National Institute on Drug Abuse (NIDA)).

- Ensure that the clinic/lab follows an established chain of custody procedure that will assist in avoiding fraudulent results.

- Decide whether a medical review officer (MRO) will be used. An MRO is a licensed physician who is trained in substance abuse and can help protect both the employer and the employee. An MRO will review the results of all drug tests, contact the employee to determine if there are any legitimate reasons for the positive results, contact the employee's medical practitioner, if applicable, and inform the employer of the final conclusion.

- Determine whether all applicants or only those for certain jobs will be tested.

- Assess the circumstances under which current employees will be tested (random, reasonable suspicion, postincident, post-rehabilitation).

- Decide whether all current employees will be included in the program, or only those in certain jobs or at certain locations.

- Determine what will happen if an employee tests positive (employee assistance program, other treatment options, suspension with or without final warning, termination).

- Determine what will happen if an employee refuses to submit to testing (termination, suspension).

Note: A drug testing program may be a mandatory subject of collective bargaining.

Most experts recommend establishing a relationship with the medical facility and/or drug lab before actually needing to use it. Visit several facilities and observe handling and testing procedures to evaluate whether they will be effective in avoiding fraudulent samples and results. Work with the facility to establish confidential reporting procedures. Examples of practices that assist in maintaining confidentiality include having a single contact for both the facility and the employer, maintaining medical records at the facility, and having only a sealed results sheet returned to the employer.

Many states have enacted provisions imposing drug-testing restrictions of various kinds. (See **Exhibit 23.4** for a state-by-state summary of state laws related to drug testing and their application.) Although testing is presumed to be lawful unless there is a specific restriction in state or federal law, legal issues concerning employee privacy and related issues continue to be raised. Any drug testing program that is not explicitly authorized by law may be considered open to legal challenge. Employers, especially those that must deal with labor-management relations, should seek counsel prior to implementing an employee drug testing program.

[F]   Evaluating and Modifying the Program

Periodic evaluation of the company's drug-free workplace program will help the employer determine whether the program is meeting the company's goals, whether any cost savings result from the program, and whether any modifications or expansion is needed.

The first step in an effective evaluation is to determine the baseline. Before beginning the program (or reviewing records prior to the implementation of the program), determine the incidence, prevalence, and/or dollar costs (if possible) of one more of the following factors that can be indicators of drug and alcohol abuse:

- Absenteeism—look for patterns, such as consistent absenteeism on Mondays and/or Fridays

- Tardiness

- Health care claims

- Workers' compensation claims

- Accidents

- Theft

- Turnover

Part of establishing a baseline is assessing employee morale. This assessment may be conducted formally or by talking informally to employees at all levels of the organization.

At the end of the program's first year, the levels of the factors listed above should be assessed and data compared with data collected before the implementation of the program. Is any improvement observable? Also, talk to employees about what they think and how they feel about the program. Do they feel they have had enough education? Has morale improved? Do they feel supervisors are trained adequately? Ask the supervisors their opinion of the program. Do they see any improvement?

A company should conduct ongoing evaluation of its anti-substance abuse program and a formal evaluation at least annually to assess the program's costs and benefits. Based on the results of the evaluation, changes may be made to the program to better reach the company's goals. Key decision makers and employees alike should be made aware of the results of the program and any changes to be made. It is recommended that a committee of employees from all levels of the company be organized to evaluate the program and recommend improvements.

Exhibit 23.1   Mandated Benefits: 2009 Compliance Guide

Exhibit 23.1
Department of Transportation Office of
Drug and Alcohol Policy Compliance
2008 Random Rate Notice

The following chart (adapted from the DOT's Web site) outlines the annual minimum drug and alcohol random testing rates established within DOT's Agencies and the USCG for 2008.

DOT Agency	Random Drug Testing Rate	Random Alcohol Testing Rate
Federal Motor Carrier Safety Administration (FMCSA)	50%	10%
Federal Aviation Administration (FAA)	25%	10%
Federal Railroad Administration (FRA)	25%	10%
Federal Transit Administration (FTA)	25%	10%
Pipeline and Hazardous Material Safety Administration	25%	Not applicable
United States Coast Guard (USCG)	50%	Not applicable

Note: Employers subject to more than one DOT Agency rule may continue to combine their covered employees into a single random selection pool. However, employers may do so only if they test at or above the highest random rates established by the DOT Agencies under whose jurisdiction they fall. For example, an employer having employees covered by both FMCSA and FRA in one pool must test, at the minimum, 50 percent for drugs and 10 percent for alcohol. Please contact the appropriate DOT Agency for additional information. (USCG-covered employees may be combined with DOT-covered employees in drug-testing pools even though the USCG is now part of the Department of Homeland Security.)

Exhibit 23.2
Information on Anti-Substance Abuse Programs

The following organizations distribute information on anti-substance abuse programs.

Organization	Phone Number	Web Site
National Clearinghouse for Alcohol and Drug Information	1-800-729-6686	http://ncadi.samhsa.gov
National Drug Information, Treatment, and Referral Line	1-800-662-HELP (1-800-662-4357)	
Division of Workplace Programs, Substance Abuse and Mental Health Services Administration		http://workplace.samhsa.gov
Substance Abuse Treatment Facility Locator		www.findtreatment.samhsa.gov
Workplace Helpline	1-800-WORKPLACE (1-800-967-5752)	http://www.workplace.samhsa.gov/Helpline/ Helpline.aspx or contact HELPLINE @SAMHSA.HHS.gov
Substance Abuse Program Administrators Association	1-800-672-7229	www.sapaa.com
Community-based substance abuse prevention groups		
Labor unions		
National Institute on Drug Abuse (NIDA)	1-301-443-1124	www.drugabuse.gov
National Institute on Alcohol Abuse and Alcoholism		www.niaaa.nih.gov
Center for Substance Abuse Prevention		www.prevention.samhsa.gov
Center for Substance Abuse Treatment		www.csat.samhsa.gov
Working Partners for an Alcohol- and Drug-free Workplace (an agency of the Department of Labor)	1-202-693-5919	www.dol.gov/workingpartners/
Partnership for a Drug-Free America	1-212-922-1560	www.drugfree.org
Community Anti-Drug Coalitions of America	1-800-54-CADCA (1-800-542-2322)	http://cadca.org

Exhibit 23.2

Mandated Benefits: 2009 Compliance Guide

Exhibit 23.2 (cont'd)

Organization	Phone Number	Web Site
Close to Home		www.pbs.org/wnet/closetohome
Department of Transportation Office of Drug and Alcohol Policy and Compliance	1-202-366-4000	www.dot.gov/ost/dapc
Substance Abuse Information Database (SAID)		http://said.dol.gov
American Council for Drug Education	1-800-488-DRUG (1-800-488-3784)	www.acde.org
Parents at Work	1-800-729-6686	www.theantidrug.com/AtWork
Addiction Action		www.Addiction action.org

Exhibit 23.3
A Sample Policy on Drug Testing and Substance Abuse

STATEMENT OF POLICY

ABC COMPANY

Purpose: To comply with federal legislation and to maintain a drug-free workplace.

Applies to: All ABC employees

It is ABC's policy to provide employees and customers with a working environment that is free from the use and abuse of controlled substances and the abuse of alcohol. ABC employees are expected to be in such mental and physical condition as will permit them to perform their assigned tasks in a professional and competent manner. An inability to meet these standards will result in disciplinary action up to and including termination. Consistent with this expectation, we have adopted a policy that all employees must report to work completely free from the presence of drugs and the effects of alcohol.

Controlled Substances

The illegal use, sale, possession, distribution, manufacture, or transfer of controlled substances at the workplace or elsewhere during work hours is strictly prohibited. Specifically prohibited under this policy is use, sale, possession, distribution, manufacture, or transfer of controlled substances during working hours or on nonworking time, and on or off company or customer property to the extent such use impairs an employee's ability to perform his or her job, or when such activities negatively affect the reputation of ABC Company to the general public or threaten the integrity of the firm.

The term *controlled substances* as used in this policy is defined to include legal and illegal drugs. The use or possession of legal drugs (i.e., those drugs for which a valid prescription is required before the drug may be used or possessed) is not prohibited by this policy unless that use or possession is inconsistent with the prescription or where no such prescription has been provided.

The term *illegal drugs* is defined to include all such drugs of which the use, sale, possession, distribution, manufacture, or transfer is prohibited by law and includes, but is not limited to, marijuana, narcotics, hallucinogens, stimulants, depressants, and so-called designer drugs.

The term *workplace* as used here shall mean any company premises or work site or customer's place of business, including firm or customer vehicles and public or private means of transportation while engaged in company business.

ABC Company personnel may not report to work or work while under the influence of illegal drugs, nor may such personnel report to work under the influence of legal drugs for which no prescription has been issued or where the use of the legal drugs is inconsistent with a prescription.

As used in this policy, *under the influence* means that the individual is affected by a controlled substance in a detectable manner.

Exhibit 23.3   Mandated Benefits: 2009 Compliance Guide

Exhibit 23.3 (cont'd)

Persons violating the ABC policy regarding substance abuse will be subject to disciplinary action, which may include termination for a first offense.

Whereas this policy does not prohibit the use or possession of over-the-counter or prescription drugs where such use or possession is consistent with the proper use of such substances, ABC personnel are encouraged to advise supervisors of such use where it may affect performance. Should performance be affected by the use of such substances, the individual may be relieved of his or her job duties under the [Occasional Absence] or [Sick Leave Programs].

ABC personnel who plead guilty or no contest or are convicted of a violation of a controlled substance statute that involves an action occurring at an ABC workplace or the workplace of a customer must inform their supervisor within five days of the conviction or plea. Failure to comply with this requirement will subject ABC personnel to disciplinary action, which may include termination for a first offense.

In compliance with a Department of Defense (DOD) regulation, ABC personnel assigned to work on contracts between ABC and the DOD may be subject to a random drug testing program. ABC will inform personnel who are subject to this requirement. Personnel testing positive on a drug test conducted pursuant to the DOD regulation are subject to disciplinary action, which may include transfer from their current positions or discharge for a first offense.

Alcohol

ABC Company expects that all personnel will maintain proper professional decorum at all times during the workday, on and off company or customer property. Expressly prohibited under this policy are reporting to work or working while impaired from the use of alcohol and alcohol consumption while on the job or at other times during the workday.

As used in this policy, *impaired from the use of alcohol* means that the individual's performance or behavior is marked by abnormal conduct or erratic or aberrant behavior, including, but not limited to, sleeping on the job, slurred words, or a significant smell of alcohol about the person.

The legal use of alcohol is not prohibited when an employee is not working and is not at the workplace.

Personnel violating the policy regarding abuse of alcohol will be subject to disciplinary action, which may include termination for a first offense.

Medical Evaluation and Implementation

All job applicants who are selected for employment must submit to a drug test. Refusal to submit or a positive confirmed drug test may be used as a basis for refusal to hire the applicant.

ABC personnel whose performance or behavior while on company property, customer property, or elsewhere during the workday gives rise to a reasonable suspicion that the individual is under the influence of a controlled substance or alcohol may be requested to undergo an immediate medical evaluation to determine fitness for work and appropriate tests designed to detect the presence of such substances.

Exhibit 23.3 (cont'd)

Consent to such tests as the Company may request constitutes a condition of continued employment. The refusal to consent to a test or to the disclosure of test results to appropriate ABC personnel will result in disciplinary action, which may include termination for a first offense.

ABC personnel testing positive for controlled substances or alcohol are subject to disciplinary action, up to and including termination. ABC, in its sole judgment, may require the employee to agree to cease all such use as a condition of continued employment. Such personnel further must agree to be tested for drug use on a random, continuous basis for a period of up to one year from the date of the positive test. If any of these subsequent tests are positive for controlled substances or alcohol, the individual will be discharged for cause. (Some states prohibit the use of random drug tests, even when part of a return-to-work program. Check with a competent attorney prior to implementing random drug testing.)

ABC Company reserves the right to transfer personnel who have tested positive for controlled substances from any positions such as those jobs involving the safety of others, positions permitting access to confidential, customer information or other valuable company property, or from positions of trust or fiduciary responsibility.

Any ABC personnel medically diagnosed as being addicted to a controlled substance or alcohol may be granted leave pursuant to the [Short-Term Disability Policy] to undertake rehabilitative treatment. Such individual will not be permitted to return to work until a release from treatment is presented to the HR department medically certifying that the individual is rehabilitated and capable of returning to work. Such individual further must agree to undergo random drug testing for a period of one year from the date of his or her return to work.

All urinalysis drug tests will utilize an initial immunoassay methodology or an equivalent. All positive results shall be confirmed by a licensed laboratory using gas chromatography/mass spectrometry (GC/MS) or an equivalent.

Enforcement

In order to enforce this policy and procedures, ABC may investigate potential violations and require personnel to undergo drug and/or alcohol screening, including urinalysis, blood tests, or other appropriate tests and, where appropriate, searches of all areas of the company's physical premises, including, but not limited to, work areas, personal articles, employees' clothes, desks, workstations, and personal and company vehicles, etc. Employees will be subject to discipline up to and including discharge for refusing to cooperate with searches or investigations or to submit to screening or for failing to execute consent forms when required by management.

Investigations and Searches

Where a manager or supervisor has reasonable suspicion that an employee has violated the substance abuse policy, the supervisor, or his or her designee, may inspect vehicles, lockers, work areas, desks, purses, briefcases, toolboxes, and other locations or belongings without prior notice, in order to ensure a work environment free of prohibited substances. An employee may be asked to be present and may remove a personal lock. The employee is hereby notified that locked areas or containers do not prevent a search, and thus employees should understand there is no expectation of privacy on company premises. Where the

Exhibit 23.3   Mandated Benefits: 2009 Compliance Guide

Exhibit 23.3 (cont'd)

employee is not present or refuses to remove a personal lock, the company may do so for him or her and compensate the employee for the lock. Any such searches will be coordinated with a representative of the HR department. The company may use unannounced drug detection methods. (To further enhance this policy, companies that provide lockers for employee use may wish to issue company locks and prohibit the use of personal locks entirely.)

Employee Assistance

ABC Company expects employees who suspect they have an alcohol or drug problem to seek treatment. The company will help employees who abuse alcohol or drugs by providing a referral to an appropriate professional organization. However, it is the responsibility of the employee to seek and accept assistance before drug and alcohol problems lead to disciplinary action, including termination. Failure to enter, remain in, or successfully complete a prescribed treatment program may result in termination of employment. Confidentiality of records and information will be maintained in accordance with all local, state, and federal laws.

Entrance into a treatment program does not relieve an employee of the obligation to satisfy ABC Company's standards regarding an employee's performance, and participation will not prevent the company from administering discipline for violation of its policies or relieve the employee of his or her responsibility to perform his or her job in a satisfactory, safe, and efficient manner.

Confidentiality

The confidentiality of all records and information relating to investigations, searches, results of drug/ alcohol testing, refusal to test, and treatment will be maintained in accordance with all local, state, and federal laws. Only those with a need to know will have access to such records and information. Those deemed to have a need to know may include management and first aid and safety personnel in emergency situations.

Employees, including management, who release confidential information to those without a need to know will be subject to disciplinary action, up to and including termination.

Exhibit 23.4
State-by-State Summary of Drug Testing Legislation

(States not listed here have no statutes governing drug testing in the workplace.)

KEY: **EAP**—Employee assistance program.
GC/MS—Gas chromatography/mass spectrometry test.
Reasonable suspicion/probable cause—States may vary on what would be required to prove either reasonable suspicion or probable cause. The law is not specific in defining these terms.
NIDA—National Institute on Drug Abuse.

ALABAMA	
Who Is Covered by Statute	Employers subject to Alabama's workers' compensation law.
Applicant Testing	Applicant testing is required to qualify for workers' compensation insurance premium discounts.
Employee Testing	Employee testing is allowed.
Conditions for Conducting Tests	Tests must be conducted by qualified testing laboratories. Employer must keep results confidential unless employee grants voluntary consent or if compelled to release results by any agency of the state, a court of competent jurisdiction, or a professional disciplinary board.
Testing Process Requirements	Testers must follow quality control and information dissemination procedures. An initial test having a positive result must be confirmed by another test.
How Test Results Are Used	Employers may establish reasonable work rules related to employee possession, use, sale, or solicitation of drugs and may take action based on a violation of those rules.
Enforcement of Statute	The Department of Industrial Relations, Workers' Compensation Division, has the authority to promulgate by rule or regulation procedures and forms for the certification of employers who establish and maintain a drug-free workplace in compliance with Alabama's drug-free workplace program law.
Employee Remedies	State has no statutory requirements.
Employer Penalties	State has no statutory requirements.
Who Pays for Testing	Employer shall pay the costs of all drug tests that the employer requires of employees. Employee or applicant shall pay the cost of any additional tests not required by the employer.
Employee Assistance Benefits	Employer must advise employees of EAP, if employer offers program, or advise employees of employer's resource file of assistance programs.
Other Requirements	One time only, prior to testing, all employees and job applicants shall be given a notice of testing.
Citations to Authority	Ala. Code §§ 25-5-330–25-5-340.

Exhibit 23.4   Mandated Benefits: 2009 Compliance Guide

Exhibit 23.4 (cont'd)

ALASKA	
Who Is Covered by Statute	Employers with one or more employees.
Applicant Testing	Applicant testing is allowed.
Employee Testing	Employee testing is allowed.
Conditions for Conducting Tests	Tests must be conducted by qualified testing laboratories.
Testing Process Requirements	Testers must follow quality control and information dissemination procedures. An initial positive result must be confirmed by use of a different analytical process than that used in the initial drug screen. The second or confirmatory test must be GC/MS. An employer may not rely on a positive test unless the confirmatory test results have been reviewed by a licensed physician or doctor of osteopathy.
How Test Results Are Used	An employer may take adverse employment action based on positive drug test or refusal of employee to provide a drug testing sample.
Enforcement of Statute	State has no statutory requirements.
Employee Remedies	Employee may bring action for defamation of character, libel, or slander if results were disclosed to a person other than the employer, an authorized agent, tested employee, or tested applicant.
Employer Penalties	Employer is not liable for monetary damages if employer's reliance on a false positive test was reasonable and in good faith.
Who Pays for Testing	Employer shall pay the cost of drug testing and all reasonable costs incurred traveling to test site, if other than employee's normal work location.
Employee Assistance Benefits	State has no statutory requirements.
Other Requirements	None.
Citations to Authority	Alaska Stat. §§ 23.10-600–23.10.699.

Exhibit 23.4 (cont'd)

ARIZONA	
Who Is Covered by Statute	All private employers.
Applicant Testing	Applicant testing is allowed.
Employee Testing	Employer may require the collection and testing of samples for any job-related purposes consistent with business necessity.
Conditions for Conducting Tests	Drug testing shall be conducted by a certified laboratory.
Testing Process Requirements	Confirmation of positive drug test results for employers shall be by use of a different chemical process than was used in the initial drug screen.
How Test Results Are Used	Test results may be used by employer to take adverse employment action against employee or applicant.
Enforcement of Statute	State has no statutory requirements.
Employee Remedies	Causes of action for defamation of character, libel, slander, and damage to reputation are available if information disclosed was a false positive result, the false positive result was disclosed negligently, and all other elements of causes of action are satisfied. Employees terminated or otherwise disciplined under Arizona's drug testing law for transportation employees of school districts are entitled to all appeal and review rights the employees would have as district employees or by contract with another person or entity that furnishes transportation services to the school district.
Employer Penalties	State has no statutory requirements.
Who Pays for Testing	Employer shall pay all actual costs for drug and alcohol impairment testing. Employer may, at its discretion, pay the costs for drug testing of prospective employees.
Employee Assistance Benefits	State has no statutory requirements.
Other Requirements	Testing for the presence of drugs shall be carried out within the terms of a written policy that has been distributed to every employee.
Citations to Authority	Ariz. Rev. Stat. Ann. §§ 23-493.01–23-493.11.

Exhibit 23.4   Mandated Benefits: 2009 Compliance Guide

Exhibit 23.4 (cont'd)

ARKANSAS	
Who Is Covered by Statute	A person or entity employing at least one person.
Applicant Testing	Applicant testing is allowed.
Employee Testing	Employee testing is allowed. A covered employer may test an employee for any drug at any time. An employee who is not in a safety-sensitive position may be tested for alcohol only when the test is based upon reasonable suspicion. An employee in a safety-sensitive position may be tested for alcohol use at any occasion.
Conditions for Conducting Tests	A covered employer that conducts drug testing or specimen collection must use chain-of-custody procedures established by federal regulations. Covered employers, laboratories, drug testing review officers, employee assistance programs, drug or alcohol rehabilitation programs, and their agents who receive or have access to information concerning drug or alcohol test results must keep all information confidential. Release of such information under any other circumstances is authorized solely pursuant to a written consent form voluntarily signed by the person tested, unless such release is compelled by a court.
Testing Process Requirements	Positive test results must be disclosed. The employee may contest the test results pursuant to rules adopted by the Workers' Health and Safety Division of the Workers' Compensation Commission.
How Test Results Are Used	If a drug or alcohol is found to be present in the employee's system at a level proscribed by statute or rule, the employer may terminate the employee and the employee would forfeit eligibility for workers' compensation medical and indemnity benefits.
Enforcement of Statute	State has no statutory requirements.
Employee Remedies	An employee or job applicant who receives a positive confirmed test result may contest or explain the result to the drug testing review officer within five working days after receiving written notification of the test result. If an employee's or job applicant's explanation or challenge is unsatisfactory to the drug testing review officer, the employee or applicant may contest the test result pursuant to rules adopted by the Workers' Health and Safety Division of the Workers' Compensation Commission.
Employer Penalties	State has no statutory requirements.
Who Pays for Testing	A covered employer must pay the cost of all drug and alcohol tests that it requires of employees. An employee or job applicant must pay the cost of any additional drug or alcohol tests not required by the covered employer.

Exhibit 23.4 (cont'd)

ARKANSAS	
Employee Assistance Benefits	If in the course of employment the employee enters an employee assistance program for drug-related or alcohol-related problems or a drug or alcohol rehabilitation program, the covered employer must require the employee to submit to a drug and alcohol test, as appropriate, as a follow-up to such program, unless the employee voluntarily entered the program.
Other Requirements	Prior to testing, a covered employer must give, one time only, all employees and applicants for employment a written policy statement regarding drug testing.
Citations to Authority	Ark. Code Ann. §§ 11-14-101–11-14-112.

Exhibit 23.4 Mandated Benefits: 2009 Compliance Guide

Exhibit 23.4 (cont'd)

CALIFORNIA	
Who Is Covered by Statute	All private employers with 25 or more employees.
Applicant Testing	State has no statutory requirements.
Employee Testing	Employee testing is allowed.
Conditions for Conducting Tests	State has no statutory requirements.
Testing Process Requirements	State has no statutory requirements.
How Test Results Are Used	Employer may refuse to hire, and may discharge, an employee who, because of his or her current use of alcohol or drugs, either is unable to perform his or her duties or cannot perform them in a manner that would not endanger his or her health or safety or the health or safety of others.
Enforcement of Statute	State has no statutory requirements.
Employee Remedies	State has no statutory requirements.
Employer Penalties	State has no statutory requirements.
Who Pays for Testing	State has no statutory requirements.
Employee Assistance Benefits	State has no statutory requirements.
Other Requirements	Employer must make reasonable efforts to keep confidential the fact that an employee was enrolled in a rehabilitation program.
Citations to Authority	Cal. Lab. Code §§ 1025, 1026.

Exhibit 23.4 (cont'd)

CONNECTICUT	
Who Is Covered by Statute	All employers, current and former employees, and applicants, but not the state or its political subdivisions.
Applicant Testing	Applicant testing is allowed only if (1) prospective employee is informed in writing, (2) test is conducted in accordance with stated methodology, and (3) prospective employee is given a copy of any positive test result.
Employee Testing	Employee testing is allowed if reasonable suspicion exists. Random testing of persons in safety-sensitive positions, as defined by the U.S. Department of Labor, is allowed. Testing must be done in conjunction with employee participation in EAP.
Conditions for Conducting Tests	Use of witnesses is prohibited.
Testing Process Requirements	Two tests are required, one by screening method and the other by GC/MS. Positive test results must be disclosed.
How Test Results Are Used	Test results may be used to screen out drug-using applicants or to discharge or discipline employees.
Enforcement of Statute	Enforcement is by private civil action and state action.
Employee Remedies	Employees may seek attorneys' fees and court costs, damages, and injunctive relief.
Employer Penalties	None.
Who Pays for Testing	State has no statutory requirements.
Employee Assistance Benefits	State has no statutory requirements. A 2001 statute provides that no state employee may be required to disclose any information or records concerning or confirming the employee's voluntary participation in an EAP sponsored or authorized by the state or any of its agencies. Nor may such a program disclose information regarding a state employee's voluntary participation therein without the prior written consent of the state employee.
Other Requirements	Statute addresses urinalysis only; it does not include other drug testing methods. Drug test results must be filed with medical records, subject to disclosure under separate statute. Preemployment drug test is required of all school bus operators.
Citations to Authority	Conn. Gen. Stat. Ann. §§ 14-276a(d), 31-51t–31-51z.

Exhibit 23.4   Mandated Benefits: 2009 Compliance Guide

Exhibit 23.4 (cont'd)

DELAWARE	
Who Is Covered by Statute	School bus drivers, Department of Corrections employees, home health agency workers, nursing home workers.
Applicant Testing	Department of Corrections employees and nursing home and home health care workers.
Employee Testing	Employee testing is allowed where a reasonable suspicion of drug use exists. Department of Corrections employees in security-sensitive positions are subject to random testing and incident-triggered testing for illegal use of drugs.
Conditions for Conducting Tests	State has no statutory requirements.
Testing Process Requirements	State has no statutory requirements.
How Test Results Are Used	Positive test results are grounds for termination. Applicants testing positive may not be hired.
Enforcement of Statute	Applicant or employer subject to fine of up to $5,000.
Employee Remedies	State has no statutory requirements.
Employer Penalties	A civil penalty of not less than $1,000 nor more than $5,000 for each violation of drug testing laws.
Who Pays for Testing	Employer pays for initial test. Subsequent test costs are paid by employee.
Employee Assistance Benefits	State has no statutory requirements.
Other Requirements	State has no other statutory requirements.
Citations to Authority	Del. Code Ann. tit. 14, § 2910; Del. Code Ann. tit. 16, §§ 1142, 1146; Del. Code Ann. tit. 21, § 2708; Del. Code Ann. tit. 29, §§ 8920 *et seq.*

Exhibit 23.4 (cont'd)

DISTRICT OF COLUMBIA	
Who Is Covered by Statute	Public employees of the Department of Human Services, Commission on Mental Health Services, and Department of Corrections.
Applicant Testing	Applicant testing is allowed.
Employee Testing	Employee testing is allowed where a reasonable suspicion of drug use exists, but only employees working in high-risk jobs may be tested randomly.
Conditions for Conducting Tests	Tests must be conducted by certified laboratories. The contractor must perform enzyme-multiplied-immunoassay technique (EMIT) testing on one sample and store the other sample. Any positive EMIT test must be confirmed with GC/MS.
Testing Process Requirements	Employees must be notified of a positive result. The employee may then authorize the sample to be sent to another qualified laboratory of his or her choice, at his or her expense, for secondary GC/MS confirmation.
How Test Results Are Used	Positive confirmed results are grounds for termination, as is refusal to submit to a drug test.
Enforcement of Statute	District has no statutory requirements.
Employee Remedies	District has no statutory requirements.
Employer Penalties	District has no statutory requirements.
Who Pays for Testing	Employees who challenge confirmed positive results must pay for the additional testing.
Employee Assistance Benefits	District has no statutory requirements.
Other Requirements	District has no other statutory requirements.
Citations to Authority	D.C. Code Ann. §§ 620.22 *et seq.*, §§ 211.22 *et seq.*

Exhibit 23.4 (cont'd)

FLORIDA	
Who Is Covered by Statute	Any agency within the state government and certain state construction contractors. An optional provision under the workers' compensation statute also applies to most private employers.
Applicant Testing	Applicant testing is allowed. All positive tests must be confirmed by GC/MS.
Employee Testing	Employee testing is allowed where a reasonable suspicion of drug use exists, or where test is conducted pursuant to routine fitness testing or follow-up testing.
Conditions for Conducting Tests	Tests must be conducted by certified laboratories.
Testing Process Requirements	Person must be informed of positive results. Within 5 working days of receipt of results, applicants and employees have the right to explain or rebut positive results. All information is confidential.
How Test Results Are Used	Test results may be used as grounds for termination of or disqualification from employment if a confirmation test is performed and if employee does not complete rehabilitation program. Test results may also be used as a basis for refusal to hire applicant. Public employees in special-risk positions may be discharged or disciplined by a public employer for the first positive result for an illicit drug. Such special-risk employees involved in an EAP or rehabilitation program may not continue to work in any special-risk or safety-sensitive position but may be reassigned or placed on leave during such participation.
Enforcement of Statute	Enforcement is by civil suit.
Employee Remedies	Employees may seek back pay and benefits, attorneys' fees, and injunctive relief.
Employer Penalties	None.
Who Pays for Testing	State has no statutory requirements.
Employee Assistance Benefits	Optional by statute. If an employee is unable to participate in outpatient rehabilitation, he or she may be placed on leave status while participating in an employee assistance program (EAP) or an alcohol and drug rehabilitation program. If placed on leave-without-pay status, the employee must be permitted to use any accumulated leave credits prior to being placed on leave without pay. Upon successful completion of an employee assistance or alcohol and drug rehabilitation program, the employee must be reinstated to the same or equivalent position that was held prior to rehabilitation.
Other Requirements	Employer with no testing program in place must wait 60 days after providing employees one-time notice before implementing such a program.
Citations to Authority	Fla. Stat. Ann. §§ 110.1091, 112.0455, 440.102; *City of Palm Bay v. Bauman*, 475 So. 2d 1322 (Fla. Dist. Ct. App. 1985). (Some provisions are part of amendment to state workers' compensation statute. Regulations establish standards for conducting tests that, if followed, provide employers with certain presumptions and benefits under the law.)

Exhibit 23.4 (cont'd)

GEORGIA	
Who Is Covered by Statute	Employees working for the state or contract workers who provide personal services for the state in high-risk jobs. Any applicant for state or public school employment.
Applicant Testing	Applicant testing is allowed for state or public school employment.
Employee Testing	Employee testing is allowed, but only an employee working in a high-risk job may be tested at random.
Conditions for Conducting Tests	Tests must be conducted by qualified testing laboratories. Testing at employer worksite is permitted using on-site kits that satisfy certain criteria.
Testing Process Requirements	Testers must follow quality control and information dissemination procedures. Positive results must be confirmed by test conducted by a qualified testing laboratory.
How Test Results Are Used	Test results may be used as grounds for termination of employment or disqualification from employment.
Enforcement of Statute	State has no statutory requirements.
Employee Remedies	State has no statutory requirements.
Employer Penalties	State has no statutory requirements.
Who Pays for Testing	The board of education of any county or independent school system may require that applicants for employment within the school system pay for the cost of preemployment testing.
Employee Assistance Benefits	If an employer has an EAP, the employer must inform the employee of the benefits and services of the program. The employer must provide the employee with notice of the policies and procedures regarding access to and use of the program. EAP must contain minimum level of core services, which include consultation, training, assistance to organization leadership in policy development, organizational development, critical incident management, problem assessment services, constructive intervention, referrals, follow-up monitoring, case management, employee education, supervisory training, and quality assurance.
Other Requirements	State has no other statutory requirements.
Citations to Authority	Ga. Code Ann. §§ 34-9-411 *et seq.*, 45-20-90–45-20-112.

Exhibit 23.4   Mandated Benefits: 2009 Compliance Guide

Exhibit 23.4 (cont'd)

HAWAII	
Who Is Covered by Statute	Any person, agency, employer, or other entity requesting an individual to submit to a drug test.
Applicant Testing	On-site testing shall be conducted according to test instructions. Applicant testing positive must report to laboratory within four hours.
Employee Testing	On-site testing shall be conducted according to test instructions. Employee testing positive must report to laboratory within four hours.
Conditions for Conducting Tests	Test must be conducted by certified laboratories only, or on-site following package directions.
Testing Process Requirements	Persons must be informed in writing of test and of which drugs are subject to detection.
How Test Results Are Used	State has no statutory requirements.
Enforcement of Statute	Enforcement is by private civil suit; state also may pursue action for injunctive relief.
Employee Remedies	Employees may recover actual damages.
Employer Penalties	Violators are subject to civil fines of $1,000–$10,000 per violation, plus costs and attorneys' fees.
Who Pays for Testing	All costs, including confirmation testing, shall be paid by employer.
Employee Assistance Benefits	State has no statutory requirements.
Other Requirements	Information from on-site testing shall be strictly confidential.
Citations to Authority	Haw. Rev. Stat. Ann. §§ 329B-1–329B-8.

Exhibit 23.4 (cont'd)

IDAHO	
Who Is Covered by Statute	All employers subject to Idaho's workers' compensation law.
Applicant Testing	Applicant testing is allowed.
Employee Testing	Employee testing is allowed.
Conditions for Conducting Tests	Statutory conditions relating to sample collection must be followed. Samples must be collected with regard to the privacy of the individual.
Testing Process Requirements	Tests must follow quality control procedures. There must be a confirmation test before the results of any positive test may be used as the basis for action by an employer. Employee must be given written notice of any positive result and be given an opportunity to discuss and explain the positive test.
How Test Results Are Used	Employer may use results of test to discharge employee for work-related misconduct or other disciplinary action, or for failure to hire an applicant.
Enforcement of Statute	The statute may be enforced by the state Industrial Commission.
Employee Remedies	State has no statutory requirements.
Employer Penalties	State has no statutory requirements.
Who Pays for Testing	All costs of conducting tests for current employees must be paid for by employer. Time spent conducting tests for current employee is considered work time.
Employee Assistance Benefits	State has no statutory requirements.
Other Requirements	Employer must have a written policy for collection and testing.
Citations to Authority	Idaho Code §§ 72-1701–72-1717.

Exhibit 23.4   Mandated Benefits: 2009 Compliance Guide

Exhibit 23.4 (cont'd)

ILLINOIS	
Who Is Covered by Statute	Any individual performing services for an employer. An employer is any person employing 15 or more employees within the state for at least 20 weeks during the calendar year of or preceding an alleged violation; any person employing one or more employees, when a complainant alleges civil rights violations as a result of discrimination; the state or any political subdivision; or any party to a public contract.
Applicant Testing	Applicant testing is allowed but not encouraged, prohibited, or restricted.
Employee Testing	Employee testing is allowed but not encouraged, prohibited, or restricted.
Conditions for Conducting Tests	Employees shall be tested in accordance with established drug testing procedures. Changes to established drug testing procedures that are inconsistent with the federal guidelines specified in the Mandatory Guidelines for Federal Workplace Drug Testing Program or that affect terms and conditions of employment shall be negotiated with an exclusive bargaining representative in accordance with the Illinois Public Labor Relations Statute.
Testing Process Requirements	State has no statutory requirements.
How Test Results Are Used	Results can be used to remove persons from safety-sensitive duties.
Enforcement of Statute	State has no statutory requirements.
Employee Remedies	State has no statutory requirements.
Employer Penalties	State has no statutory requirements.
Who Pays for Testing	State has no statutory requirements.
Employee Assistance Benefits	State has no statutory requirements.
Other Requirements	State has no other statutory requirements.
Citations to Authority	755 Ill. Comp. Stat. Ann. 5/2-101, 5/2-104.

Exhibit 23.4 (cont'd)

INDIANA	
Who Is Covered by Statute	Any individual performing services for an employer. An employer is any person engaged in an industry affecting commerce that has at least 15 employees for each working day in the last 20 calendar weeks. Corporations wholly owned by the government are exempt.
Applicant Testing	Applicant testing is allowed but not encouraged, prohibited, or restricted.
Employee Testing	Employee testing is allowed but not encouraged, prohibited, or restricted.
Conditions for Conducting Tests	State has no statutory requirements.
Testing Process Requirements	State has no statutory requirements.
How Test Results Are Used	Results can be used to remove persons from safety-sensitive duties.
Enforcement of Statute	State has no statutory requirements.
Employee Remedies	State has no statutory requirements.
Employer Penalties	State has no statutory requirements.
Who Pays for Testing	State has no statutory requirements.
Employee Assistance Benefits	State has no statutory requirements.
Other Requirements	School corporations may require contractors to provide for a limited criminal history background check of the contractor's employees. Employers for public works projects must have a written drug testing program that provides for random drug testing following specific procedures outlined in the law.
Citations to Authority	Ind. Code Ann. §§ 4-13-18, 22-9-5-9, 22-9-5-10, 22-9-5-24.

Exhibit 23.4   Mandated Benefits: 2009 Compliance Guide

Exhibit 23.4 (cont'd)

IOWA	
Who Is Covered by Statute	All employers, employees, and applicants. The state and its political subdivisions are not covered.
Applicant Testing	An employer may require applicants to submit to a drug test as a condition of employment.
Employee Testing	Employee testing is allowed. Random testing allowed where the test is administered during normal working hours. Employees may be exempted from testing pursuant to a collective bargaining agreement.
Conditions for Conducting Tests	Tests must be conducted by certified laboratories only. Only urine, saliva, blood, or breath may be tested. Samples must be collected under sanitary conditions and with regard for the privacy of the individual. Also, collection must be performed in a manner reasonably calculated to preclude contamination or substitution of the specimen.
Testing Process Requirements	Positive test results must comply with nationally accepted standards for acceptable, detectable levels of controlled substances. Positive test results must be disclosed.
How Test Results Are Used	Test results may be used to suspend, terminate, or refuse to hire a positive-testing individual.
Enforcement of Statute	Enforcement is by private civil action; state pursues violation of statute.
Employee Remedies	Employees may seek back pay, attorneys' fees and court costs, reinstatement, and injunctive relief.
Employer Penalties	State has no statutory requirements.
Who Pays for Testing	Employer.
Employee Assistance Benefits	State has no statutory requirements.
Other Requirements	Statute does not apply to persons covered under federal statutes or regulations unless such statutes or regulations are deemed unenforceable by federal court order.
Citations to Authority	Iowa Code Ann. § 730.5.

Exhibit 23.4 (cont'd)

KANSAS	
Who Is Covered by Statute	Persons taking office as Governor, Lieutenant Governor, or Attorney General, or for safety-sensitive positions in state government (state police officers who carry firearms, parole officers, state correction officers, appointed heads of state agencies, and Governor's staff). Also, employees of mental health institutions, state schools for the blind and deaf, and state veterans' homes.
Applicant Testing	Applicant testing is allowed for applicants for safety-sensitive positions in state government, but applicants must first be given conditional offer of employment.
Employee Testing	Employee testing is allowed, based on reasonable suspicion of illegal drug use.
Conditions for Conducting Tests	State has no statutory requirements.
Testing Process Requirements	The results of any test administered as part of a program authorized by the statute are confidential and must not be disclosed publicly.
How Test Results Are Used	No person may be terminated solely because of positive results of a drug test administered as part of a program authorized by the statute if (1) the employee has not previously had a valid positive test result and (2) the employee undergoes drug evaluation and successfully completes any education or treatment program recommended as a result of the evaluation.
Enforcement of Statute	State has no statutory requirements.
Employee Remedies	State has no statutory requirements.
Employer Penalties	State has no statutory requirements.
Who Pays for Testing	State has no statutory requirements.
Employee Assistance Benefits	State has no statutory requirements.
Other Requirements	Any public announcement or advertisement soliciting applications for certain positions must give notice of the drug screening program.
Citations to Authority	Kan. Stat. Ann. §§ 75-4362, 75-4363.

Exhibit 23.4   Mandated Benefits: 2009 Compliance Guide

Exhibit 23.4 (cont'd)

KENTUCKY	
Who Is Covered by Statute	Employers who are licensees of coal mines and covered by the Kentucky workers' compensation laws. Also, an employer who implements a drug-free workplace program, including preemployment, reasonable suspicion, random and post-accident testing, may be eligible for a credit on workers' compensation insurance.
Applicant Testing	Applicant testing is required.
Employee Testing	State has no statutory requirements.
Conditions for Conducting Tests	Standards, procedures, and protocols as set up by the U.S. Department of Health and Human Services' Substance Abuse and Mental Health Services Administration must be followed.
Testing Process Requirements	Positive test results must be disclosed.
How Test Results Are Used	Positive test results prevent an applicant from obtaining employment.
Enforcement of Statute	State has no statutory requirements.
Employee Remedies	State has no statutory requirements.
Employer Penalties	State has no statutory requirements.
Who Pays for Testing	Applicant pays for initial testing; if applicant obtains a job, the employer must reimburse the applicant.
Employee Assistance Benefits	State has no statutory requirements.
Other Requirements	State has no other statutory requirements.
Citations to Authority	Ky. Rev. Stat. §§ 304.13–167, 351.182–351.186.

Exhibit 23.4 (cont'd)

LOUISIANA	
Who Is Covered by Statute	Employers that are not subject to a federally mandated drug testing program.
Applicant Testing	There are no restrictions to testing. The state legislature has strongly urged public elementary and secondary schools to provide for preemployment drug screening and in-service testing of teachers, bus drivers, administrators, and any other employees who might reasonably be expected to be placed in a position of supervisory or disciplinary authority over students.
Employee Testing	There are no restrictions to testing; rehabilitation (e.g., EAP) is permitted but not required. The state legislature has strongly urged public elementary and secondary schools to provide for in-service drug testing, where reasonable suspicion exists, of teachers, bus drivers, administrators, and other employees who may be placed in a position of supervisory or disciplinary authority over students.
Conditions for Conducting Tests	Tests must be conducted by a laboratory certified for forensic drug testing by the Substance Abuse and Mental Health Services Administration. Use of witnesses is limited. Statutory requirements not applicable to an employer or employer's agent using an on-site screening test certified by the FDA to test employees or prospective employees when there are no mandatory or discretionary consequences for the tested individuals.
Testing Process Requirements	Dual confirmation is required; results go to medical review officer. Statutory requirements not applicable to an employer or employer's agent using an on-site screening test certified by the FDA to test employees or prospective employees when there are no mandatory or discretionary consequences for the employee.
How Test Results Are Used	No mandatory or discretionary consequences may result for employees or prospective employees subjected to on-site screening.
Enforcement of Statute	State has no statutory requirements.
Employee Remedies	Subject to certain requirements, employees/applicants have a cause of action for defamation, libel, slander, or damage to reputation or privacy.
Employer Penalties	State has no statutory requirements.
Who Pays for Testing	If an applicant elects to have a confirmation test of a positive result, the applicant must pay for such confirmation.
Employee Assistance Benefits	State has no statutory requirements.
Other Requirements	Testing law is subject to state unemployment compensation law and sets forth employee testing requirements in order to support a misconduct discharge and, thus, deny benefits.
Citations to Authority	La. Rev. Stat. Ann. §§ 23:1601, 49:1001 *et seq.*; La. S. Con. Res. 99 (2001).

Exhibit 23.4   Mandated Benefits: 2009 Compliance Guide

Exhibit 23.4 (cont'd)

MAINE	
Who Is Covered by Statute	All employers, employees, and applicants. (Employees at nuclear power plants are exempt.) Written policy is required. Employers with 20 or more full-time employees must establish an EAP as a condition for employee drug testing.
Applicant Testing	Applicant testing is allowed, but only after conditional offer of employment has been made. Applicants include persons on an employment agency's roster of eligibility for a work assignment with a client company to which the person has not been assigned work in the previous 30 days.
Employee Testing	Employee testing is allowed for probable cause. Random testing is permitted (1) with union-management agreement; (2) for safety-sensitive positions; and (3) if the employer: has 50 or more employees not covered by collective bargaining agreements, has established an employee committee (that includes a medical professional) to develop a drug testing policy (for which the employer must obtain DOL approval) and develops a policy that requires that employees be selected for testing by a person not subject to the employer's influence.
Conditions for Conducting Tests	Use of witnesses is prohibited. Tampering constitutes a refusal to be tested. Tests must be supervised by physicians or nurses and conducted in medical facilities. (First aid stations are medical facilities.) Chain-of-custody record (who handled sample and when) is required. Qualified testing laboratories are required.
Testing Process Requirements	Positive test results must be disclosed. Dual confirmation is required: first step is screen; confirming test method is GC/MS. Marijuana metabolite cut-off is 20 mg/ml on confirming test. Retest must be administered at testee's request. Samples must be preserved for one year.
How Test Results Are Used	Test results may be used as a factor to screen out drug-using applicants or to discharge or discipline employees; an employee's first offense results in referral to an EAP. Discharge is permitted for refusal to take test or for failure to comply with or complete a rehabilitation program within a 6-month period. Applicants and employees have 3 days after positive test to produce evidence explaining or contesting result.
Enforcement of Statute	Enforcement is by private civil action; state pursues violation of statute.
Employee Remedies	Employees may seek back pay (3 times lost wages), attorneys' fees and court costs, reinstatement, civil damages, and injunctive relief.
Employer Penalties	None.

Exhibit 23.4 (cont'd)

MAINE	
Who Pays for Testing	Employees and applicants shall pay all the costs of subsequent tests and samples taken. Employees pay all costs if the test yields a confirmed positive result.
Employee Assistance Benefits	Employer with more than 20 employees must have in existence an EAP before establishing any substance abuse testing program.
Other Requirements	Policy must be approved by state department of labor. Employees affected by new policy must be given 30 days' notice; changes to existing policy are effective 60 days after notice. Employers must consult with employees before implementing employee part of program. Employer may not require employee to sign consent form absolving employer of liability. Employers do not have to consult with employees about applicant part of program. Probable-cause finding must be written. Employee returning to workforce after drug-related absence may be tested between 90 days and 1 year following first confirmed test.
Citations to Authority	Me. Rev. Stat. Ann. tit. 26, §§ 681–690.

Exhibit 23.4   Mandated Benefits: 2009 Compliance Guide

Exhibit 23.4 (cont'd)

MARYLAND	
Who Is Covered by Statute	All employers, employees, applicants, and contractors.
Applicant Testing	There are no restrictions to testing.
Employee Testing	Employees and applicants may be tested without limitation, provided a certified laboratory is used. Legislation enacted in 2001 permits employers to conduct on-site testing of job applicants with an FDA-approved drug test kit.
Conditions for Conducting Tests	Tests must be conducted by certified laboratories only. Employers may conduct on-site preemployment testing using FDA-approved drug test kits.
Testing Process Requirements	Positive test results must be disclosed. Positive on-site tests must be confirmed by an independent laboratory and reviewed by the company's medical review officer.
How Test Results Are Used	State has no statutory requirements.
Enforcement of Statute	State pursues violation of statute.
Employee Remedies	State has no statutory requirements.
Employer Penalties	State has no statutory requirements.
Who Pays for Testing	The person requesting an independent test must pay for any related costs.
Employee Assistance Benefits	State has no statutory requirements.
Other Requirements	Principal purpose of statute is to ensure use of certified laboratories. Employer must provide a tested employee or applicant with (1) the name and address of the testing lab, if requested; (2) a copy of the test results; (3) a copy of the employer's written policy; and (4) notice of intent to take disciplinary action.
Citations to Authority	Md. Code Ann. Health-Gen. I § 17-205, 17-214.

Exhibit 23.4 (cont'd)

MINNESOTA	
Who Is Covered by Statute	All persons, independent contractors and persons working for independent contractors who perform services for compensation for an employer, and applicants for employment in such capacity. Written policy is required.
Applicant Testing	Applicant testing is allowed, but only after conditional offer of employment has been made, and is pursuant to a written policy. In addition, this test must be requested or required of all applicants. Notice of drug test during pre-employment process is required.
Employee Testing	Employee testing is allowed if reasonable suspicion of drug use exists. Postaccident and EAP-related testing is also allowed. Random testing of employees in safety-sensitive positions is permitted. Testing during routine physical examination is allowed if at least 2-week notice is given.
Conditions for Conducting Tests	Tests must be conducted by certified laboratories only; chain-of-custody record (who handled sample and when) is required.
Testing Process Requirements	Positive test results must be disclosed. Dual confirmation is required: first step is screen; confirming test method is GC/MS. Retest must be administered at testee's request. Samples must be preserved for 6 months.
How Test Results Are Used	Test results may be used to screen out drug-using applicants or to discharge or discipline employees. An employee's first offense results in referral to an EAP.
Enforcement of Statute	Enforcement is by private civil action.
Employee Remedies	Employees may seek back pay, reinstatement, and damages.
Employer Penalties	None.
Who Pays for Testing	State has no statutory requirements.
Employee Assistance Benefits	State has no statutory requirements.
Other Requirements	Nothing in the statute shall be construed to interfere with or diminish any employee protections relating to drug and alcohol testing already provided under collective bargaining agreement that exceed the minimum standards for employee protection provided in the statute.
Citations to Authority	Minn. Stat. Ann. §§ 181.950–181.957.

Exhibit 23.4   Mandated Benefits: 2009 Compliance Guide

Exhibit 23.4 (cont'd)

MISSISSIPPI	
Who Is Covered by Statute	All employees and applicants.
Applicant Testing	Applicant testing is allowed. Notice of test must be in writing on the application.
Employee Testing	Employee testing by private employers is allowed where there is reasonable suspicion. Random testing of government employees is allowed in law enforcement, public health, high-security, or drug interdiction positions.
Conditions for Conducting Tests	Tests must be conducted by certified laboratories and must satisfy chain of custody requirement.
Testing Process Requirements	Specimens must be collected in an amount sufficient for at least 2 tests. Positive test results must be disclosed in writing within 5 working days. Employees have the right to explain or rebut positive test results.
How Test Results Are Used	Test results may be used to discipline or discharge employees or as grounds for refusing employment to applicants, but only after test results are verified by confirming tests.
Enforcement of Statute	Enforcement is by private civil action; injunctive relief is available for violation of the statute.
Employee Remedies	Employees may seek damages, including attorneys' fees.
Employer Penalties	Limited to compensatory damages that are a direct result of injury or loss for violations.
Who Pays for Testing	Employer shall pay the costs of all drug and alcohol tests requested or required of employee or job applicant.
Employee Assistance Benefits	If an employer has an EAP, it must inform employees of the benefits and services of the program. An employer must post notice of the EAP in conspicuous places. In addition, the employer must provide the employee with notice of the policies and procedures regarding access to and use of the program. If an employer does not have an EAP, it must maintain a resource file of employee assistance service providers, alcohol and other drug abuse programs, mental health providers, and other persons, entities or organizations available to assist employees with personal or behavioral problems. The employer must provide all employees with information about the existence of the resource file and a summary of the information contained within the file.
Other Requirements	State has no other statutory requirements.
Citations to Authority	Miss. Code Ann. §§ 71-3-213, 71-7-1–71-7-33.

Exhibit 23.4 (cont'd)

MISSOURI	
Who Is Covered by Statute	Public and private employers covered under state employment security law.
Applicant Testing	Employer may require preemployment testing for alcohol or controlled substance use as a condition of employment if the applicant was informed of the test requirement prior to taking the test.
Employee Testing	Employer may require employee testing on a random basis, or on a reasonable suspicion basis, or following an accident in the workplace. Employee must have been notified of the policy by public posting, inclusion in a handbook, or inclusion as part of a collective bargaining agreement.
Conditions for Conducting Tests	Testing must be done by qualified testing laboratories and must satisfy chain-of-custody requirement.
Testing Process Requirements	Employee may request a confirmation test.
How Test Results Are Used	Test results may be used to show misconduct connected with the employee's work (as relates to unemployment benefits).
Enforcement of Statute	State has no statutory requirements.
Employee Remedies	State has no statutory requirements.
Employer Penalties	State has no statutory requirements.
Who Pays for Testing	Employer pays costs; employee may be required to pay costs of confirmation test if it confirms the original, positive test result.
Employee Assistance Benefits	State has no statutory requirements.
Other Requirements	State has no other statutory requirements.
Citations to Authority	Mo. Rev. Stat. § 288.045.

Exhibit 23.4   Mandated Benefits: 2009 Compliance Guide

Exhibit 23.4 (cont'd)

MONTANA	
Who Is Covered by Statute	All employers, employees, and applicants. Written policy is required, and must be made available to employees at least 60 days prior to testing program's initiation.
Applicant Testing	Applicants may be tested as a condition of hire.
Employee Testing	Employee testing is allowed if reasonable suspicion exists. Employees may also be tested if they are involved in an accident causing damage in excess of $1,500 or causing personal injury. Random testing may be allowed if the employer's written policy contains certain provisions. *See* Mont. Code Ann. § 39-2-208.
Conditions for Conducting Tests	Chain-of-custody record (who handled sample and when) is required.
Testing Process Requirements	Test results must be disclosed. Retest must be administered at testee's request.
How Test Results Are Used	Test results may be used to screen out drug-using applicants or to discharge or discipline employees. Adverse action may not be taken against a testee who presents a reasonable explanation for or a medical opinion on the test results.
Enforcement of Statute	State pursues violation of statute.
Employee Remedies	State has no statutory requirements.
Employer Penalties	Employer violations are misdemeanors.
Who Pays for Testing	Testing is at employer's expense. All employees must be compensated at their regular rate for time attributable to the testing program.
Employee Assistance Benefits	State has no statutory requirements.
Other Requirements	Drug testing for continuing employees in jobs involving intrastate commercial motor carrier transportation is permitted during biennial physical.
Citations to Authority	Mont. Code Ann. § 39-2-205–39-2-211.

Exhibit 23.4 (cont'd)

NEBRASKA	
Who Is Covered by Statute	Employees, applicants, and employers with 6 or more employees and all governmental entities.
Applicant Testing	State has no statutory requirements.
Employee Testing	State has no statutory requirements.
Conditions for Conducting Tests	Tests must be conducted by certified laboratories only; chain-of-custody record (who handled sample and when) is required.
Testing Process Requirements	Positive test results must be disclosed. Dual confirmation is required: first step is screen; confirming test method is GC/MS. Samples must be preserved for 180 days.
How Test Results Are Used	Tests may be used to discharge or discipline employees.
Enforcement of Statute	State has no statutory requirements.
Employee Remedies	State has no statutory requirements.
Employer Penalties	Violations of the statute are Class 1 misdemeanors.
Who Pays for Testing	State has no statutory requirements.
Employee Assistance Benefits	State has no statutory requirements.
Other Requirements	Employee may request a blood test. Employee refusal to submit to a test may result in denial of continued employment.
Citations to Authority	Neb. Rev. Stat. Ann. §§ 48-1901–48-1910.

Exhibit 23.4   Mandated Benefits: 2009 Compliance Guide

Exhibit 23.4 (cont'd)

NEVADA	
Who Is Covered by Statute	Only public employers are covered by Nevada's drug testing law.
Applicant Testing	Applicant testing is allowed for high-risk or safety-sensitive positions.
Employee Testing	Employee testing is allowed when there is a reasonable suspicion of violation. A law enforcement officer may be required to take a screening test if, during the performance of duties, the officer discharges a firearm, drives a motor vehicle in a manner as to cause injury to self or others, or if substantial damage to property occurs.
Conditions for Conducting Tests	Testing must be done by qualified testing laboratories. Chain-of-custody records are required.
Testing Process Requirements	Employees must be provided with the results of screening tests within three days after the results are received by the appointing authority. If an initial screening test is positive, the laboratory must conduct another test on the same sample to determine the specific substances and concentration of those substances in the sample. The appointing authority must then provide the employee with an opportunity to have the sample tested at an independent laboratory of choice that is certified by the National Institute of Drug Abuse.
How Test Results Are Used	State has no statutory requirements.
Enforcement of Statute	State has no statutory requirements.
Employee Remedies	State has no statutory requirements.
Employer Penalties	State has no statutory requirements.
Who Pays for Testing	State has no statutory requirements.
Employee Assistance Benefits	An employee who tests positive for the first time on a screening test and has committed no other acts during the course of conduct giving rise to the screening test that would subject him or her to termination must be referred to an employee assistance program. Employees who refuse to accept referrals or who fail to complete the program are subject to further discipline.
Other Requirements	State has no statutory requirements.
Citations to Authority	Nev. Rev. Stat. Ann. §§ 284.406, 284.4061–284.4069, 284.407.

Exhibit 23.4 (cont'd)

NORTH CAROLINA	
Who Is Covered by Statute	Individuals who are employees of examiner or applicants for employment with examiner and who are requested or required by examiner to submit to controlled substance examination. Controlled substance examinations required by the U.S. Department of Transportation and the U.S. Nuclear Regulatory Commission are exempt from provisions.
Applicant Testing	Applicant testing is allowed.
Employee Testing	Employee testing is allowed.
Conditions for Conducting Tests	Tests must be conducted by approved laboratories. Examiner shall use only laboratories that have demonstrated satisfactory performance in the proficiency testing programs of the NIDA or the College of American Pathology. Chain-of-custody record (who handled, labeled, and identified examination samples and when) is required.
Testing Process Requirements	Approved laboratory must confirm any sample that produces a positive result by a second examination of the sample utilizing GC/MS or an equivalent, scientifically accepted method.
How Test Results Are Used	State has no statutory requirements.
Enforcement of Statute	State pursues violation of statute.
Employee Remedies	None.
Employer Penalties	Any examiner who violates the provisions of the statute shall be subject to a civil penalty of up to $250 per examinee, with the maximum not to exceed $1,000, per investigation by the Commissioner of Labor or the Commissioner's authorized representative.
Who Pays for Testing	State has no statutory requirements.
Employee Assistance Benefits	State has no statutory requirements.
Other Requirements	None.
Citations to Authority	N.C. Gen. Stat. §§ 95-230–95-235.

Exhibit 23.4   Mandated Benefits: 2009 Compliance Guide

Exhibit 23.4 (cont'd)

OHIO
Note: Ohio does not have a general statute on the subject, but it does have administrative regulations relating to drug testing for state employees, and does allow insurance discounts for workers' compensation premiums for employers who comply with drug-free workplace requirements. Employers in Ohio that contract for public works projects must have a substance abuse program that includes drug testing. The law provides that testing should follow guidelines as outlined in the law.

Citations to Authority	Ohio Admin. Code 123:1-76-01–123:1-76-14, 4123-17-58. Ohio Rev. Code Ann. § 153.03.

Exhibit 23.4 (cont'd)

OKLAHOMA	
Who Is Covered by Statute	All employers, employees, and applicants. Written policy is required.
Applicant Testing	Applicants may be requested or required to undergo testing upon conditional offer of employment, provided testing is required of all applicants who receive a conditional offer for a particular employment classification.
Employee Testing	Employee testing is allowed when the employer has a reasonable suspicion of an employee violation, for postaccident inquiries, for postrehabilitation testing up to 2 years commencing with the employee's return to work, and as part of a routinely scheduled employee fitness-for-duty medical examination. Random testing is allowed for employees who are police officers; have drug interdiction responsibilities; are authorized to carry firearms; are involved in activities directly affecting the safety of others; or work in direct contact with inmates, juvenile delinquents, or children in state custody.
Conditions for Conducting Tests	Testing must be done by qualified testing facilities. Chain-of-custody record (who handled sample and when) is required. Use of witnesses is prohibited.
Testing Process Requirements	Dual confirmation is required: first step is screen; confirming test is GC, GC/MS, or an equivalent, scientifically accepted method.
How Test Results Are Used	Applicant refusal to undergo test or a confirmed positive test result may be used as a basis for refusal to hire. Employee may be discharged for refusal to undergo test or for a confirmed positive test. Employer cannot request or require test if an EAP is not provided.
Enforcement of Statute	Enforcement is by civil action within 2 years of the person's discovery of the alleged willful violation or of the exhaustion of any internal administrative remedies.
Employee Remedies	Employee or applicant may seek injunctive relief; compensatory damages, including employment, reinstatement, promotion, payment of lost wages, and reinstatement to full benefits and seniority rights; court costs; and attorneys' fees.
Employer Penalties	Willful and knowing violation of the statute is a misdemeanor, punishable by a fine of $100–$5,000, imprisonment for not more than 1 year, or both.
Who Pays for Testing	Employer shall pay all costs of drug testing. Employees shall be compensated at their regular rate for time involved in drug testing.
Employee Assistance Benefits	Drug or alcohol testing shall not be requested or required of employee unless employer provides an EAP.
Other Requirements	Test results are to remain confidential and kept separate from other personnel records. The employer's written policy must list the substances included in the drug and alcohol test; alternatively, the policy can reference "the substances as defined in the Standards for Workplace Drug and Alcohol Testing Act, including controlled substances approved for testing by rule of the State Commissioner of Health."
Citations to Authority	Okla. Stat. Ann. tit. 40, §§ 551–565.

Exhibit 23.4

Mandated Benefits: 2009 Compliance Guide

Exhibit 23.4 (cont'd)

OREGON	
Who Is Covered by Statute	All employees and applicants (breathalyzer test only).
Applicant Testing	Applicant testing is allowed, but breathalyzer test may be administered only if applicant consents or if employer has reasonable grounds to believe applicant is under the influence of alcohol.
Employee Testing	Employee testing is allowed, but breathalyzer test may be administered only if employee consents or if employer has reasonable grounds to believe employee is under the influence of alcohol.
Conditions for Conducting Tests	Testing by third party is required.
Testing Process Requirements	Positive test results must be confirmed by a licensed clinical laboratory using the best available technology in order to determine whether the substance identified by the first test is present in the specimen prior to reporting the test results.
How Test Results Are Used	Test results may be used to screen out applicants or to discharge or discipline employees.
Enforcement of Statute	Statute is enforced by Commissioner of the Bureau of Labor and Industries.
Employee Remedies	None.
Employer Penalties	Violation is treated as unlawful employment practice.
Who Pays for Testing	State has no statutory requirements.
Employee Assistance Benefits	State has no statutory requirements.
Other Requirements	None.
Citations to Authority	Or. Rev. Stat. §§ 659.840, 659A.300.

Exhibit 23.4 (cont'd)

PUERTO RICO	
Who Is Covered by Statute	Public and private employers are covered.
Applicant Testing	Applicant testing is allowed.
Employee Testing	Testing is mandatory for all employees working in the gunsmith business, drivers of railroads and motor vehicles, security guards, and employees whose functions include the handling and control of drugs and dangerous substances. Employers may also require testing upon reasonable suspicion of drug use, after a workplace accident attributable to the employee, or as part of a general physical-medical examination required of all candidates for employment.
Conditions for Conducting Tests	Tests must be conducted in a uniform and consistent manner for all employees and candidates for employment. The employer must give employees a written copy of the testing program.
Testing Process Requirements	Tests must be administered in accordance with scientifically accepted analytical procedures and chain-of-custody record is required.
How Test Results Are Used	Refusal to submit to testing is sufficient cause to deny employment.
Enforcement of Statute	State has no statutory requirements.
Employee Remedies	State has no statutory requirements.
Employer Penalties	Any person who knowingly and willfully divulges or makes improper use of information related to the results obtained in the administration of controlled substances detection tests or who violates provisions of the statute is guilty of a felony, and upon conviction, will be sanctioned for each violation by imprisonment for a fixed term of one year or a fine of $2,000. If there are aggravating circumstances, the penalty may be increased to up to two years in prison and/or a fine of up to $5,000.
Who Pays for Testing	The employer is not required to pay for all costs, but must defray the expenses of drug tests. The employer must deem the time needed to submit to the tests as working time and must compensate employees accordingly.
Employee Assistance Benefits	State agencies must require an employee with a confirmed positive test result to participate in a rehabilitation plan. If the employee chooses a private rehabilitation institution, he or she will be responsible for the cost of the treatment and rehabilitation.
Other Requirements	None.
Citations to Authority	3 P.R. Laws Ann. §§ 2501–2520; 29 P.R. Laws Ann. §§ 161 *et seq.*

Exhibit 23.4

Mandated Benefits: 2009 Compliance Guide

Exhibit 23.4 (cont'd)

RHODE ISLAND	
Who Is Covered by Statute	All employers and employees, except those covered by U.S. Department of Transportation regulations or other federal requirements.
Applicant Testing	Employer can require job applicant to submit to drug testing if (1) the given offer is conditioned on a negative drug test, (2) the applicant provides the test sample in private, and (3) positive test results are confirmed by means of GC/MS or technology recognized as being at least as scientifically accurate.
Employee Testing	Testing is allowed where a reasonable suspicion (based on articulable observations of an employee's appearance, behavior, and/or speech) of drug use exists and where such drug use impairs the ability of the employee to perform his or her duties.
Conditions for Conducting Tests	Use of witnesses is prohibited.
Testing Process Requirements	Positive test results must be disclosed. Dual confirmation is required: first step is screen; confirming test method is GC/MS. Retest must be administered at testee's request at employer's cost. Employee has the right to rebut or explain test result. Employees testing positive are not terminated but are referred to a substance abuse professional (e.g., an EAP professional).
How Test Results Are Used	Employees testing positive shall not be terminated on that basis but shall be referred to a substance abuse professional.
Enforcement of Statute	Enforcement is by private civil action; injunctive relief, punitive damages, and attorneys' fees are available to prevailing employee. Criminal sanction: violations are misdemeanors; penalty as noted by statute.
Employee Remedies	Employees may obtain attorneys' fees and court costs, damages (including punitive damages), and injunctive relief.
Employer Penalties	Employer penalties include criminal sanction (with a fine of up to $1,000, imprisonment for 1 year, or both).
Who Pays for Testing	Subsequent tests are at employee's expense.
Employee Assistance Benefits	State has no statutory requirements.
Other Requirements	State has no other statutory requirements.
Citations to Authority	R.I. Gen. Laws §§ 28-6.5-1, 28-6.5-2.

Exhibit 23.4 (cont'd)

SOUTH DAKOTA	
Who Is Covered by Statute	State government employees in safety-sensitive positions.
Applicant Testing	Applicant testing is allowed. Any printed public announcement or advertisement soliciting applications for employment in a safety-sensitive position in state government or for employment at the South Dakota Human Services Center, the South Dakota Developmental Center, or the South Dakota State Veterans' Home for a position in which the primary duty includes patient or resident care or supervision shall include a statement of the requirements of the drug screening program established under the statute for applicants and employees holding such positions.
Employee Testing	Employee testing is allowed if there is reasonable suspicion of illegal drug use by any such person.
Conditions for Conducting Tests	State has no statutory requirements.
Testing Process Requirements	Test results must be confidential and made available to applicants and employees who make written requests for them.
How Test Results Are Used	State has no statutory requirements.
Enforcement of Statute	State has no statutory requirements.
Employee Remedies	None.
Employer Penalties	Any person responsible for recording, reporting, or maintaining medical information required pursuant to the provisions of the statute who knowingly or intentionally discloses or fails to protect medical information declared to be confidential or who compels another person to disclose such medical information is guilty of a Class 2 misdemeanor.
Who Pays for Testing	State has no statutory requirements.
Other Requirements	State has no other statutory requirements.
Citations to Authority	S.D. Codified Laws §§ 23-3-64–23-3-69.

Exhibit 23.4

Mandated Benefits: 2009 Compliance Guide

Exhibit 23.4 (cont'd)

TENNESSEE	
Who Is Covered by Statute	All employers.
Applicant Testing	Applicant testing is allowed.
Employee Testing	Employee testing is allowed if there is a reasonable suspicion of drug or alcohol abuse by such employee. Employees may also be tested after an accident and as part of a routine fitness-for-duty physical.
Conditions for Conducting Tests	Chain-of-custody procedures established by governmental authority must be followed. Testing must be conducted at licensed laboratory.
Testing Process Requirements	Confidentiality must be ensured. Commissioner of Labor may adopt rules regarding retention and storage procedures and minimum cut-off detection levels.
How Test Results Are Used	Test results may be used for disciplinary action, including termination. Employer may not discipline, discharge, or refuse to hire on the basis of a positive test result that has not been verified by a confirmation test and a medical review officer. Employers must notify the parents or guardians of a minor of the results of any drug or alcohol test. Minors who are tested must be informed that their parents or guardians will be notified of the results.
Enforcement of Statute	State has no statutory requirements.
Employee Remedies	State has no statutory requirements.
Employer Penalties	State has no statutory requirements.
Who Pays for Testing	Employer shall pay the cost of all drug tests that the employer requires of the employee.
Employee Assistance Benefits	Employer's drug policy statement must include names and telephone numbers of EAP and drug and alcohol rehabilitation programs. Employer is not required to provide these programs.
Other Requirements	Prior to testing, employer shall give all employees and job applicants a written policy statement on alcohol and drug testing. State and local government construction contractors must submit an affidavit attesting that the contractor operates a drug-free workplace program or other drug and alcohol testing program with requirements at least as stringent as the program operated by such government entity.
Citations to Authority	Tenn. Code Ann. § 50-9-101–50-9-114.

Exhibit 23.4 (cont'd)

TEXAS	
Who Is Covered by Statute	Employers with 15 or more employees that have workers' compensation insurance coverage must adopt a policy designed to eliminate drug abuse and its effects in the workplace. A separate statute covers employees of convalescent and nursing homes and related entities.
Applicant Testing	There are no restrictions on applicant testing.
Employee Testing	Workers' compensation statute requires adoption of policies designed to eliminate drug abuse and its effects in the workplace. Regulations pursuant thereto clearly permit, but do not require, drug and alcohol testing. Employers in convalescent and nursing homes and related institutions may establish a drug testing policy for employees and may choose to adopt the Board of Human Services' model drug testing policy. The model policy requires at least one drug test per year for each employee having direct contact with residents and authorizes random, unannounced tests for such employees.
Conditions for Conducting Tests	Workers' compensation statute requires distribution of a written drug abuse policy, including a description of any drug testing program that the employer has in force.
Testing Process Requirements	State has no statutory requirements.
How Test Results Are Used	State has no statutory requirements.
Enforcement of Statute	Employers subject to the workers' compensation drug abuse policy requirement that do not have a drug abuse policy may be subject to a Class D administrative violation and may be assessed an administrative penalty not to exceed $500.
Employee Remedies	State has no statutory requirements.
Employer Penalties	Administrative penalty up to $500.
Who Pays for Testing	State has no statutory requirements.
Employee Assistance Benefits	State has no statutory requirements.
Other Requirements	Employers must provide workers' compensation officials with a copy of their drug abuse policies, for the purpose of a compliance audit, within 30 days of receiving a written request.
Citations to Authority	Tex. Health & Safety Code Ann. § 242.0371; Tex. Lab. Code Ann. § 411.091; 28 Tex. Admin. Code §§ 169.1, 169.2.

Exhibit 23.4   Mandated Benefits: 2009 Compliance Guide

Exhibit 23.4 (cont'd)

UTAH	
Who Is Covered by Statute	All employers, employees, and applicants. Employer does not include the federal or state government or any local political subdivision. Written policy is required.
Applicant Testing	There are no restrictions to applicant testing.
Employee Testing	Employee testing is allowed for the following purposes: potential impairment of individual employee, investigations of workplace accidents or theft, maintenance of safety, and maintenance of productivity.
Conditions for Conducting Tests	Chain-of-custody record (who handled sample and when) is required. Privacy of the individual being tested must be considered.
Testing Process Requirements	Dual confirmation is required: first step is screen; confirming test method is GC/MS.
How Test Results Are Used	Test results may be used to screen out drug-using applicants or to discharge or discipline employees. Employee referrals to an EAP are at sole discretion of employer.
Enforcement of Statute	Enforcement is by private civil action. Cause of action available only if test result is false positive; employer enjoys rebuttable presumption that test result is accurate if employer complied with statute; law bars damages if employer acted in good faith.
Employee Remedies	Employees may seek damages.
Employer Penalties	None.
Who Pays for Testing	Drug and alcohol testing shall be deemed work time for purposes of compensation and benefits for current employees. Employer shall pay all the costs of testing required by employer.
Employee Assistance Benefits	State has no statutory requirements.
Other Requirements	In order to be able to test employees, employers and management must submit to testing on a periodic basis. Confidentiality of all information is required.
Citations to Authority	Utah Code Ann. §§ 34-38-1–34-38-15.

Exhibit 23.4 (cont'd)

VERMONT	
Who Is Covered by Statute	All employers, employees, and applicants. Written policy is required.
Applicant Testing	Applicant testing is allowed, but only after conditional offer of employment has been made. Written notice must be given before testing. The test must be given in conjunction with a physical examination.
Employee Testing	An employee may be tested if probable cause exists and employer has an EAP available. Random testing is prohibited.
Conditions for Conducting Tests	Tests must be conducted by certified laboratories only; the subject's anonymity must be maintained; chain-of-custody record (who handled sample and when) is required. Employers must contract with or employ a certified medical review officer, who is a licensed physician with knowledge of the medical use of prescription drugs and the pharmacology and toxicology of illicit drugs, to review and evaluate all drug test results, assure compliance with state law, report results to the tested individual, and report confirmed drug test results to the employer. A certified collector must also be designated to collect specimens from applicants and employees.
Testing Process Requirements	The laboratory must provide the medical review officer with a written report of the result. Positive test results must be personally disclosed by the medical review officer. Dual confirmation is required. Retest must be administered at testee's request. Samples must be preserved for 90 days. Tests showing therapeutic levels of tested drug must be reported as negative. Employer cannot require or request a blood sample for a drug test.
How Test Results Are Used	Test results may be used to screen out drug-using applicants or to discharge or discipline employees. An employee's first offense results in referral to an EAP. The employee may be terminated if, after completion of an EAP, the employee receives another positive drug test result.
Enforcement of Statute	Enforcement is by private civil action; state pursues violation of statute.
Employee Remedies	Employees may seek attorneys' fees and court costs, damages, and injunctive relief.
Employer Penalties	Employer penalties include civil penalty (civil fine of $500–$2,000) and criminal sanction (criminal fine of $500–$1,000, imprisonment for not more than 6 months, or both).
Who Pays for Testing	Employee can retest sample at a laboratory at employee's expense.
Employee Assistance Benefits	To require, request, or conduct drug testing, employer must have available an EAP that is provided by employer or that is available to the extent provided by a policy of health insurance or under contract by a nonprofit hospital service corporation.
Other Requirements	If urinalysis is positive, testee may request, at own expense, a blood test. Results must be kept confidential.
Citations to Authority	Vt. Stat. Ann. tit. 21, §§ 511–520.

Exhibit 23.4   Mandated Benefits: 2009 Compliance Guide

Exhibit 23.4 (cont'd)

WEST VIRGINIA
Note: The West Virginia Supreme Court has held that it is contrary to the state's public policy for a private employer to require employees to submit to drug testing since such testing portends an invasion of the individual's right to privacy. However, that court has also held that prospective employees may be required to submit to testing, which is not forbidden when an employer has reasonable grounds for testing. West Virginia has an Executive Order requiring preemployment drug testing for certain state employees.

Citations to Authority	*Baughmann v. Wal-Mart Stores,* 215 W. Va. 45, 592 S.E.2d 824 (2003); *Twigg v. Hercules Corp.,* 185 W. Va. 155, 406 S.E.2d 52 (1990). Executive Order No. 5-07.

Exhibit 23.4 (cont'd)

WISCONSIN	
Note: Wisconsin does not have a general law pertaining to drug testing. However, employers for public works projects must have a substance abuse program that includes drug testing. The law provides that employers are responsible for the costs of drug testing and that testing should follow guidelines as set up by the U.S. Department of Health and Human Services' Substance Abuse and Mental Health Services Administration.	
Citations to Authority	Wis. Stat. Ann. § 103.503.

Source: John F. Buckley & Ronald M. Green, *2008 State by State Guide to Human Resources Law* (New York: Aspen Publishers, Inc. 2008).

Chapter 24
Recordkeeping

§ 24.01   AUDIT QUESTIONS

1. Are all employment applications retained for at least one year from submission date?

2. Is there a written policy regarding employee records?

3. Is job-related, medical, and payroll information kept in three separate employee files?

4. If policy exceptions are made for new employees, are they specified in writing in an offer letter?

5. Are employee records maintained for the length of time proscribed by state and federal laws?

Note: Consistent "yes" answers to the above questions suggest that the organization is applying effective management practices and/or complying with federal regulations. "No" answers indicate that problem areas exist and should be addressed immediately.

This chapter discusses the role of recordkeeping in human resources (HR) management and the reasons for establishing a formal employee recordkeeping function. It covers types of records, file setup, and record retention, security, and confidentiality. It also briefly reviews legal restrictions on and obligations of employers with regard to obtaining and maintaining preemployment reports.

§ 24.02   REASONS FOR RECORDKEEPING

Nearly every organization keeps some kind of central file of employee records. Employment data provide a valuable source of information for auditing the effectiveness of departmental functions, tracking employment-related costs, monitoring progress toward achieving departmental and company objectives, and identifying the possible causes of, or solutions to, such problems as on-the-job accidents, absenteeism, and turnover.

A formal employee recordkeeping system enables:

1. Compliance with federal, state, and, in some cases, local government recordkeeping and reporting requirements

2. Decision making regarding employment issues such as hiring, promotion, compensation, training, and discipline

3. Documenting the basis for employment-related decisions

The objective of developing and maintaining an efficient system for capturing and storing employee information is to make relevant information available, in an easy-to-use format, to the decision makers at the time that the decision is being made.

The Department of Labor (DOL) has created an Internet tool that helps employers determine which of the department's recordkeeping, reporting and notice requirements are required for their businesses. The "FirstStep Recordkeeping, Reporting and Notices" elaw Advisor can be found on their Web site at *www.dol.gov/elaws*.

[A]   Management Decisions

Prudent management decisions are based on gathering all relevant facts that can be applied to a particular set of circumstances. Employment-related decisions are facilitated if a complete employment history is maintained on each employee. Such information as positions held, pay rates, performance assessments, disciplinary action records, significant achievements, and professional development activities can be vitally important to making a sound decision.

[B]   Documentation

Employment records can be useful in justifying or defending against legal challenges to disciplinary or other HR actions. For example, a job application containing falsified information might provide the evidence needed to justify a decision to discharge an employee, whereas documentation on job performance, such as past performance appraisals, might be used to support a promotion decision. Other kinds of information retained in employment records might be cited as proof that an HR action was job related and nondiscriminatory.

§ 24.03 STRUCTURE OF EMPLOYEE FILES

A wide range of employment-related information can be maintained and used to determine individuals' qualifications for employment, promotion, training, or compensation levels and to make decisions about disciplinary actions, including termination.

It is not recommended that all employee information be stored in one file. The legal issues involved in file separation are protection of employees' rights to privacy, discrimination prevention, and confidentiality of medical, racial, and other protected information.

Separate files should be maintained for different types of employee records. Specifically, employee information should be organized into four basic types of files:

Personnel (or human resources) files:

- Personal data, such as home address, date of birth, Social Security Number, race, sex, marital status, spouse's name and employer, number and names of dependents, and education, including schools attended and degrees awarded

- Job application and resume

- Employment references or recommendations

- Results of background checks, including reports about credit, character, and work habits

- Job offer letter

- Attendance and leave records

- Performance evaluations, letters of recommendation, and merit awards

- Job descriptions, specifications, titles, and locations

- Changes in employment status, such as promotions, transfers, layoffs, or discharge

- Safety records, including accident reports (but not the medical information related to workers compensation claims–see below)

- Company-provided training and education records

- Test information, including test scores, used for selection and promotion

- Disciplinary records, such as warning notices

- Grievance records, including arbitration awards

- Notes on or results of exit interviews

Payroll files:

- Basic payroll records, including wage and salary data

- Time cards, time sheets (although these may also be kept by payroll period)

- Authorization for payroll deductions or withholdings

- Child support deduction orders

- Garnishments

Medical files:

- Results of physical examinations (periodic and/or after a job offer has been made)

- Results of drug and alcohol testing

- Occupational health and medical records

- Disability and health insurance claims records

- Medical information related to medical leaves of absence

- Medical information related to workers' compensation claims (alternatively, this might be kept in a completely separate file by claim)

Benefit files:

- Fringe benefits information, such as the name of the insurance provider and pension plan participation

- Benefit enrollment information

- Beneficiary information

Note that there are several additional files that may be needed, although generally not for every employee:

- For the participants in a group health plan: a Health Insurance Portability and Accountability Act (HIPAA) medical file containing all protected health information created, received, or maintained by the group health plan, including benefit enrollment information, claims information, and the like. (See **Chapter 6** for further information about HIPAA).

- Investigations file, as needed, containing results of past investigations of internal or external charges. (Investigations of current charges should be maintained separately and away from the employee's general HR file until the investigation is completed.)

- U.S. Citizenship and Immigration Services Form I-9 file containing the I-9s for all employees. The forms should be organized chronologically by year or alphabetically by last name, in a single file, such as a three-ring binder, to prevent a U.S. Citizenship and Immigration Services (USCIS) auditor from viewing unrelated confidential employee information.

Individual supervisors often maintain their own sets of employee files. In some cases, the HR department may not even know of the existence of such files. Although a supervisor may not consider these files part of the formal employee file, the files are considered to be so if an employee or former employee brings legal action against the employer. Thus, a formal recordkeeping function should clearly indicate to supervisors the company's policy on maintaining unofficial employee files. Supervisors should be allowed to maintain employee files containing only copies of original documentation. Supervisors' files should not contain unique data not found in the employee's master file.

Some organizations (e.g., certain federal contractors and subcontractors) are required to retain records on job applicants who have not been hired. Applicant records typically contain applicants' resumes, completed application forms, results of reference or background checks, results of drug tests or other required physical examinations, interview notes, and reasons for nonselection.

§ 24.04   RECORDS MANAGEMENT

Changes to employee information are often made in a handwritten note placed in the employee's personnel file. For example, approvals for salary increases are frequently handwritten on a separate sheet and placed in the employee's file. The net result is that it becomes necessary to find the various sheets and arrange them chronologically to see the salary progression for an employee. This is not particularly efficient.

[A]   Recordkeeping Forms

Efficiencies in employee recordkeeping can be gained through the use of the following types of forms:

- *Employee Data Form.* In a manual recordkeeping system, an employee date form summarizes each employee's employment so that important information—such as name, sex, Social Security number, and hire date—may be seen at a glance. (See **Exhibit 24.1** for a sample employee data form.). In an automated or computer-based recordkeeping system, employee data may be spread across several screens that display employment history (i.e., the job or salary screen), demographic information, and other employment records, such as employee benefits or training. Usually, there is one screen for each benefit plan in which the employee is enrolled.

- *Attendance Records.* It is important to track accurate attendance and tardiness for all employees, even for those who are exempt from overtime provisions of the Fair Labor Standards Act of 1938 (FLSA). It is particularly important to maintain accurate attendance records if the company's written policy stipulates that employees receive paid-time-off benefits that involve periodic accruals. A pattern of absences and other problem trends are easy to overlook without a comprehensive attendance record system.

- *Employee Status Change Notice.* An employee status change notice simplifies recordkeeping and creates a complete audit trail for changes to an employee's status. For changes affecting pay, it is generally advisable to include a routing to payroll to ensure that the changes are clearly communicated and implemented in a timely manner. For example, the change notice should include an acknowledgment line to be initialed and dated by the payroll administrator after a pay change is initiated.

[B]   Employee Records Policy

Every company should develop and communicate to its workers a formal, written employee records policy addressing the following major aspects of records management:

- Records description

- Information sources

- Review cycle

- Record retention

- Employee file inspection

- Adding, changing, or deleting file information

- Outside requests for HR information

- Records maintenance

- File security

Following the adoption of a policy for employee records, a company should develop written procedures to ensure compliance with the written policy.

§ 24.05   RECORD SECURITY

Whether HR records are maintained in a file cabinet or in a computer database, two concerns must be addressed: security and confidentiality.

A company should have established policies and procedures to control access to and safeguard information in employees' records. HR files should be kept in a secure area, usually in the HR department. Only those with a legitimate need to know should be allowed access to employee data. If someone other than an employee or HR administrator (e.g., a supervisor) needs to access certain file data, only the specific information required should be provided, not the entire file. Employees and, in some cases, managers and supervisors should be required to submit a request for access. **Exhibit 24.3** indicates who may have authorized access to various employee files.

Some companies notify employees of third-party requests for information; others specify the kinds of information that may be disclosed to third parties or restrict access to those with a specific need to know.

§ 24.06   RECORD CONFIDENTIALITY

Many states have legislated employee rights to inspect and copy their HR files. The definition of *HR file* generally includes any unofficial files maintained by supervisors. State laws vary, but they generally convey the right only to active employees, employees who are laid off with reinstatement rights, or employees on leave of absence. Definitions of *employee file* also vary. The definition generally includes any unofficial files maintained by supervisors.

Generally, employees are allowed to inspect any records used to determine their hiring, promotion, compensation, discipline, or termination within a reasonable time after making a request to inspect their records. Employees are generally not entitled to inspect letters of reference or records of investigation of a possible crime.

There are legal considerations regarding the confidentiality of the following types of employee information:

- *Medical and Disability Information.* Federal and state laws require that employers keep medical information confidential and not disclose it to anyone, unless there is a provable and specific need for that person to have the information.

- *U.S. Citizenship and Immigration Services Form I-9.* The personal data on the Form I-9 must be protected from accidental disclosure. The forms should be stored in a file separate from the employee history so that employees cannot claim that the information on this form was used by supervisors to discriminate against them and so that in the event of a USCIS audit, federal agents do not receive the entire employee file when they ask to review I-9 forms.

- *Protection of Private Information.* Few states have legislated employee protection from employers' divulging the contents of their personnel files; however, civil litigation in the form of common-law privacy and defamation action may result from the release of confidential information.

- *Payroll Records.* There are no specific regulations regarding the confidentiality of payroll records. However, payroll records should be confidential. An employer runs the risk of violating common-law privacy, and a defamation action may result, when negative financial information, such as garnishments for child support or bad credit reports, is divulged. Further, employee relations and morale issues are frequently involved in disclosure of payroll data and pay rates.

§ 24.07   RECORD RETENTION

[A]   Employee Recruitment Records

It is critical to maintain complete and accurate records of the recruitment process. For each job posting, the records should include the job description, the recruitment methods used, the applications received, the candidates interviewed, the candidate selected, and the reason for his or her selection.

Recruitment process records will provide evidence of the company's use of valid selection criteria in making hiring decisions in the event claims are filed against the company for discriminatory hiring practices.

[B]   Active Employee and Terminated Employee Records

Records for active and for terminated employees are generally treated the same. At a minimum, an employer should keep personnel records for the length of time required by law. The retention laws vary, however, for regular, ongoing employees and terminated employees.

A rule of thumb for retention of employee records is five years, even though most laws prescribe one to three years. The five-year retention period has advantages, as the burden of producing relevant employee records in cases of employment-related legal action is generally placed on the employer. In many cases, if the employer cannot produce a record, the law allows an employee to attest to the best of his or her recollection as to the specific information.

§ 24.08 SOCIAL SECURITY NUMBER MISMATCH

Employers report employees' Social Security numbers on the W-2 wage reports filed with the IRS annually. This is important to employees because the wages reported on W-2 are used by the Social Security Administration (SSA) to determine the amount of retirement and other benefits for which they may be eligible. In order to complete the W-2 report, employers use the Form W-4 completed by the employees. The Form W-4 requires employees to fill in their Social Security Number (SSN), full name, marital status for tax purposes, and the number of withholding deductions they are claiming.

The SSA reviews the W-2 reports, and determines if the employees' names and SSNs match their records. When an employer submits more than 10 employees with discrepancies and the number of discrepancies is more than 0.5 percent of all employees submitted, the SSA issues a "no-match letter" to the employer. Due to privacy laws, the no-match letter will only list the SSN, but no employee name.

The purpose of the letter is to obtain corrected information so that earnings can be properly posted to the employee's Social Security account. Most of the "mismatch" errors are due to name changes (e.g., when a married woman changes her name at work, but not with the SSA), and typographical, clerical, and technological errors. In addition, an individual's SSN may legally change if his or her work or residence status changes, such as when an individual obtains an SSN to comply with state driver's license requirements, and then later obtains a work permit.

The no-match letter does not imply that the employee or the employer intentionally provided incorrect information. The letters do not make any statement about an employee's immigration status and are not a basis, in and of themselves, for taking any adverse action against an employee or employer.

Each employee listed on the no-match letter also receives a similar letter. The employee letter asks him or her to check the reported information and provide SSA and the employer with corrected information. Employees may need to contact SSA by phone or in person to resolve the discrepancies. If SSA has no address for the employee, or the address is invalid, SSA will send a letter regarding the specific employee to the employer.

On June 14, 2006, the Department of Homeland Security (DHS) proposed new rules regarding the SSA no-match letters. The final rule was published on August 10, 2007. The DHS intends to prosecute employers for ignoring the no-match letters if the employees listed in those letters turn out to be unauthorized foreign workers. The final rule, published in August, provides a safe harbor process for employers to avoid prosecution.

On August 15, 2007, the Department of Homeland Security (DHS) adopted a new rule, "Safe Harbor Provisions for Employers Who Receive a No-Match Letter." The AFL-CIO and other union groups filed a lawsuit against the DHS and SSA, stating that the program violates workers' rights, places undue burdens on employers, and causes discrimination on employees who are perceived to be immigrants. On August 31, 2007, the U.S. District Court for the Northern District of California issued a temporary restraining order, and on October 15 a preliminary injunction, thereby halting the implementation of the new rule. The court has subsequently agreed to delay the case to allow the DHS an opportunity to revise the regulations.

On March 26, 2008, the DHS published a supplemental proposed rule in the Federal Register, intending to address some of the concerns raised by the lawsuit. Interested parties were invited to submit comments no later than April 25, 2008. As of this writing, there has been no action by the court to lift the restraining order.

As a result of these events, no mismatch letters were sent by the SSA in 2007 for tax year 2006. The SSA announced in May 2008 that it would not send out letters in 2008 for the 2007 tax year.

§ 24.09   FEDERAL RECORDKEEPING REQUIREMENTS

A number of pieces of federal employment-related laws and executive orders contain specific recordkeeping provisions. The statutory provisions on what should be kept and for how long vary considerably. Some laws require the use of specific forms for recording information. A formal recordkeeping process can do much to ensure that the requirements of each law are met with a minimum of duplication and that, should the employer be subject to a compliance review or DOL audit, the proper records exist and are retrievable to minimize the disruption caused by the review or audit. The following paragraphs detail the required retention period under the major employment-related law. (See **Exhibit 24.4** for a summary of major federal recordkeeping requirements.)

[A]   Age Discrimination in Employment Act

Under the Age Discrimination in Employment Act of 1967 (ADEA), which applies to companies with 20 or more employees, payroll or other records containing each employee's name, address, date of birth, occupation, rate of pay, and weekly compensation earned must be maintained for three years.

The ADEA also requires maintenance of the following types of records for one year from the date of the personnel actions to which the records relate:

- Job applications (including those for temporary personnel), resumes, other replies to advertisements, and records pertaining to failure to hire

- Promotions, demotions, transfers, selections for training, layoffs, recalls, and discharges

- Job orders submitted to employment agencies or unions

- Test papers in connection with aptitude or other employer-administered employment tests

- Physical examination results considered in connection with HR actions

- Job advertisements or notices to the public or employees regarding openings, promotions, training programs, or opportunities for overtime work

Records relating to employee benefit plans, seniority systems, and merit rating systems must be maintained for the full period that the plans or systems are in effect plus one year after the termination of such plans or systems. If the terms of an employee benefit plan or seniority or merit rating system are not in writing, a summary memorandum should be kept.

[B] Employee Polygraph Act

Under the Employee Polygraph Act of 1988, if an examiner is conducting an investigation of a workplace theft or other incident that results in economic loss to the employer, the employer must maintain the following records for three years from the date of the investigation:

- A copy of the statement provided to employees describing the activity or incident under investigation and the basis for the polygraph test

- A copy of the notice provided to the examiner and all opinions and reports that are furnished to the employer by the examiner

[C] Executive Order 11246

Under Executive Order 11246 as amended, federal contractors and subcontractors with 150 or more employees and a contract of $150,000 or more in one year must maintain employment records related to affirmative action plans (AAPs) for a minimum of two years. Federal contractors and subcontractors below those thresholds must maintain records for one year. Employment and AAP-related records include:

- Written affirmative action programs and documentation, including all required statistical analyses

- Compliance with equal employment opportunity nondiscrimination requirements, including documents on the use of tests, test validity, and test results

- Requests for reasonable accommodation

- Results of physical examinations

- Job advertisements and postings

- Applications and résumés

- Interview notes

- Any other records having to do with hiring, assignment, promotion, demotion, transfer, layoff, termination, rates of pay and other compensation, and selection for training or apprenticeship

[D] Fair Labor Standards Act

For *nonexempt* employees subject to the minimum wage and overtime pay provisions of the FLSA, an employer must retain the following records for each employee:

- Name in full as used for Social Security purposes

- Home address, including zip code

- Date of birth (if employee is under age 19)

- Sex

- Occupation in which employed

- Time of day and day of week on which the workweek begins

- Regular hourly rate of pay for any workweek in which overtime compensation is due, including an explanation of pay (indicating the monetary amount paid per hour, per day, per week, per piece, by commission or sales, or other basis) and the amount and nature of each payment that is excluded from the regular rate

- Hours worked each workday and total hours worked each workweek (hours worked may not be estimated)

- Total daily or weekly straight-time earnings or wages due for hours worked during the workday or workweek, not counting premium overtime compensation

- Total premium pay for overtime hours

- Total wages paid each pay period

- Total additions to, or deductions from, wages paid each pay period, including employee purchase orders or wage assignments; also, in individual employee records, the dates, amounts, and nature of the items that make up the total additions and deductions

- Date of payment and the pay period covered by the payment

- If the employee is working under a special certificate that allows the employer to pay the employee a subminimum wage, a record of that fact

For *exempt* employees, the FLSA requires employers to maintain the following records for each employee:

- Name in full as used for Social Security purposes

- Home address, including zip code

- Date of birth (if employee is under age 19)

- Sex

- Occupation

- Time of day and day of week on which the workweek begins

- Total wages paid each pay period

- Date of payment and the pay period covered by each payment

The FLSA requires employers to preserve all payroll records, certificates, collective bargaining agreements, individual contracts, and sales and purchase records for three years. In addition, employers must preserve all basic employment and earnings records, wage rate tables, order, shipping, and billing records, and records of additions to and deductions from wages for a two-year period.

[E] Family and Medical Leave Act

For employees who take leave under the Family and Medical Leave Act of 1993 (FMLA), the following information must be maintained for three years:

- Basic employee data (including name, address, occupation, rate of pay, terms of compensation, daily and weekly hours worked per pay period, additions to or deductions from wages and total compensation)

- Dates of leave taken by eligible employees (leave must be designated as FMLA leave)

- Hours of leave for intermittent leave taken

- Copies of employee notices and documents describing employee benefits or policies and practices regarding paid and unpaid leave

- Records of premium payments by the employee and/or employer of group health plan(s)

- Records of any dispute regarding the designation of leave.

[F] Immigration Reform and Control Act

Under the Immigration Reform and Control Act of 1986, USCIS Form I-9, Employee Eligibility Verification Form, signed by each newly hired employee and the employer, must be maintained for three years from the date of hire or one year after date of termination, whichever is later.

The I-9s must be readily available for inspection upon request. The law requires employers to examine each new hire's I-9 documents for legitimacy but does not require that they be photocopied. It is possible to accept fraudulent proof inadvertently. Therefore, in the case of a USCIS audit, an employer may be providing unnecessary proof of its acceptance of an illegal document if it makes and retains photocopies of each new hire's Form I-9 documents.

On November 7, 2007, the Department of Homeland Security (DHS), which oversees the USCIS, issued a revised Form I-9. This version should be used for all employees hired after December 27, 2007. Employers can download the latest version, available on the USCIS Web site at: *www.uscis.gov/graphics/portal/site/ uscis*, then click on "For Employers." For further information on Form I-9s, please see **Chapter 16, Section 16.10**.

The DHS has created an interim rule that allows employers to sign and retain the Form I-9 electronically. The employer may use one of a number of electronic systems as long as it complies with current IRS guidelines. Details can be found in a Fact Sheet on the U.S. Immigration and Customs Enforcement Web site at: *http://www.ice.gov/pi/news/factsheets/i-9employment.htm*.

[G]   Title VII of the Civil Rights Act

Title VII of the Civil Rights Act of 1964 requires all employers with at least 15 employees to maintain records for all employees such as application forms and records of hiring, promotions, demotions, transfers, layoffs or terminations, employees' rate of pay or other terms of compensation, and selection for training or apprenticeship (including records for temporary and seasonal personnel) for one year from the date the record is made or the personnel action is taken, whichever is later. Records relevant to a charge of discrimination must be retained until final disposition of the charge.

Employer with 100 or more employees must submit Form EEO-1, Employer Information Report, and must retain a copy of the most recent report at each reporting unit or, alternatively, at company headquarters.

[H]   Preservation of Records

According to federal government requirements regarding preservation of records, an employer must:

- Maintain records at its place of business or at an established central recordkeeping location.

- Ensure that the records are safe, accessible, and available for inspection at any time by auditors from the Wage and Hour Division. If they are kept at a central location, away from the place of business, they should be made available at the place of inspection within 72 hours after notice from the Wage and Hour Division.

- Submit to the Wage and Hour Division any extension, recomputations, or transcriptions of the records, if the auditor makes a written request.

- Request approval from the Wage and Hour Division if old records are to be converted to microfiche or microfilm. The employer must have equipment to view the records in this form, however, if it is audited by the Wage and Hour Division.

The law does not specify the form these records should take; therefore, an employer's chosen method is sufficient if it includes the information required by law. To be considered adequate, the records should be in an organized format.

A company may choose to keep its records on paper, microfiche, microfilm, or a computer hard drive (with proper disk backup).

[I]   Consumer Reports Disposal Rule

The Fair and Accurate Credit Transactions (FACT) Act disposal rule became effective June 1, 2005. The rule requires that all consumer reports and information derived from a consumer report must be appropriately disposed of when the employer no longer requires the information. Reasonable methods of disposal will depend on the format of the information (paper or electronic) and the employer's means. For example, paper documents may be burned, pulverized, or shredded; electronic documents may be wiped, overwritten, or the discs might be destroyed. Alternatively, an employer may hire a document destruction contractor. The disposal rule does not address the timing of destruction, only that the objective of the disposal of personal and financial information should be to protect against "unauthorized use of the information."

[J] Federal Rules of Civil Procedure

Amendments to the Federal Rules of Civil Procedure (FRCP) became effective in December 2006. While these rules pertain specifically to documents that must be produced during litigation, they have made it clear what employers need to do in the preservation and deletion of electronic information. Although the new rules apply to federal litigation, many states have adopted the federal rules to apply to state litigation, as well. The most important aspect of these new rules is the requirement that when an employer (as well as other parties) know or have reason to believe that litigation may occur, they must preserve all information, including electronically stored information (ESI), related to that litigation. Early in the litigation process, opposing counsel must meet to disclose important information about each party's ESI. The following information must be disclosed even before request by opposing counsel:

- A description of the ESI they possess

- The location of any ESI

- Any ESI that will not be produced because it is not reasonably accessible

The new rules define ESI broadly as "any type of information that is stored electronically." ESI includes information stored on employees' laptop or desktop computers; file and mail servers; compact disc storage; portable memory devices, such as "memory sticks" or USB "flash" drives; external hard drives; and personal digital assistants (PDAs).

The format in which the ESI is to be produced may be specified by the requesting party, but the amended rules encourage the parties to reach agreement about the format early in the process. If no agreement can be reached, the rule states that the ESI should be produced either in "a form or forms in which it is ordinarily maintained or in a form or forms that are reasonably usable."

Parties to litigation will be sanctioned for failing to meet their obligations to preserve and produce ESI. However, the rules provide a "safe harbor" exception: "Absent exceptional circumstances, a court may not impose sanctions under these rules on a party for failing to provide electronically stored information lost as a result of the routine, good-faith operation of an electronic information system." Nevertheless, employers who become parties to litigation should immediately implement procedures to prevent the loss of ESI relevant to that litigation ("litigation hold"). Previous case law has established that the duty to preserve relevant documents arises when an event occurs that would give an employer reasonable notice that litigation may begin; the litigation hold should not wait until actual notice of the litigation is received.

Employers should develop an ESI preservation and production policy prior to litigation. To develop such a policy, determine what and where all ESI currently resides or could reside in the employers' systems. Review current document and electronic document retention policies to ensure that they comply with the revised FRCP rules. Ensure that the policy includes a "litigation hold" procedure and that all impacted electronic systems are capable of implementing the procedure. Develop a litigation response policy and procedure, and identify who will implement that procedure, should the need arise.

§ 24.10 STATE RECORDKEEPING REQUIREMENTS

In addition to federal laws, many state and local laws place a recordkeeping burden on employers. In some cases, state laws mirror federal laws; in others, state law expands the scope of the federal legislation or places additional requirements on employers. When the federal and state laws have different provisions, the legislation that is most favorable to the employee usually takes precedence.

If a state requires an employer to store records from a period longer than required by federal law, only those records related to complying with the state's wage and hour requirements must be retained beyond the period specified in the federal requirements.

Exhibit 24.1
Sample Employee Data Form

Name: _____ _____ _____   Employee #: _____
          Last   First   Middle

Hire Date: _____   Social Security #: _____

Address Information

Date	Street Address	City	State	Zip	Phone

Emergency Information

In Emergency, Notify	City	State	Zip	Day Phone	Night Phone

Federal Withholding Information

Date							
Exemptions Claimed							
Additional Amount Withheld							
State Tax							
City Tax							

Exhibit 24.1
Mandated Benefits: 2009 Compliance Guide

Insurance/Benefits Data

Type	Date Eligible	Date Joined	Date Withdrawn
Life—Self			
Life—Family			
Medical—Self (HMO/PPO)			
Medical—Dependent (HMO/PPO)			
Major Medical—Self			
Major Medical—Dependent			
AD&D—Self			
AD&D—Dependent			
Dental—Self			
Dental—Family			
Pension Plan			
401(k) Plan			
Credit Union			

Wage/Salary Data

Date from	Date	Position Classification	Grade	Location	Rate of Pay Amount	Rate of Pay per (hr, week)	Reason for Change *(see codes below)

Codes*

A. Demotion
B. Discharge
C. New Hire

D. Job Re-evaluation
E. Layoff
F. Merit Increase

G. Probation Ended
H. Promotion
I. Rehired

J. Resigned
K. Retired
L. Service Increase

M. STEP Increase
N. Transfer
O. Other

Termination/Discharge Information

		Reason:
____ Resignation	Date: _____	
____ Discharge		

Exhibit 24.2
Maintenance of Personnel Files and Records

Type of File	Who May Have Access
Personnel	• Employee ——————— • Supervisors with a need to know • Former employees • Human Resources
Medical/Confidential	• Human Resources • Supervisors as needed for reasonable accommodation • Governmental/legal agencies conducting investigation relevant to medical issues
Payroll	• Payroll staff • Human Resources • Auditing/investigating agencies
I-9	• Human Resources • Auditing/investigating agencies

Source: SHRM White Paper, December 1997: *Maintenance of Personnel Files and Records.*

Exhibit 24.3   Mandated Benefits: 2009 Compliance Guide

Exhibit 24.3
Summary of Federal Recordkeeping Requirements

Employee Record Type	Maximum Retention Period
Hiring and Personnel Actions	
• Job applications, resumes, other replies to job advertisements	One year; two years if federal contractor or subcontractor with 150 employees and contract of $150,000 in one year
• Records relating to refusal or failure to hire (including test papers, medical test results, and other screening tools)	Same
• Job orders submitted to employment agencies or labor unions	Same
• Records showing impact of employment actions on protected groups, including selections, promotions, demotions, layoffs and recalls, terminations, transfers, and opportunities for training or overtime work	Same
Compensation Action	
• Documents concerning merit or seniority systems	Two years
• Explanations of any wage differences for employees of the opposite sex	Same
• Job evaluations and job descriptions	Same
• Wage rage tables	Same
• Collective bargaining agreements and individual contracts	Three years
Benefit Actions	
• All records supporting disclosures required in reports to the Internal Revenue Service, Department of Labor, and Pension Benefit Guaranty Corporation	Six years from date report filed
• Plan descriptions	One year from termination of plan
Basic Employee Data	
• Name, address, Social Security number, gender, date of birth	Four years
• Occupation or job classification	Same
• Work authorization (I-9 for all, work permits for minors)	Same for work permits; three years from date of hire or one year from date of termination, whichever is later, for I-9 forms
Compensation Records	
• Daily work schedules	Four years
• Pay rate	Same
• Weekly compensation	Same

Exhibit 24.3 (cont'd)

Employee Record Type	Maximum Retention Period
• Amounts and dates of payment; period of service covered	Same
—Daily and weekly hours	Same
—Straight time and overtime hours and pay	Same
—Annuity and pension payments	Same
—Accident and health plan payments	Same
• Benefits deductions and additions	Same
Tax Records	
• Amounts of wages subject to withholdings	Four years
• Agreements with employee to withhold additional taxes	Same
• Actual taxes withheld and dates withheld	Same
• Reasons for any difference between total tax payments and actual tax payments	Same
• Withholding forms (W-4)	Same
Employment Actions	
• Dates of hire, separation, rehiring, or return and reason for separation	One year from date of action; two years if federal contractor or sub-contractor with 150 employees and contract of $150,000 in one year
• Promotions, demotions, transfers, layoffs, recalls, training opportunities	Same
• Aptitude/ability/medical/other tests used in employment actions	Same
• Polygraph test results and records, including reasons for administering tests	Three years from date of action
Health, Medical, and Safety Data	
• Job-related injuries and illnesses	Five calendar years
• Requests for accommodation of disability	One year; two years if federal contractor or subcontractor with 150 employees and contract of $150,000 in one year
• Medical exams used for employment	30 years
• Toxic substance exposure records	30 years
• Blood-borne pathogen exposure records	30 years

Chapter 25
Human Resources Risk Management

§ 25.01   AUDIT QUESTIONS

1. Does the company know whether it runs the risk of noncompliance with regard to federal and state employment laws?

2. Are employee policies and procedures documented? Are they communicated to employees?

3. Are disciplinary actions monitored to ensure consistency and avoid discrimination?

4. Does the company have signed documentation on file from every employee proving receipt of employee handbooks and other key policy documents?

5. Does the company provide systematic training for supervisory personnel, instructing them in relevant legal issues in employment?

6. Does the company conduct a Human Resources Audit annually?

Note: Consistent "yes" answers to the above questions suggest that the organization has implemented some key risk management practices and/or is complying with federal regulations. "No" answers indicate that problem areas exist and should be addressed immediately.

This chapter discusses the overall role of human resources (HR) in risk management. It presents a model for conducting an HR risk assessment, or diagnostic review, as a process for investigating the effectiveness and legality of an organization's HR policies and practices. For the purposes of this chapter, the principal objective of the HR risk assessment process described is to ensure compliance with federal employment laws and regulations.

At the end of the chapter is a list of diagnostic self-assessment questions for managers to use in making an evaluation of the overall status of HR (**Exhibit 25.1**) and a list of federal employment law requirements by company size (**Exhibit 25.2**).

§ 25.02 THE ROLE OF HR IN RISK MANAGEMENT

The dictionary defines *risk* as "(a) the chance of loss; (b) the degree of probability of loss; (c) the amount of possible loss in full, [the] amount at risk." [*Webster's New Twentieth Century Dictionary Unabridged,* 2d ed.]

A risk manager's responsibility is usually related to insurance. He or she deals with business risks and losses by planning, directing, and coordinating activities aimed at risk avoidance, loss prevention or reduction, grouping of exposed units, and transfer of risk. However, risk management is more than just avoiding risks. It involves careful analysis and classification of possible risk, measurement of the financial impact of risk on the company, and selection of appropriate techniques to control risk.

In HR, the specific legal risks and obligations brought about by state and federal laws affect employers in many areas, including recruitment and selection, affirmative action and equal employment opportunity (EEO), performance management, compensation, benefits, safety and health, employee relations, policies and procedures, training, and termination. In today's litigious society, effective HR management equates to effective risk management for the "people side" of the organization.

From a strategic standpoint, effective HR risk management significantly and positively affects the company's financial success, growth, and corporate reputation by vigilantly addressing legal compliance issues, minimizing unnecessary exposure to liability, and avoiding capricious personnel actions. The sheer magnitude of labor law compliance suggests that risk cannot be avoided. However, if the HR manager is doing his or her job properly, company management should be well informed in advance of the risks associated with any particular course of action and should not be caught by surprise by any possible outcome of a decision, either positive or negative.

From a tactical standpoint, the HR manager as risk manager reduces exposure to liability every day by implementing equitable, safe, and legal policies, procedures, and approaches to managing the employee-employer relationship. Reduction of exposure to liability includes using confidential investigation procedures, training all levels of management to use effective HR approaches, and implementing impartial employment, evaluation, and disciplinary criteria. It also includes using methods to mitigate workplace violence and establishing and maintaining a work environment free of safety hazards.

[A] Staying Current with the Law

The best way for the HR manager to ensure legal compliance is to stay current with the law. This can be a daunting task. Fortunately, there are many ways of keeping up with HR legislation and trends. Subscribing to online HR information services, attending legal update seminars, getting on mailing lists of consulting and legal firms, joining professional HR organizations, reading reference books, and requesting publications from local government offices are all excellent ways of obtaining current HR information. Many of the larger CPA or business services firms also offer HR consulting assistance.

Establishing a relationship with an employment attorney is also a good strategy. Not all attorneys are specialists in employment law. Just as a business owner would probably not consult his or her real estate attorney on a matter concerning accounting, the HR manager should direct employment law issues to an employment attorney. The regulatory environment is so complex that an attorney needs technical expertise to provide good legal advice.

The normal role of employment attorneys is to offer legal advice in more complicated situations. In this capacity, they are reasonably compelled to present the most risk-averse course of action. Attorneys vary considerably in their approach to providing client advice. While maximum avoidance of risk is an important consideration, some business owners and managers prefer to weigh various alternatives in light of the business objectives of the organization. In this case, the company should interview several firms and select an employment attorney who is comfortable presenting an assessment of the risk associated with alternative solutions to personnel problems. This is an important relationship. Management needs to exercise good business judgment and select an attorney whose approach best fits the way in which HR is managed within the company.

[B] Employee Handbooks

For risk management purposes, a well-written and current employee handbook is important as a defense in employment litigation. It establishes the basic, written policies defining major aspects of the employee-employer relationship. Employers may use the employee handbook to communicate a consistent, nondiscriminatory method of dealing with employees—and to demonstrate that employees were notified in advance of any subsequent disciplinary action. Advance notification to employees about work rules, notification requirements, benefits, discipline, and subsequent penalties for noncompliance can strengthen the company's legal position immensely.

However, a well-written employee handbook is not sufficient in itself to protect a company from risk. For the handbook to effectively help protect the company, the company must do what it says in the handbook. Even if the handbook is constantly updated to reflect fast-breaking legal developments, in today's legal climate the employer's failure to follow the policies as written creates an opportunity for litigation.

Conversely, the absence of a written handbook does not mean a company cannot be held to established procedures, patterns, and precedents. The policies and practices are simply unwritten. Such a company's procedures are no less discoverable in the event of a lawsuit. For example, any government agency involved will simply interview enough employees to understand the current practice, determine the legality of the practice, and levy any appropriate penalties.

There is no standard rule to indicate when an organization needs an employee handbook. To determine if an organization should have a handbook, consider items such as number of employees, number (and corresponding requirements) of state and federal laws, the current employee relations climate, management and employee communication effectiveness, and the willingness to accept a certain level of risk.

A workforce of 15 employees is the point at which a number of federal laws take effect. At a minimum, it would be prudent for an employer of this size to provide written notification of specific policies to its employees. Many employers simply group employee notifications, policies, and procedures together to create a small pamphlet. As the number of employees increases, so does the number of employment laws with which an organization must comply. Communications and employee relations issues may also become more of a concern with increase in size. Thus, for an organization with 15 to 49 employees, it may become increasingly important to gather the written notifications, procedures, and policies together into an employee handbook. For example, issues such as complaint resolution, vacation accrual, absence reporting, payroll procedures, and safety rules may be helpful policies to have in addition to the legally related or required notifications and policies. Once a company exceeds 50 employees, the need for consistency, in addition to the above-mentioned issues, becomes more difficult to attain without a handbook. (See **Exhibit 25.2** for a list of federal employment law requirements by company size.)

[C] Sources of Liability

In general, employers can be held liable for the actions of employees if the actions occur on company time, if the employee is engaged in work-related activity, or if the employer provided an article or substance to the employee that caused harm.

[1] Alcohol at Company Events

Providing alcohol at a company-sponsored event may provide a risk to employers. For example, if an employee drinks alcohol at a company function and causes an accident while driving home, the employer may be held liable for resulting damages.

Because of the potential liability, many organizations have determined that they will no longer serve alcohol at company events. Employers that do provide alcohol should consider establishing clear policies that limit liability. Policies may include some or all of the following:

- Require the employee to purchase their own alcoholic beverages

- Provide free non-alcoholic beverages

- Stop providing alcohol an hour before the end of the function

- Pay for taxis or otherwise provide transportation to employees after the event

[2] Cell Phone Use

Many employers encourage their employees to maximize efficiency by utilizing a cell phone, sometimes purchased by the company. Employers should be aware of the liability they might incur.

A study by The New England Journal of Medicine found a driver's use of a cell phone increases the risk of an accident by four times. A company may be found liable for the actions of the employee (e.g. accidents) if the employee is conducting "work-related activity" or driving a company vehicle, even if the activity is not during "regular" working hours. In a number of states, it is illegal to drive while using a cell phone unless the driver is using a hands-free device. Employers are advised to draft proper policies for cell phone use, which may include:

- Prohibiting use of cell phones while driving

- Pulling over to the side of the road when placing or receiving a call

- Obeying all city and state laws

- Limiting duration of cell phone calls

- Signing a form acknowledging that employees retain all liabilities for accidents and traffic violations

Employers may also choose to require employees to maintain adequate auto liability insurance coverage.

[D] Employment Practices Liability Insurance

Many employers minimize their risks of litigation by securing employment practices liability insurance (EPLI). With EPLI, when the legal costs of a lawsuit are projected to reach a certain level, the insurance company assumes responsibility for the case in whatever manner it sees fit. EPLI carriers often seek to negotiate a settlement rather than trying the case in court. To be cost-effective, the negotiated settlement must result in an outcome that is less than the potential cost of litigation. Depending on the specific EPLI contract, some or all of the cost of the settlement is borne by the insurance company. However, the use of EPLI can become a pathway to increased litigation, regardless of how well supervisors adhere to legal discharge guidelines. Companies known to settle will often be targeted so long as they agree to mediate or turn the cases over to third-party administrators for settlement.

Before purchasing EPLI, HR directors should participate in a discussion concerning the company's strategy in limiting liability. That discussion should cover the pros and cons of EPLI, settling out of court, and going to trial.

§ 25.03 THE HR RISK ASSESSMENT

One effective way of managing HR risk is to conduct an HR risk assessment. The HR risk assessment, or diagnostic review, is a process for investigating the HR policies and practices adopted by the organization. It is important to recognize that an HR risk assessment puts the company on notice of potential problems. For risk management purposes, this assessment is a double-edged sword. It provides a good method of identifying and assessing risk: the degree of noncompliance, the anticipated risk of noncompliance, and the cost of compliance versus the possible cost of the failure to conform. However, if the company gains knowledge of a legal violation and then continues to do nothing, there is potential for increased liability. Conversely, without an HR risk assessment, the company remains blind to its risks and liabilities. It is also uncertain about the in-practice application of written policies and procedures. In a great many cases, ignorance of a law is no excuse and provides no relief for the penalties and damages resulting from failure to comply with various employment-related legislation. Such errors can be enormously costly and potentially damaging to the reputation of the employer in the marketplace.

[A] Benefits of an HR Risk Assessment

The benefits of an HR risk assessment include the following:

- The ability to create a strategy to meet the company's current and long-term business objectives

- The ability to identify the company's overall HR needs, liabilities, strengths, and weaknesses

- The ability to draft a prioritized list of recommended changes

- The ability to comply with state and federal employment laws and regulations

- The ability to identify opportunities to eliminate duplicate data processing and manual recordkeeping or unnecessary paperwork and procedures

- The ability to identify the need for improved internal controls

[B]   Who Should Conduct the HR Risk Assessment

The person conducting the HR risk assessment must understand the purpose and normal administrative policies and procedures of each major HR function, the interrelationship of such functions, and the legal environment in which all the functions operate separately and as a whole. The assessor must be sufficiently experienced to identify whether there are differences between the intended vision of the top HR policy-maker and the day-to-day HR practices of the company. If there are gaps, the assessor must be able to describe them clearly, discuss the implications, and offer prioritized recommendations for change.

Some of the major HR processes an assessor should know are the following:

- Flow of HR assets (i.e., employees) into, through, and out of the organization (e.g., selection, promotion, management succession planning, labor demand, and labor supply forecasting)

- Strategies for retention and motivation of employees (e.g., reward systems, performance management programs, and climate surveys)

- HR productivity enhancement programs (e.g., worker initiative programs, training and development programs, and job enrichment programs)

- Employment law compliance (e.g., compliance with EEO, affirmative action, the Fair Labor Standards Act, the Occupational Safety and Health Act (OSH Act), the Family and Medical Leave Act (FMLA), Title VII of the Civil Rights Act, and the Americans with Disabilities Act (ADA))

- Economics of HR programs (e.g., outsourcing, part-time workers, benefit program cost containment, and automation)

The key to obtaining meaningful data for an in-house assessment is to assure interviewees that they will not be sanctioned for providing complete and accurate information. HR staff may feel threatened if, by answering the questions, they are forced to reveal areas of weakness in their understanding of HR regulations, policies, or practices, or their difficulty in managing the pace of the function. To be successful, an in-house assessor must provide as much confidentiality as possible to individual interviewees and focus instead on the overall outcome of the assessment.

The company and/or the HR manager should not hesitate to engage the help of specialists as needed. Sometimes, these individuals or organizations can be enlisted at little or no cost. Examples of low-cost outside experts include the workers' compensation insurance carrier and the state department of commerce and community affairs. These organizations will conduct free safety consultations that simulate Occupational Safety and Health Administration (OSHA) inspections. Even if a fee is involved, the likelihood is that the reduction of liability more than justifies the expense of using a consultant or an attorney.

[C] Conducting an HR Risk Assessment

A successful HR risk assessment requires careful planning. A thorough discussion of the relationship between such an assessment and the business plan of an organization is beyond the scope of this chapter. For the purposes of this chapter, the principal objective of the HR risk assessment process described is to ensure compliance with various federal employment laws and regulations.

Following is a discussion of the major assessment steps.

[1] Developing a Strategy

Regardless of the size of the company or the industry, the following HR policies, procedures, and other general topics are typically investigated during an HR risk assessment:

- *Employment:* Recruitment and selection practices; job posting procedures; EEO and affirmative action, compliance efforts; reporting; employee orientation; the application form; management's level of awareness of employment laws; appropriate use of temporary workers and independent contractors

- *Organizational structure:* Assignment of duties and responsibilities; reporting structure procedures

- *Personnel records and administration:* File management; record retention (e.g., Forms W-4 and I-9); personnel file review; required postings

- *Compensation and performance evaluation:* Position descriptions; compensation system; compliance with wage and salary administration practices; appropriate time records for nonexempt personnel

- *Employee benefits:* Health and welfare benefit plan review (including insurance, savings, and time-off plans and requirements under the Health Insurance Portability and Accountability Act of 1996 (HIPAA), the Consolidated Omnibus Budget Reconciliation Act of 1985 (COBRA), the FMLA, and the ADA)

- *Employee relations and communications:* Methods (e.g., employee newsletters) and company philosophies and procedures (e.g., an open door policy); employee privacy protection; use of electronic communication

- *Employee training and development:* Records of legally related and/or required training (such as OSHA, age discrimination, sexual harassment) and identification of potential training needs

- *Health and safety:* Compliance with OSHA regulations and workers' compensation; use of vehicles and equipment; review of safety records

- *Disciplinary action and termination:* Procedures, forms, and documentation

- *Employee handbook review:* Handbook contents (may be reviewed with the aid of a consultant, employment attorney, or other qualified expert); annual review is recommended

[2] Determining Scope of Assessment

Determine the scope of the HR risk assessment in advance and draft a project summary for approval by company management. It is important to establish a realistic understanding of what to expect from an HR risk assessment.

An HR risk assessment is normally a representative review—a sampling of the process—not an exhaustive study. In a company of 100 or more employees, with proper preparation, an experienced HR risk assessor should be able to sufficiently review these general topics in one or two days, assuming that employee files are accessible, necessary personnel is available for interviewing, and the required paperwork is assembled in advance.

Anytime a company experiences a specific high-risk problem, it is prudent for HR to conduct targeted assessments at random times thereafter to ensure the issue is truly resolved. For example, if pervasive sexual harassment was discovered to exist in a particular department, it would be prudent for the HR manager to conduct occasional assessments of the department after the initial issue is dealt with. These follow-ups generally occur more often after the immediate resolution of the problem, then less often as time goes by. For high-risk issues, such as sexual harassment or other discriminatory treatment, an incident of workplace violence, or another highly visible situation, it would not be excessive for HR to follow up from time to time with employees involved for more than a year following the incident. It can sometimes take an employee some time to react or come to grips with a particularly serious incident he or she experienced or observed. Proactive HR risk management can provide the company with an opportunity to intercede before a secondary problem takes on major dimensions.

[3] Organizing Informational Interview

To obtain accurate information about actual HR practice, the HR assessor should use specifically con-structed diagnostic tools to conduct the review. During a risk assessment, the amount of data collected is so great that it is imperative for the assessor to be well organized.

The first major tool used to conduct the assessment is a list of preplanned questions governing each HR function, including a checklist of tasks and responsibilities by function (see **Exhibit 25.1**).

There is no specific set of questions per se about how to review the written materials, forms, and documents for each HR area. In a complex organization a set of questions should be drawn up for each functional area reviewed. The depth and complexity of the interview questions will vary, based on the size of the company and the applicability of various laws. Following are some representative questions for two specific functions within HR (these are not complete lists).

Employee Benefits

1. Are leaves of absence handled consistently from employee to employee? How is this documented?

2. Are COBRA procedures in place? How are they tracked? By whom?

3. How is unemployment insurance tracked? Are any claims contested? Are cost control measures in place?

4. How is workers' compensation tracked? How does the company follow up on old claims? What is your relationship with the insurance carrier? When is the last time you reviewed the policy or changed the policy carrier? What are the accident investigation procedures?

5. Are the benefit enrollment forms kept on file and current? Are individual medical files maintained separately? Are any claims kept on site? If yes, how are they protected? How is the confidentiality of any medical information protected?

6. Does HR understand the relationship between the FMLA, the ADA, state pregnancy leave law (if any), and other mandatory time-off programs? How are these laws coordinated and controlled? How are these coordinated with the company's other nonmandated time-off programs (e.g., vacation, sick leave, PTO)?

Compensation

1. How are salary decisions made? How often are salaries changed? Does salary change occur at other times? What is the approval process? Is it consistently followed?

2. How are salaries established? Are there salary grades and ranges? Are the salary grades and ranges current? Are employees aware of their own salary grade or range?

3. Is a distinction made between exempt and nonexempt employees? Have the distinctions been validated against federal and/or state exemption tests?

    i. Are payroll records kept confidential and current? Are payroll records separate from personnel records? Who has access to personnel records?

4. Are time cards used? If so, who completes the time cards and how frequently? Are the time cards accurate? How is the use of exempt time (such as vacation, personal days, and sick days) recorded?

5. Is payroll handled internally or by an outside service? What is the payroll interval? Are there accuracy issues?

6. Are deductions taken from the salaries of exempt employees for any reason? Under what circumstances might deductions occur?

7. Are employees paid for unauthorized overtime worked?

Information should be obtained in both written and oral form. Neither format will provide sufficient assessment information on its own.

To obtain accurate information about actual practices, the HR risk assessor must conduct oral diagnostic interviews with key individual(s) involved in HR in the company. This typically involves meeting with the key individual(s) responsible for day-to-day processing of HR paperwork and administration, files, and records as well as the person(s) responsible for establishing top-level HR policy. In addition, the HR risk assessor should interview a random sampling of managers outside HR and any other corresponding administrative functions to determine the degree to which HR practices and policies are understood and adhered to across the company.

Likely sources of written HR policy and practice information are corporate operating plans, business plans, mission statements, budgets, organizational charts, employee handbooks and policy manuals, personnel files, appraisal forms, position descriptions, employment applications, internal communication materials, posters, and other documents related to employment.

It is also important to review a representative sample of employee files for both exempt and nonexempt employees to assess the quality and quantity of documentation in the files. (See **Chapter 3** for definitions of exempt and nonexempt employees.) For example, assume there are 80 hourly, nonexempt employees and 20 exempt management employees in a typical small manufacturing company. It will not be necessary to review all 100 employee files to assess the general quality of documentation. If the assessor reviews 10 to 12 of the "thickest" hourly (nonexempt) files and three to four big salaried (exempt) files, that is generally sufficient to determine the overall quality and amount of documentation in all files and to know how well the files are maintained.

A competent assessor listens carefully, takes complete notes, and identifies gaps between written policies and procedures and actual day-to-day practices. All such gaps must be carefully examined and discussed with company management.

[4] Prioritizing the Findings

Through an HR risk assessment, employers can identify a number of projects that should be implemented to make the company function at its most effective level. Some recommendations represent major changes, and others are quick and easy. It is impossible to address all issues at once.

The findings may be structured into a list of recommendations, stated as projects, and classified in order of priority:

1. Level 1 recommendations (high priority) should be addressed over the next three months.

2. Level 2 recommendations (medium priority) should begin to be addressed over the next three to six months.

3. Level 3 recommendations (low priority) should begin to be addressed over the next six to nine months.

The priority of the projects may be determined by applying the following criteria:

- Legal liability

- Level of risk to the company

- Sequence of events that must precede it before implementation is practical

- Impact on the process

- Ease of implementation

[5] Implementing the Recommendations

For a company to realize the benefit of an HR risk assessment, it must actually implement the recommendations by taking the following steps:

1. Secure the support of top management.

2. Prioritize the list and establish a timeline.

3. Determine which recommendations are to be implemented and agree on the changes.

4. Set aside funds to implement the recommendations.

5. Stay on track by treating the recommendations as priorities.

6. Seek outside help as needed, using any of the following resources:

    a. Outsourcing HR management entirely or by function

    b. Engaging HR professionals on a retainer basis

    c. Using consultants or independent contractors on a project basis

    d. Hiring a professional HR manager with a compliance and risk management background

[D] Annual Assessments

The first internal HR risk assessment is a good start, but it is only the beginning. HR risk management is a dynamic function. Competitive, legal, and cultural changes necessitate constant review of HR policies and procedures. Laws and requirements change frequently enough that the following items should be reviewed annually:

- The employee handbook and policy manuals

- Employee personnel files

- OSHA requirements (e.g., logs and forms and required training)

- COBRA documentation

- Recent Forms I-9

- Documentation of disciplinary and employment issues

- Safety inspections and accident investigations

- Applicant flow and equal employment opportunity and affirmative action plan requirements and reporting

- Employment turnover statistics (so as to identify negative trends or hidden problems)

- FMLA and other federally or state-mandated benefit program requirements

- ADA requirements (e.g., job descriptions and reasonable accommodations)

- Required federal and state postings

- Complaints and allegations of harassment

Certainly there is an element of risk in just opening a company's door for business every day, but HR risk and liability can be minimized by making a commitment to stay abreast of employment laws and regulations and by periodically conducting HR risk assessments. It is recommended that a company conduct a complete HR risk assessment every two years to keep up with changes in the laws. However, the frequency of an audit will vary with the circumstances. In the event of a major workforce reduction, before a merger, or in any other significant event affecting employment, the company should ensure its HR practices are fully in compliance with the law. Errors tend to take on magnified proportions in such circumstances.

§ 25.04   IMPACT OF SARBANES-OXLEY ACT ON HUMAN RESOURCES

The Sarbanes-Oxley Act of 2002 [Pub. L. No. 107-204, 116 Stat. 745] (SOX) was passed by Congress and signed into law by President Bush on July 30, 2002. Sarbanes-Oxley primarily covers companies that are registered with the Securities and Exchange Commission (SEC). Created in response to a number of high profile business failures, allegations of corporate fraud, and financial statement restatements, SOX outlines significant obligations that must be met by covered organizations.

The first to be covered under this legislation were the "large" public companies, those with market capitalization in excess of $75 million. The "small" public employers were to be in compliance as of their fiscal year starting after July 15, 2005; that deadline has been extended to the fiscal year starting after December 15, 2007.

The 11 titles of SOX deal primarily with control over financial information. Initially, it appeared this legislation was going to only affect the accounting and financial personnel and the chief executive officer of the organization. However, as companies have worked to implement SOX, it has become more and more apparent that HR plays a significant role in SOX compliance. Areas of involvement and/or responsibility include:

1. Compliance—In some organizations, the HR executive is the chief compliance officer for SOX as well as other programs. In many other organizations, HR is part of a team of executives responsible for compliance.

2. Documentation of processes—As part of the compliance process, various procedures and systems need to be documented. Among the HR systems typically reviewed: payroll, HRIS data and security, compensation, benefits, selection and hiring.

3. Review of organization structure—SOX compliance may include a review of employees' ability to meet the requirements of their positions, and a review of reporting relationships.

4. Oversight of outside vendors—HR has responsibility to make sure that the work of outside vendors (such as third party administrators), as they relate to the affected internal processes of the company, are documented and controlled.

The following sections describe five of the 11 titles, and provide more detail on their impact on HR.

[A]   Section 404—Maintenance of Internal Controls

One of the most significant of the legislative mandates, Section 404 establishes the responsibility of management to maintain an adequate set of internal controls. Each organization must assess its current policies and practices to ensure that proper standards are met. The assessment includes detailed documentation of any process that results in a financial transaction. Since payroll is a financial transaction, and almost all HR activities eventually affect payroll, HR policies and practices must be part of the assessment.

To assess a company's internal control, criteria against which the assessment will be made must be identified. In 1992, the Committee of Sponsoring Organizations of the Treadway Commission (COSO) issued a report entitled "Internal Control—Integrated Framework." The report provides a definition of internal control and establishes criteria that can be utilized to evaluate a company's internal controls. The five interrelated components of effective internal control identified in the COSO report are: (1) control environment; (2) risk assessment; (3) control activities; (4) information and communications; and (5) monitoring.

[1]   Control Environment

The control environment is considered the foundation for all other components of internal controls. It sets the tone of an organization, influencing the control consciousness of its people. The control environment has a pervasive influence on the way business activities are structured, objectives established, and risks assessed. The control environment in the COSO report is discussed in terms of the following components against which an organization must assess itself (and which can, and should, be significantly influenced by HR):

- *Integrity and ethical values.* In establishing an effective control environment, management must convey the message that integrity and ethical values cannot be compromised—a message that must be received and understood by employees. Management must continually demonstrate, through words and actions, a commitment to high ethical standards.

- *Commitment to competence.* Employee job descriptions should clearly define job requirements, specify the authority given to the position, and state the reporting lines from subordinates to supervisors. Performance standards that provide the basis for employee evaluation and compensation should be developed. Sufficient corporate resources should be available for ongoing training needs. These practices, which should be more than just formalities, will help the organization attract, retain, and develop competent personnel.

- *Board of Directors or Audit Committee.* An active and effective Board, or committees thereof, provides an important oversight function. Because of management's ability to override system controls, the Board plays an important role in ensuring effective internal control.

- *Philosophy and operating style.* The philosophy and operating style of management have a pervasive effect on the way the organization is managed, including the kinds of business risks taken. An organization that has successfully taken significant risks may have a different outlook on internal control than one that has faced harsh economic or regulatory consequences as a result of taking risks. Operating style and the method and frequency of interaction between senior management and operating staff will be a function of the extent to which an organization is centralized or decentralized. For example, an informal operating style, which relies to a great extent on frequent personal contact, may be appropriate for an organization in which key functions are centered in one location.

- *Structure*. An organization's structure provides the overall framework for planning, directing, and controlling operations. Although an organization can develop different structures based on its activities, needs, and resources, significant aspects of any organizational structure include defining key areas of authority and responsibility, and establishing appropriate lines of reporting. The organizational structure should be neither so simple that it cannot adequately monitor activities, nor so complex that it inhibits the necessary flow of information. Executives should both fully understand their control responsibilities and possess the requisite experience and levels of knowledge commensurate with their positions.

- *Assignment of authority and responsibility*. The control environment should seek to balance the business environment with the need for formal policies and procedures, limits on risk taking positions, and reporting requirements. A greater level of risk normally requires a stronger control system with personnel competent to assume the responsibility of the increased risks. The assignment of responsibility, delegation of authority, and establishment of related policies provide a basis for accountability and control, and sets forth individuals' respective roles.

- *Human resources policies and practices*. HR policies are central to recruiting and retaining competent employees, and to enabling the organization's plans to be carried out and its goals to be achieved. Assessment will include the following:

  — Extent to which policies and procedures for hiring, training, promoting, and compensating employees are in place;

  — Extent to which employees are made aware of their responsibilities and what is expected of them;

  — Appropriateness of remedial action taken in response to departures from approved policies and procedures;

  — Extent to which personnel policies address adherence to appropriate ethical and moral standards;

  — Adequacy of employee candidate background checks, particularly with regard to prior actions or unacceptable activities; and

  — Adequacy of employee retention and promotion criteria and information-gathering techniques (e.g., performance evaluations) and its relation to the Code of Ethics or other behavioral guidelines.

Questions that may be asked of a company's Human Resource department during the assessment of the control environment can be found in **Exhibit 25.3**.

[2] Risk Assessment

Risk assessment at an organizational level has three components: (1) establishing objectives; (2) analyzing risk; and (3) managing change. COSO describes the risk assessment process as the identification and analysis of relevant risks to the achievement of the entity's objectives, forming a basis for determining how the risks should be managed. Because economic, industry, regulatory, and operating conditions will continually change, mechanisms are needed to identify and deal with the special risks associated with change.

[3] Control Activities

Control activities encompass a wide range of policies and related implementation procedures (including human resource processes) that help ensure that management's directives are effective. They help ensure that the actions identified as necessary to address risks achieve the organization's objectives. COSO defines control activities as policies and procedures (i.e., the implementation of the policies) to help ensure that the management directives identified as necessary to address risks are carried out. Some typical subprocesses that may be included in the documentation of the Human Resource function are:

- Hiring process (including temporary employees and contractors)

- Promotion process (performance reviews, master file updates, etc.)

- Termination process

- Disability or temporary leave process

- Drug testing process

- Disciplinary process

- Employee information security

- Vacation process

- Government withholdings on wages

- Tax process on wages

- Payroll account reconciliation to the general ledger

- Timecards and timesheet preparation, approval, and entry

- Payroll preparation

- Payroll accruals

- Payroll disbursement

- System access

This list is not exhaustive. Each organization should develop its own list of HR subprocesses based on its needs. **Exhibit 25.4** and **Exhibit 25.5** contain questions that may be used to begin documenting the various HR and payroll processes.

[4] Information and Communication

Information is identified, captured, processed, and reported by information systems. Relevant information includes industry, economic, and regulatory information obtained from external sources, as well as internally generated information.

[5] Monitoring

Ongoing monitoring occurs in the ordinary course of operations. It includes regular management and supervisory activities, and other actions taken by personnel in performing their duties that aid in the assessment of the quality of internal control performance. It is useful to take a fresh look at the internal control system from time to time, focusing directly on system effectiveness. The scope and frequency of separate evaluations will depend primarily on an assessment of risks and ongoing monitoring procedures. Internal control deficiencies should be reported to successively higher levels of management, with certain matters being reported to top management and the Board of Directors.

[B] Section 306—Blackout Provisions

Section 306 contains the following two blackout-related provisions:

1. *Insider trading provision.* This provision makes it unlawful for any Board director or executive of a publicly held company to purchase, sell, or otherwise acquire or transfer any equity security of the issuer during any blackout period if the director or executive acquired the equity security for service as a director or executive officer. Sarbanes-Oxley defines the blackout period as "A period of more than three consecutive business days during which the ability of not fewer than 50% of the participants and beneficiaries under all of the employer's individual account plans maintained by the issuer to purchase, sell, or otherwise acquire or transfer an equity security is temporarily suspended by the issuer or by the fiduciary of the plan." Blackout periods do not include:

   a. A regularly scheduled restricted trading period provided under the plan that is timely disclosed to employees before they become participants in the plan, or

   b. Any suspension in trading that is imposed solely in connection with the person becoming or ceasing to become a participant by reason of a corporate merger, acquisition, divestiture, or similar transaction.

   Employers covered by this provision are required to provide notice of the blackout period to their directors and executive officers that are subject to the requirements.

2. *ERISA provision.* This provision amends ERISA to require a plan administrator to provide notice of a blackout period for individual account plans to participants and beneficiaries at least 30 days before the blackout period begins. A blackout period in this provision means any period for which the ability of participants and beneficiaries to direct or diversify assets credited to their account, obtain loans from the plan, or obtain distributions from the plan is temporarily suspended, limited, or restricted for

a period of more than three consecutive business days. Blackout periods do not include suspensions, limitations, or restrictions that:

a. Occur by reason of application of the securities laws;

b. Are disclosed to participants or beneficiaries under the plan; or

c. Apply under the qualified domestic relations order.

The notice must be written in a manner that can be understood by the average plan participant. It must include the reason for the blackout period, identification of the investment and other rights affected, the date and length of the blackout period, and a statement that the participant or beneficiary should evaluate the current investment decisions in light of the pending blackout period.

[C] Section 402—Prohibition of Personal Loans to Executives

Section 402 makes it unlawful for any issuer to extend credit, to arrange for the extension of credit, or to renew an extension of credit in the form of a personal loan to or for any director or executive officer of that issuer. Loans that were in place on the date SOX became law—July 30, 2002—were grandfathered in; however, they cannot be modified or renewed. Certain limited exceptions have been made for loans made or provided in the ordinary course of the consumer credit business of the issuer, of the type that are generally made available by such issuer to the public, and made by such issuer on market terms, or terms that are no more favorable than those offered by the issuer to the general public for such extensions of credit.

[D] Section 406—Code of Ethics

Section 406 requires companies to establish a Code of Ethics for senior financial officers to promote honest ethical conduct, including the ethical handling of actual or apparent conflicts of interests between personal and professional relationships.

It is interesting to note that while the number of formal ethics and compliance programs has increased over the last few years, the "positive outcomes expected of those programs have not," according to the 2005 National Business Ethics Survey conducted by the Ethics Resource Center (ERC). According to their report, little change has taken place since 1994 in the extent to which employees observe misconduct in the workplace. The most significant influence of ethical behavior in the workplace is the "ethical culture" of the organization—the actions of the leaders and peers. For example, where top management displays certain ethics-related actions, employees are 50 percentage points less likely to observe misconduct.

[E] Section 806—Whistleblower Protection for Employees of Publicly Traded Companies

Section 806 prohibits officers, employees, contractors, subcontractors, and agents of publicly held companies from discharging, demoting, suspending, threatening, harassing, or in any way discriminating against an employee for providing to a law enforcement officer any truthful information relating to the commission or possible commission of any federal offense.

The Occupational Safety and Health Administration (OSHA) has the enforcement authority for this Section. On August 24, 2004, OSHA issued their final regulations providing detailed procedures for these types of cases. [29 C.F.R. Part 1980 RIN 1218 AC10] It is important to note that the whistleblower protection is intended for those employees who are subject to an "adverse employee action" because they reported fraudulent activity that might mislead or hurt shareholders. Employees who are subject to an adverse employee action for any other reason are not protected under Section 806.

A recent ruling provides additional guidelines on the types of fraudulent activity that must be reported in order to fall under the SOX protection. In *Welch v. Cardinal Bancshares Corp.* [DOL ARB, Dkt. No. 05-064, May 31, 2007], the Department of Labor's Administrative Review Board (ARB) held, in essence, that violation of GAAP (generally accepted accounting principles) was not a violation of federal securities laws, and therefore making a complaint about such activities was not a "protected activity" under SOX. This ruling overturned a 2004 ruling that was, until the ARB's decision, the first initially successful whistleblower claim under Section 806.

Companies subject to this provision should establish a whistleblower protection policy.

[F] Section 301—Complaint Procedure

Section 301 requires companies to provide "confidential anonymous submission by employees ... of concerns regarding questionable accounting or auditing matters." Employers should develop a system of receiving complaints that protects the anonymity of the employee.

[G] Privately Held Companies

While SOX was not intended to directly apply to privately held businesses, many closely held companies and not-for-profits have been significantly affected by the legislation. While the Act primarily covers companies that are registered with the SEC, the resulting standards of financial accountability are beginning to be applied more broadly. Companies most affected by SOX include those:

- Preparing for a public offering

- Preparing for a merger with a public company

- Issuing publicly registered debt

- Reporting to federal regulatory agencies

- Relying upon lenders or insurers

- Conducting business with government entities

Many private companies, both for profit and not-for-profit, are implementing many of the SOX measures voluntarily. Adopting a transparent system of financial management with built-in checks and balances is both smart business and the new standard for good governance practices that business partners expect.

Exhibit 25.1   Mandated Benefits: 2009 Compliance Guide

Exhibit 25.1
The Human Resources Risk Assessment Questionnaire

This exhibit presents a list of suggested review areas and questions for conducting an HR risk assessment. The applicability of each question may vary depending on the state in which the company is located. The list is not exhaustive.

Legal Compliance

- Has the company prepared a workforce analysis? Are any efforts made to improve the workforce use of minorities and females and other protected groups? Is the company a federal contractor (i.e., with 50 employees or a $50,000 contract)? Does the company have or refer to an affirmative action program? If yes, who developed it? Is it updated annually?

- Does the company employ someone who is well versed in and responsible for keeping current on legal regulations affecting employee relations? Required state and federal postings? Record retention?

- Has the company's management, supervisors, staff, or employees been educated concerning wage-hour issues, equal pay, child labor, occupational safety and health, civil rights (including disability rights), age discrimination, pension, garnishments, and state legislation?

- Does the company receive pertinent bulletins on state and federal labor legislation and regulations? Has experienced legal counsel been retained to advise the company in the employment area?

- Is COBRA benefit continuation explained to employees? When? How? Are terminated employees notified of COBRA continuation rights? By whom, when, and how?

- Does the company have the required federal and state posters (e.g., Federal Minimum Wage; State Safety and Health Protection; Federal Equal Opportunity Is the Law; Family and Medical Leave Act; State Job Insurance Notice; State Equal Opportunity Is the Law)?

- Is the company aware of state and federal laws and regulations, including the law prohibiting discrimination based on age? Is someone responsible for ensuring compliance? Are employees classified as exempt or nonexempt from minimum wage and overtime requirements?

- Are changes in work schedules or overtime requirements, or both, clearly communicated in advance of the need to work such hours?

- Do all supervisors have a clear understanding of overtime rules and schedules? Are nonexempt employees required to take mandatory breaks and meal periods?

- Do exempt employees regularly perform nonexempt duties? Are job duties and salary tests of exempt employees reviewed periodically?

- Is there a systematic plan regarding layoffs? Does the layoff policy include recall and reinstatement? Do you have a policy for the length of time an employee may be on layoff and still have recall rights?

Exhibit 25.1 (cont'd)

- Is pay provided for time spent in work-related activities of an unusual nature, such as training, travel, and employee meetings?

- Is new-hire information sent to the appropriate state agency?

- Does the company employ temporary workers through a staffing agency? Is there a clear distinction between employees on the payroll and staffing agency workers? Is all communication regarding compensation, time off, discipline, and termination done through the staffing agency?

- Does the company use independent contractors? Does each case get reviewed to make sure it meets the IRS guidelines for independent contractors?

Human Resource Policies, Procedures, and Records

- Are employee policies and procedures documented? Are they communicated to and understood by employees? How does HR know?

- Are policies and procedures reviewed and updated? Are management personnel and supervisors given an opportunity for input?

- Are these policies and procedures consistently applied throughout your organization? How is this monitored?

- Does the company keep adequate written records of employee complaints? How are they handled? Where are these records retained?

- Is there a designated person to whom employees turn when they have concerns?

- Are disciplinary actions monitored to assure consistency and avoid discrimination? By whom? What is reviewed?

- Are all forms of discipline promptly documented? Where are they kept and for how long?

- Does the company have a written absenteeism policy that is communicated to and understood by the employees? If so, is it specific about what is excusable? Is the policy consistently applied?

- Does the company permit an employee who is subpoenaed as a witness in a criminal case or summoned for jury duty to appear? Is the time off paid or unpaid?

- Is medical documentation for absences due to illness beyond a stated period of time consistently required? Is a return-to-work release required?

- Does the company have a medical or personal leave of absence policy? How is maternity or paternity leave handled?

Exhibit 25.1   Mandated Benefits: 2009 Compliance Guide

Exhibit 25.1 (cont'd)

- Do employees have expectations of privacy in the workplace (i.e., desk, locker, etc.) or in their communications via telephone and/or e-mail? Is any published policy distributed? Does the company conduct desk or car searches?

- Are payroll records kept confidential and current?

- Does the company keep up-to-date confidential personnel files on each employee? Who has access?

- Does the company compile information about an individual's race, sex, age, national origin, and number of dependents? Why? When? Where is the information maintained? Is it kept separate from the records that may be examined and considered by those responsible for making personnel decisions about the employee (e.g., promotion, discipline, and discharge)?

- Are security, medical, and insurance records kept separate from routine employee records and their use restricted? Does the company permit employees to examine, copy, or request corrections of their own records? Does the company have a written policy pertaining to this? Does the company have a policy for controlling internal and external use of employee information? And one for terminated employees? Are personnel records ever purged? How often?

Forms

Does the Employment Application:

- Contain any language that might be considered discriminatory, such as age, place of birth, year graduated from high school, etc.?

- Contain language preserving the employer's right to at-will employment?

- Inform the applicant that false information will result in refusal to hire or discharge?

Does the Job Description:

- List and identify essential and non-essential duties?

- Include physical requirements that are directly related to the job?

- Provide clear descriptions of job duties?

Does the performance appraisal form:

- Provide for the employee's signature, indicating his/her review of the completed form?

- Allow the employee to add comments, or indicate another method for an employee to comment on his/her appraisal?

Exhibit 25.1 (cont'd)

Safety and Health

- Does the company know whether its safety and health programs are in compliance with OSHA standards?

- Is the company aware of OSHA standards that are applicable to its business? Are copies of the standards available?

- Are OSHA Forms 300 and 301 (or an equivalent state substitute for Form 301) appropriately completed, and Form 300A completed and posted from February 1 through April 30 each year?

- Is there a procedure to put into effect immediately if and when the company receives an OSHA inspection? Is the company aware of its responsibilities and rights? Of the employees' rights and responsibilities? Has an individual been designated to accompany the OSHA inspector?

- Are all the things done (new equipment, training, safety procedures) in the safety and health area documented to demonstrate good faith to a government inspector? Are production equipment and tools in a proper state of repair and maintenance? Properly guarded? Grounded?

- Are safety and health rules clear, up to date, and reasonable? Are they in writing? Are they posted? Are supervisors well informed of the safety rules and procedures for handling violations? Is corrective action taken for violations of safety rules or for employees who refuse to wear required protective equipment?

- Does the company have an established procedure for handling employee complaints regarding safety and health?

- Is someone on each shift qualified to render first aid and CPR?

- Are local emergency (e.g., fire, police) departments well acquainted with the company's office/plant, locations, and specific hazards?

- Are all toxic and hazardous materials used in the office/plant appropriately labeled?

- Have supervisors received training on OSHA rules, regulations, and standards, including specifics of employee training and job instruction and employee rights and responsibilities under the law?

- Do supervisors understand that they have a duty under the law to provide on-the-job safety and health instruction and training? In more specific areas, have operators of industrial powered trucks, welding operators, and electrical workers been properly trained and certified under federal and state standards? Is training provided in handling toxic and hazardous substances? Are records kept on these training programs?

- If an OSHA inspector arrived tomorrow, could the company produce maintenance, injury, and training records? Would they be up to date?

Exhibit 25.1   Mandated Benefits: 2009 Compliance Guide

Exhibit 25.1 (cont'd)

- In the area of office/plant security, have policies and procedures been carefully reviewed with respect to action that is to be taken in the event of a bomb scare, riot, thefts, crimes, strikes, and extreme weather conditions and other acts of nature? Is there an evacuation plan? What is the policy or practice for paying affected employees?

- Are preemployment or periodic physical examinations required? Is an exam required upon return from an illness or injury? Is drug testing performed? Under what circumstances?

Union Avoidance

- Are supervisors trained in the strategy and tactics of union organizing efforts? How long has it been since a refresher course was completed? Are supervisors trained to recognize signs of union activity?

- Have the do's and don'ts of supervisory behavior been prepared and distributed? Do supervisors understand them and their responsibilities concerning them? Have the do's been emphasized?

- Do supervisors understand the employee's right of free speech in an organizing campaign and other legal rights and obligations? Are unionization efforts unintentionally encouraged by discriminating against nonrepresented groups, such as office employees?

- Does the company have a no-solicitation, no-distribution rule? Is it consistently enforced?

Why should a company care if it is not in compliance?

Each employment law, regulation, and rule has a different set of penalties associated with it. The repercussions for noncompliance may include payment of back wages, monetary fines and penalties, and even imprisonment for key officers and decision makers. Although compliance issues should not manage the business, they must be taken seriously. It is important for a company to manage the risk associated with noncompliance because, more often than not, ignorance is not an acceptable defense when employment law is violated.

Exhibit 25.2
Federal Employment Law Requirements by Company Size

Companies must also look into the laws of the state(s) in which they have employees for other applicable regulations. For example, several states have their own regulations concerning issues such as civil rights, wage and hour provisions, child labor, smoking, and time off to vote. It is critical to be in compliance with *both* federal and state regulations.

1 or more employees:

- Fair Labor Standards Act (FLSA) wage and hour provisions

- Child labor laws

- Equal Pay Act

- Employee Polygraph Protection Act

- Employee invention rights

- Immigration Reform and Control Act—Form I-9 Requirement

- Occupational Safety and Health Act (OSH Act)

- Hazardous Communications Act (if there are hazardous materials or chemicals on site)

- Withholding of federal income taxes

- Workers' compensation insurance coverage

- Unemployment insurance coverage

- Withholding of Social Security (FICA) and Medicare taxes

- Plan document, summary plan descriptions, and annual report (Form 5500)—required under ERISA if the company offers health plans, retirement and pension plans, severance plans, etc.

- Fair Credit Reporting Act

- New employee reporting

- Uniformed Services Employment and Reemployment Rights Act (USERRA)

- National Labor Relations Act (NLRA)

- Civil Rights Acts of 1866 and 1871

2 or more employees covered by group health plan:

- Health Insurance Portability and Accountability Act (HIPAA)

Exhibit 25.2   Mandated Benefits: 2009 Compliance Guide

Exhibit 25.2 (cont'd)

15 or more employees:

- Title VII of the Civil Rights Act of 1964 (prohibits discrimination with regard to hiring, training, promoting, compensating, and/or terminating on the basis of race, sex, color, national origin, religion, and pregnancy)

- Americans with Disabilities Act (ADA)

- Pregnancy Discrimination Act (Amendment to Title VII)

20 or more employees:

- Age Discrimination in Employment Act (ADEA)

- Consolidated Omnibus Budget Reconciliation Act of 1985 (COBRA) (continuation of health care coverage if the employer had 20 or more employees on the payroll in the previous calendar year)

50 or more employees:

- Family and Medical Leave Act (FMLA) if 50 or more employees are within a 75-mile radius

- EEO-1 Report if the company is a federal contractor or subcontractor with affirmative action plan (AAP) requirement (see below)

100 or more employees:

- Worker Adjustment and Retraining Notification Act (WARN Act) plant closure law

- Employee information reports (EEO-1) filed by September 30 of each year

Federal contractors:

- Executive Order 11246 (requires written AAP: contracts or subcontracts with the federal government totaling $50,000 or more and 50 employees or more)

- AAP for People with Disabilities: federal contracts of more than $50,000 and 50 or more employees

- Veterans AAP: federal contracts of $50,000 or more and 50 or more employees

- VETS-100 report due by September 30 of each year (if federal contracts of $25,000 or more)

- Drug Free Workplace Act: federal contracts of $25,000 or more

- Applicant flow log (if required to have an AAP)

Exhibit 25.2 (cont'd)

- Section 503 of the Rehabilitation Act of 1973 as amended: federal contractor or subcontractor with contracts in excess of $10,000

- Davis-Bacon Act wage and hour provisions for federal contractors of $2,000 or more

- Copeland Act wage standards for all government contractors, regardless of size

- McNamara-O'Hara Act wage and hour provisions for federal contractors of $2,500 or more

- Walsh-Healy Act wage and hour provisions for federal contractors of $10,000 or more

Exhibit 25.3

Mandated Benefits: 2009 Compliance Guide

Exhibit 25.3
Sarbanes-Oxley Act
Assessment Control Environment Questions

1. Do employees fully and clearly understand what behavior is acceptable and unacceptable under the company's Code of Conduct, and do they know what to do when they encounter improper behavior?

2. Does management frequently and clearly communicate the importance of integrity and ethical behavior during staff meetings and/or one-on-one discussions?

3. Has management adequately defined the knowledge and skills needed to perform jobs within your function?

4. Do individual performance targets focus on both the long-term and short-term, and do they address a broad spectrum of criteria (e.g., quality, productivity, leadership, teamwork, and self-development)?

5. Has any key personnel resigned unexpectedly or on short notice? Is employee turnover excessive in any areas?

6. Are management meetings held periodically within your function and frequently attended by senior management?

7. Do existing personnel policies and procedures facilitate recruiting and developing competent and trustworthy personnel?

8. Are employees new to your function made aware of their responsibilities and what management expects of them?

9. Do performance appraisals adequately address internal control responsibilities and set forth criteria for integrity and ethical behavior?

10. Is management's commitment to integrity and ethical behavior communicated effectively through-out the company, both in words and deeds? Does management lead by example?

11. Do rewards (e.g., bonuses and stock ownership) foster appropriate ethical behavior?

12. Does management take appropriate disciplinary action in response to departures from approved policies and procedures or violations of the Code of Conduct?

13. Do personnel appear to have the competence and training necessary for their assigned level of responsibility?

14. Does management review and make modifications to the organizational structure of the company in light of changed conditions?

15. Are there in place standards and procedures applicable to all functional areas for hiring, training, motivating, evaluating, promoting, compensating, transferring, and terminating personnel?

Exhibit 25.3 (cont'd)

16. Are there screening procedures for job applicants, particularly for positions with access to assets susceptible to misappropriation?

17. Are policies and procedures clear and issued, updated, and revised on a timely basis?

18. Are there written job descriptions, reference manuals, or other forms of communication to inform personnel of their duties?

19. Is job performance periodically evaluated and reviewed with each employee?

20. Are the lines of authority and responsibility within the company clearly defined and communicated?

21. Have key performance indicators and measurement criteria for achieving company-wide objectives been communicated?

22. Are there groups or individuals who are responsible for anticipating or identifying changes that may significantly affect the organization? Are there processes in place to inform appropriate levels of management about changes that may significantly affect the organization?

23. Are persons who report suspected impropriety provided feedback and immunity from reprisals?

24. Are good suggestions by employees acknowledged by providing incentives or other meaningful recognition?

25. Is there training/orientation for new employees and/or for employees starting a new position to discuss the nature and scope of their duties and responsibilities? Does such training/orientation include a discussion of specific internal controls for which they are responsible?

26. Is there a process for employees to communicate improprieties? Is the process well communicated throughout the entity? Does the process allow for anonymity for individuals who report possible improprieties? Is there a process for reporting improprieties and actions taken to address them to senior management, the Board of Directors, or the Audit Committee?

27. Are all reported potential improprieties reviewed, investigated, and resolved in a timely manner?

Exhibit 25.4   Mandated Benefits: 2009 Compliance Guide

Exhibit 25.4
Sarbanes-Oxley Act Assessment Human Resources Process Questions

Hiring

1. What is the current process for recruitment and hiring?

2. Are the standardized policies and procedures always used when hiring employees? Are there any exceptions to the policies and procedures (e.g., for the hiring of executives)?

3. Are hiring requisition forms used and approved for all new and existing positions?

4. Who authorizes the generation of a new position? Who are considered hiring managers?

5. How does HR determine the salary range and proposed stock options?

6. Are temporary employees used? Are copies of contracts with temporary agencies maintained?

7. Are contractors used? Are independent contractor agreements used?

8. Is a schedule that reflects employment agreements, offer letter details, and agreed-upon payment schedules (contractors and temporary), etc. used?

9. Is a payment register detailing salary or wages and other employee benefits of all employees maintained?

10. Are all new employees required to complete and sign an employment application form?

11. How are all new employees entered into the system to ensure that the most current employee information is used for payroll and benefit processing?

12. Do department managers receive payroll change reports to verify that all new hires/rehires appear in the system and are shown in the correct department?

Performance Management

Performance Reviews

1. What is the performance review process?

2. How often are performance reviews completed?

3. Are reviews discussed with the employee?

4. Are goals and objectives set by both the employee and the individual to whom he/she reports?

5. Do the reviews appropriately measure actual performance rather than traits or potentials?

6. Explain the employee career planning process.

Exhibit 25.4 (cont'd)

Merit Increases

1. What is the procedure for merit increases?

2. Are wage increases based solely on merit?

3. How is an employee's increase determined?

4. Are increases consistent throughout the company?

5. If changes are made outside of the annual review, is a hard copy of the salary adjustment sheet printed, signed, and maintained in the employee's file?

6. Are compensation rates and payroll deductions authorized in accordance with management's criteria?

7. What precautions are taken to prevent the modification of salary by unauthorized personnel?

Bonuses

1. How are bonuses calculated?

2. What measures are taken to ensure that the financial information used in the determination of a bonus and the amount of the bonus is accurate?

3. What measures are taken to ensure that the calculation of the bonus is accurate?

4. What measures are taken to ensure accurate payment of bonus?

5. What measures are taken to ensure that the payment of the bonus is correctly coded?

6. What measures are taken to ensure that bonus payments are recorded in the correct period?

7. What measures are taken to ensure that duplicate bonus payments will not be made?

8. What measures are taken to ensure that unauthorized payment of a bonus does not occur?

9. What measures are taken to ensure that bonus accruals are accurate?

10. Are bonus payments reviewed prior to being issued? Is there a process in place to ensure bonuses provided are based on approved documentation from the initiating department?

Promotions

1. What process is followed to initiate a promotion?

2. What documentation is required to substantiate a promotion?

Exhibit 25.4   Mandated Benefits: 2009 Compliance Guide

Exhibit 25.4 (cont'd)

3. What levels of sign-offs are required for promotion approval?

4. Do promotions generally occur once a year or throughout the year?

5. What measures are taken to ensure that unauthorized changes to positions do not occur?

Discipline

1. What process is followed for disciplining employees?

2. Are formal procedures established, documented, and followed for disciplining employees?

3. Is progressive discipline used?

4. How are disciplinary actions documented?

5. What levels of sign-offs are required for disciplinary action?

Terminations

1. What is the employee termination process?

2. Are formal procedures for terminating employees established? Are the procedures followed and documented?

3. Do the procedures require that supervisors immediately notify HR when an employee is terminated or when there is a change in pay rate?

4. What measures are taken to ensure that terminated employees are deleted from the payroll system?

5. Is the payroll supervisor notified when an employee is terminated to ensure that the employee is removed from the payroll system? If a payroll processing service is used, is this communicated in a timely manner to the payroll processor?

6. Are computer system access rights of terminated employees removed upon notification of the employee's termination?

7. Are exit conferences performed when an employee leaves the company?

8. Is the information secured during the exit conference documented, and are concerns voiced in the conference forwarded to senior management?

9. If an employee is terminated, what is the process for updating health insurance records to prevent unauthorized claims?

10. How is all required separation information communicated to the employee?

Exhibit 25.4 (cont'd)

11. Does HR conduct an exit interview for all terminating and retiring employees to verify their name and address and to distribute their final paychecks?

12. Is an interview checklist completed to help ensure all necessary information is relayed to the terminating employee and all necessary internal and external parties receive notice of the termination?

Benefits

1. What health, dental, and life insurance plans are available?

2. Who monitors the activity and payments to the various insurance agencies?

3. How are inactive accounts segregated from active accounts on the health insurance reports?

4. Are all required employees' personal, benefit, and payroll information obtained directly from employees? Are all employees required to attend orientation on their first day of work, during which they are required to provide proof of employment eligibility per government requirements (I-9 Form)?

5. What measures are taken to ensure that modifications of benefits do not occur by unauthorized personnel?

6. What measures are taken to ensure that all entries relating to group insurance are recorded?

7. What measures are taken to ensure that all entries relating to group insurance are properly coded?

8. What measures are taken to ensure that entries relating to group insurance are recorded in the proper period?

9. What measures are taken to ensure that payments from invoices, including administrative costs, submitted by providers are accurate?

10. What measures are taken to ensure that the proper amount is deducted from an employee's paycheck?

11. What measures are taken to ensure that certain providers automatically deduct the correct amounts from the company's bank account?

12. What measures are taken to ensure that benefits and administrative costs paid are properly allocated across all necessary entities?

13. What measures are taken to ensure that each employee receives the insurance benefits to which he or she is entitled?

Exhibit 25.4   Mandated Benefits: 2009 Compliance Guide

Exhibit 25.4 (cont'd)

14. What measures are taken to ensure that insurance benefits are not extended to terminated employees?

15. What measures are taken to ensure that group insurance accruals are accurate?

16. What measures are taken to ensure that postemployment employee benefits are properly calculated and recorded?

17. What measures are taken to ensure that employees receive the other (non-insurance) benefits to which they are entitled?

18. What measures are taken to ensure that the payment of the other benefits is correctly coded?

19. What measures are taken to ensure that the payment of the other benefits occurs in the correct period?

20. What measures are taken to ensure that duplicate payment of other benefits will not be made?

21. Is a "confirmation statement" delivered to all employees whenever a change in benefit elections are made to ensure that all personal and benefit data to be used for payroll and benefit processing has been input correctly, and that the change made was requested?

22. What are the procedures for activating and deactivating accounts within the health insurance plan(s) and other benefit plans?

23. For defined benefit retirement plans, are the record of contributions received per the pension company or fund manager regularly reconciled to records of contributions paid?

24. For defined contribution retirement plans, are employee contributions properly withheld and remitted on a timely basis? Are employer matching contributions properly calculated and made to the plan on a timely basis?

Vacation

1. How is vacation time tracked?

2. Is vacation time accrued on a monthly basis?

3. Can vacation time be carried over from year-to-year if an employee does not use all of his or her time?

4. If vacation time can be carried over, are there limits as to how much can be carried over?

5. If vacation time cannot be carried over or is not used, does the employee lose it or does he or she get paid for unused vacation?

Exhibit 25.4 (cont'd)

Workers' Compensation

1. What measures are taken to ensure that workers' compensation amounts are properly calculated?

2. What measures are taken to ensure that fictitious workers' compensation claims are not paid?

3. What measures are taken to ensure that valid workers' compensation claims are properly paid?

4. What measures are taken to ensure that workers' compensation is correctly coded?

5. What measures are taken to ensure that duplicate workers' compensation payments will not be made?

6. What measures are taken to ensure that workers' compensation payments will be recorded in the proper period?

Employee Master File

1. Is a personnel file maintained for each employee?

2. Does the personnel file contain all relevant employee information (e.g., employment application, a contract of employment, salary details, relevant tax information, job description, etc.)?

3. Is access to personnel files restricted to authorized HR staff, and is employee privacy protected?

4. How are employee records and information secured?

5. What system is used for the electronic storage of employee information (e.g., HRIS)?

6. How are electronic records secured?

7. Is access to the employee data and HRIS system properly secured? Are security procedures relating to additions and deletions of employees to or from the database in place? Is payroll processing written information subject to physical security? Are security controls that limit access to the database, including passwords that are changed frequently, in place?

8. What measures are taken to ensure that new employee information and employee information changes input into the system are accurate?

9. What measures are taken to ensure that inappropriate users do not have the ability to access, change, and delete confidential employee information?

10. Are all personnel file changes authorized by a supervisor?

11. Are payroll responsibilities properly segregated?

Exhibit 25.4   Mandated Benefits: 2009 Compliance Guide

Exhibit 25.4 (cont'd)

12. Are measures taken to ensure that individuals who develop, deliver, and maintain employee records do not prepare, disburse, or reconcile payroll?

13. Are measures taken to ensure that employee benefits, payments, and taxes are processed correctly?

14. Do retired employees appear on payroll change reports? Are retirees entered into the system with the correct termination status? How are discrepancies resolved prior to disbursing payroll?

Exhibit 25.5
Sarbanes-Oxley Act
Assessment Payroll Process Questions

Timecards/Timesheets:

1. Do hourly employees use time clocks or do they prepare manual timesheets?

2. Do salaried employees complete timesheets?

3. Who approves timesheets?

4. Do the individuals approving timesheets or timecards review hours, days, and job numbers to ensure accurate reporting and that the individuals actually worked when they said that they worked?

5. Are the salary rates for most employees documented on a Pay Rate Sheet? If so, who prepares the Pay Rate Sheet and when?

6. Who reviews and approves the Pay Rate Sheet?

7. Must a supervisor approve overtime pay before overtime is performed?

8. What measures are taken to ensure that all employee timecards have been submitted each pay period?

Payroll Processing:

1. Are the payroll procedures documented?

2. Are the payroll tax tables up to date?

3. Who processes payroll? To whom does he or she report?

4. Does the same individual process both hourly and salaried payroll?

5. Is an outside payroll service used?

6. When are salaried employees paid?

7. When are hourly employees paid?

8. Are expense reports reimbursed through payroll?

9. Is payroll processed in-house or through an outside agency?

10. Is a record of payroll adjustments made by the payroll department maintained? If so, is the record of adjustments reviewed and approved by a supervisor?

11. Are the payroll amounts subject to a reasonableness test (e.g., so that a payroll check of $1 million could not be issued)?

Exhibit 25.5   Mandated Benefits: 2009 Compliance Guide

Exhibit 25.5 (cont'd)

12. Are limits placed on variable pay items (such as overtime) so that if the limit is surpassed, the amount will be subject to a special review (e.g., a supervisory review for employees receiving over 20 hours overtime in a week)?

13. Are variances in pay for both employees and departments monitored, and are large variances investigated?

14. Have the proper amounts been accumulated for company benefit programs, such as pensions?

15. Are procedures established to promptly stop future payroll checks when an employee is terminated?

16. Is the actual payroll amount regularly compared with the budgeted amount?

Verification of Input Information/ Resolving Discrepancies:

1. How is information input in the system verified as correct (e.g., adding machine tapes, rely on system footing, etc.)?

2. Are batches logged and reconciled with batch totals in the system?

3. What happens if there are discrepancies between the system and the timesheet?

4. How do timesheets get selected for posting to the general ledger?

5. Is the system able to prevent duplicate payments from occurring? If so, how?

Employee Files and Employee Master File:

1. How are new employees entered into the system?

2. What is needed before an employee file can be added to the system?

3. Do changes to the master file need to be approved before the change is made?

4. Who can make changes, additions, and deletions to the payroll master file?

5. What documentation is required before the master file can be changed/updated?

6. How often is the master file purged (if at all)?

7. Does each employee have a paper file that agrees with the information in the payroll system?

Disbursements:

1. Are the procedures for payroll disbursements documented?

Exhibit 25.5 (cont'd)

2. How often are payroll checks disbursed from the system?

3. Is there a pre-check run report to make sure that all checks are issued and are accurate before preparation?

4. After checks are cut, what is the timeframe for mailing them out?

5. Are the payroll checks used each pay period reconciled with the number of employees on the payroll?

6. Is payroll check stock safe and secured?

7. Who has access to the check stock?

8. Are the payroll checks signed by an individual outside the group preparing the checks?

9. If signature plates are used, are they stored in a secure area?

10. Are authorized check signers able to sign their own checks?

11. Do authorized check signers have access to blank check stock?

12. Are paychecks personally handed to employees by supervisors where appropriate?

13. If funds are electronically deposited in employee bank accounts, does the employee receive a statement of pay amounts?

14. How are "voided" checks handled? Are they cancelled and the signature area cut away?

15. Do checks over a specified amount require more than one signature?

16. Is a copy of the check produced and attached to the supporting documentation?

17. How often are manual checks prepared?

18. Describe the manual check process.

19. Who approves manual checks and are they manually signed?

20. Why are manual checks prepared? Do repeat offenders cause payroll to have to prepare manual checks? If so, what is being done to prevent these individuals from doing so in the future?

21. Has responsibility been assigned for custody and follow-up of unclaimed payroll checks?

22. How often are unclaimed payroll checks reviewed and reissued or sent to the state as unclaimed property?

Exhibit 25.5   Mandated Benefits: 2009 Compliance Guide

Exhibit 25.5 (cont'd)

23. Is responsibility assigned to follow up on payroll checks not cashed after a reasonable period of time (e.g., 90 days)?

24. Are error messages produced by the payroll application corrected on a timely basis?

25. If an employee leaves or is terminated, are monies owed to the company automatically deducted from his or her final paycheck?

26. What is the ratio between actual checks and direct deposits?

27. Are deposit transfers to individual bank branches totaled and agreed to the total net pay per the payroll register?

28. Are employee requests to change bank accounts for direct deposit of pay in writing?

Other:

1. Are original timesheets, timecards, and payroll registers filed locally?

2. Are there union contracts in place? If so, what is the length of the contract, and when is the next round of negotiations set to begin?

3. Are bonuses or commissions paid periodically? If so, how and what documentation is needed?

4. If payroll is accrued, what is the accounting method, in detail, by accounts? What is the current fringe rate?

5. Are the payroll accounts reconciled on a monthly basis?

6. Are there any unclaimed wages on the outstanding check listing? If so, how long have they been unclaimed? What efforts have been made to contact the individual?

7. How are vacation and sick time tracked—manually or by the payroll system?

8. When W-2 statements are prepared for the federal government, are they reconciled with the total pay amount for the pay period?

9. Are the tax returns sent to various taxing agencies regularly reconciled with the amounts produced by the payroll system for tax purposes?

Chapter 26
Special Human Resources Situation: Merger or Acquisition

§ 26.01 AUDIT QUESTIONS

1. If a facility or plant closure is anticipated, have the requirements of the Worker Adjustment and Retraining Notification (WARN) Act been met?

2. Is the HR manager aware of state laws that affect the acquired company?

3. Has a communication plan been developed?

4. Is the HR manager prepared to conduct an HR assessment of the acquired company? If not, will the company engage the services of an expert to assist with the assessment?

Note: Consistent ''yes'' answers to the above questions suggest that the organization is applying effective management practices and/or complying with federal regulations. ''No'' answers indicate that problem areas exist and should be addressed immediately.

There is one increasingly common situation that many HR practitioners will face at some point in their career: a merger or an acquisition. This chapter provides a summary of the major HR issues to consider for the top HR officer faced with this challenge, including the need to conduct an HR assessment. In this chapter the top HR officer is presumed to be the HR manager.

A major strategic initiative such as a merger or an acquisition presents potential for major upheaval in virtually all existing systems, processes, and procedures in the company. The primary challenge presented is not purely technical. The reason for many major difficulties experienced in execution is usually described in human terms: "the culture was 'too different' "; "key people left . . . , they didn't know there were 'big plans' for them"; "merged employees were not prepared to embrace the changes."

The emergence of people problems is not hard to understand. Employees who possess a sense of mastery over their jobs suddenly feel confused. Corporate success norms in the acquired company can change radically. Key personnel may feel less secure in their positions when confronted with key personnel from the acquiring company.

In these situations senior management depends on HR to anticipate how the merger or acquisition will impact HR systems, policies, and procedures, and to provide tactical and strategic direction to design and implement necessary changes. Management also needs HR to interpret and provide insight into the perspective of employees involved in the transition and provide leadership to assist management to deal with the people issues that will arise. The better management understands how employees are reacting to the merger or acquisition, the better it can manage the transition, manage the conflict inherent in change, and increase the ability of the organization to adapt to a new operating model.

(For additional information on assessing the impact of change and increasing the adaptability of an organization to change, see **Chapter 2**.)

§ 26.02 MANAGING A FACILITY CLOSURE

Following is a general guide for planning and implementing selected layoffs, selective relocation, or closure of a facility. This is a summary of general considerations, but it is important for readers to ensure compliance with applicable state and federal laws.

This discussion focuses on a merger or acquisition involving the shutdown of the acquired site and/or layoff of some, but possibly not all, affected employees. It also assumes the added difficulty of the acquisition location in a different state. The list is to be used by the HR manager from the acquiring company.

[A] Preplanning Before Closing and Relocation

Before executing closing or relocation, identify and document the reasons for closing the site or moving operations (e.g., economic necessity). Document the alternatives explored, if any, and whether alternatives were available.

[B] Relocation, Retention, or Termination of Employees

Determine whether any of the existing workforce will relocate to the home site, or if any business will continue to be conducted at the acquired company site. If so, decide whether any current employees will be retained.

[1] Personnel File

Review each employee's personnel file to determine whether employment agreements exist and review existing employment contracts, confidentiality agreements, letter agreements, and correspondence with the employee regarding employment terms to determine if the relationship can be terminated "at will" (i.e., for any reason). Determine whether any verbal representations were made to anyone about continued employment, terminations, order of layoff, notice of layoff, and so forth. For example, under California law, if an employee has a specified term of employment that is greater than one month, the employee can be terminated only for "good cause." [Cal. Lab. Code § 2924]

[2] Company Documents

Review personnel manuals, employee handbooks, and other writings that define or govern the basis or procedures for plant closing, terminations, layoff, continued employment, and such situations. Amend such policies to increase flexibility if necessary, before taking action.

[3] Severance Policies

Review policies on severance benefits, if any. Does the company have an obligation under any contract, policy, or past practice to provide severance?

[4] Operating Needs

Review job descriptions and the organizational chart, and revise them as necessary to reflect current operating needs in the home state. Determine the number of employees, if any, who will be offered relocation. Determine the number of employees, if any, who will be retained in positions in the state of the acquired company.

[5] Organizational Chart

If some employees will be relocated to the home site, revise the organizational chart for the home location to reflect new positions. Revise the organizational chart for the acquired facility if some employees are to remain there.

[6] Independent Contractor Agreements

Review all independent contractor or consulting agreements for terms and conditions relating to acquisition, merger, termination, and so forth. It is important to check applicable state laws regarding the treatment of independent or contract wholesale sales representatives.

[7] Posters

Ensure that state-mandated employment-related posters (e.g., notice of availability of unemployment and workers' compensation insurance, Title VII) are properly posted at the acquired site.

[8] Evaluating Positions

If relocation to a new site will be offered for some positions, or if some positions will be retained in the acquired company's site, determine the value of each position the company contemplates relocating or retaining. Identify and document (1) the positions to be relocated or retained, (2) the work or tasks performed by the positions, (3) whether there are any other jobs that involve these tasks or types of work, and (4) why the positions should be retained or relocated.

Note: Top management should establish goals but not necessarily make the sole decision as to which employees will be let go and which, if any, will be offered relocation or retained in the acquired company. Top management should also formally establish the criteria for selection, but the criteria should be applied, at least in part, by lower-level managers in the company's various departments. In other words, reasonable layers of management should review and agree on the selection criteria and employees to be retained or relocated. Lower-level managers or supervisors are more likely to personally know the employees involved and to be able to comment specifically on the employees' day-to-day performance or provide other relevant information.

[C] Employee Benefits and Benefit Plans

Review all employee benefits plans for notification and closure requirements.

[1] ERISA

Review and determine if any of the company's employee benefit plans (e.g., retirement programs, severance pay programs, health insurance continuation programs) are subject to and in compliance with the Employee Retirement Income Security Act of 1974 (ERISA) and which plans are exempt to ensure that ERISA issues do not become problematic with regard to the plant closing or layoff. (See **Chapter 5** for further discussion of ERISA.)

[2] Contractual Obligation to Contribute to Benefits

Review all applicable benefit documents (e.g., qualified and nonqualified plans, stock option plans, insurance plans, profit-sharing plans). The company may have obligations to contribute to a former employee's benefits following termination based on representations in an employee handbook or other document discussing benefits.

[3] Insurance—Health, Life, and Disability

Review state laws regarding any insurance continuance rights afforded terminated employees to ensure receipt of proper notice of such rights at the time of termination. Contact the company's insurance carrier for proper notice forms to employees regarding continuation rights.

[4] Vacation Pay

Review policies and practices regarding vacation pay to determine whether employees have accrued but unused vacation time that must be paid to them. If applicable, determine the cost to the company for this payout.

[D] WARN Notice

Determine if the plant or facility closing and layoff will require notice under the WARN Act. The major criteria are as follows:

1. Is the organization a business enterprise that employs 100 or more employees (excluding part-time employees who work less than an average of 20 hours per week, or who have worked less than six of

the 12 months preceding the required notification date), or 100 or more employees, including eligible part-time employees, who in the aggregate, work at least 4,000 hours per week (exclusive of overtime)?

2. Is the event a ''plant closing''(i.e., a permanent or temporary shutdown of a single site of employment or one or more facilities within a single site, during any 30-day period for 50 or more *full-time* employees)?

If either of the above conditions applies, contact counsel to discuss WARN requirements. (See **Chapter 17** for additional information on the WARN Act.)

[E] Assistance for Terminated or Relocated Employees

[1] Counseling Services

Consider whether the company wishes to create an assistance plan or provide outplacement or career counseling services to laid-off employees. Determine the cost of such services and which service providers to contact.

[2] Relocation Expenses

Consider what type of assistance, if any, the company wishes to provide workers subject to relocation (e.g., reimbursement of moving expenses). Determine the cost of such assistance.

[3] Severance Pay

Determine whether the company wishes to offer severance pay to laid-off employees. If the company does not have an obligation to provide severance but desires to do so, it should focus on objective criteria in determining the amount of severance pay to provide (e.g., years of service, grade level). To treat employees differently for subjective reasons could result in discrimination claims against the company.

Draft a severance agreement that contains a release of all claims that the employee could have against the company in consideration for the severance payments, if the company does not have a contractual obligation to make such payments. For the release to be valid, the employee must be given sufficient time in which to consider the agreement and discuss it with legal counsel. There are also differences in settlement agreements for employees over 40 years old. Contact counsel to obtain a release and discuss any specific issues.

(See **Chapter 17** for a discussion of severance and outplacement.)

[F] Performance Reviews

If employees are subject to review before notice of closing, conduct accurate performance reviews on the basis of objective job-related criteria. Document those reviews and criteria.

[G] Communication Plan

Develop a plan for communicating organizational changes to all employees, especially those directly impacted by the changes. In some instances, communication may need to begin before the change actually takes place to diminish the impact on employees at the time of change. Prior communication may also provide middle management with the opportunity to plan for the impact of the change on their particular areas. As with all organizational changes, key messages need to be determined early on to ensure everyone in the organization receives the same information.

§ 26.03 IMPLEMENTING THE CLOSING, RELOCATION, OR RETENTION

[A] Selection for Relocation or Retention

Review current employees to determine which employees will contribute the most to positions that will be retained in the remaining facility or relocated to the home facility. To do this, establish and document *objective,* specific criteria for selecting employees for retention. For example, decide if selection will be based upon the employee's position, past performance, seniority, and other such criteria. Be sure not to consider unlawful factors such as protected-class status, including age, race, sex, and religion.

Documentation should be established illustrating that such factors *were not* considered. Avoid criteria that may contain age bias (e.g., "energetic," "new ideas," "potential"). Also ensure that there is no negative statistical impact on protected classes (e.g., not retaining any women or workers over 40). Discuss the selection criteria with managers making the recommendation. Use safeguards, such as including some protected-class members of management in layoff decision making. Alert managers to hidden discrimination.

In the performance review, the HR manager should work with management to do the following:

- Evaluate all employees who hold the same positions relative to each other.

- Assess employees on the basis of their written performance evaluations or oral supervisory assessment of their work performance (create written, signed, and dated notes) to the extent practicable.

- Ensure that the company is treating all performance appraisals consistently.

- Highlight any employee performance problems.

- Evaluate employees using job-related guidelines rather than by making subjective determinations.

- Avoid focusing on salary level to determine who should be retained or relocated; consider length of service instead. For example, if two employees are rated equally, it may be advisable to consider retraining or relocating the employee with the longest service.

- Briefly document the reason that a particular employee is selected for relocation or retention. Indicate that the company reviewed all employees for relevant positions and made the best, most objective decisions.

Senior management and HR should review layoff and relocation decisions to determine if any adjustments are needed to minimize the impact on protected classes and to achieve the intended goals. Ensure that there is no hidden discrimination.

Senior management and HR should review the list of employees to be laid off and ask the following questions:

- Did the employee selected for layoff recently exercise any public or statutory right, so that the layoff may be viewed as retaliatory or against public policy?

- Is the employee selected for layoff a union member?

- Are there protected-class issues associated with this employee?

- Can the company substantiate its reason for deciding not to relocate or retain this individual? Is the employee a long-standing employee with a good work record?

- Why was this employee not selected for relocation or retention? (Briefly document the reasons, providing an objective basis.)

Plan out what each terminated employee will be told, by whom, and where. Prepare a plan of action, including a proposed timeline up through the date of closing. Include all WARN Act and benefit notice requirements in the timeline. Identify management personnel who will be involved in the selection or decision-making process. In meeting with those individuals, emphasize the business need for the closing and the company's desire to be sensitive to employee concerns.

[B] Implementation

Implementation of the closing or relocation should include the following steps:

1. Notify the employees, state government, local government, and union (if applicable) of the plant closing in accordance with the WARN Act. Tell employees additional information will be forthcoming regarding insurance continuation and severance, if any.

2. If severance is provided, review prepared severance agreements, releases, and associated issues with counsel for particular employees.

3. Distribute written packets to employees regarding severance, signing a release, and outplacement assistance, if any. Alternatively, the company could conduct exit interviews or hold information sessions for employees and answer employees' questions regarding continuation of insurance or other benefits at that time. The company may also be able to assess the threat of litigation.

4. Obtain signed documents (severance agreements, releases, insurance forms, and so forth) from employees and obtain releases from unions, if applicable.

Note: Do not apologize for the relocation decision. In any discussions with employees, make sure more than one employer representative is present. Do not discuss the plant closing, relocation, layoff, or retention decisions with anyone except those who have an absolute need to know.

§ 26.04 ISSUES ARISING AFTER THE CLOSING, RELOCATION, OR RETENTION

[A] Determining Statutory Rights of Terminated Employees Under State Law

[1] Final Wage Payments

Determine if wages for services rendered up to the time of dismissal must be paid at the time of the employee's discharge. Determine if accrued but unused vacation time is considered part of the final wages. Determine if employers may deduct any money owed by the employee for any reason; the employee must authorize such deductions in writing.

[2] Personnel Records

Determine the conditions under which employees can review their personnel records they choose. Contact counsel before making this privilege available. Generally, a company has a responsibility to retain the personnel records for terminated employees. The retention period for various records range from six months to five years, depending on which records are retained. Consult the laws applicable to the appropriate state. (For further discussion of records retention, see **Chapter 24**.)

[3] Unemployment Compensation

Generally, laid-off employees are entitled to unemployment compensation. However, the amount of compensation available may be affected if severance pay is provided to an employee. Check the applicable state laws.

[B] Responding to Questions from Outside Sources

A company that has been acquired or is relocating should be prepared to answer questions from outside sources about terminations. The best response is usually to attribute terminations to the facility closing (i.e., there is no reflection on work performance).

§ 26.05 HR ASSESSMENT

At some point in the acquisition process, especially if the acquired company is going to remain open, it is important to determine the quality of the acquired company's HR systems and procedures. To truly assess the level of risk, this should be done before the layoff or closure takes place. This section provides a brief HR assessment overview. (See **Chapter 25** for in-depth information on HR risk management.)

The objectives of an assessment are to identify situations where the acquired company's policies and practices are potentially inconsistent with state or federal law or present other significant risks, where significant policies are missing, or where there are great contrasts between the HR policies of the two companies. It is also important to assess the culture of the acquired company to determine whether its culture will support the business goals of the acquiring company.

These findings are critical. The policies and practices define what the acquired employees expect from HR, and the sheer magnitude of differences found between the companies defines the size of the gap in expectations.

The topics assessment should generally encompass the following functions:

- Employee recruiting and selection

- Organizational structure

- Organization culture

- Personnel records and administration

- Compensation and performance management systems

- Employee benefits

- Communications

- Employee training and development

- Health and safety

- Termination procedure

It is also important to interview top management to clarify any post-merger revisions to the people-management goals and any revised expectations of the HR department. Determine the differences in HR policies between the two firms. Decide which policies will change, and determine the impact of the changes on employees.

To obtain the clearest possible picture, it is important to review forms and documents, employee files, recordkeeping, posted materials, and day-to-day practices. To do this, interview current staff to discuss written and unwritten policies and procedures. Assess management's competence in HR by interviewing key managers' understanding of employment laws. Verify the findings against lawsuits past, present, and pending. Investigate historical precedence.

[A]   Employee Handbook Review

Review the acquired company's handbook to determine how accurately it summarizes the actual HR policies of the acquired company. Review the text for inconsistencies with current state and federal employment regulations. In some states an employee handbook is considered a contractual document, so it is vitally important to know with certainty what employees have been told and how faithfully the company has honored its policy commitments.

Revise the employee handbook if necessary for legal compliance or to provide adequate flexibility in conducting the relocation, layoff, or shutdown.

[B]   Compensation and Benefits

Review all company benefit and compensation programs in light of the merger or acquisition using the following guidelines:

1. *Determine the benefits merger strategy.* Resolve differences in vacation programs, time-off policies, and so forth. Perform a savings or 401(k) plan audit.

2. *Review both sites' salary rates and ranges.* Are they compatible or competitive? Review the bonus program (if any) at the acquired company. Should it continue? Determine how compensation problems will be resolved.

3. *Decide whether or not to consolidate payroll processes.* Review exempt and nonexempt status of all employees. Contact counsel for strategy, depending on the impact of any status corrections, and correct errors.

4. *Decide which plans to continue and which to end.* Review all documentation and consult counsel before shutting down any employee benefit associated with any form of accrued compensation.

[C] HR Strategic Integration Plan

The HR strategic plan is a critical guidance document to manage the people issues in a merger or an acquisition. It integrates company culture and vision with HR policies, procedures, systems, staffing, and structure. It is used to provide the high-level framework for how HR is supposed to function within an organization. It should reflect the long-term goals and objectives of company management by describing how HR supports the company's strategic business plan.

Chapter 27
Nonqualified Deferred Compensation Plans

§ 27.01   AUDIT QUESTIONS

1. Are the participants in the company's nonqualified plan limited to members of a select group of top management or highly compensated employees?

2. Are assets that may be maintained for the purpose of funding benefits under the plan subject to the risks of the company's general creditors?

3. Has the company filed a top-hat notice and statement with the Department of Labor with respect to the plan?

4. Has the company identified all of its plans that may be subject to Code Section 409A requirements?

5. Is the company aware of the new income tax reporting and withholding requirements under Code Section 409A?

6. Has the company amended its nonqualified plans to conform to Code Section 409A?

7. Has the company been including vested benefits in the employee's wages for employment tax reporting and withholding purposes even though the benefits may not yet be includable as income to the employee?

Note: Consistent "yes" answers to the above questions suggest that the organization is applying effective management practices and/or complying with federal regulations. "No" answers indicate possible problems areas that should be addressed immediately.

Nonqualified plans are subject to a complex assortment of Employee Retirement Income Security Act of 1974 (ERISA), income, and employment tax laws. Each law sets forth its own set of definitions and rules. This chapter will discuss the framework of the laws governing nonqualified plans.

§ 27.02 GENERAL INFORMATION

A *nonqualified deferred compensation plan* is an unfunded and unsecured promise by an employer to pay compensation at some future date for current services performed by its employees.

A plan is considered "nonqualified" because it does not meet the extensive coverage, participation, vesting, funding, nondiscrimination, and distribution requirements to allow it to rise to the level of a being a "qualified" plan. For example, where a qualified plan must cover a broad distribution of employees and pass certain nondiscrimination standards, a nonqualified plan is typically used to provide retirement benefits to executives, owners, or other highly compensated employees (HCEs) in addition to their qualified plan benefits.

Since nonqualified plans do not have to meet the many requirements that qualified plans must satisfy, they are not afforded the favorable tax treatment given to qualified plans. Where an employer receives an immediate income tax deduction for contributions to a qualified plan, an employer is not allowed to take an income tax deduction for contributions to a nonqualified plan until the benefits become taxable as income to the employee. Also, while distributions from qualified plans can be rolled into an individual retirement account or another qualified plan to further defer the income tax, the same is not possible for distributions from nonqualified plans. Qualified plan benefits are not subject to employment taxes. However, nonqualified plan benefits are subject to employment (Federal Insurance Contribution Act (FICA) taxes and Federal Unemployment Tax Act (FUTA)) taxes.

The advantage of using nonqualified plans is that such plans are not subject to the minimum coverage, participation, vesting, funding, and distribution requirements. Thus, these plans can be used to cover a select group of key employees and provide "discriminatory" benefits. In fact, there is no maximum cap on the amount of benefits that can be provided to an employee by a nonqualified plan other than the limitation that the total of all compensation and benefits be reasonable compensation for the services provided.

A nonqualified plan can be designed as either a defined contribution plan or a defined benefit plan. A defined contribution plan is an account balance plan in which the amount of the employee's benefits is determined by the size of the account balance. A defined benefit plan is a non-account balance plan in which the amount of the benefits may be determined by a formula or by a fixed amount.

§ 27.03 ERISA CONSIDERATIONS

ERISA governs employee pension benefit plans and employee welfare benefit plans. (See **Chapters 5** and **8** for a detailed discussion of the ERISA provisions.) Nonqualified deferred compensation plans, although they will not generally be categorized as employee welfare benefit plans, may constitute an employee pension benefit plan. ERISA defines a pension benefit plan as a plan, fund, or program established or maintained to provide retirement income to employees, or that results in a deferral of income by employees for periods extending to the termination of employment or beyond.

Some nonqualified plans may avoid the definition of being a pension benefit plan. For example, a short-term deferred bonus plan that only provides for a deferral of two to five years followed by an immediate payout of all benefits may not be considered a pension benefit plan under ERISA, provided the deferral period and payout date do not extend to or beyond the employee's expected retirement or termination date. To determine if payment of the plan benefits is deferred until termination of employment or retirement, the specific facts and circumstances surrounding the plan must be examined. Consideration must be given to the age of the employee, the employer's employee turnover history, and the retirement age in the plan or other plans of the employer.

Nonqualified plans that provide retirement benefits or defer the payment of benefits to the expected retirement or termination date of the employee are considered employee pension benefit plans under ERISA. The two major exemptions are top-hat plans and excess benefit plans. A deferred compensation plan that constitutes a pension benefit plan under ERISA that does not meet one of these exemptions will have to comply with all of the Title 1 ERISA requirements, including funding the plan with assets held in a trust or an insurance arrangement.

[A] Top-Hat Plan Exemption

The exemption for top-hat plans is the broadest exemption and the one most often applied to nonqualified plans. This exemption is applicable to unfunded pension plans maintained by an employer for the purpose of providing deferred compensation for a select group of management or HCEs (i.e., the "top-hat" group). A top-hat plan is exempt from the requirements of Title I of ERISA that include minimum participation, vesting, and distribution rules, minimum funding standards, and fiduciary standards, including the requirement that plan assets be held in trust. Top-hat plans are technically subject to reporting and disclosure requirements; however, Department of Labor (DOL) regulations have reduced this compliance requirement to the filing of a one-time notice upon the establishment of the plan. [29 C.F.R. 2520.104-23]

Although the question as to who might qualify as being within the top-hat group is fundamental to the exemption, surprisingly, the DOL has never provided a definition. It has said that the exemption recognizes that certain individuals, by virtue of their position or level of compensation, have the ability to influence the design and operation of their deferred compensation plan and, therefore, do not need the substantive rights and protections afforded by ERISA.

The lack of guidance has resulted in varied interpretations by those who advise employers on nonqualified plans. Some advisors take the position that the group of individuals who have the influence and power to protect their own interests is very limited and does not extend beyond the most senior officers. Other advisors may use the Internal Revenue Code (Code) definition of highly compensated employees as a measure for defining who constitutes a highly compensated individual for this particular ERISA exemption—despite the fact that both the DOL and the Internal Revenue Service (IRS) have cautioned that the IRS definition of highly compensated employee in Code Section 414(q) differs from the use of the term in ERISA.

Besides the requirement that the plan only benefit a select group of employees, the plan must also be an unfunded plan (i.e., the assets of the plan must not be segregated into a trust that is protected from claims of the creditors of the employer). This does not mean, however, that no source of funding can be established for the plan. The employer can hold assets intended to help it meet its future obligations under the plan. As long as the assets it holds are subject to the claims of its creditors, the plan will be considered unfunded. In addition, the DOL has issued an advisory opinion [Advisory Opinion Letter of December 13, 1985 from

Elliot I. Daniel, Assistant Administrator for Regulations and Interpretations, Pension and Welfare Benefits Administration, to Richard H. Manfreda Chief, Individual Income Branch, Internal Revenue Service] that a special type of trust—a rabbi trust—can be utilized without jeopardizing the unfunded status of the plan. In a rabbi trust the assets of the trust remain subject to the claims of the employer's creditors. This type of trust is known as a rabbi trust because the first such trust submitted to the IRS for a ruling involved a synagogue that was establishing the trust for its rabbi.

Top-hat plans are eligible for a relaxed reporting and disclosure requirement under ERISA, including the exemption for filing Form 5500, Annual Return/Report of Employee Benefit Plan. To obtain this exemption, the plan must file a very short "top-hat notice and statement" with the DOL within 120 days of the establishment of the plan. This notice advises the DOL of the plan and the number of participants, along with some very basic information. For employers that have not timely filed the notice with the DOL and have not filed Forms 5500 annually, a delinquent filer voluntary compliance (DFVC) program is available. If the employer files under the DFVC prior to being notified by the DOL of its failure to file Form 5500 and pays a $750 penalty, it may file the "top-hat notice and statement" without having to file the past due Form 5500.

[B]   Excess Benefit Plan Exemption

The second exemption under ERISA applies to unfunded *excess benefit plans*. These are plans that are maintained by an employer solely for the purpose of providing benefits for certain employees in excess of the limitations on contributions and benefits imposed by Code Section 415 with respect to qualified plans. Under Code Section 415, for 2008, the annual amount of employer contributions to a defined contribution plan cannot exceed the lesser of $46,000 or 100 percent of the employee's pay. The annual income benefit accrued under a defined benefit plan may not exceed the lesser of $185,000 or 100 percent of the employee's average pay for the last three years of employment. These dollar amounts are indexed annually for cost-of-living adjustments. Excess benefit plans are exempt from all ERISA requirements. Although such plans do not need to be limited to "top-hat" employees, given the definition of an excess benefit plan, it would be extremely unusual for a rank and file employee to participate in such a plan.

§ 27.04   EMPLOYEES' TRADITIONAL INCOME TAX CONSIDERATIONS

One of the objectives of deferred compensation plans is to defer the income tax on the benefits being provided under the plan. Normally, employees are subject to income tax on nonqualified plan benefits upon their receipt of benefit payments. However, two longstanding doctrines under the income tax laws— constructive receipt and economic benefit—can cause the benefits to be taxable prior to the time the benefits are paid out. A basic tenet in the design of deferred compensation plans is to design the plan so as to avoid the application of either doctrine. In addition, plans must also be designed to satisfy the requirements of Code Section 409A, effective January 1, 2005 (see **Section 27.05**). Additionally, the dominion and control theory and rabbi and secular trusts are factors that affect taxation of nonqualified plan benefits.

[A]   Constructive Receipt Doctrine

Income that is not actually paid to or received by an employee will be considered to be "constructively received" in the year it is set apart or otherwise made available in a way that it may be drawn on, or could be drawn on, if notice of the intention to withdraw is given by the employee. Income is not constructively received if the employee's receipt is subject to substantial limitations or restrictions. Thus, if an employee who has performed services for the employer is given a choice to receive payment for the services now or to defer the payment until later, the compensation will be considered as having been constructively received regardless of the employee's choice. The employee will be currently taxed on the benefits whether they are paid out or deferred.

Avoiding constructive receipt has always been a key element in designing nonqualified deferred compensation plans. However, compliance with the new provisions of Code Section 409A will, in most cases, avoid the risk of constructive receipt (see **Section 27.05**).

[B] Economic Benefit Doctrine

The IRS has long held that an unfunded promise to pay deferred compensation (i.e., compensation not represented by a promissory note or secured in any way) is not regarded as a receipt of income for cash basis taxpayers. That is, the employee has not received an economic benefit. However, if a benefit is funded in a trust that is protected from claims of the employer's creditors, or if the employer's obligation is secured by promissory notes or other means, the employee may be considered as having received a current economic benefit that is immediately taxable. Accordingly, amounts funded in trusts (other than rabbi trusts), escrow accounts, life insurance policies or annuities in the name of the employee, or obligations that are secured by a security interest in the employer's assets, or in some other fashion, run the risk of being taxable currently under the economic benefit doctrine.

For these reasons, nonqualified plan documents are generally written to include clauses that clearly provide that the deferred compensation represents an unsecured obligation of the employer, and that the employee's interest in receiving payment of the obligation shall be no greater than that of any unsecured general creditor of the employer. In addition, a plan will typically include a provision prohibiting a participant from assigning, alienating, pledging, encumbering, or otherwise transferring his or her interest in the plan, as well as a "spendthrift provision" precluding its attachment by the employee's creditors.

[C] Dominion and Control Theory

The IRS has occasionally raised "dominion and control" as a theory for taxing an employee prior to actual receipt of the benefits. Under this theory, the question is raised as to whether an employee's ability to control the manner in which the funds that are being accumulated for his ultimate benefit are enough to cause the amounts to be taxable. That is, if the employee is given sufficient rights to act as if he or she owned the property, shouldn't the employee be considered the owner for income tax purposes? The issue has been presented in terms of whether amounts are "made available" to employees by reason of their ability to unilaterally elect to make deferrals and choose how they will be invested. The IRS has never asserted the dominion and control theory in court and it may now be obsolete. Regulations under Code Section 457, the section of the Code that governs the taxation of nonqualified plans in tax-exempt and certain governmental entities, make it clear that the availability of investment options does not cause any amount to be "made available" to participants, and it would seem that the result should not be different for the taxability of nonqualified plan benefits of participants in plans sponsored by taxable entities.

There are sound policy reasons behind allowing employees participating in nonqualified plans to be able to direct the investment of their account balances—including the desire to have these plans operate as much as possible like 401(k) plans in which participants can direct their investments. Nonqualified plans can be operated with similar flexibility, allowing employees to change their investment choices by communicating them to the employer or to the employer's plan representative.

[D] Rabbi Trusts

A *rabbi trust* is a trust in which the trust assets remain subject to the claims of the employer's creditors in bankruptcy. The use of a rabbi trust to hold the investments of a nonqualified plan will not cause the plan to be considered "funded" for income tax or ERISA purposes. Once assets have been placed in a rabbi trust, they become dedicated, except in the case of the employer's bankruptcy, to be used to pay benefits under the nonqualified plan. The trust assets cannot be invaded and used for some other corporate purpose; this provides plan participants some comfort and assurance that the assets are likely to be there when it comes time for the employer to pay the deferred compensation benefits to the employee.

[E] Secular Trusts

A secular trust is an irrevocable trust funded by the employer with assets that are not subject to the claims of the employer's creditors. Such arrangements are considered "funded" plans for income tax and ERISA purposes and, as such, result in current income taxation under the economic benefit doctrine as soon as the benefits are no longer subject to a "substantial risk of forfeiture." At that time, they become a current tax deduction for the employer. Secular trusts are not commonly used in nonqualified plans. While they result in current income taxation to the employee, they do not give the employee ownership of the investments. One reason for utilizing a secular trust is to prevent employees from dissipating assets intended to provide a significant part of their retirement. Where secular trusts are used, employers will sometimes gross up the income of the employee to cover the income tax cost. Depending on the design of the trust, the earnings of the trust may be taxable to the trust itself or to the participants, or possibly to the employer. Although it is not entirely clear, it appears that a plan funded by a secular trust may be subject to the Title 1 requirements under ERISA—the minimum coverage, vesting, distribution, and reporting and disclosure requirements.

§ 27.05 EMPLOYEES' INCOME TAX CONSIDERATIONS UNDER CODE SECTION 409A

The American Jobs Creation Act of 2004 [Pub. L. No. 108-357, 118 Stat. 1418], signed into law on October 22, 2004, made dramatic changes in the laws applicable to the taxation of nonqualified deferred compensation. The changes were generally effective for deferrals occurring after December 31, 2004.

The American Jobs Creation Act added Section 409A to the Code. The major substance of Code Section 409A is that nonqualified deferred compensation is taxable for income tax purposes at the earliest time the deferred compensation is not subject to a substantial risk of forfeiture (i.e., at the time it becomes "vested") unless the deferred compensation plan is documented in writing and:

1. Satisfies requirements pertaining to the initial deferral election;

2. Restricts the distribution of benefits to certain permissible distribution events;

3. Contains precise provisions governing the timing and manner of payment;

4. Precludes the acceleration of distributions; and

5. Limits the participant's ability to further extend the deferral or alter the form of distribution.

If all of the requirements of Code Section 409A are satisfied, the deferred compensation is not taxable until the time it is actually received or subject to income tax under the doctrine of constructive receipt or the economic benefit doctrine. Thus, Code Section 409A sets forth new standards and requirements for the ability to achieve deferral of income tax on nonqualified plan benefits.

[A] Plans Subject to Code Section 409A

For purposes of Code Section 409A, a nonqualified deferred compensation plan is defined as any plan that provides for the deferral of compensation, other than an ERISA qualified plan or any bona fide vacation leave, sick leave, compensatory time, disability pay, or death benefit plan. The excluded ERISA qualified plans include qualified retirement plans, 403(b) plans, eligible 457(b) plans, SEPs, SIMPLEs, and qualified governmental excess benefit arrangements under Code Section 415(m).

A plan provides for the deferral of compensation if the service provider (i.e., the person or entity performing the services, such as an employee or independent contractor) has a legally binding right during a year to compensation from the service recipient (i.e., the company or organization for whom the services were performed) that has not been received and that, pursuant to the terms of the plan, is not payable until a later year. Note that a service provider does not have a legally binding right to compensation if that compensation may be reduced unilaterally or eliminated by the service recipient after the services creating the right to compensation have been performed.

Severance pay plans were not specifically excluded from Code Section 409A. Such plans are addressed in the proposed and final regulations. **See Chapter 17 (Section 17.02[D])** for further information on how Section 409A affects severance pay plans.

Nonqualified deferred compensation plans include both elective and non-elective plans. A plan is deemed to include any plan, arrangement, or agreement, including those covering only one individual. The provisions of Code Section 409A are not limited to arrangements between employers and employees; they extend to directors, independent contractors, and partners.

Under a special exception to Code Section 409A, known as the short-term deferral exception, a deferral of compensation is not deemed to occur if an amount is actually or constructively received by the service provider by the later of the date that is 2½ months from the end of either (i) the service provider's first taxable year, or (ii) the service recipient's taxable year, in which the amount is no longer subject to a substantial risk of forfeiture (e.g., the year in which the amount is vested). Accordingly, annual bonuses or other annual compensation amounts that are paid within two and one-half months after the close of the year in which the related services were performed are excluded from the requirements of Code Section 409A. For example, under an annual employee bonus plan, if services were performed and the bonus tied to that service was "vested" in 2008, and the bonus is received by the employee by March 15, 2009, the bonus plan will not be subject to requirements of Code Section 409A.

The broad definition of nonqualified deferred compensation plans under Code Section 409A means that it will apply to traditional deferred compensation plans as well as supplemental executive retirement plans (SERPs), phantom stock plans, certain discounted stock option plans, and other similar programs. Incentive stock option (ISO) plans, Section 423 employee stock purchase plans, restricted stock plans taxable under Code Section 83, fair market value nonqualified stock option (NSO) plans, and certain fair market value stock appreciation rights plans that do not provide for the deferral of compensation are excluded from the requirements of Code Section 409A.

The final regulations contain a set of rules to be used in determining the fair market value of the service recipient's stock in order to identify whether or not a discount is involved. For stock that is readily tradable on an established securities market, the fair market value may be determined based upon the last sale before or the first sale after the grant, the closing price on the trading day before or the trading day of the grant, the arithmetic mean of the high and low prices on the trading day before or the trading day of the grant, or any other reasonable method using actual transactions in such stock as reported by such market and consistently applied. The determination of fair market value may also be determined using an average selling price (as defined in the regulations) during a specified period that is within 30 days before or 30 days after the applicable valuation date, provided that the program under which the stock right is granted, including a program with a single participant, must irrevocably specify the commitment to grant the stock right with an exercise price set using such an average selling price before the beginning of the specified period.

If the stock is not traded on an established securities market, the value must be one that is determined by the reasonable application of a reasonable valuation method. The determination of whether a valuation method is reasonable or whether the application of a valuation method is reasonable is determined on the facts and circumstances as of the valuation date. The regulations list a number of factors to be considered under a reasonable valuation method and must take into account all available information material to the value of the corporation. The regulations provide that the use of any of the following methods of valuation will be presumed to result in a reasonable valuation although the presumption may be rebutted by the IRS upon a showing that the valuation method or its application is grossly unreasonable:

1. A valuation determined by an independent appraisal that meets the requirements of Code Section 401(a)(28)(C) as of a date that is no more than 12 months before the particular transaction to which the valuation is applied;

2. Certain formula valuations that would be considered to be the fair market value of the stock pursuant to Treasury Regulation Section 1.83-5 that governs the valuation of property transferred in connection with the performance of services; and

3. A valuation made reasonably and in good faith and evidenced by a written report that takes into account all the relevant factors listed in the regulations of the illiquid stock of a start-up corporation. For this purpose, illiquid stock of a start-up corporation is stock of a service recipient corporation that has no material trade or business that it (or any predecessor to it) has conducted for a period of 10 years or more, that has no class of equity securities that are traded on an established securities market, and provided such stock is not subject to any put or call right or obligation. In addition, the service recipient must not reasonably anticipate, as of the valuation date, that it will undergo a change of control event within 90 days following the action to which the valuation is applied or make a public offering within 180 days following the action to which the valuation is applied. Such valuation must be performed by a person that the corporation reasonably determines is qualified to perform such valuation based on the person's significant knowledge, experience, education, or training. For this purpose, significant experience generally means at least five years of relevant experience in valuation or appraisal, financial accounting, investment banking, private equity, secured lending, or other comparable experience in the line of business or industry in which the service recipient operates.

This summary is simply intended to provide a broad overview of the valuation methods and standards involved under Code Section 409A. Since the rules are extremely technical, matters of this nature should be referred to someone with specialized expertise.

[B] The Initial Deferral Election

If the nonqualified deferred compensation plan is an elective plan, participants must make an election to defer compensation in the taxable year before the year the services to which the compensation relates are performed; however, this does not mean that all plans must be elective. Non-elective plans are still subject to the requirements of Code Section 409A; this particular restriction will not apply to such plans.

For existing participants, the election regarding next year's compensation must be made before the end of the current calendar year. For example, for deferred compensation to be earned in 2009, the deferred election must be made before December 31, 2008. Newly eligible participants have a 30-day window in which to make their deferral election following the date they first become eligible to participate in the plan.

An important exception relates to "performance-based compensation" for services performed over a period of at least 12 months. The election to defer such performance-based compensation must be made no later than 6 months before the end of the service period. Constructive receipt rules, however, still apply to such an election and may impose additional limitations. Performance periods of less than 12 months revert back to the general rule, requiring the election to be made in the prior year.

[C] Permissible Distribution Events

Distributions are only permitted upon the occurrence of any of the following permissible distribution events (note that termination of a plan is not one of the permissible distribution events):

1. *Separation from service.*

   a. Employees—An employee separates from service if the employee dies, retires, or otherwise has a termination of employment with the employer. The employment relationship is treated as continuing intact while the individual is on military leave, sick leave or other bona fide leave of absence if the period of such leave does not exceed six months, or if longer, so long as the individual's right to reemployment is provided by either statute or contract. If the leave extends beyond 6 months and the right to reemployment is not provided by statute or contract then the employment relationship is deemed to terminate on the first date immediately following such 6-month period. Whether a termination of employment occurs is determined based on the facts and circumstances. If the employee is not expected to provide anything more than insignificant future services for the employer then the employee will be treated as having a separation from service. An employee will not be deemed to be performing insignificant services where the services provided amount to 20 percent or more of the services rendered, on average, during the immediately preceding 3 full calendar years of employment. If the employee continues to provide services to the employer in a capacity other than as an employee, a separation from service will not be deemed to have occurred if the former employee is providing services at an annual rate that is 50 percent or more of the services rendered, on average, during the same 3-year period noted above and the annual remuneration for such services is 50 percent or more of the annual remuneration earned during such period. Levels between 20 percent and 50 percent result in no presumption; whether the employee has separated is purely a matter of facts and circumstances.

   b. Independent contractors—An independent contractor is considered to have a separation from service upon the expiration of the contract under which services are performed for the service recipient if the expiration constitutes a good faith and complete termination of the contractual relationship provided the service recipient does not anticipate a renewal of the contractual relationship or the independent contractor becoming an employee.

c. Key employees—Distributions to specified employees who are defined as "key employees" of public companies are not permitted until at least six months after their separation date. For this purpose, the Code Section 416(i) definition applies: "key employees" include (1) officers earning more than $150,000 and limited to not more than 50 employees or, if fewer than 50 employees, the greater of 3 or 10 percent of the number of employees; (2) 5 percent owners; and (3) 1 percent owners earning more than $160,000. A person is a "specified employee" if the employee meets any of these requirements during the 12-month period ending on a "specified employee identification date." The "specified employee identification date" is generally December 31. If a person is a specified employee as of an identification date, the person is so treated for the 12-month period beginning on the first day of the fourth month following the identification date.

d. With respect to a controlled group of businesses, separation from service means that the individual is no longer employed by any member of the group. For this purpose, a controlled group is defined broadly by Code Sections 414(b) and (c). Thus, it includes incorporated and unincorporated organizations.

2. *Specified time or fixed schedule.* A plan may provide that distributions will be made on a fixed date or during a specified calendar year. A plan may also provide for distribution amounts that are payable at a specified time or pursuant to a fixed schedule if objectively determinable amounts are payable at a date or dates that are nondiscretionary and objectively determinable at the time the amount is deferred. An amount is objectively determinable if the amount is specifically identified or if the amount may be determined at the time payment is due pursuant to an objective, nondiscretionary formula. This formula must be specified at the time the amount is deferred. A distribution date is not fixed if it is not currently ascertainable or is contingent on an event whose time of occurrence is not already known. Thus, for example, a plan cannot specify a payment on the date that company profits reach $1 million or the date the employee's child begins college.

3. *Change in control events.* Distributions upon a change in ownership, change in effective control of a corporation, or upon the change in ownership of a substantial portion of the corporation's assets are permitted as allowed in the final regulations. The definitions in the regulations are framed in terms of corporations, but pending further guidance the rules may be applied to non-corporate entities by analogy as follows:

a. A change of ownership is deemed to occur on the date that one person or more than one person acting as a group acquires ownership of the stock of the corporation that, together with stock held by such person or group, constitutes more than 50 percent of the total fair market value or total voting power of the stock of the corporation.

b. A change in the effective control of a corporation occurs on the date that either one person, or more than one person acting as a group, acquires ownership of stock of the corporation possessing 30 percent or more of the total voting power of the stock of the corporation, or if a majority of the members of the corporation's board of directors is replaced during any 12-month period by directors whose appointment or election is not endorsed by a majority of the members of the board prior to the date of appointment or election.

c. A change in the ownership of a substantial portion of the corporation's assets occurs on the date when one person or more than one person acting as a group acquires assets of the corporation that have a total gross fair market value equal to more than 40 percent of the total gross fair market value of all the assets of the corporation immediately prior to such acquisition.

4. *Death*. Distribution of benefits is permitted upon the death of the employee.

5. *Disability*. A permissible distribution is only allowed in the event of "disability" if a strict disability standard is met. The individual must either (1) be unable to engage in any substantial gainful activity by reason of any medically determinable physical or mental impairment that can be expected to result in death or can be expected to last for a continuous period of not less than 12 months (the definition of disability under the Social Security Act); or (2) be receiving income replacement benefits for a period of at least 3 months under an accident and health plan of the employer by reason of the medically determinable physical or mental impairment that can be expected to result in death or last for a continuous period of at least 12 months.

6. *Unforeseeable emergency*. Distributions are permitted in the event of an unforeseeable emergency, defined as a severe financial hardship resulting from an illness of or an accident suffered by the service provider or his or her spouse or a dependent, a loss of the service provider's property due to casualty, or some other similar extraordinary and unforeseeable circumstance arising as a result of events beyond the control of the service provider. A distribution made by reason of an unforeseeable emergency must be limited to the amount needed to satisfy the emergency, plus taxes reasonably anticipated as a result of the distribution. A distribution is not permitted to the extent the hardship can be satisfied by means of insurance or a liquidation of the individual's other assets (unless such liquidation itself would cause a severe financial hardship).

[D] Precise Provisions Concerning the Timing and Manner of Payment

The final regulations confirm that a distribution does not have to be made immediately on a distribution event. Payment can be made at a specified time or on a fixed schedule after a triggering event. The time may be fixed by reference to the event or may be based on a vesting date. Plans that provide for payments over a specified period of time must contain safeguards to ensure that the tax year of income recognition cannot be manipulated. As a general rule, each distribution event can trigger only one time and form of payment, but a plan may permit a different form of payment for different distribution events. Distributions do not have to occur precisely on a scheduled day. A payment is treated as timely if it is made after the scheduled date, but within the same calendar year or, if later, by the 15th day of the third calendar month following the scheduled date, as long as the service provider is not permitted, directly or indirectly, to designate the taxable year of the payment. The time and the form of distributions must be specified in the plan or elected by the participant upon entry into the plan, or if permitted by the plan, at the time of the related deferral election. Such participant elections should be documented in writing, dated, and retained in the plan's permanent file. This is critical, as Code Section 409A requires compliance in terms of both the plan documents and the operation of the plan.

[E] Acceleration of Distributions and Subsequent Changes to the Timing of Distributions

The acceleration of distributions of deferred compensation is not permitted under Code Section 409A. For example, "haircut" provisions permit an immediate payment of deferred compensation subject to a penalty forfeiture (typically 10 percent) of the deferred compensation. Such provisions, though previously included in some plans, are no longer allowed under Code Section 409A. Similarly, distributions triggered by the failure of the employer to satisfy covenants of financial creditworthiness are not acceptable. Limited relief is provided to allow a non-elective acceleration of distributions due to the occurrence of events beyond the participant's control, such as the need to comply with federal conflict-of-interest requirements or to make transfers pursuant to a court-approved divorce settlement. Accelerated distributions for administrative convenience of minimal interests, defined as an amount less than the applicable 401(k) deferral limit for the particular year (for 2009 this is $16,500), upon a permitted distribution event are allowed. Accelerated distributions are permitted upon certain plan terminations, including a plan termination that is not the result of a financial downturn and where the plan sponsor is terminating an entire category of similar plans (i.e., all non-account balance plans) provided that all payments are made between 13 and 24 months after the plan termination and no similar successor plan is adopted within three years of the plan termination. Other special rules apply to plan terminations in connection with a corporate liquidation, change of control, or bankruptcy. A plan is also permitted in certain instances to allow an accelerated distribution to cover taxes, including income, FICA, and foreign taxes, if certain conditions are met.

A plan may allow participants to make a subsequent election to further defer distributions, however, any such election must (1) not take effect until at least 12 months after the date of the election, (2) provide for an additional deferral period of at least five years from the date the payment would otherwise have been made (except in the case of death, disability, or unforeseeable emergency), and (3) if related to a payment at a specified time or pursuant to a fixed schedule, be made at least 12 months prior to the date of the first scheduled payment.

Changes in the form of the distribution are also significantly limited. If the plan provides for a lump-sum distribution and the participant wishes to receive payments in installments, the result is the equivalent of a deferral of payments. Thus, the rules restricting subsequent deferral elections apply. In contrast, if the plan provides for installment distributions, the plan may treat the entire series as a single payment commencing on the date of the first installment, or each installment as a separate payment. The latter approach allows postponement of the receipt of particular installments without the need to delay the entire series. If the installments are designated as a single payment, individual installments may not be postponed. However, the entire series may be converted into a lump sum payable no sooner than five years after the initial installment was originally due.

[F] The Consequences of Violation

If a plan fails to meet all of the requirements of Code Section 409A, or if the plan is not operated in accordance with the requirements, all amounts deferred for the participant under the plan (including earnings) for all taxable years are includible in the participant's current gross income to the extent the compensation is no longer subject to a substantial risk of forfeiture. A 20 percent penalty tax is also imposed on the amount of compensation required to be included in the participant's gross income. Moreover, the participant is subject to interest at the IRS underpayment rate plus one percentage point on the underpayments that would have occurred had the compensation been taxable when first deferred or, if later, when no longer subject to a substantial risk of forfeiture. The sum of these taxes and penalties can readily consume any benefit.

To avoid adverse consequences to plan participants, employers will have to make sure that plans comply with the Code Section 409A requirements in both form and operation. If there is a Code Section 409A violation, the adverse tax consequences would extend to all of a service recipient's plans in the same category. The final regulations provide for nine categories of plans. The categories are: (i) elective account balance plans, (ii) nonelective account balance plans, (iii) non-account balance plans; (iv) separation pay plans, (v) split dollar life insurance arrangements; (vi) reimbursement plans; (vii) stock rights; (viii) foreign plans; and (ix) all other plans.

A violation in form will result in penalties to all participants covered by the plan. If the failure to meet the Code Section 409A requirements is operational it will affect the particular participant to whom the operational failure relates, but would not impact other participants in the plan.

On December 5, 2007 the IRS issued Notice 2007-100 which sets forth a limited corrections program for unintentional operational failures under Code Section 409A. If the requirements of the Notice are met then (i) certain operational failures that are corrected during the year the failure occurs will not result in Code Section 409A violations and (ii) certain operational failures that occur before 2010 and involve only limited amounts (e.g., $15,500 or less for 2007/2008) that are corrected by the end of the second year following the year the failure occurred will result in only the amount involved in the failure being subject to immediate taxation and the 20 percent penalty (rather than all amounts the employee deferred under the plan). Note that the corrections program is very limited and only applies to certain operational failures. It does not extend to violations in the form of the plan. Examples of operational failures include unintentional failure to defer compensation, failure to delay payment for six and one-half months to or on behalf of a key employee of a public company who separates from service, excess deferred compensation, and administrative error in determining the exercise price of nonqualified stock options and stock appreciation rights. The IRS also announced it is considering a future corrections program that would apply to certain operational (but, again, not form) failures discovered after the year of the failure beyond the limited relief provided in the Notice.

[G]   Impact on the Use of Rabbi Trusts

A rabbi trust continues to be acceptable unless it is established offshore. Assets held in an offshore trust are treated as transferred to the individual under Code Section 83 at the time they are set aside or transferred outside the United States, regardless of whether they are subject to the claims of the employer's general creditors. Earnings on such assets are treated as additional transfers of property. The same rule applies to "springing" rabbi or secular trusts that become effective upon or in the event of an adverse change in the employer's creditworthiness, even where the amounts remain subject to the claims of creditors.

[H]   Effective Date and Modification of Preexisting Plans

Code Section 409A became effective on January 1, 2005 and applies to "amounts deferred" after 2004. For this purpose, an amount is "deferred" when it is both earned and vested. This means that only amounts that have vested prior to 2005 are grandfathered under preexisting law. Amounts that were deferred before 2005 but that are not vested by December 31, 2004 are subject to the new law.

In addition, if a preexisting plan is materially modified after October 3, 2004, amounts that were previously deferred under the plan become subject to the new rules. A material modification is one that adds any benefit, right or feature to the plan. The adoption of a new arrangement or the grant of an additional benefit under an arrangement existing on October 3, 2004, is presumed to constitute a material modification of a plan. The elimination of a benefit, right, or feature, or the suspension of future deferrals, does not constitute a material modification.

[I] Transition Relief

On April 10, 2007, the IRS and Treasury Department issued final regulations under Code Section 409A. The regulations are applicable to periods beginning on or after January 1, 2009. Prior to the effective date of the final regulations, taxpayers are required to operate in good-faith compliance with the statute and with Notice 2005-1 issued in late 2004 as well as certain subsequently issued notices. Compliance with the proposed or final regulations prior to January 1, 2009 constitutes good-faith compliance but is not required.

[J] Reporting and Withholding Requirements

Prior to Code Section 409A, income tax reporting or withholding was not required before the year in which the benefits became taxable to the employee. At such time, the benefits would be included as taxable income and reported on Form W-2 (even if paid following the employee's termination of employment) and the payment of benefits would be subject to income tax withholding as regular or supplemental wages, as appropriate.

Under Code Section 409A, amounts deferred under a nonqualified deferred compensation plan during a year must be reported to the IRS on a Form W-2 or 1099 for the year of the deferral (unless the amount is under the minimum amount to be specified in the regulations—provisionally $600). This is required whether or not the amount is included in the individual's income for that year. Accordingly, deferrals that comply with Code Section 409A will normally be reported twice—once in the year of the deferral and again in the year paid. An employer should report to an employee the total amount of deferrals for the year under a nonqualified plan in box 12 of Form W-2 using code Y. With respect to deferrals of non-employees, the total deferrals for the year under a nonqualified deferred compensation plan are to be reported in box 15a of Form 1099-MISC. IRS Notices 2006-100 and 2007-89 have generally suspended compliance with the above reporting requirements for calendar years 2005–2007 with respect to the reporting of annual deferrals of compensation. These Notices also include guidance regarding the calculation of amounts includable in income under Code Section 409A on account of Code Section 409A failures and the application of the reporting and withholding requirements to such amounts.

Amounts that are taxable by reason of a Code Section 409A failure are to be included as wages in box 1 of Form W-2 and are subject to income tax withholding. The IRS will be issuing further guidance that will provide a method for computing the amount includable in gross income by reason of a Code Section 409A failure. In addition, the employer should report such amounts in box 12 of Form W-2 using code Z. The amount reported in box 12 using code Z should include all amounts deferred under the plan for the taxable year and all preceding taxable years that are currently includable in gross income under Code Section 409A. New Code Section 6041(g)(2) outlines the requirements for income tax reporting and withholding for non-employees (e.g., independent contractors and directors).

[K] Getting Existing Plans into Compliance

Employers should identify and inventory the plans that are subject to the new law. Keep in mind that something as innocuous as a provision in an employment agreement may be considered a nonqualified deferred compensation plan under Code Section 409A. Employers should pay particular attention to unwritten agreements. Where existing plans may have included significant flexibility in distribution options, decisions will have to be made to establish fixed patterns that most closely conform to the various objectives of the employer and the employee while still meeting the requirements of Code Section 409A. Once the plans have been identified, an employer must determine what changes to its existing plans are required under Code Section 409A. The employer will have to consider whether to amend its existing plans or to freeze them and establish new plans. Amending a plan in accordance with IRS guidance to add the new rules for post-2004 deferrals should not jeopardize the grandfathered status of pre-2005 deferrals under the plan. Plan sponsors will also want to alert plan participants making deferral elections that the new rules will apply. As noted above, plans must be documented to conform to Code Section 409A no later than December 31, 2008.

§ 27.06   EMPLOYER INCOME TAX CONSIDERATIONS

The employer does not receive an income tax deduction with respect to contributions to or accruals into a nonqualified deferred compensation plan until such time as the benefits become taxable to the employee. When the benefits become taxable as income to the employee, they can be deducted by the employer for income tax purposes subject to the limitation that the benefits constitute reasonable compensation for the services rendered.

Employers may experience a taxable event upon sales or exchanges in the assets used to fund the plan. A taxable event may also occur upon distributions of funds in the plan. Sometimes a company establishes a nonqualified plan and designs it to operate like a 401(k) plan where the participant can direct investments between a number of investment alternatives. Employers might assume that sales or exchanges of investments, which occur when plan participants change funds, will be taxed similar to the manner in which a 401(k) plan is taxed. However, the plan assets in a 401(k) plan are held inside a tax-exempt trust so that sales and exchanges of investments will not result in an income tax consequence; that is not the case with nonqualified plans, where the assets are owned by the employer or by a taxable rabbi trust. In designing a plan, the employer should be aware of the income tax consequences that may result from the possible frequent changes in investments if participants are given free reign to direct the investments of their plan balances. For this reason, and several others, employers often utilize company-owned life insurance (COLI) to fund nonqualified plans. Sales or exchanges of investments wrapped inside a life insurance policy are not taxable sales or exchanges. The use of COLI is also favored because it provides guaranteed death benefits (if the policies are held long enough) to enable the employer to recover its costs for the plan in a tax-favored manner, since the receipt of the death benefits by the employer will generally be exempt from income taxation unless the employer is subject to the alternative minimum tax, and provided that the conditions of Code Section 101(j) are met (see below). The disadvantages of using COLI versus other investment choices, such as mutual funds, are the additional inherent mortality and administrative costs involved with life insurance and the additional complexity associated with life insurance policies.

Under Code Section 101(j), in order for the death benefits under a COLI policy to be exempt from income taxation to the employer, the policy must be issued on the life of an individual who was either an employee of the policyholder/employer within 12 months of the insured's death or who, at the time the policy was issued, was a director, highly compensated employee (within the meaning of section 414(q)), or a highly compensated individual. In addition, prior to the issuance of the policy, the employee must (i) be notified of the policyholder/employer's intention to insure the employee's life and the maximum face value for which the employee could be insured; (ii) consent to being insured under the policy; and (iii) be informed in writing that the policyholder/employer will be the beneficiary of any proceeds payable on the death of the employee. In conjunction with Code Section 101(j) requirements, Code Section 6039I established reporting requirements with respect to COLI policies. The IRS has issued Form 8925 for reporting COLI policies as required by Code Section 6039I. Every policyholder owning one or more COLI policies issued after August 17, 2006 must annually attach Form 8925 to its income tax return. The Form 8925 reports, among other things, the number of employees covered by such COLI policies, whether each employee provided advance written consent to be insured, and if the coverage continues after termination of employment.

§ 27.07 EMPLOYMENT TAX CONSEQUENCES

Besides the income tax consequences, employers and employees must understand the employment tax (i.e., FICA/Medicare and FUTA) consequences of nonqualified plans. This can be a confusing area because although amounts may be deferred for income tax purposes, they may be currently includable as wages for employment tax purposes. Unlike income taxes, where it is generally favorable from an employee's standpoint to defer the recognition of income, the current inclusion of benefits for employment tax purposes may actually be advantageous.

[A] Background

In most cases, compensation paid to employees is included as wages for employment tax purposes when paid or constructively received (the "general timing rule"). The most common example is an employee's paycheck, the amount of which is subject to FICA/Medicare taxes in the period when it is paid. Historically, compensation earned in one period and not paid until a later period was deferred for employment tax purposes until it was paid.

In 1983, Code Section 3121(v)(2)(A) was enacted to provide for a special timing rule that accelerates the time for reporting deferred amounts as FICA/Medicare wages. Under the special timing rule, such amounts are taken into account as wages for FICA/Medicare purposes as of the later of (1) when the services are performed, or (2) when the deferred amounts are no longer subject to a substantial risk of forfeiture.

Until 1994, reporting deferred compensation earnings as FICA/Medicare wages rarely resulted in FICA/Medicare tax since the wages of most employees covered by nonqualified plans were already in excess of the FICA wage base. However, in 1994, the wage limit for the Medicare portion of the FICA/Medicare tax was eliminated such that, irrespective of an employee's wages, incremental wages attributable to deferred compensation became subject to a 1.45 percent Medicare tax on both the employer and the employee. This resulted in substantial confusion, particularly with respect to defined benefit-styled deferred compensation plans, as to how and when the deferred compensation should be reported for FICA/Medicare purposes.

The IRS issued final regulations effective for amounts deferred, or benefits paid, on or after January 1, 2000, that addressed the following:

- What constitutes a nonqualified deferred compensation plan for employment tax purposes;

- How to determine the amount of deferred compensation;

- When and how to report the deferred amount as FICA/Medicare and FUTA wages;

- How a non-duplication rule prevents deferred compensation from being subject to FICA/Medicare and FUTA taxes twice; and

- How avoidance of FICA/Medicare and FUTA taxes cannot be achieved by applying excessive interest rates to deferrals.

[B]   Advantages of the Special Timing Rule

Recognizing deferred compensation accruals before they are paid, and presumably when an employee has other compensation in excess of the FICA taxable wage base, can provide a significant tax planning opportunity. For most deferred compensation arrangements described in the regulations, the special timing rule must be applied. Using the rule is not elective if the arrangement is covered by the rule. However, the provisions of an arrangement determine whether the special timing rule applies, and careful planning and design may influence the result.

While accelerating income taxes is normally not considered a desired result, in most cases, the acceleration of FICA/Medicare taxes by the special timing rule is a good plan for both the employee and employer. When compensation is deferred, the regular pay of most participating employees is in excess of the FICA wage base. In those situations, the FICA/Medicare tax on the amount deferred will be paid only at the Medicare portion rate of 1.45 percent (2.9 percent combined employee and employer) rather than at the full rate of 7.65 percent (15.3 percent combined). In addition, once deferrals are reported and employment taxes are paid, the deferred amounts and the earnings credited to them are not taxed again for employment tax purposes when the benefits are distributed.

> **Example.** An employee with a deferral of $10,000, which grows to $50,000 when distributed, would likely pay FICA/Medicare taxes of $145 ($290 combined) in the year of deferral and no additional FICA/Medicare tax when the $50,000 is distributed. If the deferral is not designed to fit within the special timing rule, that same employee could pay FICA/Medicare taxes of $3,825 ($7,650 combined) under the general timing rule when the $50,000 is distributed.

> Further, if the special timing rule should have been applied, but was not, the employer may be subject to interest and penalties for failure to timely pay the FICA/Medicare taxes due on the deferral when it was reportable as FICA/Medicare wages.

[C]   Deferred Compensation Plans Subject to the Special Timing Rule

Under the special timing rule, a nonqualified deferred compensation plan is any plan or other arrangement established by an employer for one or more employees that provides for the deferral of compensation, other than in a qualified plan.

A deferral of compensation exists if the employee has a legally enforceable right as of the last day of the calendar year to an amount of compensation which, pursuant to the terms of the plan, is payable in a later year. This broad definition of deferred compensation extends to short-term deferrals. However, regarding short-term deferrals, the regulations provide a rule of administrative convenience that allows employers to elect out of the special timing rule and instead report short-term deferrals that are earned in one year, but paid early in the next year (i.e., year-end bonuses), under the general timing rule.

Benefit plans that are specifically carved out from the definition of deferred compensation plans under the special timing rule include the following:

- Compensation paid according to the employer's customary payroll timing methods;

- Stock options and stock appreciation rights;

- Restricted property;

- Certain welfare benefits, including severance pay, vacation benefits, sick leave, compensatory time, disability pay, and death benefits;

- Window benefits or benefits paid in connection with an impending termination of employment (which will normally include any plan established within the 12-month period preceding the termination);

- Excess parachute payments under Code Section 280G; and

- Amounts paid pursuant to unwritten plans.

Benefits attributable to any of the above plans are subject to employment tax under the general timing rule.

Because the special timing rule applies only to wages deferred, nonqualified deferred compensation plans for self-employed individuals (director's plans, etc.) are not eligible for the special timing rule.

[D] Account Balance Plans Versus Non-Account Balance Plans

The regulations create a distinction between amounts deferred under an account balance plan and deferrals under a non-account balance plan. The method for determining the amount deferred and the timing for taking the deferred amounts into account as wages for employment tax purposes depends on whether the plan is classified as an account balance or a non-account balance plan.

[1] Account Balance Plans

Account balance plans are plans in which (1) principal amounts are credited to the individual account of an employee, (2) earnings are credited (or charged) to the individual account, and (3) the benefits payable to the employee are based solely on the balance in the individual's account. An example of an account balance plan is a plan established for an employee in which 10 percent of annual compensation is credited on behalf of the employee on December 31 of each year and interest is credited on the employee's account balance. This is essentially a "defined contribution" style of deferred compensation plan.

In an account balance plan, the deferred amount that is to be taken into account for employment tax purposes in a given year is generally the amount of principal credited to the individual's account that is no longer subject to forfeiture. In addition, any earnings credited on the principal prior to the time the principal is included as wages for employment tax purposes must also be included. Thus, the timing of reporting deferred compensation as FICA/Medicare wages is very significant. Earnings attributable to the period prior to the time an amount credited is included in wages are subject to FICA/Medicare taxation. However, once amounts are reported as wages, any subsequent earnings are not subject to FICA/Medicare taxes, unless an excessive rate of interest is credited to the account.

[2] Non-Account Balance Plans

Any plan that is not an account balance plan is treated as a non-account balance plan. This would include plans styled like defined benefit plans where an employee's benefit may, for example, be based on a formula tied to the employee's final average pay and years of service. An example is a plan established for an employee where the employee is entitled to a monthly life annuity at normal retirement age equal to the product of 2 percent for each year of service multiplied by the employee's highest average compensation for a 3-year period. Other examples of non-account balance plans are excess benefit plans, supplemental executive retirement plans, and early retirement subsidies.

In a non-account balance plan, the amount deferred in a given year is the present value of the vested benefit earned during the year. The present value can be determined by using any reasonable actuarial assumptions and methods. The mid-term applicable federal rate and the Code Section 417(e) mortality table can be used as safe harbor interest and mortality assumptions.

In non-account balance plans, benefits may fluctuate or even disappear, depending on changes in the employee's final compensation, or other factors such as the employee's benefits under a qualified plan, an early retirement election, and so on. Since the employee's final benefit may be uncertain under a non-account balance plan, the regulations provide the employer the option to defer taking the benefits attributable to the plan into account as FICA/Medicare wages until the "resolution date" when the benefits are "reasonably ascertainable" (i.e., when the present value of the employee's benefit is dependent only on interest, mortality, and/or cost of living assumptions). This modified special timing rule (i.e., taking the deferred amounts into account at the resolution date) reduces both the risk that an employee will pay FICA/Medicare tax on disappearing benefits and the number of required actuarial calculations.

Although an employer may elect to use the modified special timing rule and wait until the resolution date to report deferred amounts as FICA/Medicare wages, the employer can still choose to use the special timing rule and include the deferred amounts as wages prior to the resolution date (the employer can actually elect to include the deferred amounts as wages at any time between the time they would be taxed under the special timing rule and the "resolution date"). This presents a significant planning opportunity for employers. However, if an amount taken into account prior to the resolution date (plus earnings through the resolution date) is less than the resolution date amount, then the employer must "true up" by taking the balance of the resolution date amount into account as of the resolution date. If the amount taken into account early (plus related earnings) exceeds the resolution date amount, the employer may claim a refund or credit for overpayments of FICA/Medicare tax in open years.

Under the *non-duplication* rule, once a deferred amount is reasonably ascertainable and included as FICA/Medicare wages, the benefit attributable to that amount is completely excluded from further FICA/Medicare taxation.

[E] Reporting of Wages for Employment Tax Purposes

Employment taxes on nonqualified deferred compensation generally are due at the later of when the services giving rise to the deferral are performed or when there is no substantial risk of forfeiture of the rights to the deferred amount, regardless of when the deferrals are paid. Thus, it is likely that employment taxes will be due at a time other than when income taxes are due on the nonqualified deferred compensation.

Nonqualified deferred compensation for employees and former employees is reported on Form W-2. Amounts subject to employment taxes attributable to a participant's deferrals or vested accrued benefit (either elective or employer provided) are shown in Boxes 3, 5, and 11.

§ 27.08 ACCOUNTING FOR NONQUALIFIED PLAN BENEFITS

The employer must accrue an expense on its books for deferred compensation payable under a nonqualified plan. Any funding vehicles that the employer maintains (or that are maintained in a rabbi trust) are reflected as assets on the employer's balance sheet and serve to counterbalance the plan's accrued liability; they do not offset or reduce the liability. Changes in the asset value are reflected on the employer's balance sheet; however, the type of the investment may determine whether the change in value from year to year is reflected on the employer's income statement to offset that year's change in the plan's accrued expense. Employers should consult competent accountants to ensure proper accounting for nonqualified deferred compensation plan benefits.

§ 27.09 SPECIAL TAX RESTRICTIONS ON NONQUALIFIED DEFERRED COMPENSATION OF TAX-EXEMPT AND GOVERNMENTAL ORGANIZATIONS—CODE SECTION 457

An employer is not allowed to claim a tax deduction with respect to nonqualified deferred compensation until such time as the benefits become includable as taxable income to the employee (see **Section 27.06**). This results in the employer and the employee having what may be considered competing interests—with the employer seeking to obtain the tax deduction as soon as possible and the employee wishing to defer the recognition of income as long as possible. Such competing interests do not exist with respect to tax-exempt or governmental employers. In order to prevent potentially tax abusive deferred compensation arrangements, Congress enacted Code Section 457, which imposes additional requirements on nonqualified deferred compensation arrangements established by tax-exempt employers and by state and local governmental employers.

Code Section 457(b) defines what it terms an "eligible" plan, and imposes many requirements similar to those set forth for qualified plans, even though a 457(b) eligible plan is not a qualified plan. An eligible plan has the same funding limits as a qualified 401(k) plan. In 2008, the maximum amount that can be deferred to a 457(b) plan is $15,500. A 457(b) plan can begin distributions to a plan participant no sooner than the earlier of (1) the year in which the participant turns 70, (2) termination of employment, or (3) unforeseeable emergency (as described in the regulations under Code Section 457). Benefits under an eligible 457(b) plan must be paid out according to the minimum distribution requirements set forth in Code Section 401(a)(9). Eligible 457(b) plans are not subject to the provisions of Code Section 409A. Benefits under eligible 457 plans are not includible in the income of an employee until the benefits are actually or, in the case of an employee in an eligible plan of a tax-exempt employer, constructively received.

There are substantial differences between "eligible" 457(b) plans for tax-exempt organizations and governmental entities. The differences are such that it is often confusing to think of them as both being eligible 457(b) plans. Eligible plans of tax-exempt entities cannot be funded (as plan assets must remain subject to the risks of the employer's general creditors). However, an eligible governmental 457(b) plan is required to be funded. In addition, eligible plans of tax-exempt entities may only include employees who are in the "top-hat" group. Eligible plans of governmental entities can include rank and file employees in addition to the "top-hat" group. Additionally, distributions from an eligible 457(b) plan of a tax-exempt employer cannot be rolled over into individual retirement accounts or qualified plans. Distributions from an eligible governmental 457(b) plan can be rolled into an individual retirement account or, if permitted by the plan, into a qualified plan.

If a nonqualified deferred compensation plan of a tax-exempt entity does not meet the requirements for being an eligible plan under Code Section 457(b), it is governed by Code Section 457(f). A 457(f) plan, also known as an "ineligible" 457 plan, has no funding limits except that the amounts may not exceed reasonable compensation for the services rendered. In order to defer the income taxation of benefits under an ineligible 457 plan, the benefits must be subject to a substantial risk of forfeiture. When the benefits are no longer subject to a substantial risk of forfeiture (i.e., when they vest), they become includable as taxable income even though they may not be payable at that time. Ineligible 457 plans are subject to the provisions of Code Section 409A, but may be able to avoid the requirements of Code Section 409A, if the plan does not provide a "deferral of compensation." Thus, if the plan requires the payment of benefits within 2½ months following the calendar year in which the benefits become vested, it will not provide a "deferral of compensation." For this purpose, the 409A regulations apply a more restrictive definition of "substantial risk of forfeiture" than that used for purposes of Section 457. What this means is that ineligible 457 plans must provide for a short-term deferral with a risk of forfeiture that meets the 409A definition.

Appendix A
Quiz: How Many of These Acronyms/Abbreviations Do You Know?

1. ADA
2. ADEA
3. EEO
4. FLSA
5. EEOC
6. AAP
7. EGTRRA
8. ERISA
9. HIPAA
10. COLA
11. COBRA
12. BLS
13. OSHA
14. NLRB
15. FMCS
16. PPA
17. IRS
18. BFOQ
19. NMHPA
20. UIC
21. OFCCP
22. DOL
23. OJT
24. WHCRA
25. FMLA
26. ESOP
27. MHPA
28. JCWAA
29. USCIS
30. WARN
31. USERRA
32. SOX
33. VEVRAA
34. QMCSO
35. MMA
36. PDP
37. FSA
38. GINA
39. HEART
40. COLI

Answers

1. ADA: Americans with Disabilities Act (of 1990)

2. ADEA: Age Discrimination in Employment Act (of 1991)

3. EEO: Equal Employment Opportunity

4. FLSA: Fair Labor Standards Act (of 1938)

5. EEOC: Equal Employment Opportunity Commission

6. AAP: Affirmative Action Plan

7. EGTRRA: Economic Growth and Tax Relief Reconciliation Act (of 2001)

8. ERISA: Employee Retirement Income Security Act (of 1974)

9. HIPAA: Health Insurance Portability and Accountability Act (of 1996)

10. COLA: Cost of living adjustment

11. COBRA: Consolidated Omnibus Budget Reconciliation Act (of 1985)

12. BLS: Bureau of Labor Statistics

13. OSHA: Occupational Safety and Health Administration

14. NLRB: National Labor Relations Board

15. FMCS: Federal Mediation and Conciliation Service

16. PPA: Pension Protection Act (of 2006)

17. IRS: Internal Revenue Service

18. BFOQ: Bona fide occupational qualification

19. NMHPA: Newborns' and Mothers' Health Protection Act (of 1996)

20. UIC: Unemployment Insurance Compensation

21. OFCCP: Office of Federal Contract Compliance Program

22. DOL: Department of Labor

23. OJT: On the Job Training

24. WHCRA: Women's Health and Cancer Rights Act (of 1998)

25. FMLA: Family and Medical Leave Act (of 1993)

26. ESOP: Employee stock ownership plan

27. MHPA: Mental Health Parity Act (of 1996)

28. JCWAA: Job Creation and Worker Assistance Act (of 2002)

29. USCIS: U.S. Citizenship and Immigration Services (formerly the Immigration and Naturalization Service (INS))

30. WARN: Worker Adjustment and Retraining Notification Act of 1988

31. USERRA: Uniformed Services Employment and Reemployment Rights Act (1994)

32. SOX: Sarbanes-Oxley Act (of 2002)

33. VEVRAA: Vietnam Era Veterans' Readjustment Assistance Act (of 1974)

34. QMCSO: Qualified Medical Child Support Order

35. MMA: Medicare Prescription Drug Improvement and Modernization Act (of 2003), also known as the Medicare Modernization Act

36. PDP: Prescription Drug Plan

37. FSA: Flexible Spending Account

38. GINA: Genetic Information Nondiscrimination Act (of 2008)

39. HEART: Heroes Earnings Assistance and Relief Tax Act (of 2008)

40. COLI: Company-owned life insurance

Glossary

A

Adverse impact: A negative discriminatory effect of an employment action. An action is said to have an adverse impact if protected groups are not hired or promoted at the rate of at least 80 percent of the best achieving group.

Alternative Dispute Resolution (ADR): A method used by employers to clear up disagreements or conflicts between the employer and employees. Typically, ADR is the use of a neutral third party who hears both sides and works with the parties involved to arrive at an acceptable agreement, thus avoiding costly litigation.

Annuity: Periodic payment made to a pensioner over a fixed period of time or until the pensioner's death. To purchase an annuity means to pay a lump sum or make periodic payments to an insurance company. In return, the insurance company guarantees that certain periodic payments will be made to the participant, as long as he or she lives beyond the first due date of the annuity.

Arbitration: The process of submitting a dispute or an unresolved grievance to an impartial third party for a binding decision. Arbitration is often a useful alternative to court proceedings. Labor agreements typically include arbitration provisions to resolve grievances. See also Mediation; Alternative Dispute Resolution.

Automatic enrollment: The practice of enrolling all eligible employees in a savings plan and beginning participant deferrals without requiring employees to submit a request to participate. Plan design specifies how the automatic deferrals will be invested. Employees who do not want to make deferrals to the plan must actively file a request to be excluded from the plan. Participants can generally change the amount of pay that is deferred and how it is invested.

B

Benchmark job: A standard job to which other jobs can be compared as being above, below, or comparable. A benchmark job frequently refers to a job or group of jobs used for making pay comparisons in salary surveys, either within the organization or with comparable jobs outside the organization. For example, a benchmark job in the banking industry is a teller.

Blackout period: A period during which plan participants are not permitted to make changes in their investment selections, typically because the plan sponsor is switching from one plan vendor to another. During the blackout period, participants cannot direct the investments in their accounts.

Bona fide occupational qualification (BFOQ): A characteristic necessary for an employee to be able to perform a job. BFOQ is an exception to the prohibition of discrimination on the basis of gender, religion, and national origin under Title VII of the 1964 Civil Rights Act. Thus, under certain conditions, an employer may legally require persons of a specific gender, national origin, or religious affiliation to staff certain jobs. The intent of this provision is to specify that there are certain jobs for which gender, national origin or religion may be legitimate qualifications. Neither race nor color may constitute a BFOQ.

Broadbanding: In compensation, merging several pay grades into a few broad bands of pay. Broadbanding is used to overcome constraints of a rigid, hierarchical pay structure that may not mirror a flattened organizational structure relying on continuous skill acquisition.

C

Catch-up provision: A provision found in some 401(k) plans that allows eligible employees who have attained age 50 to make higher annual contributions to their retirement plans in the years prior to retirement.

Certificate of creditable coverage: A written certificate issued by a group health plan or health insurance issuer that shows an individual's creditable coverage under the plan.

Class action: A lawsuit brought on behalf of one or more persons as representatives of a particular group. Every member of the class need not be named in the suit. Members of the class must be so numerous that it is impractical to bring them all before the court, and named representatives must fairly and adequately represent the members of the class. Class action suits are designed to expedite court proceedings involving the same alleged violation.

Closed shop: A union security arrangement in a labor agreement whereby union membership is a prerequisite to employment. The closed shop was prohibited by the Taft-Hartley Act of 1947.

Coinsurance: A cost-sharing measure under a health insurance policy that requires the patient to pay a percentage of the costs for covered services.

Common law: An ''unwritten law'' based on judicial systems and customs that is recognized, affirmed, and enforced by court decisions. Common law in the United States was inherited from England and enlarged and changed by American courts.

Compa-ratio: The ratio of an employee's actual pay rate (numerator) to the midpoint of the respective pay grade (denominator). Compa-ratios can be calculated for a group of people, a department, or an entire organization. They are used to analyze the relative position of the individual or group to the pay grade.

Conciliation: Process used to settle a complaint where EEOC has found cause to believe that discrimination has occurred.

Constructive discharge: Actions of an employer or an employer's representative that make an employee's job so unbearable or onerous that the employee has no other reasonable choice but to quit. In effect, this is considered the same as a termination by the employer. An employee ''quit'' as the result of demotions involving a substantial reduction in compensation and status has been ruled in some jurisdictions to be constructive discharge.

Contingent workforce: A workforce that grows and shrinks depending on work demands. Generally, refers to temporary, contract, leased, or other nonemployee workers.

Copayment: A cost-sharing measure under a health insurance policy that requires the patient to pay a specified dollar amount for each unit of service.

Creditable coverage: Health coverage for an individual under a group health plan, including continuation coverage under COBRA, Medicare, Medicaid, a state health benefits risk pool, or a public health plan.

D

Decertification: The loss of a union's right, frequently by election, to act as the exclusive bargaining representative of a group of employees.

Deferred compensation: Compensation payable to an employee at some point in the future, including voluntary deferral of earned incentives, mandatory deferrals of earned incentives, as well as earnings and retirement plan vehicles.

Defined benefit pension plan: A pension plan that specifies the benefits, or the methods of determining the benefits, but not the level or rate of contribution. Employer and employees usually contribute a specific amount to an investment fund. The amount the employee receives at retirement is the sum that has accumulated in the investment account.

Defined contribution pension plan: An individual account pension plan in which the contributions are specified by a formula. The participant can buy benefits with the accumulated amount of money in the account.

Discrimination testing: To satisfy IRS requirements, every tax-qualified retirement plan must pass a series of tests to ensure that the plan does not benefit only owners or other highly compensated employees of the employer. The tests include the actual deferral percentage (ADP) test, the actual contribution percentage (ACP) test, and the top-heavy test.

Disparate impact: The result of an employer action or policy that does not appear unlawful on its face that affects one or more classes of employees differently than other classes of employees. In anti-discrimination law, concern with disparate impact deals with unequal treatment of members of a protected class. For example, a policy requiring that all applicants for employment possess no greater than two years of experience could have a disparate impact on persons over age 40.

Disparate treatment: An employer's actions or policies that affect one or more protected classes of employees or applicants less favorably than another.

E

Employee involvement: A management philosophy that by creating an environment in which people have an impact on decisions and actions that affect their jobs, an employer enables employees to contribute to continuous improvement and the ongoing success of their work.

Employee stock ownership plan (ESOP): A benefit provided by employers to help employees plan for retirement. With such plans, a company first borrows money from a financial institution, using its own stock as collateral for the loan. Over a prescribed period of time, the company repays the loan. Principal and interest loan repayments are tax-deductible. With each loan repayment, the lending institution releases a certain amount of stock being held as security. The stock is then placed into an employee stock ownership trust (ESOT) for distribution at no cost to all employees. The employees receive the stock value at retirement or upon separation from the company.

Enrollment date: Under HIPAA, the first day of health plan coverage or, if there is a waiting period, the first day of the waiting period.

Ergonomics: The science of how the design of jobs, facilities, furniture, and equipment affects productivity and health.

F

Fiduciary: A person who:

- Exercises discretionary authority or control over management of a pension plan, or exercises any authority or control over the management or disposition of its assets;

- Provides investment advice for a fee or other compensation (direct or indirect) as to any monies or other property of the pension plan, or has any authority or responsibility to do so; or

- Has discretionary authority or discretionary responsibility in the administration of the pension plan.

Flexible benefit plan: A plan established by an employer under Internal Revenue Code Section 125 that permits employees to select cash or benefits from a menu of options provided by the employer. In some plans, employees receive subsidies (credits) from the employer to help pay for their choices. A flexible benefit plan, also known as a cafeteria plan, includes tax-advantaged features and allows employees to select between taxable and nontaxable forms of compensation.

G

Gain sharing: A type of variable or incentive pay program designed to reduce costs and thereby improve profits. Gains made through cost-reduction efforts of the workforce are shared with the workforce.

Golden parachute: An employment contract that provides for an increase or acceleration of payments or vesting of other rights for the employee, upon change of control of the corporation as defined in the contract, or upon change of control coupled with a change in the employee's duties. Usually applied to senior executives.

Group health plan: As defined under ERISA, an employee benefit plan established or maintained by an employer or by an employee organization (such as a union), or both, that provides medical care to employees or their dependents directly or through insurance, reimbursement, or otherwise.

H

Highly compensated employee (HCE): An employee who: (1) owns 5 percent or more of the company in the current or prior year; (2) earns more than $110,000 (indexed) in the preceding plan year; and/or (3) at the employer's election, is in the top 20 percent of the organization's employees in terms of pay. The Internal Revenue Code determines the tax status of benefit programs on the basis of how the plan treats HCEs relative to other employees, by comparing their eligibility and participation rates.

I

Incentive stock option (ISO): Gives an executive a right to pay today's market price for a block of shares in the company at a future time. Although the market price could be higher by the time the option is exercised, no tax is due until the employee sells the shares, unless the individual is subject to the alternative minimum tax under the Tax Reform Act of 1986.

Individual retirement account (IRA): A personal, tax-sheltered account to which wage earners who are either not covered by an employer retirement plan (or, if covered, who exceed certain income limitations) may make elective contributions for their retirement.

J

Job analysis: The systematic, formal study of the duties and responsibilities that comprise job content. The process seeks to obtain important and relevant information about the nature and level of the work performed and the specifications required for an incumbent to perform the job at a competent level.

Job enlargement: Changes in the scope of a job so as to provide greater variety to the worker.

Job enrichment: A restructuring of the content and level of responsibility of a job to make it more challenging, meaningful, and interesting to the employee. Job enrichment builds a motivator into the job to give employees a sense of achievement.

K

Key-contributor insurance: Insurance designed to protect businesses against the possible death of a key employee with unique skills and knowledge. The business pays the premium and is normally the beneficiary.

L

Lockout: A tactic used by management after the expiration of a labor agreement in which management refuses to allow members of a bargaining unit to work.

M

Market pricing: The technique of creating a job-worth hierarchy based on the going rate paid for benchmark jobs in the labor market(s) relevant to the organization. All other jobs are slotted into the hierarchy on the basis of whole job comparison.

Mediation: A form of alternative dispute resolution where a neutral third party facilitates and expedites resolution. Unlike arbitrators, mediators are not empowered to make decisions and judgments or enforce agreements.

Money purchase pension plan (MPPP): A defined contribution plan in which employer contributions are usually determined as a percentage of pay. Forfeitures resulting from separation of service prior to full vesting can be used to reduce the employer's contributions or be reallocated among remaining employees.

N

Nonqualified plan: A plan that provides benefits in excess of those possible within IRS-qualified plans, or that does not otherwise meet IRS requirements. Nonqualified plans do not quality for tax deductibility.

O

Ombudsperson: A complaint officer with access to top management who hears complaints, investigates them, and recommends appropriate action. The ombudsperson may also mediate disputes and serve as grievance advocate.

On-boarding: The process of orienting and fully integrating a new employee into the vision, strategies and culture of the organization. Where traditional new hire orientation generally lasts days or weeks, the on-boarding process may last as long as one to two years.

Open enrollment: That period of time, generally once a year, when a group health plan and its insurance carriers, if any, allow employees to make changes to their health care coverage.

Open shop: Employment that is available on equal terms to union members and nonmembers alike. Nonmember employees do not pay union dues.

P

Paired comparison: A job evaluation technique for ranking employees. The performance of each employee is compared with every other employee in a particular group in order to evaluate each employee's performance.

Participant directed account: An account under a retirement plan for which the plan participant selects his or her own investment options. Code Section 404(c) requires a plan that wishes to be relieved of its fiduciary liability for investment performance to permit plan participants to exercise control over the investments in their accounts.

Performance management: The creation of a work environment or setting in which people are enabled to perform to the best of their abilities.

Performance share plan (PSP): A stock grant plan that requires the employee to achieve certain goals before having rights to the stock. The employee receiving the shares pays personal service income tax on the fair market value of the stock at the time of issuance.

Portability: A pension plan feature that allows participants to change employers without changing the source from which benefits will be paid.

Predetermination: An administrative procedure whereby a health provider submits a treatment plan to a third party before treatment is initiated. The third party usually reviews the treatment plan, indicating one or more of the following: patient's eligibility, guarantee of eligibility time, covered service, amounts payable, application of appropriate deductibles, copayment factors, and maximums.

Preexisting condition: A physical or mental condition diagnosed and/or treated before the effective date of medical coverage or for which a prudent person would have been treated.

Preexisting condition exclusion: A limitation or exclusion of health care benefits for a medically related condition based on the fact that the condition predated the first day of coverage.

Profit-sharing plan: An agreement between an employer and its employees that allows the employees to share in company profits. The employer makes annual contributions to a defined contribution pension plan based on company profits. Such a plan allows an employer to limit allocations to the plan in lean years.

Protected class: Any group (or member of that group) protected by anti-discrimination laws such as Title VII and the Rehabilitation Act of 1973. Protected classes include the disabled, women, people over 40, minorities, and other classifications.

Punitive damages: Punitive damages are sums of money awarded by a court to punish a party for violence, oppression, malice, fraud, or wicked conduct. They are intended to console the wronged party for mental anguish. Punitive damages are usually awarded in addition to compensatory or actual damages; they may not be covered under the provisions of insurance policies.

Q

Qualified plan: A private retirement plan that meets the rules and regulations of ERISA and Internal Revenue Code Section 401(a). Contributions to such a plan are generally tax deductible; earnings on contributions are always tax sheltered until withdrawal.

Qualifying event: A series of actions that leads to an employee's right to claim continued health care coverage under COBRA. Qualifying events include an employee's death, termination, and resignation.

R

Red circle rate: An individual pay rate that is above the established range maximum assigned to the job grade. The employee is usually not eligible for further base pay increases until the range maximum surpasses the individual pay rate.

Regular rate of pay: The regular hourly rate of pay of a non-exempt employee is determined by dividing his total remuneration for employment (except statutory exclusions) in any workweek by the total number of hours actually worked by him in that workweek for which such compensation was paid. The regular rate of pay includes bonuses, shift premiums and incentives that are non-discretionary.

S

Sexual harassment: Continued unwelcome sexual advances, requests for sexual favors, and other verbal or physical conduct of a sexual nature made by one employee to another employee against the latter's wishes.

Skill-based pay: A system of compensation that rewards employees for acquisition of specific designed skills, regardless of position or length of service.

T

Target benefit plan: A defined contribution plan that acts like a defined benefit plan. Contribution amounts are set for each year but vary according to the age of the employee. Such a plan allows older employees to receive pension amounts that are similar to those of younger employees, despite the fact that older employees have fewer years before retirement for their investments to grow.

Tort: The law of private wrongs, other than breach of contract, done negligently. Examples in employment include fraud and assault. Civil suits can be filed for such wrongs.

Total target compensation: The total cash compensation available to employees for achieving expected results. Total cash compensation includes all forms of direct compensation—base, bonus, commission, and so forth.

U

Underutilization: In affirmative action, a condition where the representation of employees of a certain gender or ethnic background in any given job group is less than what would be expected given the availability of qualified candidates for that job group.

Utilization review (UR): A health care cost containment program in which a hospital or peer review organization reviews treatment and charges by health care providers. The goal is to ensure appropriate treatment at reasonable costs and avoid unnecessary treatment.

V

Variable pay: Compensation given strictly on the basis of individual or organizational performance. Variable pay may include cash awards, profit-sharing, team incentives, or gain-sharing. Also called "pay-at-risk."

W

Waiting period: The period before an employee or dependent is eligible for coverage under the terms of a group health plan. Under the provisions of HIPAA, if an employee or dependent is a late enrollee or enrolls on a special enrollment date, any period before the late enrollment date or special enrollment date is not a waiting period.

X Y Z

Zero-base forecasting: Use of the organization's current level of employment as the starting point for determining future staffing needs.

Index

[References are to section numbers.]

A

V

Vacation
  layoffs and termination
    mandatory vacation in lieu of, 17.02[C]
    vacation accruals, 17.06[A]
  mandatory vacation, 17.02[C]
  pay. *See* Vacation pay
  policy, 11.03[A]
Vacation pay
  FMLA, 14.16[C]
  layoffs and termination, advanced pay, 17.06[B]
  merger and acquisition (M&A), 26.02[C][4]
Vacation policy, 11.03[A]
Valuation discrimination, 3.01
VBIA. *See* Veterans Benefits Improvement Act (VBIA)
VCP (Voluntary Correction Program), 8.04[O]
VEBA. *See* Voluntary employee beneficiary association (VEBA)
VEOA. *See* Veterans Employment Opportunities Act (VEOA)
Vesting
  computation period, 8.05[F]
  defined benefit plan, 8.05[G]
  defined contribution plan, 8.06[H]
Veterans
  affirmative action, 18.03[F]
Veterans Benefits Improvement Act (VBIA), 11.04[D]
Veterans Employment Opportunities Act (VEOA), 18.03[C][3]
Vets-100 report, 18.03[C][3], 18.03[F][1]
Vets-100A report, 18.03[F][1]
Vietnam Era Veterans' Readjustment Assistance Act (VEVRAA), 15.03[E], 18.03[C][3], 18.03[F]
Vietnam veterans
  affirmative action, 18.03[C][3], 18.03[F]
Violence prevention, workplace, 22.05
Vision plans, 10.03[A]
Vocational Rehabilitation Act (Section 503), 15.03[D], 18.02[C][6], 18.03[F]
Voice mail
  monitoring of, 20.03[F]
Voluntary affirmative action, 18.03[A]
Voluntary correction programs, 8.04[O]
Voluntary Correction Program (VCP), 8.04[O]

Voluntary Employee Beneficiary Association (VEBA), 5.02[D], 12.06[A]
Voluntary Fiduciary Correction Program (VFCPP), 8.04[O]
Volunteer work, 3.03[M]
Voting, 11.04[B]
V-time, 19.03[C]

W

Wage and hour laws. *See* Federal wage and hour laws
WARN Act, 17.02[B], 26.02[D]
WCRI (Workers' Compensation Research Institute), 9.04[B]
Welfare Reform Act of 1996, 4.04[A]
Wellness programs, 10.09
  ADA, 13.09[C]
  laws, 10.09[D]
  results of, 10.09[A]
  setting up, 10.09[C]
  tax regulations, 10.09[D]
  trends, 10.09[B]
  universal availability, 10.09[D]
WHCRA (Women's Health and Cancer Rights Act of 1998), 5.10, 6.06
Whistleblower protection
  SOX, 25.04[E]
Withholding
  Code Section 409A, 27.05[J]
  federal, 4.07[A]
  state, 4.07[B]
Withholding Compliance Program, 4.05[B]
Women's Health and Cancer Rights Act of 1998 (WHCRA), 5.10, 6.06
Worker Adjustment and Retraining Notification (WARN) Act, 17.02[B], 26.02[D]
Workers' compensation, 9.04. *See also* Overlapping statutes (ADA, FMLA, WC)
  ADA and, 9.04[C]. *See also* Overlapping statutes (ADA, FMLA, WC)
  benefits-related legislation interaction, 9.04[C]
  disability integration, 9.04[B]
  FMLA and, 9.04[C], 14.16[D]. *See also* Overlapping statutes (ADA, FMLA, WC)
  state laws, 9.04[A]
    compulsory coverage, 9.04[A][1]
    damages, suits for, 9.04[A][2]

    elective coverage, 9.04[A][1]
    insurance requirements, 9.04[A][3]
    notice requirements, 9.04[A][4]
    recordkeeping requirements, 9.04[A][4]
    24-hour coverage, 9.04[A][5]
Workers' Compensation Research Institute, 9.04[B]
Workforce analysis
  affirmative action plans, 18.03[E][2]
Work-life benefits, 10.07[B]
Workplace harassment
  employer liability, 21.09[C]
  hostile work environment, 21.09[B]
  investigation procedures, 21.09[D]
  other forms, 21.09
  prevention of harassment, 21.09[E]
  sexual harassment. *See* Sexual harassment
Workplace health and safety, 22.01–22.08
  audit questions, 22.01
  blood-borne pathogens, 22.02[G]
  compliance and accident prevention assistance, 22.02[H]
  employee training. *See* Safety training
  energy control program, 22.02[F][1]
  ergonomics, 22.06
  exemptions from OSH Act requirements, 22.02[B]
  Form 300/300A, 22.02[D]
  government employers, 22.07
    federal employers, 22.07[A]
    state and local governments, 22.07[B]
  hazardous waste, 22.03
  Haz-Com Standard, 22.02[E], Ex. 22.1
  home offices, 22.04
  lockout/tagout requirement, 22.02[F]
  OSH Act, 22.02
  OSHA enforcement, 22.02[I]
  recordkeeping requirements, 22.02[D], 22.02[G][4]
  regulatory changes, 22.02[J]
  safety training, 22.08
    ADA, 22.08[F]
    blood-borne pathogens, 22.02[G][2], 22.02[G][3]
    design of program, 22.08[D]
    documentation, 22.08[E]
    establishing programs, 22.08[A]
    generally, 22.02[C]